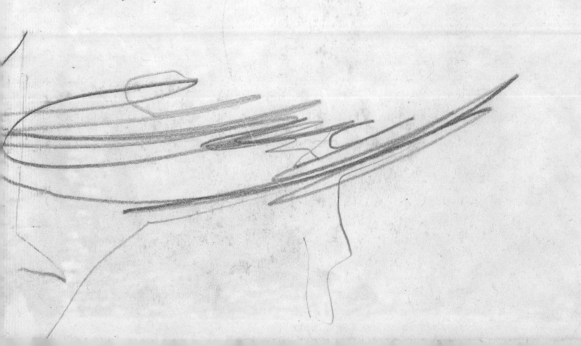

The New Book

WAR SUPPLEMENT

of Knowledge

MADE AND PRINTED IN GREAT BRITAIN BY THE AMALGAMATED PRESS, LTD.

WINSTON CHURCHILL

Photo, Fox

TO Mr. Churchill, who became Prime Minister at a time when Britain was depressed by failure of the Norwegian campaign and apprehensive about the battles just beginning in the West, the British Commonwealth of Nations owed an incalculable debt. He stimulated the people to fresh endeavours, heartened them to bear the hardships and disappointments which he foretold so frankly, and infused into all the determination to achieve final victory. He became First Lord of the Admiralty in Mr. Chamberlain's Government on Sept. 3, 1939; on Mr. Chamberlain's resignation (May 10, 1940) he became Prime Minister.

THE NEW

BOOK OF KNOWLEDGE
WAR SUPPLEMENT

Encyclopedia of World Events since Beginning of Second World War

Edited by

SIR JOHN HAMMERTON

Editor of The Second Great War, The War Illustrated, World War 1914–18
Popular History of the Great War, I Was There !
War in the Air, etc.

EXTRA VOLUME
Containing 1270 articles, 895 illustrations,
79 maps and plans, with 8 plates
in full colours and duotone

THE WAVERLEY BOOK COMPANY LTD.

Farringdon Street, London, E.C.4

The Editor Explains

THE universal confusion which Germany, blindly following a madman's lead, brought upon the world in 1939 has cut so deeply across all our ordered ways of life that to its very core the world's existence, spiritual and social, has been affected. A new world-life must somehow shape itself when the confusion of the War has done its worst in obliterating the spiritual and intellectual standards to which the mind of Man had attained through ten thousand years of history. And in this re-shaping of the world the diffusion of knowledge by means of the printed word is destined to play an even greater part than during the centuries since a countryman of the present enemies of civilization first invented the art of printing. An era of tremendous energy in every department of human life is more likely to follow the War than an era of exhaustion. The will to live and to enjoy the abundance of the Earth, together with the determination that one nation of brutalized humanity shall not again be allowed to drag the whole world into insensate conflict, will surely prevail, so that out of the evil of to-day a new and better world will emerge.

IN this new world the need to restore and apply the best that spiritual vigour, scientific devotion, and industrial activity had attained in the pre-War years will be felt in every land and will call forth a new fury of endeavour which will mark a renascence of intellectual activity such as the world has never seen. One significant sign of this new spirit is the fact that while Rommel and Auchinleck were at death grips at El Alamein the Egyptian Ministry of Education at Cairo was confirming by cable a long debated enterprise, which may yet prove historic, in deciding to proceed with an Arabic translation of the entire Universal History of the World, which the present writer had the task of editing some fourteen years ago. It is a Work of more than 2,500,000 words, lavishly documented with many thousands of authentic pictorial reproductions, and containing the original contributions of one hundred and fifty of the greatest experts in every department of historical and archaeological research. It has been chosen for presenting to the Arabic reading public in popular form as an impartial and scholarly interpretation of World-History from the earliest ages to the present day. A singular honour and a reasonable source of pride to editor and publishers alike.

WHILE a Work of history once achieved requires no revision beyond the occasional addition of new facts, an encyclopedia demands unceasing editorial vigilance to keep it up to date. Thus the greatest imaginable enemy of encyclopedia makers is surely a world war. But fortunately for THE NEW BOOK OF KNOWLEDGE its method of presenting the world of knowledge to the world (to use the slogan of a famous news reel) is so ingeniously devised that the changing world of War affects its contents far less than it would those of a conventional encyclopedia. Our tenth volume with its comprehensive Fact Index is subject to frequent change and with each new impression the Fact Index is always revised to the date of printing. But, obviously, no ingenuity will surmount the difficulty of keeping coloured maps of the countries and continents in tune with the temporary changes in the fortunes of war. Equally unavailing would be any effort to re-write the articles on the countries of the world in the unsettled conditions at present prevailing, and a multitude of other subjects that will not be capable of definitive treatment for some years to come. Meanwhile, the demand for THE NEW BOOK OF KNOWLEDGE does not slacken and some method to bring its immensely varied contents into line with the most recent developments of world affairs was essential. Hence this volume, which must be regarded as an extension of the original work, although it has all the merits of an entirely new encyclopedia of the Second World War.

THE WAR SUPPLEMENT is unique. No comparable effort has been made to bring the whole course of the War from its outbreak in 1939 to its end in 1945 within the compass of one encyclopedic volume. Used in conjunction with its companion volumes of THE NEW BOOK OF KNOWLEDGE that entire work becomes immediately up to date. All terri-torial changes, which we confidently regard as temporary, can be clearly traced in the maps of this SUPPLEMENT by comparing these with the maps in the main volumes of the work, while the governmental changes throughout the world following upon territorial conquest or occupation are all here recorded. All the important campaigns and battles since the rape of Poland are succinctly described by contributors chosen in every case for expert knowledge, and numerous personalities whom the War has brought to prominence figure in our biographical entries. The mere enumeration of the SUPPLEMENT'S contents will indicate something of the labour and resource which have gone to its making. It contains 1,270 articles, 895 illustrations, 79 maps, charts and plans, with 8 plates and maps in full colour and duotone. The articles include 255 biographies of leading soldiers, sailors, airmen, statesmen and politicians and there are over 50 special book lists added to the principal articles.

No reader will require to be told that this volume does not pretend to finality in any form. Now that the enemies of civilization have been overthrown by the tremendous exertions of the United Nations and the resistance of their Allies, a companion volume is in active preparation and, when completed, these two extra volumes in themselves will provide a unique work for immediate reference to all the outstanding events and personalities which engaged the mind of an anxious world from 1939 to 1945. But they will also form for some years to come an essential companion to THE NEW BOOK OF KNOWLEDGE so that the full enjoyment of the unrivalled contents of the main Work may be unimpaired by the multitudinous and confusing changes which the War has brought upon all books of popular instruction that are concerned in any measure with the recording of modern events and the changing conditions of our time.

J. A. Hammerton

SPECIAL PLATES IN COLOUR AND DUOTONE

Winston Churchill .. .. *Frontispiece*

Facing page

Aircraft : Camouflaged Fighters and Bombers of the R.A.F. 16

New Dive Bomber and Fighter 17

Dunkirk: The Withdrawal from Dunkirk
By Charles Cundall, A.R.A., Official War Artist 97

Homeward Bound—from Dunkirk 96

Europe : War Map of Europe and the Middle East. *Three-fold Map in full colours* .. 104

Facing page

Medals : British War Medals of the Second Great War 264

" For Indomitable Courage . . . " 265

Pacific : The Pacific War Area 336
Three-fold Map in full colours

Tanks : Four Leading Examples of British Tanks 432

How Tanks are Repaired in the Field .. 433

TABLE OF PRINCIPAL ARTICLES

In order to show the scope and variety of this Volume we present an ordered list of some 100 main articles out of a total exceeding 1,270. The actual titles of these articles as printed in the pages are given. See the end pages of this volume for a Classified Index and READER'S GUIDE to the WAR SUPPLEMENT

THE FIGHTING FRONTS

	PAGE
How the Abyssinian Empire was Reconquered	4
The Tragedy of the Balkan Countries	34
The Baltic States were Twice Invaded	36
Overrun by Nazi Hordes Belgium Falls	39
The Japanese Invasion of Burma	57
China's Stand Against Japanese Aggression	68
Strange and Grim Battle of Crete	83
Dunkirk, the Great Evacuation	97
Ending the Italian Empire in East Africa	99
Finland's Fight Against Russian Invasion	111
The Catastrophic Fall of France	120
The Glory that is Greece Today	162
Hongkong Held Out to the Last	178
Iraq, How the Axis was Forestalled	189
Java and the Battle of the Java Sea	204
How Malaya Fell to the Japanese	244
Total War Overwhelms the Netherlands	301
The Tragic Defence of the Dutch Indies	305
Ebb and Flow of the Libyan Desert War	312
Norway Under the German Heel	321
Why Japan Made the Pacific a Battlefield	332
How War Flared Up in the Pacifi	333
The Philippines Caught in the Tide of War	348
Poland, a Small Nation that Became Great	353
The German Onslaught against Russia	390
Singapore Fought On Till the End	407
Syria Was Swiftly Freed from Axis Control	426
For Two Hundred Days Tobruk Held Out	435

THE LAND FORCES

	PAGE
How the British Army is Organized and Trained	22
Commando Troops: Work and Successes	79
Gliders in Warfare	140
Home Guard: Britain's Part-time Army	176
Power of the Modern Mechanized Army	259
Parachute Troops: Their Training	338
The Development of Tank Warfare	429

WAR IN THE AIR

	PAGE
Aircraft in the Second World War	7
How Britain Thwarts the Luftwaffe	11
Modern Methods of Fighting in the Air	13
France : War in the Air	126
British Raids on Germany	137
How the Air Battle of Britain was Won	157
The Story of the Battle of London	232
Britain's Unconquerable Air Force	379

WAR AT SEA

	PAGE
Strategy of the Mediterranean Battle Front	263
Britain Wages War in the Middle Sea	264
The Merchant Navy's Part in the War	271
The Navy Magnificently Fulfils its Tasks	294
German Attempt to Control the North Sea	320
How War Flared Up in the Pacific	333
Ruthless War Under the Seven Seas	420
U-Boats and Their Deadly Work	441

SHIPPING WAR & THE BLOCKADE

	PAGE
Waging the Battle of the Atlantic	25
Convoys and Their Duties	80
Britain's Economic War against Her Foes	102
Britain Wages War in the Middle Sea	264

	PAGE
The Merchant Navy's Part in the War	271
German Attempt to Control the North Sea	320
Oil, Vital Need of Mechanized War	327
Rubber, World Supplies & World Problems	385
Ruthless War Under the Seven Seas	420

THE HOME FRONT

	PAGE
Britain's Civil Defence Goes into Action	74
How Britain Fought Nazi Fire Bombs	113
Feeding Great Britain in Wartime	117
Great Britain in the Second World War	145
Home Guard, Britain's Part-time Army	176
Britain's Mighty Output of Munitions	286
Northern Ireland	319
The Police : in War	357
The Function of Propaganda in Wartime	362
Red Cross Society	369
Scotland in the War	402
Women Answer the Challenge of War	461

THE EMPIRE AT WAR

	PAGE
Australia's Great Part in the War	29
How the Crown Colonies Answered the Call	52
Japanese Invasion of Burma	57
Canada's Contribution to the War	62
Ceylon : Gateway to Southern India	66
Gibraltar : Key to the Mediterranean	139
Hongkong Held Out to the Last	178
India's Difficult Role in World War	183
How Malaya Fell to the Japanese	244
Malta : British Bastion in the Mediterranean	249
New Zealand Fights for Empire and Liberty	310
Rhodesia	372
South Africa's Contribution to the War	412

THE ALLIED & UNITED NATIONS

	PAGE
Free Belgium	42
China's Stand against Japanese Aggression	68
The Tragedy of the Czech People	88
French Equatorial Africa	107
Free and Fighting France	126
Life in Occupied and Unoccupied France	127
Great Britain in the Second World War	145
The Glory that is Greece Today	162
Mexico	275
The Free Netherlands	304
Free Norway	325
Free Poland	356
Policy of Soviet Russia : Russia's Armed Strength	388
America Joins in the Fight for Freedom	443
Key to the War Situation in West Africa	457
Free Yugoslavia	470
See also The Empire at War	

THE AXIS AND ITS ALLIES

	PAGE
Bulgaria	56
Germany Wars against the World	132
Hungary	181
Indo-China	188
Shameful Chapter in the Story of Italy	191
War-Lords of Japan Emulate the Nazis	197
Rumania	386
Siam	404
Vichy Laid France under the German Heel	451

LIST OF MAPS, CHARTS AND PLANS
IN THIS VOLUME

	PAGE
Abyssinian Frontiers, before and after the Italian conquest of 1936	5
Adriatic Sea and its marginal coastlines	7
Air Defence : Chart	12
Alaska Road	15
Albania, Greek advance, 1940	15
Atlantic : War Zones barred to U.S. shipping	26
Atlantic : Shipping Losses, 1939–1941, Chart	27
Australia : Central Area	31
Balkans : German drive to Greece and Black Sea	35
Baltic States : German advance through Lithuania	37
Belgium : Disposition of German and Allied Forces, May 1940	40
Berlin : Military objectives for R.A.F.	44
Black Sea : Strategic ports	46
Bulgaria : Territorial claims on Greece and Rumania	56
Burma and her frontiers	58
Burma Road	59
Caucasia : Oilfields and pipelines	65
China : Areas of Japanese aggression	69
Crete : The Allied defence	83
Crimea	85
Cyprus	87
Dunkirk : Perimeter and B.E.F. withdrawal	97
Egypt : In relation to Libya and Levant	103
Europe and the Middle East Colour map f.p.	104
Finland : Invaded by Russia at eight points	112
France : German thrusts, May–June 1940	122
„ Occupied and Unoccupied	127
Germany : R.A.F. targets	138
Gibraltar	139
Great Britain : Battle of, first phase	157
„ „ „ „ second phase	158
Greece : Retreat of Imperial troops, April 1941	162
Guam : Importance as U.S. Pacific base	166
Hawaii : Strategic position	171
Hawaiian Islands : Pearl Harbour and Honolulu	172
Hongkong	178
India and Burma	186
Indo-China : Territory ceded to Siam, 1940	188

	PAGE
Italy : R.A.F. targets	196
Java : Communications, aerodromes and oilfields	206
Maastricht : Key town on R. Meuse	241
Maginot and Siegfried Lines	243
Malaya : Japanese thrusts	245
Malta : Strategic importance in Mediterranean	249
Matapan : British and Italian Fleets	257
Mediterranean Sea : Axis supply routes	263
Middle East, Axis controlled countries	276
„ „ Caucasian and Middle East oilfields	328
„ „ „ Colour map f.p.	104
Moscow and its environs	285
Murmansk : Arctic port	289
Netherlands : German points of attack and defensive lines	301
New Guinea : Dutch and British, 1942	309
North Africa : British and Axis campaigns, 1940–42	315
Norway, North : Fighting areas April-May 1940	322
„ South : Mined coastal areas	323
Oran	329
Pacific War Area Colour map f.p.	336
Pearl Harbour	172, 343
Persia : and Iraq frontiers	345
Philippines : Japanese attacks	349
„ Corregidor and Manila Bay	349
Plate, River, Battle of : Graf Spee tracked down	352
Poland : Main German thrusts, 1939	354
Rotterdam : Areas of devastation, 1940	378
Russia : German advance, July 1941	391
„ „ „ Aug. 1941	392
„ Leningrad-Murmansk front	396
„ Leningrad-Crimea front, 1941–42	397
„ Russian line, March 1942 Colour map f.p.	104
„ Urals and Ukraine industrial areas	449
Siam : General map	404
Singapore : Strategic points	408
Syria : Allied advance, 1941	428
Taranto, Battle of : 1940	431
Tobruk : Line of British advance	436
West Africa, French	458
Yugoslavia : Axis partitioning	469

VARIOUS TABLES AND CHRONOLOGIES

	PAGE
Abbreviations in the Four Services	2–4
Abyssinia : British and Italian Advances	4
Armies : Strength of, at Outset of War	22
British Army : Campaigns and Operations	24
Atlantic, Battle of : Important Incidents	26
„ „ „ Losses in Shipping	27
Bomber Command : Operations	47
Canada : War Effort	63
Coastal Command : Operations	78
Cost of the War	82
Fighter Command : Operations	110
France in the War—A Diary of Main Events	124
George Cross and Medal : Awards	132
Gibraltar : Main Events, 1940–42	140
Great Britain at War : Select Chronology	153–156, 469–740
Battle of Britain : The Big Days	158

	PAGE
Great Britain : Main Raids on Towns and Districts	161
„ „ Civilian Air Raid Casualties	161
London : Targets of Air Raiders	234
Merchant Navy : Shipping Balance Sheet	273
„ „ Allied Mercantile Marines	274
Navies : Approximate Net Strengths of the Leading Navies of the Allies and the Axis, 1941	294
„ The Allied Navies, 1941	294
Navy, Royal : Ships at Sept. 1939 with Losses to May 1942	299
Navy, Royal : British Warships Lost to May 1942	300
Royal Air Force : Attacks on Occupied Territory	383
Submarines : British Losses, 1940–42	422
Tanks : Four British Types	430
U.S.A. : Principal Types of Aircraft	446
Yugoslavia : Its Break-up by the Axis	469

Aaland Islands. Archipelago of some 300 islands at the entrance to the Gulf of Bothnia, forming one of the most important strategic points in the Baltic. They have belonged to Finland since 1921, and by an international convention remained unfortified. After the crisis of 1938 it was rumoured that the Finns had begun the work of fortification, but it was not until Dec. 4, 1939, that the Government announced its decision to do this. At the end of the Soviet-Finnish war they were demobilized and demilitarized by the terms of an agreement ratified Oct. 12, 1940. *See* Finland.

Aalborg. Seaport and city of Jutland, Denmark. It stands on the Lijm Fjord, 156 m. by sea from Copenhagen. After the occupation of Denmark by the Nazis, April 9, 1940, Aalborg was used as an air base for the campaign in Norway. The R.A.F. caused much damage to the aerodrome by a surprise attack on April 21, 1940.

Aandalsnes. This small town of Norway, on Romsdal Fjord, 120 m. S.W. of Trondheim, became a strategic centre during the Allied expedition to Norway. It is connected by railway to Dombaas, on the main line from Oslo to Trondheim. Within a week of the German invasion of Norway on April 9, 1940, British and French troops were being landed at various points on the western coast. Aandalsnes was occupied by a British naval force on April 17, and troops were landed on April 18 and 19, and advanced towards Dombaas. On May 2 it was announced that all British forces south of Trondheim had been evacuated from Aandalsnes without loss. *See* Norway.

Abadan. An important oil centre (Anglo-Iranian Oil Co.) at the head of the Persian Gulf, which was occupied by British and Indian troops from Basra with British naval and air cooperation on August 26, 1941. *See* Persia.

Abbeville. This historic town of Northern France stands on the R. Somme, 28 m. N.W. of Amiens. It was ruthlessly bombed by the enemy before German forces occupied the area on May 23, 1940. French troops recaptured the western part on May 31, but it was lost again in the new German offensive of June 5. After the Nazi occupation the aerodrome was heavily attacked by the R.A.F. on many occasions.

AANDALSNES EARLY SUFFERS THE MISFORTUNES OF WAR

This little town of Norway had an unwelcome taste of what war means when, for strategic reasons, it was chosen as a landing port for British troops coming to the aid of the Norwegians on April 17, 1940. When the expedition had to be recalled, Mr. Churchill announced that our forces were withdrawn "under the very noses of the German aeroplanes, without the loss of a single man."

Photo, "Daily Mirror"

ABBREVIATIONS USED BY THE FOUR SERVICES

The Royal Navy

A.—Admiral.
A1—First-class at Lloyd's.
A.B.—Able-bodied Seaman.
A.C.N.S.—Assistant Chief of Naval Staff.
A.F.—Admiral of the Fleet.
A.G.R.M.—Adjutant-General, Royal Marines.
A.M.C.—Armed Merchant Cruiser.
A.P.—Armour Piercing.
A.P.S.L.—Acting Paymaster Sub-Lieutenant.
A.S.L.—Acting Sub-Lieutenant.
B.—Boatswain.
C.—Captain.
Cd. R.M.G.—Commissioned Royal Marine Gunner.
Cd. S.B.—Commissioned Signals Boatswain.
Cd. S.O.—Commissioned Supply Officer.
Ch.—Chaplain.
Ch. of F.—Chaplain of the Fleet.
C.I.—Chief Inspector, Royal Marine Police.
C.M.B.—Coastal motor boat.
C.P.O.—Chief Petty Officer.
Cr.—Commander.
C.W.O. Commissioned Officer from Warrant Rank.
D.C.—Depth Charge.
D.C.T.—Depth Charge Thrower.
D.E.D.—Director of Education Department.
D.N.A.D.—Director of Naval Air Division.
D.N.E.—Director of Naval Equipment.
D.N.I.—Director of Naval Intelligence.

D.N.M.S.—Director of Naval Medical Services, R.A.N.
D.N.R.—Director of Naval Recruiting.
D.O.D.—Director of Operations Division.
D.O.T.M.—Director of Naval Ordnance, Torpedoes and Mines, R.A.N.
D. of N.—Director of Navigation.
D. of P. D.—Director of Plans Division.
D. of T. B.—Director of Tactical Division.
D.P.S.—Director of Personal Services.
D.P.T.S.—Director of Physical Training and Sports.
D.T.S.D.—Director of Training and Staff Duties Division.
D.Y.—Dockyard.
E.A.—Engineer Rear-Admiral.
E.C.—Engineer Captain.
E.D.—Education Department.
E. in C.—Engineer-in-Chief of the Fleet.
E.L.—Engineer Lieutenant.
E.L.Cr.—Engineer Lieutenant-Commander.
E. V. A.—Engineer Vice-Admiral.
G.S.P.—Good Service Pension.
H.S.—Hospital Ship.
I.D.C.—Imperial Defence College.
L.—Lieutenant.
L.A.—Lieutenant-at-Arms.
L.Cr.—Lieutenant Commander.
M.D.—Medical Dept. or Mine Depot.

M.D.G.—Medical Director-General of the Navy.
Mid.—Midshipman.
M.L.—Minelayer.
Mon.—Monitor.
M.T.B.—Motor Torpedo Boat.
M.V.—Motor Vessel.
N.A.A.F.I.—Navy, Army, and Air Force Institutes.
N.A.D.—Naval Air Division.
N.E.D.—Naval Equipment Dept.
N.I.D.—Naval Intelligence Division.
N.O.D.—Naval Ordnance Dept.
N.P.C.—Naval Personnel Committee.
N.R.D.—Naval Recruiting Dept.
N.Z.D.—New Zealand Division.
O.D.—Operations Division.
O.L.—Ordnance Lieutenant.
O.L.Cr.—Ordnance Lieutenant-Commander.
P. Boat.—Patrol boat.
P.C.—Paymaster Captain.
P. Cr.—Paymaster Commander.
P.D.—Plans Division.
P.D.G.—Paymaster Director-General.
P.L.—Paymaster Lieutenant.
P.O.—Petty Officer.
P.R.A.—Paymaster Rear-Admiral.
P.S.L.—Paymaster Sub-Lieutenant.
R.A.—Rear-Admiral.
R.A.N.—Royal Australian Navy.
R.C.N.—Royal Canadian Navy.

R.G.B.—River gunboat.
R.I.M.—Royal Indian Marine.
R.M.—Royal Marines.
R.M.O.—Royal Marine Office.
R.M.P.—R. Marine Police.
R.S.M.S.—Rendering Safe of Mines Squads.
S.A.N.S.—South African Naval Service.
S.B.—Signal Boatswain.
S.D.—Signal Dept.
Sg. C.—Surgeon Captain.
Sg. L. Cr.—Surgeon Lieutenant Commander.
Sg. R. A.—Surgeon Rear-Admiral.
Sh. L.—Shipwright Lieut.
S.H.P.—Shaft Horse Power.
Sig. L.—Signal Lieutenant.
S.L.—Sub-Lieutenant or Searchlight.
S.R.E.—Scientific Research and Experiments Dept.
T.D.—Tactical Division or Torpedo Depot.
T.L.—Telegraphist Lieutenant.
T.M.D.—Torpedo and Mining Dept.
T.S.—Training Ship.
T.T.—Torpedo Tubes.
V.A.—Vice-Admiral.
V.Y.—Victualling Yard.
Wdr. L.—Wardmaster Lieutenant.
W.O.O.—Warrant Ordnance Officer.
W.R.N.S.—Women's Royal Naval Service.
W.T.—Warrant Telegraphist.
W.W.—Warrant Writer.
W. Wdr.—Warrant Wardmaster.

The Royal Air Force and the Women's Auxiliary Air Force

A.A.F.—Auxiliary Air Force.
A.A.F.R.O.—Auxiliary Air Force Reserve of Officers.
AC—Aircraftman (followed by 1 or 2 to denote class).
A.C.A.S.—Assistant Chief of the Air Staff.
Ach—Aircrafthand.
A.C.M.—Air Chief Marshal.
A.Ct.—Air Commandant (W.A.A.F.).
Air Cdre.—Air Commodore.
A.M.—Air Marshal.
A.O.C.—Air Officer Commanding.
A.O.C.-in-C.—Air Officer Commanding-in-Chief.
A.P/O.—Acting Pilot Officer.
A.S.I.—Air Speed Indicator.
A.S.O.—Assistant Section Officer (with W.A.A.F.).
A/SRS.—Air Sea Rescue Service.
A.T.—Anti-tank.
A.T.C.—Air Training Corps.
A.V.M.—Air Vice Marshal.
(B.)—Balloon Branch Officer.
C.A.S.—Chief of Air Staff.
Ch.—Chaplain.
Cpl.—Corporal.
C.T.T.B.—Central Trade Test Board.
(D.)—Dental Branch Officer.
D.B. Ops.—Director of Bomber Operations.
D.C.A.S.—Deputy Chief of the Air Staff.
D.E.S.—Director of Educational Services.
D.F. Ops.—Director of Fighter Operations.
D.G.C.A.—Director-General of Civil Aviation.
D.G.D.—Director of Ground Defence.
D.G.E.—Director-General of Equipment.

D.G.M.S.—Director-General of R.A.F. Medical Service.
D.G.O.—Director-General of Organization.
D.G.S.—Director-General of Signals.
D.M.C.—Director of Military Cooperation.
D.M.O.—Director of the Meteorological Office.
D. of A.—Director of Accounts.
D. of I. (O.).—Director of Intelligence (Operations).
D. of I. (S.).—Director of Intelligence (Security).
D. of M.—Director of Manning.
D. of O.—Director of Organization.
D. of R.—Director of Radio.
D. of S.—Director of Signals.
D. of Tels.—Director of Telecommunication.
D.O.N.C.—Director of Operations (Naval Cooperation).
D.O.O.—Director of Operations (Overseas).
D.P.R.—Director of Public Relations.
D.P.S.—Director of Personal Services.
D.S.M.—Director of Servicing and Maintenance.
D.T.F.—Director of Flying Training.
D.T.O.—Director of Operational Training.
D.T.T.—Director of Technical Training.
D.U.S.—Deputy Under-Secretary of State.
D.W.A.A.F.—Director of the Women's Auxiliary Air Force.

(E.).—Equipment Branch Officer.
E.F.T.S.—Elementary Flying Training School.
E.O.—Education Officer.
F/Lt.—Flight Lieutenant.
F/O.—Flight Officer (W.A.A.F.).
F/O.—Flying Officer.
F/Sgt.—Flight Sergeant.
(G.).—Air Gunner-Officer.
G/C.—Group Captain.
G.O.C. (-in-C.).—General Officer Commanding (-in-Chief).
(I.).—Intelligence Officer.
(I.A.F.).—Indian Air Force Officer.
I. of R.—Inspector of Recruiting.
I.T.W.—Initial Training Wing.
J.A.G.—Judge Advocate-General of the Forces.
(L.)—Legal Branch Officer.
LAC—Leading Aircraftman.
L. of C.—Line of Communication.
L./T.—Line Telegraphy.
(M.)—Medical Branch Officer.
(Mc.)—Marine Craft Officer.
M.D.S.—Main Dressing Station.
(Met.)—Meteorological.
M.L.O.—Military Landing Officer.
M.R.A.F.—Marshal of the Royal Air Force.
(N.)—Navigation Instructor Officer.
N.T.O.—Naval Transport Officer.
(O.)—Observer Officer.
O.T.U.—Operational Training Unit.
P.A.S.—Principal Assistant Secretary.

P. Det.—Port Detachment.
(Ph.)—Photographic Officer.
(P.M.)—Provost Marshal Duties Officer.
P.M.R.A.F.N.S.—Princess Mary's R.A.F. Nursing Service.
P/O.—Pilot Officer.
P.R.O.—Public Relations Officer.
(P.T.)—Physical Training Officer.
P.U.S.—Permanent Under-Secretary of State.
R.A.A.F.—Royal Australian Air Force.
R.A.F.O.—Reserve of Air Force Officers.
R.A.F.V.R.—Royal Air Force Volunteer Reserve.
R.C.A.F.—Royal Canadian Air Force.
R.N.Z.A.F.—Royal New Zealand Air Force.
S.A.S.O.—Senior Air Staff Officer.
S.F.T.S.—Service Flying Training Squadron.
Sgt.—Sergeant.
S.I.O.—Senior Intelligence Officer.
S/Ldr.—Squadron Leader.
S.O.—Section Officer (W.A.A.F.).
S. of S.—Secretary of State.
S.P.—Service Police.
Sq.O.—Squadron Officer (W.A.A.F.).
V.C.A.S.—Vice-Chief of the Air Staff.
W.A.A.F.—Women's Auxiliary Air Force.
Wg.Cr.—Wing-Commander.
Wg. O.—Wing Officer (W.A.A.F.).
W.O.—Warrant Officer.

ABBREVIATIONS USED BY THE FOUR SERVICES

The Army

A.A.—Anti-Aircraft or Army Act.
A.A.C.—Army Air Corps.
A.A.G.—Assistant Adjutant-General.
A.A.L.M.G.—Anti-Aircraft Light Machine-Gun.
A.B.—Armoured Brigade.
A.C.C.—Army Catering Corps.
A.C.I.—Army Council Instruction.
A.D.—Air Defence or Armoured Division.
A.D.C.—Aide-de-Camp or Army Dental Corps.
Adjt.—Adjutant.
A.D.O.S.—Assistant Director of Ordnance Services.
A.D.R.—Assistant Director of Remounts.
A.D.S.—Advanced Dressing-Station.
A.E.C.—Army Educational Corps.
A.F.—Army Form.
A.F.V.—Armoured Fighting Vehicle.
A.G. & Q.M.G.—Adjutant-General and Quarter-master-General.
A. gas.—Anti-Gas.
A.I.L.O.—Air Intelligence Liaison Officer.
Air O.P.—Air Observation Post.
A.L.G.—Advanced Landing Ground.
A.L.O.—Air Liaison Officer.
A.M.G.O.—Assistant Master-General of Ordnance.
A.M.P.C.—Auxiliary Military Pioneer Corps.
A.O.—Army Order.
A.O C.—Air Officer Commanding.
A.P.—Ammunition Point or Armour Piercing.
A.P.M.—Assistant Provost Marshal.
A.P.S.—Army Postal Service.
A.P.S.S.—Army Printing and Stationery Services.
A.Q.M.G.—Assistant Quartermaster-General.
A.R.H.—Ammunition Railhead.
A.R.O.—Army Routine Order.
A.R.P.—Ammunition Refilling Point.
A.T.B.—Army Tank Brigade.
A.T. Coy.—Animal Transport Coy.
A.tk.—Anti-Tank.
A.T.S.—Auxiliary Territorial Service (Women's).
B.C.—Battery Commander.
B.M.—Brigade Major.
B.P.O.—Base Post Office.
B.Q.M.S.—Battery Quartermaster Sergeant.
B.S.M.—Battery Sergeant-Major.
C.B.—Counter-Battery or Confinement in Barracks.
C.B.O.—Counter-Battery Officer.
C.C.S.—Casualty Clearing Station.
C.F.—Chaplain to the Forces.
C.G.S.—Chief of General Staff.
C.I.G.S.—Chief of the Imperial General Staff.
C.-in-C.—Commander-in-Chief.

C.O.—Commanding Officer.
C.O.M.E.—Chief Ordnance Mechanical Engineer.
C.O.O.—Chief Ordnance Officer.
C.Q.M.S.—Company Quartermaster Sergeant.
C.R.A.—Commander Royal Artillery.
C.R.E.—Commander Royal Engineers.
C.R.O.—Corps Routine Order.
C.S.M.—Company Sergeant-Major.
D.A.A.G.—Deputy Assistant Adjutant-General.
D.A. & Q.M.G.—Deputy Adjutant and Quarter-master-General.
D.A.C.G.—Deputy Assistant Chaplain-General.
D.A.D.O.S.—Deputy Assistant Director of Ordnance Services.
D.A.M.G.O.—Deputy Assistant Master-General of the Ordnance.
D.A.P.M.—Deputy Assistant Provost Marshal.
D.A.Q.M.G.—Deputy Assistant Quartermaster-General.
D.C.M.—District Court-Martial.
D.D.M.I.—Deputy Director of Military Intelligence.
D.D.M.S.—Deputy Director Medical Services.
Decn.—Decontamination.
D.E.S.—Director of Engineer Stores Service.
D.F.—Direction Finding.
D.F.W.—Director of Fortifications and Works.
D.G.A.M.S. — Director-General of Army Medical Services.
D.G.R.—Director of Graves Registration.
D.H.—Director of Hygiene.
D.I.W.T.—Director of Inland Water Transport Service.
D.M.—Director of Mechanization.
D.M.I.—Director of Military Intelligence.
D.M.Q.—Director of Movements and Quartering.
D.M.S.—Director of Medical Services.
D.M.T.—Director of Military Training.
D.O.S.—Director of Ordnance Services.
D.P.S.—Director of Personal Services, or Director of Postal Services.
D.R.L.S.—Dispatch Rider Letter Service.
D.S.D.—Director of Staff Duties.
D.S.T.—Director of Supplies and Transport.
E.M.O.—Embarkation Medical Officer.
E.S.O.—Embarkation Staff Officer.
F.G.C.M.—Field General Court-Martial.
F.M.—Field-Marshal.
F.O.O.—Forward Observation Officer.
F.S.—Field Service.
F.S.R.—Field Service Regulations.

Fus.—Fusilier.
G.A.—Garrison Adjutant.
G.C.M.—General Court-Martial.
G.O.C.-in-C. — General Officer Commanding-in-Chief.
G.R.O.—General Routine Order.
G.S.—General Service or General Staff.
G.S.M.—Garrison Sergeant-Major.
G.S.O.—General Staff Officer.
H.D.—Horse Drawn.
H.E.—High Explosive or Horizontal Equivalent.
H.Q.—Headquarters.
H.T.—Horsed Transport.
I.A.—Indian Army.
I.M.S.—Indian Medical Service.
Int. Corps.—Intelligence Corps.
I.O.—Intelligence Officer.
I.O.O.—Inspecting Ordnance Officer.
I.T.C.—Infantry Training Centre.
I.W.T.—Inland Water Transport.
J.A.G.—Judge Advocate-General.
K.H.C.—Honorary Chaplain to the King.
L.A.D.—Light Aid Detachment.
L.M.G.—Light Machine-Gun.
L.O.—Liaison Officer.
L. of C.—Line of Communications.
L/T.—Line Telegraphy.
M.A.C.—Motor Ambulance Convoy.
M.C.—Motor Cycle or Movement Control.
M.C.O.—Movement Control Officer.
M.D.S.—Main Dressing Station.
M.F.O.—Military Forwarding Officer.
M.F.W.—Military Foreman of Works.
M.L.O.—Military Landing Officer.
M.O.—Medical Officer.
Mob. B.U.—Mobile Bath Unit.
M.P.—Meeting Point or Military Police.
M.S.—Military Secretary.
M.T.—Mechanical Transport or Motor Transport.
N.C.C.—Non-Combatant Corps.
N.C.O.—Non-Commissioned Officer.
N.S.O.—Naval Staff Officer.
O.C.—Officer Commanding.
O.C.T.U.—Officer Cadet Training Unit.
O.M.E.—Ordnance Mechanical Engineer.
O.O.—Operation Order.
O.P.—Observation Post.
O.R.—Other ranks.
O.T.C.—Officers' Training Corps.
P.A.D.—Passive Air Defence.
P.M.—Provost Marshal.
Pnr. Corps.—Pioneer Corps.
P.O.—Post Office.
P.P.—Petrol Point.
P.R.H.—Petrol Rail Head.
P.R.P.—Petrol Refilling Point.

P.S.S.—Printing and Stationery Service.
P.W.—Prisoners of War.
Q.A.I.M.N.S.—Queen Alexandra's Imperial Military Nursing Service.
Q.M.—Quartermaster.
Q.M.G.—Quartermaster-General to the Forces.
Q.M.S.—Quartermaster-Sergeant.
R.A.—Royal Artillery.
R.A.C.—Royal Armoured Corps.
R.A.Ch.D.—Royal Army Chaplains' Department.
R.A.M.C.—Royal Army Medical Corps.
R.A.O.C.—Royal Army Ordnance Corps.
R.A.P.—Regimental Aid Post.
R.A.P.C.—Royal Army Pay Corps.
R.A.S.C.—Royal Army Service Corps.
R.A.V.C.—Royal Army Veterinary Corps.
R.C.M.—Regimental Corporal-Major (Household Cavalry).
R.E.—Royal Engineers.
Recce Corps. — Reconnaissance Corps.
R.E.M.E.—Royal Electrical and Mechanical Engineers.
R.F.—Representative Fraction or Range Finder.
R.O.—Routine Order.
R.O.O.—Railhead Ordnance Officer.
R.P.—Refilling Point or Rules of Procedure.
R.Q.M.C.—Regimental Quartermaster-Corporal (Household Cavalry).
R.Q.M.S.—Regimental Quartermaster-Sergeant.
R.S.M.—Regimental Sergeant-Major.
R/T.—Radio-Telephony.
R.T.O.—Railway Transport Officer.
R.V.—Rendezvous.
R.W.—Royal Warrant for Pay and Promotion.
S.A.A.—Small Arms Ammunition.
S.C.—Staff Captain.
S.L.—Searchlight.
S.M.—Sergeant-Major.
S.P.—Starting Point.
S.Q.M.S.—Staff Quartermaster-Sergeant.
S.R.H.—Supply Railhead.
S.R.P.—Supply Refilling Point.
S.S.M.—Staff Sergeant-Major.
T.A.—Territorial Army.
T.A.N.S.—Territorial Army Nursing Service.
T.C.P.—Traffic Control Post.
T.D.—Tractor Drawn, or Territorial Decoration.
Tks.—Tanks.
T.O.—Transport Officer.
T.P.M.—Teleprint Message.
V.E.S.—Veterinary Evacuating Station.
V.I.—Vertical Interval.
V.O.—Veterinary Officer.
V.P.—Vulnerable Point.
V/T.—Visual Telegraphy.
W.D.—War Department.
W.E.—War Establishment.
Wksp.—Workshop.
W/T.—Wireless Telegraphy.

Home Defence and General

A.—Ambulance.
A.F.S.—Auxiliary Fire Service.
A.M.—Air Ministry.
A.R.P.—Air Raid Precautions.
A.R.W.—Air Raid Warden.

Aux. F.S.—Auxiliary Fire Station.
B.B.C.—Bromo-benzyl-cyanide (gas) or British Broadcasting Corpn.
B.D.—Bomb Disposal.
B.T.—Board of Trade.

C.A.P.—Chlor-acetone-phenone (gas).
C.D.—Civil Defence.
C.D.V.—Civil Defence Volunteers.
C.N.R.—Civil Nursing Reserve.

D.C.—Decontamination.
E.M.S.—Emergency Medical Service.
E.N.S.A.—Entertainments National Service Association.
F.—Auxiliary Fire Station.

[Continued in page 4]

F.A.N.Y.—First Aid Nursing Yeomanry.
F.A.P.—First Aid Post (or Party).
H.G.—Home Guard.
H.O.—Home Office.
M.A.P.—Ministry of Aircraft Production or Medical Aid Post.
M.E.W.—Ministry of Economic Warfare.
M.H. or M.O.H.—Ministry of Health.
M.O.F.—Ministry of Food.
M.O.I.—Ministry of Information.
M.O.P.—Ministry of Production.
M.O.S.—Ministry of Supply.
M.U.—Mobile Unit.
M.W.P.—Ministry of Works and Planning.
N.A.A.F.I. — Navy, Army and Air Force Institutes.
N.A.C.D.—National Association for Civil Defence.
N.D.C.—National Defence Corps or Contribution.

N.F.S.—National Fire Service.
Q.M.—Queen's Messengers.
R.C.—Red Cross.
R.O.C.—Royal Observer Corps.
R.P.—Rescue Party.
RP/H.—Repairs Heavy (or L. Light).
R.S.D.—Rescue Service and Demolition.
S.B.—Stretcher Bearer.
S.P.—Stretcher Party.
S.R.O.—Senior Rescue Officer.
S.W.—Shelter Warden.
V.A.D.—Voluntary Aid Detachment.
W.—Warden.
W.D.—War Department.
W.I.—Women's Institute.
W.L.A.—Women's Land Army.
W.O.—War Office.
W.R.—War Reserve (Police).
W.V.S.—Women's Voluntary Services.

A.B.C.D. Powers. Popular contraction indicating the four great anti-Axis countries—America, Britain, China, Dutch East Indies, particularly referring to the front against the Axis in the Far Eastern Areas before the Japanese occupation of the East Indies.

A.B.D.A. Area. Contraction indicating S.W. Pacific region in which U.S., British, Dutch and Australian interests predominated at the beginning of 1942. In Feb. 1942, Adm. Hart was appointed to command combined naval forces in this area, but on March 3, it was announced that the A.B.D.A. head-quarters in Java had been dissolved, and that henceforth control in this region would be governed by the changing military situation.

Abdul Ilah, EMIR. Regent of Iraq ; uncle of King Feisal II. In April 1941, while absent from Baghdad, he was deposed by Rashid Ali, politician with pro-Nazi sympathies, and took refuge in Transjordan. After the revolt had been put down by British intervention in Iraq (*q.v.*), Abdul Ilah was reinstated and returned to Baghdad on June 1, 1941.

Abetz, OTTO. He was a protégé of von Ribbentrop, and had been expelled from France in 1939 for subversive activities. After the fall of France he was employed by the German High Command in the Occupied area. On Aug. 5, 1940, it was announced that Abetz had been appointed Hitler's representa-

Otto Abetz, Nazi Envoy in Paris.

tive in Paris. In Marshal Pétain's negotiations with Germany the German Foreign Office insisted that all contacts between the two Governments must be made through Abetz, a supporter of Laval.

Abrial, VICE-ADMIRAL JEAN MARIE CHARLES. Before the war he was Commander of the French Fleet in the Mediterranean. He was appointed to the French Northern Command in December 1939. In charge of the French naval forces based on Dunkirk, he assisted in the evacuation of the B.E.F., and in recognition was made an honorary K.C.B. He was appointed C.-in-C. French (Vichy) Navy in Nov. 1942.

HOW THE ABYSSINIAN EMPIRE WAS RECONQUERED

In 1936, after a year of ruthless warfare, Italy annexed Abyssinia. Five years later Mussolini's armies were driven out by British and native Patriot forces, and the Emperor Haile Selassie re-entered his capital in triumph. See also Addis Ababa ; East Africa ; Gondar, etc.

Abyssinia. The Italian conquest of Abyssinia in 1935–36 was popular with all Italy. It promised land to the landless, raw materials to the industrialist. Italians in quest of a decent standard of living had had to migrate to other lands. Mussolini, himself a peasant of land-starved Romagna, dreamed of great migrations within a resuscitated Roman Empire. The victorious Abyssinian campaign explains Mussolini's hold upon his people ; the reconquest of Abyssinia by Great Britain may well be a major factor in his fall from power.

After rather more than five years of exile the Emperor Haile Selassie re-entered his capital, Addis Ababa, on May 5, 1941. The campaign which culminated, but did not actually end, with this triumphal return was short. It was, mainly, a coordinated pursuing action by four armies closing in from the cardinal points of the compass upon Addis Ababa. They were commanded by Lt.-Gen. Sir Alan G. Cunningham. Throughout, the enemy fought upon the defensive, making from strongpoints stout resistance in places, or fell back often in wild disorder.

The central weakness of the Italian position as a defending force lay in the nominal character of the so-called " conquest." The capital, it is true, was in Italian hands, and so, too, were such considerable towns as Metemma, Gallabat, Mogadishu and Dessie. But vast stretches of mountainous and well-nigh

British and Italian Marches Compared
British Advance to Amba Alagi, 1941

Rate of Advance miles/day	Place	Date	Distance miles
	Kismayu	Feb. 14	
	Juba crossed	Feb. 20	
	Brava	Feb. 25	
23 (50)*	Mogadishu	Feb. 25	250
31	Gabre Darre	March 9	370
25	Jijiga	March 17	200
5	Harar	March 26	50
6	Diredawa	March 31	30
	Bridgehead established at Awash	April 3	140
50	Addis Ababa	April 5	110
9	Dessie	April 27	200
7	Amba Alagi	May 19	150
		94 days	1,500 miles

* After crossing Juba

Italian Advance to Addis Ababa, 1935-36

Place	Occupation Date	Distance
Adigrat	Oct. 5, 1935	50 miles
Macalle	Nov. 8, 1935	
L'Amba-Aradam	Feb. 16, 1936	75 miles
Alagi	Feb. 28, 1936	
Quoram	Apr. 6, 1936	
Dessie	Apr. 15, 1936	100 miles
Addis Ababa ..	May 5, 1936	200 miles
	7 months	425 miles

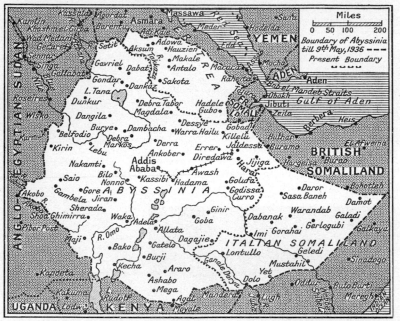

Abyssinian frontiers before and after the Italian conquest of 1936.

inaccessible country remained still under local Rases (chiefs), and the Italian hold, even before hostilities, was precarious and without security for the peasants who had been brought in to found the new Roman Empire in Africa.

Very soon after Italy declared war on Great Britain her troops invaded the Anglo-Egyptian Sudan, British Somaliland and Kenya. She also used Eritrea as the base for naval operations on our vital Red Sea communications. These contingencies had long been foreseen. In the Sudan Abyssinian refugees had been trained into the first modern Abyssinian field force under able British officers. In Kenya a similar, but smaller force had also been prepared. Thus two military units were in readiness to strike back from north and south.

Early in July 1940 a handful of British officers and N.C.O.s had crossed the borders with an important convoy of arms, and after trekking for many weeks through mountainous country and jungle reached their headquarters, some four or five hundred miles within the borders of Ethiopia, where they undertook to train Abyssinian patriots in the use of modern firearms and raise the standard of revolt. All this was accomplished under the very noses of the Italians, who failed to locate them either on the ground or from the air, and little realized that they were harbouring in their midst a hostile army.

More than six months passed. The 60-year-old British colonel in charge of the mission was able to report to the Emperor Haile Selassie that he and his staff had mobilized, trained and equipped an army of Abyssinian natives which was ready to attack the Italians, that the fire of revolt was spreading rapidly, and that the men were only awaiting the presence of their emperor.

On Jan. 24, 1941, the Emperor crossed the border with British and Abyssinian officers and men and with ceremonial and religious ritual unfurled the Royal Standard. By the end of that month drum telegraph had carried the news throughout the land and the

Patriots' revolt had become a scorching flame.

Besides the two armies of north (Patriots and Imperial troops) and south (Patriots and South African troops) two further forces attacked, one from the east and one from the south-east.

The campaign throughout was one of small numbers and of small local actions. There was continuous fighting, but no battles in the sense that Italy was experiencing them as the vanquished in Libya and Greece at this time. Our tactics were to go after the tender spots, that is, oil dumps, airfields and ammunition stores. When a defence was made by the enemy it was always in fortified towns and villages. Such points were kept perpetually under artillery fire, the R.A.F. co-operating from the air.

The Italian Commander-in-Chief, the Duke of Aosta, decided to make his last stand by withdrawing to the Abyssinian Highlands in the hope that the rains of spring would paralyse our advance (see Amba Alagi).

On April 5, 1941, the British entered Addis Ababa, a mere handful of men taking over a capital in which were 6,500 Italian troops. It was the virtual end—although Gondar (q.v.) held out until Nov. 27, 1941—of the Italian dream of an African Roman Empire.

On Jan. 31, 1942, an Agreement and a Military Convention were signed by the British Government and Ethiopia, by which diplomatic relations between the two countries were restored and Britain undertook, among other things, to finance the Emperor to the extent of £2,500,000 during the following two years, and to provide the services of British personnel to help in the restoration of his administration.

Books to Consult. Abyssinia Marches On, G. Harmsworth (Hutchinson). Mussolini's Roman Empire, T. G. Garratt (Penguin).

Achilles, H.M.S. British light cruiser (7,030 tons) belonging to the New Zealand Division. She was completed in 1933 and carries eight 6-in. guns. Commanded by Capt. W. E. Parry (q.v.) and manned chiefly by sailors drawn from New Zealand, she joined with the Ajax and the Exeter in a 14-hour attack on the German

SHE FOUGHT AN OCEAN RAIDER
H.M.S. Achilles, a cruiser of the New Zealand Division, took part in the famous Battle of the Plate against the Graf Spee, and helped to drive her to her doom.
Photo, Central Press

commerce raider, the Admiral Graf Spee, off the coast of Uruguay, Dec. 13, 1939. She received a tumultuous welcome on returning to Auckland, New Zealand, on Feb. 23, 1940. *See* Plate, Battle of.

Achtung ! German noun signifying Beware ! e.g., Achtung, Spitfeuer !—wirelessed from one Nazi pilot to another when engaged by R.A.F. fighters.

Acre. Seaport and town of Palestine. Here, in the Sidney Smith barracks, on July 14, 1941, the Syrian Convention was signed by Gen. Sir Maitland Wilson and Vichy's plenipotentiary, Gen. de Verdillac, the terms of which included the occupation of Syria and the Lebanon by Imperial and Free French forces. *See* Syria.

Adam, GENERAL SIR RONALD FORBES (b. 1887). Adjutant-General to the Forces from May 1941. He

border, the place was occupied by German and Italian forces. El Adem, which controlled east to west communications in the Western Desert south of Tobruk, was the scene of intense fighting between the British 8th Army and the German Afrika Korps during the latter part of November until mid-December 1941. A force of German tanks, estimated at 180, attempting to cut their way to El Adem on Nov. 21, was compelled to retreat towards the coast. Gen. Rommel's forces were repeatedly bombed in the El Adem area by South African and Free French airmen. On Dec. 11 it was announced that S. African and Indian troops had joined hands with the garrison from Tobruk at El Adem. Renewal of the Axis offensive in May 1942 compelled the 8th Army to withdraw on June 13. *See* North Africa.

Aden. An R.A.F. Command was established here in 1928 and was the base for attacks on Italian East Africa in 1940–41. On April 11, 1941, President Roosevelt proclaimed that the Gulf of Aden and the Red Sea were no longer combat zones and that their waters were therefore open to American shipping.

Admiral Graf Spee. German pocket battleship displacing 10,000 tons, belonging to the Deutschland class. She was launched in 1934, had a speed of 26 knots and carried six 11-in. and eight 6-in. guns. From the beginning of the war she preyed on Allied and neutral shipping, and was known to have sunk nine ships, a total of 50,089 tons. They included the Doric Star, a refrigerated meat carrier of 10,086 tons, on her way from New Zealand with a full cargo. All the sinkings took place in the South Atlantic, with the exception of the small tanker Africa Shell, caught off the coast

IGNOMINIOUS END OF THE GRAF SPEE

After a successful career of piracy in the South Atlantic, this German pocket battleship fled from a 14-hour fight with British light cruisers into Montevideo harbour. Three days later she crept out and was scuttled by her commander in the middle of the fairway.

Photo, " Daily Telegraph "

was Deputy-Chief of the Imperial General Staff, 1938–39. In France he commanded the 3rd Corps, and subsequently organized the final Allied defence of the perimeter and bridgehead of Dunkirk. He was appointed G.O.C. Northern Command in June 1940.

Addis Ababa. During the Italo-Abyssinian war the Emperor Haile Selassie (*q.v.*) fled from his capital, Addis Ababa, on May 2, 1936, and it was occupied by the Italians under Marshal Badoglio on May 5. The capital was recaptured by British and Patriot forces on April 7, 1941, and Haile Selassie made a triumphal entry on May 5, the fifth anniversary of its fall. *See* Abyssinia.

Adem, El. Formerly the largest Italian air base in Libya, El Adem was abandoned by the Italians in January 1941 as the result of heavy British bombings. After the fall of Tobruk (Jan. 22) the burnt-out remains of 25 Italian bombers and 43 fighters were found by the British. In April 1941, following the withdrawal of the British towards the Egyptian

of Portuguese East Africa. On Dec. 13, 1939, the Admiral Graf Spee was engaged near the mouth of the River Plate by three British light cruisers, Achilles, Ajax, and Exeter. For fourteen hours she was attacked and was so damaged that she fled into Montevideo harbour. From here on Dec. 17 she steamed out and was scuttled by Hitler's orders in the chief anchorage outside the port, continuing to burn until Dec. 24. Her commander, Capt. Langsdorf (*q.v.*), committed suicide on Dec. 20. *See* Plate, Battle of.

Admiral Scheer. German pocket battleship, with the same tonnage, speed and armament as her sister ship the Admiral Graf Spee. She was notorious as a commerce raider. On April 11, 1940, she was hit by a torpedo from the submarine Spearfish.

Adowa. Capital of the Abyssinian province of Tigre, and chief centre of trade between the interior and the coast. Adowa is famous as the scene of the crushing Italian defeat by the Abyssinians in 1896. The town was taken by the Italians on Oct. 6, 1935.

Adriatic Sea and its marginal coastlines.

during the conquest of Abyssinia, and recaptured by the British on April 5, 1941.

Adriatic Sea. An arm of the Mediterranean, extending N.W. between Italy and Yugoslavia; length, 470 m., breadth, 110 m. The chief ports on the west are Venice, Ancona, Bari and Brindisi; on the east, Trieste, Pola, Fiume, Zara, Ragusa (Dubrovnik), Cattaro, Durazzo and Valona. Italian troops were landed at Durazzo (Albania) on May 8, 1939. During the Italo-Greek war (1940–1941) the chief Italian bases were Durazzo and Valona, until the latter was put out of commission by British naval bombardment and bombing. British naval forces made a sweep of the

Adriatic as far north as Bari and Durazzo on Dec. 18, 1940, but "encountered no enemy shipping."

Advanced Air Striking Force. Name given to R.A.F. squadrons operating from France, 1939–40, and engaged on general flying duties under Air Marshal A. S. Barratt. They were quartered in the neighbourhood of Rheims from October 1939, to May 16, 1940, when they had to move to Central France, and thence, a few days later, to England. *See* Air Component.

Afmadu. Town in Italian Somaliland, 100 m. E. of the Kenya border. After severe bombing raids by the South African Air Force the Italians evacuated the town on Feb. 10, 1941, and fled towards Kismayu. It was occupied by the King's African Rifles on Feb. 11.

Africa. *See* Abyssinia; East Africa; Egypt; Equatorial Africa; North Africa; South Africa; West Africa.

Agheila, El. Village of Cyrenaica, one hundred miles S. of Benghazi. After the British Imperial forces had captured Benghazi from the Italians, Feb. 7, 1941, Gen. Wilson continued his advance to El Agheila, on the edge of the Sirte Desert. On March 24 a German African corps occupied the place. Early in January, 1942, Rommel's retreating forces withdrew from Jedabia towards El Agheila, where they made a stand along the road leading from the village to the oasis of Marada, 40 miles southwards.

Air Component. Section of the R.A.F. in France, engaged in army cooperation work under Lord Gort. It at first consisted of two Army Cooperation Wings, one Fighter Wing and one Bomber Reconnaissance Wing. Other units were added later. One of the main operational aerodromes was at Poix, but about May 15, 1940, this was removed to Abbeville, and after May 22 the Air Component operated from English stations. *See* Advanced Air Striking Force; France, Defeat of.

AIRCRAFT IN THE SECOND WORLD WAR

Some of the bombers and fighters, seaplanes and reconnaissance aircraft, both our own and the enemy's, incessantly waging war on all fronts, are here described and depicted. See also Colour Plate facing page 16.

Aircraft. In considering British aircraft it is fitting to take the fighters first, and pay homage to the famous Vickers Supermarine Spitfire, and the even more versatile Hawker Hurricane, four years old in 1939, but in 1941 granted a new lease of life with "cannon" (shell-guns) or bombs. But it is the eight-gun version of these fighters as used in the Battle of Britain, 1940, that will live in air and world history. The Hawker company had other single-seat fighters in hand. One of these was the Tornado, built round the equally new Rolls-Royce 1,750 h.p. Vulture engine. Two of these engines were fitted to the Avro Manchester, the largest twin-engined bombing aircraft in the world.

When war began the Short Sunderland flying-boat—a type enormously successful for sea patrol—was the only four-engined aircraft in service, but now our long-range bombing fleet is headed by the Short Stirling and the Handley Page Halifax. The Stirling has four Bristol radial engines; the Halifax, four Rolls-Royce liquid-cooled in-line engines. All these bombers,

and the older and smaller Wellingtons and Whitleys, had power-operated gun turrets in nose and tail.

Another aeroplane that will become historic is the Bristol Blenheim, put to all manner of uses as well as its basic duty of a medium bomber. From the same builder came the Beaufort torpedo-bomber of Coastal Command, and the Beaufighter. The latter was used principally for night fighting, its power (some 2,760 h.p.), speed (320 m.p.h. maximum), duration of flight, and armament (four shell-guns and six machine-guns) making it most formidable.

The outstanding Americans were the Lockheed Hudson, the Douglas Boston, probably the world's fastest bomber, and the Consolidated Catalina flying-boat. The Hudsons covered thousands of miles with Coastal Command, escorted hundreds of convoys, and settled the fate of many a U-boat. The Boston was also adapted as a night-fighter under the name of Havoc. The Catalina has the enormous range of four thousand miles with war load. Two other American aircraft were the Grumman Martlet, a

BRITISH BOMBING AND NAVAL AIRCRAFT

Twin-engined bombers are shown in : (1) Armstrong-Whitworth Whitley ; (2) Vickers Wellington ; and (3) Avro Manchester. The Saro Lerwick flying-boat (4), is in service with the Coastal Command. Aircraft used by the Fleet Air Arm are the Vickers Walrus amphibian (5) ; the Fairey Fulmar eight-gun fighter (7) ; the Fairey Albacore torpedo-plane (8) ; and the Grumman Martlet (American) fighter (9). No. 6, the Phillips & Powis Miles Magister, is a training craft.
For other British machines such as the Spitfire, Stirling and Halifax, see Vol. I, pages 42-47; also Plate facing p. 16, this vol.

U.S. MACHINES IN SERVICE WITH THE R.A.F.

Four magnificent single-engined fighter-craft are shown first : (1) Curtiss Tomahawk and (2) Kittyhawk ; (3) Bell Airacobra ; and (4) Brewster Buffalo. Then come the monster four-engined bombers : (5) Boeing Flying Fortress ; and (6) Consolidated Liberator. Of twin-engined bombers we show the Martin Maryland (7) and the Douglas Boston–1 (8). The Consolidated Catalina flying-boat (9) has done splendid work on convoy and anti-submarine duty. No. 10, the Lockheed Hudson, is a powerful reconnaissance aircraft.

Photos, British Official: Crown Copyright; L.N.A.; Central Press; Sport & General; Keystone; E.N.A.; Planet News

BOMBING AIRCRAFT OF RUSSIA AND THE AXIS

The Soviet Stormovik dive-bomber (1) attacks troop concentrations and armoured columns. A Nazi type, used for dive-attack or horizontal bombing, is shown in (3), the Junkers Ju-88. The Messerschmitt Jaguar bomber (2) was much used in the attack on Britain in 1940, while Germany's four-engined Focke-Wulf Kurier (4) did its best to harass our Atlantic shipping. Two Japanese bombers are shown in (5) and (6) : the Mitsubishi-97 heavy bomber, said to have a range of 2,400 miles ; and the Mitsubishi-98-1, a lighter type. A representative Italian twin-engined bomber, the Caproni Ca-135, is shown in (7).

Photos, Photopress; Associated; E.N.A.; Pictorial Press; Topical single-seat fighter flown from aircraft carriers, and the Consolidated Liberator, used first as a transatlantic ferry " ship," but also for coastal and bombing work.

Flying in the sub-stratosphere brought into prominence yet another American bomber—the Boeing Fortress, four-engined, fast, and capable of reaching nearly 40,000 feet, but with a comparatively small bomb load. Against it flew Germany's new single-seat fighter, the ME 109 F. This Messerschmitt was not entirely new, but appeared very different from the earlier ME 109 E. (mainly because of rounded wing tips), had a higher speed (max. about 375 m.p.h.) and, though incorporating less armament, had a shell-gun firing at 900 rounds per minute. The twin-engined ME 110 was the most successful aircraft so far tried by the Luftwaffe.

Another 1939 type was the twin-engined Junkers 88, used extensively as bomber, dive-bomber, fighter and reconnaissance plane. As a twin-engined dive-bomber it marked an advance on the JU 87 that cleared the way for the German armoured divisions.

Like almost all German bombers, the JU 88 relied on speed, and was certainly more effective than the Heinkel 111 and the Dornier bombers, all still in service in large numbers. Standardization of a few easily produced types remained the German policy.

Aircraft Production, Ministry of. This Government Department was established by Mr. Churchill on May 15, 1940, with Lord Beaverbrook as the first Minister. He held office until May 1, 1941, when it was taken over by Lt.-Col. Moore-Brabazon, who on Feb. 22, 1942, gave place to Col. J. J. Llewellin.

HOW BRITAIN THWARTS THE LUFTWAFFE

Measures against air attack include both ground and air defence, and the complex organizations which protect us from enemy bombers are outlined in this article. See also Balloon Barrage ; Civil Defence ; Fighter Command ; Observer Corps ; Royal Air Force, etc.

Air Defence. When war came in September 1939 air defence from the ground was mainly in the hands of Territorial units, who from 1935 had manned anti-aircraft guns and searchlights. These volunteers had taken up the work with enthusiasm. By April 1939 they numbered 96,000 ; in 1936 the first Anti-Aircraft Division had been completed. Through the wet summer of 1939 and the bitter winter that followed, the men of the T.A. Anti-Aircraft formations dug gun-pits, built searchlight sites and erected defensive ramparts. They also put up tents and huts.

All the while the most intense training went on, and when the Battle of Britain in the following summer brought them into action they were ready. During the year 1940 they brought down 444 enemy aircraft, and by the end of 1941 had increased their score to over 600. Mixed batteries were formed, in which women of the Auxiliary Territorial Service took over the duty of operating various directive instruments. They were trained on targets towed by aircraft, and achieved much success. Later the A.T.S. went into action with the gunners. At the end of 1941 the Anti-Aircraft Command was under Lieut.-Gen. Sir Frederick Pile.

After the conquest of the Low Countries and France, Germany had something like 2,000 miles of coastline from which attacks on Britain could be launched ; at the nearest points her aircraft could reach our coasts by a flight lasting about a quarter of an hour, and the most distant point was only some 400 miles away. Thus the enemy in his daylight raids was able to protect his bombers by fighter escorts and to maintain raids for hours. His problem at night also was easier than that of the R.A.F. bombers. Another most important advantage to the Nazis was the short time available to us for warning of impending raids. All

defences—mobile, such as the fighter units, and static, such as the ground guns and searchlights—must be in a state of alert readiness, able to come into action in a matter of seconds, almost. Over important places a balloon barrage

ANTI-AIRCRAFT UNITS AT WORK

Men of an A.A. Brigade in the South-East, some of whom are shown above firing one of their latest guns, have shot down over 200 German planes. Top left, a searchlight projector in the London area operating from its sunken sandbagged emplacement.

Photos, Central Press, L.N.A.

was constantly maintained; balloons were also employed with coastal shipping.

On the airfields pilots of "readiness flights" waited in turn through day and night, in flying kit, close by their machines. At an order they would run to the aircraft and be in the air in a few moments; even so, some minutes were needed to climb to the operating height, and more minutes to reach the danger point towards which raiders had been reported to be flying. And these same raiders might change their course suddenly, to baffle the defences; or might try to decoy our fighters while another Nazi formation strove to get through for a vital stroke on some aerodrome.

Much depended on timely and accurate information reaching both the Fighter Squadrons and the A.A. Defences. The method of communication is illustrated in the picture diagram in this page. First intelligence came from Naval patrols, from patrolling R.A.F. machines, and from posts of the Royal Observer Corps dotted about the country at vantage points. The information reached the Sector Control, which circulated

it to the A.A. batteries, to Balloon Barrages and to Fighter airfields. Simultaneously news was passed on to Group Control, R.A.F., and to Fighter Command and the Air Ministry (Headquarters, R.A.F.). From Fighter Command were sent out the warnings to Regional Commissioners of Civil Defence in the area, bringing all the local A.R.P. services into action. All this came about almost as quickly as the reader can peruse the story: a wonderful and intricate network of communications linked up all the posts, commencing with telephone and teleprinter and ending with young A.R.P. messengers on cycle or motor bicycle who risked life time after time in dashing through streets under aerial bombardment.

Fighter Command, of course, analysed the reports coming in from sea patrols and Observer Posts, plotted the ever varying location of hostile aircraft, and manoeuvred its fighter aircraft to intercept and destroy the enemy. It also gave intelligence to Anti-Aircraft formations. The latter comprised Heavy A.A. Regiments (among whose personnel were included

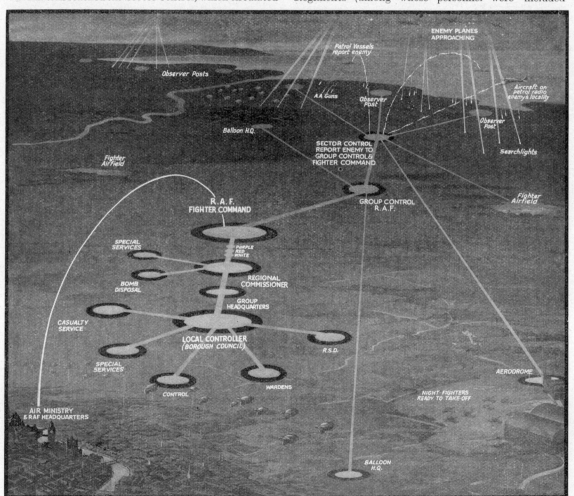

THE ENEMY APPROACHES—BUT WE ARE WARNED

The moment that a hostile aeroplane is sighted by our sea and air patrols or shore observers, warnings are swiftly transmitted by an amazing network of messages, first through Sector Control to Group Control, thence to Fighter Command H.Q. Sector Control also warns A.A. batteries and Fighter airfields; from Group Control the balloons are warned. The warnings then go on to all special services and the Local Controller.

By courtesy of "The Sphere"

women of the Auxiliary Territorial Service), with guns of 3·7-in. or 4·5-in. calibre ; and Light A.A. Regiments armed with the Bofors gun (which fired a two-pounder shell) and with light and heavy Lewis machine-guns. Spotters with powerful telescopes picked up and identified any aircraft coming within range. Then there came into operation the predictor, a remarkable apparatus combining optical and calculating mechanism. It was often worked by women of the A.T.S. (see Women's Services), who also " manned " the height-and-range finder.

Once the hostile plane was seen it could be kept in the field of view of the predictor lenses ; in the act of focusing these and keeping the aircraft clearly in view the operators set certain calculating wheels turning and caused certain resultant figures to show. Other numbers, obtained by the height-and-range finder crew, were " fed " into the predictor, and eventually, in less time than it takes to tell about it, information was secured which enabled the gunner to fire his shell in the right direction, with the proper fuse setting, to meet the aircraft in its travel.

Except in the case of the lighter guns, used against low-flying aircraft, there was no question of the gunner shooting directly at something he could see ; in order to hit a raider passing overhead at, say, 25,000 feet high with a speed of some 300 miles per hour the gunner would have to aim at some point four miles farther on the course that the raider was likely to take. That is why the predictor is employed, for by taking into account certain known facts about the approaching aeroplane it can " predict " the probable course and height. But, of course, if the enemy changes course quickly or alters height the shell will not hit the aircraft.

At night the searchlights come into play ; they rely upon the sound locator to give them information like that obtained in daylight by the predictor. The locator has gigantic ear trumpets to pick up the sound of an aeroplane engine. When the operator turning the controls hears the noise with equal distinctness in both ears the instrument will be indicating the bearing on which the aircraft is approaching. The trumpets also register the angle of elevation (from which the height can be calculated) of the enemy. A mechanism registers by a visible indication when the apparatus is correctly pointed.

The searchlights vary in type, but all near-by batteries are linked up and can criss-cross and concentrate upon an aircraft which comes into their area.

Imprisoned in a glaring field of brilliant light the enemy finds it difficult to take " evading action." And when the searchlights have him ensnared, the necessary figures are passed to the guns so that they may shoot straight at him. Here again the cooperation is instantaneous, brought about by electrically-operated and controlled mechanism connecting the giant light-projectors with the A.A. artillery.

Air Defence Cadet Corps. Founded in 1937 by Air Commodore J. A. Chamier for training British youth in airmanship, drill, discipline and technical instruction. By 1939 it numbered more than 20,000 boys between the ages of 14 and 18. In February 1941 it was merged into the Air Training Corps (q.v.).

Air Training Corps. Founded in February 1941 the purpose of the A.T.C. is to provide a large field of selection from which the R.A.F. can draw for air and ground crews. Boys of 16 and upwards wishing to serve eventually with the R.A.F. or Fleet Air Arm are organized in University, school and local units. There is thus equality of opportunity for all types of boy, and one of the main objects of the Corps is to provide such educational assistance as will enable all to reach the high standards required for air-crew candidates. The course of instruction consists first of drill, physical training, mathematics, Morse code and general lectures. In the second stage there is more specialization in two main categories, according to the duties for which the candidate is most suited : (1) *Air crew*—mathematics, navigation and Morse, aircraft identification, and administration. (2) *Technical*—courses for wireless operators and mechanics (Engine), mechanics (Airframe), instrument repairers, electricians and M.T. mechanics. Most of the squadrons are affiliated to R.A.F. stations in the vicinity. Over 180,000 boys had entered by April, 1942. Air-Commodore Chamier, Commandant 1941–42 was succeeded by Mr. W. W. Wakefield, M.P. Corps H.Q. at Stanmore, Middx.

A.T.C. cap badge.

Air Transport Auxiliary Service. This organization was formed at the outbreak of war by British Airways, for the purpose of ferrying new aircraft from factories to R.A.F. stations. The Service included a number of women pilots, among them being Pauline Gower and the late Amy Johnson (q.v.).

MODERN METHODS OF FIGHTING IN THE AIR

Great advances in the design of aircraft and the invention of new instruments have wrought many changes in the strategy of air warfare since the last war. These are discussed in the article below.

Air War. Before the Second Great War air strategy had undergone a great advance in theory, and marked changes from the aerial warfare of 1914–1918 were anticipated on both sides. One school of thought believed in the General Douhet claim that by the use of the modern bomber in huge numbers a rapid and decisive result, leading swiftly to victory, could be obtained. Shattering attacks against the industrial centres and civil population were to be the major role of an air force. Another theory was that the

heavy bomber and dive-bomber could be used with crushing effect against naval vessels at sea. There was a strong belief, too, that individual combat between opposing fighter aircraft, which was a feature of the last war, would be absent.

In the Spanish Civil War and the military operations in China the use of aircraft was not on a sufficiently large scale to confirm or refute these theories, and in the first phase of the Second Great War conditions of air warfare were almost parallel to those of 1918. One fact became plain, however. This was that the employment of great numbers of aircraft in the closest co-operation with infantry and tanks was the *sine qua non* of the German blitzkrieg. This was revealed in Poland and in the Battle of France. Coordinated attack of the air forces, army and navy was practised by Britain in the offensives in Libya in 1940, 1941 and 1942, and the swift successes obtained proved that the tactics and strategy involving massed air power and a highly-developed cooperation between aircraft and ground forces are governing factors in modern warfare. The heavy bomber which is capable of carrying a great load of bombs has immense striking power, but alongside its development a parallel advance has been made in defence measures, although the massed raids on Germany in 1942 showed that the defence could be blanketed. Night fighters with the necessary duration and special armament patrolling over the perimeter of target areas can sometimes inflict losses so severe that the cost of the assault is too high. The effectiveness of the night fighter has been greatly increased by the introduction of highly scientific means whereby the enemy machines can be tracked, intercepted and, through the skill and resolute action of the defence pilot, destroyed. Important developments to find a complete answer to the night bomber continue to be made in secrecy.

At the same time the trend in the development of the bomber is towards making sub-stratosphere operations practicable. The assumption is that by flying at heights between 38,000 and 50,000 feet the raiding aircraft is beyond the range of anti-aircraft guns, and interceptor fighters cannot reach the zone of action in time. The problems which have yet to be solved are concerned mainly with the effect of the rarefied atmosphere upon the airman, the aero engine, and the diminished accuracy of the bomb-sight as a result of great altitude.

The idea that there would be little individual fighting in the air in the present war has been shown to be wholly erroneous. In spite of the great increase in the speed of fighter aircraft, and the change in fighting tactics in which complete squadrons are engaged, situations arise when combats develop between two machines and the history of the last war in the air is repeated. Speed, altitude and firepower of the machine are the outstanding factors in which the change has been made. Besides serving as an escort for day-bombers, and as an interceptor, the fighter also assumed the role of a low-attack machine, a type fostered largely by the United States. Armed with cannon and carrying small bombs, the fighter-bomber adopted by the Royal Air Force has been employed with telling effect against enemy motorized units, tanks, ships, and in assaults at ground level upon static targets and ground troops. Low-level air attack was introduced in the later stages of the last war, when it was called "ground strafing" by the British. Its re-introduction, as seen in Libya, may result in important changes involving the production of special types of aircraft and new methods of flight operations.

Powers of Dive- and Torpedo-Bombers

So far as the dive-bomber is concerned, one opinion was formed that its striking power was limited when ground forces had become accustomed to its form of attack. It is nevertheless a formidable weapon. Germany, who placed great faith in the dive-bomber and was the first country to adopt it in strength, built up a powerful arm of parachute troops and used gliders for troop transport as well. Russia was, in fact, the originator of the plan for the employment of the glider in warfare, as well as parachute troops.

In the air war at sea the most striking advance has been in the power of the torpedo-bomber, the outstanding examples being those provided by exploits of the Royal Air Force and the Fleet Air Arm against enemy shipping both in Home Waters and in the Mediterranean. The Axis, on the other hand, appears to have been behind Britain in this field, though the serious blows struck at the Navy by the Japanese in sinking the Prince of Wales and the Repulse with torpedo-carrying aircraft showed that this country does not stand alone in this sphere of aerial warfare. Air action at sea has progressed largely because of the development of aircraft with the capacity for great range and the advance in air navigation. *See* Royal Air Force.

Books to Consult. The War in the Air, David Garnett (Chatto). Air Strategy, Capt. Norman Macmillan (Hutchinson). Alexander Seversky, Victory through Air Power.

Air War on Britain. *See* Great Britain.

Ajax, H.M.S. British cruiser of 6,985 tons, carrying eight 6-in. guns. Under the command of Capt. C. H. L. Woodhouse, and flying the flag of Commodore Henry Harwood, she, with H.M.S. Exeter and H.M.S. Achilles, attacked the German raider Admiral Graf Spee off the Uruguayan coast on Dec. 13, 1939, a glorious naval victory the story of which is told under the heading Plate, Battle of. On Feb. 1, 1940, Ajax dropped anchor in Plymouth Sound, the first home-coming after two years' service at sea. On Feb. 16 her crew, with that of Exeter were given a civic welcome by Plymouth, and on Feb. 23, 700 officers and men drawn from both ships marched through London to the Guildhall to receive their country's expression of gratitude for their share in the River Plate victory. On Oct. 12, 1940, Ajax attacked and crippled the Italian destroyer Artigliere (*q.v.*) in the Mediterranean. She was also engaged in

DIRECT PHOTOGRAPH OF AERIAL COMBAT
By means of camera-guns fitted to Hurricanes and Spitfires many remarkable photographs of air fighting have been obtained. Here a Heinkel III is caught in a hail of bullets.
Photo, British Official: Crown Copyright

the great victory over Italian cruisers and destroyers off Cape Matapan on March 28, 1941. *See* Matapan ; Plate, Battle of.

Alaska Road. Begun in mid-March 1942, this 1,200-mile highway was designed to facilitate the transport of war material to Alaska, as the spearhead of an Allied attack upon Japan. Its starting-point was Edmonton, in Alberta, terminus of the existing American-Canadian highway system.

Alaska Road, the new highway which would provide a quicker route to Russia and meet any Japanese attack on Alaska.

By courtesy of " News Chronicle "

Passing through Fort St. John and Fort Nelson in British Columbia and White Horse in Yukon Territory, it ended at the Alaskan airport of Fairbanks, where it linked up with the network of roads to the Pacific. The road was completed in 1942 and played an important rôle in the defence of Alaska against the Japanese in the Aleutian Is. *See* United States.

Albania. On Good Friday, 1939, most sacred day in the Christian Calendar, Italian troops invaded Albania, landing at Valona, Durazzo and San Giovanni di Medua. King Zog and his Queen fled to Greece ; two days later Tirana, the capital, was occupied. This was a war after Italy's own heart, one in which bribes took the place of bombs.

There was no justification for this flagrant and cynical aggression, but it may be explained. King Zog resented being directed by Mussolini. Count Ciano, the Italian Foreign Minister, sought to answer world criticism by reference to Zog's anti-Yugoslav activities and his refusal to become Italy's ally. The war, though a negligible affair in the military sense, had political repercussions throughout the world. In the Balkans little birds lay big eggs.

First, there were the local effects. Greece saw Italy at her western gate ; Turkey saw her there at one remove. Both were filled with fears. Rumania, conscious of her oil wealth and of Italy's oil needs, feared also. She had seen Germany gobble up Bohemia, and Hungary annex Transylvania.

World repercussions included Roosevelt's appeal to the aggressor states for ten years' non-aggression ; a protest from Great Britain against this violation of the Anglo-Italian Agreement (for working together for peace), and British guarantees to Greece and Turkey.

Italy at once began to impose her corporative system on the tiny

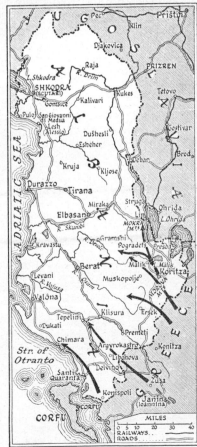

Greek advance into Albania, 1940.

state. A Constituent Assembly of Albanian chiefs was called, and these, all in the pocket of Italy, offered Victor Emmanuel III the throne, which was accepted, April 16. The Albanian Fascist Party in power, the systematic exploitation of the country began, for it has considerable mineral wealth.

In August 1940, with a notable absence of originality, Mussolini tore a complete page from Hitler's book, declared that Greece was persecuting its Albanian minority, poured troops into Albania and, on Oct. 28, crossed the Greek frontier near Janina. At that date Albania was a new and pleasant little jewel in the Crown of Italy, even if stolen property. From that day forward it became a battlefield only, for Greece flung back the invader and drove him towards the sea. (*See* Greece.)

Meanwhile, Britain at once fulfilled her pledge and sent aid to Greece by land, sea and air. Together they chased the Italian army across Albania, routing it. It was this army which had crossed the Adriatic with the ultimate intention of reaching east as far as Salonika !

The intervention of Germany, by her attack on Greece, placed Albania once more completely under Italian control. But the spirit of this small people was far from broken. Albania is a land of hills and forests, and thousands of men implacably hostile to the invader retired to these remote parts to await their opportunity to strike back.

This invasion of Albania was prompted purely by financial and commercial considerations, for Italy had invested heavily in the country. But the home need of victory was also a factor in deciding the issue. *See* Greece.

Albert Canal. Waterway connecting the R. Meuse and Maastricht with Antwerp. Before the German invasion Belgium, north of Brussels, was defended by a line of forts on this canal. On May 11, 1940, the enemy crossed it by two bridges near Maastricht which had escaped destruction by the defenders, and thus gained a foothold in Belgian defensive positions. When trying to account for the failure to destroy these bridges, it was found that the officer entrusted with the operation had been killed. A squadron of the Belgian Air

Force lost 11 out of 12 machines as it flew low to bomb one of the bridges. On May 12 six R.A.F. machines dived low and wrecked the remaining bridge. Five of the six were shot down; the sixth crashed inside our lines. *See* Garland; Maastricht.

Alcantara, H.M.S. This British armed merchant cruiser of 22,181 tons was formerly a Royal Mail Line ship. Commanded by Capt. J. C. P. Ingham, R.N., she attacked and damaged the Narvik, an enemy raider, on July 28, 1940, in the South Atlantic. The Narvik, a fast converted ship mounting four guns on each broadside, turned away on being hit, throwing out smoke screens to evade pursuit. But for a lucky shot which holed the Alcantara's engine-room and reduced her speed, the raider would doubtless have been brought to book. Permission was granted by the Brazilian Government for the Alcantara to remain at Rio de Janeiro until the slight damage she had sustained had been repaired. She left Rio on August 5 to resume her search for the raider.

ONCE A LINER—THEN A CRUISER

The Alcantara, which, as an armed merchant cruiser, attacked and damaged the fast enemy raider Narvik off Brazil, was formerly a Royal Mail liner. In this engagement she lost her foremost funnel and had to put into Rio de Janeiro for repairs.
Photo, Topical

Alderson, T. H. Detachment Leader, Rescue Parties, Bridlington, and the first civilian to win the George Cross (Oct. 1, 1940) for sustained gallantry, enterprise and devotion to duty during enemy air raids. *See* George Cross.

Aleppo. City of Syria, 70 m. E. of the Mediterranean, a great commercial centre. The Nazi-controlled aerodrome was heavily bombed by the R.A.F. during the Allied invasion of Syria, June–July, 1941.

Aleutian Islands. *See* U.S.A.

Alexander, RT. HON. ALBERT VICTOR, P.C., M.P. (b. 1885). First Lord of the Admiralty from May, 1940. When Mr. Churchill became Premier on May 10 he appointed Mr. Alexander to the office which he himself was relinquishing. This was the second time that Mr. Alexander found himself at the head of the Admiralty. The first was in 1929–1931, in Ramsay MacDonald's Government, and he was then the first politician of the left wing to win public approval as head of a service department. During that term of office he worked hard for the expansion of Britain's cruiser strength and forced the building of the Leander programme—small cruisers with 6-in. guns instead of 8-in., but firing at double the rate and having great powers of manoeuvre. The Leander was launched in 1931. In 1939 two

Mr. A. V. Alexander, First Lord of the Admiralty.
Photo, Russell

of her sister ships, Ajax and Achilles, helped to bring the Graf Spee to her doom, and in 1940 another of the Leander class, H.M.A.S. Sydney, sank Italy's battle cruiser Bartolomeo Colleoni, reputed to be the fastest ship in the world.

Alexander, FIELD - MARSHAL VISCOUNT H. R. L. G., G.C.B., D.S.O. (b. 1891), made Field-Marshal 1944, Viscount Jan. 1946. In Sept. 1939, he was in command of the 1st Division of the 1st Corps, and on Oct. 3 took over, together with the 2nd Division, the sector allotted to the B.E.F. on the Belgian frontier. After the

Field-Marshal Alexander of Dunkirk fame.
Photo, British Official

advance in May 1940, to the R. Dyle and the subsequent withdrawal towards the Channel ports, Lord Gort, who had been instructed to return to England, handed over the command of the 20,000 troops still remaining at Dunkirk to Maj.-Gen. Alexander, who was ordered to operate under Admiral Abrial. To him was certainly due a share of the credit for evacuating so many men during the last days. At midnight on June 2 he made a final inspection of the beaches with Capt. W. G. Tennant, R.N., who had organized the naval side of the evacuation. On being satisfied that no British troops were left on shore, they themselves left for England. On Dec. 10, 1940, he was appointed C.-in-C. Southern Command. On March 5, 1942, he took over command in Burma from Lt.-Gen. Hutton, and became C.-in-C. Middle East in succession to Gen. Auchinleck in August, 1942.

Alexandria. City and chief seaport of Egypt and an important British naval base. Before the collapse of France a large part of France's naval strength was concentrated in the Mediterranean at Alexandria and Oran. On July 3, 1940, all French warships lying at Alexandria, consisting of a battleship, four cruisers, and some small ships, were demobilized by the British, after peaceful negotiations with the French admiral, Admiral Godfroy. The first of many Axis raids on the city and port took place on June 22, 1940. That of June 7, 1941, did considerable damage.

Alsace-Lorraine. Immediately after the declaration of war French and German troops made contact everywhere between the Rhine and Moselle, and an artillery duel began on the Alsace-Lorraine-German frontiers. Within a few days the French had penetrated the Warndt Forest, and achieved substantial progress on a 12-mile front to the east of the Saar and Bien Wald. In retreating the Germans destroyed some of their own villages. The French communiqué of Oct. 2, 1939, reported that local enemy attacks were repulsed south of Saarbruecken. Considerable fighting continued for the next few days, which resulted in the evacuation by the Germans of villages and towns to a depth of 16 miles on the right bank of the Rhine. Various engagements, patrol encounters and artillery and air duels followed in the winter and spring and the Warndt Forest positions were evacuated. All

CAMOUFLAGED FIGHTERS & BOMBERS OF THE R.A.F.

Drawn by E. C. Mansell

These pictures supplement the photographs of Allied aircraft in pages 8 to 10. The Supermarine Spitfire (1) and Hawker Hurricane (10) are day fighters, dazzle-painted in striking contrast to the sombre-hued Bristol Beaufighter (3), as used for night interception. The Bristol Beaufort (4), a torpedo bomber, is used by Coastal Command. The Boulton Paul Defiant (6), here pictured as a day fighter, is used in other dress for night work. Of four-engined bombers, the Handley Page Halifax (2) and the gigantic Short Stirling (5) show night and day camouflage. The Handley Page Hampden (7) and Bristol Blenheim Mark IV (8) are two-engined medium bombers. The Short Sunderland flying boat (9) does convoy and anti-submarine work.

NEW DIVE-BOMBER & FIGHTER

IN many encounters with Axis forces the need for powerful dive-bombers became apparent, but for a time the British Air Ministry seemed reluctant to sanction this departure. The lower photograph shows an American-built Vultee Vengeance dive-bomber with Royal Air Force markings. Top speed is 300 m.p.h.; wing span is 48 ft. and length is 40 ft.; the engine is a Wright Double-row Cyclone of 1,600 h.p.

The Westland Whirlwind (top, seen from beneath) is a twin-engined day and night fighter with a top speed of over 350 m.p.h. Its high tail and underslung engine nacelles are unmistakable. Wing span, 45 ft.; length, 31 ft. 6 ins.; two Rolls Royce Peregrine engines of 885 h.p. Four 20-mm. cannon are mounted in the nose—deadly weapons against aircraft or ground targets.

Photo (above), " Flight "

these, however, were merely incidental or preliminary to the great clash between Germany and France which began on May 10. Breaking through Luxemburg and Belgium, the Nazis by-passed the strong fortifications of the Maginot Line in Alsace-Lorraine, and had overrun a large part of France from Havre to Orleans and Dijon by June 17, when Pétain asked for an armistice. Though the French troops continued to resist along a line from Mulhouse to Metz, they were virtually surrounded. Metz and Strasbourg surrendered. Belfort fell on June 18, and the Maginot Line was attacked in the rear on both sides of Diedenhofen, and was penetrated frontally at Saarbruecken.

On June 23 the Germans announced that the battle in Alsace and Lorraine had "ended with the capitulation of the encircled French armies," and claimed to have taken over 500,000 prisoners, including the Commanders of the Third, Fifth, and Eighth French armies ; the two French provinces were incorporated in Hitler's Germany. Their Germanization began immediately. Over 100,000 French-speaking people were deported from Lorraine and similar exile was enforced on French-speaking Alsatians. Their places were taken by German families from the Saar and Ruhr regions. All persons with French surnames not deported were compelled to Germanize them. Vichy's protest against this wholesale expulsion had no effect.

Althing (*pron.* awl-ting). This is the name given to the Icelandic Parliament. It consists of two Houses, upper and lower, and there is a responsible Ministry of five politicians. The Althing proclaimed a state of autonomy when Germany invaded Denmark, April 9, 1940.

Altmark. A large German vessel of the tanker type, the Altmark was destined to achieve notoriety as a prison ship, satellite of the Admiral Graf Spee (*q.v.*). It was her duty to carry supplies to the Nazi raider, and to take aboard any British survivors of the sinkings. On Dec. 6, 1939, in the South Atlantic, she relieved the Graf Spee of a further haul of prisoners, and with a total of 299 captives under her hatches headed northwards. Having reached Icelandic waters, she turned south and was sighted by British aeroplanes, which had been sent to search for her, on Feb. 16, 1940, off Norway.

This information was passed on to "certain of H.M. ships which were conveniently disposed," and shortly afterwards the Altmark was intercepted by H.M.S. Intrepid, one of a destroyer flotilla under the command of Capt. P. L. Vian of H.M.S. Cossack (*q.v.*). She was allowed to proceed, but later the Admiralty gave explicit orders that our ships should enter

neutral waters, search her and rescue any prisoners found. By this time the German ship, escorted by two Norwegian gunboats, had slipped into Joessing Fjord, a small inlet with a dead end, south of Egersund. Capt. Vian, in the Cossack, reached the mouth of the fjord, where the destroyer Ivanhoe was standing by, and was here assured by the captain of one of the gunboats that the Altmark was unarmed, that she had been searched at Bergen, that she had no prisoners and had permission to use Norwegian territorial waters.

The British destroyers withdrew, but, acting under further Admiralty orders, Cossack re-entered the fjord after dark, her searchlights blazing. Capt. Vian then went on board the Norwegian gunboat Kjell and asked that the Altmark be taken to Bergen under joint Anglo-Norwegian escort and the matter settled according to international law. The Norwegian captain repeated his assurances, and refused either to go to Bergen or to board the German ship. The commander of the Altmark, Capt. Dau, now took a hand and attempted to ram the British ship, but only succeeded in grounding his own vessel. By skilful handling the Cossack was grappled to the Altmark and Lt.-Cmdr. B. T. Turner led a boarding-party of two officers and 30 men, who leapt on to the enemy deck, driving the German crew before them. There ensued hand-to-hand fighting until a German shot wounded a gunner in charge of one section of the boarding-party. After this seven Germans were killed and seven wounded.

By now the prisoners had been found, battened down, locked in shell-rooms, store-rooms, and even in an empty oil tank. As they opened the holds and hammered on locked doors the rescuing party shouted " The Navy's here ! " and were answered with a roar of cheering from 299 half-starved, dishevelled merchant officers and seamen, many of whom had been over two months in captivity. Having taken them aboard, the Cossack steamed through the narrow outlet of the fjord, unmolested by the Norwegian gunboats, and set off triumphantly across the North Sea. The next day the liberated men were landed at Leith.

PRISON SHIP IS HERSELF IMPRISONED
The ill-famed Altmark, with 299 British captives aboard, was cornered in Joessing Fjord by the British destroyer Cossack, acting on information furnished by the R.A.F., who had been told to search for a vessel with a large single funnel aft.
Photo, Central Press

Amba Alagi. Situated near Magdala, west of the Eritrean border in Abyssinia, Amba Alagi was the scene of the surrender of the Duke of Aosta (*q.v.*) and his Italian army in May 1941. With this surrender the conquest of Abyssinia by British and Patriot forces was an accomplished fact. The Italians had been skilfully hemmed into the mountain fastness of Amba Alagi by the Imperial forces, who carried out an ingenious plan with great courage and determination under Generals Cunningham and Platt. As a result of these brilliant operations the enemy forces were surrounded, and the powerful fortress of Amba Alagi, situated at a height of some 9,000 ft., was rendered unserviceable to its occupants. The S.A.A.F., the R.A.F. and the Rhodesian Air Force played a vital part in Imperial operations, in addition to the splendid work of Indian troops and of the Sudan Defence Force. The object of the Italians was to resist until the last moment, in order that the rainy

PILOTS OF THE AMERICAN VOLUNTEER GROUP
The A.V.G., a body of American airmen who volunteered for service in the Chinese Air Force, performed magnificent work in Burma during the Japanese onslaught, bombing and machine-gunning enemy troops and transport and accounting for innumerable aircraft at small cost to themselves.
Photo, Graphic Photo Union

season should delay further British movements. The enemy was forestalled, however, by the rapidity of our advance, and on May 17 the Duke of Aosta sent emissaries to Gen. Cunningham, asking for terms for the surrender of his entire forces in the Amba Alagi area. The formal capitulation of the exhausted and half-starved men took place on May 19, and next day the Duke, together with his staff officers and Gen. Tressani, made a personal surrender. Prisoners numbered some 18,000, of whom about 7,000 were Italians, and considerable quantities of guns and other equipment were also captured. After the fall of Amba Alagi the only Italian stronghold to continue resistance was Gondar (*q.v.*), which surrendered unconditionally after a six months' siege. *See* Abyssinia.

Amboina (Ambon). The second largest naval and air base after Surabaya in the Netherlands East Indies, Amboina Island is situated in the Molucca group midway between Celebes and New Guinea, and

some 650 miles north of Darwin in Australia. Japanese aircraft made a heavy attack on Jan. 30, 1942, when a church and school were destroyed and the wireless station was slightly damaged. Later the same day a fleet consisting of three Japanese cruisers, six destroyers and a number of transports was sighted, and the destruction of vital points on Amboina was carried out. Enemy landings began that night and were strongly resisted by the Netherlands East Indies forces. Bitter fighting developed, and it was reported that the tide of battle was turning from one side to the other, and continued to do so until Feb. 7, when Batavia reported that the greater part of Amboina was in enemy hands. Part of the garrison, however, managed to escape. Resistance to the Japanese on the island was by no means over, and fighting went on until the whole of Amboina fell to the enemy. *See* Netherlands East Indies.

American Volunteer Group. Consisting of American airmen who resigned U.S. commissions to join the China Air Force and protect the American lease-lend convoys passing along the Burma Road, this remarkable group achieved fine work against the Japanese in Burma, notably at Rangoon, at the beginning of 1942. Under the terms of their contract with the Chinese Government A.V.G. airmen were paid 500 dollars for every Japanese 'plane destroyed. They flew Tomahawk machines and were known as Scalper Squadrons. Air Vice-Marshal D. F. Stevenson, commanding the R.A.F. in Burma, paid high tribute to these men, who up to the end of January 1942 had shot down over 100 enemy 'planes in fourteen fights at a cost of five of their own pilots killed in action and one taken prisoner. In April A.V.G. aircraft were evacuated from Lashio, western terminus of the Burma Road, to Kunming in China. On April 28 it was announced that A.V.G. fighters had shot down 11 Japanese aircraft near Lashio without loss. Maj.-Gen. Claire Chennault was in command of the Group. In all they had shot down 284 Japanese planes. In June 1942 the Group was disbanded.

Amery, RT. HON. L. C. M. S., M.P. (b. 1873). Secretary of State for India and Burma from 1940. He had travelled extensively in the Near East and in all British Dominions, and held many important posts prior to the outbreak of war.

Mr. L. S. Amery, Secretary for India. *Photo, Vandyk*

Amsterdam. Commercial city and seaport of the Netherlands. It was very heavily raided the day of the German invasion, May 10, 1940; by May 13 there was fighting in the streets, and two days later it was occupied by the Germans. After that date the R.A.F.

repeatedly bombed the harbour and oil tanks. In February 1941, following riots, the Germans imposed upon the city fines amounting to £2,000,000.

Andaman Islands. This archipelago, consisting of six main islands and some 200 small ones, lies in the Bay of Bengal, about 120 miles S.W. of Burma ; it is part of the Indian Empire. Port Blair, the capital, had a wireless station and an aerodrome. Japanese bombers flew over the islands and bombed Fort Blair twice on Feb. 24, 1942, and again on Feb. 26. Very little opposition could be offered ; the British population was therefore evacuated, and everything of value was destroyed. Japanese troops landed on March 26 and established bases from which their bombers and flying-boats could harry Indian waters and even attack the Indian coastal towns. On April 4 American Flying Fortresses, stationed in India, made a heavy attack on Japanese shipping off the Andaman Islands, sinking a cruiser and setting a troopship afire. On April 13 an R.A.F. raid destroyed or damaged 13 Japanese flying-boats, and on April 18 another R.A.F. visit destroyed two flying-boats and damaged three. These raids continued, since it was important to prevent the enemy from concentrating his forces in the Andamans and using them as an advance base for an attack on India.

Anderson, Lt.-Col. Charles Grove Wright, v.c., m.c. During the Malayan campaign this gallant Australian officer commanding a small force was sent to the assistance of a brigade holding a vital position, and succeeded in destroying ten enemy tanks. He and his men were cut off, but withstood continual attack from ground troops and from the air, and, though surrounded and suffering severe casualties, continued to fight vigorously. Lt.-Col. Anderson personally led a sally against enemy troops who were holding a bridge, and destroyed four of their guns. He gave valuable information of the enemy's dispositions by radio, and finally fought his way back to the British lines through eight miles of occupied territory. During four days of hard fighting he gave a magnificent example of leadership and courage. It was announced on Feb. 14, 1942, that he had been awarded the V.C.

Lt.-Col.
C. G. Anderson,
awarded the V.C. in
Malayan campaign.
Associated Press

Anderson, Rt. Hon. Sir John, g.c.b., m.p. (b. 1882). Lord President of the Council from Oct. 3, 1940, in succession to Mr. Chamberlain, who resigned from the Cabinet on grounds of ill health. In 1938 he was appointed Lord Privy Seal with special powers as Minister of Defence. It was while holding this office that he gave his approval to the Anderson type of small air raid shelter. From September 1939 to October 1940 he was Home Secretary and Minister of Home Security. *See* Civil Defence.

Anderson, Lt.-Gen. K. A. N., c.b., m.c. General Officer Commanding-in-Chief the Eastern Command. At the outbreak of war he was commanding an infantry brigade. He was quickly promoted to a division, with which he took part in the evacuation from Dunkirk. Later he commanded a corps, and did much to co-ordinate the work of the Home Guard and that of the field army, winning special commendation for his anti-tank measures.

Anderson Shelter. Designed and invented by Mr. William Patterson, an engineer friend of Sir John Anderson ; the patent was presented to the nation.

ANDERSON SHELTERS NEAR A CRATER
The efficacy of the Anderson shelter has been proved beyond all doubt. They withstand the impact of debris and blast and have saved the lives of countless people in the bombed areas.
Photo, Associated Press

Later the scheme was submitted to a committee of engineers which included Mr. David Anderson (no relation to the Minister), Mr. B. L. Hurst, and Sir Henry Japp. Certain modifications were made on the committee's recommendations and the shelter was then adopted. Its name was a compliment to Sir John Anderson. This took place in December 1938.

Rt. Hon.
J. M. Andrews,
Premier of N. Ireland.
Photo, Barratts

Andrews, Rt. Hon. John Millar (b. 1871). He succeeded Lord Craigavon as Premier of Northern Ireland in November 1940. Previously he was Minister of Labour, 1921–37, and Minister of Finance, 1937–40, in the Northern Irish Parliament.

Angers. French city, 212 m. S.W. of Paris. It was the seat of the Polish Government from November 1939 until this was transferred to England in 1940.

Anglo-American Naval Agreement. By this Agreement, drawn up in Washington, Sept. 3, 1940, Britain leased to the U.S.A. naval and air bases in the Atlantic, and the U.S.A. transferred to Britain fifty over-age destroyers. It was formally signed in London on March 21, 1941. *See* Atlantic Bases.

Anglo-French-Turkish Pact. Signed in Ankara, Oct. 19, 1939, this Pact provided that, in the event of aggression against Turkey by a European Power, the French and British Governments would cooperate with the Turkish Government and lend all aid and assistance.

Anglo-Polish Agreement. Signed in London, August 24, 1939, whereby Britain and Poland agreed to assist each other in the event of aggression by a European Power. *See* Poland.

Annand, SEC.-LT. R. W. Serving with the Durham Light Infantry from the outbreak of war, Sec.-Lt. Annand was awarded the V.C. for conspicuous gallantry on May 13-16, 1940, in Belgium. In command of a platoon holding the southern end of a broken bridge over the R. Dyle, he twice, single-handed, dislodged enemy bridging parties, inflicting heavy casualties with hand grenades. After obeying the order to withdraw his platoon, he returned, although himself wounded, and rescued his wounded batman.

2/Lt. R. W. Annand, awarded the V.C.
Photo, British Official

Anschluss. German word meaning "joining," applied to the Austro-German Union, March 1938.

Antelope, H.M.S. Launched in 1929 and completed in the following year, this British destroyer had a displacement of 1,350 tons and carried a complement of about 145. Her armament included four 4·7-in. guns. The Antelope scored a great success against the enemy on Feb. 9, 1940. Two U-boats which attacked a British convoy were spotted by the destroyer, and the latter, steaming to the assistance of the merchantmen, sank both German submarines. H.M.S. Antelope was commanded by Lt.-Cmdr. R. T. White, R.N.

Anti-Aircraft Defence. *See* Air Defence.

Anti-Comintern Pact. The Comintern is the name given to the international organization of the Communist Party, and is an abbreviation of the words "Communist International." Hitler's party programme having always been primarily anti-Communist, he placed the formation of an anti-Comintern bloc of states in the forefront of his diplomatic policy. The anti-Comintern Pact came into being on Nov. 25, 1936, when an agreement was signed between Germany and Japan expressing abhorrence of Communism. On Nov. 6, 1937, Italy added her signature to the Pact, and the occasion was described in the Nazi Party newspaper, "Voelkischer Beobachter," thus : " A dyke of two hundred million human beings, unwilling to be submerged by the Red flood, has been formed to protect the peace of the world from Bolshevist destruction."

Manchukuo joined the anti-Comintern group on Jan. 16, 1939, Hungary signed on Feb. 24, 1939, and Spain on April 7, 1939. The purpose of the Pact was destroyed when the German-Russian Non-Aggression Agreement was concluded on August 23,1939, and for the first 18 months of the war no reference was made to the Pact. But it was revived in June 1941, when Germany attacked the U.S.S.R., and its adherents were called upon to carry out their pledges. The Pact was, however, of propaganda value only, as was further evidenced by the adherence to it in late November 1941 of the discredited quisling governments of Norway, Denmark, Finland, Rumania,

and Croatia. Throughout, the anti-Comintern Pact was " ideological camouflage," used to mask Germany's real military purposes.

Antonescu, GEN. ION (*pron.* an-to-nesk-u). Rumanian Dictator. He was appointed Premier by

Gen. Antonescu, Rumanian Dictator.
Photo, Assoc. Press

King Carol, Sept. 4, 1940, in order to placate the opponents of the Vienna Treaty of August 30, whereby two-thirds of Transylvania passed to Hungary. He at once demanded the King's abdication and assumed dictator's powers. On Nov. 23, 1940, he signed the Axis Pact and arranged a 10-year economic agreement with Germany. He passed severe anti-Jewish laws on Dec. 4, 1940, and in February 1941 introduced very drastic measures whereby death was the penalty for possessing firearms, for criticism of the Government, and for looting or sabotage.

Antwerp. Belgian city and seaport on the R. Scheldt (Escaut). It was first bombed early in the morning of May 10, 1940, the day the Germans invaded Belgium and Holland, and its occupation was claimed by the enemy on May 18. Concentrations of enemy invasion barges here were heavily bombed by the R.A.F. in August–September, and there were repeated R.A.F. attacks on important objectives, including oil depots, in 1940 and onwards.

Aosta, AMADEO UMBERTO, DUKE OF (1898–1942) (*pron.* a-oss-ta). Second cousin of the King of Italy. He succeeded Graziani as Viceroy of Abyssinia in 1937, and became C.-in-C. Italian East Africa. At Amba Alagi, N.E. Abyssinia, on May 19, 1941, he surrendered to the British with the remainder of his forces, thus bringing major organized resistance to an end. The Duke of Aosta died in captivity. *See* Abyssinia.

Arandora Star. Blue Star liner (15,000 tons). While carrying 1,500 German and Italian internees from Britain to Canada, with a crew and British guards numbering 500, she was torpedoed and sunk on July 2, 1940, by a U-boat in the Atlantic, west of Ireland. About 1,000 survivors were landed at a Scottish port.

Ardennes. This range of wooded hills lies in both France and Belgium, either side of the R. Meuse. The enemy made heavy thrusts here against the French and the B.E.F. on May 14, 1940, piercing the Allied lines.

Arensburg. Capital of the Estonian island of Oesel, at the entrance to the Gulf of Riga. By the Pact of Sept. 28, 1939, Russia was allowed to establish a military base here. The town was captured by the Germans on Sept. 22, 1941.

Argentina. *See* South America.

Argyrokastro (*pron.* argi-rŏk-as-trō). Town in S.W. Albania, and the main Italian forward base in the Italo-Greek war. It was attacked by the Greeks in November 1940, and after much fighting was finally captured on Dec. 8. After the invasion of Greece by Germany, April 6, 1941, the town was evacuated with other positions captured by the Greeks in Albania.

Ark Royal, H.M.S. British aircraft carrier (22,000 tons), completed in 1938. Germany claimed to have destroyed her off Norway by bombing attack in September 1939, and several times afterwards. She took part in the hunt for the Admiral Graf Spee in the

South Atlantic and later served as a base for aircraft engaged in the Norwegian campaign. She was at Oran, July 1940, in action against the French Fleet; in the Mediterranean against the Italian Fleet, July 9; off Sardinia, Nov. 27, when her aircraft delivered a torpedo attack on Italian battleships. She also took part in an attack on Genoa, Feb. 9, 1941; and the German battleship Bismarck was successfully attacked in the Atlantic by her aircraft on May 26, 1941.

On Nov. 13, 1941, the Ark Royal was torpedoed in the Mediterranean, not far from Gibraltar, whither she was returning from a cruise. It was hoped to get her safely into harbour, but while in tow she took a list and sank, fourteen hours after being hit. Out of a complement of nearly 1,600 only one man was lost. On Nov. 20 the Admiralty announced that the corvette Marigold had sunk the U-boat presumed to have torpedoed the Ark Royal.

One of the most famous ships in the Royal Navy, and built at a cost of £3,000,000, the Ark Royal had sailed 205,000 miles and been engaged in 32 war operations before her tragic loss. Although she had been in almost continuous service through the war she had sustained no damage whatever from enemy action, beyond a few splinter scratches from a bomb that narrowly missed her, until the final attack that put an end to her glorious career. The loss of " The Old Ark," as the sailors affectionately called her, was a sad blow to the Royal Navy and indeed to the whole nation. The Ark Royal figured in the film " Ships with Wings."

Armed Forces Act. Enacted Sept. 6, 1939, it provided that every male British subject between the ages of 18 and 41 should become liable to be called up for service in the armed forces of the Crown. Upward age limit was later extended to 51.

Armistice, Franco-German. The terms forced upon shattered France were accepted and signed on June 22, 1940, in the Forest of Compiègne by Gen. Huntziger for France and Gen. Keitel for Germany. The Germans decreed that hostilities should not cease until six hours after the Italian Government had notified them that the Franco-Italian armistice had also been concluded. Hostilities between Germany and France therefore ceased at 12.35 a.m. on June 25.

The terms of the Franco-German Armistice are briefly outlined in the following extracts from the 24 articles.

Immediate cessation of hostilities in France, overseas and on the seas. French troops already surrounded to lay down arms. French territory north and west of a specified line to be occupied by German troops; areas to be occupied and not yet in control of German troops to be turned over to them immediately. In occupied area Germany to have all rights of occupying power, excluding local administration. The French Government to afford all necessary facilities. Germany to reduce to a minimum occupation of W. coast after cessation of hostilities with Great Britain. French Government to be free to choose for itself the seat of Government in non-occupied territory or to transfer it to Paris if desired.

French naval, military and air forces to be demobilized within a certain period, with exception of troops necessary for maintaining order. French armed forces in occupied territory to be brought back into unoccupied territory and demobilized. Germany may demand surrender of all guns, tanks, aircraft, armament, munitions, etc., in territory not occupied.

French Fleet, except those units safeguarding French Colonial interests, to be demobilized and disarmed under German or Italian control. Members of French forces not to leave French soil. No French merchant shipping to leave harbour. Aerodromes to be placed under German or Italian control and no French aircraft to leave ground. Military stores in occupied territory to be handed over intact. Ports, fortifications,

SINKING OF H.M.S. ARK ROYAL

Many times " sunk " by German propaganda, this famous British aircraft carrier was torpedoed in the Western Mediterranean on Nov. 13, 1941. She was taken in tow, but sank next day 25 miles off Gibraltar. Just before sinking she had a list to starboard of 35 degrees.

Photo British Official: Crown Copyright

communications, etc., not to be destroyed or damaged. All wireless transmitting stations in French territory to stop. Cost of maintenance of German occupying troops to be paid by France. Certain German subjects in France or French territory to be handed over. All French prisoners of war in German hands to remain so until conclusion of peace.

Armistice, Franco-Italian. This was signed on June 24, 1940, at a villa near Rome, by Gen. Huntziger for France and Marshal Badoglio for Italy. Hostilities between France and Italy ceased at 12.35 a.m. on June 25. The Italian terms were similar to the German, but also included the demilitarization by France of the Libyan-Tunisian and Algerian-Libyan frontiers, and the demilitarization of naval and air bases of Toulon, Bizerta (Tunisia), Ajaccio (Corsica), and Oran (Algeria) during the continuation of Anglo-Italian hostilities. French Somaliland coast also had to be demilitarized. Demilitarization to be achieved within 15 days. Italian troops to remain on their advanced lines in all theatres of operations for duration of Armistice.

Armies : Strengths at the Outset of War					
	Organized Force IN DIVISIONS AND MEN		Available for Field Service IN DIVISIONS AND MEN		
Nation	Active	Trained Reserve	Ready Immediately	Additional Force in Six Months	Ultimate Strength
British Empire	Divisions : 4 infantry 1 cavalry 2 armoured Men : 382,770	Divisions : 12, type not announced Men : 624,800	Divisions : 3 to 7, type not announced Men : 120,000	Men : 300,000 to 800,000	Men : 5 to 6 million
France	Divisions : 32 infantry 4 cavalry 2 armoured Men : 725,759	Divisions : 40, type not announced Men : 5,300,000	Divisions : 70 to 100, type not announced Men : 1,700,000 to 2,600,000	Men : 2 million	Men : 5 to 7 million
Germany	Divisions : 49 infantry 3 cavalry 4 armoured (Panzer) Men : 750,000	Divisions : 38, including at least 6 armoured (Panzer) Men : 3,150,000	Divisions : 80 to 110, type not announced Men : 2 to 3 million	Men : 1 to 2 million	Divisions : 150 to 200, type not announced Men : 6 to 7 million
Italy	Divisions : 46 infantry 3 cavalry Men : 917,991	Divisions : 35, type not announced Men : 6,494,177	Divisions : 60 to 90, type not announced Men : 1,000,000 to 1,750,000	Men : 500,000 to 1,250,000	Men : 5 to 6 million
Japan	Divisions : Unknown Men : 1,500,000	Divisions : Unknown Men : 4,748,000	Divisions : Unknown Men : No reliable estimate available	Men : No reliable estimate available	
Russia	Divisions : Unknown Men : 1,500,000	Divisions : Unknown Men : No reliable estimate available	Divisions : Unknown Men : No reliable estimate available	Men : No reliable estimate available	Men : 16,500,000

MILITARY STRENGTH

This chart shows under the heading, Organized Force, the total military establishment of six great nations at the outset of the war. But of this force some must be used for home defence and for training recruits. The number of men available for field service is shown at the right. Of the British Empire forces, only Great Britain's were available for field service at the start of war. The Empire's Dominion and Colonial forces, however, contributed to its six-month or ultimate strength.

HOW THE BRITISH ARMY IS ORGANIZED & TRAINED

Most of the changes in the components and organization of our Army have their origin in modern mechanization, as will be seen below. Companion articles appear under the headings Royal Navy and Royal Air Force.

Army. In organization, armament, equipment and training the British Army of 1939 onwards was very different from its predecessor of a generation earlier. Except for a few regiments retained mainly for ceremonial purposes the cavalry had discarded its horses and relied on motor transport ; it had delegated some of its traditional functions to the Air Force, now the " eyes " of the army. The infantry were no longer " footsloggers " who had to march miles and miles to reach the enemy : troops were now transported in lorries and arrived fresh and much more speedily at the focal point. In the British Expeditionary Force of 1914 there had been only 700 motor vehicles, and 60 per cent of the Force had consisted of infantry ; twenty-five years later the infantry component was only 20 per cent, and (including tanks) there were more than 25,000 motor vehicles.

Fire-power had been enormously increased by the generous provision of light machine-guns, and the rifle had come to be mainly the arm of snipers and crack shots who, furnished with the best that science could turn out in telescopic sights, were to take toll of enemy key-men. Training tended more and more to develop individual initiative and responsibility, with self-contained units whom no emergency could disconcert—who when cut off from a main body would fight on steadily and brilliantly until the end. Gone was the fear of being outflanked or encircled. Indeed, modern warfare called for units of brave and intelligent men who would penetrate between and behind enemy formations so that they might " hamstring " an invader by striking at his rear or his lines of supply.

Battle drill supplanted much of the older drill, which belonged to a past age when troops always fought shoulder to shoulder. Columns marched in threes instead of fours, allowing room for motorized units to pass. Light automatic guns for close fighting were issued—" tommy guns," as they were nicknamed after an American inventor. They fired a heavier bullet than the Service rifle, about half as big again in diameter, and were indeed deadly weapons.

"Shock troops" in formations named Commandos (*q.v.*) were recruited for special duties where endurance, skill and intelligence were prime considerations. Akin to these stalwarts were the parachute troops, transported by aircraft to the selected point and then dropped to carry out what was usually an extremely dangerous operation. Later on Airborne Divisions were formed, and great numbers of soldiers were trained as glider pilots (Glider Regt.). An R.A.F. Regiment was recruited especially for airfield defence. Grenades and mines played an important part in all fighting. Light anti-tank guns (and a heavier weapon taken over from the infantry by the artillery) were the principal defence against tanks, apart from that given by aerial bombing. Mortars of comparatively large calibre were developed for front-line use.

In the withdrawal to Dunkirk the British Expeditionary Force lost not only about 30,000 of its number in casualties and prisoners, but practically all its artillery, stores and vehicles. To make good these

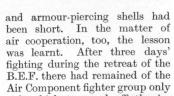

and armour-piercing shells had been short. In the matter of air cooperation, too, the lesson was learnt. After three days' fighting during the retreat of the B.E.F. there had remained of the Air Component fighter group only some fifty aircraft with which to ward off the incessant attacks of German bombers. The reorganized Army was able to count on its own air cooperation squadrons, one to each Corps. When threatened by the enemy the military commander could thus summon to his aid fighters to tackle the Nazi aircraft, and bombers to act as his artillery or to give close bombing support to his advance.

Battle training of the new armies developed initiative and instant readiness to meet the novel tactics brought about by mechanization. It also developed a tempering both physical and psychological, imparting to all ranks the ability to make swift and bold decisions in face of peril and to persist or resist to the death. Later encounters were to show that these men never knew when they were beaten.

GUNS—AND MORE GUNS

Above, anti-tank gunners in Northern Ireland are hauling their gun up a rocky hillside. Circle, a Guardsman with his tommy gun. Top right, Bren gun carriers in action. This small caterpillar vehicle can travel fast and safely over rough and boggy ground.

Photos, British Official: Crown Copyright

losses armament and equipment had to be built up at break-neck speed against the imminent danger of a Nazi invasion. This task was accomplished by the end of the year, and Britain was able also to supply the men and material needed for the Army of the Nile in its dashing invasion of Italian Libya in Dec. 1940.

Immense numbers of tanks were provided, and great reserves of shells. In the Battle of France the solitary armoured division had arrived too late to play a decisive part, and supplies of anti-tank ammunition

The "establishment" of the Army on Jan. 1, 1939, stood at between 680,000 and 690,000, and its actual strength was 575,000 all ranks. The establishment was increased by about one-third early in the year. In May the Military Training Act came into force, making training compulsory for men of 20–21; the first call-up came in July.

In September 1939 the National Service (Armed Forces) Act made military service compulsory for men of 18–41, and the various age-groups were thereafter called on to register by Royal Proclamation (20–22 in October; 22–23, October; 23–27, January, 1940). By the end of 1940 the British Army had a strength of approximately 5,000,000 and went on growing.

Though conscription had been introduced, voluntary recruiting went on concurrently for many months, and by the autumn of 1939 some 85,000 volunteers had joined the Army. Many jobs formerly done by men were taken over by women of the Auxiliary Territorial Service, which by this same period numbered 40,000 and was month by month increasing. Later, in 1941, when compulsory service for women came into effect, they could be directed to join one or other of the women's auxiliary services whose members were replacing men in the Navy, Army and Air Force. (*See* Women's Services.)

Then there was the Home Guard (*q.v.*), formed in May 1940 and numbering one and a quarter million by its first birthday. Its function was local defence, and at first its name was " Local Defence Volunteers." It became soon an integral part of the military forces and was organized on similar lines, though its local function was still insisted upon. The repelling of attack by air-borne troops (including parachutists) was one of its main duties, and it maintained continuous vigilance against invasion. At the end of 1941 it took over the manning of coastal artillery. Thus, gradually and steadily, Britain built up a mighty Army for defence of the Homeland and for offensive action oversea.

Great strides were made in the better housing of the troops and in the provision of recreation and entertainment. While the B.E.F. was in France it had received, through the Army Postal Service, some 27,000 letters and 17,000 parcels per day. Huts to accommodate 36,000 men were sent to France from Britain. " N.A.A.F.I."—Navy, Army & Air Force Institutes—provided canteen service and a hundred other comforts. " E.N.S.A."—Entertainments National Service Association—came into existence in Sept. 1939, to provide entertainment for the soldiers, and that same month ten concert parties were touring camps in Britain. Next month Ensa gave the first of many concerts to the B.E.F. in France, a series which ceased, in fact, only with the evacuation in June 1940.

From the beginning the Dominions made a mighty contribution to Britain's war effort. Australian, New Zealand and Indian troops took part in the Western Desert campaign of Wavell in Dec. 1940, while soldiers and airmen from South Africa and Rhodesia fought alongside those of Britain against the Italians in the Somaliland and Abyssinian operations. Australian and New Zealand contingents withdrawn from Libya were sent to Greece and, when our positions there had to be relinquished early in May 1941, took

Campaigns and Operations of British Army, 1940-1941	
	1940
Norway, Defence	April–June
Iceland and Faroes, Occupation ..	May
Belgium and France (B.E.F.)	May–June
Somaliland, Sudan, Kenya, Defence	August
Greece, Defence	November
Western Desert Offensive (Wavell)	December
	1941
Crete, Defence	January
Abyssinia, Eritrea, Somaliland,	
Offensive Campaign began ..	January
Iraq, Russo-British Occupation ..	May
Syria, Campaign	June–July
Libya, Auchinleck's Campaign began	November
Hong Kong, Defence	December
Malaya and Straits Settlements,	
Japanese Attack began	December
Burma	Dec.–Apl. 1942
	1942
Libya	May–June

a magnificent share in the stirring but ill-fated defence of Crete. Imperial troops were again largely engaged in the Libyan offensive that began in Nov. 1941, and thrust back the enemy to the Tripolitanian border.

The part of the Canadian troops, though they chafed against it, was to reinforce the garrison in Britain and to stand by as a guard against invasion. By the end of 1941 more than 100,000 volunteer soldiers from Canada had come to Britain (*see* Canada). But a Canadian force, which included men of the Royal Rifles and the Winnipeg Grenadiers, shared in the gallant defence of Hong Kong, surrendered to the Japanese on Christmas Day 1941.

Army Air Corps. *See* Glider Pilots.

A.R.P. *See* Civil Defence.

Arras. French town on the R. Scarpe, 38 m. N.E. of Amiens. It was the nerve centre of the B.E.F., Oct. 1939 to May 1940, and Lord Gort's rear headquarters. These were actually in the little village of Habarcq, 8 miles west of Arras. The town and surrounding area were defended by British troops, chiefly Welsh Guards, under Maj.-Gen. R. L. Petre, against an overpowering German onslaught, May 18-24, 1940, the headquarters of the British garrison being the ancient Palais St. Vaast. The whole area was heavily bombed by the enemy on May 20-22, and the British were forced to withdraw towards Douai on May 24.

Artigliere. Italian destroyer (1,620 tons). She was attacked and crippled by H.M.S. Ajax on Oct. 12, 1940, during a naval sweep in the Mediterranean. The following morning the damaged destroyer was located by aircraft of the Fleet Air Arm. She was being towed by another destroyer towards Sicily, but at the approach of H.M.S. Ajax and H.M.S. York the rescuing destroyer slipped the tow and made off at high speed. After giving the Italian crew half an hour to abandon ship, H.M.S. York sank the Artigliere by gun-fire.

Asdic. Contraction for Anti-submarine Detector Indicator Committee, by whom a special apparatus used by the Navy to detect the presence of submarines was invented. It has been fitted to all H.M. ships which hunt submarines, but further details are secret.

Asmara. Capital of Eritrea, situated 74 miles S.W. of Massawa. Heavily bombed by the R.A.F. in the East African campaign, it was taken by Imperial forces on April 1, 1941, 5,000 Italian prisoners being captured.

Assab. Coastal town of Eritrea, north of the Somaliland frontier, and once the oldest Italian possession in East Africa. Its capture by troops from H.M. ships and units of the Royal Indian Navy was announced on June 12, 1941.

Assam Road. *See* Burma.

Athenia. Donaldson Transatlantic liner (18,581 tons). She was the first U-boat victim of the war, being torpedoed without warning on Sept. 3, 1939, about 250 miles from the Irish coast, while bound from Belfast to Montreal. Her passengers included several hundred Americans hurrying home and many refugees from the Continent. The Germans asserted that she was struck by shellfire from British destroyers, " in order to draw the U.S. into the war." They even declared that " Churchill had sunk her." Of 1,418 persons on board, 128 were lost.

Athens. Capital of Greece. The Italians first bombed the city on Nov. 1, 1940, and made repeated attacks up to April 1941. German troops, converging from Thebes, Corinth and the island of Euboea, occupied it on April 27, 1941, Imperial forces having withdrawn to save the city from destruction. Piraeus (the port of Athens) was subsequently bombed by the R.A.F.

Athlone, ALEXANDER GEORGE CAMBRIDGE, K.G., G.C.M.G., 1ST EARL (b. 1874). Brother of Queen Mary. He succeeded Lord Tweedsmuir as Governor-General of Canada, April 3, 1940. He was Governor-General of South Africa, 1923–31.

Atlantic Bases. By an agreement made between Britain and the U.S.A. on Sept. 3, 1940, the U.S.A. transferred 50 over-age destroyers to Britain in return for naval and air bases in British territory in the Western Hemisphere. These included sites in Newfoundland (south coast and Avalon peninsula), Bermuda (Great Bay), and additional bases in British Guiana, the Bahamas, St. Lucia, Trinidad and Antigua. *See* illustration in page 443.

WAGING THE BATTLE OF THE ATLANTIC

Gallant ships and brave men, unceasing vigilance, heroic actions and skilled counter-measures—of such material is compiled the grim and glorious story of our Merchant Navy's campaign against the U-boat. See also Convoy ; Economic Warfare ; Merchant Navy.

Atlantic, Battle of. Barely nine hours after Britain declared war on Germany an unarmed passenger ship was torpedoed without warning some 250 miles off the Irish coast. This ruthless act was the opening theme of what came to be known as the Battle of the Atlantic, the centre of the sea struggle between the Democracies and the Axis Powers of Europe. Hitler had decided that Britain could be conquered by the dissolution of the Merchant Navy. Supplies of food, of raw materials and, later, of guns and tanks and aeroplanes and armaments, as well as Britain's flow of exports, had mainly to pass through Atlantic waters. If this supply line were cut the British would starve and war production would be paralysed.

U-boats appeared, singly at first, and during the second year of the war in packs ; raiders went swiftly like pirates to attack lone ships of poorly protected convoys. The pocket battleship Admiral Graf Spee had been responsible for many sinkings and she carried a number of merchant sailors as prisoners on board when she met her end in the southern Atlantic. The Germans used other weapons. Minefields were laid without warning, regardless of international law ; the magnetic mine appeared, sown in 30s and 40s by submarines and in twos by aeroplanes ; dive-bombers began their deadly work and later the acoustic mine its sinister action.

On Britain's side the urgent necessity was defensively to arm every merchant ship by a gun in the stern, to put into immediate operation the convoy system that

had proved decisive in the war of 1914–18 (*see* Convoy), and to find the answer to the magnetic mine. Captain Langsdorf of the Admiral Graf Spee is reported to have said that for eight years Germany had sought unsuccessfully to counter this weapon. But in the spring of 1940 the Queen Elizabeth arrived safely in New York from the Clyde with the non-magnetic girdle called the degaussing system round her hull (*see* page 92). The magnetic mine had been made harmless.

SAVED FROM NAZI SAVAGERY

Patiently awaiting the British warship which raced to their aid, these men were survivors first of a blazing rescue ship, crowded with dying and injured, and secondly of the stricken ship's lifeboats which, after launching, were mercilessly machine-gunned and sunk by circling German planes.

Photo, L.N.A.

Besides the defence of her merchant shipping, Britain had to reorganize the basis on which her merchant fleet operated. Strategy required that each ship be put to the best use. Government control, established in the first few days of the war, functioned chiefly by means of Orders under the Defence Regulations. Ten days after war began all ships had to obtain Board of Trade Licences before going to sea. Chartering committees matched essential cargoes with available ships and controlled freight rates. Building and repairs were also controlled by licence, while Government insurance against war risks operated from the first day of the war.

A form of counter-blockade declared certain cargoes to be contraband and subject to seizure if bound for

FIRST LOSS OF THE WAR

Sunk without warning the day Britain declared war, the liner Athenia was the first U-boat victim. The torpedo struck her at 7.45 p.m., and all through the night rescue operations proceeded. But, owing to the list of the ship, some lifeboats capsized, and 128 lives were lost.

Photo, G. E. Withams

enemy territory (see Economic Warfare). In October 1939 the Ministry of Shipping was formed to take over all those activities previously carried out by the Mercantile Marine and Sea Transport Departments of the Board of Trade, and experts from the shipping, shipbroking and shipbuilding industries joined the new department. From the beginning of the war merchant ships required by the fighting forces as auxiliaries—such as transports and armed merchant cruisers—were requisitioned, and towards the end of 1939 partial requisitioning of cargo ships for commercial purposes was adopted. By February 1940, however, all seagoing ships came under the requisition policy with the exception of tankers. Detailed management was left to the companies, but the voyages, cargoes and freights became Government responsibility, the owning company being paid a monthly rate of hire to cover certain expenses, depreciation and interest on the capital represented. The negative system of control by licence was thus replaced by positive Governmental

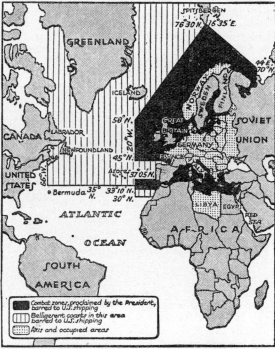

War zones barred to American shipping before the U.S. Neutrality Act was amended. *From "The New York Times"*

direction. In the autumn of 1940 coastal shipping was partly requisitioned and by January 1941 all oil-carrying vessels were under Government control. The Ministry of Shipping engaged the services of neutral ships and, in association with their national organizations, employed Allied shipping to its best advantage.

In May 1941 the Ministries of Shipping and Transport became the Ministry of War Transport with Lord Leathers as head. One result was to speed up the work in the ports through unified control.

In September 1939 the United Kingdom Register showed 1,000 British ships, 2,000,000 tons less than in 1914. During the early months of the war British losses fell from 155,000 tons gross in September 1939 to less than half that amount (see graph in facing page), while neutral losses rose from 30,000 tons gross

IMPORTANT INCIDENTS OF THE BATTLE OF THE ATLANTIC

1939	
Sept. 3	British passenger liner **Athenia** torpedoed and sunk.
Sept. 30	British cargo liner **Clement** sunk in South Atlantic, first victim of a German surface raider.
Dec. 17	German pocket battleship **Admiral Graf Spee** scuttled after naval defeat in S. Atlantic.
1940	
Mar. 7	British passenger liner **Queen Elizabeth** arrived in New York after secret maiden voyage from Clyde.
July 2	British passenger liner **Arandora Star**, carrying internees to Canada, torpedoed and sunk.
Sept. 17	British passenger liner **City of Benares**, carrying children to Canada, torpedoed and sunk.
Oct. 27	British passenger liner **Empress of Britain** sunk by torpedo while on fire from bombing attack.
Nov. 5	British armed merchant cruiser **Jervis Bay** sunk by German warship.
1941	
May 21	American liner **Robin Moor** sunk by German submarine in S. Atlantic, first U.S. ship to be torpedoed.
May 27	German battleship **Bismarck** sunk by naval forces.
July 8	Announced that U.S. forces had landed in Iceland.
Sept. 27	" Liberty Fleet Day " : 14 merchant ships of over 100,000 tons launched by American shipyards.
Oct. 17	U.S. destroyer **Kearny** torpedoed ; reached Iceland damaged.
Nov. 14	Amendment to U.S. Neutrality Act passed permitting American merchant ships to enter war zones.
Dec. 12	French liner **Normandie** seized by U.S. coastguard (later renamed **Lafayette,** caught fire and capsized in New York harbour).
1942	
Jan. 14	Panama tanker **Nornes** torpedoed and sunk off Long Island, first ship to be sunk near Atlantic coast.
Feb. 3	**Ocean Vanguard** arrived in a British port, first of 60 merchant ships ordered in America by Britain.
Feb. 7	**Fort Ville Marie,** first merchant ship of Canadian war programme, arrived in Britain.
Feb. 12	German battle cruisers **Scharnhorst** and **Gneisenau** and cruiser **Prinz Eugen** left Brest and passed through Straits of Dover.
Feb. 12	First U.S. ship, **Fluor-Spar,** after repeal of Neutrality Act, arrived with a war cargo in a British port.
Feb. 16	Tankers and Standard Oil Co.'s refinery in Aruba, Dutch East Indies, shelled by submarines.
May 9	Washington announced that Axis submarines had sunk two merchant ships in Gulf of Mexico.
May 10	Two cargo ships torpedoed in St. Lawrence River, Canada.

to nearly 100,000 in some months. This vindicated the convoy system and revealed the ruthlessness of the German campaign. And although total Allied losses by May 1940 amounted to just over 1,000,000 tons, Nazi losses were nearly 850,000 tons.

But the spring of 1940 saw serious British reverses, which profoundly altered the whole character of the Atlantic battle. Norway and Denmark were occupied by Germany. Holland and Belgium capitulated, and more than half of France, including the north and north-west coast, was enemy-occupied. Germany won valuable bases for submarines, motor torpedo boats (E-boats) and long-range bombers. The Battle of the Atlantic had now become even more definitely the centre of the struggle. The importance of the Atlantic routes was greatly increased by the loss of the near Continental sources of supply, the Atlantic now being the shortest supply route. Fortunately the heavy strain on shipping resources imposed by the greater distances to be sailed was offset by the addition of the free shipping of the invaded countries (*see* Merchant Navy).

However, Britain had lost the cooperation of the French Navy, and with Italy's entry into the war was forced to transfer many important naval units from the Atlantic to the Mediterranean. While the dangers in the Atlantic increased, protection had to be reduced. The Germans exploited their opportunities by intensified effort. The effect of these new developments was reflected in a sharp rise in losses in June 1940, and from this date the average sinkings up to February 1941 were more than doubled (*see* graph). The following three months saw an even higher rate of losses due to an intensified German campaign.

In the summer there was a turn of the tide. Throughout July and August 1941 British losses were reduced to the ratio of the first war months. There was a slight increase during the rest of the autumn, but generally the prospects appeared brighter than at any time since the collapse of France. In November the Prime Minister revealed that, making allowances for new building, the net loss of the mercantile marine, apart altogether from captures from the enemy and transfers of U.S. tonnage, had "been reduced in the last four months to a good deal less than one-fifth of what it was in the previous four months." The improvement was brought about despite the fact

BURNING TANKER OFF CURAÇAO

Shipping off the oil islands of the Dutch West Indies, in the South Atlantic, was attacked by a Japanese submarine on Feb. 16, 1942. This photograph was taken from an Allied bomber searching for the U-boat.
Photo, Keystone

that the number of U-boats and long-range bombers operating was, if anything, on the increase. It was due principally to increased convoy protection, including American naval patrols as far west as Iceland, more effective naval counter-measures, and increased aerial escorts. Other factors were the heavier bombing of European ports, U-boat bases and shipyards, and Germany's preoccupation with the attempted blitzkrieg against Russia.

The improvement, however, did not last long. Early in December Japan and the United States entered the war, and a new sea battle began.

Though there was, in the words of the Prime Minister, "a most serious increase" in our shipping losses, this was due chiefly to the sea campaigns "east of Suez." The Atlantic position was well maintained throughout December and the best part of January 1942. A new phase, however, opened with the torpedoing of the Panama tanker "Nornes" (9,577 tons) 60 miles off the tip of Long Island on Jan. 14.

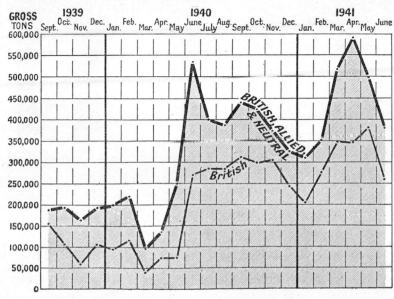

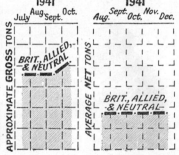

LOSSES IN SHIPPING

Following the two great peaks of 1940 and 1941, Allied shipping losses dropped. Monthly figures of gross losses can be given only up to June 1941. Thereafter the approximate gross losses are shown for the period July-September and October. The final column shows the net position (allowing for new building) for the five months August-December 1941.

TWO GREAT DEMOCRATS CONFER

In August 1941 Mr. Churchill set out in H.M.S. Prince of Wales for a four-day conference at sea with President Roosevelt, the outcome of which was the Atlantic Charter. They are here seen on the giant battleship's deck.

Photo, British Official: Crown Copyright

It was the nearest known approach so far of an enemy warship to the United States coast. Within a month 25 ships had been sunk by U-boats in the Caribbean Sea and off the Atlantic coast—American tankers and cargo vessels, a Canadian passenger liner and vessels flying the British, Panamanian, Latvian, Norwegian, Brazilian and Swedish flags. On Feb. 25 the U.S. Navy Department revealed that from the beginning of the year 114 ships of the United Nations had been attacked in the western half of the Atlantic. On the other hand, 56 attacks had been made on enemy submarines, with the known result that three had been sunk and four damaged.

The boldest of the enemy attacks was carried out by submarines against shipping off the Dutch West Indies islands of Aruba and Curaçao on the night of Feb. 16. Three tankers were sunk and four were damaged and the Aruba oil refineries were shelled.

In spite of the enemy's greater efforts, Mr. A. V. Alexander, First Lord of the Admiralty, was able to announce on Feb. 26 that " although since the beginning of the war the total number of ships convoyed is very large indeed, losses in convoy are still just under one-half of one per cent." Reviewing sea affairs he pointed out that the Battle of the Atlantic had now developed into the Battle of the Seven Seas.

Nevertheless, in regard to the most vital question of the supplying of Britain's production machine and fighting forces, the Atlantic was still the main battle-ground. In this struggle the part to be played by American shipyards, in association with the rising production of ships in Britain and Canada, was beginning to appear as a decisive factor.

A joint Anglo-American statement issued on June 27, 1942 after Mr. Churchill's return from Washington showed that shipping was still the major problem of the United Nations ; plans were in hand to reduce the heavy Axis toll of merchant shipping.

Consult Atlantic Front, Basil Woon (Peter Davies).

Atlantic Charter. Eight-point Declaration issued by President Roosevelt and Mr. Churchill after a 4-day conference at sea, August 1941, and announced by Mr. Attlee on August 14. The Declaration of British and U.S. war and peace aims comprised the following :

(1) Britain and U.S. seek no aggrandizement. (2) No territorial changes that do not accord with the freely expressed will of the peoples. (3) Right of all peoples to choose their own form of government. (4) Further trade and raw materials to all States needing them for economic prosperity. (5) Fullest collaboration between all nations in the economic field. (6) After the destruction of Nazi tyranny, a peace to ensure to all nations the means of dwelling in safety. (7) All men to traverse the high seas and oceans without hindrance. (8) Pending the establishment of a wider and permanent system of social security, disarmament of warlike nations is essential.

Although the terms of the Declaration had already been embodied, or were implicit, in recent speeches of Mr. Churchill, President Roosevelt, and other British and American spokesmen, their formal affirmation was of immense practical value in emphasizing the unity of their war aims and of their definition of the conditions necessary for peace. The contrast between the purpose of the great democracies and that of the Axis dictators, with its principle of the exploitation of enslaved countries by the so-called master race, was thus underlined before the world. Throughout the British Commonwealth the Declaration was received with enthusiastic approval. In America there were mixed praise and criticism, but all were agreed that the winning of the war was an indispensable condition.

Atlantic Ferry Service. A regular " ferry " service between the U.S.A. and Britain for flying American aircraft destined for the R.A.F. came into existence in 1940. On June 14, 1941 it was announced that Air Chief Marshal Sir Frederick Bowhill had been appointed to command the organization known as the Ferry Command. Canadian as well as British pilots were engaged in this work of ferrying. The chief machines flown included Lockheed Hudson bombers, Boeing B-17 (flying fortress), Lockheed Ventura, and Consolidated 28-5 flying-boats. In July 1941 a Lockheed Hudson was piloted across the Atlantic by Miss Jacqueline Cochran, American woman flier. A Ferry Command speed record was set up when, early in 1942, a Liberator made the west-east crossing in eight hours, one minute. Later the east-west crossing was done in even less time.

Mr. C. R. Atlee, Deputy Prime Minister.

A.T.S. *See* Women's Services.

Attlee, RT. HON. CLEMENT RICHARD, P.C., M.P. (b. 1883). Deputy Prime Minister and Dominions Secretary. He was leader of H.M. Opposition, 1935–40, and Lord Privy Seal and Deputy Prime Minister, 1940–42. As Lord Privy Seal he acted as the War Cabinet's clearing-house for questions from all Departments concerned with Britain's war effort.

Auchinleck, GEN. SIR CLAUDE, G.C.I.E., D.S.O. (b. 1884). G.O.C.-in-C. Middle East from 1941 to 1942. He served most of his career in the Indian Army. When he came home from India early in 1940 he was appointed a corps commander and was

Gen. Auchinleck,
C.-in-C. Middle East.
Photo, British Official

preparing it for service in France when operations in Norway took place, and he was put in command of the Allied forces at Narvik. He organized the capture of this town on May 28 and the subsequent withdrawal on June 10. On July 19 he was appointed G.O.C.-in-C. Southern Command. In December, the danger of immediate invasion over, he was sent back to India, this time as C.-in-C. Here he remained for six months. On July 2, 1941, he and Sir Archibald Wavell, then C.-in-C. Middle East, were switched over, each to the other's command. On Nov. 18, 1941, Gen. Auchinleck began a fresh drive into Libya, relieving Tobruk. On June 25, 1942, during Rommel's renewed offensive, he took over command of the 8th Army from Gen. Ritchie. *See* North Africa.

Augsburg. City of Bavaria, 35 miles N.W. of Munich. On April 17, 1942, twelve Lancaster bombers set out to deliver a daring daylight attack on a vital U-boat engine factory here. Four of the twelve were shot down by fighters south of Paris. The Augsburg factory had very strong A.A. defences, and three more bombers were brought down after making their attack. The five remaining aircraft loosed their bombs on the target from a low level and returned in safety, though damaged. Sqn.-Ldr. J. D Nettleton, who led the first formation, was awarded the V.C.

AUSTRALIA'S GREAT PART IN THE WAR

From the day Britain declared war Australia helped the Mother Country with every resource of her Navy, Army, and Air Force, with munitions and with food supplies. Later she herself faced the enemy at her very gates. See also New Zealand ; Pacific.

Australia. The significance and extent of Australia's war effort can best be gauged by a message which Mr. Menzies, then Prime Minister, sent to Mr. Churchill when the Battle of Britain was at its height in September 1940. Mr. Menzies telegraphed : " The Mother Country may be assured that in every part of the Empire, and in no part more than in Australia, there is a resolution to do all, bear all and spend all for the success of our most holy cause."

The news of the British declaration of war reached Australia on the Daventry Wireless broadcast at 6.15 p.m. on Sunday, Sept. 3, 1939, and the Federal Cabinet, after being in session throughout the day, authorized Mr. Menzies to make his broadcast declaring that Australia was also at war at 7.15 p.m. On June 11, 1940, a special Government Gazette declared a state of war between Italy and Australia. Finally, on Dec. 9, 1941, Mr. Curtin, the Labour Prime Minister, issued Australia's proclamation of war on Japan, and Mr. Kawa, the Japanese minister, received his dismissal.

Implementing its declaration of war, Australia had 300,000 men under arms either at home or overseas by March 1941, and it was estimated that 600,000 would be serving in the fighting services by the end of 1942—that is, one in every four men of fighting age. The first Australians to enter the European conflict were 200 men of the Royal Australian Air Force, who reached England early in 1940 and cooperated with the British Coastal Command in the defence of Britain. On Feb. 12, 1940, the first detachment of the Australian Imperial Force reached Suez. The Australians were under the command of Sir Thomas Blamey (later Commander-in-Chief of the Allied Land Forces in Australia). The second detachment of the Australian Imperial Force disembarked in Egypt on May 17 and proceeded to Palestine, under the command of Major-General Iven Mackay, and five days later Mr. Menzies announced that a third division was being raised.

The first outstanding feats of arms by Australians were in Wavell's Libyan campaign, notably in the capture of Benghazi, which was celebrated throughout Australia on Feb. 6, 1941. In April an Australian division was fighting in Greece alongside New Zealand, Greek, Serb and British troops, the sector of the line including Mount Olympus and Mount Parnassus.

Later Australian troops fought in the famous Thermopylae mountain area. Mr. Menzies, speaking on April 23, explained that his Government regarded it as unthinkable that the gallant Greeks should be left unassisted. In Crete 6,486 Australian troops took part in the fighting, and when it ended 2,887 had been evacuated, including 218 wounded, leaving 3,599 unaccounted for, most of them prisoners. Mr. Menzies admitted that the Cretan fighting represented a serious blow, but claimed that the defence of the island, by upsetting the German time-table, had enabled Britain to clear up the situation in Iraq and move troops to the threatened Syrian border. In the Syrian fighting against the troops of Vichy France the Australians again did yeoman service, particularly in

ANOTHER VICTORY SHIP LAUNCHED
Here is H.M.A.S. Lithgow sliding down the slips at Mort's Dock, Sydney, on Dec. 21, 1940, one of the many warships that were being built in Australia.
Photo, Australian Official

AUSTRALIA

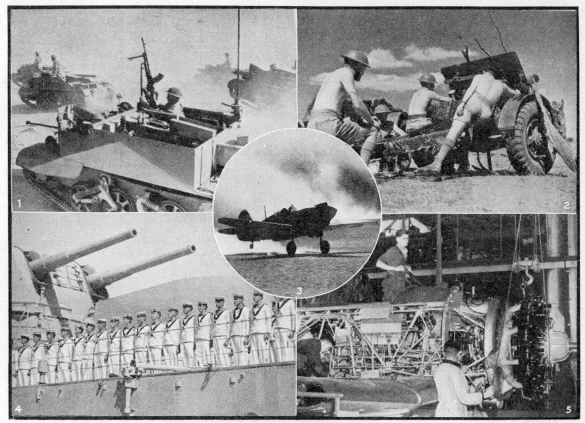

AUSTRALIA FIGHTS IN EVERY SPHERE

1. Benghazi was taken by Australian troops on Feb. 6, 1941, and here are some of the Bren carriers in which they swept to victory.   2. Gunners of an Australian field regiment practising under a hot sun.   3. Tomahawk fighter, one of a squadron in the Middle East.   4. Men of H.M.A.S. Perth stand at attention as their ship enters Sydney harbour after 177 days at sea.   5. Installing a Pratt & Whitney Wasp engine, built by the Commonwealth Aircraft Corporation.

Photos, Australian Official; Wide World

the battle of July 7, 1941, on the Damour River. By August 1941 90,000 Australians were serving abroad.

Between September 1939 and the end of 1941 the Royal Australian Air Force grew from 21 to 102 units and the personnel was seventeen times the pre-war strength, the man-power of the force in 1941 being about 60,000, including reservists. It was announced that by the middle of 1942 twenty-three Australian Air squadrons would be serving abroad. Under the British Commonwealth Air Training Scheme Australia undertook to train 16,000 men for air crews by March 1942, and 10,000 a year thereafter. No fewer than 200,000 had volunteered for air service by August 1941, of whom 20,000 passed into the air crews and 100,000 were enrolled for ground work.

At the outbreak of the war the Royal Australian Navy had a strength of 5,400 men and the ships in commission included two heavy cruisers, four other cruisers and five destroyers. Within two years the Navy men numbered twenty thousand and the fleet had a record of service in the Indian Ocean, the Pacific and the Mediterranean. Destroyers of the Tribal class were also being built in Australian ship-building yards, as well as smaller craft, such as mine-sweepers. In 1941 four or five naval ships were being launched each month in Australia. No vessel of the Royal Australian Navy had a record comparable with

that of the cruiser Sydney, which sank the Italian cruiser Bartolomeo Colleoni in the Mediterranean on July 19, 1940. The Sydney (q.v.) was sunk early in December 1941, in an action with the raider Kormoran, disguised as a merchantman. Memorable, too, was the last fight of the merchant-ship Turakina with a German raider in the Southern Pacific on August 20, 1940. The Turakina had a single gun, while the raider had armament which could be fired at all angles. The Turakina lost two-thirds of her crew of 58 before she struck her flag. The fight was one of the most glorious in the annals of the Empire's merchant marine. H.M.A.S. Vampire took part in the fight off Endau on Jan. 26, 1942, in which a Japanese destroyer was sunk and another damaged.

Scarcely less important than the contribution of man-power was the contribution of material. In the first year of the war Australia sold 56 million bushels of wheat and 150,000 tons of flour to the British Government, the shipment occupying the whole of 1940 and representing the largest wheat deal Australia had ever effected. A munitions production programme was also initiated costing £50,000,000. The Federal Government alone had 56,000 workers in its munition factories in 1941.

A thousand aircraft were produced in the first year of war, and a great increase was promised by 1942,

30

the types of aircraft including trainer 'planes, second-line fighters and Beaufort medium torpedo bombers. Rifles, Bren and Vickers guns, anti-tank guns and howitzers were also produced in Australia, while Great Britain bought the whole of Australia's wool clip for the duration of the war and a year after. In September 1941, when he was Prime Minister, Mr. Fadden announced that the Commonwealth was expending over thirty per cent of her men and materials in the war effort. As for the financial burden, Mr. Chifley, Treasurer in Mr. Curtin's Labour Government, in his Budget speech on Oct. 26, 1941, announced taxation for the year totalling £170 million, compared with £74 million in the last pre-war year.

The Labour Party had been in office only two months when Japan struck. Australia was directly menaced for the first time in its history and the Commonwealth's war plans had to be revised overnight to meet the new threat. The fighting was no longer thousands of miles away; hostilities were raging only a few hundred miles north of the continent. The Japanese attack on Malaya and the sinking of the British battleships " Prince of Wales " and " Repulse " underlined the danger facing Australia

Central area of Australia showing Port Darwin and the two sections of railway joined by a motor road.

By courtesy of the " Daily Telegraph "

and the fact that she was virtually cut off from the free countries of the world. All men between the ages of 18 and 45 were called up for service in the armed forces or were directed to essential civil work associated with the war.

On December 9, 1941, Australia had declared war on Japan. Official policy was well summed-up by Dr. E. V. Evatt, Minister for External Affairs, who said that the Commonwealth was working for full alliance with Russia and the other enemies of Japan, and for unification of control in the Pacific.

At the New Year General Wavell was appointed Allied C.-in-C. for the South Pacific, with headquarters in the Dutch East Indies; General Van Mook, the Dutch Commander, visited Sydney and promised full Dutch cooperation and the observance of a scorched earth policy; and it was understood that American help was on the way.

But in the race against time Japan had temporarily got ahead. The Allied position in Malaya went steadily from bad to worse. The Australian Imperial Force, sent there under Maj.-Gen. Gordon Bennett, had its first engagement with the Japanese on Jan. 16, and during the next week put up a fine resistance in the Muar area. But Malaya was lost, against overwhelming odds, and Singapore itself fell on Feb. 15, 1942.

Disquiet in Australia was now profound. Mr. Menzies had on Jan. 16 revealed in a broadcast that, for a whole year past, Sir Robert Brooke-Popham, with his support, had been urging that reinforcements should be sent; and Mr. Curtin, in another broadcast, said that " no single nation can afford to risk its future

on the infallibility of one man " (a reference to Mr. Churchill). When Singapore was lost he declared that this was " Australia's Dunkirk " and the opening of the Battle of Australia.

The Commonwealth now braced itself against the oncoming swarms of Japanese who were rapidly occupying island after island in the South Pacific. Recriminations which, though natural, were based on an incomplete knowledge of facts, died down, and a very different spirit might be observed in Mr. Curtin's stirring broadcast to the U.S.A. on March 3, in which he said that " looking to America " implied no belittling of the old country, which had been fully occupied in winning the Battle of Britain and the Battle of the Atlantic, and in sending supplies to Russia, and " cannot at the same time go all out in the Pacific."

Before this, the Japanese had begun attacking Australian mandated territory in the Bismarck Archipelago and New Guinea. By Jan. 26 they had landed 10,000 troops at Rabaul, capital of New Britain, but in New Guinea Port Moresby remained a centre of Allied resistance; it was repeatedly bombed by the Japanese, and with equal persistence the Allies continued to bomb Rabaul.

The first attack on the soil of Australia itself came on Feb. 19, when Japanese bombers twice raided Darwin (*q.v.*), the northernmost port of Australia.

FIRST BOMBS ON AUSTRALIA

The wrecked jetty at Port Darwin was the first damage suffered by Australia when Japan launched her air attacks on the Commonwealth on Feb. 19, 1942. The possession of this harbour would be of immense value to the Japanese.

Photo, Associated Press

In the first raid 72 bombers came over, with a strong fighter escort, and in the second raid 21 bombers with escort were employed ; they dropped 50 tons of explosive and did considerable damage, destroying some grounded 'planes and shipping. There were many subsequent raids on this town, but the damage in these was much less, and an increasing proportion of the attackers were brought down. On one occasion the enemy lost five out of seven bombers. Raids were also made on the West Australian ports of Wyndham (284 miles S.W. of Darwin), Broome (600 miles S.W. of Wyndham) and Derby (near Broome), and on Katherine, in Northern Territory, some 200 miles south of Darwin by railway.

The Battle of the Coral Sea, the area of the Pacific lying north-east of Australia, which began on May 4, 1942, is described under the heading Pacific.

On March 17 it was officially announced that America had sent General MacArthur, hero of the Philippines, to take supreme command in the South Pacific, at the request of the Australian Government and with the enthusiastic approval of all the Allied nations. It was revealed that for the past two months strong American forces had been pouring into Australia. " Now, instead of giving way, we are going to attack," said MacArthur's deputy, Lt.-Gen. C. H. Brett. The arrival of American troops and supplies continued until North Australian territory was strongly occupied, not merely for defence purposes but as a base for attack. Australia's Imperial Force was recalled from the Middle East for the defence of Australia's own shores, and its commander, General Sir Thomas Blamey, was appointed C.-in-C. of the Allied Land Forces in S.W. Pacific area. Close cooperation between Australia and America was further assisted by Dr. Evatt's mission to Washington in March. On June 4, 1942, Mr. S. M. Bruce was appointed representative of the Australian Government in the War Cabinet and the Pacific War Council. He succeeded Sir Earle Page.

It had been announced on Jan. 27 that Australia would be represented in the War Cabinet in London. On March 18 Mr. Richard G. Casey, Australian Minister in Washington, was appointed Minister of State in the Middle East, with headquarters in Cairo, in succession to Mr. Oliver Lyttelton, and was given a seat in the War Cabinet.

On the night of June 1 an attempted raid by four small Japanese submarines on Sydney harbour resulted in all being sunk. An Australian ferry boat was the only casualty. See Pacific, War in.

Auxiliary Military Pioneer Corps (AMPS). See Pioneer Corps, Auxiliary Military.

Axis, Berlin-Rome. This political collaboration of Germany was initiated during the Abyssinian War, 1936, and developed to a full political and military treaty of alliance signed May 22, 1939. It was then stated that Germany and Italy " join forces for securing their living space and maintaining peace, so as to make the foundations of European civilization safe amidst a world of unrest and disintegration."

By Articles 1 and 2 permanent touch and mutual consultation were ensured on all questions of international politics, and provided that if the security or other vital interests of one partner were threatened from without, the other partner would lend him full diplomatic and political support. Article 3 said : " If one of the two partners becomes involved in a warlike conflict with one or more other Powers, the other partner will immediately stand by him as an ally, and support him with all his military forces on land, on sea and in the air." By Article 4 there was to be immediate collaboration in military affairs and war economics. Article 5 provided that in the event of a joint war the partners must conclude an armistice and peace only in full mutual agreement. The treaty was valid for 10 years.

On Sept. 27, 1940, Japan joined the Axis by signing the Berlin Pact (q.v.), whereby she promised to assist the two European Powers to set up a New Order in Europe, while they in turn undertook to assist her in the establishment of a New Order in Greater Asia. Hungary signed her adherence to the Axis on Nov. 20, 1940, Rumania and Slovakia on Nov. 23, Bulgaria on March 1, 1941, Yugoslavia on March 29 (which led to the great revolt), and Croatia on June 14, 1941.

Bader, WING CMDR. D. R., D.S.O. Famous airman who, although he had lost both legs in a crash in 1933, " argued " his way back into the R.A.F. at the outbreak of war. He led a Canadian Squadron of the Fighter Command in the Battle of Britain, 1940, and shot down at least 15 German machines. Having played a prominent part in daylight sweeps over Northern France, 1940-41, he fell into the enemy's hands on August 9, 1941, through colliding with a Messerschmitt while pulling up from a dive-attack on another one which he had sent down in flames. One of his metal legs was damaged when he baled out, and a " spare " kept at his air station was dropped from an R.A.F. 'plane when flying over occupied territory. Wing Commander Bader had brought down 22½ German 'planes—the last being shared.

Wing Cmdr. Bader, legless pilot.
Photo, British Official

Badoglio, MARSHAL PIETRO (b. 1871). This Italian soldier had a distinguished military career. He was Governor of Libya from 1928 to 1933. Appointed C.-in-C. Italian Armies in East Africa in November 1935, he commanded operations in Eritrea,

Italian Somaliland and all occupied sectors of Abyssinia. For his services in the conquest of Abyssinia he was made Viceroy in 1936, but was later relieved of the office at his own request and created Duke of Addis Ababa. Marshal Badoglio signed the Armistice with France as Italy's representative. On Dec. 6, 1940, during the Italo-Greek war, he was dismissed from his position as Chief of the Italian Staff, which he had held since 1925.

Marshal Badoglio, Italian soldier.
Photo, Topical

Baghdad. Capital of Iraq. Baghdad stands on the R. Tigris, about 300 miles from the Persian Gulf. It is a great distributing centre for the Middle East. The Berlin-Baghdad railway was completed in 1940. During the Nazi-inspired revolt of April 1941 in Iraq, 500 British residents sought refuge in the British Embassy and U.S. Legation at Baghdad, and were held there as hostages until released by the armistice, arranged May 31, between the Iraqi authorities and the O.C. British troops in Iraq. Little King Feisal II

BADGES ISSUED FOR AUXILIARY WAR SERVICES

The examples here given are a selection from the many badges designed for the various forms of war service. Only those numbered are not self-explanatory. 1. Mechanized Transport Corps. 2. Metropolitan Police War Reserve. 3. Entertainments National Service Association. 4. Metropolitan Special Constabulary. 5. Royal Ordnance Factories. 6. National Fire Service (which in 1941 superseded 8. Auxiliary Fire Service). 7. Air Raid Precautions (replaced in 1941 by 11. Civil Defence). 9. Home Guard. 10. Ex-service men or women. 12. Navy, Army and Air Force Institutes.

Photos, L.N.A.; British Official; Mansell; Planet News

OILFIELDS AT BAKU COVETED BY HITLER

Faced by a serious depletion of the oil supplies essential for the Nazi war effort, Hitler ordered a powerful drive to be made in the autumn of 1941 towards the rich fields of Caucasia—but it was of no avail. Above are seen the great Ordzhonikidze oil-wells at Baku, from which 11,000 tons of oil are pumped daily.

Photo, Black Star

and the rightful Regent, Emir Abdul Ilah (*q.v.*), returned to Baghdad in state on June 1. *See* Iraq.

Baku. Seaport on the Caspian Sea, and capital of the Soviet Azerbeijan Republic ; it is also the name of a district within the limits of the Republic. There are vast petroleum deposits in the neighbourhood, the oil-bearing area covering more than 2,700 acres and producing 75 per cent of Soviet oil. Oil pipe-lines run from here to Batum, on the Black Sea, via Tiflis,

and to Rostov via Grozny (whence a line runs to Tuapse). The German drive into Russia to the Sea of Azov in the autumn of 1941, and the subsequent offensive against the Crimea, were directed primarily at securing the pipe-lines and oilfields of Baku.

Bali. Lying east of Java, this island was invaded by the Japanese on Feb. 20, 1942. Dutch and Balinese troops offered fierce resistance, but Bali was quickly overrun by the enemy. *See* Java.

THE TRAGEDY OF THE BALKAN COUNTRIES

Because they would not unite against Axis aggression, the Balkan countries were one by one either overrun or occupied under pressure. Here is the story of their lamentable fate. See also Albania ; Bulgaria ; Greece, etc.

Balkans. The fate of the Balkans was sealed at the signing of the Munich Pact of September 1938, although none of the Balkan countries was mentioned in it by name. The partition of Czechoslovakia, to which Britain and France agreed in that fateful document, inevitably involved the whole Balkan Peninsula. France's " iron ring " of the small allied states of Eastern and South-eastern Europe fell to pieces ; the Balkan Entente, of which Dr. Benes, Prime Minister of Czechoslovakia, had been the prime founder, dissolved ; and the seizure by Germany of the Bohemian mountain " Maginot Line " laid the whole Balkan area open to military pressure from the north.

Balkan unity having been destroyed, it remained for the Axis to attack the Peninsula piecemeal. Germany took the remainder of Czechoslovakia in March 1939. Italy fell upon Albania on Good Friday, 1939, thus gaining a foothold for the attack in the following year on Greece. In the remaining countries Germany undertook intensive " fifth column " work and the extension of an economic stranglehold over the Balkans by her system of enforced barter, whereby she imported all the valuable food and other raw materials from those countries in exchange for useless goods.

At the outset of the war the Balkans were, therefore, naked to the coming thrust, militarily and economically. Morally, they were disillusioned first by their abandonment by Britain and France at Munich, and secondly by the cynical non-aggression pact signed by Germany and Russia on August 23, 1939. The Balkan countries had had divided loyalties : their Royalty and Governments looked towards Germany, and their peoples towards Russia. The agreement of Russia to Germany's war in 1939 upset this counterpoise, and

both rulers and ruled in the Balkans were thus subjected to Nazi influence. Diplomatically, Britain and France were hopelessly outpaced and for the first year of the war had to content themselves with an economic conflict. A United Kingdom trading corporation was formed and enjoyed some success in combating German economic power in the Balkans.

Five Countries Broken Up

The principle of partition had been established first by Germany's act in dividing Czechoslovakia into the Bohemia-Moravia Protectorate, the Slovak Republic, and the small areas handed over to Poland and Hungary. The next country to be partitioned was Rumania, and in 1940 the Hungarians, supported by Germany, demanded and received Transylvania, and the Russians, not to be outdone, recovered Bessarabia, while Bulgaria, with Hitler's assistance, acknowledged receipt of the Southern Dobruja. In this way Germany bound both Hungary and Bulgaria to her side by ties of gratitude, and Rumania, whom Britain had guaranteed against Nazi aggression, was reduced to a mere cipher in Balkan affairs. King Carol fled, and after much civil disturbance General Antonescu and the Iron Guard took power there. Yugoslavia and Greece alone remained, and they became the next target. Italy began the invasion of Greece, whose leaders had proved impervious to bribes and other fifth column tactics, while Germany undertook to undermine Yugoslavia from within. Turkey-in-Europe, which is also part of the Balkan Peninsula, was ignored for the time being.

The stalwart Yugoslavs and Greeks, however, were not to be easily subdued. Greece put up a superb resistance to the Italian invasion, and indeed succeeded in driving the Italians back to the sea-coast of Albania (*see* Greece). In Yugoslavia, although the Regent, Prince Paul, and his Premier, Stoyadinovitch, were easily won over to Germany, the people and the army remained true to a belief in an Allied victory. It became evident, therefore, that the whole weight of German military power would have to be thrown into the balance. The Italian armies in Albania had to be rescued. At the end of March 1941 Prince Paul of Yugoslavia and his weak-spirited government agreed to sign away Yugoslav independence and allow German troops to pass through in order to bring relief to the Italians. On the frontiers of Bulgaria and Hungary with Greece other German armies were massing. But immediately Prince Paul's capitulation became known in Yugoslavia there was a bloodless revolution in the form of a military coup d'état, the Regent was removed, King Peter was enthroned, declared of age to rule, and the country mobilized under General Simovitch (*q.v.*).

It was too late, however, to stop the German invasion. While Yugoslavia was still incompletely mobilized, German, Hungarian and Bulgarian armies invaded her and Greece on April 6, and by the 27th the Balkan war was over. The British Expeditionary Force to Greece was evacuated and the whole Balkan Peninsula, except for certain areas in the Serbian mountains, where guerilla warfare continued on an increasing scale, came under German and Italian occupation, with all that that connotes in suffering, starvation, murder and unutterable degradation.

Free Yugoslav (under King Peter), Free Greek (under King George), Free Hungarian, Free Rumanian, and Free Bulgarian movements were formed in London, and the armed forces of Yugoslavia and Greece played heroic parts in subsequent battles in the Near East. The home governments of Hungary and Rumania provided armies to swell Hitler's hordes when he turned against Russia in June 1941.

Books to Consult. Middle East, H. V. Morton (Methuen). From the Land of the Silent People, Robert St. John (Harrap). Buffer States of the Balkans, H. Gregson (Hutchinson).

GOING UP!

Every strategic area in Britain is now protected by a balloon barrage as part of the A.A. defences. Men are here seen releasing the mooring ropes of their charge, but many Balloon Stations are manned by women.
Photo, Planet News

Balloon Barrage. Anti-aircraft defence consisting of a number of captive balloons, the metal cables of which form an obstacle to aeroplanes. Over important towns or other places likely to form targets for enemy raiders a more or less continual screen of balloons is maintained, the height being varied at intervals to suit weather conditions and the distance from the ground of the lowest cloud layer. The spacing of the balloons and their siting is such that gaps in one line are filled by the cables of balloons in other lines, and the complete barrage forms a screen through which aircraft find it very difficult —and highly dangerous— to try to penetrate.

The barrage is a defence especially against low-level attacks, whether by dive-bombers or by ordinary bombers which carry

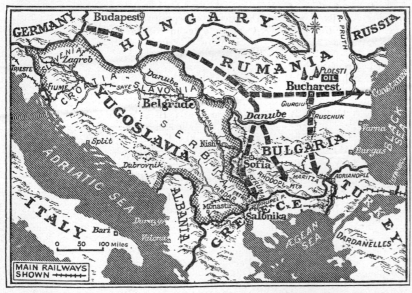

How the Nazis drove through the Balkans to Greece and the Black Sea.

delayed-action bombs. It keeps the enemy up to such a height that machine-gunning of the point guarded is not effective. Balloons are also towed by ships in convoy, and may be flown from barges for waterside protection.

A barrage balloon is not unlike the observation balloon that was much used some years ago to spot for artillery fire. It has air-filled fins which steady it in the air, while it is supported by hydrogen gas contained in the balloon body. The winding cable is made of a light but immensely strong alloy; this is extremely important, since a comparatively light cable will enable the balloon to go higher in the air than a heavier one. Hydrogen is the most convenient gas, though not the one with the greatest lifting power, and every pound of weight that can be saved is precious. The cable must be so tough and strong that it will spell destruction to any fast-flying aircraft that collides with it. The balloon is tethered to a cable drum on a winch-lorry, and the winch is worked by an engine. Over the winch operator is a strong steel network to protect him or her (women of the W.A.A.F. serve as balloon operators, as well as airmen of the R.A.F.). An indicator on the drum tells the operator the length of cable let out, and thus the height of the balloon.

The balloon is inflated from metal cylinders of gas which are carried on a special lorry; a number of cylinders is connected to the inlet pipe which goes to the balloon. The latter is never fully inflated, since the gas expands under the heat of the sun's rays and must be given room to spread out. The balloon envelope is built up of some 600 separate pieces of light but strong fabric (equal to 1,000 yards, 42 inches wide). The outside is dressed with a preparation of aluminium to reflect the sun rays and so make it cooler within.

It came to be a routine part of the German daylight raiders to attempt to shoot down balloons in readiness for a bombing attack on some key-point. On the aircraft themselves the enemy fitted V-shaped fenders, with the point of the V outward; the object was to push aside any cable which was encountered. This fender weighed some two hundred pounds, and must have been a great encumbrance. The British plan against the German barrage was to fit a number of small cable-cutters along the front edge of the aeroplane wing. But, despite anything of this nature, the balloon barrage was a powerful deterrent to hostile aircraft.

In the British defence system the Balloon Barrage was originally part of the Auxiliary Air Force, the first Balloon Squadron being formed in 1938. When, in September 1939, the Royal Air Force took over the balloons, there were 44 squadrons in being. There was a Balloon Command of the R.A.F., at the head of which from 1940 to 1944 was Air Marshal Sir E. L. Gossage, K.C.B., C.V.O., D.S.O., M.C.

Baltic Sea. Shallow inland sea, bounded N. by Sweden and Finland, E. by Russia, Estonia, Latvia and Lithuania, S. by Germany and Poland, W. by Denmark and Sweden. It includes the Gulf of Bothnia on the N., and the Gulfs of Finland and Riga on the E., and is connected with the North Sea by the Sound, Kattegat and Skaggerak. At the entrance to the Gulf of Bothnia are the Aaland Islands (*q.v.*), and many other key islands lie in the Gulf of Finland and the Southern Baltic, including Oesel (Estonia), Gothland (Sweden), and Zealand (Denmark). The Gulf of Bothnia is ice-bound from November to April, and Germany's vital iron ore supply from Lulea, the Swedish port at the head of the Gulf, was then sent round through Narvik (*q.v.*). On April 14, 1940, the Admiralty announced that a gigantic British minefield had been laid from the Kattegat along the northern coast of Germany and extending in the Eastern Baltic as far as Memel, thus blocking the N. German ports. Most of the Russian fleet is based on Kronstadt, in the Gulf of Finland. In October 1941 minefields were laid here by the Germans and Finns. *See* Finland.

THE BALTIC STATES WERE TWICE INVADED

*F*orcibly incorporated in the U.S.S.R. in 1940, then overrun by Germany in 1941—such has been the lot of Estonia, Latvia and Lithuania, the three little republics created after the First Great War. Latvia and Lithuania were made part of the German " Ostland."

Baltic States. In no instance was the insecurity of small nations more clearly manifested in an unsettled international world than in that of the Baltic States of Estonia, Latvia and Lithuania. Owing to their situation as a buffer between Teuton and Slav their strategic importance was out of all proportion to their economic value, and after the outbreak of the Second Great War Russia, desirous of securing her frontiers, speedily showed her interest in them.

When, in the summer of 1939, Britain and Russia were in negotiation for an anti-aggression front against Hitler, Russia insisted on a joint Anglo-Russian guarantee of the independence of the Baltic States. These negotiations broke down, and in June Estonia and Latvia signed pacts of non-aggression with Germany. This manoeuvre was defeated, however, by the pact between Russia and Germany.

In the autumn of 1939 the Soviet made demands on Estonia, Latvia and Lithuania for naval and air bases. A Mutual Assistance Pact with Russia was signed by Estonia on Sept. 28 and by Latvia on Oct. 5. Hardly was the ink dry on the signatures when Russian troops, planes and warships occupied strategic points on the Estonian islands of Oesel and Dago and in the town of Paldiski, in the Latvian ports of Liepaja and Ventspils, and in the Gulf of Riga. In October Lithuania signed a similar pact, but she received in return Vilna, the old Lithuanian capital, which had been taken from the Poles by the Russians.

During the autumn of 1939, too, began the great exodus of the German Balts, who, numbering about 82,000, were ordered by Hitler to return to Germany.

In the middle of June 1940 the Soviet presented the three Baltic States with ultimatums requiring a change of government and free passage for Soviet troops to guarantee the fulfilment of the existing Mutual Assistance Pacts. The formation of new Left Wing governments was followed in July by elections for new National Assemblies. In August Estonia, Latvia and Lithuania were incorporated as Soviet Republics.

Lithuania was the first of the three Baltic States through which Germany advanced towards Leningrad at the beginning of her attack on Russia in 1941.

The Germans declared Lithuania and Latvia with parts of White Russia to constitute the new German "Ostland," with Herr von Lohse as Gauleiter. The inhabitants of the Baltic States were given plainly to understand that, having made too many mistakes in foreign policy in the past, never again could they hope for independence. German wireless proclamations revealed that food was rationed, farms and hospitals had been requisitioned, that the retreating Russians had destroyed bridges, communications and manufacturing plant, and that remaining assets, even to the hospitals, had been taken over by the Germans for their own campaigning needs. Typhus was reported in December 1941. National hymns and national colours were forbidden, and executions were frequent.

But although they had been twice invaded in two years the Estonians, Letts and Lithuanians had not given up hope of independence. The accredited ministers of these States prior to their Pact with Russia were still recognized at the Court of St. James's. In the U.S.A. prominent figures of the Baltic States, like Professor Smetona, former Lithuanian President, were keeping alive their countries' claims.

A veil of secrecy descended on these small countries. British residents, deprived of their property, and those few prominent inhabitants fortunate enough to escape the vigilant Soviet naval and frontier guards, were the only sources of information for events in the Baltic States. They told of the nationalization of land, banks and large business enterprises, of the collectivization of agriculture, and of the arrest and detention of formerly prominent political leaders.

Nor was the curtain lifted on the scene when, in June 1941, Germany invaded the Baltic States as a move in her campaign against Soviet Russia and turned them into a blazing battlefield. The Germans hermetically sealed the Baltic States against the outside world. Even the Red Cross was unable to function. There were rumours of revolts in Riga and executions in Estonia. But if the Baltic States hoped to regain their independence under the Germans, they were sadly disappointed. The Germans dissolved the Provisional Lithuanian Government set up under Col. K. Skirpa with the support of 125,000 likeminded Lithuanians. In Estonia, the German General de la Roque declared Estonia a zone of military operations and threatened saboteurs with execution. In Latvia, General Dankers, presiding over a Latvian advisory council, gave a semblance of legality to the administration of the German Reichskommissar, Herr Grechsler.

Barce. Italian base in Libya, 50 m. N.E. of Benghazi. The aerodrome here was attacked by the R.A.F. early in February 1941, before its capture by British Imperial forces during the thrust to Benghazi (surrendered Feb. 7). Barce was retaken by the enemy after the British withdrawal in the first week of April 1941. Its re-occupation by Indian troops was announced on Dec. 24, 1941, but by Feb. 1, 1942, it was once more in enemy hands. (*Pron.* Bah-chay).

Bardia. Port and vital Italian base in Libya, 12 m. from the Egyptian frontier, on the coastal road to Tobruk. It was captured by the British on Jan. 5, 1941, after being surrounded by Imperial Forces. The Germans occupied it on April 12, after the withdrawal of our forces. In the British advance into Libya, which started on Nov. 18, 1941, Bardia was

OUTSIDE THE WALLS OF BARDIA
In the course of the second great drive into Libya, organized by Gen. Auchinleck, Bardia fell to New Zealand forces on Nov. 23, 1941. The picture shows troops resting near the town walls.
Photo, British Official

at first by-passed, then the outskirts were occupied by New Zealand troops on Nov. 23. Axis troops continued to hold the port until Dec. 31, 1941, when S. African troops pierced the southern section of the enemy defences. Bardia was recaptured on Jan. 2, 1942, when 7,000 prisoners were taken, and lost once more in Rommel's advance of June 1942.

Barham, H.M.S. British battleship of 31,100 tons and a main armament of eight 15-in. guns. She was completed in 1915 and later partially reconstructed. In December 1939 she was hit by a U-boat torpedo off Scotland, but was back in service within three months. She joined the Mediterranean Fleet in 1940, and took part in all the actions there, including the Battle of Matapan (*q.v.*) the great victory of March 28–29, 1941. On November 25, 1941, when operating in the Mediterranean about 200 miles off Alexandria, she was struck by a salvo of torpedoes from the submarine U-331. Her magazine blew up and she sank in four minutes with a loss of 859 officers and men. H.M.S. Barham was the only British battleship to be sunk by a U-boat. The U-boat was destroyed.

Barker, Lt.-Gen. Michael George Henry, c.b. (b. 1884). G.O.C.-in-C. Aldershot Command from 1940. He was Director of Recruiting and Organization at the War Office from 1936 to 1938, and from 1939 until the early part of 1940 served as G.O.C. British Forces in Palestine and Transjordan. Summoned home, he took over the command of the 1st Corps in Belgium from Sir John Dill in May 1940, and his force defended the Dyle position in front of Louvain.

Sir Arthur Barratt, A.O.C.-in-C. Army Cooperation Command.
Photo, Lafayette

Barratt, Air Marshal Sir Arthur, k.c.b., c.m.g. (b. 1891). A.O.C.-in-C. Army Cooperation Command from Nov. 16, 1940. He was Principal R.A.F. Liaison Officer with the French Army and Air Force, 1939, and A.O.C.-in-C. British Air Forces in France, 1940.

Barrett, F/O. John, d.f.c. One of the first five airmen to be decorated in this war. The exploit which won him the D.F.C. took place in September 1939. He and F/O. T. M. W. Smith (*q.v.*), pilots of two Coastal Command flying-boats on patrol duty over the Atlantic, rescued, by alighting on the water in a heavy swell, 34 victims of the torpedoed merchantman, Kensington Court, who were drifting in a lifeboat. *See* Kensington Court.

Bartolomeo Colleoni. Italian cruiser of 5,069 tons, carrying eight 6-in. guns. She had a speed of 37 knots and was claimed to be the fastest ship in the world. On July 19, 1940, our patrols in the Aegean, consisting of the Australian cruiser Sydney (Capt. J. A. Collins, R.A.N.) and some destroyers, sighted her and a sister ship off the N.W. coast of Crete. The enemy altered course westwards, endeavouring to escape, and a running fight ensued in which H.M.A.S. Sydney scored vital hits on the Bartolomeo Colleoni; her destruction was completed by our destroyers. Our ships rescued 545 from the sinking vessel, including the captain, but were handicapped during this work of mercy by bombing from Italian aircraft. The other Colleoni cruiser, the Giovanni delle Bande Nere, was hit but saved herself by her superior speed.

Basra. Chief port of Iraq on the R. Shatt-el-Arab, 60 m. from the Persian Gulf and 270 m. S.E. of Baghdad. Following the Iraqi revolt of April 1941, engineered by German agents, Imperial forces arrived in Basra, with the approval of the local authorities, "to open up lines of communication through Iraq." Later the Iraqi Government became hostile and on May 2 British forces occupied the air port, dock area and power station. Following an ultimatum to the Iraqi Government, fresh British troops landed here. Basra formed an important base for war supplies dispatched by Britain and U.S.A. to Russia from September 1941. *See* Iraq.

Bataan. *See* Philippine Islands.

Bath. This fine old city (*see* Vol. 1, p. 426) suffered its first big air raid on the night of April 25, 1942. For several hours high explosive and incendiary bombs rained on the town, and in the light of raging fires Nazi airmen dive-bombed and machine-gunned the streets. There were no military objectives in Bath and many people from badly blitzed areas had gone there for refuge. This "reprisal raid," as it was called by the enemy, was aimed solely at the civilian population, which suffered severe casualties, and the city's historic buildings, which on this occasion were practically unscathed. On the following night Bath was subjected to another savage attack, heavier, but shorter in duration. In the bright moonlight British

BATH AFTER A 'BAEDEKER' RAID
The ancient city of Bath was bombed on two consecutive nights in April 1942. Here are seen the damaged Regina Hotel, and, right, part of the Assembly Rooms, at the opening of which, in 1771, Sheridan was present.
Photo, Keystone

fighters intercepted the Nazi bombers and numerous dogfights raged overhead. There was a heavy casualty list, and many famous buildings, including the Assembly Rooms and some historic houses, were wrecked.

Battle Dress. Newly designed uniform, approved April 1939, to be worn by officers and men of the British Army. It is a two-piece garment of khaki serge, consisting of blouse and trousers, buttoning at wrists and ankles, the latter protected by anklets. The uniform weighs about 12 lb. When in full marching order, the infantryman carries a valise (or pack) on the back in place of a haversack, the latter being transferred to the left hip above the bayonet

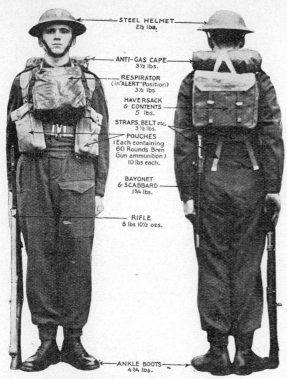

BRITISH BATTLE DRESS

Both officers and men wear the battle dress, which weighs about 12 lb. In full marching order an infantryman carries, instead of the haversack seen above, a valise holding his great-coat, a cardigan and other personal effects.

Photo, Fox, for " The War Illustrated "

and counterbalanced on the right by the water-bottle. Officers are distinguished from men by the shoulder badge. The R.A.F. and the Civil Defence forces also wear battle dress, adopted in 1941.

Batum. This town of the Soviet republic of Georgia lies on the S.E. coast of the Black Sea, and is connected with Baku, 600 m. E., by the Trans-caucasian Railway. It has a good harbour, which is of great importance in the transport of petroleum from Baku. The German thrust towards the Crimea in September 1941 was primarily directed to these pipe-lines and oilfields.

Baudouin, PAUL. Minister of State and Foreign Minister in Marshal Pétain's Cabinet after the fall of France, June 1940. On Oct. 28, 1940, his office as

Foreign Minister was given to Laval. He was no friend to Britain and belittled the B.E.F. contribution to the Allied cause. His resignation from the Cabinet was announced on Jan. 3, 1941.

Beak, MAJ.-GEN. DANIEL MARCUS WILLIAM, V.C., D.S.O., M.C. (b. 1891). He was appointed G.O.C. Malta on Jan. 9, 1942, when he succeeded Maj-Gen. Scobell.

Beattie, LT.-CMDR. STEPHEN, R.N. He was awarded the V.C. after the raid on St. Nazaire (*q.v.*).

Beaverbrook, WILLIAM MAXWELL AITKEN, 1ST BARON (b. 1879). British politician and Press magnate. He was appointed by Mr. Churchill to the newly created Ministry of Aircraft Pro-duction on May 15, 1940, and on August 2 he became, in addition, a member of the War Cabinet. On May 1, 1941, he was relieved, at his own request, of the very arduous duties as Minister of Aircraft Pro-duction, and became head of another newly created Ministry, the Ministry of State, occupying himself with the general directive work of the War Cabinet. A few weeks later, on June 29, Lord Beaverbrook was appointed Minis-

Lord Beaverbrook,
British Minister.
Photo, Assoc. Press

ter of Supply in succession to Sir Andrew Duncan, while still remaining a member of the War Cabinet. He accompanied Mr. Churchill to Washington in December 1941. On Feb. 2, 1942, he was appointed Minister of War Production, but subsequently left for America to continue work in regard to pooling the resources of the United Nations, and other special duties. Mr. Oliver Lyttelton succeeded him as Minister of Production on March 12. Lord Beaverbrook arrived home from the U.S.A. on May 5. *See* Produc-tion, Ministry of.

Beeley, RIFLEMAN JOHN, V.C. On Nov. 21, 1941, he displayed great courage at Sidi Rezegh, Libya, when he attacked single-handed an enemy post, killing or wounding the crew of an anti-tank gun position. His brave action enabled his platoon to advance, but Beeley was killed. He was posthumously awarded the V.C.

Beirut. Seaport of Syria and capital of the Lebanon. It stands on the Mediterranean Sea, about 60 miles N.W. of Damascus, and is a large commercial centre. Beirut was the headquarters of the French High Commissioner. Shipping in the harbour was attacked by the R.A.F. and Fleet Air Arm in June 1941, after the Allied armies had crossed the frontier. Australian troops entered the town on July 10, and Allied forces formally occupied it on July 15.

OVERRUN BY NAZI HORDES BELGIUM FALLS

The gallant Belgian Army strove for eighteen days, May 10–27, 1940, to hold back Germany's advancing hordes. On May 28, by order of King Leopold, the " Cease Fire " was sounded at 4 a.m.

Belgium, Campaign in. On the evening of May 9, 1940, information reached the Belgian authorities that a German attack was imminent. Although similar information had been received on other earlier occa-sions, this time it seemed more definite, and certain defence measures were put in hand at once. At 2 a.m. on May 10, following the receipt of news that German aeroplanes were flying over the Netherlands, a state

of siege was introduced in Belgium and the arrest of suspects in the eastern provinces was ordered. At 4.30 German 'planes were reported over towns near the German frontier. Half an hour later the railway station at Jemelle was bombed, and German para-chutists began to descend on the great frontier fort of Eben-Eymael, one of the Liége system ; the frontier was crossed in several places by German columns, and Brussels received its first air raid. Following these acts of war, the Belgian Government appealed to Britain and France to implement their guarantee of Belgium's independence, whereupon General Gamelin gave orders for the advance into Belgium of the B.E.F. under General Lord Gort and the French armies near the frontier to the west of Sedan. King Leopold, after issuing a proclamation to his people calling upon them to resist as their fathers resisted in 1914, proceeded to join his army, his G.H.Q. having been established at Breendonck, near Antwerp. At this time his army numbered some 900,000 men, the largest Belgian army ever put into the field.

Belgian Air Force Destroyed

In anticipation of just such an eventuality the Belgian High Command had planned to fight a delaying action along the Albert Canal from Antwerp to Liége and along the Meuse from Liége to Namur, so as to give time for the French and British to occupy the line from Antwerp through Namur to Givet on the French frontier. It had been anticipated that the Allies would be in position on the third day of the invasion, and the Belgians would then withdraw to the main defence line, Antwerp-Namur position.

At ten minutes past twelve (midnight) on May 10 the Belgian troops were ordered to take up their war stations, and from four a.m. they were exposed to the full force of the German invader. The Belgian Air Force, taken by surprise, was almost wiped out in the first few hours. Along the whole length of the outpost line the Belgian troops were pushed back by the mass of enemy infantry, tank formations, and waves of dive-bombers.

The critical point was south of Maastricht, where the forts of Liége guarded the passage of the Meuse.

Here, as in 1914, there was fierce fighting, but on this occasion the German success was amazingly swift and complete. Eben-Eymael (*see* Liége), which had been deemed impregnable, was captured by parachutists after a tremendous pounding by the German guns. Its last defenders surrendered on May 11.

An even greater disaster was the capture by the Germans of the bridges across the Albert Canal. These should have been destroyed, but whether by negligence, mishap or treachery, they were still intact. Across them poured the German tanks and motorized infantry. A squadron of the Belgian Air Force lost 11 out of 12 'planes in an attempt to destroy the bridge at Vroenhoven. Appeals to the Allies for air support met with no response until the morning of May 14, when the R.A.F. bombed the Maastricht bridges. It was then too late, however, since the Germans were already safely across. Through the gap north of Liége they stormed beyond Tongres, from where they threatened to take the whole Albert Canal position in the rear as well as Liége's western fortifications. So on the evening of May 11 the Belgian High Command gave the order to withdraw from the delaying position to the Antwerp-Namur line, and during the night troops gradually worked their way back from the Albert Canal and the Meuse to the main line of defence, which was now being supported by the B.E.F. and the French 1st and 9th Armies.

By dawn on May 13 most of the Belgian Army was already in position between Antwerp and Louvain. On their left across the Scheldt was the French 7th Army operating in Zeeland ; on their right was Gort's British Army, which had three divisions in position between Louvain and Wavre, and six other divisions lying behind between the Dyle and the Scheldt. On Gort's right was the 1st French Army holding the line Wavre-Gembloux-Namur. Namur itself was defended by the 7th Belgian Army Corps. From Namur along the Meuse to Mézières lay the French 9th Army under Gen. Corap, and to the right of this the French 2nd Army.

The Allies suffered a fresh blow when the Germans succeeded in overrunning in 48 hours the rough hilly country of the Ardennes. Thus it was that while the French 9th Army was still coming into position on the Meuse south of Namur, they were attacked by ever-increasing forces of the enemy. To the Germans' delighted surprise they found that six bridges across the river had not been blown up, and over these bridges they poured, causing a breach 50 miles wide and 50 miles deep. Then, at

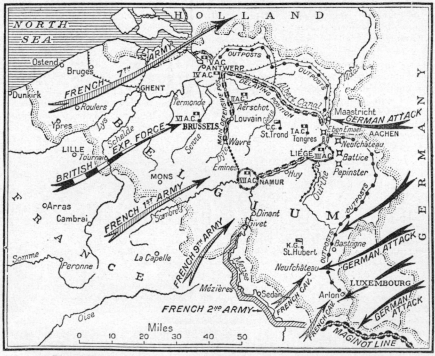

Disposition of the attacking and defending forces in Belgium, May 1940.
By courtesy of "The Times"

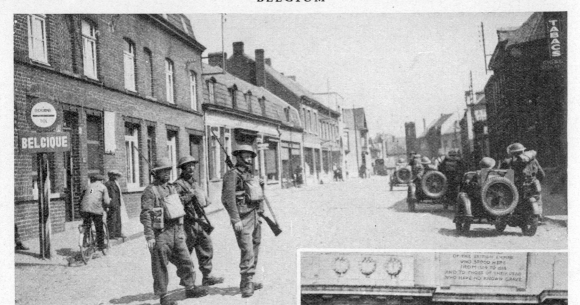

OUR MEN IN BELGIUM

Above, British troops on motor-cycles and in sidecars are seen crossing the Belgian frontier on May 10, the day of the Nazi invasion. Right, men of the 12th Lancers at Menin Gate on May 28, in the course of a famous rearguard action.
Photos, British Official

5 p.m. on May 12, the French front was breached at Sedan, and the French 2nd Army was involved with the 9th in a common rout. So vigorous was the German blow at this point that it began to appear that the operations to the north had been in the nature of a feint, designed to draw the British and French away from their well-prepared positions on the Franco-Belgian frontier.

Following the break-through at Sedan the Allied retreat from central Belgium was inevitable. After some days' fighting at Louvain Gort withdrew the B.E.F. stage by stage towards the west. Brussels was abandoned, and on May 15 General Georges, the Allied Commander on the northern front, ordered the abandonment of the Antwerp-Namur position and a withdrawal behind the Scheldt. This involved the withdrawal of the 7th Belgian Army Corps from Namur, although many of the forts, like those at Liége, continued to fight on for days more. One of the Liége forts, indeed, Pepinster, was still holding out on May 28 when the armistice was signed.

The Belgian Army was withdrawn with the rest, fighting heavy rearguard actions as it went. Already it had suffered heavily; indeed, its fighting efficiency had been seriously impaired. On May 20, when King Leopold heard that Cambrai had fallen and that Abbeville was threatened, he informed the British Government of his anxiety concerning the " possibility that the Allied front would be broken, with the result that the Belgian Army, with the B.E.F. and part of the French forces, would be cut off from Weygand's armies operating on the Somme." The next day the Germans entered Amiens, and the B.E.F. began to fall back from the Scheldt to the Lys. At the same time the Belgian left flank was exposed after the collapse of French resistance on Walcheren Island, on the north side of the Scheldt. Following the Allied Conference at Ypres on that day, it was agreed to attempt to put into operation Gen. Weygand's plan of a joint offensive from north and south, designed to close the gap which had developed. But this proved impossible, and on May 23 there was an extension of the Belgian line following the further withdrawal of the B.E.F. to the frontier positions it had occupied throughout the previous winter.

At this time King Leopold's army held a front of some 40 miles between Terneuzen and Audenarde. The only ports available were Ostend and Nieuport, and between the front line and the sea was wedged a mass—three millions, it was estimated—of terrified humanity—the civilian populace who had fled from their homes in terror of the Germans. Increasing enemy pressure compelled the Belgians to withdraw from Terneuzen and Ghent, and on May 24 the Germans forced a crossing over the Lys on both sides of Courtrai. Near Ypres a fierce German thrust threatened to sever the Belgian communications with the British, who on the next day began to withdraw to Dunkirk.

At dawn on May 25 King Leopold told his ministers that he was unshakably determined to resist to the limit of his forces and to share the fate of his army, and this resolve he repeated in an Order of the Day, in which he called upon his soldiers to fight with all their strength and supreme energy.

During the night of May 25 and in the course of the next day 2,000 railway wagons were brought up and placed end to end on the railway line from Roulers to Ypres as an anti-tank line. But on the next day the Germans thrust heavily at the Belgian front at Iseghem, Nevele and Ronsele. After some minor successes the Belgians were driven back, and their front began to crumble. At midday the Belgian Command informed the French Mission that the Belgian Army had nearly reached the limits of its endurance, and the situation became ever more desperate as the day wore on. The B.E.F. was in no fit state to counter-attack ; no further assistance was forthcoming from the French.

The King Forced to Capitulate

At dawn on May 27 the last Belgian reserves were flung into the battle, but at 11 a.m. large gaps began to show in the front. Near Thielt four or five miles of the front were exposed, thus leaving the way open to Bruges. At about 12.30 King Leopold telegraphed to Lord Gort that the Belgians were losing heart—that the time was rapidly approaching when they would be unable to continue to fight.

Later in the afternoon it was decided to send an envoy to the Germans, asking for terms. At 5 p.m. Maj.-Gen. Derousseaux, Deputy Chief of General Staff, set out for the H.Q. of the German 18th Army, asking for an armistice. At 10 p.m. he returned with the message that the Fuehrer demanded nothing short of unconditional surrender. At 11 p.m. King Leopold bowed to the inevitable and proposed that the " Cease Fire " should be sounded at 4 a.m. At that hour on May 28 firing ceased along the whole of the Belgian front, except between Roulers and Ypres, where fighting continued for some two hours more.

The terms of the agreement signed by Gen. Derousseaux and Gen. von Reichenau, for Belgium and Germany respectively, stipulated that the Belgian Army should at once and unconditionally lay down its arms and should henceforth be regarded as prisoners-of-war. All Belgian territory would be immediately occupied, and German operations against British and French troops would not be suspended. As for King Leopold, the Château of Laeken would be placed at his disposal. Thither—after one final proclamation to his troops in which he assured them that " History will relate that the Army did its duty to the full. Our honour is safe "—the King repaired. Henceforth he was the prisoner at Laeken.

Books to Consult. Official Report of War in Belgium (Belgian Min. Foreign Affairs). Belgium and the War, G. N. Clark (Oxford Pamphlet). The Prisoner at Laeken, E. Cammaerts (Cresset Press).

Belgium, Free. When the King of the Belgians was captured and the country's legislative chambers were no longer able to function by reason of the invasion of Belgium by the Germans, the government fled to France. When France fell it moved to London. It was the sole legal government of Belgium.

In London this legally-constituted Belgian government, composed of MM. Pierlot, Spaak, Gutt and de Vleeschauwer, who alone escaped, did all acts and performed all functions as the sovereign body of the invaded Belgium. To it were accredited representatives of nearly every civilized state in the world ; to them it sent its accredited representatives. The Belgian Ambassador to the Court of St. James's continued.

It is supremely important to keep well in mind that there existed no alternative governmental authority for Belgium, no puppet government that might claim to be acting in accordance with international law, for from this truth it followed that all acts done by the invader and his tools were crimes contrary to international law. This legal government of Belgium had as sole aim to rid Belgium of the invader. Therefore, the chief activities of the London government were to back up everywhere and always the British war effort.

This help and collaboration took the form of economic and financial cooperation, services and men. In May 1940 the country's gold holdings (800 million dollars) were safeguarded. This reserve, less amounts necessary for colonial purposes, was transferred to the British government against sterling.

On Jan. 21, 1941, the Belgian and British governments signed economic agreements which put the riches of the Belgian Congo at the disposal of Britain. Chief products of this Colony are copper- and tin-bearing ores, cotton, copal, palm-kernels and palm-oil, gold and diamonds. Britain sent the Belgian Congo tools, machines, fabrics and trading articles against the raw materials named above.

Belgians Continue the Fight

With regard to personal services, while the Belgian government has acted as paymaster to Belgians serving outside their native land in her cause, the men have been absorbed into the British fighting forces as airmen, officers and other ranks. Britain paid also for the aeroplanes these men fly.

Few Belgian soldiers escaped to Britain from Dunkirk, but their number was augmented by others from all parts of the world, returning to fight. Conscript classes in the unoccupied countries were also called up and, with the volunteers mentioned, were trained under the command of Lt.-Gen. van Strydonck de Burkel and General de la Chevalerie. By January, 1942 signaller corps, infantry units, artillery and armoured units had been formed.

Luckily, Belgium's important fishing fleet was saved almost intact. It is now working under the British Admiralty on patrols, sea balloon barrage service and mine-sweeping. There are also several warships manned by Belgians entirely and a Belgian section of the Royal Navy has been formed.

Belgian airmen fought in the Battle of Britain, and Belgian troops are guarding sections of Britain against invasion. Belgian troops from the Congo also fought in the Abyssinian campaign. A regular African Army is being developed.

Other activities include reorganization of administration and care of refugees (16,000) through the Central Bureau for Refugees. (Eighty per cent of Belgian men and 48 per cent of Belgian women in Britain are doing some form of war work.) Care of the men of her merchant navy and fishing fleets, the conduct of a labour exchange and training centre, publication of newspapers and magazines and the development of the diamond trade are among other activities ot this government in exile.

Belgrade. Capital of Yugoslavia, situated at the confluence of the rivers Danube and Sava. Although declared an open town, it was ruthlessly bombed by the Germans on April 6 and 7, 1941, when a great part was destroyed. A week later Belgrade was occupied.

Benes, DR. EDVARD (b. 1884). Head of the Czechoslovak Government in London. President of Czechoslovakia from 1935, he left his country in October 1938. Having settled in England, he became head of the Czech National Committee. In September 1939 he set up the Provisional Czechoslovak Government in London, which was formally recognized by Britain on July 23, 1940. *See* Czechoslovakia.

Benghazi. Capital of Cyrenaica and an important seaport, connected with Tripoli by road. It was taken by British Imperial Forces on Feb. 6, 1941. Subsequent evacuation by the British and occupation by the Germans was announced on April 3. The town was repeatedly bombed thereafter by the R.A.F., with

our mobile columns had occupied the town, but with the recapture of Benghazi on Jan. 29, 1942, it passed once more to the enemy.

Bennett, LT.-GEN. GORDON, C.B., D.S.O. (b. 1887). G.O.C. the Australian Imperial Forces in Malaya, he organized resistance to the Japanese invader during the Malayan campaign at the beginning of 1942. He was taken prisoner when Singapore fell on Feb. 15, but escaped to Johore on the Malayan mainland. After hairbreadth escapes, he arrived at Padang in Sumatra, having successfully evaded the Japanese. From here he managed to reach Sydney, Australia, Sumatra being occupied by the enemy by March 8. On March 11 it was announced that he had been appointed Acting Inspector-General of Training, and on April 3 he was made a Corps Commander under Gen. Blamey, and set up his headquarters in Western Australia. *See* Malaya; Singapore.

Berbera. Chief town and port of British Somaliland, 155 m. S. of Aden. It was evacuated by the British, Aug. 17–18, 1940, and occupied by the Italians, but was recaptured by British Imperial Forces on March 16, 1941, after the port and the aerodrome had been repeatedly bombed.

Berlin. The first raid carried out on Berlin by aircraft of the R.A.F. Bomber Command occurred on the night of August 25, 1940, eleven months after the outbreak of war. During that period British machines had flown over the German capital on a number of occasions and dropped propaganda leaflets. Political aspects rather than the prevailing air strategy were believed to have delayed bombing raids.

BENGHAZI RECAPTURED BY THE BRITISH

Four times in a year Benghazi, Libya's principal port, changed hands. This photograph of an A.A. crew on the harbour mole was taken after the re-entry of our forces on Dec. 24, 1941—a month later they withdrew again. The domed building, left, is the Cathedral which had survived all bombings.

Photo, British Official: Crown Copyright

The first raid on the heart of Germany, though not on a heavy scale, was of some importance, for, with the raids that preceded it on other objectives, it had an effect on the morale of the German population, who had been told repeatedly that the anti-aircraft defences were of such formidable power in the West that air raids would be impossible. As a military objective Berlin must always be a main target, for, besides being an industrial centre, it is a key point in the transport systems, which include canals as well as railways.

The many targets which have been bombed repeatedly include the B.M.W. aero engine works, the great Siemens electrical factory, an aircraft component factory, and the Moabit, West and Wilhelmsdorf power stations. The Danzigerstrasse, Charlottenburg and Neukolln gasworks have also been bombed, and the railway station and marshalling yards at Potsdamer, Anhalter and Lehrter have been attacked. Other targets include Tempelhof airport and railway station.

By the end of 1941 the Bomber Command had carried out more than fifty night raids on Berlin. This

great damage to the harbour, shipping, and airfields. Then on Nov. 18, 1941, the second great British drive into Libya began, and by Christmas Eve units of Gen. Ritchie's 8th Army were in Benghazi, having covered the 250 miles from Derna in five days. From here the enemy was pursued by our light forces towards Jedabia and El Agheila. But on Jan. 21, 1942, the tide of battle turned, and Gen. von Rommel not only recaptured Jedabia but pressed on to Benghazi, from which the British withdrew on Jan. 29.

Benina. In Cyrenaica, near Benghazi. The important aerodrome here was heavily raided by the R.A.F., December 1940–February, 1941. With the capture of Benghazi from the Italians on Feb. 6, Benina fell into British hands. It was retaken by the Germans in April, after the British withdrawal. On Dec. 24, 1941, it was announced that one of

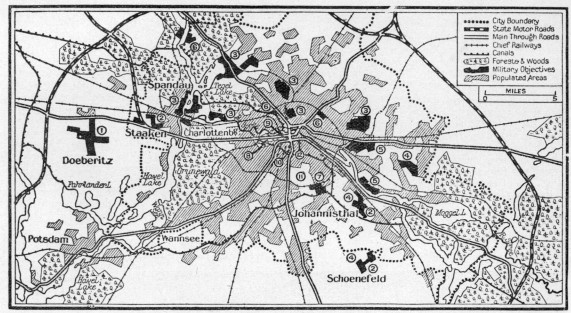

City Boundary
State Motor Roads
Main Through Roads
Chief Railways
Canals
Forests & Woods
Military Objectives
Populated Areas

MILES
0   5

MILITARY OBJECTIVES IN BERLIN FOR THE R.A.F.

In Berlin there are many objectives which are ranked as military on which the R.A.F. concentrate their bombs when raiding the city. Some of the principal ones are indicated in this map by names or numbers.

Courtesy of the "Evening Standard"

1.—Troop Centre.
2.—Air bases.
3.—Small arms and munitions works.
4.—Aircraft Factories.
5.—Electrical Plants, etc.
6.—Gas works.
7.—Telephone and wireless equipment works.
8.—Tiergarten.   9.—Reichstag.
10.—Hitler's Chancellery.
11.—Tempelhof (air port).
12.—Unter den Linden.

total would have been much higher but for the abnormally bad weather conditions which prevailed from September until the close of the year. From the accumulated reports of bomber crews engaged in assaults on the German city it was clear that the enemy had appreciably enlarged his ground defences in Berlin and its perimeter during the last six months of 1941. Hundreds of searchlights, hundreds of A.A. guns and large numbers of night-fighter aircraft have been used.

On the night of Sept. 7, 1941, Berlin was subjected to the heaviest air attack that had ever been made by the R.A.F. on the capital. Several hundreds of bombers, including the new four-engined Short Stirling and the two-engined Avro Manchester, were used. Very severe damage was done in the centre and outskirts of the city, and although a number of British machines were lost, the percentage of the number sent out was not excessive. On Nov. 7 Berlin was one of the several objectives marked down for attack by the biggest force of bombers ever detailed for night operations over enemy territory. Crews on their return to their bases reported on the great success of the raid, though the exploit was somewhat overshadowed by the fact that 37 long-range bombers were lost. These losses were mainly due to the sudden and unexpected change in the weather, which was phenomenal and resulted in numbers of aircraft losing their way and being forced down out of control through icing troubles. Weather conditions were, pending Radar developments, a ruling factor in raids upon Berlin, as was found by the Russian Air Force, squadrons of which attacked the city from far distant bases.

Berlin Pact. Also known as the Tripartite Pact, this military, political and economic agreement was signed in Berlin, Sept. 27, 1940, between Germany, Italy and Japan. By its terms Germany and Italy agreed to assist and cooperate with Japan in the establishment of a New Order in Greater Asia, Japan likewise promising to assist the two European Powers to establish a New Order in Europe. *See* Axis.

Bermudas. Group of British islands in the Atlantic, midway between the West Indies and Nova Scotia. Of some 360, only 20 are inhabited. Great Sound (area of water 5 sq. m.) and Great Bay are two of the sites leased by Britain in 1940 as air and naval bases in exchange for 50 U.S. over-age destroyers. *See* Atlantic Bases.

Bernhard of the Netherlands, PRINCE OF LIPPE-BIESTERFELD (b. 1911). Husband of Princess Juliana of the Netherlands, whom he married on Jan. 7, 1937. In 1941 he was appointed liaison officer between the Netherlands Army, Navy and Air Force and the corresponding British forces.

Berwick, H.M.S. British cruiser of the Kent class (10,000 tons). She was completed in 1928 and reconstructed 1935–38. She took part in a naval battle against the Italian Fleet off Sardinia, Nov.

Prince Bernhard of the Netherlands.
Photo, G.P.U.

27, 1940, and was the only British ship to sustain damage. She again sustained slight damage when an enemy raider attacked the convoy she was escorting in the North Sea, Dec. 25, 1940.

Bessarabia. Territory lying between the Rs. Dniester and Pruth and the Black Sea; area 17,146 sq. m. It was ceded by Russia to Rumania by the terms of the Peace Treaty, 1919. On June 26, 1940, Russia sent an ultimatum demanding its return. Soviet troops crossed the border on June 28 and occupied the country by July 1. Rumania joined Germany in attacking Bessarabia in June 1941.

Bevin, RT. HON. ERNEST, P.C., M.P. (b. 1884). Minister of Labour and National Service from May 1940. Secretary of the Transport and General Workers' Union from 1922 to 1940. He made a great recruiting drive in 1941 for women volunteers for the Services or munitions, but as numbers were too few conscription was brought in.

Mr. Ernest Bevin, Minister of Labour.
Photo, Lafayette

Bhagat, 2/LIEUT. P. S., of the 21st Bombay Sappers and Miners. He was the first Indian to receive the V.C. in this war. It was awarded for great gallantry and courage in leading mobile troops to clear the road and adjacent areas of mines after Metemma, Abyssinia, had been captured on the night of Jan. 31–Feb. 1, 1941.

2/Lt. P. S. Bhagat, first Indian V.C.
Photo, Brit. Official

Bialystok (Bielostok). Town of Poland, 45 m. S.W. of Grodno, on the R. Bialy. The Germans captured it on Sept. 16, 1939. Following Poland's collapse it was allocated to Russia, Oct. 1939. The Germans took the town during their thrust towards Minsk in June 1941.

Bickford, LIEUT.-CMDR. E. O. B., D.S.O., commanded H.M. submarine Salmon (670 tons). On Dec. 12, 1939, he sighted the German liner Bremen (*q.v.*), but, prohibited by humanity and international law from torpedoing without warning, let her go unscathed. In the same month he destroyed a large German U-boat and badly damaged the German cruiser Leipzig and another enemy cruiser. On July 21, 1940, the Admiralty announced that the Salmon (*q.v.*) was overdue and must be considered lost.

Biddle, ANTHONY JOSEPH DREXEL (b. 1897). American Minister to the Governments in London of Poland, Belgium, Norway, the Netherlands, Czechoslovakia, Yugoslavia, and Greece. From 1937 to 1939 he was ambassador to Poland; later, ambassador to Norway.

Billotte, GEN. French general who commanded the First French Army in 1940; he was also given "power of co-ordination" between the French, British and Belgian armies. He was killed on May 22, 1940, in a car accident, while returning from a meeting between the Belgian King and Lord Gort at Ypres. He was succeeded by Gen. Blanchard.

Birmingham. City in the West Midlands. It suffered many attacks by German bombers; the heaviest raid lasted nine hours, during the night of Nov. 19–20, 1940, when considerable damage was done.

Bishop, WILLIAM AVERY, AIR MARSHAL, V.C., D.S.O. (b. 1894). A famous pilot of the Great War, he was Director of Canada's Air Force Training Scheme. *See* Empire Air Training Scheme.

Bismarck. German battleship (35,000 tons). She carried eight 15-in., twelve 5·9-in. and sixteen 4·1-in. guns, and was launched in 1939. Her Commander was Admiral Luetjens. On May 22, 1941, a Coastal Command reconnaissance aircraft reported that Bismarck, previously located at Bergen, had sailed from that port with the cruiser Prinz Eugen. The next day she was sighted by the cruisers Norfolk and Suffolk and shadowed throughout the night. Early on May 24 H.M.S. Hood and H.M.S. Prince of Wales joined action with her west of Iceland. In this engagement Hood was sunk, Prince of Wales sustained slight damage, and Bismarck, though damaged, was able to escape towards the south-west. Norfolk and Suffolk again gave chase, and in the evening Prince of Wales once more engaged her. The German ship again escaped, but during the night was hit by a torpedo from an aircraft of H.M.S. Victorious.

Meanwhile, the main body of the Home Fleet was speeding from northern waters, another force steaming north from Gibraltar, and with H.M.S. Ramillies and Rodney, which had been escorting convoys in the North Atlantic, converged in the direction of the enemy. On May 26 Bismarck was located, first by a Catalina Coastal Command aircraft, and then by an aircraft from H.M.S. Ark Royal, about 550 miles west of Land's End, steering an easterly course. Shadowed by H.M. cruiser Sheffield, and successfully attacked by torpedoes from aircraft of Ark Royal and by torpedoes from H.M. destroyers Cossack and Maori, Bismarck was badly crippled but still crept towards

NAZI WARSHIP SUNK AFTER A STERN CHASE
Like a mad dog running amok, the German battleship Bismarck sank H.M.S. Hood and damaged H.M.S. Prince of Wales before she was brought to bay and finally destroyed on May 27, 1941, after a 6 day chase of 1,750 miles from Bergen, in a great sweep north, west and south of Iceland, and thence across the North Atlantic towards Brest.
Photo, Keystone

Brest. She was then engaged by our heavy ships, and finally sunk by a torpedo from H.M. cruiser Dorsetshire on the morning of May 27.

Bismarck Archipelago. *See* New Guinea; Pacific; Rabaul.

Bison. French destroyer (2,436 tons). She was sunk by German bombers in the North Sea, May 6, 1940, while convoying Allied troops from Norway, and was the first French warship to be lost by enemy action in this war.

Bittern, H.M.S.   British sloop (1,190 tons). She was set on fire by bombs from German aircraft at Namsos, May 1, 1940, and sunk to avoid becoming a danger to navigation.

Black Market.   This term was applied to describe the operations of dealers in foodstuffs and other rationed goods in very short supply.   By one means or another—by collusion with producers or by actual theft—dealers managed to obtain stocks of the goods in question and then retailed them, at prices in excess of the maximum prices laid down by the authorities, to such of the public as were willing to secure an unfair and generally illegal advantage over their fellow citizens.   Drastic measures for black market offences were announced on March 12, 1942, by Mr. Herbert Morrison.   The worst offenders would receive up to 14 years' penal servitude as a maximum penalty.

Black Sea.   This inland sea is bounded by Russia on the N., Asia Minor (Turkey) on the S., Caucasia on the E., Bulgaria and Rumania on the W.   It has great strategic importance.   Before the Russo-German war

Black Sea, showing the ports that give it great strategic value.

Germany used this route to import oil from Russia, Varna, on the Bulgarian coast, being the port of entry. Constanza, the Rumanian oil port on the Black Sea, was heavily bombed by the Russians in 1941.   Batum, another oil and petroleum base on the S.E. shore, was a vital centre for Soviet supplies in the Russo-German war, 1941, being at the end of the great pipeline from Baku.   Tuapse and Novorossiisk are two ports on the eastern shore to which run branches of the oil pipe-line from Grozny to Rostov, captured by the Germans on Nov. 21, 1941, but in Russian hands again by Nov. 29.

Blamey, GEN. SIR THOMAS, K.C.B., C.M.G., D.S.O. (b. 1884). C.-in-C. Allied Land Forces in Australia from March 1942.   In 1938 he was Controller-General of Recruiting in Australia.   Two years later he was C.-in-C. Australian Forces in Egypt, and his men formed the spearhead of Gen. Wavell's attack across the Western Desert.   When he returned to Australia to take up his new appointment under Gen. MacArthur, he was succeeded in the Middle East by Maj.-Gen. Sir Leslie Morshead.

Gen. Blamey, C.-in-C. Allied Land Forces in Australia.
Photo, Central Press

Blanchard, GEN. JEAN.   He commanded the French 1st Army in September 1939, and succeeded Gen. Billotte in May 1940, after the latter's fatal accident, assuming command of the Allied armies on the N.E. Front.   He was among the 180 French generals who were removed from the active list by the Vichy Government in August 1940.

Blimp.   Word coined in the last war when British lighter-than-air craft were divided into A—rigid, and B—limp (i.e. without rigid internal framework).   The modern barrage balloon is classed as a blimp.   The famous die-hard character, Col. Blimp, was originated by the cartoonist Low.

Blockade.   *See* Economic Warfare.

Bluecher.   German cruiser of 10,000 tons. She was sunk in Oslo Fjord, April 9, 1940, after hitting a barrier laid by the Norwegians and striking mines.

Blum, LÉON (b. 1872). Leader of the French Socialist Party.   He was Prime Minister in 1936–37 and again in March–April 1938.   Indicted by the Vichy Government in September 1940, he was "administratively interned" at Pellevoison (Indre), to await sentence by the Conseil de Justice Politique.   *See* Riom Trials.

Bobruisk.   Town of White Russia, on the R. Beresina, 105 m. S.E. of Minsk.   Stubborn fighting took place in this area in mid-July 1941, and by the end of the month the town had been overrun in the general German advance.

Bock, FIELD-MARSHAL VON. German C.-in-C. in the Smolensk sector during the Russo-German war, 1941.   He was reported to be critical of Nazi policy and was dismissed on Dec. 8 on the pretext that he was suffering from "gastric disorder," but after the death of Gen. von Reichenau, announced Jan. 17, 1942, he was given command of the armies in S. Russia.   In May he was engaged in operations based on Kharkov.

Bofors Gun.   Light automatic multi-purpose gun. Primarily an anti-aircraft weapon but also used effectively as anti-tank gun.   Used extensively in all theatres of war, and mounted on all types of ships for A.A.   Effectively employed to blast Japs out of "foxholes" in Burma. Fires tracer and armour-piercing shells.

Bomba.   Italian seaplane base in Libya, between Derna and Tobruk.   It was abandoned by the Italians in January 1941 and taken over by the British.   After the British withdrawal in April 1941 it was repeatedly bombed by the R.A.F.   Bomba was by-passed by the Imperial troops who took Derna aerodrome on Dec. 18.

Bomb Disposal Section, ROYAL ENGINEERS. Delayed action bombs dropped by German raiders are dealt with effectively by Bomb Disposal Squads, the bombs being dug up and taken away to be exploded. A powerful time-bomb was removed from $27\frac{1}{2}$ ft. below Dean's Yard, close to St. Paul's Cathedral, London, on September 12–15, 1940, and rushed at speed to Hackney Marshes by the commander of the Bomb Disposal Section, Lieut. R. Davies.   Here its explosion

BOMB REMOVAL SQUAD AT WORK

The delayed action bomb which fell near St. Paul's in September 1940 came to rest 27½ ft. below the surface. Here are men of the Royal Engineers digging it out. Inset, badge of the Bomb Disposal Section.

Photo, Topical

made a crater 100 ft. wide. At the next service in the cathedral there was a prayer of thanksgiving for "those men who performed a feat of outstanding heroism and skill, yet regarded it as their job."

Bomber Command. This is the striking force of the Home Air Force, its principal function that of attacking the enemy's war organization, military and industrial. The Command is divided into Groups, each consisting of several squadrons. It is equipped chiefly with medium and heavy bombers, the proportion of heavies tending to increase. Objectives are often suggested by the Ministry of Economic Warfare, and the Command has at various stages carried out offensives against armament works, oil refineries, aircraft factories, railways, ports, and industrial areas in Germany, Italy, France, the Low Countries, and other occupied territories. Mine-laying in enemy waters is one of its activities. The importance and the weight of its attacks have rapidly increased, and by the Spring of 1942 far surpassed all precedents in the history of air warfare. On the night of May 30–31, 1,130 bombing aircraft, all of them British, were directed chiefly against Cologne, delivering some 3,000 tons of bombs, and two nights later Essen was the principal objective, when a force of 1,036 was operated. Mr. Churchill said in a message to Air Marshal Sir A. T. Harris, Air Officer Commanding-in-Chief, Bomber Command: "This proof of the growing power of the British bomber force is also the herald of what Germany will

receive city by city from now on." Air Marshal Harris, in a recorded talk in June, said : " In the past Bomber Command was largely employed in bombing on a comparatively light scale those more immediately urgent targets dictated by the day-to-day war situation. A sort of strategic defensive. So much to do ; so little to do it with. Now we pass increasingly to the strategic offensive . . . When the storm, gathering there and here, breaks in its full fury over Germany, they will look back to the days of Lübeck, Rostock, and Cologne, as men lost in the raging typhoon think back to the gentle zephyr of a past summer." *See* Air War ; Royal Air Force.

Bonnet, GEORGES (b. 1889). French Minister of Foreign Affairs in the Daladier Cabinet, 1938–40. He was Ambassador to the U.S.A. in 1937, and Minister of Finance, 1937–38.

Bordeaux. French city and seaport, on the left bank of the R. Garonne, about 60 miles from the sea. The French Government moved to Bordeaux from Tours in June 1940. German troops entered the city June 27–28. After this it became one of Hitler's "invasion ports," in the harbour of which the R.A.F detected and bombed German troop concentrations

Bomber Command Operations

Raids on Main German Targets—Sept. 3, 1939, to August 5, 1942   ..   .. **1040**

Targets attacked—Sept. 3, 1939 to August 5, 1942   .. **248**

Main targets		1/1/40-31/12/40	1/1/41-31/12/41	1/1/42-5/8/42	Total
		Number of attacks			
Aachen ..	A B	8	6	1	15
Berlin ..	A B D E	34	18	—	52
Bremen ..	A B C D	52	39	7	98
Cologne ..	B D E	55	47	5	107
Dortmund	A B D E F	20	3	1	24
Dortmund-Ems Canal ..	C	15	1	—	16
Duisburg..	B C	34	15	4	53
Düsseldorf	A D E	20	27	2	49
Emden ..	C D F	26	39	12†	77
Essen ..	B F	33	9	7	49
Gelsenkirchen	B D F	39	3	—	42
Hamburg	B C D E	60	25	7	92
Hamm ..	B F	82	2	—	84
Hanover ..	B C D E	27	13	1	41
Kiel	C D	32	29	3	64
Lubeck ..	B C	4	2	2†	8
Mannheim	B D	34	17	6	55
Osnabruck	B F	34	4	1	39
Rostock ..	A B D E	—	1	4†	5
Ruhr ..	B D E F	3	3	22†	28
Woonemunde	C E	1	1	1	3
Wilhelmshaven	C D	37*	26	4	67
		650	332	90	1072

* 2 (September 1939)   † Include specially heavy raids.

Key to objectives bombed : A—aerodromes, aircraft factories ; B—railways, marshalling yards ; C—naval bases, shipyards, harbours, ships, canals ; D—oil refineries, dumps, fuel works ; E—munition and chemical works, power plants, blast furnaces ; F—ammunition dumps.

and fleet assemblies, while troop-carrying aircraft at Mérignac airport, close by, were also heavily raided by British bombers during 1940–41. Oil plants at Bordeaux were another target for attack.

Boris III (b. 1894). KING OF BULGARIA. Although in the early days of the war King Boris strove hard to preserve his country's neutrality, he was pro-Axis in sympathy. In November 1940 he visited Hitler at Berchtesgaden, the German News Agency stating that

" the political new order in Europe " was under discussion. King Boris had another personal conversation with Hitler at the latter's headquarters in March 1942.

Bormann, MARTIN (b. 1900). Hitler's Deputy and Nazi Party Leader. Formerly Chief of Staff to Hess (*q.v.*), the latter's duties were delegated to Bormann after Hess's flight in May 1941, the title "Fuehrer's Deputy" being changed to "Party Chancellor." Bormann became Hitler's constant companion and adviser and in February 1942 was invested with wide powers which placed him second only to Hitler in the settlement of all internal affairs.

Borneo. When the Japanese attacked in the Pacific, in December 1941, Borneo (*see* p. 599) was one of their objectives. The strategic position of the island, and its natural resources in rubber, timber, petroleum, copper and other minerals, had long been coveted by the Japanese imperialists. Situated about 1,200 miles south of Hongkong and about 400 miles east of Singapore, Borneo was also a stepping-stone to Port Darwin, N. Australia.

On Dec. 14 reports were received that Japanese troops had landed at two points, Miri and Lubong, in the British protected State of Sarawak, a territory of about 50,000 square miles, situated in the North West of Borneo adjoining British North Borneo. Having completed the total destruction of the oil refinery wells and other installations in both the Miri and Seria oilfields, our troops were withdrawn, but inflicted heavy losses on the enemy in rearguard actions. These important oilfields extend inland from a very low coast, and some of the wells are actually in shallow water, ships three miles off the shore being able to load oil from a floating pipeline. In normal times about 1,000,000 tons of some of the world's finest aviation spirit is produced from these wells. Further enemy landings in Sarawak were made on Dec. 17.

On Dec. 28 Kuching, the capital of Sarawak, and an important aerodrome, where the Japanese had landed

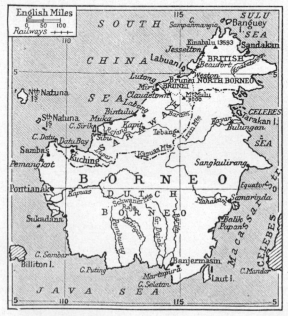

Borneo, invaded by the Japanese in December 1941.

three days earlier, was reported to be in enemy occupation. Dutch bombers inflicted heavy damage on Japanese transports off Kuching.

On Jan. 1, 1942, it was announced at Singapore that the bulk of our troops had been successfully withdrawn from Sarawak, and were in touch with the Netherlands East Indies forces in West Borneo.

British North Borneo was invaded by the Japanese, troops landing on the coast on Dec. 16. Three days previously a Dutch naval force had disembarked in this territory, at British request, and had annihilated a Japanese settlement on the coast, interning all Japanese and seizing a number of motor launches. A further enemy landing in British North Borneo was effected on Jan. 3 at Weston, about 100 miles N. of Brunei.

Tarakan, an important oil island off the N.E. coast of Dutch Borneo, stated to be, for its size, the richest oil land in the world, was raided by the Japanese on Dec. 28. Early in January 1942 the enemy again attacked it by air and sea, bringing six cruisers and six torpedo-boats to cover landings from fourteen transports, some of which were sunk by shore batteries. There was a gallant resistance for two days, when, having destroyed the oilfields and all equipment, the small Dutch garrison surrendered on Jan. 13, a few of their soldiers escaping to the main island.

Japanese troops landed at various points in Dutch Borneo during January. The great oil port of Balik Papan, on the E. coast, whose wells supplied about one-fifth of the total refined oil production of the Netherlands East Indies and produced about 8,000,000 metric tons a year, was frequently and heavily attacked by Japanese bombing planes throughout that month. On Jan. 22 the Dutch destroyed the oil wells, in accordance with their "scorched earth" policy, rendering them entirely useless to the enemy. Fighting continued in Balik Papan, both in the burnt-out town and the vicinity, for a few days, and on Jan. 24 it was occupied by the enemy. On Feb. 5 it was learned that the Dutch Commander at Balik Papan, with a number of men, had reached safety after fighting through the enemy lines.

Pontianak, the capital of Dutch Borneo, was another frequent target of the Japanese bombers. Having suffered a heavy and indiscriminate raid on Dec. 19, in which 370 people were killed or wounded, the town was subjected to further air attacks during January 1942, these being aimed chiefly at the civilian population. By Feb. 7 Pontianak was occupied by the enemy. Early in the same month several other towns in Dutch Borneo, including Samarinda, the oil port on the E. coast, and Banjermasin, an important air base on the S.E., fell to the Japanese, who claimed that the whole of Borneo, including the oil-bearing island of Tarakan, was then in their hands. *See* Netherlands East Indies.

Boulogne. Seaport and town of France, on the English Channel, 157 miles N. of Paris. In this area a medical base was installed in 1939. Following the enemy drive into France in May 1940, the rear element of British G.H.Q., till then established at Arras, was sent to Boulogne on May 17 and 18, but three days later was moved to Wimereux, owing to enemy bombing. On May 21 news was received that the Germans were advancing upon the town from the south. Before then all possible measures had been taken to put Boulogne in a state of defence, but the only troops available were labour units and personnel from rest camps. So on May 22 a contingent of

Royal Marines and the 20th Guards Brigade were rushed over from England and put up a magnificent defence until it was realized that the town could not be held.

During the night of May 22–23 4,600 British troops were withdrawn by six destroyers under the command of Vice-Admiral Bertram Ramsay. The evacuation was made while the Germans were all round the docks at a distance of about 400 yards, snipers creeping to within 50 yards. Field guns concealed on a hill overlooking the harbour fired furiously on the destroyers as they came alongside, and these replied with their guns, pom-poms and machine-guns. Meanwhile, the troops waiting to embark " stood there like rocks," apparently oblivious of the tornado of firing and of bombs from enemy aircraft swooping over the port. Boulogne was occupied on May 23. Thereafter enemy troops and barge concentrations were repeatedly bombed by the R.A.F., and shipping and harbour installations rendered unusable.

HOSPITAL SHIP LEAVING BOULOGNE

A medical base was established at Boulogne in the early days of the war, and from the quays British wounded were embarked upon hospital ships and taken to England. Here a stretcher case is being carried aboard.
Photo, British Official

In the early hours of April 22, 1942, a Commando reconnaissance raid, lasting two hours, was carried out near Boulogne, on one of the most strongly fortified stretches of the French coast. The Commandos, led by Major Lord Lovat, succeeded in penetrating the coastal defences over a frontage of 800 yards. Veiled in mist, the landing craft got silently inshore. The Commandos waded ashore and raced several hundred yards to the sand dunes before they met machine-gun fire. The Navy met with the stiffer opposition, for the Germans, taken completely by surprise and evidently not expecting a landing, concentrated their attention on the covering light naval force, which had safely brought the Commandos to the exact spot at the exact time. In the action with enemy flak ships and smaller craft, two German armed trawlers were damaged. No British ship was damaged and our naval casualties were slight. With the initiative in British hands throughout the raid, our troops drove the enemy back, contacted their strong points and cut communications to prevent reinforcements being sent for. The raid was completely successful, and every man returned with his equipment. Many of the Commandos and naval men engaged in this operation were veterans of the Lofoten and Bruneval raids.

Air Chief Marshal Sir F. Bowhill.
Photo, Bertram Park

Bowhill, AIR CHIEF MARSHAL SIR FREDERICK WILLIAM, K.C.B., C.M.G. (b. 1880). Appointed June 14, 1941, to the Ferry Command, the organization that flies across the Atlantic aircraft produced for R.A.F. in American factories. He was Air Member for Personnel on the Air Council, 1933–37, and A.O.C. Coastal Command, 1937–41.

Boyd, AIR MARSHAL OWEN TUDOR, C.B. (1889–1944). He was A.O.C. Balloon Command, 1938–1940. Appointed Deputy A.O.C. Middle East, he was taken prisoner in Sicily on his way to Cairo, Nov. 21, 1940. He escaped in 1943 but died Aug. 6, 1944.

Bracken, RT. HON. BRENDAN, M.P. (b. 1901). Minister of Information from July 19, 1941, in succession to Mr. Duff Cooper. He entered Parliament in 1929 as Conservative M.P. for North Paddington. He was chairman of the " Financial News," editor of " The Banker," and Parliamentary Private Secretary to Mr. Churchill from 1939 up to this appointment.

Mr. Brendan Bracken, Minister of Information.
Photo, Topical

Brauchitsch, FIELD-MARSHAL WALTHER VON (b. 1882). C.-in-C. of the German Army, 1938–41. He commanded in Poland in 1939, and later on the Western Front, and was one of the German representatives who attended the signing of the Armistice with France at Compiègne on June 22, 1940. He was in charge of the operations against Russia in 1941, but on Dec. 19, following serious German reverses, Hitler dismissed him and personally took over his command. It was reported in March 1942 that he had returned to Berlin for duty after an operation.

Field-Marshal W. von Brauchitsch.
Photo, Associated Press

Brazen, H.M.S. British destroyer (1,360 tons) with a speed of 35 knots and a complement of 138. She was damaged during an attack by enemy aircraft and subsequently sank while being towed into port on July 21, 1940.

Brazzaville. Capital of French Equatorial Africa. It lies on the north bank of the R. Congo, opposite Leopoldville in the Belgian Congo. In 1940–41 this town played an increasingly large part in the military history of Free France. It was on Aug. 29, 1940, that the colony declared for Gen. de Gaulle, and through Brazzaville passed Free French troops from this and other loyal African colonies on their way to the battlefields of Murzuk, Kufra, Tobruk, Keren, and as far distant as Syria. Many young soldiers of Free France were receiving their military education at the Camp Colonna d'Ornano at Brazzaville, which is able to train 125 officer-cadets at a time, and which is now the Free French St. Cyr.

Brazzaville is not only an important training camp ; it is also a receiving centre for supplies for the Free French Empire which reach it by rail from Pointe-Noire, the port in Gabun, 318 miles to the west. Through Radio-Brazzaville, a powerful station whose beams reach France, Indo-China, Syria, N. and S. Africa and N. America in a night-and-day service, it is the official voice of Free France. In April 1942 an American Consulate-General was established at Brazzaville. The town's rapid strides forward and sudden growth in numbers consequent on the foregoing factors have made it necessary to double its extent. *See* Equatorial Africa, French.

Bremen. City of Germany, on the R. Weser, about 46 miles from its mouth. It has three large harbours and is a great shipping and industrial centre. Oil storage plants, shipbuilding yards, warehouses, railway stations, armament factories and the Focke-Wulf aircraft works are among the objectives which have been repeatedly bombed by the R.A.F. On the night of Jan. 1, 1941, 20,000 incendiaries and loads of high

explosives were dropped during a 3½-hour attack. Raids increased in intensity, one of the heaviest up to then occurring on June 3, 1942. Further raids were made in June and July, including a 1,000 bomber raid on June 25 employing, as revealed later, Radar technique.

Bremen, S.S. A North-German-Lloyd liner of 51,731 tons, she was the biggest ship sailing under the Nazi flag. Before the outbreak of war she was docked at New York. She reached Murmansk on Sept. 6, 1939, after completing a voyage of 4,750 miles. On Dec. 12 she was sighted by the British submarine Salmon (*q.v.*) in the Baltic, but allowed to proceed, as both humanity and international law forbade the sinking of an unarmed vessel in such circumstances. She was burnt out at Bremerhaven on March 17, 1941.

Bremerhaven. German seaport, outport of Bremen. It stands at the junction of the rivers Weser and Geeste, about 40 miles north of Bremen. It is one of the bases of the German fleet and also a shipbuilding centre ; the docks and shipbuilding yards have therefore been repeatedly attacked by the R.A.F.

Brest. Fortified naval seaport and town of France. It lies at the extreme W. of Brittany, 155 m. from Rennes on the N. side of the bay (Brest Roads). There are great shipbuilding yards, foundries, magazines, repairing and other docks ; also a commercial harbour and manufactories. It was one of the ports at which stores and vehicles were landed for the B.E.F., and it also served as a maintenance depot. Brest was occupied by the enemy on June 20, 1940. The damaged German warships Scharnhorst and Gneisenau took shelter in the harbour early in 1941, but were discovered by British reconnaissance 'planes and were bombed 63 times between March 30, 1941, and Feb. 1, 1942. The German authorities became

NAZI WARSHIPS PLASTERED BY HALIFAX AIRCRAFT

The Scharnhorst and Gneisenau were first attacked by the R.A.F. at Brest during the night of March 30–31, 1941. Up to Feb. 1, 1942, they had been bombed 63 times. This photograph shows the daylight raid of Dec. 18, 1941. The two battleships are seen in dry dock, and the cruiser Prinz Eugen lies in one of the basins protected by anti-submarine nets.

Photo, British Official: Crown Copyright

nervous regarding the safety of these ships, later joined by the Prinz Eugen, and decided to send them out of Brest. That they were obvious targets in any port was undeniable, but the Nazis' illusions as regards the immunity of Brest had been rudely shattered by the constant R.A.F. attacks. On Feb. 11, 1942, therefore, the three great ships steamed out of the French port and prepared to run the gauntlet in the Channel. An account of their departure and the ensuing battle is given under the heading Gneisenau.

Brest-Litovsk (Polish, Brzesc Litewski). Town of Poland, on the River Bug, 180 miles S. of Grodno. It is an important railway junction. The Polish Government moved here on Sept. 11, 1939, but the Germans captured the town six days later. At the partition of Poland in September 1939 the town and fortress were handed over to the Red Army. It was again occupied by the Germans on June 24, 1941.

Bretagne. French battleship of 22,189 tons. She was heavily damaged by British shell fire at Mers-el-Kebir, Oran, July 3, 1940, and subsequently capsized. *See* Oran.

Brett, MAJ.-GEN. GEORGE H. (b. 1887). As Chief of the U.S. Army Air Corps, he attended an important conference with Gen. Wavell and Gen. Chiang Kai-shek in Chungking on Dec. 22–25, 1941. It was announced on Jan. 3, 1942, that Maj.-Gen. Brett had been appointed Deputy Supreme Commander of the South-West Pacific Area, under Gen. Wavell. He attended a secret conference on April 8, 1942, between Allied leaders when vital plans were discussed, and on April 19 it was announced that he would command the Allied Air Forces in the S.W. Pacific Area. In 1941 he had made an extensive tour of the Middle East, visiting also Britain and Moscow, to study air force organization.

Bridgeman, ROBERT CLIVE BRIDGEMAN, D.S.O., 2ND VISCOUNT (b. 1896). Director-General of the Home Guard from 1941. He was G.S.O. War Office, 1935–37. After serving as a staff officer in France, 1939–40, he organized the defence of the perimeter of Dunkirk in May 1940.

Brindisi. City and seaport of Italy, on the Adriatic. Its harbour, oil tanks and railways were attacked by the R.A.F., particularly in November and December 1940.

Brinon, FERNAND DE. Marshal Pétain's representative in Paris, appointed Nov. 4, 1940. He was a friend of Laval.

Bristol. City and seaport, mainly in Gloucestershire, but partly in Somerset. It lies on the R. Avon, 7 miles from the Bristol Channel. It was repeatedly attacked by German bombers, the first heavy raid being on Nov. 24, 1940, and considerable damage was done to docks, business premises, churches, hospitals and factories.

CENTURIES-OLD HOUSE BOMBED
Bristol was heavily raided in 1940–41, and great destruction ensued in the city. The beautiful Dutch House, built in 1676, was one of the notable buildings which suffered.
Photo, "Daily Mirror"

Among the notable buildings damaged or destroyed were parts of the University, including the library, which was burnt out, the famous Temple Church, St. Peter's Hospital, an ancient almshouse, the Old Dutch House, and certain 14th century alms-houses. From June 25, 1940, to Aug. 8, 1942 (the last heavy raid), 1,230 people were killed and 3,073 injured.

Bristowe, LIEUT.–COMDR. R. H. He commanded the boat sent into Dakar harbour to drop depth-charges under the French battleship Richelieu, July 8, 1940. *See* Dakar.

Britain, Battle of. *See* Great Britain, Air War on.

British Broadcasting Corporation. War did not take the B.B.C. by surprise. All arrangements had been made for the dispersal of staff and apparatus, and for adaptation of programmes and extension of activities to assist the war effort. The activities of the B.B.C. in war are far more numerous than the ordinary listener knows. Its work may be divided into two main parts for the Home services— to instruct and to amuse. To find out what listeners want a Listener Research Department was set up. Programmes are based on majority demand.

The B.B.C. news service is efficient, uncoloured, reliable. Its sources are manifold. Masses of material are boiled down for the news bulletin. It also gathers news, has reporters all over the Kingdom and with the Forces on all battle fronts. It seeks out men, women and children who have something interesting to tell and brings them to the microphone.

The war-time policy of the B.B.C. is the reverse of what it once was. It is no longer aloof and superior. It keeps in touch with the world of thought, imagination, and ideas in addition to the services mentioned. Religion, art, and science are given proper place.

The direct war effort of the B.B.C. takes two forms. It broadcasts in many languages to enemy and neutral countries. For example, there are eleven German transmissions daily. This work is alive and dynamic. Every time Germany's radio star performer Fritzsche lies and libels, Sefton Delmer is on the air in German, giving our version. " Frau Wernicke " is an imaginary Berlin housewife who also goes on the air to such as dare to listen in Nazi Germany. Every word uttered in any language whatsoever on wireless systems throughout the world is listened to by the B.B.C.'s Monitors. In this way much information of great value is picked up.

Critics of the B.B.C. might be persuaded to temper their acerbity by reading " B.B.C. at War " (6d.). It reveals an organization alive and alert, brave and hardworking. Twice bombed out, and with a casualty list, never once has the B.B.C. been off the air in raids.

On Jan. 26, 1942, the Director-General, F. W. Ogilvie, resigned and was succeeded jointly by Sir Cecil Graves and Mr. Robert Foot.

HOW THE CROWN COLONIES ANSWERED THE CALL

Vast have been the contributions to the Empire's war effort made by British possessions in all parts of the world. They include raw material, fighting men, strategic bases, and millions of pounds. The Dominions, Australia, Canada, South Africa and New Zealand, and India, are dealt with under their own headings.

British Colonies at War. The war efforts of the self-governing Dominions and India in the world crisis are treated in other sections in this volume.

Less spectacular, but large in the aggregate, are the contributions of the Crown Colonies. Scattered over the entire world, their products have supplemented the raw materials and manufactures of the Home Country and the Dominions, while their contribution to the fighting forces of the Crown has also been considerable. North and south, east and west, their answer to the call of Empire was full-throated when the dread significance of Totalitarianism was revealed.

When the war began it was plain that, if the full resources of the Colonial Empire were to be mobilized, the Imperial Government would have to exercise a greater degree of control over the economic life and financial policy of the units than had been necessary in times of peace. Systems of import and export control were introduced and regulations framed to conserve foreign exchange and to prevent colonial products reaching the enemy. In a dispatch to the Colonial Governors dated June 8, 1940, the Secretary of State laid down the principles governing colonial production in wartime, including emphasis upon the necessity for the maximum production of foodstuffs and other necessaries of life required to meet local needs, so that shipping might be saved.

While Germany was the only enemy the Crown Colonies were not directly involved, Germany having no colonies of her own and no overseas bases. During the first nine months the contributions from the British Colonies were financial and economic. The entry of Italy into the fighting altered this. A phase of the war began in which the African colonies were actively engaged in the fighting. Even those which were not directly attacked sent contingents to Kenya, Abyssinia and Libya, a movement which was facilitated by the fact that all of them had enlisted the youth of their territory immediately a state of war existed. In general, each African Colony made itself responsible for its own defence, unless it was plain that an Imperial garrison was needed to supplement the local defence.

West Indies. The main contribution of the West Indies to the war effort took the form of leasing a number of strategic bases to the United States for the use of the American Navy and Air Force. The value of this gesture became apparent in the winter of 1941, when the United States entered the war as a full combatant. The announcement of the lease of the Colonial bases was made on Sept. 3, 1940, the anniversary of Britain's declaration of war against Hitlerism. The leases were for 99 years and the areas concerned included Newfoundland, Bermuda, the Bahamas, Jamaica, St. Lucia, Trinidad, Antigua and British Guiana. The leases in Newfoundland and Bermuda were granted "freely and without consideration." The remainder were granted "in exchange for naval and military equipment which the United States will transfer to His Majesty's Government." In accepting the offer the United States Government transferred fifty destroyers, each of 1,200 tons, to the British Navy.

ST. LUCIA'S GIFT TO THE MOTHERLAND

The West Indian island of St. Lucia not only gave Britain indirect help by freely leasing a site to the U.S.A. as a naval base, but also made a direct practical gift in the form of scrap iron, a cargo of which is seen above being loaded on to a steamer.

Photo, "The Times"

British Guiana is the source of almost all the bauxite produced in the British Empire, bauxite being the raw material from which aluminium is extracted. Much of America's aluminium comes from the colony, and in 1941 a force of United States troops was landed in British Guiana to protect the bauxite deposits, at the wish of the British Government. British Guiana is the second largest producer of sugar in the British Empire, and her contribution to our supplies amounted to 190,000 tons a year, under war conditions.

British Honduras, our other mainland possession in America, contributed mahogany, largely used for the making of aeroplane propellers.

In the **West Indian Islands** the whole sugar crop for 1940 was purchased by the British Government at £10 5s. a ton f.o.b., and the 1941 crop was bought for £11 12s. 6d. No less valuable was the Sea Island cotton, all of which was taken over by the Home Government. The long staple cotton grown in

St. Vincent, St. Kitts and Barbados is unique, the West Indies being the only source of supply in the world. It is specially useful in wartime. Trinidad's contribution to the Empire's war effort took the form of 1,500,000 barrels of oil. After India, Trinidad is the most important oil-producing centre in the Empire. As a contribution to the fighting services the Trinidad Legislative Council established a Royal Naval Volunteer Reserve, which included the provision of war vessels. Five times the number of men required were inmediately enlisted in the R.N.V.R. Jamaica received twelve thousand evacuees from Gibraltar and established special camps for their comfort. Even St. Helena, at one time the prison-home of Napoleon, was able to make a special contribution to the Empire war effort. It took the form of the whole output of the island's flax fibre mills, which was purchased outright by the British Government.

EAST AND WEST AFRICA. When fighting began after the entry of Italy into the war, it was plain that the cost of defence would be vastly in excess of the financial capacity of the Colonial Governments. So it was agreed that 25 per cent should be added to the defence expenditure of each unit in 1939, and any excess expenditure would be borne by the Home Government. The bauxite mines in Nyasaland were put on a war footing, the deposits of the aluminium-bearing clay in this dependency being estimated at 6,000,000 tons.

FIGHTING UNITS FROM BRITAIN'S AFRICAN POSSESSIONS
No part of the far-flung British Empire has shown greater loyalty than the African colonies. Top, members of the British Somaliland Camel Corps on the Abyssinian frontier, whence they raided Italian outposts. Bottom, left, corporal of the King's African Rifles ; right, an aircraft of the R.A.F. Gold Coast Squadron, established through subscriptions from that colony, is being named after a Gold Coast town.
Photos, British Official; "Daily Mirror"

INSPECTION OF MEN FROM MAURITIUS
When the first Mauritius contingent of the Royal Army Ordnance Corps arrived in Egypt from their island, they were inspected by Lt.-Gen. Sir Henry Maitland Wilson at their camp.
Photo, British Official

Similarly, the sisal industry in Kenya was developed, in order greatly to increase the production of sandbags for the defence of Britain against the German bombing planes. A Kenya factory, canning beef from the one-time German colony of Tanganyika, produced 20,000 tins a day for the British forces in East Africa. In West Africa, Great Britain purchased the whole cocoa crop at a price £2 a ton higher than the average figure for 1938-9. The Gold Coast is the world's greatest producer of cocoa.

The shipping facilities in West Africa suggested the desirability of organizing shipyards at Lagos and Freetown for the repair of naval and other ships, and this was done, while the Nigeria Marine equipped a naval defence force which rendered valuable aid to the Royal Navy. In the Gold Coast, the Chief of the Builsa tribe volunteered to raise a battalion of infantry. Uganda immediately enlisted 1,700 men, who served with the fighting forces in East Africa. A thousand native soldiers were also recruited in Nyasaland, while Tanganyika raised an invaluable donkey corps for transport purposes. By October 1940 the European man-power in Kenya was one hundred per cent mobilized, every able-bodied man being either in the regular army or the Kenya Defence Force. Nor were the native chiefs behindhand. The Paramount Chief of Turkana offered all his young men for the King's Service, and they patrolled the Kenya frontier during the height of the Abyssinian campaign. The gallant defence of Moyale by the King's African Rifles in 1940 was recognized as one of the outstanding achievements of the African war.

RHODESIA'S first war contribution was a contingent of 700 officers and non-coms for the Royal West African Frontier Force. Many of the men had seen service in the Gold Coast, Sierra Leone, and the Gambia, and they joined the Army of the Middle East in April 1940, after a 2,000 miles' "safari" from Lusaka to Nairobi, moving in a fleet of motorized lorries belonging to the Rhodesian Government. The Rhodesian Government spent £3,000,000 upon war preparations in 1940-41, including the establishment of seven air training centres at Salisbury, Buluwayo,

and elsewhere. The climate and environment of Rhodesia are ideal for air training, and led the British Government to finance the scheme, with aid from the Government of Southern Rhodesia. Air squadrons from Rhodesia served in Kenya and elsewhere on the African fighting front, and two Rhodesian contingents aided British bombers and fighters in the Battle of Britain. More Rhodesians would have joined the army and air force if the British Government had not expressly stated that they regarded the production of copper, lead, and zinc as of primary importance. Rhodesians were, therefore, asked to stay in their jobs.

ADEN withstood numerous air raids after Italy entered the war. The Sultans of Mukalla and Lahej made generous gifts of money to the Home Government. MAURITIUS sent the whole of her exportable sugar to the Mother Country in 1940 and 1941, and, in addition, made a gift of £160,000 to the British Government. The islanders also gave £11,000 to buy a seaplane for H.M.S. Mauritius, while the Mauritius Press Association collected £28,000 for general war purposes. The principal contribution of CEYLON was her tea crop, amounting to 170 million pounds a year, but the Cingalese Government also sent £375,000 to Britain for the purchase of aircraft.

MALAYA. The fighting is the subject of special articles (see Borneo, Malaya, Singapore), but it may be noted that the Straits Settlements Government contributed £2,000,000 towards the cost of imperial defence in the first year of the war. The rulers of the Federated Malay States also gave £1,500,000 and rulers of the Unfederated Malay States £420,000 towards the general prosecution of the war. The Sultan of Brunei in BORNEO gave the British Government £23,000 and the Rajah of Sarawak £175,000, these being first and not final gifts. HONG KONG (*q.v.*), even before she was attacked, contributed three million dollars a year to Imperial funds, in addition to defence expenditure totalling six million dollars in Hong Kong itself.

Finally, in the Pacific area, the island of FIJI organized a Fiji Defence Force, including Fijian and

MAKING MUNITIONS IN RHODESIA
In the shops of the great copper mines of Northern Rhodesia munitions are now being made for the Empire's war effort. The work is done almost entirely by women volunteers.
Photo, British Official

Indian units, and sent many of her young men to New Zealand for service in the Royal New Zealand Defence Force. The people of Fiji also subscribed £50,000 towards a fund for the purchase of military aircraft.

Book to Consult: War for Britain, Donald Cowie (Chapman & Hall).

British Expeditionary Force. Under the command of Gen. Lord Gort from Sept. 3, 1939, to May 31, 1940, the British Expeditionary Force (at one time known as the British Field Force), consisting of five divisions, began its move to France on Sept. 10. The troops disembarked at Cherbourg, their stores and vehicles being dispatched to Nantes, St. Nazaire and Brest. Early in December 1940, in the course of a report of the King's visit to France, it was stated that the B.E.F. were in the front line. About a week after the King's visit the B.E.F. suffered its first battle-field casualties, the first British soldier to be killed in action being Cpl. T. W. Priday.

With the Nazi invasion of the Low Countries the B.E.F. came into action. At daybreak on May 10 motorized units sped through Flanders into the heart of Belgium, and next day British and French troops were fighting alongside the Belgians (*see* Belgium, Campaign in). With the surrender of the Belgian Army on May 28, the B.E.F., together with French troops, fought fierce rearguard actions while manoeuvring towards the coast, and wounded and troops were evacuated from Dunkirk (*q.v.*) with the assistance of Allied Navies and the R.A.F. B.E.F. losses exceeded 30,000 killed, wounded and missing, while material losses included 1,000 guns and all transport and armoured vehicles. In a statement to the House of Commons in October 1939 Mr. Hore-Belisha (*q.v.*) revealed that the B.E.F. consisted of 158,000 men, but by the end of January 1940 its strength stood at 222,200. With the embarkation of the last British soldier from France the B.E.F. ceased to exist.

British Restaurants. Communal eating centres serving quick and cheap meals to workers, particularly in bombed areas. First known as Community Feeding Centres, they were named British Restaurants in April 1941. On June 15, 1942, it was announced that there were 1,519 British Restaurants in operation. *See* Food.

Brno. Town of Czechoslovakia, capital of Moravia. It was the scene of a revolt against the German occupation in September 1939, and hundreds of demonstrators and insurgents were shot by the Germans. The town gave its name to the Bren gun, originally designed and manufactured in Czechoslovakia.

Sir Alan Brooke, Chief of the Imperial General Staff.
Photo, Fox

Brooke, GEN. SIR ALAN FRANCIS, K.C.B., D.S.O. (b. 1883). Chief of the Imperial General Staff from Nov. 25, 1941, in succession to Sir John Dill. In 1939 he was G.O.C.-in-C. Anti-Aircraft Command, but went to France with the B.E.F. and commanded the 2nd Corps in Flanders. In July 1940 he succeeded Lord Ironside as C.-in-C. Home Forces. Sir Alan Brooke is a gunnery and mechanization expert, and has special knowledge of staff work.

Brooke-Popham, AIR CHIEF MARSHAL SIR ROBERT, G.C.V.O., K.C.B., C.M.G., D.S.O. (b. 1878). He was Inspector-General R.A.F. 1935–36, Governor and C.-in-C. Kenya, 1937–39. He then rejoined the R.A.F.

as chief member of Air Missions to Canada and South Africa. On Nov. 13, 1940, he was appointed C.-in-C. Far East, but was replaced on Dec. 26, 1941, by Lt.-Gen. Sir Henry Pownall.

Brown, RT. HON. ERNEST, M.P. (b. 1881). Minister of Health from February 1941, in succession to Mr. Malcolm MacDonald. He was Secretary for Scotland, 1940–41.

Bruce, RT. HON. STANLEY MELBOURNE (b. 1883). High Commissioner for Australia in London from 1933 to 1945. On May 4, 1942, he was appointed Australian representative in the War Cabinet and on the Pacific War Council in succession to Sir Earle Page. Mr. Bruce was Prime Minister of Australia and Minister for External Affairs, 1923–29.

Bruneval. Important German radio-location centre, twelve miles north of Le Havre, the scene of a daring raid by British paratroops, supported by the Army, Navy and R.A.F., on the night of February 27–28, 1942. The paratroops, under Maj. J. D. Frost, were dropped from R.A.F. bombers, while Fighter Command carried out diversionary operations. The air troops overcame breach defences from the rear, while infantry units landed from the sea. The embarkation was covered by British light naval forces. The raid took the Germans by surprise and, although they offered strong resistance, the radio-location station was entirely destroyed, heavy casualties being inflicted on the enemy and a number of prisoners taken. Operations were completed in two hours, and all forces engaged arrived safely back in England under cover of fighter protection. Casualties were slight, and no loss was suffered by British ships or planes. A German armoured division, which appeared upon the scene, arrived after the British forces had left. This raid, the result of long and careful planning, proved the swiftness and efficiency of such combined operations upon the enemy-held coast. The Germans subsequently reinforced their garrisons, thus pinning down considerable numbers of Nazi troops upon the French coast. For their part in this daring raid, Acting Wing-Comdr. Percy Charles Pickard, leader of the aircraft which carried the paratroops, received a bar to his D.S.O., and two other officers who took troops to Bruneval were honoured, Acting Sqdrn.-Ldr. Donald Pelever gaining a bar to his D.F.C. and Sqdrn.-Ldr. James Anthony Meade receiving the D.F.C. *See* Commandos.

Brussels. Capital of Belgium. German bombers attacked it on May 10, 1940, and by May 17 enemy troops had occupied the city. King Leopold withdrew to the royal Palace of Laeken, near Brussels, and remained there as a virtual prisoner. A German Commissioner was appointed for the University and repressive measures were adopted against the Belgian students and professors. In December 1941, following a dispute between the University and the German military authorities caused by the appointment of quisling tutors, the University was closed. The Burgomaster of Brussels, M. van der Meulebroeck, who had taken office after the death of his famous predecessor, M. Max, on Nov. 6, 1939, refused, like him, to become a tool in the hands of the enemy, and was dismissed from his post in June 1941, and later arrested.

Bucharest. Capital of Rumania. It is the chief distributing centre of the country with important railway communications. German troops entered the city on Oct. 7, 1940, " to reorganize the Rumanian Army." It was attacked by Russian bombers in June 1941.

**Marshal Budenny,
Russian Commander.**
Photo, Planet News

Budenny, Marshal S. M. Russian commander in the Ukraine, 1941. He was a private in the Tsar's army, 1914–18. After the Revolution he became a cavalry general in the Civil War and defeated Denikin's White Army in N. Caucasus, 1919–20. Later he was head of the Red Cavalry and Commander of Moscow military area. He was appointed Deputy People's Commissar for Defence in August 1941. One of Russia's most famous leaders in the Russo-German war, 1941, his command was taken over in October 1941 by Marshal Timoshenko during the German thrust to Kharkov, and Marshal Budenny was charged with the formation of a new army.

Bug, River. It runs through the Ukraine and Poland and joins the Vistula 21 miles below Warsaw. It is about 440 miles long and is connected by canal with the Dnieper. The Germans first crossed the river on June 23, 1941, the day after invasion, when two main thrusts towards Kiev and Minsk developed, and Russian counter-attacks resulted in fierce fighting along its banks. Brest-Litovsk, on the Bug, fell on June 24.

Bukovina. Mountainous territory with an area of 4,030 square miles belonging principally to the Carpathian region. Before 1919 it was Austrian, but was then ceded to Rumania. The capital is Cernautzi (Czernowitz). On June 26, 1940, Russia delivered an ultimatum to Rumania demanding the cession of N. Bukovina, and this was granted. When Germany invaded Russia on June 22, 1941, Rumanian troops joined her in attacking Bukovina.

Bulgaria. At the outset of the war the Bulgarian premier, M. Filoff, and his Foreign Minister, M. Popoff, declared for neutrality, and from time to time this policy was re-stated during the first year of the conflict. The relations of Bulgaria with both sides were friendly, but, following the collapse of France in June 1940, it was evident that the belief that Germany would win the war was becoming predominant in both Court and Government in Sofia. The first overt sign of German influence in Bulgaria appeared in August 1940, when Freemasonry, one of Hitler's traditional "enemies," was suppressed, and in the same month the country was placed under an obligation to Germany when, through her good offices, the Southern Dobruja was ceded to Bulgaria by the hard-pressed Rumanians.

In November 1940 King Boris, whose sympathies were known to be pro-Axis and whose consort was an Italian princess, visited Hitler at Berchtesgaden, and thenceforward Bulgarian policy became ever more openly pro-German. Legislation against the Jews was introduced in January 1941, and a noticeable influx of German "tourists" (in reality technicians of all kinds) took place. On Feb. 15 Mr. Churchill in a broadcast speech warned Bulgaria that, if German influence increased, Great Britain would have no resource but to act as if Bulgaria were a hostile country; the report of the speech was, however, suppressed in Sofia, and its warning was ignored by the Bulgarian Government, which was by then bound body and soul to Germany. On March 1 the occupation of Bulgaria by German troops began, and on the same day the Bulgarian Government signed adhesion to the Axis Pact. Strong

representations were made by the British Ambassador, Mr. Rendel, but the situation was beyond recovery, and by the 8th German troops had taken over all strategic places, air-fields and ports, and were on the frontiers of both Greece and Turkey. On March 5 Britain broke off diplomatic relations with Bulgaria, and Russia, which was then still neutral but presumably favouring Germany, surprised the world by condemning the German entry into Bulgaria and sending a strong Note to Sofia. This was the first indication of an open rift in the accord between Russia and Germany.

Germany now began to put pressure on both Yugoslavia and Greece, and was making open preparations to invade Greece through Bulgaria. In April the Yugoslav *coup d'état* temporarily obstructed the German plans, and Bulgaria, at Germany's behest, broke off diplomatic relations with her Balkan neighbour. In May the invasion of Greece took place. Bulgarian troops gave assistance, and on May 17 the Bulgarian Government announced the annexation of certain portions of both Greek and Yugoslav territory, the reward for King Boris's assistance to Hitler.

Bulgaria and her frontiers, showing the territorial claims she made on Rumania and Greece.

Meanwhile, the Bulgarian people, the majority of whom were pro-Russian and anti-German, had become restive, and during the German occupation sporadic rioting and sabotage were reported. But the popular Agrarian Party had been suppressed in March 1941, and all forms of political liberty were abolished; it was impossible, therefore, for the people to make their desires felt, and in the face of German military and secret police activity any opposition was in the highest degree dangerous. Bulgaria had become a mere colony of Greater Germany, as Mr. Churchill had predicted; her transport system, her raw materials, her foodstuffs, her ports and harbours were taken over and administered by Germans, and she was forced, when Germany invaded Russia in June 1941, to give what assistance she could in that enterprise, in spite of the feelings of the people. King Boris successfully resisted the German demand that Bulgarian soldiers should fight against Russia alongside the Rumanians,

Hungarians and Italians, but the Bulgarian Black Sea coast became Germany's naval base against Russia, and Admiral Raeder, the head of the German Navy, took up his quarters in Sofia in September. German E-boats and U-boats, transported in sections down the Danube, were re-erected and launched at Varna, Bulgaria's Black Sea port. That harbour was employed in building invasion barges and maintaining German naval units. On Nov. 25 Bulgaria signed the Anti-Comintern Pact (*q.v.*) and in December declared war on Great Britain and the United States.

In April 1942 a new Cabinet was formed by M. Filoff. The cause of the crisis that necessitated this was considered in non-Axis countries to be the refusal of certain Ministers to follow the King in his anti-Russian policy. The official Nazi-inspired version was that the crisis had arisen on questions of internal policy.

In London, anti-German Bulgarians formed a Free Bulgarian movement, headed by Kosta Todoroff, a well-known politician who had been exiled for his opposition to Boris's regime.

Bullard, SIR READER (WILLIAM), K.C.M.G. (b. 1885). British Minister in Teheran, Iran, from 1939. He was British Minister in Jedda, Saudi-Arabia, 1936–39.

Bullitt, WILLIAM CHRISTIAN (b. 1891). American Ambassador to France, 1936–40. Early in December 1941 he was sent by President Roosevelt to the Near East, his tour to include Libya, Suez, and the Persian Gulf and Red Seas areas. He undertook this tour as the President's personal representative in order to survey the political, military, and general situation in these areas, with the object of reporting on British requirements under the Lease-Lend Act. Mr. Bullitt was U.S. Ambassador to Russia from 1933 to 1936.

Buqbuq. Egyptian town 25 miles from the Libyan frontier, on the coast between Sollum and Sidi Barrani. The Italians claimed its capture on Sept. 15, 1940. It was recaptured by the British on Dec. 10.

Burgin, RT. HON. EDWARD LESLIE (b. 1887). First Minister of Supply, 1939–40. He had previously been Parliamentary Secretary to the Board of Trade, 1932–37, and Minister of Transport, 1937–39.

THE JAPANESE INVASION OF BURMA

When the Japanese entered Mandalay on May 1, 1942, the Burmese campaign, which had lasted through six months of bitter hill and jungle fighting, was virtually over. British and Chinese fought stoutly, but reinforcements and supplies could not reach them from India and evacuation was inevitable.

Burma. Until 1937 Burma was part of British India. The separation of the two countries was a result of the Government of India Act, and during the second World War executive authority was vested in the Governor, Sir Reginald Dorman-Smith, and his Council of Ministers. The Burmese, who number between 14,000,000 and 15,000,000, came into the fighting line when Japan declared war upon Britain and the United States and marched into Thailand. The first act of war came on Dec. 11, 1941, when Japanese bomber 'planes attacked Tenasserim, Burma's southernmost province. Already it was plain that the Governor's warning, when announcing a state of war, was justified. Sir Reginald said :

" We, in Burma, will have to face a testing time. The whole future of Burma is at stake."

In April 1941 the Secretary of State for Burma announced in Parliament that the British Government was financing the extension of the Burma Railway to the Chinese border. This would link up Burma with the Chinese railway system upon which Free China was relying as its sole connexion with Britain and the United States. For the protection of this life line between China and the Democratic Alliance Indian troops were drafted into Burma during 1941, including batteries for the defence of the rugged mountain frontiers. In 1941, before the Japanese attacks upon Burma began, the Burmese Defence Force consisted of five regular battalions of Burma Rifles and six battalions of the Burma Frontier Force, apart from a territorial force and auxiliary forces, which served as nuclei for enlistment when the actual fighting began. General Wavell inspected the Burmese troops in the autumn of 1941 and expressed his satisfaction with their soldierly qualities. There is also a small Navy, manned by Burmese, but officered by Britons. Its work is mainly minesweeping and patrol services. A Burma Auxiliary Air Squadron was formed in 1940–1.

On Dec. 28, 1941, Lt.-Gen. T. J. Hutton was appointed G.O.C. Burma, and Gen. Wavell assumed military command for operational purposes.

As in India, Dominion status and home rule are a matter for controversy. Mr. U Saw, Burma's Premier, visited London in 1941, with the object of satisfying the British people that Burma had passed every reasonable test of its fitness for full self-government. Opponents of the change point out that Burma is by no means unified. The Shan States are not even within the control of the Burmese ministries, and there are. areas which are neither Shan nor British. Only the Kachins and the Karens in Burma proper have national associations. What Japan particularly wanted were the Burmese oil installations and bases for her submarines and surface raiders in the Bay of Bengal. From Burma, too, Indian industry could be crippled by air raids. Apart from oil, which provided aviation spirit for the R.A.F. operating east of Suez, the principal war exports of Burma were teak for naval construction and rice.

Japanese troops made their first incursion on Burmese soil on Dec. 15, 1941, seizing Point Victoria and the adjacent aerodrome, at the southernmost tip of Tenasserim. But with the Malayan campaign in full swing, it was still too soon to launch a full-scale attack on Burma. The preliminary air attacks were heavy and persistent. Rangoon suffered the first of many severe raids on Dec. 23, and a second one two days later; on these two occasions 40 Japanese 'planes were brought down. A Japanese attempt to infiltrate north of Point Victoria was defeated on Jan. 2, 1942, but on Jan.15 Japanese troops moved into South Burma, and four days later they captured Tavoy, a port and air base, centre of the tin industry. They were reinforced by troops from Siam. The scanty British and Burmese forces had been strengthened by a strong influx of Indians, and afterwards by Chinese, who received a notable addition on Jan. 21, under General Liu Kwan Loong.

The Japanese, however, reached the Salween River, and by Jan. 31 the port of Moulmein, which had already suffered many air attacks, had to be evacuated. The neighbouring port of Martaban fell on Feb. 10. British troops withdrew to the Bilin River, and beyond that, to the Sittang, and on Feb. 28 the key town of Pegu fell; the enemy had thus cut the Burma Road at its lower end, 80 miles N.E. of Rangoon, and also the railway which runs parallel with it from Rangoon to Mandalay and thence to Lashio. By March 3 they were in Rangoon (q.v.), which had been evacuated and demolished beforehand, in pursuance of the scorched earth policy.

Considerable Japanese reinforcements were landed in the delta of the Irrawaddy, and it was now estimated that they had at least 100,000 men in Burma. Part of these new forces moved west to the capture of Bassein, another part advanced north up the river towards Prome, parallel with the advance of those troops in the Sittang valley who were working their way up to Toungoo.

During this period air superiority had been with the Allies; they had countered the Japanese raids by attacking their bases, and had brought down 270 Japanese planes for the loss of 42. Unhappily the position deteriorated through lack of reinforcements and supplies. Ground forces, commanded by General Alexander, comprised, in addition to Indian and Burmese regiments, the K.O.Y.L.I. and the Duke of Wellington's; they put up a heroic fight against terrific odds, and splendid support was given by the Chinese armies, but the tale of retreat continued. Unhappily the Japanese had valuable help from a powerful fifth column element among the native population, engineered by the subversive Thakin party.

On the Sittang front, Toungoo was wrested from the Chinese after a four-day battle, in which the Japanese used gas; it was afterwards recaptured. South of Prome the British made an effective tank attack, but could not prevent the fall of the city on April 2. By April 17 the oilfields of Yenangyaung were in enemy hands, but the installations had been destroyed. Lashio fell on April 30, and the Japanese began to close in on Mandalay, which they entered on May 1; smouldering ruins were all that was left of the ancient royal city, and the Japanese reported that " no one— not even a dog—could be seen in the streets."

British troops, endeavouring to avoid encirclement, withdrew some 50 miles west, to the neighbourhood of Monywa, where they fought fiercely against vastly superior numbers. To the north-west, the Japanese thrust towards Bhamo, attempting a wider encircling movement, supplemented by a thrust in the south-west

Burma and her frontiers.

around Pakokku. From Bhamo they might hope to advance against an important railway line in the British rear. Meanwhile a second claw of the Japanese pincers thrust north along the Burma Road, and by the end of April Lashio had fallen to the Japanese. Following its capture the Japanese pushed along the Burma Road, passing the Chinese frontier by May 8. Meanwhile, Gen. Alexander, British G.O.C., decided to retire up the Chindwin valley to passes leading across the mountains into the Indian province of Assam. The Japanese tried to forestall this movement and during the early stages of the British withdrawal our forces fought a fighting retreat. The final battle in Burma was fought on May 10, at Shwegyin on the Chindwin opposite Kalewa, the retreating forces reaching India by May 15. Chinese forces crossed the Salween to counter-attack Japanese contingents, and some remained to harass the enemy. The R.A.F. and U.S. air forces made heavy attacks on Japanese troops and air bases continuously. British troops re-entered Burma at the end of the year.

Burma Road. Before the outbreak of the Sino-Japanese war in 1937, China, with her 4,000-mile coast-line, had a number of fine ports. By the end of her first year of resistance Shanghai fell into the hands of the Japanese. It was China's chief port. Thereafter Hongkong became the main outlet, with its railway running directly to Hankow, then the seat of the National Government of China. After the fall of Hankow in October 1938, Haiphong, in eastern Indo-China, became the main junction between China and the outside world. But China foresaw the difficulties lying ahead. Early in the war she began building a motor road to Burma. By December 1938 military supplies had already begun to stream along the road. It soon became, to all intents and purposes, the only gate to Free China through which China maintained her relations with the outside world.

The significance of the Yunnan-Burma Road, known also as the Burma Road, cannot be exaggerated. It brought to China all her military and civilian necessaries and sent abroad her exports. It has played a dominant part in the cultural and economic development of China's hinterland. Practically and symbolically, it linked up China and the British Commonwealth as never before. In October 1941 the Chinese postmaster pronounced the Burma Road to be the sole postal road carrying all mails from Free China to the outside world. Lashio, at the Burmese end of the road, became the transfer station. From mid-July to mid-October 1940 the Burma Road was closed to the transit of military supplies and certain other materials, at the request of the Japanese Government, whom Britain could not at that time risk offending.

The entire length of the road from Lashio to Kunming (Yunnanfu), the Chinese terminus of the road, is 726 miles. By May 3 the Japanese claimed, despite heavy counter-attacks, to have advanced 60 miles along the road and were thought to be preparing a major invasion of Yunnan. From Kunming the road continues to Chungking, about 1,600 miles in all. From the Chinese border town of Wanting to Lashio is 75 miles. There is a railway running between Lashio and Rangoon which is 616 miles long. This railway, at the end of 1941, was being extended beyond Lashio to the frontier at Kunming, at the cost of the Government of the United Kingdom. By car it takes 45 hours to travel from Lashio to Kunming at 25 and a half miles per hour. Heavy lorries usually did the journey in seven days. The Burma Road was fed not only by the Rangoon-Lashio railway, but by the Irrawaddy River, up which cargo steamers ply as far as Bhamo. There is another road from Bhamo which joins the Burma Road near the frontier. Along this goods brought up to Bhamo by river are sent to China.

Yunnan is the name of the province which the Burma Road traverses and into which the Japanese entered after their advance from Lashio in May 1942. With an area of 146,000 sq. miles, it has a population of only 12,000,000. Two-thirds of the province are mountains, which make the construction of the road a difficult matter. The road begins from Kunming, the provincial capital, which is also the northern terminus of the Yunnan-Haiphong Railway. Tsouhsiung, 192·3 km. away, is the centre of the silk industry. Farther west is Hsiakwan, an important town for trade between China proper and Tibet. Pao-shan is at the junction of the northern route to Burma via Teng-yiieh. Mang-shih and Che-fang, on the Chinese border, are two famous Shan towns.

A Million Builders of the Road

The idea of building a road between China and Burma was first mooted in the 1860s. Explorations were made by Colonel E. B. Sladen in 1868 and by Mr. Augustus R. Margery in 1874. The most fruitful journeys were made by Major H. Davies in 1895 and 1899–1900. Before the outbreak of the war between China and Japan in 1937, the eastern half of the road, from Kunming to Hsiakwan, was already built. It was widened and surfaced for traffic in July 1938. The remaining section was completed in December of the same year.

The Burma Road is an amazing engineering achievement. Its average height is 4,000 feet above sea level, but often it climbs up to 9,000 feet. There are about 300 bridges and 2,000 culverts. The two most important bridges are the one that crosses the 2,800-mile-long Mekong and another over the 1,800-mile-long Salween River. All the levelling of road-beds and the dynamiting of rocks were done by human hands. The road was built entirely without road-making machinery. The government employed 1,000,000 road builders, of whom many were women and children.

HIGH UP ON THE BURMA ROAD
The building of this great highway was an extraordinary engineering achievement. Here are seen hairpin bends on the Road where it climbs the side of a mountain. In some places it rises to a height of 9,000 feet.
Photo, Keystone

The Japanese conquest of Malaya and subsequent advance into Burma made it necessary to find an alternative route to the Burma Road. This possibility had already been foreseen, and plans had been made and to some extent put into action. On Feb. 17, 1942, General Chiang Kai-shek paid an official visit to New Delhi, one of the topics discussed being " new supply routes, the capacity of which will exceed that of the Burma Road."

The route chosen was probably the Assam Road, which was first projected after the Vichy surrender of Indo-China to Japan. This was to run from Free China's capital, Chungking, north-west to Chengtu, west across Sikang Province through Litang and Batang, and then south-west to Sadiya, northern terminus of the Bengal-Assam railway, which runs to Calcutta and also to the port of Chittagong, 300 miles east of Calcutta. The length of the road, from Sadiya to Chungking, would be 2,200 miles, compared with the 1,600 miles of the Burma Road. Difficult as the construction of the Burma Road was, this seemed even more formidable, involving excavation of the Himalayan ridges, sometimes at a height of 9,000 ft., buttressing of precipitous slopes, bridging of canyons, clearing of jungle growth, and the transport of the heavy material required. Normally such a task would take years to perform, but under the pressure of events miracles might be achieved. A vast army of Chinese workers,

Burma Road, highway to China captured by Japan.
By courtesy of " The Times "

men and women, some 100,000 in all, were mobilized, and in the spring of 1942 it was probable that half of the road had been constructed.

Unhappily the capture of Lashio on April 30 had a crippling effect on the project. It had been intended that the new road should link up with the Burma Road at Lashio. The Allies were hard put to it to devise some means of getting reinforcements into Burma from India. Nor would it be easy for the Chinese to send reinforcements along the Burma Road, for by May 4 the Japanese had advanced along that highway to within 25 miles of the border, and by May 5 they were over it and in Yunnan Province.

For the Allied armies, deprived of the Burma Road and the Assam Road, there was a suggested third route, through Sinkiang Province, which lies between Mongolia and Tibet. This would involve transit of supplies through Siberia to China.

 Cagliari. Capital of Sardinia, situated at the head of the Gulf of Cagliari, in the middle of the south coast. It has a fine harbour and an aerodrome, both of which have frequently been bombed by the Fleet Air Arm and the R.A.F. The British naval victory of Cagliari took place on Nov. 27, 1940. Under the command of Vice-Admiral Sir James Somerville, a British naval squadron, consisting chiefly of cruisers and the battle-cruiser Renown, was patrolling the Western Mediterranean, when about 10 a.m. messages were received from aircraft of the Ark Royal that a large force of Italian ships had been sighted 70 miles away, and about 20 miles off the coast of Sardinia. These ships were, in fact, those which had escaped damage at Taranto (*q.v.*) on the night of Nov. 11–12, and which were now seeking a safer base. The British squadron thereupon altered course and steamed at full speed to intercept them.

About two hours later four enemy cruisers were sighted and in a few minutes our advanced units opened fire. Having fired a reply salvo, the enemy turned and fled north-eastward. Half an hour later two enemy battleships—one, the Vittorio Veneto, and one of the Cavour class—accompanied by cruisers, were sighted and opened fire on the British ships, which were forced by the heavier metal of their opponents to turn aside. Soon afterwards the enemy themselves turned away and retired at speed, and our cruisers resumed the pursuit of the Italian cruisers. These were chased to within a few miles of the enemy's coast, but their superior speed enabled them to get away, and the pursuit was abandoned. Reconnaissance 'planes revealed that one cruiser had been set on fire and two destroyers hit. The Vittorio Veneto was hit by a torpedo from an Ark Royal aircraft, and other naval aircraft repeatedly attacked, harried and damaged the retreating cruisers. The only British ship to suffer damage was H.M.S. Berwick, which received two hits, but was not rendered unfit for service. A few hours later enemy bombers and fighters twice attacked the British ships, including Ark Royal, but were driven off by our naval aircraft.

Cairo. Capital of Egypt. Here were the headquarters of Britain's Middle East Command, first under General Wavell, and from July 1941 under General Auchinleck. The Middle East R.A.F. Command was also based on Cairo, the A.O.C.-in-C. being Air-Chief-Marshal Sir A. W. Tedder. *See* Egypt.

Calais, DEFENCE OF. By the end of the third week in May 1940 the supply lines of the retreating British Expeditionary Force in France had been cut by the swift advance towards the coast of German armoured divisions. In an effort to open up alternative communication, a small British force was sent to Calais to establish a route along the coast to Dunkirk. Calais Force, as it was called, was made up of one battalion each of the King's Royal Rifle Corps, Queen Victoria's Rifles, the Rifle Brigade and the Royal Tank Regiment, with an Anti-Tank Battery of the Royal Artillery— some 3,000 men, under the command of Brigadier Claude Nicholson.

Brig. Nicholson, Hero of Calais.
Photo, Universal Pictorial Press

The force landed at Calais on May 22 and 23, and almost at once found it so closely invested by the enemy as to make the original aim of the expedition impossible to achieve. An attempt to break through was in fact made by the Rifle Brigade and tanks on the night of the 23rd, but it was unsuccessful. Orders were therefore given to hold the town instead.

Calais is made up of an old town, containing the docks and Citadel, surrounded by a new town, Calais-Sud, stretching away to the south. In disposing his troops Brig. Nicholson organized an Outer Perimeter (or defence line) which roughly ringed Calais-Sud, and an Inner Perimeter girdling the old town. On arrival on the 22nd companies of Queen Victoria's Rifles established advanced posts outside the town, while the K.R.R.s and Rifle Brigade, landing on the 23rd, manned the Outer Perimeter. Meanwhile, ships were coming and going from the port, non-combatants and wounded being evacuated, and every street teeming with refugees. In this confusion a tragic mistake was made and two-thirds of the Rifle Brigade's stores were taken back to England.

By the afternoon of the 23rd Calais was being heavily shelled by the Germans, and where these batteries came within range, their fire was vigorously returned by the Royal Navy as represented by the patrolling destroyers Verity and Windsor. Enterprising tank patrols reconnoitring the immediate countryside were driven in by superior strength.

The Citadel Falls

On the 24th the Germans closed in on the town and there was continuous fighting on the Outer Perimeter. From time to time the defences were pierced by enemy tanks and infantry, which were as often thrown out again. As the day wore on the bombardment became heavier and the attack so intense that Brigade H.Q. was moved to the Citadel and, after dark, the defending troops withdrew to the Inner Perimeter, where, weary, thirsty and with little food, they stood to their posts through the night.

Some 125 men of an A.A. battery of the R.A. and 100 Royal Marines had joined the defenders by the 25th, when the assault was pressed with great determination and overwhelming numbers. Still Calais Force held out, and at 8 p.m. a demand to surrender was curtly rejected. Then, on the 26th, the Germans used dive-bombers in incessant low-level attacks on the town, Citadel and docks, following these up with infantry, tanks and mortars. It was too much : by

4 p.m. the Rifle Brigade, their meagre ammunition spent, were overwhelmed. An hour later the Citadel fell to a sudden attack and Brig. Nicholson was captured.

That night Calais was an inferno, with Germans everywhere. But here and there isolated groups of Riflemen held out to the death. R.A.F. reconnaissance planes flying over the ruins the next day could see no British troops in the town. Calais Force had been annihilated. But for four agonizing days they had engaged the whole strength of two Panzer divisions and thereby made possible the " miracle of deliverance " at Dunkirk.

After the collapse of France, Calais, only 21 miles away from the English coast, became one of the " invasion ports," the R.A.F. frequently bombing the harbour, enemy shipping, and Nazi gun emplacements.

Book to Consult : The Defence of Calais, Eric Linklater (H.M.S.O.).

Calinescu, ARMAND. Rumanian Prime Minister March 7 to Sept. 21, 1939. He was one of the strongest men Rumania has produced and, while Minister of the Interior in the previous Government, was entrusted by King Carol with the suppression of the Iron Guard, the Rumanian Fascist organization. Nevertheless, members remained at large and were responsible for Calinescu's assassination in Bucharest on Sept. 21. The murder was followed by the rounding up and execution of these Iron Guard terrorists.

Calypso, H.M.S. British cruiser of 4,180 tons. She was torpedoed in the Mediterranean by an Italian submarine on June 13, 1940. One officer and 38 ratings were reported missing out of a complement of about 437.

Cambrai. City of France, on the R. Scheldt, 37 miles south-east of Lille. The Allied armies made heroic thrusts towards the town in May 1940, endeavouring to cut off the Germans from the French coast, and heavy fighting raged between Cambrai, Valenciennes and Arras. Cambrai was captured on May 26, 1940.

Cameroons. French mandated colony in west-central Africa. In August 1940, following the example of Chad Territory, the Cameroons declared their adherence to General de Gaulle. *See* Equatorial Africa.

Camouflage. Divided into four sections, Home Security, R.A.F., War Office and Admiralty, camouflage is an important branch of war strategy (*see* pp. 786 and 787). These four sections worked independently of each other, and after the outbreak of war a committee was formed to enable the heads of the various departments to exchange ideas and to pass on valuable information as a result of experiments. One of the early tasks of the Air Ministry was temporarily to disguise vulnerable aerodromes, but with further camouflage development methods changed, and it was possible to alter the aspect of the various airfields, so that these obvious targets appeared wholly transformed when seen from a plane. Three aspects of camouflage consist of shape, texture and colour, and the outlines of targets must be disguised. In Russia experiments were carried out until extremely effective methods were evolved, as the German armies found to their cost during the bitter fighting of 1941–42. In Britain the art of camouflage was also speeded up, and intricate designs were adopted in order to produce forms of complete concealment. The aim of camouflage is to fit naturally into its surroundings, so that at a distance the various patterns blend harmoniously and do not attract the attention of the enemy.

The Ministry of Home Security adopted a black-and-green colour scheme for the tops of factories as being the most effective method, but in the case of water a problem of greater difficulty presented itself. To conceal the river Thames, for instance, from enemy bombers is an impossible task. The Germans camouflaged the Gneisenau and Scharnhorst while those ships were at Brest in 1941 by means of netting.

Book to Consult : The Art of Camouflage, Lt.-Col. C. H. R. Chesney (Robt. Hale).

Campbell, SIR GERALD, G.C.M.G. (b. 1879). Director-General of British Information Services in U.S.A. from June 1941 to May 1942, when he was succeeded by Mr. Harold Butler, former Director of the International Labour Office. Sir Gerald was previously High Commissioner for the United Kingdom in Canada, 1938–41, and British Minister in Washington, Feb.–June 1941.

Campbell, BRIGADIER JOHN CHARLES. He was awarded the V.C. in February 1942 for most conspicuous gallantry in Libya. On Nov. 21, 1941, he was in command of a small force, including tanks, in the area of Sidi Rezegh ridge and the aerodrome. They were repeatedly attacked by large numbers of tanks and infantry, and wherever the situation was

Brigadier Campbell, awarded the V.C.
Photo, "The Times"

worst he was to be seen with his forward troops, either on foot or standing in his open car, personally forming up tanks under intense fire. Next day the enemy attacks were intensified, and Brig. Campbell was always in the forefront of the heaviest fighting, staging counter-attacks and personally controlling, and twice manning, his guns. Wounded, he refused to be evacuated and remained with his command. He had already won the D.S.O., and later the bar, for gallantry in Libya in 1940. He was killed March 5, 1942.

F/O K. Campbell, awarded the V.C.
Photo, British Official

Campbell, F/O KENNETH, R.A.F.V.R. Pilot of a Beaufort aircraft, he made a daring torpedo raid on an enemy battle cruiser in Brest harbour at dawn on April 6, 1941. Despite the fierce A.A. defences, he came in almost at sea level, skimmed over the Mole and launched the torpedo at point-blank range. The aircraft did not return. Campbell was awarded the V.C. for most conspicuous bravery.

Campbell, RT. HON. SIR RONALD HUGH, G.C.M.G. (b. 1883). British Ambassador to Portugal. He had been H.M. Minister in Belgrade, 1935–39, and Ambassador to France, 1939–40.

Campbell, SIR RONALD IAN, K.C.M.G. (b. 1890). British Minister in Washington. He had previously been Minister Plenipotentiary at the British Embassy, Paris, 1938–39, and H.M. Minister in Belgrade, 1939–41.

Campinchi, CESARE (1882–1941). French Minister of Marine in the Blum Cabinet, March–April 1938 ; under Daladier, 1938–40 ; and under Reynaud, 1940–41.

Camrose, WILLIAM EWERT BERRY, 1ST VISCOUNT (b. 1879). He acted as Chief Assistant to Lord Macmillan at the Ministry of Information, and Controller of News Relations, for a period in 1939.

CANADA'S CONTRIBUTION TO THE WAR

"There is no man, woman or child whose life is not bound up with this struggle," said Mr. Mackenzie King, Premier of Britain's greatest Dominion, and Canada has given whole-hearted proof of her belief in this declaration.

Canada. Canada has surprised herself with the scope of her war efforts. Even more has she surprised the Nazi leaders of Germany. They had confidently predicted the disintegration of the British Empire upon the outbreak of hostilities. Would not Canada be foremost among the Dominions to seize the opportunity of throwing off the British yoke ? Would she not begin by declaring her neutrality, as she could do under the Statute of Westminster of 1931—the charter of the British Commonwealth of Nations ?

The Dominion of Eire did declare neutrality in September 1939, and Canada had all the more inducement to remain neutral because the President of the United States had declared that any foreign attack upon Canada would at once bring the United States to Canada's defence. Canada could thus rest secure and make profit out of the war efforts of the warring nations. Moreover—so the world was told from Berlin—Canada had suffered enough from meddling in

the war of 1914–18—it cost Canada 60,000 men killed and 155,000 wounded, and in hard cash a sum about equal to 15 years' normal national expenditure pre-war. Was it not unthinkable that Canada could or would repeat that sad experience ?

But, Berlin notwithstanding, that is just what Canada did. From the moment that Britain was at war Canada regarded herself as at war also. Her great neighbour, the United States, hesitated, and at that time stood aloof in action though not in expression of sympathy. But Canada at once threw her all into the scale. Four days after Britain began hostilities on Sept. 3, 1939, Canadian Senators and Members of Parliament—including representatives not only of British but of French, German, Italian and other former foreign descent, gathered from all parts of a widely scattered Dominion—met at Ottawa with a united resolve. On Sept. 10, 1939, following upon their almost unanimous decision, the King declared that

CANADA ANSWERS THE CALL OF FREEDOM IN PERIL

Top, left, a steel-helmeted sailor stands ready at his Lewis gun aboard a Canadian destroyer ; right, Canadian reinforcements marching into their new camp at Hongkong in November 1941. Oval, electric furnace in a Canadian arms plant. Bottom, left, pilot of an R.C.A.F. fighter squadron in England dashes to his aircraft ; right, a girl in a Canadian arsenal is checking small arms cartridge cases.

Photos, Canadian Official; British Official; Sport & General; Fox

a state of war existed between Canada and Germany. When Italy began hostilities on June 10, 1940, Canada at once declared war upon her.

Canada's population is about 11,500,000, the United States' about 130,000,000. The national income of Canada in the fiscal year 1940–41 was something less than $6,000,000,000, the national income of the United States something less than $90,000,000,000. The salient features of Canada's war effort show the following results when presented in terms of United States equivalents, figures relating to man power being translated in terms of population, figures relating to money in terms of national income :—

Canada's War Effort

	Canada	Expressed in United States Equivalents
Navy, Number of men	25,000	282,500
Army, Number of men	230,000	2,599,000
Air Force, Number of men	83,000	937,900
Sailors, soldiers and airmen overseas ..	100,000	1,130,000
Money spent on war, first two years (1939–41), including financial aid to Britain ..	$2,183,000,000	$32,745,000,000
Money spent on war fiscal year (April 1, 1941, to March 31, 1942), including financial aid to Britain ..	$2,350,000,000	$35,250,000,000
Cost to Canada of British Commonwealth Air Training Plan (three years) ..	$531,000,000	$7,965,000,000
Value of Canadian products (including war supplies and equipment) sent to Britain first two years of war	$1,071,000,000	$16,065,000,000
Value of Canadian products sent to Britain during fiscal year 1940–41	$1,500,000,000	$22,500,000,000
Federal revenue (estimated) in fiscal year 1940–41	$1,500,000,000	$22,500,000,000
Money loaned to Canadian Government by Canadian people since outbreak of war ..	$1,470,000,000	$22,050,000,000
Contributions to war charities since outbreak of war ..	$27,000,000	$405,000,000
Total value of contracts and commitments by Department of Munitions and Supply on Canadian and British account	$2,400,000,000	$36,000,000,000

Note.—To get the approximate equivalent in English pounds sterling these dollar sums may be divided by 5.

Canadians in December 1941 were paying three times as much in taxes as they did before the war, and were imposing upon themselves controls and restrictions hitherto undreamt of by a people accustomed to plenty and the freedom to enjoy it as they pleased. In September 1939 the percentage of national income allocated for defence was only 1·4% ; in September 1941 it was 40% and was fast rising.

To the 120,000 Canadians who had arrived in Britain by September 1941 was assigned the task of defending the British Isles from the foreign invader —they held the citadel of world freedom for freedom-loving peoples everywhere. Canada, while defending her Atlantic and Pacific seaboards, also had troops at strategic points—Iceland, Gibraltar, Hongkong and the British West Indies.

Small units of the Royal Canadian Air Force arrived in Britain soon after the outbreak of war. The first contingent, complete with its own 'planes and full equipment, landed here in June 1940. The Canadian aviation schools planned to turn out 25,000 to 30,000 pilots, observers, air gunners and wireless operators in a single year (*see* Empire Air Training).

Long regarded as one of the Empire's principal storehouses for food and raw materials, Canada turned herself into an Empire arsenal as well. Fourteen types of land and naval guns and mountings were being produced. Shells and small arms ammunition were being turned out at the rate of millions of rounds a year. The tank programme comprised 1,000 cruisers, 800 infantry tanks and 150,000 army vehicles. Since January 1939 the number of men engaged in aircraft construction has increased from 1,600 to more than 30,000. About £30,000,000 sterling is being spent on naval vessels, including corvettes and minesweepers.

From the end of January 1942 all munitions, foodstuffs and raw materials supplied by Canada were a free gift up to a total of one thousand million Canadian dollars, roughly £225,000,000, without charge or obligation. An outstanding sum due of £150,000,000 was converted into an interest-free loan and certain railway securities held by residents in Great Britain were purchased by the Canadian Government.

Cooperation between Canada and the U.S., already well defined at the beginning of the war, steadily increased, and many vital measures for mutual defence were put into operation. The Canadian-U.S. Joint Defence Board announced on March 18, 1941, the completion of plans for the military and naval defence of the Atlantic and Pacific coasts of both countries, and on Sept. 21 Canada and the U.S. agreed to allow their respective armed forces to cross the border freely. With America's entry into the conflict in December 1941, cooperation between Canada and her neighbour received a fresh impetus. An important agreement was reached on March 18, 1942, when plans for the construction of the Alaska Highway linking the U.S. with Alaska via British Columbia and Yukon were announced.

Books to Consult : Canada: America's Problem, John MacCormac (Cape). Canada comes to Britain, G. Beckles (Hodder & Stoughton).

Canea. Chief port and capital of Crete, situated on the N. coast of the island. It has a shallow harbour. After being heavily bombed, German parachutists landed near Canea on May 20, 1941. Their troops gained a foothold at Maleme aerodrome, ten miles S.W. of the town, on May 21, preparatory to their attack on Canea, which they captured on May 27.

Canterbury. City of Kent. On Oct. 11, 1940, a Messerschmitt dive-bombed the Cathedral and shattered some windows ; most of the ancient stained glass had been removed. The Deanery was damaged on Oct. 17, during a daylight raid. On May 31, 1942, considerable damage was caused in a raid described by the Nazis as a reprisal for ours on Cologne.

Capuzzo, Fort. Italian stronghold in Libya, S. of Bardia, on the Egyptian frontier. The Italians withdrew after bombardment of the fort by British battleships on Aug. 17, 1940, but enemy forces were reported to have reoccupied the site on Aug. 23. It was stormed and captured by British Imperial forces on Dec. 17. The Germans occupied it on April 14, 1941, after British forces had withdrawn to Mersa Matruh. On Nov. 18, 1941, the British 8th Army, under Gen. Cunningham, drove into Libya, and Fort Capuzzo was captured on Nov. 21. *See* North Africa.

A CARDIFF CATHEDRAL BOMBED
The Catholic cathedral of St. David's suffered in one of the raids on the S. Wales port. This picture shows the interior of the burnt-out building looking from the High Altar.
Photo, Topical

Cardiff. City and seaport of South Wales. The main industry is the shipping of coal, and for this there are five docks, known officially as Bute Docks, which are supplemented by Penarth Docks and Barry Docks in the neighbourhood. Cardiff suffered a violent night raid on Jan. 2, 1941, when thousands of incendiaries were followed by H.E. bombs, causing great damage and many casualties. There were further heavy night attacks.

Carinthia, H.M.S. British armed merchant cruiser of 20,277 tons, formerly a Cunard-White Star liner. Her loss, after a fight with a U-boat, was announced on June 8, 1940. Four men were killed.

Carnarvon Castle, H.M.S. British auxiliary cruiser (21,222 tons), formerly a Union Castle liner. She was in action with a heavily armed enemy raider in the S. Atlantic on Dec. 5, 1940. The fight lasted 90 minutes, during which the raider's guns were so damaged that she threw out a smoke screen and made off. The British ship also sustained damage.

Carrington, LT.-GEN. SIR R. H., K.C.B., D.S.O. (b. 1882). He was appointed G.O.C.-in-C. Scottish Command in February 1940.

Cartier de Marchienne, EMILE ERNEST, BARON DE (b. 1871). Belgian Ambassador to Britain from 1927. He was a member of the Belgian Government in London from 1940.

Carton de Wiart, MAJ.-GEN. ADRIAN, V.C. (b. 1880). He commanded the British forces in Central Norway in 1940. His V.C. was awarded in the last war, when he was wounded eight times and lost an eye and an arm. In April 1941 it was learned that he had fallen into enemy hands while on his way to the Middle East.

Casey, RT. HON. RICHARD GARDINER, P.C., D.S.O. (b. 1890). Minister of State in the Middle East. He was Minister of Supply and Development, 1939–40, subsequently becoming Australian Minister to the U.S.A. On March 18, 1942, he succeeded Mr. Oliver Lyttelton as Minister of State in the Middle East with headquarters at Cairo, and was also appointed a member of the British War Cabinet.

Mr. R. G. Casey, Minister of State.
Photo, Lafayette

Cash and Carry Act. Name popularly given to the American Neutrality Act (*q.v.*).

Caspian Sea. Inland sea between Europe and Asia. It is 760 miles long from N. to S., while the width varies from 120 miles to 300 miles. British war supplies sent to Russia in 1941 passed through Iran and were transported thence across the Caspian. Astrakhan and Guriev on the northern shore are important Russian supply centres, while Baku on the W. coast is a vital oil base.

Catania. City and seaport of Sicily. It lies at the base of Mt. Etna, 59 miles S. of Messina. The Germans used Catania as an air base from which to attack the British Mediterranean Fleet, and the aerodrome and other important military targets were heavily bombed by the R.A.F.

Catroux, GEN. GEORGES (b. 1879). High Commissioner of Free France in the Near East from 1940. He had a distinguished military career, spent largely in Morocco, Algeria and Syria, and, having reached the rank of Lt.-Gen., he was given command in 1936 of the 14th Infantry Division in Mulhouse and later of the 19th Corps in Algiers. He remained in Algeria until a few months before the outbreak of war, when he was placed on the reserve by Gen. Gamelin, with whom he was not in agreement. But in August 1939 M. Mandel, then Minister for the Colonies, made him a General and sent him to Indo-China as Governor-General. He held this post until July 1940, when, disagreeing with Pétain's policy, he was replaced by Admiral Decoux, until then commanding the Navy in the Far East.

Gen. Catroux, Free French Commissioner.
Photo, L.N.A.

Gen. Catroux arrived in England on Sept. 18, and immediately joined the Free French movement. On Oct. 27 he became a member of the French Empire Defence Council, and on Nov. 27 Gen. de Gaulle appointed him High Commissioner of Free France and Head of the Free French Forces in the Near East, the Red Sea region and the Balkans. The Free French troops who marched into Syria (*q.v.*) on June 8, 1941, were under his personal command, and it was Gen. Catroux who, with the Vichy representative, Gen. de Verdillac, drew up the terms of the Convention which, on July 14, brought hostilities to an end.

Gen. Carton de Wiart, V.C.
Photo, Planet News

Caucasia. This district of Russia, lying between the Black Sea and the Caspian, and traversed by the gigantic range of the Caucasus Mts., assumed paramount importance when the Russo-German war broke out. Hitler's great drive into the Ukraine and the Crimea in the autumn of 1941 was primarily aimed at securing the oil wells of the Caucasus and Iran, and his onslaught on Rostov to the north and Kerch to the west brought him within measurable distance both of the wells and of Russia's vital supply lines through Irak and Iran and thence from Tiflis over the precipitous Georgian Military Road to Ordzhonikidze, on the eastern slopes of the Caucasus range. The Caucasian port of Batum stands on the Black Sea near the Turkish frontier and is linked by pipe-lines with the oil-producing district east of Tiflis and that of Baku on the Caspian. Another oil port, Tuapse, lies just beyond the northern end of the Caucasus, and here come one branch of a pipe-line from the wells at Grozny and two other branches ending at Novorossiisk, north of Tuapse, and at Rostov, east of the Sea of Azov.

Cavallero, Gen. Ugo. Chief of Italian Military Forces. He succeeded Marshal Badoglio as Supreme Commander on Dec. 6, 1940, during the Italo-Greek war. On Jan. 13, 1941, he replaced Gen. Soddu in command of the Italian forces in Albania. Under him the Italians made heavy but ill-prepared attacks in the central area of the front, but were driven back by the Greeks towards the end of January. Ordered to attack again, he started a new offensive on March 9, but was again repelled and retreated on March 16. Later in 1941 he was in command of the Italian forces against Tobruk. In 1937 he had been in command of the armed forces occupying Abyssinia.

Celebes. Dutch East Indies island (*see* pp. 889–890), lying east of Borneo. Macassar is the chief port. Japanese troops landed at various points of the island on Jan. 10, 24, and Feb. 10, 1942. The Dutch, heavily outnumbered, put up a strong resistance, but by the end of February Celebes was in enemy hands. *See* Macassar Strait.

Censorship. In peacetime Britain has no censorship of Press matter or postal material. In wartime censorship is imposed, but is only partially compulsory. It may be considered under two heads : the censorship of incoming and outgoing postal letters and packages ; and the censorship of Press material in the Kingdom, and coming to or going from it.

Ordinary postal letters and packages transmitted in the normal way are handled by Post Office censors. They are not concerned with opinion ; only with the national security. For instance, a person writing abroad may criticize the Government freely.

The national security is also the touchstone of Press Censorship, which, again, does not concern itself with opinion, though the Censor may refer matter to the appropriate Government department if such action

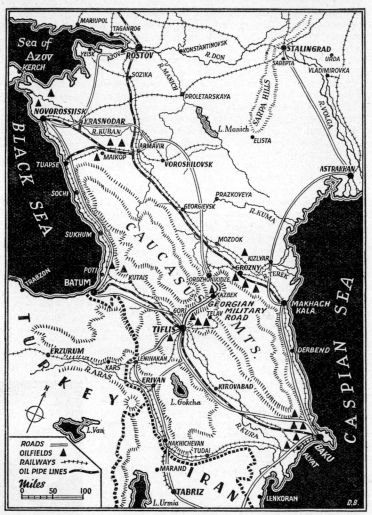

Caucasia, showing the oilfields and pipe-lines coveted by Hitler.

seems called for—for example, to the War Office, Admiralty or Air Ministry.

The Press Censorship is a division of the Ministry of Information. It is divided into nine parts, and has seven provincial branches, at Belfast, Glasgow, Manchester, Leeds, Birmingham, Bristol and Cardiff. The nine sections at the Ministry in London are Home News, Photographic, Films, Cables, Technical, Postal, Books and Periodicals, Scrutiny, and Co-ordination.

Even in wartime there exists no compulsion upon the British Press to submit material for publication to the Censor. It is voluntary. Material submitted and passed, even if subsequently found to be of use to the enemy, cannot be the subject of a prosecution of the publishing periodical or newspaper under Defence Regulation 3. The censorship of films is also voluntary.

Cable censorship is compulsory. In a single month 20 censors in the foreign department handled 1,250,000 words in sixty-two languages, including Chinese and Japanese. Seventy-five per cent of that total was handled within a minute, 20 per cent in under five minutes, the rest held longer on security grounds.

The postal section does not deal with ordinary mail, but with matter sent by correspondents in Britain to their papers outside the Kingdom. This is compulsory. The censorship of books for home publication is optional. The Scrutiny section hunts for dangerous matter already published. Editors are reminded of their responsibilities. Repeated offenders can be prosecuted under the Defence Regulations (S. 3).

Co-ordination of all sections is achieved by a 24-hour service from a directorate with four Assistant Directors. All " Stops " and " Releases " go through their hands. This section advises all others where the material is dubious from the censorship point of view.

The general direction of Press Censorship is in the hands of the Chief Press Censor, with two Assistant Directors, one for " Quick News section," the other for " Slow News section."

The Press Censorship performs a double duty. First, it must prevent information that might assist the enemy from getting into print, film or broadcast. In this it has directions from the various Government departments. Secondly, it must secure publication of the maximum amount of news, both at home and abroad. To Government departments the Censor points out the needs of the Press, and vice versa.

Cernauti (Czernowitz). Capital of Bukovina. It stands on the R. Pruth, close to the former Polish frontier. Russian troops occupied it on June 28, 1940, after N. Bukovina had been ceded by Rumania to Russia. After the German invasion of Russia on June 22, 1941, the Soviet Army repulsed many attacks on Cernauti, but by mid-July they were in retreat and Cernauti was again in the hands of the Rumanians, who were fighting alongside the Germans.

Ceylon. Of great strategical importance, the island of Ceylon (see pp. 905–906) is divided from India by Palk Strait, 40 miles wide at its northern end. This strait is almost cut into two portions by a line of coral reefs and sandbanks, over 60 miles long, known as Adam's Bridge.

When the Japanese occupied the Andaman Islands on March 23, 1942, they menaced the whole of the Bay of Bengal and were only 800 miles from Ceylon. Toward the end of March the enemy sent a powerful fleet into the Indian Ocean, and on April 4 this fleet was observed steaming in the direction of Ceylon. A large number of enemy bombers took off from aircraft carriers to raid ports and bases on the island. Colombo, capital of Ceylon and British naval base in the Indian Ocean, was their target on April 5, and it was obvious that the enemy hoped to repeat the success of his surprise onslaught on Pearl Harbour (q.v.). In this instance, however, the defences of Colombo were ready, and out of a force of 75 bombers 25 were shot down and another 25 damaged. Although the suburb of Ratamalana and the great natural harbour were dive-bombed, the damage caused was reported to be slight and the casualties few. The Japanese plan appeared to be, first, the destruction of vital bases in Ceylon, and, secondly, to effect a landing. To gain the latter objective the enemy would have had to achieve complete mastery of the Bay of Bengal. Should the Japanese invasion of the island have proved successful their forces would have menaced Southern India from across Palk Strait. On April 9 a large fleet of Japanese bombers and fighters attacked Trincomalee, the important naval and air base situated on the N.E. coast. Some damage was caused to the harbour and aerodrome buildings, and there were a number of casualties. Twenty-one enemy 'planes were destroyed.

As a result of a fierce naval battle between Japanese and British forces in the Indian Ocean, when the enemy attacked an important British convoy, H.M.S. Hermes (q.v.), British aircraft carrier, was sunk by the Japanese about 10 miles off the eastern coast of Ceylon.

Early in May East African reinforcements reached Ceylon from Kenya, Uganda, N. Rhodesia and elsewhere, all seasoned troops of the Abyssinian campaign.

Vice-Adm. Sir Geoffrey Layton was appointed C.-in-C. Ceylon in March 1942, with the acting rank of Admiral for the duration of the appointment, and Lt.-Gen. Sir H. R. Pownall assumed the military command of the island on March 14. Air Vice-Marshal J. H. d'Albiac was A.O.C. commanding the R.A.F.

Chad Territory. French colony in Equatorial Africa. On August 26, 1940, M. Eboué, the negro Governor, proclaimed Chad's adherence to Gen. de Gaulle and the Free French cause. On Nov. 16, 1940, M. Eboué was appointed Governor-General of the whole of French Equatorial Africa, and the Governorship of Chad was given to M. Pierre Olivier Lapie, formerly in charge of the Dept. of Foreign Relations at the Free French H.Q. in London. From Chad Territory came the Free French troops who made a remarkable raid on Murzuk, Libya, in late January 1941, took Kufra on Feb. 10, and joined the British forces in their prolonged attack on Keren. In March 1941 Gen. de Gaulle made a tour of inspection of the colony. *See* Equatorial Africa, French.

Chamberlain, ARTHUR NEVILLE (1869–1940). Prime Minister, 1937–40. His early political career and the part he played in the last war are described in pp. 909 and 4,592. Mr. Chamberlain's resignation on May 10, 1940, which coincided with Hitler's invasion of Holland and Belgium, was the result of outspoken and bitter criticism of the ill-conceived expedition to Norway and the subsequent evacuation, for it was felt that for some time his Government had failed to appreciate the realities of a situation which was becoming more and more grave. When Mr. Churchill took over the Premiership and formed a new Cabinet, Mr. Chamberlain served loyally under him as Lord President of the Council until his resignation in October. He died on Nov. 9, 1940. *See* Munich.

Neville Chamberlain,
Premier 1937–40.
Photo, Wide World

Chamier, AIR COMMODORE JOHN ADRIAN, C.B., C.M.G., D.S.O. (b. 1883). In 1937 he founded the Air Defence Cadet Corps for boys between the ages of 14 and 18. In February 1941 this was merged into the Air Training Corps (A.T.C.), of which Air Commodore Chamier is Commandant. He had been Secretary of the Air League of the British Empire from 1933. *See* Air Training Corps.

Channel Islands. This group of islands in the English Channel, near the coast of Normandy, has been attached to the British crown since 1066. On June 28, 1940, the Home Office announced that for strategic reasons the islands had been demilitarized and over a quarter of the population evacuated to England. Nevertheless, Jersey and Guernsey were both

GERMANS IN BRITAIN'S OLDEST POSSESSION

The Channel Islands had to be undefended and so passed into German occupation on July 1, 1940. Here a Nazi officer is seen talking to a British policeman in a street of St. Helier, Jersey.
Photo, E.N.A.

bombed and machine-gunned before the German occupation of Guernsey on June 30 and of Jersey on July 1. The Royal Militia, Island of Jersey, was afterwards re-formed as a battalion of the Hampshire Regiment.

During the winter of 1941–2 the inhabitants of Jersey and Guernsey suffered great hardships. There was a serious shortage of food, milk was practically unobtainable, and the health of the islanders was greatly impaired.

Chater, BRIGADIER ARTHUR REGINALD, D.S.O., O.B.E. (b. 1896). Commander of the British Forces in British Somaliland, 1940. He had been O.C. Sudan Camel Corps, 1927–30, and O.C. Somaliland Camel Corps in 1937.

Chatfield, ALFRED ERNLE MONTACUTE, 1ST BARON, G.C.B., O.M., K.C.M.G. (b. 1873). Admiral of the Fleet. He was Minister for the Co-ordination of Defence, 1939–1940, with a seat in the Cabinet. He resigned in March 1940, and the Ministry lapsed. Lord Chatfield had been C.-in-C. Mediterranean Fleet, 1930–32, and Chief of Naval Staff in 1933.

Cherbourg. Town, port and naval station of France, on the English Channel. It was selected as a landing-place for the B.E.F. in 1939. Cherbourg was occupied by the Germans on June 18, 1940, and was thereafter used as an " invasion " port. As such it became a constant target for the bombs of the R.A.F., the quays, oil depots and harbour installations being repeatedly attacked. It was bombarded by the British Fleet on Oct. 11, 1940, when the basin and dock area suffered great destruction. On the night of Jan. 8, 1942, bombers of the R.A.F. again heavily attacked the docks.

Cherwell, FREDERICK ALEXANDER LINDEMANN, 1ST BARON. Personal and scientific adviser to Mr. Churchill. He attended the Atlantic Conference (Churchill-Roosevelt meeting) in August 1941. Lord Cherwell, who was well known as Professor Lindemann, held the Chair of Experimental Philosophy at Oxford.

Chiang Kai-shek (b. 1888). Chinese Generalissimo. Throughout 1939 and 1940 the Chinese National Govt., under the inspiring leadership of Chiang Kai-shek (*see* pp. 1006 and 4594), continued to

AFTER AN R.A.F. RAID ON CHERBOURG

On the quays of Cherbourg British soldiers disembarked when the B.E.F. went to France in September 1939. Later British airmen had to attack this port of their former allies, for at Cherbourg the Nazis had concentrated invasion craft and supplies. The photograph shows the result of a direct hit by one of our bombers on the oil pumping station. In the same raid 20,000 tons of enemy shipping were damaged.
Photo, British Official: Crown Copyright

fight for its existence against the Japanese invaders. In 1941 his army was estimated to number more than 3,000,000 regulars. The war between China and Japan entered on its fifth year on July 7, and Chiang Kai-shek in a statement from Chungking declared that the struggle could no longer be regarded as a struggle between the two nations, since " the Asiatic and European wars have become closely interrelated." In November 1941, referring to the importance of air strength should the Japanese attack the Burma Road, he emphasized the necessity for concerted defence measures to check Japanese aggression in the Far East. The day that China declared war on Japan, Dec. 9, 1941, Gen. Chiang Kai-shek sent personal messages to Mr. Churchill, President Roosevelt and M. Stalin, and on Jan. 3, 1942, following an important military conference in Chungking between leaders of the three great Allied Powers, it was announced that he had been placed in supreme command of all land and air forces of the united nations operating in the Chinese theatre of war. On Feb. 10, 1942, he was in New Delhi for discussion with the Government of India on matters of common concern. His Chief of Staff was Lt.-Gen. Joseph Stilwell of the U.S. Army. In February 1942 Gen. Chiang Kai-shek was awarded the G.C.B. *See* China.

**Chiang Kai-shek,
Chinese Generalissimo.**
Photo, Associated Press

Chiappe, JEAN (1879–1940). French administrator. He gained notoriety for his ruthless methods as Chief of Police in Paris from 1926 to 1934. Later he became president of the Paris municipal council, and when the

Nazis entered the capital he cooperated with them. In December 1940 he succeeded M. Puaux as High Commissioner in Syria. While flying to Beirut his Air France 'plane got involved in an action between British and Italian fighters in the Northern Mediterranean, and M. Chiappe perished in the crash. His appointment was transferred to General Dentz.

Children's Overseas Reception Board. In this Government scheme for the evacuation of children between the ages of 5 and 16 to the Dominions, preference was given to children coming from areas vulnerable to air raids. Applications were received for 40,000 children attending grant-aided schools in England and Wales and about 12,000 attending other schools, and 24,130 of these applications had been approved by the Board by September 1940. Children to the number of 2,650 had reached their temporary homes in other countries when the tragic sinking of the City of Benares (*q.v.*) on Sept. 17, when 77 children bound for Canada were amongst those who perished, caused the Government to suspend the scheme. The Chairman of the Board was Mr. (later Sir) Geoffrey Shakespeare.

Chimara (Himara). Albanian port on the Adriatic, 28 miles S. of Valona. It lies on the road from Valona to Santi Quaranta, and its capture by the Greeks from the Italians was announced on Dec. 23, 1940. The Greek forces had to withdraw in May 1941, when the positions they had regained in Albania had to be abandoned in face of the German invasion.

CHINA'S STAND AGAINST JAPANESE AGGRESSION

Confronted with the terrible realities of war in her own country and those of her Allies, Britain is apt to forget that China has been fighting a powerful enemy for two years longer. See Burma Road ; Chiang Kai-shek ; Japan.

China. When war broke out between Great Britain and Germany (Sept. 3, 1939) China had been for over two years at war with Japan. Success in capturing Shanghai and Nanking in the autumn of 1937, after overrunning the north of China, had not given the Japanese their main objective—the destruction of General Chiang Kai-shek's armies and leadership. Japanese military strategy had been as inept as their diplomacy. Initial successes in the field were often insufficiently exploited. Moreover, as the result of underrating the resistance of the Chinese, the Japanese found that they had to reinforce their troops before asserting the superiority inherent in a vastly heavier armament and much better organization. Canton supplied them with an opportunity which they used more efficiently. When they were still in the process of marching on Hankow, they managed, in the short space of ten days, after landing 35,000 troops at Bias Bay, to enter Canton on Oct. 21, 1938, and so to cut off China's chief munition supply route and inflict the heaviest loss since the fall of Shanghai and Nanking. Four days later Hankow, from which the Government had retired to Chungking, was in Japanese hands. On March 27, 1939, Nanchang—General Chiang Kai-shek's " model " city—was taken, but again further Japanese advance was effectively checked,

and, in fact, the Chinese nearly retook that city. Just as the European war broke out Changsha was on the point of being captured, but in October 1939 Chinese tactics decisively outwitted the Japanese, and Changsha, despite Japanese command of the historic battle-ground of Yochow, held firm. Later, however, the Chinese suffered another severe defeat when Nanning, on Nov. 24, 1939, was taken by the Japanese albeit at much cost, and the line of communication between China and Indo-China was cut. Nanning and its province Kwangsi returned to China a year later, when, after the collapse of France in Europe, the Japanese secured from the Vichy French an agreement (signed on Sept. 22, 1940) which removed all fear of supplies reaching Chungking from Indo-China since it gave the Japanese access to bases in that French colony. Moreover, China had had another blow in the temporary closure of the Burma Road (*q.v.*) running from Lashio to Chungking.

The defeat of France and its resultant threat to Great Britain had so curtailed British defence resources for the time being that every effort had to be exerted to prevent rupture with Japan. So, with the express hope that the Japanese would take the opportunity to come to a reasonable and peaceful settlement with China, the British Government agreed to close the Burma Road for three months as from mid-July to mid-October 1940. This decision, which, as Mr. Winston Churchill frankly admitted when war with Japan came in 1941, was dictated by the hard facts of British military weakness after the fall of France, was strongly criticized by the United States of America and much resented by the Chinese, who were for that period left with only the incompletely developed and tedious highway to Soviet Russia through Sinkiang for their access to the outside world. However, to safeguard themselves after Japan's occupation of Indo-Chinese bases, they had torn up the rails on the track between the Indo-China border and Nanning on the reoccupation of that city at the end of September 1939.

No improvement in British and Japanese relations resulted from the closing of the Burma Road. Indeed, on Sept. 27, 1940, the Japanese signed a tripartite pact with Germany and Italy and thus came definitely into a closer military alliance with the Axis Powers. As Mr. Churchill put it to the House of Commons on Oct. 8, 1940, in announcing the reopening of the Burma Road on the termination of the closure agreement on Oct. 17, " instead of reaching agreement with China, the Japanese Government have entered into a three-power pact with Germany and Italy." The strain on Sino-British friendship was thus eased, and a constant stream of supplies poured into China along this highway, until the Japanese conquest of Burma made it necessary to seek other routes. (*See* Burma Road.)

This was the more important because the blockade of the China coast by Japan had been greatly tightened. Even after Japan's seizure of Hainan Island, Haichow and Lungkow early in 1939, the Chinese managed by the use of small craft and minor ports to maintain gaps.

In March 1941 the Japanese organized a series of surprise landings, and in the following month, by the capture of Ningpo and Foochow, they became masters of the only two ports left in Chinese hands. This success strengthened the Japanese in their efforts to force new currencies in occupied territories. These currencies, linked to the Japanese yen and opposed by the Chinese dollar which could not be forced out of circulation, produced considerable financial confusion. Nevertheless, Japanese economic penetration of the occupied parts of China proceeded, albeit at a slower pace than the invaders had hoped. So the elimination of leakages in the blockade by reducing China's imports to a minimum gave the Japanese their chief hope of breaking down the resistance of the Chinese dollar. The Chungking Government's pertinacity in preserving its contacts with Great Britain through Rangoon and Soviet Russia along the highways of the west gave the sole means of securing supplies from abroad and thus exploiting its command of man-power to the full.

The extent and achievements of this man-power were indicated by General Ho Ying-chin, Minister of War and Chief of General Staff, who on April 6, 1941, broadcast the following statement : " We have over 300 divisions with 3,000,000 soldiers in the field and 10,000,000 men in reserve or in training behind the lines. Over 500,000 guerillas are harassing enemy garrisons and enemy lines of communication, while more than 6,000,000 regular troops are operating behind the Japanese lines. We hold a fighting line from north to south of 2,800 miles, and hold it so well that every attempt of the enemy to break through in recent months has failed. Take, for instance, the enemy offensives in South Honan, West Hupeh and North Kiangsi when the invading forces, which made three attacks, were thoroughly defeated and routed. When we have sufficient munitions and equipment we shall at once launch large-scale counter-attacks and deal still harder blows at the enemy. . . . Meanwhile, we are successfully immobilizing more than one million Japanese soldiers in China and causing them losses of some 2,000 men a day."

The Chinese Air Force dates only from 1932, and has had to meet colossal odds. Nevertheless, in the first four years of the war it destroyed over 1,000 Japanese planes and some 3,000 airmen. It received very useful reinforcement from the American Volunteer Group, and Allied bombers helped Chiang Kai-shek's forces against the invaders on half a dozen points. New industrial bases were opened up, out of range of bombing, and up to the end of 1940 some factories for the production of planes, guns,

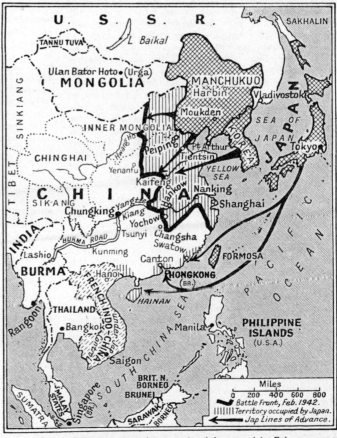

China. Extent of Japanese aggression, actual and threatened, by February 1942

CHINESE SOLDIERS IN CAMOUFLAGE

Effectively camouflaged with leaves, these Chinese soldiers are seen at practice with mine throwers which they captured from the Japanese.   This photograph was taken after the battle of Changsha.

Photo, Pictorial Press

munitions and other equipment had been moved from vulnerable areas to safety.

The chief military events of 1941 were the successful Japanese offensive in South Shansi, where in May the enemy claimed to have cut the Chinese forces in half. The capture of Ichang in June 1940 had given the Japanese an air base only 240 miles from Chungking. Of this they made ruthless use in 1941 by devastating raids on General Chiang Kai-shek's capital. These were courageously met ; although damage was done to industrial works and heavy casualties inflicted on the civil population, they failed to break Chinese morale. Indeed, later in 1941, it was reported that the Chinese had actually retaken Ichang. Preparations for the attack on the Allies led to a reduction of Japanese troops in western and central China, but although various withdrawals were reported—notably from Hankow—their extent was probably not great.

Heroic Efforts Against the Invader

In resolute tenacity inspiration was given by the leadership of General Chiang Kai-shek. Deprived of her commercial nerve centres, China rallied to the Generalissimo as to no leader in her modern history. One of the most remarkable features of this heroic effort was the mass migration of Chinese from the industrial areas of the east coast to the west, where the Chungking Government kept the people of unoccupied China together. Inspired by the example of the University of Peking and other educational and cultural centres which had established temporary and provisional headquarters in the west, the organizers of this modern exodus set up new industries and helped greatly to maintain resistance. General Chiang Kai-shek had had no easy task in maintaining his ascendancy in the earlier part of 1941. On the one hand, there was restiveness among the so-called "Communist" elements of his army, and, on the other, he had to contend with the doubts and fears of a pro-Japanese clique which was inclined to urge abandon-

ment of resistance much on the lines adopted by Wang Ching-Wei, whom the Japanese had set up as the puppet ruler of occupied China with headquarters at Nanking on March 30, 1940. The entry of Great Britain and the U.S.A. into the field against Japan in December 1941 set the seal on General Chiang Kai-shek's magnificent faith in China's ultimate victory.

China's position as an ally was quickly recognized by the British and American Governments. Negotiations were helped by the presence in Washington, at the time of Mr. Churchill's historic visit, of Chiang Kai-shek's brother-in-law, Mr. T. V. Soong, who was made Foreign Minister in place of Dr. Quo Tai-Chi. An early opportunity was taken to hold military conversations with the Chinese. Gen. Wavell—to whose command in India Burma had been returned after the Japanese invasion of Malaya, and who became Supreme Commander of the forces of the United Nations in the south-west Pacific—visited Chungking with Maj.-Gen. Brett, chief of the U.S. Air Force and later Deputy Supreme Commander in the south-west Pacific, and arrived at satisfactory conclusions with the Chinese Generalissimo. Then, on Jan. 3, 1942, it was announced from Washington that Chiang Kai-shek had accepted the supreme command over all land and air forces of the united nations which might operate in the Chinese theatre, and soon picked Chinese troops were fighting in Burma alongside British, Burmese and Indian troops.

The Generalissimo Goes to India

Chiang Kai-shek himself paid a state visit to India, arriving in New Delhi on Feb. 10, 1942, after conferring en route with Gen. Hutton, G.O.C. in Burma. He received an enthusiastic welcome, and on the 17th it was announced that the G.C.B. had been conferred upon him. The purpose of his visit was to discuss India's usefulness as a supply base, to examine the prospect of new routes in place of the Burma Road, to consider the problems of joint defence and attack, and to appeal personally to the Indian leaders for their support. Close cooperation with America was also evident when on March 10 Lt.-Gen. Joseph W. Stilwell, U.S. Military Attaché at Peking from 1932 to 1939, was made Chief of Staff under Chiang Kai-shek, while at the same time a Chinese military mission was sent to Washington.

China's resistance had been hard pressed in the autumn of 1941. The opportunity offered by the Japanese for direct and complete military association with the Allies gave her renewed hope. It was expected that the capacity of her armies for guerilla fighting would be increased by inspiration from the British military mission which, under Maj.-Gen. L. E. Dennys, had been in Chungking throughout the summer. The part played by American airmen in the defence of the Burma Road was another favourable factor in the situation, and elsewhere, too, these volunteer pilots rendered very valuable service. Mr. Churchill lost no opportunity in paying tribute to China's tenacity and in hailing China's association with the defenders of liberty. This stimulated the spirit of Chungking and brought hope to the people of occupied territory, where, despite Japanese domination of the chief towns, Chinese guerillas were still active.

In addition to military supplies, considerable financial help was arranged. It became known on Feb. 2 that the U.S.A. was making a loan of

£125,000,000 and Britain a loan of £50,000,000, and that both countries would continue the flow of supplies on a lease-lend basis.

During 1942 China scored some notable successes on several fronts. On Jan. 5 Chungking reported a major Chinese victory at Changsha, capital of Hunan. The city has great strategic value, for while the Chinese hold it, direct railway communication between Canton and Hankow, both in Japanese hands, remains impossible. It is also the centre of a great rice-growing area. From Changsha Chinese troops advanced towards the Japanese base of Yochow, 75 miles north. In various local actions they gave a very good account of themselves. On Jan. 22 and again on the 24th they heavily raided the Indo-Chinese port of Hanoy, which was seriously damaged. On Feb. 19 they started a new offensive into North Siam towards Chiengmai, and fighting also became fierce in the Shantung Province, to the north of China, near the Yellow Sea. On March 26 strong forces from the Shan States (S.E. of Burma) invaded Siam at two points.

When the Japanese overran Burma and made their way into China along the Burma Road, Chiang Kai-shek retorted with a heavy frontal attack on Japanese-occupied cities on the eastern coast and inland. Nanking, the old capital and seat of the new puppet government, was stormed by guerilla troops using Commando tactics, and there were many fires and explosions. Hongkong, Shanghai, Hangchow, Nanchang, Ningpo and the port of Amoy were also attacked, and there was much wrecking of communications, factories, power plants and supply dumps.

On May 6 Chungking announced that General Stilwell, with his Chinese Expeditionary Force practically intact, had established himself at an undisclosed base in Burma, from which he would continue to direct operations. On the 7th Chinese troops still held Bhamo and Myitkina, and it was declared that they intended to remain in Burma, in spite of Japanese attempts to eject or encircle them. Japanese troops, after occupying the Chinese border town of Wanting, advanced some 25 miles along the Burma Road to Chefang, in Yunnan Province; ahead of them waited the main Chinese armies, numbering some 4,500,000.

By June 3 Chinese forces in East China were fighting a fresh Japanese assault against Chuhsien, capital of Chekiang Province. This attack was brought about by the necessity for Japan to take prompt action against the Chekiang airfields. Long-range bombers could launch devastating raids upon Japanese cities from these airfields, and on June 7 it was reported that the battle for Chuhsien had attained some success. In July it was announced that Japanese casualties in five years of war in China were 2,500,000.

Books to Consult: China's Struggle with the Dictators, O. M. Green (Hutchinson). Dawn Watch in China, Joy Homer (Collins). Scorched Earth, Edgar Snow (Gollancz).

Christian X, KING OF DENMARK (b. 1870). He is the elder brother of King Haakon of Norway, and one of the most democratic of all monarchs. He took part in the Four-Power Conference at Stockholm on Oct. 18–19, 1939, when the three kings of the Scandinavian countries and the President of Finland declared their policy of strict neutrality. When Germany made her lightning attack on Denmark, occupying Copenhagen on April 9, 1940, King Christian broadcast an appeal to the Danes, calling on citizens to maintain a correct attitude towards the German invaders.

CHINA'S MILLIONS FIGHT THE COMMON ENEMY

Under Chiang Kai-shek's inspired leadership China put up a prolonged and heroic fight against the Japanese aggressors, inflicting great losses upon the enemy, and battling relentlessly along several fronts. China's modern army was powerfully equipped and the morale of its men remained extremely high. One desire unified all Chinese—to expel the enemy from every inch of China's soil. Here Chiang Kai-shek is inspecting recruits in a Szechwan town.

Photo, Pictorial Press

FIRE OVER CHUNGKING

On Aug. 19–20, 1940, Japanese aircraft made a devastating raid on Chungking, seat of the Chinese Government, causing great loss of life. The large numbers of incendiaries dropped started very extensive fires, which destroyed more than a square mile of the city.

Photo, Wide World

Chungking. Seat of the Chinese National Government since 1938, and headquarters of the Generalissimo, Chiang Kai-shek. Chungking is situated in S.W. China, at the northern end of the Burma Road (*q.v.*). An important conference was held here on Dec. 22–25, 1941, when a Military Council was set up, consisting of Gen. Wavell, Maj.-Gen. Brett, then Chief of the U.S. Army Air Corps, and Gen. Chiang Kai-shek, and all problems concerning joint war action were discussed. The British Ambassador in Chungking is Sir Horace Seymour, K.C.M.G., appointed Jan. 16, 1942.

Churchill, Rt. Hon. Winston Spencer, O.M., C.H. Prime Minister of the United Kingdom from May 10, 1940, till July 1945 ; First Lord of the Treasury and Minister of Defence. Born (on Nov. 30, 1874) in the political purple—his father was Lord Randolph Churchill, a leading Conservative politician of the second half of the Victorian age—he had an American mother, Miss Jennie Jerome, daughter of Leonard Jerome of New York. As told in Vol. 3, p. 1020, he was educated at Harrow, obtained a commission in the Army, and saw active service in Cuba, on the Indian frontier, and in the Sudan. There also his South African experiences and his earlier political career are recounted. In the Conservative ministry of 1924 to 1929, Mr. Churchill was Chancellor of the Exchequer, but was not included in the National Cabinet formed by Mr. MacDonald in 1931.

Between 1931 and 1939, indeed, Mr. Churchill fought a lonely battle. For some years he was most prominent because of his opposition to the Government's proposals for the extension of Home Rule to India. Then, with the growth of Hitler's power on the continent, he became a more and more pronounced opponent of Nazism. He protested against the appeasement policy which was then the vogue, and time after time warned the Government, the House of Commons, and the people that Germany was rearming fast, particularly in the air. In 1936 he was almost the only M.P. to champion King Edward VIII during the abdication crisis. In 1938 he denounced the Munich Agreement, and sided with Eden and Duff Cooper when they resigned from the Chamberlain administration.

He was still out of office when the war began, but such were his prestige and popularity with the public that Mr. Chamberlain at once called him into the Cabinet as First Lord of the Admiralty, the same post which he held at the outbreak of the war in 1914. In this post he was a great success ; his power in the country was testified to by the bitter attacks which were launched against him by the German propagandists. By his reviews of the war at sea given in the House of Commons and over the wireless he achieved fresh renown. By friend and foe alike he was regarded as a man in the great tradition of English politics ; and when, following the disasters of Norway, Mr. Chamberlain's Government fell, it was a foregone conclusion that Mr. Churchill should obtain the succession. So at long last he crowned his career with the Prime Ministership of Britain at a supreme crisis in our history.

Through the terrible months of the Battle of France and, still more, of the Battle of Britain, Mr. Churchill showed all the qualities of a supremely great leader.

LEADER OF AN EMPIRE

"I have nothing to offer but blood, toil, tears and sweat," Mr. Churchill told his newly-formed Government in May, 1940, and the whole nation, as well as Parliament, has followed him with enthusiasm and trust.

Photo, Walter Stoneman

He promised the people no easy things—only " blood, toil, tears and sweat," to quote from his famous broadcast on May 13, 1940—but his matchless oratory found an echo in the hearts of the people high and low, at home and abroad. There were many, however, who regarded his election as Leader of the Conservative Party in October 1940 as a mistake, since they feared that this would entail his identification with the political caucus which had been in power for many years, with far from glorious results.

In the third year of the war there was some criticism of the way in which he handled—or permitted to be handled—the home front, but every critic was careful to affirm his enthusiastic allegiance to the man who in Britain's "finest hour"—another of his phrases—was at the helm. In August 1941 he met President Roosevelt in the Atlantic and became the joint father of the Atlantic Charter (*q.v.*); at Christmas he went again to America and was given a great reception at Washington and Ottawa (*see also* United States, p. 448).

Mr. Churchill married in 1908 Miss Clementine Hozier, daughter of the late Col. Sir H. M. Hozier, K.C.B., and has four children : Randolph, M.P. for Preston, and in 1941 given a position at G.H.Q. in Cairo ; Diana, wife of Duncan Sandys, M.P., and a member of the W.R.N.S.; Sarah, an airwoman who married Vic Oliver, the music-hall star ; and Mary, in the A.T.S. He was made C.H., 1922, F.R.S., 1941, and received the O.M. in Jan. 1946.

Churchill, H.M.S. This name was given to the leading destroyer of the first flotilla of 50 over-age destroyers transferred from the American Navy to the British Fleet September 1940. *See* Anglo-American Naval Agreement.

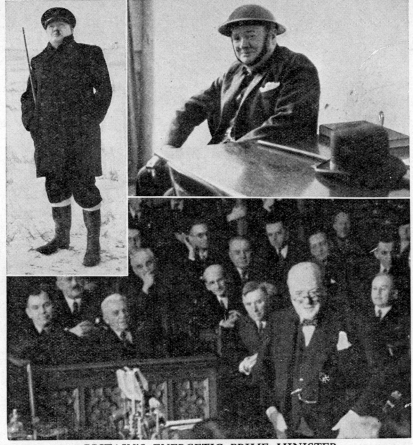

BRITAIN'S ENERGETIC PRIME MINISTER
On Dec. 31, 1941, Mr. Churchill delivered an historic address to members of the Canadian Legislature at Ottawa. Top, left, the Premier watching an A.A. demonstration at a Royal Artillery establishment ; above, right, during a visit to the " front line " at Dover and Ramsgate.
Photos, British Official

Ciano, COUNT GALEAZZO (b 1903). Italian Foreign Minister and Mussolini's son-in-law. He served in the Abyssinian War as a pilot, commanding the Disperata air squadron. Regarded as representative of Axis policy, he signed the Anti-Comintern Pact in 1937 and the Italo-German military alliance on May 22, 1939. He was in attendance on the Duce at most of the latter's meetings with Hitler, and in June 1940 took part in the talks at Rome which preceded the signing of the Franco-Italian Armistice. He led the Disperata Squadron in one of the first raids on Salonika in November 1940, an act which was recognized by his promotion to Lieut.-Col. of Aviation.

Count Ciano, Italian Foreign Minister.
Photo, Topical Press

Citrine, RT. HON. SIR WALTER MCLENNAN, P.C. (b. 1887). General Secretary of the Trades Union Congress from 1926. He led the British Council of Labour Delegation to Sweden and Finland in February 1940, and attended the Anglo-Soviet Trade Union Council at Moscow in October 1941, which examined at first hand Russian industrial effort.

In February 1942 Sir Walter became Chairman of the Committee on Regional Boards in the Ministry of Production. In May this Committee issued a White Paper on its aims and activities.

City of Benares. British steamer of 11,081 tons, flagship of the Ellerman Line. She was torpedoed by a U-boat on Sept. 17, 1940, about 600 miles from land in the Atlantic, while conveying among her passengers 90 children to Canada under the evacuation scheme of the Children's Overseas Reception Board. Only 13 of these children, together with six more travelling privately, were rescued. Out of a total ship's company of 406 persons, 248 were drowned. The U-boat's attack was made without warning,

SURVIVORS FROM THE CHILDREN'S SHIP

The story of the sinking of the City of Benares, in which 90 children were being evacuated to Canada, is one of tragedy and heroism. Only 13 of these children were rescued, and here are some of them aboard H.M.S. Hurricane, wearing clothes lent by the crew while their own were being dried.

Photo. "Daily Mirror"

after dark, when most of the children were in their cots or bunks, and the work of rescue was greatly hampered by heavy seas. After 24 hours adrift in boats and on rafts in bitterly cold weather, during which many of the passengers, both children and grown-ups, died of exposure, 112 survivors, including only seven children, were picked up by a warship. It was feared that all the rest had perished, but on Sept. 26 a Sunderland flying-boat reported having sighted an open boat full of people, and another Sunderland flew to the place and found it. Having collected all the food in the aircraft and dropped it by parachute, the Sunderland flew off to fetch a destroyer forty miles away, and led her to the lifeboat. Here were found 46 more survivors of the City of Benares, including six children—all boys—and Miss Mary Cornish, one of the escorts, the only woman aboard. The crew had kept the boat moving east through the stormy seas, sometimes by sail, sometimes by a pedal

screw, at which the boys had taken their turn to help them keep warm. When found after eight days' ordeal they had no almost water and their food was almost gone.

City of Flint. American steamer, commanded by Capt. J. H. Gainard. She first came into the news as one of the ships which helped to rescue survivors from the Athenia, torpedoed on the night of Sept. 3, 1939, in the North Atlantic. Having landed them at Halifax, Nova Scotia, she went about her own business and eventually sailed with a full cargo from New York on Oct. 3. On Oct. 9 she was stopped by a warning shot from the German raider Deutschland, which sent aboard her an armed prize crew of 18 and 39 captives from the British steamer Stonegate, which had been sunk by the Deutschland. The Germans painted out all the American insignia, and on Oct. 21 hoisted the German flag as the ship entered Tromsoe. Here the Stonegate's crew were landed, and then the City of Flint was taken to Kola Bay, near Murmansk. Ordered to "move on" by the Russian authorities, she returned to Tromsoe on Oct. 31, but after a few hours' stay was escorted away by a Norwegian warship. Still controlled by the German crew, but under Norwegian escort, she steamed down the Norwegian coast and, although forbidden to enter Haugesund, the commander anchored there on Nov. 3. Here the prize crew were interned by the Norwegians, as the Nazis had violated international law. To the fury of Germany, the ship was then released, in charge of the original American crew, and returned to Bergen under the American flag.

City of Rayville. American cargo steamer of 5,883 tons. The first U.S. ship to be sunk in this war, she struck an enemy mine off Cape Otway, on her way from Adelaide to Melbourne, her loss being announced on Nov. 9, 1940.

BRITAIN'S CIVIL DEFENCE GOES INTO ACTION

Men and women of this vital Service have been in the front line since the first air raid, and their courage, fortitude and resource have earned the admiration of the community, and many decorations from the Government. See also Fire Service, National.

Civil Defence. The meaning of this term is the passive protection of the civilian population against air raids. It is thus quite distinct from armed defence. The subject is still a novel one. It has developed rapidly, efficiently, almost incredibly. This peculiarly grim kind of war has meant that our enemies have aimed, not only at the destruction of military objectives, but at disorganizing all our civilian life by means of air attacks.

An Air Raid Precautions Act was passed in 1937. This empowered local authorities to organize a general

precautions scheme, so that matters were well under way before the outbreak of hostilities.

The country has been divided into twelve regions, each in charge of a Regional Commissioner. Thus, after a severe air raid, urgent matters can be immediately settled without the possible delay of consultations in London. Each Regional Commissioner is responsible to the Minister of Home Security, and under him is an extensive organization.

By December 1941 the number of Civil Defence workers in Britain had reached the imposing total of

CIVIL DEFENCE IN SOME OF ITS MANY ASPECTS

1. Roof-spotter in the City of London.   2. A stretcher case has been brought during a raid to an Ambulance and A.R.P. station in Westminster.   3. Shelter warden in Westminster distributing " season " tickets.   4. Rescue squad clearing away the debris of a demolished house beneath which they may find survivors.   5. Notice placed on Police Boxes for the benefit of motorists who may not have heard the sirens.

Photos, Wide World; "Daily Mirror"; "News Chronicle"; Keystone; Fox

REHEARSAL FOR GAS ATTACK
Civilians and A.R.P. workers are seen wearing their gas
masks in a London street during a tear gas test in the City.
They are fully prepared for any emergency
Photo, Sport & General

more than a million, excluding members of the
National Fire Service. Amongst these workers were a
large number of women, and more and more women
were continually coming in and proving of essential
value.

It is a heartening fact that the voluntary workers
far outnumber the paid ones. Some are part-time and
some are full-time, and they are in every town and
borough in the Kingdom. Amongst them are railway
men, dock workers, lorry drivers, and followers of
almost every other occupation.

Under the National Service Bill of December 1941 it
was enacted that men of 35 and over might apply for
Civil Defence duties instead of Army Service.

About four thousand awards have been made,
including George Crosses, British Empire Medals, and
commendations, and that number is steadily increasing.

In September 1939 some of these devoted workers
wore uniform, and some did not. Then, in the winter of
1940, they were provided with a uniform, but not an
adequately thick one. In December 1941 all were
being speedily equipped with a smart blue battle-dress.
The women wear skirts or trousers, jackets, and
berets and shoes, and all the men have battle-dress,
great-coats, boots and berets.

Members of the Civil Defence Services are trained
to perform a dual job; thus, a decontamination worker
may be a stretcher-bearer, or possibly a warden, such
is their versatility.

What the Warden Does
AIR RAID WARDENS. First of the Civil Defence
Services is that of the Air Raid Wardens. These, as
may be readily imagined, need to be brave people,
possessed of marked individuality, and their task is to
assist their harassed neighbours, and to serve as a
link between the public and the authorities. Each
local area is provided with sectors and posts which are
supervised by a Chief Warden. It is the lot of the
Warden to report every incident, including unexploded
bombs, to help to estimate the extent of air-raid
damage, to help the A.R.P. Services which are sent
to deal with it, and to assist the public always, in
every imaginable dilemma. He is closely linked up
with the police, and the Wardens' Service is, in some

areas, under the executive control of the Chief
Constable. In others a Chief Warden is responsible
to the Local Authority through its Emergency or
Civil Defence Committee.

AMBULANCE SERVICE. A circular issued on Jan 10,
1939, to local authorities by the Ministry of Health,
which controls all Ambulance work, pointed out that a
regulation large type of ambulance should be employed
for the transport of serious casualties to hospital,
whilst a smaller kind would suffice for moving less
urgent cases to a First Aid Post, or for those who,
after attention, are able to walk home.

The ambulances used for collecting casualties from
air-raid incidents and conveying them to casualty-
receiving hospitals are equipped to take two or four
stretchers. When large numbers of patients are transferred from one hospital to another, passenger buses are
employed. These are converted to take either stretchers
or sitting cases. If the distance over which patients are
to be sent is great, ambulance trains are used.

By Jan. 31, 1942, there were 14,863 ambulances
available in England and Wales (8,785 whole-time
and 6,078 part-time) and 18,474 cars for sitting cases
(3,387 whole-time and 15,087 part-time). The personnel of this service numbered 32,867 men (9,348
whole-time and 23,519 part-time) and 43,490 women
(13,765 whole-time and 29,725 part-time).

Each ambulance has a driver and in most cases an
attendant who must hold a First Aid Certificate. The
Ambulance Service has functioned very effectively
during air raids, and the part-time personnel has done
very good work.

Rescuing the Bombed
RESCUE PARTIES. The Rescue Service consists of
squads of skilled workmen, who are under a foreman,
and whose task is to release those who are trapped in
bombed buildings. This is work that needs skill,
technical knowledge and very great care, for debris
that is unskilfully shifted is liable to collapse both
upon the rescuers and those who are to be rescued.

During the Battle of Britain the Rescue Service
devised new methods of succour. With the arrival
of the blitz there came a clearer realization of the
whole problem, and much was achieved by the aid of
tunnelling operations.

DEMOLITION AND REPAIR WORK. Following upon
an air raid much demolition work may need doing;
there are craters to be filled, fractured gas, water and
electricity mains and sewers must be put into working
order, streets must be cleared. This work is undertaken by parties who are requisitioned from the staffs
of local authorities, from contractors, or from the
staffs of the Public Utilities which are concerned.

DECONTAMINATION SQUADS. All areas wherein persistent gas has fallen are dangerous until that gas has
either been neutralized or dispersed. Decontamination
squads have been recruited chiefly from the street-
cleansing services.

FIRST AID POSTS. These are usually situated in
buildings which are specially equipped. They are
supported by Mobile Units, made up of vehicles in
which full medical equipment and staff are taken to
areas where casualties have occurred, so that temporary
First Aid Posts may be set up as near as possible.

In country districts First Aid Points consist of a
First Aid box in some central building.

There were in 1942 383 fixed and 187 mobile First
Aid Posts in London, and 1,904 fixed and 995 mobile

in the Provinces (England and Wales). The total staff employed was: whole-time, 4,516 men and 19,720 women; part-time, 16,475 men and 76,323 women. In charge of posts or on call were 3,750 doctors, while 2,800 trained nurses were either on whole-time or part-time service.

FIRST AID PARTIES. Quite frequently there are injured who need attention where they lie; some of these must be removed for further treatment. For this work there are First Aid (or Stretcher) Parties, each consisting of four men with a driver and transport for themselves and vehicles for the injured, provided by the Ambulance Service.

Work in First Aid

STRETCHER PARTIES. These were inaugurated some time before the war. They consisted of four men and a car driver, one man being appointed to act as leader. Each local authority was subject to a Medical Officer of Health, and thus the Stretcher Party was directly under his jurisdiction. The parties were usually based on depots, and these were in close contact with ambulance depots. These again were linked up with Rescue Parties and with the National Fire Brigade Union. The work of the stretcher parties was to deal with the casualties at the spot where they occurred and to pass them on to the appropriate organization. This would often be the St. John Ambulance Association or the British Red Cross Society, or, in Scotland, the St. Andrew's Ambulance Association. Classes were held by local authorities and certificates taken in First Aid Party work. There was much collective training, and combined exercises were held. The stretcher parties were only expected to deal with minor casualties, but, as time went on, these were found to be fewer than the severe ones, so that the Rescue Parties were having a more strenuous time. It was found that the stretcher workers, when they were first on the scene in a bombed area, would naturally begin to extricate those who had been bombed, so the authorities accordingly decided to equip them in rescue work. Then it was found best to give special training to both First Aid and Stretcher Parties, so that they were qualified, when necessary, to augment the Rescue Parties.

In January 1942 the term Stretcher Parties was discontinued in the London Region, and, so as to effect really satisfactory team-work, the whole organization was amalgamated with that of Rescue Parties. Broadly speaking, the " Light " Rescue Service has now absorbed the original Stretcher Parties. At the same time (January 1942) the Stretcher Parties came to be known as First Aid Parties outside the London Region. All over the country these stretcher workers are now receiving a far more comprehensive training, and are now able to deal in an expert manner with all light Rescue Work.

Messengers, Clerks and Telephonists staff the Report Centres from which the dispatch of the various services is organized.

FIRE GUARDS. Air warfare brought about two changes in Britain's fire-fighting organization. First, all brigades became unified as the National Fire Service (q.v.); secondly, all able-bodied persons not on other war-work were compelled to act as fire-guards.

The compulsory fire-guarding of business premises came in during January, 1941.

The Compulsory Enrolment Order made it obligatory on all persons liable to register with their local civil authority for this duty, but the use of such enrolled persons was left to the local authority, some of which organized for fire-defence throughout their areas, while others did not do so.

Long before this order came into force, residents of suburbs and residential districts had formed voluntary fire guards, usually working by streets and areas.

When the Compulsory Order came into force (August 1941) local authorities had at hand these voluntary organizations. They were not upset, but extended and brought within the compulsory rule. The order was extended to cover women between 20 and 45 August 20, 1942.

Usually street or road parties worked by rotas and in many districts zone commanders were placed in charge of areas for purposes of organization.

LONDON COUNTY COUNCIL. In London the Ambulance Service and the Rescue Service are administered by the London County Council.

There already existed in peacetime a London Ambulance Service, and an Auxiliary Ambulance Service was set up during the latter part of 1938 to deal, together with the peacetime service, with the expected large number of casualties in the event of war. All kinds of vehicles were requisitioned. Furniture lorries and laundry-vans were improvised as ambulances, and there were many makeshift vehicles, but these were quickly replaced by proper vehicles; more and more improvements were made, until in December 1941 a very high standard of equipment and efficiency had been attained. Each vehicle has stretchers, first aid kit and gas kit, and is manned by a driver and an attendant, who are trained in First Aid.

Up to December 1941 there had been twelve fatal casualties among the personnel of the London Ambulance Service. Thirty-five had received serious injuries, and there were many minor injuries. Twenty-three of the personnel were killed while off duty. On April 16, 1941, when London received the heaviest

SPOTTING AN INCENDIARY

These fire fighters have just spotted an incendiary on the roof of the building they are guarding during a raid, and are taking instant action.
Photo, " Daily Mirror "

of all blitzes, there was not one casualty in the ambulance service, although nearly every vehicle was out.

At the end of 1941 London had 113 Auxiliary Ambulance stations, 5,500 full-time workers and 1,000 part-time workers (unpaid). Three George Medals, eight British Empire Medals, and five commendations had been awarded to members of the London Ambulance Service.

The Service had dealt with large numbers of casualties, taking them to hospitals or to first aid posts where it was decided whether hospital treatment was necessary. The work of building up a Rescue Service in London began about the middle of 1939. The personnel of the Service at the end of 1941 numbered 8,000 and there were 90 depots and 460 lorries. Seventeen of the workers had been killed, 71 seriously injured and 320 received minor injuries. Awards to personnel comprised 40 George Medals, 54 British Empire Medals and 52 commendations.

Books to Consult : Dusk to Dawn, "A Warden" (Constable). Post D: Experiences of an Air Raid Warden, J. Strachey (Gollancz).

Clodius, Dr. Karl. As Nazi Economic Adviser he set up an economic drive in the Balkans in the autumn of 1939, exerting the previously acquired German hold on Balkan trade. It was largely owing to Clodius that Germany received oil from Rumania, for this German " commercial traveller " headed an

Coastal Command Operations—1939–42

Miles flown on operational sorties—approx. 55,000,000		
(To Sep., 1942 ; does not include distances covered by units away from home bases.)		
Convoys escorted		4,947
U-Boats attacked		587
Daily Patrols to protect shipping over } Area 5,500,000		
seas Iceland to Gibraltar .. .. }		sq. miles

Outstanding Actions, 1939–42	Date
Two Sunderlands rescue crew of torpedoed *Kensington Court* in Atlantic .. .. ..;	21/9/39
U-boat sunk by Hudson (first attack on sub.)	8/12/39
Altmark prison ship located ..	16/2/40
Beauforts and Hudsons bomb *Scharnhorst* off Norway	21/6/40
Bismarck tracked by Hudsons, Sunderlands and Catalinas	23–27/5/41
Beaufort torpedo attack on pocket battleship *Lützow*	13/6/41
U-boat attacked and captured by Hudson	7/9/41
Air escort to Commando raid on Vaagso	27/12/41
Beauforts' torpedo attack on *Scharnhorst*, *Gneisenau* and *Prinz Eugen*	12/2/42
Participated in 1,000-bomber raid on Bremen	25/6/42

Note.—Coastal Command aircraft in 1942 flew over 25,000,000 miles. In 12,000 patrols over 300 U-boat attacks were made and over 4,000 on shipping. The number of assaults on German naval units and supply ships to June 1942 totalled 932.

economic mission to Rumania in November 1939. In March 1940 he was again in Bucharest and, after a month's negotiations, signed a trade protocol that achieved little save confirming existing arrangements.

Coastal Command. One of the nine Commands into which the R.A.F. is divided, this Command has the primary tasks of reconnaissance and of protecting the merchant shipping that brings war supplies to Great Britain. To these tasks have been added many others, mostly of an offensive nature, such as the attack on enemy supply shipping and the continuous bombing of his docks and U-boat bases and fortified zones on the coasts of occupied territory. During the first three years of war the Coastal Command flew a total of approximately 55,000,000 miles on operations over the sea. More than 4,900 convoys, most of them deep sea, were given air escort. Enemy naval units or supply ships were attacked more than 4,000 times. Many enemy aircraft were destroyed approaching convoys, and many hundreds put to flight. Aircraft of the Coastal Command were concerned in finding the prison ship Altmark, in attacks on the Scharnhorst, in locating the Deutschland, in protecting

COASTAL COMMAND AIRCRAFT ON OPERATIONS

One of the duties of the Coastal Command is to escort convoys and give protection to individual vessels, driving off attacks from the air and reporting any danger that threatens from the sea. Here an aircraft is circling a freighter bound for a British port.

Photo, Fox

the B.E.F. at Dunkirk, in attacks on invasion ports, in tracking the Bismarck, in torpedoing the Lützow, and in the capture from the air of a U-boat. Types of aircraft used in the Coastal Command include Sunderland and Catalina flying-boats, Lockheed Hudsons, Beauforts (some equipped to carry torpedoes), Blenheims, Wellingtons, and Beaufighters. The nickname " Kipper Kites " was given to coastal patrol 'planes detailed to protect British herring fleets in the North Sea from German raiders. *See* R.A.F.

Coastguard Service. Control of this service was taken over by the Admiralty on May 28, 1940. In war, besides their ordinary duties, coastguards watch for enemy 'planes, surface ships and submarines approaching the coast. For coastguard purposes Britain is divided into twelve divisions, each in charge of a Captain or Commander of the Royal Navy, and the Service is maintained by naval pensioners and men with a knowledge of local conditions.

Codreanu, CORNELIU ZELEA. Leader of the Rumanian Iron Guard. Early in 1938 King Carol and his premier, M. Calinescu, set about suppressing this movement, and in May Codreanu was sentenced to 10 years' imprisonment for plotting against the social order and for planning a revolt. Many of his followers were also sent to gaol. The agitation continued, however, and in November 1938 it was announced that he and thirteen supporters, while being conveyed from one prison to another, had been shot by their guards " while attempting to escape."

Colijn, HENDRIKUS (b. 1869). Prime Minister of the Netherlands 1925–26 and 1933–39. He resigned on June 29, 1939, and was succeeded by Jonkheer de Geer. In February 1941 a tightening of Press control was followed by the resignation of Dr. Colijn from the editorship of the Conservative paper " Standaard." On July 26 he was arrested, together with 60 other members of the recently dissolved Anti-Revolutionary Party, and was sent to a concentration camp at Limburg. On Dec. 17 he was deported to Germany.

Gen. Collet.
Free French leader.
Photo, British Official

Collet, GEN. PHILIBERT. Free French leader. He had been stationed in Syria since 1918 and had gained the whole-hearted fidelity of the native troops under his command and of the famous squadron of Circassian cavalry which he founded. He was former Chief of Staff to Gen. Catroux. In June 1941, although ordered by Vichy to proceed with his troops to Damascus, he led them instead across the border into Palestine, to join the Free French forces there. On June 22, accompanied by members of his staff, he made the first formal entry into Damascus pending the official entry of Gen. Legentilhomme.

Collishaw, AIR COMMODORE RAYMOND, D.S.O., O.B.E. (b. 1893). A.O.C. Egypt Group, Middle East Command. He directed R.A.F. cooperation with the Imperial forces in the Western Desert in 1941 until succeeded in November by Air Vice-Marshal Coningham. Air Commodore Collishaw served as senior R.A.F. officer in the Courageous, 1929–32, and later commanded various R.A.F. stations in England.

Cologne. City of Western Germany, on the Rhine. It is a great railway junction and river port,

and a large industrial centre. It was repeatedly bombed by the R.A.F. By the end of April 1942 Cologne had been raided 98 times. On May 30 the R.A.F. delivered the first of their 1,000-bomber raids, when enormous damage was done. Casualties were estimated at 20,000, and whole districts were destroyed. Three-fifths of the inhabitants were evacuated from the devastated city. The majority of Cologne's chemical and fine machine-tool industries were wrecked.

Columbus. German liner of 32,581 tons. She left Vera Cruz on Dec. 14, 1939, and was stopped by a British warship on Dec. 19 off the coast of Virginia. Rather than submit to capture, her captain scuttled his ship. This was Germany's third largest liner, and the 18th German vessel to be scuttled.

Commandant Teste. French seaplane carrier of 10,000 tons. She was intended to act as tender to the aircraft carrier Béarn, and as reserve from which aircraft supplies could be drawn by cruisers which carried 'planes. She was heavily shelled and set on fire at Oran on July 3, 1940.

Commando Troops. This " hush-hush " force was raised in 1940, and came into being during the Norwegian campaign when certain contingents were formed to carry out special tasks. These groups were formed into battalions after Dunkirk and were em-

COMMANDOS IN ACTION
Specially trained raiding troops, known as Commandos, have scored many dramatic successes against the enemy, notably in Libya and Norway. Here they are seen attacking under cover of a smoke screen.
Photo, British Official

ployed as raiding parties that cooperated with the Navy and R.A.F. The Commandos represented a new conception of warfare, and their operations were carried out by the three services, the R.A.F., Army and Navy, working in close collaboration. The general standard was extremely high, for the men were shock troops, drawn from almost every regiment in the Army, and were selected individually. For almost a year after their inception the Commandos remained a secret force. The men were trained not only to operate independently on land for long periods without the assistance of the supply and maintenance organizations which normally minister to the needs of the fighting soldier, but also in amphibious warfare, training for which was carried out with the Royal Navy.

Both officers and men were familiarized with the life of ocean-going ships and trained in the use of small craft, including practice in rapid embarkation and disembarkation. Most of this latter training was carried out with assault landing craft and motor landing craft. On land the Commandos were trained to march long distances over difficult country and to become experts in explosives and guerilla warfare. They fought against the Germans in the Libyan campaigns in 1941 and were also in Syria during that year.

On Nov. 17, 1941, the eve of the second British offensive in Libya, Lt.-Col. Geoffrey Keyes, son of Sir Roger Keyes, led a daring Commando raid on Gen. Rommel's H.Q., hoping to capture or kill him, and so paralyse the enemy. On Nov. 15 thirty men were landed 200 miles in enemy-held territory, and lay for two days in a dried river bed. A small detachment then approached the H.Q., shot their way inside, using revolvers, tommy guns and hand grenades, and searched the building. But Rommel was absent (at a birthday party) and the raiders at length withdrew to the agreed meeting-place with the rest of the band, 20 miles away. The next day they were discovered and attacked by German and Italian forces. The Commando then broke up into small parties which set off separately for the British lines. Lt.-Col. Keyes lost his life in this raid. On June 19, 1942, he was posthumously awarded the V.C.

The spectacular Lofoten raids (q.v.) were largely the work of Commandos and also that on Vaagso (q.v.). The most spectacular Commando raid was made against the docks at St. Nazaire (q.v.) on March 28, 1942, in which furious fighting occurred.

In the raid near Boulogne on April 23 the Commandos attacked one of the most strongly defended positions on the German-occupied coast of France.

On Nov. 16, 1941, it was announced that Sir Roger Keyes had relinquished his post as Director of Operations of the Commandos; on April 13, 1942, Mr. Churchill stated that Lord Louis Mountbatten (q.v.) had succeeded him as Chief of Combined Operations.

Coningham, AIR VICE-MARSHAL ARTHUR, D.S.O., D.F.C., A.F.C. (b. 1895). He was appointed A.O.C. Western Desert in succession to Air Commodore Collishaw shortly before the opening of the Libyan campaign on Nov. 18, 1941. Born in Brisbane, Coningham was educated in New Zealand, and began to fly at an early age. He served in the last war, first as an infantryman, then as a fighter pilot.

Air Vice-Marshal Arthur Coningham.
Photo, British Official

Constanza. City and principal port of Rumania. It stands on the Black Sea, its docks covering 150 acres, and is a very important oil port. When Germany incorporated Rumania into her " New Order," Constanza came automatically under the control of the Nazis, and after the outbreak of the Russo-German war it was heavily bombed by Soviet aircraft.

Convoy. The convoy system of protection for mercantile shipping proved its worth when adopted after much opposition in 1917. In that year 99 per cent of the ships convoyed across the Atlantic reached port safely. In this war there was no delay in making the

decision, although, with ships scattered, a little time elapsed before the organization of the convoy system was completed.

A convoy consists usually of 40 to 50 ships, but sometimes numbers 100. At its best it has a surrounding wall of escorts, destroyers and corvettes ; at its worst it consists of the cargo vessels themselves arranged in formation and depending on their own guns and speed.

Convoy conferences are held before the ships sail. The masters, first officers, chief engineers and radio operators attend. The captain in charge explains the sailing orders. The commodore—a naval officer who is responsible for the convoy—gives some details of how he intends working the convoy, times of signalling, etc. Each master is given his station, although if there is a gale blowing or there is fog it may take 48 hours for the convoy to get into position. Given adequate protection the success of a convoy is largely due

ON WATCH
Look-out man on an escort vessel guarding a convoy through the English Channel.
Photo, Associated Press

to the adaptability of the ships' masters, who soon learned to keep station with something of the accuracy of naval units, and steadily increased their efficiency in signalling and general manoeuvrability.

As well as the submarine menace, convoys have had to face mines and raiders and a later terror, the bombing and " spotting " aeroplane. After the capture of the French ports and aerodromes by the Germans in the summer of 1940 spotting 'planes could locate ships, and bombers sweep half-way across the Atlantic and back. But by the end of 1941, with more numerous escort ships and perfected cooperation between the members of the convoy itself and the R.A.F. Coastal Command, both aeroplanes and U-boats appeared more loath to attack. During the first 16 months of the war aircraft of the Command escorted about 4,700 convoys, entailing some 16,500 separate sorties of flying boats and land 'planes. With adequate escorts the success of the convoy system appears undeniable. An Admiralty statement made in July 1940 points out that nearly 100 million tons of shipping had been escorted, losses being about one-quarter of 1 per cent of the total.

Convoys fall roughly into two categories, the ocean-going and the coastwise. During 1940 the latter were given barrage balloons as additional protection. Ocean-going convoys at a later date carried aeroplanes, which were catapulted from the ships' decks when air attack was imminent.

High losses at sea have not meant failure of the convoy system, but scarcity of escorts. To counteract this deficiency, numbers of small anti-submarine vessels were built with the anti-submarine powers of a destroyer and a fairly high speed. Called corvettes, these seaworthy little ships soon proved their worth. They could be built quickly by small yards normally producing coastal vessels, and in the yards of Canada.

CONVOY UNDER BRITISH ESCORT IN THE NORTH SEA

The twenty-four merchantmen, mostly colliers, comprising this convoy, are among the many thousands of Allied and neutral ships escorted safely to their destinations since the outbreak of war. The lifeboats are swung out, ready for instant use if necessary.

Photo, Central Press

During November 1941 Admiral Burges Watson, a Commodore who had escorted some 20 ocean-going convoys, stated that he considered the so-called Battle of the Atlantic won " for the present."

Cooper, RT. HON. ALFRED DUFF, P.C. (b. 1890). Chancellor of the Duchy of Lancaster from July 1941. In the autumn of 1941 he toured the Far East on

Mr. Duff Cooper, Chancellor of the Duchy of Lancaster.
Photo, Lafayette

behalf of the War Cabinet, pulling together political and diplomatic departments scattered about the Pacific, and was at Singapore when Japan started war on the United States. On Dec. 19 it was announced that he had been appointed Resident Minister of Cabinet rank at Singapore for Far Eastern Affairs, but in January 1942, following the appointment of Gen. Wavell to the Supreme Command of the Pacific, the post lapsed and he returned to England on Feb. 16. He was Minister of Information, 1940–41.

Copenhagen. Capital of Denmark. Shortly before dawn on April 9, 1940, a large body of German troops crossed the Baltic to Copenhagen. While aeroplanes roared overhead, scattering leaflets which announced the completion of the Nazi invasion of Denmark, the troops occupied the Citadel and the radio station, and by 8 a.m. the capital was in their hands. Shots were fired at the invaders by the Royal Guard outside the Amalienborg Palace, and in the result some Danes lost their lives, but otherwise the German victory was bloodless.

Corap, GEN. French general. In May 1940 he was in command of the French 9th Army holding positions in the Ardennes. When the German tanks broke through at Sedan the French defenders were unprepared, the 9th Army became disorganized, and Gen. Corap was captured.

Corinth. City of Greece situated on the isthmus between the Gulfs of Corinth and Aegina. Connecting these two gulfs is the famous Corinth ship canal, 4 miles long. In their advance upon Athens in April 1941 the Germans approached from three directions, one being from Corinth, which was captured on April 26 by German parachutists, dropped from 35 troop-carrying 'planes, after an aerial blitz lasting three hours. A number of British troops, covering the retreat southwards of the last convoy, were surrounded and taken prisoner.

Cornwall, H.M.S. This British cruiser had a displacement of 10,000 tons and carried a complement of 679. Completed in 1928, she sank the German raider Pinguin in the Indian Ocean at the beginning of 1941. On April 9, 1942, it was announced that the Cornwall had been sunk by Japanese aircraft in the Bay of Bengal.

Cornwallis, SIR KINAHAN, K.C.M.G. (b. 1883). British Ambassador to Iraq from 1941. To him fell the duty, in April 1941, of informing the Iraqi Government of the British Government's decision to land British troops at Basra to counter the German-inspired revolt of Rashid Ali.

Corregidor. Island fortress at the mouth of Manila Bay. First bombed by the Japanese on Dec. 28, 1941, its magnificent defence by U.S. and Filipino troops under Gen. MacArthur continued until Feb. 22, 1942, when Gen. MacArthur (*q.v.*) transferred his H.Q. from the Philippines to Australia. Gen. Wainwright was left to carry on the heroic fight. Japanese bombardments and aerial attacks became incessant from April 29 ; there were numerous casualties among the U.S. troops and severe damage was inflicted on military installations. On May 5 the Japanese made landings from steel invasion barges, and on May 6 it was stated that the defenders' resistance had been overcome. *See* Manila ; Philippine Islands.

H.M.S. COURAGEOUS—FIRST NAVAL LOSS IN THIS WAR

The aircraft carrier Courageous was struck by an enemy torpedo at five minutes to eight on the evening of Sept. 17, 1939. Almost at once she began to list to port, and she foundered within 20 minutes of being hit. The submarine was believed to have been sunk immediately by depth charges from destroyers which hastened to the scene and picked up survivors from the Courageous.
Photo, Associated Press

Corvette. By the beginning of 1941 there were many of these anti-submarine vessels in commission and many more under construction. They were more speedy than trawlers, thoroughly seaworthy, possessed an excellent armament, and were of great value as escorts to convoys. The corvette crew consisted of three officers, besides the captain, and about 50 ratings. In the old navies a corvette was a flush-decked ship of war with one tier of guns. *See* Convoy.

Cossack, H.M.S. British destroyer (1,870 tons) of the Tribal class. Commanded by Capt. P. L. Vian, she pursued the German prison ship Altmark into Joessing Fjord, Norway, on Feb. 16, 1940, and rescued 299 British prisoners. Cossack was one of the vessels of the 2nd Destroyer Flotilla, which, with H.M.S. Warspite, sank seven German destroyers at the Second Battle of Narvik, April 13, 1940. In May 1941 she was in action against the German battleship Bismarck. Her loss was announced on Nov. 10, 1941. *See* Altmark.

Cost of War. By March 1942 the cost of the war to Britain had reached £12,500,000 a day (see table). It was calculated that the total war expenditure for the first three years to August 1942 would be £10,000,000,000.

	Total War expenditure per day	Fighting & Supply Services
1940	£	£
March..	5,000,000	4,000,000
July ..	7,500,000	6,500,000
Oct. ..	9,000,000	7,500,000
1941		
Feb. ..	10,250,000	8,000,000
June ..	10,500,000	8,000,000
Oct. ..	11,000,000	9,000,000
Dec. ..	11,750,000	9,000,000
1942		
Mar. ..	12,500,000	9,750,000

Courageous, H.M.S. British aircraft carrier of 22,500 tons. She was built in 1915–16 as a shallow-draught cruiser to operate in the Baltic, and was later converted into an aircraft carrier. During the night of Sept. 17, 1939, she was torpedoed by a U-boat, and of the ship's complement of some 1,200 officers and men, 518 were lost. Her commanding officer, Capt. W. T. Makeig-Jones,

went down with his ship. This was the Royal Navy's first loss in this war.

Coventry. City of the Midlands. The German "terror" raid of Nov. 14–15, 1940, caused great devastation. In a 12-hour attack the Luftwaffe dropped 1,200 high-explosive bombs, 50 parachute mines and 30,000 incendiaries. The famous 14th-century cathedral, many hospitals, hotels, clubs, cinemas, large stores

COVENTRY CATHEDRAL DEVASTATED

When German raiders bombed Coventry on the night of Nov. 14–15, 1940, they left behind them an almost unexampled trail of ruin. The beautiful 14th-century cathedral is now a mere shell.
Photo, Fox

and office buildings in the centre of the city were destroyed. The Germans coined the word "coventrate" as the result of the raid. Between Aug. 1940 and Aug. 1942 the raids killed 1,252 persons, seriously injured 1,859 and destroyed or damaged 54,373 houses and several thousand shops.

Cracow, City of Poland, on the R. Vistula. It was a busy commercial centre before the outbreak of war. The Germans captured it Sept. 6, 1939. After the partition of Poland on Sept. 29 the city became German.

Craigavon, JAMES CRAIG, 1ST VISCOUNT (1871–1940). Prime Minister of Northern Ireland, 1921–40. He endeavoured to get Mr. de Valera to agree to a joint defence of all Ireland, but stated on July 11, 1940, that his offer had been rejected.

Craigie, RT. HON. SIR ROBERT, P.C., G.C.M.G. (born 1883). British Ambassador to Japan, 1937–1941. In an endeavour to keep on good terms with Japan he negotiated, in January 1940, for the release of nine out of 21 German seamen who, in accordance with international law, had been taken by a British cruiser from aboard the Japanese steamer Asama Maru.

Cranborne, ROBERT ARTHUR JAMES CECIL, BARON (b. 1893). Secretary for the Colonies from February 1942. He was Parliamentary Under-Secretary for Foreign Affairs, 1935–38, Paymaster - General in 1940, and Dominions Secretary, 1940-1942.

Creagh, MAJ.- GEN. SIR MICHAEL O'MOORE, M.C. (b. 1892). He commanded the British armoured division which made a spectacular dash across the Western Desert in December 1940. He had been promoted to divisional commander after the present war started, and trained the armoured forces for the Libyan operations.

Crerar, LIEUT.-GEN. HENRY DUNCAN GRAHAM, D.S.O. Former Chief of the Canadian General Staff, he was appointed, in December 1941, G.O.C. Canadian Corps in Britain during the absence on sick leave of Lieut.-Gen. McNaughton (*q.v.*).

STRANGE AND GRIM BATTLE OF CRETE

Driven from Greece by overwhelming German forces, British, Imperial and Greek troops withdrew to Crete, where for ten days some fought against airborne troops with sublime courage and resource, while the rest made their retreat to Egypt.   See Greece ; H.M.S. Kelly, etc.

Crete. After Greece fell to the Nazis in the spring of 1941 Crete, where many Greek and British soldiers had retreated, became the next German objective. On May 20 Mr. Churchill announced that a heavy attack by Nazi airborne troops had begun early in the morning of that day. Fifteen hundred Germans had landed from troop-carriers, gliders and by parachute in the Suda Bay and Maleka areas. Most of these were accounted for by members of the Imperial and Greek forces under General Freyberg, V.C.

But the Germans continued to arrive in large numbers. The next day about 3,000 dropped from the sky in the regions of Canea, Suda Bay, Heraklion (Candia) and Retimo, though many machines crashed on landing, and some were shot down by A.A. fire. The enemy having subjected the few airfields in Crete to heavy bombing, rendering them unusable, it was decided to withdraw our remaining aeroplanes from the island. The R.A.F. was then at the disadvantage of operating from North African bases, the nearest being 400 miles distant, whereas the Nazis had at least eight aerodromes available on the Grecian mainland and the island of Melos, the latter being only 90 miles away. The struggle for Heraklion, Retimo and Suda Bay continued furiously and indecisively, the enemy throwing in airborne reinforcements regardless of cost. Mr. Churchill, speaking on May 22, said the war in Crete " is a most strange and grim battle . . . . Our side has no air support because they have no aeroplanes. The other side have very little or nothing of artillery or tanks."

While the Army was taking toll of the enemy's airborne troops, the Navy intercepted and dispersed two enemy transports, an Italian destroyer and a number of caiques ; a second convoy of thirty vessels was attacked and driven away towards the Greek Archipelago by British destroyers and light forces.

Though the fight for Heraklion and Retimo, mostly hand-to-hand, persisted with the greatest heroism, new German landings here and at Maleme, at the west end

Crete—where Allied troops fought heroically for ten days in May 1941.

of the island, strengthened the enemy positions. On May 25 it was announced that King George of the Hellenes had left Crete for Egypt, escaping all Nazi attempts to capture him and the Greek Prime Minister, M. Tsouderos. By now there were 25,000 to 30,000 Nazis on the island, in battle formation and marching against Canea and Suda Bay. The Allied position had become serious, owing to our limited air support and the sheer weight of German reinforcements. The enemy penetrated the British defences west of Canea, and captured the city on May 27. Military operations on the island continued until the end of the month, the fighting attaining " a severity and fierceness which the Germans had not previously encountered in their walk through Europe." On June 1 a War Office communiqué announced in the following terms that the British and Empire forces had withdrawn from Crete :

"Although the losses we inflicted on the enemy troops and aircraft have been enormous, it became clear that our naval and military forces could not be expected to operate indefinitely in and near Crete without more air support than could be provided from our bases in Africa. Some 15,000 of our troops have been withdrawn to Egypt."

In all, 17,000 men were got away and were landed in Egypt. Our losses in killed, wounded, missing and prisoners amounted to 15,000 men, exclusive of Greek and Cretan casualties. Losses in ships included the cruisers Gloucester, Fiji and York, the destroyers Juno, Kelly and Greyhound, and the submarine Usk, units of Admiral Cunningham's Mediterranean fleet which patrolled Cretan waters under continuous bombing.

The German casualties, according to precise inquiries made by the Commanders-in-Chief on the spot, were believed to be about 5,000 drowned in attempting to reach the island, and 12,000 killed or wounded on the island itself ; 180 fighter and bomber aircraft were destroyed and 250 troop-carrying aeroplanes.

On June 10 Mr. Churchill, in the House of Commons, taking the fullest personal responsibility for the decision to fight the Cretan campaign, disposed of his critics in a comprehensive review of the whole proceedings. "What would happen," he asked, "if you allowed the enemy to advance and overrun without cost to himself the most precious and valuable strategic points ? Suppose we had never gone into Greece and had never attempted to defend Crete ! Where would the Germans be now ? Suppose we had simply resigned territory and strategic islands to them without a fight ! Might they not at this early stage of the campaign in 1941 already be masters of Syria and Iraq and preparing themselves to advance into Persia ? "

As events proved Crete was a brilliant rearguard action which enabled Britain to consolidate her hold on the Nile Valley and Eastern Mediterranean.

After the Nazis occupied Crete they were continually harassed by Cretan guerillas. These intrepid fighters have been famous throughout the ages and they gave the Nazis little peace. Ranging the island from one end to the other, they nightly attacked the enemy's posts and lines of communication. So unsuccessful were the German attempts to restrain them that strong Axis forces had to be sent to Crete in February 1942 and harsh measures of repression adopted. The usual Nazi retaliation was inflicted on the people and hundreds were arrested, being held as "hostages." This drastic action did not break their spirit, however, and the guerilla bands, with fresh recruits joining them daily, went about their task of harrying the invader.

The aerodromes in Crete were heavily bombed by the R.A.F. after the enemy occupation of the island.

Crimea. This famous peninsula of South Russia, joined to the mainland by the isthmus of Perekop (*see* pp. 1176–1177), was the objective of the furious

GERMAN PARACHUTE TROOPS DESCENDING UPON CRETE
Following the heavy bombing of Heraklion aerodrome, and covered by ground strafing from Messerschmitts, Nazi troop-carrying aircraft arrived over Crete and dropped parachute troops, over 60 per cent of whom were killed before reaching the ground. The parachutes in clusters are carrying heavy articles such as machine-guns, field guns, small motor vehicles, etc.
Photo, British Official

German thrust in S.E. Ukraine in September 1941. The Nazi invaders had penetrated deeply into the Novoskaya Steppe to the north of the Perekop isthmus by Sept. 17, thus paving the way for a direct attack on the Crimea. Not only would their capture of the peninsula have provided an excellent winter base for von Runstedt's armies, but it would also have put out of action one of Russia's richest sources of raw materials and have yielded a jumping-off place for an attack on the Caucasian oilfields.

On Sept. 19 it was reported that fierce fighting was going on in the Perekop isthmus, in which the Germans were stated to have suffered heavy casualties. The Black Sea Fleet Air Arm bombed enemy positions and supplies, and the Russians defended their territory with stubborn persistence, but it was evident that, with the German capture of towns on the mainland north of the Sea of Azov, the enemy ring was steadily closing round the Crimea. Large-scale air operations were launched by the Germans at the beginning of November and savage fighting continued relentlessly. The Russians evacuated Kerch, which the Germans captured on Nov. 16. Feodosia, on the Black Sea coast, had already fallen, and the Germans claimed that they were besieging Sevastopol. Simferopol, some

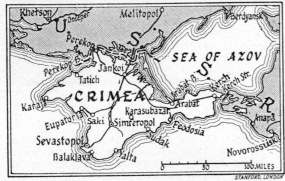

Crimea, scene of violent fighting in the Russo-German war.

30 miles from Sevastopol, had likewise been captured by the Nazi forces.

After their recapture of Rostov-on-Don and their subsequent thrust along the mainland coast of the Sea of Azov, the Russians made successful landings across the Kerch Straits and, after stubborn fighting against German and Rumanian troops, recaptured Kerch and Feodosia. German supplies were repeatedly bombed by the Russians, and on Jan. 5, 1942, it was reported that the latter had landed at Eupatoria. Meanwhile, the Sevastopol garrison launched heavy attacks, aided by aircraft and the guns of the Black Sea Fleet, the Soviet forces endeavouring to trap and annihilate the enemy troops as they retreated to the mainland.

A new phase of the battle in the Crimea opened in the middle of March 1942 with a violent Soviet attack launched from the Kerch peninsula. Fierce fighting continued throughout March and April, the Russians making a series of heavy attacks, aided by warships of the Black Sea Fleet. After four days' fighting Soviet troops captured the powerfully fortified height of Golden Ridge on April 24. Early in May the Germans admitted that heavy Russian attacks, with strong tank support, aimed at breaching their main positions in the Crimea. The Germans suffered serious losses in men and materials in their effort to stem the advance.

The Nazis renewed their attacks against Sevastopol at the beginning of June. These were repelled by the Russian garrison, and it was reported that Hitler was personally conducting the enemy offensive. On June 9 it was announced that in a single day's fighting the Nazis had lost 2,500 men. German pressure against Sevastopol was maintained regardless of losses, and on July 3 it was announced that after eight months of heroic defence the city had been evacuated although fighting continued in the Khersonese peninsula.

Cripps, RT. HON. SIR (RICHARD) STAFFORD, P.C., K.C. (b. 1889). Lord Privy Seal and Leader of the House of Commons; Labour M.P. for East Bristol from 1931. Youngest son of the 1st Baron Parmoor, Sir Stafford practised as a barrister and was Solicitor-General from 1930 to 1931. In May 1940, when it became desirable to negotiate a Trade Agreement with the U.S.S.R., he was sent to renew the exploratory talks which had been broken off after the Russian invasion of Finland. The Soviet Government refused to negotiate unless he was given ambassadorial status. He was

Sir Stafford Cripps, Leader of the House of Commons.
Photo, Central Press

therefore appointed in place of Sir William Seeds, and remained Britain's Ambassador to the U.S.S.R. until January 1942. During this period he did a great deal to improve relations between the two countries, and negotiated the Anglo-Russian Pact of Mutual Assistance on July 12, 1941. He then resigned at his own request, in order to embark on a special mission to India, and in the interim was appointed Lord Privy Seal and Leader of the House in succession to Mr. Attlee. Arriving in India on March 23, 1942, he had talks with leaders and delegates representing every point of view, and it was hoped that a working agreement could be found for the mobilization of defence, pending the formation of the new Constitution on which India's Dominion status would be based after the war. Unhappily the mission failed (*see* page 187), but much had been done towards the establishment of goodwill. Cripps returned on April 13.

Croatia. Following their advance into Northern Yugoslavia and the occupation of a large part of Croatia, the Germans established on April 10, 1941, an independent Croat state, with Anton Pavelitch at its head and Gen. Kvaternik as Vice-Premier and Minister of War. On May 18 Pavelitch, accompanied by a Croatian delegation, arrived in Rome and offered the crown of Croatia to the House of Savoy. At a ceremony at the Quirinal, and in the presence of Mussolini and Ciano, King Victor Emmanuel nominated the Duke of Spoleto, younger brother of the Duke of Aosta, as King of Croatia. He later took the title of King Aimone. On June 14, at Venice, Pavelitch signed Croatia's adhesion to the Axis Pact.

Cross, RT. HON. SIR RONALD HIBBERT, P.C. (b. 1896). British High Commissioner in Australia from 1941. He was Minister of Economic Warfare, 1939–40, and Minister of Shipping, 1940–41.

Csaky, COUNT STEPHEN (1895–1941). Hungarian Foreign Minister, 1939–41. He was a strong supporter of the Axis, and constantly tried to bring his country into closer relation with Germany and Italy. He signed the Tripartite Pact in November 1940.

Cudahy, JOHN (b. 1887). American Ambassador to Belgium, 1939–40. He was summoned home by President Roosevelt in August 1940 after being publicly reprimanded for an indiscreet interview given in London to the Press Association.

Cumming, LT.-COL. ARTHUR EDWARD, M.C. This officer, of the 12th Frontier Force Regiment, Indian Army, was awarded the V.C. in February 1942 for

Lt.-Col. Cumming, Awarded V.C.
Photo, Assoc. Press

outstanding bravery displayed while wounded and under enemy fire. On Jan. 3, 1942, while brigade head-quarters and a battalion were being withdrawn in Malaya, a strong enemy force penetrated the position. Lt.-Col. Cumming with a small party of men immediately counter-attacked and prevented any further penetration until his whole party had become casualties and he himself had received two bayonet wounds in

the stomach. Later, in spite of severe pain and weakness, and under heavy fire, he drove in a carrier for over an hour, collecting isolated detachments of our men. He was wounded twice more and lost consciousness while attempting to collect a further detachment. He recovered consciousness, however, and would not retire until he discovered that he and the driver of the carrier were the sole survivors in the locality. His bravery, initiative, and devotion to duty were largely responsible for the safe withdrawal of the brigade.

Cunningham, LT.-GEN. SIR ALAN GORDON, K.C.B., D.S.O. (b. 1887). Appointed G.O.C. newly established Eighth Imperial Army which advanced into Libya on Nov. 18, 1941, he had to relinquish the command to Maj.-Gen. Ritchie on Nov. 26, owing to ill health. Gen. Cunningham, an artillery expert, is a brother of Admiral Cunningham. Commander of the 5th Anti-Aircraft Division, T.A., in 1938, he was sent, shortly after the outbreak of war, to command the Imperial troops in East Africa, and it was his brilliant leadership there which brought the campaign to a

Gen. Cunningham, Victor in East Africa.
Photo, South African Official

successful conclusion. His skilful operations in Italian Somaliland were crowned by the capture of Mogadishu on Feb. 26, 1941. He later achieved notable successes at Keren and Amba Alagi, his column performing one of the greatest marches in history. *See* Abyssinia; East Africa.

Cunningham, ADMIRAL OF THE FLEET VISCOUNT ANDREW BROWNE, G.C.B., D.S.O. (b. 1883). C.-in-C. Mediterranean, 1939–42 and C.-in-C. Allied Naval Forces, Mediterranean, 1943, made Admiral of the Fleet 1943. Much of Cunningham's early career was spent in command of destroyers. His good services during the Gallipoli campaign brought him the D.S.O. In the last year of the war he commanded destroyers in the Dover Patrol; in 1919 he was in H.M.S. Seafire in the Baltic. For his work at Dover and in the Baltic he was awarded two bars to his D.S.O. In 1930 he was appointed to the battleship Rodney, and promoted to flag rank in 1932. From 1934 to 1936, a period which included the Italo-Abyssinian war, Admiral Cunningham commanded destroyers in the Mediterranean Fleet. In November 1938 he became Deputy Chief of Naval Staff at the Admiralty. In 1939

Admiral Cunningham, C.-in-C. Mediterranean.
Photo, Vandyk

he succeeded Admiral Sir Dudley Pound as C.-in-C. Mediterranean, and after Italy's entry into the war he achieved many victories over the Italian Fleet in Mussolini's "Mare Nostrum." On July 9, 1940, his squadron of light cruisers, supported by many battleships, had a running fight with the enemy in the Ionian Sea, west of Crete, the Italian ships fleeing at full speed to harbour. On the night of Nov. 11–12, with the cooperation of the Fleet Air Arm, Admiral Cunningham struck a crippling blow at Italy's navy in port at Taranto (*q.v.*). Flying his flag in H.M.S. Warspite, he won another great victory over the enemy battle fleet on the night of March 28, 1941, south of Cape Matapan (*q.v.*). In May 1942 Cunningham became head of the Admiralty delegation in Washington, and was created baronet, being succeeded as C.-in-C. Mediterranean by Sir H. Harwood (*q.v.*). Made Viscount 1946.

Curtin, JOHN (b. 1885). Premier of Australia from Oct. 5, 1941, in succession of Mr. A. W. Fadden. and Defence Minister from April 14, 1942. He was strongly in favour of a military alliance with the U.S.A., and on Dec. 28, 1941, published an article in the "Melbourne Herald" stating that the Australian Government regarded "the Pacific struggle as primarily one in which the United States and Australia must have the fullest say in the direction of the democracies' fighting plan. Australia looks to America, free from any pangs as to traditional links or kinship with the United Kingdom.

John Curtin, Australian Premier.
Photo, Australian Official

We know the problem that the United Kingdom faces, but we know that Australia can go and Britain still hold on. We are determined that Australia shall not go." This article aroused considerable discussion and criticism in Australia, but Mr. Curtin replied that he did not mean any weakening in the interrelationship of British peoples or any political alliance with the U.S.A., but considered a geographical and military alliance inevitable. He emphasized Australia's loyalty to the Empire.

On March 13, 1942, he broadcast a stirring speech to America in which he stressed the immediate and pressing need of first-hand contact between the two countries, and Australia's determination to hold and hit back at the enemy. "Australia is the last bastion between the West Coast of America and the Japanese. If Australia goes the Americas are wide open."

Mr. Curtin was appointed a member of the Privy Council on April 3, 1942, and on April 14 he assumed the title of Defence Minister, instead of Minister for Defence Coordination, the object of this change being to facilitate discussions with General MacArthur, between whom and the Government Mr. Curtin acted as link. Before his accession to the Premiership in 1941 he led the Australian Labour Party for ten years. *See* Australia.

Curtis, MAJ-GEN. HENRY OSBORNE, D.S.O. (b. 1888). G.O.C. British forces in Iceland. In France he commanded the 46th Division, defending the canals between Aire and Carvin. It was known as Polforce, having been intended to hold St. Pol, Frevent and Divion.

Cutler, LIEUT. ARTHUR RODEN. Officer in the Australian Military Forces who was awarded the V.C. in November 1941 for conspicuous gallantry during the Syrian campaign, and for outstanding bravery during the fighting at Merj Ayoun. He was the fourth Australian to win the V.C. in the war.

Cuxhaven. Seaport and naval base in Germany, at the mouth of the R. Elbe. On Sept. 4, 1939, the R.A.F. started hostilities with a lightning raid on the German fleet in its harbours at Wilhelmshaven, Cuxhaven and Brunsbüttel.

Cyprus. The island of Cyprus is only 40 miles from the coast of Turkey in Asia, and thus came into the thick of the fighting in the Mediterranean Basin which followed Italy's entry into the war in 1940. Cyprus has been administered by the British Government since 1878, but was only formally annexed in 1914, when Turkey fought with Germany in the last war. The population of about 360,000, however, is pro-British to the core, and warmly welcomed the formation of the Cyprus Regiment, which King George approved a few months after the present war began. Most of the inhabitants of Cyprus are of Greek extraction and have had no military tradition since the Turkish conquest in 1571. Yet 19,000 Cypriots at once volunteered for service and a large percentage of the male population of the island was soon in uniform. In addition, 5,000 other Cypriots joined the British armies in the Middle East. The air attacks which followed the German invasion of Greece made the Greek-speaking inhabitants of Cyprus all the more eager to serve the Democratic Alliance.

A Pack Transport (mule) Company was organized directly the war began. When it landed in France in January 1940 it was the very first Colonial unit to join the British Expeditionary Force. It did yeoman service during the retreat upon Dunkirk and also in the Libyan, Syrian and Greek campaigns and the fighting in Crete, where its losses were heavy.

After the bitter lesson of Crete in May 1941 everything possible was done in the following year to prevent Cyprus suffering a similar fate. Many new airfields were laid out, so that enemy aircraft approaching the island from the nearest Axis aerodromes at Castellorizo, 250 miles away, and Rhodes, 300 miles, could be promptly attacked by British fighters based here. The garrison, made up of troops from Great Britain and India, as well as Cypriot forces, had learnt, from Crete

ON GUARD IN CYPRUS

The Cyprus Regiment, composed of natives of the island led by British officers, was formed shortly after the outbreak of war. Here a squad is seen receiving instruction in the use of a mortar.

Photo, British Official

and Tobruk, the art of defending a comparatively small area against simultaneous air and land attacks. An intricate system of subterranean defence sectors honeycombed the island, which became an almost impenetrable fortress, ready to withstand any Axis attempt at invasion.

Cyrenaica. One of the two provinces into which Libya was divided for administrative purposes, the other being Tripolitania. Cyrenaica borders Egypt, and the capital is Benghazi. *See* North Africa.

Cyrene. Town of Cyrenaica, lying between Derna and Benghazi. Here were Graziani's headquarters. British forces captured the place on Feb. 3, 1941, but had to withdraw in April. On Dec. 21, 1941, British troops again took the town, and its port, Apollonia, in the course of their drive on Benghazi. It fell once more to Rommel in Feb. 1942.

Czech Legion. This military unit was formed in France and Britain in September 1939. It fought with the French Army in France and took part in the great

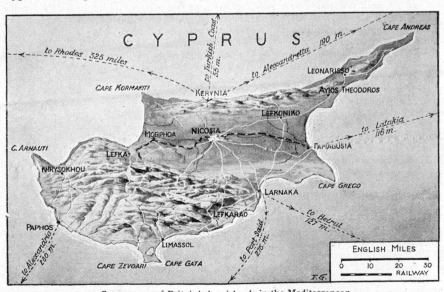

Cyprus, one of Britain's key islands in the Mediterranean.

retreat of May–June 1940. Many Czech soldiers eventually escaped to England on British warships. On Oct. 25, 1940, a military agreement was signed whereby Czech forces were organized under the command of a Czechoslovak C.-in-C. for cooperation with the Allied forces. Moscow announced in August 1941 that Czech forces under Gen. Blaha had been organized in Russia, and by a Russo-Czech military agreement, signed Sept. 30, it was arranged that Czechoslovak forces would fight under their own military leaders in collaboration with the Russian High Command.

THE TRAGEDY OF THE CZECH PEOPLE

After twenty years of freedom—1918-1938—the republic of Czechoslovakia was broken up, and in March 1939 became a German protectorate. Thenceforth it was subjected to a sinister regime of terror and tyranny.

Czechoslovakia. When the present war broke out the so-called Protectorate of Bohemia and Moravia and the so-called independent Slovak State had been in existence for six months. During that time the inhabitants of Czechoslovakia had the fullest opportunity of discovering what it meant to be under German domination. The appointment of Baron von Neurath as Reich Protector at the outset was no doubt intended to produce the impression that the Protectorate would be governed in a civilized manner, for the Baron, who had been the German Ambassador in London from 1930 to 1932, was a professional diplomat of the former regime and was not one of Hitler's cruder henchmen. In actual practice, however, most of the power passed into the hands of State Secretary Karl Hermann Frank, one of the most rabid anti-Czech Sudetic Germans. Dr. Hacha, who under duress had signed the document at Berlin by which the Czech nation was deprived of its freedom and much more besides, was allowed to continue in office as State President, his ostensible function being to form a link between the German authorities and his fellow-countrymen. This was another pretence by which the Germans sought to persuade opinion abroad that they intended to govern the Czechs in a spirit of justice and moderation.

Nazis Aimed at Economic Ruin

The real German purposes soon proved to be quite different. What the Germans aimed at was to ruin the Czechs in an economic respect, and, politically, to reduce them to a condition of abject servility. With the former object in view, they at once proceeded in a systematic manner to gain possession of Czech property, and they did this by methods which ranged from commercial trickery to undisguised pillage. These activities were accompanied and, indeed, reinforced by anti-Semitic measures, as the presence of a single Jew on the managing board of a Czech industrial or business concern sufficed to make it a Jewish undertaking and, therefore, subject to the process of Aryanization which, bluntly speaking, meant that the Germans helped themselves to it without much ado. In this way the Germans acquired Czech factories, banks and various other economic resources to a value exceeding three hundred million pounds sterling. There was also an enormous amount of looting, pure and simple. For months at a time goods trains and lorries, filled with plunder, plied between the Protectorate and Germany.

It is known that 40,000 truck-loads of wheat were, under this particular scheme, removed from the granaries belonging to the Czechoslovak State, and the Germans stole much else of which there is no detailed record, but which included works of art, contents of libraries, scientific equipment, and so forth.

In order to bring about the political subjugation of the Czechs numerous devices, wide in scope, were adopted. All democratic institutions were, of course, at once abolished. The Czech press passed under direct German control, one of the results being that within a few months 520 periodicals, including nine out of the 18 daily papers, were suppressed. Those that survived contained little more than the German official news bulletins, translated into defective Czech, although now and then an ingenious Czech journalist contrived to insert, in veiled language, a reference to the Germans which, if detected, would not have met with approval.

Mass Attack on Czech Culture

The Czech wireless service, too, underwent a similar transformation. But the German influence on press and wireless was a trifling matter compared with the removal of the Czech system of justice and the introduction of a German code which reduced the rights of the Czechs to vanishing point. The Germans took specially drastic measures against the Czech labour organizations, seizing their funds, imprisoning their leaders and exploiting their members, 300,000 of whom were sent to Germany to work there under conditions of slavery. Then, too, as part of the scheme for the progressive Germanization of the Protectorate, thousands of Czech land-workers were deprived of their soil, in order that it might be handed over to German settlers or used for purposes beneficial to the Germans.

Over and above all these encroachments on their personal freedom and material possessions, the Czechs became the victims of wholesale arbitrary persecution, involving the arrests of thousands of them for no specific reason. Thus, between March 15, 1939, and the following September no fewer than 55,000 Czechs were thrust into concentration camps, at the mercy of the German Secret Police. As far as these mass arrests followed any method at all, their purpose was to deprive the Czech nation of its leaders, or potential leaders ; hence the large percentage of Czech politicians, writers, professors and other prominent personalities of the Republic detained at Dachau, Buchenwald and other notorious camps.

The same sinister purpose can be discerned in the attack on the Czech universities, which, in the late autumn of 1939, were closed by the Germans for a period of three years. This was a sequel to the events of Oct. 28, 1939, when the Czechs celebrated their Independence Day in spite of German prohibitions. At Prague this led to clashes between Czech students and German police and Black Guards. Several of the students were wounded, and one of them, Jan Opletal, subsequently died of his injuries. On the day of his funeral there were further demonstrations, and by Hitler's express orders the student quarters at Prague

DR. BENEŠ SALUTES THE FLAG OF THE FREE CZECHS

Like other enslaved countries of Europe, Czechoslovakia has set up a "Free" Government in London, under Dr. Beneš. The Free Czech Army consists of several thousand troops trained to fight by their own military leaders.

Photo, Wide World

few days hundreds of Czechs, on the flimsiest of pretexts or on no pretext at all, were executed, while thousands more went to join those already languishing in German concentration camps.

On May 27, 1942, Heydrich was badly injured in an attempt on his life in Prague. Immediate reprisals were taken on the population, and when Heydrich died on June 4 the number of Czech citizens executed since the attack totalled 157. The Nazis continued their savage toll and by July 3 1,133 had been executed. In addition, all the men (some 200) of the village of Lidice, near Kladno, were shot on suspicion of harbouring the fugitives, the women were sent to a concentration camp, the children deported to reformatory schools, and all the buildings of the village razed to the ground. The village of Lezocky was similarly treated.

Czechoslovakia was one of the Allied countries in German occupation whose representatives signed a declaration in London on Jan. 13, 1942, placing among their principal war aims the punishment of those responsible for atrocities against civilian populations.

FREE CZECHOSLOVAKIA. While Czechs in the Protectorate were resisting and frustrating German aggression, thousands of Czechs who succeeded in escaping became organized in an official movement with headquarters in London. Their leader was Dr. Beneš, once again President of the Republic. His timely departure from Czechoslovakia in the autumn of 1938 was cleverly arranged by his nephew, Bohuš Beneš. In London Dr. Beneš joined Jan Masaryk, who in consequence of the Munich agreement resigned his post as Czechoslovak Minister to this country. The collapse of France was followed by a large influx of Czechs, many of whom had taken part in the fighting there.

Finally, on July 23, 1940, the British Government granted recognition to Dr. Beneš and his colleagues as an Allied Government and as the sole authorized representatives of the Czech people. Dr. Beneš himself was President of the Republic, Jan Masaryk was Minister of Foreign Affairs, while the post of Prime Minister was occupied by Jan Šrámek, a former Prime Minister, and one of those who, thanks to the devoted help of Czech railwaymen, managed to find his way from the Protectorate into Poland before the outbreak of war. When the full story of these escapes is told, it will contain many examples of self-sacrifice on the part of Czech workers who risked, and, only too often, incurred, the harshest of punishments for helping their fellow-countrymen across the frontier to freedom.

The Czech army consists of several thousand troops who (*see* Czech Legion) reached this country after the collapse of France, together with many others who rallied to their country's ranks from far and wide, in some cases after long and difficult journeys across

were surrounded and attacked with machine-guns by the vilest ruffians at his disposal. Large numbers of students were murdered in cold blood, while the remainder, male and female, were packed into lorries and driven to an Air Force barracks on the outskirts of Prague, where they were subjected to bestial tortures.

The Germans also increasingly curtailed Czech elementary and secondary education. By the end of 1940 more than 6,000 elementary teachers out of 20,000 had lost their employment, and tens of thousands of Czech children were deprived of education, although more than adequate provision was made for the needs of German children. The conditions as regards secondary education were even worse, and there is every reason to suppose that, in this respect, the Germans intended to proceed to the same lengths as in the case of the Czech universities.

Powerful Underground Movement

The fate of the Czech students in November 1939 taught the Czechs that it was useless for them to attempt any open revolt against the Germans—yet. They did, however, perfect an underground opposition, which operated in various ways, and was so effective that the Germans could not cope with it, although they had half a million soldiers, police, Black Guards and other exponents of brute force on special duty in the Protectorate. This Czech opposition took the form mainly of sabotage and go-slow methods in factories and on railways, deliberate interference with agricultural output, illicit newspapers, leaflets and wireless transmitters, together with whispered propaganda which utilized news items obtained from the Czech broadcasts of the B.B.C. How powerless the Germans were against this dogged and elusive resistance was plainly demonstrated when, on Sept. 27, 1941, Baron von Neurath ceased to be Reich Protector and his place was taken by Reinhard Heydrich (*q.v.*), a degenerate with a criminal record and an intimate of the notorious Himmler. The arrival of Heydrich in Prague was marked by a declaration of martial law which formed the prelude to terrorism on a wider scale and of a more ruthless character than any hitherto. Within a half the globe. The Czech squadrons serving with the R.A.F. have distinguished themselves in operations against the enemy. The available figures show that up to the end of May 1942 they had carried out more than 1,000 raids over Germany, including 113 on Brest, 97 on Cologne, 85 on Bremen, 80 on Hamburg, 65 on Kiel, 53 on Mannheim, and 36 on Berlin. In this connexion it should be borne in mind that any Czech airman who falls into the hands of the Germans is liable to be executed for serving the British cause. The night fighters of the Czech air force have also given an excellent account of themselves in the defence of this country against German raiders.

A preliminary agreement of federal union between Czechoslovakia and Poland was signed in London on Jan. 23, 1942.

Books to Consult : A German Protectorate, Sheila Grant-Duff (Macmillan). Volcano under Hitler, J. Hronek (Czechoslovak Independent Weekly).

THE HARBOUR AT DAKAR

Still in the control of Vichy France at the beginning of 1942, Dakar is a naval and air base of great strategic value, and was greedily coveted by Hitler as a base for Atlantic raiding.
Photo, Dorien Leigh

 Dakar. On the West African coast, about 1,000 miles N. of the Equator, lies the port of Dakar, which, following the French collapse in June 1940, suddenly became of major strategical importance.

Capital of French West Africa, Dakar with its dependencies covers 700 sq. miles and has a population of approximately 93,000, of which more than a third are French, 1,500 are other Europeans, and the remainder negroes.

The factors controlling the strategical importance of Dakar can be summed up thus :

(1) Dakar is the only naval and air base of importance on the French West African coast.

(2) It is the most westerly port in Africa, being only 2,000 miles from Pernambuco, in Brazil.

(3) The vast territory of which Dakar is the capital and centre of maritime, air, road and rail communications, connects by land French North Africa on the north and British and Free French territories on the south and east.

(4) Hostile sea, submarine and air forces based on Dakar would constitute a grave threat to Allied Atlantic shipping.

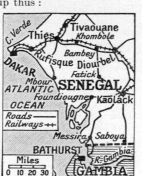

Dakar, seaport of Senegal.

(5) Dakar could be used as a " jumping-off " place for Axis attacks on Latin America, a matter of vital interest to the United States.

With these considerations in mind, the events which occurred at Dakar in July and September of 1940 follow logically.

The first of these was the British naval and air attack on the new and powerful French battleship Richelieu, which at the time was lying in the Naval Basin at Dakar. This attack was part of British strategy to prevent the French fleet from falling into enemy hands, being similar to the grim naval attacks on French naval units at Oran (Algeria) on July 3.

Arriving off Dakar with a strong naval force on July 7, the Flag Officer entrusted with the mission succeeded after some difficulty in conveying to the French Admiral honourable proposals similar to those made at Oran. No satisfactory reply being received, a motor-boat under the command of Lieut.-Commander R. H. Bristowe skilfully penetrated the boom defences

of the harbour under cover of darkness. With almost unprecedented daring depth charges were dropped which disabled the Richelieu's rudder and propellers. On her return journey the motor-boat broke down and lay helpless for a time. She was discovered, but the crew got one engine going and she escaped by crossing the defence nets, which held up her pursuers.

The battleship was then attacked by aircraft of the Fleet Air Arm ; subsequently, air reconnaissance showed her listing to port and down by the stern. She was later repaired, but was stated in 1942 not to be fit for sea duty.

In September 1940, believing that a large part of the population favoured Free France, and fearing the possibility of German annexation of the port, Gen. de Gaulle arrived at Dakar at the head of an expeditionary force, military, naval and air, with considerable British naval forces forming a supplementary protection. He informed Admiral de Laborde, in command of the naval base, that he was about to send emissaries ashore under a flag of truce. The Admiral refused to receive them, and when they nevertheless set out, unarmed and in an unarmed boat, they were fired on and two were seriously wounded.

Summoning his followers in Dakar to rally to his cause, de Gaulle then made an attempt to land troops peacefully, but the Dakar forts again opened fire and they were forced to retire. Following this, shore batteries were turned on one of de Gaulle's warships, and this, despite British efforts to avoid it, led to a severe bombardment between H.M. ships and the shore batteries, supported by guns from the Richelieu and other French warships and submarines. Two submarines were sunk and there were many casualties.

When it was seen that Dakar could be taken only by " a major operation of war," the action was discontinued and the Allied Forces withdrawn. In effect, much harm was done to the Allied cause in French West Africa and many critics considered that, once begun, the attempt to take Dakar should have been carried through. Further difficulties arose over the British blockade of Dakar and the coast, and the stopping of all Vichy convoys. There was evidence in 1941 that U-boats were using Vichy-controlled bases on the Dakar coast. *See* West Africa, French.

Edouard Daladier, French politician.
Photo, British Official

Daladier, EDOUARD (b. 1884). He was Prime Minister of France from 1938 to 1940, and was succeeded by Reynaud on March 20, 1940. During France's great national crisis brought about by the German onslaught he became Foreign Minister on May 25, 1940. He was Minister of National Defence and War in the Reynaud Cabinet, and resigned on June 6. Daladier's power was considerable while he was Prime Minister; the Communist Party was suppressed and some of its representatives were arrested in the Chamber of Deputies. It was the public disgust over failure to help Finland that brought about Daladier's resignation. After the formation of the Pétain cabinet in mid-June 1940, and the subsequent French armistice, a number of ex-Ministers, including Daladier, made an attempt to set up a Government in French North Africa. They sailed from the Gironde on June 19, but on reaching Africa they were refused permission to land by the acting Governor and shipped back to France, where they were placed under arrest. On Sept. 9 it was reported that Daladier had been detained in the Château de Chazeron and was to await trial by the "war guilt" Court. He was subsequently moved to Pellevoisin, and in February 1942 was tried at Riom (*q.v.*).

D'Albiac, AIR VICE-MARSHAL SIR JOHN HENRY, K.B.E., D.S.O. (b. 1894). He was appointed Commander of the British Air Force in Greece in November 1940. In May 1942 he became A.O.C., R.A.F. Ceylon.

Dalton, RT. HON. HUGH, P.C. (b. 1887). President of the Board of Trade from Feb. 22, 1942. He was Minister of Economic Warfare from May 1940,

Damascus. Capital of Syria. On June 18, 1941, ten days after British and Free French forces crossed the Syrian frontier, the Allies were fighting in the orange groves and amongst the canals surrounding Damascus. That night the C.-in-C., Gen. Sir Henry Maitland Wilson, sent a message over the Palestine wireless to Gen. Dentz, commander of the Vichy forces in Syria, appealing to him to avoid damage to the historic city by declaring it an open town and withdrawing his troops. No reply was given to this ultimatum within the time specified, so Gen. Wilson gave the order to advance and by the evening of June 20 the Mezze aerodrome had been taken by Indian troops, a force of Free French troops and two batteries—one Indian and the other British—had

driven off the French tanks barring the road from Kuneitra, and the main Vichy forces had withdrawn from the city under machine-gun fire from Royal Australian Air Force fighters. The next morning Damascus was stormed by Gen. Legentilhomme's Free French from the south, Gen. Collet's Circassians from the east, and by Imperial troops from the west. By 11 a.m. on June 22 Vichy resistance collapsed and Gen. Collet led his Free French troops into the city. *See* Syria.

Danube, RIVER. A long stretch of this river, forming the greater part of the frontier between Rumania and Bulgaria, came under the control of the Germans when they occupied Rumania on Oct. 4, 1940. Immediately before the signing of the Tripartite Pact by Bulgaria on March 1, 1941, German troops and mechanized units, which had been massing for some weeks on the north bank of the Danube, crossed by pontoon bridges to the Bulgarian side of the river at Ruschuk, Nikopol and Vidin, preparatory to their onslaught on Greece in April.

Danzig. From 1919 until Sept. 1, 1939, Danzig was a Free City, under the protection of the League of Nations. Poland held special privileges in the port (*see* Westerplatte), and controlled the foreign relations of the little State. Predominantly German, Danzig resented League rule, and resident Nazis, under the leadership of Albert Forster, instituted a reign of terror against Jewish merchants of the city. By the end of 1937 the Nazis had gained complete control. In 1938 Danzig's reincorporation in the Reich had become a matter of immediate political interest. Forster proclaimed himself Head of the State of Danzig on August 24, 1939. This was a signal for the Nazis to threaten Poland, and for Germany no longer to conceal her real intentions. Three days later Hitler demanded that Danzig and the Polish Corridor be returned to the Reich. The Corridor was entered by German troops on September 1, the day of the invasion of Poland, and Hitler made his triumphal entry into the city on September 19. On that date he opened his "peace" offensive, declaring to the world in a frenzied speech that Germany's aims were "strictly limited." In 1941 it was reported that Danzig was in a state of economic ruin.

Darlan, ADMIRAL JEAN FRANÇOIS (1881–1942). When war broke out Admiral Darlan, then Chief of the French Naval Staff, was made C.-in-C. of the Fleet, and to begin with there was close and cordial cooperation between him and Sir Dudley Pound.

ALLIED FORCES ENTER DAMASCUS
Free French and Imperial troops took part in the capture of Damascus, ancient city of Syria, when it was found necessary to counter German intrigue in the Levant by taking over the whole country.
Photo, British Official

After the fall of France, however, Darlan evinced a strong anti-British attitude and was said to be in favour of handing over the entire French Fleet to Hitler, despite the terms of the Armistice. On Feb. 9, 1941, Marshal Pétain announced that he had appointed Darlan Vice-Premier in succession to Laval, now out of favour, Minister of Foreign Affairs in place of Flandin, and Minister of the Interior. Darlan acted as envoy between Vichy and Abetz, German Ambassador in Paris, and by June was definitely pro-Hitler. In July he resigned from the Ministry of the Interior, and on August 12 Marshal Pétain issued a decree appointing him Minister of Home and Empire, with supreme control of the Ministries of War, Air, the Navy and the Colonies.

Admiral Darlan, C.-in-C. of French Armed Forces.
Photo, Wide World

When Laval returned to power as "Chief of the Government" on April 14, 1942, Darlan resigned his post as Vice-Premier and Minister of National Defence, Foreign Affairs and Marine. The Ministry of National Defence was abolished and its functions divided between the Army, Marine and Aviation ministries. Darlan's resignation was the outcome of German pressure on the Vichy Government to appoint Laval at the head of affairs in Unoccupied France. Darlan was excluded from the newly formed Cabinet, but remained head of the French armed forces. On May 5, following the British landing in Madagascar, he sent a message to the Vichy forces there, urging them to defend the island, and vilifying Britain. He was assassinated Dec. 24, 1942. *See* Vichy.

Darwin. Port and chief town of Northern Territory, Australia, Darwin was of great importance in the Pacific strategy: first, because of its great oil installations set up by the Navy ; secondly, because the R.A.A.F. established at Darwin a permanent operational station ; and thirdly, because it is a military centre for both the Home Service force and the A.I.F. Darwin has a splendid harbour, but no docks. Until comparatively recently communication with the rest of Australia was either by air or by sea. Now a railway runs southwards as far as Birdum. The railhead here is linked with that at Alice Springs by the Central Australian road, 621 miles long, now taken over by the Army, along which there is a constant traffic of men and supplies.

The Japanese began their attack on Australia by bombing Darwin on Feb. 19, 1942. This first raid is described in pp. 31–32. Minor attacks were made thereafter at intervals until June 13, when a strong force of 27 heavy bombers, escorted by fighters, raided the aerodrome. Damage was, however, negligible. The next day Allied fighters intercepted a force of Japanese aircraft, destroying four fighters and causing the bombers to turn back, but on June 15 the enemy got through and an extensive raid was made, again by 27 bombers escorted by fighters, which followed the shoreline of the harbour, bombing as they went. *See* Australia ; Pacific, War in.

Déat, MARCEL. A former French Deputy, Déat was editor of the pro-German L'Œuvre, a newspaper published in German-occupied Paris, which expressed the quisling point of view and attacked Germany's enemies. On August 27, 1941, during a ceremony at Versailles, attended by German officers

and a number of leading French Fascists, including Laval (*q.v.*), Déat was seriously wounded by a Frenchman, Colette. Another unsuccessful attempt on his life was made on March 27, 1942, at Tours.

Decoux, VICE-ADMIRAL JEAN. He succeeded Gen. Catroux as Governor-General of French Indo-China in July 1940, and conducted the Vichy-Japanese negotiations at Hanoi which were concluded on July 23, 1941—very much to Japan's advantage.

De-Gaussing. This term was given to the process of fitting British ships with a device which rendered them immune from magnetic mines by neutralizing the ship's own magnetic field by means of an electrically charged cable. News of its use was officially released when the British liner Queen

DE-GAUSSING CABLE ON A LINER

When the 85,000-ton s.s. Queen Elizabeth made her maiden voyage to New York early in 1940, her hull was protected by a gigantic cable (shown by arrow) designed to neutralize the attraction of the metal in the ship for magnetic mines.
Photo, Wide World

Elizabeth arrived at New York on March 7, 1940, with her hull girdled by an anti-magnetic cable. The device is known as de-Gaussing because it is based on a law discovered by the German scientist, K. F. Gauss (1777–1855). *See* Mines and Minelaying.

Degrelle, LÉON (b. 1906). Leader of the Rexist (Fascist) Party in German-occupied Belgium from 1940. He had been arrested by the Belgian Government in May 1940, but was released by the Germans the following month.

Denis, LT.-GEN. HENRI. Belgian Minister of Defence, 1939–40. After King Leopold's capitulation in May 1940 he went with the Belgian Cabinet to Bordeaux, and at a meeting there on June 18 declared himself in favour of remaining in France and following the French Cabinet to Vichy, rather than establish a Free Belgian Government in England.

Denmark. Picture tall King Christian of Denmark taking his morning ride through Copenhagen's streets, with his subjects cheering him, while bewildered German soldiers look on. This happened on King Christian's birthday anniversary on Sept. 26, 1940. Picture again Danish Nazis being chased through the streets and beaten by indignant loyal Danes, while the armed and booted German invaders, friends of the Danish Nazis, are helpless to intervene.

After the outbreak of the Second Great War little Denmark was the first country to experience the heel of the German invader and Germany wished to keep Denmark as a show-piece of " benevolent " Nazi rule. The Germans began well. For one day only, from 6 a.m. on April 9, 1940, when German warplanes flew over Copenhagen and mechanized troops violated the frontier near Flensburg and Tonden, while naval units landed at Copenhagen, Körsor, Nyborg, Gjedsen and other places, did the Germans display force.

Germany pretended that in breaking her Non-Aggression and Trade Treaties with Denmark she was forestalling an invasion by Britain and France. King Christian was allowed to continue his reign and the Rigsdag (Parliament), under the Prime Minister, Hr. Stauning, who informed members on April 10 that both the King and the Government had decided to accept Germany's pledge of political independence for Denmark, continued to function.

Then began the German requisitions of food, petrol and clothes from Denmark's well-stocked stores. Ten per cent of Denmark's milch cows, 150,000 or one quarter of her young cattle, $1\frac{1}{2}$ million pigs, eight million chickens were slaughtered in September and October, 1940, first to provide food for Germany, secondly because no fodder could be imported to feed them. At the end of October, 1940, Germany owed Denmark 300 million kroner for goods requisitioned. Bread, butter, cheese, eggs, meat—all foodstuffs became scarce, and horse-drawn vehicles replaced motor buses and cars. Germany even impressed ten Danish torpedo boats into her service in February, 1941, and forced a customs union on Denmark.

Through accepting Nazi rule so meekly Hr. Stauning speedily found himself surrounded by Nazi hirelings, and political independence became a farce. Gradually the Nazi yoke was forced on the Danes. Outspoken and fearless political leaders, like Christian Moeller (Conservative) and leaders of the Liberals and Social Democrats, were forced from office. Odious quislings like Hr. Scavenius, who brought Denmark on Nov. 25, 1941, into the Anti-Comintern Pact, and Dr. Fritz Clausen, chief Danish Nazi, increased their power in spite of the contempt of their countrymen. Denmark's first concentration camp, that at Horseroed, was established on August 21, 1941.

Outside Denmark, however, in the United States and the United Kingdom, independent Danes were combining in a movement to free Denmark. In March 1942 Count Reventlow, Danish Minister in London, was officially recognized as responsible for all Danish interests outside enemy control and as head of the Free Danish movement in Britain.

Book to Consult: Denmark: Fight Follows Surrender, T. M. Ferkelson (Danish Council).

Dentz, GEN. HENRI. He took over the Military Governorship of Paris on June 13, 1940, from Gen. Hering, who, after declaring it an open town to save it from destruction by air bombardment, departed to assume an army command. The next day the Germans marched in. Dentz became French High Commissioner in Syria on Dec. 7, 1940, in place of M. Chiappe (*q.v.*), killed while flying to Beirut to take up the post. It was he who on July 11, 1941, sued for the cessation of hostilities in Syria between Vichy and the British and Free French forces. He was interned with 35 other Vichy officers on August 7, because of the Vichy failure to release, as provided under the Armistice Convention, 75 British and Indian officers, some of whom were in Axis-occupied territory. Released at Jerusalem on Sept. 5, he went to France.

Depot Ship. A depot ship is a vessel set apart to attend upon a destroyer or submarine flotilla. These ships are really floating workshops. They comprised at the outbreak of war 8 submarine and 4 destroyer ships. H.M.S. Forth and Medway, two noted vessels that act as depot ships for submarines, came into prominence in 1940–41. H.M.S. Forth has accommodation for the crews of 12 submarines, and contains plant for charging batteries, machine shops, foundry, plate shop and smithy, etc., enabling repair work to be undertaken at sea. The submarine crews live in special quarters aboard the parent ship when in port. H.M.S. Medway (14,650 tons), based at Singapore in March, 1941, can " mother " 18 submarines.

Depth Charge. This is a formidable weapon employed against hostile submarines. It consists of a thin-walled cylindrical container, resembling an oil drum, holding a large high-explosive charge and firing mechanism. Charges are either dropped overboard or fired from a special gun resembling a trench mortar. Depth charges sink so as to form a ring of explosions round the place where the submarine is judged to be. The firing mechanism can be adjusted to function at a pre-determined depth. The explosion of the charge within a certain range of the submarine damages or destroys it by the passage through the water of the explosion shock, which may break open the submarine's plates at quite considerable distances.

Derna. This Libyan town, situated on the coast, 100 m. W. of Tobruk, together with its important aerodrome, changed hands several times during the course of the North African campaign. On Jan. 30, 1941, it was captured from the Italians by British Imperial troops, who drove out the Italian garrison, about 10,000 strong, the majority of whom, it is

DERNA, LIBYAN COASTAL TOWN

The little port of Derna is about 100 miles west of Tobruk. Its chief importance to the contending armies lies in the ample supply of fresh water found there. British troops are here seen taking over in December 1941.

Photo, British Official

believed, escaped. The R.A.F. helped considerably in the capture of Derna by their repeated heavy bombings of the aerodrome. Retaken by German and Italian forces on April 7, 1941, Derna fell once again into British hands on Dec. 19, 1941, captured by the Eighth Army. In a new forward drive Rommel recaptured Derna in Feb. 1942. *See* North Africa.

Dessie. The Italian Army in retreat from Addis Ababa made a stand at Dessie, a strong defensive position astride mountains. The ensuing battle was one of the fiercest in the East African campaign. The Italians were routed by South African forces, and Dessie fell on April 26, 1941. *See* Abyssinia.

Deutschland. Originally the name-ship of the class to which the Admiral Scheer and Admiral Graf Spee belonged, this pocket battleship had a displace-

DEUTSCHLAND, NOTORIOUS NAZI RAIDER
Launched in May 1931 by Hindenburg at Kiel, the Deutschland was the first of Germany's "pocket battleships." When Hitler formally took over Memel on March 23, 1939, he proceeded to that port in this warship.
Photo, Central Press

ment of 10,000 tons and a complement of 926. She captured the American City of Flint (*q.v.*) in October 1939, and sank the British Rawalpindi (*q.v.*) off Iceland in November 1939, after heroic combat on the part of the British vessel. During intense naval activity off Norway in April 1940 the Lützow, as she had been renamed, was beached 50 miles W. of Trondheim on April 25. In June 1941 it was reported that she had been hit by R.A.F. 'planes when trying to escape into the Atlantic as a commerce raider. In December the Lützow was reported in the S. Atlantic, off the coast of Argentina.

De Valera, EAMON (b. 1882). Prime Minister and Minister for External Affairs in the Government of Eire from 1937. Some months before the outbreak of war he declared that in the event of war Eire would remain strictly neutral. While reaffirming this policy of neutrality on several occasions, he made it clear that if Eire were attacked she would defend herself to the utmost. Speaking in Dublin, June 16, 1940, to a large audience, he emphasized the nation's danger and stressed the need for greater defence. On July 5, 1940, he urged the union of N. Ireland with Eire, and in May 1941 protested to the British Government against their proposed conscription plans in N. Ireland. In a speech at Mullingar, Oct. 5, 1941, he declared that the Irish

would be ready to "join in any world organization of free people designed for the general welfare of mankind and the maintenance of peace." He strongly opposed the lease of Irish ports to Britain. He also denounced the activities of I.R.A. terrorists. He protested in January 1942 against the presence of U.S.A. troops in Northern Ireland. *See* Eire; Northern Ireland.

Dill, FIELD-MARSHAL SIR JOHN GREER, G.C.B. (b. 1881). Governor of Bombay in succession to Sir Roger Lumley, the appointment being announced on Nov. 19, 1941. He went to France at the beginning of the war as commander of the First Army Corps of the B.E.F. under Lord Gort. On May 26, 1940, he succeeded Lord Ironside as Chief of the Imperial General Staff and retired from that position on Dec. 25, 1941. In April 1941 he visited Athens and Egypt on a tour of the Middle East, accompanying Mr. Eden. He was present at the Atlantic Conference (Churchill-Roosevelt meeting) in August 1941. He was one of the experts who travelled with Mr.

Sir John Dill,
Governor of Bombay.
Photo, Fox

Churchill to the U.S.A. for a further conference with President Roosevelt on Dec. 23, 1941, remaining there for some time to help in co-ordinating joint British-American military strategy. It was his duty to put forward to the U.S. Government the views of Sir Archibald Wavell, Allied C.-in-C. in the S.W. Pacific.

Diredawa. This Abyssinian town was captured from the Italians by a South African force on March 29, 1941. In taking it, the British cut the Addis-Ababa–Jibuti railway and closed the net round the Abyssinian capital. *See* Abyssinia.

Dnieper, RIVER. This great river rises in the Valdai plateau, flows south through White Russia and the Ukraine, and is navigable almost from its source. On July 5, 1941, the Germans claimed that their forces east of Minsk had successfully crossed the river, but the Russians later denied this report.

DNIEPER DAM DESTROYED BY ITS OWN BUILDERS
The retreating Russians blew up their most famous engineering achievement to prevent it from being used by the Nazis, and this striking air photograph shows the vast gap through which the water is surging, while in the right bottom corner can be seen the gap made in the bridge leading to the dam.
Photo, Associated Press

A violent struggle ensued between the two armies for the possession of the industrial Ukraine. On August 16 the Russians withdrew east of the river, and continued to retreat, the Germans capturing the town of Dniepropetrovsk (q.v.) on August 26. Two days later the retreating Russians, in accordance with their "scorched earth" policy, destroyed the famous Dnieper dam. On Sept. 24 Marshal Budenny launched a counter-attack against the German forces at Kherson, on the Dnieper. See Russia.

Dniepropetrovsk. This great iron and steel town on the W. bank of the R. Dnieper is about 250 m. S.E. of Kiev. It was captured by the Germans on August 26, 1941. The Russian troops defending the town had orders to destroy all machinery and industrial plant before making an attempt to join their comrades on the E. bank of the river. See Russia.

Dniester, RIVER. Rising in the Carpathians, this river traverses Poland and the U.S.S.R. and falls into the Black Sea midway between the mouths of the Danube and the Dnieper. It was the scene of violent fighting during the German thrust to Odessa in July 1941. On July 19 German-Rumanian forces crossed the Dniester at several points, the Russians retreating to lines behind the river. Ten days later Rumanian troops reached the mouth of the Dniester, occupying the town of Akkerman. See Russia.

Dobbie, LIEUT.-GEN. SIR WILLIAM GEORGE SHEDDEN, D.S.O. (b. 1879). Governor and C.-in-C. of Malta from June 1940 to May 1942, when he resigned owing to ill health. On May 11 he was given the G.C.M.G. Lord Gort succeeded him at Malta (q.v.).

Sir Wm. Dobbie, Governor of Malta. *Photo, Walter Stoneman*

Dobruja. This district of the Balkans is bounded W. and N. by the R. Danube, E. by the Black Sea, and S. by Bulgaria. On August 21, 1940, the southern part of the territory, an area of 2,956 sq. miles, was ceded by the Rumanian government to Bulgaria. The new frontiers followed those of 1912, running from just north of Silistria on the Danube to the Black Sea, south of Mangalia.

Dodecanese. Twelve Italian islands situated in the Aegean Sea are known by this name. Close to them, and usually included in the group, is the island of Rhodes (q.v.). From the time of Italy's entry into the war her bases and aerodromes in the Dodecanese were bombed by the Fleet Air Arm, while British warships bombarded important military objectives. Enemy shipping off the Islands was also attacked by our 'planes.

Dombaas. This vital Norwegian railway junction was the scene of fierce fighting in April 1940, when the Germans invaded Norway. Nearly two hundred German parachutists landed here and made frantic, but unsuccessful, efforts to

destroy the junction. They were either killed or captured by the Norwegians. Later the Norwegians made a series of counter-attacks against the Germans near the town. British troops arrived to join up with them and put up a heroic resistance. In the face of strong enemy attacks the British and Norwegian troops were forced to withdraw, and on May 1, 1940, it was announced that they had evacuated the area. See Norway.

Doran, F/O. KENNETH CHRISTOPHER, D.F.C. This officer was one of the first five British airmen to be decorated in the war. Early in September 1939 he led an attack against an enemy cruiser. In face of heavy gunfire and under extremely bad weather conditions he pressed home a successful low attack with great determination. For this gallant exploit he received the D.F.C. on Nov. 2, 1939.

Dorman-Smith, COL. RT. HON. SIR REGINALD HUGH, P.C., G.B.E. (b. 1899). He was appointed Governor of Burma on Dec. 24, 1940, succeeding Sir Archibald Cochrane on the expiry of the latter's term of office in May 1941. He was Minister of Agriculture and Fisheries 1939–40, and Liaison Officer between the Home Defence Forces and Government Depts., 1940.

Dormer, SIR CECIL FRANCIS JOSEPH, K.C.M.G. (b. 1883). Appointed British Ambassador to the Polish Govt. in London on March 26, 1941, in place of Sir Howard Kennard. He was Envoy Extraordinary and Minister Plenipotentiary to Norway from 1934 to 1940.

Dorsetshire, H.M.S. Sister ship of H.M.S. Norfolk, this British cruiser was completed in 1930. The Dorsetshire had a displacement of 9,975 tons, and carried a complement of 650. In May 1941 she took part in the chase of the Bismarck (q.v.), sinking her by torpedo on May 27. In December she sank a German commerce raider of 10,000 tons in the South Atlantic. On April 9, 1942, it was announced that she had been sunk by Japanese air attack in the Indian Ocean.

Dortmund. This Prussian town, situated 50 m. N.E. of Düsseldorf, is the largest town on the Ruhr coalfield. Important objectives in this area were repeatedly bombed by the R.A.F. during 1940–41.

Dortmund-Ems Canal. This vital link in the German transport system, connecting the industrial area of the Ruhr with N.W. Germany, and running into the sea at Emden, was frequently bombed by the R.A.F. Between May and November, 1940, various parts of the canal, in particular its lock gates and docks, were heavily attacked no fewer than sixteen times. An

H.M.S. DORSETSHIRE—FEARED BY ATLANTIC RAIDERS
This British cruiser carried an armament of eight 8·9-in. guns, eight 8-in. guns, eight 4-in. guns, four three-pounders, and sixteen smaller guns. She also carried eight 21·9-in. torpedo tubes, and one aircraft with catapult. It was H.M.S. Dorsetshire that finally sank the Bismarck. She herself was sunk by the Japanese in the Indian Ocean, April 1942
Photo, British Official

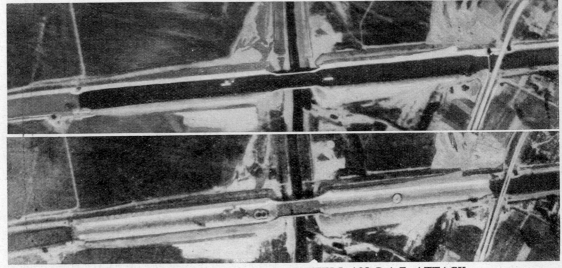

THE DORTMUND-EMS CANAL SUFFERS AN R.A.F. ATTACK

This important link in Germany's internal transport system has been a frequent target for our bombers. The photographs of a stretch north of Münster show (above) the aqueduct with barges proceeding along it, and (below) after an air raid, when it will be seen that the water has drained away and that there are large craters in the canal bed on either side.

Photo, British Official

especially vulnerable point, just N. of Münster, was the double aqueduct that carried the canal across the R. Ems. This was the objective of several raids, including a determined low-level attack on August 12–13, for which Fl.-Lt. Learoyd (*q.v.*) won the V.C.

**Marshal of the R.A.F.,
Sir W. Sholto Douglas**
Bertram Park

Douglas, MARSHAL OF THE R.A.F. SIR WILLIAM SHOLTO, G.C.B., M.C. (b. 1893). A.O.C.-in-C. Fighter Command, 1940. He was promoted Air Marshal in 1940, and was Air Chief Marshal 1942–46.

Dover. The Kentish seaport of Dover was repeatedly attacked by German aircraft and bombarded by German guns from the French coast. During a particularly heavy daylight raid on July 29, 1940, seventeen out of the eighty attacking German 'planes were shot down in a fierce air battle. Not a single bomb fell on shore on this occasion. There was another heavy mass raid on August 12, 1940. During the Battle of Britain many aerial battles took place over this district. On August 13, 1940, Dover was bombarded for the first time by German guns from Gris Nez. Cross-Channel shelling on August 22 caused damage to a church and buildings near the sea front. It was bombarded many times afterwards. Although daylight air attacks became less frequent in 1941, the town and harbour were frequent objectives of the German night bombers. *See* Great Britain, Air War.

[**Dowding**, AIR CHIEF MARSHAL LORD HUGH CASWALL, G.C.B., G.C.V.O. (b. 1882). A.O.C.-in-C. Fighter Command from 1936 to 1940, when he was succeeded by Air Marshal Sir W. Sholto Douglas (*q.v.*). He was seconded to the Ministry of Aircraft Production for special duty in the U.S.A. in November 1940. Retired Oct. 1941 he was recalled Nov. 1941, to review R.A.F. home establishments. He retired July 15, 1942; created baron 1943.

Dublin. Capital of Eire. In the early hours of May 31, 1941, German aircraft dropped bombs on this neutral city. In protesting to Germany, the Eire

Government announced that 27 people were killed and 80 injured, but the figures subsequently proved higher. Until the bombs were proved to be of German origin, the Nazis put the blame on Britain for this outrage.

Duda, El. Eighteen miles S.E. of Tobruk, this was the most advanced point reached by the Tobruk garrison in December 1941, and constituted a keypoint against the German forces. Three heavy enemy attacks were launched at the beginning of December, and in their third attack the Germans gained some ground, which was subsequently recaptured in a British counter-attack. After the raising of the siege of Tobruk, announced on Dec. 9, 1941, mopping-up operations were carried out in the El Duda area. It fell to the Germans with Tobruk in June 1942.

Duisburg-Ruhrort. This city and river port of Germany, situated between the Rhine and Ruhr, with which rivers it is connected by canal, was a frequent target of the R.A.F. Its railway junctions, marshalling yards, oil plants and blast furnaces were first attacked by British bombers May 15–16, 1940, after which repeated attacks, inflicting heavy damage, were made. On July 13 Duisburg suffered its fiftieth raid and in the same month the devastating new 4,000 lb. bombs were rained on the city, doing immense damage.

Duke of York, H.M.S. British battleship of 35,000 tons, sister ship of H.M.S. Prince of Wales. She was launched a fortnight after war was declared, and the first intimation that she was in service was when it was announced that Mr. Churchill had travelled in her to the United States in December 1941.

Dunbar Castle. This 10,000-ton Union Castle liner, while sailing in convoy for the Cape, struck a mine and sank off the S.E. coast on Jan. 9, 1940. The liner had 48 passengers aboard and, although she sank in about fifteen minutes, they were all rescued. The commander, Captain H. A. Causton, a storekeeper, and a seaman were killed by the explosion, but the rest of the crew were saved.

HOMEWARD BOUND
—FROM DUNKIRK

EXHAUSTED after their terrible ordeal on the blazing beaches of Dunkirk, these men of the B.E.F. crowd to the rail of the transport which is taking them to safety, for a final glimpse of the French coast smothered under the smoke of war. They represent but a handful of the thousands who were rescued in this, the greatest evacuation in history. In such quick succession did the rescue ships arrive at British ports that they were often two deep alongside the quays.

Photo, British Official

THE WITHDRAWAL FROM DUNKIRK, May 26 to June 2, 1940

Duncan, Rt. Hon. Sir Andrew Rae, p.c. (b. 1884). Re-appointed Minister of Supply on Feb. 2, 1942. He was Controller of Iron and Steel under the Ministry 1939–40, President of the Board of Trade from the beginning of 1940, and Minister of Supply, October 1940 until June 30, 1941, when he was succeeded by Lord Beaverbrook (q.v.), and again became President of the Board of Trade.

Dunkerque. This French battleship, a sister ship of the Strasbourg, was completed in October 1935, and put into service in 1937. She had a displacement

DUNKERQUE, ONCE AN ALLIED WARSHIP
This stately French battleship, which was to be seriously damaged by the British Navy at Oran, is here seen in happier days, paying a courtesy visit to the port of Liverpool.
Photo, Keystone

of 26,500 tons, a speed of 29·5 knots, and carried a normal complement of 1,381. Her main armament included eight 13-in. guns. During the Graf Spee action, Dec. 13, 1939, she was on patrol outside Montevideo harbour. Heavily damaged and driven ashore by the British Navy during the attack on the French Fleet at Oran (q.v.), July 3, 1940, she was bombed and put out of action by the Fleet Air Arm, July 6, 1940.

Dunkirk, Evacuation. As the month of May 1940 drew to a close the position of the Allied armies in Northern France became increasingly difficult, and even before the Belgians laid down their arms on May 28 Lord Gort had made plans for the withdrawal of the B.E.F. to a bridgehead to be established at Dunkirk—the only port of any consequence not in enemy hands—with a view to its evacuation (if possible).

To permit this to be done the Dunkirk Perimeter was organized, a shallow salient, 15 miles wide and less than 10 miles deep at its deepest, extending from a point on the coast about five miles west of Dunkirk to Nieuport. As soon as might be the units of the B.E.F. were withdrawn into the Perimeter, whose outside edge was fiercely defended. The task of organizing

the bridgehead was entrusted by Lord Gort to Lieut.-Gen. Sir Ronald Adam. The naval arrangements were placed by the Admiralty in the hands of the Dover Command, and steps were taken to collect nearly 1,700 ships—light warships, yachts, lifeboats, London fire floats—and boats for taking troops from the beaches out to the ships. These were rushed across the Straits of Dover, and a start was made in the embarkation on May 26. Embarkation beaches were organized at La Panne, Bray Dunes, and Malo-les-Bains, one being allotted to each of the three British corps. Dunkirk was heavily bombed that same day, with the result that, though the outer mole could still be used, the inner harbour was now blocked except to small ships. Since there were no quays or piers except at Dunkirk, the embarkation had now to be done entirely from open beaches.

The Armada of Little Ships

By the afternoon of May 28 10,000 men had been already taken off, chiefly from Dunkirk, but some 20,000 more were waiting to be taken off on the beaches. Moreover, the area was congested with French and Belgian troops with their transport, as well as a horde of refugees. However, it was thought that, given a reasonable measure of immunity from air attack, the troops could gradually be evacuated and supplies landed. But if intensive enemy air attacks continued, the beaches might easily become a shambles.

The next day the naval arrangements for the evacuation were in full swing, and an armada of little ships, manned for the most part by eager volunteers, was passing backwards and forwards across the Channel.

By May 30 there remained to be evacuated some 80,000 British troops out of a total of 250,000, but in addition there were many thousands of French soldiers who were now swarming into the Perimeter. All this time hospital ships were working continuously, though incessant bombing made their berthing difficult.

On the night of June 2 Lord Gort, on instructions from the British Government, sailed for England, leaving Maj.-Gen. Alexander in command of the British troops still unevacuated. Before leaving, Lord Gort had the satisfaction of knowing that, whatever happened to the rearguard, sufficient men had been withdrawn to enable fighting units of the B.E.F. to be quickly re-formed at home. The evacuation continued, although at 3 a.m. on June 2 it was temporarily stopped to prevent casualties in daylight; at that time there remained in the Dunkirk area about 3,000 men of

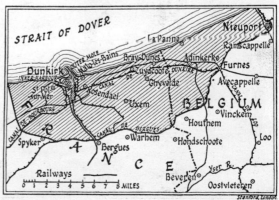

Dunkirk Perimeter, to which the final withdrawal was made.

various artillery and infantry units, with seven anti-aircraft guns and 12 anti-tank guns. This little force held the outskirts of Dunkirk throughout June 2 with little interference, save for heavy shelling and bombing of the beaches. By midnight on June 2/3 all the remaining British troops had been embarked. Maj.-Gen. Alexander, accompanied by the Senior Naval Officer (Capt. W. G. Tennant, R.N.), made a tour of the beaches and harbour in a motor-boat, and on being satisfied that no British troops were left on shore, themselves left for England.

Altogether, of the B.E.F. 211,532 fit men and 13,053 casualties were embarked at Dunkirk and the beaches, as well as 112,546 Allied troops, chiefly French. So ended what Mr. Churchill was soon to call a "miracle of deliverance achieved by valour, by perfect discipline, by dauntless service, by resource, by skill . . ." *See* Colour Plate facing page 97.

Up to the end of April 1942 the port of Dunkirk was bombed 91 times by the R.A.F.

Books to Consult : The Nine Days' Wonder, John Masefield (Heinemann). Return via Dunkirk, "Gunbuster" (Hodder & Stoughton).

Durazzo. Situated on the Adriatic, this is the chief port of Albania. On April 7, 1939, its people witnessed the humiliating spectacle of Italian troops landing to rob the country of its independence. During the Italo-Greek War, October 1940–April 1941, it was used as a port of disembarkation by the Italians. It was heavily attacked by the R.A.F. during November-December 1940. *See* Albania.

Düsseldorf. This industrial city of Germany, situated on the Rhine, 24 m. N.W. of Cologne, was one of the many targets in the Ruhr subjected to heavy and frequent bombing by the R.A.F. By the end of June 1940 oil tanks had been set on fire, a steel works completely destroyed, and almost a whole district burnt. On the night of Dec. 4, 1940, Düsseldorf was bombed, for the first time in force, for twelve hours. On Dec. 7, 1940, it was again severely raided. In later raids, which, up to Dec. 31, 1941, numbered 47, the station and factories, warehouses, etc., were damaged.

Dutch Indies. *See* Netherlands East and West Indies.

DUNKIRK EVACUATION

British troops wading out from the beach to be taken to safety aboard a transport. While waiting their turn they had been subjected to constant shelling, bombing and machine-gunning from the enraged enemy. Left, paddle steamer, typical of the vessels of all kinds which raced across the Channel and snatched over 337,000 men from the jaws of death.

Photo, G.P.U.

Dyle, RIVER. Louvain and Malines are two of the towns lying on this Belgian river. In May 1940 it was a factor in the strategic plans devised by Lord Gort in conjunction with the French High Command. It is the most easterly of three rivers flowing roughly parallel, the other two being the Dendre and the Scheldt. On May 10 the B.E.F. crossed the Belgian frontier and advanced to positions on the Dyle stretching from Wavre to beyond Louvain. This operation was completed on May 12, and here until May 16 the British divisions held back the Germans, who had advanced swiftly from Maastricht. Enemy penetration south-west of Louvain was pushed back, but the French 1st Army on the British right flank had lost ground irretrievably, so on the night of May 16 Lord Gort was ordered to withdraw to defences on the Scheldt (*q.v.*), and on May 17 the Germans' thrust through the French armies to the south had turned the line of the Dyle, and Louvain was in their hands. One of the first V.C.s of this war was awarded to Second-Lt. R. W. Annand (*q.v.*) for an act of gallantry in defending a bridge over the Dyle.

Eagle, H.M.S. British aircraft carrier (22,600 tons), carrying 21 aircraft and a complement of 748. She took part in the British naval victory over the Italian Fleet at Taranto, Nov. 11-12, 1940.

Eagle Squadrons. First formed officially on Oct. 8, 1940, from American volunteers, some of whom had already fought in the Air Force in France, they were trained as squadrons in March 1941. They became an operational unit of the R.A.F. Fighter Command and headed the list for Fighter Command successes in October 1941. Flying-Officer C. W. McColpin

Badge of U.S. Eagle Squadron.

of the First Eagle Squadron, was awarded the D.F.C. on Nov. 10, 1941. By Dec. 1, 1941, there were three Eagle Squadrons. In Sept. 1942 they were transferred to the U.S. Army Air Force in Britain.

ENDING THE ITALIAN EMPIRE IN EAST AFRICA

Britain attacked Mussolini's African Empire at several points. The campaign in Abyssinia is described under that heading; here we give a bird's-eye view of the operations on the northern and southern fronts. See also Asmara; Juba River; Keren; Massawa; Mogadishu; Somaliland, etc.

East Africa. Italy's campaign in the summer of 1940 against Great Britain in East Africa was fought over land dry and often waterless, with occasional escarpments, and rivers knee-deep or in spate, in a tropical climate of heat and seasonal torrential rains. In men, machines, equipment, pack animals, guns, and stores of all kinds Italy was incomparably superior to the British. Yet in a far shorter time than the Commander-in-Chief, General Sir Alan Cunningham, had dared to hope, Italy was overwhelmingly defeated.

Why, with two difficult campaigns already on her hands, did Italy launch this African war?

She did so for a number of reasons, strategic and military, and political. The conquest of British Somaliland meant control of the south of the Gulf of Aden and a door to the East.

Eritrea, a triangular territory having a long eastern coastline on the Red Sea, with the fine port of Massawa capable of taking the largest ships, had a very special place in the total African dream of Il Duce. A waterless and torrid zone, it was of first importance as a " jumping-off ground " for military operations. If the Italians were able to penetrate so swiftly into the Sudan, into Kenya, and to annex British Somaliland, it was because in Eritrea they had three divisions, and in East Africa altogether no fewer than 64,000 well-equipped and well-trained troops.

The Italians launched their assault out of the Abyssinian highlands and massed 20,000 men and 48 guns on the River Juba, capturing Moyale on June 28, 1940.

By August 1940 the Italian forces had entered the Sudan and British Somaliland and had occupied Gallabat and Kassala (July 4). Kurmuk, south of Gallabat, fell on the 7th and British Moyale on the Kenya border on July 14, the Italians invading Kenya 30 miles south.

On August 4 the Italians invaded British Somaliland. This move coincided with a change of command in French Somaliland, due to the negotiations that were going on between France and Italy for an armistice— a serious adverse development for Allied strategy in this part of the world. The armed forces of French Somaliland constituted more than half of those on which the Allies had counted; and the Franco-Italian negotiations had immobilized them. The Italians advanced in considerable strength in three columns, one moving on Odweina, another on Hargeisa, the third towards Garagara. They occupied Zeila on August 5 without opposition, our troops having previously withdrawn. Next day Odweina fell. Hargeisa was captured by a strong Italian force which included tanks, artillery, machine-guns, and aircraft; and the Italian advance continued towards Berbera. Our forces were comparatively weak, but as they fell back they did the maximum damage possible to the enemy. The R.A.F. kept up attacks from the air, and units of the British navy bombarded Italian positions near Zeila. On August 19 the British evacuated Berbera, and the Italians marched in. Two days later it was reported that the British force had reached Aden safely with the bulk of its equipment and material.

For the time being, land fighting in that area was at an end, but air activity continued. At Mogadishu, in Italian Somaliland, 1,000 motor lorries were destroyed in one raid by the South African Air Force. Agordat, Asmara, Massawa, Assab, Kismayu, Diredawa, Javello, Dessie, Metemma : these places and others were constantly attacked by our bombers.

The end of the rainy season brought renewed land fighting. At the beginning of November Gallabat was recaptured by the British, and though it changed hands again half a dozen times, it fell finally to our forces on Jan. 21, 1941. In early November 1940 Italian shipping in the Juba River (Italian Somaliland) was bombed. A little later British naval forces were bombarding Mogadishu and Kismayu. On Dec. 16 El Wak, a small but important enemy forward position on the Italian Somaliland frontier, was captured by African troops. Patrol activity was intensified in the Gallabat region, and on Jan. 19 the British re-occupied Kassala. The Italians, evacuating not only Kassala but strongly defended positions round about it, began to retreat into Eritrea, closely followed by the British. On Jan. 26 it was reported in Cairo that the British had captured Biscia and were pressing on towards Agordat, which fell on Feb. 1, and Barentu, evacuated by the Italians on Feb. 2. At Agordat the hundreds of prisoners, many guns, and much mechanical transport captured indicated that this action was much more than an affair of frontier patrols.

In January, too, began the rising in the Gojjam (western Abyssinia) of Abyssinian Patriots, trained and organized by a small band of British officers who had been in the country secretly since the previous July. Enemy detachments which had established themselves on the Kenya side of the Abyssinia-Kenya border were driven back across the frontier by intensive patrol activities, and before January was out South African troops had captured Gorai and Hobok, some ten miles inside the Abyssinian border from Kenya.

In February 1941 the East African Force went into action to retrieve the main situation. Far from formidable, it possessed one quality the enemy lacked, namely, the will to victory. All concerned with this brief war are unanimous : the Italian morale was exceedingly low, so that the advantage of superior numbers and equipment was more or less cancelled out.

Other factors also came into play—for example, the supremely fine work and high technical standard of the South African Sappers, who everywhere performed miracles of engineering. The South African troops and the Nigerian Brigade also turned out first-class fighting men, the King's African Rifles adding fresh laurels to its colours.

Basing his strategy on the logic of the relative strength of the two forces, the British commander-in-chief decided to make the port of Kismayu, in Italian Somaliland, his objective. By the end of March the campaign was completed.

It began with the re-occupation of Kurmuk in the Sudan on Feb. 14, after which no Italians remained on the soil of Egypt, the Sudan, or Kenya except as prisoners. Afmadu (Italian Somaliland) was captured on the 11th. At Kismayu, captured on the 14th, five Italian merchant ships fell into our hands, four others scuttled themselves, and two German ships were destroyed. A week later the Juba River had been crossed by the 12th African Division, and Jumbo at its mouth was captured. " Hit them ; hit them hard and hit them again," was Lt.-Gen. A. G. Cunningham's order of the day at Juba River, and hit them again and again the British forces did. Brava, some 100 miles up the coast, was taken on Feb. 24 by West African troops. South Africans of the 11th African Division captured Gelib, about 60 miles up the Juba River. Mogadishu fell on the 25th, and resistance in Italian Somaliland came to an end. By bombarding to a carefully arranged time-table important Italian positions along the coast, the Navy had been able to render considerable help. The fall of Mogadishu brought release to a number of interned British seamen whose ships had been sunk by raiders based on that port.

From Mogadishu our troops turned northwards into Abyssinia, capturing Dagga Bur on March 10 and Jijiga on the 17th. On March 16 British troops, in cooperation with the Royal Navy and the R.A.F., made two successful landings by moonlight at Berbera, and took that port. Hargeisa was recaptured on the 20th by troops advancing from Abyssinia, and four days later it was announced in Cairo that British Somaliland was again under British control, and the road from Hargeisa to Berbera was open.

The tactics employed were simple, but effective. Our forces followed the retreating enemy and, whenever he came upon a prepared position and occupied it, they cut off his retreat and dealt with him.

Meanwhile, British troops continued to advance in Eritrea. Mersa Taclai and Karora were occupied. Cub-Cub was captured with the cooperation of Free French forces on Feb. 23. Keren fell on March 27.

The natural stronghold of Keren was regarded by the Duke of Aosta as essential to resistance in Eritrea. To it he sent his finest troops — Bersaglieri, Alpini, Grenadiers. The British force faced appalling natural obstacles, for Keren is pitched in a cup of rock on the Eritrean escarpment ringed by towering ridges rising nearly perpendicularly from the plain and topped by arrow-head peaks. It was up these ramparts that our troops had to make their assault.

Lines of British advance in Italian East Africa.

INDIAN TROOPS TAKE OVER IN ERITREA

Asmara, the capital of Eritrea, was captured on April 1, 1941, when British and Indian infantry swept victoriously down the road from Keren in the wake of the retreating Italians.

Photo, British Official

Italian engineers had blasted roads through this rock mass to the hidden town above. And Keren had to be taken by assault against fire from the dominating peaks, which carried gun positions covering every point below. The battle opened with an intense barrage and bombing on March 15, 1941, the R.A.F. unloading 120 tons of bombs on the town in 12 days. Luck was with the British, for fog cloaked their assault on the seven main peaks. The heights once stormed, the town surrendered.

British armoured troops followed the broken Italian army across the Eritrean escarpment as fast as wheels could take them. Asmara, the capital, fell on April 1, nearly 5,000 prisoners (4,000 of them Italians) being taken. With the fall of Massawa on April 8 resistance ended in Eritrea, and all the Imperial and Allied forces at Lt.-Gen. Cunningham's disposal could be concentrated on the Abyssinian campaign, which had already been progressing rapidly. (*See* Abyssinia.) It was concluded in effect with the fall of Amba Alagi (*q.v.*) on May 20, and Italy's East African Empire had crumbled like an insubstantial dream.

Had the Italians given battle on the Juba they might have driven the British from the river bridgehead and thus halted the dry-rot which was already weakening their troops. By their lack of enterprise on the Juba they virtually threw away the campaign.

Campaigns fought over terrains of this kind, and in tropical conditions, commonly involve major problems of hygiene, for some of the country over which our troops had to fight was fever-laden. They had, moreover, to endure campaigning in the dreaded rainy season. Yet care, plus initial physical fitness, proved that white men can come through the worst tropical conditions with good health.

Two other factors played an important part in the dramatic success of this campaign. The first was the outstanding handling of the Q (quartermaster's) branch. At no time did Q fail to mobilize all necessary transport for big moves, and never once was strategy embarrassed by lack of mobility. Last, the campaign was fought by troops of outstanding fighting qualities, backed by the South African Air Force and highly specialized details such as road-builders, water-finding companies and first-class medical services. It may be said, and with truth, that the East African campaign, under the generalship of Cunningham, owed much if not almost everything to South Africa's contribution.

In December 1941 it was decided that Eritrea should be used as a United States war base, particularly for the assembly, maintenance and repair of U.S. aeroplanes and tanks, but there was no question of America taking over the colony. Partial control of the Eritrean railways would facilitate U.S. activities under the Lease-Lend Act.

Eastbourne. Up to the end of May 1942 Eastbourne had suffered more than sixty raids of the tip-and-run variety, during which a total exceeding six hundred high explosive bombs were dropped. The death roll was relatively slight. During the daylight raids in May 1942 certain of the main streets were subjected to machine-gunning, and a church was destroyed by fire.

Eastwood, LT.-GEN. THOMAS RALPH, D.S.O. (b. 1890). G.O.C.-in-C. Northern Command from May 17, 1941. He had been Director-General of the Home Guard from 1940.

E-boat. This term, standing for the German "Eilboot," meaning speed-boat, is applied to German and Italian motor torpedo craft used by the enemy to

SPOILS OF WAR AT NAIROBI

Italy's losses in the campaign that resulted in the end of her East African Empire were enormous, both in men and materials. Here captured enemy guns, guarded by native soldiers, are being shown to the interested population of Nairobi.

Photo, British Official

NAZI E-BOAT AT SPEED

Germany's motor torpedo boats, which on occasion were troublesome in the Channel, had the advantage of low visibility and high speed. They were able to sight even a small coasting vessel while remaining inconspicuous themselves, and were clever at using smoke screens for both attack and escape.

attack British convoys in the English Channel and the Mediterranean. German E-boats are designed to carry a crew of 19 officers and men. They lie very low

in the water. In addition to torpedoes, they are armed with 1½-in. automatic shell guns, have a range of about 600 miles and are driven by Diesel engines. They were particularly active around Britain in July 1940, and were met in the Channel on many occasions. Italian E-boats are of a type classed as Motoscafi Anti-Sommergibili (Anti-Submarine Boats). They have a range of some 250 miles, are manned by a crew of about 12, and carry an armament of shell-firing automatic guns, in addition to two side-firing torpedo tubes. Their speed is about 45 knots.

Éboué, ADOLPHE FÉLIX SYLVESTRE (b. 1884). Negro Governor - General of French Equatorial Africa from Nov. 16, 1940. In 1936 he was Governor of Guadeloupe, having the distinction of being the first native functionary to rise to this rank. He became Governor of Chad in 1938, and while holding this post declared, on August 26, 1940, for Gen. de Gaulle and the cause of Free France. *See* Equatorial Africa, French.

A. F. S. Éboué,
Governor-General
of French
Equatorial Africa.

BRITAIN'S ECONOMIC WAR AGAINST HER FOES

Paralysis of the enemy's war machinery by blockading and buying up raw materials and supplies of every kind constituted a weapon of a very deadly potency used by the Allies. It included R.A.F. attacks on industrial plants and centres. See also Atlantic, Battle of.

Economic Warfare. One of Britain's chief offensive weapons against Germany was put to use from the first day of the war—the weapon of blockade. Under the more comprehensive, and more correct, name of economic warfare, its function was to starve the enemy of economic resources of every sort—raw materials for munitions, oil, grain, fats, cotton, and every imported commodity that might be useful to the enemy's war machine. It aimed at " attacking the industrial, financial and economic structure of the enemy, and thus so to cripple and enfeeble his armed forces that they can no longer effectively carry on the war." That was the description given by Mr. (later Sir) Ronald Cross, first head of the Ministry of Economic Warfare, a Government department set up Sept. 3, 1939.

The ability to wage economic warfare was provided principally by Britain's undisputed command of the sea. At the beginning of the war a number of contraband control stations was established at which Allied and neutral ships were searched for enemy-destined goods that had been declared contraband of war. Such cargoes were seized and dealt with by the Prize Court under international law.

At first the blockade applied only to goods imported by Germany, but at the end of November 1939 an export blockade was announced as a reprisal for Germany's many violations of international law at sea. From Dec. 4 German exports in neutral ships were liable to confiscation. At this time, except for her North Sea coast and the frontier with France, Germany was bounded by neutral countries whose good will Britain was anxious to retain. Every effort was made not to interfere with the legitimate trade of these countries, and, with a view to avoiding shipping

delays and simplifying the work at the contraband control stations, a system of control at the port of shipment was instituted in the case of certain countries. This enabled traders to give advance information concerning cargoes and to obtain a form of passport, called a navicert, for legitimate cargoes. In addition, war trade agreements designed to fulfil the same purposes were negotiated with some countries. However, in spite of the vigilance of the Royal Navy and the control authorities, with so many possible loopholes through the neutral countries—which included Italy—there were leakages in the blockade.

A secondary arm of economic warfare at this stage was the buying up of supplies in neutral European countries so as to prevent their going to Germany.

With the German conquests in Europe in the spring of 1940, and Italy's entry into the war, the methods of the blockade had to be completely altered. At the same time Germany's economic position was greatly eased in many ways, some only temporarily, by her acquisition of considerable stocks of imported materials as well as the natural products of the conquered countries. But the blockade of enemy-occupied Europe became almost complete. The conquered countries and their industries had to be run without the overseas supplies they were formerly permitted.

The spring and summer of 1940 saw another extension of Britain's economic warfare—the attack on the enemy's industrial resources in direct form, for the steadily increasing offensive of the R.A.F. had begun. Some of the targets of the night bombers were purely military, but others were planned in close cooperation with the Ministry of Economic Warfare—transport, oil refineries and other industrial plant. The positive arm in the form of bombs struck where the indirect arm of blockade had created a weak point for the blow.

The adjustment of the blockade machinery to the new European situation involved an extension of the ideas which had led to the introduction of navicerts. Control at the source became the fundamental principle. The contraband control stations that had been set up in the Orkneys and at the Downs on the south-east coast of England were closed at the end of May 1940 and two months later a compulsory navicert system was introduced. All cargo bound for European and North African ports not covered by navicerts was declared liable to seizure. When navicerts had been obtained for all items of cargo, a ship's navicert was granted at the last port of loading, and any neutral vessel sailing without this document was presumed to be carrying contraband and was treated accordingly. At the same time a new system of " ship-warrants " was established.

This ensured that only those shipowners who guaranteed to carry navicerted cargo should enjoy world-wide British facilities such as bunkering, insurance, etc. If one ship of a fleet tried to run the blockade, the warrants for the whole of the fleet were cancelled.

Europe Isolated from the World

As Germany added to her land conquests and penetrations in 1941, so the isolation of the continent of Europe from the rest of the world became complete, the last contact being closed with the attack on Russia in June 1941. By the end of the year neutral shipping trading to Europe had practically disappeared, for the Greek and Yugoslav fleets were in Allied service, Finland was an enemy, and Sweden had long since been permitted by the belligerents to conduct only a strictly limited trade through the North Sea. With such complete constriction many important commodities were in short supply, and others were unobtainable once stocks had been consumed. And for the first time Germany embarked on a reckless expenditure of materials in the Russian war, while the force of the British bombing increased. The situation resembled, except in tempo, that described in memorable words by the American naval historian, Admiral Mahan, in reviewing the Napoleonic war after Trafalgar:

Amid all the pomp and circumstance of the war which for ten years to come desolated the Continent, amid all the tramping to and fro over Europe of the French armies and their auxiliary legions, there went on unceasingly that noiseless pressure upon the vitals of France, that compulsion whose silence, when once noted, becomes to the observer the most striking and awful mark of the working of Sea Power.

Books to Consult: Economic Warfare 1939–40, Paul Einzig (Macmillan). Battle for Supplies, E. V. Francis (Cape).

Anthony Eden,
Foreign Secretary
Photo, Topical Press

Eden, Rt. Hon. (Robert Anthony, p.c. (b. 1897). British Foreign Secretary. He succeeded Viscount Halifax in December 1940. In February 1941 he went to Cairo, Ankara and Athens with Gen. Sir J. Dill for discussions with military chiefs on the war in the Near and Middle East. In December 1941 he was in Moscow discussing war plans with Stalin and Molotov, and in May 1942 he negotiated the Treaty of Alliance between Great Britain and Russia. Mr. Eden had served as Secretary of State for Dominion Affairs, 1939–40, and as Minister for War in 1940.

Edmondson, Cpl. John Hurst, v.c. Australian soldier. One of a party of seven that made an attack on April 13–14, 1941, on German infantry which had penetrated the wire defences at Tobruk, Cpl. Edmondson, though wounded, continued to advance under heavy fire and killed one enemy with his bayonet. Later he saved his officer's life by killing two more of the enemy, but he himself died of wounds. For this heroic act Cpl. Edmondson was posthumously awarded the V.C., the first to be won by an Australian during the present war.

Edwards, Actg. Wing-Cmdr. Hughie Idwal, v.c. Though handicapped by a physical disability resulting from a flying accident, Wing-Cmdr. Edwards repeatedly displayed gallantry of the highest order. On July 4, 1941, while leading an important daylight attack on the port of Bremen, he brought his formation 50 miles overland to the target, flying at a height of little more than 50 feet,

Wing.-Cmdr. Edwards,
Awarded the V.C.
Photo, Wide World

although aware that he had been sighted. After passing through a formidable balloon barrage he was met with a hail of fire over Bremen, and all the aircraft were hit, four being destroyed. Wing-Cmdr. Edwards, however, made a successful attack, and with great skill and coolness withdrew the surviving aircraft without further loss. He was awarded the V.C.

Egypt. Egyptian affairs during the Second World War were largely determined by the Treaty of August 26, 1936, which ended the British occupation and

Egypt, showing its relation to Libya and to the Levant. *By Courtesy of "The Manchester Guardian"*

substituted an alliance based upon the idea of Egypt for the Egyptians.

The country, including the Libyan Desert and the region between the Nile and the Red Sea, covers about 380,000 square miles, but the cultivated and settled area covers only about 14,000 miles on the banks of the Nile. The war area was practically confined to the Libyan Desert country, though occasional air raids were staged by the Germans and Italians upon Alexandria and the suburbs of Cairo. These caused some damage and loss of life, and the British Government announced that they would make reprisals upon Rome if Cairo was bombed.

Under the terms of the Treaty of 1936 Britain retained an army of 10,000 troops and 400 aircraft in the Canal zone, and provision was also made for military cooperation in the Sudan, under the condominium proclaimed in 1899, whereby the British and Egyptian flags were flown jointly in the Sudan. With the outbreak of war the British garrison defending the Suez Canal was greatly increased, particularly by expeditionary forces from Australia and New Zealand. In compliance with the Treaty Egypt also put her ports, Alexandria and Port Said, at the disposal of the British fleet, and Germans were interned. Thus Egypt was not a neutral State, though she was not formally at war with Germany.

How Marshal Balbo Died

Active warlike operations in Egypt began after June 10, 1940, when Italy entered the conflict. At first there was frontier fighting on the Libyan-Egyptian border, an early incident being the death of Marshal Balbo, Governor of Libya, who was officially stated on June 29, 1940, to have been killed " during an air battle near Tobruk." In fact, Balbo was shot down by Italian gunners and this was later admitted.

The Italian army was massed on the Egyptian frontier in August 1940 and crossed the frontier in September, occupying the Egyptian settlements of Sollum and Sidi Barrani, while the British defending force fell back to Mersa Matruh. These relative positions were held until General Wavell's surprise attack was launched in December, 1940, obviously anticipating an attack upon Egypt which Marshal Graziani, the Italian commander, had been ordered to execute. After the German counter-offensive of April, 1941, the Italo-German forces under General Rommel were halted at Sollum and Fort Capuzzo. Danger to the frontier and the Canal zone temporarily ceased when General Auchinleck launched the second Libyan campaign in November 1941. For Rommel's advance into Egypt in June 1942 *see* North Africa.

Early in February 1942 a Cabinet crisis arose over the question of the Royal prerogative, the King claiming that he had not been properly consulted when the Government broke off relations with Vichy early in January. The Prime Minister, Hussein Pasha Sirry, thereupon resigned. Nahas Pasha, leader of the Wafdist Party, took office as Prime Minister, the appointment giving great satisfaction in both British and Egyptian circles. In his new Cabinet he also held the offices of Minister of Foreign Affairs and Minister of the Interior. At the elections in March the Wafdists scored a sweeping victory. *See* North Africa.

Eire. Six months before war came Mr. de Valera stated that Eire had no commitments to Britain and that his Government would follow any course which

Irish interests seemed to dictate. That was on Feb. 19, 1939. On May 2 he repeated that the whole responsibility for peace or war rested on the Irish themselves (unlike 1914, when it rested on the Government in London), and " it was a very heavy responsibility indeed." In accord with these declarations of policy Eire remained a neutral from Sept. 3 onwards, the Nazi Minister staying in Dublin with a large and active staff of spies and stirrers-up of trouble. As a countermeasure Sir John Maffey was sent from London to be " British representative in Ireland."

An Emergency Powers Act was passed by the Dail ; there was a partial mobilization. But the existing forces soon appeared insufficient. In 1940 a Local Security Force was enrolled on the lines of the British Home Guard. Part of this was in 1941 absorbed into the Regular army. The other part was reported towards the end of that year to consist of some 250,000 men. The size and equipment of the Regular army can be judged by its total cost being $3\frac{1}{2}$ million pounds a year. Yet Mr. de Valera declared in a radio address on Dec. 25, 1940, that the island could defend itself if attacked.

An all-party Conference (May 20, 1940) came to no particular conclusions. The idea of a Coalition Ministry was dismissed. Plans were made for regional, county and parish commissioners to take charge in case of invasion, but the suggestion of a joint defence scheme was rejected by Mr. de Valera as impossible while Ireland was divided. If the North came under the Dublin Parliament, the position would change.

In August 1940 a Nazi aircraft dropped bombs at Wexford. Two ships were machine-gunned. Berlin apologized. But in May 1941 there was a raid on Dublin in which 34 were killed and 88 badly injured, while 500 were rendered homeless. Shortages of grain, for bread, of fuel, butter, sugar, tea and cocoa were the subject of a speech by Mr. de Valera on March 29, 1941. He urged extension of cultivated land. Rationing and price fixing were introduced. The U.S. Red Cross Relief Fund sent £100,000 worth of food, but America refused to sell armaments. On Nov. 7, 1941, the suggestion that the West Coast ports handed over by Mr. Chamberlain—Cobh (Queenstown), Berehaven and Lough Swilly—should be leased either by Britain or the U.S.A. was dismissed by Mr. de Valera as out of the question. His Minister in Washington said on Jan. 7, 1942, he hoped the United States would not press Eire to grant the Allies naval or air bases—which showed that some notion of this sort was in the air.

Eisenhower, Lt.-Gen. Dwight D. In command U.S. Forces in Europe, June 1942 (*see* p. 448).

Elias, Gen. Alois. Prime Minister of the Czech puppet Govt. of Bohemia and Moravia. Following the appointment of Gen. Heydrich as Deputy Protector in September 1941, in succession to Baron von Neurath, Gen. Elias was arrested on a charge of " plotting high treason." He was taken to Berlin and tried by the National Court. Sentence of death was passed but was not carried out until June 19, 1942.

Elizabeth, Queen Consort of King George VI (b. 1900). Long before war broke out the Queen was actively engaged in furthering the cause of Britain, and the alliance of the North American Continent with our country may owe much to the visit made by the King and Queen to Canada, Newfoundland and the United States in May and June, 1939. Her Majesty's

WAR MAP OF EUROPE &
THE MIDDLE EAST

GREAT BRITAIN
GERMAN OR GERMAN OCCUPIED TERRITORIES PRIOR TO SEPT. 1939
AXIS COUNTRIES 1942 WITH DATES OF ADHESION TO AXIS
GERMAN & AXIS OCCUPIED TERRITORIES 1942 WITH DATES OF CONQUEST
VICHY FRANCE
PRO-ALLY COUNTRIES
NEUTRAL "
RUSSIA (U.S.S.R.)

SCALE 100 50 0, 100 200 300 400 500 MILES

Specially prepared for this work

STANFORD, LONDON.

ready sympathy, lack of ceremony, and true understanding endeared her there to men and women in every walk of life, and these qualities have been in still greater evidence during the hazardous days of war. In September 1940 bombs fell on four occasions on her London home, Buckingham Palace, and with the King she replied to a Cabinet message : " Like so many other people we have now had a personal experience of German barbarity which only strengthens the resolution of us all to fight through to final victory."

The Queen was untiring in her efforts to help the national cause and made several visits to the poorer London districts that had suffered from air raids. With the King she toured many of the large provincial areas that had been bombed, comforting the sufferers by the sincerity of her sympathy and receiving an enthusiastic welcome wherever she went. The Queen made several broadcasts to women. On Nov. 11, 1939, she addressed a message full of understanding to all women of the Empire engaged in national service of whatever kind ; on June 14, 1940, she spoke (in French) to the suffering mothers and wives of France ; and on August 10, 1941, she broadcast to the women of America, thanking them for their work on behalf of Britain. As Commandant-in-Chief of the Women's Navy, Army and Air Force Services, the Queen made many inspections of units belonging to these Services. *See* illustration, page 131 in this volume.

Elles, Maj.-Gen. Sir Hugh Jamieson, k.c.b. (b. 1880). Regional Commissioner for S.W. England. He was Chief of Operational Staff of the Civil Defence Services in 1940.

Elliot, Rt. Hon. Walter, p.c., m.c. (b. 1888). He was Minister of Health from May 1938 to May 1940. In January 1941 he was appointed Director of Public Relations at the War Office. This position he relinquished in December 1941, as it was decided to amalgamate it with that of Senior Military Adviser to the Ministry of Information, and Maj.-Gen. the Hon. E. F. Lawson was appointed to the combined post.

Elverum. Town of Norway, at the mouth of the Oesterdal, the easternmost of the great Norwegian valleys. It is an important railway junction on the Oslo-Trondheim line. German bombers reduced the town to ruins in mid-April 1940 as an act of vengeance following King Haakon's refusal to hand over Norway to Nazi control. The King removed to Elverum from Hamar with the Norwegian Government on April 11, narrowly escaping bombing and machine-gun attacks by the enemy, for 50 people were killed and 100 wounded during an intense raid.

Emden. Seaport and town of Germany, near the mouth of the R. Ems. It is the terminus of the Dortmund-Ems canal (*q.v.*), and is an important naval base. Emden was repeatedly attacked by the R.A.F., and was the first place in Germany to receive the new type of heavy bomb. Two were dropped on the night of March 31–April 1, 1941. On June 6, 19 and 20, 1942, Emden was heavily bombed, the raid of June 20 being the 76th R.A.F. attack on the town.

Emden. This German light cruiser of 5,400 tons was named after the successful German commerce raider in the last war. Built in 1925, she was one of Germany's first attempts to create a new navy, and latterly was used as a training ship for cadets. It was reported on April 10, 1940, that she had been sunk by the Norwegian minelayer Olav Tryggvason.

Emergency Powers Act. An emergency session of Parliament, following on the Cabinet communiqué of August 22, 1939, took place on August 24, when statements on the international situation were made by Mr. Chamberlain in the House of Commons and by Lord Halifax in the House of Lords. Both Houses passed the Emergency Powers Act, conferring wide powers on the Government in time of emergency, through all its stages. Defence regulations under this Act were issued on August 28.

Emirau. This island in the South Seas, north of the Bismarck Archipelago, off New Guinea, came into the news in December 1940. Six British ships and one Norwegian had been caught by German raiders in the South Pacific during the last four months of that year. These ships were : Komata, Rangitane, Holmwood, Triona, Triaster, Triadic, and the Norwegian Vinni. Some 500 survivors were imprisoned for weeks in a German supply ship, the Tokyo Maru, where, it was admitted, their treatment was fairly good. On Dec. 21 they were landed on Emirau, the German commander making sure that there was a plentiful supply of fresh

CASTAWAYS ON A SOUTH SEA ISLAND
About 500 survivors from ships sunk in the Pacific by German raiders were landed on the island of Emirau on Dec. 21, 1940, where for four days they led a primitive life. This photograph, taken by a member of the Rangitane crew, shows the impromptu huts made along the foreshore by the victims and friendly natives.
Photo, Sport & General

EMPIRE AIR TRAINING IN PROGRESS

Contingent of Royal Canadian Air Force pilots at Camp Borden, Ontario, marching past a line of Yale training 'planes after the presentation of their wings. At the outbreak of war the R.C.A.F. comprised 3,800 officers and men. In less than two years this was increased to 68,000, of whom 30,000 were under the Air Training Scheme.

Photo, Sport & General

Employment Order. The first registration of women for war work under this Order took place on April 19, 1941, when 429,820 women of 20 years of age registered. One purpose of the registration was to find recruits for the nursing and auxiliary services, N.A.A.F.I. and Women's Land Army. On May 3 281,961 women of 21 registered. On Oct. 10 it was announced that registration for women would be fortnightly. Mr. Bevin stated on Sept. 5 that 200,000 women would be needed for the A.T.S. and another 500,000 for vital war work during the next 12 months.

Empress of Britain. British liner of 42,348 tons, the flagship of the Canadian Pacific fleet. She was attacked on Oct. 26, 1940, by German aircraft, first with machine-guns and then with incendiary bombs which set her afire amidships, before being finally sunk by a U-boat. Her commander, Capt. Sapsworth,

water on the island. Food and shelter proved inadequate, for there are only a little over 200 inhabitants on Emirau, but the natives helped to build emergency huts for the castaways. The marooned passengers were rescued four days later and landed at a North Australian port.

Empire Air Training Scheme. An important agreement between Great Britain, Canada, Australia and New Zealand was signed three months after the declaration of war. It provided for the training of airmen from these Dominions and Britain at stations established in New Zealand, Australia and Canada, but principally the last, owing to its size and proximity to Britain. In Canada the air-training establishments were subdivided into elementary and service flying-schools, observer, navigation, bombing and gunnery schools, engineering and technical training schools. The first pilots completed their training during October 1940, and arrived in England for operational training in December. Australian and New Zealand schools cater only for pupils in those two countries. The Scheme in Canada has four commands, at Toronto, Winnipeg, Montreal and Regina. At Trenton, Ontario, instructors are turned out from the central training school. It was estimated in February 1941 that at full output the Training Scheme would produce 20,000 pilots and 30,000 air crews a year. In May 1942 it was announced that this figure had been considerably exceeded. The United Nations Air-training Conference was held at Ottawa in May, and marked an important stage in the development of Allied air planning and strategy.

END OF A FAMOUS LINER

The Empress of Britain, the stately Canadian Pacific ship which brought the King and Queen back to England after their visit to the U.S.A. and Canada in 1939, was set on fire by enemy aircraft and finally sunk by a U-boat on Oct. 26, 1940.

Photo, Keystone

remained on board until the decks were awash. In 1939 she brought King George and Queen Elizabeth back to England after their tour in Canada and the U.S.A.

Ensa. (Entertainments National Service Association). At the outbreak of war this organization was ready to begin its work, the headquarters being at Drury Lane Theatre, London. By Sept. 25, 1939, twelve fully equipped concert parties were touring camps in Britain. Four camp halls equipped for cinema and living performances were opened in 1939. Today it is possible for Ensa companies, presenting all types of entertainment, to spend more than nine months in visiting these semi-permanent entertainment halls without repeating a single visit. An ever larger number of companies go to the smaller units, playing in hired halls, N.A.A.F.I. hostels, or wherever it is possible to gather the men together. The total number of entertainments given in France was roughly 5,500, attended by 2,242,559 persons. A regular service of cinema and living entertainment is maintained for troops in Iceland, Gibraltar, West Africa and the Middle East. *See* Badges, page 33.

Equatorial Africa, French. Forming a vast block of territory of over 900,000 sq. miles, with a population of nearly 3,500,000, French Equatorial Africa consists of Gabun (cap. Libreville), Middle Congo (cap. Brazzaville), Ubangi-Shari (cap. Bangui) and Chad (cap. Fort Lamy). Adjoining on the north-west is French Cameroons, 166,000 sq. miles, with a population of some 2,500,000. The whole of this vast area forms part of the Empire of Free France, having broken with the Vichy Government in August 1940.

This African group of colonies is of great strategical interest. Its coast-line stretches for some 600 miles, and it contains a number of up-to-date ports such as Libreville, Port Gentil, Pointe Noire and Douala. The two latter are equipped with jetties and quays in deep water. With British West and East Africa this group forms a solid block of Allied territory across the continent from the Atlantic to the Red Sea, thus providing a vital life-line from Britain and America to the Middle East. After the break-away from Vichy, it was possible to move men and war materials by motor-truck and aeroplane from one side of the continent to the other without fear of effective enemy interference.

After the autumn of 1940 several great strategic roads were built in the colony, the most important of these being (a) from Douala through Ubangi-Shari and Fort Lamy to Khartoum, and (b) from Douala through Ubangi-Shari to Bahr-el-Gazal in the Southern Sudan. A further important link was the road running from Douala through Bangui to Juba, whence supplies could be diverted through Kenya to Mombasa on the Indian Ocean. These roads provided routes by which the Allies could be reinforced, not only in Egypt, but as far south as Kenya. Stores and equipment landed at Douala could be dispatched to the Middle East across the vast stretch of territory instead of

by the long and more hazardous route round the Cape. Two tributaries of the Congo were also spanned by concrete bridges, and these ambitious constructional works constituted a "Burma Road" across Africa, supplementing the existent aerial route. The result was that the interior of French Equatorial Africa, hitherto impenetrable, could be reached from the coast by car or lorry in four or five days in all seasons.

Commercially this great colony is of immense potential importance, for it abounds in rich tropical produce. The principal crops are cocoa, coffee, cotton, palm kernels, palm oil, ground nuts, and timber. There are also minerals such as tin ore, plumbago, wolfram, mica, iron ore and gold. Gabun is rich in timber, and in normal times exports some 400,000 tons per annum, almost all of which before the war was sent to Germany. In October 1940 agreements were entered into by the British Government with Gen. de Gaulle's representatives for the purchase of a large part and, in certain instances, of the whole yield of crops. Owing to this arrangement not only were all sections of the native community ensured a livelihood, but the Allies were guaranteed considerable quantities of essential goods. Some of the food supplies derived from French Equatorial Africa were conserved in readiness for the day when France herself would be liberated.

In August 1941 it was reported that Gen. de Gaulle had invited America to make use of the ports of Pointe Noire, Douala and Port Gentil. Fort Lamy, situated south of Lake Chad, constituted the strong point of the territory. It was from Fort Lamy that roads stretched out to Kano, railway terminus from Lagos, port in British Nigeria, to Abeche, Fort Archambault, Carnot and Yaunde. The Axis recognized the importance of this centre and attacked it with aircraft. These attacks were both long and costly to the enemy, however, for the nearest Axis air base was at Ghadames, about 1,500 miles distant.

Situated in the territory were numerous air bases and modern aerodromes, enabling Britain to maintain

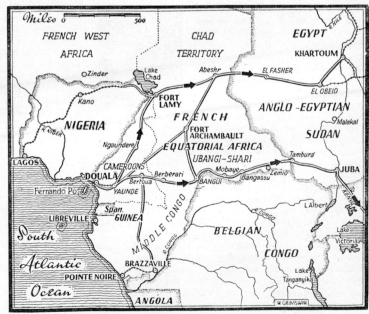

French Equatorial Africa, showing ports and roads

regular communication between West Africa on the one side, and Egypt, Kenya and the Sudan on the other.

When France capitulated to Germany in June 1940 military preparedness in the French Cameroons and French Equatorial Africa was extremely weak. After August 1940, however, that deficiency was made up rapidly. Brazzaville (*q.v.*), capital of the Free French Middle Congo, became the receiving station for ever-increasing supplies of men and materials. From Brazzaville, too, went the Free French troops who distinguished themselves in Libya and Eritrea.

Book to Consult : Watch Over Africa, Denis Saurat (Dent).

Eritrea. *See* East Africa.

Ervine-Andrewes, CAPT. HAROLD MARCUS, V.C. (b. 1911). This officer of the East Lancs. Regiment was awarded the V.C. on July 30, 1940, for outstanding bravery, tenacity and devotion to duty at Dunkirk.

Capt. H. M. Ervine-Andrewes, awarded V.C. after Dunkirk.
Photo,
"Daily Mirror"

On the night of May 31–June 1 Capt. Ervine-Andrewes took over about a thousand yards of the defences in front of Dunkirk. For over ten hours, despite artillery, mortar and machine-gun fire, and in the face of superior enemy forces, he and his company held their position. He himself accounted for 17 of the enemy with his rifle and for many more with a Bren gun. When the house from which he was engaging the enemy was set alight, and all his ammunition was gone, he sent back his wounded in the one remaining carrier, collected the remaining eight men from this forward position and, although almost completely surrounded, led them safely back to cover.

Escaut. French name of the River Scheldt (*q.v.*).

Esmonde, LIEUT.–COMMANDER EUGENE, V.C., D.S.O. Decorated by the King for a previous exploit only the day before the action which cost him his life and for which he was awarded a posthumous V.C., this gallant officer's supreme courage is made clear from the following extract from the official announcement of the award : " On the morning of Feb. 12, 1942, Lieut.-Commander Esmonde, in command of a squadron of the Fleet Air Arm, was told that the German warships, Scharn-horst, Gneisenau (*q.v.*), and Prinz Eugen, strongly escorted by some 30 surface craft, were entering the Straits of Dover, and that his squadron must attack before they reached the sandbanks N.E. of Calais. Lieut.-Commander Esmonde knew well that his enterprise was desperate. He and his squadron of six Swordfish set course for the enemy, and after ten minutes' fight were attacked by a strong force of enemy fighters. Touch was lost with his fighter escort, and in the action which followed all his aircraft were damaged. He flew on, cool and resolute, serenely challenging hopeless odds, to encounter the deadly fire of the battle-cruisers and their escort, which shattered the port wing of his aircraft. Undismayed, he led his squadron on straight through this inferno of fire, in steady flight towards their target. Almost at once he was shot down, but his squadron went on to launch a

Lt.-Cmr. Esmonde, awarded the V.C.
Central Press

gallant attack in which at least one torpedo is believed to have struck the German battle-cruisers, and from which not one of the six aircraft returned."

Essen. Situated in the Ruhr district, 22 m. north of Düsseldorf, this important industrial town and railway centre is the seat of Germany's armament manufacture. The great Krupp iron and steel works (*see* p. 1841), on which practically the whole of Essen depends, were bombed heavily by the R.A.F. on many occasions. On March 25, 1942, while our bombers were over Germany they obtained photographic confirmation of severe damage done in earlier raids at Essen. On June 1 Essen was the centre of a mass raid on the Ruhr by 1,036 R.A.F. bombers, and was again bombed by a powerful force on June 2.

Estonia. *See* Baltic States.

Europe at War. When War broke out in September 1939 the German Reich had already extended its boundaries by the forcible incorporation of Austria on March 12, 1938, and the piecemeal annexation of Czechoslovakia in 1938–9 (*see* colour map facing p. 104). In September 1939 came the lightning campaign against Poland, followed by the partition of that country between Germany and the U.S.S.R. Beginning on April 9, 1940, the flood-tide of Nazi invasion swept over Scandinavia and the Low Countries, and one by one Denmark, Norway, Luxembourg, Holland and Belgium fell victims to Nazi aggression. Then came the turn of France, which, compelled to capitulate in June 1940, saw half its land occupied by the conqueror and a puppet Government set up at Vichy in the unoccupied area.

Without declaring war the Germans invaded both Greece and Yugoslavia on April 6, 1941. Greece, which had for months successfully resisted the Italian invader, fell to this powerful new enemy at the end of April. Yugoslavia was forced to surrender after twelve days' total war.

On June 22, 1941, came the staggering news that Germany had invaded Soviet Russia, whose territory had been increased by the acquisition in June 1940 of the Baltic States of Estonia, Latvia and Lithuania. This move was a turning-point of the war. Instead of the quick victory promised by Hitler, terrific battles were fought on Soviet soil, and the Nazis, who had advanced considerably in the early months of the war, were, through the winter of 1941–42, slowly but surely pushed back by the Russians with enormous losses in men and equipment. In the summer of 1942 fighting was renewed on a tremendous scale.

Of the remaining countries in Europe, Bulgaria, Hungary and Rumania, all signatories of the Axis Pact, were entirely under Nazi domination. Hungary and Rumania both declaring war on Russia immediately after the German invasion of that country. Finland, too, which had been at war with Russia from November 1939 to March 1940 (the Russo-Finnish War), came in on Germany's side and declared war against her former enemy. Spain, while proclaiming neutrality, was definitely pro-Axis in sympathies, being linked to the Axis in the Anti-Comintern pact. Sweden remained neutral, though to an extent dominated by Germany, who found the iron ore, timber, and meat and dairy produce of Sweden extremely valuable.

But although Hitler had virtually conquered most of Europe by 1941, throughout that year and during the spring of 1942 a war was fought inside Europe—

a desperate war waged by saboteurs and guerillas against the hated invaders. The following powerful passage from the " Economist " gives a vivid picture of the wave of sabotage that spread over Europe, despite ruthless repression and ferocious reprisal. " It is a moving and terrible spectacle—a darkened Europe through which the tramp of the Nazi guards re-echoes and their voices ring into the night, challenging every sound and movement ; and behind this façade of vigilance a host of nameless men, working in silence with pliers and saws and acetylene flares, pulling at the proud structure, dislocating here a line, there a dynamo, there a storage plant, like death-watch beetles in the floor of Europe." *See* separate countries and campaigns under their own headings *and* Colour Map *facing* page 104.

Evacuation of Schoolchildren. On Sept. 4, 1939, the exodus of schoolchildren from the London area began. For four days the great migration continued, and 376,652 schoolchildren, accompanied by their teachers, left the metropolis. In addition, 275,895 young children went away to safety areas under the care of their mothers. In the movement away from danger zones in the Provinces there were 757,583 schoolchildren, and 445,580 young children with their mothers. *See* Children's Overseas Reception Board ; City of Benares.

Evzones. Famous kilted soldiers, crack troops of the Greek Army. The bodyguard of the King of the Hellenes was drawn from this regiment. They fought heroically against the Italians in Albania, 1940–41, and against the Germans in Greece in 1941.

GREECE'S FAMOUS KILTED TROOPS
Derived from the ancient Greek term, " euzonoi," meaning " well-girt," the name Evzones is given to a front line regiment of the Greek Army. These were the men who took Koritza at the point of the bayonet.
Photo, Keystone

Exeter. County town of Devonshire (*see* p. 1579). Towards the end of April 1942 the Germans threatened " reprisal " raids on England for the R.A.F.'s heavy bombing of military objectives in Germany. These raids were to be directed against our peaceful and beautiful towns of great historic interest, and not against military targets. Exeter was chosen for the first of these " terror " raids, and on the nights of April 23, 24, and May 3, 1942, it was savagely and ruthlessly bombed by the enemy, who later gloated over the loss of life and damage caused.

EXETER SUFFERS A REPRISAL RAID
This ancient West Country City was bombed three times in the course of Hitler's "Baedeker" raids and many beautiful buildings, including the Cathedral, were damaged. Here are firemen at work in a ruined street.
Photo, Sport & General

The attack on May 3 was particularly heavy ; there was a high casualty list, and many famous buildings, as well as countless homes, were wrecked.

Exeter, H.M.S. British cruiser (8,390 tons). She was completed in May 1931 and recommissioned at the outbreak of war. She carried six 8-in. guns, six 21-in. torpedo tubes, and two aircraft with catapults. Commanded by Capt. F. S. Bell, she took part in the famous action against the Admiral Graf Spee at the Battle of the River Plate, Dec. 12–13, 1939. In company with the British cruisers, Achilles and Ajax, she was engaged in a running fight against the German pocket battleship for 14 hours. Early in the action she was hit by an enemy salvo which knocked out two of her four turrets, and smashed three of her 8-in. guns. She was forced to reduce her speed of 32·5 knots, but succeeded in eventually coming up with the other two cruisers, which by that time were maintaining a nocturnal vigil outside Montevideo harbour, in which the Graf Spee had taken refuge. The next morning she witnessed the ignominious end of the German battleship. On Feb. 15, 1940, Exeter, bearing her heroic crew, steamed into Plymouth Sound, there to receive a great civic welcome and the personal

H.M.S. EXETER—SMALL BUT GALLANT
At the battle of the River Plate, Exeter was hit over 40 times by shells three times the weight of her own. She was lost in the battle of the Java Sea, March 1, 1942.

congratulations of Mr. Churchill. On Feb. 23 officers and men of the Exeter were entertained by the Lord Mayor and Corporation of London. In the fierce battle of the Java Sea, which opened on Feb. 27, 1942, she was hit on the first day, and on March 1, when steaming at half speed, reported sighting enemy cruisers. No further news was received of Exeter, or her companion destroyer Encounter. *See* Java.

Fadden, RT. HON. ARTHUR (b. 1896). Treasurer and former Premier of Australia. He succeeded Mr. Menzies as Premier on August 28, 1941, and resigned from that office five weeks later, after the rejection of his Budget, being succeeded by Mr. Curtin. He became the leader of the Country Party in 1939. After the General Election of September 1940 he was entrusted by Mr. Menzies with the Treasury, a post that he retained on his resignation from the Premiership.

Falkenhorst, GEN. NIKOLAUS VON (b. 1885). German army chief in Norway. C.-in-C. German armies in the northern sector of the Russian front, 1941. In 1939 he fought the Polish campaign, and in 1940 was General of German infantry and C.-in-C. of the German Army in Norway.

F.A.N.Y. (FIRST AID AND NURSING YEOMANRY). *See* Women's Services.

Far East. Geographically a term of some vagueness, it is, for the purposes of this Supplement, to be taken as including that part of the eastern hemisphere east of longitude 60° to a line drawn midway down the Pacific Ocean. The countries or places therein included, which are affected or threatened by war due to aggression of the Japanese, are dealt with under their own headings : Australia ; Borneo ; Burma ; China ; Hong Kong ; India ; Indo-China ; Japan ; Malaya ; Netherlands East Indies ; New Zealand ; Pacific ; Philippines ; Siam ; Singapore. A general discussion of the major campaigns and fighting in the Far East appears under the heading Pacific.

Faroe Islands. This group of 21 islands belong to Denmark, and are situated in the N. Atlantic, about 195 m. N.W. of the Shetlands. They cover an area of 540 sq. m. The largest is Stromo, with the capital, Thorshavn. These islands, of great strategic importance, were occupied by British forces on April 11, 1940, after the German occupation of Denmark.

Fascists, British Union of. On July 11, 1940, it was announced that the Home Office had made an Order banning the British Union (Fascists). The order made it an offence to summon, attend, or advertise meetings of the British Union, or to invite support for the organization. This followed the arrest in May 1940 of Sir Oswald Mosley and many members of the organization. Seven hundred Fascists rioted at their internment camp at Peel, Isle of Man, on Sept. 20, 1941.

Capt. E. S. F. Fegen, V.C., of H.M.S. Jervis Bay.
Photo, J. Hall

Fegen, CAPT. E. S. FOGARTY, V.C. One of the outstanding heroes of the war, Captain Fegen commanded the British auxiliary cruiser H.M.S. Jervis Bay (*q.v.*). Badly wounded in the Jervis Bay's gallant battle against the German raider, he stayed on the bridge until the last, going down with his blazing ship. For his heroic conduct he was awarded a posthumous V.C. on Nov. 16, 1940.

Feisal II. King of Iraq (b. 1935). He succeeded to the throne when his father, King Ghazi, died as the result of an accident in 1939. Until the king comes of age the country is under the regency of his uncle, Emir Abdul Ilah (*q.v.*). He was reported to have been kidnapped by Rashid Ali (*q.v.*) during the Iraqi revolt, but returned to Baghdad on June 1, 1941.

Fifth Column. This phrase dates from the siege of Madrid in the Spanish Civil war, 1936–39, when the Nationalists under Gen. Franco attacked the Republicans in four columns from the outside, while their adherents organized uprisings, espionage and sabotage within the Republican ranks. These secret fighters behind the front were called the fifth column. The activities of such persons in countries attacked or occupied by Axis forces were particularly noticeable in the Netherlands and Norway (*q.v.*), but existed to a greater or less degree in all countries.

Fighter Command. Fighter Squadrons provide the air-borne element of the defence of Great Britain against air attack. Into the headquarters comes all information concerning air war over this country, and out of them go the orders and the warnings that set the air defence system in motion. Fighter Command co-ordinates not only the operations of the Fighter Squadrons, but every other weapon used against the Luftwaffe, including the A.A. guns, balloon barrage, searchlights, and the warnings that go to the Civil Defence system.

The aerodromes under the Command are ranged in sectors which are under the control of Group Headquarters, the Groups themselves being under Command H.Q. An elaborate system of communication connects the whole, and by radio-telephony each sector can control the movements of all fighter pilots in the air.

Operations Rooms at Sector, Group and H.Q. plot all information about hostile machines and at Command H.Q. provide a complete picture of the entire air battle front, there being present representatives of Bomber

Fighter Command Operations
(In and near Britain, 1939–1942)

Date	German losses	British losses	Pilots saved
Oct. 1939–May 1940	57	1	1
1940			
June	24	—	—
July	237	50	6
August	1,101	297	149
September	1,124	319	168
October	246	118	67
November	221*	53	28
December	51	9	8
1941			
January	26	1	—
February	36	6	—
March	71	6	2
April	112	3	—
May	207	18	9
June	52	2	1
July	47	1	—
August	15	—	—
September	11	—	—
October	23	1	—
November	18	—	—
December	13	2	—
1942			
January	10	5	—
February	10	26	—
March	7	28	—
April	30	100	1
May	84	62	2
June–Sept. 3	760 (about)	650 ?	?
Total	4,710 (about)	1,758 ?	442 ?

* Including 20 Italians

and Coastal Commands in direct communication with their own H.Q. In all Operational Stations a squadron is kept in readiness with pilots waiting, able to be in the air three minutes after receiving an order from the Controller. Fighter Command shares with Coastal Command the duty of protecting shipping.

After the decline of the daylight offensive against Britain Fighter Command began to attack, and has continued to attack the enemy in Northern France with increasing force. Daylight sweeps are the principal activity, but the work of the Command includes night raids. The scale of the operations is shown by the fact that as many as 1,000 aircraft in a day have been engaged. Attacks on enemy shipping by fighters armed with shell-firing guns, escorts for bombers, reconnaissance, and opposition to night bombers are among the functions of the Command.

Many Hurricane and Spitfire fighters have been adapted for low-level high-speed bombing, and they carry out effective raids. In May 1942 alone the Command was responsible for 57 daylight operations, each involving one or more squadrons.

Air Chief Marshal Sir Sholto Douglas (q.v.) was appointed A.O.C.-in-C. Fighter Command in 1940. *See* Air Defence; Royal Air Force.

Fiji, H.M.S. This 8,000-ton British cruiser, completed in 1940, was sunk by German aircraft off Crete in May 1941. The Mediterranean Fleet was intercepting convoys of German troops destined for the enemy invasion of Crete. German dive-bombers concentrated furiously on the British ships, and a direct hit forced the Fiji to reduce speed. She went down fighting to the end.

Fiji Islands. *See* Pacific, War in.

FINLAND'S FIGHT AGAINST RUSSIAN INVASION

After the Red Armies crossed the frontier on Nov. 30, 1939, the Finns withstood their onslaught for over three months. The underlying causes are here discussed, as well as the Russian strategy. In 1941 Finland sided with Germany against the Soviet. See Hangö; Karelian Isthmus; Mannerheim; Russia, etc.

Finland. Why did Russia attack Finland in November 1939? Some observers saw in it blatant Russian Imperialism. Others saw Russia's fear of German aggression, against which she was guarding by the acquisition of further strategic bases in the Baltic, like those she had already obtained in the States of Estonia, Latvia and Lithuania. Some people felt that the Russian attitude was justified in view of the proximity to Leningrad of the Finnish frontier, with its immense fortifications, and the dangerous Russophobe tendencies of Finland's military leaders. Yet another view was that Stalin perceived the military

weakness of the democracies and felt that Russia would have to rely entirely on her own strength and what advantages she could acquire without a major conflict to safeguard her future, whatever the outcome of the war between the Allies and Hitler.

Certain it is that Russia's attack on Finland brought her very nearly into war with Britain. Had the war lasted a few weeks longer, considerable British armies might have been helping the Canadian and British airmen sent to the aid of the Finns.

Later historians will speak with greater precision on Soviet policy. The first announcement of the

PART OF THE SPOIL AFTER A FINNISH VICTORY
The Finns' greatest triumph of the war was their destruction of the Soviet 44th Division on the Suomussalmi front, when they also captured an enormous amount of war material, including 40 tanks, some of which are shown above, 100 field guns, 278 motor-cars, armoured cars, field kitchens, and hundreds of small arms, together with ammunition.
Photo, Planet News

FINLAND INVADED AT EIGHT POINTS

Russia launched her invasion along the entire frontier from the Karelian Isthmus to the Rybachi Peninsula in the Arctic Circle, attacks being made on the eight strategic places indicated by arrows. The main and decisive attack was that on the Mannerheim Line. The map also shows, by vertical shading, the areas ceded to the U.S.S.R. at the conclusion of peace   *By courtesy of "The Times"*

negotiations between Russia and Finland came from Helsinki on Oct. 8, 1939. They were resumed on Oct. 21, and, although the conversations were secret, Finland proceeded at once partly to evacuate Helsinki and to mobilize her army.

Russian demands were : (1) A mutual assistance pact with Finland. (2) The moving back of the Finnish frontier on the Isthmus of Karelia. (3) Lease as a naval and air base of the port of Hangö and cession of certain Finnish islands in the Gulf of Finland. (4) Lease of the Rybachi peninsula with Finland's only ice-free port, Petsamo.

Finland's reply was in keeping with the country's tradition. In most of the demands, especially that involving abandonment of her fortifications on the Karelian Isthmus (the so-called Mannerheim Line) and the lease of Hangö, she saw her neutrality and independence menaced. The Soviet offer of compensation in the shape of 2,134 square miles of territory in Soviet Karelia was considered worthless. On Nov. 28 M. Molotov, Soviet Foreign Commissar, who had concluded the Non-Aggression Pact with Germany, denounced the Non-Aggression Pact between Finland and Russia. Two days later, in spite of mediation by the United States, Russia began a military campaign against Finland.

The Russians were superior in man-power, artillery, air and sea-power. In Finland's favour were her highly defensible country, with its numerous lakes, marshes and forests, a belt of fortifications 20 miles deep and excellently designed on the Karelian Isthmus (the most likely approach for the Russians), and soldiers, experts in Arctic warfare, imbued with militant patriotism.

Finnish Army Dispersed

With the single-track Murmansk railway as a supply line, the Russians combined seven simultaneous attacks at various points along Finland's frontier with an attack against the Mannerheim Line in the Karelian Isthmus. The Finnish Army, with its 300,000 front line troops, was dispersed to meet these attacks.

The Finns abandoned the unfortified approach zone between the frontier and the Mannerheim Line. The other Russian attacks fared as follows :

Salmi (on the north-eastern bank of Lake Ladoga) : the Russians advanced 40 miles into Finnish territory.

Suojärvi (60 miles north of Salmi) : the greater part of the three Russian divisions employed fell into an ambush on Dec. 13, and suffered heavily.

Lieksa (Liekaa) on Lake Pielis : Russians advancing towards Nurmes routed.

Kuhmo (50 miles north of Lieksa) : stalemate.

Suomussalmi : Soviet 163rd Division and 44th Division defeated with heavy losses as much by the Arctic weather as by the Finns.

Salla : captured by Russians.

Petsamo : Russians threatened Finland's communications with Sweden by the capture of Petsamo and a 60-mile depth of country south of the port in the first month of the war.

Had the Russian forces achieved an easy break-through on any of these fronts they would perhaps have abandoned the more costly frontal attack on the Mannerheim defences. But victory was not to be so easily obtained.

Meanwhile, in spite of spirited Finnish counter-attacks, they had been testing the Mannerheim Line for its weakest point and concentrating their men, tanks and munitions on the Karelian Isthmus. After attacks at various points to divert the attention of the Finnish C.-in-C., General Mannerheim, notably a six-day battle along the north shore of Lake Ladoga, the Russian General Meretskov launched his main attack on Feb. 2, 1940, on the Finnish right centre sector of the Mannerheim Line—the Summa front. The Finns, blasted by 300,000 shells a day, crushed by 70-ton tanks and hopelessly outnumbered in the air and on the ground, yielded Kotinen fortress and Koivisto fortress, and Viborg was gravely threatened. The Mannerheim Line was broken. The Finns sued for peace, and on March 13, 1940, after 104 days of war, the cease-fire was sounded at 11 a.m. The Red Army lost 48,745 killed and 158,863 wounded. The Finns 60,000 killed and 250,000 wounded.

Russia obtained her desired bases in Finland, but the Finnish High Command longed for revenge. The German invasion of Russia in June 1941 seemed to give the opportunity.

Although Finland could ill afford to lose more men, and in spite of warnings by the United States and Britain, who was allied with Russia, the Finns helped the German attack. Finnish soldiers fought outside Leningrad and Moscow with the Germans, Finland provided a base for German operations against Murmansk and Kandalaksha, and Finns took Kexholm

on August 23, Viipuri the next day, and Petrazavodsk on Sept. 30.

The Russians fought back bitterly, and at the end of November 1941 the tide began to turn with the retreat of the German armies from around Moscow and Leningrad. Finland was also threatened with famine.

The Finnish armies suffered intense hardships during the bitter winter of 1941-42. Heavy fighting occurred round Lake Ladoga, and many villages fell into Russian hands. At the beginning of April 1942 the Red Army, particularly its strongly equipped guerilla bands, inflicted severe casualties upon the Finnish forces. Early in June Hitler paid a visit to Marshal Mannerheim, apparently inspired by the necessity of encouraging war-weary Finland.

In attacking Russia the Finnish generals said that they desired only a removal of the dangers which threatened Finland's existence, without specifying definite war aims. A Russian offer to discuss peace with Finland on a basis of territorial compensation to the Finns in August 1941 had been rejected. The Russophobe sentiments of General Mannerheim and his colleagues forfeited U.S. friendship for Finland and made her an enemy of Britain—an enemy because Britain could not stand idly by while Finns and Finnish territory were used to attack the Murmansk port and railway, which constituted the main route for Allied supplies of arms to Russia in her struggle with Germany.

Book to Consult : The Soviet-Finnish Campaign, W. P. and Z. Coates (Eldon Press).

Fire Guard. In September 1941 all male British subjects between 18 and 60 were obliged to register for Fire Guard service, the only exceptions being members of the Services (including the Home Guard and the Royal Observer Corps), the police and special constables, doctors, seamen, and blind or insane persons. Exemptions might be claimed for persons already in the Civil Defence services doing 48 hours duty per month, or on grounds of excessive hardship. Although three out of four men claimed exemption, an adequate body of fireguards was established. On August 20, 1942, the order was extended to cover women from 20 to 45. All had to undergo training.

HOW BRITAIN FOUGHT NAZI FIRE BOMBS

The regular Fire Brigades, and the voluntary A.F.S. detachments that sprang into being a year before the war, were, on August 18, 1941, incorporated into one great fire-fighting system, operating under a central control. See also Civil Defence.

Fire Service, National. When war was declared in September 1939 there were over 1,400 regular Fire Brigades situated in different parts of England, Scotland and Wales controlled by local authorities. These Brigades (composed of about 80 per cent ex-Servicemen of whom some 45 per cent were ex-Navy) had attached to them members of the Auxiliary Fire Service, namely the men and women who had voluntarily joined up from September 1938 onwards and who were necessarily only part-time, unpaid, and still in course of training, the men as fire-fighters, the women for watchroom telephone work and as car drivers, and youths as messengers, dispatch riders, etc.

The A.F.S. were called up for full-time service on August 31 and thousands responded. Recruiting also progressed so rapidly that before long the combined Brigades (not yet nationalized) totalled high figures. A.F.S. predominated, and in London alone there were

approximately 32,000 compared with 2,000 to 3,000 men of the regular Fire Brigades, though this difference was not so marked in other parts of the country. Training was intensified, every opportunity was given A.F.S. men to attend fires whether due to enemy action or not, and the new and old sections of the Brigades became more closely interlocked almost daily. By this time the full-time members of the A.F.S. were paid, but the part-time service rendered by hundreds of men and women was then, and continued to be, an important and valuable side of the organization.

At last the time came for nationalization. This event took place on August 18, 1941, and the 1,450 local authorities' Brigades in England, Scotland and Wales were welded into a National Fire Service under the Home Secretary, and comprising 32 Fire Forces plus five covering the London Region, organized in 200 divisions. As a first result nationalization

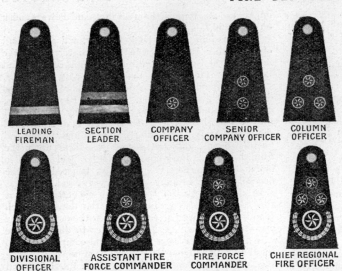

LEADING FIREMAN   SECTION LEADER   COMPANY OFFICER   SENIOR COMPANY OFFICER   COLUMN OFFICER

DIVISIONAL OFFICER   ASSISTANT FIRE FORCE COMMANDER   FIRE FORCE COMMANDER   CHIEF REGIONAL FIRE OFFICER

Badges of Rank in the National Fire Service.

N.F.S. firemen did much besides fire-fighting. Besides all the work in ensuring water-cover, they built their own stations and establishments and made the Service self-contained in every way. They manned field telephone and radio vans, mobile control rooms and kitchens, mobile and static workshops, fire-boats and barges. During their little spare time fire-stations were busy, principally in the London area, in voluntarily manufacturing small parts and items of military equipment for the Army.

After the first big raids in 1940 there was a great shortage of turntable ladders. Many of these valuable appliances were destroyed, often with their special crews, in the raids on London. To meet this the N.F.S. designed and manufactured its own in two models; one machine operated, and one a smaller ladder of 65 feet, extended by hand.

The gallantry of the British firemen is now known the world over. They rose magnificently to every test, however fierce. Long before the Battle of Britain the men of the East and South Coasts had known what it meant to fight enemy-created fires. But Londoners undoubtedly had the most strenuous time of all, even when compared with the savage onslaughts on such places as Bristol, Coventry, Plymouth, Southampton, Liverpool, Bootle, Hull, Sheffield, Clydebank and Belfast. In September 1940 London men went through a continuous ordeal which lasted day and night for nearly a month. Despite water shortage, nights without sleep, days without rest and constant bombs over and around them, they saved London then—and yet again and again in the many raids which followed in the months between October 1940 and May 1941.

In addition, in company with brigades from many parts of the country, London men were rushed to the rescue of other towns. These towns, in their turn,

ensured standardization of uniform, equipment, ranks, and conditions of service, and gave greater opportunity for men and women to obtain high positions or undertake special work. Training was also standardized, and an important development was the establishment of an N.F.S. Training College for both men and women.

The most important result of nationalization was a vastly improved system of mobilisation. Any threatened point or burning town could at once receive sufficient pumps and appliances from the surrounding Fire Forces, while no single division was left weakened. With the reinforcing pumps went the new N.F.S. mobile kitchens and workshops.

The standard equipment was based on the tender towing a trailer-pump. These were mainly in two sizes. The major trailer-pump gave a flow of 350–500 gallons per minute, the light pump 120–350 gallons per minute. The latter could also be dismounted from its chassis and manhandled over debris and into burning buildings.

It was found in practice that the greatest difficulty in air raid fire-fighting was water-shortage caused by the fracture of mains. A great part of the work of the N.F.S. in lull periods consisted in the preparation of static water supplies in towns. These were made by waterproofing and flooding the basements of demolished buildings, or erecting sectional steel tanks at strategic points. All open water in the country was mapped and sign-posted, and access prepared for pumps. The rank of Water-Officer was appointed for specialists in this department. Towns were covered further by a system of dry surface mains, the sections of which could be quickly replaced during raids.

Hydraulics, engineering and allied subjects figured largely in programmes of N.F.S. training schools. Drills were devised and practised in water-relaying, and in a short while any town in Britain could be defended from fire independent of its own water mains.

SUPPLIES FOR THE FIREFIGHTERS

The frequent breaking of mains in air raids led to the storing of vast quantities of water by the N.F.S. It was kept in the basements of demolished buildings and in steel tanks, and these 'dams' became a familiar sight in London and other towns. In this photograph of part of Shoe Lane, London, a cellar is seen containing 500,000 gallons, flooded after the ruins were cleared.

New York Times photo

ACTUAL FIRE-FIGHTING IN HEAVY LONDON RAIDS

1. From fire floats on the Thames vast jets of water are played on burning warehouses along the riverside.   2. Air-raid control room where, on a large map of the local area, the situation during a raid is presented and kept up to the minute by means of coloured flags and studs.   3. Fire station officer using an oxy-acetylene cutting plant to cut through a girder and so rescue victims entrapped beneath.   4. Firemen endeavouring to save burning buildings in Newgate St. after the great Fire of London on the night of Dec. 29, 1940.   5. Fight to control a blazing building in the City area.

Photos, Sport & General; Fox; Daily Mirror; Planet News; Central Press sent their quota of help to their neighbours. The most striking effort, perhaps, was the dispatch of men and equipment across the Irish Sea to Belfast.

Firemen suffered, too. Many were injured or badly burned ; some were invalided out of the Service ; many died " on the job." There were outstanding deeds of heroism, some recognized in official quarters. The list of awards which were made up to January 1942 to men and women of the Fire Service comprised : George Cross, 2 ; George Medal, 85 ; Empire Awards (O.B.E., M.B.E., B.E.M.), 188 ; and Commendations, 331. But there were countless more deeds of bravery and self-sacrifice known only to a few.

Books to Consult : Ordeal by Fire, Michael Wassey (Secker). The Bells Go Down, An A.F.S. Man (Methuen). Fire and Water, various authors (Lindsey Drummond).

Fisher, SIR (NORMAN FENWICK) WARREN, G.C.B. (b. 1879). Special Commissioner for London Region from 1940 to 1942. He was Regional Commissioner for Civil Defence, N.W. Region, 1939–40. From 1919 to 1939 he was Permanent Secretary of the Treasury and Official Head of the Civil Service, and his signature appeared on Treasury notes.

Flak. Contraction of the composite German name *Flugabwehrkanone,* meaning " the aeroplane-warding-off-gun," and signifying anti-aircraft guns. There are two kinds of flak, light and heavy. Light flak are guns from $\frac{3}{4}$-in. to 2-in. calibre, and fire shells weighing from $\frac{1}{2}$ lb. to $3\frac{1}{3}$ lb. Heavy flak range from $3\frac{1}{2}$-in. guns firing 15 rounds a minute and throwing shells to 20,000 ft., to the 4·7-in. firing ten 32-lb. shells a minute to a height of 30,000 ft.

Flaming Onions. Incendiary shells used primarily with a view to setting fire to aircraft. Two projectiles strung together hurtle into the air, leaving a trail of fire.

Flandin, PIERRE ÉTIENNE (b. 1889). French Right Wing politician. He held many posts in the French Cabinet ; was Prime Minister, 1934–35 ; Minister without Portfolio under Laval's premiership, 1935–36 ; and Foreign Minister, 1936. Before war broke out he worked for a rapprochement between France and Germany, and was in favour of sacrificing the alliance with Britain. After the fall of France he lived for a time in retirement in the occupied area, though he made speeches stressing the need for " wholehearted and loyal collaboration with Germany." He was appointed Foreign Minister in the Vichy Government, December 1940, but resigned on Feb. 9, 1941, being succeeded by Adm. Darlan.

Fleet Air Arm. Formerly a branch of the R.A.F. administered by the Navy when afloat. The Navy contributed three out of four of the pilots and all the observers. In 1939 the Command was taken over by the Royal Navy. The training stations of the Fleet Air Arm are " His Majesty's Ships," though they may actually be islands or even land aerodromes (*see* Kestrel, H.M.S.). Fleet Air Arm Machines are designed to land on and take off from aircraft carriers.

Its first important engagement was on April 11, 1940, when a number of German warships were attacked in Trondheim Fjord in Norway. In the Battle of France, June 1940, the Fleet Air Arm launched a series of strong attacks on enemy positions along the French and Belgian coasts. In the highly successful attack on the Italian fleet at Taranto, Nov. 11–12, 1940, torpedo-carrying 'planes achieved spectacular triumphs. The Fleet Air Arm played an important part in the victory over Italian ships at Matapan, March 28, 1941. These were followed up by many other successful attacks on the enemy.

Machines used by the F.A.A. included the Fairey Fulmar, the Walrus, and the American Grumman Martlet and Albacore (*see* Aircraft).

Uniforms of the Fleet Air Arm are those general in the Royal Navy, but officers are distinguished by the letter A in the curl of their sleeve stripes, and a small pair of wings above the sleeve stripes denotes a pilot.

Florina. This town of N.W. Greece, on the road to Salonika, was bombed by the Italians soon after the outbreak of the Italo-Greek conflict at the end of October 1940. The Italians launched an attack from Koritza, in Albania, in the direction of Florina, having crossed the Albanian frontier on Oct. 28. By the end of the first fortnight, however, the Italian attack had been held and in part thrown back by the Greeks.

On April 11, 1941, Empire forces drove the attacking Germans back near Florina after all-day fighting. The town was occupied by the Bulgarians in the same month.

Flushing. Seaport of Holland, situated on the island of Walcheren at the mouth of the R. Scheldt. After the German conquest of Holland in May 1940, Flushing became one of the German invasion ports, the extensive basins of the port making it adaptable for the purpose. The R.A.F. attacked it frequently, the raids becoming extremely heavy in September 1940, and by June 1, 1942, Flushing had been attacked seventy-two times. Considerable damage was done to barges, shipping, harbour installations, oil tanks, and to the aerodrome.

Folkestone. Seaport and resort of Kent. On August 26, 1940, a great many enemy bombs were dropped during a heavy daylight attack. Much damage was caused, and houses were destroyed on the sea-front. German raiders made repeated attacks during the summer and autumn of 1940 and throughout 1941 and 1942.

FEEDING GREAT BRITAIN IN WARTIME

The Ministry of Food faced an onerous task when it took over the control and distribution of supplies. That this task had been successfully performed was shown by the high standard of health prevailing in the community in the third year of war.

Food : in Wartime. At the end of the first year of the war the Ministry of Food measured the nation's total intake of calories and found the national diet within 1 per cent of the pre-war calorific level. At the end of the second year a similar measurement revealed almost identical results. In other words, two years of a war whose objective was, from the start, the starving-out of the British Isles, made no difference scientifically to the nation's diet ; and, in consequence, the national health was unexpectedly maintained at a high level. What the war did to the national diet was to introduce alternative and, sometimes, unaccustomed foods, and to substitute for one familiar food another less familiar.

Wartime rationing may be conveniently considered under these heads : what foods are available, what foods are lacking, where they come from, how they are distributed, and, last, how communities dislocated by heavy enemy air bombardment are catered for.

Wheat is mainly supplied by Canada, to whom the biggest orders in the history of the grain trade have been given—120,000,000 bushels at a time. Grain also comes from Australia and South America. Canada is the best wartime source because it has the shortest sea haul. Wheat supplies have not fallen short.

Meat comes mainly from South America (Argentine, Brazil, Venezuela). At the beginning of the war Australia and New Zealand were sources of supply, but the long sea haul and shipping losses indicated the shorter S. American sea route in the third year of the war.

Bacon formerly came mainly from Denmark. To offset this loss, Canada increased her pig production to maintain our supply. In 1941 we also got bacon from the U.S.A. and Eire. Sugar comes from the West Indies and the Queensland crop of Australia. Great Britain produces in wartime 40 per cent of her total sugar consumption from the sugar-beet crop.

Cheese comes from New Zealand and Canada and, in 1941, from Canada and the U.S.A. also. Tea comes from India, Ceylon, and the Dutch East Indies ; butter from Australia and New Zealand ; dried milk from Australia, New Zealand, the U.S.A., and Canada.

FOOD FROM AMERICA

Bags of Canadian wheat being unloaded at a British port from a transatlantic freighter. The cargo, which also included cheese, dried milk and lard, was sent partly under the Lease-Lend Act, partly by the American people.

Photo, Planet News

BRITISH RESTAURANT

By June 15, 1942, there were 1,519 of these restaurants, run on cafeteria lines, where good food could be obtained cheaply and quickly. The one shown above is at Memorial Hall, Farringdon St., London.

Photo, Keystone

Margarine, composed of vegetable oils and whale oil, comes, as oil or oil seed, from West Africa and South America, and (but less) from India. Whale oil was still being brought to us by Norway's fishing fleet.

The chief foods that were off the national menu were

all imported fresh fruits, formerly from the Empire and Italy ; and all proteins (meat, eggs) were strictly rationed. Coffee was abundant because we had the cargoes of French ships carrying it when France fell.

The task of the Ministry of Food was to maintain the national intake of food at a level necessary to keep the people healthy. This involved an alternative make-up of diet. For example, proteins being one of the staples of which the country was short, instead of meat, potatoes and vegetables had to be used. The proteins are less, the carbohydrates more, in the average diet. Even so, after three years of war, the people of Great Britain enjoyed a bigger protein intake than many other countries.

There was less meat, less fish, less fats, less sugar.

Milk has had a peculiar war history in Great Britain. At first people were encouraged to " drink more milk," and milk bars multiplied. Consumption went up 20 per cent in the first year of the war. But by the second year of the war, when cuts in cattle feed were necessary, production fell away and the policy of encouraging milk drinking had to be revised.

In July 1940 the Ministry of Food introduced a National Milk Scheme under which all children under five and expectant and nursing mothers became entitled to one pint a day at twopence, against the 4d. or 4½d. normal price. In six months 3,000,000 people had taken advantage of the scheme. The milk production was able to meet this added demand upon it during the summer, but in the autumn of 1941 the rationing of milk was introduced. Under this scheme young people up to eighteen, and invalids, were added to priority consumers.

Fair distribution of the national larder was assured by ration books to each individual and registration with the retailer. Local Food Offices kept registers of all customers and their ration retailers. Rationed foods could be obtained only against coupons, and these were valid only when produced uncut in the customer's ration book. Miners, farm labourers, roadmen, and others unable to take a proper midday meal got preferential rations in the form of larger cheese rations.

Points rationing was introduced in the autumn of 1941. It differed from coupon rationing. Rationing proper prescribes a fixed amount of one food for a fixed period. The Points scheme covered a group of foods, each with a given number of points, and the period was a four-week one. There was no registration—no compulsion to buy from a single retailer. Points rationing applied to tinned foods, certain cereals, dried fruits, etc., points allotted to a particular food varying with demand, an excess of which was countered by raising the number of points.

The greatest obstacle to food imports was the shortage of shipping space. The scientists were consulted and much ingenuity shown in overcoming this. First, there was a great intensification of home farming, more land being put under the plough and greater crops

FOOD CONCENTRATED

The 2½ lbs. of raw carrot, after dehydration, becomes the 4 ozs. of dried carrot in the bottle. Soaking for a few hours makes it soft and ready to cook.

Fox photos

raised. Then all unnecessary imports, such as tinned fruits and bananas, were cut out. Next, new processes of drying and dehydrating reduced bulk and hold space without impairing food values. Formerly 3,000,000 tons of water had been imported annually with our food imports. Fresh milk weighs 41 oz. per quart while the same quantity as milk powder weighs 5.3 oz., and the bulk is reduced from 15·6 to 7·7 cubic in. This discovery made it practical to store the rich spring and summer milk for winter use. In 1942 100,000 tons of dried egg were imported. In shell, the weight would have been 500,000 tons and the space needed six times as great. Dehydration, too, solves the problems of storage. Refrigeration is not needed and the food values and vitamins are not affected. Meat and vegetables are supplied dehydrated to the Forces and their transportation and cooking in the field is simplified. A test showed that an Army mess derived more vitamin C from dried cabbage than from fresh, with the added advantage of winter use.

In the three months January-March 1941, imports of food dropped to half of the peak period of 1940, due to enemy action. The deficiency was made up from stocks. Yet such was the improvement in the second six months, that by December 1941, stocks were built up to 30 per cent higher than in 1940.

By March 1942, 80 per cent of the miners had canteen facilities, and workers' canteens were functioning in two categories : A, serving double rations to heavy manual workers, were dealing with 15,000,000 meals weekly ; and B, serving half over the normal ration, 28,000,000 meals weekly.

Community feeding was the child of the raids. The L.C.C. organized it, using school staffs and buildings. The scheme was known as the London Meals Service. It now became nation-wide and known as the British Restaurants. On June 15, 1942, there were 1,519 of them, and 275,000 or more meals are served every day. The Ministry of Food centralized equipment for emergency use, and helped local authorities to organize their communal feeding with funds, equipment, and expert advice. There were also 5,500 workers' canteens and school canteens feeding about 650,000 children daily. In March 1942 the Ministry pointed out that the nation had not until then been called on for any serious sacrifices, but that the world war situation would cause a reduction in food imports and a simplification of diet was to be expected with an extension of the points system. In 1941 price control covered 60 food commodities and very few were uncontrolled. At the same time sterner measures against those operating in the " black market " were announced.

After 3 years of war Britain's food, and Britain's health, showed little sign of Hitler's starve-Britain policy. There was enough, and a little for Russia, too.

Book to Consult : Britain's Food in Wartime, Sir John Russell (Oxford Pamphlet).

Food, Ministry of. Established on Sept. 8, 1939, to place the nation's food supply under Government control. The first Minister was Mr. W. S. Morrison. He was succeeded on April 3 1940, by Lord Woolton.

Forbes, Admiral of the Fleet Sir Charles Morton. G.C.B.,D.S.O.(b.1880). C.-in-C. Plymouth from May 1, 1941. He was Vice-Adm. commanding the 1st Battle Squadron and Second-in-Command Mediterranean Fleet,1934–36, and C.-in-C. Home Fleet from 1938 to Dec. 2, 1940, when he was succeeded by Adm. Sir John Tovey.

Forbes, Air Commandant Katherine Jane Trefusis (b. 1899). Director of the W.A.A.F. from 1939. She was Chief Instructor to the Auxiliary Territorial Service School of Instruction for Officers, ranking as Company Commander, 1938, and was attached to No. 20 Royal Air Force Company A.T.S., 1939.

Formidable, H.M.S. This 23,000-ton British aircraft carrier of the Illustrious class, completed in 1939, has a complement of 1,600 and carries sixteen 4·5-inch (dual purpose) guns. Bomb and torpedo-carrying dive bombers of the Fleet Air Arm launched from H.M.S. Formidable attacked and severely damaged the Italian battleship Vittorio Veneto and bombed the Italian cruiser Pola at the Battle of Matapan (q.v.), March 28, 1941.

Forster, Albert. German Reichsstatthalter of West Prussia, appointed after the German conquest of Poland, 1939. This territory, including Danzig and the Polish Corridor, from which Poles were ejected to make way for German refugees from the Baltic States,

FIRST GERMAN AIR RAID ON BRITAIN

It was on Oct. 16, 1939, that the first German 'planes flew over our territory. About twelve of them attacked ships of the Royal Navy lying in the Firth of Forth, and the photograph shows the splash made by the bomb that fell near H.M.S. Edinburgh. The raider is being driven off by heavy A.A. fire.

Photo, Associated Press

was occupied by the Germans after the subjugation of Poland. On Oct. 27 Forster declared, " Whoever belongs to the Polish nation must leave this country." Before the outbreak of war he was the Nazi leader in Danzig and stirred up anti-Polish feeling there. Early in 1938 Forster declared that Berlin had resumed control of the city's foreign policy. *See* Danzig.

Forth, Firth of. Estuary of the R. Forth, on the east coast of Scotland. The first German air raid on Britain occurred in daylight on Oct. 16, 1939, in this area, the raid lasting upwards of an hour and a half. Twelve, or possibly more, German 'planes, in waves of

H.M.S. FORMIDABLE SHARED THE VICTORY OF MATAPAN

Britain's new aircraft carrier Formidable, commanded by Capt. A. Bissett, played a vital part in bringing the Italian fleet to action at the Battle of Matapan. This was said to be the first occasion in history in which skilful coordination of naval operations with attacks launched by aircraft resulted in the enemy's speeds being so reduced that the Fleet's main units were able to force action upon a reluctant combatant.

Photo, Central Press

two or three at a time, dived down on to the ships of the Royal Navy lying in the Firth off Rosyth. One raider swooped almost as low as the topmost span of the Forth Bridge and machine-gunned two cruisers. Then it turned again towards the warships and dropped bombs, none of which hit the bridge itself. Several bombs were dropped at Rosyth. One glanced off the cruiser Southampton, causing some damage. Others fell into the sea near the destroyer Mohawk and the cruiser Edinburgh, splinters causing a number of casualties. Only four civilians were slightly injured, but the naval casualties were seventeen killed and forty-four wounded. R.A.F. 'planes made contact

with the raiders and were responsible for destroying three of the German 'planes, while a fourth was brought down in flames by anti-aircraft fire. Other German machines were badly damaged.

Four-Power Conference. Held at Stockholm on Oct. 18–19, 1939. The Kings of Denmark, Norway and Sweden and M. Kallio, President of Finland, together with their Foreign Ministers, met at the invitation of King Gustav of Sweden. The conference was called owing to the situation created by Russian demands on Finland. The three Kings and the President made broadcasts on Oct. 19, when solidarity between the four countries was emphasized.

THE CATASTROPHIC FALL OF FRANCE

For more than eight months France, behind her Maginot Line, watched the invasion of Poland, of Scandinavia, and finally of the Low Countries. Five weeks only were to elapse between the Nazi crossing of the frontier and France's surrender. A separate section deals with Free France. This review is by Maj.-Gen. Sir Chas. Gwynn, K.C.B., D.S.O. See Armistice ; Belgium ; Maginot Line ; Vichy, etc.

France : DEFEAT OF. On Sept. 3, 1939, two days after Poland had been invaded, France and Britain declared war on Germany, but rather with the object of calling a halt to German aggression than of moving at once to Poland's assistance. Isolated geographically, Poland could not be directly helped, and only if Germany were forced to withdraw part of her armies to meet an attack from the west could she hope to resist the German onslaught for long.

But Britain and France were unprepared and ill situated to take immediate offensive action. They had started late and half-heartedly in the armaments race which Germany had provoked, and only at sea did they hold a dominating superiority of force. That superiority, however, gave them access to all the material resources of the world and enabled them to exclude Germany from the same sources of supply. These conditions gave rise to the over-confident belief that time was on the side of the Allies, and that by remaining on the defensive while maintaining the stranglehold of the blockade they could deliberately prepare for an ultimate offensive. France, confident that the experiences of the last war had proved that modern weapons gave the defence mastery over the attack, felt secure meantime behind her Maginot Line should Germany attack her.

Why France was Inactive

Such was the background of what was known in America as the " phoney " war of the autumn and winter of 1939–40. General Gamelin, C.-in-C. of the Allied Armies, was probably right in refusing to launch a large-scale offensive on account of the incomplete condition of his armaments and the nature of the frontier with Germany. On half its length of 200 miles the great obstacle of the Rhine blocked the way, and on the other half the enemy had constructed the formidable Siegfried position in a terrain which lent itself to defence. Since neutral territory on either flank prohibited turning manoeuvres a direct frontal attack was the only course open, and to have attempted it without great superiority of material might have led to disastrous failure—especially after the fall of Poland set the German Army free to counter-attack.

It is less easy to justify the extreme policy of inactivity General Gamelin adopted both in the air and on the ground, while he remained on the defensive.

No bombs were dropped on German munition factories, rapidly approaching peak production, and aircraft were employed only on reconnaissance, photographing enemy defences and dropping propaganda leaflets. This policy may in part have been due to the Allied resolve not to drop bombs on any targets where civilian life would be endangered and partly to save their own munition factories, especially in France, where they were extremely vulnerable, from hostile reprisals.

On the ground after the first weeks of the war operations were confined to infrequent skirmishes between patrols in No-Man's-Land, and troops confined to defensive positions suffered from boredom, lost offensive spirit and got little training for serious encounters. The Allied Governments on their part were infected by the same lassitude and displayed little appreciation of the necessity of developing their potential munition production.

Peace in the Maginot Line

The story of the phoney war can be briefly told. The blockade was at once established and effective measures to counter the U-boat menace were taken. The French Army, having deployed behind the Maginot Line, advanced across the frontier, driving back German advanced posts. Some sharp encounters occurred, but their importance was probably exaggerated in official communiqués, and since they were not followed by any attempt against the German main positions, they were merely a gesture which brought no relief to Poland and served rather to reassure the enemy that he had little to fear on his western front.

Early in October all pretence at offensive action was abandoned, and when, on the final defeat of Poland, German counter-attacks threatened, the French withdrew to an outpost line covered by the guns of the Maginot Line, and they were not followed up. Henceforward, during the winter, hostilities took the form of desultory patrol encounters in the wide No-Man's-Land which separated the outposts of the adversaries.

The enemy was thus left with the initiative to strike at his chosen place and time. It was expected that under the pressure of the blockade he would be unable to face a long war and was bound to seek a decision in the spring. But, confident in the power of defence and in the belief that the static conditions of the last war would develop, Gamelin, ignoring the experiences of Poland, was prepared to await attack. Yet there was no certainty where and how the attack would come. Would the enemy at all sacrifice of life hurl his armies against the Maginot Line ? Should he do so he might seek to outflank it through Luxemburg and Switzerland, and Italy, abandoning her non-belligerent policy, might cooperate. Gamelin was forced to keep adequate forces in the south to meet that contingency.

On the other hand, Germany, ignoring pacts and neutral rights, might again attack through the Low Countries, in which case the Allies were committed to come to their assistance, although Belgium, determined to maintain her policy of absolute neutrality, refused to enter into any consultations as to what action should be taken. All that Gamelin could do, therefore, was, in the first instance, to strengthen the

line of defence marked by the River Dyle. This line was to be held by the 7th Army on the left, the B.E.F. in the centre and the 1st Army on the right, while the 9th and 2nd Armies were to extend their front along the line of the Meuse between Dinant and Montmédy, and thus form the pivot of the wheel forward. This plan entailed an advance of some 60 miles, and it was calculated it would take the whole force about ten days to reach their positions.

It was considered that the Belgian defences were strong enough to impose a deliberate advance on the Germans, and east of the Meuse French cavalry were to support Belgian delaying action. It will be observed, however, that Gamelin adhered to his defensive policy and intended only to take up a defensive position. He had decided on the Dyle line mainly because it provided the shortest front to hold.

Such was the general situation and such the plans made during the period of the phoney war, and in the spring it became evident that Germany had massed her armies along her frontiers from the North Sea to Switzerland in readiness to take the offensive, though where the main blow would fall was still uncertain.

Then, on May 10, in spite of treacherous assurances, came the invasion of Holland, Belgium and Luxemburg.

The King of the Belgians called for assistance, and the Allies put their prearranged plans into operation. Their mechanized cavalry reached the Dyle line the same evening, followed by the leading infantry divisions in motor transport. By the 12th the

ON THE FRENCH FRONT

These scenes are from the early days of the positional war, described by Americans as "phoney." Above, men of a machine-gun post near the front line about to open fire. Bottom right, anti-aircraft gun and crew in action during the winter of 1939-40.

Photos, French Official

defences on the Belgian frontier from Montmédy, where the Maginot Line terminated, to the sea, and, secondly, to make his plans for moving to the assistance of Belgium.

The non-committal attitude of the Belgian Government made it difficult to decide how assistance could best be given, but it was known that Belgium had strengthened the defences of her northern and eastern frontiers. Connecting those works with the Maginot Line at Montmédy, the Meuse, running through a deep gorge, formed a strong defensive line with the hilly, afforested Ardennes district lying between it and Germany. No heavy attack was expected through the Ardennes, for there were few roads and railways to facilitate the passage of large forces, and the terrain lent itself to delaying tactics.

In view of these conditions Gamelin decided, in the event of Belgium calling for assistance, to swing the left wing of his armies forward to a line between Antwerp and the Fortress of Namur on the Meuse, where it was understood the Belgians had prepared a second

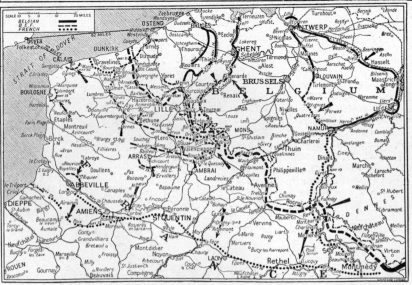

The BATTLE of FRANCE

German thrusts from the invasion of Holland and Belgium on May 10, 1940, to the cessation of hostilities in France on June 25.

Left, the successive defence lines of the Allies in northern France and Belgium. The broken black line indicates the Belgian frontier defences, once called the Maginot Line extension. The Belgians fell back to the Antwerp-Namur line on May 11–12, the French and British conforming. After the German break-through on the 13th the Allies withdrew to the Scheldt (May 16–17). Above, the enemy was now pressing on to the Channel ports, and soon the Allied armies in Belgium were cut off. Then came the retreat to Dunkirk, and evacuation. The Belgian army had surrendered on May 28. On June 5 there began the Panzer drive into France which in 11 days brought France to peace negotiations. Italy entered the war June 10.

line was fairly strongly held, and by the 16th the whole Northern force had reached its position. The Belgian main position had, however, been penetrated at Maastricht on the first day and the Germans flowed through the gap, turning the Liége defences. The Belgians fought gallantly and the Liége forts held out, but their army was forced to retreat and rally on the left of the British. A counter-attack by French tanks and cavalry slowed up the enemy's advance, but the French advance troops then had to withdraw to their main position between Wavre and Namur, where heavy fighting took place. The B.E.F. and Belgians were not strongly attacked and held their positions.

In the meantime Dutch resistance had been broken; the Dutch Army had surrendered on the 14th (*see* Netherlands). On the next day still worse occurred. German mechanized columns, advancing with unforeseen speed through Luxemburg and the Ardennes, had driven back the Belgian delaying troops and the French cavalry before the 9th French Army had reached its allotted front on the Meuse. Confronted only by weak detachments, and supported by masses of dive bombers, the Panzer troops forced crossings over the Meuse between Sedan and Mézières and at Dinant. In some cases bridges had been left standing, either by neglect or by fifth column treachery. Exploiting their success with great rapidity, the German tanks and dive bombers spread confusion in the 9th Army.

No Answer to German Tactics

This was a new form of warfare of which the skirmishes on the Lorraine front and the experiences of the last war had given no warning. The lessons of the Polish campaign had not been grasped, and there seemed no answer to the novel tactics employed by the Germans. French anti-tank guns produced little effect on the tanks. They were hardly powerful enough to penetrate thick armour, and French soldiers had not learnt to use them against the vulnerable parts of the monsters. Belief in the invincibility of the Germans spread, destroying morale, a disaster always liable to happen when troops find themselves opposed to adversaries better armed.

Moreover, the Germans had learnt much in Poland, and during the winter had made good defects in their organization and armoured vehicles. Rapidly gaps formed in the French front, through which more Panzer divisions poured, supported by motorized infantry. The gaps united to become a swelling bulge, and as the Germans advanced they found fewer and fewer formed bodies of troops to oppose them. Further, the civil organization of the country broke down. Local authorities had no instructions to control the movements of growing streams of refugees, or to destroy petrol and other stocks invaluable to the Germans, whose chief difficulty was to maintain a flow of supplies.

At first there was doubt as to the Germans' intentions. Was their object to push on direct to Paris or did they aim at taking the Maginot Line in the rear? It soon became apparent, however, that the Panzer thrust was heading west, intent on severing the communication of the armies in Belgium. Realizing their danger, those armies were ordered to retreat to the line of the Scheldt, and the withdrawal began on the night of May 16–17. Even before that the 7th Army, part of whose mission it had been to support the Dutch, had been ordered back to the support of the 9th Army, leaving the 1st Army, the B.E.F. and the Belgians to oppose the Germans advancing from the north. The retreat to the Scheldt was successfully accomplished by the night of May 18–19, but by then the Germans had captured Amiens, through which the main communications of the B.E.F. ran.

General Weygand, who had been recalled from the Middle East to supersede Gamelin, was endeavouring to organize a force with which to counter-attack the German thrust and thus prevent the northern armies from becoming isolated. But reserves were hard to collect, for their movements were interfered with by the streams of refugees on the roads and by the damage done to railways by bombing. All he could therefore establish was a weak defensive line on the Somme.

The Germans, on their part, pressing on towards the coast, were satisfied to obtain a footing at a few points across the Somme, and in the main used the river for the protection of the left flank of their thrust, holding it with infantry brought up in lorries. Much was being left to the initiative of individual commanders of Panzer divisions, who avoided centres where strong resistance was probable and boldly dispersed in small parties in order to cause the maximum of confusion. On May 21 they reached the coast in force, finally interrupting British communications with bases in the south. Turning north, they captured Boulogne and Calais and threatened to cut off Arras, which had been held by the British as a bastion projecting into the German corridor. From Arras it had been hoped to launch a counter-attack to join hands with Weygand in the south. But no well-co-ordinated operation could be arranged, and though on May 20 and 21 a partially successful counter-attack was made by two divisions of the B.E.F., it could not progress far in the absence of a corresponding attempt by the French on the south.

Allied Armies in a Trap

In the meantime the German armies in the north were pressing the Allied retreat, directing their main attacks chiefly on the Belgians, now nearing exhaustion, and on the 1st Army, which had been driven into a small area in the neighbourhood of Valenciennes and was also much exhausted. It will be seen that the Allied Armies of the north were now in a trap from which they could not hope to escape unless Weygand from the south could assist them to break out; for, running short of ammunition and holding off the Germans in the north, they were in no condition to launch a strong attack southwards. Dunkirk had become the only base from which the armies in the north could obtain supplies, and communication with it was threatened from both sides. While plans for a break-out to the south were still being made, pressure against the Belgians in the north intensified and their front was broken. To save the situation reinforcements had to be sent to them, and with that the last hope of escape south was abandoned. Retreat towards Dunkirk commenced, at first in order to shorten the defensive perimeter and to maintain communications, but finally for evacuation of as much of the Army by sea as possible.

The wonderful story of the evacuation of the B.E.F. and of a considerable part of the 1st French Army through Dunkirk is retold under its own heading. The enemy was foiled in his attempt to surround and make prisoners the whole of the Allied armies in the north, but by capturing practically all their equipment he had temporarily eliminated them as a factor in the situation.

The evacuation at Dunkirk was completed on the night of June 2–3, but already the German armies were

FOR THE SECOND TIME

On June 14, 1940, the Germans marched into Paris—70 years after their first triumphal entry. Troops are here seen passing beneath the Arc de Triomphe. Of Pétain it was said : He saved Paris—but he lost France.

Photo, E.N.A.

making preparation for their blow against the heart of France itself. General Weygand, though unable to collect a large enough force for a major counter-attack, had been able to establish a defensive position across France from Montmédy, whose Maginot forts had withstood all German attacks, to the mouth of the Somme. This " Weygand line " followed generally the course of the Aisne and the Somme and their inter-connecting canals. But the Germans had already secured bridgeheads at Amiens and Abbeville, which counter-attacks failed to recover. The position consisted mainly of villages prepared for defence and other hastily constructed defences. No solid permanent works existed and there was no time for their construction. The position had, however, considerable depth, and the villages especially provided pivots capable of resisting tank attacks. In the east the Maginot Line, still unattacked in front, protected the position from being taken in reverse.

With astonishingly little delay, considering the length of their communications and the opposition they had met in Flanders, the Germans, on June 5, opened their attack on this position. The bombing attacks which the R.A.F. and French aircraft made on roads and railways, both at the front and right back into Germany, had failed to stop or seriously delay advancing columns. Possibly the attacks might have had greater effect if they had been more concentrated on targets in the forward areas.

After two or three days of attacks designed to make contact, to discover weak spots and to gain jumping-off positions, the Panzer divisions, on June 8, were

France in the War—A Diary of Main Events

1939		
Sept.	3	Lord Gort assumed command of the B.E.F.
	6	French troops penetrated German territory in direction of Saarbruecken.
	10	Move of B.E.F. into France began.
	12	First meeting of Allied Supreme War Council.
	13	French War Cabinet formed under Daladier.
	25	French artillery first bombarded Rhine fortifications.
Oct.	3	British 1st Corps took over sector Maulde-Gruson on Belgian frontier.
Dec.	9	British troops now in Maginot Line in contact with enemy.
1940		
March	20	Daladier resigned ; succeeded by Reynaud.
	28	Allied Supreme War Council issued solemn Declaration of United Action.
May	10	Germany invaded Holland, Belgium and Luxemburg. Allied troops crossed into Belgium and took up positions on R. Dyle.
	11	Germans crossed Albert Canal at Maastricht. Enemy thrust against French 9th Army in Ardennes.
	14	Great mechanized battle taking place near St. Trond. Netherlands High Command ordered Cease Fire.
	15	Louvain evacuated. Enemy crossed Meuse between Sedan and Mézières. Gen. Corap's 9th Army shattered.
	16	B.E.F. began withdrawal from R. Dyle to R. Scheldt.
	19	Weygand replaced Gamelin.
	20	Heavy fighting east of Cambrai. Germans captured Laon and occupied Amiens.
	21	Railway at Abbeville cut. Enemy approaching Boulogne. Capture of most of Liége forts claimed.
	22	Enemy 9 miles from Calais.
	23	Allied forces withdrew to behind R. Lys. Calais isolated. Boulogne occupied.
	26	Evacuation from Dunkirk began.
	27	Courtrai evacuated. Calais fell.
	28	King Leopold ordered Cease Fire.
	29	French and British armies fighting rear-guard action to coast.
	31	Lille captured.
June	1	German planes bombed Marseilles, Lyons and other towns in Rhône Valley.
	2-3	Evacuation from Dunkirk completed.
	5	Germans launched new offensive along Somme and Aisne.
	7	Enemy thrust north and east of Soissons, where they crossed the Ailette Canal.
	8	New German attack between Aumale and Noyon.
	9	Enemy reached outskirts of Rouen. New attack in Champagne.
	10	Italy declared war. French Govt. left Paris for Tours. In Champagne Germans reached R. Retourne.
	11	French withdrew south of R. Marne.
	12	Germans crossed Marne near Château Thierry. Rheims captured.
	13	Germans attacked south of Rouen. Montmédy captured. Paris declared an open town.
	14	Germans entered Paris.
	15	Verdun captured. Maginot Line pierced near Saarbruecken. French Govt. went to Bordeaux.
	16	Enemy crossed Seine south of Paris. British Govt. submitted draft Declaration of Solemn Act of Union. Reynaud Cabinet resigned.
	17	Pétain announced appeal for Armistice. Violent fighting at Orléans. Germans entered Dijon. Fortress of Metz surrendered.
	18	Germans reached Cherbourg and Rennes, and claimed capture of fortress of Belfort. Strasbourg occupied.
	19	Nancy and Lunéville occupied.
	20	Lyons occupied. Brest captured.
	22	Armistice with Germany signed at Compiègne.
	23	French troops still holding part of Maginot Line. Gen. de Gaulle announced formation of National Committee.
	24	Armistice with Italy signed in Rome. Italians occupied Mentone.
	25	Cease Fire sounded 12.35 a.m.

launched to break right through. The chief thrust was made from the Abbeville bridgehead, where the British 51st Highland Division and Armoured Division played a notable part in the defence. In the following days other attacks developed. notably on the Aisne, where the French offered a gallant resistance. But weak points were discovered. and as more and more Panzer divisions were brought into action they penetrated deep into and through the position, often by passing centres of resistance, leaving them to be dealt with by infantry and artillery. The fighting became very confused and rumours of tanks everywhere— often false reports spread by agents—led to retirement as troops found their line of retreat threatened. At first resistance was fierce and withdrawals were to an extent co-ordinated, but with the breakdown of means of communication troops were often without orders. Resistance weakened and soon the Weygand line was completely overrun. By June 12 the Germans had reached and crossed the Seine between Rouen and Paris ; the Aisne had been passed and Rheims captured, while in the centre German troops were reported to be 12 miles from Paris.

A Government Without Leadership

It was still hoped that the line of the Marne would be held, and the Government declared that Paris would be defended at whatever cost. But if the plight of the Army was bad, that of the Government was worse. On June 10 it left Paris for Tours. Never strong, its nerve had gone and, paralysed, it failed to give orders or show any quality of leadership. The unfortunate civil population, without control or direction, drifted southwards, blocking roads which troops might have used and suffering from ruthless air attack as well as from fatigue, hunger and thirst. On this day, too, when France was already in extremis, Mussolini delivered his stab in the back in order to stake his claim to a share of the spoils. The treacherous blow probably had little effect on the immediate

military situation. but later it may have confirmed France n the belief that Britain must inevitably share her downfall.

The German wave swept forward. On June 12 it crossed the Marne from Château Thierry eastwards, occupying Châlons. Paris, n spite of earlier protestation. was on the 13th declared an open town, and on June 14 the Germans entered it, the French troops which were to have fought in its streets withdrawing on both sides of the city.

Delusion of the Maginot Line

The principal German drive now began to develop south-eastwards between Paris and the Maginot Line. Verdun was captured on June 15, and the Maginot Line itself was attacked and penetrated near Saarbruecken by a frontal attack, the troops which should have held the intervals between the main works having been withdrawn. Though the garrisons of the forts held out gallantly, and in some cases were the last of the French Army to surrender, these great works, on which the French had pinned such reliance and on which such great sums had been lavished, had proved only a snare and a delusion.

French resistance had by now practically ceased, and masterless troops made their way southwards mingling with streams of refugees. There was talk of rallying on the Loire, but nothing came of it, though a contingent of Czech troops made a gallant fight in the sector assigned to them. Nor did the landing of fresh British troops in Normandy have any effect. Lacking French support, they had to be withdrawn before they came into collision with the Germans, now sweeping practically unopposed through western France, determined to secure control of the coast.

Weygand himself had given up hope and was obsessed with a fear of a Communist revolution. Marshal Pétain, who had been recalled from his Embassy at Madrid to be War Minister in the hopes that the name of this national hero would miraculously restore

READING THE TERMS OF THE FRANCO-GERMAN ARMISTICE

The Armistice terms were presented and signed on June 21 and 22 respectively, at Compiègne, in the railway coach in which Marshal Foch had received the German plenipotentiaries in 1918. This picture, based on a photograph taken on June 21, shows General Keitel reading the preamble. Facing him are the French representatives, Gen. Huntziger and Adm. Leluc. On Keitel's right are Hitler, Goering, Raeder and Ribbentrop (back to camera) ; on his left (seated) are von Brauchitsch and Hess.

the fighting spirit of the Army, was, on June 16, called on to accept the Premiership in succession to Reynaud, but this time in order to accept responsibility which the politicians did not dare to assume. On June 17, persuaded by Weygand that surrender was the only alternative to revolution, he opened negotiations with Germany for an Armistice, and five days later, in all the humiliating conditions Hitler could devise, the Armistice was signed. Yet it was not till June 25, when Italy had also granted an armistice, that hostilities actually ceased.

Books to Consult : The Road to Bordeaux, Denis Freeman and Douglas Cooper (Cresset Press). A Thousand Shall Fall, Hans Habe (Harrap). Return via Dunkirk, " Gun Buster " (Hodder & Stoughton). What Happened in France, Gordon Waterfield (Murray). Chronology of Failure, Hamilton Fish Armstrong (Macmillan). Berlin Diary, William Shirer (Hamish Hamilton).

France : AIR WAR IN. For the first eight months of the war the air conflict between the opposing air forces was insignificant in the Western Front campaign. Between September and the end of December 1939 the R.A.F. losses totalled only five, and the enemy lost but fourteen aircraft. In the period January–April 1940 the R.A.F. lost six machines and the Luftwaffe lost twenty-three. Though heavy attacks by bombers were expected on both sides, these did not develop, and many of the air operations were concerned with photographic reconnaissance. Such work was done jointly by the R.A.F. and the French Air Force.

In the opening stage of the war the strength of the R.A.F. serving in France consisted of one Fighter Wing, one Bomber Reconnaissance Wing, and two Army Cooperation Wings, the whole forming the British Air Component. In January 1940 the number of squadrons was increased and a new Command, known as the British Air Forces in France, was formed, under Air Marshal A. S. Barratt.

Something of the strength of the German Air Force was revealed when the enemy invaded Holland and Belgium. Dive-bombers, heavy bombers, troop-carrying aircraft and fighters were employed on a huge scale. The bombing of aerodromes was a marked feature of the German air onslaughts, as were the highly developed cooperation and support which aircraft provided for the German tanks. Both the British and French Air Forces were heavily outnumbered. On May 10 only 50 fighter aeroplanes were available in serviceable condition.

The superiority of the British machines, and the skill and desperate courage of the pilots, were thrown into relief during the fateful days of May and June 1940, and this can be discerned in the official figures of air losses sustained at the time. In May the R.A.F. lost 271 aircraft in contrast with 701 lost by the enemy. In June the latter's figures were 219 and the R.A.F. losses were 98. The German advance and bombing attacks forced the R.A.F. to change its main operational bases from Poix to Abbeville in May, but this too became untenable, and the headquarters of the Air Component (which came within the newly-formed Command) were transferred to England.

One of the outstanding exploits of the R.A.F. in the Western campaign was that in which Fairey Battles bombed a bridge over which the enemy was moving his mechanized army in his thrust through at Maastricht (*q.v.*) on May 11. The V.C. was posthumously awarded to the pilot and gunner, Flying Officer R. E. Garland (*q.v.*) and Sergeant T. Gray, of one of the machines. They were the first air V.C.s of the war.

The last main phase of the war in the air in France was linked with the B.E.F. withdrawal from Dunkirk. In the evacuation every available aircraft was thrown into that epic trial of strength. Viscount Gort, in his dispatches, stated that the evacuation would have been almost impossible but for the fighter protection afforded. His reports also refer to the individual superiority of the British pilot in combat.

Books to Consult : Diary of a Staff Officer, Air Intelligence Liaison Officer (Methuen). Fighter Pilot, Anon. Flt.-Lt. (Batsford).

FREE FRENCH SET UP THEIR STANDARD OF LIBERTY

France, Free. Free France is not a geographical area but a spiritual unit, though an ever-increasing part of the French Empire overseas proclaimed its " freedom " during 1941. Free France represents the body of Frenchmen who maintain loyalty to the Third Republic and refuse to follow the defeatist policy which rejected the British alliance after Dunkirk.

General de Gaulle (*q.v.*), who founded the Free French movement, was Chef du Cabinet Militaire in the Reynaud Government, and established a French National Committee in London on June 23, 1940, when the defeatist attitude of the Pétain administration became plain. The purpose of the Committee was to counter the total capitulation embodied in the armistice terms. De Gaulle believed that the French powers of resistance were far from exhausted, though arms, 'planes, warships and gold were being handed over to Germany and Italy. " France has a vast empire behind her. She can unite with the British Empire and utilize the immense industrial resources of the United States." This was the policy of Free France throughout 1940 and 1941.

As the military and economic difficulties of Germany and Italy were revealed the supporters of Free France increased, and at the end of 1941 almost all Frenchmen were De Gaullist at heart, any doubts being due to the varying degrees of uncertainty regarding the Allied victory. In particular, the French trade unionists supported Free France, their support taking the form of sabotage in the factories, under-working, and attacks upon German officials and soldiers.

With the assent of De Gaulle French ships in Portsmouth, Plymouth, Sheerness and Alexandria were taken over by the British in June 1940 and became the nucleus of a Free French Navy under Admiral Muselier. With the aid of these ships De Gaulle organized risings in Africa and elsewhere, in particular at Dakar. De Gaulle reached Dakar on Sept. 23, 1940, accompanied also by some British warships. Certain French battleships and cruisers, which were under the orders of Vichy, had been allowed to pass the Strait of Gibraltar, and these opened fire. As this made it plain that Dakar could only be taken by a major operation of war, hostilities ceased (*see further under* Dakar).

De Gaulle was better informed regarding the wishes of the people in French Equatorial Africa and the

The Cross of Lorraine.

manuated territory of the Cameroons. Here the Chad Territory linked British Nigeria with the Anglo-Egyptian Sudan. On August 26, 1940, the Territory declared for Free France, but it was not until Nov. 11 that Libreville, in the Gabun area, surrendered. Important arterial roads were at once built or extended, connecting Nigeria and the Sudan. Aided by these communications, De Gaulle organized a Free French force which did noteworthy service in the Libyan, Abyssinian and Syrian campaigns. When General Dentz asked for an armistice in Syria on July 11, 1941, Free French negotiators approved the terms, as well as the proclamation of Syrian independence on September 28.

The first anniversary of the foundation of the Free French Empire was celebrated by De Gaulle in Brazzaville (q.v.) on August 26, 1941. In the course of his speech he referred to the forty French vessels commanded by Admiral Muselier, the hundred French merchantmen navigating for the war, the 2,000 airmen training or trained, and the 60,000 soldiers led by his younger generals.

De Gaulle announced on Sept. 23, 1941, the creation of a de facto Cabinet to share his authority. Two new bodies were set up : one, a Free French National Committee of eight or nine members with executive duties ; the other, a National Advisory Council drawn from French organizations all over the world. Gen. de Gaulle remained in supreme command of the Free French forces, which, apart from naval and air units, were concentrated in Africa. The commander of the Free French Air Force is Gen. Valin. On Dec. 12, 1941, Gen. Odic, formerly Chief of Staff of the Air Force and Air C.-in-C. in North Africa, joined the Free French.

On Christmas Eve 1941 Free France surprised and captured the islands of St. Pierre and Miquelon, off the coast of Newfoundland, the expedition being led by Admiral Muselier. The population at once voted in favour of alliance with the De Gaullist movement.

In July, 1942, the U.S. Government recognized Gen. de Gaulle's position and that of the Free French National Committee. On July 14 Free France became Fighting France (see De Gaulle, Gen.).

LIFE IN OCCUPIED & UNOCCUPIED FRANCE

France, Occupied and Unoccupied. Under the armistice concluded on June 22, 1940, between conquered France and the victorious Nazis, the industrial half of France, all territory north and west of a line connecting Tours and Geneva, remained in German occupation, while the south-eastern agricultural half was left in French possession, under a Government headed by Marshal Pétain.

For administrative purposes the Germans divided Occupied France into six zones. The two Northern areas were designated A and B, and the others the Central, Western, Eastern and Paris regions. As the Eastern area, including Alsace and Lorraine, was administered from Berlin as part of the Reich, it would seem that Hitler's plan was to add the region to the Greater Germany he hoped to reconstitute after the war. The A and B regions in the North (the " Prohibited Zone "), with Lille and Rheims as their foci, are the centres of textile manufacture and engineering, and they were compelled, under force of arms, to

contribute to the Nazi war effort during the period of occupation. Similarly, the western and northern coasts gave bases for Germany's submarine warfare against the British shipping and also the aerodromes whence intensive bombing was possible during the Battle of Britain in the summer of 1940 and the winter of 1940–41. Among the disabilities suffered (though cheerfully) by Frenchmen in the occupied areas were the British bombing of such ports as Brest, Cherbourg and Dieppe and of railway centres and marshalling yards in France's industrial North.

When the Pétain Government was first established in Unoccupied France the chief executive authority belonged to the lawyer, Laval; he was dismissed from the premiership on Dec. 13, 1940, and his successor, Flandin, resigned on Feb. 9, 1941. Admiral Darlan then became Premier, and on August 12, 1941, was created Minister of National Defence.

On August 27 a young Frenchman, Colette, attempted to murder Laval and his associate Marcel Déat at Versailles. Following the attempted assassination courts of repression were set up in the occupied areas, and, when similar attacks upon German officers and officials followed, savage reprisals were attempted by Germany. When a German officer was shot and killed at Bordeaux in October 1941 fifty French hostages, arrested at random, were shot. Only an angry protest from the people of France, Occupied and Unoccupied, saved fifty other hostages from a similar death.

Always conquered France was subject to political blackmail, owing to the fact that 1,500,000 soldiers were in Germany held as hostages, that is, one in three of all Frenchmen between 20 and 40 years of age. Originally, Germany had 1,800,000 French prisoners. About 300,000 of the older men were allowed to return to France during 1941. Germany was fully aware of the value of the 1,500,000 prisoners as blackmail, knowing their labour was essential if French industry and agriculture were to be restored.

The financing of conquered France during 1940 and 1941 proved simpler than might have been expected. During 1941 the Vichy Government spent

Occupied, Unoccupied and Demilitarized zones in France.

133 milliards of francs, 68 milliards being raised by taxation, while 65 milliards represented a deficit. In addition, 146 milliards a year were paid to the German army of occupation. The total deficit in 1941 thus exceeded 200 milliards. A few French business-men who were helping the German war effort profited, but the rest were being steadily deprived of their material wealth, in exchange for what would eventually be worthless paper francs. There was paper money in plenty, but, all the time, the material assets were being sucked up by Germany and industry was being slowly strangled by the loss of raw material and the lack of man power. Many factories in Occupied France closed, and at one time a million unemployed were registered, two-thirds being in the Paris region. Food was taken to Germany in such quantities that millions of French people suffered semi-starvation.

During 1940 and 1941 the German-controlled Paris wireless was indefatigable in sending out propaganda,

HUNGER QUEUE IN UNOCCUPIED FRANCE

It is Germany's rule to pillage the countries she conquers, and France, even the Unoccupied part, was not spared. Hence the food queues that formed up in cities such as Grenoble, seen above, where a distribution of bread provided by the Vichy Winter Relief Fund is being made to needy families.

Photo. Fox

at times denouncing Marshal Pétain as one who favoured the policy of only limited cooperation with victorious Germany. There were, however, numerous Free French repercussions, among them the clandestine news-sheet circulating from Paris. At times, in 1941, there were twenty such broadsheets attacking the Nazi regime, and a special branch of the police force was recruited to track down the clandestine newspapers.

In an effort to weaken anti-German agitation, the Vichy Government (q.v.), on Aug. 24, 1940, dissolved all the ex-service-men's associations in France, replacing them with their own Légion Française des Combattants. Within a year the Légion claimed to have enrolled 1,200,000 war-veterans. Germany made use of the treacherous Laval (q.v.), who returned to power as " Chief " of the Vichy Government in April 1942, and under the cloak of a Franco-German " friendship "

the Nazis were enabled to press ever greater demands upon France.

Books to Consult: Report on France, Thomas Kernan (Bodley Head). Thro' Occupied Territory, Polly Peabody (Cresset Press).

Franco, GEN. FRANCISCO (b. 1892). Spanish dictator. He organized the military uprising in July 1936 which led to the Spanish Civil War, and on Oct. 1, 1936, pro-claimed himself Leader (Caudillo)

General Franco, Caudillo of Spain.
Photo. Associated Press

of the State and C.-in-C. In May 1939 he joined the Anti-Comintern Pact. In August 1939 the second Government of the New State was formed and Gen. Franco was proclaimed President and Prime Minister. In an official declaration on July 18, 1940, he stated that " the possession of Gibraltar is, for Spain, an imperative claim." On Oct. 23, 1940, he met Hitler on the Franco-Spanish border, the German dictator being particularly anxious to have Spain's cooperation in his "New Order." Franco conferred with Mussolini at Bordighera on Feb. 12, 1941, establishing, according to a brief official communiqué, " identity of viewpoints." The next day he met Marshal Pétain and Adm. Darlan at Montpelier, France, before returning to Spain. When addressing the National Council of the Falange on July 17, 1941, he made a strongly pro-German and anti-British and anti-American speech, in which he declared that the battle for the New Order had first been fought in Spain, and ended his speech with a declaration of solidarity with the German Army.

Frank, DR. HANS. First German Governor-General of Nazi-occupied Poland. He was installed at Cracow on Nov 8, 1939, and immediately imposed measures of oppression. One of his first decrees made a sharp distinction between the Germans and the native Poles, the latter being stigmatized as belonging to an inferior and subject race. Another decree introduced com-pulsory labour for the whole of the Polish population between the ages of 17 and 45. Large numbers of Gestapo inquisitors and spies were let loose on the population, and Poles were arrested wholesale. Looting was intensified. During the first year alone of Dr. Frank's cruel and barbaric rule as Governor-General, thousands of innocent men and women were killed, and hundreds of thousands were evicted from their homes. On Jan. 30, 1942, he issued a decree depriving the Polish nation of nationality. *See* Poland.

Frank, KARL HERMANN. State Secretary for the German Protectorate of Bohemia and Moravia from 1939. Frank and his band of Sudeten agents provo-cateurs were responsible for much bloodshed among the Czechs in Prague on Oct. 28, 1939 when, despite German prohibitions, the national Independence Day was celebrated. On that occasion 17 Czechs were reported to have been killed and some 3,500 arrested.

Frankfort-on-Main. This great German railway, manufacturing and commercial centre was frequently bombed by the R.A.F. On the night of June 4, 1940, it was raided for one and a half hours, the oil tanks being the chief target on this occasion. In subsequent raids considerable damage was done to railway communications, factories, warehouses, etc.

Lt.-Gen. Franklyn, led Frankforce.
Photo, Bassano

Franklyn, Lt.-Gen. HAROLD EDMUND, C.B., D.S.O. (b. 1885). In May 1940 he was placed in charge of all the British troops operating in and around Arras. He had commanded the 5th Division since 1938, and this contingent, together with the 50th Division of the 1st Army Tank Brigade, Petreforce, and the force under the O.C. 12th Royal Lancers, was known as Frank-

force. On May 21 Gen. Franklyn attacked the Germans, inflicting heavy losses, but enemy opposition proved strong. Frankforce was eventually withdrawn as it was in danger of being hemmed in. It withdrew in an easterly direction, thus delaying the enemy attack on Arras.

Fraser, RT. HON. PETER, P.C. (b. 1884). Prime Minister of New Zealand from April 1940. He succeeded Mr. M. J. Savage. From 1935 to 1940 he was Minister of Education, Health, Marine and Police.

Freeman, AIR CHIEF MARSHAL SIR WILFRID RHODES, K.C.B., D.S.O. (b. 1888). Vice-Chief of Air

Peter B. Fraser, Premier of N. Zealand.
Photo, Topical

Staff from November 1940. In May 1940 he was appointed Tempy. Air Chief Marshal, having become Air Marshal in 1937. He was present at the Churchill-Roosevelt meeting in the Atlantic in August 1941.

Freyberg, Lt.-Gen. SIR BERNARD CYRIL, V.C., K.B.E. (b. 1890). C.-in-C. 2nd New Zealand Expeditionary Force from 1939. On May 5, 1941, he was appointed C.-in-C. of British, New Zealand and Greek forces in Crete. After the evacuation he commanded the New Zealand forces in Egypt.

Frisian Islands. A chain of islands lying from 3 to 20 m. from the mainland and extending from the coast of N. Schleswig to the Zuider Zee. The N. Frisian Islands include Sylt and Fohr, and the E. Frisians include Norderney and Borkum. *See* Norderney; Sylt.

Lt.-Gen. Freyberg, C.-in-C. N. Zealand Expeditionary Force.
Photo, British Official

Funk, WALTHER (b. 1890). President of the German Reichsbank from January 1939. He succeeded Dr. Schacht, who had held that post for 6 years. Funk also became Minister for Economic Affairs for the Reich and Prussia.

Furious, H.M.S. British aircraft carrier with a displacement of 22,450 tons, a complement of 748 (about 1,200 with R.A.F. personnel), and an official complement of 33 aircraft. She underwent refitting and alteration from 1921 to 1925, having been originally completed in 1917 as a cruiser. The Furious carried out valuable work near Tromso, Norway, in

April 1940, when Fleet Air Arm machines made attacks against German 'planes. Snow and ice coated her deck on this occasion, making landing conditions difficult.

Gabun. One of the four colonies of French Equatorial Africa, and the last to rally to the flag of Free France. Refusing at first to follow the example of Chad Territory, which announced its adherence to Gen. de Gaulle on Aug. 26, 1940, Gabun put up resistance and on Oct. 27 Free French Forces under Gen. de Larminat advanced on the village and fortress of Lambaréne. On Nov. 6 these were captured, and five days later Libreville, the capital, surrendered, and units of the Free French Navy entered the harbour. On Nov. 12 Port Gentil, the second port of Gabun, capitulated, and thus the whole of the Colony became anti-Hitler. *See* Equatorial Africa, French.

Gafencu, GREGORY (b. 1892). Rumanian Foreign Minister at the outbreak of war. He held pro-Ally sympathies and was eventually dismissed by King Carol on June 1, 1940, his successor being M. Gigurtu, a friend of Goering.

Gallabat. Fortified village on the Sudan-Abyssinia frontier. The Italians advanced from Eritrea and captured Gallabat on July 3, 1940; a short-lived success, for it was retaken by British forces on Nov. 6 and though it fell again into enemy hands on the 9th, was finally retaken by our forces on Nov. 10. *See* East Africa.

Galway, GEORGE VERE ARUNDELL MONCKTON-ARUNDELL, VISCOUNT P.C., G.C.M.G. (b. 1882). Governor-General of New Zealand from 1935.

Gambier-Parry, MAJ.-GEN. M. D. He led the British Military Mission to Athens early in November 1940 and became chief British Liaison Officer with the Greek Army. He was in Libya in 1941 and was taken prisoner in April at Mekili after the British withdrawal from Benghazi. Two other senior British officers—Lt.-Gen. O'Connor and Lt.-Gen. Neame—were captured during the same retreat.

Gambut. It was at this Italian base in Libya, situated between Sidi Aziz and Sidi Rezegh, that Gen. Rommel established his main forward supply of fuel and ammunition when the British evacuated the place in March 1941, after holding it for a month. Thereafter Gambut was a target for repeated attacks by R.A.F. bombers, until New Zealand forces wrested it from German and Italian troops on Nov. 24, 1941, in the course of the second great British drive into Libya. After the German capture of Tobruk on June 21, 1942, during the fifth Libyan campaign, Gambut once more fell into enemy hands as Rommel's forces pressed on to Bardia. *See* North Africa.

Gamelin, GENERAL MARIE GUSTAVE (b. 1872). French C.-in-C. of the Allied forces, 1939–40. On May 19, 1940, during the disastrous retreat of the French armies, he was succeeded by Gen. Weygand (*q.v.*). A firm believer in the efficiency of the Maginot Line, Gamelin was among those soldiers and statesmen on whom the

General Gamelin, C.-in-C. Allied Forces, 1939–40.
Photo, Fox

Vichy Govt. put the blame for the defeat of France at the hands of the Germans. On Sept. 9 he was arrested and detained in a fortress by order of Marshal Pétain to await trial and sentence. *See* France, Defeat of; Riom Trial.

Gardner, CAPT. PHILIP JOHN. Officer of the Royal Tank Regiment. He was awarded the V.C. for courage, determination and complete dis-

Capt. Gardner, awarded the V.C.
Photo, British Official

regard for his own safety displayed on Nov. 23, 1941, south-east of Tobruk. Capt. Gardner led two tanks to the aid of two armoured cars of the King's Dragoon Guards which were out of action and under fire at close range. Dismounting under intense fire, he secured a tow rope to the first car, lifted into it a wounded officer and gave the order to tow. The rope broke, and Capt. Gardner returned to the armoured car, being immediately wounded in the arm and leg. Despite this, he lifted the other officer out of his car and got him back to safety. The first London V.C. of the war, Capt. Gardner became a prisoner in 1942.

Garland, F./O. RONALD EDWARD, V.C. He piloted the leading aircraft of the five R.A.F. bombers which destroyed two bridges over the Albert Canal near Maastricht on May 12, 1940. They had not been destroyed in time because the officer entrusted with this operation was killed. Another officer sacrificed his life in blowing up a third bridge, but meanwhile over the other two came pouring hordes of enemy tanks. Both bridges were heavily defended, and although eight attacks had been made by the

F./O. Garland, awarded the V.C.
Photo, G.P.U.

R.A.F., no direct hit had been scored. The C.O. at the Squadron H.Q. accordingly called for volunteers to finish the job, and all the pilots stepped forward. Lots were drawn and five crews chosen. Diving low through an inferno of A.A. fire, they bombed and destroyed the remaining bridge, but of the five machines one only returned. For leading this heroic assault the V.C. was awarded posthumously to F/O. Garland and to his observer, Sergt. Thomas Gray. *See* Maastricht.

Garrod, AIR MARSHAL ALFRED GUY ROLAND, C.B. (b. 1891). Air Member for Training from July 1940.

Gaulle, GEN. CHARLES ANDRÉ JOSEPH MARIE DE (b. 1890). Head of the Free French Government and leader of the Free French forces fighting beside Britain. He is a specialist in mechanized warfare, the claims of which he urged upon his Government, and in 1940, before the fall of France, commanded, with the rank of Maj.-Gen., the 4th Armoured Division. He was one of the few French generals to win any success; in May he launched successful counter-attacks at Laon and later at Abbeville. Soon afterwards Reynaud made him Under-Secretary of State for National Defence and War. A man not only of great military experience, but also of military imagination, de Gaulle had been several times in London as military adviser for France, and it was he who took back to Bordeaux Mr. Churchill's famous offer of an Anglo-French Union. When the Pétain Government appealed for an Armistice he came to London, and on June 22 issued his

call to Frenchmen in the Colonial Empire, to the French Navy, and to all his compatriots outside the jurisdiction of the Bordeaux Government to continue to fight on for France. On June 28 the British Government recognized him as head of the Free French National Committee, and on Aug. 21 an Allied Forces bill was introduced, giving "any foreign Power allied with His Majesty" power to discipline and administer its force according to its own laws.

Gen. Charles de Gaulle, Leader of Free France.
Photo, Fox

In September 1940 Gen. de Gaulle made an expedition to Dakar (*q.v.*) in order to raise the standard of revolt against Vichy, but his landing was resisted and he had to return. In the autumn of 1940 and the summer of 1941 he made extensive tours of the Middle East and the French West African colonies, where he inspected all the Free French units. On his return in September 1941 he announced far-reaching modifications in the control of Free French interests. On Bastille Day, July 14, 1942, Gen. de Gaulle announced that Free France would be known as Fighting France (La France Combattante). *See* France, Free.

Gayda, VIRGINIO (b. 1885). Italian publicist and editor of the Italian newspaper " Giornale d'Italia " from 1926. Acting as Mussolini's mouthpiece in the Italian controlled press, he did much to stir up anti-British feeling during and preceding the present war.

Gazala, EL. Libyan coastal town, between Bomba and Tobruk. The town was captured from the Italians by Imperial British forces in February 1941, after repeated raids by the R.A.F. on the aerodrome, where a great number of Italian 'planes were destroyed. Abandoned by the British in April 1941, it was then occupied by German troops. El Gazala was heavily bombed in the ensuing months by the R.A.F., and after the British started their second great sweep into Libya in November 1941 it was captured by New Zealand forces on Dec. 15. In Jan. 1942 Gen. von Rommel attacked and in Feb. our forces, which had driven him beyond Jedabia, withdrew to Gazala. On June 14 the South African division holding Gazala was evacuated to Tobruk. *See* North Africa.

Gdynia (Nazi name, Gotenhafen). Port of the former Polish Corridor. Situated on the Baltic coast, 12 miles N.W. of Danzig, Gdynia was originally a fishing village. By 1932 two-thirds of Poland's trade went by the sea routes commanded by Gdynia and Danzig, but despite the prosperity of the latter there was great rivalry between the two ports, Danzig being predominantly German. After Hitler's accession to power in 1933 German resentment against the Polish port increased. Gdynia was forced to surrender on Sept. 14, 1939, as it was entirely cut off from the Polish army. Three hundred out of 350 Polish hostages seized when the port was occupied by the Germans were shot in batches without even the suggestion of a trial. When Poland was partitioned, Gdynia was emptied of its Polish citizens and of all Jews, and the houses from which they were ejected had to be left in good order for the return of the Baltic Germans, repatriated to the Reich from Latvia and Estonia. It was stated that at the end of 1941 the population of 130,000 had shrunk to 17,000. In May 1942 the Gneisenau took shelter in the port from R.A.F. bombing.

Geer, DIRK JAN DE (b. 1870). Former Premier and Minister of Finance and General Affairs in the Netherlands Government in London. In May 1940 he left Holland with the Dutch Cabinet for London, following the German invasion. He resigned in August 1940 for reasons of ill-health, and was succeeded in September by Prof. Gerbrandy.

Gelsenkirchen. Town of Westphalia, 27 miles W. of Dortmund, on the Duisburg-Hamm railway. It is a great industrial area, and the large oil refineries and plants had in the first two years of the war been bombed 42 times by the R.A.F.

Genoa. City and seaport of Italy. It stands at the head of the Gulf of Genoa, 74 miles S.E. of Turin. The first R.A.F. raid was carried out on June 11-12, 1940, when Whitleys from England reached Genoa and bombed the docks and Ansaldo works. The Alps had to be crossed twice by the British bombers to make this attack. By the end of August British raids had caused considerable panic in the city, and it was reported that evacuees fled in such numbers as to cause serious congestion on the roads and in the country villages. On Feb. 9, 1941, the British Western Mediterranean Fleet bombarded military targets in and around the great port, over 300 tons of shells being

fired. On the night of April 12, 1942, Genoa was bombed by home-based aircraft of the R.A.F.

Gensoul, ADM. French naval officer. He was in command at the French naval base of Oran when, on July 3, 1940, Vice-Adm. Sir James Somerville arrived at the head of a British squadron and presented honourable terms for safeguarding the French fleet from falling into German or Italian hands. Parleys continued all day, and then Adm. Gensoul, acting probably on instructions received from Wiesbaden, where the Franco-German Armistice Commission was sitting, announced his intention of fighting. *See* Oran.

George II, KING OF THE HELLENES (b. 1890). In April 1941, when Greece capitulated to Germany, the King went to Crete with members of the Greek Government. They narrowly escaped capture by the Germans when Crete was invaded in May, but escaped to Egypt. King George arrived in England in September 1941 from South Africa, accompanied by the

King George of the Hellenes.
Photo, Hay Wrightson

Crown Prince and Princess and the Greek Prime Minister, and made London his headquarters.

George VI, KING OF GREAT BRITAIN (b. 1895). From the outbreak of war his Majesty was tireless in his war work. In addition to shouldering the arduous responsibilities of his State duties, he found time to pay many visits to the Army, the Navy and the Air Force, and to inspect the work of war factories. In December 1939 he paid a 5-day visit to the Western Front, when he saw both British and French troops in

THEIR MAJESTIES TOURING A BLITZED AREA IN THE EAST END

King George and Queen Elizabeth, whose London home was bombed several times, were indefatigable in visiting raid-scarred districts, whether in London or the provinces, and everywhere their sincere sympathy and cheerful optimism warmed the hearts and buoyed up the spirits of those who had suffered in the raids, bringing comfort to the bereaved and courage to those whose homes or livelihood had been lost.

Photo, Central Press

the line, inspected trenches, visited a Fighter Station, examined a sector of the Maginot Line, and talked with M. Lebrun, M. Daladier and military leaders of both armies. The King was indefatigable in touring bombed areas in Britain, and in showing in the most practical way his sympathy with those who had been rendered homeless or bereaved. He broadcast many messages to the nation, one notable address to the Empire being made from Buckingham Palace on Sept. 23, 1940, during the Battle of Britain, when he emphasised the unconquerable spirit of the British peoples and announced his institution of the George Cross and Medal (*q.v.*). On Dec. 10, 1941, he sent a personal message to President Roosevelt, with whom he had become well acquainted during the Royal visit to the U.S.A. in May and June 1939, in which he stressed that Britain stood at America's side against Japanese aggression.

George Cross and Medal. King George VI chose the design for the George Cross and the George Medal, the honours which he created on Sept. 23, 1940, " for men and women in all walks of civilian life."

Awards of George Cross and Medal
(*From Sept. 23, 1940, to June 23, 1942*)

	George Cross	George Medal
Navy	16	83
Army	12	150
Air Force	7	60
Civilians	12	637
Totals	47	930

Note.—Civilians includes Civil Defence workers, Police and National Fire Service.

E.G.M. (Empire Gallantry Medal) was awarded from 1923 to 1940 to 129 persons (61 military and 68 civilians). Holders living in September 1940 received the George Cross in its place. Posthumous awards of the E.G.M. made during the war were also replaced by the G.C.

(There is also a military division.) Both decorations are in silver. The Cross was designed and modelled by Mr. Percy Metcalfe, C.V.O., R.D.I., the artist responsible for the King's Coronation Medal. It has four equal limbs and in the centre is a circular medallion bearing the design of St. George and the Dragon, taken from the reverse of the gold coinage, surrounded by the inscription " For Gallantry." In the angle of each limb are the letters G VI. The reverse of the Cross is plain, and on it will be inscribed the name of the recipient and the date of the award. The ribbon is dark blue, threaded through a bar adorned with laurel

leaves. The Medal is 1·42 in. in diameter. The obverse shows the crowned effigy of the King, surrounded by the inscription GEORGIUS VI D.G. BR. OMN. REX ET INDIAE IMP., and is identical with that of service medals in general. The reverse depicts St. George slaying the Dragon, a design adapted by Mr. George Kruger Gray, C.B.E., A.R.C.A., F.S.A., after the bookplate designed by Mr. Stephen Gooden, A.R.A., for the Royal Library at Windsor. The ribbon is red with 5 narrow vertical stripes of blue. The King announced the creation of the new honour for civilians in a broadcast to the nation from Buckingham Palace on Sept. 23, 1940. The first civilian to receive the George Cross was Mr. T. H. Alderson (*q.v.*). In April 1942 it was awarded to the heroic island of Malta (*q.v.*).

See also colour plate facing p. 264.

Georges, GEN. ALPHONSE JOSEPH (b. 1875). Second in the military hierarchy of France at the outbreak of war, he bore the title of Commandant of the French Army. He was a member of the French Supreme War Council and Commander of the French Armies of the North-East. The B.E.F. was under his control until the task of coordinating the French, British, and Belgian Armies in a common defence scheme was assigned to Gen. Billotte (*q.v.*) in May 1940.

Gerbrandy, PROF. P. S. He was Prime Minister in the Netherlands Government in London from September 1940, succeeding Jonkeer de Geer in that office. On Dec. 9, 1941, he broadcast Queen Wilhelmina's proclamation declaring that the Netherlands Government was at war with Japan. In May 1942 he became head of the new Ministry for Coordination of Warfare.

Prof. Gerbrandy,
Dutch Prime Minister
in London.

German Freedom Party. The Anti-Nazi movement was given fresh impetus by the establishment of the German Freedom Party, which first came into prominence in April 1937. It circulated a manifesto which was unwittingly delivered by Nazi postmen. This party claimed to represent all classes in Germany, all former political parties and chief religious bodies. Hitler singled it out for direct attack in October 1937, and after the outbreak of war the mysterious voice of the German Freedom Party was heard on the air, broadcasting from some unknown place. The first issue of " Die Zeitung," a Free German newspaper, appeared in London on March 12, 1941.

GERMANY WARS AGAINST THE WORLD

Almost every country in Europe knows by painful experience the meaning of Hitler's attempt to set up his " New Order." In this article are described the conditions obtaining within Nazi Germany and the daily life of her enslaved population.

Germany at War. In war, when normal avenues of information are shut off, countries engaged get knowledge of each other's life and activities through the reports of neutral travellers, their intelligence services, and from the close study of the texts of broadcasts, newspapers and journals, lay and scientific.

Verbal reports are often contradictory, being coloured by violent racial, national, or political bias, and, in the case of Jewish refugees, by terrible personal sufferings.

From such sources we get our knowledge of Germany during, and at the close of, three years of total war on her own pattern. What, then, is daily life like in a country that can show conquests comparable with those of Philip of Macedon and his son, Alexander the Great ?

At once we uncover the first great paradox of this strange war. The enslavement of small neighbour States and the looting of their treasures in man power, in foods, in commodities and raw materials have not produced a well-clothed, well-fed, and well-provided ordinary German, but the contrary. As Nazi aggressions proceeded from outrage to outrage, the well-being of the German people declined. At the start of 1942 they were short of many essentials.

As with most paradoxes, the explanation is a simple one. Germany has stolen from her neighbours and has enslaved their people only to squander this wealth upon the manufacture of munitions of war and for the maintenance of her vast armies of aggression.

She steals the dairy produce of Holland to feed her troops, and all the fecundity of France is requisitioned to that end. She takes bauxite from France in order to make, not the much-needed pots and kettles for the " herrenvolk, " but fighter aeroplane parts. She takes the fish and timber of Norway and all that can be moved from Denmark to the same end.

All these transactions, it will be realized, have small effect on the daily life of Frau Schmidt and her "Mann." What, then, is daily life like for them ?

Germany, far more than with us, is housed in large city flat blocks. Normally central-heated (for Germany has, it must be remembered, a severe winter), they are unheated today. When Frau Schmidt goes shopping she carries, not one ration card, but fourteen, each of a different colour. She is entitled, for instance, to 8 ounces of fats per week, the word fat including margarine, oils, and cheese. The shops she passes have gay windows, and the food shops appear to be laden with good things under the bright lights : fruits, cakes, goodies of all kinds. All are dummies.

Hausfraus who demonstrate in Germany are dealt with by the S.A. (Sturm Abteilung). One method is to put the demonstrators in lorries, drive them ten miles out of town, and leave them to walk home. The response of the State to every attempt of the individual to criticize is force and repression. Never in the whole history of Germany has its people made such extravagant claims of racial superiority while so supinely submitting to a virtual serfdom.

Take, since this human impulse is important for all humanity, the practice of religion. The official programme of the Nazi Party, according to its authorized publication following the Weimar Council of 1926 (Gottfried Feder), contains these words : " Our Party as such takes its stand upon the basis of positive Christianity." No existing Christian community, however, meets with Nazi approval, the Roman Catholic and German Confessional Churches being alike the subject of sequestration and persecution.

FROM A GERMAN PROPAGANDA FILM

This picture, from the film " Victory in the West," purports to show the demolition of Hangest railway station, south of the Somme. The gun crew, protected by a heavy armoured shield, crouches down behind the tractor on which the gun is mounted. On the right is the raised level crossing barrier.

The clash between Churches and State is upon a clearcut issue, namely, the right of prelates and pastors to preach the Gospel of Christ and to animadvert upon anti-Christian activities in the State. Two Evangelicals, the brothers Niemöller, and two Catholic Archbishops, Faulhaber and Innitzer, provide well-known examples of such persecution.

No German Has Freedom

It is not easy to estimate to what extent the ordinary German submits willingly to the conditions under which he is living today, as the inheritor of the Nazi earthly paradise. All ordinary channels of criticism are closed to him, even that of expressing himself freely at his own hearth. He may listen in only to German broadcasting stations, and he tunes in to any other at the risk of his head. He may read only newspapers or journals under Nazi direction. Freedom of speech and freedom to write have been taken from him. Moreover, he moves in a land of spies. In the café, where he sips his substitute coffee, his neighbour may well be a Gestapo spy. Indeed, children are taught to spy upon parents and cases of denunciation of parents by children are on record. Under this pernicious system the smallest children are inculcated, not with a Christian philosophy of life, but with Nazi ideas of aggression and hatred towards the world at large, and especially towards Germany's oppressed victims.

Such a system of wholesale spiritual and intellectual enslavement can be enforced, even on a people so docile and subservient as the Germans, only by draconian laws. Justice has undergone a striking but symptomatic change, with the change in judicial personnel. The old-type German judge, upright and learned, has been ousted by Nazi placemen. These, often political bigots, and dependent upon the Party for their place, administer Nazi laws of ferocious severity and in a spirit of ferocity.

By the reintroduction of the death penalty for a whole range of venial offences, Nazi Germany has put back the judicial clock three centuries. One example of Nazi law will suffice to reveal its quality. Death is the penalty for listening-in to foreign stations, and the official judicial justification is as follows : " Foreign broadcasts may produce a rift or crack in the listener's mind which might develop into a rift in the mind of the community. It is not only a crime to mutilate your body to render it useless to the community, it is criminal to mutilate the mind, the soul, to the detriment of the German people."

Nevertheless, people continue to tune-in, a fact well known to Dr. Goebbels, the Minister of Propaganda. In this department Nazi Germany has shown a remarkable virtuosity, both at home and abroad. Propaganda has been conducted by the spoken, the broadcast and the written word, pictorially, and by the cinema. The cumulative effect upon the mind of young people has been formidable. It has produced, together with the Hitler cult, a generation of fanatics.

Under the Imperial regime Germany became a leading cultural and scientific centre. Its universities attracted students from all over the world. No small part of that distinction was due to the contribution made to applied science, literature, music and art by her Jewish nationals. It is enough to mention such names as Ehrlich, Einstein, Freud and the brothers Mann.

Today, universities, technical schools and hospitals are staffed entirely by Nazi placemen. Some are competent, more are mediocre or incompetent. The result is the inevitable one—a general decline in the standard of work. This deterioration is being felt already where it touches war production.

Nazis Ruined Germany's Railways

One example of how the guidance of Nazi technicians is affecting Germany after three years of war may be cited. Under Nazi technical advice Germany's industry and transport had been adapted to war purposes. Industrial plants were first equipped for, and then put into, war production on a mammoth scale. It was the Nazi view that the day of the railway was past. A scheme for a network of magnificent arterial roads (autostrasse) was inaugurated. The production of railway rolling stock and locomotives was cut down. The formerly fine railway system was allowed to get out of condition. Today, when it is seen that motor roads cannot handle the terrific problems of wartime transport, Germany's railways are proving seriously deficient, a fact indicated by the enormous increase in railway accidents.

To what extent has opposition to the iron rule of the Nazis been organized ? It is not easy to discover this. That such opposition exists we know from the secret German radio station and from the circulation of secret news-sheets.

The Pact of Friendship with Russia probably disturbed a large body of opinion in the Reich, since it constituted so complete a turn-about. The subsequent war has served further to obscure the outlines of Nazi world policy. For the German workers the Russian alliance was a natural enough alignment. The present war may prove a yeast that will produce a ferment in which the Nazi system will dissolve.

Speculation as to the relations existing between the Nazi Party itself and the fighting services provides food for thought. That feeling is not always or everywhere too cordial is probable. Hitler, as actual Commander-in-Chief, can no longer sacrifice scapegoats when things go wrong. He stands or falls.

MOB HYSTERIA IN BERLIN

Hitler is here seen leaving a munitions factory after making a vitriolic speech in which he boasted that Nazi Germany could beat the world, including the United States. On his left is Ley, Minister of Labour ; behind him walks Goebbels, Minister of Propaganda.

Photo, Keystone

HOW THE WAR FEVER GRIPPED GERMANY

In the top photograph, Ribbentrop gives Press correspondents the pretexts for Germany's treachery in breaking her pact with the Soviets. Centre, left, women workers test shells ; right, civilians queue up to gloat over the historic railway carriage used in the Forest of Compiègne for the capitulation of German delegates in 1918 and that of French delegates in 1940. Below, left, girls are working on the envelopes of barrage balloons, and, right, a U-boat crew is lined up for an official godspeed.

Photos, Wide World, Keystone, Associated Press

After three years of war, in short, the actualities of Nazi Germany are somewhat different from the conventional picture offered to the world. The German is a docile, disciplined and sub-servient being. He makes a good soldier as he makes a good waiter, because obedience and servility are instinctive with him. Far from being innately a herrenvolk (super-race) the Germans are, by instinct, slaves. They have produced no heroes or adventurers comparable with those of Portugal, Spain, Italy, France or England.

Is such a race the predestined master of the world? Already the world war has answered that question.

What were, at that time, the possibilities of an internal break-up in Germany? Such questions are always difficult to answer. Consider the morale which sustained the German people and it is plain that it differs fundamentally from British morale. It is based on resignation. It is not the spiritual resilience for which the French have the word *élan*. It is the passive acceptance of evil and suffering. Would any other race have accepted the abrogation of parental authority by the State, and, worse, the transference of childish loyalty from parents to State save, perhaps, the Japanese?

CONVOY OF GERMAN PANZERS IN RUSSIA

On the move to another part of the line, these tanks are approaching what was once a Russian village—now a ruin of flame and black smoke. The enemy's advance into Russia was chiefly due to his preponderance of armoured divisions

Photo, Associated Press

While Hitler won great victories such degradations were tolerated. But the invasion of the U.S.S.R. changed the war pattern. At a moment when victory appeared to be in sight, the people saw unfolded the dread prospect of a long and bitter campaign against a powerful foe.

The implications of peace were changed, and it was seen that the war had become a life-and-death struggle without the use of those words in any hyperbolic sense. The Nazi-controlled press hammered home this point : it was fight and work and go hungry, or die. Before there was consciousness of an alternative—peace proposals, negotiations. Russia meant a struggle to the final death.

Perhaps the most significant event in Germany in these circumstances was the necessity which prompted Hitler to ask for and take such powers in the State that no human individual ever assumed in history Supreme commander of the armed forces on land, at sea, and in the air, he constituted himself the embodiment of the law and absolute autocrat in all departments of government. That measure was taken to quash any possible opposition when the Russian campaign yielded a harvest of death that sent a wave of horror throughout Germany.

Hard upon the heels of this political humiliation, for Hitler's act implied mistrust of the people he claimed to lead, came the fresh trial and, perhaps, greatest test of German morale, namely the opening of the great British air offensive upon the war-producing plants of the Reich, with the Cologne 1,000-bomber raid of May 30, 1942, followed on June 1 by an even heavier attack on Essen with 1,036 bombers. Mr. Churchill's promise of continued devastation " city by city " emphasized the severity of the strain upon the Nazis.

Books to Consult. Behind the Nazi Front, J. M. Raleigh (Harrap). Berlin Diary, W. Shirer (Hamish Hamilton). Pattern of Conquest, J. Harsch (Heinemann). Hitler's War Machine, W. Necker (Lindsay Drummond). Last Train from Berlin, H. K. Smith (Cresset Press).

Germany, British Raids On. In the first three months of the war the R.A.F. carried out a number of daylight bombing attacks on German territory, and amongst the more outstanding were those made at very low level on Wilhelmshaven, Brunsbüttel, Cuxhaven, Borkum and Heligoland. The assaults on Brunsbüttel and Wilhelmshaven were executed a short time after the declaration of war Compared with later raids these preliminary operations were on a small scale, and the losses were high.

British bombing attacks on Germany from the beginning have been directed against the industrial basis of the enemy's war effort, against his shipping and transport systems. The targets selected vary from time to time, the changes and degree of concentration depending on information received through various means, including reconnaissance and aerial

Targets of the Royal Air Force in Germany

than 80 times by the close of 1941. In that year squadrons of R.A.F. Bomber Command were equipped with new heavy bombers of the four-engined class and an increase of 200 per cent in the bomb load compared with that of the earlier bomber types was made possible. Bigger bombs with an intensified destructive power were also adopted.

In June 1941 some resumption of day raids over enemy territory was made by the R.A.F., and in these operations partial support was given to the bombers by new types of long-range fighters. A number of attacks were carried out also in daylight by four-engined American Boeing sub-stratosphere bombers. These aircraft, flying at an altitude of some 36,000 feet, successfully evaded detection and fire from the ground and experienced no interception by German fighters.

In addition to drastic changes in equipment and the adoption of heavier bombs and improvements in armaments, a marked increase in Britain's bomber strength was accomplished in 1941. The latter factor was thrown into relief on Nov. 7, 1941, when hundreds of machines were in action in raids on Berlin and Cologne. Weather conditions, however, caused the loss of 37 machines on this night. In the winter months of 1941 abnormal weather seriously curtailed the operations of the Bomber Command. Otherwise the scale of attacks on Germany would have risen in proportion to the greater striking power with which the R.A.F. was now endowed.

photography. Daylight raids over enemy territory, which formed the earlier actions, were found to be costly ; the anti-aircraft ground defences and fighter strength of the enemy prevented the British bombers, which had no fighter escorts, from penetrating deep into Germany in daylight without serious losses. Long-distance flights over enemy territory were made by R.A.F. bombers early in 1940. In January reconnaissance flights were made as far as Austria and Bohemia, and " leaflet raids " in March were carried out on Prague and Vienna as well as Berlin.

On March 19, 1940, raids which were the biggest that had so far been made on Germany, were accomplished by a considerable force of Wellingtons, Hampden and Whitley bombers on Hornum, Sylt and the Hindenburg Dam. During August 1940 particular attention was given to the bombing of the Dortmund-Ems Canal, and on August 25 military objectives in the Berlin area were bombed for the first time. By Sept. 3 five raids had been made on the capital in nine days, and on Oct. 7 British night-bombers were over Berlin for four hours and some of the machines flew as low as 5,000 feet. The twenty-fourth Berlin attack was executed on Oct. 27, and on the same date assaults were made on objectives as far distant as Stettin, Politz and Pilsen.

Another field of persistent activity for Bomber Command was the Ruhr, where at different periods attacks were made nightly on the heavy-industry area and on railway centres such as Hamm, Osnabrück, Soest, Schwerte, and Krefeld. Hamm was raided more

In the spring of 1942 R.A.F. attacks on Germany increased, both in weight and numbers. A particularly heavy raid took place on March 28, when Lübeck was the chief target. On April 17 a daring daylight attack was made on Augsburg by 12 of our newest bombers, seven of which were shot down. Rostock was reduced to ruins by four successive night raids, April 23-26. Mannheim suffered heavy damage in a large-scale raid in May. On May 30 the first of the " 1,000 bomber " raids took place, with Cologne as the chief target. This was followed on June 1 by a still heavier attack on Essen, with 1,036 machines. Of this total 35 planes were lost. These " 1,000 bomber" raids marked a new phase in the air offensive against the war industry of the Reich. The raid on Cologne was an experimental test of new tactics employing the use of radiolocation (q.v.) navigational aids.

Radar, or radiolocation, was originally devised as a defensive measure, to detect the approach of enemy aircraft, but had now been developed as an offensive aid for carrying the air war, with greater intensity, to all parts of Germany. The need for more accuracy in bombing had become apparent in 1940-41, when the whole policy of Bomber Command, in carrying out night raids, gave cause for grave anxiety. Results had not come up to expectations, as only experienced air crews were able to find the target in darkness. A bomber force of 1,000 or more was projected, but the shortage in personnel of the required ability and experience was acute at this time. British science provided the answer by adapting Radar to the needs of night bombing. The experimental stage had occupied the whole of 1941, but in the spring of 1942, Bomber Command had achieved their object, a concentration of time and space, whereby hundreds of bombers could be handled over a single target in the matter of minutes. The average time for a six hundred bomber raid had been narrowed down to 20 minutes.

Two of the devices used enabled a bomber to locate accurately its position at all times regardless of the weather. A later development improved on this and actually gave the signal, from a base in Britain, when the bombs were to be dropped.

Radar also resulted in the " Pathfinder " (q.v) force being formed. This system of pathfinding was carried out with marked success. Using navigational aids it was possible for a bomber to indicate accurately a target area, marking it with flares or bombs, on to which the main force dropped its bombs.

The introduction of Radar and the use of these tactics resulted in an immense step-up in the striking power of Bomber Command which was becoming very apparent during the last few months of 1942, although by the year's end there had been only one more 1,000 bomber raid, making a total of three for the year. The target on this occasion was Bremen, which was visited on the night of June 25. The stepping-up of the offensive against German industry, although in progress, could not reach anything like the intensity planned until 1943, as the need for heavy bombers was acute. But this latter raid, together with other heavy attacks, was a good augur of things to come and for the fulfilment of Mr. Churchill's promise that German " cities of war production would be subjected to an ordeal the like of which had never been experienced in any country for continuity, severity and magnitude."

In June 1942, Bomber Command turned its main attention to Emden, where on the 6th, 19th, 20th and 22nd they dropped a total of 1,300 tons, causing severe damage to the U-boat yards. In July, Hamburg, one of the main centres of U-boat building and oil refining, received its heaviest raid to date, when 400 aircraft dropped 740 tons during the night of the 20th, inflicting severe damage. Saarbruecken was raided on the 29th, when 350 tons resulted in serious damage to the railways and railway buildings. Several factories, and the

Defries works, Germany's most important machine tool factory, were put out of action. Apart from Cologne, this town was the most damaged at this time. Although attacks in August included two on Mainz, August 11 and 12, when 100 acres were devastated, which covered parts of the industrial centres and shipyards. Osnabrück in Prussia was raided on August 9 and 17 and again on Oct. 6. It possessed nine factories on Bomber Command's priority list and all received hits, and in addition, warehouses, factories, railway targets and military barracks received damage. Kassel, another important industrial town, turning out locomotives, tanks and other war equipment, received attention on August 27, when 550 tons went down from 300 aircraft.

R.A.F. BOMBER RAIDS ON GERMANY, 1942

1942	Industrial towns	Naval targets	A/c. factories	Specific industries	Misc. targets	Total tons	No. of mines laid
Jan.	853	1,219	82	—	138	2,292	62
Feb.	285	376	36	—	314	1,011	306
Mar.	1,711	298	32	510	124	2,675	356
Apl.	2,667	847	243	397	279	4,433	569
May	2,383	231	304	211	105	3,234	1,023
June	6,087	223	390	36	109	6,845	1,167
July	5,246	896	99	22	105	6,368	897
Aug.	3,828	110	34	15	175	4,162	968
Sep.	5,256	103	125	16	95	5,595	1,101
Oct.	3,124	394	183	37	71	3,809	982
Nov.	1,700	662	8	9	44	2,423	1,156
Dec.	2,497	24	7	88	98	2,714	987
Totals	35,637	5,383	1,543	1,341	1,657	45,561	9,574 =6,367 tons.

It is convenient to note here that during the whole of 1942 Bomber Command dropped a total of 45,561 tons, the vast majority falling on industrial areas; this was more than the total dropped in 1940-41, a striking achievement which would never have been possible had not new navigational aids and strategy been forthcoming. The loss in personnel was almost double that of 1941, which resulted mainly from the fact that concentrated raids had increased, of necessity, the efficiency of the German defensive system. In trying to overcome these new methods of bombing, Germany had to improve her night fighter strength and employ new tactics, as it became apparent that A.A. defence, although it remained a menace, could never cope with massed formations of planes. Besides achieving striking success with their attacks against the German power to wage and sustain war, air supremacy had been won. See Table above and also that in page 47.

Germany: Soviet Pact with. This non-aggression pact was signed between Germany and Russia on August 23, 1939, after two meetings between Molotov and von Ribbentrop in Moscow. The two countries agreed to refrain from any act of force against each other and engaged that neither would join any other group of Powers which directly or indirectly menaced one of the two. The agreement was concluded for the duration of ten years and was to come into force immediately. Great surprise was expressed in Britain at the apparent volte-face of German and Russian policy, but all sections of the press and public opinion united in expressing determination to uphold Britain's pledge to Poland should that country be attacked. As events proved, Germany, assured of Russia's neutrality, invaded Poland on Sept. 1, 1939. On June 22, 1941, without any denunciation of the Pact, Germany invaded Russia. See Poland ; Russia.

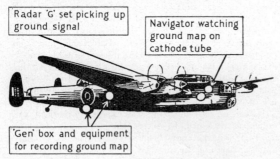

Radar 'G' set picking up ground signal

Navigator watching ground map on cathode tube

'Gen' box and equipment for recording ground map

RADAR AGAINST THE ENEMY

After the air war against Germany was ended it was revealed that the great increase in 1942 of the R.A.F. bomber attacks was due to the help of Radar. Here is a Lancaster showing the arrangement of the Radar equipment.

Eichdudlingen Iron Works received hits. On July 31, Düsseldorf, one of Germany's larger industrial cities, was attacked with a considerable weight, receiving extensive damage. About two-thirds of the Schiess

Gestapo. Contraction of Geheime Staatspolizei, the German Secret Political Police. It was organized immediately after Hitler's advent to power in 1933, to deal with the enemies of the Nazi regime, and rapidly became one of the terrors of the German population and the chief support of the Nazi regime. The Gestapo was notorious for its barbaric cruelty, and possessed countless agents all over Germany supervising the behaviour and utterances of the people and making immediate arrests whenever they heard a word of opposition. The chief of this organization, Himmler (*q.v.*), who was put in that position by Hitler, also became head of the SS or Black Guards. After Germany had occupied Denmark, Norway, the Netherlands, Belgium, France and Greece, the network of the Gestapo was flung far in an intensive search for victims. Its activities were particularly notorious in Czechoslovakia and Poland, where thousands of people were brought to trial for so-called acts against the State. Many of its victims were either sent to concentration camps or shot.

G.H.Q. Liaison Regiment. This specialized force of the British Army began as a very small unit in Belgium, in 1940, to form a direct link between field communications and the C.-in-C. Where normal communications were constantly being wrecked by swift German assaults it was found that the only way of sending news of a battle to French or British H.Q. was by means of a small motorized detachment. This method proved invaluable in Greece in 1941. All members were picked men, and included many expert rough-riders in motor-cycle trials. All were trained in map-reading and military observation. The regiment's fleet of fast cars, which were equipped with wireless and even with small aircraft piloted by the men themselves, achieved splendid work in both the Belgian and Greek campaigns.

Gibraltar. Occupying a vital strategic position on the southernmost point of Spain is Gibraltar. Known as "The Rock," it is the world's finest fortress and is considered impregnable. It is $2\frac{3}{4}$ miles long, $\frac{3}{4}$ mile broad, and is connected with the mainland by a promontory. The population normally is about 20,300, four-fifths being civilians.

As well as its Admiralty Harbour of 440 acres, protected by three moles, Gibraltar has three large graving docks. Boom defences protect the two harbour entrances. The fortifications, already formidable, were recently strengthened. New extensive tunnelling, to accommodate underground emplacements,

hospitals, barracks and stores, was carried out deep into the Rock.

Innumerable guns of every calibre are mounted, including big naval guns and automatic A.A. guns working from a secret "electric eye." Cunningly hidden, they are so placed that every approach to the Rock is guarded. Fresh water, collected by giant catchments and stored in reservoirs, is plentiful, and enough food is stored to last three years under siege conditions. With the addition of an air base, numerous 'planes and thousands of troops, Gibraltar stood prepared. On July 25, 1940, the evacuation began of some 15,000 women and children ; and later it was announced that accommodation had been provided in London for 11,000 refugees from Gibraltar.

The factors governing Gibraltar's vitally important strategic position are :

(1) It is the base of naval and air operations controlling shipping passing through the Straits, along trade routes to South America, Africa, and the Cape, and to the East and Australasia, and is therefore an essential factor in maintaining Britain's economic blockade.
(2) Following the loss of French naval bases, it is the only Allied naval and air base linking Britain with Malta.
(3) It is doubly important as a result of the menace created by the newly fortified ports of Algeciras, Ceuta and Tangier.

Up to the spring of 1942 Gibraltar's war role was a quiet one, the major events being the raids by French aircraft on Sept. 24 and 25, 1940, as a reprisal for the Allied attacks on Dakar. On Sept. 24 20 'planes bombed the Rock for four hours, dropping 100 bombs. Four people were killed and 12 injured. One hundred 'planes took part in the second attack (Sept. 25), in which two powder magazines exploded and fires were started. One aircraft was shot down.

Axis threats to Gibraltar, which were voiced frequently, failed to materialize, partly because of

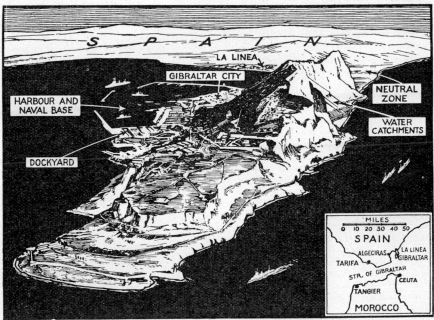

GIBRALTAR, KEY TO THE MEDITERRANEAN

Gibraltar, a natural fortress, was very strongly fortified against the threat of Axis domination in the Mediterranean. It bristled with guns and was a well-equipped air base. Thousands of troops were stationed there, stated to be provisioned with enough food and water to stand a three years' siege.

Axis pre-occupation in Libya, Russia, etc., and partly because the time for such a venture had not come—yet. Gibraltar is a key position which Britain must hold at all costs. The greatly increased defences, some of which have been developed fivefold since the beginning of the war, have made Gibraltar virtually impregnable from both land and sea.

Gen. Lord Gort was appointed Governor and C.-in-C. of Gibraltar on April 25, 1941, succeeding Lt.-Gen. Sir C. Liddell. Lord Gort held this office until May 7, 1942, when he went to Malta to succeed the retiring Governor, Gen. Dobbie. Lt.-Gen. Mason MacFarlane became the new Governor of Gibraltar.

Gibraltar, Main Events, 1940–1942

1940	Sept. 4	Many French aircraft landed from Morocco, making a total of 36.
„	Sept. 24 & 25	Gibraltar bombed by French aircraft (see text).
„	Oct. 30	Italians attempted to torpedo ships in harbour by means of special device. No damage done.
„	Dec. 25	Unidentified plane crashed into sea off La Linea after being fired on by British and Spanish A.A. batteries.
1941	Jan. 1	Governor broadcast warning reminding population that Gibraltar was now exposed to attack.
„	June 12	Gibraltar bombed (Italian communiqué).
„	July 13	Press reported bombs dropped on La Linea by Italian planes on previous day. Six people killed and 18 injured.
„	July 14	Bombs dropped near a village between La Linea and Algeciras by two Italian aircraft.
„	Sept. 20	Attack by Italian motor torpedo-boats. Enemy's exaggerated claims discounted by Admiralty, which admitted sinking of hulk used as coal depot.
1942	May 7	Lord Gort transferred to Malta; succeeded at Gibraltar by Lt.-Gen. Mason MacFarlane.

Giffard, Gen. Sir George James, K.C.B., D.S.O. (b. 1886). G.O.C.-in-C. West Africa from July 1941. Military Secretary to the Secretary of State for War in 1939, he was appointed G.O.C. British Forces in Palestine and Transjordan in 1940.

Gigurtu, Ion. Rumanian politician. An industrialist of pro-Nazi sympathies, he was made Foreign Minister on June 1, 1940, in place of Gafencu (q.v.), and on July 4 succeeded Tatarescu as Prime Minister. This was shortly after Rumania had renounced the Anglo-French guarantee of her frontiers. Under the Premiership of Gigurtu places were found for Horia Sima, leader of the Iron Guard (q.v.), and Cuza, a notorious anti-Semite. In an endeavour further to placate the Axis and to get its support against the territorial claims of neighbouring countries, the Government expelled 22 British engineers and oil experts from Rumania, and on July 24 took over control of the Astra Romana Oil Company, which was owned by British and Dutch interests. But the Axis, which had supported the cession of Bessarabia and Bukovina to Russia in June, ordered the handing over of the Dobruja to Bulgaria and of northern Transylvania to Hungary in August. Alarmed at these concessions, the Rumanians united in opposition, Gigurtu's Cabinet fell, the Iron Guard demanded the King's resignation, and Antonescu became Premier and virtual Dictator.

Gilmour, Sir John (1876–1940). In October 1939 he became the first head of the newly established Ministry of Shipping, and was at work in his department until the day before his death, April 30, 1940.

Glider Pilots Regiment. Incorporated in the Army Air Corps, the formation of which was announced by the War Office on March 24, 1942. This corps was created in order to simplify the administration of Army airborne units in such matters as records, pay, family allowances, etc.,

Army Flying Badge for Glider Pilots.
Photo. British Official

hitherto controlled by their own regiments. The Glider Pilots Regiment was brought within its scope, further units to be included progressively. In May 1942 the U.S. Army started to train large numbers of glider pilots.

Gliders in Warfare. A glider is an engineless aeroplane launched into the air by catapult, or by towing by means of a winch, a motor-car or some other method of providing the initial lift. Once in the air it stays aloft by utilizing the support afforded by air streams, but must, of course, continue in flight or lose its lift. Apart from the lack of engine controls, its controls resemble those of an aeroplane.

Quite apart from the use of gliders in sport or as a means of giving training and experience to would-be aeroplane pilots, some experiments had been made before 1939 in the towing of gliders by engined aircraft and the casting loose of the tow after reaching the neighbourhood of a landing ground. Not only single gliders but " trains " of several were taken into the air behind the towing 'plane. Since much of this experimental work was done for a military object few details were made public. The German attack on Crete (May 20, 1941) showed that the technique of glider towing had been brought to a high pitch of efficiency.

The gliders used were of simple construction and varied in size, carrying 4, 6, 12 or 20 men. They were towed by aircraft of different kinds, with two, three or four engines. Sometimes an aircraft would have three gliders attached by separate cables so that they spread out fanwise behind; on other occasions the

CRASH-LANDING IN CRETE

A large number of gliders were used for the German invasion of Crete. They were capable of holding four to 20 men with equipment, and were towed by planes. Gliders are very easy targets, and many of them were lost.
Photo. British Official

'plane would tow several gliders one behind the other. Many were shot down by the defences, but they were brought in in such numbers, and so persistently, that eventually enough enemy troops were landed to take and hold vantage points where engined aircraft could alight with impunity. Aid was given by clouds of troops descending by parachutes, while transport 'planes brought yet more. So in the course of twelve days the Germans conquered the island, and British troops were obliged to be withdrawn.

In North Africa the Germans used gliders for bringing arms and armament to their troops, and it was calculated that the craft employed could carry up to three tons of men or material. Such gliders were of more elaborate construction than those employed for Crete, which bore the appearance of having been improvised from simple material and designed for that particular operation. On the Russian front gliders were employed to reinforce and supply German troops encircled, or others left in frontal positions by the enemy retreat and difficult to supply by other means. In 1942 the United States Navy Air Service was said to be employing gliders of even more ambitious design, with a capacity as great as that of a large air liner and with a standard of aerodynamic efficiency almost as high as that of the modern aeroplane. *See* illus. p. 1881.

Glorious, H.M.S. A sister ship of the Courageous (*q.v.*), this British warship was launched in 1916 as an armoured cruiser, her conversion into an aircraft carrier being completed in January 1930. She had a displacement of 22,500 tons and carried 48 aircraft. Her complement, including R.A.F. personnel, was 1,216. The Glorious was sunk during naval operations covering the withdrawal of the Allied forces from Norway, the Admiralty announcing her loss on June 10, 1940. *See* Navy, Royal; Norway.

Gloucester, H.R.H. HENRY, DUKE OF, G.C.V.O. (b. 1900). Brother of H.M. King George VI. From 1939 to 1940 he acted as Chief Liaison Officer to the B.E.F. in France, and on Aug. 12, 1940, was appointed Chief Liaison Officer, G.H.Q. Home Forces. In May and June 1942 he made an extensive tour of the Middle East and India.

Gloucester, H.M.S. This famous British cruiser of 9,400 tons belonged to the Southampton class and was completed in 1939. Her complement was

LOST IN ACTION OFF THE NORWEGIAN COAST

The Glorious, originally built as a cruiser, was converted into an aircraft carrier in 1930. She was sent to Norway to cover the withdrawal of Allied forces there and was lost in the course of naval operations. Her sister ship, Courageous, was sunk in September 1939.

Photo, Wright & Logan

700, and she carried twelve 6-in. guns and three aircraft with one catapult. Under the command of Flag Capt. H. A. Rowley, she was in action in the great battle of Matapan (*q.v.*) on March 28, 1941. H.M.S. Gloucester formed part of Vice-Admiral Pridham-Wippell's squadron which had been sent to intercept a strong Italian naval force on its way to attack British convoys between Egypt and Greece. She was engaged by three enemy cruisers at a range of about 23,000 yards, the Italian cruisers then making off and being pursued by the Gloucester until the latter was attacked by the Vittorio Veneto (*q.v.*). During this engagement she suffered no damage. On May 22, 1941, she was dive-bombed by the Luftwaffe off Crete during the German attempt to invade that island by sea. She had closed in to support British destroyers racing to the assistance of H.M.S. Greyhound. Wave after wave of enemy bombers concentrated on the Gloucester, and finally a direct hit finished her off. She sank with guns blazing upwards. Her loss was announced on May 27.

Glowworm, H.M.S. British destroyer of the Greyhound class. Her displacement was 1,335 tons and she carried a complement of about 145. The Glowworm accompanied a large British mine-laying force off Norway on April 8, 1940, the day before

H.R.H. The Duke of Gloucester,
Chief Liaison Officer
Home Forces.
Photo, British Official

END OF H.M.S. GLOWWORM

Taken from the deck of an enemy destroyer, this photograph shows the Glowworm laying a smoke-screen in a vain endeavour to escape destruction. A shell has just fallen short of her, but a subsequent one broke her in half. She was outnumbered by three to one.   Her crew were saved.

Photo, Planet News

the German invasion of that country. Having lost a man overboard, she stopped behind to rescue him and was hurrying to rejoin her force when two German destroyers appeared. She engaged them, but a third enemy ship joined in the attack, and the odds became too heavy. The British destroyer was overwhelmed by shells and a violent explosion broke her in half. All the survivors, it was announced, were picked up by the German cruiser. *See* Norway.

Glubb, MAJ. JOHN BAGOT (b. 1897). Commander of the Arab legion in the Middle East, a small Arab

Major Glubb, "Second Lawrence of Arabia."

Photo, Planet News

force that did valuable work in Iraq in protecting the oil pipeline during the revolt of 1941. Maj. Glubb had lived for 22 years among the nomadic Beduins in Transjordan and Iraq and in 1941 earned the popular reputation of a second "Lawrence of Arabia." He succeeded Col. Peake as right-hand man to the Emir of Transjordan in 1939 and administered law among the nomad tribes of that country.

Gneisenau. Famous German battle-cruiser which was used as a surface raider. She was completed in 1938. Her displacement was 26,000 tons, she carried a main armament of nine 11-in. guns, and had a complement of 1,461. When the R.A.F. bombed Kiel district on Oct. 25, 1939, it was reported that a bomb fell down the funnel of the Gneisenau. During the naval actions between the Germans and British at the time of the Norwegian invasion in April 1940 it was persistently rumoured that she had been sunk—according to one report, sent to the bottom by the fire of Norwegian coastal batteries. At the beginning of 1941 the Gneisenau, in company with the Scharnhorst (*q.v.*), was raiding in the Atlantic, and after a fairly successful foray, during which they sank some 20 British and Allied merchantmen, took refuge in Brest. The Gneisenau entered dock on March 28, 1941, and was first attacked by R.A.F. aircraft on 30–31 of that month. After this she was attacked repeatedly, from all heights. On the night of April 4–5 one of our aircraft hit her with a 1,900-lb. bomb from 1,000 ft. Another attack, from 900 ft., was made on June 13–14. There were reports in neutral newspapers that she had been heavily damaged and that one bomb killed 128 of her crew. During many critical months Hitler was unable to use this powerful battleship on the high seas, where she would have added considerably to Allied shipping casualties. Up to February 1942 over 83 raids had been made on the docks at Brest where the Gneisenau was sheltering.

The severity and persistence of these raids forced the Germans to move their ships to more sheltered waters. Meteorological reports were carefully studied, and during the night of Feb. 11, 1942, the Gneisenau and Scharnhorst, with the 10,000-ton cruiser Prinz Eugen, slipped out of port, escorted by a large number of destroyers, torpedo-boats, E-boats and minesweepers, and protected overhead by a strong force of fighter 'planes. It was a pitch-dark night with heavy clouds, enabling the enemy squadron to escape detection. When daylight came, the weather continued to favour them ; a thick sea-mist, heavy banks of cloud and squalls of rain provided a most effective screen.

Hugging the coast and continually protected by an air umbrella of fighters sent in relays from shore bases, the German ships managed to get nearly to Cap Gris Nez before they were spotted by a couple of Spitfires on patrol which evaded pursuit and brought back this valuable information. It was then 11 a.m.

Soon afterwards the British attack began. First to go into action were six Swordfish torpedo-carrying 'planes from the Fleet Air Arm, under the leadership of Lt.-Commdr. E. Esmonde, D.S.O. The heroic pilots must have known that they were a veritable suicide squad, for their machines, built some six years ago, were too lightly armoured to be able to survive the inferno of flak and fighter attack that awaited them. A larger formation of British torpedo-bombers took

GNEISENAU BEFORE ATTACK

This notorious German battle-cruiser was used as a surface raider and, with her sister ship, the Scharnhorst, menaced Allied shipping in the Atlantic until, in 1941, they entered Brest for re-fitting. Constant R.A.F. attacks kept them bottled up there for nearly a year.

Photo, H. Greenhalgh

up the fight, escorted by some fifty fighters. The sky became a pandemonium of battling 'planes. Hurricanes and other R.A.F. machines kept up a steady bombing of enemy vessels, often from mast height, in the teeth of furious gunfire. The new Beauforts of Coastal Command proved their mettle, hurtling through the formidable barrage to release their torpedoes against the German battleships, on which undoubtedly they inflicted serious damage.

Meanwhile, the Fleet was not idle. A swarm of M.T.B.s was on the scene by 12.30, pertinaciously harrying the German convoy with torpedoes and gunfire. Destroyers, summoned from their station in the North Sea, made contact with the enemy at 3.45, by which time they were off the Belgian coast. There was no time to clear the heavily mined waters for the British vessels ; they steamed straight ahead to reach their quarry, defying the great guns of the German warships and releasing their torpedoes at close range.

Despite these sustained attacks, the enemy was able to withdraw under cover of darkness. When last seen, they were about 175 miles from the Heligoland Bight, and with little difficulty reached their own harbours.

The attempt to intercept them cost the British forces 20 bombers and 16 fighters, in addition to the 6 Swordfish. The enemy lost some 20 fighters and a number of E-boats ; the Gneisenau, Scharnhorst and Prinz Eugen received direct hits, one of them being observed to be listing considerably. Subsequently the Prinz Eugen was badly holed by the British submarine H.M.S. Trident.

The three ships were later located at different ports —the Scharnhorst at Kiel, the Gneisenau at Gdynia, in Poland, and the Prinz Eugen at the Norwegian port of Trondheim. Aerial reconnaissance photographs issued at the end of June established that the Gneisenau was severely damaged along the whole length of her forecastle and was partly dismantled for very extensive repairs.

Public opinion in Britain, shocked by the success of the German sortie, demanded an explanation. In particular, it was asked what was the use of the frequent bombing of Brest if this was the result ? Mr. Churchill, in the House of Commons, admitted that 3,299 bomber attacks had been made and 4,000 tons of bombs had been dropped, with a loss of 247 men and 43 'planes, but, he pointed out, these raids, though they had not sunk the ships, had immobilized them for nearly twelve months.

Goebbels, DR. PAUL JOSEPH (b. 1897). German Minister of Propaganda and National Enlightenment, Goebbels was one of the most fanatical of the Nazi leaders. He entered the Nazi movement in 1922, when he first heard Hitler speak at a public meeting. In 1926 the Fuehrer appointed him organizer for the Nazi party in Berlin, and Goebbels became Minister of Propaganda when Hitler came to power in 1933. He had absolute control of the Press, wireless and theatre in Germany, and was responsible for public book burnings that disgusted the more enlightened countries. In 1939, on the outbreak of war, he directed Germany's propaganda, both at home and abroad. After Hitler and Goering, Goebbels became one of the most important men in the Reich. His propaganda machine, which he built up when Germany began her policy of expansion, was unscrupulous, and truth had no consideration in this system. As adviser to Hitler, he is said to have advocated a radical course in domestic as well as foreign policy. He played a leading part in the Nazi anti-Jewish policies, despite the fact that his wife was the adopted daughter of a Jew named Friedlander. *See* Germany.

Dr. Goebbels,
Hitler's mouthpiece.

Goering, FIELD-MARSHAL HERMANN WILHELM (b. 1893). He joined Hitler's party when it was first founded and took part in the abortive Munich "putsch" in November 1923, fled to Italy and returned to Germany in 1927. He reorganized the Nazi storm-troops, was elected to the Reichstag in 1928, and was its president from 1932. On Hitler's advent to power in 1933 Goering was appointed Prussian Prime Minister and Minister of the Interior, thus gathering into his hands the executive power in the most important State of Germany. His name was widely mentioned in connexion with the Reichstag Fire on Feb. 27, 1933. He became General and Air Minister, and was later appointed Commissioner of the Four-Year Plan and for raw materials. As economic dictator he supplanted Dr. Schacht. Goering was made Field-Marshal in 1938 and was responsible for the expropriation of Jews in that year. He was known for his grandiose display of splendour and for his love of luxury, and it was he who coined the phrases "Guns instead of butter" and "When

Field-Marshal Goering,
created the Luftwaffe.
Photo, Paul Popper

I hear the word culture, I reach for my revolver."
At the outbreak of war in 1939 Hitler declared
to the Reichstag that Goering was to succeed him as
dictator of Germany in the event of his death. By then
Goering was Reich-Marshal of Greater Germany. As
chief of the German Air Force he did much to build up
the Luftwaffe, and it was one of his many boasts that
the Ruhr was immune from British bombs—a boast
that, like so many, proved empty. In February 1940
Goering signed a decree confiscating agricultural
areas and goods in Poland, and ordered all available
stocks and reserves to be removed from Polish factories
and transported to the Reich. On June 22, 1940, he
attended the signing of the French Armistice in the
Forest of Compiègne. In 1941 there were rumours
that he was out of favour with the National-Socialist
Party, and, in particular, with Hitler. These rumours
proved groundless, however, for he appeared in his
customary splendour at one of the Nazi functions that
had been staged to disprove the many stories of his
decline from power.

Gojjam. This N.W. province of Abyssinia was one
of the chief centres of anti-Italian feeling following the
conquest of Ethiopia by Italy in 1936. On the outbreak
of war with Italy in 1940, Britain recognized Haile
Selassie as Emperor and promised full support for the
Ethiopian cause. A British Military Mission trekked
through the western Abyssinian lowlands with the
object of making contact with the Abyssinian chiefs,
and, although pursued by the Italians, established its
headquarters in the heart of the highlands of Gojjam.
Leading chiefs in the east of the province stirred up
trouble for the Italians, and Patriot guerillas continually harassed every movement of the enemy. The
R.A.F. bombed Italian positions in western Gojjam
with the greatest effect. Finally, the speed of the
Italian retreat from the Sudan frontier, and the
auspicious start of the British offensive, convinced the
Ethiopians that liberty would be restored. Following
the successes of the Somaliland campaign the Gojjam
revolt grew stronger every day, and the province was
practically abandoned by the Italians by the beginning
of March 1941. *See* Abyssinia.

Gomel. On Aug. 19, 1941, the mention of Gomel,
half way between Smolensk and Kiev on the central
front in Russia, made plain a fresh German drive to
outflank Marshal Budenny's army from the north and
separate him from Timoshenko in the centre. The capture of the town by the Germans on Aug. 21 gave the
enemy command of railways and roads leading north-
east towards Moscow and south towards Kiev. Gomel
was the scene of intensely bitter fighting and casualties
on both sides were heavy. *See* Russia.

Gondar. Capital of the province of Amhara,
Abyssinia, the town lies 24 miles N.E. of Lake Tsana.
A British drive in the direction of Gondar was first
indicated in Feb.–March 1941, when Gen. Wavell's
forces advanced into Abyssinia from the Sudan-
Ethiopian border. With the Duke of Aosta's surrender in May at Amba Alagi (*q.v.*), the conquest
of Abyssinia by British and Patriot forces was an
accomplished fact. The Italians, however, continued
to put up resistance at Gondar, the last Italian stronghold in E. Africa. On Nov. 27, 1941, Argyll and
Sutherland Highlanders took part in the final assault,
which, under Maj.-Gen. Cyril Fowkes, ended in the
unconditional surrender of the fortress after a siege
lasting six months. The mountainous country was

UNION JACK FLIES OVER GONDAR
This old Portuguese castle was the headquarters of the Italian
General Staff, and became the last stronghold of Italian resist-
ance in Abyssinia. It surrendered, after a six months' siege,
on Nov. 27, 1941.
Photo, British Official

favourable to the defending force, which, it was
reported, exceeded 23,500, half of whom were Italians.
Highland, Indian, Sudanese, South African and
West African units, with small numbers of Free
French, took part in preliminary operations. The chief
credit for the final battle went to East African and
Abyssinian Patriot troops. A final heavy raid was
carried out by bombers and fighters of the S.A.A.F.,
supported by the R.A.F. The capitulation of Gondar
marked the end of the highly successful campaign
conducted by the Air Forces in E. Africa, resulting
in the complete destruction of the Italian Air Arm.
The latter had been reduced to one fighter and one
bomber. Enemy prisoners taken at Gondar numbered
approximately 11,500 Italians—including the commander, Gen. Nasi—and 12,000 native troops. *See*
Abyssinia.

**J. H. Gordon,
awarded the V.C.**
Photo, Australian Official

Gordon, Pte. James
Heather, v.c. The action which
won this member of the Australian forces the V.C. took place
on the night of July 10, 1941,
when Pte. Gordon's company was
held up by intense machine-gun
fire near Jezzine, Syria. Creeping forward over an area swept
by machine-gun and grenade fire,
he charged the enemy post from
the front and killed the four machine-gunners with the
bayonet, completely demoralizing the enemy and thus
enabling the company to advance and take the position.
During the remainder of that night and on the following
day Pte. Gordon fought with equal gallantry.

Gordon-Finlayson, Gen. Sir Robert, k.c.b.
(b. 1881). He was G.O.C.-in-C. Western Command,
1939–41, and retired under the age-limit on Nov. 24,
1941. From 1939 to 1940 he was Adjutant-Gen. to
the Forces.

Gort, Gen. John Standish Surtees Prender-
gast Vereker, 6th Viscount, v.c., g.c.b. (b. 1886).
When war broke out Lord Gort was Chief of the
Imperial General Staff. He was given command
of the British Expeditionary Force and left England

General Lord Gort,
Governor of Malta.
Photo, Planet News

for France on Sept. 14, 1939. Landing at Cherbourg, he proceeded to Le Mans, where G.H.Q. was first established. Gort, whose forces consisted so far of four British divisions and the French 51st Division, acted under the direct control of General Georges, who himself served under General Gamelin, in supreme command of the Allied Forces in France. On Oct. 2 Gort established his headquarters at Habarcq, 8 miles west of Arras. His first dispatch, which covered the period Sept. 3, 1939, to Jan. 31, 1940, dealt with events before the opening of the great battle and described the construction by our troops of an elaborate system of field defences and the arrangement by which infantry brigades of the B.E.F. successively completed short tours of duty on the Saar front to give them some preliminary experience of actual contact with the enemy. His second dispatch, published with the first on Oct. 10, 1941, covered the operations of the B.E.F. up to the final evacuation of Dunkirk (*q.v.*).

An account of Gort's activities in the period February–May 1940 is, in effect, the story of the Battle of Flanders, culminating in the tragic but glorious withdrawal to Dunkirk at the end of May. Having completed his plans for the evacuation, and superintended much of their carrying out, Lord Gort, in accordance with instructions received from London, handed over his command of the 1st Corps to Maj.-Gen. H. R. L. G. Alexander and embarked for England in the early morning of June 1. On July 19 he was appointed Inspector-General of Training to the Forces and the Home Guard, a post which he held until April 25, 1941, when he became Governor and C.-in-C. of Gibraltar, in succession to Lt.-Gen. Sir Clive Liddell. On May 7, 1942, it was announced that Lord Gort had been appointed to succeed Sir William Dobbie as Governor and C.-in-C. of Malta. *See* British Expeditionary Force; Dunkirk; France, Defeat of; etc.

Gossage, AIR MARSHAL SIR ERNEST LESLIE, K.C.B., D.S.O. (b. 1891). He was appointed A.O.C. Balloon Command in October 1940. From 1936 to February 1940 he was A.O.C. No. 11 (Fighter) Group, and then became Inspector-Gen. of the R.A.F. He was subsequently selected as Air Member for Personnel.

Gower, PAULINE. Appointed First Officer of the Women's Section of the Air Transport Auxiliary Service in December 1939. Their duty is to fly aircraft from factories to aerodromes.

Gowrie, BRIG.-GEN. ALEXANDER GORE ARKWRIGHT HORE-RUTHVEN, V.C., G.C.M.G., 1ST BARON (b. 1872). Governor-General of Australia from 1936. He was formerly Governor of South Australia and of New South Wales.

Graf Spee. *See* Admiral Graf Spee.

Gray, SGT. THOMAS, V.C. The act of valour for which a posthumous V.C. was awarded to this airman is described under the name of the pilot with whom he was serving, F./O. R. E. Garland.

Sgt. Gray, V.C.,
R.A.F. hero.
Photo, G.P.U.

Graziani, MARSHAL RODOLFO (b. 1882). Chief of Staff of the Italian Army when Italy entered the war, he commanded the forces that invaded Egypt in 1940, succeeding Marshal Balbo as Governor and C.-in-C. of Libya. Following the capture of Tobruk by British forces he was recalled by Mussolini on Jan. 27, 1941. The series of Italian defeats in Libya gave rise to the report that he had been arrested in Rome after his dismissal.

Marshal Graziani,
Italian soldier.
Photo, Associated Press

According to the Marshal it was Mussolini who had devised the invasion of Egypt and planned its conduct. Despite cogent proofs that the Duce was to blame, Mussolini had ordered the advance and ignored all adverse arguments. Marshal Graziani thereupon resigned from the Fascist Party, but was later reported to have been reinstated. On March 25, 1941, it was announced officially that he had resigned at his own request. Graziani was one of Italy's ablest soldiers, and was largely responsible for the rapidity of the Italian conquest of Abyssinia in 1935–36. For this he had been appointed Viceroy of Abyssinia, a position he relinquished to the Duke of Aosta in 1937, when he was awarded the title of Marchese di Neghelli.

GREAT BRITAIN IN THE SECOND WORLD WAR

Peace-loving and unprepared for war as she was, Great Britain succeeded in marshalling her enormous resources and maintaining her morale, to the astonishment of her critics. Here is a study of development and progress in her war activities. The separate campaigns are dealt with under their own headings.

Great Britain at War. Any brief account of the causes that led up to the war involves the danger of suffering falsification through over-simplification. With that necessary warning to the reader, it is broadly true to say that the following were the factors immediately responsible for the final catastrophe.

First, the extension to the sphere of foreign policy by Nazi Germany of the use of force as a political instrument. Secondly, the jettisoning by the Nazis of the Law of Nations as expressed in solemn treaties, pacts and agreements to which Germany had freely subscribed. Thirdly, the disinclination of the British Government, and, in particular, of its leader, Mr. Neville Chamberlain, to believe in the essential wickedness of their Nazi opponents, and, indeed, an apparent failure to recognize either Hitler and his conspirators, or Mussolini and his gangsters, as antagonists at all. That a nation could will and work all-out for total

LONDON IN THE BLACK-OUT

Starting from Sept. 2, 1939, strict black-out regulations were imposed. Curtains and blinds screened every light ; traffic, with lamps reduced to the minimum, crept about in the dim streets. The photograph shows Regent Street, on the edge of Piccadilly Circus.

Photo, Fox

war was a proposition unacceptable to the large majority of British thinkers. So it was that when the climax came two races aspiring for twenty years to a permanent world peace—the French and British—found themselves opposed to a people pledged to the use of force as the instrument for achieving world domination.

As the apostle of " appeasement," Mr. Chamberlain, with M. Daladier, the French Premier, met Hitler and Mussolini at Munich on Sept. 29, 1938. The Agreement then signed gave, temporarily, promise of peace, an illusion reinforced by the following visit of Mr. Chamberlain and Lord Halifax to Rome on Jan. 10, 1939.

Realists in England, the greatest of them being Mr. Winston Churchill, were not deceived at all by these shallow exchanges between the British Red Riding Hood and the European two-headed Wolf. While Mr. Chamberlain smiled his way through Rome, Sir John Anderson produced the first of the steel garden shelters named after him. A.R.P. activities were speeded up. A Schedule of Reserved Occupations was issued. It covered seven million workers.

Appeasement prompted recognition by the British Government of Franco, contrary to established international usage. On Feb. 15 the Chancellor of the Exchequer called for from 400 to 800 millions for defence purposes. Regional Commissioners were ap-

pointed to administer twelve zones in the event of war. Deep air-raid shelters versus surface shelters caused a great controversy.

On March 10, 1939, Hitler massed his troops on the Czechoslovak frontier and four days later invaded. The Prime Minister and Foreign Secretary told the country that the Czechs had invited German occupation. This aggression was the real starting point of the World War. It was followed, on April 7, by Mussolini's invasion of Albania.

On May 1 the Military Training Bill was introduced, the Labour Party opposing compulsion. The Government's foreign policy was for a so-called Peace Front, a combination strong enough to hold Germany. Essential for success was a Russian alliance, in order that, in the event of war, Hitler would have the dreaded two-front war he was destined to venture on his own account. Negotiations had begun in the spring, and on August 5 a military mission went to Moscow to negotiate. Russia, however, was conducting simultaneously secret negotiations with Nazi Germany. On August 18 a commercial treaty between the two countries was announced and three days later a Non-aggression Pact.

Indications of war were marked, and a cold wind blew about the world, chilling men's hearts. Japan, encouraged by Berlin, began a blockade of the French and British Concessions at Tientsin, and at home the British began to gird up their loins for the war that loomed ever nearer.

The Emergency Powers Act (*q.v.*), providing for unheard-of powers in the event of war, brought the grimness of the situation home to the most thoughtless ; and the appeals made by the King of the Belgians, Queen Wilhelmina, the Scandinavian Powers, the President of the United States and the Pope, Pius XII, underlined the seriousness of the moment.

Poland was the obvious next objective of the Nazi grab, and Britain was tied by her joint pledge with France to go to that Republic's aid should Germany strike. On Sept. 1 Mr. Chamberlain gave a last warning in these terms to Germany, and on Sept. 3 declared that a state of war existed.

The First Months of War, 1939

On August 9 England had her first black-out and mimic large-scale air raid. Hitler, by direct message, assured us of his desire for friendship while refusing to defer the solution of what he termed the " Polish problem." That war was inevitable was now obvious. The country went at once on to a war footing. The three fighting Services went to their stations and on Sept. 1 the children's evacuation scheme (*q.v.*) was put into operation. On that day Germany invaded Poland. For two days Britain and France, pledged to aid Poland, did not move. Then, on Sunday, Sept. 3, the Prime Minister told the country by radio that we were at war with Germany. This was the beginning of what became known as the " sitzblitz, " or war of inaction. For, though we had kept faith with Poland, we were, with France, practically impotent to help her.

In the Four Years' War the problem of the enemy alien had been simple. But in 1939 it was complicated by the fact that thousands who were technically enemies were virtually excellent friends, being refugees from Nazi intolerance and cruelty. Tribunals were set up to examine cases, but later, unhappily, many potentially valuable friendly aliens were interned.

The repercussions of the war were felt first through the social changes involved at home, actual hostilities being sporadic events, such as the raid on Kiel, the sinking of the Athenia, and so on. On land, the French army, under whom our own fine force was placed, rested content in the Maginot Line.

National registration came into force on Sept. 29 ; income tax was raised to 7/6 in the £ ; the Prices of Goods Bill was introduced to check profiteering ; but of all such changes in daily life that which followed evacuation was the most radical. The evacuation of large sections of the population from areas exposed to air assault to places of comparative security involved the greatest mass migration of England's population since the Industrial Revolution. Its effects will be permanent. In 1939 it created a complex problem, including the housing of the evacuated women and children and the education of the latter. But the danger of air bombardment did not materialize at once, and there began a drift back to the danger areas. This drift was due to the inability of the women to accommodate themselves to the new life. The children of the towns were happy enough in the country, but not their mothers. City schools had been closed, and therefore they had to be reopened. But for a lengthy period large numbers of children were running wild.

The introduction of rationing (Nov. 1) with butter and bacon, and the National Savings drive, were two more wartime measures that touched Everyman.

The land campaign remained unchanged. But Russia had acted by going into Poland at the moment of Germany's " victory " to secure restoration of the former Russo-Polish boundary. By sea general excitement was caused by a new weapon, the magnetic mine (see Mines and Mine-laying), whereby the Germans claimed they would starve Britain out. The danger

was quickly countered by British science, and then, as now, there was food for all in the land.

By the end of the year there had been no air raids, and although abroad there had been such spectacular isolated actions as the scuttling of the defeated Graf Spee off Montevideo, and the unequal sea battle between the P. & O. liner Rawalpindi and the battleship Deutschland, the only major event that had changed the general war scene was the violation of the Finnish frontier by Soviet Russia and the vigorous Finnish resistance to that aggression.

One economic change that was by that time making itself felt in many homes was the disappearance of thousands of one-man businesses throughout the country, coupled with the unemployment of large numbers of " black-coat " workers.

The end of 1939 was the period when people began to talk of a " phoney war " ; but it saw Britain sitting snug and slowly limbering up for giant efforts.

Economic Aspects of Early 1940

One of the first steps taken by the Government in 1940 was the subsidization by £1,000,000 a week of bread, flour, meat and milk. The object of this measure was to check the ten per cent rise which had taken place after the start of war.

Despite the intensification of unrestricted U-boat war, Britain's larder was still adequately supplied, thanks largely to the resumption of the convoy system which had worked so well in the Four Years' War. But the importation of foodstuffs was only one of the tasks of our Merchant Marine. War supplies of all kinds were called for. They had to be paid for, and the problem for the Treasury was : How ? There was only one way : by exporting goods against our imports. Thus the fostering of our export trade was

DEFENCE PRECAUTIONS IN GREAT BRITAIN

As a defence against possible invasion or Fifth Column activities, barricades composed of concrete and barbed wire were erected across the roads in certain areas, to impede the progress of enemy motor-cyclists or tanks. Motorists were stopped by armed sentries and were asked to show their credentials. This photograph is from a British Movietone News film.

BRITISH BOMBERS IN PRODUCTION

These are Whitley long-range bombers, a type of aircraft used effectively in hundreds of British raids on Germany and Italy. They are two-engined and have a speed of 245 miles an hour. This North of England factory worked by night as well as by day ; note the careful black-out, the windows being entirely screened.

Photo, Central Press

revealed as a war measure of prime importance and an Export Trade Council was set up under the Board of Trade to push exports to the limit.

By early spring and after one of the coldest winters on record, a Supreme War Council was called for and met in London. It was then that the British and French made a solemn declaration not to conclude armistice or peace save by mutual agreement. When, so soon after, she collapsed, France asked to be released from her promise before suing for an armistice. It was then that Mr. Churchill made the first of his many subsequent inspiring broadcasts and revealed himself unmistakably as the symbolic figure about which all the virtues of the race would shine forth before men.

Even amid these shattering events in the military scheme, the economic side of war obtruded itself upon the Government. To combat German trade infiltration in the Balkans and Turkey the Government formed the English Commercial Corporation. Its activities were the extension of the armed conflict to the spheres of international trade war.

The first of the chain of events which resulted in the invasion of Norway also reveals the all-embracing character of modern war. That country became a battlefield because from Norway's northern port, Narvik, was shipped the iron-ore essential to German munitions production from the Swedish-Lappish iron-ore mountain at Kiruna. War being based upon unlimited supplies of iron-ore, we had to stop this traffic. Minefields were laid, and this action resulted in accusations by Norway's jurists of a breach of international law. The Battle of Narvik (*q.v.*) closed that port. But the whole operation was negatived by the action of Sweden, which carried the supplies to Germany by rail and across the narrows of the Baltic.

At home the great events of May were the resignation on May 10 of Mr. Chamberlain and the speech of his successor, Mr. Winston Churchill, in which he promised his countrymen, not victories, but those things which must always go before them : " blood and toil and tears and sweat." The whole nation welcomed the new Premier, but it had not entirely forgotten in the hour of his eclipse the fact that the retiring Premier had striven nobly to preserve the peace of the world.

The swiftness of the German advance and those terrible events that reached their culmination on the beaches of Dunkirk (all of which events are described under their own headings such as Belgium, Dunkirk, France, Netherlands, etc.) had repercussions at home. First, they brought an understanding of the part played by machines in the new warfare. Secondly, they made clear the menace of invasion. Thirdly, they produced in the national mind preparedness for all sacrifices.

The Bill, introduced on May 22, 1940, under which Parliament was to assume vast and wide-sweeping powers over life and property, was made law. Its passage illustrates the seriousness of that moment, for it persuaded the people to surrender, for the time being, rights and privileges for which, through long centuries, their forefathers had fought and died.

The Defection of France

The cardinal psychological fact was, of course, the terrific shock to Britain of the French collapse in the field on June 22. It was at once followed by a worse blow : the revelation that M. Reynaud's successor as Premier, Marshal Pétain, was hostile to his former comrades-in-arms, and ready to work hand in glove with the nation which had thrice ravaged France.

On June 10 Italy, deeming the moment apposite for the stab in the back, declared war on France. Six days later the whole country was electrified by the Premier's dramatic offer of a Solemn Act of Union with France. It was, however, too early and too late. It was too early in history : too late in the swiftly changing kaleidoscope of war.

It was decided to intensify preparations against invasion. The Local Defence Volunteers were reconstituted and renamed the Home Guard. Government propaganda included a drive to make everyone realize what the German massacre of the civilian population fleeing before their armies in France meant to us by way of lesson. All were told, at all costs, to keep the roads clear for the troops. The policy of the authorities was to prepare the country for a defence in depth, in contradistinction to the French system of the Maginot Line, a single shallow system of deep, heavily armoured defences. Everywhere concrete erections and barbed wire sprouted.

While Britain prepared to welcome the invader in the British tradition, a big scheme was launched to ship overseas large numbers of children. In three weeks 52,000 applications were received and the first children sailed. The torpedoing of the City of Benares (q.v.), upon which were many children, determined the Government to abandon the scheme.

In May, while the turmoil of war was seething to some apparent climax, the role played by the treacherous, both in Norway and in France—the Quislings, fifth columnists or simple traitors—produced a short-lived wave of hysteria in Britain, and the cry " Intern the lot ! " The Government permitted popular feeling to govern its actions, and thousands of good friends of

Britain, who were enemies only in that they had German or Austrian nationality, were thrown into internment camps completely unsuited to receive them. Some were shipped to Canada and lost their lives in the Arandora Star, torpedoed on July 3, 1940.

This extremist policy, which put behind bars scientists, doctors, literary men and artists, engineers and chemists, was soon changed. On July 31 " enemy aliens " were divided into 18 categories eligible for release, and those who remained in confinement were transferred from the War Office to the Home Office.

Hysteria was subsiding, but there were elements of it in the proposal to set up new courts with sweeping powers, including that of the death sentence. The fate of that scheme provides an interesting illustration of how a free Parliament prevents, by vigilance, the extinction of a free people's constitutional rights. For the right of appeal from these tribunals was insisted upon by the House as a whole.

The last symptom of that brief phase was the attempt to equate criticism with defeatism by the newly constituted Ministry of Information, and the ridiculous prosecutions for " spreading gloom and despondency " which resulted. Thereafter the historian will look in vain for symptoms of unbalance in the people of Britain or in their leaders.

The continued success at sea of the convoy system did not, however, prevent a fearful toll being taken of our merchant shipping, and at home, with the prospect of a long war, it became clear that more food should be grown. On July 11 the Ministry of

NEW CRUISER FOR ROYAL NAVY NEARING COMPLETION

One of Britain's latest cruisers has just left the slipway (seen in the foreground) and been towed to her fitting-out berth. In September 1939 the Royal and Imperial Navies had 61 cruisers ; of these sixteen had been lost up to March 1942. The First Lord of the Admiralty, speaking on Feb. 26, said that casualties to the Fleet had been and were being well replaced, and that a much larger number of building berths were in operation than existed in 1939.

Photo, E.N.A.

Agriculture set up County Agricultural Committees to direct what crops should be grown in their areas.

On August 8 a vast battle was fought over the Channel in which the small, fast E-boats went into action against us together with the Luftwaffe. It was, clearly, prelude to invasion. But the R.A.F., who had already earned from the Prime Minister the historic eulogy " Never in the field of human conflict was so much owed by so many to so few," brought down sixty Nazi machines and smashed the attack. The "greatest day" was Sept. 15, when 185 machines were shot down for the loss of only 25 of our own. After that defeat the German Luftwaffe concentrated on night attacks (see Great Britain, Air War on ; and London).

Towards the end of the year an increase in U-boat activity revealed the justification of the agricultural policy of the Government, for in the week ending Oct. 22 no less than 198,000 tons of shipping were sunk by the enemy. By October, however, 2,000,000 added acres were ready to produce food.

Abroad, the chief events of the dying year were Italian activity in North Africa, with its obvious objective, the invasion of Egypt and seizure of the Suez Canal ; and the action of the Jervis Bay (q.v.) converted merchantman, which engaged a Nazi warship while her convoy escaped.

The end of the year showed that one great advantage had flowed from the defection of France and the revelation of her political rottenness, namely, the extinction of the legend of British decadence. The common people were revealed as the worthy successors of Elizabethan England who, under an inspiring leadership, had found fortitude to suffer and strength to endure.

British Sea Power Predominates, 1941

By January, 1941, the main great outline of the war picture had become clear. First, Nazi Germany straddled all Europe, but had yet come to resemble a beleaguered city cut off from the supplies of fertile surrounding plains. Once more British sea power had emerged in war as a dominant factor, one wresting from the enemy freedom to choose a strategy not tied to considerations of raw material supply and food.

It was the success of the British blockade of the long European seaboard that was the determining factor of Germany's policy in the East. Her people, despite their army's vast territorial gains, were worse off than the British, whose total annihilation, promised them by their Fuehrer, had yet to satisfy the Teutonic appetite for hate. Hitler had to have oil and wheat, and it was that factor which decided him on his winter Russian campaign gamble, perhaps the greatest and most wickedly reckless military gamble in all history.

The Royal Navy had much to do beside attend to the sealing of the European coasts, for it had to keep clear the sea paths along which material aid, such as munitions and foods, came to Britain. To understand the war at that point a clear picture of the world's raw materials, produce, machines and man-power must be in the mind. If the dire need of wheat and oil drove Hitler over the Russian frontier, Britain's dire need of foods and all manner of raw materials and manufactured munitions of war determined her internal economy. By the early months of 1941 there was a growing shortage in Britain of such commodities as pottery, distilled spirits, leather goods, woollens and a vast range of manufactured articles. All these, however, were being manufactured on a reduced scale and were

absent from the shops because they were all made for export, and were exported to offset our vast American commitments.

The process was one that could not go on indefinitely. Roosevelt, for the third time President of the United States, realized this. He realized, too, that Britain was fighting America's battle, and, indeed, the battle of all free nations. On March 8, 1941, he steered the Lease and Lend Bill through the American Senate. This marked a turning-point in the war and was as important as a victorious campaign. It placed the whole resources of the most highly industrialized country in the world at our disposal.

But it is one thing to produce, another to deliver. So, once again, Roosevelt acted with true statesmanship and characteristic courage, and on July 6 put American troops and naval units into Iceland and ordered American naval craft to shoot U-boats at sight. In a word, the United States, without declaring war on Germany, was actively assisting the Atlantic convoy. The arming of American merchant ships followed naturally in due time. These events were of prime importance because they meant the inevitable failure of the German blockade of Britain and the end of the threat of starvation.

With this mobilization of materials of all kinds went the intensification of the organization of Britain's man-power. On April 19 all women were required to register. The conscription of women was a revolutionary measure, but it was accepted with practically no opposition. Women workers were required mostly for the auxiliary services of the three fighting Services and for munitions. The policy of moving young girls from their own home towns to industrial centres was criticized and was open to criticism. One million women were drafted into munition factories.

As 1941 wore on the armchair advocates of a western front diversion multiplied. They suggested an invasion of the French, Belgian, Dutch and Danish coasts. They pointed to the large and ever-growing army in Britain. Wisely, the Government ignored this clamour. It would have been possible to invade, but the practical problem was at that time insoluble, namely, to maintain in the face of the air strength of the enemy a cross-Channel transport system to support the army of Continental invasion.

At home another problem made its appearance, namely, the handling of an army highly trained over a long period and with only one battle to fight—boredom. By the end of the year Britain had become an armed camp, the whole countryside bristling with military encampments of men drawn from the Dominions. This formidable army was kept intact against the possibility of an invasion in force, the probability of which was throughout the year a constant theme of governmental warning.

All Aid to Russia

Beside this army stood the Home Guard, mainly men too young or too old for army service, but sprinkled with men of wide war experience and everywhere imbued with zeal for the protection of Britain's soil.

On June 22, 1941, Germany invaded Russia and on that day Mr. Churchill promised all aid to the Soviet Union. In a war which even by that date had produced a number of surprises, the alignment of Britain beside Russia made necessary a very radical political readjustment. It involved a forgetting of old mutual abuse, mistrust and ill-will, and the mutual effort

BRITISH INDUSTRY GOES TO IT IN MANY SPHERES

Men and women alike came forward splendidly to help in the huge industrial drive, thus playing a vital part in the war effort. Top, left, we see a shipyard worker operating the giant hydraulic riveter during the construction of a new warship ; centre, a W.A.A.F. mechanic is working on the cockpit of a Hurricane ; right, a girl telephonist, wearing a steel helmet, remains at her switchboard during a blitz.   Centre, left, a woman engine-cleaner is at work in a railway depot.   Below, a big bundle of waste-paper for salvage.   Right, scrap-iron, melted down in a 90-ton ladle, is being emptied into moulds.

Photos, Central Press, Sport & General, L.N.A., Planet News, Fox to sink all differences for the attainment of a common end. Subsequent events revealed how much may be accomplished where men of good will work together. The Three-Power Conference held in Moscow in late September was successful, and it was followed up by Mr. Eden's visit at the close of the year, when the Prime Minister was making his historic speech at Washington.

The great destruction wrought by indiscriminate air raids, amounting in some cases—Plymouth, for example—to the virtual wiping out of an historic town, had one unforeseen good result. It focused attention on the need for planning. The smashing-up of wide areas of closely-built-up urban districts, the personal aspect set aside, was revealed as a good in that it provided opportunities for the rebuilding of the people's homes on healthy and aesthetic lines. Britain became extremely " plan-conscious " and many books appeared dealing with this immediate post-war problem. Another war-born revelation showed the inadequacy of haphazard agriculture and the imperative need for agricultural planning on national lines.

Food rationing had also added to the general pool of knowledge. It proved that with a restricted diet the nation's health had not deteriorated, but, on the contrary, had actually improved. This unexpectedly pleasant result was due to the care with which the national diet was drawn up. The rationing system was further extended on December 1, when " Points " rations were introduced for tinned goods. The central idea of this simple and clever system is to vary the " points cost " of goods to regulate supply and demand.

Perhaps the central fact of the close of 1941 was the change wrought by the events of the year upon the morale of the populations of Britain and Germany respectively.

The United Nations Come Into Line

The entry of America into the war, and the formation of the Grand Alliance of . the British Empire, the United States, the Soviet Union and the Chinese Republic, made ultimate victory certain in the minds of the vast majority. This great central fact well offset any local reverses, such as the loss of H.M.S. Prince of Wales and H.M.S. Repulse in the East, or our Ally's disaster at Pearl Harbour, when by Japanese treachery the American Pacific Fleet in that harbour was badly battered by air.

For Germany the end of 1941 brought the mammoth Russian disaster, coupled with the advent of new and powerful enemies, and the growing realization of the fallibility of Hitler and the probability of defeat.

The year 1942 may hereafter be seen as the point in time when the war swung slowly and almost imperceptibly from the defensive to the offensive. Not that the first months brought naval or military triumphs. Far from it, they brought many setbacks and reverses for British arms. The change, nevertheless, existed, and it may perhaps be characterized as a psychological change that was produced, in part, by the growing knowledge of internal difficulties and of an increasing war-weariness in Germany.

At sea, Hitler intensified the Atlantic battle, and losses, which had been described by Mr. Churchill (at Ottawa) as decreasing from August to December 1941, began to rise once more. While attacks on convoys became increasingly heavy, the whole character of the Atlantic battle was modified by Germany's decision to extend its scope to include the United States coastal waters and such French possessions as Curaçao, which was shelled by a U-boat to destroy its oil refineries and the shipping lying at anchor.

In February, while the country was still smarting from the blows rained upon it by Japan in the East, yet another reverse profoundly disturbed the people. Germany's crack battleships, Scharnhorst and Gneisenau, and the smaller Prinz Eugen, long at Brest and there subjected to persistent bombing from the air, escaped, and did so in a manner that suggested some oversight on the part of the British defence organization. These ships, which had been watched for months, slipped out under cover of darkness on the night of Feb. 11 and, instead of taking the route round the British Isles, made a bold dash up Channel. Visibility on that day was bad, and this circumstance has been advanced to account for the failure to locate these ships, with their hundreds of fighter-planes escort, until four hours after daybreak—11.35 a.m. An account of the actions that then ensued is given under the heading Gneisenau. An Inquiry, under Mr. Justice Bucknill, was ordered by the Government.

India Rejects the Cripps Proposals

Another blow to fall on the country was the failure of the Indian parties to come to a compromise and accept the plan placed before them by Sir Stafford Cripps. On April 11 Sir Stafford broadcast to the Indian people, stressing the peril to the country which must result in failure to consolidate for defence. This appeal failed, and India declared for a defence policy of non-violence on lines made familiar by Gandhi.

A feeling that much of our trouble in the various spheres of battle on land and at sea was the result of lack of unification of grand strategy much exercised the popular mind in the early months of 1941. The appointment, on April 13, of Lord Louis Mountbatten as Chief of Combined Operations foreshadowed the form likely to be taken by a Combined General Staff, advocated by the War Minister, Sir James Grigg. The main change here was the proposal for the sweeping away of three separate and distinct Services for one great Service : Army, Navy and R.A.F. all operating under a single unifying master mind.

On April 15 the Chancellor of the Exchequer brought in his Budget. It called for an additional £150,000,000 in taxation. He then revealed the fact that the United States was lending Great Britain £100,000,000 a month. Increased taxation affected farming profits, purchase tax, tobacco, alcohol, and entertainment.

The unification of munitions production control was again to the fore, both in the public mind and in Parliament. On his return from America the Prime Minister had introduced a White Paper conferring vast powers on Lord Beaverbrook as Minister of Production. It met with an icy reception and, reluctantly, the Prime Minister was obliged to accept the adverse verdict of . the House upon this appointment. Mr. Lyttelton, formerly Minister of State, was next appointed to the great task of coordinating all war materials production. This appointment was generally approved.

See further under Great Britain, Air War on ; *also* Atlantic, Battle of ; *the different campaigns such as* North Africa, Malaya, etc. ; *general headings, such as* Air Defence, Civil Defence, Food, Munitions, etc., British Colonies *and the various Dominions.*

GREAT BRITAIN AT WAR: SELECT CHRONOLOGY

Principal Events, September to December 1939

Sept. 1939
1 Britain stands by Guarantee to Poland.
2 Military Service Bill passed.
3 **Ultimatum to Germany expires**—Athenia sunk by U-boat.
4 R.A.F. drops 6 million leaflets over Germany. Wilhelmshaven raided.
12 British troops stated to be in France.

Sept. 1939
17 **Courageous**, aircraft carrier, sunk.
30 First R.A.F. casualties over Germany.

Oct.
2 R.A.F. over Berlin.
12 Hitler's "peace" proposals rejected.
14 **Royal Oak** sunk in Scapa Flow by enemy submarine.
16 First enemy raids on Britain over Firth of Forth.

Oct. 1939
31 First British fight with German bombers over France.

Nov.
3 Roosevelt's Neutrality Bill passed. Huge British orders for war supplies in America.
12 King George replies to Dutch-Belgian peace appeal.
21 Rawalpindi auxiliary cruiser sunk in Atlantic.
22/24 German air attacks on Shetlands.

Dec. 1939
3 R.A.F. attack on Heligoland warships.
13 **Admiral Graf Spee** attacked by Achilles, Ajax and Exeter in Battle of River Plate.
17 Graf Spee scuttled. First Canadian Forces land in Britain.
26 First squadron R. Australian Air Force lands in England.

Principal Events, January to December 1940

Jan. 1940
5 Hore-Belisha resigns Sec. for War ; Oliver Stanley apptd.
8 Rationing of bacon, butter and sugar.
10 Seaplane base at Sylt raided.

Feb.
3 Trade agreement with Turkey.
16 **Altmark** prison ship boarded by H.M.S. Cossack. 299 British seamen freed.

Mar.
8 R.A.F. machines over Posen, longest flight to date.
28 Supreme War Council in London agreed no peace without mutual consent.

April
8 British mines laid off Norwegian coast ; H.M.S. Glowworm sunk.
9 **Norway and Denmark invaded by Germany** ; H.M.S. Gurkha sunk.
10/13 British destroyers attack at Narvik. Second battle of Narvik
14 **Allied troops land at Namsos.**
15 **British troops land at Harstadt**, near Narvik.
16 Faroe Is. occupied by Britain.
17 **Allied troops disembarked at Aandalsnes** ; advance from Namsos checked at Stenkjer.
19/23 British forces from Aandalsnes held at Lillehammer.
26/30 Fighting in Dombaas-Storen area ; German columns from Oslo reach Trondheim.

May
2/3 **British troops evacuated** from Aandalsnes and Namsos.
7/8 Debate in Parliament on Norwegian campaign ; in division Govt. majority only 81 votes.
10 **Mr. Chamberlain resigns ; Mr. Churchill forms Govt. Germans invade Luxemburg, Holland and Belgium** ; British troops go to Belgium.
13 British troops in Iceland ; Dutch Royal Family and Govt. come to London.
14 Local Defence Volunteers formed ; **Dutch army capitulates.**
16/19 B.E.F. on Escaut line.
21 British counter-attack towards Arras ; Germans at Abbeville ; B.E.F.'s communications with supply bases cut.
22/23 Allies retreat to Lys ; Calais and Boulogne invested.
24 Germans break through on Lys ; Germans take Boulogne, after British troops had been withdrawn.
26 B.E.F. withdraws behind Lys ; Dunkirk evacuation begins.
27 King Leopold asks for armistice ; **Enemy takes Calais.**
28 **Belgian capitulation** ; Allies capture Narvik.
30 **B.E.F. within Dunkirk defence perimeter** ; 170,000 British and French troops evacuated.

June
1 Lord Gort leaves for England.

June 1940
2 **Evacuation from Dunkirk complete** ; 211,523 fit men and 13,053 casualties of the B.E.F. were saved, besides 112,546 Allied troops.
3 51st (Highland) Division in the Bresle-Aulne region.
7/8 British 1st Armoured Division holds line N.E. of Rouen.
9 1st Armoured Division protects Seine crossings.
10 **Italy declares war on Britain and France** ; final withdrawal of troops in Norway ; King Haakon and Govt. reach London ; **loss of aircraft carrier Glorious** announced.
11/12 R.A.F. raids on Italy. Part of 51st (Highland) Division embarked for Britain.
13 Remainder of 51st Division captured at St. Valery.
14 Germans enter Paris.
16 Britain proposes **Act of Union with France** ; French Cabinet decides for peace negotiations ; Reynaud resigns ; Pétain asks for armistice.
17 French Government reminds Pétain of French obligation not to make a separate peace ; Pétain tells the French they must "cease to fight."
18 General de Gaulle broadcasts from London an appeal to the French to continue resistance.
21 French plenipotentiaries meet German leaders at Compiègne.
22 **Franco - German armistice signed**, conditional on an armistice with Italy.
24 French plenipotentiaries sign armistice in Rome. Night, first air-raid alert London area since Sept. 3, 1939.
25 Hostilities cease between France and Germany, . and France and Italy.
28 British Government recognize De Gaulle as leader of the "Free French." Channel Islands demilitarized.
30 **Germans occupy Guernsey.**

July
1 Germans land in Jersey. Rumania renounces the Anglo-French guarantee. German daylight raids over Britain.
3 Arandora Star sunk by U-boat. **British naval action against French fleet at Oran.**
4 French warships in British ports taken over. Italians occupy Gallabat and Kassala.
5 French Govt., now at Vichy, breaks off relations with Britain. Rumania joins Axis.
8 Naval action to immobilize French battleship Richelieu at Dakar.
9 British and Italian fleets in action off Calabria. French warships at Alexandria demilitarized.
11 German air attacks on Channel convoys begin. Pétain becomes "Chief of State."
13 Italians attack Moyale.
15 British withdraw from Moyale.

July 1940
18 Britain stops transit of war materials for China by Burma Road for three months ; also transit through Hongkong.
19 Italian cruiser **Bartolomeo Colleone sunk** in Mediterranean by H.M.A.S. Sydney.
23 Formation of Provisional Czech Government in London.
24 French liner Meknes, with French troops for repatriation, sunk off Portland.
25 Mass air attack on British convoy in Channel.
29 **German air attack on Dover Harbour** repulsed.
31 Armed merchant cruiser Alcantara in action with German raider off Brazil.

Aug.
2 Lord Beaverbrook appointed to War Cabinet.
4 **Italians invade British Somaliland** and take Hargeisa and Zeila.
5 Anglo-Polish military agreement.
6 Italians capture Oadweina.
7 British Government signs military agreement with General de Gaulle. Widespread air raids over Britain.
8 **Battle of Britain opens.** German attacks on Channel convoys.
[See further under Great Britain, Air War, pp. 158 and 161.]
16 **R.A.F. bomb factories at Milan and Turin.**
17 R.A.F. begins extensive attacks on enemy oil refineries and aircraft factories. Invasion ports also raided.
19 **British withdraw from Somaliland.**
24 Germans resume mass attacks. Air battle near Maidstone, in which raiders fled.
25 Air attacks on Portsmouth and Southampton, Kent and Thames Estuary ; 54 raiders destroyed.

Sept.
3 **Agreement with U.S.A. for transfer of 50 American destroyers** to Britain, in exchange for bases in Br. W. Indies and British Guiana.
4 Hitler threatens "air reprisals."
6 46 German aircraft destroyed over Britain.
7 **German raiders strike at London** and other industrial targets ; formations of bombers with equal fighter escorts.
12 **Signs of German preparations for invasion of Britain** ; single German raider drops bombs on Buckingham Palace.
13 Italians take Sollum.
15 **Greatest day of aerial Battle of Britain** ; in morning and afternoon 250 enemy raiders came in over S.E. coast, 185 raiders destroyed.
17 **City of Benares**, bound for Canada with British child evacuees, **sunk by U-boat.** Italians occupy Sidi Barrani.

Sept. 1940
18 18 German raiders destroyed over Britain.
22 Franco-Japanese Agreement about Indo-China.
23 King George institutes George Cross and Medal. De Gaulle's expedition reaches Dakar. British night raid on Berlin.
25 De Gaulle withdraws from Dakar.
27 Germany, Italy and Japan sign ten-year pact.

Oct.
1 First award of George Cross.
3 Naval sweep announced in Mediterranean ; Mr. Chamberlain resigns ; Sir Kingsley Wood and Mr. Bevin join War Cabinet ; Mr. Herbert Morrison, Home Secretary.
4 Sir Charles Portal becomes Chief of Air Staff.
6 **Final stage of Luftwaffe's attack on Britain** ; fighters and fighter-bombers now employed at great heights, and attacks by night increased.
8 Announced that ban on Burma Road was to be lifted.
9 British naval bombardment of Cherbourg.
15 Three Italian destroyers stated sunk in Mediterranean.
21 Purchase Tax of 25 per cent comes into force in Britain.
25 British military agreement with Czech Govt. in Britain.
26 Liner Empress of Britain sunk by U-boat off Ireland.
28 **Italy sends ultimatum to Greece** and invades the country. British aid to Greece promised.
31 **End of Luftwaffe's 84-day attack on Britain** (see pages 158 and 161).

Nov.
1 R.A.F. bombers raid Naples.
2 British military, naval and air forces in Greece.
4 Two Italian submarines destroyed ; two others take refuge at Tangier. Spain takes over government of Tangier. R.A.F. bombs Naples.
5 Roosevelt re-elected for a third term. Enemy surface raider attacks Atlantic convoy. Auxiliary cruiser Jervis Bay sunk.
6 British loan of £5,000,000 to Greece.
7 R.A.F. bombs Essen.
8 **British bombers attack Munich**, where Hitler was making anniversary speech.
9 **Death of Mr. Chamberlain.** Italians take Gallabat.
10 R.A.F. raids Danzig and Dresden. **British regain Gallabat.**
11 Italian airmen in raid on Britain ; 13 Italian aircraft destroyed, no British losses. **British Naval 'planes torpedo Italian warships in Taranto harbour.**
13 Air Marshal Sir R. Brooke-Popham appointed C.-in-C. Far East. British bombers raid Berlin area.
14 **Massed air attack on Coventry.**

153

Nov. 1940
17 Army Cooperation Command of R.A.F. set up, with Air Marshal Sir A. S. Barratt in command. Air Vice-Marshal W. S. Douglas becomes C.-in-C., Fighter Command.
18 R.A.F. bombs Pilsen.
26 R.A.F. bombs Cologne (26/27).
27 R.A.F. bombs Cologne, second night. Naval brush with Italians off Sardinia.

Nov. 1940
29 British naval brush with Germans in Channel.
Dec.
5 **Auxiliary cruiser Carnarvon Castle** in encounter with German raider in S. Atlantic.
9 **Wavell opens offensive in Western Desert.**
11 Army of the Nile captures Sidi Barrani, over 20,000 prisoners taken.

Dec. 1940
12 Big raid on Sheffield (night of 12/13).
14 Flandin replaces Laval as Vichy Foreign Minister.
15 R.A.F. bombs Berlin area.
16 R.A.F. bombs Mannheim (night of 16/17).
17 **British capture Sollum** and Fort Capuzzo. Mannheim bombed (17/18).

Dec. 1940
18 Mannheim again heavily bombed (18/19), also Milan and Genoa.
20 Naval sweep in Mediterranean.
23 Lord Halifax becomes Ambassador to Washington, Mr. Eden Foreign Secretary, and Capt. Margesson Secretary for War.
29 **Second " Great Fire of London "** at night (29/30).

Principal Events, January to December 1941

Jan. 1941
1/2/3 R.A.F. bombs Bremen.
5 **Bardia surrenders** to Imperial forces.
9 German bombers attack British warships in Sicilian Channel. H.M.S. **Southampton sunk** and aircraft carrier Illustrious damaged.
15 Haile Selassie enters Ethiopia. Wilhelmshaven bombed.
18 Malta attacked by dive-bombers.
19 **Kassala reoccupied** by British.
20/21 At Malta, 37 Axis dive-bombers brought down. Compulsory enrolment for Civil Defence and Fire Prevention.
22 **Tobruk captured.**
26 Mr. Wendell Willkie in Britain.
29 Imperial troops cross frontier into Italian Somaliland.
30 British capture Derna.
Feb.
1 Imperial forces capture Agordat.
3 **Capture of Cyrene.**
6 **Capture of Benghazi.**
8 Capture of El Agheila ; Mr. Malcolm MacDonald appointed High Commissioner in Canada.
9 Naval **bombardment of Genoa.**
10 British Government breaks off diplomatic relations with Rumania. Night attack in Calabria by British parachutists.
14 Kurmuk recaptured.
15 Kismayu taken by our forces.
19 Australian contingent lands at Singapore.
20/21 Juba river crossed ; Mr. Anthony Eden and Sir John Dill in Cairo.
21 Lord Harlech appointed High Commissioner in South Africa.
26 **Mogadishu captured** by Imperial troops ; Mr. Anthony Eden and Sir John Dill at Ankara.
28 Sir Stafford Cripps visits Ankara to confer with Mr. Eden.
March
1 Mr. Winant, American Ambassador, reaches London.
2 Mr. Eden and Sir John Dill in Athens to confer with Greek authorities.
3 Raid on Cardiff.
4 **British raid on fish-oil plants in Lofoten Islands.** Cardiff again raided.
5 British Government breaks off diplomatic relations with Bulgaria ; heavy raid on Malta.
6 Imperial forces from Somaliland enter Abyssinia.
7 Abyssinian Patriots in action on Gondar road.
8 Heavy night raid on London.
9 London raided again ; heavy raid on Portsmouth ; Italian auxiliary cruiser Ramb I sunk in Indian Ocean by H.M.S. Leander.
11 **Lease-lend Bill becomes law.**
12 Mr. Roosevelt asks for a first Lease-Lend appropriation amounting to 7,000,000,000 dollars. Jamaica granted a new Constitution. On Berlin, Bremen and Hamburg, at night, the R.A.F. delivers the heaviest raid of the war.
14 R.A.F. raids Düsseldorf and Lorient.

March 1941
16 **Berbera recaptured** by Imperial forces ; very heavy air raid on Bristol.
20 Hargeisa taken.
21 **Capture of Jarabub.**
23 Capture of Negelli ; Berlin, Kiel and Hanover raided by R.A.F.
24 Imperial troops secure Marda pass, W. of Jijiga. Our troops withdraw from El Agheila.
26 **National Service Bill,** making civil defence duties compulsory, passes second reading ; War Damage Bill becomes law.
27 Capture of Keren and Harar. Agreement signed for lease to U.S.A. of bases in Caribbean and Atlantic.
28 British naval **victory of Cape Matapan ;** three Italian cruisers and two enemy destroyers sunk.
29 Imperial troops occupy Diredawa.
30 Air attack on Brest, where battleships Scharnhorst and Gneisenau sheltered.
31 Heavy R.A.F raid on Emden.
April
1 Capture of Asmara. Iraqi Premier resigns.
2 British evacuate Mersa Brega.
3 British **withdraw from Benghazi.** In Iraq, Rashid Ali el-Gailani seizes power and displaces the Regent.
4 Air raid on Bristol.
5 **Capture of Addis Ababa** by Imperial troops.
6 **Germans invade Yugoslavia and Greece ;** Belgrade bombed. British and Imperial forces enter Greece. R.A.F. bombs Sofia.
7 Germans force back southern Yugoslav army, and break through towards Salonika. Germans retake Derna. Income Tax increased to 10s. R.A.F. raids Kiel.
8 Germans recapture Doiran, in Libya ; surrender of Massawa, in Eritrea. Heavy raid on Coventry.
9 Germans enter Salonika. R.A.F. bombs Berlin.
10 British and Imperial forces in Greece engaged. Germans take Monastir and Yannitza. Hungary invades Yugoslavia. U.S.A. takes Greenland under her protection.
12 In Greece Imperial forces withdraw to Olympus line.
13 Enemy in Libya captures Bardia and encircles Tobruk. Heavy air attack on Malta.
15 Navy sinks three enemy destroyers and five supply ships off Sicily.
16 British forces in Greece abandon Olympus line.
17 **Imperial troops enter Iraq,** at Basra ; Yugoslav army capitulates. Heavy raid on Berlin by R.A.F.
19 First batch of women registers under Employment Order of 1941. Heavy raid on London.

April 1941
22 Imperial forces begin withdrawal from Greece.
23 Greek King and Government go to Crete.
25 Lord Gort apptd. Governor and C.-in-C., Gibraltar.
26 German parachutists take Corinth and Isthmus. British take Dessie, in Abyssinia.
28 **Sollum captured by Germans.**
May
1 **Cabinet changes :** Lord Beaverbrook, Minister of State ; Lt.-Col. Moore-Brabazon, Minister of Aircraft Production ; Mr. (later Lord) Leathers, Minister of Shipping & Transport.
2 Evacuation from Greece completed—43,000 got away. Iraqi troops attack R.A.F. cantonment at Habbaniya.
3 R.A.F. bombs Iraqi troops and aerodromes.
5 Maj.-Gen. Freyberg appointed to command Allied forces in Crete. Emperor Haile Selassie enters Addis Ababa. Mannheim bombed. German raid on Clyde area.
6 Habbaniya recaptured.
8 Bremen bombed.
10 **Rudolf Hess, Hitler's deputy,** lands by parachute near Glasgow. General Sir H. Maitland Wilson appointed C.-in-C., Palestine and Transjordan.
15 German aircraft en route to Iraq utilize Syrian airfields therefore R.A.F. bombs aerodromes at Palmyra, Damascus and Rayak. **Imperial forces recapture Sollum.** Hanover bombed.
16 Iceland proclaims her independence.
18 Syrian airfields bombed. Kiel bombed.
19 **Amba Alagi surrenders.**
20 **Germans invade Crete** by air, landing 1,500 troops. Falluja, in Iraq, occupied by Imperial troops. Sir W. Dobbie apptd. Governor and C.-in-C., Malta. In Britain, Bill passed to constitute National Fire Service.
21 In Crete, Germans take Maleme aerodrome.
22 R.A.F. withdrawn from Crete.
23 Regent returns to Iraq and rallies loyal elements.
24 **Loss of battleship Hood** while pursuing German battleship Bismarck and cruiser Prinz Eugen off Greenland. British take Soddu in Abyssinia.
26 Bismarck hit by aeroplane torpedo and attacked by our destroyers ; stops 400 miles W. of Brest.
27 **Bismarck** engaged by King George V and Rodney **sunk** by torpedoes fired by Dorsetshire. Germans capture Canea ; loss of two British cruisers and four destroyers off Crete announced.
29 In Crete, British withdraw E. of Suda Bay.
30 **Collapse of Iraqi revolt ;** Rashid Ali goes to Persia.
31 Armistice signed in Iraq.

June 1941
1 **Imperial forces withdraw from Crete ;** cruiser and two destroyers lost. Imperial troops enter Baghdad. Air Vice-Marshal A. W. Tedder appointed A.O.C.-in-C., Middle East. Clothes rationing introduced in Britain.
3 General Sir J. H. Marshall-Cornwall appointed G.O.C.-in-C., Egypt.
4 Imperial forces occupy Mosul.
7 R.A.F. bombs Brest (first of many attacks on German warships).
8 **British and Imperial troops,** with Free French formations, **enter Syria.**
9 Our forces occupy Tyre.
11 Luftwaffe drops propaganda leaflets in Britain. R.A.F. attacks Ruhr, Rhineland and N.W. Germany.
12 Capture of Assab.
13 Air-Marshal Sir P. Joubert A.O.C.-in-C., Coastal Cmd.
15 Imperial forces take Sidon and Kiswe, in Syria.
21 Free French forces occupy Damascus. King Peter of Yugoslavia in England.
22 **Germany invades Russia :** Mr. Churchill states that " we shall give whatever help we can to Russia."
27 **British Military Mission** arrives **in Moscow.**
29 Changes in British Cabinet : Lord Beaverbrook, Minister of Supply ; Sir Andrew Duncan, President of Board of Trade ; Mr. Oliver Lyttelton to be Minister of State in Middle East.
July
1 General Sir Archibald Wavell appointed C.-in-C., India ; General Sir C. Auchinleck apptd. G.O.C.-in-C., Middle East. R.A.F. raids Brest and Cherbourg ; also begins series of daylight sweeps over Channel and Northern France.
3 In Syria, **Palmyra surrenders** to Imperial forces ; Debra Tabor (Abyssinia) captured.
7 **American Naval forces in Iceland,** Trinidad and British Guiana. Southampton raided.
8 Russian Military Mission arrives in London.
9 In Syria, General Dentz asks armistice terms. R.A.F. raids Naples.
10 R.A.F. raids Naples. Beirut occupied by Imperial troops.
11 **General Dentz accepts British terms** and hostilities cease in Syria.
12 **Anglo - Soviet Agreement signed :** mutual assistance and no separate peace.
14 R.A.F. raids Hanover and N.W. Germany.
15 British control Syria and Lebanon.
16 British raid on Hamburg.
18 Britain recognizes Czechoslovak Govt. in London ; Agreement between Soviet and this Govt. ; Dr. Benes President.

July 1941

19 British Cabinet changes : Mr. Duff Cooper, Chancellor of Duchy (on mission to Far East) ; Mr. Brendan Bracken, Minister of Information.

21 R.A.F. raids Mannheim and Frankfort.

22 U.S. Loan to Britain : £106,000,000 at 3 per cent for 15 years.

23 German battleship Scharnhorst bombed at La Pallice (moved from Brest). Japan demands bases in Indo-China.

25 Japanese assets in Britain and Dominions " frozen." R.A.F. bombs Berlin.

26 M.T.B. attack on Valetta harbour. Britain denounces commercial treaties with Japan.

28 Japanese troops land in Indo-China. R.A.F. raids aerodromes in Sicily, destroying 84 aircraft.

29 Vichy govt. announces pact with Japan giving latter Indo-China aerodromes.

30 Soviet - Polish Agreement signed ; Polish army to be formed in Russia. Joint British and Russian air attack on Kirkenes and Petsamo.

Aug.

1 British relations with Finland broken off. British naval raid on Kirkenes ; Kiel bombed ; R.A.F. raids Crete.

2 R.A.F. raids Berlin, Kiel and Hamburg.

3 Italian cruiser torpedoed and two supply ships sunk.

4 R.A.F. raids Hanover and Frankfort.

5 Reinforcements reach Singapore. Vichy govt. recalls Gen. Weygand from N. Africa.

6 Mannheim and Karlsruhe raided by R.A.F.

8 R.A.F. attacks Corinth Canal.

10 British and Soviet Govts. renew pledges to Turkey and promise assistance in attack. H.M. Queen Elizabeth broadcasts to women of America.

11 R.A.F. raids places in S. Italy.

12 Daylight raid on Cologne ; night raid on Magdeburg.

14 Announced that **Mr. Churchill and Pres. Roosevelt met** in American waters on board battleship Prince of Wales ; declaration of joint peace aims (" Atlantic Charter ").

15 Message from Mr. Churchill and President Roosevelt to Mr. Stalin presented in Moscow ; maximum help promised and Moscow meeting suggested.

16 Day and night raids on Syracuse by R.A.F. ; also Cologne and Rhineland by day.

17 Mr. Churchill visits Iceland on return from U.S.A. R.A.F. bombs Bremen.

18 Mr. Churchill lands in Britain.

19 Lord Beaverbrook, in Washington, meets Pres. Roosevelt.

20 Canadian Premier, Mr. Mackenzie King, in England.

25 **British troops from South and Russian troops** from North enter Persia.

26 British occupy Abadan ; Russians enter Tabriz.

27 British troops occupy Shahabad in N. Persia ; Persian government resigns.

28 In Australia, Mr. Menzies resigns Premiership. Succeeded by Mr. A. W. Fadden.

29 **End of hostilities in Persia.** Mr. Harriman to lead U.S. Mission to Moscow.

30 Raid on Cherbourg by R.A.F.

31 Junction between British and Soviet forces in Persia at Kasvin. Bremen bombed in daylight by Fortress aircraft.

Sept. 1941

1 R.A.F. raids Italy and Sicily ; also Cologne.

2 R.A.F. raids Berlin and Frankfort ; also carries out offensive sweeps over Occupied France and Channel ; daylight raid on Bremen.

3 R.A.F. raids Brest.

4 Axis raids on Malta recommence.

6 R.A.F. bombs Rhineland.

7 Our bombers attack Palermo, Kiel, Boulogne.

8 **Combined raid on Spitsbergen** by British, Canadian and Norwegian units ; coal mine installations destroyed and population brought to Britain. U-boat surrenders to British flying boat in Atlantic.

9 Mr. Churchill reviews war and explains Atlantic Charter ; British Naval attack on German supply ships near Murmansk ; Mr. Duff Cooper at Singapore. Heavy night raid by R.A.F. on Messina.

11 Axis convoy in Mediterranean broken up by air attack.

12 R.A.F. raids St. Nazaire.

14 **Wing of R.A.F. operating in Russia.**

15 British Mission to Moscow : Lord Beaverbrook, Capt. Harold Balfour, Maj.-Gen. Sir H. Ismay, Maj.-Gen. G. N. Macready. R.A.F. heavy raids on Hamburg and Havre.

16 **British and Russian troops advance on Teheran ;** Shah abdicates, succeeded by Crown Prince. Enemy raid on Cairo. R.A.F. raids Karlsruhe.

18 Submarines sink two Axis Libya troopships.

22 King George of Hellenes, with Crown Prince and members of Govt., arrives in England.

24 **Conference of Allied Govts.** affirms adherence to Atlantic Charter.

26 Surrender of Wolchefit, Abyssinia. Gen. Wavell in Baghdad. Mr. Oliver Lyttelton in London. R.A.F. raids Dunkirk and Calais.

28 British and American delegates in Moscow. General Catroux (De Gaulle's representative in Lebanon) proclaims independence of Syria. R.A.F. raids Palermo.

29 Negotiations for exchange of wounded British and German prisoners.

Oct.

1 Successful termination of Three-Power Conference at Moscow. Stuttgart raided.

2 Our forces in Middle East reorganized : Ninth Army, in Palestine and Syria ; Eighth Army, in Western Desert. Both Commands under C.-in-C., Middle East. R.A.F. raids Brest.

3 Mr. A. W. Fadden resigns, his Govt. defeated on Budget.

4 Benghazi raided by R.A.F. (first of 15 raids during month) ; other bombers raided Sicily airfields.

5 Tripoli raided by R.A.F. (ten raids during month).

6 New Australian Govt. formed, Mr. Curtin Premier (Labour Party). Our bombers attack Piraeus.

9 In Iraq new Govt. formed, under Gen. Nuri es Said.

7 Plan for exchange of British and German prisoners breaks down.

10 Lord Beaverbrook and Mr. Harriman reach London from Moscow ; Britain will supply Soviet's requirements. Burmese Prime Minister, Mr. U Saw, in London asks for Dominion Home Rule for Burma.

Oct. 1941

12 R.A.F. raids Nuremberg and Bremen.

13 Our bombers raid Düsseldorf.

16 New Japanese Cabinet, under Gen. Tojo. Gen. Gamelin and former French Ministers, Blum, Daladier, Mandel and Reynaud, arrested by Vichy government. R.A.F. raids Naples.

17 R.A.F. attacks airfields in Sardinia.

20 R.A.F. attacks Wilhelmshaven docks.

21 R.A.F. raids Lorient ; other squadrons attack Naples (continued three following nights).

22 Britain resumes diplomatic relations with Mexico. R.A.F. raids Mannheim, Rhine territory and Le Havre.

23 Kiel and Hamburg raided by R.A.F. ; chemical works at Cotrone, in S. Italy, also attacked.

24 Italian auxiliary cruiser sunk by Navy in Mediterranean. Naples and places in Sicily bombed.

26 Cherbourg raided.

27 R.A.F. attacks near Cotrone, Pres. Roosevelt, in Navy Day broadcast, says America is at her battle stations.

29 British Naval aircraft raid Comiso, Sicily ; R.A.F. bombs objectives in S. Italy.

31 Air attacks on Naples, Palermo and Licata.

Nov.

1 R.A.F. carries out **daylight sweeps over France** and the Channel ; night raid on Kiel.

2 Off S. African coast our Naval units capture five Vichy ships carrying contraband.

3 Mr. U Saw, Burmese Premier, leaves Britain, mission unsuccessful.

4 R.A.F. attacks Dunkirk, Ostend, Rhineland and Ruhr.

6 Hamburg, Le Havre and Wilhelmshaven raided by R.A.F. ; other formations attack Naples (in all, nine times during month).

7 Announced that Hurricane aircraft adapted to carry bombs had been used in **daylight sweeps over Channel and France.** At night, very heavy attacks on Berlin, Cologne and Mannheim : owing to extremely severe weather 37 aircraft lost out of 300. Raids also on Brindisi and Sicily.

8 Düsseldorf and Essen raided.

9 In the Mediterranean, off Taranto, Navy sinks nine enemy supply ships and three enemy destroyers.

10 **Mr. Churchill**, at Mansion House, stated that Britain had **air parity in size and numbers with Germans** ; also that **if Japan made war on U.S.A., Britain would join in within the hour.** Loss of destroyer Cossack announced.

14 **Aircraft carrier Ark Royal sunk** off Gibraltar, in tow after being torpedoed by U-boat on 13th.

15 Canadian troops at Hongkong. R.A.F. raids Boulogne and Emden.

17 **British commando raids German H.Q. in Libya,** 200 m. behind enemy lines.

18 **In Libya Gen. Cunningham's army advances 50 miles.** Gen. Sir Alan Brooke apptd. C.I.G.S., replacing Sir John Dill (apptd. Governor of Bombay). Lt.-Gen. B. C. T. Paget C.-in-C., Home Front.

19 Imperial troops **capture Sidi Rezegh.** H.M.A.S. Sydney sunk in action with German raider, all on board lost.

Nov. 1941

20 Great tank battle with Rommel's force near Sidi Rezegh.

21 **Tobruk garrison sallies out** to join Imperial forces at Sidi Rezegh. Our troops capture Fort Capuzzo.

22 H.M.S. Devonshire sinks German raider in S. Atlantic.

23 **Bardia captured** by our troops. R.A.F. raids Brest and Lorient. British mechanized column reaches Aujila.

25 **Rommel makes drive over Egyptian frontier :** then attacks our forces in rear. R.A.F. raids Cherbourg. Benghazi bombed by our Libyan Air Force.

26 Gen. Cunningham (in command Eighth Army) is replaced by Maj.-Gen. Ritchie. British force from Tobruk takes El Duda and joins advanced units of Eighth Army 4 m. from Sidi Rezegh. General Catroux proclaims Lebanon independent.

27 **Gondar, Abyssinia, surrenders** to our forces.

29 British mechanized advanced forces reach coast between Jedabia and Benghazi ; Gen. von Ravenstein, of 21st German Panzer Division, captured. Submarines Tigris and Trident sink supply ships in Arctic waters.

30 Germans surround Tobruk again by penetrating narrow " corridor " between port and Sidi Rezegh. Japanese fleet reported from N. Borneo steaming south. 1,000th air raid alert at Malta.

Dec.

1 Connexion with Tobruk restored, but enemy again cuts off town. Submarine Aurora sinks Italian destroyer, supply ship and tanker in Mediterranean. " Stand-by " ordered in Hongkong ; state of emergency proclaimed in Malaya. Rear-Adm. Sir Tom Phillips apptd. C.-in-C., Eastern Fleet.

2 Battleship Prince of Wales at Singapore as Rear-Adm. Phillips' flagship. Australian sloop H.M.A.S. Parramatta lost off Australian coast. Daylight sweeps by R.A.F. on Channel and France (made on 20 days during month).

4 Gen. Sir Henry Maitland Wilson apptd. G.O.C., Ninth Army, Middle East.

5 Emergency war measures in Australia. R.A.F. raids Naples.

6 Roosevelt sends personal message to Emperor of Japan asking for his efforts for peace. **Britain at war with Finland,** Hungary and Rumania.

7 **Japan attacks** by air **U.S. bases in Hawaii** (Pearl Harbour, etc.) and Manila, International Settlement, Shanghai ; Hongkong ; places in Malaya and Thailand (Siam). **Japan declares war on Britain and U.S.A.** as from dawn. At night, Japan bombs Singapore and lands troops in N.E. Malaya and Siam.

8 **Britain, America, Canada and Netherlands Govt. declare war on Japan.** Japanese air attacks on Guam, Midway and Wake Is. and on Philippines. Land and sea attack on Hongkong. Siam gives passage to Japanese troops. British retake Sidi Rezegh and effect junction with Tobruk.

10 **Loss of Prince of Wales and Repulse** by air attack off Malaya.

Dec. 1941

11 **Germany and Italy declare war on U.S.A.** U.S. military aircraft sink Japanese battleship Haruna off Philippines. R.A.F. raids Brest, Le Havre, Cologne and West Germany; also Crete and S. Greece.

12 British destroyers sink two Italian cruisers in Mediterranean. R.A.F. raid on Sicily and N. Italy.

13 Beginning of five-day battle in Libya, in which Rommel makes stand S.W. of Gazala. Britain at war with Bulgaria.

14 Ten-year treaty signed between Japan and Siam.

Dec. 1941

15 **British withdraw from mainland at Hongkong;** enemy gains ground in Malaya; Victoria Point, Burma, evacuated. Loss of submarine Tetrarch. R.A.F. raids Ostend.

16 Ostend again raided; Bremen and Wilhelmshaven bombed.

17 **Japanese land in N. Borneo.** Rommel retreats from Gazala. British cruiser Dunedin sunk in Atlantic by U-boat.

18 Dutch and British forces occupy Portuguese Timor. Kedah, Malaya, evacuated. **Japanese land at Hongkong.**

Dec. 1941

19 British evacuate Penang. Derna and Mekili recaptured.

22 Gen. Wavell at Chungking, meets Chiang Kai-shek.

23 **Anglo-U.S. Council in Washington:** Mr. Churchill, Lord Beaverbrook, Sir John Dill, Sir Dudley Pound and Sir Charles Portal. British recapture Barce and Benina.

24 We recapture Benghazi. St. Pierre and Miquelon occupied by Free French.

25 **Hongkong surrenders.** Japanese land at Kuching.

26 Lieut.-Gen. Sir R. Pownall becomes C.-in-C., Far East,

Dec. 1941

vice Sir R. Brooke-Popham. British combined **raid on Lofoten Islands,** off Norway.

27 **British combined raid on islands Vaagso and Maaloy,** off Norway. Axis air raid on Malta. R.A.F. raids Boulogne and Düsseldorf.

29 Mr. Churchill in Ottawa. British withdraw from Ipoh, Malaya. R.A.F. raids La Pallice.

30 All-India Congress declares for participation in war effort; Gandhi, resigns. Mr. Churchill addresses Canadian Parliament at Ottawa.

Principal Events, January to April 1942

Jan. 1942

1 British withdraw from Sarawak.

2 **Bardia surrenders** to Imperial forces. Fall of Manila; Chinese troops arrive in Burma.

3 **Gen. Chiang Kai-shek in supreme command** United Nations' forces in Chinese theatre. Gen. Wavell apptd. to unified command in S.W. Pacific area; Gen. Pownall his Chief of Staff.

6 Our forces withdraw on Perak front; Kuantan evacuated.

7 Rommel fights delaying action at Jedabia; withdraws towards El Agheila.

8 Heavy fighting along Slim River, Malaya.

11 Kuala Lumpur evacuated.

12 **Sollum recaptured;** Japanese enter Negri Sembilan; fierce fighting at Selangor.

13 Rommel entrenched between El Agheila and Marada. Seven enemy raids on Malta. **Inter-Allied War Conference in London.**

15 Australian troops in action at Negri Sembilan. Balkan Union Pact signed in London between Greece and Yugoslavia. British and Indian land forces in Iraq and Persia come under Gen. Auchinleck, C.-in-C. Middle East.

17 Mr. Churchill back from U.S.A. New Japanese landing at Muar, Malaya. Halfaya surrenders to Imperial forces.

18 Japanese land in Batu Pahat area, Malaya. Detention of Mr. U Saw, Premier of Burma, who had been in contact with Japanese authorities.

22 Rommel takes Jedabia.

23 Agreement for federal union between Poland and Czechoslovakia. Successful British air and sea attack on large enemy convoy in Cent. Mediterranean. Libya, fierce fighting in triangle Jedabia, Antelat, Saunna.

25 Heavy fighting at Kluang, Malaya. Chinese reinforcements in Burma. Libya, heavy engagement near Msus.

26 Rommel captures Msus.

27 Mr. Churchill opens three-day war debate in Commons. Heavy raids on Singapore.

28 Rommel takes Benghazi.

29 Mr. Churchill winds up debate in Commons; on vote of confidence, 464 for Govt. and 1 against. Anglo-Iranian treaty signed.

31 Germans in Libya reach Maraua area.

Feb.

2 Rommel captures Barce.

4 **General attack on Singapore begins.** British Cabinet apptmts.: Ld. Beaverbrook, Min. of Production; Sir A. Duncan, Min. of Supply; Col. Llewellin, Pres. Bd. of Trade.

Feb. 1942

5 Rommel's forces reach Derna.

6 **Chiang Kai-shek visits India.**

8 Singapore naval base evacuated, floating dock sunk; Japanese cross Johore Straits in force.

11 Japanese reach outskirts of Singapore.

12 Singapore, our forces resist to utmost but are driven back. **Scharnhorst, Gneisenau and Prinz Eugen leave Brest,** shielded by enemy fighters, and proceed up Channel; our aircraft and Naval units attack, but warships, though damaged, get to German port in North Sea.

14 Japanese occupy naval base at Singapore; they shell Kalang Fort.

15 **Singapore. Gen. Percival surrenders unconditionally.**

16 Japanese enter Singapore.

17 Chiang Kai-shek sees Mr. Jinnah at Delhi. Japanese mass in Burma and N. Siam.

18 Chiang Kai-shek sees Mr. Gandhi.

19 British Cabinet apptmts.: Mr. Attlee, Dominions Sec. (Deputy Premier); Sir Stafford Cripps, Ld. Privy Seal & Ldr. of Hse. War Cabinet: Mr. Churchill, Mr. Attlee, Sir Stafford Cripps, Sir John Anderson, Mr. Eden, Mr. Oliver Lyttelton, Mr. Bevin. In Libya, Rommel's forces hold line Tmimi-Mekili.

20 Japanese cross Bilin River; British withdraw to Sittang.

22 British Ministerial apptmts.: Sir James Grigg, War Sec.; Ld. Cranborne, Colonial Sec.; Mr. Hugh Dalton, Pres. Bd. Trade; Ld. Wolmer, Min. Economic Warfare; Ld. Portal, Min. of Works & Bldgs.; Col. Llewellin, Min. of Aircraft Prodn. (War Cabinet of 7 members.)

26 Submarine Trident secures torpedo hit on Prinz Eugen.

27 **British combined attack on radiolocation station at Bruneval,** 12 m. N. of Havre; our parachute troops land and destroy station. Two Japanese transport fleets approaching Batavia and Sourabaya attacked by Allied Naval and air forces, but Japanese landed in strength.

March

3 **R.A.F. bombs factories in France** working for enemy: Renault works at Billancourt; factories at Neuilly and Boulogne-sur-Seine. Fierce fighting around Pegu, Burma.

5 National Service Act Proclamation: men between 18 and 45; women between 20 and 30.

7 Bandoeng taken by Japanese.

8 **Japanese take Rangoon** and Payagi.

9 General Sir H. R. Alexander apptd. G.O.C. Burma.

March 1942

11 In Fezzan, Free French units capture Temessa. **Sir Stafford Cripps to go to India** to satisfy himself that certain proposals agreed by War Cabinet for present and future action would achieve their purpose.

12 Mr. Oliver Lyttelton apptd. Min. of Production.

13 Japanese occupy Medan, in Sumatra.

14 Large contingents of U.S. troops now in Australia.

17 **General MacArthur (U.S.A.) apptd. to supreme command** of United Nations' forces in S.W. Pacific.

19 Lt.-Gen. Stillwell (U.S.) apptd. commander of 5th and 6th Chinese Armies in Burma. Mr. R. G. Casey, Australian Minister at Washington, apptd. British Min. of State in Middle East.

20 Heavy air attack on shipping in Malta harbour.

22 Convoy in Mediterranean attacked, but our Naval forces secure shell hit on Italian battleship of Littorio class.

23 Battle S. of Toungoo, in Burma. Sir Stafford Cripps in Delhi.

25 Japanese occupy Andaman Islands, British garrison withdrawn on 12th. Heavy and continuous raids on Malta. Sir Stafford Cripps meets Maulana Azad and Mr. Jinnah.

26 Very heavy raids on Malta.

27 **Combined night attack on submarine base at St. Nazaire:** dock gates rammed by H.M.S. Campbeltown, bows filled with explosives; troops carry out demolition; M.T.B. torpedoes entrance to U-boat basin. Sir Stafford Cripps meets Mr. Gandhi and other Indian leaders.

28 **British Draft Proposals for India** published. Mass raid on Lubeck.

April

1 Enemy air raid on Gibraltar. In Libya Rommel concentrates forces in triangle Martuba-Mekili-Bomba. Large Japanese forces reach Rangoon; British retire from Prome. Pacific War Council meets at Washington.

4 U.S.A. recognizes authority of Free French throughout French Equatorial Africa and Cameroons.

5 Japanese aircraft raid Colombo.

6 Japan bombs harbours in Madras Province. Mr. Harry Hopkins and General Marshall arrive in London from U.S.A.

7 In Burma British take up new positions N. of Thayetmo. Destroyer Havoc lost off Tunis. **2,000th air raid alert at Malta.**

April 1942

9 **H.M. aircraft carrier Hermes sunk** off Trincomalee by Japanese aircraft; cruisers **Dorsetshire and Cornwall also sunk.** Italian cruiser sunk in Mediterranean.

10 British Naval units sink two Italian supply ships and two schooners in Mediterranean. In India the Congress Working Party Committee rejects British proposals.

13 Appointments announced: Adml. Sir James Somerville, C.-in-C. Eastern Fleet; Vice-Adml. Lord Louis Mountbatten, Chief of Combined Operations.

14 Torpedo-planes attack Axis convoy in Mediterranean. Libya, enemy sets up a line of strong points on line Gazala-Bir Temrad-Sidi Bregesch. Burma, British forces retire from Migyaungwe; Japanese advance from N. Siam and threaten flank of Chinese in Shan states. New British Budget.

17 **Daylight raid on Augsburg** by Lancaster bombers, flying roof-top height. Germans report British attempt to land on island S. of Crete. British forces on Irrawaddy withdraw N. of Magwe; Yenangyaung oilfields destroyed.

18 Japanese report **air attacks on Tokyo, Yokohama, Kobe and Nagoya.** Free French submarine Surcouf reported lost.

19 Chinese recapture Yenangyaung and relieve surrounded British troops. Fierce fighting on Pinchaung and Sittang rivers.

22 British Commando raid S. of Boulogne for reconnaissance. Australian destroyer Vampire lost in Bay of Bengal.

23 In Burma, British forces withdraw from Taungdwingyi. 23/24, German "reprisal" raid on Exeter. **Heavy R.A.F. raid on Rostock,** in Baltic (first of four in succession); enormous damage.

24 Heavy fighting at Yamethin, on Sittang river.

25 American troops land in New Caledonia. Reprisal raid on Bath; also 26th.

26 Japanese enter Yamethin. Loss of destroyer Southwold.

27 German "reprisal" raid on Norwich; also 29th.

28 Announced that U.S. warships operating in Mediterranean. Reprisal raid on York.

29 Japanese occupy Lashio on Burma Road. Allies bomb Lae and Kupang. Second "reprisal" raid on Norwich.

30 German attack on our convoys to Russia in Arctic. Cruiser Edinburgh torpedoed. Scattered enemy raids on N.E. coast of Britain; 11 raiders destroyed.

HOW THE AIR BATTLE OF BRITAIN WAS WON

The whole might of the Luftwaffe was loosed against Great Britain in a series of mass air-attacks. She was shielded by the valour of her small band of R.A.F. heroes, who brought down more than 2,000 of the enemy machines.

Great Britain, Air War On. As soon as hostilities became inevitable in September, 1939, mass air attacks on Britain were envisaged, but a very considerable time had elapsed before raids were made by bombers of the German air force on what may be adjudged a large scale. Indeed, months passed before a single bomb was dropped on British soil, and then the attacks were sporadic and in the form of what was called " armed-reconnaissance " flights.

Before any assaults were made by Germany, the general plan for the defence of the civil population was brought into play. Over a million children were evacuated from London and provincial cities to camps and other centres arranged in parts of the country where it was thought that they would be safe from bombing raids. The A.R.P. organization which had been evolved, trained and tested before the war, was in a state of readiness, as were the Observer Corps and the R.A.F. Fighter Command and Group Headquarters, all of which worked to a closely co-ordinated system. The defence system also involved the allocation of barrage balloons to key points throughout the country (*see* Air Defence).

The initial attacks made by the Luftwaffe were carried out in daylight on the Firth of Forth and Scapa Flow, the targets obviously being British warships. The first occasion when bombs were dropped on land targets was on March 16, 1940, near

Scapa Flow, and it was then that Britain sustained her first air-raid casualty. Before these attacks were made preliminary reconnaissance flights had been carried out by the enemy. In these and all the early raids of the war R.A.F. fighters were notably successful in destroying the raiders, and at the end of 1939 twenty-nine German machines had been shot down when over British soil or British waters, while the R.A.F. losses were nil. On April 3, 1940, a Supermarine Spitfire fell as a result of enemy action. It was the first home-based fighter machine to be vanquished by the enemy. Up to June, 1940, the Luftwaffe had not been engaged in night attacks on this country and there was an erroneous impression that this indicated that Germany had not developed night bombing technique.

The scene was set for the great air offensive in August, 1940, eleven months after the outbreak of war. In clear weather huge, unwieldy formations of bombers and dive-bombers were thrown into action, escorted by large numbers of fighters. The raids were, in the first instance, upon coastal towns, such as Weymouth, Dover, and Portland. These attacks on land targets coincided with dive-bombing attacks on shipping in the Channel. The number of enemy machines detailed for these assaults varied between 150 and 400. Within a week the raids had been so frequent that the citizens of London and the people of the home counties had

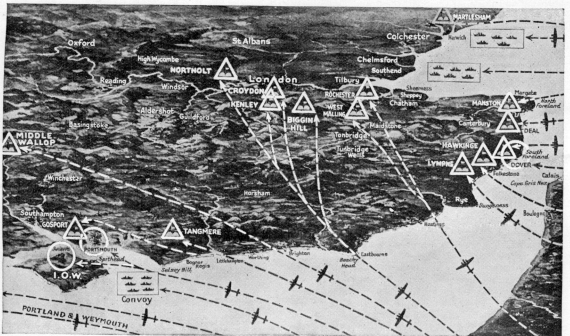

FIRST PHASE OF THE GREATEST AIR BATTLE

On August 8, 1940, Germany opened her air offensive with a 10-day attack on the South of England ports and Channel shipping. This met with magnificent resistance from the R.A.F., which inflicted very heavy casualties (totalling 697 aircraft) upon the Luftwaffe. Part of their plan was heavy attacks on South-east aerodromes, shown as triangles in this picture plan.

From " The Battle of Britain " (H. M. Stationery Office)

become used to the sound of the air-raid sirens and the sight of the tracery of vapour-trails left by aircraft as they sped, climbed, and fell in combat.

In this first stage of the Battle of Britain the German losses were very considerable. In the daily air battles which occurred it became clear that in spite of inferiority in numbers the British fighters were able to wield such power that the enemy could not maintain his offensive unless a change in his plans and tactics was made. From the German point of view the first necessity was the immobilization of the R.A.F. fighter units. This entailed a deeper penetration by the Luftwaffe bombers in order to seek out and bomb the aerodromes where our fighter squadrons were stationed. Therefore, while raids were made on shipping and ports on the South-East and East Coast areas, intensive attacks were carried out on R.A.F. stations such as Northolt, Biggin Hill, Martlesham, Croydon, Kenley, and Middle Wallop.

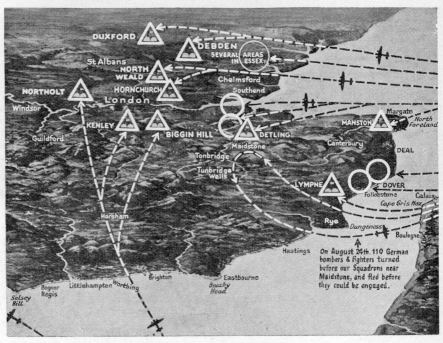

SECOND PHASE OF THE BATTLE OF BRITAIN

After a 5-day lull, some 35 major attacks were made in the period from August 24 to September 5, the objectives being inland fighter aerodromes and aircraft factories in S.E. England and Hampshire. At least 562 German 'planes were lost. Circles represent ports.

From " The Battle of Britain " (H. M. Stationery Office)

This widening of the arena in the battle of the air added to the ferocity of the offensive and defensive actions. The British losses rose, yet the punishment inflicted on the enemy was of the same proportions as that which marked the initial stage of the conflict. In the ten days which had passed from the beginning of the German air offensive 153 British fighter aircraft had been shot down. The German losses then amounted to no fewer than 697.

A further phase of the Battle of Britain came in the second week of September 1940, when the enemy made concerted attacks on London. Machines flying in many formations of about 40 bombers with fighter escorts came towards the capital from various directions and at heights of 15,000 feet and more. The brilliance and courage of the British pilots, flying Spitfire and Hurricane eight-gun fighters, in the tremendous battles which ensued increased in intensity as the struggle went on without respite. On September 7 the Luftwaffe made a tremendous onslaught on London with the intention of destroying the docks. Hundreds of bombers were used in daylight as well as at night, and enormous damage was done. This attack was the gravest blow that had been struck by the enemy in the great battle of the air.

The final scene in this great struggle began in October 1940, when the enemy threw into action fighter-bombers and fighters carrying small bombs in place of the twin-engined long-range heavy bombers he

had used before. This replacement was made in order to combat the R.A.F. with faster and more manoeuvrable machines. This last move was unsuccessful, however, and the British defences remained as formidable and invulnerable as they had been from the beginning. The Battle of Britain had ceased by the end of October and the Luftwaffe was soundly defeated Between Aug. 8 and Oct. 31, 2,375 German aeroplanes had been destroyed in daylight alone. (See also p. 383.)

The realization that their air strategy was at fault and that the day raids had failed to achieve their object, led the Nazis to turn to night bombing. Concentrated attacks against single, localized objectives were made on an intensive scale in the long winter

Big Days in the Battle of Britain, 1940

Aug.	Germ.	Btsh.	Pilots Saved	Sept.	Germ.	Btsh.	Pilots Saved
8	60	16	3	1	29	15	9
11	60	26	2	2	66	20	12
12	61	13	1	4	57	17	12
13	78	13	10	5	38	20	9
14	31	11	12	6	46	19	12
15	181	34	17	7	103	22	9
16	74	22	14	9	52	13	6
18	150	22	12	11	89	24	7
24	50	19	12	15	185	25	14
25	54	13	4	18	48	12	9
26	47	15	11	25	26	4	3
28	29	14	7	26	33	8	5
30	62	25	15	27	133	34	17
31	93	37	26	30	48	22	12

Note.—To save space, only days on which 20 or more German machines were destroyed are included. The totals for August were: **German 1,110**, British 310 ; September : **German 1,114**, British 311. Between Aug. 8 and Oct. 31 **2,375 German 'planes were destroyed in daylight.**

HISTORIC BUILDINGS RAVAGED BY THE HUN

Favoured by brilliant moonlight, Nazi bombers were able to drop several bombs on the Houses of Parliament. The Debating Chamber was ravaged by fire, and a delayed action bomb demolished one of its outer walls. The top photograph shows all that is left of the other outer wall. Below, the Hall of the Middle Temple, a priceless Elizabethan gem, is seen to be badly damaged. Blast from a bomb carried away the minstrels' gallery and the lovely carved screen supporting it.

Photos, G.P.U. and Fox

TRACKS OF THE ROUTED HUN IN BRITAIN'S SKY

On a lovely September day in 1940, a hundred German planes set out to bomb London. This particular raid failed to reach its objective, being driven off by gunfire and by R.A.F. fighters. Vapour trails from British fighters and fleeing Luftwaffe machines produced a curious seamed effect in the sky. These aerial patterns were a familiar sight during the Battle of Britain.

Photo, Topical Press

nights of 1940. One of the most vicious raids was centred on Coventry on Nov. 14, when several hundred bombers caused widespread havoc. A prolonged attack was made on Southampton on the night of Nov. 30, and also on the following night. Bristol, Birmingham and Cardiff, Merseyside, Sheffield, and many other industrial centres were heavily bombed by the enemy in November and December 1940, and January 1941.

A particularly savage attack, in which thousands of incendiary bombs were dropped on the City of London, took place on the night of Dec. 29, 1940. This raid was one of the most serious that had been inflicted on the capital, and immense damage was done by fire to historic buildings, churches and offices. This raid drew attention to the pressing need for greater organized vigilance in cities in order to counter the fire-bomb menace. In Sept. 1941 Herbert Morrison, Home Secretary, introduced compulsory fire-watching measures.

From the opening phase of the Battle of Britain the effectiveness of our fighter aircraft operating by day was abundantly proved. Defence against the night raider was less successful, however. The difficulties of locating and intercepting bombers in darkness are great, and, judging by the results, at one time were insuperable. Nevertheless, intensive research and development work had been going on in secret, so that by means of special and highly scientific equipment R.A.F. night fighters could track more readily enemy machines at night. The most notable system evolved was called " Radiolocation " when it was first referred to by Mr. C. R. Attlee, Lord Privy Seal, in June 1941. The introduction of this means of helping British fighters to make contact with the enemy coincided with a great increase in the number of night-fighter squadrons and

the production of formidable night-fighter aircraft.

The growth of effectiveness of Britain's night defence in the air was revealed in the spring of 1941. In the first ten days of May 96 German machines were destroyed at night. Thirty-four of these were shot down on a single night (May 10–11), and twenty-four on May 7–8.

On June 22, 1941, a new phase of the war opened when Germany invaded Russian territory, and it was not long before this gigantic new venture of the enemy was reflected by a change in the air war on Britain. Night bombing raids continued but were on a lessening scale, and as the weeks and months passed it became evident that the commitments of the Luftwaffe on the 1,800-mile Russo-German front had necessitated the transfer of a big proportion of both fighter and bomber strength to the East. By the end of 1941 the enemy raids on Britain had dwindled to a scale reminiscent of those in the early months of the war. They continued as such in the opening weeks of 1942.

At this time some evidence was forthcoming that the Germans were placing in service a new type of bomber, the Dornier 217. But this machine, though having a performance in advance of that of its predecessors, showed no superlative qualities.

It was anticipated by the Government that some new and perhaps surprise operations by the Luftwaffe might be expected in the spring of 1942. Plans were set in motion to prepare for these. One possibility, for which counter-measures were drawn up, was air invasion and tactics involving the capture of aerodromes. A strategy was planned incorporating special co-ordination of the Army and the R.A.F. to repel airborne enemy troops, and a new force called the R.A.F. Regiment was formed for aerodrome defence.

List of Main Raids on Towns and Districts of Great Britain

1939
Oct. 16 Firth of Forth, *First on Great Britain.*
Nov. 13 Shetland Is. *First bombs on British soil.*

1940
May 24 N. Riding, first English casualties.
June 18 Cambridge, E. Anglia, and Yorkshire. *First large-scale raid.*
Aug. 8 Battle of Britain opens—Channel shipping.
11 Dover and Channel ports; Weymouth, Portland.
12 Dover, I. of Wight, Portsmouth.
13 Thames Estuary and S.E. coast. Southampton.
14 Dover, Southampton, Hastings.
15 Mass attack, Plymouth to Tyne. **169 down.** Croydon airport.
16 Thames and airfields, 500-600 raiders.
18 S. and S.E., Croydon, outer London. **140 down.**
24 Ramsgate, Portsmouth. *First bombs on central London.*
26 Longest night raid to date, London.
30 Inland aerodromes; London by night, 800 raiders.
Sept. 7 London mass raid, Thames-side, 88 down.
11, 12, London and Home
13 Counties.
15 S.E. and London. **185 shot down.**
18 S.E. Eng., London, Merseyside.
25 London, S.E. and S.W. England.
27 S.E. Eng. and London. **133 shot down.**
Oct. 1 Liverpool, Midlands town.
5 London.
7 London, Liverpool, Welsh town.
9 London (night).
11 London, Liverpool (night).
13 London, Provinces (night).
15 London (day and night), Midlands.

1940
Oct. 21 Liverpool (200th raid), London, N.E. coast towns, Midland town.
25 London (day and night), Mid. town.
Nov. 4 London (night), S.E.
6 Southampton.
7 London, Midlands.
10 S. coast town.
11 Italian raiders in Thames Estuary.
14 Coventry (heavy), London.
15 London (*heaviest night attack*).
16 S. coast town.
18 Liverpool.
19 Birmingham (heaviest to date), London.
21 Liverpool.
22 W. Midland town, London.
23 Birmingham, Southampton (*heaviest*).
24 Bristol (heavy).
26 Bristol.
27 Plymouth.
28 Liverpool, other towns.
30 Southampton (heavy).
Dec. 1 Southampton, London.
2 Bristol.
3 Birmingham, London.
5 S. coast town.
6 S.W. town.
8 London.
11 Birmingham, W. England, W. Midland.
12 Sheffield, Liverpool, London.
15 Sheffield, N. England town.
20 Liverpool and Merseyside, N.W. town.
21 Liverpool and Merseyside.
22 Manchester.
23 N.W. town.
27 London.
29 London, *heaviest incendiary raid.*

1941
Jan. 2 Cardiff.
3 Bristol.
4 Bristol.
9 London, Merseyside, N.W. England.
10 Portsmouth.
12 London.

1941
Jan. 17 S. Wales.
19 London, S.W. England.
Feb. 17 London.
19 Swansea.
20 Swansea.
21 Swansea.
Mar. 3 Cardiff.
4 Cardiff.
8 London.
9 London, Portsmouth.
12 Merseyside. 9 night raiders down.
13 Clydeside. 13 night raiders down.
14 Clydeside and N.E. town. 5 down (nt.).
16 W. town.
29 Bristol Channel.
April 3 Bristol.
7 General raids. 5 night raiders down.
8 Coventry, Birmingham, N.E. towns. 7 night raiders down.
9 Coventry, Birmingham, London. 13 night down.
10 Coventry, Birmingham. 10 night raiders down.
11 Bristol. 6 night raiders down.
15 Belfast. 9 night raiders down.
16 London, fierce raid. 6 night raiders down.
17 Portsmouth. 3 night raiders down.
19 London, E. 2 down.
22 Plymouth.
23 Plymouth.
28 Plymouth. 3 night raiders down.
29 Plymouth. 5 down.
May 1 Liverpool. 1 night raider down.
2 Liverpool. 6 night raiders down.

1941
May 3 Merseyside. 16 night raiders down.
4 Merseyside, N. Ireland. 9 night raiders down.
5 Clydeside. 9 down.
6 Clydeside. 9 down.
7 Merseyside. 24 night raiders down.
8 Humber, N. Midlands. 14 down.
10 London. 34 night raiders down.
11 Widespread, but light. 12 night raiders down.
30 Merseyside, Dublin. 2 night down.
31 Widespread, not severe. 3 down.
June 4 Widespread. 5 night raiders down.
13 Many small raids. 7 night raiders down.
21 S. England town. 4 night raiders down.
July 4 Midlands and S.W. town. 3 down.
7 S. England town. 6 night raiders down.
8 Midlands, South and Scotland. 5 night raiders down.
17 N.E. town.
27 London, S.E. England. 4 night raiders down.
Oct. 2 N.E., S.E. coasts. 3 night raiders down.
Nov. 1 Merseyside, S. coast. 6 night raiders down.

1942
April 23 Exeter, heavy.
24 Exeter.
25 Bath, heavy.
26 Bath.
27 Norwich, heavy.
28 York.
29 Norwich.
May 3 Exeter.

Civilian Air Raid Casualties—1939–1942

	Killed	Injured	Totals
Sept. 3, 1939–July 31, 1940	310	410	720
Aug.–Dec., 1940	22,837	28,535	51,372
Jan.–Dec., 1941	20,520	21,451	41,971
Jan.–March, 1942.. ..	155	95	250
April, 1942	938	998	1,936
	44,760	51,489	96,249
Battle of Britain			
Aug. 8–Oct. 31, 1940 ..	14,281	20,325	34,606
(Of these by night) ..	(12,581)	(16,965)	(29,546)

Note: Raids included in this list are, in general, main raids with considerable damage and casualties. After Oct. 5, 1940, raids listed were mostly night attacks. London had no raid between July 27 and December 1941. In 1942 up to March 31 very few raiders, mostly coastal, were reported. In April-May there were the so-called "Baedeker" reprisal raids. For Battle of Britain *see also* table in p. 158.

Intensification of R.A.F. big-scale raids in depth into Germany culminated in a declaration of reprisals by Goebbels on April 20. By threats to destroy Britain's historical monuments and treasures it was hoped to temper the increasing fury of R.A.F. raids.

On April 25 a large-scale raid was made on Bath; great damage was done and the beauties of that fine town were destroyed. Both H.E. and incendiaries were used. Five bombers were destroyed. Exeter was attacked on April 23 and 24, and May 3. On April 27 Norwich was attacked and had its worst raid of the war. Many parts of the city were damaged and there were many fires. The following night York was bombed, with loss of life and much damage, some to ancient buildings. Of the 20 raiders, five were "clawed down." That night Norwich had a second raid. In addition to these heavy attacks on our "Baedeker" cities the Luftwaffe carried out many one- or two- machine raids on the south-west, south, south-east and north-east coasts. Usually the attackers tipped and ran, machine-gunning as they fled.

Germany justified this destruction of objectives without military value on grounds that we had done likewise in Hamburg, Bremen, Kiel, Augsburg, Cologne, Lübeck and Rostock. But among these are those old Hanseatic towns which were largely used as equipment and reinforcing bases for the Russian front.

Books to Consult. The Battle of Britain, J. M. Spaight (Bles); The Battle of Britain (M.O.I.); Britain Under Fire (Country Life).

L II

THE GLORY THAT IS GREECE TODAY

This small nation utterly routed the Italian raiders, but was unable to withstand the German Juggernaut. Defeated but uncowed, the Greeks await the hour when they can strike for freedom again.

Greece. On Oct. 27, 1940, the Italian Minister to Greece gave a party at the Italian Legation. One Greek notable, the Prime Minister, M. Metaxas, was unable to attend. At 2.30 a.m. the host excused himself and left his guests. At three o'clock he was with the Prime Minister, but not to inquire about his health. M. Metaxas was presented with an ultimatum. Greece was told to hand over, within three hours, certain strategic points to Albania. The Minister did not even know what points were involved. M. Metaxas described the ultimatum as a declaration of war by Italy on Greece, and forthwith called for general mobilization. In this way, and in keeping with the methods of Fascism, Italy, the sedulous ape of Nazi Germany, played the role of cynical aggressor.

The events which led up to this break began when Italy invaded Albania and the rumour spread through Greece that she would next attack Corfu. It was in British interests that the situation in the Mediterranean should remain unchanged; Greece was therefore promised British support should she be attacked. France gave a like undertaking.

On Sept. 20, 1939, Mussolini undertook to withdraw the troops which he had amassed on the Greco-Albanian frontier, and made many protestations of good faith in keeping with the Pact of Friendship signed by both countries in 1928. But beneath these blandishments were distrust and trickery.

Greece under the Metaxas Government was approximating closely to the political models of Italy and Germany, yet her sympathies, when the clash came between the Western Powers and the Reich, were with Great Britain.

The war brought Greece new trials and suffering. Her ships were sunk by U-boats and there were, until British action remedied the position, difficulties with her foreign trade with Germany, to whom she sent tobacco. As early as April 1940 Greece had six meatless days a week.

A month later Greece saw plainly that the flames of war were licking in the direction of her territory and that the logic of events indicated eventual war. Metaxas again made a declaration that Greece would fight only to preserve her neutrality and independence, and called up large numbers of officers and men for special training. He had read the writing on the wall, and when he addressed the National Youth Organization in June he told his young countrymen of war's imminence.

In August Italy began a campaign of words against Greece, the basis of which throws a strong light upon the completely immoral character of Italy's leaders. Twenty years ago a price was put on the head of a notorious Albanian brigand, Daut Hodja. He was murdered in Greece, and two Albanians living in that country confessed to the murder. Just as Germany exalted the degenerate Horst Wessel into a symbol of patriotism, Italy now declared the brigand Hodja to have been a patriot. Greece offered to surrender the two implicated assassins for trial before Italian courts. Rome, no doubt embarrassed by the correctitude of this procedure in the neighbour with whom she desired a quarrel as prelude to war, ignored the offer.

The next intimation of Italian intentions came over the air from the radio station of Tirana and from the Stefani Agency (the Reuter of Italy). Both vilified Greece, repeated the calumny with regard to Hodja, and generally tried to create a warlike atmosphere.

On August 15 the Greek light cruiser Helle was anchored off the island of Tinos while members of her crew attended the Festival of the Assumption. As she had chosen Good Friday to invade Albania, so Italy chose this great day in the calendar of the Greek Orthodox Church to torpedo this ship, while still ostensibly at peace with Greece, and without warning or pretence of justification.

Greece from this moment onward was subjected to the concerted blackmailing of the Axis partners. Italy began troop movements which could

Greece : showing the successive lines where Imperial troops made a stand during their retreat to the Piraeus in April 1941.

be regarded by Greece as being aimed at her frontiers and their violation. Germany began to press for barter trade agreements, in which her own interests were the sole consideration. She also demanded peremptorily facilities for her air lines and for permission to fly over the Greek islands. Metaxas had seen the flames, he now felt their fiery breath.

We come again to October 1940 and the invasion that followed within a few hours of the official reception in Athens in the Italian Legation. Actually, the invasion began before the three hours demanded had expired, Italian troops pouring over the frontier on the Pindus Range, and in the coastal regions looking towards Corfu, and north at Koritza.

GREEKS ON THE WAY TO BATTLE IN ALBANIAN SNOWS
The heroic Greeks made short work of the Italian invasion, driving the interloper back over the frontier within a fortnight. By the end of 1940 they were in occupation of about a third of Albania, and this they held until, in the spring of 1941, Germany launched her Panzer divisions. Then the Greeks were driven, fighting all the way, out of Albania and their own country.
Photo, Black Star

The invasion, on the Hitler pattern, was remarkable for the cynicism that scarcely troubled to conceal the bogus character of the alleged offences of the victim.

Albania had proved a " walk-over "; Greece was to be a campaign on similar lines. To the consternation of the Italian command, and the satisfaction of the whole non-Axis world, it found itself faced by an army which both outgeneralled and outfought it.

For a fortnight the Greeks held the superior numbers which faced them, and then, with a heroism that astonished the world, they began to press the invader back. Faced, for the first time, by an army imbued with a tradition whose roots thrust far back to antiquity, Italy's levies ran. Ammunition dumps, guns by the hundred and stores of all kinds were abandoned; and the prisoners taken numbered many thousands.

The Invader is Driven Off

The Greek troops chiefly responsible were the famous kilted Evzones, who secretly scaled heights in the Florina sector, 5 miles inside Albanian territory, and took the enemy by surprise. If the Italians could claim any victory it was in the air, since, until the R.A.F. could come to their aid, the Greeks were heavily outnumbered. The enemy's air attacks were directed chiefly against the civilian population. Salonika was heavily raided on Nov. 1, 40 civilians being killed and 80 wounded. This was one of several raids in which Ciano's Disperata squadron was engaged.

By Nov. 22 the last trespasser had been driven off the soil of Greece, and the war, now a pursuit or general rout, was on Albanian soil. It had taken precisely twenty-three days to rid the country of the invader. On Nov. 22 the Greeks took Koritza and many prisoners, and by the end of the year they were in occupation of about a third of Albania.

Great Britain had pledged herself to aid Greece in the event of the violation of her territory after Italy made such guarantee necessary by her invasion of Albania. Our contribution was by sea and by air in the zone of operations and elsewhere by financial assistance. The British Navy operated from Suda Bay, Crete, and on one occasion our ships, with those of Greece, got into the Adriatic as far as Durazzo. Valona was bombed from the sea and air. The Italian navy hid.

By the end of the year, and even more so in the first months of 1941, it was plain that Italy was being very thoroughly beaten by Greece, despite her superiority in men and arms. And thus, once again, Germany found herself embarrassed by a military ally who could always be relied upon to lose battles.

Germany then intensified her war of nerves against the small Balkan states. On March 4, 1941, Sofia, capital of Bulgaria, was celebrating with festivities the anniversary of her Independence Day. On the same date the last units of the German army made their dispositions in what was the virtual total occupation of that country.

Germany's next move was to frighten Yugoslavia into a mood of complaisance and to win over Turkey to her side. Italy, meanwhile, attempted a " comeback," throwing masses of men against the numerically inferior enemy, who had been suffering intense hardships during the winter campaign in the Epirote Mountains. This attack was expected to turn the tide in Italy's favour, and it was launched with regular troops and Fascist crack units to synchronize with the massing of German troops on the Thracian frontier of Greece.

On March 24 Germany brought her nerve-war against Yugoslavia to a climax with the blunt demand for the use of her railways for the transport of soldiers and war material. The next day Yugoslavia signed. This back-down by her neighbour before the bully was a heavy blow for Greece, since it was in effect the act of an enemy, for those who help our enemies are of their company.

But Yugoslavia had not said her last word. The situation changed with dramatic suddenness. The Government, which had brought dishonour on the country, was driven out; the Senior Regent, Prince Paul, fled. King Peter assumed power; the army took control.

On April 2 Germany demanded the demobi-

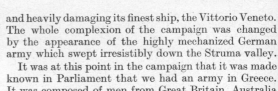

FRIENDS AND FOES OF GREECE

Here we see, above, British troops assembled in lorries near Athens. Below, left, ancient civilization and modern barbarian meet : the Nazis are photographed, for propaganda purposes, near the Erechtheum, on the Acropolis.

Photos. British Official and German Official

and heavily damaging its finest ship, the Vittorio Veneto. The whole complexion of the campaign was changed by the appearance of the highly mechanized German army which swept irresistibly down the Struma valley.

It was at this point in the campaign that it was made known in Parliament that we had an army in Greece. It was composed of men from Great Britain, Australia and New Zealand, many of whom were seasoned by the Libyan campaign. But, numerically and mechanically, our forces were vastly inferior to those of Germany, and the thrust made by the Nazi Panzer columns continued until the vanguard of that monstrous cavalcade roared, firing its guns, into Salonika on April 9.

The British fought under the command of General Sir Henry Maitland Wilson. The action, a continuous one, was virtually a rearguard engagement in which men were pitted against machines. By April 26 it had become a case of " backs to the sea."

On April 27 the Nazis entered Athens. Germany had defeated Greece, but it was a victory already stigmatized by world opinion as among the most ignoble in history. Throughout, the Panzer divisions and Luftwaffe had a superiority over their valiant opponents which made the war, while it lasted, the massacre of heroes. Greece, among the smallest of the world's nations today, and today under the iron heel of Nazi Germany and Germany's creature, Italy, was revealed as no less glorious than the Greece of antiquity, whose virtues of valour, endurance and loyalty had come down the centuries unimpaired.

Even when their own battle was lost, the Greeks did not desert their comrades in arms, the British. For it was after further resistance to the Nazi tanks was impossible, when the British were fighting, foot by foot, towards the coast, that their Greek comrades revealed their quality. Without this loyal cooperation it would not have been possible for our troops to leave Greece

lization of the Yugoslav army. Four days later, without a declaration of war, Hitler invaded Yugoslavia simultaneously with the crossing of the Thracian frontier and the launching of a terrific air war upon both countries.

The German intervention came at a moment when Italian prestige stood about at its lowest. Not only was Italy's army proving completely unequal to the spirit of the Greeks, but her navy, too, was suffering reverses upon what Mussolini liked to refer to as " Mare Nostrum." At Matapan, on March 28, the British Navy had thrashed the Italian fleet very thoroughly, sinking three cruisers and two destroyers, and, even so, their ordeal under perpetual air bombardment, which made embarkation possible only under cover of darkness, was no less terrible than that suffered by our men at Dunkirk (*q.v.*).

In this epic work of rescue the Royal Navy played a magnificent role, but paid a terrible price. Ships of every kind, from warships and cargo ships down to lighters and even sailing caiques, were used. The bulk of our army got away. And while the embarkation proceeded, Australian sappers, showing incredible courage and self-sacrifice, destroyed our stores.

With Athens in the enemy's hands, her own army overwhelmed by vastly superior numbers and the army of her ally thrown into the sea, with both King and Government fled and all hope of further resistance futile, Greece faced what was, perhaps, the most honourable defeat in history. By turning over this gallant people to the Italians, Germany revealed her utter lack of chivalry towards a defeated foe.

On March 9, 1942, Britain agreed to supply equipment to the Greek forces on a lease-lend basis. This agreement was signed in London by Mr. Eden and M. Tsouderos. In May 1942 M. Kanellopoulos became Vice-Premier of the exiled Greek Government and Minister of State in the Middle East. Kanellopoulos escaped from his country in the spring of 1942 and joined the Greek Government in Britain. On May 4 it was announced that Britain had given 4 destroyers to the Greek Government.

On Jan. 15, 1942, a far-reaching agreement between the Greek and Yugoslav Governments had been signed in London, in which detailed plans were laid for federating the two countries as a basis for a wider association of States to be called the Balkan Union.

Starvation reached terrible levels in Greece. In March 1942 it was stated that from 150,000 to 200,000 Greeks had died since the enemy occupation of the country. These deaths were caused by hunger or diseases due to malnutrition. Food prices rose to preposterous heights. In Athens the Italians installed a civil governor and a military commander, and a curfew was imposed in the city. There were no trams, buses, or taxis. People disobeying the curfew were shot on sight. The country was stripped by the Germans not only of her own food productions, but also of the small stocks remaining after the invasion.

Books to Consult. Greece Against the Axis, Stanley Casson (Hamilton) ; Short History of Modern Greece, E. S. Forster (Methuen) ; The Greek White Book, Royal Greek Ministry for Foreign Affairs (Hutchinson).

Greenland. On May 1, 1940, it was announced in Washington that the U.S.A. and Greenland had agreed to the mutual establishment of consulates, in view of the German occupation of Denmark. There were some 17,000 Danish colonists in Greenland who were cut off from their mother country. On April 10, 1941, the United States took Greenland under its protection after learning that German aircraft had been flying over the territory. The next day President Roosevelt signed an agreement with de Kauffmann, the Danish Minister in Washington, acting in the name of the King of Denmark, providing for the establishment of U.S. air bases. The agreement recognized Danish sovereignty over Greenland and asserted that " the defence of Greenland against attack by any non-American power is essential for the preservation of the peace and security of the American Continent."

Greenwood, Rt. Hon. Arthur, p.c., m.p. (b. 1880). Minister without Portfolio from May 1940 to February 1942. At the outbreak of war in September 1939 he was Deputy Leader of the official Labour Opposition and Secretary of the Labour Party Research Dept.

Arthur Greenwood British politician. *Photo, L.N.A.*

Grenville, H.M.S. Launched on Aug. 15, 1935, this British destroyer had a displacement of 1,485 tons. Her peacetime complement was 175, but this was increased after the outbreak of war. On Jan. 21, 1940, it was announced that she had been sunk by mine or torpedo in the North Sea. There was no time to lower the boats, but other ships were near, and these at once engaged in the work of rescue. One hundred and twenty-three officers and men were landed at an East Coast port, eight men were killed and 73 missing. The Grenville was commanded by Capt. G. E. Creasey.

Sir James Grigg, War Minister. *Photo, P.N.A.*

Grigg, Sir James, k.c.b., k.c.s.i. (b. 1891). Secretary of State for War from 1942. He had been Permanent Under-Secretary at the War Office since 1939, and succeeded his own former political chief, Capt. Margesson, when Mr. Churchill reconstructed his Cabinet on Feb. 22, 1942.

Gripenberg, Georg Achates (b. 1890). He was Finnish Minister in London from 1933 to 1941. On Aug. 1, 1941, the British Government decided to break off diplomatic relations with Finland in view of the fact that the latter was a co-belligerent with Germany in the war against Russia.

Gris Nez, Cap. In August 1940 the Germans mounted heavy guns on the French coast at Cap Gris Nez (between Boulogne and Calais), and the first shells to arrive on British soil from across the Channel killed two A.R.P. workers and wrecked some houses in the Dover area on August 13. A few days later (August 22) the German guns not only shelled a convoy of 18 merchantmen in the Straits of Dover, past " Hell's Corner," scene of some of the greatest enemy air raids, but also again bombarded the Dover area. The R.A.F. repeatedly raided the gun emplacements, but the Germans continued their spasmodic shelling of the Dover region with resulting damage to property and some loss of life. *See* Dover.

Gristock, Sgt.-Maj. G., v.c. (b. 1906). On May 21, 1940, when his company was holding a position on the line of the R. Escaut in Belgium, the enemy broke through and threatened the right flank. Realizing the danger to his company, Sgt.-Maj. Gristock, with one man as connecting file, advanced and put an enemy machine-gun out of action, kill-

Sgt.-Maj. Gristock, awarded the V.C. *Photo, Sport & General*

ing the crew. Severely wounded, he dragged himself back to the right flank position, from which he refused to be evacuated until contact with the battalion on the right had been established. He died from his wounds and was posthumously awarded the V.C.

Grodno. Before the war this town of N.E. Poland was regarded by the Lithuanians as being in their country. The Poles put up a desperate resistance against the Russians when the latter marched into Poland on Sept. 17, 1939, but the town was captured, the Polish garrison being defeated. On June 23, 1941, Grodno was taken by the Germans.

Guam. This U.S. Pacific naval base, situated at the southern extremity of the Mariana Archipelago, was repeatedly attacked by Japanese dive-bombers early in the morning of Dec. 8, 1941. Tokyo claimed that all large buildings on Guam were on fire, and Japanese warships surrounded the island. Two days afterwards Imperial Headquarters in Tokyo

on the future mechanized war some years before. Hitler accepted Guderian's advice with regard to tanks, and the Panzerdivisionen were created. In France and Flanders in 1940 he directed tank operations from an aeroplane, but in the campaign against Russia he met with reverses, and sixteen Nazi divisions under his command were routed at Kaluga in December 1941.

Gunn, 2ND LT. GEORGE WARD, V.C. This officer was posthumously awarded the V.C. for an act of great courage at Sidi Rezegh, Libya. On Nov. 21, 1941, he attacked a large number of enemy tanks with a single unarmoured gun. So accurate was his aim at a range of about 800 yards that two were set on fire and others damaged before he fell dead.

Gurkha, H.M.S. The first destroyer of this name, belonging to the Tribal class, had a tonnage of 1,870, a speed of 36·5 knots, and carried a complement of 190. Commanded by Cmdr. Buzzard, she was attacked during the Norwegian campaign by twelve waves of enemy bombers in the North Sea and sunk on April 9, 1940. The name Gurkha was then given to another destroyer just coming into service. The loss of this ship, commanded by Cmdr. C. N. Lentaigne, was announced on Feb. 19, 1942.

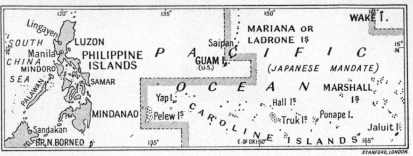

Guam : its importance as an American base in the East Pacific.

stated that Japanese army and navy units, acting in close concert, had successfully landed on Guam. The island has an area of 210 sq. miles. It is 1,300 miles from Japan and only 40 miles from the Japanese Saipan group of strongly fortified islands. The U.S. Navy had made continual demands that Guam and other Pacific islands should be developed as naval bases, but Congress rejected them until Feb. 18, 1941, when it was announced that Guam would be fortified as a naval and seaplane base. The construction of defence works was apparently under way when the Japanese forces began their attacks against the island, and if they had been completed these attacks would have been extremely difficult.

Japanese forces landed at the port of Apra, in Western Guam, at dawn on Dec. 10 and, attacking a number of strategic points, took prisoner 30 naval officers and men, including the captain of a corvette. They also seized a 3,000-ton tanker. On Dec. 11 Agaña, the capital of Guam, was occupied, and 350 Americans, including Admiral George McMillan, Governor and Commander of the Naval Station, the Vice-Governor, and many officers, were taken prisoner. From American sources it was learned that only a small force, consisting of less than 400 naval personnel and 155 marines, was stationed at Guam. *See* Pacific.

Guderian, GEN. HEINZ. Inspector of the Nazi tank divisions and C.-in-C. of German mechanized troops. Guderian was born in Poland and the Germans called him " Liberator of his Fatherland " after their Polish campaign in 1939, when he led the vast army of tanks that defeated the Polish divisions. His strategy and technique were based on Gen. de Gaulle's theories, the latter having written a book

General Guderian, created Panzer divisions.
Photo, Wide World

Haakon VII, KING OF NORWAY (b. 1872). Second son of Frederick VIII of Denmark, he is a brother of Christian X of Denmark. In October 1939 he attended the Four-Power Conference (*q.v.*) held in Stockholm. On April 9, 1940, when the Germans invaded his country, King Haakon and the Royal Family, together with the Norwegian Government and Parliament, left Oslo

NORWAY'S KING IN EXILE

King Haakon escaped in the nick of time from the clutch of the German armies invading Norway. He firmly refused to abdicate and, with his son, Prince Olav (centre), was tireless in furthering the cause of Free Norway in Britain.

Photo, British Official

for Hamar. He refused to yield to the German demand that he should appoint a Norwegian Government enjoying the confidence of the Nazis and nominated by Hitler. The Germans systematically bombed towns and centres such as Elverum (*q.v.*), where the King had taken up his headquarters, and he had many escapes.

It was not until April 27, 1940, that the Germans published the announcement in Berlin that a state of war existed between the two countries and thereupon appointed a Reich Commissioner for the German-occupied Norwegian territories. King Haakon sent a message to Herr Christensen, President of the Oslo Administrative Council, on April 24, that neither he nor his Government could agree to anything but the complete withdrawal of German forces then holding parts of Norway. Following the Allied withdrawal from the Trondheim area the King issued a Proclamation to the Norwegians on May 7, reaffirming this resolution. On June 10 the Allies withdrew from Narvik and King Haakon and the principal members of his Government left Norway in a British warship, arriving in London the same day. In July German pressure at Oslo attempted to force the King to abdicate, but he refused.

On Oct. 4, 1941, the King approved his Government's decision to reintroduce the death penalty in Norway for crimes against the State, to be judged after the war, a measure obviously aimed at the Quisling Government and its supporters. *See* Norway; Quisling.

Habbaniyah. This R.A.F. training centre of some years' standing is about 60 miles west of Baghdad (*q.v.*). At the outbreak of war five squadrons, mostly in training, were quartered there. On May 2, 1941, the guns of the rebel Iraqis opened fire on the aerodrome and destroyed some of the machines, inflicting a small number of casualties. R.A.F. bombers attacked the guns and frustrated an attempt on the part of the Iraqi air force to raid the aerodrome. By May 4 shelling of the aerodrome had become slight owing to vigorous offensive patrols by the R.A.F. The besiegers were thrust back and the aerodrome was in constant use during operations. *See* Iraq.

Hacha, DR. EMIL (b. 1872). He was appointed President of Czechoslovakia on Nov. 30, 1938, succeeding Gen. Sirovy, who had acted as President after the resignation of Dr. Benes on Oct. 5. His attempts to maintain the independence of Czechoslovakia failed, and when German troops marched into the country in March 1939 he was summoned to Berlin to see Hitler. Under German threats he signed a declaration whereby Czechoslovakia came under German " protection." Hacha remained in office as a puppet " State President " of the " Protectorate of Bohemia and Moravia." During the Czech disturbances against the brutal German regime in the summer of 1941 Hacha made the comment on June 24 after Germany's attack on the U.S.S.R.: " The Fuehrer's decision to square accounts with Bolshevism is an historic milestone in the effort to reconstruct Europe." *See* Czechoslovakia.

Hague, The. Political capital of the Netherlands. German parachute troops who landed from the air near the city during the German invasion of Holland on May 10, 1940, were surrounded by the Dutch forces and destroyed. Hundreds of enemy planes landed at low tide on the Dutch coast at a number of points, and troops disembarked with the object of pushing on to The Hague and capturing Queen Wilhelmina and the Dutch Government. Enemy raids were made on the city and damage was caused. Meanwhile energetic action was taken against fifth columnists. German civilians who had been resident in Holland opened fire on Dutch soldiers from the windows of houses, and over 100 Germans and Dutch Nazis attempted to take possession of strategic points in the centre of the city. They were destroyed or captured and the houses from which they fired were stormed. The Germans entered the city on May 15. *See* Netherlands.

Haifa. Important port in Palestine, a terminus of the pipe line from the Kirkuk oilfields in Iraq. A British contraband base was established here in 1939. The first Italian air raid on Palestine occurred at Haifa on July 15, 1940. The town was raided again in September 1940. Further enemy bombing attacks took place during 1941. *See* Palestine.

Haile Selassie, EMPEROR OF ABYSSINIA (b. 1891). Haile Selassie (*see* Vol. I, pp. 15–18) left Abyssinia in May 1936, following the Italian conquest

ABYSSINIA'S RULER RETURNS
The royal city of Addis Ababa gave a gala welcome to the Emperor Haile Selassie (inset) on his return from five years of exile. Peace and prosperity followed the ejection of the Italian invaders.
Photos, British Official and Hay Wrightson

and shortly before the fall of Addis Ababa (*q.v.*), but renounced none of his rights. At the outbreak of war with Italy in 1940, Britain recognized him as Emperor and promised full support for the Ethiopian cause. After nearly five years' exile, spent chiefly in England, Haile Selassie crossed the Sudan frontier into his own country on Jan. 15, 1941. He re-entered Abyssinia at the head of his troops, accompanied by his two sons, the Crown Prince and the Duke of Harar. In solemn religious ceremony he personally hoisted the red, green and gold flag of Ethiopia on his native soil. On May 5, 1941, the Emperor was welcomed back to Addis Ababa with traditional ceremony. A treaty with Great Britain was signed by him on Jan. 31, 1942. *See* Abyssinia.

Halfaya Pass. Known by the troops as " Hell-fire " Pass, this important area on the Egyptian-Libyan border, close to Sollum, was the scene of fierce fighting during the Western Desert campaign at the end of 1940. The Italians, who had entrenched themselves across the Egyptian frontier, stubbornly defended the rocky walls of the escarpment against advancing British forces. The Royal Navy repeatedly bombarded enemy defensive positions, blowing away a 150-yard stretch of the escarpment leading to the Pass known as " Hell-fire Corner." This constituted the only line of retreat for the Italians and enemy casualties were accordingly heavy.

In April 1941 a combined German-Italian force entered Halfaya, directly menacing Egypt once more, but on May 15 British troops thrust into the steep valley and took a large number of prisoners belonging to Gen. Rommel's Afrika Korps. Meanwhile heavy raids were carried out on enemy concentrations by the R.A.F. and S.A.A.F. in this area. Throughout the summer of 1941 the Germans fortified Halfaya, and by November the enemy positions extended from Halfaya to Sidi Omar, 30 miles S.W. of Sollum. This line was encircled by the British 8th Army from Nov. 18 to Nov. 21, effectively cutting off the enemy. Nevertheless, with German and Italian occupation of this vital pass, British supplies from Egypt to the Imperial forces in Western Cyrenaica—for by that time Gen. Rommel had retreated across Libya south of Benghazi—were constantly threatened, and although it was merely a matter of time before the enemy force at Halfaya capitulated owing to shortage of supplies, particularly water, a prolonged siege would have been to the disadvantage of the British. Intensive

bombing raids were therefore carried out on the enemy garrison.

Halfaya surrendered on Jan. 17, 1942, to Gen. de Villiers, commanding the 2nd South African Division. Some 5,500 prisoners were taken, together with two Italian generals. The fall of Halfaya opened the coastal route for supplies from Buqbuq on the Egyptian coast to Sollum, and thence to the front. In Rommel's sweeping advance in June 1942 Halfaya was evacuated after the loss of Bardia on June 21. *See* North Africa.

Halifax, EDWARD FREDERICK LINDLEY WOOD, K.G., P.C., 3RD VISCOUNT (b. 1881). British Ambassador to U.S.A. from Dec. 22, 1940, in succession to the late Lord Lothian. Lord Halifax was Lord President of the Council from 1937 to 1938, and Leader of the House of Lords in 1940. From 1938 to December 1940 he was Secretary of State for Foreign Affairs, being a member of the War Cabinet formed by Mr. Winston Churchill.

Lord Halifax, Ambassador to U.S.A.

Hamar. Some 80 miles N. of Oslo, this town was chosen as the headquarters of the Norwegian Royal Family, Government and Parliament on April 9, 1940, when the German occupation of Oslo took place. It

THE FAMOUS 'HELL-FIRE' PASS

Halfaya Pass, on the coastal area from the Egyptian frontier to Sollum, was the scene of many violent attacks and counter-attacks during the Libyan campaigns, being continually under fire from land, sea and air. On Jan. 17, 1942, Germans in Halfaya surrendered to Gen. de Villiers, and thereafter the coastal route from Egypt to Sollum was open for supplies to the front.

Photo. British Official

THE OFT-RAIDED MARSHALLING YARDS AT HAMM

This favourite target for the R.A.F. was attacked 80 times in one year.   In the photograph bombs may be seen falling.   Hamm is an extremely important railway junction in the Ruhr, and its yards are the biggest in Germany, accommodating some 10,000 goods wagons.   The dislocation of traffic was very considerable.

Photo. British Official

was the scene of fierce fighting between the German and Norwegian forces, the Germans relying chiefly on their powerful air force.   Hamar was occupied by the enemy on April 20.   *See* Norway.

Hambro, C. J., Dr. (b. 1885).   President of the Norwegian Storting (Parliament) at the time of the Altmark incident in February 1940, Dr. Hambro protested violently against what he termed the gross violation of Norwegian neutrality by the British (*see* Altmark).   On Oct. 4 Quisling announced that the Storting would be replaced by a Rigsting, recruited on the cooperative principle.   Members of Dr. Hambro's Government had their property seized and many of them were themselves placed under police supervision.

Hamburg.   This famous city, before the War Germany's greatest port and one of the largest in Europe, was bombed by the R.A.F. so frequently and heavily that the docks became almost unusable. The raids began early in May 1940 and from that time up to May 1942 the city was bombed 87 times; extensive damage was caused.   In October 1940 advertisements appeared in German newspapers for " workmen to be employed on the rebuilding of Hamburg."   By November the docks, quays and equipment were practically non-existent and a number of submarines under construction were badly damaged. The raids continued, factories, oil works, goods yards and the enormous Blohm and Voss shipyards being battered.   Great damage was caused in the districts of Altstadt and Neustadt.   In spite of the terrific anti-aircraft barrage encountered over Hamburg the R.A.F. raids often lasted for hours, the 'planes swooping low over their targets.

Hamm.   Having the largest marshalling yards in Germany (daily capacity 10,000 wagons), Hamm is a

vitally important junction for railways from Münster and Hamburg to Dortmund.   It stands at the N.E. corner of the Ruhr, and with Osnabrück, Soest and Schwerte regulates almost all the rail traffic movement between the Ruhr, Central and Eastern Germany. Hamm was a frequent target of the R.A.F.   In one year alone, from June 1, 1940, to June 12, 1941, the place was raided over eighty times.   Dislocation and congestion in goods traffic were considerable.

Hangö.   A Finnish port and island commanding the entrance to the Gulf of Bothnia, Hangö was included among the concessions which Russia demanded from Finland on Oct. 31, 1939.   On Nov. 30 Russian forces attempted a landing.   This was on the first day of the Russo-Finnish conflict, when Russia invaded Finland, bombing the latter's towns and bombarding her islands.   Hangö was heavily raided by Russian bombers on Jan. 21, 1940, and on Jan. 29 50 people were killed and 200 injured.   On Mar. 12, 1940, Hangö was leased to Russia by the Finns for 30 years as a military base, under the terms of the Peace Treaty   On Dec. 4, 1941, during the Russo-German war, the Russians evacuated it.   *See* Finland.

Hankey, Rt. Hon. Maurice Paschal Alers, p.c., g.c.b., 1st Baron (b. 1877).   On July 20, 1941, it was announced that Lord Hankey would relinquish the Chancellorship of the Duchy of Lancaster, a position he had held from May 1940, but would continue to perform special duties assigned to him, including the chairmanship of a number of War Cabinet Committees.   He was Paymaster-General from 1941 to March 1942.   Lord Hankey was raised to the peerage in 1939 and was Minister without Portfolio from September of that year until 1940.

Sgt. Hannah,
airman V.C.

Photo, Topical Press

Hannah, Sergt. John, v.c. (b. 1922). On the night of Sept. 15, 1940, a British bomber successfully attacked enemy barge concentrations at Antwerp. An enemy shell which burst inside set the British plane on fire. The navigator baled out, but the wireless operator-air gunner, Sergt. Hannah, fought the flames for ten minutes and extinguished the fire. His "courage enabled the pilot to bring the aircraft safely to its base," and for this he was awarded the V.C.

Hanover. The railway station at Hanover was damaged by R.A.F. bombs early in May 1940, this being one of the first British raids on the German city. By the first week in July the chief motor factory ceased to work for some time on account of the damage inflicted. In subsequent raids (it was raided 40 times in the first two years of war) the main passenger railway station was put out of use, while Germany's largest rubber factory, the Continental Gummiwerke, and the chief naphtha plant were severely damaged. An important target close to Hanover was Misburg, where oil refineries were effectively bombed.

Hansson, Per Albin (b. 1885). Swedish Prime Minister in the Socialist Govt. from 1932. In February 1940 he reaffirmed Sweden's policy of neutrality. Swedish neutrality in the Russo-German war was officially announced on June 25, 1941.

Harar. This ancient Abyssinian town, standing at an elevation of 6,000 ft., was captured from the Italians by British Imperial troops. its fall being reported on March 27, 1941. After their triumphs at Kismayu and Mogadishu in Italian Somaliland (*see* East Africa), the South African forces struck northwards along the desert road to Daggabur. Capturing Jijiga on Mar. 17, one column turned west along the road to Harar. The capture of Harar greatly facilitated the occupation of Addis Ababa (*q.v.*) by the Imperial forces. *See* Abyssinia.

Hardy, H.M.S. Leader of the British Second Destroyer Flotilla, the Hardy was an Admiralty type leader with a displacement of 1,505 tons. She was one of eight destroyers of the Hero class, and had a wartime complement of 200 men. On April 10, 1940, the Hardy, leading the destroyers Hotspur, Hostile, Havock and Hunter, headed up the narrow channel

H.M.S. HARDY, LOST AT NARVIK
This ship sank a large enemy destroyer, set three ablaze, and sank seven supply ships and transports before being put out of action. Her commander, Capt. Warburton Lee, was posthumously awarded the V.C.
Photo, Abrahams, Devonport

into Ofot Fjord at Narvik, the Norwegian ore port. Here German naval forces had concentrated. The dangerous passages through the fjord having been successfully accomplished. the Hardy entered the harbour alone and the bay appeared to be full of German ships. The flotilla leader fired at a large enemy destroyer, and the first battle of Narvik began. The Hardy then engaged a number of German warships and was badly damaged, Capt. Warburton Lee (*q.v.*), the commander of the British force, being mortally wounded. Paymaster Lieut. Stanning courageously steered the ship into shallow water in spite of fierce enemy attacks, and grounded the Hardy on the rocks. The survivors got ashore, where they were given shelter by the Norwegians until they could be rescued by British warships. *See* Narvik, Battle of.

Hargeisa. This town of British Somaliland was captured by the Italians on Aug. 4, 1940, and reoccupied by the British on Mar. 20, 1941. *See* East Africa.

Hargest, Brigadier James, d.s.o., m.c. (b. 1891). Comdr. 5th Infantry Brigade, 2nd N.Z. Expeditionary Force, from 1940, he arrived in Britain with his contingent in June 1940.

Harlech, William George Arthur Ormsby-Gore, p.c., g.c.m.g., 4th Baron (b. 1885). High Commissioner for South Africa. He was appointed High Commissioner on Feb. 21, 1941, for the duration of the war. He was Secretary of State for the Colonies from 1936 to 1938, and North-East Regional Commissioner for Civil Defence in 1940.

Harriman, William Averell (b. 1891). American industrialist. He was President Roosevelt's special envoy to Britain from 1941, to expedite the delivery of all types of war material under the Lease-Lend Act. He was present at the Churchill-Roosevelt conference in August 1941 (*see* Atlantic Charter) and was American delegate to the Three-Power

William Harriman,
U.S Lease-Lend
representative.
Photo, Associated Press

Talks held in Moscow from Sept. 29 to Oct. 1, 1941. In February 1942 he was appointed U.S. Government representative on the Combined Shipping Adjustment Board in London.

Harris, Marshal of the R.A.F. Sir Arthur, k.c.b., a.f.c. (b. 1892). C.-in-C. Bomber Command from Feb. 19, 1942. He was appointed A.O.C. in Palestine and Transjordan in 1938, and in September 1939 was given command of a bomber group. From November 1940, until his appointment for special duties with the British Air Staff at Washington in May 1941, he was Deputy Chief of the Air Staff.

Hart, Admiral Thomas Charles (b. 1877). On January 4, 1942, it was announced that Admiral Hart would assume command of all the naval forces in the South-West Pacific area, but on Feb. 11 he resigned on grounds of ill health and was succeeded by Adm. Helfrich. He later returned to his former post as C.-in-C. of the U.S. Asiatic Fleet. Washington regarded him as a "first class strategist" and as having a unique knowledge of the Japanese mentality. In August 1940 Adm. Hart outwitted the Japanese by making a surprise trip to Shanghai in order to prevent their exploitation of the situation caused by Britain's withdrawal of troops from the International Settlement.

Gen. Sir Alan Hartley, former C.-in-C. India.
Photo, Walter Stoneman

Hartley, GEN. SIR ALAN FLEMING, K.C.S.I., C.B., D.S.O. (b. 1882). On Jan. 16, 1942, he was appointed C.-in-C. India in succession to Gen. Sir Archibald Wavell (q.v.), a member of the Gov.-General's Executive Council, and A.D.C. to the King, and on Feb. 24 Burma was placed under his command. In March Wavell was reappointed to the Indian command, which included responsibility for operations in Burma, and in May it was announced that Gen. Hartley had been made Deputy C.-in-C. From 1933 to 1936 Gen. Hartley had been Director of Military Operations in India ; he commanded the Rawalpindi District from 1939 to 1940.

Harwood, REAR-ADM. SIR HENRY, K.C.B., O.B.E. (b. 1888). On Oct. 17, 1940, he was appointed a Lord Commissioner of the Admiralty and Assistant Chief of Naval Staff in succession to Vice-Adm. Sir Geoffrey Blake. He was in charge of the British cruisers Exeter, Ajax and Achilles at the Battle of the River Plate (q.v.). In May 1942 he succeeded Adm. Cunningham as C.-in-C. Mediterranean, with the rank of Acting Admiral.

Haugesund. It was to this Norwegian port that the German prize-crew brought the City of Flint (q.v.) in 1939, although forbidden to anchor there. She was subsequently freed at Haugesund. R.A.F. raids took place in the vicinity in December 1941 and January 1942.

Rear-Adm. Harwood, winner of the River Plate Battle.
Photo, Sport & General

Havock, H.M.S. A British destroyer of the Hero class with a displacement of 1,340 tons, the Havock was launched in 1936. She was the only one of the five destroyers to remain undamaged at Narvik on April 10, 1940. At Matapan in March 1941, under the command of Lieut. G. R. G. Watkins, the Havock attacked the Italian cruiser Pola. On April 7, 1942, it was announced that the Havock had been wrecked off the Tunisian coast and was a total loss. It was believed that all but one man were saved. *See* Matapan ; Narvik, Battle of.

Havre, Le. This famous French port was used as a B.E.F. base, the British holding a sector in that part of France in 1940. The Germans captured Le Havre on June 14, 1940, after repeated enemy bombings, when considerable damage was done to the quays. Shortly after they had captured the town they converted it into one of the " invasion ports." Concentrations of barges and shipping in Le Havre were frequently and heavily bombed by the R.A.F. in 1940–41, there having been 48 raids up to September 1941.

Hawaii. The Hawaiian Islands or Sandwich Islands lie about 2,000 miles west of San Francisco and 3,000 miles south-east of Yokohama. For this reason they seemed to the United States authorities ideal for the establishment of a military, naval, and aeroplane base for the defence of the vital trans-Pacific link between the United States and Australasia. The principal (although not the largest) Hawaiian island, Oahu, with its capital Honolulu, was decided on, and the base was established at Pearl Harbour, about seven miles from Honolulu, soon after the group was annexed in 1898. In view of the distance from Japan, Pearl Harbour was judged safe from a surprise attack, as the American advanced bases at Guam, Wake and Midway (qq.v.) islands made it possible for patrol 'planes to cover a wide extent of ocean and thus gave promise of ample warning of approaching attack.

Mortal Failure at Oahu

Events on Sunday, Dec. 7, 1941, proved that the American calculations were ill-judged. Japanese bombers and torpedo-carrying aircraft, based upon two aircraft carriers, unexpectedly attacked Oahu at 7.55 a.m. and the bombing continued until 9.25 a.m. From 50 to 150 Japanese 'planes were in the air at a time and, owing to the absence of due warning, the defending American 'planes were heavily handicapped. It would seem that Lt.-Gen. Short, commanding the Hawaii Army Dept., and Admiral Kimmel, commanding the U.S. Pacific Fleet, each regarded the other as responsible for the timely detection of invasion by air. Even the presence of a hostile submarine on the fateful Sunday morning was not regarded as justifying a " general alarm." Indeed, when the first Japanese 'planes approached, a junior officer concluded that they were friendly and nothing was done. The surprise was complete. Admiral Kimmel and Lt.-Gen. Short, together with Maj.-Gen. Martin, commanding the Hawaii air force, were later superseded and their actions were the subject of a Court of Inquiry at Washington. Admiral Ernest King, who had commanded the Atlantic Squadron, took over the Pacific command from Kimmel in mid-December.

In the attack upon Pearl Harbour (q.v.) the battleship Arizona (32,600 tons and completed in 1916) was sunk, together with six other warships, the naval casualties

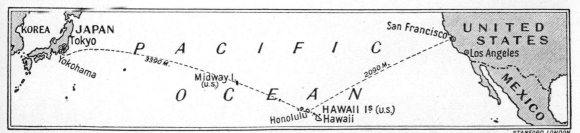

Hawaii : its strategic position in mid-Pacific relative to the United States of America and to Japan.

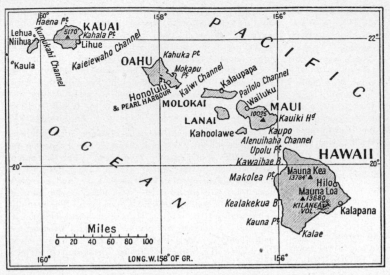

Hawaiian Islands, showing the situation of Pearl Harbour and Honolulu.

'Haw-Haw, Lord' (said to be William Joyce, a British Fascist). One of Berlin's English wireless announcers. The news-broadcasts in English of this British Fascist earned him a nickname which became a household word soon after the outbreak of war. Joyce's appointment as chief expositor of the German point of view to English-speaking listeners was a psychological blunder on the part of the Nazis, for the majority of people in Britain regarded "Haw-Haw" as being merely amusing.

Hazebrouck. This town, situated between Calais and Béthune in Northern France, formed part of Lord Gort's main line of communications with the French coast in the middle of May 1940. When the B.E.F. fell back upon the coast the town was taken by the Germans and became one of their military bases. It was repeatedly attacked by the R.A.F. in their offensive sweeps over Northern France, and the marshalling yards there were bombed.

totalling 91 officers and 2,638 men killed and 656 injured. The large number of dead was due to the fact that the old battleship Oklahoma capsized. The other ships lost were the target ship Utah (19,800 tons), three destroyers, Cassin, Downes, and Shaw, and the minelayer Oglala.

In this initial attack other military and naval targets on the island of Oahu were bombed, and in Honolulu there was considerable damage and many casualties. On Dec. 16 a Japanese submarine shelled Maui, another of the Hawaiian group, and on Jan. 1. 1942, Honolulu reported further shelling on the port of Hilo (Hawaii) and elsewhere on the islands.

Judged in the light of history, the disaster of Pearl Harbour would seem to arise, in part, from the policy of naval limitation laid down by the Washington Conference of 1921. This was intended to give Britain and the United States naval supremacy in the ratio of 3 : 3 : 2 over Japan, but, in fact, improved Japan's relative position as compared with her pre-Conference position. In particular, the United States debarred herself from developing any Pacific naval base during the currency of the Four-Power Pact. Thus Guam (q.v.) and the other advanced bases were never developed in a manner needful if the surprise attack upon Pearl Harbour was to be rendered impossible. The dry dock at Pearl Harbour was opened in 1919 and the naval station had been in existence since 1898, so there was small excuse for the surprise, but, strategically, the safety of Hawaii was endangered, as stated above, by the policy of naval limitation in the Pacific embodied in the Washington Agreement. The margin of safety was not sufficient to enable America satisfactorily to patrol two oceans, particularly as Japan consistently developed her own advanced bases in the Pacific.

From mid-December 1941 Oahu island was strongly garrisoned by the Americans, so that, should the Japanese attempt another attack on the Pearl Harbour scale, they would meet with powerful resistance. The need for air reinforcements was stressed by the authorities at the beginning of 1942, though up till then Hawaii's air power had prevented the enemy from seizing outlying islands of the group as bases from which to attack Oahu.

POLAND'S LAST FIGHT ENDS

After heroic resistance, Rear-Adm. von Unruh was forced to yield Hel, the last Polish stronghold, to enormously superior German forces. Here he is seen signing the capitulation, under the wolfish eyes of German officers.

Photo, Keystone

Hel (HELA). The last Polish stronghold that fell to the Germans was the Peninsula of Hel. On Oct. 1, 1939, the Polish garrison of 4,000 men under Rear-Adm. von Unruh laid down its arms, having held out against attack from sea, land, and air for 30 days. *See* Poland.

Helfrich, VICE-ADM. C. E. L. (b. 1887). C.-in-C. of all Netherlands and Netherlands East Indies forces at sea, in the air, and on land in the Far East, from April 1942. A native of Java, Vice-Adm. Helfrich

Admiral Helfrich,
C.-in-C. of all Dutch forces in
the Far East.
Photo, Keystone

succeeded Admiral Hart as Chief of Allied Naval Services, W. Pacific, when the latter resigned through ill-health on Feb. 11, 1942. Vice-Adm. Helfrich was also C. in-C. of the Netherlands East Indies navy, and an expert in submarine and destroyer operations. Before that he held the post of Commander of the Naval Air Arm in the Netherlands East Indies. In March 1942 he went to Ceylon. Soon after that his new appointment was announced.

Heligoland. This strongly fortified German island in the North Sea belongs to the Northern group of the Frisians (*q.v.*). The first attack on the German

GERMAN NAVAL STRONGHOLD
Heligoland is one of the strongest German fortresses, bristling with guns. An inscription chalked on the wall in this photograph states that the gun is pointed " Against England," and Mr. Churchill is depicted underneath, complete with cigar.
Photo, Keystone

fleet in Heligoland Bight was launched by the R.A.F. on Sept. 29, 1939. On Dec. 3 a strong formation of R.A.F. bombers attacked German warships near Heligoland and scored direct hits with heavy bombs. There was a great aerial battle in the vicinity on Dec. 18, 1939, when nearly 100 aircraft were engaged. After this date German warships and submarines off Heligoland, which became known to our airmen as " the Hornet's Nest," were attacked on many occasions. The Gneisenau, Scharnhorst, and Prinz Eugen returned here from Brest on Feb. 13, 1942.

Helsinki. Formerly known as Helsingfors, Finland's capital resorted to air defence measures during the tension between Russia and herself, before the outbreak of war in November 1939. Soviet 'planes bombed the city on November 30, the first day of war, when considerable damage was done. Russian raids increased in severity throughout December, inflicting heavy casualties and causing much damage. Compulsory evacuation of citizens took place in the depth of the Finnish winter. The majority of Russian raids occurred during daylight, and life in the city gradually returned to normal after four months of war, peace

being concluded in the middle of March 1940, a peace that was to be of comparatively short duration, for on June 22, 1941, hostilities broke out afresh between the two countries, Finland having thrown in her lot with Germany. Three days later Russian 'planes again attacked Helsinki, German aircraft and troops in the vicinity being the main objective. Subsequent raids by the Soviet Air Force resulted in considerable damage. *See* Finland.

Henderson, RT. HON. SIR NEVILE MEYRICK, G.C.M.G., P.C. (1882–1942). British Ambassador to Berlin, 1937–39. He strove for peace with the Germans until the last in September 1939, and in 1940 he published " Failure of a Mission," an account of this struggle. He left Berlin on Sept. 4, 1939, the day after the declaration of war by Great Britain. An attempt was made by a U-boat to torpedo the Dutch liner Batavia in which,

Sir N. Henderson,
Ambassador to Berlin,
1937–39.
Photo, Topical

escorted by British destroyers, Sir Nevile and his Embassy staff were returning to England on September 7. In 1941 he became Group Commander in the Home Guard. He died Dec. 30, 1942.

Henlein, KONRAD (b. 1898). After the German annexation of Czechoslovakia in March 1939 Henlein, who had been leader of the Sudeten German party and chief agitator in the events leading up to the crisis of September 1938, became Gauleiter of Sudetenland and Civil Administrator of Bohemia.

Heraklion (CANDIA). The battle of Crete (*q.v.*) began on May 19, 1941, when a large formation of German bombers swept

Konrad Henlein,
leader of Sudeten Nazis
against Czechs.
Photo, Wide World

across the narrow sea from their aerodromes in Greece and subjected Heraklion, a key-point on the north coast of Crete, to intense bombing. On May 20 the first German parachutists arrived, and some 3,000 landed near Heraklion. Of these it was reported that 1,800 were taken prisoner, wounded or killed. The Greeks held out for six days. This heroic defence enabled the British troops to hold the aerodrome without interference. On May 24 the town suffered a ferocious raid by German aircraft, heavy bombs being used. The British withdrew from Crete on June 1, and Heraklion was then occupied by the Germans.

Hermes, H.M.S The first British aircraft carrier to be designed for that function, the Hermes displaced 10,850 tons. Her armament included six 5·5-in. and three 4-in. A.A. guns ; she operated 15 aircraft. In April 1942, when under the command of Capt. R. F. J. Onslow. D.S.O.. she was sunk about ten miles off Ceylon by Japanese dive-bombers. 305 lives were lost.

Hertzog, GEN. HON. JAMES BARRY MUNNIK (1866–1942). Prime Minister of the Union of South Africa, 1924–39. He resigned from the Premiership in September 1939, owing to his policy of neutrality for South Africa, and was succeeded by Field-Marshal Smuts (*q.v.*). On November 6, 1940, he resigned from the South African Nationalist Party, of which he had been leader from 1933 to 1939. As leader of the Opposition, Gen. Hertzog brought forward a peace motion on August 29, 1940, which was rejected. He resigned his seat in Parliament in December. On March 6, 1941, he was elected Leader of the new Afrikander Party at Blomfontein. He died Nov. 21, 1942.

Hess, WALTHER RICHARD RUDOLF (b. 1894). As long ago as 1920 Hess had been a member of the Nazi Party in Germany, and in 1923 he became Hitler's secretary. Before the war he was Hitler's personal deputy in the Reichstag and in 1939, at the outbreak of war, was named as the Fuehrer's successor in second rank after Goering. On May 10, 1941, " Nazi No. 3," as Hess was called on his appointment as Deputy Fuehrer, flew from Augsburg in Germany and landed some eight miles S.W. of Glasgow, a distance of 900 miles. He baled out of his Messerschmitt by parachute, his plane crashing in flames. Hess suffered nothing worse than a broken ankle.

Rudolf Hess,
" Nazi No. 3."
Photo, Associated Press

The news of his arrival in Scotland was received with amazement throughout the world. The Nazi press declared that papers left behind by the Deputy Fuehrer revealed that he suffered from mental disorder, and laboured under the delusion that a step taken on his personal initiative with Englishmen whom he knew would lead to an understanding between Germany and Britain. It was subsequently proved that Hess was perfectly sane. On May 14 it was made known that Hess had wished to land on the estate of the Duke of Hamilton, whom, as Lord Clydesdale, he had met in Germany before the war. Goebbels followed up this announcement by declaring that Hess had come to Britain on an unofficial peace mission.

The British authorities offered no explanation and Hess remained as a prisoner of war. It was not until Jan. 27, 1942, that Mr. Churchill, in the course of a speech in the House of Commons, confirmed Goebbels' announcement. " When Rudolf Hess flew over here some months ago," said the Premier, " he firmly believed that he had only to gain access to certain circles in this country for what he has described as the ' Churchill clique ' to be thrown out of power and for a Government to be set up with which Hitler could negotiate a magnanimous peace. The only importance attaching to the opinions of Hess is the fact that he was fresh from the atmosphere of Hitler's intimate table." He was succeeded in February 1942 as Hitler's deputy by Martin Bormann (*q.v.*).

Heydrich, REINHARD. On Sept. 28, 1941, the German authorities in Prague announced that the Czechs would have a new master, " Higher Group Leader Heydrich," and that he had already assumed his duties in Prague Castle as Deputy-Protector of Bohemia and Moravia. Heydrich, whose reputation in Europe was one of the most unsavoury, was Himmler's deputy, and he succeeded Baron .von Neurath (*q.v.*). Heydrich's first act was to visit the puppet President, Dr. Hacha, to inform him of the arrest of the Prime Minister of the Protectorate, Gen. Elias. A reign of terror rapidly developed under Heydrich's rule. After he returned in May 1942

from France, on a visit to increase rigours against the French, he was attacked and shot near Prague on May 27. Heydrich died on June 4 ; over 180 people had already been executed in reprisal and the terror was expanding. *See* Czechoslovakia ; Gestapo.

Himmler, HEINRICH (b. 1900). Chief of the Gestapo, Himmler was responsible for the defence of Nazi rule against opposition in Germany and, accordingly, for innumerable outrages and murders carried out in the name of the Gestapo. He was also charged with maintaining " order " in Hitler's occupied countries. Himmler grew up with the National Socialist movement, and joined the party at the age of 19. When he was 23 he took part in the unsuccessful attempt to destroy the Bavarian Government. He escaped arrest and joined Hitler. After the Fuehrer's rise to power Himmler carried out the " purge " of former storm troops in 1934. At that time he was put in charge of the newly created Gestapo, or secret police, and the Black Guards. He was responsible for Hitler's life. After the Nazi conquest of Poland in 1939 Himmler's activities became even more ruthless, the executions of unfortunate Poles soaring to diabolical heights. Not only in Poland and Czechoslovakia were horrors perpetrated by Himmler, but also in Norway, the Netherlands and France, Yugoslavia and Greece. At home Himmler and his deputy Heydrich (*q.v.*) controlled the so-called cultural organizations, and supervised all the activities of Germans. *See* Gestapo.

Heinrich Himmler,
Gestapo Chief.
Photo, Keystone

Hinton, SGT. JOHN DANIEL, V.C. Fourth member of the New Zealand military forces to be awarded the V.C., Sgt. Hinton won it in recognition of his daring action on the night of April 28, 1941, when, in spite of an order to retreat in face of a column of German armoured forces converging on a large force of British and New Zealand troops awaiting embarkation at Kalamai, Greece, he advanced to within several yards ot the nearest gun and hurled two grenades, completely wiping out the crew. German troops retreated into two houses, followed by Sgt. Hinton and a crowd of New Zealanders, who attacked the garrison with the bayonet. The guns were held by the New Zealanders until overwhelming German forces arrived. Sgt. Hinton was wounded and taken prisoner.

Sgt. J. D. Hinton,
awarded the V.C.
Photo, British Official

Hipper. Germany's Hipper class of fast modern cruisers consisted at the outbreak of war of 5 ships : the Blücher, Adm. Hipper, Prinz Eugen, Seydlitz and the Lützow. Of 10,000 tons displacement they mounted eight 8-in. guns and carried 830 crew. The Adm. Hipper was completed in April 1939, and the Blücher, completed in August 1939, was sunk by mines in Oslo Fjord after being disabled by Norwegian forts on April 9, 1940. The Lützow was formerly the Deutschland (*q.v.*). The Prinz Eugen took refuge at Brest (*q.v.*).

ADOLF HITLER, MAKER OF WORLD WAR

Germany's Fuehrer, whom Nazi Party propaganda had made the object of feverish adulation, developed the nation's resources to the utmost, only to harness them to his senseless purpose—war, and the domination of the world. See also Axis; Europe; Germany; Gestapo; Goering, etc.

Hitler, ADOLF (b. 1889). An outline of Hitler's life up to the beginning of September 1939 is given in Vol. 5, pp. 2094–5, and Vol. 10, p. 4673. The Fuehrer's career may be said to have reached its climax when, in one of those maniacal outbursts for which he had long been notorious, he plunged Germany and Europe into war on Sept. 1, 1939. His invasion and conquest of Poland provoked what was to be a Second World War, but on Oct. 6 Hitler launched his " peace proposals." Neville Chamberlain, British Prime Minister, rejected this typical volte-face : " Peace conditions cannot be acceptable which begin by condoning aggression . . ."

The Fuehrer narrowly escaped death on Nov. 8, 1939. He had attended a celebration of the Nazi Party in the famous Munich beerhouse (once the scene of an abortive revolt by Hitler and his followers in 1923), and shortly after he had left the building a bomb exploded, killing several people. Hitler's megalomaniac dream of conquering Europe and ultimately the whole world, with the Germans as the " master race," was revealed in brutal clarity during 1940. The Germans invaded Denmark and Norway in April,

and the Low Countries and France were conquered in May and June.

Of Hitler's various conferences with fellow-dictators and others, the first took place on March 18, 1940, when he met Mussolini on the Brenner Pass—a meeting repeated on Oct. 4, 1940—" to discuss future plans." On Oct. 21, 1940, Hitler met Laval near Paris, and then went on to Hendaye, facing the Spanish frontier in the Pyrenees. He had two conferences in his special railway coach with Gen. Franco. On his return journey the Fuehrer met Pétain somewhere in Occupied France. All these meetings pointed to the fact that Hitler, cheated of a quick victory over Great Britain, was attempting to consolidate his " New Order " in Europe.

Hitler's triumph over defeated France was elaborately staged. On June 21, 1940, he received the French armistice delegates at Compiègne (*q.v.*) in the same railway carriage in which, on Nov. 11, 1918, France had dictated to Germany the terms of the armistice.

Having failed to subdue Britain in the summer and autumn of 1940, he launched a fierce drive in the Balkans, and German troops soon occupied Rumania and Bulgaria. By March 1941 the stage was set for

THE FUEHRER WITH HIS DUPES

(1) In an armoured train on the Brenner Pass, Hitler confers with his arch-dupe, Mussolini. (2) He inspects wounded soldiers. (3) He acknowledges the organized " Heils " before a speech. (4) He is visited by King Boris of Bulgaria. (5) He is greeted by supporters at Munich. Hitler's gloomy expression throughout is worthy of note.

Photos, Wide World, Planet News, Associated Press, Sport & General further German aggression. Greece was vanquished in May, and in June Hitler turned his attention to Russia. Disregarding the non-aggression pact made in August 1939, and his alliance preceding the partition of Poland, he launched a sudden and furious attack upon the U.S.S.R. on June 22. Month after month Hitler's armies battled against the Russian forces. The struggle assumed terrific proportions, and the German losses were enormous. The Russian winter, terrible in its intensity, was largely responsible for the slowing up of the German advance, and then the Soviet troops pushed them back from their positions. Already holding the title of Supreme Commander of the German Armed Forces, Hitler dismissed several generals and took over the post of C.-in-C. from von Brauchitsch on Dec. 19. It was a desperate bid to regain the confidence of the ill-equipped and half-frozen armies. Hitler made his headquarters at Smolensk, but in January 1942 he moved to Minsk in the face of the Russian advance. Later it appeared that he had made his peace with the Military Party, and Gen. von Bock, one of the disgraced officers, was given command of the southern armies.

On April 26, 1942, Hitler made a speech to the Reichstag in which he demanded absolute power over everyone and everything in Germany, including the setting-up of himself as "Supreme Law Lord." The Reichstag yielded immediately and the new decree put into the Fuehrer's hands the entire machinery of Germany, bestowing upon him the right to get rid of generals, judges, or any officials in any capacity, regardless of their position. The speech was regarded by the United Nations as an offensive against the German people and an excuse for Hitler to bolster up his defeats on the Russian front. On April 29 and 30 Hitler and Mussolini met for conferences at Salzburg.

Hitler Youth. This was a compulsory organization for all Germans from the ages of 14 to 21. Its members wore brown uniform, carried a dagger, and received Party and military training. The organization ensured that young people were thoroughly conditioned to the National Socialist movement, and that on reaching the age of 21 they would be completely obedient to the Nazi system. The Hitler Youth movement glorified militarism and mass regimentation. The Young Folk, a junior movement, consisted of children from the ages of 10 to 14.

Hoare, SIR REGINALD HERVEY, K.C.M.G. He was British Minister to Rumania, 1935–41. On Feb. 10, 1941, Sir Reginald handed a Note to Gen. Antonescu conveying the British Government's decision to break off diplomatic relations with Rumania.

Hoare, RT. HON. SIR SAMUEL JOHN GURNEY, P.C., G.C.S.I. (b. 1880). British Ambassador Extraordinary to Spain from June 1940. Sir Samuel became Home Secretary in 1937, Lord Privy Seal in 1939, and on April 3, 1940, Air Minister, an office he held only until the following month.

Holland. *See* Netherlands.

Homburg. R.A.F. 'planes first bombed Homburg, near Frankfort, in June 1940, scoring direct hits on railway tracks. Subsequent attacks set oil refineries ablaze at this once famous German spa.

Home Guard. First known as the Local Defence Volunteers, this great force of part-time soldiers, numbering over 1,500,000 men, was Britain's Citizen Army. Raised in May 1940, it was mainly intended to combat the possible activities of enemy parachute troops in the event of invasion, the threat of which

was then imminent. Throughout the anxious summer and autumn months of that year each unit of L.D.V.s kept watch and ward over its own locality, thus covering the length and breadth of Great Britain with a protective network of vigilant patrols.

In August 1940 the name of the force was changed to the Home Guard, and its hitherto improvised organization was placed on an established basis. Sorely needed equipment slowly but surely began to reach its eager members, and a co-ordinated scheme of training was put into operation. By the end of the year its personnel constituted 1,200 battalions, 5,000 companies (or 25,000 platoons), a large proportion of which was adequately armed and clothed in regulation serge battle-dress. Early in 1941 Home Guard officers were granted the King's commission, and non-commissioned ranks adopted on the Army model.

The problem of providing effective training for hundreds of thousands of men in the restricted time available in their leisure hours, however gladly given, proved a difficult one. Of great value were the special schools of instruction established at first independently and later under War Office supervision, where officers and N.C.O.s received intensive instruction in field training, which they subsequently imparted to their units. Cooperation with the Regular Army, developed on an increasing scale, was also an outstanding help to efficiency. After long and patient waiting the Home Guard was equipped with a variety of powerful arms, including grenades, automatic rifles, light and heavy machine-guns, mortars and anti-tank weapons, all of which they were well qualified to handle.

The Home Guard was unpaid, receiving only a nominal subsistence allowance when on long periods of duty. Its original terms of enrolment permitted resignation at a fortnight's notice and stipulated that members should not be required to leave their own localities.

Early in 1942, however, drastic changes were made. After Feb. 16 no member could resign unless in exceptional circumstances, and power was given in event of invasion for units to be moved outside their own areas. A maximum training period of 48 hours per month was required, and the Home Guard became liable for Civil Defence duties. Part-time Civil Defence workers were invited to enrol with the Home Guard. On March 12 it was announced that enrolment of all men exempted from military service was to be made compulsory in certain areas within the East, South-east and South Commands. On the 27th compulsion was extended to the whole country. A further development occurred on April 16, when it was decided that A.A. sites were to be manned by the Home Guard during the hours from dusk to dawn, thus releasing a very useful number of trained infantrymen for the Army. In coastal districts the experiment has already been tried with success. Plans were also put in hand for a Home Guard Corps of Signals and a Medical Corps.

Up to May 1942 the Home Guard as a whole had not been called upon to go into action, but during the months of heavy air bombardment in the autumn and winter of 1940 many units gave invaluable help to civil defence and individual members were honoured by H.M. the King for their courage and devotion to duty while under fire.

On May 14, 1942, the Home Guard celebrated its second anniversary and the King honoured it by becoming Colonel in Chief.

Book to Consult. Home Guard Warfare, J. Langdon Davies (Routledge).

BRITAIN'S PART-TIME ARMY MAKES GOOD

The special function of the Home Guard (originally known as Local Defence Volunteers) was to keep patrol and to deal with possible invaders. (1) Bulmer Home Guard off to manoeuvres on their bicycles. (2) "Invasion," staged by a Canadian battalion in the City of London, meets with H.G. resistance. (3) Lord Bridgman, Director-General of the Home Guard. (4) Members of the Home Guard handling a projector in exercises. (5) Reading the King's Regulations to the H.G. mounting guard outside Buckingham Palace.

Photos, Planet News, Fox, Topical Press

HONGKONG HELD OUT TO THE LAST

The defenders of Hongkong were outnumbered by five to one ; naval and air support, equipment and supplies, were all inadequate. When finally the Japanese captured the reservoirs, the island had to be surrendered, after seventeen days of heroic resistance.

Hongkong. Including the leased territories and Kowloon, the Crown Colony of Hongkong covers an area of 391 sq. miles, the island of Hongkong itself being situated off the south-east coast of China near the mouth of the Canton River. The island is 32 sq. miles in area, and possesses an excellent natural harbour, on which stands Victoria, the capital. One of the most densely populated areas in the world, the island had a population of approximately 9,900 non-Chinese and 450,300 Chinese, while the population of the whole colony, excluding 750,000 Chinese, was about 1,071,900.

In an economic sense Hongkong was of great importance both to the British Empire and the United States, being not only the main centre but also the distributing centre of world commerce in the Far East.

Strategically it was of still more vital importance. In a nutshell, it was the Allies' most advanced base (excluding Russian bases in Siberia) from which to strike at Japan, being only 1,580 miles from Tokyo. It also guarded sea commerce in the South China Sea and helped thereby to maintain British and American prestige in the East. Japan's seizure of the naval bases of Cam Ranh and Saigon in Indo-China gave her, with the aid of bases in Formosa, a stranglehold of this sea, consequently threatening Allied communications with Hongkong.

As a fortress, Hongkong was immensely powerful. Concrete fortifications and gun emplacements were built for 20 miles along the coast ; the beaches were protected by barbed wire, and, strategically located in three ranges of granite hills behind, natural barriers in themselves, scores of powerful batteries of naval, mobile and A.A. guns commanded both sea and air approaches. Air-raid protection for the thousands of

civilians was provided by giant tunnels dug into the hills, one of them capable of holding 50,000 people. The harbour itself, which faces Kowloon, was strongly protected by minefields and boom defences as well as by powerful shore batteries, while naval patrols kept watch day and night.

As a result of the gradual deterioration of Anglo-Japanese relations, strong reinforcements of British, Canadian and Indian troops arrived from time to time to strengthen the garrison. Chinese sappers and British and American volunteers gave additional assistance. Though the colony had but few aerodromes, limited air support was given by both the R.A.F. and the Fleet Air Arm.

The epic story of the tragic heroism, superb endurance and unconquerable spirit of the defenders of Hongkong today ranks with the finest recorded in our history. Displaying amazing tenacity and courage, they fought against 5 to 1 odds for 17 days, defending a fortress strong, but inadequately supported in the air and on the sea.

The story begins on Dec. 8, 1941, when, following the outbreak of war with Japan, two divisions of Japanese, supported by dive bombers, launched an attack on the colony from the land side. Strong British artillery fire repulsed this first attack.

On Dec. 10 General Chiang Kai-shek, the Chinese Generalissimo, launched the 4th Chinese Army on the enemy's rear, 100 miles to the north-west, to relieve Japanese pressure on Kowloon. Nevertheless, enemy attacks increased during Dec. 11 and 12, compelling our forces at Kowloon to withdraw to the island.

The next day the Japanese issued an ultimatum, which the Governor of the colony, Sir Mark Young, rejected. Then came three days of intense air,

THE ISLAND OF HONGKONG SEEN FROM THE WEST

Victoria, the so-called City of Hongkong, is dominated by the Peak (1,825 feet), which was heavily armed and encircled by roads cut into the slopes for armoured cars. Both the sea and mainland sides were heavily fortified. The native quarter was normally crowded with a population of over a million, to which some 750,000 refugees were added before the siege, creating a very difficult food problem. Kowloon, on the mainland, was a model city, with some fine buildings and an aerodrome.

Courtesy of " News Chronicle "

HONGKONG PREPARES FOR THE JAPANESE ATTACK

Air-raid shelters (left) were built in the walls of Hongkong, penetrating deeply into the rocky foundation on which the city stands. On the right is seen an Indian gun crew working one of the defence guns which wrought havoc among the invaders before the garrison was overwhelmed and forced to surrender on Christmas Day, 1941.

Photos, British Official and Associated Press

naval and artillery bombardments, followed by a second Japanese ultimatum, which also was rejected.

On Dec. 18 the enemy succeeded in crossing the narrow strait and penetrated our defensive positions in the Tai Koo area and Lyemun, and from there soon overran Saiwan, Mount Parker, Mount Butler, Jardine's Island and the Wong Nei Chang Gap. Despite a number of desperate British counter-attacks the enemy held their captured positions, and, taking advantage of the defenders' growing difficulties of supplies and communications, by Dec. 22 had landed fresh troops on the north-east coast.

A second British attempt to retake the vital Wong Nei Chang Gap on Dec. 22 was repulsed with heavy losses to Canadian troops. With their forces split up, without the essential support of strong air and naval forces, and lacking supplies, ammunition and water, the British troops faced a position so grave that there could be only one end.

The water situation was indeed desperate. Important reservoirs had fallen into Japanese hands and the water mains were destroyed by bombardment. The Public Works Dept. struggled bravely to effect a remedy, but the enemy destroyed the pipes again and again. The troops grimly held out for a further

two days, with only one day's supply of water remaining, and on Dec. 25 " the military and naval commanders informed the Governor that no further effective resistance could be made." Hongkong was therefore surrendered unconditionally at 7.5 p.m. on Christmas Day. On Dec. 28 the Japanese marched into Hongkong, and thus ended Britain's century-old domination of this vital outpost—the guardian of British interests in China.

On March 10, 1942, Mr. Eden made a terrible statement in the House of Commons about the atrocities proved to have been committed by the Japanese on prisoners of war and civilians, both men and women, after the fall of Hongkong. The Japanese Government had refused to permit visits by a representative of the Protecting Power (Argentina) or of the International Red Cross Committee, but stated that at the end of February the number of prisoners in Hongkong were : British, 5,072 ; Canadian, 1,689 ; Indian, 5,829 ; others, 357.

Hood, H.M.S. A famous British battle cruiser, the largest in the world, H.M.S. Hood was completed in March 1920. She had a displacement of 42,100 tons and carried a complement of 1,341. During 1929–30 the Hood was refitted, and her outstanding

H.M.S. HOOD, ONCE THE WORLD'S LARGEST BATTLE CRUISER

This famous warship, completed in 1920 and refitted in 1929–30, was considered impregnable, so strongly was she built and armoured.   But she was sunk off Greenland on May 24, 1941, by the German battleship Bismarck, having received a direct hit in the magazine.   There was a terrific explosion, Hood's bow tilted vertically in the air, and she sank within a few minutes.

Photo, Central Press

feature was the huge areas covered by heavy armour, strong framing, etc. On July 3, 1940, as one of Vice-Admiral Somerville's squadron, the Hood took part in the British naval action against French ships at Oran. On July 9 she carried out an offensive sweep in the Central Mediterranean in company with H.M.S. Ark Royal (q.v.). On May 24, 1941, she was sunk by the German battleship Bismarck off the coast of Greenland. The Admiralty communiqué, referring to this loss, described the Hood as receiving an " unlucky hit in the magazine." Capt. Ralph Kerr, C.B.E., R.N., was in command of the ship. The casualty list was heavy owing to the sudden and violent explosion ; the ship went down with her guns firing. The loss of this splendid ship was quickly avenged, as is described under the heading Bismarck.

Hopkins, HARRY (1890–1946). Pending the appointment of a new American ambassador in London, Mr. Hopkins, formerly U.S. Secretary for Commerce, became on Jan. 4, 1941, President Roosevelt's personal representative in Britain for the interim period. He remained until Feb. 10, when he left for America. On April 15 he was made supervisor of the Lease-Lend programme (q.v.) and was given the title of Special Assistant to President Roosevelt. In July he visited Russia, where he discussed with Stalin and Molotov the expediting of American war material to the Soviet Union. He was present at the Churchill-Roosevelt talks in Washington, Christmas 1941. In February 1942 Mr. Hopkins was made head of the Munitions Assignment Board recently set up in the United States. In April he arrived in England for consultations with the British authorities.

Harry Hopkins, supervisor of Lease-Lend programme.
Photo, Topical Press

Hore-Belisha, RT. HON. LESLIE, P.C. (b. 1893). He was Secretary of State for War from 1937 to 1940. Under his rule at the War Office in April 1939 conscription was for the first time introduced into Britain during peacetime. His resignation on Jan. 5, 1940, and the appointment of Mr. Oliver Stanley, caused a political sensation. He was offered the Presidency of the Board of Trade, but refused, and it was accepted by Sir Andrew Duncan.

Hornum. This German seaplane base, at the southern extremity of the island of Sylt (q.v.), was first heavily bombed by 49 machines of the R.A.F. on March 19, 1940. Hits were secured on sheds, oil tanks, dumps and barracks. Forty-five tons of 500-lb. and 250-lb. bombs were dropped. German propaganda was very active after this raid, and American journalists were conducted over the island and shown certain areas carefully selected for them by the Germans.

Horthy de Nagybanya, ADMIRAL NICHOLAS VITÉZ (b. 1868). Regent of Hungary from 1920. On March 1, 1940, Hungary celebrated the 20th anniversary of the regency of Adm. Horthy. On Nov. 8 a plot by Nazi intriguers to kidnap him and to assassinate certain members of his entourage was unmasked. Although he fostered friendship with Italy and Germany before 1939, at the outbreak of war he adopted a neutral attitude. His country's

adhesion to the Tripartite Pact on Nov. 19, 1940, however, made Hungary a satellite of Germany. On April 12, 1941, Adm. Horthy issued a statement seeking to justify Hungarian action in Yugoslavia, Hungarian troops having marched into that country the day before. He conferred with Hitler at the latter's headquarters on the Eastern front from Sept. 8 to 10, 1941, on the military and political situation. On Feb. 16, 1942, Adm. Horthy announced to the Hungarian Parliament that he intended to retire from office, and nominated as Deputy-Regent his son, Stephen Horthy. The latter was elected to the post on Feb. 19. He was killed in action, Aug. 1942.

Hostile, H.M.S. Belonging to the Hero class, this British destroyer was completed in 1936. She had a displacement of 1,340 tons with a complement of 145 and a speed of 36 knots. With four sister ships she took part in the gallant attack on German destroyers in Narvik Bay on April 10, 1940, and was damaged as a result of the action. Four months later the Hostile was sunk by an enemy mine, her loss being announced on Aug. 26, 1940. She was under the command of Lt.-Comdr. A. F. Burnell-Nugent, D.S.C., R.N. *See* Narvik, Battle of.

Hotspur, H.M.S. A sister ship of H.M.S. Havock and belonging to the Hero class, this British destroyer has a displacement of 1,340 tons and carries a complement of 145. She was completed in 1936. The Hotspur was in the Second Destroyer Flotilla at the First Battle of Narvik (q.v.) on April 10, 1940.

Hudson, RT. HON. ROBERT SPEAR, P.C. (b. 1886). Minister of Agriculture and Fisheries from May 10, 1940. From 1937 to 1940 he was Secretary of the Department of Overseas Trade, and on April 2, 1940, succeeded Sir John Gilmour as Minister of Shipping.

Hull. One of Britain's chief ports and situated close to the shores of the North-East coast, Hull provided a tempting target for the Nazi 'planes, which attacked it repeatedly, causing heavy damage and casualties. The city was continuously under attack from the autumn of 1940 and by the autumn of 1942 there had been 70 raids and scarcely a street had escaped damage.

Hull, CORDELL (b. 1871). American Secretary of State from 1933. Mr. Hull was an ardent supporter of the Lease-Lend Bill. On June 20, 1940, speaking at Harvard, he uttered a strong warning against the belief in isolation and on Nov. 26, at Washington, condemned the aggressor States. On Aug. 12, 1941, it was announced that Mr. Hull and Adm. Nomura, Japanese Ambassador to the U.S.A., had had conversations at Washington, and the Japanese Govt. had been warned that any Japanese action threatening Siamese independence would be a matter of direct concern to America and Britain. Mr. Hull was in conference with Adm. Nomura and Mr. Kurusu, Japan's " peace negotiators," on Dec. 7, when the news came through that Japan had bombed U.S. bases in the Pacific. Mr. Hull afterwards declared, referring to Japan's reply to America's basic

Cordell Hull, U.S. Secretary of State.

principles : " In all my 50 years of public service I have never seen a document that was more crowded with infamous falsehoods and distortions on a scale so huge that I never imagined that any Government on this planet was capable of uttering them."

On May 5, 1942, the American Government issued a statement in support of the British landing on the Vichy-occupied island of Madagascar, and Mr. Cordell Hull promised that U.S. warships would join in such actions if need arose. Vichy rejected the American Note supporting the British landing, but Mr. Hull declared that the U.S. warning called for a further reply.

Sgt. A. Hulme, awarded the V.C.
Photo, Central Press

Hulme, SGT. ALFRED, V.C. Sgt. Hulme of the New Zealand Force was awarded the V.C. for heroic conduct during operations in Crete. He " displayed outstanding and inspiring qualities of leadership, initiative, skill, endurance and devotion to duty from the commencement of the action on May 20, 1941, until he was wounded in the field eight days later."

Hungary. Though pro-Axis in sentiment, Hungary made efforts in September 1939 to keep out of the war. The mounting of A.A. guns in Budapest and the banning of Nazi meetings were merely precautionary measures. She tried to preserve her friendship with both Germany and Poland, and resumed diplomatic relations with the Soviets. On March 16, 1940, Count Csaky deplored the activities of Dr. Benes and Czechoslovakian committees working abroad for the restitution of the Czechoslovak state, and warned the Western powers that Hungary might have to intervene if these activities endangered the Hungarian nation.

The dispute between Hungary and Rumania over Transylvania, which had embittered relations between the two countries since the end of the First Great War, was settled by Axis dictation under the terms of the Vienna Award, whereby Hungary gained 45,000 kilometres of Transylvanian territory and a population of 2,300,000. Hungary agreed to export to Germany 50 per cent of her surplus wheat and other produce. On Dec. 12, 1941, Hungary signed a pact of eternal friendship with Yugoslavia.

Count Teleki, Hungary's Foreign Minister, committed suicide on April 3. In his farewell letter he said that he could not carry on in the difficult and unhappy task owing to far-reaching German demands for cooperation against Yugoslavia, with whom Hungary had concluded a treaty of friendship. It was obvious that the Axis had determined that Hungary should take a more active part in the war. Diplomatic relations between Britain and Hungary were broken off.

Hungary's declaration of war on Russia on June 27 was a logical result of Axis policy, though her excuse was that the Soviets had bombed Hungarian territory. There was also an explosion at Nagyteteny Arsenal and a fire at Almasfuzito oil refinery, Budapest, attributed to communist elements. On Sept. 6 Admiral Horthy, Regent of Hungary, was called to Hitler's headquarters on the Eastern front, where he remained from Sept. 8 to 10 discussing military and political questions. The Hungarian army took part in the great battles on the southern front in the neighbourhood of Kiev. Britain, through the United States' State Department, handed Hungary a note on Dec. 6, as a result of

which M. Bardossy, Hungarian Prime Minister, stated that Britain had declared war on Hungary as from one minute past midnight on Dec. 6, 1941. In February 1942 Nicolas Kallay, a former Minister of Agriculture, succeeded Bardossy as Premier.

There was no enthusiasm in Hungary for the alliance with Germany, but in order to retain the territory gained by the Vienna award she needed the authority of the Axis on her side. Were Germany to lose the war, the Czech-Polish and Greek-Yugoslav federations, recently formed in London, would have been strong enough to enforce another partition of Hungary. Meanwhile, her entire resources were pledged to the Axis.

Hunter, H.M.S. Sister ship to H.M.S. Havock, this British destroyer had a displacement of 1,340 tons and carried a complement of 145. She was launched in 1936. H.M.S. Hunter took part in the First Battle of Narvik (*q.v.*) on April 10, 1940, and was sunk in action with German destroyers on that date.

Huntziger, GEN. (1880–1941). One of the principal signatories of the French-German and French-Italian armistice conventions, Huntziger first came into prominence in 1940. Prior to this he was commander of one of the French armies and had a distinguished colonial record. In France's downfall his main concern was to resist German encroachments and to foster the French military spirit in unoccupied France. He attempted to rebuild the French army, and opposed Laval's efforts to allow French ports to be thrown open to the Germans. In this he succeeded in influencing Pétain in Dec. 1940, when he was War Minister for the Vichy Government. On Jan. 3, 1941, he was made Defence Minister. On Aug. 27 he was appointed to command all French (Vichy) forces in French North Africa, and began a tour of 10,000 miles on Oct. 10. The 'plane in which he was returning to report to Pétain crashed at Le Vigan, 50 miles from Nîmes, on Nov. 12, and he was killed, as were all the other occupants of the machine. Huntziger had gone to Africa in order to ascertain what Gen. Weygand, at that time French Commissioner in N. Africa, intended to do if France's African bases were attacked. *See* Weygand.

Gen. Huntziger, French patriot.
Photo, Planet News

Hussein, ABDULLAH IBN. *See* Abdullah Ibn Hussein.

Hussein, SIRRY PASHA. Egyptian Premier and Minister of the Interior from Nov. 15, 1940, to Feb. 2, 1942. He was completely loyal to the Anglo-Egyptian Treaty. In July 1941 he broadened the base of his Cabinet, which meant a less full representation of the Wafdist Party. On Feb. 2 the Cabinet resigned owing to trouble between King Farouk and the Prime Minister over the severing of diplomatic relations with Vichy France. He was succeeded by Nahas Pasha, leader of the Wafd.

Hyperion, H.M.S. Belonging to the same class as the five British destroyers that took part in the First Battle of Narvik (*q.v.*) on April 10, 1940, the Hyperion and her seven sister ships were all completed in 1936. She had a displacement of 1,340 tons and a main armament of four 4·7-in. guns and eight 21-in. torpedo tubes. Her speed was 36 knots, and her normal complement was 145. On Jan. 22, 1941, it was announced that she had sustained damage by torpedo or mine in the Mediterranean, and had subsequently to be sunk by British forces. The Hyperion formed part of light naval forces which, sweeping the Adriatic as far as Durazzo, were then detailed to carry out a sweep some miles ahead in order to deal with any enemy E-boats or submarines which might appear.

I **Iceland.** On April 10, 1940, the day after the German invasion of Denmark and Norway, the Althing (Parliament) took over the powers exercised by King Christian X in Iceland, and also the conduct of foreign affairs, declaring that this was a temporary measure. It was announced on May 10 that British troops had landed in the island in order to prevent its seizure by Germany for a naval base, an assurance being

given that they would be withdrawn at the end of the war. On May 20 Iceland became an independent State. One of the chief reasons for this decision was on account of the difficulty of maintaining communications with Denmark. German propaganda put out a story that it had been brought about under British pressure, but the British Government once more declared that it had not the slightest intention of interfering with the internal affairs of Iceland. American forces landed in Iceland in July, 1941, to reinforce the British garrison. The American Navy was ordered to ensure the safety of communications between Iceland and the U.S.A., and American planes were provided for defensive purposes. In April, 1942, an American general assumed command of the garrison. It was off the west of Iceland that the first American warship was lost—the destroyer Reuben James being sunk by a U-boat on Oct. 30, 1941.

ICELAND GARRISONED BY FRIENDLY ALLIED TROOPS

To forestall a German occupation of Iceland, British troops were sent to garrison this strategically important Danish island. American troops arrived later. (1) Line of Hurricanes, based on Iceland, ready to play their part in the Battle of the Atlantic. (2) Troops for the garrison come ashore in tenders. (3) Bren-gun carriers take a plunge in manoeuvres. (4) British warships in the harbour ; in the foreground is a typical Icelandic pony with a milk-float.
Photos, British Official, B.I.P.P.A., Associated Press

Illustrious, H.M.S. This famous British ship belonged to a class of six 23,000-ton aircraft carriers laid down between 1937 and 1939. She carried a complement of 1,600 and her speed was 32 knots. Illustrious was in action at the battle of Taranto on Nov. 10–12, 1940, when planes of the Fleet Air Arm inflicted heavy losses on the Italian Fleet. She was commanded by Capt. Denis Boyd, and

ONE OF BRITAIN'S NEWEST AIRCRAFT CARRIERS

H.M.S. Illustrious (23,000 tons) came into service in 1940, in time to play an important part in the Fleet Air Arm's devastating attack at the Battle of Taranto, Nov. 10–12. Two months later she was violently and persistently attacked by German bombers in the Mediterranean, nine of which were shot down, and another attack was made in July 1941, again without success.
Photo, Topical Press

mention of her name in the official communiqués was the first public intimation of her completion. On Jan. 9, 1941, she was attacked six times by German bombers in the Sicilian Channel, between Sicily and Tunis. Nearly 100 enemy planes were beaten off and nine of them were shot down during the engagement. Several bombs struck the ship and started fires, inflicting some casualties. In July, when Illustrious was at Malta, German bombers unsuccessfully tried to attack. Capt. Boyd was promoted Rear-Admiral and Lord Louis Mountbatten became her commander. *See p. 252.*

Imperial Transport. On Feb. 11, 1940, this British oil tanker was cut in two by a U-boat in the Atlantic. The crew hurriedly took to the boats, but, finding that the stern still floated, they returned to what remained of their ship, and after an adventurous voyage of three days, during which they covered over 170 miles, they were rescued by a warship and landed safely at a Scottish port on Feb. 18. Capt. Smiles, the skipper, and 41 survivors of the crew of 44 were rescued ; in the process of getting into the lifeboats two men were drowned.

MIRACLE OF NATIONAL SALVAGE AND REPAIR WORK

Torpedoed amidships in the Atlantic, the Imperial Transport, a British tanker, broke in two. The crew took to the boats, but as the stern half remained afloat Capt. Smiles ordered their return. This pertinacious Yorkshireman, with the aid of a school atlas, brought his maimed vessel safe home to a Scottish port, and a new bow portion was constructed. Left, the stern offshore ; right, the new bow portion being launched ; and, centre, the dovetailing of the two.
Photos, J. Hall

INDIA'S DIFFICULT ROLE IN WORLD WAR

A medley of races and creeds, India, despite some political discords, made widespread efforts in support of the Allied cause, and her contributions in the Services, in industry, and in financial aid augured well for her future development as a Dominion. See also Burma ; Ceylon.

India at War. India was declared to be at war with Germany on the day that Britain broke off relations with the Nazis, Sept. 3, 1939. At once declarations of loyalty began to pour in from all quarters. Even Mr. Gandhi said his sympathies " from the purely humanitarian standpoint " were with Britain and France.

Already there existed a body which was prepared with plans for war work. This was the Eastern Group Supply Council at Delhi, on which India was

represented by an Indian, and which included in its duties the assessing of the requirements of all forces that could be served from the East, the surveying of the capacities in this direction of Australia, New Zealand, South Africa, and the rest of the Commonwealth east of Suez, and, finally, the allocation of orders. To keep this body in close touch with the needs of the British war effort the Ministry of Supply in London sent out Sir Alexander Roger and a technical staff. Immediately India began to expand industrially, and the process which had been going on for a number of years at a moderate speed was greatly accelerated. The training of mechanics was undertaken on a vast scale and young Indians were found to be very apt pupils. Munitions of many descriptions were turned out from factories that had never done this kind of work before.

There was a rush to enlist in the rapidly expanded army, of which the numbers went up from 210,000 to half a million. The rulers of Native States came forward, as they had done in the First Great War, with offers of help. From Nepal, 8,000 Gurkha troops were sent. Hyderabad and Bihar, Nizam and people combining, gave two Fighter Squadrons of aircraft. When the need for sandbags became urgent in Britain, the jute industry was able to ship seven hundred million for use in air raids and for protection against bombs.

For a short time it seemed that Indians were going to unite against the threat of Nazi domination, that divisions would be closed up, old animosities dropped. But this prospect soon faded. The first note of discord came from the Working Committee of the Indian National Congress, which asked that the British Government should declare its war aims concerning democracy and imperialism, should explain how these would apply to India, and should give effect to them in India at once. Three days after a message from the King-Emperor had been read to the Central Legislature, expressing deep satisfaction at the " widespread attachment of India to the cause in which we have taken up arms," that request was put forward by the Working Committee, and it was affirmed a month later by the All-India Congress Committee, which also complained that the country had been proclaimed a belligerent without the consent of the people, and demanded independence. This was in spite of Mr. Gandhi's declaration at the start of the war that Indian cooperation ought to be unconditional. He had soon reverted to his former attitude of pacifism and preached a campaign of civil disobedience.

Conflict Between Moslem and Hindu

The Viceroy, Lord Linlithgow, had a hard task before him—the reconciling of the totally divergent views of Hindus and Moslems as to how a new system should be fashioned, and the treatment of the active opposition to the war effort which was now being made by the former. An Act had been passed in London giving the Viceroy power to authorize provincial Governors to take over the duties of provincial elected bodies, and this was done in several areas. Large numbers of the " civil disobedients " were imprisoned or fined. At one time four-fifths of the leading Indian politicians were under lock and key, with thousands of the rank and file. This did not to any serious extent hinder the war effort. Production went up, munition factories increased in number and size ; work was done with cheerfulness, if not with enthusiasm.

The Liberal elements in the Legislature and outside it were heartily with the Government. The mass of the four hundred millions comprising the population of India appeared to be little interested in the internal political struggle. What a section of the Moslems asked for, through their leader, Mr. Jinnah, were independent Moslem States carved out of India in the north-east and north-west, where there are Moslem majorities, these States to be known as Pakistan and to control their own foreign policy, defence, customs and finance. To this the Congress leaders (Hindus) flatly refused to agree. In Aug. 1940 the Viceroy said that, after discussing matters with leaders of all shades of opinion, he must leave Indians themselves to decide what sort of constitution they wanted. As they did not get any nearer a decision, he announced in Nov. 1940 that his attempts to bring Parties together would cease.

During 1941 the industrialization of India went on apace. The output of war material rose steadily. Indian troops in Libya distinguished themselves by their skill and courage. The population generally carried on as usual. Then towards the end of 1941 there came closer and closer the moment of Japan's entry into the war, which now threatened to spread

INDIAN HEAVY INDUSTRY IN ACTION
In the large-scale production of iron and steel India is not backward. These workmen muffle their faces as a protection from the fierce heat given off by the hot metal, just as the desert tribesmen muffle themselves against the heat refracted by the scorched sands.
Photo, Sport & General

FIGHTING FORCES OF INDIA ON MANY FRONTS

Indian forces played a magnificent part in the war, not only in the Middle East and the Far East, but in other theatres of conflict.
(1) Naval ratings are seen at gunnery practice. (2) Units of an Indian regiment are being trained in the erection of barbed wire entanglements in the desert. (3) A pilot officer of the Royal Indian Air Force about to enter his plane. (4) Pack-mule contingent out on exercises somewhere in England.

Photos, British Official, Indian Film Unit, Sport & General

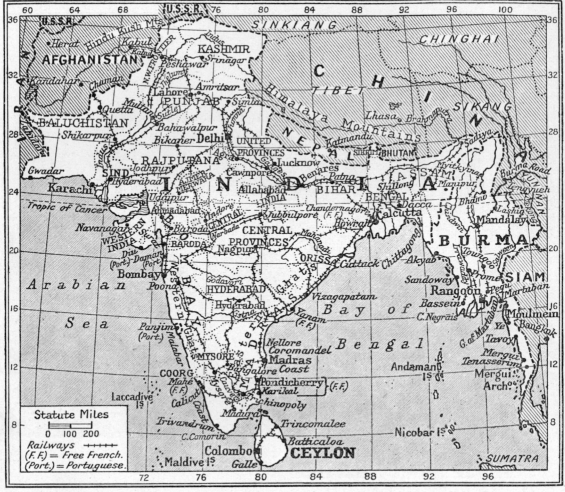

India and the adjacent country of Burma, the overrunning of which threatened the great Indian Empire.

to India. A further endeavour was made to remove the obstacles to the union of all Indians in the fight against tyranny and barbarism. Numbers of prisoners were released, including Pandit Jawaharlal Nehru. On the other hand, it was necessary to make two noteworthy arrests. On October 10, 1941, J. P. Narain was found in possession of plans for the establishment of a subversive Congress Socialist Party; Congress itself denied cognizance of this. On Nov. 10 it became known that Subhas Chandra Bose, who had disappeared from Calcutta in January, 1941, was visiting Berlin and Rome to arrange for Fifth Column activities. His brother, Surat Chandra Bose, was found on Dec. 11 to be in contact with the Japanese.

But in the meantime the Indian people had subscribed nearly £2,000,000 to the War Purposes Fund; the country was manufacturing nine-tenths of its own military supplies; Indian soldiers were winning glory in more than one theatre of war; Indian merchant seamen, numbering one-quarter of the crews of all the ships of the British Empire, were facing no less willingly and bravely the dangers of the war at sea. If anything had been needed to concentrate and intensify India's contribution to the Allied cause, Japan's rush into the arena would have supplied it. From that instant

Indians realized that they were in the war zone, that their hope of avoiding slavery under German " masterfolk " lay in Allied victory, and that they must exert their whole strength in the common cause.

The Malayan débâcle and the Japanese invasion of Burma made it urgently necessary to organize Indian resistance. On March 11, 1942, Mr. Churchill told Parliament that Sir Stafford Cripps, Lord Privy Seal, was to head a special mission to India. Recalling that in August, 1940, India had been promised full Dominion status under a constitution to be framed by the Indians in agreement among themselves, he said that Sir Stafford was to put forward the Government's proposals and to exchange views with all sections of Indian opinion. It was generally felt that Sir Stafford was the best possible choice for this difficult task; his recent mission to the U.S.S.R. had paved the way for better understanding there. He had made a special study of the Indian problem, and was a long-standing friend of Pandit Nehru, who had stayed at his home when he visited England and had invited Cripps to India as his guest in December 1939.

On March 23 Sir Stafford arrived in India, and during the following two weeks he engaged in a series of talks with Indian leaders and delegates, including Gandhi,

Nehru, Azad and Rajagapalachari (all of the Congress Party), Jinnah (Moslem League), Savarkar, Dr. Moonje and Dr. Mookerjee (of the Hindu Mahasabha), and Sir Tej Bahadur Sapru (Liberal), in addition to the Indian Princes and delegates from the Sikhs and other races (not omitting the Untouchables) '; he was, of course, in consultation with the Viceroy, with Gen. Wavell, C.-in-C., and with the representatives of British interests in India, also with Col. Louis Johnson, who was in India on a special mission from President Roosevelt.

The Government's proposals were published on March 30, to the effect that, directly after the war, a body of Indians, elected by Indians, should frame a constitution on which the new Dominion could be based, in treaty with the British Government. Any province which wished to secede from the new Dominion was to have the right to do so. During the present emergency the British Government was to have the responsibility and control of defence, which would be organized in full cooperation with the Indians. In a statesmanlike broadcast, Sir Stafford spoke of the difficulty of setting aside the existing constitution in time of war ; he assured the Indians that the new constitution would be whatever they themselves decided, and that meanwhile a representative of India was to have a seat in the War Cabinet and in the Pacific Council, and later in the Peace Conference.

Britain's Plan for India Rejected

Unhappily, in a sub-continent comprising so many races and religions, it was not possible so soon to reach agreement or to obliterate old distrusts. On April 1 the Mahasabha rejected the plan, alleging that the secession clause would partition India and that defence ought to be in Indian hands. The Sikhs also objected vehemently to the secession clause. On April 3 Congress raised the same objections, and next day the Moslem League expressed its disappointment that Pakistan had not been recognized. After a welter of discussion the Government's proposals had to be withdrawn on April 11. Sir Stafford, in another notable broadcast, summarized the prevailing opinion that " such an effort, inspired by goodwill and sincerity, will leave its mark upon the history of our relations and will cast its beneficent light forward into the future." He left Karachi on April 13. Later he explained to Parliament, on April 28, that the breakdown in negotiations was not on the question of defence, since all parties agreed that the British C.-in-C. should remain in control. The difficulty was that far-reaching constitutional changes, curtailing the power of the Viceroy, were demanded, to which Britain could not safely agree in time of war.

Meanwhile Pandit Nehru, in a spirited interview with the press on April 13, accused the politicians in England of living in a world of their own, " which has nothing to do with the realities in India." But, he declared, " it would be a tragedy for the world if Germany and Japan won this war and dominated the world." India would not surrender to the invader. She would, where necessary, use scorched earth tactics. Maulana Azad, Congress President, also preached defiance to the invader, " even at the cost of our lives." Proposals for a compromise with the Moslem League were brought forward by Mr. Rajagapalachari, ex-Premier of Madras, but were heavily defeated on May 2, though Dr. Azad expressed his willingness to initiate discussions between Congress and Moslem delegates. In contrast with this activity, Mr. Gandhi in his paper " Harijan " continued to advocate passive resistance, and even tabled a motion, which he afterwards postponed, that Congress should declare for neutrality.

While these talks were in progress, events moved relentlessly on. The capture of the Andaman Islands (*q.v.*) on March 28 was the first inroad on Indian territory. On April 4 came the first air raid—on Colombo, capital of Ceylon. Based on aircraft-carriers, 75 Japanese planes made the attack ; 27 were certainly and 5 probably shot down, and 25 damaged. Two days later, raids were made on Vizagapatam, 400 miles N.E. of Madras, and Coconada, 100 miles S.W. of Vizagapatam, but damage was slight On the same date British aircraft, sent to attack the enemy aircraft-carriers, were lost in the attempt, and a fierce naval battle took place off the coast of Orissa, resulting in the loss of two British cruisers and of the British aircraft-carrier Hermes, besides several merchant ships in convoy.

GURKHAS IN THE MALAYAN JUNGLE

These sturdy Nepalese troops are splendid fighters whose favourite weapon is their native kukri, a curved knife. Here they are seen training for modern warfare in the jungle. It was thought that tanks could not be used in Malaya, but the Japanese proved otherwise.

Photo, British Official

Evacuation began along the coast of Orissa. On April 9 the naval base of Trincomalee in Ceylon was raided, with a loss of 21 planes certainly and 12 probably.

In a broadcast on April 21 General Wavell voiced his unshakable confidence in the ultimate victory of the Allies, and paid tribute to the gallant defenders of Burma, who were also the defenders of India. He warned the Indians to expect intensified air attack. The following day, Col. Johnson announced that American troops were already in India, that American air forces were in action, and more were coming.

Books to consult. India at War (M.O.I.). India, L. F. RUSHBROOK WILLIAMS (Oxford Pamphlet).

Indo-China. Up to the date of the collapse of France in June 1940 relations between French Indo-China and Japan had been regulated by those of the Quai d'Orsay (French Foreign Office) with Tokyo. As soon as Marshal Pétain had become supreme ruler the Japanese began negotiating with Vichy for assistance in their preparations for war in the Far East. They wanted air bases and they hoped for permission to

Indo-China : frontiers and areas ceded to Siam in 1940.

move troops through French territory. If they had virtual control of the area adjoining Thailand (Siam) and could frighten or cajole the Siam Government into giving their army free passage into Malaya, they would be in a very strong position for attacks on the Peninsula which has at its foot Singapore, and on Burma as well; and so it proved.

At first the overtures made by Japan, member of the Axis Pact and therefore ally of the enemy before whom France lay defeated and helpless, came as a shock to French officials both in Vichy and in Indo-

China itself. But, when German urging was added, Vichy weakened and the local French rulers were told that they must not wholly refuse the Japanese requests, which were becoming more and more like demands. Before long all opposition to these demands ceased and the Japanese got what they required.

Their troops passed over into French territory from China ; large numbers were reported to have been concentrated there by August 1941. They built air bases which were to be of great value to them when they decided to enter the war. Further, it was announced that Vichy and Japanese officials were cooperating for the reorganization of the export trade in rubber, rice, etc., which meant that Japan was taking as much as she could get of these commodities, necessary to her war effort and the feeding of her people in wartime.

At the same time as Tokyo began to press for these advantages, the Japanese Navy Department sent a fleet to the coasts of Indo-China ostensibly to watch the transport of goods through French and Siamese ports to China. The Japanese had, as soon as they invaded China in 1937, taken great pains to stop communication between the Chinese and these ports, and had induced the French to close the railway between Haiphong and Yunnanfu on the Burma Road to the transit of war materials. At that date it was not so clear as it became later that they were anxious for a firm foothold in this region not only for the purposes of their war against China, but because it was essential to them to have airfields and ports there when they carried out their long-cherished plan of attacking Malaya and the Dutch East Indies.

For many years Japanese propagandists had been busy in French Indo-China and Siam. They posed as photographers, barbers. dentists. Thus they picked up gossip while they shaved or cut hair ; they could take almost any photographs their paymasters in Tokyo asked for ; while, as dentists, they might wriggle into acquaintance with people in authority and leaders of big business. Gradually they grew more and more outspoken about their ambitions. A radio talk from Tokyo in 1940 made an appeal to all who were " related culturally, racially and economically " in East Asia and the South Seas to prepare for being united " under a single sphere." This aim had been known to those who studied Japanese policy. Now it was proclaimed to the world and warning given that, whenever the moment seemed favourable, Japan would attempt to carry it out by armed force.

Britain and the United States made efforts to persuade the Siamese government to stand in with the democratic countries. They told Japan that any threat to Siam's independence would be " of direct concern " to both. Siam then declared that it would not yield an inch of territory without a struggle. But on Dec. 7, 1941, when Japan struck, Siam collapsed, offering no resistance. French Indo-China had also been well and truly absorbed by the Japanese, who thus gained at the outset an advantage of which full use was made. Troops streamed down from Siam into Malaya, having passed through French Indo-China, and Japanese bombers were on airfields within reach of Singapore.

Information, Ministry of. At the outbreak of war Lord Macmillan was appointed Minister of Information, having held the same office in 1918, during the last war. For a short time Lord Camrose was his Chief Assistant and Controller of News Relations. There was widespread dissatisfaction regarding the Ministry at the beginning of 1940, and Mr. Chamberlain, at that time Prime Minister, made certain changes in its personnel. Lord Macmillan was replaced on Jan. 5 by Sir John Reith, who was himself succeeded by Mr. Duff Cooper on May 10. In July the Ministry again came in for adverse criticism owing to its plan of making the censorship of the Press more severe. This measure was abandoned, however, on consultation with the Press Advisory Committee. When Mr. Duff Cooper was appointed Chancellor of the Duchy of Lancaster in July 1941, the post of Minister of Information was given to Mr. Brendan Bracken, until then Parliamentary Private Secretary to the Prime Minister. The Director-General was Mr. Cyril Radcliffe, K.C., who succeeded Sir Walter Monckton in December 1941. The Ministry worked in close association with the Service departments, advisers being appointed by the Admiralty, War Office and Air Ministry to cooperate in all matters of censorship (*q.v.*) and news in their respective affairs.

Ingr, GEN. S. He was in charge of all military affairs on the Czechoslovak National Committee which was set up in France after the outbreak of war. In 1940, after the collapse of France, as C.-in-C. of the Czechoslovak forces, Gen. Ingr arrived in England with the final contingent of Czech troops, the first contingent having been evacuated from France by two transports of the Royal Navy.

Inönü, GEN. ISMET (b. 1884). A friend of Kemal Ataturk, he became President of Turkey on the latter's death in 1938. After the collapse of France, when Turkey was faced by an aggressive Axis policy in South-East Europe, President Inönü affirmed Turkish non-belligerency and friendship for Britain. On Nov. 2, 1941, he reaffirmed friendship for this country and at the same time stressed the fact that the German-Turkish treaty of non-aggression which was signed on June 18, 1941, had created an atmosphere of mutual confidence.

Invalided, King's Badge for. This badge was instituted by the King in 1941 for those invalided from the Naval, Military and Air Forces and the Merchant Navy and Fishing Fleet through wounds or war disablement attributable to service from September 1939. Designed by Mr. Percy Metcalfe, the badge consists of the Royal and Imperial Cypher, surmounted by a circular band bearing the inscription "For Loyal Service." *See* illustration page 33, No. 10.

Ipoh. Centre of Malaya's tin-mining industry, Ipoh was captured by Japanese forces after the British had withdrawn from the town on Dec. 29, 1941. The next day it was announced that our troops had formed a new line south of Ipoh, and that heavy fighting was in progress. *See* Malaya.

Iran. *See* Persia.

Iraq. The history of this new Arab kingdom is outlined in pp. 2244–45. After the first king of Iraq, the Emir Feisal, died in 1930 Iraq was ruled

IRAQ'S BOY KING VISITS OUR TROOPS

Feisal II became King at the age of four. His uncle the Regent, Emir Abdul Ilah (seen here with him), safeguarded him when the pro-Nazi Rashid Ali seized power. British intervention sent Rashid Ali packing and restored the boy king.

Photo, Sport & General

by his son Ghazi, who was killed in a car crash in April 1939. When the war broke out the throne was held by Ghazi's infant son, Feisal II (b. 1935). His Prime Minister, Nuri es Said Pasha, was a pan-Arab who held progressive political views, while fully recognizing Iraq's obligations to the 25-year Treaty of Alliance made in 1930, which included special trade relations, a military mission, a police force with British inspectors and squadrons of the Royal Air Force occupying special aerodromes. In accordance with its Treaty obligations, Iraq severed relations with Germany on Sept. 7, 1939.

From the beginning of the war German intrigue in the country was general. Early in April 1941 a military coup d'état placed Sayid Rashid Ali, a former Prime Minister, at the head of the Government. His pro-German sympathies were well known, so, acting under her Treaty rights, Britain landed troops at Basra, on the Persian Gulf. Though Rashid Ali declared his friendly intentions, Iraqi troops attacked the R.A.F. aerodrome at Habbaniyah, west of Baghdad, on May 2, forcing the British troops to seize the docks and airport at Basra. From Basra the British contingent moved upon Baghdad. First Faluja on the Euphrates was occupied and then Rutba, on the oil pipeline near the Transjordan frontier. On June 1 Baghdad was occupied and Rashid Ali fled. The Regent, Emir Abdul Ilah, thereupon returned to Baghdad with the young king. Rashid Ali went first to Turkey and then to Berlin, and was living there when he was sentenced to death by an Iraqi court-martial, together with other rebels.

When the German intrigue spread to Persia, and the British and Russian forces moved upon Teheran, Iraq assumed importance as a centre whence British and American war material could be distributed to Russia. A railway line ran from Basra to Khanikin on the Iraq-Persian border, and quickly the harbour facilities at Basra were improved and the

General Inönü, Turkish President.
Photo. Dorien Leigh

PRISONERS CAPTURED IN IRAQ
Considerable numbers of Iraqi rebels were rounded up during the revolt by the use of low-flying R.A.F. planes. Some are seen above in the camp at Habbaniyah, obviously on good terms with their captors.
Photo, British Official

capabilities of the railway extended. The chief handicap to Iraqi cooperation in the British and Russian war effort was the absence of a railway bridge at Baghdad, all freight having to be carried across the Tigris by a primitive rail ferry.

In February 1942 it was stated that an American military mission under General R. A. Wheeler of the U.S. Army was working in Iraq and Persia to speed up war supplies to British and Russian zones in this part of the Middle East. An organization including 5,000 technicians had been established, and docks, railways, roads and pipe lines were to be built and factories to assemble aircraft, tanks and motor transport.

Ireland. *See* Eire ; Northern Ireland.

Irish Free State. *See* Eire.

Iron Duke, H.M.S. Once a battleship, the Iron Duke was demilitarized under the London Treaty, 1931–32, and became a gunnery training ship. Her displacement was 21,250 tons and she carried a complement of 589 (exclusive of boys under training). She retained six 13·5-in. and twelve 6-in. guns. On Oct. 17, 1939, German aircraft dropped two bombs near the ship in a raid on Scapa Flow. The Iron Duke sustained certain damage, but there were no British casualties. One of the German planes was shot down and another was damaged.

Iron Guard. Fascist organization of Rumania, the Iron Guard caused strife and bloodshed in the stormy years of Rumanian politics shortly before the war. It was an agency of German Nazism, and its leader Codreanu (*q.v.*) encouraged anti-Semitic feeling and the repression of liberal movements. In the autumn of 1938 Codreanu and a number of other Iron Guard leaders were shot " while attempting to escape." The Iron Guard was responsible for the death of Calinescu (*q.v.*), who had been appointed Prime Minister in March 1939.

After the collapse of France Rumania was unable to pursue her policy of neutrality, and members of the Iron Guard played a leading part in the formation of the new National Party in July 1940. Horia Sima, notorious Iron Guard leader, was given a place in

the Cabinet. On Sept. 4 Gen. Antonescu (*q.v.*) succeeded Gigurtu as Prime Minister, and immediately the Iron Guard began an agitation for the abdicatio1 of King Carol, an event which took place two days later.

On Nov. 27 opposers of the Iron Guard were arrested and 64 were shot, including a number of prominent Ministers and statesmen. This was the signal for savage anti-Jewish pogroms and massacres by the Iron Guard, when thousands of people were killed. Owing to quarrels among the organization itself Antonescu disbanded the Iron Guard police and placed Rumania under military control on Dec. 11. The following day the Iron Guard was disarmed and Cristescu was appointed Inspector-General of the Police. The organization then comprised two elements, those who supported Antonescu and those representing the extremist party. On Jan. 21, 1941, serious disorders broke out, and the next day street fighting occurred in Bucharest and many Rumanian towns. By Jan. 25 the revolt was broken and Antonescu, supported by the Army and the Germans, was once more in control. Rebel losses were stated to be between 1,500 and 2,000, while deaths throughout the country were estimated at about 6,000.

Ironside, FIELD-MARSHAL EDMUND, 1ST BARON, G.C.B. (b. 1880). At the outbreak of war he was Governor of Gibraltar. In September 1939 he was appointed Chief of the Imperial General Staff, which position he held until May 1940, when he was succeeded by Gen. Sir John Dill (*q.v.*). Ironside became C.-in-C. Home Forces in May 1940, relinquishing that appointment in the following July. He was raised to the peerage on Jan. 1, 1941, and took the title of Lord Ironside of Archangel and of Ironside.

ROUGH-RIDERS TO THE FORE
Here a group of Ironsides are negotiating a difficult road as part of their training. Reconnaissance units have been formed consisting of armoured cars, Bren-gun carriers and motor cyclists, to forge ahead and harass the enemy, pending the arrival of the main forces.
Photo, Topical Press

'Ironside.' The armoured cars which were given this nickname as a tribute to Lord Ironside (commanding the Home Forces in 1940) were light armoured vehicles with which mechanized cavalry were equipped during the summer of 1940. These cars were not only very fast, but could negotiate the roughest country. *See* Mechanization.

Ismay, MAJ.-GEN. SIR HASTINGS LIONEL, K.C.B. (b. 1887). He was appointed Senior Staff Officer to Mr. Churchill as Minister of Defence in the War Cabinet, 1941. In 1938 he had been appointed Secretary of the Committee of Imperial Defence.

Isolationism. At the outbreak of war America was bound by the Neutrality Act of 1937. On Sept. 21, 1939, President Roosevelt sought to modify the embargo on the sale of munitions, and on Nov. 3 Congress repealed this embargo against shipments of arms to belligerent nations. The amendment was made after several weeks of opposition from those favouring an isolationist policy. On June 10, 1940, President Roosevelt declared that the U.S.A. would aid the Allies with all the material resources at her disposal and the President's declaration was attacked by Col. Lindbergh on June 15. As one of the chief Isolationists Lindbergh addressed a large meeting of his supporters on August 5, urging that America should keep aloof from war and build up her own defences. His speech was severely criticized throughout America, and, although still powerful, the influence of the Isolationists began to wane towards the end of the year. In the spring of 1941, however, they became particularly active, since they were strongly opposed to the Lease-Lend Act (*q.v.*) and were ill-disposed to America convoying shipments of war material to Britain.

The year 1941 saw an ever-increasing flow of war supplies to this country despite the obstructionist methods employed by the Isolationists at home. It was in December, however, that Isolationism received its coup de grâce. By Japan's aggressive action in bombing American naval bases in the Pacific before the actual declaration of war against the U.S.A. and Great Britain on Dec. 7, even the most confirmed of Isolationists changed his views, since it was clearly seen that America could no longer avert war.

SHAMEFUL CHAPTER IN THE STORY OF ITALY

Since the days of Garibaldi Italy had been Britain's staunch ally. Fascism changed all that, and Mussolini was responsible for the disastrous policy of support to Hitler, not foreseeing that it meant Italy's subjugation to Germany. See also Abyssinia ; East Africa ; Greece ; Mediterranean ; Mussolini ; North Africa.

Italy at War. For more than a month before Mussolini—the jackal, as Mr. Churchill called him—decided to enter the war on Hitler's side, reckoning that this would pay him better than keeping in with Britain, the Italian public was assured through the Press and radio that Britain was finished. Up to this time Mussolini had been afraid to make up his mind. The Italian air force had been seriously weakened by the Spanish war and had not been brought up to date. Corruption on a vast scale pervaded the munitions industry. The anxiety of business men was to make as much as they could as quickly as possible and transfer it to the United States. Officials in public departments also robbed the Government. The armaments turned out were often of poor quality : steel of inferior grade was purchased for the armour-plating of warships, for example. However, some progress was made and by all the signs Mussolini's opportunity had come when France collapsed. After months of dejection he pulled himself together and resolved to stir.

The Italians were told that all Mussolini's demands for French territory, Corsica, Tunis, the eastern Riviera including Nice, could be enforced without any fighting. Demonstrations by order took place outside the British Embassy in Rome, the demonstrators being mostly lads of fifteen or so. Hymns of hate were taught to children. Every effort was made to work up hostile feeling and to persuade the Italian people that their war would be a walk-over. A diplomat in Rome remarked that Mussolini " did not want to fight a sick man ; he wanted to gouge the eyes out of a corpse." The people did not, however, respond as the Fascists hoped they would. So doubtful were the latter about the loyalty of the army that military police (*carabinieri*) were secretly drafted into a number of regiments. Measures were taken to prevent any expression of the popular fear and dislike of war. These were successful, but nothing could make the people enthusiastic or even hopeful. They were lukewarm, gloomy, depressed. They were told of the million and a half men under arms, the 2,000 first-line aircraft with 400 reserve, the navy with two new 35,000-ton battleships and a hundred submarines. They remained cold.

The early successes in Somaliland did a little to cheer them, but the harvest was poor and coal scarce, though the Nazis were sending some in exchange for vegetables and fruit, while every month made it more apparent that the Duce had to do whatever the Fuehrer told him, putting German interests before Italian. So much of a commonplace did this become that a saying was current : " How well off we used to be under Mussolini ! " The death of Marshal Balbo in a 'plane (June, 1940) was consequently the source of many rumours. It was given out that his 'plane had been shot down by the wicked British, but the shells were actually fired, as was later admitted, by Italian guns, whether accidentally or on instructions will probably never be known. Balbo had been known to be very doubtful about the wisdom of going to war. Apparently others shared his view.

At the end of 1940 high military and naval officers were dismissed as a result of the defeats suffered by the Italian army invading Greece, which came as a specially unpleasant shock, since Mussolini had promised a very short campaign and complete success. He hoped for this as a means of checking the defeatist tendencies of the nation, which were becoming more evident, but it had the opposite effect ; and following hard on this, the rapid sweep of Wavell's Nile army through Libya and the steady expulsion of Italian forces from Abyssinia sent the spirits of the nation down lower still.

Reassuring statements were issued after Mussolini's meeting with Hitler in January 1941, but these had less effect than the turn of the tide in Libya, when the British were compelled by German stiffening of Italian troops and German planning to give up all the ground they had taken. In March the British Navy followed up its success of the previous November at Taranto, in which harbour half the Italian fleet was put out of action, with an engagement off Cape Matapan, which

ITALIAN TRENCHES NEAR TOBRUK

Tobruk, once the stronghold of Graziani's military and naval forces, was captured by the British in January 1941, and the subsequent German campaign failed to dislodge them. General Auchinleck succeeded in driving back the Axis forces at the close of the year. An Italian division was cut off and the survivors surrendered.

Photo, Associated Press

culties he had to meet, " not in the Mediterranean only, but above all on the widely separated fronts of the war against British world-power." The Italian people could not forget that a few years earlier he had been on friendly terms with those who administered that world-power, any more than they forgot his 1939 and 1940 guarantees of safety to the Greeks, and his testimonials to their loyalty and gallantry, which were so soon followed by his treacherous attack on them.

It was made plain now that the Italians' attitude towards Fascism was entirely different from that of the Germans towards Nazism. They endured it without believing in it. They felt no personal enthusiasm or gratitude to Mussolini, such as Hitler aroused. The Italian soldiers were anything but eager to sacrifice themselves for an idea or a personality. It was said in Italy that they " sat down and declined to fight." Italians at home spoke of the army being "on strike." Dissatisfaction was widespread, indeed universal, except among Fascists in positions which enabled them to get rich at the public expense. Numbers of industrialists had been almost ruined. They had to submit to hastily vamped rules, to pay heavy taxation, to part with skilled workmen in order that these might be sent to Germany, to make desperate efforts, often unsuccessful, to secure their raw materials. They and the large landowners complained savagely that, having put the Fascists in power, they ought to have been well looked after, but were actually being victimized like the working men. They declared their belief that Hitler wanted to destroy Italian industry and make the country agricultural, a supplier of German needs and not a possible rival. Some industrial leaders and some landowners had got themselves into the position of local chiefs, which gave them great authority, but not much influence with the central Government. They mostly consulted their own interests, not those of the locality or the nation. Others, not so cunning or so pushful, denounced the whole system, which they were too timid however, to oppose openly. As for the middle classes, they were crushed by taxation which, they muttered, was for the benefit of Hitler only.

resulted in several Italian ships being sunk, and this again lowered Italian morale, while the re-entry of the emperor Haile Selassie into Addis Ababa in May, five years after he had been driven into exile, and the accelerated clearing-up of the Italian forces still in Abyssinia, made it clear to the home front that Italy would get nothing out of the war but disaster.

The death penalty was now threatened for defeatist talk and also for hoarders of food, which had become still more scarce. Four meatless days a week were ordered, while oil, macaroni, sugar, coffee, butter, soap and flour were meagrely rationed, and many small luxuries, to which the people in towns at any rate were accustomed, disappeared altogether. Taxation mounted higher, and many welcomed the loss of Abyssinia, which would relieve them of the expense of administering and developing the country. Another cause of bitter resentment against Fascism was the sending of Italian artisans and labourers to Germany to work for the Nazis. This was the way in which Hitler insisted on being paid for the war materials and food he was allowing Italy to have. At first the agreement provided for 150,000 of these being furnished, but later (February 1941) the number was increased to 350,000.

Mussolini by this time had changed his cheerful note for one of melancholy stoicism. He broadcast to the Italian people and the world a lament over the diffi-

Thus Mussolini became more and more unpopular with all except the young people brought up as Fascists and not yet capable of understanding what Fascism was or how the rest of the world regards it. The monarchy shared in the unpopularity of the dictator to whom the king had ceded his powers, and whom the royal family treated with admiring respect. Minds turned in many

NO GLORY OR GAIN FOR ITALY IN HITLER'S WAR

When Italy entered the war she thought that the worst was over, but British resistance upset her calculations. (1) Mussolini is seen reviewing a motorized division in Northern Italy, soon to be strafed by the R.A.F. (2) Italian prisoners working on the land somewhere in England pause for a meal. (3) The Duke of Aosta (second from left) surrenders after stubborn resistance in Abyssinia. (4) An Italian battleship, the Vittorio Veneto, fires a salvo to cover her retreat during the Battle of Matapan.

Photos, Keystone, Press Portrait Bureau, British Official

quarters to the establishment of a republic. This thought was strengthened in October 1941 by the enforcement of bread rationing. There was rioting in Sicily, where the R.A.F. had created terror by its frequent raids, and where living was especially hard. In December as many as seventy-one persons were charged with conspiracy to spread alarm and discontent. Yet no prospect of any large movement against Mussolini and Fascism could be discerned. Underground activities of a revolutionary character had little chance of making headway until a considerable part of the army could be counted on to support them.

Relations between Italian and German soldiers were bad, but not so hostile as those of the civilian population and the Nazi troops. The commander of the latter had to admit in an order blaming them for drunkenness, housebreaking, and assaults on civilians, that "the reputation of the German forces had been seriously damaged by shocking incidents."

THE SWASTIKA HAWKED IN ROME

Axis propaganda required that Mussolini should boost the Nazis in Italy, but Italians were never enthusiastic. As time went on, growing Nazi exploitation of the country aroused strong hostility, and special measures were necessary, as seen here, to popularize the Nazi symbol.

Photo. E.N.A.

The second British offensive in Libya at the end of 1941 and in the early part of 1942 caused even greater hopelessness among Italians in Italy than had prevailed at any time before, but, according to reports by foreigners who came out of the country, it was into a state of collapse rather than rebellion that this latest catastrophe had plunged them.

The British retreat, when von Rommel attacked soon afterwards, gave them a little encouragement, but not much. They knew the Germans had a contempt for their forces. When they were left to themselves the Italian troops, feebly led and with no stomach for fighting, made a poor show. At Halfaya, where few Nazis supported them, they were so weak for want of food and water that they were glad to surrender, and two Generals of Division, who were among the prisoners, made no secret of their discontent.

The continuous bombing of Malta was undertaken almost entirely by German planes, based on Sicily, the Italian airmen being pushed contemptuously aside as third-rate. This was attributed not to want of skill or courage, but to lack of interest in the operations planned by their Nazi masters.

Life became more difficult, too. Many suffered from cold as a result of the shortage of fuel. No private cars were permitted to run because petrol was scarce. All entertainments and restaurants were compelled to close at 10 p.m., and the food obtainable in the latter was diminished. Small wonder that "sowers of doubt, uncertainty and disappointment" had to be officially denounced, or that rumours suggested action on the part of the king and certain Generals who had not bowed the knee to Mussolini. It was considered significant also that Farinacci, once secretary-general of the Fascist Party, should come out with an attack on the corporative system sustained by that Party as "lopsided and rigidly bureaucratic" and, therefore, incapable of handling food supplies efficiently or regulating prices.

Mussolini kept very quiet all through these unquiet times. He signed a military convention with Hitler and Japan ; he sent Ciano to meet Darlan, one of the French quislings, who nevertheless shied at handing over Savoy and Corsica to Italy ; he met Hitler again in the spring, not, as before, at the Brenner, which signified some sort of equality between the two rulers, but at Salzburg, whither he was summoned peremptorily to receive fresh instructions, including the order to get ready to send Italian troops to Russia. In Hitler's address to the Reichstag at the end of April there was the customary compliment to the Duce, but it had a formal ring. One result of Hitler's speech, in which he proclaimed himself supreme Law Lord, was that Mussolini called a conference of judges and magistrates, who were told to make alterations in the penal code of Italy, though, as the Gestapo was in full authority there and made laws for itself, this hardly seemed to Italians to be necessary.

About the same time Mussolini ordered Italian officials to spend as little as possible so as to avoid the danger of inflation, and said they must not apply for promotion during the war. This deepened the gloom in Rome and other cities, because it showed that greater sacrifices must be faced. The bad effect was heightened by the Duce's ban on all "frivolous amusements," variety shows and dance halls being ordered to close before the end of May.

An exchange of sick and disabled prisoners of war, arranged through the Red Cross, was carried through according to agreement, unlike that which the Germans refused to complete. Ships carrying the men selected met at Smyrna, and the passengers were transferred from one to the other on April 7. Next day two Italian liners left Gibraltar, where they had been permitted to anchor under the Red Cross, for what had been Italian Somaliland. They were sent to take back to Italy 11,000 of the civil population of that former Italian colony, and of Eritrea and Abyssinia.

Many Italians, eager for any sign of possible escape from their unhappy position, thought these arrangements between the British and Italian Governments might perhaps be indicative of an approach to some sort of wider understanding. They were the same who said to one another sarcastically and in whispers, " How well off we were under Mussolini ! " suggesting that there was now no Mussolini, only a shadow of Hitler. But the hope they cherished was a very faint one. They knew the United Nations had declared that no peace would be made until both Nazism and Fascism had been destroyed, and as yet (April 1942) both held Italy down in a cruel grip.

Italian spirits were raised at home with the news of Rommel's advance into Egypt in May 1942. Mussolini, with an impressive staff, flew to Africa for the triumphal entry into Alexandria. But the elation was doomed to be short-lived and the speedy retreat of the Axis and the blatant desertion by Germans of Italian units in the field intensified the growing distrust of the Nazis (see N. Africa). Meanwhile the domestic crisis in Italy was deepening. The budget for 1941–42 showed a deficit of 65,000,000,000 lire and inflation was a constant danger. Control of prices meant the disappearance of goods from the market. By a decree of March 1942 all war profits had to be invested in three per cent state war loans and registered in the holder's name. But the value of the lira continued to fall.

In April 1942 there was another meeting between Hitler and Mussolini. The report stressed that the talks took place in " a spirit of close friendship and brotherhood of the two nations." The results of this brotherhood were soon apparent to the disillusioned Italians. The demand for Italian workers for German factories increased, and thousands were sent into Germany. There they enjoyed the status, not of allies, but of inferior alien labourers. Signor Gayda announced that " Italy must supply more men and more material for the gigantic German economy." The scanty rations of bread, oil and fats were still further reduced, and all open spaces in the cities were ploughed and sown with wheat. Any remaining

WHEAT GROWING IN MILAN CITY
In the summer of 1942 the shortage of bread in Italy was such that wheat had to be supplemented by maize flour and potatoes. Even in busy cities open spaces were ploughed up and sown for corn, as seen in this photograph taken in Milan.
Photo, Associated Press

doubts that Italy was becoming a mere vassal state were dispelled with the arrival of a large detachment of German police. Even the Blackshirt militia now functioned under the orders of the Gestapo.

The walling up and protecting of Rome's ancient monuments, the digging of air-raid shelters, the growing strength of the R.A.F.'s raids on Germany, all were portents for the future. More and more it was realised that Germany was dragging Italy to disaster.

For all this discontent Fascism had its usual panacea. France was humbled and broken, and could not resist any demands supported by Hitler. So the Fascist Party once again raised the demand for the cession to Italy of Nice, Corsica and Tunisia. On May 26, 1942, King Victor and the Crown Prince reviewed 300,000 troops in a provocative demonstration on the French Alpine border near Piedmont. But the campaign aroused no enthusiasm, and was soon dropped ; on Hitler's orders, it was said.

Discontent with Mussolini and the trend of Italian policy now grew so strong that it invaded the Fascist Party itself. In May 1942, after a meeting between Mussolini and the party directorate, it was announced that the party would be subject to a drastic purge. This was taken as an official acknowledgment of the prevalence of anti-German feeling and of abuses within the party.

In May 1942 appeared yet another incident to show the people how Italy was losing her independence. The northern provinces of Bolzano, Trento, Belluno

AFTER A MEETING WITH HIS MASTER
Mussolini was summoned to meet Hitler at Salzburg at the end of April 1942. Despite the report of talks "in a spirit of friendship and brotherhood," Hitler's demands for Italian labourers and materials caused dismay. Here, Mussolini (Ciano behind him) reads the document incorporating Hitler's demands, while Ribbentrop (right) displays his customary self-satisfaction.
Photo, Associated Press

and Udine contained large German minorities, and by Hitler's orders a plebiscite was held to determine how many of them wished to return (with generous compensation from Italy) to the Fatherland. Some 180,000 voted for Germany, and Italy, with all her financial difficulties, was forced to pay them compensation for 244,400 hectares of land, 40,000 houses and estates and 7,040 business undertakings.

In the autumn of 1942 the thoughtful and patriotic Italian was beginning to consider secretly that the best interests of his country could be served only by breaking the bond with Germany and making peace with the United Nations.

Books to Consult. Italy Militant, E. Hambloch (Duckworth). Italian Foreign Policy, Barbara Ward (Oxford Pamphlet). Italy in Africa, Christopher Hollis (Hamilton).

Italy, Air War on. Britain made her first air attack on Italy on June 11, 1940, one day after that country had declared war on the Allies. The raid was carried out by bombers of the Middle East Command and the objective was Turin, where the big Fiat motor and aeroplane works and other industrial centres were the main targets. This raid marked the opening of assaults from the air upon the Fascist State which, in spite of the great distances involved, unfavourable weather, and the limited number of aircraft available at the time, were persistently made.

Attacks on industrial targets in northern Italy were shared between R.A.F. squadrons in the Middle East and others which were based in England. The home-based aircraft were Vickers-Armstrong Wellington heavy bombers, which have a range of 3,500 miles and a duration of 18 hours. These were the machines which carried bombs to Turin, Genoa and Milan. By August 27, 1940, certain factories engaged in the manufacture of armaments and war material had sustained severe damage. In these earlier actions it was noticed by the R.A.F. raiders that Italian defences were poor, and little opposition was encountered from fighter aircraft of the Regia Aeronautica. On a number of occasions the attacks were made from a height of a few hundred feet. From June 1940 until September 1941 the R.A.F. had singled out for bomb attack thirty-two objectives. The targets were mainly power-stations, railways, and certain manufacturing centres which were of vital importance to the enemy.

One British air attack which stands as an epic of daring, skill and courage was the shattering raid by torpedo-carrying aircraft upon the naval base at Taranto (*q.v.*). This was made on the night of Nov. 11, 1940, when Fairey Swordfish naval planes, operating from the aircraft carriers Illustrious and Eagle, dived down in the moonlight and struck three battleships, two cruisers and two fleet auxiliaries with torpedoes. Two days later heavy bombers of the R.A.F. dropped high-explosive and incendiary bombs on the Taranto docks and inner harbour. Bombers had struck heavy blows at Naples three nights previously, when they bombed an oil refinery and a railway junction and station.

During 1941 Naples was constantly bombed by the R.A.F., and this was particularly noticeable when the Imperial Air Forces had gained command of the air in Libya. These raids, which were carried out to frustrate the Axis move to send reinforcements and fresh supplies across the Mediterranean, were all part of the British plan of action which prefaced the Libyan offensive.

The re-equipment of the R.A.F. with big four-engined bombers (the Stirling and the Halifax) and such high-performance twin-engined machines as the Manchester and Beaufighter, increased its striking power in operations over Italy in 1941.

Italian targets of the Royal Air Force bombers.

R.A.F. OBJECTIVE IN NORTH ITALY

Turin was attacked many times. The chief targets were the Fiat motor works and aeroplane factory, and railway sidings. In this flashlight photograph we see incendiaries falling, the streaky effect being due to exposure after the flash.

Photo, British Official

Many of the raids carried out over Southern Italy were made in daylight, and a large proportion of these attacks started from R.A.F. stations in Malta. Aircraft using the island as a base dropped no fewer than one million bombs on Italian targets in a single month in 1941.

On Jan. 2, 1942, and again on Feb. 3, night attacks were made on Naples. Reconnaissance showed that half the Royal Arsenal here had been destroyed by repeated R.A.F. raids, and extensive damage done to military and industrial objectives. On the night of April 12, 1942, a strong bomber force crossed the Alps and raided Genoa, Turin and other places, the first raid on Italy from home bases since September 1941. All our 'planes returned safely.

Ivanhoe, H.M.S. This British destroyer aided H.M.S. Cossack during the latter's dramatic rescue of British seamen from the German ship Altmark (*q.v.*, in Joessing Fjord, Norway, on Feb. 16, 1940. The Ivanhoe was completed in 1937 and belonged to the Intrepid class. Her displacement was 1,370 tons and she carried a complement of 145. In company with ships of her class she was fitted for minelaying and cost £320,000. On April 13, 1940, the survivors of H.M.S. Hardy were rescued and taken aboard the Ivanhoe (*see* Narvik, Battle of). She herself was sunk by mine in the North Sea on Sept. 1, 1940.

 Jackman, LT. (T/CAPT.) JAMES JOSEPH BERNARD. He showed outstanding heroism on Nov. 25, 1941, at El Duda, Libya. In command of a machine-gun company of the Royal Northumberland Fusiliers during an enemy tank attack, he led machine-gun trucks up the El Duda ridge in the face of intense enemy fire, and by his courageous action enabled the brigade to maintain its hold on the position. He was subsequently killed, and was posthumously awarded the V.C.

Janina (Yannina). This Greek city of Epirus was one of their main objectives when the Italian forces crossed the Albanian frontier into Greece on Oct. 28, 1940. One of the three main columns of the invaders headed towards Janina, but the stubbornness of the Greek troops prevented the enemy from approaching this vital point. The town was bombed by the Italians on Nov. 2, when a number of casualties occurred. On April 6, 1941, Germany invaded Greece and Yugoslavia, and by April 21 Janina formed part of the new line held by the Allied forces during their retreat from Mt. Olympus. Two days later a further withdrawal had to be made, the heroic Greek Epirus army surrendered, and the enemy occupied Janina.

WAR-LORDS OF JAPAN EMULATE THE NAZIS

While the Allied resources were being concentrated on the crushing of Hitler, Japan treacherously launched her long-prepared attack. From a flying start she swept all before her, and was at the threshold of Australia on one hand and India on the other before she was halted. See also Burma ; China ; Malaya ; Pacific, War in ; etc.

Japan. That the Japanese Government, or at any rate the military and naval elements which controlled it, had the widest ambitions towards a Pacific Empire was well known. These ambitions were revealed in the memorandum of General Count Tanaka, at one time head of a Ministry, in which he claimed " special rights and interests " for his country in Manchuria and Mongolia, and gave warning that these would be defended, if necessary, " no matter whence the menace comes." He did not attempt to conceal, nor did other Japanese spokesmen, that this was part of the design which was intended

eventually to secure Chinese Pacific ports and also Vladivostok ; or that the same " rights and interests " would be insisted upon elsewhere as soon as Japan was in a position to assert them.

Mr. H. L. Stimson, former American Foreign Minister, pointed out that this marked a complete change from the policy defined by Mr. Sidehara, the advocate of friendship with the Western Powers. He had not demanded political or sovereign rights, only economic and contractual. That Japan was threatening trouble was pointed out also by Mussolini's Under-Secretary of State for the Italian colonies, who

called the Far Eastern Empire "a great danger to
Europe" and described Japan's demands and strength
as the points on which Far Eastern politics turned.

At that time (1934) Japanese agents were active in
Abyssinia, and it was thought that Mussolini might
find himself checked there by Japan. Two years later
Adm. Takahashi warned the United States that, if
they continued to aim at expanding their foreign
trade under protection of the Navy, Japan's naval
policy, which in the past had been defensive, might
have to be altered. Japan, he emphasized, must
expand into the South Pacific.

This area attracted the Japanese because they needed
the oil, rubber, tin, copra, pepper, palm oil and spices
of Java and Sumatra. For ten years the Dutch had
been nervous about Japanese intentions. In 1935 the
chairman of the Japanese Society in the United States
said it was highly questionable whether Holland
could retain much longer its East Indian possessions;
it was uncertain, too, how long India would remain a
British possession. There was no time to be lost.
Japan must make its way southward without delay.
On the gold, iron, manganese and chromium (used
for armour plating) of the Philippines the Japanese
also looked with longing eyes. Here they followed

a policy of peaceful penetration. Large numbers of
Japanese settled in the Philippines. Davao was
described as being like a Japanese town. Street
names were put up in Japanese, there were Japanese
schools and societies. There went on a large export
of hemp from the Philippines, which received in
return cheap textiles. Every Japanese looked forward
to the day when the Americans would be driven out
by them. The Americans did not, however, feel any
apprehension, as the Dutch did. They despised Japan.

Yet ever since the annexation in 1910 of Korea, a
strategic point in the mastery of the Far East, it
had been clear that Japan was advancing step by step
towards the goal of its rulers' ambitions. When
they were given mandates over some fourteen hundred
Pacific islands comprised in the Marshall, Caroline
and Marianas groups, they had reason to be very
grateful to the Peace Conference in Paris. Some of
these islands were merely coral reefs with no inhabitants
on them, but others were of considerable value. It
was laid down that none of them should be fortified,
but this was soon forgotten. Although an American
commission of inquiry did not find any proof of the
persistent report that fortifications existed, the persistent dogging of the footsteps of visitors by police
made it plain that there was
something to hide. In 1936
Mr. Mikami, Japanese M.P.,
let out the secret when
he urged the necessity of
"making the islands a strategic base for Japanese policy
in the South Seas."

In 1937 came the invasion
of China, following a local
clash between Chinese and
Japanese soldiers. From
1931, when Lord Simon,
as British Foreign Secretary,
had excused Japanese overrunning of Manchuria in a
speech which the Japanese
representative on the

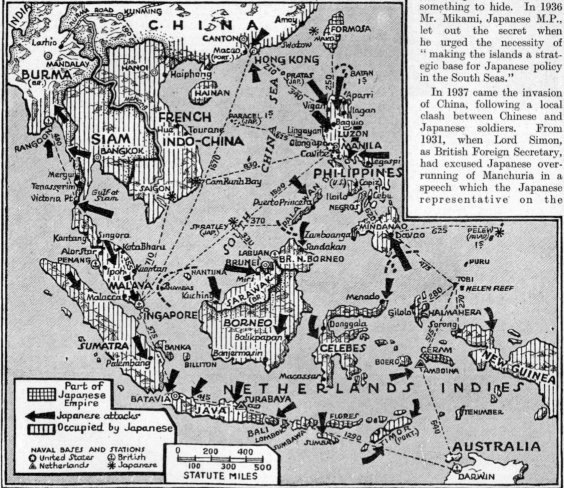

Showing the direction of Japanese attacks in the S.W. Pacific, the occupied territories and naval bases.   *"New York Times"*

League of Nations Council welcomed as stating his own arguments better than he could have stated them himself, the path Japan intended to pursue had been clear. Yet nothing was done to stop its aggressive acts. The Tokyo Cabinet was convinced therefore that no obstacle would be put in the way of their dealing with China as they pleased. They knew they had the sympathy of many throughout Europe and America who thought, as Lord Simon did, that China was going to pieces and had become a nuisance to the world, needing the firm hand which Japan promised to apply. Actually Japan seized this moment to attack China just because, instead of going to pieces, the country was pulling itself together. Unity was coming into sight and reorganization being carried out in many directions. The Japanese were resolved to stop both these developments if they could. They were afraid of the stirring of the Chinese national spirit as evidenced by the New Life and the People's Economic Reconstruction Movements.

ANTI-SPY PROPAGANDA IN TOKYO

Japan, like every other country, has her quota of fifth columnists, and this row of placards in a Tokyo suburb was posted up during an anti-spy week. The one of the girl with a hand over her mouth is obviously a version of our " Careless Talk Costs Lives."

Photo, Keystone

The New Life, which was to be characterized by self-respect and a sense of the value of personality, by even-handed justice for all classes, by honesty in government and private transactions, by good-will and tolerance all round, and which was beginning to show itself in the daily lives and habits of the people, was viewed by the Japanese militarists as a danger to their imperialist plans. They felt they must strike, and strike hard, before China had time to grow in strength and determination. Prince Konoye, then Premier, expressed this feeling when he said, on Aug. 28, 1937, that " the Chinese were about to be beaten to their knees, so that they would no longer have the energy to fight."

No hand, no voice even, was raised to hinder this wanton and, as it appeared at the time, cowardly aggression. The Chinese seemed to be far below their enemy in military resources. Their air force was less than five years old. Their armies were loosely held together and inadequately trained. Their armaments were insufficient for war on a vast scale. For a time the Japanese had it almost all their own way. The Chinese turned for help to the United States, Britain and France, but none was given. The world looked on. Even among the European business men in China itself were some who considered the country chaotic, incompetent, and in need of stern discipline.

Gradually, as the methods of Japanese " discipline " became known, American opinion changed in favour of giving the Chinese the help that had so far been refused. In the systematic destruction by the Japanese of schools, colleges and universities many American institutions suffered. American business interests began to see that the Japanese were not only ruining their own best foreign market, but were ruining at the same time those of their competitors. The atrocities perpetrated by the invaders were given prominence in the American Press and caused fierce indignation. A boycott of Japanese goods was attempted—without great success, it is true—and it was suggested that the Government should prohibit the export of materials Japan relied on for the supply of its troops.

In Britain also feeling against the Japanese rose. When a train-load of people, most of them mothers trying to take their children out of danger, was bombed from the air at a low altitude, the leading British newspaper in China, the " North China Daily News," said it was " as wanton a crime against humanity as could well be conceived," while the leading American journal declared " there are no words in the dictionary to describe such deeds." Another example of Japanese methods of making war on defenceless populations was given at Changsu, where aircraft flying near the ground bombed and machine-gunned first one side of a street crowded with people and then the other.

The events of the war are recorded under the heading China. As these turned slowly against the Japanese hope of winning a quick victory, so did their efforts increase, while their plans in other directions were speeded up. They were disappointed when they failed in their powerful attempt to cut off Chiang Kai-shek's supplies. The Chinese made a mass removal of industries. Four hundred factories, blast furnaces, chemical and electrical works were shifted westwards

IN A TOKYO ARMAMENT FACTORY

Special war demands have led in Japan to a vast expansion in the heavy industries, of which Tokyo, with its population of six millions, is the chief centre. Cheap labour, and child labour, are abundant, working hours are long and the conditions often extremely bad. Here two operatives are pushing a trolley-load of shells.

Photo, Wide World

hope to win in the long run.

Their only chance lay in making a tremendous effort and gaining their objects before the Chinese could bring their immense resources into play. But from this they were dissuaded by Hitler's cry for help when his Nazi hordes in Russia began to be rolled back. Not that they were anxious to help him. They knew that in his mind they were classed with negroes and Jews and other "non-Aryans" in the Nazi jargon. They were aware that his world-empire aspiration clashed with theirs, and that if the Axis Powers could be victorious there would very soon be a fight between Japan and Germany for the Far Eastern spoils.

But the Japanese militarists saw that their own interest demanded they should at once enter the con-

to provinces still free from the enemy. This, with the aid of material from Russia, made it possible for the Chinese to keep up their stubborn resistance, even when the Burma Road was closed and nothing reached Free China from the United States. But they were hard put to it, and they rejoiced when the Japanese triumph over British objections to closing the Burma Road was seen to be short-lived. In the same month that the Tokyo Government was incensed by its reopening, the Mikado's Ministers were equally perturbed by the United States letting their trade agreement with Japan expire, cutting off supplies of iron, steel and aviation petrol, and granting China a very large credit for the purchase of war material.

All through 1941 the relations between Japan and Washington seemed frequently to be approaching a critical phase. In the autumn a special Japanese mission was sent to the United States Government for discussion of all matters at issue between them. At this time it was expected that, if Japan did make war on Hitler's side, it would not be until the spring of 1942, when weather conditions would be favourable. Also it was supposed by many that Japan was too deeply embroiled in China to engage in warfare on other fronts. The number of Japanese troops in China was reckoned at one million. They were said to have lost a million on the fields of battle. Chiang's armed and trained forces were stated to be two millions, with another million irregulars and twenty millions in training. At such a disadvantage in point of numbers it seemed impossible that Japan could

flict. If Hitler were beaten in Europe, they argued, their opportunity would have passed. For them it was "now or never." They determined to make it "Now," and on Dec. 7, 1941, while the Japanese Mission was still in Washington, prophesying smooth things, both Britain and the United States were attacked at the same moment and with temporarily unpleasant results. Hostile aircraft raided a number of places and did great damage. Pearl Harbour (q.v.) in Hawaii was bombed, the battleships Arizona and Oklahoma being sunk, with three destroyers, a mine-layer and a target-ship. It was stated that 2,459 of the crews were killed, including 91 officers. The attack came as a complete surprise. Thailand (Siam) was invaded and immediately gave way, in spite of declarations by its rulers that it would resist to the bitter end.

The enemy's chief objectives appeared to be Manila and Singapore. The former fell quickly. It was declared an open town in the hope that it might not be bombed. But it was bombed mercilessly, and very large numbers were killed. The Japanese entered on Jan. 1, 1942. The defences of Singapore began at the top of the Malay Peninsula, where it joins Siam and Burma. Outnumbered and lacking protection from enemy bombers, British troops were compelled to retreat day after day. The position was made worse at sea by the loss of the new battleship Prince of Wales and the old battle-cruiser Repulse, sunk on Dec. 10 by torpedoes launched from Japanese aircraft which, in the absence of British fighter 'planes, were

GLIMPSES OF THE JAPANESE BATTLE FRONTS

These photographs come, of course, from enemy sources. 1. Japanese infantry and one-man tanks, at the approaches to Singapore Causeway. 2. Ship's crew carrying out manoeuvres in the Pacific. 3. Soldier at an artillery outpost using the stereo-telescope. 4. Japanese officers, armed with swords, go over the top after landing at Miri, Sarawak. The huge blaze that confronts them comes from the oilfield, set alight by the defending troops in accordance with their "scorched earth" policy.

Photos, Keystone; Black Star

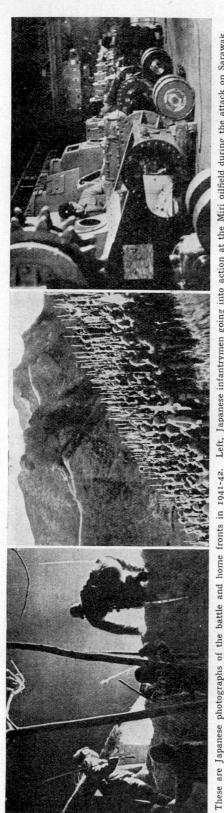

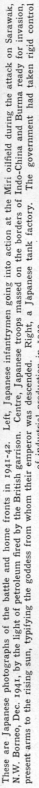

These are Japanese photographs of the battle and home fronts in 1941-42. Left, Japanese infantrymen going into action at the Miri oilfield during the attack on Sarawak, N.W. Borneo, Dec. 1941, by the light of petroleum fired by the British garrison. Centre, Japanese troops massed on the borders of Indo-China and Burma ready for invasion, present arms to the rising sun, typifying the goddess from whom their emperor was descended. Right, a Japanese tank factory. The government had taken rigid control of industrial production in 1939.

THE JAPANESE PHOTOGRAPHED THEIR TREACHEROUS ATTACK ON PEARL HARBOUR FROM THEIR OWN BOMBERS

This striking photograph from enemy sources is one of a series taken above Pearl Harbour on December 7, 1941 when, without warning or declaration, Japanese bombers made their crippling attack on the American naval base. In this photograph the first bombs are falling upon battleships and cruisers, all stationary, close together and near the shore —an easy target and one that was practically undefended. (See also page 342.)

Photos. Associated Press, Keystone

202

able to fly low and take careful aim. Hongkong held out gallantly against heavy assaults, but was obliged to capitulate on Christmas Day. Penang was abandoned and, although a "scorched earth" policy had been promised, after the Russian example, much of value was left both on land and in the harbour.

So serious was the state of affairs in this theatre of war that Mr. Churchill decided to go to Washington for conferences with President Roosevelt and his naval, air and military advisers. On Dec. 23 his arrival there was announced, and soon there followed the good news of unified command in the south-west Pacific, Sir Archibald Wavell being Supreme Commander, with the American Major-Gen. Brett as second and General Sir H. Pownall as Chief of Staff. As a consequence of Wavell's appointment, Mr. Duff Cooper, installed a few weeks earlier as Resident British Cabinet Minister at Singapore, was recalled. Air Chief Marshal Brooke-Popham was deprived of his command.

Japanese losses were heavy in spite of their advances. They were defeated with disastrous results at Changsha by the Chinese at the beginning of the year, and on all fronts in the Pacific fighting they were thrown in regardless of casualties, the Japanese object being to gain as many vital points as possible, particularly Singapore, before the United States and Britain could summon up their strength and become ascendant in the air. The Dutch did very good work against the common enemy, especially at sea, torpedoing a number of Japanese transports and supply-ships. The rapidity of the Japanese penetration, their lightning seizure of air bases, the combined cleverness and daring of the methods their troops used in jungle fighting, the carefully-worked-out plan for widespread operations, all with the same end in view, surprised the world.

The Americans especially got a shock at finding so redoubtable a foe in a people they had despised and underrated. That they were able to win a signal advantage by taking both the U.S. and Britain by surprise was blamed on the diplomats and politicians, but, as they went on week after week driving British and American forces before them, the feeling of alarm and anger, especially in Australia, became more and more vigorously voiced. After the middle of January the R.A.F. were more active, having received reinforcements of bombers and fighters both. The Americans, too, held fast in Luzon, which they made a stronghold after the loss of Manila, and for a long time held the Bataan Peninsula against very heavy attacks.

One of History's Most Heroic Episodes

But when Gen. MacArthur early in March gave up the command of the U.S. and Filipino troops to fly to Australia and take over command of all land forces there, it looked as if the end were not far off. Gen. Wainwright succeeded him, and for weeks longer what Mr. Stimson, American Secretary for War, described as "one of the most heroic episodes in military history" was prolonged, with heavy loss to the Japanese troops and airmen. But on April 7 there began a desperate attack on land, at sea and from the air. The Japanese were determined to clear up this pocket of resistance before the rainy season started. They had so vast an advantage in numbers that the defenders were swamped. They surrendered on April 10, and the enemy took prisoner 35,000 serving soldiers, including sixteen generals, 3,500 sick and wounded, with 25,000 civilians. Next day they landed on the Philippine island of Cebu and established themselves there. The fort of Corre-

SAILOR AIRMAN OF JAPAN
Naval pilot of Nippon, armed with pistol and Samurai sword —the hilt is seen on the left—ties a Japanese flag around his head before taking off on a bombing raid.
Photo, Keystone

gidor in Manila Bay still defied capture, but this was compelled to give up the unequal struggle early in May.

By that time the Japanese had subdued, in addition to the Philippines, both Malaya and the Dutch East Indies. Their drive down the Malay Peninsula from the bases they had been able to establish in Siam was very ably planned and carried out with unhesitating resolution. Never did the British troops have the opportunity to make a stand and meet the enemy in battle. The whole operation was one of skirmishes, jungle rushes, fighting by small detachments in forest and swamp. The lack of air support was fatal to the British effort, but the surrender came as a shock to the nation, which had not been allowed to realize how strong the Japanese were in machines and men, nor how carefully their plans had been prepared. Now they threatened both Australia and India, and their rapid progress in Burma was not less spectacular than their successes in other parts. Again the British found themselves vastly outnumbered; again the enemy had a marked superiority in the air; again, as in Malaya, they received valuable help from the local populations.

The Chinese sent in troops to save, if possible, the stoppage of supplies to their capital, Chungking, along the Burma Road. This was explained by General Tojo, the Japanese Premier, to be one of the main objects of the Japanese invasion of Burma, and they had gained it by the end of April. Almost the whole of the country was then in their hands, though a "scorched earth" policy had left them little to take over in the way of materials they badly needed. The machinery at the oilfields of Yenangyaung had been systematically destroyed. Rangoon and Mandalay were largely in ruins. The enemy courted the good-will of the Burmese by promising them, as he promised the Filipinos, independence if they " showed under-standing " towards Japanese troops and readiness to cooperate in reconstruction.

Against Australia and the Dutch East Indies Gen. Tojo vowed vengeance if they persisted in their resist-ance and their " misunderstanding of Japan's true intentions." He warned Australia and New Zealand against relying on the help they hoped to get from Britain and the U.S., and thus " causing useless war." At the same time, however, he virtually admitted that the war had been begun by Japan and that for him it had definitely " useful " aims. Japan intended, he said, to set up for Greater East Asia " a new order of co-existence and co-prosperity on ethical principles," and in this each country and people would take its proper place ; he did not add " under Japanese orders," though that was clearly his meaning.

What this new order would be like Mr. Eden explained in the House of Commons, London, on March 10, when he gave his shocked and fiercely angry hearers an account of the hideous atrocities committed by the Japanese after their capture of Hongkong. Soldiers were tied together and bayoneted. Others were made to run, and killed as they ran. Hospital nurses were raped in the presence of doctors with whom they had worked. Whole districts were turned into brothels for troops. It was clear, Mr. Eden said, that the Japanese commanders were aware of all this and must be held responsible. One consequence of his appalling recital was that no pity could be felt for the people of Tokyo when it became known that on April 18 the city had been bombed by American aircraft, and the ports of Yokohama and Kobe as well. Giving an account of the raid, Brig.-Gen. J. H. Doolittle, a famous flier of the 'twenties, said it was made in the middle of the day and took the enemy unawares. Little opposition was met with. In the Navy Yard a battleship or cruiser in course of construction was hit and set on fire. At Nagoya " one of our bombers strewed incendiary bombs along a quarter of a mile of an aircraft factory," and in each place visited extensive fires were caused, the smoke from which could be seen by observers on ships from 25 to 30 miles distant. The Japanese complained bitterly of the " inhumanity " of this attack. They heard little about the commando raids

on a dozen Chinese cities supposed to be firmly in their grasp. These began with bomb throwing by people inside ; then, under cover of the confusion caused by fires, Chinese soldiers rushed in from outside and did as much damage to the enemy as possible.

An internal event which created some stir in Britain and America was the exchange of diplomatic represen-tatives between the Mikado and the Pope as well as between the Pope and China. Both Powers expressed their concern at this public recognition by the Vatican of an aggressor Government. How aggressive the aims of the Japanese were was hardly realized until the Chinese captured a map of what Tokyo called " the Co-prosperity sphere," in other words, the future Japanese Empire. This was to include the whole continent of Asia with the exception of Arabia ; India, China, and Siberia thus becoming Japanese. The Philippines and the Dutch East Indies, the northern part of Australia with Darwin and Cape York, and the whole of New Guinea, would also have to acknowledge the sovereignty of the Mikado. This was considered by the Chinese Government to be as important as the Tanaka Memorial, already mentioned, in which the first steps towards these aims were laid down. That the successes quickly gained by their forces in the Pacific had gone to the heads of many Japanese was shown by the address of a University professor in Tokyo, who claimed that almost the entire world was Asiatic and therefore ought to be ruled by Japan !

For a general view of Japanese aggression and naval, military and air action in the Pacific area, see Pacific.

Books to Consult. Japan Unmasked, Hallett Abend (Lane). Japan's Kampf, Jaya Deva (Gollancz). How Strong is Japan ? Noel Barbour (Harrap). Japan's Purpose in Asia, Sir Frederick Whyte (Royal Inst. of Internat. Affairs).

Jarabub. This desert settlement in Libya lies about 150 miles south of Bardia and 50 miles north-west of Siwa. In January 1941 an Italian army, reported to number between 20,000 and 30,000 men, was surrounded at Jarabub by the British Imperial forces, these having cut the lines of communication with Tobruk and Derna. This enemy force had been concentrated at Jarabub by Graziani to make a drive through the Siwa Oasis towards the Nile Valley in Egypt. After a siege lasting 15 weeks the Italians surrendered on March 21. On Nov. 18, 1941, Jarabub was the southern end of the line of the British advance into Libya.

JAVA AND THE BATTLE OF THE JAVA SEA

In their victorious sweep through the South-West Pacific Japan had captured Java by March 7, 1942. But before the capitulation there had been fought, north of the island, one of the most gallant, tragic, and forlorn naval actions of the war. See also Netherlands East Indies ; Pacific ; Sumatra ; etc.

Java, Invasion of. The simplest way to appreciate the position of Java on Feb. 18, 1942, is by the visual method of considering the strategic position of the Japanese air, land and sea forces at that date (*see* Netherlands East Indies). These forces, in great numbers, were safely in occupation of bases in Sumatra, Borneo and the Celebes and, of course, Singapore was also in their hands. The disposition of these forces forms, roughly, a crescent above Java : north, Pontianak in Borneo ; north-west, Palembang, Sumatra ; north-east, Banjermassi, Borneo ; and

Macassar at the south tip of Celebes. All these striking points are within 400 miles of Java, and ad-mirably situated for a combined sea and air operation.

That is the first thing the student of the situation at that date has to carry in his head. The second is the hard fact that the Dutch, by that time, were fighting virtually single-handed against an enemy who had been preparing his attack, not over months, but over a period of years.

From their bases the Japanese had been bombing Surabaya and Batavia, while the Dutch, aided by a

BATAVIA, EVACUATED CAPITAL OF NETHERLANDS EAST INDIES

Batavia, chief city of Java, is divided into two parts : the old town, intersected by numerous canals, situated on low ground near the sea and flanked by the shipping quarters ; and the new city of Weltvreden, standing high some two miles from the water-front. The photograph shows part of Weltvreden before the Japanese occupation, with its sports clubs and racecourse (top, right), Government and business offices, and the railway station (left). It was evacuated to avoid useless massacre of civilians.
Photo, G.P.U.

limited number of American bombers, took offensive action against the enemy's numerous shipping. On Feb. 19 one transport and many landing barges were sunk ; the Japanese next day carried out mass attacks on Javanese air bases. It is worth noting here that the Japanese strategy aimed at the destruction of Java's aerodromes as the prerequisite to large-scale landings. On Feb. 22 a big naval battle developed off Bali, the small island at the eastern end of Java. Two days later that island was overrun and its aerodrome at Den Pasar was in enemy hands.

During the night of Feb. 27–28 the Japanese broke through sea and air defences (*see* Java Sea, Battle of) and landed troops at three points on the N. coast of Java : at Bantam, 50 miles west of Batavia ; in the Bay of Indramayu, about 100 miles east of the capital ; and near Rembang, some 200 miles farther east of Batavia. They were resisted by Dutch, British, Australian and U.S.A. units. The method employed was that of infiltration, plus speed. Cycles were used and light mortars were carried. The air support was one hundred per cent, and met with practically no opposition. Within 24 hours they had made considerable headway, having reached Soebang, 40 miles from Indramayu and halfway to Bandoeng, and pushed 16 miles south of Rembang. Bandoeng, the Allied headquarters in the mountain spine of the

island, was heavily bombed on March 3, and next day 10-ton tanks—again an illustration of Japanese pre-occupation with light, mobile war material—were in action.

By March 5 battles were raging all over the island, the Japanese capturing centres of communication and threatening to cut off the great naval base, Surabaya. The following day Batavia was declared an open town and evacuated ; and the Japanese were nearing Bandoeng. Strong reinforcements were reported to have arrived, and it was stated that the Japanese in Java outnumbered the Allied forces by about five to one. At this point in a resistance that became hourly more hopeless, the Dutch, with the sort of stubborn courage which had already sent Admiral Doorman's ships to destruction, decided to fight in the hills, adopting full guerilla tactics. But they faced utterly hopeless odds, for one of the greatest armadas ever to sail the seas was at their door.

On March 7, at 12.55 p.m., the radio station of Bandoeng closed down with this final message to the outside world. " We are now shutting down. Long live our Queen ! Good-bye till better times ! " Soon followed news that Surabaya was surrounded. Tokyo announced the end of resistance and, later, the surrender of 93,000 Dutch troops, 5,000 British, Australian and United States troops.

Java with the smaller islands of Bali and Bankalang. Road and rail communications and the sites of aerodromes and oilfields are shown. The Strait of Sunda separates Java from Sumatra.

By courtesy of "The Daily Mail"

Why did the Dutch yield? The answer has been supplied by them, and, in face of the known modern practice of the Japanese army in the field, it is a sufficient one. Had the Dutch fought on, they feared that the invaders would have carried out a ruthless, indiscriminate massacre of the people of the island. It was to avoid that horrible consequence that these brave men laid down their arms.

With the conquest of Java Japan became, for the time, undisputed mistress of Eastern Asia and the holder of the gateway between East and West. It was, doubtless, knowledge of the magnitude of the strategical catastrophe which such a conquest would represent to the United Nations that determined the desperate attempt by the small fleet under Admiral Doorman to attack the vast Japanese armada of invasion.

Java Sea, Battle of. The lesson of this disastrous naval engagement is the plain one that the days of sea romance in war are gone. It is no longer possible for a force, comparable to the little Revenge of Sir Richard Grenville, to challenge the might of a vast fleet. Yet in the waters off the coast of threatened Java that is what the Dutch Admiral Doorman, acting on the orders of Admiral Helfrich, did. The result was the total annihilation of the United Nations' fleet, including the Exeter, made illustrious for her part in the Battle of the River Plate (*q.v.*).

On the afternoon of Friday, Feb. 27, 1942, a fleet composed of the following ships sailed from Surabaya to engage the convoyed Japanese armada heading for Java: *Cruisers:* Exeter (British), Perth (Australian), Houston (U.S.A.), De Ruyter and Java (Dutch); *Destroyers:* Electra, Jupiter, Encounter, Stronghold (British), Pope (U.S.A.), Kortenaer, Witte de With and Evertsen (Dutch).

The enemy was sighted midway between Surabaya and the island of Bawean. It was known that the enemy was in strength, but that these thirteen ships were heading for a fleet said to be over a hundred strong was not known. The Japanese had assembled this

AT THE NAVAL BASE OF SURABAYA

Surabaya is the largest city in Java and was also the chief military and naval base of the Dutch East Indies. Although stated to be well fortified against attack, its capture was claimed by the Japanese on March 10, 1942. The photograph shows Dutch sailors boarding a battleship in the harbour.

Photo, Paul Popper

MARINES OF THE DUTCH INDIES WHO FOUGHT IN JAVA

Java is an island of great natural beauty, rising in the interior to heights ranging between 6,000 and 9,000 feet. The south coast is bold and rugged, but in the north it is indented by numerous bays affording sheltered harbours. Allied headquarters, under the command of Gen. Ter Poorten, were at Bandoeng, in the western part of the island.

Photo, Keystone

armada in order to protect some hundred or more troop-carrying transports. It included over twelve cruisers with ships carrying 10-in. guns that outranged the 8-in. guns of the United Nations' ships.

Under orders to go in, Admiral Doorman was faced by two alternatives to attain his objective—the destruction of the troopships. He had to try to dodge the screen of ships, with their deadly fire power, or attempt to go through, a completely desperate expedient.

Thus opened out the first phase of the battle. It was one of attack by unnumbered destroyers supported by aircraft on a vast scale. In a moment Admiral Doorman found his ships in a sea sown with leaping death from which he strove to escape by serpentine manoeuvre. The first victim was the Kortenaer, torpedoed. Next, a shell hit Exeter's boiler room. Their destroyer attack delivered, the Japanese destroyer flotillas retired behind smoke screens. They were pursued by the three British destroyers, which passed through that smoke screen into history. Not until March 19, when 54 members of Electra's crew were rescued by an American submarine, was anything known of the action subsequent to that mad dash.

The second phase of the battle opened when the Japanese fleet turned and steered on a north-easterly course with the remaining handful of United Nations' ships on their heels. Night fell ; and out of the darkling sky came the flares of the enemy's sea-borne bombers, for which the pursuing ships had no air answer.

Undaunted, Admiral Doorman, like a persistent hound, still sought round this death-dealing protective screen of warships for the troop-carrying convoys. But in the darkness he lost touch and

therefore turned about and steered off the coast 12 miles from shore on a westerly course, hoping thus again to come up with the enemy. Twelve miles north of Rembang contact was made at 11.30 p.m. by this little fleet, which had suffered meanwhile the loss, by torpedo or mine, of Jupiter.

The Japanese opened up with a torpedo attack and sank both the flagship De Ruyter and the cruiser Java in a matter of minutes. The cruisers Perth and Houston, after making for Tanjong Priok, were ordered to get out of the Java Sea. This they attempted via the narrow Sunda Strait. It was guarded by Japanese cruisers. They were never heard of again. Exeter, Encounter and Pope, the first limping, left Surabaya only to meet greatly superior enemy forces and they, too, went to a certain fate by unascertained ways.

Epic, in terms of human courage and dogged endurance, the Battle of the Java Sea must become subject for many a debate. Were both lives and ships thrown away ? In Time's perspective may lie the true answer to these questions. The total allied loss was 13 warships ; precisely what damage was done to the Japanese was not revealed. At least one heavy cruiser was said to be sunk and other ships damaged. Later indications were that Japanese losses were considerably heavier.

Javelin, H.M.S. Completed in June 1939, this British destroyer was the name-ship of the Javelin class. Her displacement was 1,690 tons, and she carried a complement of 183. The Javelin was armed with six 4·7-in. guns and ten torpedo tubes. Commanded by Comdr. A. F. Pugsley, R.N., she was damaged by a torpedo fired from an enemy destroyer during a naval engagement in the English Channel on Nov. 29, 1940.

Jedabia (AGEDABIA). Scene of heavy fighting between the British and Italo-German forces, this village on the Gulf of Sirte in Western Cyrenaica, about 100 miles south of Benghazi, was taken by British Imperial forces in February 1941 after the Italians had retreated south following the fall of Benghazi. By February 9 clearance by our forces of the areas in the Jedabia region as far south as El Agheila proceeded satisfactorily. In April 1941 the British withdrew from this area following an Italo-German advance from the south towards Benghazi. Jedabia was again the scene of operations during December 1941 and January 1942, when Gen. Rommel was brought to bay. It was reported on Jan. 1 that British forces were closing round the concentration of German troops there, and by Jan. 8 Rommel's forces had moved off under cover of a sandstorm in an attempt to make their way round the Gulf of Sirte and thence to Tripoli. They were closely pursued by British mobile columns to El Agheila, and the British occupation of Jedabia was announced on Jan. 13. But on Jan. 21 three strong mechanized enemy columns drove our light forces back from the area south of Mersa Brega, and the next day they reoccupied Jedabia, our troops having withdrawn to the north-east. The enemy retained the initiative in this area for some while after the recapture of Jedabia, but were hampered by the R.A.F., who, during February, March, and April, successfully bombed their troops, tanks, and motor transport.

Jersey, H.M.S. Belonging to the Javelin class, the British destroyer Jersey was completed in April 1939. Her displacement was 1,690 tons, and she carried a complement of 183. She managed to reach port safely on Dec. 7, 1939, after being damaged by a mine. The Jersey took part in the British naval bombardment of Genoa on Feb. 9, 1941. She was sunk by a mine May 2, 1941.

Jervis Bay, H.M.S. Built in 1922, the Jervis Bay was a passenger steamer of 14,164 tons, speed 15 knots. She was commissioned as an auxiliary cruiser and armed with eight 6-in. guns and anti-aircraft pieces. She was commanded by Capt. E. S. Fogarty Fegen (q.v.). On Nov. 5, 1940, the Jervis Bay was in mid-Atlantic protecting a convoy of 37 homeward-bound merchantmen. She sighted a warship, later proved to be the German Admiral Scheer, which opened fire with 11-in. salvos, concentrating on the Rangitiki, whose impressive appearance caused her to be mistaken for the leader or escort. The Jervis Bay gallantly turned towards the German ship and immediately gave battle in order that the merchantmen under her protection might escape. The contest was palpably unequal, for the six 11-in. guns of the Admiral Scheer were credited with an extreme range of 30,000 yards, and her eight 5·9s would carry very much farther than the British 6-inchers. Eleven knots faster than the Jervis Bay, the enemy could choose the range. There could be but one result to the action. Direct hits were received and a shell started a fire. Capt. Fegen kept his ship in pursuit of the enemy with all the steam he could raise, knowing that every minute was giving the convoy a better chance to escape. The crew served their guns steadily until they were awash. All boats but one had been destroyed by shellfire. As the liner went down by the stern, life-saving rafts floated off her deck but were fired on by the German ship. A few survivors were picked up by one of the ships in the convoy. This heroic action on the part of the Jervis Bay saved 33 out of 37 ships of the convoy, and the posthumous award of the V.C. was made to her commander.

Jews, Measures Against. Almost the first act of Hitler's Government, which took office in March 1933, was to organize for April 1 a general boycott of Jewish shops and enterprises. This lasted four days in Berlin. After that Jews went on with their businesses as before, though on April 7 it was decreed that all office-holders under Government must be "Aryan," without any Jewish blood in their families for three generations (i.e. no Jew great-grandfather or grandmother). In June this was followed up by the expulsion from the Government service of all who were married to Jews, and the prohibition of such marriages in future. At the same time it was made more difficult for Jews to engage in any profession, to make a living by authorship or painting, to take part in theatrical or film work, to be composers or teachers of music. Yet at the Nuremberg Conference in September 1933 Rosenberg, chief exponent of the doctrine of "Nordic" racial supremacy, denied that these measures were due to race hatred or that there was any wish to stir up such hatred. The idea was that each race should remain "pure," since Nazis believed that from the mixture of races resulted, "not nations, but ethnic chaos."

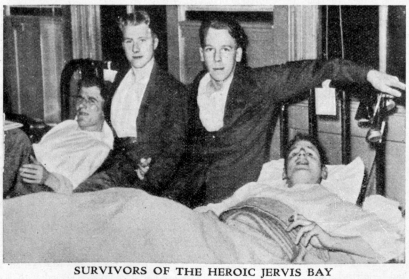

SURVIVORS OF THE HEROIC JERVIS BAY

Having saved thirty-three of the thirty-seven ships of her convoy by engaging and pursuing their attacker, the powerfully armed pocket battleship Admiral Scheer, the Jervis Bay went down in mid-Atlantic with all her guns firing. There were few survivors, but a Swedish freighter picked up the four men shown and brought them safely to a Canadian port.

Photo, Wide World

Nevertheless, "Stürmer," the obscene organ of Julius Streicher, prophet of anti-Semitism, continued to abuse and defame Jews in violent terms, and, though it was for a short time suppressed, its editor retained Hitler's confidence and was allowed free rein for his slanderous and filthy accusations. It may be mentioned here that Fritz Thyssen, the millionaire, who was so largely instrumental in bringing Hitler to power, declared his belief, after he broke with the Fuehrer, that Hitler's father was the illegitimate son of a Rothschild and that this accounted for his fury against the whole Jewish race. At any rate, the pretence that no special animus existed in Nazi leaders' minds was dropped.

Goebbels, in July 1935, contradicted Rosenberg flatly,

UNENVIABLE LOT OF THE JEWS

All Jews in Germany are branded by the compulsory wearing of a yellow star on the left side of the outermost garment. Left, caricature of the former Jewish owner of a shop in Vienna. To ensure against his reopening the premises, the padlocks have been filled with concrete.

Photos, Associated Press; Keystone

them to give their children any names except those to be found in the Bible, and they were deprived of any share in the Winter Relief Fund. By this time the half-million Jewish inhabitants who were in Germany in 1933 had been reduced by about 150,000.

In 1942 it was estimated by the New York Institute of Jewish Affairs that only 255,000 remained. Their flight from Austria, after Hitler seized that country, was even more headlong and multitudinous, for the reason that the persecution there was more brutal and pitiless. They were beaten, robbed, murdered. Thousands, including old people and men distinguished in many walks of life, were herded into prisons or camps, Jewish institutions were suppressed and every effort made to carry out Goering's order that "Vienna must be free from Jews." In Hungary the Horthy Government declared that a Jewish problem existed, but beyond limiting the numbers who might benefit by higher education, and preventing Jews from holding national key positions, not much was done to injure them.

In Italy, on the other hand, Mussolini was induced by his Nazi masters to attack, not "loyal Italian Jews, but international Jewry, which is anti-Fascist." He ordered all foreign Jews to be expelled; Jewish teachers were dismissed from schools and universities; the numbers of Jewish students were restricted, though they were given special schools; many were prevented from carrying on business, especially banking. In Poland there had been considerable persecution by the Polish authorities, but under the Nazis they were to suffer hideous cruelties. In Rumania the German influence caused the feeling against Jews which had long been smouldering to break into flame. There were riots and the same kind of anti-Jewish

comparing Jews to fleas and saying, "We do not want them any more; they have no longer any place in the community." In September 1935 they were deprived of their citizenship by law. They became merely subjects. "For the protection of German blood and honour" no Jew was allowed to employ for household duties any woman not Jewish under 45. Schools and universities were closed to Jews and mixed marriages declared illegal. A later ordinance forbade egislation as elsewhere. Even in France the dotard Pétain was persuaded to agree to anti-Semitic measures for the non-occupied regions, while in those held down by the Nazis Jews had, of course, much more to endure. Efforts to find new homes for the hundreds of thousands who had become refugees (as many as 600,000 was an American estimate) were made at a conference begun at Evian-les-Bains in 1939 and continued in Washington. San Domingo and the Philippines were discussed. A survey of British Guiana was also made.

Jijiga. Town in S.E. Abyssinia. After the capture of Mogadishu (*q.v.*) on Feb. 26, 1941, Gen. Cunningham's troops drove the Italians northwards along the road which links Mogadishu, capital of Italian Somaliland, with Jijiga, a town of considerable importance on the railway from Jibuti to Addis Ababa. Jijiga was captured from the Italians by South African forces on March 17. *See* Abyssinia ; East Africa.

Johnson, Amy. British aviation lost one of its most daring exponents in the death of Amy Johnson (*see* p. 2356) on Jan. 5, 1941. She had been working as a ferry pilot for the Air Transport Auxiliary and left the airfield on Jan. 5 in unfavourable weather, on a short flight. That was the last that was seen of Miss Johnson. Her 'plane came down over the Thames Estuary. It was presumed that she lost her course owing to bad flying conditions, and after cruising round for several hours crashed owing to lack of petrol. Lt.-Comdr. W. E. Fletcher, R.N., of the naval trawler Haslemere, saw Miss Johnson baling out and dived, fully clothed, into the icy water to rescue her. He reached her, but was unable to support her, and he died from exposure and exhaustion on arrival at hospital. He was posthumously awarded the Albert Medal.

Johnson, MAJ.-GEN. D. G., V.C. He commanded the 4th Division of the B.E.F. from 1939 to 1940. In October 1940 he was appointed C.-in-C. Aldershot Command.

Jones, GLYN. He was the first Home Guard to receive a military decoration. His job was to defend a vital point. The post in question was bombed, one man being killed. Jones, unhurt, first carried his wounded comrade to safety and then returned to his post and continued on guard, heedless of further bombs and much debris which fell round him. For his devotion to duty he was awarded the Military Medal.

Air Chief Marshal Joubert de la Ferté.
Photo, Howard Coster

Joubert de la Ferté, AIR CHIEF MARSHAL SIR PHILIP BENNET, K.C.B., C.M.G. (b. 1887). He succeeded Sir Frederick Bowhill as Air Officer C.-in-C. Coastal Command on June 13, 1941. One of the greatest British authorities on long-distance flying over sea, he was A.O.C. in India, 1937–39, and in February 1940 was appointed to the Department of the Chief of Air Staff as Adviser on Combined Operations.

Jowitt, SIR WILLIAM (b. 1886). Paymaster-General from March 4, 1942, in succession to Lord Hankey. It was stated that he would be engaged on work in preparation for post-war reconstruction, such as demobilization of men and women from the Services, reversion of industry to peacetime production, etc.

Juba, River. Flowing from the mountains of Southern Abyssinia in a southerly direction through Italian Somaliland to the Indian Ocean, the Juba

provided the Italians with a strong defensive position against the British troops advancing from Kenya in February 1941. Jumbo, the port at the mouth of the river, was captured by British forces on Feb. 22. Meanwhile a second British column cut eastwards straight through the bush and arrived at the Juba nearly 100 miles north of its mouth. The retreating Italians destroyed as many bridges as possible, but the South Africans waded across the stream, and enemy resistance on the farther bank was overcome. Pontoon bridges were then constructed and the British cars and trucks poured across. The South Africans moved up the river and captured Margherita and Jelib on Feb. 23. The S.A.A.F. cooperated in the attack on Jelib and machine-gunned transport. The east bank of the Juba was thus cleared up. Large quantities of guns and ammunition of all kinds were taken together with a great number of prisoners. *See* East Africa.

Juliana, OF THE NETHERLANDS, PRINCESS (b. 1909). On May 13, 1940, it was announced that Princess Juliana, heiress to the throne of the Netherlands, with her husband Prince Bernhard and their two children, the

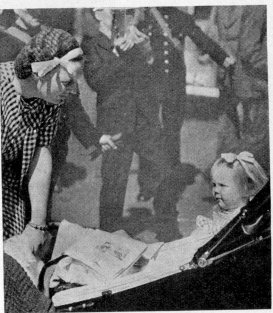

DUTCH PRINCESSES IN LONDON

Princess Juliana, heiress to the throne of the Netherlands, escaped with her husband and two children to England early in May 1940. Here the Princess and her elder daughter are seen the day after their arrival in London.
Photo, Wide World

Princesses Beatrix and Irene, had left Holland in a British warship and taken refuge in England. The Princess's mother, Queen Wilhelmina (*q.v.*), followed shortly afterwards. But for the timely aid of the destroyer Princess Juliana would undoubtedly have been captured by the Germans, or killed during the fierce and incessant air raids that the Germans had launched over Holland. A magnetic mine was dropped by an enemy 'plane only a few hundred yards in front of the British ship. The mine exploded immediately on hitting the water, and the destroyer passed on its way unscathed. In June 1940 Princess Juliana took her children to Canada.

Kain, F.O. EDGAR, D.F.C. An intrepid New Zealander, familiarly known as "Cobber," Kain was one of the first British air aces of the war. On March 26, 1940, he brought down two German Messerschmitt 109s over the Western Front before he himself was shot down in flames and escaped by parachute at the last moment, to land half a mile from the German lines. This was but one of Kain's many successes over the Western Front in 1940. He was killed in a flying accident on June 7, 1940, at the age of twenty-one.

Michael Kalinin, President of the U.S.S.R. *Photo, Planet News*

Kalinin, MICHAEL IVANOVICH (b. 1875). President of the Presidium of the Supreme Council of the Soviet Union from 1938. Originally a metal worker, he joined the "Union for struggle for the freedom of the working class" in 1895, and did party work in St. Petersburg, Reval, Tiflis and Moscow, being several times imprisoned and exiled, before the Revolution. He was President of the Executive Committee of the U.S.S.R. in 1923.

Kalinin. Key city on the Moscow-Leningrad railway, 100 miles N.W. of the Soviet capital, Kalinin was the scene of fierce fighting between the German and Russian forces during the German thrust for Moscow in October–December 1941. On Oct. 29 it was announced that the Germans had lost some 5,000 men and large quantities of equipment during fighting in the approaches to the city. They then brought up reinforcements, furious fighting continued, and by Nov. 5 they claimed to be holding the greater part of the town. The situation remained extremely grave for the Russians throughout November, but enemy pressure in the Kalinin area was eased by Dec. 3, and on Dec. 16 it was announced that the Russians had recaptured the town. Six German divisions were routed in the battle.

Kallio, KYÖSTI (1873–1940). President of Finland from 1937 to 1940. Of peasant extraction, Kallio entered politics in 1904 and quickly rose to important positions. He was three times Premier. In October 1939 he attended the Four-Power Conference (*q.v.*) at Stockholm to discuss the demands made by Russia on Finland. Throughout the Finnish war he constantly visited the fronts to encourage his gallant armies in their struggle against overwhelming odds. In 1940, worn out and grief-stricken at the fate of his country, he decided to retire from public life and return to his farm. On Dec. 19 Risto Ryti, his Prime Minister, was elected President. That same night, as Kallio was being given, at Helsinki railway station, a remarkable demonstration of the nation's affection and good will, he died from heart failure.

Kyösti Kallio, Finnish President. *Photo, Fox*

Kaluga. This Russian town, 110 miles S.W. of Moscow, was occupied by the Germans on Oct. 16, 1941, after fierce fighting and heavy casualties. Russian counter-attacks were ceaselessly repulsed, and the Germans used Kaluga as one of the bases for

"Cobber" Kain, New Zealand air ace. *Photo, British Official*

their drive from the south-west to Tula and thence towards Moscow. Crossing the River Upa in December, the Russians prepared for their advance on Kaluga, employing a special concentration of shock troops. In order to surprise the enemy they avoided main roads, using forest tracks instead. By Dec. 20 they had driven a wedge towards their objective almost 40 miles in length. On Dec. 21 Kaluga was attacked, and until Dec. 30, when the place was finally captured, the Russians fought innumerable street battles. Sixteen Nazi divisions under Gen. Guderian (*q.v.*) were routed in this episode of the campaign. *See* Russia.

Kandahar, H.M.S. This destroyer of the Javelin class was completed in 1939. She had a displacement of 1,690 tons and carried six 4·7-in. guns, six smaller ones, and ten 21-in. torpedo tubes. She took part in May 1940 with H.M.S. Kelly (*q.v.*) in a thrilling episode off the coast of Germany. On Jan. 3, 1942, the Admiralty announced that she had been damaged by a mine in the Mediterranean and was subsequently sunk by our forces.

Kandalaksha. An important Russian base on the White Sea, Kandalaksha was a vital point on the Murmansk railway, the main line of transport between Leningrad and the Arctic Ocean. During the Russo-Finnish war, 1939–40, the Finns made several raids upon this railway, their ski patrols being particularly active and threatening the town at the beginning of March 1940. *See* Russia.

Karelian Isthmus. Finland's Mannerheim Line (*q.v.*) formed a strong line of defence across the Karelian Isthmus behind the frontier separating Finland from the U.S.S.R. This famous defensive area was included in the Soviet demands to Finland in November 1939, the Russians insisting that Finland should immediately withdraw her troops in the frontier region of the Isthmus to a line 12 to 16 miles from the border. During the war which subsequently broke out between the two countries and which lasted from Nov. 30, 1939, to March 12, 1940, violent fighting continued with unabated fury throughout the entire area. The whole of the Karelian Isthmus passed to Russia by the Peace Treaty of March 12, 1940, the Finns evacuating their villages and towns before the Russians marched in. In December 1941 the Red Army made a great drive against Karelia and there was fierce fighting inside the Finnish positions on the northern bank of the R. Svir. *See* Finland; Russia.

Karlsruhe. Capital of Baden, Karlsruhe is situated 39 miles from Stuttgart. After the outbreak of war its important machinery works were converted into armament factories. On the night of Aug. 5 and 6, 1941, despite unfavourable weather conditions, R.A.F. aircraft launched a fierce attack on the city, when bombs of the heaviest type were used. Karlsruhe's proximity to the large manufacturing area of Stuttgart rendered it a vital target, and great fires were caused.

SUNK BY A BRITISH SUBMARINE

The German cruiser Karlsruhe, taking part in the invasion of Norway, was damaged off Kristiansand by a hit from the coastal batteries. H.M.S. Truant, after worming her way through a Nazi minefield, fired a torpedo which struck the vessel amidships and sent her to the bottom of the Skagerrak.

Photo, Central Press

Karlsruhe. This German cruiser, sister ship to the Königsberg, had a displacement of 6,000 tons and carried a complement of 571. She was sunk by H.M. submarine Truant on April 9, 1940, off Kristiansand, Norway.

Kassala. A well-known Sudanese frontier post, 260 miles S.E. of Khartoum and about 15 miles W. of the Eritrean frontier, Kassala was occupied by the Italians on July 4, 1940, the weakness of the British forces in the Sudan making it impossible to hold the frontier against the enemy. On Jan. 19, 1941, Kassala was recaptured by the British, and the Italians all along this front were in retreat. *See* East Africa.

Katowice. This Polish industrial town was the first to be raided by the Germans. A wave of Hitler's bombers attacked it on Sept. 1, 1939, causing great damage and many casualties among the civilian population. The chief town of the Silesian coalfields, with iron works, foundries, and machine-shops, Katowice passed to Germany in the partition of Poland on Sept. 29, 1939.

Kaunas (Kovno). Capital of the former independent State of Lithuania, Kaunas passed into Russian control in August 1940, when the little country was forcibly incorporated into the Soviet Union. One of Germany's first actions at the beginning of the German-Soviet war was to bomb Kaunas on June 22, 1941. The town proved an easy objective for the Nazi Panzer divisions, since it was near the East Prussian frontier, and it was occupied by the Germans on June 24, 1941, two days after Hitler had attacked the U.S.S.R.

Keitel, FIELD-MARSHAL WILHELM (b. 1882). Supreme Chief of the German High Command from 1938, when he succeeded von Blomberg. It was Keitel who, against the advice of his staff, urged Hitler to attack through Holland and Belgium, and at the weakest point of France's defences. Submarine and air bases in the Low Countries as well as in France were necessary, he maintained, for the success of the long-contemplated attack on Britain by land, sea and air. He signed the French armistice for his country at Compiègne on June 22, 1940. Keitel was much in evidence after the French capitulation. He was said to have been one of Hitler's favourite

Field-Marshal Keitel, German soldier.
Photo, Planet News

WITH THE ITALIANS ON THE SUDANESE FRONTIER

Kassala, a Sudanese frontier post, stands at the foot of the Abyssinian highlands, about 15 miles from the Eritrean border. Soon after Italy entered the war in June 1940 she invaded British territory from her East African colonies, and for about six months Kassala was in enemy hands. The photograph shows an Italian breastwork near the river Gash on which Kassala lies.

Photo, E.N.A.

HOW H.M.S. KELLY CROSSED THE NORTH SEA TO ENGLAND

In May 1940 a Nazi communiqué claimed, with customary exaggeration, that a British destroyer had been torpedoed and sunk off the German coast by an E-boat. Kelly was indeed torpedoed, but she was not sunk. The story of her remarkable 91-hour journey home with decks awash is told in the text. This photograph, taken just after Kelly was hit, shows members of the ship's company on her deck, calmly waiting on events. The gallant destroyer met her end a year later, off Crete.

Photo, Fox

generals, and took part in the Fuehrer's triumphant return to Berlin in mid-June, 1940. In January 1942 Keitel visited Budapest. Following close on the visits of Ribbentrop and Ciano it was thought that the purpose of his journey was to urge more active Hungarian participation in the war with Russia.

Kelly, H.M.S. At the outbreak of war the Kelly, only just completed, was one of the newest and best armed destroyers in the British Navy. She belonged to the Javelin class, her displacement was 1,695 tons, and she carried a complement of 183. In May 1940 the Kelly, commanded by Lord Louis Mountbatten, was leading a destroyer flotilla operating against a German minelaying force off the enemy coast. An escorting aircraft having reported a submarine ahead, the Kelly and a sister ship, the Kandahar, proceeded to hunt her. As twilight fell a torpedo struck the Kelly, blowing a hole in her side and killing men in the foremost boiler room, which was blown open to the sea. The damaged ship was taken in tow by H.M.S. Bulldog, the wounded being transferred next day to the Kandahar. German bombing attacks upon her were carried out repeatedly and beaten off, but eventually, owing to her heavy list and the likelihood of her sinking, it was decided to send everyone out of the ship not required to man the guns. The whole ship's company volunteered to remain, and from these 18 officers and men were chosen.

Attempts at towing had to be abandoned, owing to the heavy seas, and when aircraft reported two enemy submarines in Kelly's direct path, her captain transferred his volunteer party to the Bulldog. Throughout that night Kelly lay abandoned, while escorting destroyers steamed round her in an endless patrol. At dawn the volunteer party returned aboard and, because the electrical system was out of action, worked the guns

by hand whenever hostile aircraft arrived to attack. Eventually, after having been 91 hours on tow or hove-to, the Kelly and her escort arrived safely at a repair yard, which six months later returned her to service.

In May 1941 Kelly, leading the Fifth Destroyer Flotilla, was bombarding enemy-occupied positions in Crete and also preventing the approach of enemy shipping. German dive-bombers dropped hundreds of bombs in the area and finally hit the Kelly with a thousand-pounder. She turned turtle and sank 50 seconds after being hit, but some 3½ hours after the explosion H.M.S. Kipling reached the scene and, despite continued enemy dive-bombing, got survivors safely away.

Kennard, SIR HOWARD, G.C.M.G. (b. 1878). He was British Ambassador to Poland from 1935 until the Polish collapse in September 1939. In March 1941 he was succeeded by Sir Cecil Dormer as ambassador to the Polish Government in London.

Kennedy, JOSEPH PATRICK (b. 1888). He was appointed American Ambassador to Great Britain in January 1938. On Oct. 22, 1940, he went back to the U.S.A., and a week later spoke on the radio on the war situation in Europe. He returned to America, he said, " renewed in the conviction that this country must and will stay out of the war." On Dec. 1 Mr. Roosevelt accepted his resignation.

Kensington Court, S.S. Bound for Birkenhead from the Argentine with a cargo of wheat, this 4,863-ton ship was sunk by a U-boat when nearing the English coast on Sept. 18, 1939. After sending out an S O S her crew of 34 took to the one lifeboat still available. Soon after they had pushed off, a flying-boat arrived on the scene and alighted near by, quickly followed by a second. The officer of the first plane said he could take 20 men aboard, and, having opened a door in the side of his craft, pushed out a

FLYING-BOATS RESCUE A SHIP'S CREW

A most dramatic example of life-saving at sea occurred when the entire crew of the freighter Kensington Court was picked up from their lifeboat by two R.A.F. flying-boats which alighted on the water near by. This photograph was taken from one of the aircraft.

Photo, British Official

small, collapsible rubber boat. In this the crew of the Kensington Court were ferried across two or three at a time, first to one plane and then to the other. A few hours later they were safe in England.

Kent, H.R.H. DUKE OF, PRINCE GEORGE, K.G., G.C.M.G., G.C.V.O. (1902–1942). Fourth son of the late King George V and brother of H.M. King George VI. He was indefatigable in visiting sea and shore establishments and inspecting training schools and coastal defences. He particularly identified himself with the activities of the R.A.F., in which he held a pilot's certificate, and Allied air forces. In July 1941 he flew to Canada to inspect the Empire Air Training Schools and made an arduous tour of every province of the Dominion. He afterwards crossed into the United States, visited the President, and inspected naval facilities and aviation factories. He was killed on Aug. 25, 1942, on active service when his Sunderland flying boat on a flight to Iceland crashed in N. Scotland.

Kerch. The Kerch peninsula, easternmost point of the Crimea, is one of the most important sources of iron ore in Russia. In the German drive for the Crimea and Caucasus in November 1941, Timoshenko's armies held the inner defences of the town of Kerch, which was intended by the Germans to be a jumping-off place for the Caucasus. The Germans claimed to have captured it on Nov. 16, and three days later the Russians admitted having evacuated Kerch,

after destroying industrial equipment, power works, factories and quays. They maintained that during the battle for Kerch the Germans had lost over 20,000 killed. On Dec. 30 it was announced that Soviet troops, landing under cover of the Soviet Black Sea Fleet and the Red Air Force, had crossed the Straits of Kerch, stormed and recaptured that town and Feodosia, and were pursuing the enemy westward. On May 12, 1942, the Germans started a smashing onslaught along the 15-mile front of the Peninsula. The Russians evacuated the town of Kerch on May 17, and by May 24 overwhelming enemy air power had forced them to withdraw, in good order, from the peninsula. *See* Crimea.

Keren. Seventy miles N.W. of Asmara, capital of Eritrea, Keren was strongly defended by the Italians when they withdrew here after their defeat at the hands of the British at Agordat in February 1941. The place, a natural fortress, being situated on top of a plateau rising 6,000 ft. above the plain, was of considerable strategic importance, since it guarded Asmara and the route to the Eritrean coast. The siege of Keren began on Feb. 6. A formidable array of armoured cars, tanks, Bren-gun carriers and convoys of motor lorries were brought to the foot of the plateau. After a month's preparation two columns of Imperial troops began the attack by advancing from the west along both sides of the railway from Agordat. A third column, chiefly Free French, approached from the north-east. On March 15 Imperial troops under the command of Gen. Platt (*q.v.*) fought their way up the sides of peaks commanding Keren and carried them by assault. The R.A.F. and S.A.A.F. kept up a violent bombardment of Italian positions and over 120 tons of bombs were dropped in the Keren area. Furious fighting raged for days among the wild jagged slopes. The enemy put up the most desperate resistance,

H.R.H. Prince George, Duke of Kent.

Photo, British Official

KEREN, ITALIAN STRONGHOLD IN ERITREA

The town of Keren lies at the top of a plateau, surrounded by precipices and rugged peaks, the only normal approach being through a steep gorge. At this key point the Italians made a determined but unavailing stand against Imperial and Free French troops who advanced from three directions. They captured the place after more than six weeks of the most furious fighting among the foothills and jagged slopes.

Photo, E.N.A.

but without avail, and the fall of Keren on March 27 finally sealed the fate of the Italian colony. *See* East Africa.

Kerr, Sir Archibald Clark, k.c.m.g. British Ambassador to Soviet Russia from January 1942, in succession to Sir Stafford Cripps. He was our Ambassador in Baghdad, 1935–1938, and held the same post in China until he went to Russia.

Kestrel, H.M.S. Fleet Air Arm land establishment in Hampshire. Recruits for this branch of the Service are trained in H.M.S. Kestrel, for all the

FLEET AIR ARM MECHANICS AT WORK

One of the land establishments for recruits in the Fleet Air Arm is H.M.S. Kestrel, in Hampshire. Here numbers of naval ratings undergo an intensive course of training, some as riggers and fitters and ordnance artificers.

Photo. Fox

training stations of the Fleet Air Arm, like those for sailors undergoing special courses, are " His Majesty's Ships," though they may actually be islands or even land aerodromes. A Goebbels-inspired broadcast in the autumn of 1939 claimed that the Germans had sunk H.M.S. Kestrel !

Keyes, Admiral Sir Roger, g.c.b., k.c.v.o., d.s.o., m.p. (b. 1872). As Conservative member for South Portsmouth, and famous as the commander of the Zeebrugge raid in 1918 (*see* p. 4702), he made it known during a debate in the House of Commons in May 1940 that he had offered to lead a naval raid on the Germans at Trondheim in Norway. His intervention in the debate was largely responsible for the fall of the Chamberlain administration. Shortly afterwards he was made British liaison officer to King Leopold of the Belgians, and it was largely through his advocacy that the King was in some measure rehabilitated in popular

esteem after the surrender of Belgium. From July 17, 1940, until Oct. 19, 1941, Sir Roger was responsible for the organization of the Commandos (*q.v.*). When it became known that he had resigned, the matter was raised in the House of Commons on Nov. 25. The Admiral complained that he had been frustrated " in every worthwhile offensive action I have tried to undertake as Director of Combined Operations." Sir Roger Keyes' son, Lt.-Col. Geoffrey Keyes, was reported on Jan. 1, 1942,

Adm. Sir Roger Keyes, organized the Commandos.

to have lost his life while leading a Commando raid on Gen. Rommel's headquarters on Nov. 17, 1941. *See* Commando.

Kharkov. The German thrust in the Ukraine developed fiercely towards the end of October 1941, and on Oct. 25 the invaders claimed to have captured this important centre. Later, the Russians announced that they had evacuated the city, and that the principal factories and plants, railway rolling stock, raw material stores and other valuables had been removed. It was stated that the Germans had lost nearly 120,000 killed and wounded, over 450 tanks and armoured cars, nearly 3,000 lorries with supplies, and over 200 guns, in the fighting for Kharkov.

On May 13, 1942, the Russians, under Marshal Timoshenko, launched a full-scale drive on Kharkov, taking the enemy by surprise, and thereby forestalling Hitler's summer offensive in the Ukraine. The Soviet forces, in spite of torrential rain, quickly broke through the Nazis' winter defence lines, and threatened the city from north and south. Within a few days, after winning one of the biggest tank battles in history, they reached the second line of the enemy defences. The Germans

DEVASTATION IN KHARKOV

This great industrial city of the Ukraine was twice wrecked, first by dive-bombing Nazi 'planes before its capture, and then by the Russians themselves, who carried away all machinery from the factories and burnt the buildings.

Photo, Associated Press

made a number of fierce counter-attacks, but could not stem the Russian advance. They retreated, leaving behind them large quantities of war material. By May 20 advanced Soviet units were within fifteen miles of the centre of the city. By June 1 the Russians were consolidating on recaptured ground and it was clear that, despite fantastic German claims, Timoshenko had both frustrated a planned German offensive on Kharkov and defeated heavy counter-attacks on the huge Russian salient south of Kharkov. Losses on both sides were heavy. The drive to the Caucasus had not begun and the stalemate was in effect a German defeat.

Kianta, LAKE. Scene of a Finnish victory on Dec. 21–30, 1939, when the Soviet troops were advancing against Suomussalmi, a town on Lake Kianta. When the Russians reached the westernmost of the two northern arms of the lake fifteen thousand were trapped. After ten days, during which the Russian power of resistance was enormously reduced by the intense cold, the Finns attacked. They claimed that the 163rd Russian Division of 18,000 men had been virtually destroyed. Twenty-seven guns, 11 tanks, 650 vehicles, besides much ammunition, were reported captured. The Finns also suffered heavy casualties. *See* Finland ; Suomussalmi.

Kiel. Important German naval base, particularly for U-boats, at the Baltic end of the Kiel Canal. The devastation caused by R.A.F. raids on the harbour and shipyards was considerable. The heaviest attacks were made on the nights of April 7–8 and 8–9, 1941, when enormous numbers of incendiaries, as well as

many tons of high-explosive bombs, were dropped in the area. These bombs included some of a new heavy type, and the damage was unprecedented. It was after these April raids that complaints were made in Germany about the inadequacy of their A.R.P. and fire-fighting services. In June 1941 the R.A.F. again battered Kiel, then being used for vessels operating against the Russians in the Baltic. Up to Feb. 1, 1942, Kiel and the Canal area had been raided 61 times. After the return of the German warships Gneisenau and Scharnhorst, in February 1942, following their dramatic escape from the French naval base of Brest, the docks at Kiel were again heavily raided by the R.A.F. on many occasions. On the night of April 28 there was a particularly heavy attack by our bombers against this strongly defended base, where it was believed that the Scharnhorst was sheltering in dock. Large fires were left burning, and although no definite damage to the German warships was reported, the raid was considered a successful one.

Kiel Canal. This vital waterway (*see* p. 2381), was first attacked by British aircraft on Sept. 4, 1939, the day after the declaration of war, when ships of the German Fleet were bombed at Brunsbüttel, at the west entrance to the canal. During the rest of that year many air fights occurred between German and British planes in the Kiel Canal area, and throughout 1940 and 1941 the whole of this important district became a target for British bombers.

Kiev. This great industrial centre (*see* p. 2382), capital of the Ukraine, was bombed by the Germans from the outbreak of the Russo-German war, June 22,

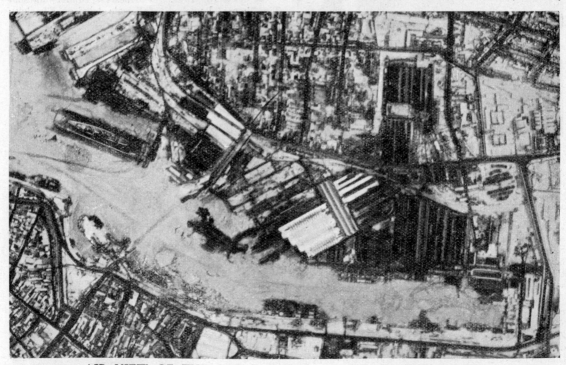

AIR VIEW OF THE GREAT DOCKS AT KIEL IN THE BALTIC

Kiel is one of Germany's most important naval bases. Besides the docks, which cover many acres, there are great ship-building yards, such as the Deutsche Werke and the Germania shipyard. On the left in this photograph can be seen the battle cruiser Gneisenau, which escaped from Brest, crept along the Channel and reached Kiel on the night of Feb. 21, 1942. On May 3 it was stated that she had been located by the R.A.F at Gdynia. The Scharnhorst was then at Kiel.

Photo. British Official

NAZI CONQUERORS ENTER KIEV

By a vast encircling movement the Germans obtained possession of the capital of the Ukraine. Here troops are seen passing through the gateway of the historic citadel.

Photo, Keystone

1941. The battle for the city began by what the Germans described as a " great encircling movement " about 125 miles east of Kiev on Sept. 13. Employing vast numbers of troops, aided by a host of tanks and armoured cars and supported by dive-bombers, the Germans surrounded Kiev with a ring of fire and iron. The offensive for the city, which had temporarily halted while Von Runstedt's and Von Bock's armies joined hands, was resumed on Sept. 17. German divisions moving up the east bank of the Dnieper attacked from the north, while others advanced up the western bank from the south. On the night of Sept. 18 enemy infantry swam across a little river to the south of Kiev and stormed the concrete casemates defending the inner city, and two days later the Germans announced that they had captured the city.

Kindersley, ROBERT (MOLESWORTH), 1ST BARON, G.B.E. (b. 1871). He was President of the National Savings Committee during the last war, and resumed that office after the outbreak of the present conflict, leading Britain's War Savings Campaign. *See* National Savings Campaign.

King, ADM. ERNEST J. (b. 1878). On Dec. 21, 1941, he was appointed C.-in-C. of the U.S. Navy, and supreme commander of all naval forces operating in Atlantic, Pacific and Asiatic waters. His former position as Commander of the Atlantic Fleet was assigned to Rear-Adm. Ingersoll. Adm. King saw service with the Air Corps and also served with submarines. He attended the Churchill-Roosevelt Atlantic Conference in August 1941.

King, RT. HON. WILLIAM LYON MACKENZIE, P.C., C.M.G. (b. 1874). Prime Minister of Canada from 1935. In April 1940 he went to Washington and held informal conversations with President Roosevelt, Mr. Cordell Hull and Lord Lothian, and on August 17 he again met the American President at Ogdensburg near the Canadian-U.S. border. Shortly after this latter meeting it was announced that a Permanent Joint Defence Board would

Mackenzie King,
Canadian Premier.
Photo, Topical Press

be set up by Canada and the U.S.A. for the immediate study of sea, land, and air problems relating to the defence of the northern half of the Western Hemisphere. Mr. Mackenzie King arrived in England on August 20, 1941, for discussions with the Government. In December he was again in Washington, taking part in the discussions of the Anglo-American War Council. He travelled back to Canada with the British Prime Minister, and was present when the latter gave his famous broadcast at Ottawa on Dec. 30. On May 11, 1942, Mr. Mackenzie King introduced the Conscription Bill, shortly after a plebiscite on this issue had been taken. The affirmative vote released him from his former anti-conscription pledge. *See* Canada.

King George V, H.M.S. Launched on Feb. 21, 1939, this powerful battleship was one of five ships of her class, displacing 35,000 tons and having a speed of over 30 knots. Her armament consisted of a main battery of ten 14-in. guns mounted in two quadruple turrets and one double turret. Designed to meet intensive air attack, the King George V cost about £8,000,000 and carried a complement of 1,500. Lord Halifax sailed in her in January 1941, when he went to America to take up his duties as British Ambassador. In May 1941 she was in the Atlantic and took part in the hunt for the German raider Bismarck (*q.v.*), and in company with H.M.S. Rodney engaged the already damaged enemy ship.

Kirke, GEN. SIR WALTER MERVYN ST. GEORGE, G.C.B. (b. 1877). He was C.-in-C. of the Home Forces from 1939 to 1940, when he retired. From 1936 to 1939 he was Director-General of the Territorial Army.

Admiral E. J. King,
U.S. Naval C.-in-C.
Photo, Sport & General

Kirkuk. Important oil wells lie around this town of Iraq, situated about 90 miles S.E. of Mosul. Pipelines run from here to Haifa and to Tripolis. The Kirkuk oilfields attracted covetous glances from Germany, and British troops guarded them in April 1941. On May 3, during the Iraq revolt, the pipe-line to Haifa was reported to have been cut by the rebels, but by May 20 this revolt was collapsing as the result of firm British action.

Kishinev. The capital of Bessarabia, Kishinev was occupied by the Russians on June 28, 1940, having been ceded by Rumania. On July 17, 1941, after their invasion of Russia, the Germans took the town, and the Russians had withdrawn from Bessarabia by July 21. The Germans reported on July 22 that every building in the place was found to be destroyed, each house having been systematically dynamited and then set on fire.

Kismayu. British troops and Abyssinian Patriot forces rapidly advanced against the Italians in Italian Somaliland after the capture of Afmadu (*q.v.*), and on Feb. 14, 1941, the King's African Rifles marched into Kismayu and hoisted the Union Jack in the main square. The Italian garrison, two battalions with some artillery, had evacuated the place two days before, after having destroyed everything that might have been of military value, but five Italian ships were captured in the harbour. *See* East Africa.

Kleffens, DR. E. N. VAN. He was Dutch Foreign Minister at the time of the German invasion of the Netherlands in May 1940. On May 11 he arrived in England, and on May 15 gave graphic details of how Holland's entire bombing force of about 50 machines had been lost in the fighting. He prepared the official statement "The Rape of the Netherlands" covering the German conquest.

Kleist, GEN. VON. He commanded the German forces when the latter occupied Belgrade on April 13, 1941. During the German-Soviet war he was appointed, under Marshal von Runstedt, to command German armoured forces on the Southern Front, and in December 1941 suffered a humiliating setback at the hands of the advancing Russian troops, after having pushed his forces as far east as Rostov-on-Don. *See* Russia.

Gen. von Kleist, German soldier.
Photo, Associated Press

Klisura. A strongly fortified key-point in central Albania, the town was evacuated by the Italians and its capture announced by Athens on Jan. 10, 1941, during the Italo-Greek war. By that date the steady advance of the Greek forces had been greatly accelerated and Italian losses were particularly heavy in this sector of the front. Klisura had been the Greeks' objective for many weeks; since, indeed, the fall of Argyrokastro early in December 1940. It lies in a defile surrounded by steep cliffs, and everything possible had been done by the Italians to make the place impregnable. From here the enemy retreated towards Tepelini (*q.v.*). After April 6, 1941, when the Germans marched into Yugoslavia and subsequently thrust into Greece, the Greek forces were compelled to withdraw from all Albanian towns. *See* Albania; Greece.

Sir Hughe Knatchbull-Hugessen, British Ambassador to Turkey.
Photo, Wide World

Knatchbull - Hugessen, SIR HUGHE MONTGOMERY, K.C.M.G. (b. 1886). British Ambassador to Turkey from Jan. 11, 1939, succeeding Sir William Seeds. He had been British Ambassador in China from 1936 to 1938, and

was attacked in 1937 by a Japanese aeroplane.

Knightsbridge. A track centre 12 m. S. of Acroma, Libya. Here Rommel overran the British 150th Brigade, June 3, 1942. Furious tank battles ended in a British withdrawal after serious losses on June 15, Rommel then being free to assault Tobruk. *See* North Africa.

Knox, COL. FRANK (b. 1874). Secretary of the U.S. Navy from June 1940, Knox had always advocated a large U.S. navy and, following the outbreak of war in 1939, he maintained that America should help the Allies in every way save that of dispatching an expeditionary force. On Oct. 1, 1941, he declared that the "Totalitarian forces must be defeated." He provided for great increases in the American fleet.

Col. Frank Knox, U.S. Sec. of Navy.
Photo, Wide World

Mrs. Jean Knox, Head of A.T.S.
Photo, Fox

Knox, JEAN (b. 1908). Chief Controller of the A.T.S. from July 8, 1941, in succession to Dame Helen Gwynne - Vaughan. She joined the Service before the outbreak of war and was appointed Inspector of the A.T.S. in March 1941, her work then consisting of touring the country to investigate the personal side of A.T.S. life. *See* Woman's Services.

Koeln. This German cruiser gave her name to a class which included her two sister ships Karlsruhe and Königsberg. The Koeln was completed in 1930 and had a displacement of 6,000 tons, carrying a complement of 571. When H.M. submarine Ursula sank a German cruiser in the Heligoland Bight on Dec. 14, 1939, it was announced that the victim was either the

THE GERMAN CRUISER KOELN

Thought at first to have been the victim of a torpedo from H.M. submarine Ursula in December 1939, the Koeln was later proved to have been sunk following a bombing attack by the R.A.F. in April 1940.
Photo, Central Press

Koeln or one of her sister ships. This report as regards the cruiser herself proved incorrect, for on April 9, 1940 (the date of the German invasion of Norway), the R.A.F. attacked German warships in Bergen harbour and bombed the Koeln. She was hit amidships and sank ten minutes after the explosion.

Koivisto. Fortified island and mainland town in the Gulf of Finland, south of Viipuri. Here, in March 1940, Finland suffered her first real reverse at the hands of the Russians. After three months of warfare the guns of the island forts at Koivisto were silenced, having either been blown up or carried away by the survivors of the garrison to fresh positions on the mainland. From captured Koivisto the Russians were able to deliver a flanking fire on the Finnish defences between the Gulf of Finland and Lake Muolaa, and this hastened the Finnish retreat on the Karelian Isthmus. At the conclusion of the war in March 1940 Russia stipulated that Finland should cede the whole of the Karelian Isthmus " to ensure the safety of Leningrad." This demand included the island of Koivisto and the town. *See* Finland.

Prince Konoye, Japanese Premier.
Photo, Wide World

Konoye, PRINCE FUMIMARO (b. 1891). He became Prime Minister of Japan for the second time on July 17, 1940, succeeding Admiral Yonai, and under his administration Japan subsequently exacted military concessions in Indo-China, under threat of invasion. Konoye furthered Axis collaboration, fostering the Fascist point of view. In August 1940 a large number of the Government's liberal representatives abroad were recalled home. In October 1941 it was announced that owing to internal differences of opinion on national policy the Konoye Cabinet would resign. On Oct. 16 the Premier's resignation was made public after several days' conferences, during which the Emperor received in audience both Prince Konoye and Lieut.-Gen. Tojo. On Oct. 17 Gen. Tojo was entrusted with the formation of a new Cabinet, himself becoming Prime Minister. *See* Japan.

Koo, DR. VI KYUIN WELLINGTON (b. 1887). Formerly Chinese Ambassador to France, Dr. Wellington Koo (*see* p. 4705) after the collapse of France continued as Ambassador to the Vichy Government. On April 24, 1941, he was appointed Ambassador to Britain in succession to Mr. Quo Tai-chi.

Dr. Wellington Koo, Chinese Ambassador.
Photo, Sport & General

Koritza (KORCHA). One of the chief Italian bases in Albania at the beginning of the Italo-Greek war. On Nov. 1, 1940, the Greeks crossed the Albanian frontier and drove towards Koritza. Strategically of great importance, the heights dominating the town were captured by the Greeks at the point of the bayonet, and over 1,000 prisoners were taken. The town itself was captured on Nov. 22. Koritza was an Italian stronghold, and after the place had been abandoned the Greek soldiers found great quantities of guns, ammunition, and other stores which the Italians had left behind them in their flight. This was one of the most important Greek victories of the campaign, and Koritza was held until the German invasion in April 1941, when all the Greek positions in Albania had to be abandoned. *See* Albania.

Koryzis, ALEXANDER. Formerly Governor of the Bank of Greece and Minister of Social Welfare, he succeeded Gen. Metaxas as Prime Minister on Jan. 29, 1941. On taking office he declared that the government would resolutely pursue the policy laid down by Gen. Metaxas. Koryzis survived his predecessor by only three months, dying suddenly in Athens on April 18. Mr. Tsouderos, Foreign Minister, then took over the Premiership. *See* Greece.

Kota Bahru. Capital of Kelantan, one of the Unfederated Malay States, Kota Bahru lies near the mouth of the Kelantan River, the port being Tumpat. The latter is the terminus of the east coast railway and the only port on this coast of Malaya. Shallow cargo boats are able to navigate the Kelantan River for 60 miles. Japanese forces landed in this area on Dec. 7, 1941, and attempted to capture the aerodrome. The enemy landings were made north of Kota Bahru and consisted of five transports escorted by warships. The Japanese were at once engaged by British forces and severe fighting developed, Indian troops distinguishing themselves in the defence of the aerodrome. Heavy

ALBANIAN TOWN OF MANY VICISSITUDES

Koritza, whose misfortune it was to be strategically important, was first occupied by the Italians in 1939. It was captured from them by the Greeks in November 1940, and finally overrun by the Germans in April 1941.
Photo, G.P.U.

KRONSTADT, RUSSIA'S GREAT NAVAL BASE

Situated on an island at the head of the Gulf of Finland, Kronstadt has played a very important part in the defence of Leningrad. In the foreground of this photograph is the breakwater south of the harbour, which is generally ice-bound for five months of the year.

Photo, E.N.A.

Japanese pressure led to a reorganization of the British line on Dec. 10 south of Kota Bahru and heavy fighting continued in the Kelantan area. The Japanese gained possession of the airfield, which had been rendered unserviceable. On Dec. 22 it was announced that the British lines had been withdrawn from the Kelantan area to Kuala Krai, 45 miles southward. *See* Malaya.

Kowloon. Mainland suburb of Hongkong, Kowloon was dive-bombed and machine-gunned by Japanese planes on Dec. 8, 1941. On Dec. 15 it was announced that British troops were being withdrawn from Kowloon to Hongkong, and subsequently that Chinese troops on the mainland were keeping up pressure in the rear of the enemy some 30 to 40 miles from Kowloon. By Dec. 19 Japanese guns had been mounted at Kowloon, facing Hongkong, and these, together with dive-bombers, carried out non-stop attacks on the Hongkong garrison strong points. *See* Hongkong.

Kristiansand. The Germans landed at this Norwegian port on the Skagerrak, 150 miles S.W. of Oslo, on April 9, 1940, the first day of their invasion of the country. The place put up a determined resistance to the invaders, who attacked from both sea and air. It was here that the German cruiser Karlsruhe (*q.v.*) was sunk by the British submarine Truant. The large airport was captured by the enemy and subsequently used as a base. *See* Norway.

Kronstadt. This important seaport and naval base of Russia was bombed by the Finns on Jan. 22, 1940, during the Russo-Finnish war. Thirty-one miles W. of Leningrad and connected with that city by a canal, Kronstadt contained the State dockyard and was the base of the Russian Baltic Fleet. When the Germans sought to invest Leningrad during October and November 1941 Kronstadt played a prominent part in the fierce Russian defence, being used by the Soviet forces as a key point from which they raided the Finnish coast and interrupted supply traffic on the roads along the Gulf of Finland, thus striking in the rear of both Germans and Finns. Great stores of ammunition and food were accumulated by the Russians in the fortress of Kronstadt in the eventuality of a long siege. East of the fortress were constructed seven artificial islands built on concrete granite, all powerfully armed and stretching north towards the Finnish coast. *See* Finland.

Kuala Lumpur. Capital of the Federated Malay States, Kuala Lumpur was bombed by the Japanese on Dec. 27, 1941. Damage was done to Government offices, and among other buildings hit was the Mosque, one of the chief in Malaya. Three of the worshippers were killed during the raid, and this profoundly shocked the Indian Moslem community in Kuala Lumpur. By Jan. 9, 1942, Kuala Lumpur was stated to have been cleared for action. A strict curfew was imposed on the population and everything of value was withdrawn from the town. Two days later the Imperial forces were compelled to withdraw to the south, and the Japanese marched in. *See* Malaya.

Kuantan. Capital of the province of Kuantan on the east coast of the Malay Peninsula, Kuantan, about 200 miles N. of Singapore, was the scene of Japanese landings on Dec. 10, 1941. The enemy force disembarked just north of Kuantan and were engaged by the British. It was off Kuantan that the British warships Prince of Wales and Repulse (*q.v.*) were sunk on Dec. 10, 1941. By that date a small Japanese force had secured a foothold, and on Jan. 7, 1942, it was announced that the Japanese had captured the aerodrome. *See* Malaya.

Kuhmo. The Finns launched a vigorous offensive against the Russians north of Kuhmo in Central Finland on Jan. 30, 1940, and in a series of battles the Russians were reported to have lost 1,500 men. Victory lay with the Finnish forces, and on February 18 it was announced that the Russians had sustained further heavy losses, their 18th Division having ceased to exist. *See* Finland.

Kuibishev. On the R. Volga, 540 miles E. of Moscow, Kuibishev (ancient name Samara) became Russia's wartime capital when part of the Central Administration withdrew here from Moscow in October 1941.

SEAT OF RUSSIAN GOVERNMENT

Kuibishev, which became the wartime capital of the U.S.S.R., is an important industrial centre. The Government withdrew here as a precautionary measure in the autumn of 1941.

Photo, Planet News

Kurmuk. This Abyssinian-Sudanese frontier post was captured by the Italians on July 7, 1940, when the small garrison of Sudanese police withdrew after inflicting 50 casualties on the enemy. Kurmuk was recaptured by British forces on Feb. 14, 1941. *See* East Africa.

Kurusu, SABURO. On Nov. 5, 1941, it was announced in Tokyo that the Japanese Government had decided to send Kurusu, former Ambassador to Berlin, to Washington to aid Adm. Nomura, the Japanese Ambassador to the U.S.A., in his talks with the U.S. Government on the tense political situation. Kurusu arrived at San Francisco on November 14 by Clipper from Manila. The U.S. State Dept. emphasized that his mission had not been suggested by the U.S. Government, and that the latter had merely placed facilities for the journey at his disposal. While the two envoys were still conferring with Mr. Cordell Hull, news reached Washington of the Japanese attacks, without warning, on the U.S. base at Pearl Harbour and on bases in the Philippines. Kurusu was immediately handed his passport.

Kuusinen, OTTO. When Soviet troops marched into Finland on Nov. 30, 1939, the Finnish Government, led by Prof. Cajander, resigned. The next day Dr. Risto Ryti, till then Governor of the Bank of Finland, formed a new Government of National Union. The Russians, however, refused to recognize its existence, and set up a puppet creation of their own at Terijoki, just within the Karelian frontier, putting at its head Otto Kuusinen, a Finnish revolutionary leader of the civil war of 1918. This so-called Government accepted a treaty with the Soviet Union in which Russian demands were granted, but it was entirely ineffectual in all its activities. *See* Finland.

L **Laake,** MAJ.-GEN. K. (b. 1875). He was C.-in-C. of the Norwegian Army from 1931 to 1940. When the Germans invaded his country on April 9, 1940, he was made responsible for Norway's campaign against the Nazi forces, being appointed Commandant-Gen. of the Norwegian Army.

Ladoga, LAKE. The largest lake in Europe, situated in both Russia and Finland, a few miles north of Leningrad, Lake Ladoga was the centre of fierce fighting between the Finns and Russians during the war of 1939–40. By the terms of the Peace Treaty, March 12, 1940, the Finns were forced to cede to Russia the territory north and west of Lake Ladoga, including the towns of Sortavala and Suojärvi, a condition which had not been presented by the U.S.S.R. in the pre-war negotiations. The Finnish armies had made a very successful resistance and had scored many victories in this area, particularly at Sortavala and Kitelae, but the whole of it passed to the U.S.S.R. After Germany invaded Russia on June 22, 1941, there was again heavy fighting around Lake Ladoga. Finnish troops under Mannerheim advanced along the northern shore and captured Salmi on July 27 in an attempt, coinciding with the German push from the south, to encircle Leningrad. In August there were fierce engagements for the possession of Kexholm on the western shore. On Nov. 10 the Germans claimed the capture of Tikhvin, south of Lake Ladoga, but its recapture was announced by Russia on Dec. 8.

Lady Shirley, H.M.S. This minesweeper, formerly a Hull fishing trawler, commanded by Lieut.-Comdr. A. H. Callaway, in a gallant action sank a German submarine—the U. 111 — by shellfire near Gibraltar on Oct. 4, 1941, capturing 45 of the crew. Her commander won the D.S.O. On Jan. 17, 1942, it was announced that the Lady Shirley was overdue and presumed lost.

Lampson, SIR MILES WEDDERBURN, G.C.M.G. (b. 1880). British Ambassador and High Commissioner for the Sudan from 1936. *See* p. 4708.

Lancastria, S.S. This Cunard liner of 16,243 tons, one of the most famous cruising ships, became a troopship after the outbreak of war. On June 17, 1940, while lying at anchor in St. Nazaire harbour, she was sunk by a salvo of bombs dropped by a formation of Junkers 87 dive-bombers. When she met her end the Lancastria had completed the embarkation of a large number of B.E.F. personnel and of the R.A.F. from France. There were some 5,000 people on board.

TRAGIC END OF THE TROOPSHIP LANCASTRIA AT ST. NAZAIRE

Few sea disasters can surpass in human suffering the sinking of the Lancastria by enemy bombers. A survivor said that soon after she was struck the ship gave a terrific lurch and men were thrown into the sea, where they struggled to swim in the thick oily water until they could hold out no longer, or were killed by the machine-guns of the continually swooping Nazi 'planes In this photograph scores of men can be seen in the water.

Photo, Associated Press

including French refugees. Of these more than 2,000 British were lost, while about 2,477 were known to have been rescued. The Navy picked up many survivors.

Langsdorf, CAPT. HANS. He commanded the German battleship Admiral Graf Spee (*q.v.*) and, by Hitler's order, scuttled his ship outside Montevideo on Dec. 17, 1939. On the evening of Dec. 19 he spent three hours in consultation with his staff officers. He then wrote his last letters and dispatches, and gave away his more valuable personal effects. The following morning he was found shot.

La Pallice. Situated close to La Rochelle in the Bay of Biscay, this French base, taken over by the Germans after the collapse of France in June 1940, was repeatedly bombed by the R.A.F. Shipping, docks and oil stores were among the many targets hit. One of the most successful operations took place on July 23 and 24, 1941, when the German battle cruiser Scharnhorst (*q.v.*), which had been discovered at La Pallice by a reconnaissance aircraft of the Coastal Command, was attacked by Stirling and other bombers and damaged. She later returned to Brest.

Larissa. On March 1, 1941, this Greek town, south of Mt. Olympus, was devastated by an earthquake, most of the public buildings and private houses suffering either complete or partial destruction. Immediate help was forthcoming from detachments of the R.A.F. then in the area. The number of casualties were, however, twice increased by Italian raiders, which dropped bombs on the stricken town. On the occasion of the second raid the enemy bombers were intercepted by fighters, and four were brought down near Larissa. The fifth machine made a forced landing, and the crew were captured. On April 21, 1941, British forces with their Greek allies took up new positions south of Larissa, the town itself having been evacuated. Fierce fighting took place in the streets between Australian troops retreating from Mt. Olympus and Germans who had meanwhile occupied the town.

Larminat, GEN. DE. High Commissioner of French Equatorial Africa. He joined the Free French movement during the summer of 1940, and became a member of the Council of Defence set up by Gen. de Gaulle in Britain. On August 29, 1940, it was announced that he would be Governor-Gen. of French Equatorial Africa, which post he filled until November 9, when he was succeeded by M. Eboué, former Governor of Chad. Gen. de Larminat was second-in-command, under Gen. Catroux (*q.v.*), of the Free French forces in Syria and the Lebanon in June 1941.

Latvia. For the physical features and other details of this country the reader is referred to pages 2445–46. Its political misfortunes in this war are dealt with under the heading Baltic States (*q.v.*).

Laurentic, H.M.S. Before she was taken over by the Navy and commissioned as an armed merchant cruiser, the Laurentic belonged to the Cunard White Star Line. She was built in 1927 and displaced 18,724 tons. On Nov. 4, 1940, it was reported that she had been sunk by a U-boat.

Laval, PIERRE (b. 1883). A former Premier and Foreign Minister of France, Laval, who had suffered a political eclipse, climbed to power again after the defeat of his country. During the critical phase of early June 1940, when the French armies were being rapidly pressed back and the Germans were advancing on Paris, it was Laval who took up a thoroughly defeatist

attitude and succeeded in preventing President Lebrun and his Ministers from transferring the seat of Government to North Africa. On June 23 he was appointed Vice-Premier and Minister of State, and on July 22 took over the French censorship department.

Pierre Laval,
French politician.
Photo, Associated Press

By a Constitutional Act signed on Sept. 25, Marshal Pétain designated Laval as his successor as Chief of State, should circumstances arise making the change n e c e s s a r y, and on Oct. 28 made him Foreign Minister in place of Baudouin. All this time Laval was hurrying to and fro between Vichy and Paris, to c o n f e r w i t h Goering, Ribbentrop and even Hitler (on Oct. 21), on what were termed the principles of Franco-German collaboration. Always anti-British, by this time Laval had become in the highest degree pro-Nazi. But he overstepped the line and Pétain was suddenly made aware of his treachery. On Dec. 14, without previous warning, the Marshal broadcast to the French nation that Laval was no longer a member of the Government, that the portfolio of Foreign Affairs had been taken over by Flandin and that the Constitutional Act which nominated Laval as his own successor had been cancelled. "It is for high reasons of internal policy that I have taken this decision," added the Marshal, and gave no further explanation. Thereupon rose a storm of protest and vilification of the Vichy Government by the German-controlled Parisian press and radio, which became particularly violent after a meeting between Pétain and Laval on Jan. 18, 1941, at La Ferté, when a reconciliation was said to have taken place, but which was not followed by any change in the Government or its policy. So great was German indignation that Hitler himself intervened, the apparent result being that on Feb. 8 Pétain invited Laval to enter the Cabinet as Minister of State and a member of the Directing Committee. But Laval, who aspired to be head of the Government with powers which would make the Chief of State no more than a figurehead, declined the offer.

On Aug. 27, 1941, during a ceremony at Versailles of presenting colours to members of the Fascist Legion proceeding to the Eastern front, Laval and his colleague, Marcel Déat (*q.v.*), were shot at by a young Frenchman, Paul Colette. Both were seriously wounded, but were later stated to be recovering. Thereafter it seemed that the Nazis had to a considerable extent lost faith in Laval as an effective collaborator, although it was understood that he remained in close touch with Nazi authorities in Paris.

On April 14, 1942, Berlin and Vichy announced that Laval would return to office as "Chief of the Government with special powers," and that Pétain had decided to "reconstruct the Cabinet on a new basis." At the same time Laval declared that his policy aimed at establishing friendly relations with Germany and the U.S.A. His appointment led to disturbances in Paris and elsewhere. *See* Vichy Government.

Layton, VICE-ADM. SIR GEOFFREY, K.C.B., D.S.O., R.N. (b. 1884). From 1939 to 1940 he was Vice-Adm. commanding 1st Battle Squadron and Second-in-Command, Home Fleet. In July 1941 he was appointed C.-in-C. China Squadron, and on Dec. 11 he succeeded Adm. Sir Tom Phillips as C.-in-C. of the Eastern Fleet, the latter having gone down with his flagship, H.M.S. Prince of Wales (*q.v.*). Early in January 1942 he left Singapore " to reorganize the Eastern Fleets," and in March his appointment as C.-in-C. Ceylon was announced.

L.D.V. *See* Home Guard.

Leahy, ADM. WILLIAM D. (b. 1875). American Ambassador to the Vichy Govt. from January 1941, in succession to Mr. William Bullitt. Admiral Leahy was formerly U.S. Chief of Naval Operations and Governor of Porto Rico. Details of his activities at Vichy were not disclosed, but it was clear that by representing the attitude of the U.S.A. in such matters as Franco-German collaboration, the Far East, contraband, imports of food-stuffs, and so forth, he did much to maintain a balance between Vichy and Germany. He was in constant touch with Darlan as well as Pétain, expressing the interest of the U.S.A. in all important aspects of the world war, and remained at Vichy after the outbreak of war between Germany and America. He was recalled after Laval was reinstated in 1942.

Admiral Leahy, American Ambassador to Vichy.
Photo, Wide World

Leander, H.M.S. A British cruiser of 7,270 tons, the Leander was completed in March 1933 and was a sister ship of the Ajax and Achilles of River Plate fame. Her main armament consisted of eight 6-in. guns, eight 4-in. A.A. guns and one aircraft. It was announced on March 9, 1941, that she had sunk the Italian armed merchant cruiser, Ramb I, in the Indian Ocean.

Learoyd, FL.-LIEUT. R. A., V.C. The first bombing of the Dortmund-Ems Canal (*q.v.*) was announced on July 17, 1940, and Flight-Lieut. Learoyd was engaged in these operations. On the night of August 12 he was detailed to attack a special objective on this canal. He made his attack at 150 ft., his aircraft being repeatedly hit. He subsequently brought his 'plane home and was awarded a V.C. for his courageous exploit.

Fl.-Lieut. Learoyd, awarded the V.C.
Photo, L.N.A.

Leary, VICE-ADMIRAL HERBERT F. On Feb. 8, 1942, he was appointed to a new, but short-lived, naval command comprising the combined naval forces in the Australian-New Zealand area, and known as the Anzac Forces.

Lease-and-Lend Act. The Lease-and-Lend Act, which became American law on March 11, 1941, was rendered to some extent supererogatory by the entry of the United States into the war. It was a legislative device to make possible unneutral acts by a neutral State in aid of a friendly belligerent. Lease-Lend arrangements were continued in a modified form after the U.S.A. entered the war, but the original Act had a real historical interest.

On Nov. 4, 1939, a Neutrality Act became law in America, under which, so soon as the President declared a foreign State to be at war, no American arms, ammunition or other war materials might be supplied to it save upon the basis of " cash-and-carry." Further, the Act forbade the United States merchant marine to

ply between her own and belligerent ports, and also the arming of such ships. Britain, therefore, as a buyer of vast quantities of war materials from America, had to pay cash for them and contrive delivery. This method was pursued until Britain had spent four billion dollars (in cash) for American war material.

Two facts then became clear on both sides of the Atlantic. First, Britain's capacity to continue cash payments was beyond her financial power ; secondly, that her own merchant marine was inadequate to cope with the tremendous demands made upon it by arms deliveries while still bringing to Britain essential foods.

The Lease-and-Lend Bill was successful in meeting and overcoming this difficulty. It was passed despite fierce opposition from the Isolationists, sentiment in its favour crystallizing in a remarkable way at the moment of success. It was approved by the House of Representatives in March by 260 votes for and 165 against. Fourteen days later the Appropriation Bill, implementing it, had a six to one majority.

The chief provisions were as follows : The President to be empowered to have made in American factories

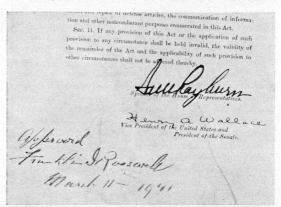

SIGNING THE LEASE-AND-LEND BILL
President Roosevelt's signature, seen on the left in the reproduction above, made the Lease-and-Lend Bill law. By its means America, while still neutral, was able to give complete financial and material aid to Britain.
Photos, Wide World

or shipyards any defence material needed by a country whose defence he deemed vital for the defence of the United States. Such material to be handed over by lending, exchanging, transferring, selling or leasing. Tests, inspections and repair work to be undertaken on behalf of friendly foreign Governments at war; and such assisted Governments to have access to plans and blue-prints and other relevant information when in the interest of the United States.

The first financial allotment under the new Act was $7,000,000,000 on March 27, 1941. In August a further $6,000,000,000 followed.

So far, so good. Britain could get title to this abundant supply of war materials from America, but could she ship them without American aid ?

The answer being No, the repeal of those provisions of the Neutrality Act of 1939 touching transport to, and use of, sea lanes and ports in the zone of war operations was required. This the President successfully accomplished by a Repealing Act which became law Nov. 13, 1941.

At that date, then, the position was complete aid, bar actual naval and military intervention.

The entry of Russia into the war brought the extension of the Lease-and-Lend Act to that country, $1,250,000,000 being allocated for Russian aid. On Dec. 8, 1941, the U.S.A. herself became a belligerent.

On Feb. 24, 1942, a White Paper, issued in London, announced a new and far-reaching Lease-Lend Agreement between Britain and the U.S.A. The new Agreement reaffirmed the intention of both countries to continue to supply defence articles, services and information for each other's defence.

On the long view (rational action for the abolition of war) even more important was the extension of the cooperative efforts to general world economic problems by providing for conversations to examine the best means of solving world economic problems (now generally accepted as the major cause of wars). Both Governments " declare that they are engaged in a cooperative undertaking, together with every other nation of like mind, to the end of laying the bases of a just and enduring peace security order under law to themselves and all nations."

By the end of January 1942 Lease-Lend aid had totalled more than £500,000,000. *See* Harriman, W. A.

Lord Leathers,
Minister of Transport.
Photo, Barratt's

Leathers, FREDERICK JAMES, 1ST BARON. On May 2, 1941, it was announced that he had been appointed Minister of Shipping and Minister of Transport, the combined Ministry to be known as the Ministry of War Time Communications.

Lebensraum. This German word, meaning " living space," was a slogan adopted by Hitler and the Nazi Party to justify both his annexation of neighbouring States and his demand for the return of colonies on the ground of the overcrowded and highly populated condition of Germany.

Lebrun, ALBERT, G.C.B. (b. 1871). President of the French Republic from 1932 to 1940. After the collapse of France in June 1940 he resigned from the Presidency. On July 11 it was announced that Pétain, newly constituted Chief of the French State, had taken over the powers of both President and Prime Minister.

Leeb, FIELD-MARSHAL RITTER VON. German commander. He was placed on the retired list during 1938, but was brought back to the German Army at the outbreak of war in 1939. In May 1940 he commanded the large army group of some 30 divisions that attacked Holland and Belgium. Von Leeb took command of the German forces in the Leningrad sector of the Russian front after the Nazi invasion of the Soviet Union from June 1941, his forces, estimated at about 1,000,000 men, being opposed to those of Voroshilov. *See* Leningrad.

Field-Marsh. von Leeb,
German commander.
Photo, Planet News

Legentilhomme, GEN. PAUL LOUIS. National Commissioner for War in the Free French Govt. Until the Franco-German armistice in June 1940 he was in command of the Allied forces in French and British Somaliland under Gen. Sir Archibald Wavell (*q.v.*). When the Armistice was declared Gen. Legentilhomme did his best to persuade officials in Somaliland to support Britain. For this he was dismissed by the Vichy authorities, and thereupon left Jibuti and went to Egypt. He arrived in Britain in October 1940, and placed himself at the disposal of Gen. de Gaulle. From June to July 1941 he commanded Free French forces in Syria. On Sept. 5, 1941, he was condemned to death in absentia by a Vichy court-martial.

Gen. Legentilhomme,
Free French War
Minister.
Photo, British Official

Le Mans. This town of N.W. France, 77 miles S.W. of Chartres, was the headquarters of Lord Gort at the beginning of the war. He arrived at the Château de la Blanchardière, placed at his disposal by the French Government, on Sept. 14, 1939. British troops arrived at Le Mans on Sept. 22, and on the same date Lord Gort left the place for Amiens. Le Mans was occupied by the Germans in their thrust towards Brittany in June 1940, and after the signing of the Franco-German armistice on June 22 the town was included in Occupied France.

Leningrad. Second largest city of the U.S.S.R., situated at the mouth of the R. Neva on the Gulf of Finland, Leningrad became one of Russia's chief naval bases in recent years. The proximity of the city to the Finnish frontier in the Karelian Isthmus provided one of Stalin's pretexts for the invasion of Finland on Nov. 30, 1939. In December the Finns flew over Leningrad showering down leaflets, which stated the Finnish case with regard to the bitter war by that time raging between the two countries. By the peace treaty of March 12, 1940, Finland had to cede the whole of the Karelian Isthmus.

In June 1941, when the Germans attacked the Soviet Union, German bombers at once began to raid the Leningrad area, and by June 24 a Nazi drive was being made through the Baltic States towards the city. Fierce air battles between the opposing forces frequently took place and the Germans suffered heavy

SCENES DURING THE SIEGE OF LENINGRAD

1. Sappers at one of the approaches to the city where they set up defence works.   2. Girls of a first-aid squad drawn from students of the Medical Institute.   3. German soldiers passing through a blazing suburb of Leningrad.   4. Peaceful view of the city, much of which is built on islands and intersected by reaches of the R. Neva.   A Soviet submarine is here seen manoeuvring her way along one of the reaches that penetrate far into the capital.

Photos, Ministry of Information; Associated Press

losses. By mid-July the invaders were making determined efforts to break through the Soviet lines in order to speed up their thrust towards Leningrad, and by Aug. 23 were attempting to cut the Leningrad-Moscow railway in order to isolate the two largest Russian cities. All able-bodied men were mobilized in Leningrad itself and in adjacent towns and villages in accordance with Marshal Voroshilov's proclamation to defend the city to the uttermost. At the beginning of September the Germans were within 30–50 miles of Leningrad and air attacks increased in violence.

On Sept. 2 Voroshilov personally took over operations in its defence. Furious fighting continued without abatement in the area, the Germans throwing in large masses of men and materials in an attempt to encircle the city, for Gen. von Leeb (q.v.), commanding the German forces in this sector, had received orders from Hitler that he must capture Leningrad at all costs. Meanwhile, the whole population was mobilized and heavy blows were inflicted on the Nazis by guerilla troops operating behind their lines. Dive bombing, incessant air attacks and shelling of the city had no effect on the stubborn morale of the defenders. From October until December 1941 strong counter-attacks were delivered by the Russians, and the German forces suffered thousands of casualties. The invaders' grip on Leningrad was loosened by Red Army pressure in the Volkhov and Lake Ilmen region, E. of Leningrad, supported by sallies of the city's garrison. On Dec. 22 a junction was effected between two Russian armies advancing towards Leningrad, while the beginning of 1942 saw increasing Russian pressure against the Germans. Early in February 1942 strong, fresh Russian forces were brought into action around Leningrad. Soviet cavalry, followed by infantry, widened the breaches in the German defences in the Schlusselburg zone. The beleaguered garrison cooperated with these forces in their effort to loosen the enemy's grip. Savage fighting continued throughout the month, deep wedges being driven into the German first and second defence lines by infantry and ski troops, strongly supported by tanks.

On March 26, following counter-attacks by the enemy, the Russians resumed their offensive on a large scale in an effort to free the city before the spring thaw should cut the supply line over the ice of Lake Ladoga. This great highway had enabled food, fuel, and military and medical supplies to reach the city, both by lorry and in propeller-driven sledges. Refugees had been brought to safety, and machine tools collected from Leningrad's factories, which had continued their output in spite of bombing attacks. With the capture of two villages in April the Russians cut the Leningrad-Novgorod and Leningrad-Dno railways. Early in May the enemy were forced to abandon several strong positions on the Leningrad front.

Leopold III, KING OF THE BELGIANS (b. 1901). On Aug. 21, 1939, King Leopold (*see* p. 2479) broadcast an appeal for peace on behalf of Belgium, Denmark, Finland, Luxemburg, Holland, Norway and Sweden. On Aug. 29, as war loomed nearer, he made, with Queen Wilhelmina of the Netherlands, a joint offer of mediation. It was subsequently announced that the Belgian and Dutch Sovereigns had decided to address telegrams to the rulers of Great Britain, France and Germany, with the object of facilitating possible negotiations. On May 11, 1940, the day after the Germans invaded Luxemburg, Holland and

Belgium, King Leopold declared in a proclamation to the Belgian people : " Like my father in 1914, I have placed myself at the head of my troops, and with the same faith and confidence." Great was the astonishment, therefore, when he capitulated with his Army on May 28. By that time most of the Belgian Cabinet were in Paris, and at a meeting held the same day they declared that the King, being under foreign control, was, according to the Constitution, no longer in a position to govern. King Leopold was branded as a traitor, largely owing to a misleading statement made by Reynaud (*q.v.*) that he had surrendered

Leopold III,
King of the Belgians.
Photo, Topical Press

without having consulted the Allied commanders, thus exposing the B.E.F. and the French Army to great danger. The contumely heaped upon him was great, but in the light of subsequent evidence his action was vindicated.

This evidence was made public by Sir Roger Keyes, formerly Special Liaison Officer at Belgian H.Q., during the hearing on June 13, 1941, of a libel action brought by him against a London newspaper which had commented adversely on his recommendation that judgement on King Leopold's surrender should be suspended until the facts were known. It was then proved that the King informed the British and French authorities at 5 p.m. on May 27 that he intended at midnight to ask for an armistice ; that, although this message was received in London and Paris, all communications with the British Army had been cut ; and that wireless messages, which were repeatedly sent out, had not reached the Commanders-in-Chief.

After the Armistice the Germans made considerable efforts to obtain King Leopold's cooperation, but he insisted on regarding himself as a prisoner-of-war and withdrew from public life. He lived in the palace of Laeken, situated in a suburb to the N. of Brussels, where he remained virtually a captive in the hands of the Germans.

At the time of the invasion the King's three children, then in France, were taken to Portugal. On Aug. 2 it was announced that they had returned to Brussels, travelling in a German 'plane. On Sept. 11, 1941, King Leopold married as his second wife Mlle. Mary Lilian Baels, daughter of a former Belgian Minister. She took the title of Princesse de Réthy and renounced all claim to royal rank. *See* Belgium ; France, Defeat of ; Netherlands ; Wilhelmina, Queen.

Leuna. This industrial town near Leipzig, important chiefly by reason of its large synthetic oil works, became one of the main targets in central Germany for R.A.F. bombers, the object of the raids being to cause a breakdown in the enemy's production.

Ley, DR. ROBERT. He was head of the German Labour Front, the organization set up in Germany in place of the trade unions. It was on Dec. 2, 1939, that he declared at a Party Congress in Prague that the former capital of Czechoslovakia was once again " a centre of German culture." Shortly before the outbreak of war Ley, by his utterances to the Hitler Youth movement, went far in the attempt to convince his audiences that the Fuehrer had a " divine mission."

Early in 1942 he toured the whole country in the course of a great production drive, inciting the people to a more intensive effort, and telling them that, although he was aware that they often worked 16 hours a day, they must demonstrate to the world that, " like the soldiers of the Reich, they were the best in the world."

Liardet, Maj.-Gen. Claude Francis, c.b., d.s.o. (b. 1881). On Jan. 8, 1942, Mr. Attlee, Lord Privy Seal, announced that aerodrome defence was essentially a part of land defence and must henceforth be the task and responsibility of a military commander. Maj.-Gen. Liardet, recently Inspector of Aerodrome Defence, was therefore appointed to the newly created post of Director-General of Ground Defence in the Air Ministry. As senior officer of the Royal Air Force Regiment, though not exercising operational control, he was given the title of Commandant.

FREE BELGIUM REARS HER HEAD

Here is reproduced part of the front page of No. 9 of Free Belgium's secret monthly newspaper. The ironic humour of editor and publisher is shown in the particulars given of the journal's staff : the publishing office is stated to be at the H.Q. of the German Command, while the editor bears the name of Peter Pan. *Photo, G.P.U.*

Libre Belgique, La. Secret newspaper produced by Belgian patriots in Belgium shortly after the Germans took over their country. It bore the same name as its forerunner in the last war, and its purpose was to expose the cruelties of the enemy and to foster the spirit of freedom among the Belgian people. *See* Belgium, Free.

Libreville. Capital of Gabun, one of the four divisions of French Equatorial Africa which declared for Gen. de Gaulle's Free French cause in August 1940. In spite of this declaration, Vichy resistance continued as a retrogressive power at Libreville, but on Nov. 10, 1940, Free French headquarters announced that the officer commanding the garrison at Libreville, the last centre of Vichy supporters in Gabun, had surrendered to Gen. de Gaulle, and that the Free French warships Savorgnan de Brazza and Commandant Domine had entered Libreville harbour. *See* Equatorial Africa.

Libya. The physical features and early history of Italy's colony in North Africa are described in pages 2483–85. For the purpose of administration Libya is divided into two provinces : Cyrenaica, bordering Egypt, the capital of which is Benghazi ; and Tripolitania, the western portion, with its capital at Tripoli. Libya entered the orbit of the Second Great War on June 10, 1940, when Mussolini decided to come in on Germany's side against France and her Allies.

The Libyan campaigns are dealt with under the heading North Africa. *See* also Bardia ; Benghazi ; Derna ; Halfaya ; Tobruk, etc.

Liddell, Lieut.-Gen. Sir Clive Gerard, k.c.b. (b. 1883). He was Governor and C.-in-C. of Gibraltar from 1939 to 1941, being succeeded, on April 25, by Field-Marshal Lord Gort (*q.v.*). Sir Clive Liddell was then appointed Inspector of Training in the United Kingdom.

Lidice. Village near Kladno, Czechoslovakia. Following Heydrich's death on June 4, 1942, (*see* p. 89 this vol.) all the men of the village were shot, women and children deported and all buildings razed. The deed roused world wide condemnation and a village in U.S.A. (Illinois) and a town in Quebec province were renamed Lidice to preserve its memory. A Lidice settlement in Palestine was also planned. The Czech M.C. was conferred on Lidice, July 14. Few of the children were found after the war.

Liége. This Belgian city (*see* p. 2486), lying in the valley of the R. Meuse, was the centre of fierce fighting when the Germans invaded Belgium in May 1940. Liége stood as the pivot of a powerful system of fortifications, extending over a vast area the most modern being Eben-Eymael, covering 200 acres. Although it put up a gallant resistance, inflicting heavy losses

DESOLATION IN LIBYA

Since 1940 the campaign in the Western Desert has twice surged from west to east and back again. In the course of fierce battles many towns have been battered first by one side, then by the other, and now lie in ruins. The photograph shows British Bren-gun carriers passing buildings shattered by shelling near Fort Capuzzo.

Photo, British Official

HOW BELGIUM'S GREAT FORT OF EBEN-EYMAEL AT LIÉGE WAS CAPTURED

These shots from the German film " Victory in the West " purport to show how the Nazi troops reached the base of this bastion of Liége to link up with the attackers dropped into the fort by parachute. 1. Shock troops set out in a rubber boat at dawn to cross the Albert Canal. 2. They paddle furiously across under heavy protecting fire. 3. They land under cover of a smoke-screen and establish a bridgehead, the boat returning for another load. 4. They advance, still protected by the smoke-screen, to take up positions for the final assault.

on the enemy, the German thrust proved too powerful, and this great fortress system was outflanked and isolated. Tremendous attacks were developed by German heavy artillery, by bombing planes, and by waves of infantry. The bastion of Eben-Eymael fell quickly, victim of surprise and daring novelty. Some German gliders landed on the roof of the fort while it was yet dark, and their crews put the defensive armament out of action by explosives and bombs flung through the casemates. Then, entering through the breaches made in the massive walls, they destroyed the galleries. The remaining forts held out for many days, despite repeated air attacks and the fact that the Germans had penetrated beyond the town. On May 15 King Leopold broadcast the following message to the gallant defenders : " Resist to the end for your country. I am proud of you." On May 21, 1940, the Germans claimed that all the inner forts of Liége were in their hands. *See* Belgium.

Liepaja (LIBAU). This port of Latvia on the Baltic was leased to Russia after the U.S.S.R. consolidated her position in the Baltic States (*q.v.*), and became an important Russian naval base. After the outbreak of the Russo-German conflict the Germans claimed to have captured Liepaja on June 30, 1941.

Lifeboat Institution, Royal National. During the last war Sir Doveton Sturdee, victor of the battle of the Falkland Islands, called the lifeboat service " a sister service to the Navy." From the outbreak of war in September 1939 the lifeboats became a sister service, not to the Navy only, but to the Army and Air Force. The greatest of their many services to the fighting forces was in helping to bring the B.E.F. from Dunkirk at the end of May 1940. Nineteen lifeboats took part in this, the " most extensive and difficult operation in naval history " ; all the nineteen were damaged and one was lost. During the first two and a half years of war this admirable service rescued over 4,600 lives, an average of 35 lives a week. In this work lifeboatmen faced the same perils at sea as the fighting services. They were bombed and machine-gunned by the unscrupulous enemy ; their work had to be carried on in waters full of mines. One of the most valuable services the lifeboat crews performed was the help given to the crews of aeroplanes which had crashed in the sea round the coasts of Britain. Many hundreds of merchant ships also received valuable assistance.

Coxswain Parker, of Margate, and Coxswain Knight, of Ramsgate, were awarded D.S.M.s for their courageous gallantry at Dunkirk. Coxswain Blogg, of Cromer, was again awarded the Gold Medal of the Royal National Lifeboat Institution, a decoration equivalent to the V.C. Blogg was largely instrumental in saving 119 lives when six ships were stranded on the Haisborough Sands during a gale. Seven medals, 18 vellums, and £117 were awarded to the coxswains and crews of five lifeboats which took part in the rescue. In addition to his having been awarded the Gold Medal three times, Blogg also received the Silver Medal three times, and the B.E.M.

Of the 43 lifeboat rescues up to February 1942 for which the Institution awarded medals for gallantry, two of the most gallant were concerned with ships of the Royal Navy. One of these was a minesweeper and the other a trawler on submarine patrol. The first service was by the Whitby lifeboat, which went alongside the minesweeper in the darkness and rescued all her crew of 18. The other, carried out by the Dover lifeboat in a full gale, was the rescue of the trawler's crew from the middle of a minefield, when 16 men were saved.

Lightships, Bombing of. Some of the most determined of the German attacks on inoffensive shipping were those delivered on lightships soon after the outbreak of war. On Jan. 9, 1940, the Reculver, a Trinity House vessel, unarmed and engaged on the relief of lightship personnel off the East coast, was bombed and machine-gunned, at least 30 on board being injured, of whom two died. Later, other vessels were attacked, including the East Dudgeon lightship, stationed off the Norfolk coast, which was attacked by a Nazi 'plane on Jan. 29, 1940. The crew took to their boat, which, unfortunately, capsized near the shore. The men were thrown into the water and only one reached safety. Again on May 25 the East Dudgeon lightship was reported to have been bombed off the East coast. On August 14, 1940, another lightship was attacked off the S.E. coast by six German dive-bombers. Two of the crew were killed and the rest injured. Owing to these repeated attacks automatic crewless lightships, known as floats, were substituted.

Lille. The important industrial city of Lille was the last stronghold to be held by the French in the North of France. It fell to the Germans on May 29, 1940. After the defeat of France R.A.F. aircraft made heavy attacks upon the steel works and power station at Lille and considerable damage was done. Lille was the centre of a prohibited zone in the northern part of Occupied France.

Lillehammer. This Norwegian town, situated between Dombaas and Hamar, was the scene of stubborn fighting between the Allied forces and the Germans in April 1940. It lies on the Oslo-Trondheim railway, and the Germans made many attempts to cut communications. Increased enemy pressure necessitated a British withdrawal by April 25.

Lindbergh, CHARLES AUGUSTUS (b. 1902). One of America's foremost Isolationists, this famous airman strongly advocated a " negotiated peace " policy and American non-intervention in European affairs. One of his most outspoken speeches was made on Jan. 23, 1941, when he criticized the Lease-and-Lend Act (q.v.). His attitude provoked a sharp reaction throughout America, and numerous supporters of Britain, including President Roosevelt, condemned his point of view. Lindbergh resigned from the U.S. Army Corps on April 28, 1941. After the Japanese attacks on U.S.

bases in the Pacific on Dec. 7 he offered his services to the American War Dept., and they were accepted in a civilian capacity. On March 25, 1942, he took up a position in the engineering department of the huge new bomber building plant of the Ford Motor Company. See Isolationism.

Linlithgow, VICTOR ALEXAN-DER JOHN HOPE, 2ND MARQUESS, P.C., G.C.S.I. (b. 1887). Viceroy of India from 1936. On Oct. 25, 1940, Lord Linlithgow opened the Delhi and Eastern Group Conference attended by delegates from three continents representing eleven British territories, with a view to ensuring the best use being made of their resources in the war. His term of office as Viceroy was extended on Sept. 22, 1941, until April 1943. See India.

Lord Linlithgow,
Viceroy of India.
Photo, Central Press

List, FIELD-MARSHAL WILHELM (b. 1880). In the last war this German general commanded the regiment in which Hitler served as a corporal, and after the Nazis seized power he became Director of Military Training in Germany, being responsible for the iron discipline to which German youth found itself subjected. As military commander in Moravia in March 1939 he became notorious for the large number of death-warrants he signed, and during Germany's blitzkrieg campaign in Poland in September 1939 he lived up to his sinister reputation, for his name became a byword among Polish women and children for typical Nazi cruelties. In this campaign it was he who led the German forces from Slovakia into Poland on the first day of war, Sept. 1, 1939. List arrived in Bulgaria from Rumania at the end of February 1941, and took command of the German troops then pouring into the country. On April 6, 1941, he invaded Yugoslavia, and had at his disposal some twenty-five divisions, comprising nearly a million men. At the outbreak of the Russo-German conflict in June 1941 he commanded the German-Rumanian army attacking Bukovina and Bessarabia. He replaced Field-Marshal von Bock (q.v.) on Dec. 8 as C.-in-C. in the Smolensk sector of the Russian front, prior to Hitler's assuming supreme command of the German armies on Dec. 19, 1941. See Poland ; Russia.

Field-Marshal List,
German soldier.
Photo, Planet News

Lithuania. The chequered history of this European State, up to the time of the Second Great War, is outlined in pages 2523-24. Its temporary extinction after that date is described under the heading Baltic States.

Littorio. This Italian battleship gave its name to a class which included the Vittorio Veneto, the Imperio and the Roma. The Littorio was completed in May 1940. Each of these ships had a displacement of 35,000 tons and carried a complement of 1,600. They were laid down between 1934 and 1938. Their main armament consisted of nine 15-in. guns, twelve 6-in. and twelve 3·5-in. A.A. guns. Their speed was 30 knots, and they carried four aircraft with two

PROUD BUILDINGS LAID LOW IN ONE OF BRITAIN'S GREAT PROVINCIAL CITIES

The area near the waterfront at Liverpool suffered badly in the raids of 1940–41. In the above photograph the numbers indicate: 1, Mersey Tunnel ventilating towers (left and right sides of photo); 2, twin towers of the Royal Liver Building; 3, India Building; 4, Queen Victoria monument; 5, Town Hall. Top, panoramic view from offices in South Castle Street, near the Pierhead, showing how this devastated area is being gradually cleared.

Photos, Topical Press; Associated Press

catapults. They were the largest and most modern ships in the Italian Navy. The Littorio was badly damaged by the Fleet Air Arm at Taranto on Nov. 11, 1940, when she was left with her forecastle under water and a heavy list. At the end of February 1941 she was still in the same position, but was later towed to Venice for repairs. *See* Taranto.

Litvinov, MAXIM MAXIM-OVICH (b. 1876). Soviet Am-bassador to the U.S.A. from Nov. 6, 1941, in succession to Oumansky. On Nov. 11 he was appointed Deputy-Commissar for Foreign Affairs. Litvinov was Soviet Foreign Commissar from 1930 to 1939. On May 3, 1939, he was succeeded by Molotov.

Maxim Litvinov,
Soviet Ambassador
to U.S.A.
Photo, Keystone

Liverpool. The important city and immense port of Liverpool were frequently attacked by German raiders in 1940 and throughout 1941, and both Liverpool and Mer-seyside suffered considerable damage. The majority of the raids occurred at night, one of the heaviest being on Dec. 20, 1940, when a large force of enemy machines bombed targets for several hours, and extensive damage was also caused by fire. The city was subjected to heavy raids for five consecu-tive nights at the beginning of May 1941, when great damage was again inflicted. One area which suffered particularly was in the lower part of the city, near the Pierhead, and included South Castle Street, the bottom of Lord Street, and the church of St. Nicholas.

Llewellin, COL. JOHN JESTYN, P.C., C.B.E. (b. 1893). Minister of Aircraft Production from Feb. 22, 1942, in succession to Col. Moore-Brabazon. He was Parliamentary Secretary to the Ministry of Supply, 1939–40; to the Ministry of Air-craft Production, 1940–41; and to the Ministry of War Transport, 1941–Feb. 4, 1942. He was then given his first office of Cabinet rank as President of the Board of Trade, but held this for three weeks only before being appointed to the Ministry of Aircraft Production.

Col. Llewellin,
Minister of
Aircraft Production.
Photo, Sport & General

Lloyd, GEORGE AMBROSE, P.C., 1ST BARON (1879–1941). He was appointed Secretary of State for the Colonies in 1940 and became Leader of the House of Lords on Jan. 10, 1941, in succession to Lord Halifax. The latter office he never exercised, for his illness pre-vented him attending any sittings. His death occurred on Feb. 4, 1941. Lord Lloyd represented the Crown as Governor of Bombay and as High Commissioner in Egypt during two long and critical periods.

Lloyd's War Medal. At the beginning of 1941 Lloyd's decided to add to their medals and, with the approval of the Admiralty and the Ministry of Shipping, struck one to be awarded to officers and men of the Merchant Navy and fishing fleet, in recogni-tion of exceptional gallantry at sea in time of war. It is known as "Lloyd's War Medal for Bravery at Sea." The ribbon is blue and silver, similar in design to that of the ribbon for Lloyd's Meritorious Medal, but with the colours reversed. *See* Colour Plate of Medals *facing* p. 264.

Lodz. Known as "the Manchester of Poland," this former industrial city was heavily attacked from the air on the first day of the German invasion of Poland, Sept. 1, 1939. By September 8 the Poles had retreated from the Lodz area. When the parti-tion of Poland took place between Russia and Germany Lodz passed to Germany. The names of the streets were Germanized, and Polish schools, newspapers and all educational books in Polish were abolished.

Lofoten Islands. This group of rugged islands off the north-west coast of Norway form the seaward side of the Vest Fjord, which leads to the iron ore port of Narvik. They are important for their position on one of the richest fishery grounds in the world, and are a great centre for cod-liver oil extrac-tion. The fish oil plant was one of the Nazis' biggest sources of glycerine for making explosives, for more than half Norway's annual output of 8,000,000 tons was produced there. Svolvaer, which is the chief trading port of the Lofotens, is built on a number of rocky islets off the island of Ost-Vago. The Germans occupied the Lofotens during their Norwegian campaign.

British forces made a daring raid on the islands on March 4, 1941, with Commando troops and Nor-wegian marines, accompanied by Norwegian guides. They landed at Svolvaer with three objects in view : (1) to destroy the plant used for the production of fish oil ; (2) to sink any German ships, or ships under German control, in the vicinity ; (3) to capture Ger-mans concerned in the control of fishing industries, and also local quislings. All these aims were carried out with conspicuous success. Nine German merchant vessels and one Norwegian ship under German con-trol were sunk by our light forces, and also a German armed trawler, the total tonnage being 18,000 tons. The largest unit sunk, a German ship of 10,000 tons, was fully laden. Meanwhile Commandos and Norwegian marines were landed before anyone ashore had time to discover what was happening. They first took control of the telegraph station, post office and police station. Their next step was to destroy the oil, cod-liver oil and cod-fishing factories, and six of these went

GERMAN PRISONERS FROM LOFOTEN
When British commandos returned from their famous raid on the Lofoten Islands in March 1941 they brought with them a number of German air force personnel, here seen blindfolded, as well as many Norwegian volunteers.
Photo, British Official

BURNING OIL PLANT ON THE LOFOTEN ISLANDS

Dense clouds of black smoke are seen rising from the oil storage tanks detonated by the British raiding party on March 4, 1941. The fish oil plant on the islands was one of the Nazis' biggest sources of glycerine for making explosives, for more than half of Norway's annual output of 8,000,000 gallons was produced here.

Photo, British Official

up in smoke and flames. Three petrol storage tanks and a power station were also destroyed. The German prisoners taken numbered 215, including 17 air force personnel who were engaged on preparations for building a naval air station. Ten quislings were detained. A number of eager volunteers for the Norwegian Navy were among the 300 Norwegian patriots who accompanied the landing party back to their ships. The opportunity was taken to supply the local population with consignments of foodstuffs, soap, cigarettes, clothing and other comforts which could be disposed of without immediate danger of being diverted to enemy use. In this raid of March 4 invasion barges were used for the first time by the British. Practically no opposition was encountered, and no casualties were suffered by either British or Norwegian troops. A German naval officer and six ratings were killed.

A second and more extensive joint British and Norwegian raid on the Lofoten Islands took place on Dec. 26, 1941. Our light naval forces, which included Norwegian and Polish units, were under the command of Rear-Adm. L. H. K. Hamilton. For three days the islands were in control of the British forces, and our warships were able to use enemy-occupied harbours for re-fuelling. The enemy's sea communications were completely disorganized, shipping brought to a standstill, and a Nazi patrol vessel sunk. Commando and Norwegian troops, under Lt.-Col. S. S. Harrison, landed at four different points on the islands, meeting with no opposition. They quickly obtained control of post offices, a radio mast, radio equipment and telephone cables, which were demolished, and took some German prisoners and several quislings. About 100 men and women decided to come to Britain rather than stay under German occupation. Some bombing attacks were made by the Germans, but they did no damage, and one machine crashed. This raid coincided with one on Vaagso (*q.v.*). *See* Commando Troops.

THE STORY OF THE BATTLE OF LONDON

For over eight months, beginning towards the end of August 1940, London suffered almost continuous attacks by the Luftwaffe, chiefly at night. Irreparable damage was done to historic structures, thousands of other buildings were reduced to ruin, but Londoners remained undaunted. See also Great Britain, Air War on.

London, Battle of. An aerial invasion of Great Britain, designed as prelude to invasion by sea, was launched on August 11, 1940, three days after a considerable sea engagement in the English Channel. In its initial phase this was a legitimate enterprise of war, with military objectives on the south-east coast as Luftwaffe targets. But it failed, for our fighters brought down on August 15 alone—when over a thousand machines crossed, or attempted to cross, our coasts—no fewer than 169. London thereafter became one of the enemy's main targets.

On August 24 the enemy set about London in earnest, using the night attack method at which, up to that date, his air experts had sneered. This first raid on the capital went on continuously for two weeks, being interspersed with daylight raids.

In that month over a thousand Londoners were killed. Little damage of military importance was done. The capital emerged from its baptism of fire with a stout heart. It comforted people to know that our magnificent fighters had accounted for 586 enemy 'planes, and that this brilliant achievement had been accomplished with a loss of 238 machines and the escape of 129 pilots.

There was, nevertheless, a general feeling that too many Nazi machines were getting through our defences, that our anti-aircraft gunnery and our system of warning needed looking to. This last problem was pressed home by a direct factory hit at Croydon, when 50 were killed and no warning had been sounded.

From September onwards it was clear that the Germans had decided upon a policy of night bombing. It was tantamount to confessing their preference for dropping bombs upon a blacked-out city rather than for engaging the R.A.F. in the blue—the fact that they lost 185 machines, and probably more, in one day, Sept. 15, perhaps forced the decision. On Sept. 7 the Surrey Docks were fired, and that was the real start of systematic night bombing that continued until May 1941.

The object of these gruelling raids was a twofold one : first, to strike terror into the heart of the civilian population ; secondly, to smash transport and docking.

In the first, there was complete failure to terrorize the Londoners, who met each disaster with coolness, courage and even grim humour.

The city suffered heavily, particularly by the grievous loss of historic buildings. But though the most severe raids slowed up the tempo of the great city's heart, they never did more than that. It was as though a criminal setting out to murder a man had succeeded only in scratching his face.

London's Anger Rises

London's defences were improved by the extended use of the predictor, by means of which the air paths of the raiders were gauged and fire directed at them with greater precision. Unfortunately, when the enemy found himself in a hail of steel he sometimes jettisoned his bombs and fled, causing terrible havoc. Even more effective in later months in combating the night raider was the night fighter. Specially trained pilots in Defiants accounted for many Nazi bombers in the spring of 1941.

This was the trial of the Civil Defence Forces, and they emerged from it with such honour that the King instituted two new decorations, the George Cross, to rank after the V.C., and the George Medal.

The wantonness of these onslaughts now roused the anger of London's sorely-tried citizens and there arose a demand for reprisal raids against Berlin. The Government did not accede to this popular demand, and the R.A.F. continued to confine its attention to military objectives.

Experience revealed the defects of a shelter system designed on theory alone. The city had plenty of cover to go to, but it had nowhere to sleep. Lack of sleep became the major and dominant problem for London's working millions. Under the advice of Lord Horder the Government put a million bunks into the shelters. The public, ignoring the Government's prohibition, next occupied the Tube System by night and proceeded in orderly fashion to organize their strange troglodyte existence.

On Oct. 7 a particularly heavy raid—450 aircraft— was staged by day and proved to be the last of its kind. In that month there were over a hundred hit-and-run raids by single craft or small formations. Contact with the R.A.F. was never courted.

A large-scale evacuation scheme was introduced in October. The L.C.C. canvassed parents, but found

LONDONERS GO TO WORK AS USUAL

In their efforts to dislocate the City's communications and business life Nazi bombers tried, but failed, to hit London Bridge, although buildings in the vicinity suffered heavy damage, as will be seen in this photograph taken from the corner of King William Street.

Photo, Planet News

IN ONE OF LONDON'S TUBE DORMITORIES

Many thousands of Londoners regularly spent the night in the Underground railway stations, bringing their own bedding and food. Later the authorities, whose prohibition of this use of the Tubes had been disregarded, themselves provided bunks and introduced a highly organized system of weekly bunk tickets, canteen meals and medical attention.

Photo, Planet News

everywhere an aversion from sending the children away. Yet in November 1940, 1,750 London civilians were killed and 2,900 wounded.

On the night of the last Sunday of the year (December 29), when the city's commercial buildings were unwatched, the Nazis made a gigantic fire-raid on the City of London.

Thousands of incendiaries were showered upon the square mile of the City that evening in a raid which ended before midnight and included, for reasons never made clear, no organized high explosive attack. The results were disastrous, and throughout the first hours of the night there raged over all the City and in

London Targets of Nazi Air Raiders
Destruction and Damage in the Period Sept. 12, 1940, to May 1941

HOSPITALS
Charterhouse Clinic
Great Ormond Street
London Hospital
Queen Mary's Hospital
St. Bartholomew's Medical School
Guy's
St. Thomas's
Swiss Relief Centre
St. Dunstan's Headquarters

CHURCHES
Westminster Abbey
St. Paul's Cathedral
St. Martin-in-the-Fields
St. Clement Danes
St. Giles's, Cripplegate
St. Swithin's, Cannon Street
St. Augustine, Watling Street
St. Boniface, Adler Street
St. Dunstan-in-the-East
St. Clement's, Eastcheap
Jewin Chapel
Dutch Church, Austin Friars
Swedish Church, Rotherhithe
St. Magnus the Martyr
St. Mary-at-Hill
St. Mary Woolnoth
St. Margaret's, Westminster
Christ Church, Westminster Bridge Road
St. John's, Smith Square
St. John's, Kensington
Our Lady of Victories, Kensington
St. Mark's, Regent's Park
Islington Parish Church
St. George's R.C. Cathedral, Southwark
St. Lawrence Jewry
St. Mary the Virgin, Aldermanbury

St. Andrew by the Wardrobe
St. Stephen's, Coleman Street
St. Vedast, Foster Lane
Christ Church, Newgate Street
St. Anne & St. Agnes, Gresham Street
St. Bride's, Fleet Street
St. Mary-le-Bow
St. Martin's, Ludgate Hill
City Temple
St. Andrew's, Holborn
Chelsea Old Church

HALLS OF CITY COMPANIES
Coopers'
Girdlers'
Haberdashers'
Saddlers'
Stationers'

EMBASSIES
American (time bomb removed)
Japanese (evacuated)
Spanish

PALACES
Buckingham Palace
Kensington Palace
Lambeth Palace

OTHER IMPORTANT BUILDINGS
British Museum
Law Courts
Tate Gallery
Imperial War Museum
Somerset House
Wallace Collection
Burlington House

Tower of London
Westminster Hall
Temple
Inner Temple Library
Royal College of Surgeons
Houses of Parliament
Guildhall
Central Criminal Court
Trinity House
General Post Office
St. George's Hall
Guildhall School of Music
Royal Hospital, Chelsea
Hogarth House
Holland House
Radnor House, Twickenham
Statue of Richard Coeur de Lion
Australia House
Bank of England (near)
County Hall
Madame Tussaud's
National City Bank of New York
Public Record Office
South Africa House
University College Library
Yokohama Specie Bank
Y.M.C.A. Headquarters
The Zoo
Indian Students' Hostel
Italian Tourist Company
Wimbledon Centre Court

NEWSPAPER OFFICES
Associated Press of America
Daily Telegraph
Daily Express
Daily Herald
Daily Mail
Daily Mirror
Daily Sketch
Daily Worker

Evening Standard
Glasgow Herald and Bulletin
New Statesman and Nation
The Times

SQUARES AND STREETS
Berkeley Square
Leicester Square
Kensington Square
Sloane Square
Smith Square
Berwick Market
Bond Street
Burlington Arcade
Bruton Street
Carnaby Street
Lambeth Walk
Maddox Street
Oxford Street
Park Lane
Piccadilly
Regent Street
Rotten Row
Royal Arcade
Savile Row
Watling Street
Elephant and Castle

STORES
Austin Reed (Piccadilly)
Bourne and Hollingsworth
Ford Showrooms, Regent Street
Gamage's, Cheapside
John Lewis
Peter Robinson
Selfridge's

CLUBS
Arts (Dover Street)
Carlton
Reform

Note.—This list includes only buildings allowed to be mentioned by the censorship. One small attack only on London was reported between May 1941 and May 1942; it was on the night of July 27–28, 1941.

SCENE FROM LONDON'S SECOND GREAT FIRE

That the City of London was not all laid in ruins on the night of Dec. 29, 1940, is primarily due to the bravery of the firemen who, with unwearied skill, fought the terrible sheets of flame enveloping so many areas and prevented them from spreading. Exposed to the falling bombs and to the imminent danger of collapsing buildings, they continued their heroic struggle throughout the night. Many lost their lives, others were badly injured, but London was saved.

Photo, Keystone

THE SCARRED FACE OF THE CITY OF LONDON

This photograph, taken from St. Paul's Cathedral, looking east, shows the wanton destruction wrought in one part of the City by bombs and fire. The lovely spire of St. Mary-le-Bow (3) rises from the wreckage. Behind is the Bank of England (4), and to the right is the Mansion House (5). Some of the principal streets are indicated : (1) Gresham Street ; (2) King Street, Cheapside ; (6) Bow Lane ; (7) Milk Street ; (8) Cheapside ; (9) Bread Street. The photograph shows only a portion of the ruin caused by this particular raid.

Photo, Keystone

One result of the destruction wrought by Hitler's bombers was the unusual view of well-known buildings presented by the removal of intervening structures. Top, is one of Holborn Viaduct from the north, with the bombed-out shells of the City Temple and St. Andrew's; the towers of both churches escaped serious damage. The debris in the foreground lies between Shoe Lane and Farringdon Street. Below, a new aspect of St. Paul's Cathedral, seen from the south-east rising clear of warehouse and other buildings, beyond the devastation bordering Cannon Street.

Photos, Topical Press; Keystone

SENSELESS DESTRUCTION WROUGHT IN THE CITY DURING THE SECOND GREAT FIRE OF LONDON

No military targets were included in most of the Luftwaffe's attacks on the capital. 1. The interior of London's beautiful and historic Guildhall is still burning, while the Union Jack flies defiantly above. 2. Havoc following a night raid. 3. Converging streams from hose-pipes above a blazing gas main. 4. The burning nave of St. Bride's, Fleet Street. This was one of the loveliest of the City churches built by Wren after the Great Fire of 1666, so many of which were destroyed or damaged in that of 1940.

Photos, Topical Press; Fox; "Daily Mirror"

Southwark an inferno which was only too correctly entitled " The Second Great Fire of London." Some 150 'planes took part, and dropped at least 10,000 incendiary bombs. Before dawn more than 10,000 firemen had got the fires under control, but by the Monday there were blackened ruins everywhere. The ancient Guildhall seemed to be but a shell, although it was, in fact, later re-roofed and brought into use again. Eight Wren's churches were destroyed or gutted, and round St. Paul's Cathedral fire had raged in many of the wholesale warehouses, while most of Paternoster Row and Warwick Lane, for the best part of a century the home of publishers and booksellers, was but a series of smoking ruins. The Cathedral itself, thanks largely to the devoted work of the Cathedral watchers and firemen, was unharmed, but of the Chapter House only gaunt brick walls remained. The eight Wren churches destroyed included St. Lawrence Jewry, Gresham Street, and St. Bride's, Fleet Street. Those who were in Fleet Street on that terrible night will not easily forget the tiered Wren steeple flaming like a monstrous torch. Other famous buildings damaged included Trinity House, Dr. Johnson's house in Gough Square, and the Central Criminal Court, Old Bailey. The less-known buildings which suffered in this wanton and savage attempt to burn out the centre of London were numbered by the score. It was stupid as well as savage, for, though the material damage it caused might be calculated in millions of pounds, it had no great effect upon the life of the City and none whatever on the morale of the Londoner.

This raid showed the incendiary as a worse danger than the high explosive, and revealed the inadequacy of the city's fire protection measures, then voluntary, later compulsory.

On Jan. 4, 1941, shelter control was made the joint responsibility of the Ministries of Home Security and Health. Regional Commissioners were appointed.

April 16 saw what was probably the greatest raid of all on the city. Germany justified it as a reprisal. Eight great hospitals were hit, hotels, churches, departmental stores, theatres, restaurants and hundreds of homes.

Throughout the rest of 1941 and up to the spring of 1942 the raids ceased and London worked hard to clear away the debris. The basements of demolished big buildings were turned into water reservoirs for fire fighting. Air raid shelters were improved and the number continually increased.

Of all the buildings destroyed during the period, Sept. 1940 to May 1941, a number of the best known are listed in p. 234.

Books to Consult. Hell Came to London, Basil Woon (Peter Davies). London's Burning, Maurice Richardson (Hale). History Under Fire, J. Pope-Hennessy (Batsford).

Longmore, AIR CHIEF MARSHAL SIR ARTHUR MURRAY, G.C.B., D.S.O. (b. 1885). Inspector-Gen. R.A.F. from July 1941 to March 1942. In July 1939 he took over the Training Command of the R.A.F. and in May 1940 became A.O.C.-in-C., Middle East Command. On March 3, 1942, it was announced that he had retired from the R.A.F.

Loraine, RT. HON. SIR PERCY (LYHAM), P.C., G.C.M.G. (b. 1880). British Ambassador to Italy from 1939 to 1940. He arrived back in England on June 30, 1940. From 1933 to 1939 he was British Ambassador to Turkey.

Lorient. This important French naval base on the S. coast of Brittany (*see* p. 4720) was occupied by the Germans on the collapse of France and became one of the chief bases from which U-boats carried out their war against British shipping. Its shipbuilding yards, magazines, docks and armament works soon felt the effect of the heavy counter-offensive by our Bomber Squadrons, which in the months following the German occupation attacked Lorient almost daily.

Los Angeles. A highly important base of the U.S. Navy, Los Angeles (*see* pp. 2570-2571) is situated some 126 miles south of San Diego, chief American naval base on the Pacific coast. A rigid black-out was imposed throughout the city immediately after the Japanese attack on the U.S. naval base at Pearl Harbour in the Pacific on Dec. 7, 1941. The Japanese quarter contained about 30,000 people, and a police ring was placed round it. A large concentration of aircraft works is centred at Los Angeles.

Lothian, PHILIP HENRY KERR, P.C., 11TH MARQUESS (1882-1940). British Ambassador to U.S.A. 1939-1940. His death, which occurred at Washington on Dec. 12, 1940, came as a shock to millions of people both at home and in the U.S.A. His term of office as Ambassador was outstandingly successful, for he liked Americans and they liked him. He did much to foster Anglo-American understanding and friendship at a critical moment, so that later they developed into a whole-hearted alliance. Lord Lothian was succeeded at Washington by Lord Halifax.

Lord Lothian, British Ambassador to U.S.A.
Photo, Topical Press

Lotta Svard. This was the name of the Finnish women's national organization which played a useful part in the Russo-Finnish war. It had over 100,000 members who undertook every sort of non-combatant duty in support of the Army. Service was voluntary and unpaid. The name was derived from a woman whose heroism during the war of 1808-9, in which Sweden lost Finland to Russia, made her one of the most popular characters in the poems of J. L. Runeberg, Finland's national poet.

Louvain. This world-famous city of Belgium (*see* p. 2577), which was burnt by the Germans in the last war, suffered again at their hands in May 1940. The B.E.F. and the Belgians held the town, and by May 14 most of its civil population had been evacuated. German bombers destroyed the railway station and many other public buildings, preparatory to an attack. The Germans captured the station and two other points on the outskirts of the town, but the British drove them from their positions by a powerful counter-attack. By May 16 there was sharp fighting, and house-to-house sniping went on in the suburbs and on the western side of the city near the river Dyle (*q.v.*). At one or two places the Germans crossed the river. In the fighting in Louvain itself exceptionally good work was done by an Irish regiment and a battalion of the Grenadier Guards. By May 17 the German thrust through the French armies to the south had turned the line of the Dyle, and the B.E.F., though unbroken in action and capable of continuing resistance on the line which had been chosen, was

LOUVAIN DEVASTATED A SECOND TIME
The Germans laid waste the beautiful Belgian city of Louvain in the First Great War. It was rebuilt and restored, only to fall a victim to the Nazis in May 1940. British tanks are seen passing along a ruined street during the counter-attack in which they temporarily drove out the enemy.
Photo, British Official

which contained large armament works, became German. Shortly afterwards Hitler's plan for the establishment of a Jewish reserve in the province of Lublin was set up, and by the end of 1939 some 50,000 Jews, mainly from Western Poland, but including a number from Vienna and Prague, had been transferred to the town and its neighbourhood. *See* Poland.

Ludlow - Hewitt, AIR CHIEF MARSHAL SIR EDGAR RAINEY, G.C.B., C.M.G., D.S.O. In 1937 he left India, where he had commanded the R.A.F. since 1935, and came to England as A.O.C.-in-C., Bomber Command. In April 1940 he relinquished the Bomber Command to become Inspector-Gen. of the R.A.F., with the rank of Air Chief Marshal.

Ludwigshafen. Situated opposite the German industrial city of Mannheim (*q.v.*) on the Rhine, Ludwigshafen was bombed by the R.A.F. from June 1940, oil refineries, marshalling yards and factories being heavily attacked. On June 4–5, 1940, the French made a fierce raid on the town as a reply to the German raid on Paris on June 3. Air attacks by the R.A.F. increased in severity throughout 1941 and the damage inflicted was considerable.

compelled to withdraw as part of the Allied strategical plan. After an encircling attack Louvain fell to the Germans on May 17. It was reported that only 15,000 volumes survived out of the 900,000 in the library of Louvain University, destroyed by the Germans. *See* Belgium ; France.

Loyd, LT.-GEN. HENRY CHARLES, C.B., D.S.O. (b. 1891). G.O.C. Southern Command from March 1942, in succession to Gen. Sir Harold Alexander. In 1940 Lt.-Gen. Loyd had followed Gen. Paget as C.G.S. Home Forces.

Lübeck. Important German port in the western Baltic, handling the supply of iron ore and other raw materials from Sweden, and used for sending troops and supplies to the North Russian Front. Of the R.A.F. attacks on Lubeck the heaviest was that delivered on March 28, 1942, when 340 tons of bombs were dropped and the whole port left ablaze.

Lublin. A few days after Germany's aggressive action against Poland on Sept. 1, 1939, the Polish Government removed from Warsaw to Lublin (*see* p. 4721), 95 miles to the south-east. The town was stated on Sept. 15 to be in flames as the result of merciless air bombardments by the Germans. On Sept. 29, when the " final partition " of Poland was concluded between Russia and Germany, Lublin,

Lulea. This important Swedish port at the head of the Gulf of Bothnia shipped, in normal times, 9,000,000 tons of iron ore a year from the great mines in Swedish Lapland to Germany. From the outbreak of war Britain declared iron ore to be contraband, and took determined steps to interrupt the supply of a commodity badly needed by Germany for the prosecution of the war. During the winter months, when Lulea was ice-bound, the iron ore was dispatched to the North German Baltic ports via Narvik and the Norwegian coast, and it was the mining by Britain of Norwegian waters, to stop this traffic, that precipitated the invasion of Norway. *See* Narvik.

Luxemburg. The Germans invaded this little undefended country on May 10, 1940. The invasion by land and air forces occurred without warning at 3 a.m., and a large part of Luxemburg was immediately overrun by the enemy. The hereditary ruler, the Grand Duchess Charlotte, and the Government left the country and arrived safely in Northern France, taking with them the official archives and the national gold reserve. The German invaders built pontoon bridges across the river that separates the Grand Duchy from Germany, and over these poured great numbers of troops and mechanized transport for their attack on Belgium and Holland.

Luzon. *See* Philippine Islands.

Lwow (LEMBERG). This Polish city was one of the most severely bombed by the Germans. Nazi 'planes destroyed the waterworks, station, and numerous factories, and then flew low over the city and bombed the civil population indiscriminately. On September 29 Lwow was finally assigned to Russia at the partition of Poland, being surrendered by the Germans. On June 30, 1941, the Germans claimed the recapture of the city from the Russians.

Lyons. This French city (*see* p. 2593) was occupied by the Germans on June 20, 1940. On the same day Marshal Pétain broadcast to the French people that he had asked the enemy to put an end to hostilities. Under the terms of the armistice Lyons remained in Unoccupied France, thus coming directly under the jurisdiction of the Vichy Government.

Lyster, REAR-ADM. ARTHUR LUMLEY ST. GEORGE, C.V.O., D.S.O. (b. 1888). Fifth Sea Lord, and Chief of Naval Air Services from 1940. At the battle of Taranto (*q.v.*) he commanded the aircraft carriers which scored outstanding successes against the Italian Navy.

Lyttelton, OLIVER, P.C., D.S.O. (b. 1893). At the outbreak of war he was appointed Controller of Non-Ferrous Metals in the Ministry of Supply. On Oct. 3, 1940, he succeeded Sir Andrew Duncan as President of the Board of Trade, but relinquished this post on July 1, 1941, when he was appointed Minister of State in the Middle East, where, it was announced, "he would represent the War Cabinet and concert on their behalf the measures necessary for the prosecution of the war, thereby relieving the G.O.C.-in-C. of many responsibilities unrelated to the actual conduct of military operations." On Feb. 19, 1942, when Mr. Churchill reorganized his War Cabinet, Mr. Lyttelton was made Minister of State with general supervision over production.

Oliver Lyttelton,
Minister of Production.
Photo, Planet News

On March 12 the Prime Minister announced that Mr. Lyttelton would be appointed Minister of Production, with chief responsibility, on behalf of the Cabinet, for war production as a whole. He would undertake the duties hitherto discharged by the Production Executive and would direct the work of the British representatives on the combined bodies set up here and in the United States to provide for the most effective use of the joint resources of the United Nations in munitions and raw materials. He would organize, in cooperation with the Dominions and other Empire Governments, the general planning of the production of raw materials, machine tools and finished munitions in the Empire. He would be responsible for planning the development of home resources, for arranging the import programme and for

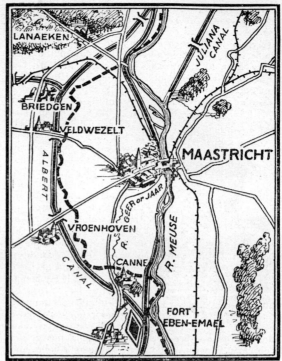

Maastricht, key town on the R. Meuse, and the Albert Canal, just over the Belgian border, 2½ miles west. By a tragic misadventure two of the three canal bridges on the Belgian side were left undestroyed and over them the enemy's tanks poured into Belgium on May 11, 1940.

allocating stocks, and would control the building programme. *See* Production, Ministry of.

 Maastricht. Situated on the river Maas (Meuse) in Limburg, southernmost province of Holland, at the junction of the Dutch, Belgian, and German frontiers, this town was of vital strategic importance at the beginning of Germany's invasion of the Low Countries on May 10, 1940. Limburg, sometimes termed the "Maastricht appendix," most of which lies east of the river, was overrun in a few hours, and the Germans, equipped with a tremendous mechanized force, threatened on that first day the crossings of the Maas in the town itself and the parallel waterway (2½ miles W.) of the Albert Canal, which formed the main line of Belgian defence in the north. The Dutch bridges in the town had been blown up by the defenders.

On May 11 the enemy succeeded in crossing the Albert Canal by two bridges which had not been destroyed in time because the officer entrusted with this operation was killed. Another officer had sacrificed his life to blow up the third and remaining bridge, but the enemy had advanced over the others, hordes of tanks being supported by enormous numbers of aircraft. The two bridges left open were wrecked next day by the R.A.F., the leading machine in the second attack being piloted by Flying Officer Ronald Garland, under whose name an account of this heroic exploit appears. *See* Netherlands.

MacArthur, GEN. DOUGLAS, D.S.C., D.S.M. (b. 1880). G.O.C. American land and air forces in the Far East. He was the virtual creator of the Filipino Army, in which he held the rank of Field-Marshal, and served with the Philippine Division of the U.S. Army from 1922 to 1936. He retired in 1937, but in July 1941 President Roosevelt, anticipating a dangerous situation arising in the Philippines owing to Japan's aggressive attitude, sent Gen. MacArthur back there. When war broke out on Dec. 7, 1941, he had under his command more than 10,000 American troops, 20,000 Filipino regulars, and 130,000 reservists.

Gen. Douglas MacArthur, G.O.C. American Land and Air Forces in the Far East.
Photo, Associated Press

After the Japanese landings particularly heavy fighting took place north-west of Manila, and here Gen. MacArthur himself took the field. Late in December he declared Manila an open town, but this did not save it from heavy enemy bombing, and by Jan. 2, 1942, he had withdrawn his troops to Corregidor (*q.v.*) and later occupied strong positions in the Bataan peninsula. Here, in January and February, he withstood violent Japanese attacks, and himself made many successful counter-attacks against the enemy.

On February 22 he received President Roosevelt's directions that he should proceed to Australia. He obtained permission to carry out a planned attack on Japanese positions, and then, leaving Maj.-Gen. Wainwright in command, he escaped to Australia with his wife and son by motor torpedo-boat and air. Here it was announced on March 17 that he had been appointed to the supreme command of the S.W. Pacific area, including Australia and the Philippines, an appointment hailed with satisfaction by the United Nations. *See* Australia; Manila; Philippine Islands.

Macassar Strait. Situated between the islands of Borneo and Celebes, the Macassar Strait connects the Celebes Sea on the north with the Java Sea on the south, and has a length of about 550 miles, with a breadth varying from 80 to 240 miles. In January 1942 this strategically important seaway was the scene of a seven-day battle between U.S. and Dutch ships and bombers and a large Japanese troops transport convoy, which was attempting to pass southward through the Strait. On Jan. 23, the first day of attack, a large enemy warship was sunk, a heavy cruiser was set on fire and left listing, and another cruiser, four large transports and a destroyer were set ablaze. Next day a large transport was sunk, a passenger liner hit, a destroyer struck four times, and four Japanese aircraft shot down. On Jan. 25 a heavy cruiser was struck, listed and probably sank, a second cruiser and troopship were set on fire, and three fighter aircraft were shot down. The Allied attacks continued up to Jan. 29, when American Flying Fortresses destroyed one transport and set another ablaze off Balik Papan. During the seven days 29 (probably 34) ships were definitely destroyed, including one battleship, and over 25,000 Japanese were killed. *See* Borneo; Pacific, War in.

Malcolm MacDonald, High Commissioner for U.K. in Canada.
Photo, Lafayette

MacDonald, RT. HON. MALCOLM, P.C., M.P. (b. 1901). High Commissioner for the United Kingdom in Canada from February 1941. He was Secretary of State for Dominion Affairs, 1938–39, and Minister of Health, 1940–41.

MacFarlane, MAJ.-GEN. F. N. MASON, C.B., D.S.O. (b. 1889). He succeeded Lord Gort as Governor and C.-in-C. of Gibraltar in May 1942. In May 1940, in France, he commanded what was known as Macforce. This mixed unit, which consisted of the 127th Infantry Brigade, a Field Artillery Regt. and the Hopkinson Mission, was organized to cover the crossing over the River Scarpe between Raches—three miles N.E. of Douai—and St. Amand, thus guarding against an immediate enemy threat to the right flank of the B.E.F. In the summer of 1940 he was appointed Military Commander at Gibraltar, where he remained until the early summer of 1941. On June 27 he arrived in Moscow at the head of a British Military Mission.

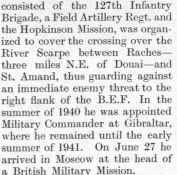

Maj.-Gen. MacFarlane, Governor and C.-in-C. of Gibraltar.
Photo, British Official

Macmillan, HUGH PATTINSON, P.C., G.C.V.O., 1ST BARON (b. 1873). He was Minister of Information from September 1939 to Jan. 5, 1940, when he tendered his resignation, and Sir John Reith was appointed as his successor. In July 1941 Lord Macmillan returned to the Court of Appeal.

Lt.-Gen. McNaughton, commanding Canadian Army in Gt. Britain.
Photo, Fox

McNaughton, LT.-GEN. ANDREW GEORGE LATTA, C.B., C.M.G., D.S.O. He commanded the First Canadian Army Overseas and arrived in Britain with the first contingent in December 1939. From December 1941 to March 1942 he toured Canada and the United States. At Washington he had conferences with President Roosevelt. Headquarters of the 1st Canadian Army in the United Kingdom of two army corps was established on April 6, 1942. The Army was stated to be strong in armoured units. Gen. McNaughton had been Chief of the Canadian General Staff from 1929 to 1935.

McPherson, FLYING OFFICER ANDREW, D.F.C. He carried out reconnaissance flights early in September 1939, and on one occasion was forced by extremely bad weather conditions to fly close to the enemy coast at very low altitudes. These flights made possible a successful raid on German naval forces. He received the D.F.C. from the King on Nov. 2, 1939, and was one of the first five airmen to be decorated.

Madagascar. French island in the Indian Ocean, lying 240 m. off the E. coast of Africa, and covering an area of 241,000 sq. m. (*see* p. 2603). With the object of forestalling a Japanese move against Madagascar, which would have imperilled the Allies' supply lines to the Middle East, India, Australia and Russia, strong British naval and military forces landed at Courier Bay at the northern end of the island on May 5, 1942, an action preliminary to crossing the isthmus to the important naval base of Diego Suarez. They were supported by carrier-borne naval aircraft which covered their landing, during which little opposition was encountered, and attacked the aerodrome, depriving the defence of air power. Simultaneously with this landing the British force commanders, under instructions from H.M. Government, made certain proposals to the French authorities, making it clear that the United Nations had no intention of interfering with the French status of the territory, and urging them to accept their offer to help in the defence of the island against Axis aggression. Marshal Pétain sent a message to the Governor-General, M. Annet, instructing him to resist, while Adml. Darlan, in a message to the Vichy forces, declared : " Fight to the limit of your possibilities and make the British pay dearly for their act of highway robbery."

Acting on these instructions the French put up a determined resistance, but on May 6 Antsirana, the chief town in the harbour of Diego Suarez, was captured, and on the following day the French naval and military commanders surrendered, and the town of Diego Suarez fell, the British Fleet entering the port. During the operations two French submarines, a sloop and an auxiliary cruiser were sunk. British casualties were just under 500. On May 13 it was announced that the Free French National Committee was to play its due part in the administration of liberated Madagascar. It was not until late in the year that fighting in the island ceased.

Magdeburg. One of Germany's important industrial cities, situated 75 miles S.W. of Berlin, Magdeburg was frequently attacked by the R.A.F. in 1940 and throughout 1941. Great damage was done to industrial buildings, and oil refineries, railway lines and stations were bombed repeatedly.

Maginot Line. This world-famous line of French fortifications, named after its designer, André Maginot, ran from the Swiss frontier south-west of Basle along the left bank of the Rhine to a position opposite Karlsruhe. Thence it turned north-westward to the southwest corner of Luxemburg, where it terminated at Montmédy. From here an extension ran to Dunkirk but it consisted of little more than concrete surface posts strung out across the plain. The Maginot Line proper was the world's most modern defence system, the work of many years and of the most careful planning by expert military engineers. Most of the fortifications were below ground, only a mound or a cupola reaching up

from out of a tangled expanse of barbed wire. There were guns by the thousand, moved and operated by electricity ; vast subterranean passages along which regiments could march in unseen security ; soldiers' quarters as capacious as they were comfortable, situated 100 or 150 ft. below ground ; first-rate sanitation and hospital facilities ; huge storehouses which a siege of many months would not empty. From the Swiss frontier to Karlsruhe the Maginot Line faced the German Siegfried Line. In between the two Lines was a No-man's-land, from three to thirteen miles wide, a region hilly and well-wooded, dotted with villages and farms. When war broke out the inhabitants were evacuated, some to France, some to Germany.

Because France believed that the Maginot Line was impregnable her war effort became essentially defensive. But the Line served the purpose of allowing France to mobilize unmolested, and it is a moot point whether the Germans could ever have got through if, instead of stopping short where it did, it had extended along the whole Belgian frontier. As it was, the enemy

Course of the two great fortified lines which protected the frontiers of France and Germany.

security among military leaders as well as in the public mind, the Maginot Line contributed to France's downfall or at least her weakness, others held that its conception was sound but vitiated by the failure or refusal of the Belgian authorities to permit similar defences continuing westwards.

For the similar German fortifications facing the Maginot Line, *see* under the heading Siegfried Line.

Magnetic Mine. This new type of sea mine, sown by aircraft, is described and illustrated under the heading Mines and Mine-laying. *See also* De-Gaussing; Ouvry.

Ivan Maisky, Soviet Ambassador to Great Britain.
Photo, Photopress

Maisky, IVAN (b. 1884). Soviet Ambassador to Great Britain from 1932. His name was prominent in 1939 at the time of the British-Soviet negotiations, and again in 1941, when he attended talks in December between Mr. Eden and Stalin at Moscow.

Malan, WING COMMDR. A. G., D.S.O., D.F.C. A South African, he was credited by March 1942 with having destroyed 32 enemy aircraft, as well as numerous others believed to have crashed. He was the first airman in this war to win bars to both his D.S.O. and D.F.C.

Wing-Cmdr. Malan, S. African airman.
Photo, Sport & General

MAGINOT LINE INSIDE AND OUT

One of the munition storage galleries in the vast underground system below the fortifications. Top, gun emplacements, like gigantic molehills, behind a protective line of small trees.
Photos, French Official

broke through north of Montmédy, outflanked the Line and finally took it in reverse. In places the Maginot defences held out for a considerable time, but, being encircled, they had eventually to surrender. While some critics considered that, in creating a false sense of

HOW MALAYA FELL TO THE JAPANESE

The invasion of Malaya began, not, as was expected, by a naval onslaught on Singapore, but by an overland attack from Siam. Tragically outnumbered, the British fought a desperate rearguard action down the Peninsula until they reached Singapore and were forced to surrender. See Pacific, War in; Siam; Singapore.

Malaya. On July 28, 1941, Japan occupied French Indo-China. It gave her many air bases, landing-grounds, and flying-boat bases. It was, clearly, the first step in a large-scale naval and military operation that could have only one objective—an attack upon the Malay Peninsula and on the Netherlands East Indies (*q.v.*).

The war in the Pacific was waged on the greatest battlefield in all history, and unless one keeps in mind the vastness of the distances over which the contending

armies and navies were fighting it is not possible to understand the reason for the movements made.

Japan had to secure Indo-China in order to secure Siam (Thailand), and she had to secure Siam in order to attack down the Malay Peninsula from the north. Military theory before the war held that attacks upon the Malay Peninsula, and upon the Island of Singapore at its southern end, were possible only from the sea. For that reason £30,000,000 was spent upon the Singapore naval base. What had been overlooked was the possibility of an over-land attack from the north through Siam, and down through the open rice- and rubber-planted country, an operation which got round the almost insuperable difficulties of landings on the jungle-clad coasts of Johore, Pahang and Trengganu.

The possibility of an attack by Japan had long been fore-seen. In August 1941 troops and R.A.F. units were sent East. On Oct. 19 the formation of a Cabinet by the Nazified General Tojo made war inevitable. On Nov. 2 Gen. Wavell visited Malaya to confer with defence chiefs. On Nov. 10 Mr. Winston Churchill announced large eastward movements of naval units. The expected attack came, Dec. 7, 1941, but it was by way of the back door, and it caught Britain unprepared.

The actual operation was a twofold one : over the Siamese frontier, and by sea, by way of the Gulf of Siam. By Dec. 9 there was already fierce fighting in North Malaya. The next day the Prince of Wales and the Repulse were sunk by Japanese air attack, a naval disaster that revealed at once the basic weakness of the British, namely, lack of air cooperation for her naval forces.

This naval tragedy was the greater since both ships

Where the Japanese landed in Malaya and thrust south to Singapore.
"New York Times"

INDIAN TROOPS MASSED IN MALAYA TO MEET THE JAPANESE

Prior to Dec. 7, 1941, when Japan struck simultaneously at many points in the Far East, large numbers of Imperial troops had arrived at Singapore, men from Australia and India, as well as from Great Britain. Many of them proceeded north up the peninsula and were in action against the Japanese, who succeeded in making landings on the beaches and fighting their way through swamps and jungle down to Singapore.

Photo, Keystone

Outnumbered, and lacking the air support enjoyed by the Japanese, the British moved down the Peninsula in what was really a continuous rearguard action. By the end of the year they had withdrawn from Ipoh.

On Dec. 8, 1941, Singapore had its first air raid, and on that date the British left Sarawak. On Jan. 5 General Wavell was appointed to the supreme command of the South-west Pacific area. Two days later the Kuantan area was evacuated, the "scorched earth" policy being applied, but in such modified form as to defeat its own purpose. On Jan. 8 the Japanese launched violent attacks on Lower Perak. Next day the British countered with heavy air raids on Bangkok, Siam.

On Jan. 10 a battle for the possession of Kuala Lumpur entailed

had no chance to go into action on the high seas against the naval forces of Japan, or to perform their logical function of intercepting Japanese troopships between the Japanese Isles and Indo-China. Both ships, under the command of Rear-Admiral Sir Tom Phillips, recently arrived in Singapore, put out to sea on Dec. 9. They were shadowed by Japanese aircraft and, having no air protection, put back. Next morning both ships were attacked from the air and sunk with great loss of life. This major sea disaster left Britain with naval forces completely inadequate for the task of barring the China Seas to Japanese troop-carrying transports, and the Japanese were, consequently, able to pour in troops and munitions from the north, impeded only by the small but very gallant Dutch naval forces.

On Dec. 13 Japanese bases in Siam were heavily bombed ; tanks made their appearance and a tank battle was fought at Kedah. Penang was raided on that day. Between Dec. 16 and

GRIM SCENES FROM THE MALAYAN BATTLE FRONT

The Australians fought magnificently in Malaya. Above is seen some of the punishment they inflicted on the enemy : one tank completely smashed, another put out of action. In the foreground lies one of the dead Japanese crew. Top, left, Army transport negotiating a heavily flooded section of road in northern Malaya.

Photos, British Official; G.P.U.

19 severe fighting proceeded in the rice-fields in N.W. Malaya. The British withdrew from Kedah to a line on the Perak frontier.

On Dec. 19 the Dutch, who had at once declared war on Japan, seized the port of Timor, which was being used by the Japanese as a submarine base. The same day Penang was evacuated and the principal line was made at Perak, where the British stood on Dec. 23.

intense fighting on both sides, with heavy casualties. Meanwhile, the R.A.F. continued to strafe the Japanese bases in Siam, wrecking trains and railway depots. By Jan. 14 it was clear that Kuala Lumpur, lacking air support, was lost, and the British carried out a further orderly withdrawal. In this great battle the Japanese used large numbers of light tanks very effectively.

On Jan. 15 General Wavell arrived in the Netherlands East Indies. A new Malaya front was drawn for a

stand; and Dutch troops went into action in Sarawak. But the advance continued, and the following day the Japanese advanced into Johore. On that day began the evacuation of Singapore. On Jan. 19 the enemy landed south of Malacca, using troop-landing barges. Singapore oil depot was set on fire. Next day the Imperial forces were threatened on their west flank and the Japanese landed reinforcements at Batu-Pahat. The Australian Imperial Force attempted to stabilize the line, and the Australian Air Force succeeded in smashing up a tank attack. On Jan. 22, with the Japanese keeping up a constant and intense pressure, it was necessary for the Australians to retreat further. Their losses were heavy; their fighting magnificent. Japanese raiders destroyed Singapore's air defences. Now

'SCORCHED' EARTH POLICY IN MALAYA
Unable to withstand the Japanese onslaught from the north, the retreating British forces left behind a systematic trail of destruction. Above is seen a blazing rubber factory near Kuala Lumpur. Top, right, Indian sappers and miners are preparing to blow up a bridge in the same area.
Photos, British Official

On Jan. 29 opened the real battle for Singapore Island, and two days later the Japanese were only 30 miles from the Causeway that links the Island of Singapore to the Malay mainland. In Borneo and the Celebes the Dutch put up a stubborn resistance. On Feb. 2, smarting under the memory of Pearl Harbour, the United States Navy delivered an attack on the Japanese Marshall Islands (q.v.) bases and the Gilberts (both groups mandated after the last war). On that day began the siege of Singapore. Australian engineers breached the Causeway, though, as events proved, not sufficiently to prevent the enemy sappers making a very swift repair for the passage of his troops.

On Feb. 5 General Wavell announced the coming of big reinforcements. Singapore was heavily and continuously bombed with considerable loss of life. Her Governor, Sir Shenton Thomas, announced a No Surrender battle-cry. The Dutch naval base at Surabaya was heavily bombed.

came the Battle of Johore, opening on Jan. 23. On Jan. 24 the Solomons, Australian islands, were invaded and Canberra sent out an SOS to London.

On Jan. 26 the Japanese landed in New Ireland, near New Guinea, but the Malayan positions were being held. But next day the Japanese captured Batu Pahat, on the west coast, using cyclists in this operation. More landings were effected by them in the Solomons.

On Feb. 10 the Japanese made a landing in force on the Island of Singapore along a 10-mile front. Flame-throwers were used, and the defenders were forced back by sheer weight of numbers and superior mechanization. Three days later fighting was taking place outside the city and resistance was plainly hopeless. On Feb. 16 the city capitulated unconditionally. The number of troops made prisoners of war was

H.M.S. MALAYA, THE GIFT OF THE FEDERATED MALAY STATES

This fine battleship, which fought in the Battle of Jutland, was the fifth of the Queen Elizabeth class to be built. She was armed with eight 15-in. guns, twelve 6-in., and eight 4-in. A.A. guns, beside a large number of smaller ones. She also carried four aircraft, with catapult. In the early hours of Feb. 9, 1941, the Malaya took part in operations off Genoa, when she plastered the Ansaldo electrical and boiler works with shells from her heavy guns.

Photo, Charles E. Brown

variously estimated, but was not known. Japanese H.Q. reported the capture of 30,000 British and Austra'ians. The British Commander, General Percival, himself became a prisoner of war.

Malaya, H.M.S. Belonging to the Queen Elizabeth class of battleship, the Malaya had a displacement of 31,100 tons and carried a complement of 1,124–1,184. She was completed in 1916, but her armour was subsequently modified and improved. The Malaya was the gift of the Federated Malay States and cost nearly £3,000,000. From August 31 to Oct. 12, 1940, a series of extensive sweeps of the western and eastern Mediterranean were carried out

by the British Navy as a result of the threat of an Italian invasion of Egypt. In these actions the Malaya played a conspicuously successful part.

Maleme. Situated at the western end of Crete, Maleme was the scene of desperate fighting between the German invaders and Greco-British forces in May 1941. Ceaseless German bombing attacks were kept up and the enemy landed some artillery at Maleme. The aerodrome was captured by the Germans on May 21. *See* Crete.

Mallet, VICTOR ALEXANDER LOUIS, C.M.G., C.V.O. (b. 1893). British Minister to Sweden from 1940. He was Counsellor at Washington from 1936 to 1939.

MALEME AERODROME AFTER THE GERMANS INVADED CRETE

It was at Maleme, 10 miles south-west of Canea, that the main body of enemy air-borne troops landed in May 1941. From this vital centre they could attack both Canea and Suda Bay, where British warships were lying. The photograph shows the aerodrome cluttered up with Junkers transport planes, many of which crash-landed in an effort to get the aircraft down quickly.

Photo, British Official

MALTA: BRITISH BASTION IN THE MEDITERRANEAN

*In less than two years Malta suffered and withstood over 2,000 raids.
Despite these unceasing attacks the island is still a great naval base,
convoys continue to arrive safely, and the inhabitants accept with
equanimity a life lived partly underground.   See Mediterranean.*

Malta. Malta is a rock. Geographically, it is African ; culturally, it is European. It is the most exposed place in the British Empire in time of war, and it was the first place in the Empire to be attacked. It has suffered grievously, having had more than 2,000 heavy air raids in under two years. But it is a rock and still stands. Napoleon described it as " the strongest place in Europe."

Malta (*see* pages 2628–29) lies in the Mediterranean sixty miles from Sicily, on the Gibraltar-Alexandria ship lane. It is also on the sea route of Italy and Tripoli. How this geographic fact affects Italian operations in North Africa was put recently by an Italian writer. " Italy," he wrote, " is like a man who has to cross a path on a more or less urgent errand, but who suspects that at any time he may be attacked without knowing by how many enemies and from what direction."

It is the natural fortress or bastion from which we can organize sea war in the Mediterranean and its fall would be a military disaster of the first order for us. Thanks to the superb courage of its population it resisted successfully every attack from 1940 onwards.

From a strategic point of view Malta leaves a good deal to be desired. It is within 20 minutes from enemy airfields. But this vulnerability carries with it power to operate by air against the nerve centres of Italian war industry. Twenty-five years ago it would not have been true to say that. For then Malta had to do in war with ships, and it is an island whose fine harbours have been the envy of sailors since the day when Phoenicians, Greeks and Romans took the island by force of arms.

Very different is the position of Malta when for both defence and attack the air arm offers the logical form of combat. In air war it is difficult to defend a small area, for it becomes a clearly defined target from the air from which the population cannot be evacuated, and Malta has 250,000 inhabitants. It is equally handicapped for air attack, however, since it offers few facilities for airfields. Despite this limitation, in one month alone in 1942 R.A.F. aircraft, using Malta, dropped 1,000,000 bombs on enemy objectives, and flew 250,000 miles on these operational flights.

From the moment Italy came into the war it may be said with truth that Malta has been living in a state of siege. It has been invested from the deep blue vault of the Mediterranean sky.

On Jan. 16, 1941, German dive-bombers in force attacked the harbour, where the aircraft-carrier Illustrious and the destroyer Gallant lay after the great action six days earlier in the Sicilian Channel, when both ships had been damaged by enemy dive-bombers while escorting a convoy. The defence put up at Malta was heroic and brought congratulations to the islanders from Mr. Winston Churchill. In July 1941 large formations of Italian bombers made a terrific air assault on Grand Harbour, the island's chief anchorage. With the night air attack they used fast E-boats and torpedo-boats. It was a long-thought-out attack which was to end the island's obstinate resistance. Rome boasted the exploit—but not one Italian ship returned to tell the tale.

The Nazis Could Not Finish Malta

When the Germans sent squadrons south to stiffen the discredited Italian Air Force, they based their air force on Sicily. They told their Italian comrades that they would finish Malta in sixty hours. But they did not ; nor in six hundred. Malta, it became clear, could take punishment. But, more marvellous still, the battered island struck back, again and again, inflicting heavy losses on the raiders.

The Maltese are of mixed racial origin. In their veins runs the blood of Phoenicians, Greeks, Romans, Goths, Arabs and Latins. They are dark, sturdy and volatile and formerly were regarded as indolent. The present ordeal has revealed a hard unsuspected streak in the Maltese character which has drawn the admiration of the world. In one respect, even so,

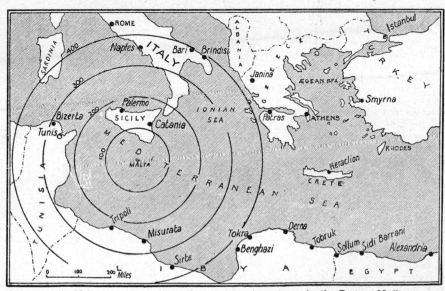

Showing how Malta controls seaways of paramount importance in the Eastern Mediterranean.

British subjects by their own will since 1814, when they refused to become subject to the crown of Sicily, have many sons in the King's Own Malta Regiment, of which the first contingent left for active service overseas on May 5, 1940.

For a long time it has been Italian policy to plant in the simple Maltese mind the idea that they are culturally and racially Italianate. For years before the war the Italian Government conducted an intensive propaganda drive in the island, endeavouring to persuade the people of their natural Italian affiliations. Scholarships were offered to Maltese lads to Italian schools and colleges, and students were given financial aid. All this propaganda effort was negatived when the first bomb fell from an Italian aeroplane, and since then whatever Italian sentiment may have existed on the island has been obliterated.

The Lieut.-Governor, Sir Edward Jackson, who administered the civil side of the island under the then Governor, Lieut.-General Sir William Dobbie, revealed the

Malta compares well in the matter of civil defence with other territories in the war zone. It has the finest natural deep air-raid shelters in the world. These are the famous Catacombs traditionally supposed to have once been used by early Christians. They resemble the Phoenician tombs in Syria and are probably of Phoenician origin. In them hundreds of families have made their homes, leaving the pellucid light of the Mediterranean for the damp and darkness of excavations that were old when Nero put a torch to Rome.

Thanks to these shelters, and to the resilience of the Maltese people, the island has withstood every air and sea assault made upon it. Perhaps nothing reveals the quality of these astonishing islanders more than a recent charitable appeal made to them to which they responded in the most generous way. It was an appeal for the bombed people of East London! Maltese absent from the island have organized a Maltese Relief Fund. The British Government gave £1,000,000 for Maltese relief.

Malta's contribution to the Empire's war effort does not end with her magnificent defence of the island. The Maltese, who are

AN AIR ATTACK ON MALTA
The A.A. barrage is here seen bursting in the sky during a raid on this island citadel; Malta's gunners are famed for the accuracy of their marksmanship. When a raid is imminent a red flag is hoisted high on a building (top, left), and sometimes flew there for six hours at a stretch.
Photos, Associated Press

MALTA'S REPLY TO THE ENEMY'S ONSLAUGHT

1. Hurricanes lined up ready to take off in the defence of the island ; in the background is Valetta, the ancient capital.
2. Wreckage of an Italian aircraft shot down by the South African Air Force in Malta. 3. Policemen, wearing battle-dress,
clear away debris after a raid. 4. View across the island during an air raid, showing German bombs bursting in the distance.
In April and May 1942 the Germans so intensified their air attacks on the island that it was temporarily put out of action as
a raiding base for the R.A.F. against enemy supply vessels proceeding to Libya.

Photos, British Official

WHEN THE BATTLE OF MALTA WAS AT ITS HEIGHT IN 1941

This informative painting by Joseph Galea, a Maltese artist, depicts one of the final attacks by Stukas when the aircraft carrier H.M.S. Illustrious (see pp. 183 and 249) had reached Malta Harbour. Beginning on January 10, 1941, no fewer than six determined dive-bombing attacks were made on the aircraft carrier. Hit repeatedly by heavy bombs, she

MANCHESTER CLEARS UP AFTER THE GERMAN BOMBING

One of the great provincial cities which suffered heavily from enemy air raids was Manchester. The photograph shows how a devastated area in the centre of the city has been cleared of debris. On the left is Deansgate leading to the cathedral, one chapel of which was destroyed on the night of Dec. 22, 1940. Across the picture in the foreground runs St. Mary's Gate.

Photo, Topical Press

quality of the Maltese in a broadcast tribute to their courage and endurance. " Is it not a very great thing," he asked, " that so many hundreds of men and women have proved to themselves that they can look in the face of danger undismayed, that they can have torn from them in an instant all that they possessed in the world except the courage to get up out of the dust and begin all over again ? And is it not something to have shown the world that the people of Malta have that courage ? "

According to the General Officer Commanding the troops, Maj.-Gen. D. M. W. Beak, V.C., the Malta raids are not comparable to England's worst : it is the duration of the air bombardment which challenges the island's spirit. On Jan. 3, 1942, paying a warm tribute to the gallantry of the people, he said : " The enemy is evidently attempting to make it very difficult for us to use it, trying to neutralize the dockyards and airfields. The damage is insignificant despite continual bombings, and, as I said before, Malta is well able to look after itself. I am full of faith in the gallant peoples of the island."

In recognition of this heroism and devotion in face of ceaseless enemy attacks, the King bestowed the George Cross on the island on April 16, 1942. Malta thus had the distinction of receiving the first such award to be made to any part of the British Commonwealth.

On May 8, 1942, Malta had its 2,300th raid. The Germans and Italians appear to have been prepared to face any losses in their effort to subdue the island, for the A.A. defences of Malta were remarkably effective. In April 1942 alone, when 6,000 tons of bombs were dropped, 101 enemy planes were shot down. During the four months ending April 5 the Axis lost 199 planes, in addition to many more damaged.

It was announced on May 7 that Lt.-Gen. Sir Wm. Dobbie, Governor and C.-in-C. Malta, who was suffering from severe overstrain which necessitated a period of rest, had tendered his resignation and that he would be succeeded by Gen. Viscount Gort, Governor and C.-in-C. Gibraltar. Lord Gort arrived in Malta the next day. Sir William Dobbie received the G.C.M.G. on his retirement.

Manchester. This great industrial centre (*see* pp. 2640–41) was frequently attacked by the Luftwaffe. The first severe raid occurred on December 22–23, 1940, when the Royal Exchange and the Military Chapel of the 14th-century cathedral were wrecked, and there were many casualties. Attacks were continued in 1941, and a heavy night raid on June 1 caused considerable damage. Public buildings, factories, churches and office blocks were among the many objectives that the German airmen selected haphazard, and numerous fires were started.

Mandel, GEORGES (b. 1885). At the outbreak of war he was Colonial Minister in the Daladier Cabinet, and became Minister of the Interior in March 1940, under Reynaud. He was also one of the nine members of the Inner War Cabinet. At the time of the collapse of France in June 1940 he went to French North Africa, but was sent back and accused by the Vichy Government of being one of the Ministers responsible for France's downfall, and proceedings were taken against him before the Supreme Court of Riom (*q.v.*).

Manila. Capital of the Philippines, on the west coast of Luzon Island, Manila (*see* pp. 2643–2644) was raided by Japanese bombers for the first time on Dec. 9, 1941, when the southern part of the city was the main target. Already on Dec. 8 Fort William McKinley and Nichol's Field, the large air base near the capital, had been attacked, and Clark's Field, the military aerodrome, 40 miles north of the city, also suffered bombing raids. Japanese landings on the west coast of Luzon, at a point about 200 miles north of the city, were made on Dec. 9, and by Dec. 11 the Cavite Naval Yard in Manila Bay had been raided and great damage caused. Despite the fact that Manila had been declared an open city, and every A.A. gun and all other weapons of defence, as well as troops, removed, Japanese bombers savagely attacked the capital for three hours on Dec. 27, killing over 40 people and destroying many buildings. These included the former palace of the Spanish governors and the church of Santo Domingo. Another ruthless attack was made on Dec. 28, when Corregidor, the island fortress at the

to recapture the territories yielded up to Russia at the conclusion of the earlier struggle, looked to Mannerheim once more as her supreme military leader. On July 11, 1941, he declared in an Order of the Day that the objective of the Army was a "great Finland" and "the liberation of the Karelian people" on both sides of the frontier. It was suggested that when, in October 1941, Great Britain declared that

MANILA PREPARES FOR ATTACK

That apprehension was felt in the Philippines before the Japanese invasion of Dec. 9, 1941, is indicated by these two pictures, one showing a practice black-out in Manila, the other four Filipino girls inspecting gas masks during a civilian defence demonstration.

Photos, Planet News

entrance to Manila Bay, was also bombed. The U.S. War and Navy Depts. announced on Jan. 2, 1942, that the evacuation of Manila and the Cavite naval base had taken place after all American and Filipino troops had been withdrawn. Advanced elements of Japanese forces then entered the city, but U.S. troops continued to hold Corregidor and certain powerfully defended positions to the north-west of the city, and against these areas a relentless air offensive was carried out by the Japanese. *See* Corregidor; MacArthur, Gen.; Philippines.

Mannerheim, FIELD-MARSHAL CARL GUSTAV EMIL, BARON (b. 1867). One of Finland's most famous and enterprising figures, the leader of the "Whites" against the "Reds" in the Civil War of 1918, Mannerheim was appointed by President Kallio "Defender of Finland" and C.-in-C. of the Finnish Army on Nov. 30, 1939, the first day of the Russo-Finnish war. Throughout that winter he directed the valiant Finnish armies, winning many victories against troops far greater in number and better equipped, although it became clear at the close of the campaign that the victories had little effect upon the result of the war, as explained under the heading Finland. In February

Field-Marshal Mannerheim, Finnish soldier.
Photo, Wide World

1940 it was reported that he had taken over command on the Karelian front, where the fiercest fighting was now concentrated. In March he was forced to advise the Finnish Government to accept Sweden's offer of mediation between Finland and Russia. War again broke out between the two countries when Germany invaded the U.S.S.R. in June 1941. Finland, throwing in her lot with Germany and wishing

Finland allied with Nazi Germany had become an enemy nation, it was Mannerheim's influence that stiffened the Finnish Government. *See* Finland.

Mannerheim Line. Named after Finland's famous Field-Marshal, the Mannerheim Line was a series of strong defensive fortifications designed to protect Finland against Russian attacks. It stretched across the Karelian Isthmus from the Gulf of Finland to Lake Ladoga, being based on the water system of the Vuoksi River. This section constituted one branch. The other branch extended from Taipale to Sortavala, thus covering the greater part of the western and northern banks of Lake Ladoga in Finnish territory. The Russian frontal attack on the Line showed that the strongest fortifications of this nature were not impregnable to modern methods of assault. The Russian peace treaty of March 12, 1940, stipulated that the whole of the Mannerheim Line defences in the Karelian Isthmus should pass to the U.S.S.R. From June 1941, when the Finns joined the Germans in attacking Russia, the Line was again a war zone. *See* Finland.

Mannheim. Chief industrial centre of the Upper Rhine, Mannheim was frequently raided by bombers of the R.A.F. in 1940–1942. The first heavy raid occurred on Dec. 4–5, 1940 ; it was repeated on the next night and again on the night of 20–21 on a smaller scale. During the first raid a bomb gravely affected the work of the fire-fighting services in the city ; marshalling yards were brought to a standstill by the lack of electricity and water. Armament works, oil plants and docks were subsequently attacked. During the first week of August 1941 bombs put out of action one of the railway lines for some days, sidings and warehouses were destroyed and a gas container exploded, while considerable losses were inflicted on rolling stock. In 1940 and 1941 the city was bombed 51 times. Some particularly heavy raids occurred during February 1942. On May 19 a large force of R.A.F. bombers carried out a concentrated attack on Mannheim, using the heaviest H.E. bombs and thousands of incendiaries.

J. F. Mantle, awarded the V.C.
Photo, G.P.U.

Mantle, LEADING SEAMAN JACK FOREMAN. A posthumous award of the V.C. was made to this sailor on Sept. 3, 1940, for acts of gallantry on July 4. When his ship, H.M.S. Foylebank, a 5,000-ton motor vessel of the Bank Line, was attacked by enemy aircraft, Mantle, who was in charge of a pom-pom, had his left leg shattered. Nevertheless, he remained at his gun, and when the ship's electric power failed he continued to fire with hand gear only. He was wounded many times, but his courage bore him up to the end of the fight. He later succumbed to his wounds.

Marblehead, U.S.S. Completed in 1924, this 7,050-ton U.S. light cruiser carried a main armament of ten 6-in. guns and a complement of 458. The Japanese repeatedly claimed to have sunk her in the Battle of Java Sea, but on May 6, 1942, she arrived at an American E. coast port, having made her voyage half way round the world after being bombed three times and severely damaged.

Margesson, CAPT. DAVID, P.C., M.C. (b. 1890). He was Parliamentary Secretary to the Treasury and Govt. Chief Whip from 1931 to 1940, when he became Joint Chief Whip with Sir Charles Edwards in Mr. Churchill's National Coalition Government. In December of that year he was appointed Secretary of State for War in succession to Mr. Eden. He was the fourth to hold this post since the outbreak of war. When Mr. Churchill reorganized his Cabinet on Feb. 22, 1942, Capt. Margesson was replaced by Sir James Grigg (*q.v.*). He was later given a Viscounty.

Capt. Margesson was Secretary for War.
Photo, Sport & General

Maritime Regiment. Established in May 1941, but kept secret until 1942, the Maritime Regiments operate the air defence of merchant ships. In May 1942 there were four regiments, officially part of the Royal Artillery, about 12,000 strong, mostly volunteers from the Army. Trained at naval gunnery schools, they are acquainted with every type of weapon. They wear an Admiralty badge—a red anchor with the letters A.A.— and are on ordinary Army pay. Formed after the fall of France, when a number of men were transferred from the Army to supplement the force of the Defensively Equipped Merchant Ship ratings (the D.E.M.S.), they at first operated in British waters, but later helped successfully in the Battle of the Atlantic. Thus the 17th Century Maritime Regiments were revived after nearly 300 years.

Mariupol. Situated in Southern Ukraine, between Taganrog and Melitopol, north of the Sea of Azov, this town was evacuated by the Russians on Oct. 14, 1941, after fierce fighting. The Germans, under Von Kleist, continued their thrust eastward towards Rostov-on-Don, a distance of about 100 miles, but suffered great losses, and fighting continued in this area without respite throughout October. Timoshenko's forces succeeded in routing the enemy in the Rostov and Taganrog areas in November, and pursued them back to Mariupol. Von Kleist's troops fell back on the town on Nov. 30. Their chief concern then was to avoid encirclement if the Soviet forces should drive farther west along the shores of the Sea of Azov. By Feb. 3, 1942, the Russians had driven a wedge between the German forces fighting south of Kharkov and those operating along the Sea of Azov. They by-passed Mariupol in order to avoid exhausting frontal attacks, and in so doing they cut the Mariupol-Dnepropetrovsk railway, the main line of supply for the Germans in the whole of the area.

Marshall, GEN. GEORGE CATLETT (b. 1880). Chief of Staff of U.S. Army from Sept. 1, 1939. He attended the Churchill-Roosevelt Atlantic Conference in August 1941. In April 1942 Gen. Marshall arrived in England for talks with British leaders on questions of strategy, and to see something of the development of British forces.

Gen. George Marshall, C. of S., U.S. Army.
Photo, Sport & General

Marshall-Cornwall, LT.-GEN. SIR JAMES HANDYSIDE, K.C.B., D.S.O. (b. 1887). G.O.C.-in-C. Western Command from November 1941, when he succeeded Gen. Sir Robert Gordon Finlayson. He was Director-General of the Air and Coast Defence at the War Office from 1938 to 1939, and G.O.C. British Troops in Egypt in 1941 until he took over the Western Command. As chief of the British Military Mission in Egypt in 1937 he helped to modernize the Egyptian Army.

Marshall Islands. Formerly owned by Germany, the Marshall group of islands, situated S.E. of the Caroline Islands in the Pacific, was placed under a Japanese mandate after having been surrendered by Germany at the end of the last war. On Jan. 31, 1942, the American Pacific Fleet and air units struck a fierce blow at Japanese shipping and shore establishments in the islands. The principal attack centred on the anchorage at Kwajalein Island. Sixteen ships in all were destroyed, including a converted 17,000-ton aircraft carrier, a light cruiser, a destroyer, three large tankers, two submarines, five cargo vessels, and some smaller ships. Other ships were badly damaged. Aircraft destroyed included two large seaplanes, 15 fighters, 11 scout bombers, and 10 bombers of other types. Shore establishments demolished were hangars, ammunition dumps, fuel storage tanks, four radio stations, A.A. batteries, and some industrial buildings. The cost

U.S. RAID ON JAPANESE ISLANDS
American gunners open fire during a raid on the Japanese base in the Marshall Islands, North Pacific.
Photo, Wide World

to the attacking forces comprised the loss of five scout aeroplanes and some damage to a cruiser.

Martel, LT.-GEN. GIFFARD LE QUESNE, C.B., D.S.O. (b. 1889). Commander of the Royal Armoured Corps from 1940. He was Deputy Director of Mechanization at the War Office, 1938–1939, and afterwards commanded the 50th Division of the B.E.F. He arrived in France in February 1940, and was in charge of the British counterattack at Arras on May 23.

Lt.-Gen. Martel, Commander of Royal Armoured Corps.
Photo, British Official

Martinique. A French island in the West Indies, lying between the British islands of Dominica and St. Lucia, Martinique (*see* p. 2669) came into prominence after the collapse of France in 1940. Admiral Robert, in command of French warships at Martinique, declared that he felt it his duty to obey the orders of the Vichy Government and make for France. This he could not do without coming into contact with British warships, which maintained a strict blockade of the island. It was obvious that had these French warships, which included the aircraft carrier Béarn, returned to France, they would have come under the control of the Germans, and fears were expressed that the Axis Powers might use Martinique as a base. President Roosevelt sent Admiral Greenslade to the island in August 1940, and after a few days it was understood that a compromise had been effected. The ships were virtually decommissioned and laid up in the harbours of the island and their crews demobilized. No satisfactory arrangement, however, was made regarding the ownership of American-built 'planes ordered when France was fighting as Britain's ally. On Dec. 20, 1941, it was announced that a naval agreement had been reached between the French High Commissioner and the U.S.A.

After Laval's return to power in the Vichy Government in April 1942 America decided to forestall any Axis attempt to use Martinique as a base. U.S. representatives negotiated with Admiral Robert, and on May 15 it was reported that agreement had been reached. The negotiations concerned the immobilization of French warships and merchant ships, control of wireless stations and the dismantling of fortifications. America would safeguard French interests in return for assurances that Martinique and other Caribbean islands would "furnish no aid or comfort to the Axis forces."

Martuba. Important landing-ground, S.E. of Derna, Libya, used by the enemy during Rommel's campaign in the spring of 1942. It was constantly attacked by British mobile columns and by the R.A.F. and S.A.A.F., and on April 9 it was reported that, in order to protect it from further land assaults, Rommel was attempting to establish a line of strong points southwards from Gazala.

Masaryk, JAN. Deputy Premier in the Czechoslovak Government established in London. At the time of the Czechoslovak Government's formal recognition by the British Government in July 1940 he was appointed Minister of Foreign Affairs.

Jan Masaryk, Czech Foreign Minister.
Photo, Wide World

Massawa. Chief port of Eritrea on the Red Sea, Massawa was captured by British Imperial forces on April 8, 1941. Its surrender by the Italians sealed the fate of Italy's oldest colony, for it meant that Mussolini had lost his last port on the Red Sea, and that shipping in that sea would no longer be menaced by the Italians. *See* East Africa.

Massey Shaw. This famous fire float of the London Fire Brigade took part in the evacuation of the B.E.F. from Dunkirk in May 1940. Manned by a

LONDON'S FIREFLOAT MASSEY SHAW
The Massey Shaw was one of the gallant band of little vessels sent to help in the evacuation from Dunkirk. Her crew consisted of regular firemen and A.F.S. men, all of whom volunteered for the job.
Photo, Wide World

Naval lieutenant and a volunteer crew, she crossed to the French port and brought home 60 men. Returning again, the Massey Shaw ferried 500 men from shore to ship, and then came back to England with another load.

Matapan, CAPE. The great naval battle fought between British and Italian forces off Cape Matapan—the southernmost point of Greece—was one of the most outstanding naval engagements of the war. On March 27. 1941, air reconnaissance reported Italian cruisers at sea S.E. of Sicily. This enemy naval force was presumably steaming towards the Eastern Mediterranean to harass British convoys between Greece and Egypt. Adm. Sir Andrew Cunningham (q.v.) was at Alexandria, and made the following disposition of his forces : H.M.S. cruisers Orion, Ajax, Gloucester, H.M.A.S. Perth and some destroyers were ordered to a position south of Crete. Meanwhile the Warspite, accompanied by the battleships Valiant and Barham, the aircraft carrier Formidable, together with a destroyer force, steamed in a N.W. direction in the hope of intercepting the enemy ships and bringing them to action.

On March 28 air reconnaissance reported a considerable force of Italian ships, consisting of the battleship Vittorio Veneto, six cruisers and seven destroyers. The enemy was later reported to be 35 miles south of Gavdo Island, south of Crete, and was there joined by two more cruisers and two destroyers. The British cruisers, under the command of Vice-Adm. Sir Henry Pridham-Wippell (q.v.), contacted the enemy cruisers, after which, turning S.E., they attempted to draw the Italians towards the main British fleet. A torpedo attack was launched on the Vittorio Veneto by the

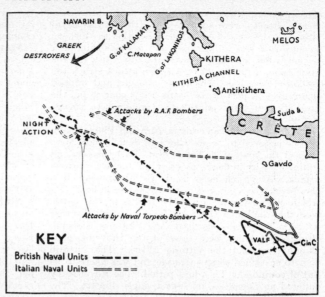

HOW THE BATTLE OF MATAPAN WAS FOUGHT
Map showing the attempt of Vice-Admiral Pridham-Wippell, VALF (i.e. Vice-Admiral Light Forces), to draw the Italian cruisers towards the main British fleet ; also the long chase, during which the enemy ships were under repeated air attack, and the night engagement off Cape Matapan.
Admiralty Chart

Fleet Air Arm operating from H.M.S. Formidable, and one hit was claimed. Shortly afterwards, Pridham-Wippell's force met the main British fleet and all the British warships set off in pursuit of the Italians, the latter by then having headed towards their bases.

A second enemy fleet was reported 80 miles west of Gavdo island. This comprised two battleships of the

A NEAR MISS ON THE BRITISH CRUISER GLOUCESTER
Not one of H.M. ships was hit at Matapan, March 28, 1941, and there was not a single casualty, although two Fleet Air Arm machines were lost. The enemy, on the other hand, lost three cruisers—Fiume, Pola and Zara—and two destroyers, Maestrale and Vincenzo Gioberti. The cruiser Giovanni delle Bande Nere and destroyer Vittorio Alfieri were probably sunk, and the Vittorio Veneto badly damaged. The Gloucester, seen in this photograph, was sunk off Crete, May 22, 1941.
Photo, " News Chronicle "

Cavour class, three cruisers and four destroyers. Heavy attacks were again launched by British naval aircraft, in which three hits were scored on the Vittorio Veneto, two hits on a cruiser, and probable hits on a second, while a destroyer suffered a direct hit. At the same time, a further Fleet Air Arm attack struck the Italian cruiser Pola, which was damaged and stopped three miles to port of the battle fleet's course, and the main British force immediately prepared to engage this enemy unit.

Suddenly the Italian cruisers, Zara and Fiume, and a cruiser believed to be the Giovanni delle Bande Nere, crossed the bows of the British fleet. Both the Zara and Fiume blew up in flames as a result of the fierce British attack. A possible move by the enemy to escape into the Adriatic was covered by a force of Greek destroyers which steamed westward. The results of this battle were that the Fiume, Pola and Zara were sunk, together with the destroyers Maestrale and Vincenzo Gioberti. Probable sinkings were those of the Giovanni delle Bande Nere and the Vittorio Alfieri. The Vittorio Veneto sustained serious damage and was likely to be out of commission for a long period. The Royal Navy suffered no casualties, nor was a single ship hit. The only British losses were two Fleet Air Arm machines.

Some 55 Italian officers and 850 seamen, as well as 35 German naval officers and ratings, were picked up from sunken enemy warships. About 3,000 Italian officers and men, including Adm. Cantoni, who commanded the Italian heavy cruiser squadron, perished. Some hundreds more survivors would have been saved had not German bombers attacked those engaged in the work of rescue.

Cape Matapan was described later as "the most momentous naval victory since Trafalgar." This victory without loss was a triumphant vindication of the Admiralty's policy of giving the most careful training in night fighting.

Matchek, DR. VLATKA. Leader of the Croatian cause in Yugoslavia, he became first Vice-Prime Minister in the Yugoslav Cabinet which was formed under the Premiership of Gen. Simovitch in March 1941. As leader of the Croat Peasant Party, Matchek called for Croat unity against the Germans when the latter invaded Yugoslavia on April 6, 1941. On June 30, after the German occupation of Croatia had been effected and enemy reprisals were being carried out in a savage fashion, Dr. Matchek was taken to Germany on the pretext that his life was " endangered." In April 1942 he was released from a concentration camp and sent home in a grievous condition.

Mathews, MRS. VERA LAUGHTON, M.B.E. At the outbreak of war in September 1939 she became Director of the W.R.N.S. (Women's Royal Naval Service). During the last war she organized the first unit of the W.R.N.S. and under her leadership the "Wrens" rapidly became one of the most efficient of the Women's Services (q.v.).

Matsuoka, YOSUKE (b. 1880). He became Foreign Minister in Prince Konoye's pro-Fascist Cabinet in July 1940. On Aug. 1 Matsuoka declared that Japanese foreign policy aimed at constructing a " new order " in greater Eastern Asia. It was he who ordered the arrest of a dozen well-known British citizens on the charge of espionage. In March 1941

Y. Matsuoka, former Foreign Minister of Japan.
Photo, Wide World

Matsuoka left Tokyo for a series of visits in Europe, his stated object being " to make a substantial contribution towards lasting peace and the New Order of the world." He first had conversations at Moscow with Stalin and Molotov, and then went to Berlin. Here, between March 26 and 29, he had conversations with Hitler, Ribbentrop, Goering, Keitel and Funk. From March 31 to April 3 he stayed in Rome, conferring with Mussolini and Ciano, and being received in audience by the King and the Pope. Back in Berlin, he was again received by Hitler before leaving once more for Moscow. Here, on April 13, a pact of friendship and neutrality was signed between Japan and the U.S.S.R. Some nine weeks later Germany invaded Russia, and on July 16 Matsuoka was replaced by Admiral Toyoda. *See* Japan ; Russia.

Maubeuge. A strongly fortified town on the Maginot Line in N.E. France, close to the Belgian frontier, Maubeuge played a vital part in the

LAST FORT OF MAUBEUGE CAPITULATES

Here is seen the cupola of Des Sarts after the brave defenders had been forced to hoist the white flag. One of the outlying forts, it continued to offer a determined resistance after the fall of the main fortress at Maubeuge, until most of its turrets were out of action and its guns silenced.

" Battle of the Bulge " in May 1940. A salient was formed in the Allied line near Sedan on May 16, and widened out until it extended by May 18 as far as Maubeuge. The Germans turned westwards and the town was taken by their storm troops on May 21. In this sector enemy 'planes destroyed numbers of tanks with which the French had hoped to stay the fierce German onrush. Had the main fortress been able to offer a prolonged resistance the course of this battle might have been different. The various forts resisted valiantly, but were overwhelmed by superior forces, the last to capitulate being Des Sarts. With most of its turrets out of action and its guns silenced by the terrific hail of shell fire, the garrison had then to meet the frenzied onrush of Nazi troops   *See* France.

Maulde. This place constituted the right-hand limit of the first dispositions of one of the main B.E.F. sectors in Northern France in 1939, Halluin being the left-hand limit. On Oct. 3, 1939, the 1st Corps under Field-Marshal Sir John Dill took over the sector Maulde-Grison on the Belgian frontier.

Max, ADOLPHE (1869–1939). Burgomaster of Brussels from 1909, Max was one of the heroic figures of the last war. Because of his courageous resistance to German demands in the early days of the occupation, he was arrested in September 1914 and imprisoned. In November 1918 he was reinstated in his former position at Brussels. Max died on Nov. 6, 1939, at a time when Germany was again preparing an invasion. He was succeeded by M. van der Meulebroeck (*q.v.*).

POWER OF THE MODERN MECHANIZED ARMY

The days of marching infantry and trench warfare seem far away. Today an army, and all its equipment, moves swiftly in motorized vehicles, mobility has taken on a new meaning, and mechanized warfare annihilates both time and space beneath its caterpillar wheels.
See Army; Tanks.

Mechanization of Armies. Mechanization is the provision of self-propelled transport and fighting machines. Its development can be seen from a comparison of the number of self-propelled vehicles and machines possessed by the British Expeditionary Force which went to France in 1914 and the number taken with the B.E.F. of 1939. The 1914 force numbered 148,000 men; the force sent to France in September 1939 was bigger by 10,000. In 1914 there were only 800 mechanized vehicles with the Army; twenty-five years later our expeditionary force required more than 25,000 mechanical vehicles and self-propelled fighting machines.

Now let us look at another army—that of the United States of America. An armoured corps was formed in 1940, largely modelled on the pattern of the German Panzer (" armoured ") divisions. There were four divisions, each of some 9,000 men, and each was composed of :

> Observation aircraft squadron
> Reconnaissance battalion
> Tank brigade
>> 272 light tanks; 110 medium tanks; 201 armoured scout cars
> Mechanized field artillery regiment
> Field artillery battalion
> Motorized infantry regiment with its own ordnance.
> The artillery of a division included 8 guns of 75 mm. calibre; 12 guns of 105 mm.; and 24 howitzers of 75 mm.

This American force did not carry mechanization so far as the German organization, but its composition gives an idea of the nature of a modern army, moving on wheels and able to cover 100 miles a day.

The part formerly played by cavalry in reconnaissance and scouting is now performed by aircraft and light motorized units—troops on motor cycles; others in motor-cycle " combinations " (machine-gun in sidecar); other troops in lightly armoured machine-gun carriers on caterpillar tractors, able to go at fair speed over rough country. The division can summon to its aid squadrons of dive-bombing or assault aircraft, which act as a spearhead in attacking opposing armoured formations. In the U.S. army referred to, armoured " scout " cars act as aggressive reconnaissance units, making swift attacks at vital points and withdrawing rapidly. Light armoured cars of the

British divisions did similar work in Libya, harassing the enemy and securing valuable information which they radioed to their base.

The field artillery is towed by tractors or, in the case of lighter guns, by special tenders which carry the gun crew also. The same method of transport is used for the many types of anti-aircraft guns, dual-purpose quick-firers, or tank guns. Heavy artillery in the main is carried on railway mountings, but today quite big guns travel by road and travel fast.

Infantry travel in lorries with their arms and special equipment, reaching the striking point fresh and unfatigued. Similarly, if strategy calls for a mass transfer of units to a sector miles away, the movement is carried out swiftly and, quite as important, with a fair measure of secrecy. It follows from this very

ROUGH-RIDERS OF THE ARMY
A Bren carrier climbs to the top of a heather-covered hill to take up a fighting position during severe training tests undergone by a Reconnaissance Unit in the Northern Command
Photo, Topical

LEARNING THE NEW WARFARE

Ambushed " enemy " dispatch riders fire their automatic rifles from the shelter of their motor-bicycle during manoeuvres in Britain. The invading troops were distinguished by the white cross on their crash hats or by wearing steel helmets.

Photo, Planet News

mobility of the ground troops that a competent general can do more with a given strength of men than was possible a generation ago. Motorization has endowed the bold and resourceful commander with enormous powers, but he has had to learn his profession anew in order to employ these powers to advantage. The tempo has quickened, and all ranks nowadays have to think quickly and act rapidly.

The tactics of the armoured army are briefly to attack in column of tanks, driving in what seems a reckless manner at the enemy line, breaking through by sheer momentum and weight of metal and, once through the main opposing forces, fanning out behind and taking the defenders in the rear. Given a distant objective of crucial importance, a column may push on at utmost speed towards it, leaving to other formations the task of covering flanks and mopping up isolated bands of defenders.

The old conception of a continuous defence line, the piercing of which was regarded as a grave and maybe mortal wound, has gone. Defence now is zonal and extends deeper back from the point of contact with the enemy. Defending formations cut off from their neighbours or even surrounded entirely still fight on, and in this swift war of movement may fight a way out to join other bands and turn the tables on their foe. Isolated armies may be provisioned and supplied from the air by resolute airmen ; they may be reinforced in the same way, and even gliders (*q.v.*) have come into use for this latter purpose.

As to strategy, the campaigns in Europe and in North Africa have given object lessons of what may be accomplished with the new machines and new methods. Poland was overrun in three weeks ; five days sufficed to bring the Netherlands armies to terms ; Belgium's King sued for an armistice on the eighteenth day of the German invasion ; the British Expedi-

tionary Force in Belgium was withdrawn by the twenty-fourth day. A bare month later France signed an armistice. Much of this lightning success was due to surprise and unpreparedness, it is true, but the inherent character of the Panzer war made recovery almost impossible once grave wounds had been inflicted on the Allied armies.

In Libya the ebb and flow of mechanized war was remarkable, but behind this kaleidoscopic change there lay the menace of a swift enemy dash in force over the many miles of desert to Alexandria and the Suez Canal —an operation possible only to the new army of today, to which the desert is no longer a barrier.

On the other hand, it has to be remembered that the virtues of mechanization in war can be exaggerated. A multiplicity of motorized vehicles entails complicated systems of both supplies and repairs, and gadgets may assume too great an importance. Behind the mechanized forces must come the infantry, the greater bulk of the army, who will occupy and hold the ground fully won and exploit the partial successes of their armoured comrades, completing their work. Vitally important as the tanks and highly mobile forces are in modern fighting, experience in both Russia and the East has shown that simpler methods can achieve great successes. The Cossack horses in winter and Japanese bicycles in Malaya are examples.

Books to Consult: War on Wheels, Capt. Liddell Hart (John Lane). Engines of War: Mechanized Army in Action (A. & C. Black).

Mechanized Transport Corps, Women's. Formed as a voluntary corps in February 1939, its members did notable service in France in 1940, more especially in association with the French Forces, and in the civil defence of Britain during the autumn and winter of 1940. An organization for women drivers for transport work in wartime, the M.T.C. was given official recognition by the Government in December 1941, when it was brought under the supervision of the Ministry of War Transport. Mrs. G. M. Cook is the Commandant.

FUSILIERS GO INTO ACTION BY LORRY

The Royal Scots Fusiliers took part in the training exercises, and here some of them are seen leaping to the ground from their lorry on arrival at the scene of action. They are armed with light machine-guns.

Photo, British Official

PRACTICE AT HOME & THE REAL THING IN LIBYA

The training of instructors for our mechanical army is an important factor today. The officers, N.C.O.s and picked men are selected by the Military College of Science and undergo a gruelling intensive course of instruction, both theoretical and practical, before being passed out. In the top photographs are seen trainees attached to the Western Command hauling a gun to a mountain summit. Below, a British armoured car column in the Western Desert, near Tobruk.

Photos, British Official; Sport & General

STRATEGY OF MEDITERRANEAN BATTLE FRONT

Italy's advantageous position in what Mussolini called "Mare Nostrum," her temporary control of the Libyan seaboard, and Germany's grip on Greece and the French ports, created a difficult situation for Britain, despite possession of the central stronghold, Malta. See also Alexandria ; Gibraltar ; North Africa ; Toulon, etc.

Mediterranean, Strategy of. Before the advent of the submarine and the developments of aviation Britain's strategic hold on the Mediterranean was immensely strong. Gibraltar and Malta provided bases for the Fleet, and a comparatively small army sufficed to ensure the safety of the Suez Canal. Sea power enabled us to reinforce our Mediterranean garrisons at will, and Egypt was well protected from invasion by armies of marching men who would be encumbered with animal transport, for to them the Sinai desert on one side and, to a greater extent, the Western and Libyan deserts on the other were almost impassable obstacles.

The appearance of German submarines in the Mediterranean in the First Great War, and the toll they took of our shipping, gave the first indication that our strategic position was deteriorating. It was also realized that, with the increased range of modern guns, the fortress of Gibraltar, while retaining its impregnability, could no longer be looked on in all circumstances as a safe naval base. Malta, for this reason, as well as from its central position, became all the more important to the Navy.

It was not, however, till aviation attained its modern power that the situation gave cause for serious anxiety and, in particular, directed attention to the strategic advantages it gave Italy. Her aircraft, operating from shore bases, could combine with submarines and surface

vessels to render passage through the Sicilian Channel and adjacent waters dangerous, almost to a prohibitive degree, for all except warships ; and Malta itself might become unusable as a base for the British Fleet.

Mussolini was not slow to exploit the inherent advantages of Italy's geographical position. While Britain was still committed to a policy of unilateral disarmament he expanded his army, developed a powerful air force, and embarked on an ambitious programme of naval construction in which a high proportion of submarines and fast torpedo craft were included. In the design of cruisers and battleships speed was given first place, making them particularly capable of employing evasive and harassing tactics. But, trusting to the cooperation of shore-based aircraft, no aircraft carriers were included in the naval programme, an omission which cost Italy dear.

Combined with his military policy Mussolini entered on one of colonial expansion, which culminated in his Abyssinian adventure. Prior to that he had fortified and strongly garrisoned the Dodecanese Islands and had begun to expend vast sums on Libya. There, although the methods employed in subduing native resistance were barbarous, many legitimate enterprises were started, such as the development of roads and water supplies and the establishment of agricultural settlements. Yet all these enterprises had a strategic significance, especially the construction of a great

Mediterranean Sea, with its islands, adjacent countries, and Axis supply routes attacked by the British.

motor road skirting the coast for over 1,100 miles from the Tunisian to the Egyptian frontiers. Libya had, in fact, become a potential base for operations either against Tunis or Egypt.

Italy was maintaining in Libya a powerful army (far exceeding what was required for internal security) and in completing the subjugation of Libya Italy had successfully employed a mechanized column to cross a formerly impassable desert in order to capture the headquarters of the Senussi sect at the Kufra oasis. This raised the question whether the desert still afforded Egypt complete protection from invasion by land from the west.

Such was the general strategic situation in the Mediterranean when the outbreak of war in 1939 found Italy, though a non-belligerent, in close alliance with Germany. Counter-measures to offset the potential hostility of Italy were necessary. France strengthened her Tunisian defences, and the reinforced French and British forces in Syria, Palestine and Egypt were placed under General Weygand. The British and French Mediterranean Fleets came under the control of the British Admiralty and used Alexandria as their main base in the Eastern Mediterranean. By compelling such large Allied detachments to stand idle Mussolini rendered valuable assistance to Germany.

With the collapse of France and Mussolini's declaration of war, Italy had wonderful opportunities. Having no danger on the Tunisian front, the whole of the Libyan army, estimated to consist of over 250,000 men, could concentrate against the comparatively small British contingent in Egypt. The Italian navy was considerably stronger numerically and in material than the Fleet which Britain could now spare for the Mediterranean. The French navy had gone out of action, and the loss of Bizerta and other French ports markedly reduced the operational range of British squadrons.

The air situation was even worse, for there were no adequate air bases—apart from Malta, itself under constant attack—from which offensive action could be taken against Italy or air protection be given to ships through the Sicilian Channel. For air protection, outside a limited range from Egypt, Britain had to rely on anti-aircraft armaments and on aircraft carriers, themselves very vulnerable to air attack.

On the naval side Admiral Cunningham (as is apparent from the article following this) had established an increasing ascendancy over the Italian navy.

This, then, was the situation before Wavell's brilliant Libyan campaign at the end of 1940. The fighting in Libya was to swing to and fro in 1941 and early 1942, but it seemed clear that a serious threat to Egypt had been averted (*see* North Africa). Malta (*q.v.*) remained a strong point, a thorn in the side of the combined Italo-German air forces in that part of the Mediterranean, and a base for offensive air action against Sicily and Southern Italy.

German plans for an overwhelming spring offensive in 1942 to strike from Gibraltar to Suez and through, or by-passing, Turkey, to Syria and the oilfields of the Near East were bruited. Turkey's position as the one remaining neutral of strategic importance seemed to offer, despite her alleged military weaknesses, a considerable obstacle to such schemes.

BRITAIN WAGES WAR IN THE MIDDLE SEA

Some of our most important naval victories of this war have been won in the Mediterranean, although the Italian fleet was always difficult to find, but when Germany entered this battle area Britain engaged a sterner foe. See Mediterranean Strategy, and also Adriatic Sea ; Crete ; Malta ; Matapan ; Sicily ; Taranto, etc.

Mediterranean, War in. When war broke out in September 1939 Britain had a considerable fleet in the Mediterranean. A large part of the French navy was also there, so that, although it was necessary to keep a careful watch on Italy on account of her close friendship with Germany and because she had recently been expanding her fleet while vowing vengeance on Britain for her part in the sanctions at the time of the Abyssinian trouble, it was felt that the Allies had a comfortable margin of safety.

In addition to the French bases on both sides of the Western Mediterranean, Britain was well supplied. Gibraltar's defences were being strengthened, although it afterwards turned out that they were still very far from ready, and this base was regarded as of particular importance. It still controlled the western exit to the Mediterranean, and it was an obvious bait to persuade Spain to enter the war. Malta was in a fine state of defence, but it had been subjected to intensive Italian fifth-column activities for many years and its possession was admitted to be an Italian aim. It was completely isolated and many British observers considered that it would be indefensible against large forces, while the Italians openly boasted that they could reduce it in a few days. Alexandria was used under the agreement with Egypt, and had been well equipped during the Abyssinian trouble in 1935.

Cyprus was well situated strategically, but very little had been done towards making it a base, and an entirely new artificial harbour was necessary.

The Italian fleet was a considerable one, and it was generally understood that its efficiency had been vastly improved since the last war. For several years it had, however, been following the policy of the jeune école, ignoring battleships and building up a large fleet of cruisers, destroyers, submarines, and motor torpedo-boats, whose most conspicuous quality was their high speed. Only in 1933 had the Italian Government decided that battleships were still necessary, and in 1939 the Navy had two of the latest type completing and four old ships being reconstructed out of all recognition. In addition, Italy had a huge air force, most of it attached to shore bases, as she did not believe in air-craft carriers.

The Italians were also very well supplied with strategic bases, which existed all round their coast. They had complete control of the Adriatic, except for a weak naval power on the opposite shore whose flank had already been turned by the seizure of Albania. Offshore they had the island of Pantellaria in the Central Mediterranean, a small-scale Malta which was understood to have had a good deal of money spent on it ; the Dodecanese Islands, with excellent harbours, in the east ; and, in the west, a strong hold of the

Balearic Islands, which they had obtained as a price for their help during the Spanish Civil War.

For many years the Fascist Party had been carrying on intensive propaganda, with the whole Mediterranean as " Mare Nostrum," while the central section had been latterly described as " Mussolini's Lake," and the people had been assured that no enemy force would be allowed to exist there, or to traverse it, in the event of war. Egypt was marked on propaganda maps as a future Italian possession, uniting their East African colonies with the Mediterranean, and for years the country had aimed at a controlling interest in the Suez Canal, although they had refused to take part in its construction or financing.

The German triumphs in France brought Italy into the war on June 10, 1940. This was expected, but it put the British Navy in a very difficult position through the withdrawal of the French Fleet, and later through Vichy France importing supplies for Germany. Italian submarines started operations immediately, following the German policy against merchant shipping, and Malta was raided by Italian aircraft the day after war was declared. After that few days passed without one or more raids. The British immediately retaliated by an air raid on Tobruk, in Northern Africa, hitting the old cruiser San Giorgio and two submarines, while four Italian submarines were definitely sunk in the Mediterranean area within six days of the outbreak. On June 26 Rome announced the opening of an intensive war against the Royal Navy, and next day the destroyer Espero was sunk while attempting it.

Italians Boast of Avoiding Battle

It had been anticipated that, enjoying a large numerical superiority over the British Mediterranean Fleet, the Italian Navy would adopt an aggressive attitude even if it were only to save face after the propaganda campaign, but it soon proved that their naval command was still held by the fetish of preserving material at all cost, especially the larger ships, to whose construction the Italian taxpayers had always been inclined to object. The propaganda continued, but before very long the Italians were quite openly congratulating themselves on avoiding action, and boasting that they would give battle when it suited their convenience. The first occasion was on July 9, when surface squadrons came into contact to the east of Malta and the Italians immediately fled to the shelter of shore batteries, having a battleship and cruiser hit. That started a long series of unfounded claims to have inflicted serious air damage on British ships, the Hood and Ark Royal being the favourite victims. Actually one cruiser had been slightly damaged, which was immediately admitted, and after that there was a fairly regular succession of destroyer losses reported and submarines overdue, although not nearly sufficient to give the Italians the command which they claimed. Soon afterwards Rome officially stated that their purpose was to keep powerful British squadrons employed in the Mediterranean in order to help Germany in the North Sea.

On July 19, 1940, the Italian cruiser Bartolomeo Colleoni (q.v.), a ship famous for her extraordinary speed, was sunk in a few minutes by H.M. Australian cruiser Sydney, carrying the same armament. British naval men had long maintained that Italy had sacrificed far too much for the sake of speed by giving her ships very

END OF AN ITALIAN DESTROYER

This great pillar of smoke was the result of a shell from H.M.S. York (from which the photo was taken) hitting the magazine of the Artigliere, a destroyer which had already been crippled by H.M.S. Ajax on Oct. 12, 1940. The crew were helped to escape before the coup de grâce was given

Photo, G.P.U.

BRITISH WAR MEDALS OF THE SECOND GREAT WAR

Drawn by E. C. Mansell

R.A.F.—(**1**) Distinguished Flying Cross (D.F.C.) ; (**2**) Distinguished Flying Medal (D.F.M.) ; (**4**) Air Force Medal (A.F.M.) ; (**5**) Air Force Cross (A.F.C.). **Army, Navy and General.**—(**3**) Victoria Cross (V.C.) ; (**6**) Distinguished Service Order (D.S.O.) ; (**7**) Military Medal (M.M.) ; (**8**) George Cross (G.C.) ; (**9**) Distinguished Conduct Medal (D.C.M.) ; (**11**) George Medal (G.M.) ; (**13**) Military Cross (M.C.) ; (**14**) Medal of the Order of the British Empire ; (**18**) Meritorious Service Medal (Army, Navy and R. Marines) ; (**20**) Officer of The Order of the British Empire (O.B.E.). **Navy.**—(**10**) Distinguished Service Cross (D.S.C.) ; (**17**) Distinguished Service Medal (D.S.M.) ; (**19**) Conspicuous Gallantry Medal (C.G.M.). **Merchant Navy.**—(**12**) Lloyd's War Medal for Bravery at Sea. **Police.**—(**15**) King's Police Medal for Gallantry. **Women.**—(**16**) Royal Red Cross.

6

'FOR INDOMITABLE
COURAGE . . .'

DURING his numerous visits to R.A.F.
Fighter Stations in Britain the
King decorated airmen for brave
deeds performed in the defence of their
country. The above scene is typical
of such an occasion. Flt. Lt. A. C. Deere
stands smartly to attention as His Majesty
presents him with the D.F.C. This young
airman took part in offensive patrols
over Northern France and was engaged in
seven combats against superior enemy
forces. He was responsible for the
destruction of five German aircraft, and
assisted in the shooting down of others.
On one occasion his 'plane was attacked
by twelve Messerschmitt 109s.

Photo, Topical Press

REMARKABLE EFFECT OF A STICK OF BURSTING BOMBS

This photograph, taken from a near-by vessel, shows an attack by Axis aircraft on H.M.S. Malaya, a ship of the Mediterranean Squadron, the exploding bombs creating a curious resemblance to a forest fire. The great battleship continued steadily on her course both during and after the raid. Italy's air bases are favourably situated for sudden attacks in the Mediterranean.

Photo, Associated Press

light hulls; the whole fore part of the Colleoni was blown off by a 6-inch salvo.

On Oct. 28 Italy attacked Greece (*q.v.*), whose army was ill-equipped and appeared to be an easy victim, although its wonderful gallantry and striking successes against the Italians, until they were reinforced by German mechanized troops, astonished the world. The Greek Navy was small but remarkably efficient and very keen. The small craft in particular, submarines and destroyers, were handled with the greatest dash and skill. The new campaign added to the responsibilities of the Fleet in backing the Greek Navy and keeping the land forces supplied with reinforcements and munitions, but the Greek bases and merchant ships were of the greatest assistance to the Allied cause.

The necessity of protecting their lines of communication across the Adriatic caused the main Italian fleet to be concentrated on Taranto (*q.v.*), where, on Nov. 11, a conspicuously successful night raid was carried out by torpedo-dropping 'planes from the carriers Ark Royal and Illustrious. Three battleships and two cruisers were put out of action and the dash of the attack caused a panic; the fleet was immediately withdrawn farther west and the lines of communication were left protected only by small craft. Full advantage was taken of this. The surviving ships that had been withdrawn were encountered by the main British Fleet off the Sardinian coast and immediately fled to the protection of their shore batteries after sustaining damage.

Naval cooperation was invaluable to the advance of the Army from Egypt through Libya; the Fleet not only undertook bombarding and transport duties, but constantly harassed the Italian supplies When the Army retreated, leaving a garrison at Tobruk, communications were maintained by the Navy. Axis supplies were handicapped by constant raids and by the very successful naval bombardment of Genoa on Feb. 9, 1941. At the same time a powerful attack by enemy aircraft failed to stop a munitions convoy to Greece, although the cruiser Southampton was so badly damaged that she had to be sunk to avoid delaying the convoy, and the aircraft carrier Illustrious was damaged

by continuous air raids, although she succeeded in reaching Malta, where she was repaired.

The Italian Navy was making such a poor exhibition that the German and Italian naval authorities met towards the end of February and German control officers were placed in Italian warships to stiffen up the personnel. Later reports showed that Italian submarines working in the Atlantic had German officers on board, and there was evidence of very natural ill-feeling. German aircraft had already been sent to the Italian bases and had greatly increased the attacks on British ships, especially by dive-bombing. For a time they entirely replaced Italian machines in attack.

Heavy Losses in Greek Waters

In April 1941 the arrival of a large number of German mechanized troops turned the scale in Greece, and the final evacuation of the mainland, under cover of the Royal Navy, which lost the destroyers Diamond and Wryneck, was completed on May 1. Greek naval losses were heavy, but the remaining ships joined the Royal Navy and continued the fight. A gallant stand was made in Crete, the Royal Marines distinguishing themselves, but the troops suffered from lack of equipment and were forced to retire. The cruisers Gloucester, Fiji and York, and four destroyers, were lost in these operations.

On March 27, 1941, the Eastern Division of the Mediterranean Fleet, under the Commander-in-Chief, Admiral Cunningham, received information from aircraft that a considerable Italian fleet was at sea steering for Crete. While the light forces kept touch and torpedo-carrying aircraft and bombers attacked, he got his battle squadron to sea from Alexandria. The 10,000-ton Italian cruiser Pola was disabled off Cape Matapan (*q.v.*) by a 'plane's torpedo, and after nightfall the British battleships detected other cruisers with lighter forces going to her assistance. Two 10,000-ton cruisers, Zara and Fiume, and two big destroyers were blown out of the water with 15-inch salvoes without the slightest damage to the British ships, and the disabled Pola was destroyed at leisure. Unfortunately the Italian battleships, getting under fire at 13 miles' range

OUR WARSHIPS SMASH AN ATTACK ON A CONVOY

1. H.M.S. Rodney keeps guard over a convoy in the Mediterranean carrying supplies to our armies in the Middle East.
2. Torpedo-carrying enemy planes are sighted, Rodney's guns are manned, and from pom-poms like those on the right of the picture the flak goes up.   3. The attack has been beaten off, the merchantmen steam steadily on, and one more convoy has got through, thanks to the British Navy.

Photos. G.P.U

and one of them being hit by a 'plane, turned tail and contrived to reach safety by their superior speed.

In the meantime the Navy continued to bombard enemy strongholds on the North African coast and to harass their communications. Submarines and aircraft were constantly active, with occasional raids by surface ships, and by October 1941 it was estimated that between 20 and 30 per cent of the ships on the Libyan supply service were being sunk, and 20 per cent more were being damaged. When the British advance for the recapture of Libya started in November 1941 the Navy cooperated as before, and with even better results. (*See* North Africa.)

In June 1941 German operations in Syria, with the connivance of the Vichy authorities, had forced the British and Free French forces to take action. Several Vichy men-of-war attempted to interfere and suffered losses and damage ; the remainder were allowed to escape to Toulon without molestation.

Two Great Losses in the Middle Sea

Naturally the activities of the Navy both on and under the surface caused a steady stream of losses, which were duly acknowledged by the Admiralty, although care was taken not to reveal useful facts to the enemy by mentioning the exact place and time. The greatest loss was the sinking of the famous aircraft carrier Ark Royal (*q.v.*) in the Western Mediterranean by German submarines in November 1941, but happily the loss of life was negligible.

On Nov. 25 H.M. battleship Barham was torpedoed and sunk off Sollum, a loss that was not announced until Jan. 27, 1942.

In November the urgent needs of enemy forces in Libya increased their naval activities, and the British Navy took advantage of them. Light forces under Captain Agnew cut up two convoys and sank four destroyers, drowning a large number of German and Italian troops. Early in December 1941 light forces sank another destroyer and a supply ship, and a few days afterwards two cruisers were sent to the bottom by an Anglo-Dutch destroyer force. On Dec. 15 the

Admiralty reported further sinkings by British submarines in the Mediterranean, including a 12,000-ton liner believed to be the Italian S.S. Virgilio (used as a troopship), two supply ships, and other vessels. Two days later it was announced that the destroyer Farndale had sunk the new Italian submarine Ammiraglio Caracciolo, which was attempting to evacuate 20 Italian officers from Bardia.

Successes in January 1942 included the sinking of three U-boats (two German and one Italian) off Libya, a large troop transport and a supply vessel in the Ionian Sea, and a surfaced U-boat and an Italian troopship by H.M. submarine Talisman. On Jan. 23 R.A.F. bombers and naval aircraft carried out prolonged attacks on a large convoy, almost certainly sinking a 20,000-ton liner, and damaging a cruiser, a destroyer and two merchant ships.

From the end of January 1942 the military position in North Africa and the Axis preparations to invade Egypt dominated the naval situation throughout the Mediterranean. Enemy convoys across the central area were constantly attacked by surface ships, submarines and aircraft, and it was to save them that Malta was subjected to a series of air raids unprecedented in history. It was necessary to revictual the garrison and to restore the supplies of ammunition which were being used at a prodigious rate against aircraft, and for this reason large British convoys were sent from Alexandria and were the target of determined enemy attack. Such other naval activity as took place was entirely subsidiary to this main operation, although patrols were constantly maintained all over the sea, attacks were made whenever the opportunity offered, and President Roosevelt announced at the end of April that units of the United States Navy were cooperating with the other Allies. In view of the attitude of the Vichy Government it was necessary to maintain forces in the Western part of the Sea to prevent the French North African ports being put completely at the disposal of the Axis.

Two particularly heavy attacks on British convoys from Alexandria to Malta were noteworthy. The

MUSSOLINI LOSES ANOTHER OF HIS SUBMARINES

An Italian U-boat in the Mediterranean, engaged on a raiding cruise, was detected by British naval units. She crash-dived, but was soon forced to the surface again by depth charges. In this photograph her crew is seen lining the deck awaiting rescue by boats sent by the British warships standing by. The submarine sank a few minutes later.

Photo, Keystone

first started on Feb. 13 and continued for three days. The enemy claim was that the greatest part of the convoy had been sunk and the rest turned back, seven merchant ships, one destroyer and a torpedo boat sunk, and eight merchant ships, five cruisers and two destroyers damaged, at the cost of one Italian submarine. The Admiralty reported that superficial damage was caused to one man-of-war and that two damaged merchant ships had to be sunk to avoid delaying the operation. Torpedoes dropped by British aircraft scored hits on two Italian cruisers and a destroyer, and a submarine scored two hits on a 10,000-ton cruiser, while at least five enemy aircraft

HER SHIPS WERE THE PRIDE OF FRANCE

Shortly before the entry of Italy into the war in 1940, France reinforced her navy in the Mediterranean, and this scene in Alexandria harbour gives some idea of French naval power before France's collapse. A sailor is cleaning an A.A. gun against a background dominated by a large battleship.
Photo, Keystone

were definitely destroyed. The remainder of the large convoy reached Malta safely.

The second attack started on March 21. The convoy was sighted in bad weather, which reduced its speed, and swarms of aircraft and an Italian surface squadron attacked. It was claimed that two cruisers, three destroyers and many merchantmen had been sunk. The British convoying force consisted of five light cruisers and a number of destroyers under Rear-Admiral P. L. Vian, D.S.O., of Altmark fame, and they were attacked by the 35,000-ton battleship Littorio, two 8-inch and four light cruisers and a flotilla of destroyers. Our vessels made the utmost use of smoke screens, in and out of which the destroyers dashed and into which the enemy dared not penetrate for fear of the forces that might be waiting behind them. The Italian ships withdrew damaged and left the attack to aircraft. One British cruiser and four destroyers were damaged, and one freighter sunk.

Saga of the Cruiser Penelope

The cruiser was the Penelope, and her subsequent adventures were extraordinary. She reached Malta with the rest of the convoy on March 26, and went into dry dock. There she became the special target of constant air attack beginning on April 5. Many near misses were scored and some damage was caused. Her guns joined in the defence until there was difficulty in maintaining the ammunition supply. On April 6 over 200 bombers concentrated on her. She left Malta two days later and was attacked at sea by waves of torpedo-dropping and bombing aircraft all the way to Gibraltar. She went to America for repair and her captain received the C.B.E. and two of his officers the D.S.O.

While the Penelope was a special target, the enemy attacks on the town, dockyard and airfields of Malta

were continuous. Great damage was admittedly done although casualties were comparatively light, but the enemy checked the activities of the base in preventing supplies getting to Libya at a very heavy cost. On May 12 it was announced that 507 'planes had been definitely shot down since the beginning of the offensive. Most of the attacks were by the Germans, the Italians being exhausted, and they claimed to have destroyed many warships. The defence of Malta aroused the admiration of the whole world and on April 16 the King awarded the island the George Cross in recognition of the gallantry of its people.

Apart from the two big attacks, the Axis claimed successes against British warships and supply vessels between Alexandria and the Libyan front almost daily —a British battleship and sixteen cruisers between the latter part of January and the middle of May, in addition to numerous smaller vessels, submarines and transports. The R.A.F., Navy and Fleet Air Arm were relentless in their attacks, and while the claims they made were more moderate they were far better substantiated, and were indeed often admitted by the Italians themselves.

On May 4 it was announced that 1,273,000 tons of Axis shipping had been sunk in the Mediterranean between June 1940 and the end of April 1942. Latterly the rate had slackened owing to the preoccupation of the forces at Malta, but the attack was never completely relaxed, and on April 13 Rome officially gazetted a scale of cash awards for merchant seamen who succeeded in slipping past the British cordon. There was other evidence of lowered morale in face of the constant attacks on supply ships and their naval escorts in which our submarines were particularly successful, often penetrating close up to the Italian shore batteries. Successes, not all claimed as sinkings owing to the impossibility of waiting to observe results,

'MOST BOMBED SHIP STILL AFLOAT' AT MALTA

H.M.S. Penelope, described by her commander, Capt. Nicholl, as "the most bombed ship still afloat," is seen entering Malta harbour. For a fortnight this ship was subjected to some of the heaviest raids in Malta's experience. Despite severe damage she put to sea, and after withstanding further enemy attacks reached port safely, en route for the U.S.A.

Photo, British Official

hero of the River Plate, had been made an acting Admiral and Commander-in-Chief of the Mediterranean in place of Admiral Cunningham, who was to lead the British Naval Mission to the United States.

After he left the Mediterranean Sir Andrew Cunningham, who had held the command since January 1939, gave a brief review of the conditions in that area. He maintained that the Fleet could never have enough torpedo planes, but our strength was growing daily.

He revealed what had not been fully realized outside Service circles —the reliance on the French Fleet in the Mediterranean before the surrender, the nearness of Italy to complete collapse, and the manner in which German air power had saved the situation for the Axis. But he maintained that ultimate victory could only be won by the foot-slogging soldier in his thousands, and to transport and supply him sea power was necessary, as had been shown in the Mediterranean in 1941 and in the Far East in 1942. The air was an indissoluble ingredient in sea power in modern war, but in confined spaces like the Mediterranean aircraft could be shore based. The loss of Tobruk and the retreat to El Alamein and the threat to Alexandria in June 1942 further restricted naval movement.

included a cruiser and destroyer, reported on March 3 to have been set on fire by the R.A.F., a 10,000-ton cruiser and a patrol boat, which the Italians admitted on April 2 to have been sunk by submarine, and a large transport from a convoy reported on April 17, which turned out to be the Galilea (8,040 tons), in which 768 lives were lost.

In the Eastern Mediterranean air attacks on Alexandria, as the base of the British forces in Libya, recommenced. On Feb. 15 the Fleet Air Arm sighted an Italian squadron of three cruisers and about 20 destroyers in the Ionian Sea and attacked for twenty hours, hitting two cruisers and at least one destroyer. On May 11 four British destroyers with a few Beaufighters were attacked south of Crete by a large number of enemy planes, and the Kipling, Lively and Jackal were destroyed by dive-bombers, although most of their crews were saved.

On June 17 it was announced that two large British convoys, one going east from Gibraltar to Malta, and the other west from Alexandria to Tobruk, had been attacked by Axis naval and air forces. Extravagant Axis claims to have destroyed some 30 merchant ships were proved false. A fierce sea-air battle took place off Pantellaria, the Italian island situated between Sicily and Tunis, on June 15. The Italian fleet, which had steamed out of Taranto to challenge British naval supremacy in the Mediterranean, suffered heavy losses. Two enemy battleships were hit by torpedo planes of the R.A.F., and by Liberator bombers, manned chiefly by U.S. Army personnel. Enemy losses also included the sinking of a cruiser of the Trento class and two destroyers, while two cruisers and two destroyers were also hit.

Between January and May it was necessary to make several changes in the commands. Air Vice-Marshal Lloyd took over the command of the Royal Air Force in the Mediterranean, with his headquarters at Malta. General Dobbie was succeeded by Lord Gort, V.C., as Commander-in-Chief at Malta, and on May 16 it was announced that Rear-Admiral Sir Henry Harwood,

A review of the military situation at that period of the war, taking in Europe, showed that the giant Nazi pincers, with Rommel at Alamein in the South, and Von Kleist driving for Caucasia in the North, could never close unless Malta succumbed to the air assault she was being subjected to at this time. The whole Mediterranean had evolved itself into a battle for this resolutely defended island.

The Axis aims were the maintenance of supplies to their armies in N. Africa and the cutting of the Allied life-line to Malta. In their latter aim the waiting game could be played and large forces of U-boats and E-boats, strongly supported by the Luftwaffe from N. Africa and Sicily, could be mustered for attacks on the Allied convoys.

The Allied Navies and the R.A.F. could not afford the waiting policy, but had to operate largely as separate entities which added a greater strain on their resources. It had become apparent that Allied superiority and complete domination could only be attained by the coordination of air and sea power.

In the convoy battle of June the Navy lost the cruiser "Hermione" and the destroyers "Hasty," "Grove" and "Airedale" as well as the Polish destroyer "Kujawiak."

Early in July it was revealed that the U.S. aircraft carrier "Wasp" had successfully ferried planes through to Malta, and on one mission the R.A.F.

DESPITE THE ENEMY'S HEAVIEST ATTACKS THE MALTA CONVOYS WENT THROUGH

For nearly three years Malta, from 1940 to 1942, was exposed to the full fury of Axis attack and the Mediterranean convoys on which her existence depended, and in fact the whole strategy of the Mediterranean, were subject to every assault from above and below the sea. One of the biggest battles was that of August 11 to 13, 1942, when an aircraft carrier and other warships were lost. Here is a Malta convoy of 1942 approaching the end of a hazardous journey.

British Official, Crown Copyright

had flown the planes from her decks into combat, so great was the need. The battle for Malta was maintained with the same intensity throughout July. Axis air losses had reached 100 in the first two weeks.

The seeking out and destroying of Axis supply vessels continued by both the Navy and the R.A.F. On July 9 a British submarine sank a supply vessel and naval auxiliary in the West and on the 18th South African patrol vessels accounted for a U-boat. Three more supply vessels were sent down on the 23rd.

The R.A.F. maintained attacks on Rommel's supply bases at Tobruk, Benghazi and Bardia and Sollum, and accounted for numerous Axis supply vessels. But with all the vigilance by the Navy and R.A.F., supplies were still reaching Rommel. Much went by air.

Enemy activity throughout July had been mainly concentrated on Malta. Bardia, Sollum and Tobruk were heavily bombed by the R.A.F. on August 2, 3 and 6. On the 5th the Italian S.S. "Adda" was sunk by gunfire from a British submarine off the E. Sardinian coast.

R.A.F. activities were mainly directed against Axis shipping in the ports. A 10,000-ton transport was sunk at Tobruk, August 8. U.S. heavy bombers had also been active, and on the 11th three Italian cruisers were attacked at Navarino, the Greek base used by the Axis for transporting supplies to N. Africa.

Towards the West one of the biggest convoy battles was in progress. The British naval operations were under the command of Vice-Admiral E. N. Seyfret in H.M.S. "Nelson." The enemy attacked with dive-bombers, bombers, torpedo planes, fighters and U-boats. The carrier-borne planes brought down 39 enemy aircraft on the first day. E-boats attacked in the night of 12th-13th and two were sunk. On the 13th the enemy resumed his attack, but by this time the battle had moved towards the central Mediterranean and fighter support from Malta resulted in 27 planes being shot down, making a total of 66 certain. The convoy successfully reached Malta but had sustained severe losses, which included the aircraft carrier "Eagle," and H.M. ships "Cairo," "Manchester" and "Foresight." The enemy suffered heavily.

On August 22 it was announced that the British submarine "Upholder," before she was lost, had accounted for 122,000 tons of enemy shipping in the Central Mediterranean in 23 successful attacks.

Throughout the month the Axis attack on Malta was reduced in intensity, and 52 aircraft had been brought down by the island's defences, bringing the total to 939, of which 227 were due to A.A. fire.

Rommel's supply lines had been constantly harassed by the Navy and R.A.F., but sufficient reinforcements had got through for him to launch an offensive against the Allied positions on August 31.

On August 27 Admiral Sir Henry Harwood, C.-in-C. Mediterranean Fleet, announced that a new organization had been created for better co-operation between the British naval and air forces in the Mediterranean.

Books to Consult. Mediterranean Front, Alan Moorehead (Hamish Hamilton). From Gibraltar to Suez, Lord Strabolgi (Hutchinson).

Meknes, S.S. A French liner of 6,127 tons, belonging to the Compagnie Générale Transatlantique, the Meknes was torpedoed off Portland at close range by a German E-boat on the night of July 24, 1940. She carried some 1,200 French naval officers and ratings for repatriation in Unoccupied France and was unarmed and brilliantly illuminated. Nearly a thousand survivors were rescued by British warships; nine officers and 374 men were lost.

R. G. Menzies,
Australian Premier
1939–41.
Photo, Wide World

Menzies, RT. HON. ROBERT GORDON, P.C. (b. 1894). He was Prime Minister of Australia from 1939 to 1941. The Federal Labour Party rejected his offer of an all-party Government on August 26, 1941, and two days later he resigned the Premiership. He was succeeded by Mr. A. W. Fadden (*q.v.*). He also held the post of Minister for Coordination of Defence in 1939 and again during Mr. Fadden's short term of office, August-October 1941. During 1940 he was Minister for Information and Minister for Munitions.

THE MERCHANT NAVY'S PART IN THE WAR

Facing daily peril, contending, sometimes alone, with sudden attack from sea or air, doing an essential and highly dangerous job with matter-of-fact heroism—such are the men of the Merchant Service. See also Atlantic, Battle of; Convoy.

Merchant Navy. Her Merchant Navy is essential to Britain's economic existence because she is an island and a manufacturing country, not a producer of raw materials. In war it is the most vital and potentially the most vulnerable link in the British chain of defence ; it is also the basis of her offensive power, because every soldier, weapon and piece of equipment for striking at an enemy must be carried across the sea in ships. The Merchant Navy is vulnerable because every ship scattered over the seas may be a target for attack by submarine, raiding warship or converted merchant ship, and before it can reach a home port it is exposed to enemy aeroplanes, motor torpedo boats and sometimes long-range coastal batteries. In addition, there is the ever-present danger from mines. If the supply line maintained by merchant ships were sufficiently interfered with by an enemy the British population would be faced with starvation and the factories with idleness ; the offensive and defensive power of Britain would be gradually extinguished. That was the aim of German military policy from the first day of the war. (*See* Atlantic, Battle of.)

Badge of the
Merchant Navy

At the outbreak of the war in September 1939 the British Mercantile Marine was made up of 7,000 ships of 18,000,000 tons gross, smaller than the fleet of 1914 by over 1,000 ships and more than 1¼ million tons. British Dominions and Colonies possessed a further 2,500 ships of 3,200,000 tons. These totals included ships of all sizes and types of 100 tons and more— harbour craft, dredgers, coastal ships, tankers for carrying oil, ocean tramp ships (carrying bulk cargoes from any part of the world), cargo liners (carrying mixed, or " parcel " goods on a fixed schedule), and mail and passenger liners. The ocean-going ships consisted roughly of 1,000 liners (cargo and passenger) of 8,640,000 tons gross, 700 tramp ships of 3,360,000 tons, and 350 tankers of 2,586,000 tons. The liners and tramps together were smaller than the 1914 ocean-going fleet by 1,000 ships and 2,000,000 tons gross.

In the first few weeks of the war Germany succeeded in sinking British ships at the rate of over 150,000 tons a month, but, chiefly owing to the convoy system (*see* Convoy), this was later halved. Losses were, however, greatly increased when Germany acquired submarine and bomber bases in Norway, Denmark, Holland, Belgium and France in the spring of 1940. (*See* Atlantic, Battle of.) By June 1941—when the Admiralty ceased publishing the figures—losses of British ships totalled 4,377,000 tons gross and of British, Allied and neutral 6,789,000 tons. In the spring months of 1941 the total sinkings by enemy action had reached a level of over 500,000 tons per month. The seriousness of this can be seen if measured against the production capacity of Britain's shipyards. While ships were being sunk at a rate of 6,000,000 tons a year, replacements from British yards—governed partly by the demands on facilities and labour of the naval programme and ship repairs—were in the region of 1,200,000 tons per annum.

In subsequent months, however, losses were reduced to a monthly rate of between 150,000 and 200,000 tons and the largest shipbuilding programme in history was gathering momentum in the United States. The improvement in the war at sea was due to several factors. The strength of convoy escorts was steadily increased, particularly from September onwards, when the American Navy began convoying in the Atlantic. Escort organization was improving. New anti-submarine methods were being introduced as a result of constant planning, research and experiment. Officers and crews of naval and merchant ships were becoming more skilled in their different duties. And, not least, air escorts were considerably and steadily strengthened.

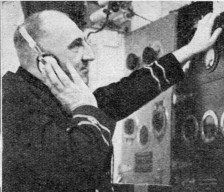

ALL ON THE ALERT FOR POSSIBLE ENEMY ATTACK

No longer are the anxieties of a master and his crew limited to those occasioned by the forces of Nature. Left, a British merchant captain on the bridge of his ship scans the sky for hostile aircraft. Centre, the wireless operator is all keyed up as a message comes over the radio. Right, George Elliott, a 21-year-old gunner serving on a collier, who fired a shell at a big German bomber with such effect that the raider made off with smoke pouring from its tail.

Photos, British Official; Keystone; Fox

Control of the Mercantile Marine was exercised by the Government through the Ministry of War Transport (originally the Ministry of Shipping). All vessels except coastal tramp ships were requisitioned, their employment being directed by the Ministry, who paid owners a monthly rate of hire. Many were taken over by the Admiralty and other departments for service as minesweepers, troop transports, supply ships, armed merchant cruisers, and so on.

The term Merchant Navy describes not only the ships but the men who man them, without whose indomitable courage and resourcefulness the German blockade might well have succeeded. These gallant men wear no uniform—except the officers—but during the war they adopted a badge bearing the letters M.N. The heroism of English sailors is renowned, but never in history have there been so many heroic stories, so many individual exploits. It is invidious possibly to tell one story rather than another, but each has a double significance as a record on its own and as an incident reflecting the spirit

At the end of 1940 the Coastal Command of the R.A.F. had passed under the operational control of the Admiralty. Aeroplanes flew farther westwards, protecting convoys from air attack and spotting and destroying U-boats. In addition, 'planes of the Bomber Command struck at U-boat bases, enemy shipyards and potential enemy raiders in harbour. Fighters also played their part : in protective patrols over convoys and shipping during a period of twelve months they flew out on more than 50,000 sorties.

On a bare tonnage basis, the total losses of British ships at this stage were more than made good by the support of the shipping of the countries Germany had conquered, amounting in all to 8,000,000 tons, and by additional ships purchased, captured from the enemy, and built. But against that addition had to be set the longer voyages to be made following the loss of European supply sources.

By the end of the year, however, the scene had vastly changed. A new, grim phase opened with the Japanese attack on Pearl Harbour in Honolulu on Dec. 7, 1941. As the tempo of the war in the Far East increased, Germany redoubled her U-boat offensive in the Atlantic. At the end of February 1942 the Prime Minister stated : "In the past few months there has been a most serious increase in shipping losses." Fortunately there was also gain in deliveries, for the first batch of many hundreds of standard emergency ships was being handed over by the American shipyards. In later months U-boats sought new battlefields along the Atlantic seaboard, in the Caribbean Sea and even in the mouth of the St. Lawrence River, as well as further afield in South Atlantic waters.

LIFE IS DANGEROUS IN THE MERCHANT NAVY

One of the crew of an East Coast trawler crouches behind the deck-house as a German plane sprays bullets at a range of 200 yards. Men of these small vessels are known locally as the " suicide gang." Top, left, a British merchant ship's gun crew at practice.
Photos, British Official; " Daily Mirror."

and quality of the entire Merchant Navy. The sea must be in the merchant seaman's blood. Shipwrecked, torpedoed, bombed, wounded, perhaps rescued only after weeks of torture in a lifeboat or on a raft, the seaman is soon anxious again to join a ship. It is recorded that after 43 days in an open boat, the last week without water, a sailor after ten days at home signed on because he " couldn't stick it."

Sailors are notoriously adaptable, and this was proved with the defensive arming early in the war of as many merchant ships as possible. At first the armament consisted of an all-purpose gun mounted in the stern, but when the war came closer to Britain's shores after the German occupation of France and Belgium protection against dive-bombing and attacking aeroplanes became essential. The merchant ship had to be given a sting in many places as well as her tail. During 1941 no fewer than 13,000 anti-aircraft guns of one kind and another were fitted in British and Allied ships. More

Shipping Balance Sheet

The figures are in tons gross and are approximate
(in some cases estimated)

British Tonnage, September 1939		17,890,000
Gross additions up to December 1941—		
Captures (enemy & Danish) ..	730,000	
Purchases & Transfers	900,000	
Building	2,000,000	
		3,630,000
Allied Tonnage (escaped enemy):		
Norwegian	3,810,000	
Dutch	2,620,000	
Greek	1,230,000	
Free French	570,000	
Belgian	370,000	
Polish	130,000	
		8,730,000
	Total	30,250,000
LESS:		
British Losses, etc. (war):		
1939	424,000	
1940	2,397,000	
1941	1,835,000	
(to June 30)		
	4,656,000	
Allied Losses to June 30, 1941 ..	1,500,000	
British & Allied Losses		
June 30, 1941–Dec. 31, 1941	1,250,000	
Marine Losses	1,000,000	
		8,406,000
BALANCE		21,844,000

N.B.—U.S. shipping = 9,000,000 tons gross.

than 4,800 ships were fitted with " anti-aircraft devices other than guns "—a description that might cover barrage balloons as well as ship-borne fighter aircraft. Thus the sailor had to become an anti-aircraft gunner. Gunnery courses had been started for men of the Mercantile Marine before the war. These new circumstances made fresh demands. In April 1941 special firing courses were made available at various ports, but as the sailor in port had little spare time, motor-buses were fitted up as anti-aircraft schools, one form of instruction being given in the lower deck and another on the upper. Every man completing the course satisfactorily received a certificate and 10s.

With various anti-aircraft guns manned by expert gunners, every merchant ship became a formidable target. By the end of 1941, the First Lord of the Admiralty revealed, merchant ships and fishing vessels alone had shot down 76 enemy 'planes, with another 40 " probables," and had damaged a further 89. Sinkings by enemy aircraft had fallen to one-twelfth. The element of guerilla warfare was not lacking in the encounters, as when the mate of a small ship alone on the ocean chased off an enemy 'plane from the fo'c'sle armed only with a portable machine-gun and a stream of abuse.

Although the convoy system greatly reduced losses and casualties, attacks and sinkings by U-boats continued. In November 1940 the Jervis Bay (*q.v.*), a solitary armed merchant cruiser escorting a large convoy of 38 ships from the United States, won fame by her sacrifice in challenging a German battleship raider to a duel, thus giving her charges time to escape. The Jervis Bay was sunk, but her courageous action became known as the Jervis Bay epic. In the forefront of this convoy steamed a tanker, the San Demetrio, loaded with petrol. After the sinking of the Jervis Bay the San Demetrio received a direct hit and the order to abandon ship was given. Some 36 hours later members of the crew again boarded the ship and fought the fires. The bridge had gone, compasses, charts, steering gear, etc., were destroyed, but the second officer navigated her safely home some 700 miles with his diminished crew of 15. The sequel came about in the Admiralty Court when salvage remuneration was awarded, the costs of the claim being guaranteed by the owners, an unprecedented occurrence. The Judge, commenting on the " splendid story of the Jervis Bay," added that the " tale of courage, resource and skill with which the salving of the San Demetrio was accomplished will afford a fitting and not unworthy sequel to . . . one of the great English stories of the sea."

The possibilities of salvage have always been present and desirable in the sailor's world, but the more usual story of the war at sea was the sudden torpedoing

PROTECTING A CONVOY FROM LOW-FLYING RAIDERS

Barrage balloons are frequently flown from ships in a convoy to protect them from enemy dive-bombers and from aircraft which fly low over the convoy and machine-gun the decks. There are also special balloon barrage vessels, manned by R.A.F. crews, which accompany and guard convoys moving up and down the Channel and see them safely into port.
Photo, L.N.A.

without warning at night and without assistance after-wards, as in the case of the City of Benares, which was carrying a number of children to the U.S.A. under the British Government's evacuation scheme. If the mid-Atlantic has its additional terrors of storms and cold, warmer seas have sharks and octopuses and the horrible manthir. Insanity hovers near all shipwrecked mariners. There can scarcely be a more terrible story than that described by a young army officer who was on a raft for five days pursued by man-eating sharks, after his ship was sunk by a raider. Nine of his twelve companions went mad and jumped into the water, their violence capsizing the raft. Splashing kept the sharks at bay, but they were there to devour each man as he lost his reason and jumped into the water. In each case reason appeared to return at the shark's bite. An Indian hanging on to the raft was consumed by a manthir, which hugs its victim like a bear.

In another ship a survivor described an explosion which broke the ship in two, men trying to lower life-boats from a listing deck, men dying of exposure and being buried at sea by their mates with one thought in their minds, " I wonder who is the next to be put overboard." Nine days of competition with the ele-ments, a flying-boat passing by without seeing them, and then land at night, six survivors out of 41 struggling to land on the rocks through the breakers, and in the morning only one left to tell the terrible tale.

But it was not always the British ship that was sunk. The gun in the stern accounted for many U-boats, sometimes while in convoy.

Women were among those decorated in the Merchant Navy. The awarding of the M.B.E. to a woman engineer is probably unique. When her ship was attacked by

A.A. GUNNERY TAUGHT IN A BUS

A number of London's omnibuses have been transformed into mobile A.A. gunnery schools for the Merchant Navy. Here an officer is seen undergoing training with a Hotchkiss gun, the class being held on the lower deck of the bus.

Photo, Central Press

Allied Mercantile Marines
Ships and Tonnage in Service of the Allies, July 1941

	Free France*	Norway	Nether-lands	Poland	Greece	Belgium	Totals
Ships in Service, July, 1941 : No.	92	719	480	32	240	54	1,617
Tonnage	400,000	3,250,000	2,250,000	100,000	1,000,000	200,000	7,200,000
Losses to the end of June, 1941 : No.	34	121	77	4	65	34	335
Tonnage	174,667	562,061	371,714	29,210	233,050	131,691	1,502,393

*Part of tonnage sailing under British flag.

RESCUED AFTER ELEVEN DAYS

After eleven days adrift at sea in two small open boats, the crew, numbering 27, of a small Allied merchantman sunk in the South Atlantic by a submarine were picked up and brought to safety.

Photo, Planet News

dive-bombers this brave woman sent the engine-room staff above and, although wounded, remained alone in the engine-room coaxing more speed from the engines in order to elude the enemy. Another woman to be decorated was the stewardess of a sinking ship who regardless of her own safety jumped into the sea with a girl and supported her for two hours until rescued. Over 1,500 officers and men of the Merchant Navy lost their lives by enemy action during the first year of war.

There was no conscription and no compulsion to join the Merchant Navy and men were always available. The problem lay in the distribution of personnel. Mainly to facilitate this a measure of control over merchant seamen, officers and engineers was introduced on May 26, 1941, under the Essential Work (Merchant Navy) Order. Though it entailed restrictions, the scheme was described as the " Seamen's Charter " because of the benefits it included, chief of which was continuous employment and holidays with pay for the seaman. On discharge from his ship the officer or sea-man automatically came into the Merchant Navy Reserve Pool and was paid his basic wages until he signed on again. Meanwhile he might have to under-take any work on the direction of the Pool manager, or undergo training.

No more important, more gallant part was played in the fight for freedom than by the seamen—seamen from the British Isles, 40,000 from India, others from the Dominions, America, the West Indies, China and Africa ; Norsemen, Danes, Poles, Dutch, French, Belgians, Greeks, Russians, Yugoslavs and Egyptians— the Brotherhood of the Seas fighting side by side.

Books to Consult. The Merchant Navy at War, A. C. Hardy (Murray). Red Duster at War, Warren Armstrong (Gollancz). The Merchant Navy Fights, A. D. Divine (Murray).

Mersa Matruh. Situated on the Egyptian coast between Alexandria and Sidi Barrani, this strong point in the defence of Egypt was the terminus of the railway from Alexandria. Gen. Sir Archibald Wavell concentrated large forces of British Imperial troops at this vital strategic centre against Graziani's Libyan army during the summer of 1940. The Italians invaded Egypt on Sept. 13, 1940, and it was from Mersa Matruh that the Imperial forces launched their attack on Sidi Barrani on Dec. 11, preparatory to their lightning advance into Libya. The Italians were thus checked in their thrust towards the town which, should they have captured the place, would have thrown open to them a long stretch of Egyptian coast-line. The town was once again threatened when, at the end of April 1941, combined German and Italian forces occupied Sollum on the Libyan-Egyptian frontier. Heavily fortified, with the sea on one side and on the other the enormous Qattara depression, it was hoped that Mersa Matruh would prove an insurmountable barrier to the enemy tanks aiming for Alexandria. An attempted enemy advance on May 12 was checked, and three days later Sollum was again in British hands. In Rommel's June advance Mersa fell on June 27, 1942. *See* North Africa.

Mers-el-Kebir. Military port adjacent to Oran (*q.v.*) on the Gulf of Oran in Morocco.

Gen. Metaxas,
Greek Dictator.
Photo, G.P.U.

Metaxas, Gen. John (1871–1941). One of the most dynamic Greek personalities, he played an important part in the restoration of King George II of the Hellenes (*q.v.*) in 1935, and established a virtual dictatorship on August 4, 1936, when the Greek Parliament was dissolved. In 1938 he became Prime Minister, and two years later, on Oct. 28, 1940, when Greece presented a united front to Italian aggression, Metaxas rejected the Italian ultimatum, declaring it to be " tantamount to a declaration of war." In her gallant struggle for freedom against the aggressor, he led his country with an indomitable resolution and skill. His death occurred on Jan. 29, 1941, following an operation. His successor was Alexander Korizis (*q.v.*).

Metemma. Town of N.W. Abyssinia, a few miles east of Gallabat, just inside the Abyssinian frontier. As a result of aggressive action by British patrols and artillery, the Italians evacuated Metemma on Nov. 24, 1940, but it was not captured until Feb. 1, 1941.

Meulebroeck, M. van der. Burgomaster of Brussels. He succeeded M. Max (*q.v.*) on the latter's death in November 1939. After the German occupation of Brussels in May 1940 he refused to become a tool in the enemy's hands and, like his courageous predecessor, was punished by the Germans for his loyalty to his country. In June 1941 the Nazis,

incensed by his resolution, dismissed him, declaring that he had voluntarily retired. Van der Meulebroeck protested against this violation of the Hague Convention in a proclamation which was posted on the city walls. The posters were torn down by the enemy, only to be replaced. Thereupon the Burgomaster was arrested and a fine of 5,000,000 francs imposed on the population.

Meuse, River. This important river (*see* pp. 2717–18) rises in N.E. France, flows north into Belgium and enters the North Sea some 20 miles below Rotterdam in Holland, where it is known as the Maas. On May 11, 1940, the Germans crossed the Meuse to the north of the Albert Canal, the waterway that formed the main line of Belgian defence in the north. By May 14 the Germans had reached the stretch of the river west of Liége and their advance guards were within sight of the fortress of Namur. From Namur to Sedan they were within striking distance of the Meuse bridgeheads. The French evacuated Sedan and the battle extended from the Meuse at that point to the Moselle north of Metz. The enemy breakthrough on the Meuse confounded French predictions and frustrated their hopes, for the terrific German onslaught in the Sedan sector was responsible for the eventual outflanking of the Maginot Line. *See* Albert Canal ; Maastricht.

Mexico. During the early part of 1941 Mexico declared her determination to cooperate to the full with other American States in the defence of the Western Hemisphere from external aggression and to develop Mexican defences. On Dec. 21, 1940, the Mexican Senate approved the creation of a separate Navy Ministry, and on Jan. 24, 1941, the Government decided to recondition the naval bases of Vera Cruz and Laguna del Carmen, Acapulco and Margarita Island. Relations were broken off with Japan on Dec. 9, 1941, and Mexico dispatched strong troop reinforcements to her Pacific coast. The U.S. Government agreed to the passage of Mexican troops through Arizona to reinforce the defences of Lower California. Relations between Mexico and the Axis Powers steadily deteriorated from the beginning of 1942, and on May 30 Mexico declared war, the first major Latin-American state to enter the present conflict.

Michael I, King of Rumania (b. 1921). Son of King Carol II and Princess Helena of Greece, he was proclaimed King on Sept. 6, 1940, on the abdication of his father. This was the second time that Michael became King, for when his grandfather King Ferdinand died in 1927 he succeeded to the throne, his father being then in exile. In 1930, however, he was supplanted by Carol, the latter having made a dramatic return to Rumania.

King Michael
of Rumania.
Photo, Wide World

Although proclaimed King for the second time in 1940, Michael held little authority, the real power that ruled the country having been transferred to Antonescu (*q.v.*) and his followers, in their turn subject to German control.

Middle East. For the purposes of this work, and following military observance, the terms Middle East and Near East cover approximately the same areas.

MEETING OF THE MIDDLE EAST WAR COUNCIL IN CAIRO

Sessions of the Middle East War Council take place at regular intervals, presided over by the Minister of State, to discuss questions of policy and strategy. In the photograph, reading from left to right, are seen Air Marshal Sir A. W. Tedder, Gen. Sir Claude Auchinleck, Mr. Oliver Lyttelton, then Minister of State (succeeded by Mr. Casey), Sir A. Rucker, of the Minister of State's office, Sir Miles Lampson, British Ambassador in Cairo, and Sir Harold MacMichael, High Commissioner for Palestine. Another important member of the War Council is the C.-in-C. Mediterranean.

Photo, British Official

The Middle East Command, held by General Auchinleck (1941–1942), comprises Libya, Egypt, East Africa, Palestine, Transjordan, Iraq and Persia. Under him were the Eighth and Ninth Armies and the newly formed Tenth Army, commanded by Lt.-Gen. E. P. Quinan. Turkey comes within the older definition of the Near East.

Early in 1942 it was disclosed that new railway tracks were in course of construction in various parts of the Middle East, planned to meet the Army's present needs, and, after the war, to help to open up Egypt, Palestine, Transjordan, Syria and Eritrea. These new routes include a 175-mile railway between Palestine and Syria, a railway by-pass of the Nile shallows, a railway from the Sudan to Eritrea, a steel swing bridge across the Suez Canal, and a 108-mile extension of the Western Desert railway.

Another enormous enterprise in the Middle East is the outcome of a mission sent by the U.S. Army, under Gen. Wheeler. The aim is to create a vast U.S. supply centre, and to this end the construction and extension of harbours in the Persian Gulf were put in hand, which greatly speeded up the delivery of seaborne war supplies from the U.S.A. to Russia and Turkey. A gigantic organization was created for the assembly and repair of 'planes, tanks and transport.

In 1941 it was decided to appoint a Minister of State in the Middle East, and on July 1 Mr. Oliver Lyttelton was given the post, " to represent the War Cabinet and concert on their behalf the measures necessary for the prosecution of the war in that theatre other than the conduct of military operations, thereby relieving the G.O.C.-in-C. of many responsibilities." After Mr. Lyttelton's recall to take up the post of Minister of Production, Mr. R. G. Casey, then Australian Minister in Washington, was appointed Minister of State in the Middle East.

Midway Island. Situated north-west of the Hawaiian Group in the Pacific, this U.S. naval base was first raided by the Japanese on Dec. 8, 1941. The small American garrison put up a determined resistance, and held out successfully, suffering four further raids up to June 4, 1942, when the Japanese launched a large scale attack known as the Battle of Midway Island (*see* p. 336). Admiral Nimitz's forces repelled it, causing heavy losses to the enemy. See Pacific, War in.

Milan. Second largest city of Italy, Milan (*see* pp. 2737–2738) was bombed by the R.A.F. for the first time in mid-June 1940, the British 'planes

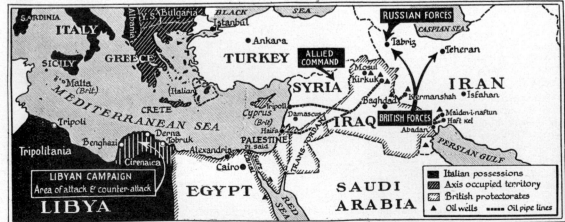

Middle East, showing the countries controlled by the Axis and the coveted British protectorates.

operating from Salon in France. This was the last bombing operation undertaken by the R.A.F. from French soil. Long-distance raids were carried out in August 1940, when big fires and heavy explosions occurred at the Caproni aircraft works. Attacks became more frequent towards the end of October and during November, and raids were also made on the city by British 'planes operating from bases in the Middle East. Large stocks of rubber in the Pirelli works were destroyed and for some time the Fiat works were unable to guarantee delivery of anything as a result of these attacks. *See* Italy, Air War on.

Milch, GEN. ERHARD (b. 1892). Inspector-Gen. of the Luftwaffe. After the Nazis came to power in 1933, Goering made him Secretary of State at the German Air Ministry. Milch was responsible for transforming the German " Air Sport League " into the Hitler Flying Youth, which numbered about 100,000 members. Under his organization the Luftwaffe became one of the deadliest forces of destructive air power.

Milne, FIELD-MARSHAL GEORGE FRANCIS, G.C.B., D.S.O., 1ST BARON (b. 1866). Col. Commandant of the A.M.P.C. (Auxiliary Military Pioneer Corps) from July 1940. He was Chief of the Imperial General Staff, 1926–1933.

Mines and Minelaying. The modern sea-mine is not, as so often supposed, a product of the ingenuity of science applied to destruction peculiar to this war. It was used over a century ago. And even the magnetic mine dates back to the last war, though then it was neither perfected nor extensively used.

Every weapon has produced its antidote. The sea-mine is no exception. There are three main types of sea-mine: the contact mine, exploded by collision with the ship; the magnetic mine, exploded by the magnetism of the adjacent ship itself; the acoustic mine, detonated by the vibrations set up by the propeller of a near-by ship.

On Nov. 2, 1939, a German aircraft was seen to drop two magnetic mines near Shoeburyness. The novel feature was the magnetic device for setting off the detonator. This comprised a delicately poised magnetic needle which was deflected by the iron of a ship passing over or near the mine; by this means an electrical contact was effected, thus closing a circuit and firing the mine.

Acoustic mines and magnetic mines are laid at the bottom of the sea; contact mines are submerged and moored. At sea mines are laid by surface ships and by aeroplanes. Before the end of 1940 the R.A.F. had laid more than 30 minefields, some within a stone's throw of enemy quays and wharves.

The general routine method of dealing with mines, which are laid singly or in fields, is by minesweeping, work done by trawlers manned almost entirely by amateur yachtsmen with temporary naval ranks. The British Admiralty has certain secret methods in addition to these for dealing with mined areas. The magnetic mine was heralded by Hitler as the secret weapon that was going to defeat Britain. Until its secrets were revealed through one (1,500 lb.) which was washed ashore at Shoeburyness, examined and understood, the magnetic minefields of the East Coast took terrible toll of British naval and merchant ships, and also of neutral shipping. Science almost at once produced the magnetic mine antidote—the de-

MINE-LAYING AND MINE-REMOVING

Top, some of the mines carried by a vessel which has been converted from a holiday transport ship to a mine-layer. Below, the boat's crew from a lightship, having sighted a drifting mine, have put out to take it in tow, remove it from the shipping fairway, and then render it harmless.
Photos, Charles E. Brown; G.P.U.

Gaussing girdle for ships, neutralizing their magnetism. When the Queen Elizabeth arrived safely in New York on March 7, 1940, it was seen that she had been fitted with this non-magnetic girdle coiled round the entire length of the hull, high above the water line (*see* p. 92).

In September 1941 Mr. Churchill stated that 30 or 40 enemy 'planes were laying mines in British waters every night, and that 20,000 men and 1,000 vessels were employed on anti-mining work.

The use of mines on land is, likewise, nothing new. In the First Great War mining operations were carried on by both sides, tunnels being driven by miners turned soldiers under No-Man's-Land to focal points to be packed with heavy charges of T.N.T. They were also used in a variety of ways, chiefly by the Germans, as booby traps, or devices left by retiring troops to kill

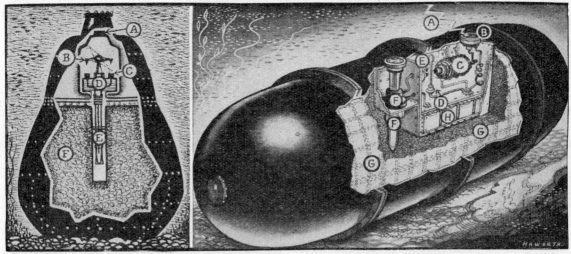

TWO KINDS OF SEA MINE SOWN BY NAZI AIRCRAFT

Left, sectional diagram of the magnetic mine. It remains harmless until the seal, A, has dissolved. Then a ship passing over it attracts the small balanced magnet, B, upwards until the opposite end completes an electric circuit at C. A weak current strengthened by the relay, D, fires the detonator, E, which sets off the 700 lb. of explosive, F. Right, operation of an acoustic mine. Sound waves, A, from a ship's propellers affect the hydrophone, B, and set in vibration the trembler, D, and the electromagnet, C. When the ship is near enough the trembler touches the contact, E, and sets off the detonator, F, which in turn explodes the massive charge, G. The battery is shown at H.

Drawn by Haworth

without combat men hungry, thirsty or exhausted. This method is also popular with the Italian troops in North Africa, and it is in that theatre of war that the mine has been employed most fully. The defenders of Tobruk used mines, and large reaches of the desert were mined. The chief British type is the Pancake,

fired either by the weight upon it of the passing tank or by electric impulse. The chief German mine is the Teller, also detonated by depression.

The detection of land-mines presented difficulties. The electro-magnetic principle is used, the presence of concealed metal revealing to the sweeper the presence

THE GERMAN TELLER MINE AND METHODS FOR ITS REMOVAL

This type of field mine has both a top and bottom plate which, on depression, fire the charge ; the safety catch, when locked, prevents the plunger from being depressed. Tellers were used in great numbers in both Russia and Libya. The Russians had an ingenious device for detaching them : a magnetic ring on a pole was waved over the suspected area and the presence of a mine was shown on a dial at the handle end of the pole. Right, a South African sapper in Libya removing Tellers.

Diagram, by courtesy of " The Sphere "; photo. British Official

of the buried mine. In Russia, minesweeping is done by passing a pole fitted with a magnetic ring at the end. The mine is revealed by an indicator actuated by its presence. The German Teller mine has a safety device not unlike that of the Mills bomb. In Libya our men removed thousands of these mines from desert minefields, rendering them harmless. In addition to the contact mines described, electro-pneumatic mines are set in groups, coupled up to a single battery which detonates the group simultaneously.

The limitation of the ordinary mine is that which many people in Britain now appreciate with regard to aerial bombs, namely, that, unless very large, the damage is localized. The group system is employed to enlarge the land area mined, and thus to ensure widely spread detonation. *See* De-Gaussing; Ouvry.

Minsk. The capital of White Russia, Minsk was an important centre of communications, being 15 miles over the Stalin Line on the road to Moscow. It is situated on the River Svisloch, a tributary of the Beresina. Minsk was the centre of one of the largest battles ever fought when the Germans, advancing eastwards from Bialystok in Poland, captured the town from the Russians on June 30, 1941. When the Russians made their great drive towards Smolensk at the end of December 1941, Hitler moved his headquarters from that town back to Minsk. *See* Russia.

Mittelhauser, GEN. EUGENE (b. 1873). He was C.-in-C. of the French forces in Syria from the outbreak of war until June 1940, having succeeded Gen. Weygand in that post. After the collapse of France on June 22, Syria was no longer a belligerent, and her relations with France became indefinite, despite the declaration of the C.-in-C. that, whatever might happen in France, it was the determination of the French forces in Syria to fight on. Before her collapse France maintained an army of 100,000 men in Syria, and this force was rapidly affected by the chaotic conditions at home. Weygand tried to persuade Mittelhauser to adhere to the policy of the Vichy Government, but evidently without success, for Gen. Mittelhauser was recalled and left for France on July 16, 1940. He was succeeded by Gen. Fougère.

Modlin. This Polish fort to the north of Warsaw heroically held out against savage German attacks to the last. Enemy aerial bombardments reduced the fort to ruins and on Sept. 28, 1939, Modlin was forced to surrender.

Moerdyk Bridge. Spanning the chief estuary of the River Maas (here known as the Hollandsch Diep), which separates North Brabant and South Holland, this great bridge was of major importance to the Germans when they invaded Holland in May 1940, since it carried the main railway link between Dordrecht and the North

MOERDYK BRIDGE AT WILLEMSDORP

This vast railway bridge, which was begun in 1868, has fifteen arches. It spans the waters of the Hollandsch Diep, part of the estuary of the Maas, which separated the two Dutch provinces of North Brabant and South Holland. When the German tanks swarmed across it on May 14, 1940, Holland could no longer hold out against the enemy.
Photo, E.N.A.

and Antwerp. The bridge was crossed by enemy armoured columns on May 14, and its capture, through the treachery of Fifth Columnists, was one of the deciding factors in the Dutch decision to cease fighting, for the Germans were thus enabled to thrust rapidly into the very heart of the country.

Mogadishu. Capital and chief port of Italian Somaliland, Mogadishu was bombarded by light forces of the British Navy in November 1940. It was announced on Nov. 17 that hits were scored on targets ashore and shipping in the port. Enemy shore batteries replied ineffectively. The town was captured by

NATIVES OF MOGADISHU WATCH A BRITISH CRUISER

The capital of Italian Somaliland was taken by British forces in February 1941, and the campaign in this part of East Africa soon afterwards came to an end. The native population (more than four-fifths of the total of 50,000) were thankful to exchange Italian for British rule.
Photo, British Official

British Imperial forces on Feb. 25, 1941, when the place was largely undefended owing to the Italians falling earlier in the campaign into Gen. Cunningham's trap at Jelib on the River Juba. With the capture of Mogadishu the whole of Italian Somaliland was imperilled. *See* East Africa ; Somaliland, Italian.

Mohawk, H.M.S. Belonging to the Tribal class and completed in 1938, this British destroyer had a displacement of 1,870 tons and carried a complement of 190. She sustained damage in the Firth of Forth on Oct. 16, 1939, as a result of the first German raid on Britain. A bomb fell near the ship and casualties were inflicted by bomb splinters among men standing on deck. Among those killed was the commanding officer, Comdr. R. F. Jolly.

Mojaisk. Sixty-five miles west of Moscow, Mojaisk constituted the key town to the Russian capital, and it was here that the Germans, after having captured the place on Oct. 14, 1941, concentrated more war material than at any other point of the front. Of great strategical importance, it was converted by the Nazis into a bastion with three general lines of defence, including strongly fortified villages, concrete blockhouses, earthworks and barbed wire. Having seriously defeated the Germans at Dorokhovo, south-east of Mojaisk, on Jan. 13, 1942, the Soviet forces hurled them back on the Mojaisk defences. The battle for the town began on Jan. 14. The object of the Russians was to encircle the German forces, and with the reduction of the Mojaisk fortifications and incessant dive-bombing attacks on enemy columns, the Russian pincer movement north and south of the town made such good headway that, under threat of being surrounded, the Germans were compelled to evacuate Mojaisk, leaving only a rearguard to cover their retreat. Soviet infantry entered the south-west suburbs, occupied the railway station, and wiped out defending bodies of the enemy. Other Russian units entered the northern suburbs and street fighting raged fiercely. On Jan. 19 Soviet troops finally penetrated the western part of the town and the Red Flag once more flew over the building of the City Soviet. The German threat to Moscow was virtually ended by the recapture of Mojaisk. *See* Moscow.

Molde. Situated 20 miles N.W. of Aandalsnes at the entrance to Romsdals Fjord in Norway, Molde was the port from which King Haakon (*q.v.*) embarked for Britain with the Norwegian royal family and Ministers on June 10, 1940. The Germans bombed the town and caused considerable damage.

Molotov, VYACHESLAV MIKHAILOVICH (b. 1890). People's Commissar for Foreign Affairs from May 3, 1939, when he succeeded Litvinov (*q.v.*). It was announced on May 6, 1941, that he had, at his own request, been relieved of his concurrent duties as Chairman of the Council of People's Commissars—a position which is, in effect, that of Prime Minister, and which he had held from 1930—and that Stalin had taken it over, Molotov being made Vice-Chairman.

On Oct. 31, 1939, he made a declaration on Russia's foreign policy in the European war to the Supreme Council of the U.S.S.R. He said that since the signing, on Aug. 23, of the Soviet-German non-aggression pact, an end had been put to the abnormal relations that had existed for years between Russia and Germany, and that a further improvement in the new good relations had been made by the German-Soviet Amity and Frontier Treaty signed in Moscow on Sept. 29. (This

V. M. Molotov,
Soviet Foreign Minister.
Photo, Planet News

latter was, of course, the treaty by which Poland was abolished.) Molotov at the same time accused Britain and France of being war-mongers, approved the measures by which the three little Baltic States became vassals of the U.S.S.R., and justified the proposals to Finland which, a month later, led to the Finnish-Russian war.

On March 29, 1940, reaffirming Soviet neutrality in the war in the west, Molotov again showed a violent anti-British attitude and accused the Allies of many acts of hostility to the Soviet Union. On Aug. 1 he reiterated that the good relations existing between Russia and Germany were based on the fundamental interests of both countries. At the same time he admitted that the appointment on June 5 of Sir Stafford Cripps as Ambassador to Moscow might foreshadow improved relations with Britain. On Nov. 12, at the invitation of the German Government, Molotov, accompanied by a number of officials, arrived in Berlin, was given an effusive welcome, and had conversations with Hitler, Ribbentrop, Goering and others. It was hinted in Berlin that his visit was the outcome of the signing of the Tripartite Pact on Sept. 27.

On April 13, 1941, a week after Molotov had received Matsuoka, the Japanese Foreign Minister, for the second time, a Russo-Japanese Friendship and Neutrality Pact was signed in Moscow, being hailed in Germany and Italy as an Axis victory, although shortly afterwards " Pravda " stated that when Molotov was in Berlin suggestions had been made that Russia should adhere to the Tripartite Pact and thus transform it into a Four-Power Pact, but that Molotov had refused. Two months later, on June 22, Germany invaded Russia, and Molotov, broadcasting to the nation, indignantly denied that the Soviet Union had in any way provoked " this robber attack . . . without example in the history of civilized nations."

On Sept. 29, 1941, Molotov headed the Russian delegation at the Three-Power Conference held in Moscow (*q.v.*), when full aid for Russia was discussed with the British and U.S. Missions. On Nov. 25, 1941, he sent a Note to all non-Axis Powers, protesting against Germany's barbaric treatment of Russian Army prisoners. In December he attended conferences at Moscow with Stalin and Mr. Anthony Eden, when the conduct of the war and post-war organization, peace and security in Europe were the principal matters discussed. In a Note broadcast to the Powers on April 27, 1942, Molotov charged the German Government with a premeditated policy of atrocities in Russia carried out by the High Command.

Monastir (Bitolj). Town of Yugoslavia, 130 miles N.W. of Salonika. The Germans captured Monastir on April 10, 1941, and by their occupation of this strategic point brought overwhelming forces to bear against the Greek forces fighting the Italians in Albania. *See* Greece ; Yugoslavia.

Monckton, SIR WALTER TURNER, K.C.V.O., M.C. (b. 1891). Head of Propaganda and Information Services under the Minister of State in Cairo from November 1941. He was Director-General of the Press and Censorship Bureau from 1939 to December 1940, when he succeeded Mr. Frank Pick as Director-General of the Ministry of Information. He visited the U.S.S.R. Oct.–Nov. 1941, and had conversations at Kuibyshev with Lozovsky, head of the Soviet Information Bureau, which resulted, on November 11, in an agreement for Anglo-Soviet collaboration on propaganda and information. He was Acting Minister of State in the Middle East between the departure of Mr. Oliver Lyttelton and the appointment of Mr. R. G. Casey.

Sir W. Monckton,
Head of Propaganda
in Middle East.
Art Photo Service

Montevideo. The capital of Uruguay, Montevideo (*see* p. 2793) lies at the mouth of the River Plate, and is famous for its harbour, six sq. miles in area. It was here that the damaged Admiral Graf Spee (*q.v.*) sought refuge on Dec. 13, 1939, after her encounter with three British cruisers. On June 21, 1940, a Nazi plot was revealed at Montevideo, proving the existence of a German political organization with cells in all parts of Uruguay. Following a secret session, the Minister of the Interior was empowered to ban societies which spread anti-democratic ideas, and Nazi agents were rounded up. *See* Plate, Battle of.

Montgomery, FIELD-MARSHAL VISCOUNT BERNARD LAW, K.C.B., D.S.O. (b. 1887). He was appointed G.O.C.-in-C. South Eastern Command in November 1941, in succession to Lt.-Gen. Paget. From 1938 to 1940, when he became specially employed, he was a Divisional Commander. Field-Marshal 1944, Viscount 1946.

Mook, DR. HUBERTUS VAN. Dutch Colonial Minister from May 1942, succeeding Professor Gerbrandy. At the end of 1941 he had been appointed Colonial Minister in the Netherlands Government in London, but, in view of the situation in the Far East, was sent instead to the Netherlands East Indies as Lieutenant Governor-General. He arrived in Sydney on Jan. 6, 1942, and conferred with members of the Australian Government ; on Jan. 14 he was in Washington for conferences with President Roosevelt. He then went to Java. When that island was overrun by the Japanese in March 1942, Dr. van Mook escaped with 14 other members of the Government to Australia. He arrived in London in April.

BRITISH TRAWLER WHICH CAPTURED A U-BOAT

H.M.S. Moonstone, here seen entering Aden harbour, chased the Italian submarine Galileo Galilei in the Gulf of Aden, hit the conning tower with a shell from her 4-in. gun, and, after a few more exchanges of shots, secured the U-boat's surrender and brought her in triumph into harbour.
Photo, British Official

Moonstone, H.M.S. On June 19, 1940, the British trawler Moonstone, while on patrol in the Gulf of Aden, sighted an enemy submarine. The Moonstone attacked with depth charges and the Galileo Galilei came to the surface, dead astern of her, about a mile away. The enemy began steaming in the opposite direction, so the trawler swung round and chased her, opening fire with her 4-inch gun. The second round burst inside the submarine's conning tower. The Galileo Galilei now returned the fire, but the trawler overhauled her to within half a mile and by heavy fire from Lewis guns forced the Italian gunners to abandon their own 3·9s. Another hit from the Moonstone's 4-inch gun was scored, and the range closed rapidly. After two more hits on the conning tower, the Italian crew of three officers and 37 ratings surrendered, and Boatswain W. J. H. Moorman, in command of the Moonstone, brought his prize into Aden harbour, the British flag flying above the Italian. For this gallant exploit Mr. Moorman was awarded the D.S.C. and recommended for promotion to Lieutenant.

Moore, SIR HENRY MONCK-MASON, K.C.M.G. (b. 1887). Governor and C.-in-C. Kenya from 1939. He was Assistant Under-Secretary of State for the Colonies at the Colonial Office, 1937–1939, and Deputy Under-Secretary of State for the Colonies in 1939.

Moore-Brabazon, LT.-COL. RT. HON. JOHN THEODORE CUTHBERT, P.C., M.C., M.P. (b. 1884). From May 1941 to February 1942 he was Minister of Aircraft Production, in succession to Lord Beaverbrook. On Feb. 23, 1942, it was announced that he had been succeeded by Col. J. J. Llewellin. Moore-Brabazon was Minister of Transport from October 1940 to May 1941. A pioneer of aviation, he held the first certificate granted by the Royal Aero Club for pilots. In March 1942 he was given a barony, taking the title Lord Brabazon of Tara.

Brigadier Morgan,
commanded at
Aandalsnes.
Photo, L.N.A.

Morgan, BRIG. H. DE RIMER. He commanded the first British troops—from the 49th (West Riding) Division—to land at Aandalsnes (*q.v.*) in Norway, on April 18–19, 1940. In response to an appeal for help from the Norwegians who were hard pressed by the Germans at Lillehammer, he dispatched two lightly armed Territorial battalions down the Gudbrand valley. These joined up with the Norwegians, but were soon forced to withdraw with them up the valley in the face of increasing German pressure. De Rimer Morgan was formerly in command of the Northumberland Fusiliers.

Morrison, RT. HON. HERBERT STANLEY, P.C., M.P. (b. 1888). Home Secretary and Minister of Home Security from October 1940, in succession to Sir John Anderson. On Jan. 18, 1941, in consequence of the disastrous Fire of London on Dec. 29, 1940, he announced details of the new Government compulsory fire-fighting scheme. On May 13, 1941, he introduced a Bill, which shortly became law, by which fire brigade resources throughout Britain came under the control of the Home Secretary and the

Herbert Morrison,
Home Secretary.
Photo, B.B.C.

Secretary of State for Scotland. Mr. Morrison had been Minister of Supply from May 10 to Oct. 3, 1940, and was the originator of the poster slogan, "Three words to the Nation : Go to it ! " In a broadcast on May 22 he called on all firms working on Ministry of Supply contracts to "work at war speed" and announced a 7-day week for all Royal Ordnance works engaged on the Ministry's contracts. In January 1941 he suppressed the Daily Worker on the grounds that it sought to undermine public morale. In March 1942 he threatened the Daily Mirror with the same fate, a warning which led to much controversy in Parliament and the Press. Mr. Morrison was Leader of the L.C.C. from 1934 to 1940. In 1939 he did work of the greatest value in organizing the evacuation of mothers and children and the speeding up of air-raid precautions.

Morrison, RT. HON. WILLIAM SHEPHERD, P.C., K.C., M.P. Postmaster-General from 1940. He was Minister of Food from April 11, 1939, to April 3, 1940, in addition to being Chancellor of the Duchy of Lancaster. From 1936 to 1939 he was Minister of Agriculture and Fisheries.

Morshead, MAJ.-GEN. SIR JAMES, C.M.G., K.B.E., D.S.O. (b. 1889). An Australian soldier who served in the first Great War, he was in command of Tobruk *(q.v.)* during its seven and a half months' siege in 1941. In November he collaborated with the newly formed 8th Army under Gen. Cunningham sent to relieve Tobruk, and pushed his forces out to meet it. Morshead had also taken part in the British offensive that drove the Italians out of Libya in 1940–41. On March 27, 1942, it was announced that he had been appointed G.O.C. Australian forces in the Middle East in succession to Gen. Blamey, who had been made C.-in-C. of Allied land forces in Australia.

Maj.-Gen. Morshead
withstood siege of
Tobruk.
Photo, British Official

Moscicki, IGNACE (b. 1867). He was President of Poland from 1926 to 1939, being re-elected in 1933. He resigned in September 1939, after his country had been overrun by Germany and Russia. His successor was Wladyslaw Raczkiewicz, who became President of the Polish Government in exile in France. A famous chemist, Moscicki made discoveries in connexion with oxygenation of nitrogen in air. On Sept. 25, 1939, it was reported that Moscicki had been interned in Rumania.

Moscow. The capital of the U.S.S.R., Moscow *(see* pp. 2809–2810) was first raided by the Luftwaffe on July 21–22, 1941, little damage being done. Further raids were carried out by the Germans during the summer and autumn, but many of the Nazi 'planes were prevented from penetrating the city owing to the efficiency of the A.A. defences. The threat to Moscow developed throughout September and October. The German capture of Vyasma and Briansk was followed up by attacks by enemy aircraft on railway communications round the capital. These were made presumably with the object of paralysing the Soviet transport system, and the Germans lost many 'planes during this period. But Soviet reinforcements continued to arrive at the front. Both sides suffered heavy losses in the Orel and Kalinin sectors, but the Germans continued to advance inexorably towards the capital. The fighting grew ever fiercer, the Russians defending every inch of ground. The Germans made their thrust from four main directions —Kalinin from the W., Vyasma and Orel from the S., and Kaluga from the S.W. Most of the diplomatic missions, including the British Military Mission, were reported to have left Moscow. Preparations were made to defend the city, street by street. Home Guards were raised and intensive military instruction was given to the citizens. On Oct. 20 it was announced that the Soviet Government and the Diplomatic Corps had left the city and established themselves at Kuibyshev *(q.v.)*, and certain State departments were stated to have been transferred to Kazan and Sverdlovsk (Ekaterinburg).

In the city itself there was no attempt to hide the gravity of the situation from the people. The Muscovites realized, as their comrades at Leningrad had realized, that they might have to fight for their native town and defend it street by street, house by house. On Oct. 19 Stalin issued a decree, proclaiming a state of siege in Moscow and the surrounding districts. The city was placed in a state of defence. Everyone capable of handling a rifle was enlisted in workers' battalions, and thousands of people were engaged in digging trenches and raising ramparts. On Oct. 23 Hitler's chiefs claimed that their troops had broken through the outer defences—a claim that was unsubstantiated.

The Germans continued to throw in huge forces on the Moscow front regardless of losses. On Nov. 3 a fifth offensive was begun by them against Moscow, and this was met by strong Russian counter-attacks launched in bitterly cold weather. At the same time the Nazis maintained their air attacks upon the city. Enemy pressure increased throughout November ; desperate efforts were made to capture Moscow at all costs, for, the Russian winter having begun in earnest, the Germans sought to entrench themselves in favourable positions, and threw into the battle more than half their tank divisions. At the beginning of December fighting went on in 36 degrees of frost, and the severe cold took a heavy toll of the German infantry, many of whom were found frozen to death. The most serious threat came from the Tula sector, south of Moscow, where fighting was at its fiercest. By Dec. 13, however, the initiative had passed into Russian hands. Although the position was still grave, German pressure against the capital had been eased in several sectors. Gradually the Russians pushed back the enemy from Moscow's outer defences, reoccupying important centres and inflicting further losses until an area many miles in extent had been completely cleared of Nazis.

Though Moscow was repeatedly attacked from the air, its A.A. defences proved to be remarkably efficient. Details are, of course, not available, but the system appears to consist of zonal defences in concentric rings. Hundreds of batteries surround the city, ring within ring ; hills have been honeycombed with passages linking bombproof store-rooms, dormitories and clubrooms and leading to the great guns and the predictors.

MOSCOW FENDS OFF THE ENEMY'S ONSLAUGHT

1. Foreign journalists inspect a Nazi 'plane shot down during a raid on the Soviet capital. 2. Members of the Young Communists' League digging anti-tank defences at the approaches to the city. 3. Reconstruction in Gorky Street after damage by German raiders. 4. Gun crew of a Red Army anti-aircraft battery which has effectively repelled German air raids on Moscow, and has many Luftwaffe bombers to its credit.

Photos, British Official; Associated Press

THE MUSCOVITES TRIUMPH OVER HITLER

In the second year of war, Moscow, having beaten off Hitler's savage onslaught on the capital, by which he confidently expected to bring the Russian State to its knees, celebrated something of its triumph. In the Gorky Central Park of Culture and Rest in Moscow they put on show Nazi warplanes and other trophies captured by the troops who saved Moscow.

Here, a Guard of Honour of the famous Moscow Regiment composed of members of the Red Guard, marches past Mr. Churchill and Mr. Averell Harriman, with Mr. Molotov at the Moscow airport. It was the men of this Red Guard who, in the autumn of 1941, vowed that they would "stop Hitler or die." The occasion was Mr. Churchill's visit to Moscow, August 12-16, 1942.

Photos, U.S.S.R. Official and British Official

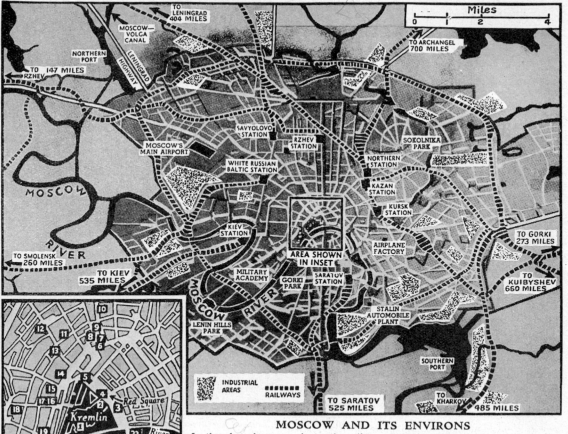

MOSCOW AND ITS ENVIRONS

In the plan above are shown the railway communications, stations, airports, and the chief industrial areas. Left, enlarged plan of the central section, about one mile square. 1. Grand Palace. 2. Headquarters of the Central Executive Committee. 3. Cathedral of St. Basil. 4. Lenin's tomb. 5. Historical Museum. 6. Theatre Square. 7. Mostorg (central department store). 8. Grand (Bolshoi) Theatre. 9. New Government House. 10. State Bank. 11. Moscow Art Theatre. 12. Moscow Soviet (City Hall). 13. Central Telegraph and Post Office. 14. U.S. Embassy. 15. Moscow University (First). 16. Kalinin's office. 17. Kremlin Hospital. 18. Central Market. 19. Lenin Public Library. 20. Palace of Soviets (under construction). 21. Kamerin Bridge. 22. Tretiakov Art Gallery. 23. Moscow Bridge. 24. Main power plant.

By courtesy of the New York "Journal-American"

Of the guns, it has been revealed that no Nazi 'plane has a higher ceiling, and they can fire an average of 400 shells an hour, with an unlimited supply of ammunition. Few German 'planes could penetrate this "wall of fire," and of those that did get through, few survived.

See Kalinin; Moscow: Three-Power Conference; Russia; Tula.

Moscow : Three-Power Conference. Following the Roosevelt-Churchill Atlantic Conference (*q.v.*) it was announced that Britain and America had suggested to Stalin on Aug. 15, 1941, that a Three-Power Conference on the vital question of arms supply to Russia should be held in Moscow. The next day Stalin accepted the offer. Mr. Harriman headed the American delegation and Lord Beaverbrook was the leader of the British. The Russian delegation was headed by Molotov, and included Voroshilov. After the formal opening of the Conference at Moscow on Sept. 29 six committees were appointed. These were concerned respectively with army, navy, air, transport, raw material and medical supplies. Lord Beaverbrook

and Mr. Harriman announced that an agreement had been reached to place at Russia's disposal virtually every requirement for which the Soviet military and civil authorities had asked. Russia in turn had agreed to supply Britain and the U.S.A. with urgently required raw materials.

At another Conference early in Aug. 1942, including Mr. Churchill, Mr. Stalin and Mr. Harriman, together with Mr. Molotov, the British Ambassador, Sir Alan Brooke, C.I.G.S. and Sir A. Cadogan, joint decisions on the war against Hitlerite Germany were reached. The determination was expressed to carry on the war of liberation until the complete destruction of Hitlerism had been achieved.

Mosul. Town 220 miles north of Baghdad in Iraq, the centre of a great oil-field. On May 15, 1941, following an appeal by Rashid Ali, who had temporarily usurped power, a number of German aircraft arrived at Mosul. They were subjected to heavy bombing until May 30, when the rebellion collapsed. Mosul was occupied by British troops on June 4, 1941.

Moulmein. Southern Burmese port, situated on the estuary of the Salween River, about 100 miles from Rangoon across the Gulf of Martaban. Moulmein was raided by Japanese 'planes on Jan. 17 and 19, 1942, when the R.A.F. base was attacked. Heavy fighting between British forces and the Japanese invaders was reported in the Kawkareik area, about 45 miles east of Moulmein, on Jan. 21, and on Jan. 27, having captured Tavoy and occupied the port of Mergui, the enemy advanced on Moulmein in three columns. On Jan. 30 fighting took place to the east of the town, and the next day our forces evacuated it and took up positions west of the Salween River. *See* Burma.

Lord Louis
Mountbatten,
Chief of Combined
Operations.
Photo, Hay Wrightson

Mountbatten, VICE-ADMIRAL, LORD LOUIS, G.C.V.O., D.S.O. (b. 1900). A cousin of King George VI, he commanded the destroyer H.M.S. Kelly (*q.v.*) and the 5th Destroyer Flotilla in June 1939. In May 1940 he brought the Kelly home after she had been 91 hours on tow or hove-to, following severe damage by an enemy torpedo. For this achievement he was awarded the D.S.O. Lord Louis was in H.M.S. Javelin (*q.v.*) when that destroyer was torpedoed in the English Channel on Nov. 29, 1940. In command of H.M.S. Kelly he was among the survivors when his ship was sunk during the evacuation of British forces from Crete in May 1941. On his return to England he was given the command of the aircraft carrier H.M.S. Illustrious. In October 1941 he was promoted Commodore, first class, in succession to Sir Roger Keyes as adviser of Combined Operations. On March 15, 1942, he was made Chief of Combined Operations with the acting rank of Vice-Admiral and hon. ranks of Lt.-General and Air Marshal. *See* Commando.

Moyale. Small British frontier post on the Kenya-Abyssinian border, important because of the fresh-water wells lying outside its fortified walls. Across the frontier lay a settlement of the same name, Italian Moyale, which was bombed by 'planes of the S.A.A.F. on June 11, 1940. The capture of British Moyale was hailed by the Italians as a momentous victory when they entered the place on July 14, 1940, the attack having lasted from June 28. On Jan. 25, 1941, both frontier posts of Moyale were recaptured by the South Africans. *See* Abyssinia.

Moyne, WALTER EDWARD GUINNESS, 1ST BARON, P.C., D.S.O. (b. 1880). He was Secretary of State for the Colonies from 1941 to 1942, and Leader of the

House of Lords from 1941. On Feb. 23, 1942, it was announced that he had been succeeded in both appointments by Lord Cranborne (*q.v.*).

Mufti of Jerusalem. The part he played in furthering Axis intrigue in the Middle East is outlined under the heading Palestine (*q.v.*)

Munich. Capital of Bavaria and one of the most famous of German cities, Munich (*see* pp. 2841–2843) was the place chosen for the signing of the Agreement of 1938 between Great Britain, Germany, France and Italy. The city had been associated with the Nazi party from the beginning of that movement in Germany, the headquarters of the Party being established at the "Brown House." It was at Munich, in the Bürgerbräu beer cellar, scene of the famous 1923 Putsch, that Hitler delivered an anniversary speech to his followers every November. On Nov. 8, 1939, the Fuehrer gave his address here as usual, and shortly after he and his platform supporters had left a bomb exploded, killing and wounding many people. This exploit was later thought to have been engineered by the Nazis themselves, and to be comparable to the burning of the Reichstag in 1933. On June 18, 1940, Munich was the scene of a triumphant meeting between Mussolini and Hitler, when the dictators discussed armistice terms for defeated France. The first R.A.F. raid took place on Sept. 1, 1940, and considerable damage was done. A daring raid by British 'planes occurred on Nov. 8 in that year, but Hitler had sent Hess to take his place in the celebrations, and these were held far from the famous cellar, which was hit during the raid. Railway stations, electric installations and goods yards were vigorously attacked on this and subsequent occasions by the R.A.F. *See* Munich Agreement.

Munich Agreement. This Agreement constituted the final act of appeasement adopted by the Western Powers towards Hitler. It was made between Great Britain, Germany, France and Italy, these Powers being represented by Chamberlain, Hitler, Daladier and Mussolini, and was signed on Sept. 29, 1938, at Munich. It provided for the cession to Germany of the Sudeten-German districts of Czechoslovakia. All the areas stipulated by Hitler to be returned to Germany were ceded without a plebiscite, and the agreement provided for a guarantee of Czechoslovakia's new boundaries by all signatories. Hitler broke the Agreement in characteristic fashion by his subsequent seizure of what was left of Czechoslovakia in March 1939, and by that act of aggression brought Europe yet closer to war.

BRITAIN'S MIGHTY OUTPUT OF MUNITIONS

The making of munitions was gradually organized on mass-production lines, so as to enable supplies to be sent to Russia and to the many other regions where they were urgently required. Only by a steady expansion of output could the Allies gain sufficient strength to mount a shattering offensive.

Munitions. War at once brought State control of a very wide range of activities, including finance, transport, commerce, agriculture, heavy industry and the man power without which none can function. In the last war the need for co-ordination of production of war material was met by a Ministry of Munitions. Since that time the lessons then learnt have been slowly, if imperfectly, digested.

On August 1, 1939, a Ministry of Supply was set up under Mr. Burgin, who had been studying the problems involved for months. The task of this Ministry was to speed up arms for the Army. Nothing else. The Navy and the R.A.F. were not at first within its purview. The powers of this new Ministry were very wide. It could exercise control over all industry and also over all raw materials. On Sept. 22 a Supply Council was

set up with four Directors for munitions, chemicals, explosives, tanks, and equipment and stores. At the same date industrial rationing was introduced.

Before the war an "Industrial Doomsday Book" had been in preparation. Its object was to make an inventory of all firms capable of producing war material of any kind. There were 9,000 such, and, in addition, 6,500 firms of contractors capable of handling big munitions orders. For purposes of war material production the country was divided into 13 zones under a Director-General of Munitions Production. There were 28 national factories at work within a few months, and 700 firms making shells.

The attitude of Labour to this assumption of power by the Government was hostile, as expressed through Trade Union leaders. But before long they were to accept in a good spirit the inevitability of total economic mobilization for total war. On Jan. 25, 1939, a provisional schedule of reserved occupations was published, the Conscription Act following on April 27.

The Minister of Labour, Mr. Ernest Brown, acquired wide powers under the Control of Employment Act, giving him authority over all manner of labour. Again the Trade Unions were hostile, an agreement being reached whereby the Minister's orders were subject to amendment by unions and employers. National Registration came into force Sept. 20, and within a month the organization on a national scale of man power was nearing completion. Many novel changes then took place. For example, all Merseyside and Clydeside dock workers found themselves the employees of the Ministry of War Transport, while shipyard workers became the servants of the Admiralty.

In the sphere of labour two forces were at work, sometimes in opposition. For while the stepping-up of munitions production called for more and more labour, so did the fighting Services demand men—men and women. The War Cabinet has an analysis of the man-and-woman power of the country, which is secret. The Prime Minister, however, told the House of Commons that more than a million more munitions workers were "going to it" than had been the case in

FOR DELIVERY TO THE AXIS

1. An outsize bomb leaving the factory. 2. Girls painting 500-lb. bombs. 3. Workmen beside a casting furnace arranging 13-lb. bombs after the milling process.

Photos, British Official; Keystone; Fox

GIRLS AT WORK PRODUCING SHELLS

In a munitions factory under the Ministry of Supply, girl workers are fitting caps to shells, which will then be dispatched for filling. British output was progressively stepped up until it had overtaken that of Germany and her satellites.

Photo, Sport & General

When war broke out there were 1,000,000 unemployed. By Sept. 1940 there were still 613,000. At that time Mr. Bevin stated that we should need a million more men and women on war work before August 1941.

This Minister exercised vast power, since he could say who should and who should not be released for the fighting forces. In practice, when men were released in increasing numbers for the fighting forces, their places were taken by labour from non-essential industries and by drawing on the pool of woman labour.

A problem which caused much bitterness was the lack of organization for large bodies of labour shifted to often isolated districts for building work. No accommodation existed for these men in many cases, and no facilities for feeding them. There were also transport difficulties for such workers.

The need for increased production became an urgent and pressing problem on June 22, 1941, when Germany invaded Russia and the Prime Minister pledged Britain to " all-out " aid. On June 29 Lord Beaverbrook, who had just left the Ministry of Aircraft Production for the Ministry of Supply, went

1918. The Ministry of Labour and National Service by then had a million women on war work. By July 1940 1,300,000 men were registered for National Service, and munitions production was stepping up briskly.

For some time pressure was put on workers to work long hours, and many did so. But longer hours, it was found, did not produce a proportionate increase in output. The fatigue factor had been overlooked, and the seven-day week was proved bad policy. Therefore, in Royal Ordnance Factories working hours were gradually decreased for efficiency, and the method was recommended to the 1,500 factories engaged on munition work.

On July 30, 1940, the relief system was introduced whereby shifts maintained the machines. The training scheme which had been set up in the early days revealed certain defects. There was a lack of Government training centres. The scheme was expanded to handle 400,000 workers per annum and not restricted, as formerly, to the unemployed. Small factories were converted into training centres. These changes were made by Mr. Bevin.

A practical problem touching output arose when bombing became severe. Were workers to take cover and thus reduce output ? It was finally agreed that workers should carry on, but with such protection as roof watchers could give of the approach of enemy aircraft. This they readily did on the understanding that their families would not suffer in the event of injury or death.

with Mr. Harry Hopkins, U.S.A. representative, to confer with M. Stalin and received from him a long list of essential war material urgently required. At the end of the year Parliament extended powers of labour compulsion to meet new demands.

On Feb. 11, 1942, a White Paper defined the functions of Lord Beaverbrook as Minister of Production, an arrangement under which the Ministries of Labour, Supply and Aircraft Production retained a general autonomy. But on Feb. 19 it was announced that he was returning to the U.S.A. to carry on work in regard to pooling the resources of the United Nations, and that Mr. Oliver Lyttelton, Minister of State, was to take his place in exercising general supervision over the whole field of war production.

In March the formation of a Joint War Production Staff was announced by Mr. Lyttelton during a debate on war production. The complexity of modern aircraft and war equipment had created a division between the Services and those who supplied them, and there was danger of makers and users being out of touch. Much had been done to remedy this weakness. The Joint War Production Staff would also be responsible for dovetailing our raw materials and munitions output into American programmes. Plans were laid for this coordination by Mr. Churchill and Lord Beaverbrook during their visit to the U.S. at the end of 1941. The Citrine Committee, called together by Lord Beaverbrook before Mr. Lyttelton's appointment in March, evolved a scheme whereby small firms were grouped under local organizations responsible for supervising allocation of orders to prevent wastage. These firms were vital to production—out of a total of 27,000 engineering firms 26,000 employed 500 or less—and, to stimulate production by substituting personal for "paper" contacts, each local organization would have only such firms attached as the Staff could easily visit. The Government was determined to carry the war production organization to the highest possible level.

Münster. One of the most heavily bombed cities of Western Germany, Münster, 80 miles N.E. of Cologne, was the R.A.F.'s reply to the German blitzing of Coventry (q.v.). The city was bombed for five successive nights from July 6 to 10, 1941. It was twice set on fire from end to end, and became known throughout Germany as "the unhappy town." The port area on either side of the Dortmund-Ems Canal (q.v.) suffered exceptionally heavy damage. Münster is an important railway junction in addition to being a garrison town. On the occasion of a factory being destroyed in the Dortmund-Ems canal area, the barracks were also heavily damaged.

Murmansk. Russian seaport and base on the Kola inlet of the Murman coast on the Arctic Ocean. It is situated at the head of the inlet and is the terminus of the Leningrad-Murmansk railway. Perpetually

Murmansk, Russia's ice-free port in the Arctic.

ice-free, Murmansk played an important part during the Russo-Finnish war, 1939–1940, when the Soviet forces made their thrust to the Finnish nickel port of Petsamo. Murmansk had already been in the news, for on Sept. 6, 1939, the German liner Bremen (q.v.) arrived at the port after a hazardous voyage of some 4,750 miles from New York. War flared up again in the Murmansk region in 1941, when Finland threw in her lot with Germany and attacked Russia. The Germans claimed to have captured Murmansk on July 1, 1941, after dive-bombing the port with Stukas. They were soon ejected by the Russians, the latter forestalling an enemy flank attack on Leningrad by the landing of a strong force of Soviet storm troops under cover of the guns of the Soviet-Arctic Fleet. German and Austrian Alpine troops under Gen. Dietl suffered heavy losses in an unsuccessful attempt

to reach Murmansk on Sept. 23, 1941. On March 31, 1942, the Russians announced the destruction of an enemy transport and a U-boat in the Barents Sea off Murmansk. Two great convoys bound to and from Murmansk were heavily attacked by air and sea for several days from April 30 ; only four ships were sunk, but the cruiser Edinburgh was lost. It was stated on May 7 that 90 per cent of Russian supplies were safely delivered.

Murmansk Railway. Running from Leningrad to ports on the White Sea and thence to Murmansk, this line was of great strategic value to the Russians during the Russo-Finnish war of 1939–1940, for it provided the only link between Leningrad and Russia's northern army of some 10,000 men based on Murmansk. A Finnish general, Tavela, with fifty men, undertook to attack this difficult objective, and on Dec. 29, 1939, tore up a section of line. After the peace treaty had been signed on March 12, Finland agreed to help to extend a railway through Märkajärvi to link up with the Leningrad-Murmansk line at Kandalaksha, the Russian port on the White Sea. After the Russo-German war broke out in 1941, the section of line near Murmansk was the scene of bitter warfare in September, and German troops suffered heavy losses in an unsuccessful attempt to reach Murmansk. In the Petrozavodsk area, where the railway ran N.E. of Lake Ladoga, heavy fighting occurred between German-Finnish and Russian forces.

Murzuk. Free French forces made a daring raid on this town in the desert province of Fezzan, South-West Libya, in January, 1941. The Italians had established an air base at Murzuk, and the French force, composed of units of the Free French Camel Corps, was dispatched from the Chad territory, a distance of about 200 miles. The Italian garrison, 500 strong, was completely taken by surprise. They withdrew into the fort and the French troops, consisting of soldiers from the Tibesti and Tuareg native tribes of the Sahara under French officers and N.C.O.s, worked havoc in the aerodrome. The French took back some Italian prisoners with them into Chad. Details of this raid, which covered a distance of 400 miles, were given by Gen. Catroux (q.v.) on January 28, 1941.

Muselier, EMILE, VICE-ADM. National Commissioner for the Navy and Mercantile Marine in the Free French Govt. from Sept. 1941 to April 1942. After the last war he commanded the Second Cruiser Squadron of the French Mediterranean Fleet and was also in charge of the naval and coast defences at Marseilles. On June 10, 1940, he was at Bordeaux in charge of factories working for national defence. As soon as he heard of the impending armistice he drove to Paris and destroyed several important secret plans before the Germans arrived in the city. Having escaped from Paris, he went to Marseilles. Here he rallied several naval officers and men, manned a warship and sailed to Gibraltar. Thence he was flown to Britain in an R.A.F. machine, and joined forces with Gen. de Gaulle. On July 1, 1940, he was appointed Commander of the Free French Naval Forces and became a member of the Council of Defence.

Admiral Muselier, former Head of Free French Navy. *Photo, Associated Press*

On Dec. 24, 1941, acting on instructions from de Gaulle, Muselier landed from Free French naval vessels on the small islands of St. Pierre and Miquelon, off the mouth of the St. Lawrence River, Canada. His first steps were to dismiss the Governor, de Bournat, a supporter of Vichy, and to close the wireless station. The coup gave rise to a diplomatic incident involving the U.S. Government and Vichy, but was later smoothed over. A plebiscite showed that the population was in favour of joining the Free French. Admiral Muselier returned to England early in March 1942. In April he resigned from the Free French Naval Command.

Mussolini, BENITO (b. 1883). An account of this dictator's career up to 1939 is given in pp. 2861–2862. Mussolini played a waiting game after the declaration of war between Britain, France and Germany. He enjoyed the role of " peacemaker " in Europe during the early part of 1940, but when Germany brought France to her knees in June of that year it seemed a propitious moment for Italy to strike and seize what booty she could. Hitler was determined that Mussolini should play his part in the Axis partnership, and the Brenner talks on March 17, 1940, when the two dictators met to discuss respective war policies, had been directed to this end. Italy therefore declared war on France and Britain on June 10, 1940. Another meeting took place at the Brenner Pass on Oct. 4, 1940, at which final arrangements were discussed for an Italian invasion of Greece. The Duce launched his attack on Oct. 28, and that day he again met Hitler, this time at Florence. But all did not work out according to plan, and by November 17 the last Italian invader had been driven from Greek soil, and a series of disasters, involving Italian forces fighting the Greeks

MUSSOLINI, HITLER'S JACKAL

1. Italy's dictator, tempted by the chance of loot, declares war on the Allies : a study in truculence. 2. He confers with two of his officers after the Albanian fiasco. 3. With Hitler, he is cheered by German troops on the Eastern front.

Photos, Associated Press; Sport & General

in Albania, caused Mussolini to sack several of his prominent generals and produced tension and unrest at home.

One of his boasts had been that he would make Egypt the granary of Rome. In December 1940 Britain began a powerful thrust against Italian infiltration at Sidi Barrani and drove Mussolini's legions across Libya beyond Benghazi. The Duce became increasingly dependent upon Nazi power to bolster up his undermined regime. British naval victories in the Mediterranean, Greek triumphs in Albania, and the subjugation of the whole of Italian East Africa by British forces threw Mussolini upon the dubious mercy of the Fuehrer. Italian prestige was at its lowest ebb at the end of 1940, and April

and May 1941 saw a " come-back " in Libya and Albania solely owing to German victories in Libya and Greece. Close cooperation between the two countries was maintained to the end of that year, Germany playing the dominant role.

On Feb. 12, 1941, Mussolini had conferred with Gen. Franco at Bordighera, when it was stated that the two men " established identity of viewpoints." It was widely believed that a primary cause of the meeting was the situation created in the Mediterranean by the Italian disaster in Libya. On Dec. 11, 1941, Mussolini announced, from the Palazzo Venezia, in Rome, Italy's declaration of war against America.

As a result of Hitler's surprise Reichstag speech on April 26, 1942, in which the Fuehrer arrogated to himself powers of arbitrary legal control, nervousness was apparent throughout Italy. To restore confidence to the people and to bolster up his tottering regime, Mussolini met Hitler at Salzburg on April 29–30, when "renewed expression was given to the stern determination of Germany, Italy and their allies to ensure final victory by all means in their power."

Mussolini's two sons, Bruno and Vittorio, were in the Italian Air Force. In November 1940 they took part in a raid on Salonika, in Greece, which killed 200 civilians. Bruno was killed on August 7, 1941, while testing a new bomber near Pisa. Vittorio gained notoriety by writing a book describing his experiences in the Abyssinian war. Mussolini's daughter Edda married Count Ciano in 1930.

N.A.A.F.I. The Navy, Army and Air Force Institutes, a great wartime catering concern, commonly known as N.A.A.F.I., provides canteens and entertainment halls at camps and ports for all three Services. Its motto, "Servitor Servientium"—"servant of those who serve"—is admirably chosen. Among other activities N.A.A.F.I. had in 1942 over 5,000 institutes, or canteens, in Great Britain, and over 1,000 in other parts of the world where British troops were serving. During the Battle of France in 1939–40 N.A.A.F.I. sent out companies to play to the troops and established canteens for the Forces. Some 90 N.A.A.F.I. establishments were set up along the lines of communication.

Namsos. This port on the Namsen Fjord, 320 m. N. of Oslo, and the most northerly point of the main Norwegian railway system, was used as an Allied base during the Norwegian campaign. On April 14, 1940, a British naval detachment landed here, followed, a few days later, by British troops and French Chasseurs Alpins. It was from Namsos that the

FLAMING RUINS OF NAMSOS
From this Allied base the British and French troops in Norway were evacuated on May 2, 1940. For several days it was heavily attacked by German bombers with incendiaries and explosives, which reduced it to ruins.
Photo, Mrs. T. Muir

whole of the British and French forces in the sector N. of Trondheim were successfully evacuated on May 2. After repeated bombing raids by the Germans from April 29 to May 2, this small town, from which, fortunately, the civilian population had been evacuated by order of the British commander, became a scene of complete devastation. *See* Norway.

Nantes. Seaport in Occupied France, 35 m. up the estuary of the Loire. Nantes was one of the ports at which stores and vehicles were landed by the B.E.F. early in September, 1939. It also served as a maintenance depot. After the German occupation the R.A.F. bombed oil refineries and storage depots at Nantes. On Oct. 20, 1941, Lt.-Col. Dr. Karl Holtz, the German Military Commander of the Nantes region, was shot and killed by two men, supposedly French patriots, who subsequently escaped. Many people were immediately arrested, German troops surrounded the town and, by order of Gen. Stülpnagel, German Commander in the occupied zone, fifty "hostages" were shot. A few days later, when bombers of the Coastal Command attacked the docks at Nantes, the population welcomed them by displaying lights, some of which were arranged in the "V" sign. *See* France.

Naples. One of Italy's most famous and beautiful cities, Naples (*see* p.p. 2868–9) was visited on many occasions by the R.A.F., who bombed military targets in the vicinity. The first attack took place on the night of Oct. 31, 1940, when Wellington bombers scored direct hits on oil refineries, a railway station and an important junction. In subsequent frequent and heavy raids much damage was done to the Royal Arsenal, a torpedo factory, the Alfa-Romeo works, the I.M.A.M. air-frame factory, docks, shipping, warehouses, railways, engine sheds and oil storage tanks. Great fires were caused and, after one particularly heavy raid on Oct. 21, 1941, a large area of the city was left in flames. The aerodrome at Capodichino was also bombed. *See* Italy; Sicily.

Narvik. Why did an obscure Norwegian port, far north of the Arctic Circle, and of no more than 6,000 inhabitants, become, early in 1940, one of the most talked-of towns in the world? The answer is that this bleak town, remote from the open sea, at the head of Ofot Fjord, and huddled at the foot of precipitous, wooded mountains, happened to be the entrance to Vulcan's Forge for Germany. Over the spine of the peninsula, from Kiruna, Swedish Lapland, came through Narvik the unlimited supplies of iron-ore vital to the making of war material.

For long (*see* Norway At War) the Germans had been securing their supplies by this route, using the device of hugging the Norwegian coast, contrary to international law. If Britain secured possession of Narvik that source of war materials could be cut off. But Britain was not at war with Norway and had, perforce, to content herself by mining the poached waters. Germany's invasion of Norway made possible an assault on this all-important port; and it was in the icy waters of the Ofot and Rombaks Fjords that two of the most gallant naval actions of the war were fought.

On Tuesday, April 9, 1940, the Second Destroyer Flotilla, then in those waters, was ordered to blockade Narvik. The port was already in German hands and six German destroyers, one U-boat and numerous supply ships were known to be in the Fjord; batteries were also known to be in position ashore. The

BRITISH WARSHIPS VICTORIOUS IN NARVIK FJORD

Two glorious naval actions were fought in Narvik Fjord, after the German capture of the port. On April 10, 1940, a flotilla of five British destroyers, led by H.M.S. Hardy, dashed in and destroyed six German supply ships and one destroyer. Three days later, the battleship Warspite with escorting destroyers sank seven enemy destroyers. This photograph shows the Warspite with two destroyers after the second action. Narvik was recaptured, but the Luftwaffe laid it in ruins.

Photo, "The Times"

attackers had to get to the port through the West Fjord, sixty miles long, but linked to Ofot Fjord by a narrow channel. The weather was bad, with heavy snow and bad visibility. All these factors were known and appreciated when, in the Admiralty, London, the First Lord, Mr. Winston Churchill, and high naval officers considered the hazards at 1 a.m. on April 10, and finally left the decision to attack, or not to attack, to the commanding officer, Captain Warburton-Lee.

Captain Warburton-Lee decided to attack, and led his flotilla, composed of Hardy, Hotspur, Hostile, Havoc and Hunter, into the channel at 3 a.m. in heavy snow. At 4.30 a.m. the ships were off Narvik, Hardy, commanded by Captain Warburton-Lee, entering the Fjord alone. At first she could see only a merchant ship, but a little later a whole mass of shipping hove into view.

Only One Officer Left on the Hardy

The action which followed was fierce and fast, and, during the operation, Hardy thrice withdrew and thrice came in again to attack. Her gallant commander received mortal injuries, and his ship was grounded in a sinking condition, by Paymaster Lieut. Stanning, the only officer remaining. Hunter was sunk and Hotspur and Hostile were damaged. Six German supply ships were sunk, one destroyer torpedoed by Hardy, and three set on fire.

Three days later the second naval action at Narvik took place. This attack was made at midday, April 13. It was led by the battleship Warspite, flagship of Vice-Admiral Whitworth, supported by the destroyers Cossack, Punjabi, Foxhound, Icarus, Hero, Eskimo, Bedouin, Forester and Kimberley. The action which ensued in Ofot Fjord, and the waters about it, has been described as a series of dog fights in which ships paired and fought running fights, and the Warspite hammered at the shore batteries, while the Fleet Air Arm joined in at 1.30 p.m.

From the log-book of one destroyer the entries made in twenty minutes, at the height of the action, indicate its intensity. They read: 1.58 p.m. Enemy badly hit; 2.02 p.m. Shore batteries firing; 2.03½ p.m. Enemy destroyer on fire; 2.05 p.m. German destroyer hit by torpedo; 2.10 p.m. Enemy fired torpedo; 2.14 p.m. Another enemy destroyer on fire. By 4.20 p.m there were only two German destroyers afloat, and one sank later, leaving only the Hans Lüdemann. Later, landing parties had little trouble in securing Germans ashore, 120 surrendering.

Since both these actions were fought in the first week of the German invasion of Norway, it may be asked: How came it about that the Germans had shore batteries and possession of the port ?

How the Nazis Sneaked into Narvik

The explanation is simple. The Germans used at Narvik the same methods they used at Bergen and Stavanger. Before the actual invasion German naval ratings were landed dressed as merchant seamen from merchant ships. Each was armed with hand-grenades. In the Fjord lay a 10,000-ton ship, the Norge, ostensibly a whale-oil tanker, actually a camouflaged troopship. When the local Customs officials went aboard this ship they were detained. Only connivance ashore could have covered this action, and such connivance there was, the officer in command, Colonel Sundlo, being a quislingite in contact with the invaders. His second-in-command, Major Omdam, was ordered to arrest his commanding officer ; but it was too late. Later Major Omdam distinguished himself in the land fighting which developed after the two naval actions, driving German detachments back behind Djuduik station ; but treachery doomed the port. The British naval actions put Narvik in the hands of the Allies, but it was not to survive, and within a week Dorniers had reduced the town, largely built of wood, to ashes.

At home, the opening phase of the Norwegian invasion war was marked by bitter criticism in the House of Commons and in the Press of the tardiness of the authorities in despatching an expeditionary force. The criticism was ill-founded, for a force was despatched with the minimum of delay, troops intended for the aid of Finland being diverted so soon as plans for their successful landing could be worked out. With British troops were French Chasseurs Alpins, and a Polish Highland Brigade, commanded by General Bohusz-Sztszko. These troops were landed at Harsted and other coastal points and made long forced marches under bitter conditions. The land fighting in the bleak, mountainous country about Narvik was in the nature of widely-scattered, small-scale actions, pitched battles being out of the question because of the character of the terrain. Had not events elsewhere made imperative a drawing-in of British naval and military resources, the north of Norway would, it is highly probable, have remained firmly in British hands. *See* Norway.

Books to Consult. With the Foreign Legion at Narvik, Capt. Pierre O. Lapie (Murray). I Was One of Them, Z. Lytinski (Cape).

National Registration. The National Registration Act was passed on Sept. 1, 1939, and the National Register taken on Sept. 29, identity cards being issued to every man, woman and child in the country during the following few days. This registration provided material for up-to-date man-power and other population statistics, and formed the basis for the issue of ration cards. Under Ministry of Labour Orders there were further registrations for industrial service, affecting certain age groups of men and women as well as all skilled men in specified trades.

National Savings. The encouragement of savings for war purposes, begun in the first world war and maintained in the interval between the two world wars, was launched as a new campaign in November 1939. The King is Patron of the Movement, Lord Kindersley, G.B.E., the President, Lord Mottistone, C.B., C.M.G., Chairman, and there are four Vice-Chairmen.

The National Savings Committee under these leaders extended the movement until, in May, 1942, there were more than 1,300 local committees and 273,306 Savings Groups in places of employment, schools, streets and the Services in Great Britain and N. Ireland, with a total membership of about 15 millions. Savings were obtained by means of vigorous propaganda encouraging the public to lend money to the Government for war purposes in the forms of National Savings Certificates (purchased at 15s. and maturing in ten years at £1 0s. 6d.), 3 % Defence Bonds (of which only £1,000 could be held by any individual) and increases in the deposits of the Post Office and Trustee Savings Banks. These were known as "small savings," representing money actually saved by the people as a whole, and in October 1941 these savings had passed the thousand million pounds mark. In addition to this there were the "large savings," representing investments in War Loan, 2½% National War Bonds, 3% Savings Bonds and loans free of interest. By March 1942 these investments exceeded £2,030,000,000.

Enthusiasm for the movement was kindled by many special efforts such as the War Weapons Weeks of 1940–41 and the Warships Weeks of 1941–42, when cities, towns and villages aimed at large sums of money to be raised in one week to be lent to the Government. Rivalry and competition led to spectacular figures in many cases, reaching from £20 to £200 per head of population in one week, although critics pointed out that big investment figures in some of these results overshadowed the real savings.

At the end of the Warships Weeks Campaign, March 31, 1942, 1,245 local committees out of 1,294 in England and Wales had held these special weeks, producing a total of over £475 million pounds, the London Warship Week itself producing £146,000,000. Analysis showed that of this big figure, 12¾ million pounds represented the small savings of the London people as a whole. Per head of population the small savings in the London week were £2 14s., compared with £7 4s. in Halifax. Possibly the main value of these drives was the wide-scale opportunity provided for the continuation of propaganda and the stimulation of enthusiasm for this important aspect of the war economy.

In his Budget Speech of April 15, 1942, Sir Kingsley Wood pointed out that the personal savings were £473,000,000 in 1940, and £665,000,000 in 1941. The invaluable work of the National Savings Movement, which had then raised £1,400,000,000 in small savings, was entitled to much of the credit for the gratifying increase during 1941.

An important aspect of the campaign was propaganda for the reduction of consumption by the people of non-essential goods. There was no doubt, in the main, of its success both as a thrift campaign and as an important factor in the prevention of dangerous inflation.

National Service Acts. On Sept. 1, 1939, two days before the declaration of war, the National Service (Armed Forces) Act was passed. It provided that every male British subject in Great Britain between the ages of 18 and 41 should, from time to time by proclamation, become liable to be called up for service in the armed forces.

On Dec. 18, 1941, the National Service (No. 2) Act was passed. This raised the age for compulsory military service for men from 41 to 51. Unmarried women, also, between the ages of 18 and 31, with certain exceptions, became compulsorily liable to serve in the uniformed Auxiliary Services of the Crown or Civil Defence.

Nauru. British S. Pacific island. Formerly German, Nauru was mandated by the League of Nations under the joint control of Britain, Australia and New Zealand, and demilitarized under the League Covenant. It is well-known for its rich phosphate deposits. At daybreak on Dec. 27, 1940, Nauru was heavily shelled by a German raider which approached the island disguised under a Japanese name and bearing Japanese colours. Just before opening fire she hoisted the Nazi flag. Great damage was done to plant, stores and fuel tanks, making the production of phosphates impossible for many months. After Japan entered the war, Nauru was attacked several times, from Dec. 8 to 12, 1941, by Japanese bombing 'planes.

Navicert. *See* Economic Warfare.

Navy League, Sea Cadet Corps. Recruits of the most promising type were secured for the Royal Navy from the Navy League's Sea Cadet Corps. Some of those who underwent training before the War were among the ratings granted temporary wartime commissions in the R.N. Cadets at nautical training schools became officers in the Royal Navy or the Mercantile Marine. The late Lord Lloyd, former President of the League, stated of the Cadets that in "the uneasy years of peace they had produced a highly efficient, disciplined and well- organized body of many thousands of men and boys." Lord Beatty became President of the League in December 1941.

THE NAVY MAGNIFICENTLY FULFILS ITS TASKS

*The navy's duties in time of war are manifold. It is Britain's bulwark
against attack ; it convoys her transports of troops, her traffic of
foodstuffs, munitions and other vital supplies across the waters of the
world. It has to keep a ceaseless watch on the enemy's activities,
harry his shipping from the seas, and maintain the blockade of his
overseas supplies.*

Navy, Royal. The War at Sea falls into four different phases, for all of which the Navy was more or less unprepared owing to insufficient time to build up the necessary material after the policy of appeasement. The first was the German campaign to starve out Britain by all forms of commerce destruction. The second was the overrunning of the neutral countries and the extension of the enemy's coastline to the North Cape. The third was the total collapse of France and the entry of Italy. The fourth was the extension of the war to the Pacific. In September 1939 the superiority of the combined British and French Navies over the German in the bigger types was undeniable, and on paper most impressive. The complete modernization of the principal British capital ships was nearly finished, and in the event of the British Navy alone meeting the German in action there could be no doubt as to the result. Unfortunately the German Navy had not the least intention of fighting a fleet action, but had already planned to rely on commerce destroyers and the submarine campaign against merchant ships in spite of Hitler's personal pledge. As there was no hope of successful sea attack on the short and well

Approximate Net Strengths of the Leading Navies
June 1, 1941 (Principal Ships)

	Under-age	Over-age	Ready 1942	Building		Under-age	Over-age	Ready 1942	Building
British Empire :					**Japan :**				
Battleships	16	—	5?	2	Battleships	12	1	2	3?
Aircraft carriers ..	6	2	—	2	Aircraft carriers ..	7	—	?	2
Cruisers, heavy ..	14	1	—	—	Cruisers, heavy ..	12	5	?	—
Cruisers, light ..	27	23	—	8	Cruisers, light ..	15	8	—	5
Destroyers	173	—	?	?	Destroyers	118?	—	?	?
Submarines	51	—	—	?	Submarines	64?	—	?	?
Germany :					**Russia :**				
Battleships	3	2	—	2	Battleships	3	—	—	4
Aircraft carriers ..	2	—	—	?	Aircraft carriers ..	2	—	—	1
Cruisers, heavy ..	4	—	—	?	Cruisers, heavy ..	5	—	—	3
Cruisers, light ..	6	—	—	2	Cruisers, light ..	2	—	—	?
Destroyers	38	12	—	30	Destroyers	91	—	—	9
Submarines	100?	—	—	70?	Submarines	170	—	—	30
Italy :					**United States :**				
Battleships	3	—	—	2	Battleships	14	3	4	11
Aircraft carriers ..	—	—	—	—	Aircraft carriers ..	6	—	1	11
Cruisers, heavy ..	3	1	—	—	Cruisers, heavy ..	18	—	—}	47
Cruisers, light ..	11	2	—	2	Cruisers, light ..	17	2	7}	
Destroyers	44	—	—	8	Destroyers	86	95	46	138
Submarines	120?	7	—	6	Submarines	48	68	19	50

Note.—Disposition of the French Navy is believed to have been as follows: **Sunk or out of action :** Battleships, 3. **Under British control :** Battleships, 3 ; heavy cruisers, 4 ; light cruisers, 3 ; destroyers, 8 ; submarines, 12. **Remaining under French control :** Battleship, 1 ; aircraft carrier, 1 ; heavy cruisers, 4 ; light cruisers, 7 ; destroyers, 55 ; submarines, 60 ? In general the specific information given in this table is based upon pre-war statements.

The Allied Navies
Ships Manned (August, 1941)

Class of Ship	F.N.F.L. Free French Navy	Royal Norwegian Navy	Royal Netherlands Navy	Polish Navy	Royal Hellenic Navy	Royal Yugoslav Navy	Royal Navy Section Belge	Totals (excluding Hellenic and Yugoslav Navies)
Cruisers	–	–	1	–	Not Disclosed		–	1
Destroyers and Torpedo Boats	3	6	4	6			–	19
Submarines				Not Disclosed				
Gunboats, Sloops and Corvettes	11	4	4	–	Not Disclosed		–	19
Minesweepers, Patrol and Small Convoy Vessels	3	37	24	–			6	70
Smaller Fighting Vessels ..	15	9	1	3			–	28
Harbour Service Vessels	10	2	5	–			–	17
Totals	42	58	39	9			6	154*
PERSONNEL : Officers	290	250	315	200	140	20	12	1,230 (appx.)
Men	4,100	2,500	3,000	1,350	1,600	200	200	13,500 (appx.)

*Grand Total of all Allied Vessels (including categories undisclosed above) : 187. Personnel figures approximate.

protected German coast, the Navy's rôle, apart from clearing the seas of enemy commerce, was defensive.

From the early days the Admiralty were faced with the problem of spreading the Fleet to cover all actual and potential danger spots in European waters, and at the same time sparing important units for convoying in special cases. It was very necessary to deceive the enemy as to the exact position of many ships, so that the 1914 scheme of a " dummy squadron " of merchant ships carefully disguised as warships was revived with the former mistakes avoided. Three fast cargo liners were excellently converted, two as battleships of the Royal Sovereign class and the third as the aircraft carrier Hermes. They were never actually brought into action, but they were very active and influenced enemy dispositions and plans for some time. When their functions were regarded as complete, and merchant tonnage was dangerously short, they were paid off and returned to trade. The dummy Hermes was torpedoed on her way to a dockyard for reconversion, and was beached on the Norfolk coast where her wreck caused the enemy to waste many torpedoes and bombs.

For the defensive work, covering a colossal area in which the enemy always had the advantage of choosing the point of attack, the British Navy was woefully short of cruisers, which necessitated the immediate commissioning of a number of armed liners whose vulnerability to modern weapons was admitted. Against the submarine menace, which developed very rapidly, the shortage of destroyers and other small craft was crippling, in spite of the help of the French Navy with a large number of minor vessels. Efforts were already being made by the Admiralty to remedy this shortage when war broke out, but the submarine-hunting fleet, which could only be really effective by numbers, suffered under a great handicap for a long time; and it was not until early in 1941 that the necessary small craft were delivered in quantity.

American naval critics, forgetting the improvements that had been made, have often stated that Britain started the war against submarines with the methods of 1918, but that is incorrect in at least one very important point. In spite of the economy regime the anti-submarine school had secured the money to evolve the " Asdic " gear for detecting and locating submarines, Britain's closest-guarded secret which proved most effective in the early days. It was the most striking innovation of any of the combatant fleets, and resulted in the destruction of a large number of U-boats. The convoy system, so far as was permitted by numbers, and the defensive arming of merchant ships, were put in hand at once and also proved very satisfactory, so that for some time in 1940 the submarines almost concentrated on unprotected neutrals.

BRITISH GUNNERS ON THE ALERT FOR ENEMY AIRCRAFT

Unidentified aircraft have been spotted, and the gun-crew of this destroyer are eagerly awaiting developments. Behind, the anti-aircraft guns are ready for an engagement. A very great number of enemy planes were brought down by the deadly fire of British destroyers and other craft. The Luftwaffe at first attacked from a high level and did little damage, but later they took to dive-bombing and aerial torpedo attack ; this, though more menacing, provided better targets for our gun crews.
Photos, British Official

Radar was another defensive instrument which was still in the experimental stage in 1939, but which was rapidly improved and vastly increased in its scope in the early days of the war. For some time these new functions were apparently unsuspected, although the Germans were working more slowly on similar lines, but finally they sent three expeditions of senior ranking scientists into the Atlantic in U-boats to investigate. It is not known how much they discovered for all three were destroyed in a very short time.

Under the 1939 Estimates the Navy was building two entirely new types. One was the 900-ton sub-destroyer design, the Hunt class, which the Navy promptly dubbed the "Woolworth destroyers," similar to those already built for practically every big navy. The second was first referred to as the "patrol vessel on whaler lines" but soon after became world-famous as the corvette. With the extreme handiness—and incidentally the lively motion—of the whale-catcher, these little ships have a reasonable speed, excellent sea-keeping qualities and a fair armament. They were designed on the simplest lines to be built in large numbers by shipyards which were not accustomed to naval work, both at home and in the Dominions. Owing to the simplicity of their design, which was at first criticized, the output of these little vessels exceeded all estimates, and without them the losses by submarine would have been infinitely greater.

Even with the French Navy's help, the "mosquito" fleet was quite inadequate, and, although steady progress was made on big ships being built, more attention was paid to small craft. When, one after the other, at very short interval, Italy entered the struggle, the French Navy's help was withdrawn, and Germany seized the West coast of Europe from

that score, but pending the completion of several dry docks in various parts of the Empire it raised serious questions of repair facilities and the work of completing the docks was hurried forward as quickly as possible. Destroyers and ships of all the smaller types continued to be turned out rapidly, and, contrary to fears, the quality was excellent. Simplification was sought in every direction in which it would not impair efficiency, and output was greatly accelerated. The Admiralty's control of all ship-building, naval and mercantile, permitted men and material to be allocated according to the needs of the moment. While the new ships were being built, welcome relief was obtained by the transfer of fifty over-age U.S. destroyers to the Royal Navy in September 1940, followed by ten ocean-going U.S. Coast Guard cutters.

The submarine fleet was also small compared with those of the Axis powers, and suffered heavy losses after the surrender of France, when the enemy presumably secured the secrets of the Asdic gear. All details of our reinforcements were naturally secret, but mention in official reports and casualty lists of several hitherto unknown names beginning with U, characteristic of the smallest and handiest modern pre-war type, and the numbered submarines P-31 and P-32, suggested that the yards had been busy in that section. In spite of small numbers, British submarines, together with aircraft, maintained constant and successful attack on enemy warships and on the lines of sea communication off the occupied coasts and in the Mediterranean.

Many secrets of naval shipbuilding, from the earliest days of the war, were successfully kept until the end. In a number of big ships projected and laid down all work was suspended, but the enemy obtained a steady stream of spies' reports of their progress towards commissioning and in some cases, apparently, even of their joining the Fleet. They also received details of ships which had never even been authorised and these, doubtless, had a considerable influence on their operations and plans. In the case of the new "light fleet aircraft carriers" of the Glory class, ships of 14,000 tons with a speed of 25 knots, they do not

the North Cape to the Pyrenees, the need for numbers became more and more urgent, and Italy's new capital ships demanded the completion of our battleships.

An appeal was made to the shipbuilding industry for a tremendous effort and proved very successful. The 35,000-ton King George V, Prince of Wales and Duke of York were completed in good time. Those ships were so far advanced that any major alterations in their design were impossible without causing long delay in their commissioning, but in the ships which were still in their early stages immediate steps were taken to embody the lessons of the war and the changes made greatly increased their displacement. The international agreement for limiting the displacement of each type was dead, so that there was no trouble on

TWO NEW TYPES OF U-BOAT HUNTERS

Designed on simple lines, for rapid production in large numbers, these vessels achieved very considerable successes in the war against submarines. The corvette, of which an example is seen above, was a very handy little ship on whaler lines which became famous in all convoys. Below, H.M.S. Lauderdale, a 900-ton sub-destroyer of the Hunt class, built in 1940 and known to naval men as "Woolworth destroyers"
Photos, Planet News

SAILOR'S LIFE AFLOAT IN BRITAIN'S WARSHIPS

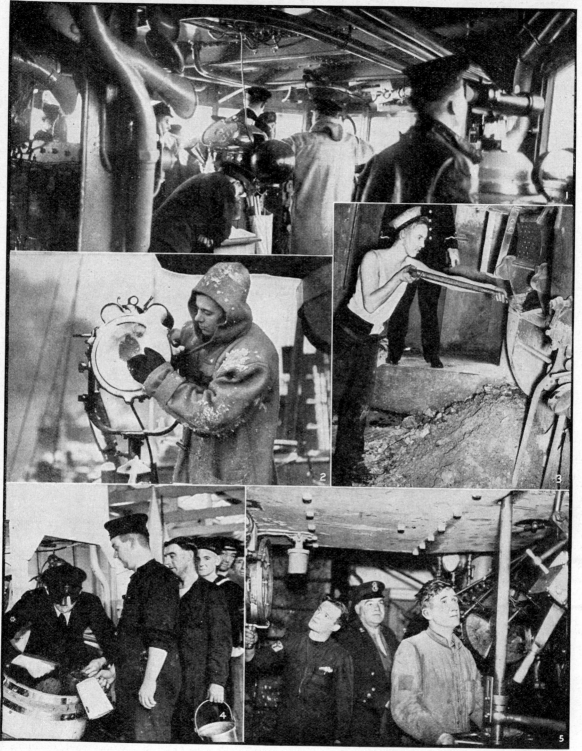

1. Action stations are continually manned and on the alert for enemy vessels, submarine attack or roving planes. 2. In wintry weather the signalman has to scrape away snow from his lamp. 3. Down in the stokehole the boilers must be fed. This photograph was taken on a trawler. 4. Ratings line up for the rum ration, ⅛ pint diluted. Some of these men represent a mess of perhaps twenty, hence the size of the receptacles. 5. Staff of the engine-room of a corvette.

Photos, British Official; Fox; Topical Press

appear to have received any information until the ships were actually in commission.

The same successful secrecy in building operations appears to have been maintained in the case of the steam gunboats, miniature destroyers of 250 tons with a speed of 35 knots and quite a heavy armament, which were built by the specialist yards to give a stiffening to the light coastal forces of motor gunboats and motor torpedo boats, and of the preparations to build a number of convoy frigates, bigger, more powerful and with greater radius of action than the corvettes, by prefabricated methods. The parts were constructed in general engineering works in various parts of the country and sent to non-specialist yards for assembly. As in the case of American prefabricated merchant shipping the preliminaries took a long time, but later the actual construction was very rapid indeed.

The development of the magnetic and then the acoustic mine by the Germans demanded a new mine-

CAMOUFLAGED FOR CONVOY DUTY

This close-up view of the destroyer Javelin shows the dazzle painting of zigzag bands adopted for modern camouflage to break up the outlines of ships. It may be difficult to spot a ship so disguised, to know her type or even her direction. H.M.S. Javelin distinguished herself in spectacular attacks on enemy convoys in the Mediterranean once, with another destroyer sinking eleven ships in three hours.

Photo, British Official

sweeping fleet and a new technique, for the normal A sweep, dragging a wire between two sweepers to catch and cut the moorings of the old type of mine, was useless against the new type, although moored mines still had to be considered. Wooden-hulled sweepers were needed for the magnetic mines, and there were comparatively few of the old type of wooden shipwright left at work in the country. They were all put to the job and were joined by a number of highly-skilled veterans who had long retired. With the help of American and Canadian shipwrights accustomed to building wooden hulls they were soon producing diesel-driven minesweepers of very efficient design. For other forms of mine sweeping numbers of steel vessels were built, many on a somewhat distant adaptation of a fishing trawler's lines.

Repairs and alterations to H.M. ships also demanded the most careful organization, largely in yards which normally only undertook mercantile work. Careful watch was kept for every opportunity of embodying the lessons of the constantly changing war into the design of existing ships as well as new ones and it often entailed radical changes. Many features, for instance, had to be sacrificed in a number of ships in order to install additional anti-aircraft defence without dangerously overloading, and this would occasionally make them almost unrecognisable.

In personnel also the effort of revival had not proceeded far enough by 1939. Unusual numbers were under training and an unduly large proportion of the crews afloat were very young, but they stood the strain magnificently.

Many of the older men who came back to the Service proved unable to bear the physical strain and had to be invalided, but the flow of recruits, both volunteers and under the Military Service Act which gave a man the choice of his Service, was most satisfactory in quality and embarrassing in number. Many who selected sea service were put through a course of intensive training for merchant ships on the supply services.

After the first immediate demand had been satisfied, commissioned rank in the Royal Naval Volunteer Reserve could only be reached through the lower deck, except for specialist work; several months sea time under close observation was necessary.

As these amateur officers became qualified, and by their enthusiasm and patriotism did much to make up for their lack of practical sea experience, it began to be possible to demobilise a number of professional officers from the Royal Naval Reserve and to let them return to their normal work of handling the transports, supply ships and food carriers, in which heavy casualties had made their skill and experience an urgent need.

At the other end of the scale the traditional system of promotion from Captain to flag rank by seniority only—all those senior to the officer who was wanted being retired next day—was abolished at the end of 1940 and any Captain within five years of the top of the list could be promoted.

Instead of relying entirely on disguised merchantmen for commerce destruction, Germany used some of her armoured ships, from the "pocket battleship" Admiral Graf Spee to the 26,000-ton Scharnhorst and Gneisenau and the 35,000-ton Bismarck. Most of the regular warships which ventured out were accounted for, and many of the disguised auxiliaries, but it meant an extension of the convoy system and a serious dispersal of the British forces, which was very embarrassing.

As in the early days of the last war, British cruisers and destroyers proved superior to the enemy whenever they met, but it was necessary to make many alterations for new duties and to meet the air attack which developed in 1940 and 1941 to an extraordinary degree. At first it was principally high-level bombing, which did little harm to ships of any size. Later dive-bombing and torpedo-dropping were adopted, and proved far more dangerous. The thick armoured decks of big modern ships like the Rodney and Illustrious proved capable of resisting very heavy bombs, although the swift destruction by Japanese dive bombers and torpedo planes of the new Prince of Wales off Malaya made the danger even more clear and the losses among the smaller types mounted rapidly. The strengthening of anti-aircraft batteries was obviously demanded, but it was clear that the protection of fighter planes was absolutely necessary.

The first important British losses came as a shock to laymen : the battleship Royal Oak, sunk by submarine inside the protected waters of Scapa Flow, and the aircraft carrier Courageous by the same means in the open sea. The Navy itself expected such ships to show little resistance to modern explosives ; the Royal Oak belonged to a class which had proved impossible to modernize, while the Courageous was a conversion which had never been satisfactory, and was due for scrapping. Both ships were over-age by international agreement, as was also the battleship Barham, later sunk by torpedoes in the Mediterranean, the only ship of the Queen Elizabeth class which had not undergone a complete modernization before the war.

Ships Lost and Ships Repaired

For a long time the later ships proved capable of offering a very stout resistance. Light cruisers, destroyers and smaller craft were lost in a steady succession, but it was to be expected from the work that they were doing and the risks they had to run owing to inadequate numbers. The loss of the battle cruiser Hood in action with the new German battleship Bismarck, and of the battle cruiser Repulse in the Pacific, was also partially explained by the age of the ships, but the manner in which the new Prince of Wales succumbed to Japanese torpedo planes, although the weight of the attack was admitted, was a very serious matter and caused grave public concern in the absence of authoritative information as to the circumstances, which obviously could not be given. It was also necessary to hide from the enemy damage sustained by H.M. ships and the manner in which it had been repaired. Mr. Churchill, speaking on the loss of the Prince of Wales and Repulse in the absence of aircraft protection, revealed that all but one of our aircraft carriers were under repair at the time, and Mr. A. V. Alexander, First Lord of the Admiralty, stated that a large number of our heavy ships which had sustained major damage had been safely brought into harbour and repaired.

On the same occasion, the debate on the 1942–43 Naval Estimates, the First Lord stated that the Admiralty had arranged a special investigation into the losses of all important ships since the war began, in order to make quite certain that there should be no question of missing any lesson, large or small, which ought to be learned and acted upon. The Scientific Advisory Panel had made reports on these investigations, and a number of improvements had already been put into effect.

From the very outbreak of war events fully justified the scheme of training followed since 1919, although certain changes had to be made to meet changed enemy methods. The Engineering Branch received the highest praise for the colossal distances steamed by the ships without breakdown. The condenser trouble which was such a handicap during the last war was practically eliminated. The gunnery of the Fleet was excellent in all branches, long range as well as anti-aircraft. The anti-submarine work, both in convoying and attack, was as good as the shortage of material permitted, and the much-discussed attention which had been given to training in night actions was amply

repaid by the obvious superiority of the British personnel on many occasions, particularly over the Italians.

Cooperation with the other Fighting Services was another matter which had received great attention before the outbreak of war, and although there was a good deal of bitter comment, both inside and outside Parliament, on the lack of close cooperation with the R.A.F. in Home Waters and the Far East, various combined operations on the Occupied Coasts and in North Africa, as well as the evacuation of France, Greece and Crete, showed what good work could be done and confirmed the wisdom of letting the personnel of each Service see the work of the others.

When Seventy Destroyers Were Out of Action

The German invasion of Norway in April 1940, and the taking of the Continental coast as far as the Spanish border, greatly increased the difficulties of the Navy, as they provided so many more jumping-off places for enemy attack. In spite of this, nearly half the ships which attempted to run the blockade from enemy territory in 1941 were intercepted. As a compensation it gave Britain the use of a large number of merchant ships. Italy's entry and the collapse of France demanded an entire rearrangement, with fewer ships available ; apart from the loss of the French Navy, the repairs after Dunkirk lasted several months, during which seventy destroyers were out of action. The first clashes showed that the Italians suffered from their old anxiety to preserve material at all costs, and that their design was generally defective. One of the most distasteful jobs which the Navy had to undertake was immobilizing the French ships after they had refused to move out of reach of Axis seizure.

The growing hostility of Japan became more and more plain, and all possible concessions were made to keep her out of the war. It was obviously impossible for the Navy to spare ships to cover the Pacific ;

Ships of the Royal Navy Including Australian, Canadian and Indian Ships		
	At September 1939	Losses Announced to May 31, 1942
Battleships	12	3
Battle Cruisers	3	2
Aircraft and Seaplane Carriers	9	4
Cruisers	61	19
Auxiliary Cruisers, etc. ..	—	27
Anti-Aircraft Ships	4	1
Destroyers and Flotilla Leaders	191	72
Minelayers	8	2
Minesweepers	40	13*
Monitors	3	1
Escort Vessels	42	10
Patrol Vessels	10	4
Submarines	60	37
Motor Torpedo Boats	21	—
Tugs	12	2*
Trawlers	118	133*
Drifters	21	17*
Corvettes	—	11
River Gunboats	20	3
Seagoing Depots	9	—
Repair Ships	1	—
Surveying Ships	10	—
Netlayers	2	—
Hospital Ships	1	—
Small Craft	8	2
Whalers	—	3
Yachts	—	11
Armed Boarding Steamers ..	—	2

*Including Auxiliaries.

Note. No new construction, nor any ships of Allied Navies, are included in the first column of this table.

British Warship Losses
To August 31, 1942

Battleships

Barham	Prince of Wales	Royal Oak

Battle Cruisers

Hood	Repulse

Aircraft Carriers

Ark Royal	Eagle	Glorious
Courageous	Hermes	

Cruisers

Bonaventure	Effingham	Neptune
Calcutta	Exeter	Perth
Calypso	Fiji	Southampton
Canberra	Galatea	Sydney
Cornwall	Gloucester	Trinidad
Dorsetshire	Hermione	York
Dunedin	Manchester	
Edinburgh	Naiad	

Anti-Aircraft Ships

Cairo	Curlew

Destroyers

Acasta	Gipsy	Kingston
Acheron	Glowworm	Kipling
Afridi	Grafton	Legion
Airedale	Grenade	Lively
Ardent	Grenville	Maori
Basilisk	Greyhound	Margaree
Bedouin	Grove	Mashona
Belmont	Gurkha (1)	Mohawk
Berkeley	Gurkha (2)	Matabele
Blanche	Hardy	Nestor
Brazen	Hasty	Punjabi
Broadwater	Havant	Southwold
Campbeltown	Havock	Stanley
Codrington	Hereward	Stronghold
Cossack	Heythrop	Sturdy
Dainty	Hostile	Thanet
Daring	Hunter	Valentine
Defender	Hyperion	Vampire
Delight	Imogen	Venetia
Diamond	Imperial	Vimiera
Duchess	Ivanhoe	Vortigern
Electra	Jackal	Wakeful
Encounter	Jaguar	Waterhen
Escort	Jersey	Wessex
Esk	Juno	Whirlwind
Exmoor	Jupiter	Whitley
Exmouth	Kandahar	Wild Swan
Fearless	Kashmir	Wren
Foresight	Keith	Wryneck
Fraser	Kelly	
Gallant	Khartoum	

Large Auxiliaries

Audacity	Hector	Rosaura
Andania	Jervis Bay	Salopian
Banka	Lady Somers	Scotstoun
Camito	Laurentic	Springbank
Carinthia	Manistee	Terje Viken
Chakdina	Patia	Tonbridge
Cormorin	Patroclus	Transylvania
Crispin	Queenworth	Vandyck
Dunvegan Castle	Rajputana	Voltaire
Forfar	Rawalpindi	

Hongkong was regarded as doomed in the event of war, but Singapore was expected to hold out with the assistance of Dutch East Indian forces. Japan's treacherous attack on the United States had the advantage that it brought America into the struggle immediately.

The high opinion held of the Dominion Fleets, small though they were, was fully justified, and their remarkable expansion after the outbreak of war exceeded expectations. After two years of war there were nearly 200 ships, from cruisers to small craft, of the occupied countries cooperating with the British, manned by nearly 15,000 trained officers and men.

Books to Consult. The Royal Navy at War, Vice-Adm. J. E. T. Harper (Murray). Action Stations : The Royal Navy at War, Rear-Adm. H. J. Thursfield (Black).

Neame, Lt.-Gen. Sir Philip, v.c. (b. 1888). Commanding the British Forces in Palestine and Transjordan from August 1940, Lt.-Gen. Sir Philip Neame

Lt.-Gen. Sir P. Neame, served in Middle East.
Photo, Vandyk

was taken prisoner, with Generals O'Connor and Gambier-Parry, by the Germans in Libya, April 1941. He was Commandant of the Royal Military Academy, Woolwich, 1938–9, and Deputy Chief of the General Staff, 1939–40. *See* North Africa.

Near East. *See* Middle East.

Neghelli. Important Abyssinian town, from which Graziani (*q.v.*) took his title of Marquis. The Italian aerodrome here was first attacked by S. African bombers, June 18, 1940, enemy aircraft on the ground being destroyed. Neghelli was captured from the Italians by Imperial (African) troops on March 22, 1941. *See* Abyssinia.

Nehru, Pandit Jawaharlal (b. 1889). Indian nationalist leader. Educated at Harrow and Cambridge, he later practised as a lawyer at Allahabad High Court. He was several times President of the Indian National Congress, and was often imprisoned for furthering its cause. In October 1940 he was sentenced to four years under the Defence of India Act, but was released in December 1941. He opposed the terms of the British draft scheme for Indian dominion status presented by Sir Stafford Cripps in March–April 1942, but was foremost in advocating Indian resistance to Japan. *See* India.

Nelson, Donald. An American expert in organizing output and distribution, Mr. Donald Nelson was, on Jan. 16, 1942, appointed Chairman of the new War Production Board which was to coordinate and develop American war production. Mr. Nelson was to have the final word on all questions arising out of the allotment of supplies and the rate and direction of output. Mr. Churchill soon afterwards appointed Mr. Oliver Lyttelton as Minister of Production, with similar powers.

Mr. Donald Nelson, in charge of U.S. Production.
Photo, Topical Press

Nelson, H.M.S. This British battleship, of the class to which she gave her name, has a displacement of 33,950 tons, a complement, as a flagship, of 1,361, and as a private ship, of 1,314, and a main armament of nine 16-in. guns. She was completed in June 1927. In the early part of December 1939 she was damaged by a magnetic mine, but was able to return to harbour under her own steam. H.M.S. Nelson was one of the naval units which, towards the end of July 1941, successfully protected an important convoy of merchantment through the Sicilian Channel in the face of intense enemy attacks by bombers and E-boats.

Neptune, H.M.S. British cruiser of the Leander class. Completed in February 1934, she had a displacement of 7,175 tons and carried a complement of 550. Her main armament was eight 6-in. guns. In Dec. 1941 the Neptune, commanded by Captain R. C. O'Conor, was sunk by enemy mines in the Mediterranean. The destroyer Kandahar, cruising near, went to the rescue, but was damaged and had to be sunk.

TOTAL WAR OVERWHELMS THE NETHERLANDS

With supreme disregard for the law of nations and the principles of civilization Hitler flung his legions on Holland. In a five-day campaign Germany's war machine, long prepared and ruthlessly employed, shattered the independence of yet another of Europe's peace-loving countries.

Netherlands, Invasion of. At nightfall on May 9, 1940, there was little to suggest that the clouds of war were about to burst over Holland. True, for months past there had been rumours of war, but it was still hoped that the menace, so often and so long threatened, would be averted.

That evening the Dutch authorities received through their Intelligence Service the message : " Tomorrow at dawn ; hold tight." At once the Commander-in-Chief, General H. G. Winkelman, and his two principal lieutenants, Lieut.-Gen. Van Voorst tot Voorst and Vice-Admiral Fürstner, commanders of the field army and the naval forces respectively, were ordered to put into operation the plans against invasion already prepared. At 3 a.m. air observer posts reported large numbers of German 'planes flying over the country. A quarter of an hour later the military aerodromes of Schiphol, Waalhaven, and Bergen de Koog had been bombed. Immediately afterwards it was reported that German troops had actually crossed the frontier. It was not until three hours later that the German Minister at The Hague, Count von Zech, visited the Netherlands Ministry of Foreign Affairs to tell the Minister, Dr. Van Kleffens, that Germany had irrefutable evidence that the British and French were about to invade the Ruhr from the Low Countries with the connivance of the Netherlands and Belgium. The German Government, therefore, found itself compelled to occupy the Netherlands, and expressed the hope that the Dutch would accept the " protection " of the German Reich. Only one reply was possible in the circumstances : " The Netherlands considered themselves at war with the German Reich."

The bombardment and machine-gunning of the military aerodromes was followed by attacks of parachute troops in large numbers. Three aerodromes near The Hague were swiftly captured and German transport 'planes landed. By 5 a.m. The Hague, the headquarters of the Court and Government, was encircled by considerable enemy forces. The parachutists and air-borne troops, all too ably supported by members of the Fifth Column, continued to arrive, with the result that the First Army Corps, mainly stationed in the province of South Holland and there intended to hold the fortifications of the new Dutch water line (i.e. the eastern edge of the " Fortress of Holland "), became involved in a welter of confused fighting in the heart of the country, especially around Rotterdam and The Hague.

The German attack was threefold: (a) through the provinces of Groningen and Friesland to the Zuider Zee dyke connecting Friesland with North Holland ; (b) on the Grebbe line in the centre of the country, and beyond this against the new Dutch water line ; and (c) through Limburg and North Brabant in the

The Netherlands, showing German points of attack and successive defensive lines.

THE GERMAN ADVANCE HAMPERED BY HOLLAND'S GALLANT DEFENDERS

German troops reached the Dutch first line of defence along the Yssel and Maas early in the short-lived campaign. Among the bridges on the latter river blown up by the Dutch to impede the aggressors' advance was the fine Wilhelmina Bridge at Maastricht. As seen above, the Nazis were thereby compelled to use rubber boats in order to reach the western bank.

Photo, Keystone

direction of the Moerdijk bridges, Zeeland and Belgium. The Moerdijk bridges, which cross the estuary of the River Maas separating the province of South Holland from North Brabant, were seized, and thus the principal channel of communication between the central and southern provinces was cut, although it was not until three days later that Nazi armoured divisions were able to overcome the opposition in North Brabant and pour over the Moerdijk (*q.v.*) into Fortress Holland. Meanwhile, other German air troops were fiercely attacking Dordrecht and its bridge across the Waal—unsuccessfully, since the river crossing at Dordrecht was not forced until the end of the five days' campaign. Then at Rotterdam, on the morning of May 10, German parachute troops seized the aerodrome of Waalhaven and extended their hold along the southern bank of the Meuse. An attempt to take Delft by parachutists was foiled, all the attackers being killed or taken prisoner. The same fate befell the parachutists at The Hague.

So far the Dutch resistance had been unexpectedly strong. From papers found on the dead body of the German General von Sponeck, commanding the troops operating against The Hague, it was learnt that he had been ordered to take the Dutch capital on the first day. Accordingly, fresh waves of parachutists descended in the neighbourhood of The Hague in the late afternoon of May 10, while a number of transport 'planes came down on beaches. In many a place in Fortress Holland and, indeed, throughout the country the parachutists and Fifth Columnists were working confusion and havoc.

During the night of May 10 and the early hours of May 11 parachute troops round The Hague were again reinforced, and again their activities were suppressed.

In Rotterdam the invaders had more success. Although the bridges across the Meuse which they had seized were recaptured by Dutch Marines, a fresh wave of Germans, landed on the Waalhaven aerodrome, appeared on the scene, and the Dutch, after suffering severe casualties, were forced to withdraw again to the north bank. Since it was obvious that the Dutch had not the force to recapture Waalhaven, a request was sent to the British R.A.F. that it should be destroyed. So on the nights of May 10, 11 and 12 British bombers subjected the aerodrome to an intensive bombardment. The Dutch Navy was also in action against the ubiquitous parachutists. Considerable enemy forces were now on the south bank of the Meuse.

Rotterdam a Shambles in Half an Hour

In Rotterdam itself fighting continued for days with changing fortune. Since R.A.F. bombers had rendered Waalhaven aerodrome untenable, the Germans landed their air-borne troops on the parking space of the Feyenoord Stadium. Then on the third day German artillery opened fire against Dutch artillery brought up from Rotterdam. So there developed on the fifth day a lively artillery duel across the river.

The German armoured columns which had crossed the Moerdijk bridges and crushed the fighting at Dordrecht were by then in the outskirts of Rotterdam. On the afternoon of May 14 the city became the victim of a ruthless air bombardment. Two squadrons of 27 aeroplanes each, dropping 400-kg. high-explosive bombs and incendiaries, converted the city into a shambles. Thirty thousand people, almost all civilians, perished during this half-hour.

While this fierce and strange struggle was proceeding in Fortress Holland the Germans were sweeping all before them on what might be described as the front. In the north the Dutch forces, in the late afternoon of May 10, retreated in orderly fashion in the direction of the Zuider Zee dyke and took up new defensive positions at Den Helder. On the eastern bank they maintained a bridgehead at Kornwerderzand, and this was fiercely assailed by the Germans on May 12 and 13.

Both times they were beaten off, so the Germans then attempted to cross the Yssel Lake from the little harbours on its eastern shore. To meet this new threat of invasion a small force was hurriedly concentrated on the Zuider Zee, reinforced by French and British motor torpedo boats. In this, the first battle to be fought on the Zuider Zee since 1578, the honours went to the Dutch : the dyke remained untaken to the end.

To the south the Germans swept rapidly ahead, however. The Dutch frontier battalions fought a delaying action against vastly superior forces, falling back to the Yssel line. This line, too, was only thinly held (as had been intended), but such was the Dutch resistance that it took the enemy three days

to cover the 50 miles separating the frontier from the Grebbe line, the main line of resistance. This was assailed on Sunday, May 12, when a serious situation developed, and on May 13 such was the German strength in tanks and 'planes that the defences were swamped. The Dutch retreated to their final positions behind the inundations of the new Dutch water line, i.e. the eastern front of Fortress Holland. There were no reserves. The Dutch defenders were sorely battered and exhausted after their fighting retreat. It was hardly surprising that on May 14 the Germans broke through the last line of defence and penetrated Fortress Holland. Already the southern wall had been breached, following the occupation of the Moerdijk bridges. Further resistance was clearly useless, and it was the realization of this, and not the effect on morale of the ferocious bombing of Rotterdam a few hours before, that decided the Dutch G.H.Q. to capitulate.

In North Brabant and Zeeland the struggle went on. The Dutch had to abandon the Peel-Raam position on May 10, since it was rendered untenable by the retreat of the Belgians on their right flank behind the Albert Canal. Yet they resisted bravely and made the Germans pay dearly for their passage of the Meuse-Waal Canal and the Meuse itself. All four of their armoured trains which crossed the frontier were destroyed, one after crossing a bridge at Gennep.

The bridge at Gennep it should be noted, was the only important one near the frontier not destroyed in time by the Dutch. Though one bridge near Maastricht was not destroyed—an omission which had disastrous effects on the Allied defences—this structure was across the Albert Canal, which nowhere runs through Dutch territory. The three bridges at Maastricht (*q.v.*) in Dutch territory were all blown up in time.

Pursuing their advantage, the Germans forged ahead through North Brabant and their armoured

AFTER THE NAZI RAIDERS HAD PASSED

History holds no parallel to the coldly calculated mass murder committed by the Luftwaffe in Rotterdam on May 14, 1940. Two square miles of the heart of the city were laid waste in thirty minutes, and 30,000 lives were lost. Top, Rotterdam in flames ; below, Waalhaven, the city's airport, after the bombardment.

Photos, Wide World; E.N.A.

LANDING OF BRITISH TROOPS

Although the swift Nazi onslaught prevented powerful military aid being sent to Holland, the Allies helped effectively in evacuating civilian refugees and troops, and destroying everything likely to be of value to the enemy. Above, a British demolition party arrives at a Dutch port.

Photo, Keystone

columns crossed the Moerdijk bridges on May 14. Still to the west, however, Dutch forces (reinforced now by French troops from Flushing and the south) continued a strong resistance. For some days after the capitulation of Fortress Holland on May 14 the Dutch and French in the island province of Zeeland kept up a fierce resistance, ably supported by ships of the Netherlands and British navies.

Just before the final surrender the surviving naval forces in the north and centre were ordered to get across the North Sea to England. On the way they were repeatedly attacked by dive-bombers, and the Johan Maurits van Nassau was lost.

Meanwhile, Queen Wilhelmina and the Royal Family had been an enemy objective. At 4 a.m. on May 10 German 'planes attacked the palace outside The Hague. The Queen's situation was rendered precarious when the palace was surrounded by parachute troops who were landing continuously. Prince Bernhard manned a machine-gun on the roof and maintained a heavy fire against low-flying 'planes and snipers. Late in the afternoon the Queen and her family removed to the Noordeinde Palace in the centre of The Hague. But this at once became an enemy target, and towards 8 o'clock in the evening of Sunday, May 12, Princess Juliana, with Prince Bernhard and the two children, left The Hague and went on board the British destroyer Codrington (Commander Creasy).

On the morning of the next day, May 13, General Winkelman informed the Queen and her Government that he could no longer hold himself responsible for their safety. The Queen decided to proceed to Zeeland, but dangers from parachutists and bombers compelled her to sail for England, followed later by members of the Dutch Government. By the evening of May 14 the Commander-in-Chief, General Winkelman, considered that the military situation of Fortress Holland " had become impossible " and entered into negotiations with the Germans for surrender.

Holland had been overthrown ; after a campaign of but five days her army had been overwhelmed and bludgeoned into capitulation. But Holland was still at war. Her Queen and her Cabinet were safe in England, and from the Dutch Indies, East and West, the Netherlands Government continued the struggle.

Books to Consult: Rape of the Netherlands, E. van Kleffens (Hodder & Stoughton). Holland Fights the Nazis, L. de Jong (Lindsay Drummond). The Netherlands at War, H. S. Ashton (Routledge).

Netherlands, Free. Holland, like Sweden, but with less luck, pinned her faith to the abracadabra " Neutrality." That was why, when Mr. Churchill invited the Netherlands to join all other threatened Democracies alongside Britain, Dr. Van Kleffens, her Foreign Minister, declined. Fear of Germany stained Dutch foreign policy, and fear has a power to bring to the fearful the evil feared.

When, on May 13, the Queen and Royal Family and Government were forced to accept British sanctuary, Holland set about resisting the Nazi aggressor from a foreign capital. Since then the Netherlands Government has functioned from London, and from

QUEEN WILHELMINA INSPECTS HER TROOPS IN ENGLAND

Queen Wilhelmina named this Free Dutch Regiment " The Princess Irene Regiment " after her grandchild, the daughter of Princess Juliana and Prince Bernhard. She is here seen, accompanied by Prince Bernhard, visiting her troops at their camp in the Midlands, on the occasion of her presenting colours to the regiment. There were many fighting men of the Netherlands in Britain, awaiting the day which should release their Motherland from the grip of Nazi tyranny.

Photo, Wide World

London the Netherlands East Indies possessions have been controlled.

The Dutch are solid, stolid people, little given to "nerves," and they set about organizing their Free people in a businesslike manner. With very large gold resources to draw upon from America, the Free Dutch were able to work with a large degree of independence of their friendly host.

A Free Dutch Legion was created at once, and fitted into the pattern of Britain's great new armies. A Fleet Air Arm was organized to cooperate with the British Navy, and was assigned duties with the Coastal Command. The Netherlands Navy remained intact after the German invasion, for it was based on the overseas Dutch Empire. This navy is small and not important, since it has few modern ships. Nevertheless, in action, it has already done surprising things, and shown against the Japanese aggressor in the

Pacific a fine fighting spirit, cooperating with the British and American Fleets in those waters.

More important is the Dutch Merchant Marine of 3,000,000 tons, for this fine fleet is intact and now serves the common interests of the Allies. On June 12, 1941, a great Inter-Allied Conference was held in London together with the Dominions, and all present pledged themselves to mutual assistance. On Sept. 24 Holland, with all other Free Allies, adhered to the Atlantic Charter. On May 10, 1942, as a tribute to the Dutch people, Britain and the United States raised the status of their Ministers to the Netherlands Government to that of Ambassador ; the corresponding Dutch Ministers were similarly raised in rank.

An interesting illustration of the reality of the Free Dutch is provided by the Dutch Courts set up in London. Never before have foreign courts administered foreign law under foreign judges on British soil.

THE TRAGIC DEFENCE OF THE DUTCH INDIES

Against overwhelming odds the Dutch fought gallantly to stem the lightning advance of the invader. The " scorched earth " policy, ruthlessly carried out by the defenders, prevented many of the riches so long coveted by Japan from falling into the aggressors' greedy hands. See Java ; Pacific, War in ; Sumatra ; etc.

Netherlands East Indies. The Netherlands East Indies (*see* pages 1362–64) form a vast Aladdin's cave of natural wealth, supplying 31 per cent of the world's copra, 17 per cent of its tin, 33 per cent of its rubber, 20 per cent of its sisal (fibre-producing aloe), 29 per cent of palm oil, and large quantities of tea, cane sugar, coffee and quinine.

Holland, enlightened and progressive, accepted the trusteeship of these islands and administered them in such a way that their great natural wealth was at the disposal of mankind. But the rich man's house is the magnet for the eye of the robber. For long years Japan, over-populated (73,000,000) and poor in natural resources, cast covetous eyes upon the archipelago. When, on May 15, 1940, Holland, overrun by Nazi Germany, capitulated and this great colonial possession became the financial, commercial and economic centre of the kingdom of the Netherlands, Japan prepared to act.

Bogus Missions of the Japanese

On June 29 Mr. Arita, Foreign Minister, proclaimed the Japanese New Order for Asia and ushered it in in true totalitarian fashion by a series of bogus " economic " missions, the blackmailing character of which later became plain. Japan's aspirations in East Asia were no longer in doubt : she sought after a self-sufficient East Asia in which a dominant Japan would stand at the centre of satellite countries under her economic direction.

For the Netherlands, the hour struck when the first bomb descended upon Pearl Harbour. On Jan. 8, 1942, Dr. Van Mook, Lieutenant-Governor of the N.E.I., conferred with Australia's Premier and got promise of full aid should Japan strike. There could have been no other answer, since a Malay Peninsula in Japanese hands ended Australian security from a menace now nearly forty years old.

Japan's main strategy was quite clear to the Dutch. She would consolidate positions in the Philippines and Malaya and thereafter " present an ugly face to the N.E.I. in the hope of getting the oilfields and industries

intact." For more than a year the Dutch had been preparing for this eventuality, and if war involved them in swift defeat the prime factor therein was not that which undid the British, namely, a state of unpreparedness, plus the element of surprise, but inferiority of numbers and—this above all—inferiority in air combat. The N.E.I., like the British Malay possessions, were lost on the seas and in the skies.

Crowded Heroic Weeks of the Airmen

Four days after the conference between the Lieut.-Governor of the N.E.I. and Mr. Curtin, Japan struck. Japanese parachute troops landed on the Dutch island of Tarakan, north-east of Borneo and near Minahasa (Celebes). Already the Dutch command had become active. Dutch ships were already moving northwards to join their British comrades and already sinking enemy shipping. With this fleet went the aircraft that, outnumbered throughout, raised the prestige of the Dutch in a few crowded, heroic weeks.

Australian bombers gave concrete evidence of the value of Australia's pledged word, as soon some of her finest fighting men were to do. From N.E.I. air bases the Australians took off to give battle to that unending stream of shipping which flowed, like a poisoned stream, from the islands of Japan through the China Sea to Malaya. Naval craft of the United Nations laid mines to impede the path of these invasion fleets, whose spearhead was composed of bombing aircraft and naval ships, and whose shaft was one continuous line of troop-carrying transports. Already the salients of a campaign, short, sharp and bitterly fought, were articulated for all to see.

The Japanese outnumbered their victims, and in the air had sheerest preponderance. Moreover, they had abandoned the battle technique of the text books, now pathetically out-dated by the new war of combined sea, land and air arms. They struck swiftly. They moved swiftly. They marched light. They left cumbrous artillery behind ; used light, easily-handled mortars, giving them magnificent fire power,

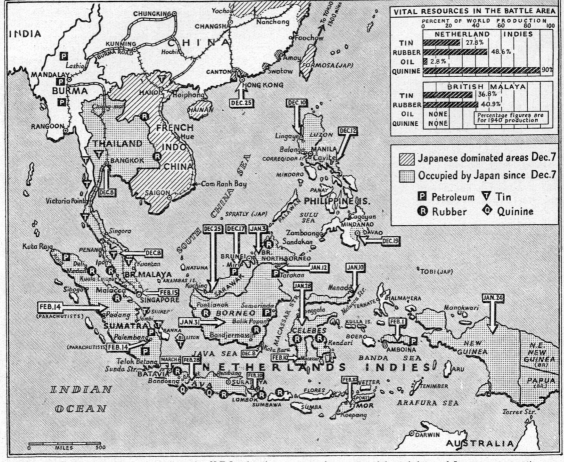

The Far Eastern war zone, including the N.E.I., showing sources of raw materials and dates of Japanese occupation.

plus the element of surprise. They infiltrated, on foot, in armoured cars, but mostly on a hitherto completely ignored means of battle locomotion—the cycles they stole from the native population.

The Dutch military and naval authorities foresaw the end. Only one thing could save the N.E.I.—immediate. large-scale reinforcements of men and materials, materials meaning mainly fighter and bomber aeroplanes. The war became a race against time. And time favoured the Japanese and determined an issue whose repercussions must echo down the years for decades, perhaps for centuries.

On Jan. 15 General Wavell arrived in the N.E.I. as Commander-in-Chief, with the American Lieut.-Gen. G. Brett as his second in command. Already the Dutch were displaying an offensive spirit, attacking the first invaders upon Dutch soil along the Sarawak border. On that day the Japanese delivered a heavy bomb attack on Balik Papan, Borneo. Hard fighting developed in Minahasa, near Lake Tondano ; and next day Amboina suffered the first of the many attacks which ended with the loss of the Molucca Islands. Amboina was important, for it lies only 300 miles west from New Guinea and the South Molucca Passage between Celebes and Halmahera.

The Japanese method of attack is most easily understood from the map above (see also p. 198, this volume). Singapore was supremely important as the key to Sumatra—most valuable island in the whole group for raw materials. But Sumatra was vital also strategically for the larger Japanese plan, for who holds Sumatra (and Singapore) controls the Strait of Malacca, and who controls that Strait controls the channels to Burma, India, the Red Sea and Africa.

By Jan. 16, on which date the Japanese were already striking in force by air across the Strait of Macassar, the strength of the enemy was being realized. Three days later Japanese troops secured a foothold on the south bank of the Muar river, south of Malacca. On Jan. 22 they had fanned out to take into the zone of battle the Bismarck Islands. The following day the Dutch, who never shrank from the deliberate destruction of stores, equipment and plant, applied this policy to Balik Papan.

From the United Nations point of view the battle for the N.E.I. was one that involved perpetual and vigorous attacks on the enemy's long-drawn-out lines of communication, and, in particular, upon her transports at sea. On Jan. 24 Dutch aircraft got four direct hits on enemy battleships and four upon transports concentrated in the Macassar Straits ; two days later a forty-eight-hour attack was staged successfully in the same area with U.S. Flying Fortresses.

On Jan. 26, nevertheless, such was their persistence and such their numerical superiority that the Japanese made landings at Balik Papan, Borneo. This phase of the war was in the nature of a perpetual running of the gauntlet by the enemy to make landings, and the perpetual strafing of him by bomb, torpedo and shell fire. On Jan. 28 a naval engagement accounted for a large enemy warship, cruisers and destroyers, and eight laden transports. This three-day battle was fought with ferocity and cost the Japanese dear. But despite this resistance, and the sea-fighting which ensued sheer weight of numbers prevailed, and Japanese troops landed on Balik Papan.

From the end of January onwards Japanese aircraft ranged over the N.E.I. skies without let or hindrance, for the hoped-for help had not come, and Japan became master of the eastern skies. The Dutch had sworn to fight to the last, and despite a quite hopeless situation on land, sea and air, they kept their word. The method adopted was that of guerilla war. But in Borneo this method could not prevail against the superior numbers of the enemy, who landed upon the coast and descended locust-fashion by the thousand.

On Feb. 1 the Japanese, who the previous day had launched an intense sea attack on the naval base of Amboina, landed troops near the aerodrome and took the western capital. On Feb. 3 the aerodrome at Surabaya was badly bombed and the naval establishments also suffered heavily. U.S. naval units sank two more transports in the Macassar Strait. Bombings of Malang, Madioen, Magilang and Rembang took place within the week. On Feb. 5 violent air raids were delivered against Surabaya, 31 being killed and 131 injured, and many modern buildings being destroyed. From that point on the raids became a daily feature. Landings on a large scale followed on Feb. 9. The Pacific War Council met in London on Feb. 11, and next day Admiral Hart, U.S.N., was succeeded by the Dutch Admiral Helfrich, a native of Java, 55 years old, vigorous and enterprising.

Parachutists in Thousands

On Feb. 16 Singapore fell, and thus the Japanese were able to concentrate in full force upon the N.E.I. Sumatra was invaded by sea and air (parachutes). Landings were made at Palembang, the great oil-refining centre. The Anambas groups of islands off the Malaya coast were occupied. On Feb. 16 Palembang was taken, the Dutch first destroying the wells and refineries capable of producing 4,200,000 tons of oil a year. Parachutists in thousands were dropped on the town. With the capture of Palembang, the only oilfields left to the United Nations were those in north Sumatra, near Medan. With bases secured by the enemy in Sumatra, Borneo and the Celebes, the spectre of defeat loomed large in the absence of reinforcements, particularly by air. The Dutch were fighting virtually single-handed against a numerically superior, victory-drunk aggressor. And that enemy was astride the isles. On Feb. 20 the first air raids were launched against Java's airfields, and it may be said that from that point on the task of the Japanese command was a matter of placing the flourish to a completed lightning campaign. By March 9 Java also was in enemy hands and the war was over.

The loss of these islands involved major problems of world-war strategy, for they lie, like a series of forts, between the Pacific and Indian Oceans. They lie athwart air and sea lanes, and thus today stand locked against the United Nations' shipping. At the end of March 1942 Japan had command of communications between the Indian Ocean and the China Sea, and the Pacific. Allied naval craft—all Allied shipping—was forced to take the Australian route.

Next, this victory exposed Australia's 10,000 miles of coast-line to those attacks against it that followed. Air communications were likewise crippled, since the normal route used by Imperial Airways and the Dutch K.L.M. Lines flew over 1,200 miles of N.E.I. territory, using Rembang, now in enemy hands.

The loss of the N.E.I. must rank among the major military catastrophes of the world war. Not least in assessing the damage wrought by the Allied cause is the tremendous fillip given to Japanese morale, by these initial successes, so swift and so brilliant, against the White man on Asiatic soil. The prospect looked black, but the appointment of Gen. MacArthur (*q.v.*), as generalissimo in the S.W. Pacific, and his declared intention of not only defending Australia but of taking the offensive against the Japanese, lent rays of hope. In June 1942 a guerilla leader from the N.E.I. reported to the S.W. Pacific Command in Australia that Dutch forces were maintaining effective resistance, keeping the enemy tied to occupied coastal areas in the islands.

Netherlands West Indies. These Dutch possessions comprise the colonies of Surinam, or Dutch Guiana, in S. America, and Curaçao, two groups of islands off the coast of Venezuela. Of this latter colony, Curaçao and Aruba, 30 m. to its W., are the two largest islands.

Dutch Guiana exports much tropical produce, and its bauxite mines furnish more than 60 per cent of the requirements of the U.S. aluminium industry. In November 1941 a contingent of the U.S. Army was sent to protect these mines.

Curaçao's chief industry is oil-refining. On May 11, 1940, the refineries, including those on Aruba, which are the largest in the western hemisphere, were taken under the protection of Allied troops. In July 1940 an attempt by a landing party from a Nazi raider to destroy the refineries at Curaçao failed, the raiders suffering casualties. American troops and air-craft were sent to the islands in February 1942 to assist the Dutch defending forces. On Feb. 16 enemy submarines shelled the oil installations, causing no serious damage, and torpedoed seven tankers. American 'planes destroyed at least one submarine.

Nettleton, Sq.-Ldr. J. D. He led the first section of Lancaster bombers in the R.A.F. daylight raid on Augsburg on April 17, 1942. His formation flew for many miles at an altitude of 25–30 ft., and engaged enemy aircraft in running fights. Of the six machines that composed his section, Nettleton's was the only 'plane to return. He was awarded the V.C.

Neurath, Baron Constantin von (b. 1873). From March 18, 1939, until his resignation on Sept. 27, 1941, officially stated in Berlin to be " on account of ill-health," von Neurath was Reich Protector of Bohemia and Moravia. He was succeeded by Reinhard Heydrich (*q.v.*). During his protectorship von Neurath ruthlessly carried out, with the aid of Gestapo agents and by brutal Nazi methods, the Germanization of the country. *See* Czechoslovakia.

Neutrality Act, 1939. American Law, Nov. 4, 1939. Under it countries designated as belligerent by President could buy war materials from United States only on a cash-and-carry basis (i.e. pay in dollars and take away in their own ships). U.S. citizens were forbidden investments in wartime issues of belligerents, or to make loans to such. American ships were forbidden to handle war cargoes, be armed, or enter war zones. No U.S. citizen was allowed to travel on a belligerent ship. Licences were required for all arms exports. (The Act excluded American Republics.) The object of the Act is clear from the foregoing : it was an attempt to keep clear of war by preventing U.S. citizens securing vested interests in the war by trade or money loan.

Neutrality legislation was first adopted in 1935, and was renewed in 1937, when war was plainly nearer. That Act forbade all arms supplies and permitted other supplies only on a cash-and-carry basis. The framers overlooked the handicap the Act put upon the Democracies by precluding arms buying in the States, thus, in effect, helping Germany. Therefore, in 1939 the present Neutrality Act was passed. It was modified March 12, 1941, by elimination of the cash clause and became obsolete with the entry of the United States into the war, December 1941. *See* Lease-and-Lend Act.

Sir Cyril Newall,
Gov.-Gen. of
New Zealand.
Photo, Russell

Newall, MARSHAL OF THE ROYAL AIR FORCE SIR CYRIL LOUIS NORTON, G.C.B., O.M., G.C.M.G. (b. 1886). Governor-General of New Zealand from February 1941 in succession to Viscount Galway. On Oct. 29, 1940, he received the Order of Merit, being the first airman to be admitted to this very exclusive order. He was Chief of Air Staff from 1937 to 1940.

Newfoundland. At the outbreak of war the Dominion of Newfoundland, Britain's oldest colony (*see* pp. 2942–3), again proved her loyalty by her contributions to the Empire's efforts. Many of the fishermen crossed the Atlantic to join the Royal Navy or to serve in minesweepers, the first contingent arriving in December 1939. A fine body of sailors, known as the Royal Newfoundland Naval Reserve, kept in being during the peace, did valuable work. A contingent of Newfoundlanders was serving in H.M.S. Jervis Bay (*q.v.*) at the time of her loss. Newfoundland was well represented in all three Services, the first artillery contingent arriving at a British port, where they were greeted by Mr. Anthony Eden, on April 25, 1940. Another contribution to manpower from Newfoundland was the arrival of a number of lumbermen, whose services in meeting the country's needs in timber from British forests proved invaluable.

In July 1941 it was announced in a Budget speech that Newfoundland had decided to reserve $2,300,000 as an interest-free loan to Britain for the duration, and to make a gift of $500,000 for a fighter squadron manned by Newfoundlanders.

Vice-Adml. Sir Humphrey Walwyn was Governor of the Dominion from 1936.

New Guinea. This large island of the Pacific lies in the East Indian Archipelago. New Guinea (*see* pp. 2943–2946) was divided between the Dutch and the British. The western half of the island was included in the Dutch possession of the Molucca Islands. The south-eastern part, Papua, with a number of groups of small islands, passed into Australian control in 1906. Port Moresby, on the south coast, is the capital. The Mandated Territory of New Guinea, held by Australia since 1921 by decision of the League of Nations, consisted of north-eastern New Guinea, the Bismarck Archipelago (which includes New Britain, New Ireland and the Admiralty Islands) and certain of the Solomon Islands group. The Torres Strait, between Papua and Cape York Peninsula, Queensland, is about 100 miles wide.

Japan's attacks on New Guinea began on Jan. 4, 1942, with two long-range air raids on the R.A.A.F. aerodrome at Rabaul, capital of New Britain. These bombing attacks on Rabaul, on Kavieng, in New Ireland, and on a number of other points in the Bismarck Archipelago continued at intervals until Jan. 23, when the enemy made landings at both Rabaul and Kavieng. Their purpose was obviously to obtain bases from which to strike farther south. From Jan. 24 there was heavy fighting in New Britain, and Gasmata fell into Japanese hands. The R.A.A.F. repeatedly bombed enemy shipping in the harbour at Rabaul. It was officially announced in Melbourne that about 1,100 white women and children had been evacuated from Rabaul to Australia by a fleet of airliners during the ten days before the Japanese attack.

On Feb. 3 Port Moresby, in Papua, suffered the first of many severe raids. On March 7 the enemy attacked from the air Lae on the E. coast of New Guinea and the mining town of Bulolo inland. Next day, preceded by shelling and bombing and protected by cruisers and destroyers, a considerable Japanese force landed on the

NEWFOUNDLAND'S STALWART SONS IN ACTION

"Prepare to move." Here are seen Newfoundland gunners limbering up a 25-pounder battery on a range somewhere in England. Time and again this loyal colony has proved her devotion to the Motherland, and in this war she has played her part as magnificently as ever in the defence of the Empire.

Photo, Central Press

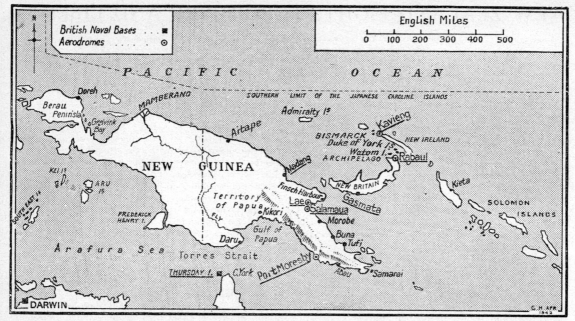

Dutch and British New Guinea, showing centres of air fighting in early 1942.

mainland and captured the ports and airfields at Lae and Salamaua, a few miles to the south. Port Moresby lies about 180 miles south of Salamaua; in between is the Owen Stanley mountain range, rising in places to 13,000 feet. On March 10 the Japanese made a third landing in New Guinea, this time at Finsch Harbour, 70 miles east of Salamaua. The R.A.A.F. strove gallantly to stem the invasion by damaging enemy cruisers, destroyers, and transports, particularly at Salamaua. Here, on March 11, they dropped 18 tons of bombs. Three days later enemy bombers extended the range of their offensive by raiding islands near Thursday Island in Torres Strait, off Cape York, when low-level machine-gun attacks were made.

On March 18 it was announced by the U.S. Navy Department that a Japanese armada had been severely battered in an action off New Guinea. The operations were carried out by combined American and Australian island-based forces against land installations as well as ships, in and near Salamaua and Lae. The result was that 23 enemy ships were sunk or damaged, including the certain destruction of two heavy cruisers and five transports. The same day as this announcement Allied aircraft carried out daylight raids on shipping at Rabaul and secured a direct hit on a heavy cruiser.

Missionaries as Fifth-column Agents

Meanwhile the Japanese land forces in New Guinea were pushing forward from Lae along the Markham Valley, 200 miles N.W. of Port Moresby. Their probable objective was said to be the establishment of airfields from which to operate. In their quest for these the Japanese were stated to be receiving considerable help from pro-Nazi Lutheran missionaries, whose fifth-column activities before the war had been well known. At Salamaua they had taught the natives German. They possessed fast motor boats and wireless sets, and, because all road systems in New Guinea are poor and most communications are made by air, they also possessed aeroplanes and landing-grounds.

As the month passed the air war intensified. On March 22 Allied bombers made a smashing attack on Lae, where 15 enemy aircraft were left in flames, and another on Rabaul, where Fortress aircraft sank a heavy cruiser. On this and the following three days further heavy raids were made on Port Moresby, the town which the Japanese ardently desired to capture, so as to use it as a springboard against Australia, whereas, if left in Allied hands, it might be made the base of an Allied offensive.

At the end of April 1942 a Japanese advance was expected to take place in the important Markham Valley. Enemy guerillas showed signs of becoming active and preparing to make their way through the rough, jungle country towards Port Moresby (q.v.). The Japanese invasion base at Lae, where the Allies maintained superiority, was raided six times in one week from the end of April to the beginning of May. American machines dropped hundreds of bombs, damaging or wrecking aircraft on the ground, oil dumps, stores and buildings. These raids resulted in large fires which destroyed enemy equipment. On July 21 a small invasion force landed near Buna, 120 miles N. of Port Moresby.

It was on Port Moresby that the enemy directed his numerous air attacks. It was reported that even after three weeks of constant bombing by Allied aircraft of the Japanese bases, the latter still had sufficient forces to send 170 bombers and fighters against this important target during the last nine days of April. Meanwhile fighting in the New Guinea area became fiercer, and the Japanese suffered heavy losses in men and materials. Aerial activity increased on both sides and the enemy lost a large number of planes. Persistent Allied air attacks almost wiped out Salamaua—the Japanese had selected it as a base for their attacks upon Australia. The enemy aerodrome of Vunakrnau, south of Rabaul, was also successfully bombed. On July 21 an invasion force of 1,500 landed at Gona, 120 miles N.E. of Port Moresby.

NEW ZEALAND FIGHTS FOR EMPIRE AND LIBERTY

From the first day of war New Zealand wholeheartedly joined the crusade against the forces of Fascist tyranny and oppression, her airmen, soldiers and sailors distinguishing themselves in many successful engagements against the enemy.

New Zealand. When war broke out on Sept. 3, 1939, New Zealand cabled her entire concurrence with the action taken by Mr. Chamberlain's Government, stating that the people of the Dominion regarded it as inevitably forced upon the British Commonwealth, " if the cause of justice, freedom and democracy was to endure in the world." At once steps were taken to speed up primary production. The British Government purchased the entire wool clip for the duration of the war and one year after. Mutton, butter, cheese and pigs were covered by similar agreements. Thus New Zealand was assured of a market for her products and funds to cover interest upon overseas debts and essential imports.

The military results of the wartime speed-up were seen when a New Zealand contingent landed at Suez on Feb. 12, 1940, under Major-General Freyberg, V.C. By this time 5,000 airmen were serving in the New Zealand Air Force, and a draft reached Britain in July 1940 and served during the Battle of Britain. The brilliant work of Flying-Officer Kain (*q.v.*)

attracted widespread attention and his early death was greatly regretted.

The New Zealand Squadron of the Royal Navy, including the cruisers Achilles and Leander, an armed merchant cruiser, several minesweepers and armed trawlers, cooperated with the British Navy in the Pacific and Atlantic. Achilles (*q.v.*) played a glorious part in the Graf Spee battle on Dec. 13, 1939. The services of the New Zealand ships of war were recognized by King George when, on Sept. 10, 1941, he approved the naval forces of the Dominion receiving the title Royal New Zealand Navy, the ships being designated " His Majesty's New Zealand Ships." In 1941, 50,000 New Zealanders were serving overseas.

The most important services rendered by what was known as the Second New Zealand Expeditionary Force (the first being that of 1914) were in Libya, Greece and Crete. Some 16,500 New Zealanders served in Greece and Crete. The detailed casualties were : in Greece, killed, 126 ; wounded, 516 ; prisoners, 41 ; missing, 1,892 ; in Crete, killed, 87 ; wounded,

OFFENSIVE AND DEFENSIVE AT HOME AND ABROAD

1. Coastal guns are ready in the event of a Japanese attack upon New Zealand's shores. 2. Armed with Bren guns, New Zealanders are seen training in Britain. 3. A fire-fighting display staged in a New Zealand town by men of the Emergency Precautions Scheme. 4. German infantry are surrendering to men of a New Zealand Bren carrier ; a wounded German rides at the back of the carrier. Inset : reloading the guns in the wing of a Spitfire.

Photos, British Official; Associated Press; Keystone; Sport & General

671 ; unaccounted for, 2,450. Mr. Fraser, the Prime Minister, visited the contingent at its desert camp in Egypt after the evacuation from Crete, and told the men, " You were blasted out of Crete by an air attack no flesh and blood could stand." The rested and rearmed New Zealand contingent rendered sterling service in the second Libyan campaign, particularly on Dec. 4, 1941, when the German-Italian army attempted to re-establish communications between its two panzer divisions near Tobruk. The New Zealanders bore the brunt of this attack. The Maori battalion earned the highest praise for two daring bayonet attacks in the fighting at Suda Bay, Crete.

Mr. Savage, who was Prime Minister when the war opened, died in March 1940 and was succeeded by Mr. Fraser. Mr. Fraser formed a Coalition Cabinet in July 1940, including Mr. Adam Hamilton, Leader of the Opposition, and Mr. J. G. Coates, a former Prime Minister. The Coalition Government's Budget for 1940–41 exceeded £50,000,000, a great effort for a community of only 1,500,000 people. New Zealand's war expenditure in 1940–41 included £30,000,000 for the Army, £1,500,000 for the Navy and £6,000,000 for the Air Force. The second wartime Budget, for 1941–42, totalled £69,000,000, £50,000,000 being on behalf of the Army, £9,000,000 for Air Defence and £4,200,000 for the New Zealand Navy, the remainder being on account of the repayment of debts to the British Government. Whereas taxation in New Zealand was £37 10s. in 1940–41, it was £39 per head in 1941–42.

The increasing tension with Japan culminated in a declaration of war on Dec. 9, 1941. Mr. Fraser announced that the Air Force was fully mobilized, and other steps included the calling up of Territorials and the National Reserve. The Prime Minister said that the people of Britain had set New Zealanders a noble example. He ended, " We will fight a good fight, we will keep the faith and we will win."

On March 12, 1942, following consultations with the Australian War Advisory Council on common war strategy, Mr. Fraser announced the formation of a Defence Construction Council, with himself as chairman.

Book to Consult ; New Zealand Now, Oliver Duff (Dept. of Internal Affairs, Wellington, N.Z.).

L./Cpl. Nicholls, awarded the V.C.
Photo, " Daily Mirror "

Nicholls, LANCE-CORP. HARRY, v.c. (b. 1915). One of the Army's first two V.C.s to be won in the war was awarded to L./Cpl. Nicholls of the Grenadier Guards for an act of great gallantry. On May 21, 1940, he was commanding a section on the banks of the Scheldt (*q.v.*) when the company was ordered to counter-attack. At the very start of the advance he was wounded in the arm, but continued to lead his section forward. As the Company came over a ridge the enemy opened heavy machine-gun fire at close range. L./Cpl. Nicholls immediately seized a Bren gun and dashed forward, firing from the hip, and succeeded in silencing three of the machine-guns. He then engaged the German infantry, causing many casualties and, in spite of being severely wounded at least four times, continued to fire until no more ammunition was left. This gallant action enabled his Company to reach its objective and caused the enemy to retreat across the Scheldt.

Believed killed, L./Cpl. Nicholls was reported later to be a prisoner-of-war.

Nicholson, BRIGADIER CLAUDE. This gallant British officer was in command of the heroic troops which in May 1940 made such a glorious stand at Calais. Refusing to surrender to the Germans, he defended the citadel to the end and was eventually taken prisoner. A former commander of the 16th/5th Lancers, Brig. Nicholson was, in 1939, in command of the Imperial Defence College. *See* portrait under the heading Calais.

S./L. J.B. Nicolson, V.C.
Photo, Keystone

Nicolson, SQUADRON LEADER JAMES BRINDLEY, v.c. (b. 1917). It was announced on Nov. 14, 1940, that Flight Lieut. (afterwards Squadron Leader) Nicolson of 249 Squadron had been awarded the V.C. The official account stated that " during an engagement near Southampton on Aug. 16, F./Lt. Nicolson's aircraft was hit by four cannon shells, two of which wounded him, while another set fire to the gravity tank. When about to abandon his aircraft owing to flames in the cockpit, he sighted an enemy fighter, which he attacked and shot down, although, as a result of staying in his burning aircraft, he sustained serious burns to his hands, face, neck and legs . . . By continuing to engage the enemy after he had been wounded and his aircraft set on fire, he displayed exceptional gallantry and disregard for the safety of his own life." S./L. Nicolson was the first fighter pilot to win the V.C.

Niemöller, MARTIN, (b. 1892). Lutheran pastor. Once a U-boat commander and later leader of the German Protestant Confessional Church, Dr. Niemöller was imprisoned in a concentration camp for his determined efforts to defend the Lutheran faith. Arrested in July 1937, he was sentenced to seven months' imprisonment after a secret " trial " in March 1938. He made a heroic stand in prison and refused to alter his views. At the end of this term he was not released, but kept further in " protective custody." In spite of interventions by prominent people Hitler refused to free him.

Nimitz, ADML. CHESTER. C.-in-C. U.S. Pacific Fleet from Dec. 17, 1941, in succession to Adml. Husband Kimmel. At one time Adml. Nimitz was Commander of the first American submarine flotilla.

Noble, ADML. SIR PERCY LOCKHART HARNAM, K.C.B. (b. 1880). C.-in-C. Western Approaches. The appointment was announced on March 14, 1941. From 1938 to 1940 he commanded the China Station. He was Director of Operations Division, Admiralty Naval Staff, 1928–30, and Director of Naval Equipment, 1931–32.

Noguès, GEN. Governor of French Morocco. At the time of the French Armistice Gen. Noguès was also C.-in-C. of the French N. African forces. On June 25, 1940, he proclaimed the determination of French Morocco not to yield to the enemy. Soon after, however, he gave his support to the Vichy Government. In July 1940 he was placed on the

Gen. Noguès, Governor of French Morocco.
Photo, Topical

GIANT LINER GUTTED BY FIRE AT NEW YORK

The Lafayette, formerly the Normandie, is seen lying on her side at her New York pier after a fire had raged furiously for thirteen hours throughout this famous ship. The Normandie captured the " Blue Ribbon " of the Atlantic in 1935.

Photo, Wide World

with Mr. Cordell Hull, news reached Washington of the Japanese attacks on Pearl Harbour and the Philippines on Dec. 7. Both envoys were immediately handed their passports. *See* Japan.

Norderney. One of the E. Frisian Islands (*q.v.*). The German seaplane bases established here were many times attacked by the R.A.F. In April 1941 British bombers carried out a daring daylight raid on Norderney in which, after dropping bombs on their target, they descended to below rooftop level and machine-gunned boats in the harbour and troops drilling on a barrack square. In subsequent raids barracks and gun positions were bombed and machine-gunned in daylight and other damage inflicted

retired list, while still retaining the Governorship. *See* North Africa, French.

Nomura, ADML. KICHISABURO (b. 1877). Former Foreign Minister, Adml. Nomura was appointed Japanese Ambassador to the United States in November 1940. In a highly rhetorical speech on Dec. 19, 1940, he called on his compatriots to " guard the peace of the Pacific." In November and December 1941 Adml. Nomura was one of the Japanese envoys to Washington, Mr. Kurusu (*q.v.*) having been sent from Japan to aid him in his talks with the U.S. Government. While they were still conferring at the State Dept.

Adml. Nomura, Japan's U.S. envoy. *Photo, Wide World*

Normandie, S.S. This famous French liner (*see* p. 3687), lying in New York harbour at the outbreak of war, was taken into protective custody in May 1941, and seized in December 1941 by U.S. coastguards. She was then taken over by the U.S. Navy as an auxiliary vessel, and renamed Lafayette. On Feb. 9, 1942, when 2,200 workmen were on board, a fire started on the promenade deck. The men made dramatic escapes, but many were injured. After burning furiously for thirteen hours the Normandie capsized. She was raised and taken to a berth at Brooklyn but despite prolonged salvage work her refitting was finally abandoned.

North, ADML. SIR DUDLEY, K.C.V.O. (b. 1881). He was Admiral commanding the N. Atlantic Station from 1939 to 1940. From 1934 to 1939 he commanded H.M. Yacht.

EBB AND FLOW OF THE LIBYAN DESERT WAR

From General Wavell's successful drive to Benghazi in 1940-41 to the enforced withdrawal to Egypt of General Auchinleck's 8th Army in June 1942 there had been six British and Axis campaigns swaying to and fro in the desert. Here the story of the bright hopes of 1940 that ended in the failure of 1942 is told by a writer of authority.

North Africa : THE CAMPAIGNS OF 1940–42. Not till the Fascist regime was established did Italy make any serious attempt to develop the strategic potentialities of her Libyan colony acquired in 1912. Mussolini, however, saw that it furnished a base in which a powerful army and air force could be maintained within easy reach of the mother country. This, combined with the growing strength of Italian naval and air power, which might render passage through the Mediterranean precarious, provided a

menace to the British position in the Middle East, particularly as the Western Desert of Egypt presented no impassable obstacle to mechanized forces. While France and Britain were allied Italy could not safely exploit these strategic advantages, for the Allies maintained superior naval forces in the Mediterranean; France could attack Libya from Tunis and Italy's East African colonies would be isolated. In the light of these facts Mussolini's decision to remain non-belligerent is understandable.

POINTS OF EPIC RESISTANCE

British troops are seen advancing towards Tobruk to relieve their besieged comrades who held out against the Axis forces for many months. Right, an artillery observation post in a captured fort at Derna.

Photos, British Official

When, however, France collapsed, Italy ceased to be vulnerable. Her Fleet was more powerful than the one Britain could spare for the Mediterranean; relieved of danger from Tunis, she could concentrate her whole Libyan army against the small British force in Egypt, and from her East African colonies she could threaten the adjacent weakly garrisoned British possessions. It seemed that Italy's hour had come when she declared war on June 10, 1940.

General Wavell, C.-in-C. in the Middle East, was in a desperately precarious position. Not only were the forces under his command far inferior numerically to the Italians, but they were widely dispersed, and their equipment had not been raised to modern standards. Britain, threatened with invasion and depleted of equipment at Dunkirk, could spare neither men nor material to reinforce him. Only from India and Australasia could he hope for help, but India could not spare any large numbers. The Australasian Dominions were raising new forces, but they were still in the earlier stages of training, and both they and the Indian troops were incompletely equipped. Fortunately, summer heat in Libya and the rainy season in East Africa prohibited large-scale operations before the autumn; and good use was made of the respite. The British Government, accepting great risks, decided to send reinforcements of men and material, though, owing to the dangers of the Mediterranean route, they had to go round the Cape. India, Australia and New Zealand also sent all that were available—the Dominion troops completing their training in Palestine—while South Africa reinforced the Kenya garrison.

Meantime, General Wavell and Admiral Cunningham, commanding the Fleet based on Alexandria, were not content to adopt a passively defensive policy. The admiral, by constantly seeking to bring it to action, established a moral ascendancy over the Italian navy to an extent that, before the crisis matured, enabled convoys with further reinforcements to reach Egypt by the direct route. The R.A.F., similarly, with

obsolescent aircraft, achieved ascendancy over their more numerous adversaries. The primary task of Wavell's army was, of course, to establish a defensive position on which to meet an invader, and in particular to cover approaches to the naval base at Alexandria. This was constructed at Mersa Matruh, where ample water supply was available and the railway from Alexandria provided good rearward communications.

But 70 miles in advance of his main position Wavell maintained a screen of mobile troops on the frontier, and their role was essentially offensive. This screen was furnished by an Armoured Division, equipped with light tanks and armoured cars, supported by mechanized artillery. These troops soon had many exploits to their credit, and time after time they broke through the formidable wire obstacle, backed at frequent intervals by defended posts, which the Italians had constructed along the frontier for 100 miles inland.

In the latter half of the summer Graziani began to concentrate a considerable force in the frontier area

VICTORIOUS AUSTRALIANS ENTER BENGHAZI

The inhabitants of the city crowd to the windows to watch the entry of the Australians through Benghazi's streets. This Army lorry moves between two lines of infantry. The capital of Cyrenaica was captured twice in 1941 by the Imperial forces—on Feb. 6 and on Dec. 24.

Photo, British Official

made good; fortunately Admiral Cunningham's action enabled convoys to arrive when most needed. Meantime, however, the active harassing policy had prepared the ground, for it made the Italians neglect patrol activities and caused them to shut themselves up in a line of fortified camps stretching out into the desert. The line extended from Maktila on the coast, some 10 miles east of Sidi Barrani, to Bir Rabia, 40 miles inland. But between the latter camp and Nibeiwa camp there was a gap of 15 miles which the Italians had intended to fill but had been prevented from so doing by British mobile parties. It was this gap that Wavell proposed to exploit.

By November he was almost ready to strike, but he had still to wait some weeks. Not till Dec. 9 did Press representatives in Cairo learn that the offensive had begun that morning, though they were still left in doubt as to whether it was not merely a raid in force, for the invasion of Greece had necessitated postponement of plans.

Wavell's plan hinged on a surprise attack on the Nibeiwa camp by tanks and infantry, which, passing through the gap in the Italian position, would take the camp from the rear. If this succeeded the force would swing northward towards Sidi Barrani, capturing the intervening camps as it progressed. Meanwhile, Maktila on the coast would be engaged by a smaller body advancing from Matruh, while another small force engaged the outlying camps at Rabia and Sofari. At the first opportunity a tank detachment would leave the main striking force and move westwards in order to cut the line of retreat from Sidi Barrani and to deal with reserves, especially of tanks, believed to be about Buqbuq and Sollum.

The main problem was: How could the striking force achieve surprise, seeing that it had to traverse some 80 miles of desert devoid of cover? Movement could be made by night, but the distance was too long to be covered in a single night.

The striking force, composed of an Indian and the Armoured Division, started on the night of Dec. 7–8. Motionless and camouflaged, it spent the next day unobserved. The following night it reached its position of deployment, S.W. of Nibeiwa. Before dawn a brigade of infantry had crept close up to the stone walls and wire that surrounded the camp. Suddenly, while the Italians were thinking of breakfast, through the unmined opening used by supply vehicles came the British tanks, followed by infantry. Surprise was

about Bardia, and Wavell withdrew his tanks for overhaul while continuing active patrolling with artillery, motorized infantry and some armoured cars.

Finally, on Sept. 13, 1940, Graziani advanced across the frontier. Due warning of the move had been given, and Wavell withdrew his frontier screen, leaving only mobile detachments to harass the enemy's advance. Graziani's advance was slow and cautious, preceded by motor cyclists followed by tanks and infantry in lorries. His caution did not save him from casualties, however, for guns and aircraft took their toll of his troops as they descended the steep and narrow road of the Halfaya Pass (*q.v.*). By Sept. 16 Graziani reached Sidi Barrani, where a fair supply of indifferent water was available, but there he halted, still some 70 miles from Mersa Matruh. A pause might have been understandable in order to give time for the construction of a good road for his supply services, for the formation of advanced depots and improvement of water supplies. But when more than two months elapsed, and Graziani still remained motionless with his troops deployed in defensive positions, it was evident that he had misgivings about his task. He has himself told us that, having appealed for reinforcements in vain, he was preparing to seek the victory Mussolini demanded when Wavell's thunderbolt struck him.

It had never been Wavell's intention to fight purely on the defensive, but to counter-attack at the first opportunity. When, however, his enemy halted at such a great distance covered by wide stretches of desert, the opportunity had to be created rather than awaited. But before Wavell could take the offensive it was essential that he should receive further reinforcements, and that defects in his equipment should be complete, and the tanks were in the camp before the Italians could man their weapons. Some guns and machine-guns came into action, and a confused mêlée ensued. But resistance was unorganized and was quickly overcome. General Maletti, in command of the camp, fell dead whilst himself firing a machine-gun. Over 2,000 prisoners and great quantities of material were captured. Part of the Armoured Division then set off towards Buqbuq, while the main force attacked northward, capturing two more camps before nightfall. Next morning the attack on Sidi Barrani itself was delivered. After a heavy artillery duel the defences were penetrated by tanks and by three British infantry battalions. The action lasted till evening, but a bayonet charge by the Argyll and Sutherland Highlanders settled the issue.

The battle of Sidi Barrani, brilliantly conceived and brilliantly executed, left some 40,000 prisoners and immense quantities of material in British hands, and removed all immediate danger to Egypt, but it remained to exploit success. Immediate pursuit, led by the tank detachment at Buqbuq, was undertaken in order to secure Halfaya Pass and to round up such Italians as were still across the frontier. Many more prisoners were captured, and after a sharp fight the plateau was gained by Dec. 15.

Then followed a pause, for the stronghold of Bardia, with a large garrison, blocked the road ahead. To carry it by assault fresh troops and guns were required; and, moreover, the long line of communication with Mersa Matruh had to be organized. On Jan. 3, 1941, after two days' intensive bombardment from sea, air and land, the attack was delivered by the freshly arrived Australian Division, led by tanks. By the end of the first day decisive progress was made, though it took two more days to bring about complete surrender. Another great haul of prisoners was made, bringing the total to 80,000.

Now came a rapid advance to Tobruk, a strongly fortified post, and by Jan. 6 our advanced troops had surrounded the 30 miles of its defensive perimeter, but again the necessity of bringing up supplies and water, and repairing vehicles, delayed the attack. But on Jan. 21 it took place on much the same lines as at Bardia, the Australians again finding the main part of the attacking

infantry. In two days it was captured, with another 15,000 prisoners. Furthermore, at Tobruk we had secured a good harbour, which greatly eased supply and evacuation problems.

By Jan. 30 Derna was occupied after some sharp fighting with Italian rearguards, who took advantage of the hilly country which had now been reached. It was still doubtful, however, whether Graziani meant to make a final stand at Benghazi, the capital of Cyrenaica, or was merely fighting delaying actions to cover the retreat of the remnants of his army to Tripolitania. In either event his retreat, to complete his destruction,

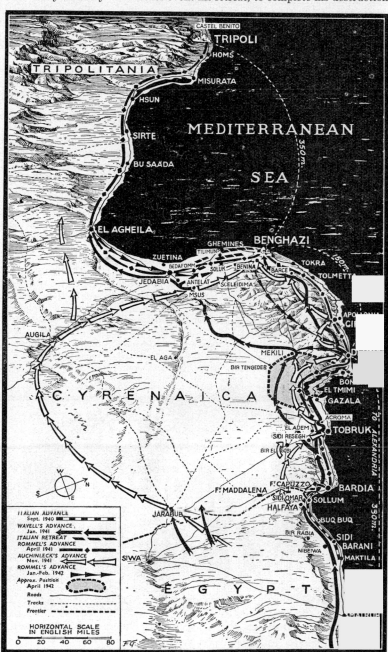

Five British and Axis campaigns in Libya from September 1940 to April 1942.
Drawn by Félix Gardon

must be cut off. While, therefore, the Australians continued the pursuit along the coastal roads, the bold decision was taken to send the Armoured Division by a rough desert track south of the Akhdar hills to reach the Tripoli road south of Benghazi, its first task being to drive an Italian armoured detachment out of Mekili on the desert track and there collect supplies for an advance synchronized with that of the Australians.

An Amazing 150-Mile March

When, however, news was received that the Italians were evacuating Benghazi, the Division was given orders to make for the coast with all speed. Headed by the most mobile vehicles, the Division started at midday on Feb. 4, and in spite of appalling conditions the advanced guard reached the Tripoli road within 24 hours after an amazing march of 150 miles, while the main body was still far behind. In $1\frac{1}{2}$ hours the Italians came in sight, unconscious of their fate. Though immensely outnumbered, the advanced guard attacked the 10-mile-long enemy column in front, flank and rear.

Thus began the battle of Beda Fomm, which was the hardest fought of the campaign, and lasted, with many critical moments, for 36 hours. The enemy had missed his chance of breaking through when first surprised, and the whole force surrendered—20,000 prisoners, 216 guns, and 112 tanks being destroyed or captured.

So ended the first Libyan campaign, in which, in 62 days, Graziani's Cyrenaica Army was destroyed, with the loss of over 123,000 prisoners and 1,300 guns.

The threat to Egypt had for the moment vanished, but Wavell's small army, with its men exhausted and its vehicles worn out, was in no condition to undertake the invasion, across another 400 miles of desert, of Tripolitania, which remained an enemy base. Leaving only a small force to hold the conquered territory, the Army of the Nile withdrew to refit. Then, almost before it was fit to take the field again, came the call from Greece for assistance.

This was the enemy's chance, and under German inspiration he was not slow to seize it. At least one German Panzer Division and other reinforcements

had reached Tripoli. A formidable force had been collected, and it suddenly attacked and overwhelmed the single light armoured brigade in Western Cyrenaica. Retreat of the whole occupying force became inevitable. But retreat did not entail the complete abandonment of Cyrenaica. Wavell decided that Tobruk should be held, and there the retreat of the Australian Division ended.

Rommel, who in practice commanded the Axis forces, decided to by-pass the place and to press on to Bardia and Halfaya, thinking that under air bombardment and lack of supplies Tobruk would eventually fall. But at the frontier he met fresh opposition, and while Tobruk stood, a thorn in his side, on his main line of communication, he could go no farther. All through the summer Rommel remained halted at Bardia and Halfaya, organizing and strengthening a naturally formidable position, to form either a base for a further advance or for defence; and he succeeded in beating off such attacks as were made on him. The Tobruk garrison, Australians, and the British troops who by degrees relieved them, safely convoyed by the Navy, maintained an active defence.

In the autumn of 1941 it became evident that both sides had received reinforcements, and the only question was whether General Auchinleck, who had exchanged places with Wavell, or Rommel, would strike first. On Nov. 18 the answer was given when the former struck. He aimed at achieving surprise by making a wide turning movement with his now powerful armoured force round the south flank of the Halfaya position. Passing round the southern flank of the Halfaya position his mobile forces made straight for Tobruk, seeking to join hands with the garrison and to defeat Rommel's armour if it intervened. It was not until Jan. 1942, two months later, that the Sollum, Bardia and Halfaya positions were reduced.

Rommel, who had been on the point of staging a decisive attack on Tobruk, quickly recovered from his surprise and, concentrating his armoured forces, soon initiated counter-attacks. After hard fighting he recaptured from a South African brigade the position at Sidi Rezegh, struck at his opponents' line of com-

GERMAN GUN CREW AT WORK IN THE WESTERN DESERT

Fighting conditions in the Western Desert taxed troops to the utmost, and in the wastes of Libya, where water was short and the heat excessive, only the strongest could survive. Nevertheless, the fighting was tenacious over a constantly changing front, Rommel relying for the most on swift movement and surprise attacks. Here is a German gun crew in action in Libya.

Photo, Associated Press

ever, he counter-attacked, and it was only the magnificent conduct of an Indian Division at Gazala which prevented his securing an important success. Having failed, and with his line of retreat to Tripoli threatened, as Graziani's had been, he retired rapidly to Jedabia. Benghazi was reoccupied on Christmas Eve 1941, and by the end of the year practically the whole of Cyrenaica was in our hands, though Bardia and Halfaya still held out.

Thus the first phase of Auchinleck's campaign had regained the territory captured by General Wavell, but Rommel's army had not been completely destroyed. He had been severely defeated, and over 30,000 prisoners had been taken with great quantities of material, but his army remained in being. When 1942 opened a fresh phase of the campaign began. Rommel, when he retired to Jedabia, did not continue, as was expected, his retreat to Tripolitania.

munication and attempted to relieve his troops in the frontier position. Much confused fighting took place with varying fortune. Some of the German tanks had heavier armament than the British and American vehicles, though the latter had the advantage of speed. But Rommel's greatest asset was the admirable system developed for the recovery of damaged vehicles, which time and again enabled him to escape complete defeat. Meanwhile, however, the New Zealand Division swung round Halfaya and, destroying many enemy depots, recaptured Sidi Rezegh, for a time joining hands with a sortie from Tobruk. Again Rommel counter-attacked and again secured Sidi Rezegh, though he failed to recover the important ground gained by the Tobruk sortie. Pressure on him was continued and, probably running short of supplies and fearing for his line of communication, he fell back west of Tobruk. Again, how-

SWEET WERE THE FRUITS OF VICTORY

New Zealand infantry are seen in the top photograph, smilingly greeting the crews of British tanks. The latter dashed out from Tobruk to meet them at the Duda position on the "Axis Highway," already captured by Imperial forces. Enemy tanks and armoured vehicles, below, are left ablaze after having been captured by the South Africans.

Photos, British Official

Instead, presumably hoping for reinforcements, he took up a strong defensive position. There, partly on account of exceptionally wet and stormy weather rendering supply difficult, and partly because after weeks of intensive action vehicles were in need of overhaul, Auchinleck could not attack him decisively. It was now more than ever necessary to clear up the situation on the frontier, where Halfaya and Bardia closed the main motor road.

During the first fortnight in January 1942 Bardia, after intensive bombardment by land, sea and air, fell to assault, somewhat more easily than was expected; and on Jan. 17 Halfaya surrendered, chiefly through lack of water, after South African troops had taken Sollum, and before the projected main assault was delivered. The position was immensely strong, and would probably have cost many lives to storm.

Rommel Returns to the Attack

Meanwhile, under cover of bad weather, Rommel had retired a further stage to an even stronger position at El Agheila, where he had protection by marshy ground, and where he could more easily receive reinforcements from Tripoli, in spite of constant attacks by the R.A.F. on the intervening road. Still hampered by wet weather and the necessity of reorganization, contact with Rommel could be maintained only with light forces. Then, suddenly, with characteristic daring, Rommel returned to the attack, having evidently received reinforcements. The move achieved remarkable success, driving Auchinleck's light forces rapidly back and overrunning some of his forward supply depots. By Jan. 30 Benghazi had changed hands for a fourth time. The issue still hung in the balance, for Auchinleck's main strength had not yet been engaged. Rommel continued to advance with his main body north of Akhdar range, till by the middle of February he had recaptured Derna with its airfields, and, in the south, Mekili. General Ritchie, who commanded the 8th Army in Libya, had been content to delay the enemy's advance with rearguards and harassing parties while concentrating his main force in the strong Gazala position. His withdrawal had been effected without serious losses except of material, but he was not able to undertake counter-offensive operations on a large scale.

On May 25–26 a new Axis offensive opened with dive-bombing attacks on our positions in the north. In the south an enemy armoured force moved towards Bir Hakeim—the British forward line in Libya at this date roughly extended from Gazala on the coast to Bir Hakeim some 40 miles inland—and on May 27 this force split into two columns, one moving towards El Adem, whence it was headed off and later joined the other column at " Knightsbridge," a track centre some 12 miles S. of Acroma. Furious fighting developed over a vast area and both sides suffered heavy losses. Rommel planned a double thrust at Tobruk (q.v.), but this plan was disrupted by British counter-attacks in the Knightsbridge-Acroma area. A great tank battle raged for four days and nights in which the Germans lost some 600 vehicles and many aircraft. Meanwhile Free French forces defending Bir Hakeim withstood numerous attacks but, despite a valiant defence, had to be withdrawn on June 10–11. Following a disastrous tank action S. of Acroma on June 13 the 8th Army later withdrew from the Gazala position, and also from El Adem and Sidi Rezegh, retreating in good order to the Libyan-Egyptian border. Rommel then hurled his full strength against the garrison left behind at Tobruk (q.v.), and on June 20 the outer perimeter was breached. At 7 a.m. June 21 Tobruk fell. On the same date the enemy also claimed to have taken Bardia. Weakened by the fall of Tobruk our troops fell back to Mersa Matruh. Here and southwards fighting was fierce on June 27 ; on June 29 Matruh was evacuated.

Auchinleck took his stand at El Alamein, 65 miles west of Alexandria ; here, on July 2, the second great battle with Rommel's forces began. Rommel endeavoured to exploit his success to the utmost of his strength, but on July 6 it was stated that the British positions were held while the R.A.F. and the S.A.A.F. maintained fierce and constant attacks on German supply lines and armoured forces. The threat to our naval base at Alexandria and to Egypt was serious. On July 10 a five-mile advance was made at El Alamein, the station at Tel el Eisa being captured, and on the 18th Ruweisat ridge in the centre sector was occupied, followed on July 22 by a general attack by Auchinleck on the 30-mile front from El Eisa to the Qattara depression, Rommel's right flank.

There is no denying that the Libyan campaigns, after brilliant initial success, ended in disastrous failure. We aimed primarily at removing the threat to Egypt by defeating Graziani's army and, more remotely, but equally important, at driving the Axis out of Libya altogether in order to regain control of sea communications in the Central Mediterranean. General Wavell's campaign achieved the first object and by capturing the Cyrenaica airfields partly achieved the second. General Auchinleck's offensive for a time retrieved what was lost in Rommel's first counter-offensive, but Rommel's second counter-stroke not only deprived us of almost all we had regained but shattered all immediate hopes of our full object. But it was not until Rommel struck for a third time that we had to admit severe defeat, which revived the threat to Egypt.

Reasons for the Defeat

To what can this shattering result be attributed ? In the first place we never had the reserve of strength necessary to exploit success to the full. Our first reverse may certainly be attributed to the diversion of forces to Greece. Our second reverse was mainly due to Rommel's daring seizure of a fleeting opportunity. A complete explanation of the defeat of General Ritchie's Eighth Army, which led to the capture of Tobruk and retreat into Egypt, may never be given, but it should be recognized that the diversion of reinforcements and material to the Far East imposed a defensive attitude. Throughout the campaign, after the appearance of German troops, our troops were handicapped by relatively inferior armament. For that our initial unpreparedness for war and the continuing effects of the disaster in France and the loss of equipment at Dunkirk were largely responsible.

These are general considerations, but the fundamental reason for Rommel's rapid recovery after reverses and our slowness in developing our potential strength was, of course, his possession of immensely shorter lines of sea communication and the Axis ability to protect them with shore-based aircraft. Desert warfare lends itself to the maximum use of mobile mechanized forces, for it admits great liberty of rapid movement and thereby the difficulty of water supply is reduced. On the other hand, it places limits

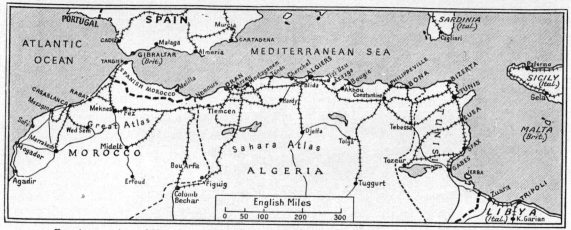

French possessions of Morocco, Algeria and Tunisia in North Africa, with rail and road communications.

on the employment of less mobile elements. The great spaces of the desert place a further handicap on the side compelled to adopt a defensive attitude, for there must always be open flanks. Defensive positions can be no more than pivots of manoeuvre. The more lightly armed force tends to evade decisive collision and to concentrate on harassing its opponent's supply services, relying on artillery and powerful anti-tank weapons to defend its pivot of manoeuvre.

These tactics General Ritchie appeared to have employed with considerable success until his armoured strength was fatally reduced in the action of June 13, in which Rommel proved that the anti-tank gun is not solely a defensive weapon. Desert warfare, which admits the use of greatly dispersed formations, reduces the value of air superiority, which, in general, the R.A.F. retained.

Books to Consult: Wavell in the Middle East, Maj.-Gen. H. Cowan-Robinson (Hutchinson). Destruction of an Army (M.O.I.).

North Africa, French. French North Africa includes Morocco, Algeria, and Tunisia. The three possessions not only represent important negotiating assets in peace discussions between Germany, Italy and France, but Bizerta in Tunisia and Oran in Algeria, if held by the Axis powers, would do much to assure naval supremacy in the Central Mediterranean.

Tunisia became a French protectorate in 1881 and when the war began in 1939 there were about 90,000 Italians in Tunisia, compared with 110,000 Frenchmen. Hence the cries raised in the Italian Chamber in November 1938, " Tunisia, Corsica, and Nice ! "

Italy's entry into the war in the summer of 1940 brought French North Africa into the battle-ground. Some 23,000 Italians were interned. The downfall of France, however, was too speedy to allow of any invasion of Tripoli, such as the Allies had planned. Under the Armistice terms the defences between Tunis and Tripoli (Mareth Line) were dismantled, and a demilitarized zone between Libya and Algeria established.

When the Armistice was signed a French Fleet lay in Oran harbour consisting of two battleships and several cruisers, destroyers and submarines. A British squadron under Admiral Somerville arrived off Oran (*q.v.*) on July 3, 1940, and gave the French Fleet six hours in which to join the British cause or sink their ships. As the ultimatum was disregarded, Somerville attacked, sank one battleship, damaged another,

drove the Dunkerque, a battle-cruiser, ashore, and sank some destroyers and a seaplane carrier. The action, necessary though it was, greatly angered the Vichy Government and particularly Admiral Darlan.

The necessity for holding on to French North Africa was always plain to Vichy, and Marshal Pétain's first step was to send Marshal Weygand as commander-in-chief in September 1940. Weygand controlled North African affairs until December 1941, when he was retired in consequence of pressure from Germany. His position had become increasingly difficult during 1941, owing to German agents, tourists, technicians and so-called members of the Axis Armistice Commission, who threatened to take possession of the key positions. There were also feeding difficulties, though the United States allowed food vessels to reach North Africa regularly until the dismissal of Weygand made it plain that Germany would profit by the further food licences. When Weygand left, his military commands were given to General Juin (North Africa) and General Barreau (West Africa), both under Darlan's orders.

Shortly after the Hitler-Mussolini meeting at Salzburg on April 29–30, 1942 the Italians resumed their anti-French cries of " Nice, Corsica and Tunisia ! " It was thought that Hitler had offered these French possessions to Mussolini as a bribe for extensive Italian military help in Russia. He was also able to exert further pressure on Vichy. *See* Equatorial Africa.

Northern Ireland. The division of Ireland into Eire and Northern Ireland (Ulster) created a peculiar problem in strategy. Eire (Premier, De Valera), Catholic and nationalistic and living remote from the grim realities of power politics, affirmed neutrality and supported, in Dublin, the presence of Nazi representatives. Northern Ireland (Pop. 1,300,000) became in feeling and in war effort part of England. Early in the war her Premier, Lord Craigavon, (d. Nov. 23, 1940), conferred with the War Cabinet in London on defence. He was succeeded by Mr. J. M. Andrews, who had shared his views on a-hundred-per-cent cooperation with Britain for victory. The proposal for conscription in Northern Ireland was abortive, however, owing to the opposition of Nationalists.

The neutrality of Eire gave her almost complete freedom from air raids ; but Belfast had to pay the price of her steadfast loyalty. The great dockyards there were throbbing with war activity, a circumstance well known to the enemy, and on April 7, 1941, the first

THEY WERE WELCOME VISITORS

The driver of this typically Irish cart is an interested spectator as American troops march through the cobbled street of a Northern Ireland town en route for the parade ground. Inset, Maj.-Gen. R. P. Hartle, who commanded the U.S. troops in Northern Ireland.

Photos, Wide World

the first American contingent, Milburn Henke, stepped ashore. Later this private broadcast from Northern Ireland to the U.S.A. The American troops were commanded by Major-General Russell P. Hartle, a Marylander. That afternoon squadrons of German bombers came over, indicating plainly the activities of the Nazis in Dublin. Despite the obvious use being made of the Eire capital by the enemies of Britain, and despite the plain need for Irish defence, Mr. De Valera, the greatest of all the Isolationists, spoke of the "American invasion" with resentment, though himself American-born of mixed racial descent.

Behind that resentment lay the story of negotiations in the form of a suggested "deal" initiated by Dublin when America entered the war. The terms were that the U.S.A. Government should bring pressure to bear on the British Government to coerce Northern Ireland into union with Eire. That done, there would be, Dublin assured Washington, no further difficulty about the use of Eire ports as naval bases. Washington treated the proposal with the contempt it deserved. Therefore, when De Valera protested about American troops in Northern Ireland, Washington expressed " surprise."

Throughout Northern Ireland, which has many commercial affiliations with America, the arrival of American troops was hailed with joy, and they were everywhere received with enthusiasm. Another large contingent of U.S. troops, with artillery, arrived at a Northern Ireland port on May 19, 1942. At Londonderry a naval base, one of the best equipped in Europe, was constructed by U.S. technicians and was in use from Feb. 5, 1942.

air raid was made on Belfast. Raids were continuous for ten days, particularly severe attacks being made on April 15–16 and again on May 4.

On Jan. 6, 1942, President Roosevelt told the people of the United States that America would take up stations in the British Isles on land, sea and air. At that date there were, in fact, units of the American Marines already in London. Many Americans were also serving with British Dominions forces and with the R.A.F. After the passage of the Lease-and-Lend Bill the British Government engaged American technicians in Northern Ireland for a wide range of important defence works. These technicians, though Americans, were the employees of the British Government.

On Jan. 27, 1942, at dawn, troopships docked in Northern Ireland and the first American soldier of

NAZI ATTEMPT TO CONTROL THE NORTH SEA

The North Sea, no less than the Atlantic, was a vital area of naval and air operations from the outbreak of war. The enemy-occupied coastline extended from Norway to Belgium and German aircraft and submarines constantly attacked British shipping in its waters.

North Sea. Enemy naval and air activities in the North Sea differed entirely during the two wars, necessitating a complete recasting of British measures to counter them. The only major similarity was that Germany repeated in this war her policy of keeping her main surface fleet intact behind its defences, and only operating small craft, backed by a very large number of aircraft, against the British Navy, merchant shipping and coasts.

The development of material and the progress of the war to date accounted for the change. There was no longer any chance of Britain hemming the enemy in with a great minefield between the Allied coasts of the Channel and from Scotland to the edge of Norwegian territorial waters in the North, as was done before the end of 1918. That practically confined naval operations outside the North Sea to submarines and a few raiders ; they were important, but neither capital ship nor sizable cruiser contrived to get outside.

With the High Seas Fleet keeping to the German coast the operations inside the North Sea were then restricted, except for one or two sorties, to the submarines and small craft, but on this occasion the huge defensive minefield, laid parallel to the East Coast soon after the outbreak of war, practically eliminated the danger from these types. They were replaced by aircraft—bombing, torpedo-dropping, gunning and minelaying—and the motor torpedo boats known as E-boats. They could pass over the minefields without danger from them and were constantly attacking the trade lane inside them, but the main area of enemy raiding was transferred to the open sea through the protected but still dangerous passages along the occupied coasts.

Risks of the North Sea Patrol

The motor torpedo boats and aircraft contrived considerable success in the North Sea area and forced the Navy to keep large numbers of men and ships there to defend the trade lane and to act as an outpost line and protection against the threatened invasion. With such a long coastline from Norway to Ushant available as a jumping-off place, constant patrols of all kinds were necessary. Casualties in the British Fleet were therefore greater than in the German, waiting its opportunity in protected waters, although enemy losses in the bigger types were heavy when they undertook long-distance operations, and a steady toll was taken of their small craft and 'planes.

Germany's pre-war plan was to control the North Sea completely with aircraft and submarines, and the first attack was made about three weeks after the outbreak of war, when a squadron of British capital ships with an aircraft carrier, cruisers and destroyers were attacked by about twenty German aircraft. Their radio claimed great success, but actually they hit nothing, and one 'plane was brought down. At the same time, it showed the obvious risk from a more determined attack by more numerous and better 'planes, and the Navy could not afford unnecessary risks for no apparent advantage. Since then most of the reports of ships operating in the North Sea have concerned cruisers and the smaller types, except if there was a definite object in view, when there was no hesitation in using capital ships.

It would obviously have been madness to maintain a standing naval patrol in the Skagerrak to prevent German forces reaching Norway, with Danish airfields seized and equipped with large numbers of bombers.

Constant patrols by enemy reconnaissance 'planes also hampered raids in force on the lines of communication through the Skagerrak by robbing them of all chance of surprise. In addition, the narrow waters and the distances were all in favour of the enemy.

The Chance of the Small Craft

As the Navy started the war with quite inadequate numbers of cruisers and destroyers, the types which would be used principally for such work, they always had to consider the value of possible results against probable losses, and to decide each case on its merits. Dunkirk in 1940, and several of the operations on the Norwegian coast in 1940 and 1941, some of the latter backed by capital ships, were considered worth the risk, and they were carried out with reasonable or light losses, but the gibes of the enemy showed how disappointed he was that we did not throw away ships by engaging him on his terms. The loss of the cooperation of all but a few French ships in 1940 increased the necessity for care.

Small craft of all kinds, on the other hand, had their chance in the North Sea and took advantage of it daily. Their main purpose from the first was protecting essential commerce against constant attack; it was reduced on the East Coast route as much as possible in 1940, but some had to use the North Sea to London—North-East Coast coal for the public utility companies, and the like. The Fleet had to deal with constant attacks on these ships, by aircraft in daytime and motor torpedo boats at night, and with minelaying of all varieties by both. Destroyers of all kinds, escort vessels, corvettes, armed yachts, trawlers, drifters, motor launches, motor torpedo boats and a host of other types were constantly at this work, few of their officers above the rank of Commander. They worked in close cooperation with shore-based aircraft.

Several combined naval and air expeditions, with or without Commando troops, crossed the North Sea to Norway in 1941, and secured striking successes, while it was constantly crossed by the air raiders of both sides en route for their land targets and running the gauntlet of the anti-aircraft fire of numerous small ships. In addition, big British 'planes made, after the German occupation of the coasts, almost daily attacks on their seaborne supply services, in spite of their heavy convoys, causing so many losses that they were seriously handicapped in relieving the overworked enemy railways. By July 15, 1942, over a million tons of Axis shipping had been sunk or captured in the North Sea.

NORWAY UNDER THE GERMAN HEEL

Germany's occupation of Norway was a long-laid plan of campaign, and it was no magnanimous gesture on the part of Hitler that Norwegian neutrality was not violated until it suited Germany's purpose. When that violation took place on April 9, 1940, it was accompanied by the usual protestations of innocence.

Norway. The Norwegian coast, with its innumerable lurking places for U-boats and other craft from which to attack Britain, was sure to become an objective of the German High Command. The Nazis had been using Norwegian territorial waters in 1939 and 1940 and the flow of Swedish iron ore through Narvik to Germany had become intolerable to the Allies. Our grievance was illuminated by the Altmark incident

(*q.v.*) in the Joessing Fjord, when, on Feb. 16 1940, the Royal Navy rescued British seamen from the Nazi prison ship. The howl of Nazi fury and indignation that followed sounded very hollow when the world was told that neutral Norway had already lost through German action 49 ships and 327 sailors.

It was palpably absurd, therefore, for Germany to accuse Britain of violating Norwegian neutrality.

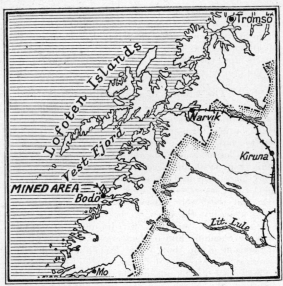

Here the areas of northern Norway concerned in the fighting of April and May 1940 are shown. The southern fields are given in the opposite page.   *By courtesy of "The Times"*

Neither on the sea nor in their own homeland were the Norwegians safe from Nazi cruelty and conspiracy. Hitler already had his Fifth Column plotting in Norway under command of Major Vidkun Quisling. The traitor paid a visit to Berlin early in April 1940, and returned to Oslo with final instructions on the 6th of that month.

At 4 a.m., April 9, 1940, Dr. Bräuer, Nazi Minister to Norway, presented a Note to Dr. Koht, Norway's Foreign Minister. It was a brutal demand calling for absolute non-resistance to Nazi occupation of the kingdom. Its terms included the surrender of all coastal fortifications, the immobilization of merchant marine and navy, control of all transport and of all radio stations.

Four hours earlier, however, four German warships steamed past Faerder, at the entrance to Oslo Fjord. Soon after the forts of Bolaerne opened fire, and were supported by those of Rauer. By the time these attacking ships had reached Filtuet and the guns of Oscarsborg were in action, similar naval operations, carefully synchronized, were in progress elsewhere. At 3.30 a.m. two Nazi warships passed Agdenes and steamed into Trondheim Fjord. At Bergen no fewer than five warships had passed the outer fortifications two hours after midnight.

When Dr. Koht asked for time to consult with his Government, Dr. Bräuer informed him that the Nazi navy had orders to seize the Norwegian ports by, at latest, 10 a.m. These places were attacked before the Nazi Note was presented. The exact chronology of these events is important, since it fixes precisely both clear intent and act of aggression.

Germany had determined upon the military occupation of Norway. If it could be accomplished without resistance, so much the better.

To avoid capture, and not as an act of flight, King Haakon and the Government, headed by the Premier, Johan Nygaardsvold, left the invaded capital in order to function from Hamar. From that town next day King Haakon broadcast to his people, characterizing the aggression as " a crime condemned by the whole civilized world."

Thus Norway, completely pacific, and with a traditional foreign policy of absolute neutrality, was sucked into the vortex of world war.

Hitler's invasion had already begun, for merchant ships fitted as transports, full of Nazi soldiers concealed below decks, were steaming through the Kattegat and Skagerrak towards Oslo and Norway's Atlantic ports. On April 8 the Allies had informed the Norwegian Government that Britain was laying mines in Norwegian territorial waters owing to their abuse. It was after these operations that the destroyer Glowworm (*q.v.*) was sunk on April 8 and Gurkha on the 9th. The Germans attempted to make this an excuse for their aggression against Norway, but the enemy's plans were in fact so far advanced that Nazi troops landed at Bergen, Trondheim, Stavanger, Kristiansand and even as far as Narvik in the north on April 9. Simultaneously, German transports had arrived off Oslo, and landings had been made two hours before the German minister in that city at 4 a.m. presented Dr. Koht with the ultimatum. Through a faked order, requiring the commander of the naval base near Oslo to allow German ships to pass unmolested, some of the Norwegian batteries held their

SYMBOLS OF NAZI AGGRESSION IN OSLO

The peace of Oslo was shattered when the Germans occupied the city on April 9, 1940, and the citizens of the Norwegian capital were to grow accustomed to such a sight as this—German tanks stationed outside one of Oslo's modern buildings.

Photo, Keystone

fire; but the mine-layer cruiser Olav Tryggvason, failing to receive these forged instructions, fired on the Germans and sank the cruiser Emden.

Nazi 'planes landed troops at Fornebu, Oslo's airport, and other enemy 'planes roared over the city to terrorize the population. Thus Oslo, a city of 30,000 bewildered inhabitants, was occupied by about 1,500 Nazis the same day. While heavily armed units took possession of the key-points of the city German bands played cheerful music to the astonished citizens. Nor did the people know that their King and Government were at that moment being murderously pursued by Hitler's airmen, and that Major Quisling was the head of a Nazi-controlled party ready to administer their betrayed fatherland.

The Germans rapidly consolidated their power in the region of the capital, meeting with little opposition. The hastily mobilized Norwegian army, near Kongsvinger, east of Oslo, tried to make a stand, but was beaten back towards Hamar and Elverum on the Swedish frontier. The Nazis were also strengthening their

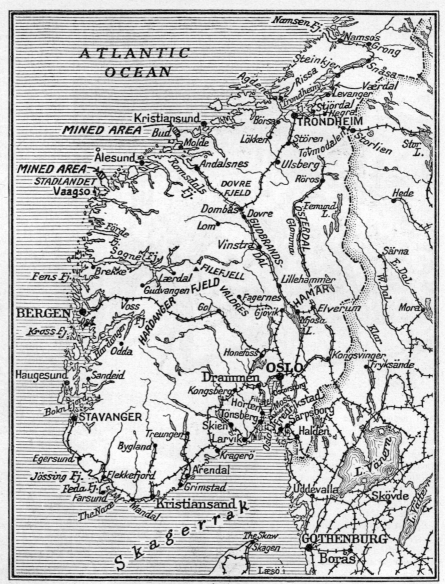

This map covers the central and southern portions of the Norwegian battlefield. It shows the sites of mined coastal waters and also the two great valleys, Gudbrandsdal and Oesterdal.

By courtesy of "The Times"

positions on the Atlantic coast, though their troops and supply ships were being heavily attacked by the R.A.F. and Fleet Air Arm.

The war was short, sharp and cruel. By Sunday, April 7, already British intelligence knew that a vast Nazi armada was on the high seas for Norway. That evening a battle fleet sailed from Scapa and Rosyth; on the 8th it was joined by the 1st Cruiser Squadron.

An expeditionary force under General Paget was embarked. Both naval and military aspects of the campaign presented great difficulties. At sea, the difficulties arose from the character of the Norwegian coast, which offered innumerable hiding places for the enemy. On land, the difficulty arose from lack of aerodromes which had been seized by the Germans, whose attack towards the north was by way of the parallel Gudbrand and Oester valleys.

On April 9 H.M.S. Renown, with destroyers, was diverting neutrals from our minefields off Narvik (*q.v.*) when she engaged the Scharnhorst, inflicting considerable damage in an engagement under very bad weather conditions. Meanwhile, British destroyers discovered that German warships had entered Narvik Fjord under cover of a blinding snowstorm. Next day, under the command of Captain Warburton-Lee, posthumously awarded the V.C., the British destroyers entered the fjord and inflicted heavy damage on the German naval craft and other shipping in the fjord.

Narvik, whence came the iron ore from Sweden, was regarded as a key town. A British and French force landed there on April 15.

British strategy was afterwards outlined by the Prime Minister, Mr. Chamberlain, in Parliament on May 2, when he said: ". . . the objects we had in view

Germans had control of the aerodromes and air superiority which made it impossible to land either tanks or heavy guns. In the last week of April, therefore, a withdrawal began, the whole expeditionary force being embarked and cleared under the noses of the Luftwaffe without the loss of a man.

Up to this date, in three weeks of fighting the British naval forces had badly damaged two German capital ships, had sunk three or four cruisers, eleven destroyers and five U-boats. In addition, submarines operating in the Skagerrak sank German troopships and drowned over 8,000 men whose bodies were washed ashore at Oslo.

The withdrawal, however, meant that the fight for Central Norway

were, first, to give all the support and assistance in our power to the Norwegians ; second, to resist or delay the German advance from the south ; and third, to facilitate the rescue and protection of the Norwegian King and Government."

The gallant naval action in Narvik Fjord so completely crippled the German naval power there that troops earmarked for the holding of the port were released to implement the other objects indicated in the Prime Minister's speech.

The Nazis were already in Trondheim, but it was decided to attempt the capture of that port by attacks at Namsos in the north and at Aandalsnes (q.v.), to the south. On April 14 naval forces landed at Namsos (q.v.), followed by British troops, 16th–18th, and, a few days later, French Chasseurs Alpins. The Norwegians were holding Stenkjer and this force went in support of it. On April 17 a naval party landed at Aandalsnes, and troops on the 18th–19th, and advanced to the important railway junction of Dombaas (q.v.), a contingent going to Lillehammer, where Norwegian forces were striving to hold the main German thrust from the south.

These attempts failed, and they did so because, as the Prime Minister later told the country, the

PREPARING TO MEET THE ENEMY

Within a week of the German invasion of Norway Allied troops, British and French, were disembarked at various points. Namsos, on Namsen Fjord (top left), was one site of a British landing. The Norwegians showed great hospitality to our troops, and above are seen some of the B.E.F. receiving welcome refreshment from an old lady.

Photos, Topical Press

was at an end. It was a reverse, and although the British had less than a division engaged, it was a blow to British prestige.

At the same time King and Government moved north. In the south, the government of Quisling, leader of the Nazi Nasjonal Samling party (National Union) and the creature of his German masters, had failed and the invaders were trying to administer the occupied territory through the Administrative Council set up by the Supreme Court as an administrative council and not as the government into which the Nazis tried to convert it. This attempt to oust the constitutional authority failed, and by Decree, April 24, Hitler appointed as German Reich Commissioner Terboven, former Essen bank clerk.

Narvik was recaptured on May 27, and that might well have been the turning point in the campaign had not disasters elsewhere made imperative the withdrawal of our forces. With that withdrawal Norwegian resistance was at an end. On June 7 King Haakon and his Government sailed to England on H.M.S. Devonshire, there to continue the struggle.

These events precipitated a political crisis in Britain which resulted in the resignation of Mr. Chamberlain and the premiership of Mr. Winston Churchill, May 11.

Books to Consult: Norway and the War, G. N. Gathorne-Hardy (Oxford Pamphlet). Odds Against Norway, E. O. Hauge (Lindsay Drummond). Norway Fights the Nazis, J. Worm-Müller (Lindsay Drummond).

Norway, Free. When the Norwegian Government came to England they placed the Norwegian merchant fleet (about 1,000 ships totalling 4,000,000 tons) at the Allies' disposal, organized a Norwegian army under the C.-in-C. General Fleischer, and established a training camp for Norwegian airmen in Canada. Norwegian naval units played a valuable part in convoy and patrol work with the Royal Navy.

The King's hold on Norwegian affections remained unimpaired, and information supplied by patriotic Norwegians was instrumental in ensuring the success of many raids on the Norwegian coast, notably at Lofoten (March 1941) and Vaagso (December 1941).

Norway, Occupied. When the Norwegians had recovered from bewilderment at finding their country overrun, they began in every way to oppose the Nazis. Acts of sabotage, notably the cutting of the Oslo-Bergen railway in various places in the autumn of 1940, were frequent. There were many persecutions, especially among trade unionists who had burned their books and membership lists rather than allow their members to be exploited by the Nazis. Altogether hundreds of Norwegians faced firing squads or were tortured to death in concentration camps.

On Feb. 1, 1942, the traitor Major Vidkun Quisling (*q.v.*) was made Prime Minister. He announced that his first aim would be peace with Germany, and that Norwegians needed a severe schoolmaster. An outburst of sabotage in many districts signalized the occasion, and on the following day Norway's Government in London denounced Quisling and proclaimed that there could be no peace until Norway was liberated. On Feb. 8 Quisling arrogated to himself the powers hitherto vested in king and Storting (Parliament), and the further power of overriding the Constitution. He visited Germany Feb. 13–18.

It was, of course, Germany's aim to Nazify the country. The appointment of puppet judges and magistrates had led to the resignation of the Supreme Court of Justice on Dec. 12, 1940. On Feb. 17, 1942, it was decreed that all lawyers must belong to the Norwegian Advocates' Association, under Nazi leadership. Hundreds of them resigned from their profession.

The Church had repeatedly condemned the Nazi rule as lawless and godless. On Feb. 1, 1942, Nazi interference came to the point of requisitioning Trondheim Cathedral for a service conducted by one of their few supporters, and refusing to allow the

Dean to preach afterwards. On this same day Quisling had decreed that all children between the ages of 10 and 18 must be enrolled in a Youth Organization similar to the Hitler Youth. Bishop Berggrav, Norway's Primate, supported by other bishops, protested, and on Feb. 24 they resigned in a body. Their Deans refused to step into the vacant places and were deposed. The Primate, who had meanwhile protested against the Nazi attempt to control education, was on April 3 (Good Friday) prevented from preaching in his own Cathedral. A mass resignation of the clergy followed on April 5 (Easter Sunday). The Nazi Commissioner, Terboven, did not hesitate to arrest Bishop Berggrav on April 10 and send him to a concentration camp; on April 26 he was removed to an isolated cottage surrounded by barbed wire, and watched day and night by 20 armed guards.

Following the clergy's lead, most of the schoolteachers refused to make themselves the instruments of Nazi propaganda, and nearly 2,000 were arrested on March 31. They were deported to labour camps and given until May 1 to reconsider their attitude, but stubbornly resisted. On May 3 it was announced that the teachers would be given the opportunity of reinstatement, with an official undertaking that they would not be required to go against their consciences. Terboven had tried to fill the places of these brave clergy and teachers, but the people defeated him by boycotting his nominees.

During the German occupation Norway was a ruined country. She was forced to find £25 per head of the population to support the occupying armies. Local industries, except those commandeered for the German war effort, perished for lack of raw materials and fuel. Collective fines were imposed on the slightest pretext. In spite of the death penalty imposed for attempted escape from the country, some 4,000 Norwegians made the perilous voyage across the sea in tiny boats to Britain.

Norwich. The Germans carried out "reprisal" raids on this ancient cathedral city on the nights of April 24–25 and 27, 1942, these constituting the worst attacks suffered by Norwich. The enemy used 25 'planes in the first raid and caused heavy damage in residential districts.

Novgorod. Russian city about 100 miles S. of Leningrad. After a week's tenacious fighting the Russians evacuated Novgorod on Aug. 25, 1941. They launched a new offensive around it on Dec. 18. Bitter fighting continued in this area throughout January 1942, when the Russians advanced slowly down the Volkhov valley towards Novgorod. In order to form new defensive positions, the retreating Germans dynamited the ice on the Volkhov river. In February fierce fighting took place in bitter cold in the approaches to Novgorod. *See* Russia.

Lt.-Gen. Sir A. Nye, Vice-Chief of I.G.S.
Photo, Bassano

Nye, Lt.-Gen. Sir Archibald Edward, k.c.b., m.c. Vice-Chief of Imperial General Staff from Nov. 18, 1941, in succession to Lt.-Gen. Sir Henry Pownall. In December 1941 he took part in the Eden-Stalin-Molotov talks in Moscow on questions relating to the war and to post-war organization. He was Director of Staff Duties at the War Office from Nov. 1940 to Nov. 1941, and before then he commanded every type of formation of the British Army, from a section of eight to an infantry brigade.

Nygaardsvold, JOHAN (b. 1879). Head of the Free Norwegian Government in London, Nygaardsvold was Norwegian Premier from 1935, and a member of the Storting from 1916. Speaking on April 11, 1940, of the refusal of King Haakon to yield to the German request for a Norwegian Government nominated by Hitler, he said, " The Nygaardsvold, which has led the country for five years in collaboration with the Storting, is still the only legal Government." He called upon the people to retain the country's traditional liberty and to continue the struggle to that end. After the withdrawal of Allied troops from Norway Nygaardsvold came to England with the King and Government, arriving in London June 10, 1940. He was outlawed, with King Haakon and the Free Norwegian Government, when Terboven, Reichskommissar, announced his New Order for Norway on Oct. 1, 1940. Nygaardsvold represented Norway at the historic meeting in St. James's Palace, London, on June 12, 1941, when the leaders of the Allied Powers reaffirmed their determination to " fight on to victory." *See* Norway (Free).

Observer Corps, Royal. A civilian corps transferred to the Air Ministry on the outbreak of war, but not officially part of the R.A.F., the Royal Observer Corps performs services on which the success of interception of enemy aircraft by the R.A.F. largely depends. Formerly known as the Observer Corps, the title Royal was conferred on it in May 1941, in recognition of valuable services rendered over a number of years.

Its object is to track and report the movements of all hostile aircraft flying over this country. This enables fighter aircraft to be sent to the correct position to make an interception, and air-raid warnings to be issued in advance of the direction in which the raiders are proceeding. This ground observation system consists of observer posts, manned by personnel living in the vicinity and trained in observing duties and the recognition of aircraft. Normally, a number of posts, covering an area of a medium-sized county, are connected to a centre ; a centre with its posts is called an observer group. Posts are connected in bunches of three, so that any two posts can overhear reports from the third.

Speed of reporting is essential and every observer post has a permanent telephone connexion to its centre. The post crews are supplied with binoculars, instruments to ascertain height and direction of flight, and gridded maps. At each observer centre there is a gridded map around

Badge of Royal Observer Corps.

which are seated the plotters, who receive plots from the post crews. By placing counters on the grid squares reported by post crews, tracks of aircraft are obtained. Tellers overlooking the table " tell " these tracks to the Royal Air Force. A continuous watch

THEIRS ARE EVER-WATCHFUL EYES

The duties of members of the Royal Observer Corps include the tracking of all aircraft, Allied and hostile alike, and a night and day service is maintained. Here is an officer inspecting and sighting up the plotting table of an East Coast observation post.
Photo, Planet News

is maintained day and night, and every aircraft, friend or enemy, is tracked whilst flying across country up to the capacity of the organization.

Members of the Royal Observer Corps are recruited from all classes of the community and are carefully selected. Some are full time " professionals," but the majority perform their duties in their spare time. Quite a number of women are now doing valuable work in the corps.

The commandant of the R.O.C. is responsible to the C.-in-C. Fighter Command for operational work and to the Air Ministry for administration and equipment. *See* Air Defence.

O'Connor, LT.-GEN. SIR RICHARD NUGENT, K.C.B., D.S.O. (b. 1889). He was in direct command of the Imperial Army in the Western Desert and played a prominent part under Gen. Wavell in the operations which led to the conquest of Cyrenaica in February 1941. When the British troops withdrew in face of heavy enemy attacks, Lt.-Gen. O'Connor, with Generals Neame and Gambier-Parry, was captured by the Germans in Libya, April 1941. *See* North Africa.

Odessa. The great Russian grain port and naval base of Odessa (*see* p. 3033) on the Black Sea was heavily bombed by the Germans in June 1941, during the first days of the Russo-German war. Early in August eighteen Rumanian divisions, comprising almost half the entire Rumanian Army, with a stiffening of Nazis, made a thrust towards Odessa and set about its capture. At the approaches to the outer defences of the city the enemy was repulsed with very heavy losses, but by August 23 Odessa was encircled. Fierce fighting continued and, having received substantial reinforcements of German artillery, bombing 'planes and mine-throwers, the Rumanians delivered a fresh onslaught on Sept. 17 on a narrow sector of the front. The defenders stood fast until, after two months' heroic resistance in which enormous casualties were inflicted on the Rumanian and German troops, it was decided, for strategic reasons, to evacuate the city. All factories and important works and buildings likely to be of value to the enemy were blown up, the civilian population was safely got

CHEERING THEM ON THEIR WAY TO THE BATTLE

Odessa was abandoned by the Russians after enormous losses had been inflicted on the German and Rumanian troops besieging the great Black Sea port. Little was yielded to the enemy on its capture, for every important building was destroyed by the Russians. Here is a scene in one of the city's boulevards, showing a group of the inhabitants greeting soldiers of the Red Army

Photo, P.N.A.

away, and troops and war equipment transported to Sevastopol, while a mere handful of soldiers held the outer defence line. They, too, followed, and when the enemy marched into Odessa on the next day, Oct. 16, 1941, they found an empty and burning city. *See* Russia.

Odic, GEN. JEAN CLAUDE. After the Franco-German Armistice Gen. Odic was appointed Chief of Air Staff, and later served under Gen. Weygand as Commander of the French Air Force in N. Africa. On Nov. 23, 1941, it was announced by the Free French that he had rallied to Gen. de Gaulle, and on Dec. 12 he arrived in London from the U.S. to join him.

Odlum, MAJ.-GEN. VICTOR WENTWORTH, C.B., C.M.G., D.S.O. (b. 1880). Appointed Canadian High Commissioner in Australia, Nov. 6, 1941. He commanded the 2nd Canadian Division in Great Britain from April 1940.

Odweina. The Italians occupied this small town in British Somaliland on August 6, 1940, two days after invading this territory from Abyssinia. Odweina was retaken by the British in March 1941. *See* East Africa.

Oesel (Saaremaa). Estonian island in the Baltic. By the pact of Sept. 28, 1939, the Estonian Government allowed Russia to garrison Oesel and Dagö, a neighbouring island, and to maintain naval bases and lease aerodromes on them. A German attempt to land troops on Oesel was repulsed on Sept. 14, 1941, an enemy destroyer and four transports being sunk and other vessels damaged. A week later a large-scale German attack developed, but the Russians exterminated the 15,000 troops who landed, and recaptured the island on Sept. 26. About a month later Oesel was evacuated by the Russians, who went to Hangö. On Dec. 4, 1941, when the Russians withdrew from Hangö, they evacuated a number of the survivors of the Oesel garrison.

Oflag. One of the three types of prison camps in Germany and German-occupied territory, Oflag, an abbreviation of Offizierslager, denotes a camp used for officer prisoners of war. *See* Prisoners of War.

Ohqvist, GEN. H. At the outbreak of the Russo-Finnish war Gen. Ohqvist was second in command of the Finnish Army. He was responsible for the determined defence of Viipuri in March 1940.

Oil. Modern war is based on machines and the mobility of machines. The natural limits of movement of marching men and galloping horses do not exist

OIL IS AN ESSENTIAL PRODUCT

Having brought the oil to Britain's shores the ship's crew is seen connecting the land pipe-line which carries the precious liquid to safety after its long and hazardous journey in a tanker across the seas.

Photo, Keystone

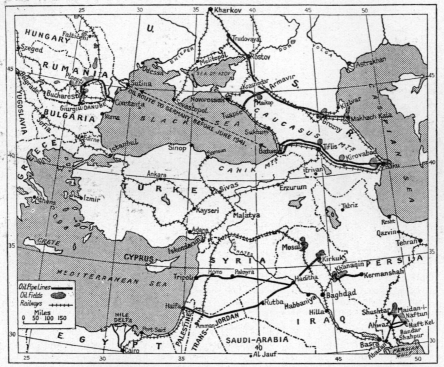

Caucasian and Middle East oilfields ; Kirkuk, in Iraq, is one of the most productive.

U.S.A., 170,432,000 metric tons ; U.S.S.R., 30,112,000 ; Venezuela, 28,112,000 ; Iraq, 10,358,000 ; Dutch East Indies, 7,394,000 ; Rumania, 6,871,000, and so on, to a grand total of 280,276,000 metric tons. Germany's contribution represents roughly $\frac{1}{467}$ of that total.

For the supply of her vast Panzer (armoured) divisions her own oil production is totally inadequate. What part, then, of the world supply can she tap from overseas, or from Rumania, Iraq or U.S.S.R. ?

The answer is : very little, while the British blockade effectively cuts off from her seaborne supplies from the great New World sources of supply, the United States and Venezuela, Mexico, Colombia, Trinidad, the Argentine, Canada, etc. Oil, then, is a major problem for the directors of Germany's great war of aggression. She is meeting the problem with characteristic cleverness and ingenuity.

for the tank. It can go practically anywhere where its steel caterpillar track can bite earth. The tank is a land ship which has made obsolete the war text books of 1939 by creating on land war conditions similar to those of sea fighting. The aeroplane has taken the mobility factor in war into the air and has made necessary a rescaling of all previous estimates of possible speed.

Both these prime agents for the prosecution of modern war are completely dependent on oil. Therefore adequate supplies of petrol and lubricants are absolutely essential, for without them tanks, armoured cars, mechanically hauled guns, lorries, cars and fighter and bombing aeroplanes would soon be immobilized.

What, then, of the respective "oil strengths" of the Aggressor States and the Allies ? Here two things must be kept in mind : first, the geographical distribution of the world's oil supply ; secondly, power to draw upon it.

Germany produces oil, some 609,000 metric tons a year. She is seventeenth among the chief oil-producing countries, the most important of which are the

Now petroleum, which is the crude material from which all the needful oils are fabricated, is stored in

GUARDING THE OIL EN ROUTE FOR BRITAIN

Taken aboard an oil tanker on the high seas, this photograph shows a British destroyer guarding the all-important convoy on its homeward journey. Oil is one of the most vital essentials in war, and every precaution is taken against enemy 'planes and U-boats when it is sent across the sea.

Photo, Keystone

vast subterranean lakes under immense rock roofs. It is a mineral in a treacly, greenish, evil-smelling form. Its chemical composition is similar to that of coal.

If the scientific German likes one thing more than another it is imitating Nature. Faced with the possibility—now a certainty—of an oil shortage, Germany set about making synthetic oil. At Leuna, Gelsenkirchen and Poelitz great plants were built to produce synthetic oils so that, cut off from the world's main supplies, Germany could still operate her vast land fleets of tanks and armoured cars. These towns, and certain others, are the constant targets of the R.A.F., so that Germany's independent supplies of oil shall be destroyed and the efficiency of her vast oil-consuming Panzer divisions be impaired.

Though a fanatical hatred of Communism was probably Hitler's prime motive in ordering the invasion of the U.S.S.R., the need for access to the oil of the U.S.S.R. and the Near East was also a large factor.

Very different is the position of the Allies, for they had not only the bulk of the total world supply, but, what is as important in war, the means of transporting it where it is needed for war purposes, for tanks, aeroplanes and ships. Here is a single fact which is most significant in calculating the chances of the Aggressor States' victory : the U.S.A. has today proved oil reserves of 2,500,000,000 metric tons.

For sea transport the great oil industry has built up a big tanker fleet. Britain has the largest oil tanker fleet in the world, and can use it. It also controls practically the whole of the Norwegian tanker fleet, the third largest in the world, and it cooperates with the tanker fleet of the U.S.A., the second largest.

What, it may be asked, is the effect upon the oil resources of the Allies of the Japanese conquest, for the time being, of the Far Eastern sources of supply ? The answer is that such temporary reverses would not take one British tank off the battlefield nor one fighter out of the sky. Given the sea routes, the oil resources of the Allies are illimitable. By contrast, Germany is a pauper in oil. She has only the small fleet of Danubian barges, and that river freezes up in winter and has the bottle-neck of the Iron Gates. Germany controls Rumanian oil. But there is no pipe-line to the west, and that is a job not even German engineers could accomplish under three years.

Oliphant, Sir Lancelot, k.c.m.g., c.b. (b. 1881). British Ambassador to Belgium and Minister to Luxemburg from 1939 until the German occupation of those countries. While proceeding from Belgium to France to join the Belgian Government, he was captured by the Germans and was interned in Germany from June 2, 1940, until Sept. 27, 1941, when he was released by an arrangement for the exchange of diplomatic officials. He resumed his duties in London on Oct. 1, 1941.

Oliver, Dame Beryl. Chief of the V.A.D. (Voluntary Aid Detachment). Wife of Admiral of the Fleet Sir Henry Oliver. *See* Women's Services.

Oran, Action at. In the Western Mediterranean the key points of French naval defence were Toulon in France and Bizerta in Tunis, with Ajaccio in Corsica and Oran in Algeria as supporting bases. Oran lies at the head of the Gulf of Oran, about 220 miles east of Gibraltar. It has been in French possession since 1831 and has a population of about 150,000, most of them Europeans.

When the Pétain Government signed the Armistice on June 22, 1940, the greater portion of the Mediterranean fleet was at Oran, and the action fought on July 3 was designed to prevent it being handed over to Germany, in defiance of solemn obligations entered into both by the Reynaud and the Pétain governments. On June 16 Reynaud, then Prime Minister, asked that France should be released from her treaty obligation with Britain not to negotiate a separate peace with Germany. Churchill agreed on condition that the French fleet should be sent to British ports while the armistice was negotiated. When Reynaud resigned, the Pétain Government, then at Bordeaux, was reminded of this condition and gave Britain solemn assurances that under no circumstances would the French warships be handed over to Germany or Italy.

In fact, Article 8 of the Armistice terms made it clear that the French warships were to pass to Germany or Italy fully armed. Immediately Churchill addressed a protest to France and later informed the House of Commons, "with sincere sorrow," that French warships in British and Egyptian ports had been seized and those in the port of Oran had been sunk or damaged by a British battle-squadron under Vice-Admiral Somerville.

The action at Oran took place on July 3, 1940. In the port were two French battleships, two up-to-date battle-cruisers, as well as light cruisers, destroyers, and submarines. Somerville offered the French commander, Admiral Gensoul, conditions which would have prevented the Oran fleet getting into German hands, but they were refused. Somerville, therefore, gave Admiral Gensoul six hours' notice to sink his ships, and, when the notice was disregarded, he attacked. The action was short and sharp. The battle-cruiser Dunkerque (26,000 tons) was badly damaged and had to be beached, while its companion ship, the Strasbourg, was hit by a torpedo and damaged. It was able, however, to slip out of Oran in the night and reached Toulon. A 22,000-ton battleship was sunk in Oran harbour and another battleship of the same tonnage was badly damaged by gunfire and torpedoes. The aircraft-transport vessel, Commandant Teste, of 10,000 tons, was sunk after being set on fire, together with two destroyers and other small craft. The British fleet suffered no material damage in this unhappy affair. Casualties were two wounded and two missing.

The fact that the first naval engagement in the Mediterranean during the Second World War should have been between British and French ships furnished a grim commentary upon the course of events.

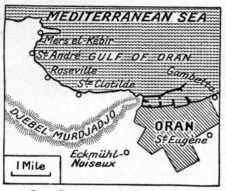

Oran, France's naval base in Algeria.

Historically, Oran was the equivalent of the Battle of Copenhagen, which Nelson fought in order to stop the Danish fleet helping Napoleon. At Alexandria the French and British commanders were able to arrange terms for the internment of the French ships until the end of the war and thus avoid fighting. It was pitiful that Admiral Gensoul at Oran was not equally wise. The officers and men of the Strasbourg, the Dunkerque, and other doomed vessels in Oran harbour were the victims and earned the deep sympathy of their companions in arms. The seamen of the De Gaullist party in particular fully approved of British action at Oran. In 1942 it was understood that the Dunkerque had reached Toulon.

Orbay, HUSSEIN RAUF. He was appointed Turkish Ambassador in London, February 1942, in succession to Dr. Rüstü Aras. M. Orbay was a former Prime Minister of Turkey.

Orbay, GENERAL KIAZIM. Leader of the Turkish Military Mission to London which arrived on Oct. 3, 1939, to discuss matters of common interest between Britain and Turkey.

Orel. After very heavy fighting, which raged for three days, this Russian town, an important railway junction 75 m. S.E. of Bryansk, was evacuated by the Russians on Oct. 7, 1941. The city had changed hands several times during the course of the fighting, and was only abandoned on the arrival of strong enemy reinforcements. Later in October ceaseless Russian counter-attacks led to the weakening of enemy pressure in this sector, and the Germans suffered a heavy defeat, in which they lost much material. At the end of December the Soviet troops advanced in the direction of Orel, which the Germans then used as a supply centre. In January 1942 the Russians attacked heavily, and fighting was reported in the eastern suburbs of Orel.

At the beginning of February the Germans announced that fierce fighting was raging north-east of Orel. Timoshenko's forces reoccupied Trosna, 42 miles south-west of the city, the Red Army making considerable progress in this sector. Late in February the Russians entered the province of Kursk, situated between Orel and Kharkov. There they were held and in June retreated east. *See* Russia.

Orion, H.M.S. This 7,215-ton British cruiser of the Leander class, completed in January 1934, has a complement of 550, carries eight 6-in. guns, and has a speed of 32·5 knots. In the Battle of Cape Matapan (*q.v.*) she acted as a decoy ship. Flying the flag of Vice-Adml. H. D. Pridham-Wippell off the coast of Crete, she made contact with enemy cruisers on the morning of March 28, 1941. The Vice-Admiral, who had with him the cruisers Ajax, Perth and Gloucester, and some destroyers, decided to lure the Italians on until they came within range of Adml. Cunningham's main battle fleet which, 120 miles away to the east, was speeding westwards to meet them. The enemy fell into the trap and gave chase, firing at a range of some 16 miles, but although a number of shells fell close to the Orion she escaped without a scratch. The Orion also helped in the evacuation of troops from Crete in May 1941. *See* Matapan, Battle of.

Orkney Islands. Group of islands off the North of Scotland (*see* p. 3071). At Kirkwall, a town on Pomona, the largest island, a contraband control station was established at the beginning of the war.

A METHOD OF MINESWEEPING

Here we see the use of the Oropesa float. It remains attached to the minesweeper by a wire, and is operated from a safe distance, combing the waters at the required depth.
Photo, Planet News

It was closed in May 1940 owing to the changed situation on the Continent. The Orkneys were attacked on several occasions by German bombers, the first raid taking place in daylight on Oct. 17, 1939. *See* Scapa Flow.

Oropesa Float. This apparatus enables a single ship to sweep mines. It is shaped like a torpedo and streams out at an angle from the ship towing it on a wire cable. The wire is kept down to the required depth by a multiplane kite. Having put out the float with kite line and sweep wire attached, the vessel, herself remaining outside the mined area, can clean up "lanes" in the minefield, rather like a reaper cuts swathes from the side of a cornfield. The name Oropesa was that of a trawler in the war of 1914–18, in which this form of minesweeping was first tried out. *See* Mines and Minelaying.

Orzel. When Hitler invaded Poland in September 1939 the Orzel (which means Eagle), a Polish submarine of 1,110 tons, was trapped in port at Gdynia. The sixty daring men on board declined to surrender, and took her to sea in spite of an attack from the Nazi fleet. On Sept. 15 she put into the neutral port of Tallinn to land her sick captain, and the first lieutenant, Lt.-Comdr. John Grudzinski, took command. The Estonian authorities, fearing unpleasant repercussions from the Nazis who had meanwhile taken over the port of Gdynia, made an attempt to intern her and confiscated her charts, small arms, breech-blocks and most of her torpedoes. Two Estonian guards were mounted, but the crew had planned an escape and at midnight overpowered the guards, cut the mooring ropes and made their way to sea. They were discovered, but, blinded by search-

THE POLISH SUBMARINE ORZEL

This gallant vessel made her way, without charts, guns or torpedoes, out of the Baltic and across the North Sea to offer her services to the British Navy. Her commander, Lt.-Cmdr. John Grudzinski, is seen, right, looking out of the conning-tower.

Photo, Central Press

lights and with bullets spattering round them, they slipped through the harbour entrance.

After this dramatic escape they were hunted incessantly by German warships. They managed, however, to release their Estonian guards near the Swedish coast and watched them row safely to shore. At last their water supply ran dangerously low, and they decided to try to reach England. In spite of lack of charts, constant enemy attacks and damage caused by running ashore five times on shoals and rocks, they threaded the intricate channels from the Baltic to the North Sea. Their wireless apparatus had been damaged, but on Oct. 14 a faint message indicating their position reached a British wireless station. A few hours later a British destroyer found them and led them triumphantly into harbour. The Orzel thereafter joined the Royal Navy, and later sank a German transport carrying troops to Norway. When Gen. Sikorski, the Polish Premier, visited England in November 1939, he conferred decorations on Lt. Grudzinski and all the members of the crew. In June 1940 this gallant ship was presumed lost. Three months later news came that part of her crew had been rescued by the Germans and sent to hospital at Gdynia.

Oslo. The capital of Norway, Oslo (*see* pp. 3074–5) stands at the head of the Oslo Fjord, about 80 miles from the Skagerrak. At daybreak on April 9, 1940, the day of the Nazi invasion of Norway, German warships steamed up the fjord and landed troops in the vicinity of Oslo. At the same time troop-carrying 'planes landed at Fornebu, the airport just outside the city. Other German 'planes roared above the housetops in order to terrorize the populace into surrender and the authorities into inaction. As news reached Oslo of the rapid approach of the Germans, the evacuation of civilians was at once undertaken. People poured out of the city and the Government and the Royal Family removed to Hamar, 80 miles to the north. By four o'clock in the afternoon a small force of approximately 1,500 German troops marched in unopposed and seized the city.

During the German occupation there were several disturbances in Oslo. Many students and lecturers were arrested in October 1940, following anti-German

demonstrations in the University. On Sept. 10, 1941, the Nazis declared a state of emergency in Oslo on the grounds that Trade Unionists had been plotting strikes. Two days later Heydrich (*q.v.*) arrived on a " visit of inspection " and over 1,000 persons were arrested by the Gestapo. So much anger was caused, both in Norway and abroad, by the severity of these measures and by the recent executions that the Germans became alarmed, and on Sept. 16 decided to lift the state of emergency. Later revelations of Gestapo brutality to Norwegians impelled the Free Norwegian Government to issue a statement in March 1942.

Military targets at Oslo were bombed by the R.A.F. on a few occasions. At the end of April 1940 British bombers attacked the German air bases established here, and on Sept. 6, 1941, Flying Fortresses made a daylight raid on the harbour, causing considerable damage. *See* Norway.

Osnabrück. Situated on the R. Hase, 70 miles W. of Hanover, this was one of the first German towns to be bombed by the R.A.F. From June 1940 onwards Osnabrück was frequently attacked in force. The main targets of the British bombers were the railway yards and locomotive sheds, supply depots, industries, and communications, which were all heavily damaged. Supply and ammunition trains were also wrecked.

Osservatore Romano. This Vatican newspaper, the Papal organ, was directed by Count Della Torre, who earned the enmity of the Fascist Press by his unbiased reports of the international situation that were published in it. The Osservatore Romano denounced Nazi aggression and, after the German invasion of the Low Countries in May 1940, wrote : " The total war launched by Germany has clearly revealed itself as a pitiless war of extermination conducted in defiance of the laws of war." When Italy came into the war its independence disappeared, a compliant editor being appointed.

Ostend. Important Belgian port. When the Germans invaded Belgium on May 10, 1940, they bombed the aerodrome at Ostend, and on May 28 their bombers attacked the city again, destroying the American hospital and killing many wounded men. After the Germans occupied Belgium they established a seaplane base here. The large number of barges and other craft assembled at Ostend made it one of the most important of the " invasion " ports, and thus it became the object of particular attention from bombers of the R.A.F. From September 1940 onward the R.A.F. made frequent raids, mostly on the docks. On Feb. 11, 1941, units of the Royal Navy bombarded the harbour at Ostend, causing many fires.

Ostrov. Situated just inside the Soviet frontier from the Latvian border, this Russian town was the centre of fierce fighting in the German thrust to Leningrad. It was captured by the enemy in July 1941.

Ouvry, Lt.-Cmdr. J. G. D., D.S.O. One of the five men who solved the secrets of the magnetic mine, Lt.-Cmdr. Ouvry, of H.M.S. Vernon, Mine and Torpedo School, Portsmouth, received the D.S.O. for his outstanding skill and courage in performing

Lt.-Cmdr. Ouvry, D.S.O., **fought magnetic mines.**
Photo, Topical Press

this hazardous task. In November 1939 he went to Shoeburyness, with four other experts from the school, to examine a magnetic mine that had been dropped on the foreshore six hours previously by a German aircraft. He volunteered to go out by himself and dismantle the mine by moonlight. He left with the party details of the exact parts which he proposed to remove first. Thus, had this mine exploded, those who came after him would have had some clue to guide them in tackling the next one secured. Lt.-Cmdr. Ouvry first removed a fitting which appeared to be the detonator ; then, working all day, the whole party slowly dismantled this perilous machine. At one point they were startled to find yet another detonator. Finally the mine was safe enough for removal to the

Mine Experimental Dept. at Portsmouth, where every secret of its device was revealed. *See* Mines.

 Paasikivi, DR. J. K. At the outbreak of war in September 1939 he was Finnish Ambassador to Sweden, and during the Russo-Finnish discussions in October 1939 —brought about by the U.S.S.R.'s demands for Finnish territory—he headed the Finnish delegation in Moscow. He returned to his country after long but inconclusive talks with Molotov, and the Moscow conferences were resumed on Oct. 21. Russian demands, however, were severe, and at the end of November 1939 the Russo-Finnish war broke out.

WHY JAPAN MADE THE PACIFIC A BATTLEFIELD

Japanese strategy in the Pacific aimed first at capturing the great archipelago of the Dutch Indies. Owing to conditions under which the enemy launched their attack it was inevitable that the situation in the Far East should develop adversely for the Allies in the opening stages.

Pacific, Strategy of. Strategically, the Pacific can be considered as a gigantic triangle, subdivided into three smaller triangles by lines drawn from its centre to the three corners.

If we look at a Mercator projection of the world we can see the apex of the Pacific triangle in the Bering Strait. Its base is half the length of the 60th parallel of South latitude, and its sides are the coast lines of the Asiatic mainland and of North and South America. Just a little to the north and east of the exact geometric centre of the triangle lies Pearl Harbour, the great U.S. naval base in the Hawaiian Islands. Pearl Harbour is the strategic focus of the Pacific war area. Lines drawn from here to the corners of the main triangle—in the Bering Strait, at Cape Horn, and a point in the Indian Ocean south and west of Australia —subdivide the Pacific into its chief strategic zones.

The triangle Bering Strait–Pearl Harbour–Cape Horn may be thought of as the rear, or supply, zone and main defence area for the west coast of the Americas. The triangle Pearl Harbour–Cape Horn–Australia is the forward zone. Within it are to be found most of the advanced bases needed by the Allies for the counter-offensive against Japan. Approximately on the line from Pearl Harbour to the south-western corner of the triangle beyond Australia lie the "stepping stones of the Pacific," the island bases of Wake and Guam, which linked Pearl Harbour with Manila and Singapore, and, with Pearl Harbour, were the first objects of Japanese offensive action.

From the Allied strategic point of view the area bounded by the lines Bering Strait–Pearl Harbour–Australia and the Asiatic coast-line may be called the " Pacific offensive triangle."

THE PACIFIC WAR COUNCIL MEETS IN WASHINGTON

President Roosevelt is seen presiding at the first conference of the Pacific War Council in Washington, April 1, 1942. It was attended by representatives of the seven Pacific Powers. Left to right : Dr. Soong, Chinese Foreign Minister ; Mr. W. Nash, New Zealand Minister ; Dr. H. Evatt, representing Australia ; Lord Halifax, British Ambassador ; Mr. H. Wrong, Counsellor of Canadian Legation ; Dr. Loudon, Netherlands Minister ; and Mr. Harry Hopkins, special assistant to the President.
From a radioed photo, Planet News

Half-way up the long side of that triangle lie the islands of the Japanese archipelago, whose subjugation by starvation, invasion, or air attack is necessarily the final objective of Allied strategy.

The very shape of that triangle, and the central location of the Japanese islands within it, explains more simply than words the chief reasons for the initial Japanese successes. Though, judged by European standards, the Japanese lines of communication to the various strategic points on the boundaries of that triangle are long, they are short compared to the immense distances to the nearest Allied sources of military, naval, and air strength and production in Britain and in the United States.

The whole basis of Pacific strategy must be essentially that of communications and supply, and the bases by which they may be maintained.

Japan's Main Objectives

Japan's initial strategy was, therefore, unconcerned with the occupation of territory or even the capture of raw material resources. These were only secondary considerations. Primarily the Japanese objectives were the bases held by the Allies—Singapore, Manila, Surabaya, Amboina, Guam, Wake, Midway.

Only by capturing these and pushing outwards the two sides of the triangle of Allied and U.S. bases which enclosed them, could the Japanese hope to establish naval and air supremacy within the triangle and to protect the necessary lines of communication.

In this light the progress of events in the early stages of the war in the Pacific becomes clear. The first blow had to be delivered at the key position, at the strategic hinge and pivotal point, Pearl Harbour. At all costs the U.S. Battle Fleet had to be immobilized for long enough to allow the attacks on the bases along the southern edge of the triangle to achieve their purpose.

The first blow was successful. The U.S. Fleet was taken by surprise, and though the damage inflicted upon it by the Japanese carrier-borne bombers and torpedo-planes was probably less serious than was at first thought, it prevented effective interference by the U.S. Fleet in the subsequent Japanese attacks on Wake Island, Guam, the Philippines, and Malaya.

Fanning outward rapidly from their main advanced bases on the island of Formosa and in French Indo-China, the Japanese effected landings on the coasts of Luzon and Malaya, while other expeditions seized strategic points in Sarawak, Borneo, and other islands.

Though in the Philippines a small mixed force of Americans and Filipinos were able to maintain a sturdy resistance in Bataan and Corregidor, Manila itself was lost and its use as a base denied to the Allied naval forces. And when Singapore fell, after only ten weeks, the way was open to the Dutch East Indies.

With the capture of Sumatra and Java, and the consolidation of their positions in Borneo, Celebes, Timor, and elsewhere in the East Indian Archipelago, the Japanese had succeeded, after four months of war, in swinging back the southern base-line of the triangle a thousand miles or more to the northern shores of Australia itself, so that the Allied line of communications now ran from Australia to Hawaii to the west coast of America, with a precarious gap beyond Australia in the Indian Ocean, where Allied shipping routes were menaced by Japanese submarines and raiders operating out of Singapore and Rangoon.

Basis of Allied Strategy

The task of Allied strategy was clearly to reverse the process by which the Japanese achieved their successes, and, pivoting upon Pearl Harbour, to push inwards upon the Japanese islands the two arms of the offensive triangle. To do this, it was necessary not only to hold Australia inviolate, but to convert it into a major advanced base for Allied offensive operations of all kinds.

Pushing forward the northern side of the triangle—the line from Pearl Harbour through the Aleutian Islands to Bering Strait—presents other difficulties, for beyond a certain point its northern end sweeps Russian territory.

However, if Pearl Harbour be held, and the lines of communication maintained from the United States to the advanced bases in Australia and Alaska, with the help of the Chinese it would eventually be possible for the Allies to force the Japanese on to the defensive on all three sides of the triangle, and to close it in gradually until the Japanese Islands are at the Allies' mercy.

HOW WAR FLARED UP IN THE PACIFIC

The Pacific offered immense possibilities for Japanese aggression— the Philippines, Malaya, Borneo and the Netherlands East Indies were obvious targets. By April 1942 the enemy was dominant over a vast expanse of the world's largest ocean. See also Australia ; Borneo ; Japan ; Java ; Netherlands East Indies ; Philippine Is., U.S.A., etc.

Pacific, War in. The war in the Pacific started on Dec. 7, 1941, when, without warning, Japan attacked Pearl Harbour, the American naval base in the Hawaiian Islands, and Manila in the Philippines. One hour after the attack on Pearl Harbour the Japanese Ambassador in Washington delivered to Mr. Cordell Hull, U.S. Secretary of State, a message saying that the establishment of peace in the Pacific and the world was the " cherished desire " of the Japanese Emperor. In the attack on Pearl Harbour, America lost one battleship, the Arizona, and five other warships, with 2,340 killed and 946 wounded (Roosevelt, Feb. 23, 1942). Japanese losses in the action were three submarines (two small) and 41 aircraft.

On the same day the Japanese seized the international settlement at Shanghai, and entered Siam

from Indo-China. Next day they invaded Malaya from Siam, where resistance collapsed immediately and was transformed to assistance ; an attack on Hong Kong began ; an attempt was made to land at Kota Bharu in northern Malaya, and the U.S.A. and Great Britain declared war on Japan.

Immediately on the outbreak of hostilities Admiral Sir Tom Phillips, Commander-in-Chief of the Far East Fleet, put to sea from Singapore with the object of intercepting the Japanese forces attacking northern Malaya and the warships covering them. H.M.S. Prince of Wales (35,000 tons), one of the newest British battleships, and H.M.S. Repulse (32,000 tons), a battle-cruiser built in 1916, were sunk on Dec. 10 by attack from the air. Anti-aircraft fire accounted for seven of the attacking 'planes, but lack of fighter support made the great ships indefensible. 2,330 survivors out of a total of 2,925 reached Singapore, but Admiral Phillips was lost.

HONG KONG. The attack on Hong Kong, begun on Dec. 7, 1941, was intensified on the 11th, and during that night the British forces withdrew from the mainland to the island. A demand for its surrender was made on the 13th, but, buoyed up by hopes of relief from the Chinese forces striking at the Japanese rear and flank in the area, the Governor, Sir Mark Young, held out until Christmas Day, when, the water supply having given out, the island surrendered.

MALAYA. After severe fighting the Japanese secured Kota Bharu aerodrome, and began a relentless push southward down the peninsula. In numbers the invaders greatly exceeded the defenders, and the forests, which had always been regarded as impenetrable,

Singapore, which he later described as " the scene of the greatest disaster to British arms which our history records." The British had lost a naval base that cost something like £60,000,000 to construct and, like the Maginot Line, never came fully into action. All the dock installations, and the oil stored in the island— enough to fill Japan's wartime needs for three months— were destroyed. The Japanese claimed the capture of 15,000 British, 13,000 Australian and 32,000 Indian troops, a probable figure, for Mr. Churchill said that we had managed to reinforce Singapore by more than 40,000 men, together with large quantities of A.A. and anti-tank artillery, all withdrawn from other areas where they were sorely needed—nine convoys in all.

PHILIPPINES. Manila on Luzon in the Philippines (U.S.), bombed on Dec. 7, was bombed again on the 9th. Despite the sinking of the 29,000-ton Japanese battleship Haruna off the north coast of Luzon on the 11th, landings were effected near Aparri, and parachutists seized an airport 80 miles to the south. On the 12th landings were made in the extreme south of the island. At least 40 enemy aircraft were destroyed over the Philippines on the 14th, on which day submarines of the Netherlands East Indies naval forces sank four laden troopships, one cargo boat and a tanker, and U.S. aircraft sank four enemy troopships. On the 22nd a third invading force, armed with tanks, began to land at Lingayen on the east of Luzon. Davao, on the island of Mindanao, 600 miles from Manila, was occupied. Manila, declared an open city on the 26th, was savagely bombed on the 27th and 28th. By the 30th it was estimated that 200,000 Japanese troops had landed in the Philippines.

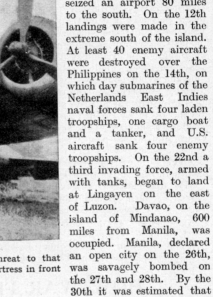

READY FOR THE JAPANESE AGGRESSOR
America sent powerful reinforcements to Australia as the Japanese threat to that continent increased. Here are members of a U.S. Army Air Corps Flying Fortress in front of their four-engined bomber at an Australian airfield.
Photo, Planet News

seemed to offer little hindrance. The British evacuated the State of Kedah on Dec. 18, and on the 19th all Europeans were evacuated from Penang, where the Prai power station and the tin-smelting works had already been destroyed. The British continued a fighting withdrawal southwards, keeping their forces substantially intact. Ipoh, capital of Perak and centre of the tin industry in Malaya, was evacuated on Dec. 29.

The Japanese occupied Kuala Lumpur, capital of Selangor, heart of the rubber-growing region, on Jan. 12, 1942. By the 19th Japanese troops were filtering down the peninsula and were also landing on the S.W. coast near Batu Pahat.

SINGAPORE. On Jan. 30 the enemy was approaching Kulai, 18 miles from Singapore Island. Raids on Singapore city, which had no shelters, were already frequent. Next day the British forces withdrew to the island, and the causeway was breached. The siege began on Feb. 1. On the 8th the Japanese landed on the north-west of Singapore Island itself.

On Feb. 15 Mr. Churchill announced the fall of

The new year opened with the fall of Manila, and on Jan. 4, 1942, Gen. MacArthur, commanding the U.S. and Philippine military forces, withdrew to the Bataan Peninsula, where he conducted an heroic and masterly defence. After General MacArthur's departure to Australia (*see below*) the gallant defence of Bataan was taken over by Maj.-Gen. Jonathan Wainwright, who held out until April 8, when, after a final ten days of intense and continuous assault by land, sea, and air, the exhausted defenders gave in. Some 35,000 military and 25,000 civilian prisoners were captured. Gen. Wainwright himself, some thousands of troops, and all the Army nurses on the peninsula, rowed or swam across to the island fortress of Corregidor, which, though repeatedly bombed, continued to hold out. A week after the fall of Bataan 13 American bombers based on Australia caused great destruction to Japanese bases in the Philippines, and brought off 44 passengers who had escaped from Corregidor.

BURMA. While the Japanese were overrunning Malaya, they were also making some headway in

Burma. In face of air attack a small British garrison withdrew from Port Victoria on Dec. 18, 1941. Tavoy, a port and tin centre in lower Burma, was lost on Jan. 19, 1942; and Moulmein was evacuated on Jan. 31. But in Burma the Japanese did not have it quite all their own way in the air. Between Dec. 23, when Rangoon was raided for the first time, and Jan. 30, 110 enemy aircraft certainly, and another 50 probably, were shot down in battles over and around Rangoon. Another 50 were destroyed over Rangoon on Feb. 25 and 26. By cutting the road to Prome in the defenders' rear, however, the Japanese forced the evacuation of Rangoon on March 7, thus closing the seaport end of the Burma road.

Chinese forces, first reported in Burma on Jan. 3, were now described as "pouring in," and heavy fighting near and in Toungoo began on March 18. Unfortunately the Allies lost command of the air, and the British were forced northwards along the Irrawaddy, the Chinese along the Sittang. The oilfields at Yenangyaung were destroyed on April 17. Japanese hordes (numbering at least 100,000 and repeatedly reinforced) continued their prong-like thrust northwards, with the aim of separating British and Chinese forces. On April 26 they captured Taunggyi, capital of the Shan States, and three days later were in Lashio, key town of the Burma Road and linked by rail also with Mandalay. Their troops then began to converge on Mandalay.

The Andaman Islands, in the Bay of Bengal, abandoned by the British a few days before, were occupied by the Japanese on March 23. At the beginning of April American Flying Fortresses attacked Japanese shipping in Port Blair, and in an R.A.F. raid on the same place reported on April 15 thirteen Japanese flying boats were destroyed or damaged.

The Japanese lost 27 aircraft in their first air attack on Ceylon on April 5, another 21 in a second attack a few days later. The Indian mainland was attacked for the first time on April 6, when the ports of Vizagapatam and Cocanada were raided from the air. April 10 brought news of the loss of two British cruisers, the Dorsetshire and the Cornwallis, in an engagement off Ceylon against superior Japanese forces. Next day it was learned that the aircraft carrier Hermes had also been lost.

BORNEO. The first enemy landings on Borneo were made at Miri and Lubon in Sarawak on Dec. 17. British troops were withdrawn from Sarawak after the complete destruction of all installations in the oilfields. On Jan. 3 the enemy landed at Weston in British North Borneo. Parachutists were dropped in north Celebes on the night of Jan. 10–11. Tarakan, off Dutch Borneo, attacked by overwhelming numbers of seaborne troops and parachutists, surrendered on Jan. 13. In anticipation of attack, Balik Papan, the biggest oil centre in Dutch Borneo, was destroyed on Jan. 22.

On Jan. 23 began a five-day sea and air battle in the Macassar Straits (between Borneo and Celebes) in which nine enemy transports were sunk and others set on fire; five or six bomb hits were scored on cruisers; an American submarine claimed a large cruiser or aircraft carrier. On Jan. 30 U.S. aircraft sank two more transports in the Macassar Straits, and probably a third.

NETHERLANDS EAST INDIES. Amboina, Dutch naval base in the Moluccas, raided for the first time on Jan. 7, was mainly in enemy hands by Feb. 8, after bitter fighting in which a Japanese cruiser was sunk, and another cruiser and a transport were hit.

Parachutists landed in the island of Sumatra (Netherlands East Indies) on Dec. 28, 1941, at a point opposite Perak (Malaya). On Feb. 3, 1942, Surabaya and other places in Java were raided. Batavia (Java),

DEFENDER OF CORREGIDOR AT CANBERRA
General MacArthur, Supreme Allied C.-in-C. in the S.W. Pacific, arrived in Australia on March 17, 1942. At Canberra he attended a sitting of the House of Representatives, and subsequently conferred with members of the Australian War Council. He is seen with Mr. Curtin, Australian Premier, during an important discussion.
Radio photo, Associated Press

capital of the Netherlands East Indies, had its first air attack on Feb. 9. On Feb. 14 some 700 parachutists were dropped at Palembang (south Sumatra), one of the world's most important oil centres and the main supply centre for the allied navies. Next day large-scale landings began, but the vital oil installations at Palombang had been destroyed. Of a great fleet sent to conquer Bali, a small island one mile from the east end of Java, 19 warships and transports were destroyed on Feb. 20 and only one ship escaped undamaged. But part of Bali, including the only good aerodrome at Den Pasar, was overrun. A week later the Japanese landed at three places on the north coast of Java, occupying a large area of the Indramaya district. In an engagement on Feb. 27 against much superior enemy forces, which included about 20 warships, 17 Japanese transports were hit, at least one being sunk; 2 cruisers were sunk or put out of action; 1 warship was blown up; 5 other cruisers were damaged, and 5 destroyers put out of action. The enemy fleet retreated to the north. But on March 2 a new invasion fleet appeared off Java. In these battles of the Java Sea 12 allied ships were lost and one had to be beached. Without even the most primitive port, and with no tackle but that of their ships, the Japanese landed in Java an army estimated at 100,000 strong. On March 2 industrial plant at Batavia was destroyed by the Dutch ; so was the great naval base at Surabaya.

During the early part of January the headquarters of the Unified Allied Command in the south-west Pacific, under General Wavell, had been established in Java. The loss of Malaya and the entry of the Japanese into Sumatra separated the Netherlands East Indies from Burma, and on March 2 command of the allied troops in the Netherlands East Indies passed to Lieut.-Gen. H. ter Poorten, commander-in-chief of the Dutch forces, General Wavell returning to India.

On March 7 the Dutch asked for an armistice in the region of Bandoeng, the emergency capital. But fierce resistance in Java, Sumatra, Borneo, and other islands of the Netherlands East Indies continued to be reported. The Japanese claimed the fall of Medan, capital of Sumatra, on March 13.

AUSTRALIA. On March 17 Gen. MacArthur arrived in Australia, to take over, at the request of the Commonwealth of Australia, supreme command in the south-west Pacific. It was revealed that for two months U.S. army units, ground and air, together with supplies, had been arriving in Australia.

Australia Comes Under Fire

A direct threat to Australia began when the Japanese occupied Rabaul (Solomon Islands) on Jan. 23. The first of many heavy raids on Port Moresby, New Guinea, was made on Feb. 3. On March 8 the Japanese landed at Lae and Salamaua, in British New Guinea. A Japanese convoy was heavily attacked by U.S. and Australian "land based forces" off New Guinea on March 18, when two heavy cruisers and five transports were sunk, a total of 23 ships being sunk or damaged. The first bombs fell on the Australian mainland when Darwin was attacked on Feb. 19. Air attacks on Darwin continued. Broome and Wyndham were raided on March 3 ; Thursday Island, off Cape York, on March 14 ; Katherine, 200 miles south of Darwin, on March 22. In late March floods drove the Japanese out of Markham Valley, along which they were penetrating from Lae towards Port Moresby ; but they continued to raid Port Moresby from the air. Meanwhile, U.S. and Australian air units kept up attacks on the Japanese-occupied bases of Lae, Rabaul, and Kupang (Dutch Timor).

The U.S. navy carried out surprise attacks on Japanese bases in the Marshall and Gilbert Islands on Feb. 1, and, towards the end of March, on Wake and Marcus Islands.

General Wavell, summing up the campaign in the Pacific to the middle of March, said that in Java we lost a race against time "by some four or five weeks. The Japanese moved quicker than we had hoped, and our reinforcements were rather later than expected." He asked that judgement should be suspended, pointing out that the allies were not ready for war in the Far East, where readiness would have been possible only "by taking forces from places which were more immediately threatened, like the Middle East Command and Great Britain herself, or by withholding from Russia those supplies which enabled her to stage her great recovery. . . . Our enemy

made the most detailed preparations . . . But undoubtedly from the Dutch East Indies we did strike the enemy some heavy blows on sea, land, and in the air."

On April 1 the Pacific War Council met at Washington for the first time. This consultative body included representatives of the Pacific Powers : Great Britain, U.S.A., Canada, Australia, New Zealand, Netherlands and China. "We are getting pretty near to the stage of an offensive," declared Mr. Stimson, United States Secretary for War, on April 17 ; and next day the world was thrilled to learn that Tokyo, Nagoya, Kobe, and Osaka, four of the most important towns of Japan itself, had been raided from the air.

The Japanese Navy had carried out most of its early moves in the Pacific in defiance of all accepted theories of strategy and had escaped very lightly, but in May and June 1942 the pendulum swung. On May 4 a big fleet of transports, covered by aircraft carriers, cruisers and light craft, apparently working towards Australia, was intercepted by the Americans in the Coral Sea and scattered with heavy loss, the operation being at least seriously delayed. The action was noteworthy for the dashing use of aircraft from carriers and shore. Most of the fighting fell to them and they had a major part in sinking the Japanese carrier Ryukaru and, almost certainly, four cruisers, two destroyers and eight of the transports and supply ships. The speed and confusion of a modern air battle makes it very difficult to observe exact results. The Americans had the big carrier Lexington set on fire so that she had to be sunk ; the destroyer Sims and the tanker Neosho were sunk.

Undeterred by their losses the Japanese, on June 4, launched an attack on Midway Island, the U.S. outpost 1,300 miles from Honolulu. A force of four aircraft carriers supported by battleships, cruisers and destroyers was overwhelmingly defeated, after three days of ineffective assaults, solely by American air power, without a ship's gun being fired. The opposing fleets were never within 200 miles of each other. The Battle of Midway Island cost the Japanese four carriers sunk, two big cruisers sunk and three others damaged, three battleships heavily damaged and ten other warships sunk or damaged (not included in table). About 275 Japanese aircraft and 4,800 naval personnel were lost. This complete victory finally removed the threat of invasion from Hawaii. U.S. Navy losses were the carrier Yorktown which was bombed and torpedoed, and a destroyer, the Hammann which was torpedoed in the last hours of the battle on June 6. (See also separate countries and islands, as Australia, Borneo, Java, Netherlands East Indies, U.S.A., etc.)

Consult : The Fight for the Pacific. Mark Gayn (Lane).

Japanese & U.S.A. Losses in the Pacific
Dec. 7, 1941–June, 1942

	Sunk		Prob. Sunk	Damaged		Total Hit	
	Japan	U.S.	Japan	Japan	U.S.	Japan	U.S.
Battleships ..	1	1	—	5	1	6	2
Cruisers ..	15	1	5	33	2	53	3
Aircraft Carriers	6	1	2	4	1	12	3
Destroyers ..	19	10	6	13	4	38	14
Transports ..	25	—	4	11	—	40	—
Auxiliaries ..	46	15	10	24	1	80	16
Submarines ..	7	3	—	1	—	8	3
Totals	119	31	27	91	9	237	41

Based on figures issued by U.S.A. Navy and War Departments

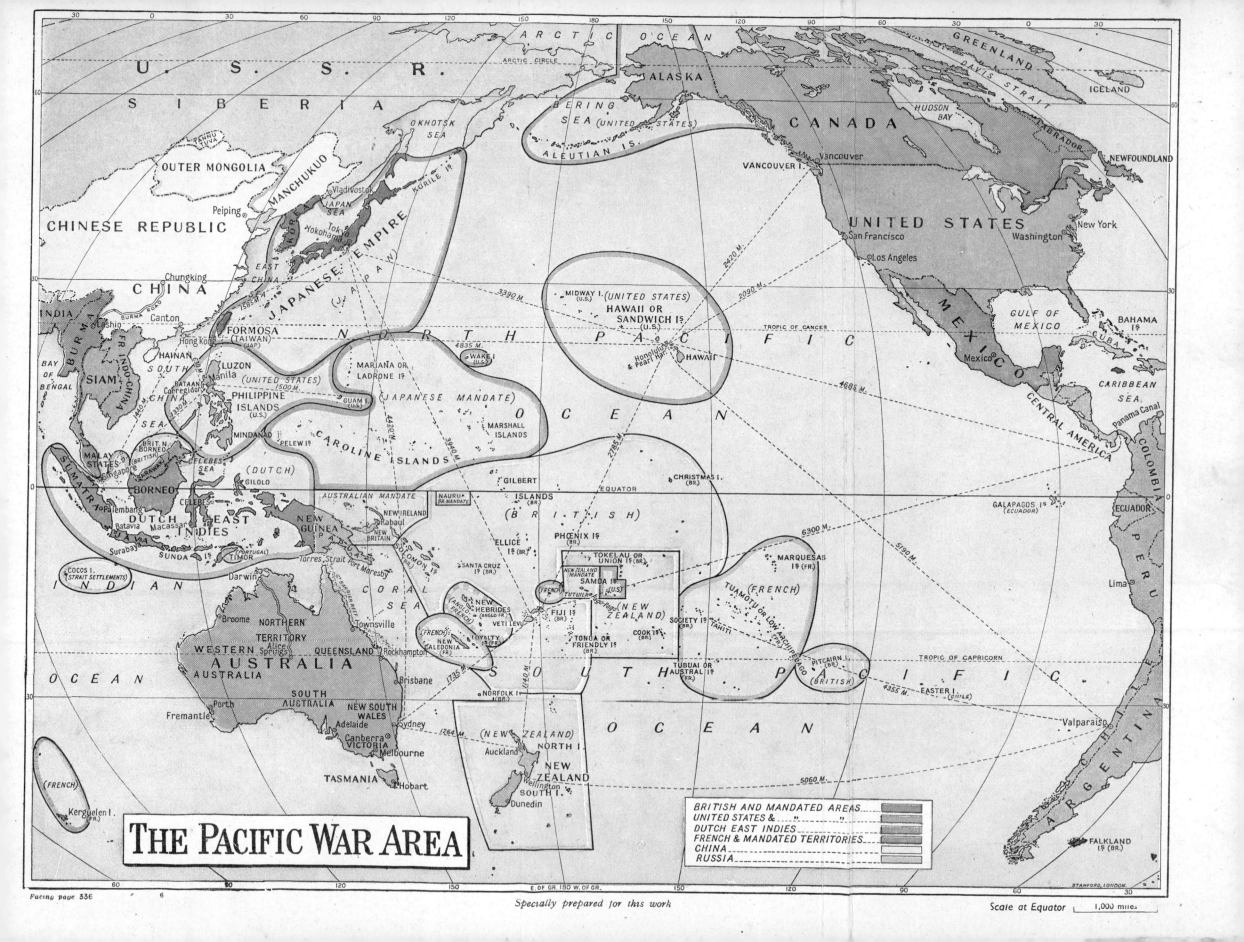

THE PACIFIC WAR AREA

| BRITISH AND MANDATED AREAS |
| UNITED STATES & " " |
| DUTCH EAST INDIES |
| FRENCH & MANDATED TERRITORIES |
| CHINA |
| RUSSIA |

Scale at Equator ___ 1,000 miles

Specially prepared for this work

STANFORD, LONDON.

E. OF GR. 180 W. OF GR.

Sir Earle Page, Australian representative in London.

Page, RT. HON. SIR EARLE, C.H., P.C., G.C.M.G. (b. 1880). Australian representative in London from September 1941 to May 1942, his function being to establish personal Cabinet liaison between the British and Commonwealth Governments. He was succeeded on June 4, 1942, by Mr. S. M. Bruce (*see* p. 32 of this volume), who had represented Australia in London since 1933. Sir Earle Page was Minister of Commerce in the Australian Government when the Prime Minister, Mr. Lyons, died suddenly in April 1939. At the request of Lord Gowrie he then acted as Premier of a temporary administration until the United Australian Party chose a new leader (Mr. Menzies) on April 24.

Paget, LT.-GEN. SIR BERNARD CHARLES TOLVER, K.C.B., D.S.O. (b. 1888). He succeeded Gen. Sir Alan Brooke as C.-in-C. Home Forces on Nov. 18, 1941. During the fighting in Norway between the Germans

Lt.-Gen. Paget, C.-in-C. Home Forces. *Photo, British Official*

and the Allied forces in April 1940 he was in command of the British land forces in the Trondheim-Aandalsnes area. It was largely due to his determination and the skilful dispositions of his troops that the whole of the British forces in the area were enabled to withdraw from Aandalsnes at the end of April. On June 5, 1941, it was announced that he had been appointed C.-in-C. of the South-Eastern Command. Later, as C.-in-C. Home Forces, General Paget introduced new realistic methods into Army training. Live ammunition instead of blank was used for sham battles, mines were exploded, and the noise and smell of real warfare was reproduced. He also founded G.H.Q. Battle School, where specialists from every combatant branch of the Army assembled to cooperate.

Mohammed Pahlevi, Shah of Persia. *Photo, E.N.A.*

Pahlevi, MOHAMMED RIZA KHAN. When Crown Prince of Persia he married Princess Fawzieh, a sister of King Farouk of Egypt, in 1939. He became Shah of Persia on Sept. 16, 1941, on the abdication of his father, Riza Khan Pahlevi (*q.v.*). It was declared that the new Shah would "carry out his duties according to the law of the Constitution," and on Sept. 17 it was formally announced that Mohammed Riza Khan would reign as a constitutional monarch.

Pahlevi, RIZA KHAN. He served as a private soldier in the Persian Cossack Brigade as a young man, and became C.-in-C. of the Army in 1921. Minister of War and Prime Minister, he

Riza Khan Pahlevi, ex-Shah of Persia. *Photo, E.N.A.*

took control of Persia in 1923. The Shah, Sultan Ahmad, was dethroned in 1925, and a provisional Government, headed by Riza Khan, was set up. The following year he was crowned Shah of Persia. During the early years of his reign a centralized administration was evolved and Persian industry and communications were greatly improved. Though outwardly subscribing to constitutional methods, the Shah exercised complete and despotic control over the affairs of the country and imposed heavy taxation.

After the Nazi menace declared itself in the Middle East he adopted a vacillating attitude and, in spite of repeated warnings from the Allies, he was unable to control the German infiltrations into Persia. His War Minister, who urged collaboration with Britain and Russia, received scant consideration and was imprisoned. Riza Khan abdicated on Sept. 16, 1941, following insistent demands for internal reforms and the subsequent entry of British and Soviet troops into Persia. He was succeeded by his son, the Crown Prince Mohammed Riza Khan (*q.v.*).

Riza Khan left Teheran for Ispahan, and on Sept. 21 it was announced that his estates had been transferred to the State; these consisted of immense private properties acquired by him during his reign. He arrived on Oct. 18, 1941, in Mauritius, where, owing to the war situation, it was considered desirable he should remain temporarily. On March 4, 1942, it was reported that he had been granted permission by the Canadian Government to live in Canada with his family. *See* Persia.

Palembang. Situated on the south-east coast of Sumatra, and one of the world's most important oil centres, Palembang was first attacked by the Japanese on Feb. 14, 1942, when some 700 parachutists were dropped from the air. The next day large-scale operations began from the sea. It was supposed that these forces made their thrust from Pontianak in Dutch West Borneo, where enemy concentrations had been reported some days previously. Dutch, British and American bombers and fighters attacked the invading enemy warships and transports in the Banka Strait, scoring direct hits on two cruisers and five transports, and also setting one of the cruisers on fire. Fierce fighting raged around Palembang, and the Japanese suffered heavy losses, a great number of the parachutists being mopped up. But on Feb. 16 the enemy captured the place, although he was robbed of his rich prize, the wells and refineries—which produced 4,200,000 tons of oil a year—having been blown up. Fighting continued in the area for some days. *See* Java; Netherlands East Indies; Sumatra.

Palestine. After the outbreak of war in September 1939 Palestine (*see* pp. 3105–3108) at once declared her loyalty to Britain. Arabs and Zionists composed their differences and offered their services to Britain, since they realized that the latter was ready to defend them against Hitler. The Palestine troubles, carefully fomented by emissaries of the Axis Powers, disappeared, and members of the Palestine Labour Corps, consisting of Jews and Arabs, fought with the B.E.F. in France in May 1940. The country was placed on a war footing on June 23, 1940, with the publication of a decree empowering the High Commissioner to mobilize its entire resources in manpower and property. Coastal defences were permanently manned, fifth column activities vigorously cleaned up and a black-out imposed in Jerusalem. Strategic centres in Palestine were the scene of great activity in June 1941, when British and Free French forces launched their drive upon Syria. Allied troops entered Syria from Palestine on June 8. Haifa (*q.v.*), Acre and Tel Aviv were raided by Vichy French and German 'planes, but little damage was done.

After his expulsion from Palestine in 1937, Haj el Hussein, the former Grand Mufti of Jerusalem, continued to try to stir up anti-British feeling among the Arabs. He lived in Syria until his surreptitious arrival in Baghdad on Oct. 16, 1939, and proceeded to rally about him leaders of the Pan-Arab movement. Hitler used this movement as a propaganda weapon against Britain in the Middle East. After the collapse of the Iraqi revolt in May 1941 he fled to Persia, which in turn he left after the Anglo-Russian occupation in August of that year. By this time the prestige he once enjoyed in the Arab world had greatly diminished, for all were convinced that he had sold himself to the Axis. This was borne out by his arrival in Rome from Albania on Oct. 27, 1941, and his departure a week later for Berlin. It was said he and Rashid Ali, the unsuccessful Iraqi rebel leader, were planning to set up an Arab government in Tripolis as soon as the Axis started an attack on the Middle East. *See* Iraq ; Syria ; Transjordania.

Palmyra (Tadmor). Situated 150 miles N.E. of Damascus in the Syrian desert, Palmyra (*see* p. 3111) is an important point on the oil pipe-line which runs from the oil fields of Iraq to Tripolis. The aerodrome was extensively used by the Germans and was bombed by the R.A.F. in May 1941. During the Syrian campaign in June 1941 the Allied forces advancing from Iraq reached Palmyra and there encountered stiff resistance from a Vichy column. Saba Biyar, some 60 miles S.W. of Palmyra, was captured by the British by June 28, and though the garrison at Palmyra still held out, they were finally encircled and surrendered on July 3, 1941. *See* Syria.

Panama Canal. The tolls of the Panama Canal (*see* pp. 3112–3121) during the financial year ending June 30, 1940, were reduced by over two million dollars, and cargo handled by 567,611 tons, as a result of the war. The decline of shipping under European flags was offset by a rise in American tonnage. No German ships used the canal after the outbreak of war, and on Italy's entry into the conflict in June 1940 Italian shipping was also stopped. America spent large sums in improvements in the Panama Canal Zone after the outbreak of war in 1939. A third set of locks was planned, large enough for the biggest ships, a new air base at Rio Hato, Panama, a new A.A. post on Gatun Lake, and barracks to be enlarged for a garrison of 25,000.

Papagos, GEN. ALEXANDER. On the outbreak of the Italo-Greek conflict in October 1940 he became C.-in-C. of the Greek Army, having been responsible for reorganizing that army into a splendid fighting force which routed the Italian armies. On March 16, 1941, it was announced that he had received the Grand Cross of the British Empire from King George VI for his distinguished leadership. He resigned when the Hellenic Government removed to Crete on April 23, 1941, and was subsequently arrested by the quisling Tsolakoglu regime after they had signed an armistice with the Germans. *See* Greece.

General Papagos,
Greek C.-in-C.
Photo, British Official

Franz von Papen,
German Ambassador
to Turkey.
Photo, Topical Press

Papen, FRANZ VON (b. 1879). German Ambassador to Turkey. As Nazi Minister in Vienna in 1938, he helped to pave the way for the Anschluss. On April 18, 1939, he was appointed Ambassador to Turkey, and three weeks after his arrival in the Turkish capital the Anglo-Turkish agreement was announced. This pact of mutual aid between Turkey and Britain was strengthened and enlarged by the Anglo-French-Turkish pact (*q.v.*) in October 1939. Both agreements caused serious misgivings in Berlin. It was said that von Papen was not a favourite with Hitler, and he made repeated journeys between Ankara and the German capital, having been " recalled " several times by the irritated 'Fuehrer ; his position was a curious one, half veiled by mists of propaganda of which he was himself a master.

An insidious propaganda campaign was launched by Germany in November 1939, and at the same time von Papen strove to obtain concessions from the Turkish Government. These efforts bore fruit, for on Jan. 24, 1940, it was announced that Turkey had concluded an agreement with Germany providing for an exchange of goods. Trade agreements were also concluded between Turkey, Germany and Britain, that of the British being signed on Sept. 29, 1941. The Turko-German agreement was concluded on October 9 by Sarajoglu, Turkish Foreign Minister, von Papen and Dr. Clodius (*q.v.*), head of the German trade delegation. When walking with his wife in an Ankara street on Feb. 25, 1942, von Papen narrowly escaped being blown to pieces by a bomb which exploded close by. Both he and his wife were unhurt. Following a police investigation, it was stated on March 8 that the outrage was directed against von Papen, and was the result of a conspiracy among persons of " Communist leanings." He was active throughout the early months of 1942 furthering Nazi intrigues in the Balkans in preparation for the heralded "spring offensive."

Badge of British Parachute Troops.

Parachute Troops. Reports that Soviet Russia was training parachute jumpers (*see* illus. p. 3131) as an arm of offence reached Western Europe some time before the Second World War started in September 1939, but these reports were not taken very seriously until Russia actually used parachute troops in her war against Finland at the end of 1939. On the same day that hostilities started Russian troops thought to have been dropped by parachute were fighting near Petsamo. Other parachutists landed during the next few days at Petchenga, and at Vitmannstrand on the Karelian Isthmus, the latter equipped with machine-guns. Some 200 Russian soldiers, believed to have been parachuted from six big Soviet aeroplanes, " appeared from nowhere " near the village of Salmijärvi.

The precise objectives of these Russian parachutists, and their success or failure in achieving them, have not so far been authoritatively stated. But the

READY TO EMBARK FOR FLIGHT

British paratroops wear jackets cut close to the hips and trousers strapped round the ankles, crash helmets (to which they will finally add goggles) and very thick-soled boots. Part of their equipment is dropped with them ; the heavier part is dropped by accompanying parachutes.

Photo, "Daily Mirror"

Germans had clearly been impressed by the value of parachute troops in attack, especially against an unprepared foe, for German parachutists took a prominent part in the invasion of Norway. On April 16, 1940, fifty landed near Dombaas, an important junction, but were reported to have been destroyed by the Norwegians. Another group taken prisoner was equipped with bicycles, cameras, a wireless transmitter, welding instruments, and food for

GERMAN PARATROOPS MAN THEIR GUN

This photograph, taken during army manoeuvres in Germany, shows parachute troops who have just landed and set up a machine-gun post, to safeguard the landing of further troops. Parachutists played an important part in the German aggressive campaigns.

two days, including a special ration of sugar. A third group was well equipped with automatic weapons. Obviously, some of these German parachutist were intended to act as spies, others to fight. Three weeks later a considerable body of parachute troops landed near Narvik with the object of attacking the main Norwegian force in the rear, and this contingent was continually reinforced during the Norwegian campaign.

Germany attacked the Netherlands early on May 10, 1940, and within a few hours parachutists were dropped

A TRAINEE MAKES THE DROP

Here we see the parachutist suspended by his belting and guiding his parachute earthwards in a perfect descent, during a training course with the Polish Army stationed in Scotland. Parachutes are made of very strong oiled silk.

Photo, by courtesy of the Polish Ministry of Information

at a number of points well inside the country. Many were destroyed immediately, but others escaped to act as spies and saboteurs. After the capitulation of the Dutch army on May 15 Hitler in an order of the day paid tribute to the courage of his troops, " particularly the heroism of the death-defying parachutists." In France, parachute troops armed with incendiary equipment and explosives appear to have taken a leading part in the German attack launched north of the Somme on May 20. Immediately on landing they made for road junctions, police stations, and telephone exchanges.

A year later, to the day, the German onslaught on Crete began with an airborne attack, troops being

in Celebes on the night of Jan. 10-11, and contributed to the fall of Tarakan off Dutch Borneo on Jan. 13. Twice—the first time in December 1941, the second in February 1942—Japanese parachutists were dropped in Sumatra. But parachutists do not appear to have been a decisive factor in Japan's advance.

The world first learned that Great Britain had parachute troops when, in the middle of February 1941, it was announced that British parachutists had landed in a lonely part of Calabria in southern Italy. According to Italian official statements, all were captured before they could carry out their aims. A German spokesman commented, "This imitation of German methods is one of the worst examples of stealing ideas in war." Five months later a picked body of

landed by gliders, parachutes, and troop carriers. Early reports, quoted by Mr. Churchill in the House of Commons, stated that the German parachutists landed in New Zealand battledress. This statement was afterwards corrected, with the explanation that the German airborne troops had captured a hospital and forced New Zealand walking wounded to precede them as they advanced. Next day German parachutists were reported to be landing "in swarms," baling out with tommy guns in sparsely populated districts, and it is certain that they contributed largely to Germany's success in occupying Crete.

Germany invaded Russia on June 22, 1941, and three days later a Russian official announcement stated that the invaders were landing groups of five to ten parachutists in the uniform of Soviet militiamen, and that "extermination battalions" had been formed in the rear of the Russian forces to destroy them. Two months later a Soviet report stated that a large body of German parachutists with three whippet tanks had landed in the vicinity of an unnamed bridge, but that Red Army troops and a Soviet extermination battalion had wiped the whole party out. Twenty light tanks were also reported to have been landed near a Ukrainian town.

Japan started war with the United States of America and Great Britain on Dec. 7, 1941, and six days later she landed parachutists in Luzon. They were landed

PARATROOPS TAKE TO THE AIR

Top left, a mass descent of Soviet paratroops during manoeuvres. In Soviet Russia, earlier than elsewhere, parachute flights were enthusiastically adopted, not only by the Red Army but by the civilian population. Below, American parachute troops are seen entering a transport 'plane for mass jumping at Fort Benning. These 'planes carry twelve men apiece.

Photos, Planet News; Keystone

British parachute troops gave a demonstration before Canadian ministers and soldiers in England. On the night of Feb. 27–28, 1942, British parachutists went into action again: they landed at Bruneval (*q.v.*), on the northern French coast, and destroyed an important radiolocation station. Paratroops also played a vital part in the combined British raid on St. Nazaire (*q.v.*) on March 28. *See* Commandos.

Paris Under the Nazis.

Except for a black-out — less stringent than London's —and fairly frequent short alerts due to the visits of German reconnaissance 'planes, Paris did not greatly change her peacetime aspect during the first eight months of the war. So little did she sense the approach of disaster that as late as May 10, 1940, when the Low Countries were invaded, arrangements for the Paris Fair were still going forward. A week later Paris was included in the army zone. Everybody wishing to leave the city had to be provided with a special pass, and officials of the broadcasting services were authorized to carry firearms. Hordes of refugees, fleeing before the advancing Germans, poured into the city and passed on. Hundreds of Parisians joined them in the flight south, and before long German families evacuated from the Ruhr and the Rhineland to escape British air raids were put into their abandoned apartments.

NAZIS TROOPS AS SIGHTSEERS IN PARIS
In Occupied Paris German troops went the rounds as tourists. In Montmartre they would visit the beautiful Cathedral of Sacré Coeur and eat *chez* Mère Cathérine, the open-air restaurant seen on the right. They despoiled the shops for souvenirs, which they bought with worthless paper money.
Photo, Planet News

On June 3 Paris had her first and only German air raid. It lasted about 50 minutes. Casualties were 254 killed, 652 injured. Eighty-three bombs fell on the city, 997 on the western outskirts. A number of fires were started, and five schools were hit. The battle drew nearer, and eleven days later the Military Governor, General Hering, declared Paris an open town to save it from destruction. The French army retired south of the city and the Germans marched in. Two days later the French army stopped fighting —and thenceforth France had to be included in the British blockade.

Paris a Month Later

According to an American observer, the city was " almost normal " in appearance at the beginning of July 1940, except for the ubiquitous German soldiers. Many of the small shops were shuttered, and food was scarce, but street vendors of fruit, vegetables, and flowers were about again, children were sailing their boats in the Luxembourg Gardens, and the Punch and Judy shows had reopened. So had the Museums, and there was talk of reopening the Opéra. But the Métro was the only means of transport. Tramcars, omnibuses, and all petrol-driven vehicles were prohibited. Many bicycles appeared on the streets, and a former French champion cyclist, Dominique Lamberzac, was seen riding a tricycle dating from 1890. Another American observer described the behaviour of the Germans as " correct but arrogant."

The German Military Governor imposed a curfew from the outset, at first beginning at 10 p.m., extended on July 9 to 11 p.m. Many of the Paris factories had been blown up or otherwise deliberately damaged in face of the German advance. Some were hastily put in order again, and German specialists were introduced to get them re-started. But unemployment rose steadily, and by the end of the year industry was almost at a standstill. Even the large stores were beginning to put up their shutters : as stocks were exhausted, they could not be replaced. Many clerks and shop assistants joined the growing body of unemployed. So bitter was the workers' plight that some accepted the conquerors' invitation to go and look for work in Germany.

Conditions Worsen, Resistance Stiffens

The food and fuel situation grew steadily worse. By January 1941 bread, though not in short supply, was very dark. Eggs were scarcely to be found, meat was very unequally distributed, vegetables non-existent, and butter scarce. There was no coal, and for fuel the Parisians uprooted trees in the parks and public gardens. By August 1941 poor families were on the verge of famine. Tea, coffee, chocolate, oil, soap, rice, and all confitures were unobtainable, and a black market sent prices soaring. The large hotels had been requisitioned by the Germans, and many cinemas, restaurants, and theatres had been taken over exclusively for German use. All the famous restaurants had fallen on evil days, except Maxim's, which had been taken over by the Restaurant Hoerscher of Berlin. In February 1942 it was reported that the dearth of foodstuffs in Paris was very great, the markets sometimes being virtually empty. All bed linen and mattresses had been requisitioned by the German authorities.

As conditions worsened, French resistance stiffened. Factory workers adopted go-slow tactics. Walls were covered overnight with Vs and Lorraine crosses. The Métro was inscribed with such phrases as " Mort à Hitler " and " A bas Darlan." German attempts to win the friendship of the Parisians met with less and less success. The French did what they could to snub the Germans, the Parisians' proverbial wit proving an effective weapon. The feeling against Britain began to grow less, and it was said that there were two parties —the Anglophiles who prayed that " Les Anglais " might win, and the Anglophobes who prayed that

THE TRAGEDY OF PEARL HARBOUR UNITES A MIGHTY NATION

The treacherous blow dealt by Japan in her surprise attack on Pearl Harbour served to unite the American people overnight. In this remarkable picture the artist portrays the scene with vivid realism. Formations of dive-bombers have just begun to blast the Fleet, the naval 'planes on Ford Island, the oil storage tanks, and the Army's Hickham Field above the narrows.

From a drawing in "Life" Magazine, December 22, 1941

"ces cochons d'Anglais" might win. Actual attacks on German soldiers began in September 1941, when an officer was struck with a truncheon and an N.C.O. was ridiculed and molested by a group of youths. Two German N.C.O.s were shot, one of them dying. Stulpnaegel, the Nazi Military Governor of Paris and commander of the Nazi occupation troops in France, introduced more and more repressive measures; but attacks on German soldiers continued, and in December a bomb exploded actually in the Gestapo headquarters of a Paris suburb, killing six people. Shortly afterwards another bomb exploded in a German military police mess.

The great Paris factories were taken over from the beginning of the German occupation for the production of war materials. One of the most extensive of these enemy-controlled works, the Renault motor factory at Billancourt, in the south-western suburbs, was heavily bombed by the R.A.F. on the night of March 3, 1942, and great destruction wrought as shown later by photographs smuggled out. These works were the largest in France for making transport vehicles, tanks and aero engines. The adjacent Farman and Salmson factories were heavily damaged in the same raid. On March 8 the R.A.F. made a successful daylight raid on the Matford army lorry works at Poissy, ten miles north-west of Paris. The Matford works were again raided on the nights of April 1–2 and 2–3. On April 29 the R.A.F. attacked the Goodrich works at Geunevilliers. On June 12 a Beaufighter pilot made a daring midday roof-top flight and dropped a French tricolor flag over the Arc de Triomphe.

Fruitless negotiations for the return of the French Government to Paris were carried on from time to time, but Germany's demands were such that Marshal Pétain could not accede to them. In May 1941 Paris became the headquarters of Axis military operations.

Parry, CAPT. W. E., C.B. He was in command of H.M.S. Achilles (*q.v.*), one of the three famous British cruisers that damaged the Admiral Graf Spee and chased the German ship into Montevideo harbour. Capt. Parry was awarded the C.B. for his gallantry in this great British naval victory. During the First World War he served as torpedo officer in H.M.S. Birmingham.

Patras. One of the chief seaports of Greece, situated on the Gulf of Patras, 13 miles S.W. of Lepanto and at the entrance to the Gulf of Corinth, Patras was bombed by the Italians on the first day of the Italo-Greek war, Oct. 28, 1940. Many people were killed and wounded, the number of casualties being all the greater on account of the Italian planes having been disguised with Greek markings and the streets accordingly filled with spectators. The town was immediately evacuated and subsequent enemy raids caused fewer casualties. On April 21, 1941, fifteen days after the German invasion of Greece, the Greek hospital ship Ellenis, anchored near the port, was sunk by German aircraft, despite the fact that her Red Cross identification was clearly observable. After the capture of Corinth by German parachute troops on April 26, Patras was taken over by the enemy.

Paul, of Yugoslavia, Prince (b. 1893). After the assassination of his cousin, King Alexander I, at Marseilles in 1934, he became Chief Regent for the young King Peter II (*q.v.*) until the latter should attain his majority. The Council of Regency consisted of Prince Paul, Dr. Stankovitch and Dr. Petrovitch. From the outbreak of war Yugoslavia endeavoured

Prince Paul,
Regent of Yugoslavia.
*Photo.
"Daily Mirror"*

to protect herself against her powerful neighbours, Italy and Germany, and adhered to a policy of strict neutrality. Nevertheless, the Germans sent thousands of "tourists" into the country during the spring of 1940, thereby causing great uneasiness among the population. After Italy entered the war on the side of Germany in June 1940 it became increasingly difficult for Yugoslavia to remain a detached spectator. German demands became inordinate, and the crisis came in March 1941, when the Premier, Tsvetkovitch, and his Foreign Minister, Cincar Marcovitch, pledged their country's adhesion to the Tripartite Pact. This agreement provoked a rebellion and a dramatic *coup d'état* took place in Belgrade on March 27. Both Premier and Foreign Minister were thrown out of office and put under arrest. Prince Paul and the other Regents placed their resignations in the hands of the King. Accompanied by his wife—Princess Olga (a sister of the Duchess of Kent)—and their three children, Prince Paul subsequently left Yugoslavia and arrived in Athens on March 28. It was announced on Jan. 2, 1942, that he and Princess Olga had been deprived of membership of the Yugoslav Royal Family under a decision of the Royal Family, of which King Peter II—then in Britain—was head. The Prince and his wife were by this time in Kenya. *See* Yugoslavia.

Pearl Harbour. Chief U.S. naval base in the Pacific, situated in Oahu, principal island of the Hawaii group. Here, at about 8 a.m. on Dec. 7, 1941, Japan struck the first blow in a new world war. Without warning or a declaration of war (that was to be made some hours later), from 150 to 200 Japanese aircraft, operating from aircraft carriers, heavily attacked Pearl Harbour and other military and naval targets on the island for two hours, causing severe damage and casualties later estimated to number 3,000, of which half were fatal. This was the first of a series of almost simultaneous attacks on a number of American and British possessions in the Pacific, which were all the more treacherous in that, when they were launched, the two Japanese envoys, Nomura and Kurusu, were still holding talks in Washington with Mr. Cordell Hull.

The Japanese onslaught must have been prepared long before. Pearl Harbour lies nearly 4,000 miles from Japan, and some 2,000 miles from the nearest Japanese

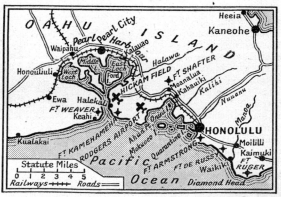

Plan of Pearl Harbour, U.S. Pacific base.

bases in the Caroline and Marshall Islands. For over a week the aircraft carriers must have been creeping nearer and nearer, until they had come within striking distance. Their object was so to cripple the American fleet that it would be unable to sail out and join the British Far Eastern squadron at Singapore.

The results of the attack on Pearl Harbour, though grave, were at first wildly exaggerated. On Feb. 23, 1942, President Roosevelt gave in a broadcast some authenticated figures of losses. "The number of our officers and men killed," he said, "was 2,340, and the number wounded 946. Of all combatant ships based on Pearl Harbour only three were permanently put out of commission. Very many ships of the Pacific Fleet were not even at Pearl Harbour. Some that were there were hit very slightly. Others that were damaged have either rejoined the fleet or are undergoing repairs. The report that we lost more than 1,000 aeroplanes at Pearl Harbour is as baseless as the other rumours." (Later it was officially stated that Army casualties were 226 killed and 396 wounded.) One of the ships lost in the attack was the 32,600-ton battleship Arizona,

submarines, two of these being of a small type. On Dec. 17 it was announced that Admiral Husband Kimmel (C.-in-C. Pacific Fleet) and Lt.-Gen. Walter Short (commanding the Hawaiian Dept.) had been relieved of their commands. A special Commission was appointed next day to inquire into the facts of the attack on Pearl Harbour. In its findings, published on Jan. 24, 1942, the Commission accused the two responsible Commanders of "dereliction of duty." The report stated that they had received many warnings of possible hostilities for months past, that Admiral Kimmel was warned by Admiral Harold Stark, Chief of Naval Operations, ten days before the attack that Japan was expected to make an aggressive move within a few days, and that on the same day the Chief of Military Intelligence advised Army officials in Hawaii that peace negotiations with Japan "have practically ceased, that hostilities might ensue, and that subversive activity might be expected." There were subsequent warnings in the next few days, but these "did not create in the minds of responsible officials in the Hawaiian area apprehension as to the probable imminence of air raids." It was said that they failed to confer and consult with one another about the warnings and the appropriate measures of defence required by the imminence of hostilities. The permanent installation of aircraft warning systems had not been completed on Dec. 7, the Commission said, but some temporary installations had been made. The systems shut down at 7 a.m. on the fateful Sunday, but one non-commissioned officer, who had been training, remained at one station, and at 7.02 a.m. he discovered that there was "a large flight of aeroplanes" about 130 miles away. This was reported to an army lieutenant 18 minutes later, but the lieutenant assumed that the aeroplanes were friendly and took no action.

On March 1, 1942, the U.S. War and Navy Departments announced that Admiral Kimmel and Lt.-Gen.

sunk by what Col. Knox, U.S. Navy Secretary, called "a lucky hit." The 29,000-ton battleship Oklahoma capsized but did not sink. The aerodrome at Hickham Field was severely damaged, as were oil installations on the island. American A.A. batteries went into action and shot down a number of the attacking 'planes, and during the raid bomber reinforcements arrived from San Francisco. Japanese losses were reported to be 41 'planes and three

SALVAGE OF AN AMERICAN WARSHIP

Victim of the savage bombing attack on Pearl Harbour, the U.S. destroyer Shaw, reported sunk by Japan, and three months later made seaworthy, is seen above blazing after a direct hit ; top left, being repaired in dry dock.

Photos, Associated Press

Short would be court-martialled on charges of dereliction of duty, the courts-martial to be postponed "until such time as public interest and safety permit." *See* Hawaii ; Pacific, War in.

Book : Pearl Harbour, Blake Clark (Lane).

A.C.M. Peirse,
A.O.C.-in-C., India.
Photo, Howard Coster

Peirse, AIR CHIEF MARSHAL SIR RICHARD EDMUND CHARLES, K.C.B., D.S.O.. A.F.C. (b. 1892). In 1937 he became Director of Operations and Intelligence and Deputy Chief of the Air Staff. He followed Air Chief Marshal Sir Charles Portal (*q.v.*) as A.O.C.-in-C. Bomber Command in October 1940. It was announced on Feb. 20, 1942, that he had been succeeded by Air Marshal A. T. Harris (*q.v.*) and on March 9 that he had been appointed A.O.C.-in-C., India, in succession to Air Vice-Marshal Sir Patrick Playfair (*q.v.*).

Penang. Situated at the north end of the Straits of Malacca off the west coast of Malaya, the island of Penang, with Prov. Wellesley on the mainland, formed one of Britain's Straits Settlements. The Japanese, who invaded Malaya on Dec. 7, 1941, raided Penang on Dec. 11. The enemy aircraft made a heavy attack, considerable damage was done. A further raid occurred on Dec. 12, when fires were still raging from the previous day's attack. Three attempted Japanese attacks were driven off by R.A.F. fighters on Dec. 14. Some 600 European evacuees arrived in Singapore from Penang on Dec. 15. Heavy Japanese forces pushed back the Empire troops on the N.W. Malaya front, an enemy advance which necessitated the evacuation of Province Wellesley. The Japanese were thus in control of the strip of coast opposite the island and cut off Penang itself on Dec. 17. *See* Malaya.

Perak. One of the most thickly populated of the Federated Malay States, Perak in N.W. Malaya is rich in tin and rubber—highly prized commodities in war. On Dec. 18, 1941, it was reported that the Japanese were making drives southward down two main roads into Perak. The British had withdrawn to the River Krian, which forms the boundary between the Unfederated Malay State of Kedah and the Federated State of Perak. This withdrawal meant that the fertile rice-growing areas of Kedah and Province Wellesley, most northerly of the Straits Settlements, had been abandoned to the vastly superior forces of the enemy. The centre of the Malayan tin-mining industry was at Ipoh, capital of Perak, and by Dec. 21 the Japanese were making fierce thrusts towards the town. Meanwhile British troops held positions at Kuala Kangsar, 15 miles north of Ipoh. The capital was abandoned on Dec. 29 in order to avoid an enemy pincer movement from the north and south-west. On Jan. 4, 1942, the Japanese claimed to have crossed the Bernam River, which forms the boundary between the States of Perak and Selangor. Heavy enemy pressure subsequently caused a British withdrawal in Lower Perak, south of the Slim River (*see* Kuala Lumpur). With the swift development of fighting in Selangor and the steady Japanese thrust towards Singapore the whole of Perak fell into enemy hands. *See* Malaya.

Percival, LT.-GEN. ARTHUR ERNEST, C.B., D.S.O. (b. 1887). From 1939 to 1940 he was Brigadier, General Staff, 1st Corps B.E.F. On April 8, 1941, he was appointed G.O.C. Malaya, succeeding Lt.-Gen.

L. V. Bond. Under his command the Empire troops put up an heroic resistance against overwhelming Japanese forces at Singapore in February 1942. On Feb. 15, 1942, Gen. Percival was forced to accept the demands of Gen. Yamashita, Japanese C.-in-C., for an unconditional surrender. The meeting to sign the necessary documents took place in the Ford motor plant at Bukit Timah.

Gen. Percival,
G.O.C. Malaya.
Photo, L.N.A.

Peregrine, H.M.S. One of the Fleet Air Arm Schools, which, though on land, are named like ships. This school trains carefully selected men, an important part of the course dealing with the recognition of British and enemy 'planes, for which scale models are used. Air gunnery also plays a vital part in the training.

Persia (Iran). During the First World War Persia was not strong enough to protect her neutrality, and British troops entered the country to expel the Turks who endangered the Anglo-Iranian oilfields. In the Second World War the cause of the British invasion was the folly of Riza Khan, the Kemal Pasha of Persia, who had made himself Prime Minister and later Shah, under the title Riza Khan Pahlevi (*q.v.*). Aided by huge sums of money paid into his treasury by the Anglo-Persian Oil Company, Riza Pahlevi subdued the Persian tribesmen and entered upon a generous policy of road and railway building. In particular, he com-

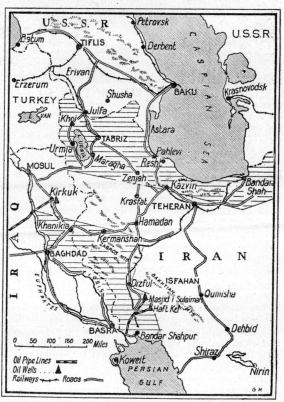

Shaded areas in this map of Persia and the Iraq frontier represent those areas first occupied by Soviet troops in the north and British troops in the south. Later all Persia was occupied by the Allies.

pleted a railway line joining the Caspian with the Persian Gulf at a cost of £30,000,000, Persian capital being used throughout, and ninety-five per cent of the workers being Iranian.

Wisdom should have dictated to Riza Pahlevi the folly of intrigues with Germany and the desirability of working with Russia and Britain. Instead, he brought numerous German engineers and agents into key positions in Persia. When Hitler invaded Russia in the autumn of 1941, Persia was the centre of anti-Allied propaganda in the Near East. The Mufti of Jerusalem took refuge there ; so did Rashid Ali, after the British occupation of Iraq. Many warnings were given by Britain, but they were disregarded. When the German panzer divisions reached the Ukraine and threatened the Donetz Basin at the end of August 1941 Britain and Russia were forced to act. The oil industry in Persia was a product of British capital and enterprise, and this could not be risked. Moreover, the annual output of ten million tons of oil was an important factor in the Allied war effort. Lastly, the Persian Gulf was the best headquarters and route for the war supplies which the United States and Britain were sending to Russia.

Iraq, under the direction of Gen. R. A. Wheeler, of the U.S. Army. Its task was to speed up the supply of war weapons to the Soviet and British forces in the regions north and west of the Persian Gulf, and to assist in the rapid development of communications by road, rail and water in those areas. An enormous organization had been established and much of the equipment was already in use. Some 5,000 technicians were at work.

Perth, STRATHALLAN JAMES ERIC DRUMMOND, P.C., G.C.M.G., 16TH EARL (b. 1876). After the outbreak of war he was Chief Adviser on Foreign Publicity to the Ministry of Information until July 28, 1940, when he resigned. From 1933 to 1939 he was British Ambassador to Italy, retiring from that post in April 1939. His successor in Rome was Sir Percy Loraine (*q.v.*).

Perth, H.M.A.S. Completed in 1936, having a displacement of about 6,830 tons and carrying a complement of 550, this Australian cruiser was among the British Light Naval Forces of the Mediterranean Fleet commanded by Vice-Adm. Sir Henry Pridham-Wippell at Matapan (*q.v.*) on March 28, 1941. The Perth did splendid work during the evacuation of the Allied troops from Crete in May 1941, when some 1,200 men were taken aboard. As soon as they had been successfully embarked the cruiser set sail, but before she reached port she was bombed by the enemy for seven hours one day, and thirteen hours on another On March 14, 1942, the Admiralty reported that a great naval battle had been fought in the Java Sea at the time of the Japanese invasion of Java on Feb. 27, 1942. The Perth, commanded

LOST IN THE BATTLE OF THE JAVA SEA
H.M.A.S. Perth, a cruiser of the Australian Navy, was sunk during the action off Java. In the words of Admiral Sir W. James, C.-in-Chief, Portsmouth, this battle was " among the fiercest and bloodiest ever known . . . the Dutch, British and American sailors fought to the last gun against impossible odds."
Photo, Keystone

On August 25, 1941, a British force crossed the southern frontier of Persia, while a Russian army entered from the north, and both marched upon Teheran. The Persian resistance was small. Within a week the Iranian army was ordered to cease fire and negotiations were opened between a new Prime Minister and the British and Russian diplomats at Teheran. In four more days complete agreement was reached. The German Legation at Teheran was closed, the so-called German experts were surrendered, and as Riza Khan continued recalcitrant he was forced to give up his throne on Sept. 16.

The ex-Shah's harsh and dominating character had left him few friends, in spite of the manifest services he had rendered to his country in restoring order, political and economic. He was succeeded by his son, Mohammed Riza, who took an oath to respect the constitution of Persia and accepted a Government formed by the Prime Minister Ali Faroughi. The ex-Shah had invested £10,000,000 abroad and this was confiscated. It was made available for the expansion of public works, including the extension of the Trans-Iranian Railway.

In February 1942 it was announced that an American military mission was then at work in both Persia and

by Capt. H. M. L. Waller, D.S.O., in company with U.S. and Dutch cruisers, was at sea north of Surabaya on that date when contact was made with a large force of Japanese destroyers, and she received some damage. She reached Tanjong Priok on Feb. 28, and left the same day with the intention of passing through the Sunda Strait during darkness. During the night a report from the Perth indicated that she had come into contact with a force of Japanese ships off St. Nicholas Point. No further news was received from her, and she was presumed lost. *See* Java.

Pétain, MARSHAL HENRI PHILIPPE (b. 1856). He became Prime Minister of France on June 17, 1940, at the age of 84. Probably Pétain's advanced age is the explanation of strange inconsistencies in his dealings with the Nazi authorities after the armistice of June 22, 1940. Pétain's patriotism was never open to serious doubt, but his politics continually revealed a personality of lath-and-plaster rather than the strong man whom the Republic looked for when it accepted Pétain as wartime dictator. Helped by the President's age, unscrupulous advisers and flatterers took advantage of occasional lapses of memory and judgement to be expected in a man of his years, especially when he

Marshal Pétain,
Vichy Chief of State.
Photo, Wide World

was unfamiliar with the tortuous methods of French politicians.

As a soldier Pétain made his name in the French offensive near Arras in May 1915, and in the stubborn defence of Verdun after 1916. His courage and grim determination led to his appointment as Commander-in-Chief, until Foch took over the control of the Anglo-French forces. He was Minister of War in the Doumergue ministry of 1934, but took no steps to inaugurate the big programme of armament building which the advent of Hitlerism plainly demanded. This fact was commented upon continually by the defendants in the Riom trial (*q.v.*).

Marshal Pétain held Fascist views long before the collapse of France. In his opinion democratic government did not encourage the stern discipline which, as a Catholic and a Conservative, he felt to be in the true interests of his country. To understand this attitude and that of many Frenchmen who supported Pétain after the Armistice, it is necessary to remember the events of 1936, after the Confédération Générale du Travail enjoyed a sudden popularity and its membership rose from one million to more than five million. By this time, May 1936, the cost of living index in France was 486 compared with 100 in 1914. The threat of Communism frightened France. To deal with the situation Blum, Prime Minister in the first Socialist Government France had known, organized the so-called Popular Front. Its task was to prevent the French trade unions going Communist. The alternative was a Fascist government of the Italian type, based upon fear of Communism. Pétain preferred a Fascist dictatorship to either Communism or any revival of the Front Populaire. Hence the authoritarian regime which he established at Vichy (*q.v.*) and which he described as " destined to permit a far more perfect realization of the ideals dear to Frenchmen than was possible under Parliamentary institutions."

The formula which Pétain approved was the replacement of the familiar Republican phrase, Liberté, Egalité, Fraternité, by the words Famille, Travail, Patrie. His underlying purpose was to revive the ancient regime, with its insistence upon a " back to the land policy " and the virtues of the simple life. In fact, Pétain was usually the tool of careerists and in particular of Admiral Darlan (*q.v.*), who succeeded Laval and Flandin, the first administrative officers at Vichy. A term of office as ambassador at Madrid, when he was persona grata with Franco, the Fascist dictator of Spain, emphasized the anti-democratic instincts of the old Marshal.

Frequently Pétain stood out against other members of his entourage in their endeavours for more active collaboration with Nazi Germany. When he met Goering in the Occupied Zone on Dec. 1, 1941, Pétain refused to hand over the French Fleet, though at Montoire a year earlier he had agreed that French factories should supply war material to Germany despite the old-time alliance with Britain. In general, Pétain's practice was to exploit the glories of 1914 to 1918 and thus veil the disgraceful surrender of 1940. In his first broadcast after he took office the old marshal revealed a touching faith in the chivalry of the German victors, which argued badly for his success as a statesman in an hour of international crisis. He said : " I have appealed to our opponent to ask him if he is ready to sign with us, as between soldiers after the fight and in honour, a means to put an end to hostilities."

In February, 1941, Pétain invited Laval (*q.v.*) whom he had previously dismissed, to enter the Cabinet, but it was not until April 14, 1942, that Pétain, submitting to Hitler's threat of occupying all France and requisitioning all food, agreed to Laval becoming head of the Cabinet and so gaining effective power in France.

Peter II, KING OF YUGOSLAVIA (b. 1923). Eldest of the three sons of King Alexander I and Queen Marie —sister of ex-King Carol of Rumania—he succeeded to the throne on the death of his father in 1934, King Alexander having been assassinated at Marseilles on Oct. 9 of that year. Before he returned to his country, in 1934, King Peter was at school in Surrey. During his minority the Royal power was vested in a Council of Regency headed by his uncle, Prince Paul (*q.v.*). Following the revolt brought about by the Cabinet's decision on March 25, 1941, to " collaborate " with Germany, the army, led by Gen. Dusan Simonovitch (who became Prime Minister), compelled the Regency Council to resign and installed Peter as King. Great public rejoicing took place throughout the country as a result of the dismissal of the pro-Axis Cabinet, a satisfaction that was to be short-lived, for without warning and a declaration of war Germany invaded Yugoslavia on April 6. On April 21 it was reported that the King and members of his Government had arrived by 'plane in the Middle East from Athens. Before leaving Yugoslavia King Peter issued a proclamation thanking all Yugoslavia for defending the country and pledging himself and his Government to continue the fight for national freedom.

Peter II,
King of Yugoslavia.
Photo, Topical Press

He arrived in Britain on June 21, accompanied by members of the Cabinet, and on Sept. 16, 1941, attended a special service at St. Paul's Cathedral, London, on the occasion of his coming of age. This ceremony was attended by His Majesty King George VI and Queen Elizabeth and the heads of the Allied Governments. *See* Yugoslavia.

Petre, MAJ.-GEN. RODERIC LORAINE, C.B., D.S.O., M.C. (b. 1887). In 1939 he commanded the 12th Division, and was entrusted with the defence of Arras in May 1940. At this crucial period an emergency force, led by Maj.-Gen. Petre, was improvised to meet the extremely serious situation in which the B.E.F. was placed owing to the German thrust to Amiens by May 18. This force was known as Petreforce, and consisted of the troops holding the Canal du Nord and those of the garrison of Arras, including the 23rd Division and the 36th Infantry Brigade. Gen. Petre's troops held Arras in the face of greatly superior enemy forces and fought heroically against terrific odds until May 24, when they withdrew from the city. *See* France, Defeat of.

Petsamo. Finland's ice-free port on the Arctic, west of Murmansk (*q.v.*), was ceded by Russia to Finland by the Treaty of Dorpat in 1920. In October 1939 the U.S.S.R. made demands on Finland, and it was reported that an exchange of territory near Petsamo for a considerable area in the Karelian isthmus, facing Leningrad, had been proposed by Russia. Finland refused, since by giving up Petsamo she would have been virtually cut off from the Arctic, which in summer afforded an alternative exit to the Baltic. In the ensuing conflict between the two countries the Russians achieved a victory over the Finns at Petsamo in November 1939, but were subsequently driven out. Fighting raged throughout the region in conditions of the utmost rigour. Finnish

counter-attacks inflicted heavy losses among the Soviet troops. Russian aircraft bombed the port, and the main road connecting the town with Enare was also bombed. Despite intense wintry conditions fighting continued fiercely through December.

Petsamo changed hands repeatedly and was finally left by the Finns as a burning ruin. On March 12, 1940, at the conclusion of hostilities, Russia agreed to withdraw her troops from the Petsamo area, but stipulated that Soviet citizens must have free transit through that region into Norway and back, and that a consulate must be established at Petsamo. The adjacent Rybachi Peninsula—the "Fisherman's Peninsula"—became Soviet territory.

Petsamo was again the scene of military activity when Finland threw in her lot with Germany in June 1941 and attacked Russia. Fighting then developed along the Murmansk front. *See* Finland.

THE PHILIPPINES CAUGHT IN THE TIDE OF WAR

With lightning rapidity Japan swooped on the Philippines. Forced to retreat to the rock fortress of Corregidor, the defenders put up a gallant and determined resistance that lasted for months—a resistance that was a source of inspiration to the United Nations.

Philippine Islands, Invasion of. The Philippines (*see* page 3205) form an archipelago of 7,000 square miles about 500 miles off the south-east coast of Asia. North of them lies the China Sea; east of them, the Pacific Ocean; south, the Sea of Celebes. The islands are mountainous, with extensive coastal plains.

DEFENDING THEIR HOMELAND

The Filipinos were outstandingly loyal and courageous in the defence of their islands against the Japanese. Here are seen Filipino scouts at one of their anti-aircraft machine-guns during Army manoeuvres.
Photo, Keystone

Directly after she had struck her blow at the United States at Pearl Harbour, Dec. 7, 1941, Japan put into action a major military operation for which preparations had been going forward for more than ten years. This operation, with the conquest of the Philippines as its first (but by no means final) objective, was feasible only with uninterrupted lines of sea communications. From the point of view of those who had the defence of the islands in charge—the President, Manuel Quezon, and his American field-marshal, Douglas MacArthur—any sustained defence of the islands against Japan depended upon uninterrupted supply lines. Pearl Harbour, with its great naval harbourage and works, both menaced an aggressive Japan and protected the exposed Philippine Islands.

Its loss, advantageous to Japan, since it made her communications relatively secure, marooned the Philippines, a fact which explains why MacArthur (who reverted to the rank of U.S. General from the moment of war) declared the freeing of the islands his first task as commander-in-chief of Australia (March 18, 1942). For while the Japanese held the Philippines they had a base from which to prosecute their major military designs : the conquest of all "white" Asia and, say some, the domination of the whole world.

While it is essential to use maps in order to understand conflicts between nations, it is important not to equate military strength with territorial dimensions. For example, the Isles of Japan on the map look like a few chips broken off the mass of Asia's mainland, while Australia occupies a considerable part of the globe's land surface. Yet Japan has a population of over 100,000,000, many times that of Australia. It is this vast reservoir of man-power, backed by the most intense system of industrialism in the modern world, that menaced the Pacific and realms far beyond it.

If there is one land that can plead with justification for lebensraum (living space), it is Japan. Her methods of acquiring it, unfortunately, are patterned on the banditry of Nazi Germany, her ally and admired model.

Japan wants the Philippines (population 10,000,000) because the islands are rich in rice, coconuts, sugar

Sites and dates, so far as officially stated, of Japan's attacks on the Philippines.

have to fight at a severe numerical inferiority as to men, arms and aeroplanes.

The attack developed very swiftly and extended from San Fernando, on the north-west coast, through Vigan and round to Aparri. By Dec. 13 landings were made also in the south of Luzon, and it was plain that this pincer tactic was to be used by vast masses of invading troops, landing from invasion barges under cover of air and naval bombardment.

General MacArthur had a desperate situation to handle, since he had to withstand this mass attack without hope of outside help, and with quite limited air resources. To increase the handicap further, it was soon seen that the enemy were landing light tanks in large numbers. Even so, from the start there was developed an offensive defence that was maintained throughout fighting which continued as a war of action until, outnumbered, out-gunned and out-flown, the combined American and Filipino forces retired for their last great stand in the island fortress of Corregidor at the mouth of the Bay of Manila.

From the start, and throughout the campaign, the fighting was severe and bitter, the Filipinos being imbued with the sense that they were fighting for their native land. On Dec. 16 there was fighting north, north-west, south-east and south on land, and many gallant air attacks were carried out on Japanese transports. But by that date it was clear that sheer weight of numbers was going to

cane, Indian corn, tobacco, cacao, coffee and such minerals as gold, silver, iron, copper, manganese, coal and petroleum shale. The islands, moreover, are situated handily for Japanese colonization. They represent the first step in realizing an imperial dream of a Japan whose possessions will hang, like a pendant, from Nippon to Sydney Harbour.

The attack on the Philippines was expected by the United States. On Dec. 7, 1941, at a Tokyo meeting to celebrate the first anniversary of the treaty between Tokyo and Nanking, a message was read from General Tojo, leader of the Japanese expansionists. In it these words occur: "Unless Great Britain and the U.S.A., which form the A.B.C.D. encirclement front whose acts are an offence and an injustice to God and humanity, correctly understand Japan's ideal and cease from hampering her mission, we are strongly resolved to crush them. Asia for the Asiatics."

On Sunday, Dec. 7, Manila, capital of Luzon, the northernmost island of the group, was bombed. The two fine airfields, Clark Field and Nichols Field, were swooped on, and many machines put out of action on the ground—and this within three days of the first landing, made at Aparri, on the north-east tip of the island of Luzon. The situation for the defenders was a perilous one, for Japan had a clear run from her home bases, and Pearl Harbour lay stricken from the great attack of Dec. 7. It was clear that vast forces would be employed in the invasion and that the defence would

Strategic position of the fortress island of Corregidor at the entrance to Manila Bay.

make it impossible to hold Manila, the capital, and on Dec. 27 General MacArthur declared Manila, already heavily bombed, an open town. This withdrawal from the capital was made necessary by the enormous numerical superiority of the enemy, 80,000 of whom had formed an invading party on Dec. 23. By Dec. 27 the Japanese had no fewer than seven beach heads. Despite the declaration of Manila as an open town, and the blaze of lights put on by night to emphasize the fact, the Japanese continued to bomb the town. On Dec. 29 Tokyo broadcast a message calling on the Filipino troops to down arms and help them turn out the Americans. By Jan. 1, 1942, the Japanese claimed that Manila was encircled, and intensified their drive from the north and south with terrific air bombardment. This air activity made the roads almost impassable and thus hindered the retirement of the defending forces.

'GIBRALTAR' OF THE PACIFIC

Guarding the waters of Manila Bay was Fort Corregidor, extending 500 ft. into the island's volcano rock. Left, is a view of its ammunition stores. The top photograph shows a 12-in. gun firing into Manila Bay from Fort Mills, on the north of Corregidor.

Photos, Paul Popper; Planet News

Much of the fighting was in dense jungle. The Japanese high command cared not how many men were sacrificed. Every foot they gained cost them dear. By the New Year the world was asking : What will MacArthur do if Manila falls ? He had two alternatives. To retire to the mountains, as the Filipinos did during the insurrection, or to retire into the Gibraltar-like fortress of Corregidor, with its rock-hewn air-raid shelters, vast supplies of provisions and ammunition and water, its 12-inch guns, commanding the seven-mile-wide entrance to Manila Bay, and its fine anti-aircraft defences. The successful holding of Corregidor made an attempt to use the bay by the enemy a hazardous enterprise, since the field of vision embraced the whole terrain. On Jan. 3 Manila surrendered. Troops destroyed all defence works in the city. Cavite, the naval base, fell also, but ships and stores were safely got away. North of the town troops continued to resist.

On Jan. 5 Corregidor was attacked. In Manila the Japanese treated all whites with brutality. On Jan. 6 an air attack on enemy naval units accounted for a Japanese battleship. North-west of Manila the defenders attacked and drove the enemy back in places five miles. On Jan. 8 the enemy attacked the whole Bataan Peninsula from the air. Panay, the third largest island, was invaded in April.

On Jan. 23 Japanese troops made landings at Davao on the island of Mindanao. The estimated number of Japanese on the islands at that date was 300,000. On Jan. 26 MacArthur staged a heavy attack with artillery preparation and charges. But the defenders were now tired and hard-pressed. From that date forward the main defence (for guerilla warfare continued throughout the island of Luzon) was concentrated on Corregidor. On March 18 General MacArthur arrived in Australia to take supreme command of all Australian and American forces. His successor in the Philippines was Maj.-Gen. Jonathan Wainwright. Gen. MacArthur announced his first intention to recapture the Philippines, and, still thinking in terms of attack, he stated as his reason the supreme importance of the islands for an attack on the Japanese Isles. By March 31 the fortress was still holding out. But Japanese penetration had extended to other islands: to Masharu, Homma and many smaller members of the group. Fighting of a determined character was still reported in Mindanao on March 25, and on May 6 the enemy landed at Malabang, near Cotabato in Mindanao. The Japanese also exerted heavy pressure near Digos.

On May 5 the enemy succeeded in making landings on Corregidor after heavy artillery and aerial bombardment, and the next day it was announced that the resistance of the defenders of the fortress had been overcome. From April 29 to May 6 Corregidor had been incessantly bombarded by enemy batteries installed on Bataan, and also pounded from the air. With the capitulation of Corregidor and the Manila Bay forts, effective Allied resistance virtually ceased.

Obu, the second city of the Philippines, was razed to the ground on May 22 in reprisal for guerilla activity.

Adm. Sir T. Phillips, British sailor.
Hay Wrightson

Phillips, VICE-ADM. SIR TOM SPENCER VAUGHAN, K.C.B (1888–1941). From 1938 to 1939 he was Commodore Commanding the Home Fleet Destroyer Flotillas. Shortly before the outbreak of war in September 1939 he succeeded Adm. Cunningham as Vice-Chief of Naval Staff. On Nov. 27, 1941, it was announced that he had been appointed to a sea command, and on Dec. 1 that he had been made C.-in-C. Eastern Command. Admiral Phillips was aboard H.M.S. Prince of Wales (*q.v.*) when that battleship was bombed and sunk by the Japanese off Malaya on Dec. 10. On Dec. 11 Mr. Winston Churchill paid this tribute to him : " I regret that Adm. Phillips is among those missing. . . . He was undertaking a thoroughly sound, well-considered offensive operation, not, indeed, free from risks, but not any different in principle from many similar operations we have repeatedly carried out in the North Sea and the Mediterranean."

Phipps, RT. HON. SIR ERIC, P.C., G.C.B. (b. 1875). He was British Ambassador in Paris from 1937 to 1939, and left the French capital on Oct. 23, 1939. From 1933 to 1937 he had been Ambassador in Berlin.

Pierlot, HUBERT. Premier of the Free Belgian Government in London. He became Prime Minister and Foreign Minister of Belgium on the resignation of M. Spaak (*q.v.*) on Feb. 20, 1939, and resigned on Feb. 27. In April of the same year he formed a new Cabinet, following a general election. There was a reorganization of the Cabinet on Sept. 4, 1939, M. Pierlot giving up the portfolio of Foreign Minister in order to devote all his energies to the office of the Premiership. By May 28, 1940, after the Germans had overrun Belgium, most

M. Hubert Pierlot, Prime Minister of Free Belgium.
Photo, Wide World

members of the Belgian Cabinet were in Paris, and on the German conquest of France the Pierlot Ministry eventually succeeded in establishing itself in London. M. Pierlot, after many adventures, arrived in London from Spain on Oct. 22, 1940, and joined his fellow Ministers. *See* Belgium.

Pigeons, Carrier. They were adopted as message carriers by the British Army during the last war, in 1916. The Royal Corps of Signals trained hundreds of pigeons in 1940, and the birds proved particularly valuable when telephonic communications were broken as a result of the German raids on this country. Some pigeons are able to fly over a mile a minute and to travel over 100 miles a day. Pigeons also serve with the R.A.F., two of them accompanying both fighter and bomber pilots on their flights, so that if a forced descent is made and the 'plane's radio is out of action, the birds form a valuable link with the airman's station.

Pijeaud, LT.-COL. CHARLES FÉLIX (d. 1942). He escaped from France shortly after the French armistice and reached Gibraltar, subsequently becoming Chief of Staff of the Free French Air Force. At the beginning of December 1941 he was on active service over Libya and was shot down on Dec. 20. Badly wounded, he was sent to a hospital at Derna and

during the swift advance of the British forces towards that town he managed to escape from the Italian hospital. For four days and nights he wandered through the desert in company with two R.A.F. men until he was picked up by a British patrol. Col. Pijeaud died as a result of his wounds in January 1942.

Pile, GEN. SIR FREDERICK ALFRED, K.C.B., D.S.O., M.C. (b. 1884). G.O.C. Anti-Aircraft Defences from 1939. Sir Frederick commanded the Canal Brigade in Egypt from 1932 to 1936. From 1937 to 1939 he commanded the 1st Anti-Aircraft Division, T.A.

Pilsen. City of Bohemia famed for its beer. It was the centre of Czechoslovakia's steel industry, the Skoda works being situated near the town. After Hitler's occupation of Czechoslovakia in March 1939, the Nazis converted these works into a huge armament-producing centre for Germany's benefit. R.A.F. 'planes bombed the Skoda works on Nov. 19–20, 1940. This flight was made in severe weather conditions and the distance covered was some 1,400 miles. Another highly destructive raid was made on the night of April 25, 1942.

Pioneer Corps, AUXILIARY MILITARY (Amps). Formed Oct. 25, 1939, the Corps consists of men aged from 30 to 50 who undertake work such as bridge-building, road and railway construction, trenches and fortifications, etc. Men of this Corps were invaluable in France in 1940, where they distinguished themselves in many engagements and were the last of the B.E.F. to leave Boulogne on May 24, after valiantly defending the harbour under severe enemy fire. Maj.-Gen. L. W. Amps was, appropriately enough, made G.O.C.

Badge of the Pioneer Corps.

Pius XII (b. 1876). Eugene Pacelli was elected Pope in 1939. During the fateful weeks before the outbreak of war he made continual efforts for peace. He broadcast a moving address to the world on Aug. 24, 1939, in which he declared that " A grave hour is striking for the great human family . . . The danger is vast, but there is still time. Nothing is lost by peace. Everything is lost by war." Such an appeal fell on deaf ears in Germany, and Hitler struck at Poland on Sept. 1. On Oct. 27, 1939, the Pope stated in his first encyclical that denial of universal morality had become a radical evil. In his customary Christmas address in 1939 he enumerated five postulates for a just and honourable peace, and at Christmas 1940 he followed them up with what he described as five indispensable prerequisites of a new order. This speech was broadcast from the Vatican, and translated into many languages. On Easter Sunday 1941 he broadcast from the Vatican an appeal for world peace.

His Holiness Pope Pius XII.
Photo, Keystone

Plate, Battle of the. At the beginning of the war Germany had three 10,000-ton pocket battleships at large, operating as surface raiders against Allied shipping. It was important that they should be brought to heel. At daybreak on Dec. 13, 1939, the Admiral Graf Spee, newest of the trio, was nosing along the coast of Uruguay towards the estuary of

How the Graf Spee was hunted down off Uruguay.
By courtesy of the "Evening Standard"

the River Plate when she was sighted by the British light cruiser Ajax, which, though heavily outmatched, did not hesitate to attack, and was soon joined by the Exeter and afterwards by the Achilles. These three ships formed part of Commodore Henry Harwood's squadron, on patrol duty in South Atlantic waters, where several British merchant vessels had recently been sunk. According to plan, the Exeter took up position on one flank of the Graf Spee, preventing an escape seawards, while the Ajax and Achilles took the other flank. Though beset by three resolute and skilful adversaries, the Graf Spee still had the advantage, for she carried heavier guns, and her broadside weighed half as much again as that of the combined British ships. Her deadliest fire was concentrated against the Exeter, which came to within 8,000 yards' range and gave her shot for shot, receiving heavy damage but not failing to inflict it in return.

Exeter was eventually crippled by the silencing of her guns and serious damage to her structure, including the steering-gear, but the remaining two cruisers continued the fight. The German ship, exchanging terrific salvoes with her intrepid attackers, put up a series of smoke-screens and steamed at top speed towards the harbour of Montevideo, which she entered at nightfall, after a running fight lasting fourteen hours, in which she had been outfought and outsailed by three comparatively small ships. Her own commander, Captain Hans Langsdorf, spoke of the "inconceivable audacity" of Ajax and Achilles in coming to such close range.

Though safe in harbour, she had gained no more than a breathing-space, for international law does not allow a belligerent ship to remain in a neutral port for a period longer than is required to make her seaworthy. It was reckoned, by British prisoners aboard the Graf Spee, that she had been hit at least sixteen times, and photographs taken in Montevideo harbour show that the damage was indeed considerable, but it was argued that the ship was certainly not unseaworthy, since she had been able to retreat at such speed. The Uruguayan Government gave her 72 hours, and, being strongly pro-Ally, the native population rendered little assistance in re-fitting her. It seemed, then, that the choice before her captain was either to come out and fight or to submit to internment for the duration of the war. Three British cruisers (the Exeter had been replaced by the Cumberland) waited in the estuary for Captain Langsdorf's decision.

On the evening of December 17 the Graf Spee steamed out, with only a skeleton crew, the remainder being transferred to the German oil tanker Tacoma. To the amazement of the onlookers, Graf Spee cast anchor just beyond the three-mile limit and her men took to the boats. There was a violent explosion, and flames lit up the deserted ship. Following secret instructions from Nazi headquarters, she had been scuttled—a course which has been well described as "ignominy to order." Captain Langsdorf, unable to survive the disgrace, shot himself three days later. The battered hulk lay half submerged in shallow water, right in the channel used for shipping in this neutral port, where she remained a menace until she was dynamited.

In the three months during which she had ranged the ocean the Graf Spee had sunk nine British merchant vessels, with a total tonnage of 50,089 tons. Several of their captains, together with members of their crews, were aboard her at the time of the action, and were disembarked at Montevideo.

An enthusiastic reception awaited Ajax and Exeter at Plymouth on Feb. 16, 1940; and Achilles, a New

GRAF SPEE IN MONTEVIDEO HARBOUR
Battered by the British cruisers Exeter, Ajax and Achilles, in the splendid victory of the River Plate, this German battleship was allowed to shelter in Montevideo for 72 hours. On Dec. 17, 1939, she steamed out, not to give battle but to scuttle herself ingloriously.
Photo, Associated Press

BLITZED PLYMOUTH TIDIES UP

Plymouth was one of the most heavily raided of Britain's cities, presumably because it is the chief port of the West Country. Vast areas were devastated, but the spirit of the people remained unbroken, and here we see the rubble cleared away, ready for rebuilding.

Photo, Keystone

Zealand ship, had a similar welcome when she put in to Auckland. Commodore Harwood, who was flying his flag on the Ajax, was made Rear-Admiral and K.C.B., and Captain F. B. Bell of the Exeter, Captain W. E. Parry of the Achilles and Captain C. H. L. Woodhouse of the Ajax all received the C.B.

Lt.-Gen. Sir W. Platt, C-in-C. East Africa.
Photo, British Official

Platt, Lt.-Gen. Sir William. G.O.C.-in-C. of the East African Command from Aug. 26, 1941. He was in command of the Sudan Defence Force from 1938, and in January, 1940, he commanded the Imperial Army that invaded Italian Eritrea from the Sudan. During February, 1940, he led his army through a series of swift, triumphant achievements before joining with Cunningham's forces, with whom he was responsible for the successful Abyssinian campaign. Sir William won special distinction for his work at Keren (*q.v.*) in Eritrea, and was the first to enter the fortress after the British tanks had broken through. *See* East Africa.

Playfair, Air Vice-Marshal Sir Patrick Henry Lyon, k.b.e., c.b., m.c. (b. 1889). In 1936 he was appointed A.O.C. No. 3 Bomber Group, and in 1938 commanded No. 1 Bomber Group. At the outbreak of war in September, 1939, he became A.O.C. Advanced Air Striking Force in France. He went to India in August, 1940, as A.O.C.-in.-C. It was announced on March 9, 1942, that he had been succeeded by Air Marshal Sir Richard Peirse (*q.v.*).

Ploesti. Situated 35 miles north of Bucharest in the centre of the famous Rumanian oil fields, Ploesti was first bombed by the Russians on July 5, 1941, when great damage was done to the oil plants.

Plymouth. World-famous city and seaport. Plymouth (*see* p. 3296) welcomed men from the Ajax and Exeter on Feb. 16, 1940, on their return from the Battle of the River Plate (*q.v.*). The city suffered heavily in the intensive German air raids. The Luftwaffe inflicted a severe battering upon the commercial and residential districts of both Plymouth and Devonport. The raids began towards the end of 1940, the night raid of Nov. 27 being particularly fierce. Throughout 1941 and 1942 attacks were made repeatedly. There were considerable numbers of casualties and hundreds of homes were wrecked. The busy shopping areas suffered acutely, but the savage German attacks were unable to break the spirit of Plymouth's inhabitants. King George and Queen Elizabeth visited the city on March 20, 1941, just before a concentrated raid was made that night. During the many night attacks hospitals, churches, schools, famous public buildings and house property were bombed indiscriminately.

Pogradets. After five days of fighting this Albanian town, 20 miles N.W. of Koritza on the shores of Lake Ochrida, fell to the Greeks on Dec. 1, 1940. They captured quantities of munitions, together with a number of tanks and lorries which the Italians had abandoned as they sped along the road to Elbasan. Pogradets was evacuated by the Greeks subsequent to the German attack on Greece and Yugoslavia at the beginning of April, 1941.

POLAND, A SMALL NATION THAT BECAME GREAT

The first of Germany's war victims was Poland, invaded without warning on September 1, 1939. Previous Nazi aggressions had gone unchecked, but this time Britain and France could not forbear to intervene, since they had guaranteed the independence of Poland. Defeated on her own soil, she continued to resist from overseas.

Poland, Conquest of. No nation had more reason to be alarmed at German rearmament than Poland. As a poor country she could not hope to compete in munition production with her highly industrialized neighbour, who also possessed more than double her man-power. Moreover, geographically her strategic position was desperately unfavourable and became even more so after the rape of Czechoslovakia. The whole of western Poland was enclosed by German or German-dominated territory in which

invading armies could deploy, ready placed to carry out the strategy of envelopment at which the German army always aimed.

The length of frontier threatened was too long to admit of elaborate fortification, and it presented no natural defensive features. Only by abandoning the whole of west Poland and falling back to the lines of the Vistula, and its tributaries the Narew, Bug and San, could a strong defensive position be found. Such a course would, however, have meant the sacrifice

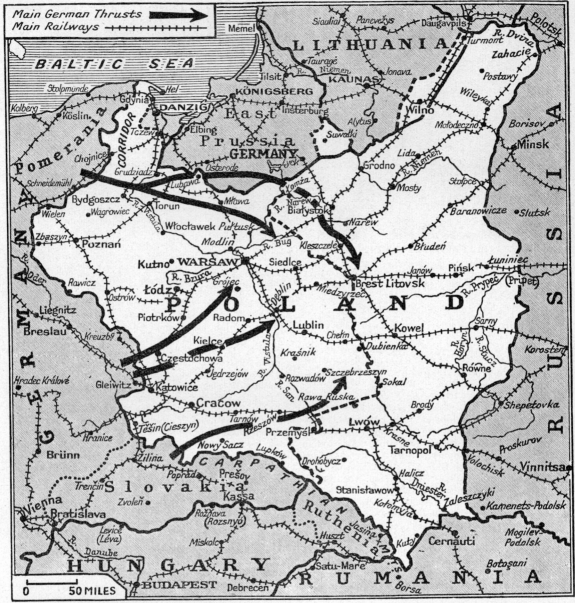

Map showing the direction of the main Nazi thrusts which resulted in the complete overrunning of Poland, September 1939.

of the most highly industrialized and populous part of the country, and was unthinkable except as a last resort. Nor could Poland rely on receiving assistance if she were attacked. With Russia, the only Power which could intervene directly, her relations were not good, and when Hitler concluded a pact of friendship with Russia the possibility of assistance from that quarter disappeared. The guarantees given by France and Britain, if they failed to have a deterrent influence on Germany, were of little practical value strategically, for the Siegfried Line blocked the only front where France could take offensive action, and no large part of the German Army would be required to hold it, leaving the bulk free to be directed against Poland.

After the occupation of Czechoslovakia in March 1939, tension over the Danzig and Corridor questions

increased rapidly, and it was evident that Hitler intended to make Poland his next victim, though it was possible that he still trusted to achieving his object by threats rather than face the danger of a war with France and Britain. Anxious to maintain peace, and in view of the negotiations in progress, Poland therefore did not mobilize her Army, even when, as the crisis approached, German armies began to concentrate on her frontier. On Aug. 31 mobilization orders were at last given, but before they could take effect Germany launched her attack.

Before dawn on Sept. 1 the Luftwaffe crossed the frontier and bombed every Polish aerodrome. The pitiably small Polish Air Force of not more than 500 aircraft, taken by surprise, was shattered by the blow. Such machines as had not been destroyed sought improvised landing-grounds, where equipment, and in many cases petrol supplies, were lacking. The little remnant at times were able to take effective action, but Germany gained complete supremacy in the air in the first hour. She employed it to disrupt immediately the processes of Polish mobilization, interrupting railway traffic and destroying telephone communications. Her aircraft took a prominent part in ground conflicts, in particular co-operating with armoured columns, warning them of dangers and locating objectives. Lamentably deficient in anti-aircraft weapons, the Poles, civilian and soldiers alike, had not even the small amount of protection these might have afforded.

Closely following the initial air attack the German armies advanced in two groups. The northern group, commanded by von Bock, consisted of two armies, one in East Prussia, the other in Pomerania. These

GERMAN TRANSPORT BOGGED

In spite of their overwhelming numbers, the Germans did not find it easy to conquer Poland. Horse transport and mechanized vehicles alike were bogged in difficult terrain. Unluckily for the Poles, the weather was, on the whole, dry and favoured the use of armoured cars and tanks.

Photo, Wide World

two armies co-operated in an attack on the Polish Pomorze army at the base of the Corridor, but the main attack from East Prussia was towards Warsaw and on the crossings of the R. Narew. Between von Bock's and von Rundstedt's groups there was an interval of nearly 100 miles, in which no considerable attack was made, and the main operation of penetrating the centre and enveloping the left of the Polish Army was entrusted to von Rundstedt. He had three armies, of which von Reichenau's in the centre was particularly strong in armoured divisions, though List's on the right was numerically the larger, since it had to operate on a wider front. Including reserve divisions brought into action as the campaign progressed, the Germans employed some 70 divisions in all, of which 10 were light or heavy armoured divisions. In addition they had regiments of tanks co-operating with their normal infantry divisions.

Against this great force Poland could mobilize only 30 regular and 10 reserve divisions, and she had practically no tanks. Her sole armoured formation, a mechanized cavalry brigade, was chiefly equipped with armoured cars. Moreover, she was still without an adequate supply of anti-tank guns.

The immense disparity between the two armies both numerically and in equipment is obvious, but owing to the interruption of Polish mobilization by the German onslaught the disparity was even greater than figures reveal. Some divisions never completed mobilization, others were overwhelmed in early encounters, so that at no time had the Poles more than 18 complete divisions in action. The Polish soldiers, including reservists, were thoroughly well trained in the weapons they possessed, and in the fighting they displayed the gallantry for which they were always famous, but the cavalry, on which much reliance had been placed, neither in mobility nor offensive power could match armoured vehicles—particularly as the latter throughout the campaign were favoured by exceptionally dry weather.

The main features of the campaign can be briefly told. The Poles, without any permanent fortified line, intended to conduct a war of manoeuvre, and with that

POLAND BRAVELY RESISTED

The Polish troops fought like heroes, but they could not oppose more than eighteen divisions to the seventy which Germany sent against them, and they lacked mechanization. Some of their few armoured cars are shown moving through a village near Warsaw.

Photo, Planet News

NAZI GENERALS DICTATE TO POLES

At the conclusion of the Polish campaign a conference was held to decide the future of Warsaw. In mocking memory of Versailles, a railway carriage, halted near the capital city, was made the scene of this conference, at which the Nazi generals imposed their demands upon the Polish commanders (seen in the foreground).

Photo, Wide World

of retreat, and one of his Panzer divisions, recalled from Warsaw, struck the Poles in the flank. The Poznan and the Pomorze Armies after some days of desperate fighting in the Bzura valley were encircled, only a small part succeeding in cutting their way through to Warsaw, already besieged.

All hope of establishing a defensive front on the Vistula and the other river lines had now gone, for there were insufficient troops to hold them, while in addition a thrust in the south towards Lwow, and another in the north by Panzer columns from East Prussia, had already turned them. There were, however, elements of the Polish Army east of the Vistula still determined to fight on, and Warsaw was resisting magnificently in spite of ruthless bombing and increasing artillery bombardment. There was yet a hope that a defensive front might be found on the Dniester and its tributaries, where, with their backs to Rumania, the remnants of the Army might make a stand till autumn rains and winter would immobilize the German onslaught.

On September 17 that hope was crushed by the Russian invasion, and no course was open to the troops in the east but to take refuge in Rumania, trusting to the eventual victory of the Allies. Warsaw and the little garrison of the Hel peninsula at Gdynia fought on. But on September 27 Warsaw, and some days later the Hel garrison, surrendered, having added a glorious page to Polish history.

The world stood in wonder at the rapidity of the German campaign, but drew the false conclusion that it could not happen again when the scales were more evenly balanced. It failed to realize that mechanization had revolutionized warfare.

Poland, Free. On Sept. 17, 1939, after being chased by German bombers in the course of a fortnight from Warsaw to the Rumanian frontier, the Polish Government crossed into Rumania, arriving at Bracau two days later. The presence of a fugitive belligerent Government in neutral Rumania put that country in a very delicate and dangerous position. M. Moscicki, President of Poland, and Colonel Beck, Prime Minister, eased the situation by resigning, and a new Polish Government was constituted in France on Sept. 30, with M. Ladislas Raczkiewicz as President and General Ladislas Sikorski as Prime Minister and Minister of War.

Before the formation of the new Government General Sikorski had begun the recruiting of a Polish army in France. At that time he was 55 years old. He had been one of the chief organizers of the Polish

aim they deployed their armies in five groups, though actually only a small number of their divisions had reached their war stations when the blow fell.

On the first day collisions were mainly between German advanced detachments and Polish frontier guards. Then followed two days' heavy fighting, which in the north resulted in the two German armies joining hands on the lower Vistula and driving back the Pomorze Army. The Polish Poznan Army facing the gap between the main German groups was not, however, seriously engaged. In the south, where to meet the three German there were only two Polish armies, those of Lodz and Cracow, resistance was stubborn. But it was here that the Germans had planned to penetrate the Polish front, and Reichenau's Panzer divisions broke through the left of the Lodz Army at Czestochowa. Heading straight for Warsaw, overrunning or by-passing such resistance as they encountered, in eight days they reached the outskirts of the capital. There, however, they were held up.

Meantime, on September 3 the Polish Army was ordered to retreat to the Vistula, but a well co-ordinated withdrawal was impracticable; the Cracow Army was closely pursued, and although it resisted on successive river lines, its left was continually outflanked by part of List's Army, which had crossed the Carpathian mountains from Slovakia. The Lodz Army, pursued by the main bodies of Reichenau's Army and by the left army of Rundstedt's group, reached the Vistula in a shattered condition. In the north, pressure on the Pomorze Army and on the Narew front was unrelenting, and the enemy was closing in on Warsaw. Only the Poznan Army was not yet heavily engaged, and it was slow to commence retreat. When it moved it launched a hastily staged counter-attack towards Kutno against the left of Rundstedt's armies. The counter-attack, gallantly delivered, had some initial success, but Reichenau's Army, swinging northwards, threatened the line forces in 1914–1918, and in 1920 his generalship contributed to the success of the Poles against an earlier Russian invasion. In 1922 he became Prime Minister, and afterwards served as Minister of War and Chief of the General Staff. On Oct. 2, 1939, the United States of America announced its recognition of the continued existence of the Government of Poland.

All Poles in Great Britain were mobilized for service, and by the end of October many thousands of Poles in France, Great Britain, and other countries had responded to General Sikorski's call. Arrangements were made for units of the Polish Navy to cooperate with the British Navy. Among the ships that came into service was the submarine Orzel (q.v.), whose escape was one of the great exploits of the war. Polish ships cooperated with the French and British Navies in the evacuation from Dunkirk. A Polish ship, the Piorin, was the first to sight the Bismarck in June 1941.

Polish Divisions Escape to Switzerland

By an agreement between M. Daladier, the French Premier, and General Sikorski, signed on Jan. 4, 1940, the Polish army and air force were reconstituted in France. In April General Sikorski and M. Zaleski, the Foreign Minister, represented Poland on the Allied Supreme War Council. A detachment of the Polish army served in Norway, being afterwards withdrawn to Great Britain. The French army ceased fighting on June 16, and four days later President Raczkiewicz arrived in England and was met by the King. General Sikorski and the rest of the Polish Government and staffs followed. So did the two divisions of the Polish army which had been training in western France. Of two Polish divisions in the battle line in eastern France, some 18,000 men with 2,300 horses and 500 wagons succeeded, on General Sikorski's orders, in escaping to Switzerland, where they were interned. The Polish army in Great Britain was established in Scotland, and towards the end of the year took over the defence of a section of the Scottish coast. Polish troops shared in the stubborn defence of Tobruk.

Polish airmen fought side by side with British pilots in the Battle of Britain. One Polish squadron claimed 150 victims, 127 between August and October; and a Polish squadron which flew Hurricanes in defence of London destroyed 28 enemy machines in 3 days. Five members of this squadron won the D.F.C. and three the D.F.M. A Polish bombing squadron was formed towards the end of the year and shared with British airmen in the raids on Germany and the occupied ports.

The German invasion of Russia in June 1941 produced an immediate change in the relations between Poland and Russia. On July 30 an agreement was signed in London by which the Soviet-German Treaty of 1939 regarding territorial changes was declared invalid, the Polish and Russian Governments agreed to render each other support of all kinds, and a Polish army was to be raised on Russian soil. Polish prisoners of war in Russia were simultaneously amnestied. A week later General Ladislas Anders was appointed Commander of the Polish army in Russia, and on August 15 a Polish-Russian military agreement was signed in Moscow. In September the two Governments exchanged ambassadors. Later in the year General Sikorski visited Russia, and on Dec. 3 he and General Anders met M. Stalin. By this time six Polish divisions, to be equipped by Great Britain and America, had nearly completed their training; and Stalin promised that the 1,500,000–2,000,000 Polish men,

women, and children scattered about the Soviet Union should be brought together and given temporary settlement in the warm and fertile district between Tashkent and Alma Ata.

On Jan. 23, 1942, an agreement that should prove of great value in the rebuilding of Europe was signed in London between the Polish and Czechoslovak Governments : it provided for post-war economic confederation between their two states, to include at their own

POLISH SHIPS FOUGHT GERMANY
Polish ships rendered valuable service in cooperation with the British Navy. When the destroyer Grom was bombed and sunk off the Norwegian coast, the British Government handed over the Piorin to replace her ; this was the ship which first sighted the Bismarck in June 1941. Here we see Polish naval officers on her bridge.

wish other states vitally linked in the economic sphere with Poland and Czechoslovakia.

General Sikorski visited Washington on March 23 and had talks with President Roosevelt. He announced on April 2 that 40,000-60,000 Polish troops, equipped in Russia, were to take up positions in Persia.

Poland, Occupied. Of all the conquered countries Poland suffered the most from Germany's barbaric terrorism. On July 9, 1942, it was stated in London that the number of Poles brutally murdered had reached a total of 400,000. Jews in the ghettos were systematically massacred or deported to concentration camps. Thousands died from starvation or sickness. The population of 35,000,000 had been reduced by over 2,500,000 since 1939, and Germany evidently aimed at its gradual extermination.

Books to Consult : It Started in Poland, U. Dragomir (Faber). I Saw Poland Suffer, A Polish Doctor (Harrap). They Fought for Poland, ed. F. B. Czarmonski (Unwin).

Police : In War. When war broke out all police pensioners were called up ; this included all county and metropolitan retired police officers. Next, the Police War Reserve was mobilized. There already existed the institution of special constables, the last war having familiarized the Home Office authorities with the problem of John Citizen acting as " Robert " for a time. It was arranged for the specials to undertake more duties than they did in the last war owing to the greater calls on the police generally following the blitz.

The most radical change in police working for war was the formation of the Women's Auxiliary Police Corps. The position of members of this Corps is somewhat analogous to that of women members of the Civil Defence Services. Their duties mainly consist in rendering assistance to the Police Force in such matters as driving motor vehicles, maintenance and repair of cars and other police equipment; and all kinds of clerical work. They also act as telephonists. A proportion in London and the provinces do regular duty on the beat like their male comrades. Women also act as military police in the A.T.S. and the W.A.A.F.

Poorten, Lt.-Gen. Hein ter. On March 2, 1942, it was announced from Downing Street that, owing to the changed situation in the Far East, Gen. Wavell had resumed the appointment of C.-in-C. India, and that the command of all operations in the Netherlands East Indies would pass to the Dutch. Two days later Gen. ter Poorten, C.-in-C. of the Dutch forces in the Netherlands East Indies, was placed in supreme command of all land forces in the South-West Pacific area, while Acting Rear-Admiral J. J. A. Staveren was given command of the Allied naval forces. On Oct. 24, 1941, Gen. ter Poorten had succeeded Gen. Berenschot as C.-in-C. of the Royal Netherlands East Indies Army. After the fall of Surabaya on March 9, 1942, Gen. ter Poorten was taken prisoner.

Viscount Portal,
Chief of Air Staff
Photo, Bertram Park

Portal, Air Chief Marshal Viscount Charles Frederick Algernon, o.m., k.c.b., d.s.o. (b. 1893). Chief of Air Staff from October 1940. In August 1937 he became Director of Organization, and was appointed Air Member for Personnel in February 1939. He succeeded Sir Edgar Ludlow-Hewitt in March 1940 as A.O.C.-in-C. Bomber Command, and received the K.C.B. Visct. 1946.

Portal, Wyndham Raymond Portal, d.s.o., m.v.o., 3rd Baron (b. 1885). Minister of Works and Planning from Feb. 22, 1942, in succession to Lord Reith (*q.v.*). In 1939 he was Regional Commissioner for Wales under the Civil Defence Scheme, and Chairman of the Coal Production Council from 1940.

Portland. During August 1940 German aircraft launched large-scale attacks against the Channel coasts and shipping. A determined day raid was carried out by Nazi bombers against Portland on August 11. Over 200 enemy planes took part, and during the attack two of H.M. ships sustained slight damage from splinters. Bombs falling on shore caused damage to naval buildings, including a hospital, but few of the casualties were of a serious nature. This attack was met by intensive opposition from R.A.F. fighters and ground defences. On August 25 strong enemy forces attempted to cross the Dorsetshire coast. They encountered heavy air and ground opposition, and in a fierce aerial battle over Portland 43 German planes were destroyed and the attacking formations broken up and driven off.

Port Moresby. In Papua, the British portion of New Guinea, the administrative centre is Port Moresby, built on a wooded headland encircled by hills which in the North West rise to a lofty mountain range 12,000 ft. high. The strategic importance of Port Moresby lies in the fact that it is only 350 miles

LONDON'S POLICE IN THE EMERGENCY

During the blitz period London's splendid police force coped imperturbably with their unaccustomed duties. 1. City workers have to show their identity cards before entering a devastated area. 2. A notice is posted up to give warning of an unexploded bomb. 3. A policeman and a fireman, at work among debris, lie flat as more bombs fall around them.

Photos, Fox; L.N.A.; Planet News

HARBOUR AT PORT MORESBY

This little town, strongly held as Australia's outpost against Japanese attack, became, as Allied strength mounted, the advance base for counter-attack. It was frequently bombed, but increasing toll was taken of the enemy planes.
Photo, E.N.A.

from Cape York, the northernmost tip of Australia. Allied troops therefore made a determined effort to hold it as the outer bastion of Australia's defences against Japanese attack. The town was repeatedly bombed, and the Japanese, landing at Lae and Salamaua on the north-west coast, attempted to infiltrate across the mountains, but were checked and largely mopped up. Enemy transports were heavily attacked by the growing air strength of the Allies, and their bases, especially Rabaul in New Britain, suffered severely in March and April 1942. These counter-measures emphasized the importance of Port Moresby since it would serve as an Allied base when the time came to sweep away the Japanese menace.

Portsmouth. During the Battle of Britain in 1940 Portsmouth, along with other famous British naval bases and seaports, was fiercely attacked by German aircraft. Two hundred Nazi planes set out to bomb the town on August 12, but only about 50 got through the barrage. An attack on the Dockyard was made, but this had little success. Bombs were dropped on the outskirts of the Dockyard area, setting fire to a store and causing minor damage to a jetty. Two small harbour service craft were damaged and subsequently sank. In other areas of the town a railway station was hit, and a number of buildings set on fire. Further heavy attacks were made during both August and September. As a result of these raids, several working-class and residential districts suffered badly and hundreds of people were homeless.

Ferocious night raids developed towards the end of 1940 and continued with determined savagery throughout the winter and into the spring of 1941. Shops and private houses were among the chief targets hit on Oct. 29, 1940, when two concentrated attacks were made. The full weight of Nazi ruthlessness was directed at Portsmouth on Jan. 10, 1941, but the city was saved from the worst consequences by the terrific anti-aircraft fire put up by the Royal Navy and by the help that the Navy gave to the A.F.S. Among the numerous buildings destroyed during this raid were six churches. On March 10, 1941, Portsmouth was raided by relays of planes for six hours, when thousands of incendiaries and many H.E. bombs were dropped. One street was almost wiped out. In all raids from 1940 Portsmouth suffered 930 persons killed, 2,837 injured, 6,625 houses destroyed and 73,425 damaged.

Portugal. The Portuguese Republic is the fourth colonial power in the world, with possessions extending from the Atlantic to the Pacific and including Angola in Africa, Timor in Malaya and Macao in China, all prizes which Germany and Japan would gladly share. The role of Portugal in the Second World War was, therefore, one of an anxious watcher, neutral, in spite of a centuries-long alliance with Great Britain, which has been the surest factor in assuring the security of the Portuguese empire overseas.

Happily, Portuguese international relations were in safe hands from 1939 onwards. For sixteen years after 1910 Portugal suffered eighteen revolutions and *coups d'état*, and had forty different governments. In 1926 the chiefs of the Portuguese Army seized power, and in 1928 Dr. Salazar became Finance Minister. His rule was so salutary that he soon added to his office that of Prime Minister, Minister of War and Foreign Minister, and he held all these offices when war broke out. Under Salazar's tolerant but firm rule the Portuguese budget was balanced, and for ten years the national finances showed a surplus. In 1940 the national receipts were £25,980,000 and the outgoings £24,240,000.

The state of war reduced Portugal's foreign trade, but made little difference to her productivity. The proximity of Republican Spain, with its strong pro-German sympathies, always made neutrality difficult, but Dr. Salazar was not to be moved. He was invariably friendly towards his ally, Britain, but did nothing which would justify a German attack. The coming of Japan into the war, however,

PORTSMOUTH'S RUINED GUILDHALL

Only the façade remains of the imposing Guildhall; its interior was completely gutted by fire after a severe blitz. Portsmouth was continually and savagely attacked
Photo, Keystone

forced Portugal into unwilling participation. When a Japanese invasion of Timor was threatened, a Dutch and Australian force entered the Portuguese territory on Dec 18, 1941, to assist the small Portuguese force, as this was plainly insufficient to counter a Japanese landing. The Portuguese authorities made a token protest, but were soon persuaded of the rightness of the Allied action, which did not disturb the ancient friendship of Portugal and Britain. Later Portuguese forces were sent to take over the defence, but Japanese troops had already landed on the island. *See* Timor.

Admiral Sir Dudley Pound, First Sea Lord.
Photo, G.P.U.

Pound, ADMIRAL OF THE FLEET SIR DUDLEY, G.C.B. (b. 1877). First Sea Lord and Chief of Naval Staff from 1939. From 1941 he was First and Principal Naval A.D.C. to the King. From 1936 to 1939 he was C.-in-C. of the Mediterranean Fleet, and became Admiral of the Fleet in 1939. He was present at the Roosevelt-Churchill Atlantic conference in August 1941 (*see* Atlantic Charter), and in December 1941 he attended conferences between Mr. Churchill and President Roosevelt in Washington.

Pownall, GEN. SIR HENRY ROYDS, K.B.E., D.S.O. (b. 1887). Appointed on March 14, 1942, to the Ceylon Army Command under the C.-in-C., Admiral Sir Geoffrey Layton. After the outbreak of war in September 1939 he became Chief of General Staff under Lord Gort in France. In September 1940 he was appointed Inspector-General of the Home Guard, and continued to hold this position until May 1941, when he became Vice-Chief of the Imperial General Staff under Gen. Sir John Dill. It was announced on Nov. 19, 1941, that he had been selected for a "special appointment." This was revealed on Dec. 26, 1941, to be that of C.-in-C. Far East, in succession to Air Chief Marshal Sir Robert Brooke-Popham. On Jan. 3, 1942, however, he was appointed Chief of Staff to Gen. Wavell in the South-west Pacific area. When later Wavell returned to India, Pownall received the Ceylon Command.

Gen. Sir Henry R. Pownall, C.-in-C. Ceylon Army.
Photo, British Official

Poznan (Posen). The city of Poznan lies 170 miles west of Warsaw on the River Warthe and was an important industrial centre of Poland. It was one of the first places to be occupied by the Germans after they attacked Poland on Sept. 1, 1939. At the end of the first week of war the enemy had established himself in Western Poland, and in the final partition of that country between Russia and Germany on Sept. 29, 1939, Poznan passed to Germany. The conquerors displayed the greatest cruelty and injustice towards the unhappy inhabitants. In the province of Poznan some 5,000 persons were reported to have been executed. National monuments were destroyed in the city itself, and repressive measures adopted against all those guilty of patriotism. *See* Poland.

Prague. On Sept. 1, 1939, the day that Germany attacked Poland, some 800 Czechs were arrested in Prague. In the streets of this ancient city (*see* pp.

3349-3350) machine-guns were mounted, and soldiers and Black Guards marched about with a view to cowing the populace. Everywhere there were spies and informers. On Sept. 17 fighting broke out in Prague and as a result hundreds of people were shot by the German authorities. On Oct. 28, the twenty-first anniversary of the day on which Czechoslovakia achieved her independence, workers demonstrated in the streets and German armoured cars fired at the crowds. Hundreds of patriots were arrested, and many received brutal treatment at the hands of the Germans. In November the Nazi oppressors occupied Prague University. Two thousand students and many professors were arrested, and of these only 800 were released after interrogation.

Martial law was proclaimed in the city on Nov. 18. The first Nazi public meeting was held in Prague on Dec. 2, 1939, when Henlein (*q.v.*), the German Governor of Sudetenland, declared that " wherever the swastika flies it flies for ever." Nevertheless, throughout 1940 the Czechs put up a prolonged and determined resistance to German oppression, and the Nazis failed in their clumsy attempts to Germanize either the citizens of Prague or their national institutions. Following the resignation of Baron von Neurath, Reichs-Protector of Bohemia and Moravia, and the appointment of Heydrich (*q.v.*), Himmler's second-in-command of the Gestapo, as Deputy-Protector on Sept. 27, 1941, a state of emergency was proclaimed in Prague. Arrests and executions in the city constituted a reign of terror during October 1941, and the victims comprised Czechs in every walk of life. When Heydrich was assassinated in May, 1942, hundreds of the citizens of Prague were put to death, and the city as a whole was severely penalized. *See* Czechoslovakia.

Priday, CPL. THOMAS. First British soldier to be killed in action in the war. Cpl. Priday, King's Shropshire Light Infantry, was killed on Dec. 9, 1939, while leading a patrol in France against the German lines.

Pridham-Wippell, VICE-ADM. SIR HENRY DANIEL, K.C.B., C.V.O. (b. 1885). Second in Command of the Mediterranean Fleet from December 1940. He commanded the naval squadron that made an outstandingly successful sweep of the Adriatic on Dec. 18, 1940. This squadron, consisting of cruisers and destroyers, swept the Adriatic as far north as Bari and Durazzo—vital ports in the Italian conflict with Greece. In command of the British naval light forces at Matapan on March 28, 1941, Pridham-Wippell flew his flag in H.M.S. Orion (*q.v.*), the ship which acted as a decoy and drew the Italian naval forces to their doom. *See* Matapan.

Prince of Wales, H.M.S. Laid down in 1937 and launched in 1939, this famous and powerful battleship was a sister ship of H.M.S. King George V. She had a displacement of 35,000 tons, a speed of about 30 knots and a main armament of ten 14-inch guns. These guns had a range greater than that of the 15-inch guns mounted in earlier ships. The Prince of Wales was one of the most powerful battleships in the world and took a prominent part in the pursuit of the German battleship Bismarck in May 1941. On May 24 contact was made with the Bismarck and during the ensuing engagement H.M.S. Hood (*q.v.*) was hit at extreme range and blew up. The Prince of Wales (commanded by Capt. Leach, R.N.) sustained slight damage, but continued to shadow the fleeing German ship until May 25, when contact was lost owing to low visibility, about 350 miles S.S.E. of Greenland.

It was aboard the Prince of Wales that the Churchill-Roosevelt Conference took place in August 1941 (*see* Atlantic Charter).

It was reported on Nov. 22, 1941, that the presence of the Prince of Wales at Cape Town indicated that she was on her way to reinforce Britain's naval strength in Far Eastern waters. She was sunk off Malaya on Dec. 10, 1941, three days after the Japanese attack on Pearl Harbour. The great battleship was attacked by Japanese bombers and torpedo aircraft while she was endeavouring to smash Japanese transports intended for the enemy invasion of Malaya. With her was H.M.S. Repulse, likewise a victim of the Japanese torpedoes and bombs. Admiral Sir Tom Phillips (*q.v.*) and Capt. Leach went down with the ship. Survivors were picked up and taken to Singapore. At least seven enemy planes were destroyed as a result of this action, but the loss of the Prince of Wales was a serious injury to British naval power.

Prinz Eugen. German 10,000-ton cruiser of the Hipper class, used as an Atlantic raider. With the Bismarck (*q.v.*) she left Bergen on May 22, 1941. After a long chase she reached Brest, where she was later joined by the Scharnhorst and Gneisenau. In February 1942 she escaped with them along the Channel to a German port, but was badly damaged by H.M.S. Trident while on her way thence to Trondheim. On May 17 she was hit with torpedoes by R.A.F. aircraft off Norway while proceeding, under escort, to Kiel. *See* Gneisenau.

Prisoners of War. At the end of 1941 there were over 76,000 British and Dominions prisoners of war in German and Italian war prisons. In Germany camps are Oflags (officer camps), Stalags (for other ranks), Dulags (temporary camps), Luftlags (for airmen), Marlags and Milags (for naval ratings).

By International convention signed by 61 powers, including Britain and Germany, prisoners of war have certain rights, which are safeguarded by the International Red Cross Committee at Geneva. The chief of these rights are : food on the same scale as the captor country's backline troops ; clothing, underwear and footwear ; medical attention, access to medical officer and periodical examination ; correspondence, both in and out ; parcels of food and reading matter.

It is believed by the Red Cross and St. John War Organization that Germany is applying the terms of the International Convention referred to above, save that the food is nearer German civilian scale than that laid down, and that the clothing provisos have been reduced to the issue of overcoats. British prisoners, therefore, stand in need of food parcels, which are sent through the Red Cross at the rate of one per week per man, for distribution through Geneva. Adequate supplemental clothing is sent through the same organization. Prisoners seriously ill are eligible, under the Convention, for repatriation, after a medical board on which two of three doctors must be neutrals. There are, however, many prisoners who are ill but not permanently incapacitated as fighting men. These men are in hospitals in Germany and occupied France. Some are wounded, others suffering from diseases contracted in camp. These men are the especial care of an Invalid Comforts Section of the Red Cross (*q.v.*) and receive invalid foods and disinfectants.

Camp inspections are carried out by delegates of the International Red Cross and by delegates of the

BRITISH AND ENEMY CAPTIVES

1. British soldiers in Germany's Stalag XXI, equipped by the International Red Cross. 2. Captured German and Italian naval officers on the quarter-deck of a battleship ; note distinguishing marks on the clothes. 3. Exhausted German soldiers taken prisoner in the Libyan Desert awaiting transport.
Photos, Central Press; British Official

ORGANIZING RELIEF FOR PRISONERS

In Geneva the International Red Cross looks after the interests of prisoners. Details are filed according to a card-index system. Here we see part of the section dealing with Poles.

Photo. Wide World

"Protecting Power." Until December 1941 the latter was the U.S.A., but is now Switzerland.

Prison-camp life in Germany may be summed up as monotonous and dreary : it is life, but it is not living. Therefore, while every effort is made to supply lacking material needs—including adequate supplies of vitamins against scurvy—the psychological factor is also considered. Prisoners receive reading matter and games of all kinds.

The German aptitude for discipline manifests itself in the prison camps. These are, generally considered, well organized.

Italy holds far fewer British and Dominions prisoners of war. The chief camp centres are at Sulmona in the Abruzzi, south-east of Rome, Prato all' Isarco, Fiesole, Rezzanello and Gruppignano. All reports received indicate that prisoners in Italy are well treated and letters home indicate this.

A great number of British and Allied prisoners were captured by the Japanese, notably at Hongkong and Singapore, and aid to them and to interned civilians in the Far East was held up for a time owing to the lack of Japanese cooperation.

For prisoners of war today there are two main safeguards against ill usage. The first is the very wide power to inspect possessed by neutral delegates of the International Red Cross and of the Protecting Power, and the right of every prisoner to speak direct with them. The second is the obvious one that in war, where all engaged have prisoners, any policy of ill-treatment would involve the risk of reprisals. *See* Red Cross, International.

Production, Ministry of. On Jan. 29, 1942, the Prime Minister announced in the House of Commons his intention to create an office more or less corresponding to that of the newly-appointed Minister of Production in the United States, Mr. Donald Nelson (*q.v.*). This decision had been made as a sequel to the Anglo-American agreement to pool shipping, munitions, and raw materials. On Feb. 2 Lord Beaverbrook, then Minister of Supply, was appointed Minister of War Production, and seven days later Mr. Churchill presented to Parliament a White Paper setting out the duties of his new Minister. On Feb. 19 the Prime Minister reconstructed his War Cabinet. Lord Beaverbrook was invited to join it, but declined on grounds of ill health (he had been suffering from asthma), and it was then announced that he would proceed to America and, after a period of recuperation, would carry on the work already begun in regard to the pooling of the resources of the United Nations, but no longer remain a member of the Government.

Mr. Oliver Lyttelton, Minister of State, then on his way home from Cairo, was charged with the general supervision of production, and on March 12 was appointed Minister of Production. In a review of his task which Mr. Lyttleton made in Parliament on March 24 he said that he was setting up a general staff of war production which would consist of Sir Walter Layton, his chief adviser on programmes and planning, the assistant chiefs of staff of the three Services, and the highest technical officers of the three production Ministries. This general staff would be the servant on war production of the Defence Committee. As a member of the Defence Committee he was in constant touch at the highest level with strategical plans and developments.

THE FUNCTION OF PROPAGANDA IN WARTIME

Chiefly by wireless broadcasts, the warring nations did their best to stimulate the efforts of their own people, influence neutral opinion, and undermine the morale of their adversaries. The Press gave further publicity to their efforts. Allied propaganda won credence by eschewing the absurd perversions of fact to which the Nazis were always prone. See B.B.C. ; Information, Ministry of.

Propaganda. Propaganda in wartime is best regarded as national advertising. Its function is two-fold. At home, its purpose is to increase the war effort ; abroad, it seeks to persuade other nations that the cause of the propagandist is a righteous one and that victory is assured. In view of its special function the material of propaganda differs widely from ascertained fact, such as historians seek and perpetuate. Hitler expressly recognized this difference when, in " Mein Kampf," he wrote : " Scientific

exposition is for the intelligentsia and propaganda for the masses." He added : " By clever persistent propaganda even Heaven can be represented to the people as Hell." Elsewhere in " Mein Kampf " Hitler set the standard of Nazi propaganda in the famous aphorism, " The bigger the lie the greater its value as propaganda," a standard which his henchman, Goebbels, adopted in its entirety.

Characteristic of the lengths to which the Nazi regime went in its efforts to hoodwink the German and neutral peoples was a broadcast play in which Mr. Churchill, as First Lord of the Admiralty, was represented as making a profit of £4,000,000 on the Stock Exchange in a few hours by withholding the news of alleged damage done by the Germans to H.M.S. Nelson. In the play Mr. Churchill was represented as stuttering with rage over the losses of British shipping ; another scene represented the sounding of the Lutine Bell at Lloyd's, as someone announced to "the terrified members" the loss of one ship after another. This farrago of nonsense continued for half an hour, and is only worthy of mention as evidence of what Hitler meant when he maintained that the bigger the lie the greater is its value for propaganda purposes.

Among the methods open to propagandists during the Second Great War wireless broadcasting was far and away the most potent. Fifteen million people in Britain alone listened to the 9 p.m. news bulletin from British stations every night, and when Mr. Churchill or President Roosevelt was making a big speech the audience, the world over, must have numbered hundreds of millions. During 1940 Mr. Churchill made ten broadcasts, six of them as Prime Minister, and in each case was heard all over the world. The broadcasts of King George on Empire Day 1940 and Christmas Day 1941 were equally valuable. Memorable, too, were Queen Elizabeth's message to the Women of France on the Fall of Paris, in French on June 14, 1940, and Princess Elizabeth's very first broadcast, that to the Children of the Empire in October 1940.

The 'Voice of Britain'

In British wireless propaganda the outstanding feature was the "Voice of Britain" broadcasting of war news in foreign languages. The earliest B.B.C. broadcasts in French, German and Italian dated only from the Munich Crisis of 1938. During 1940 "The Voice of Britain" was broadcast in 32 languages and 250,000 words were sent out every day. By the end of 1941 forty different languages were being used daily. Thus hope was sustained in the countries occupied by Germany, and a sense of the difficulties with which Britain was grappling was implanted the world over.

On July 20, 1941, "Colonel Britton," of the Ministry of Information, launched the "V for Victory" (q.v.) wireless campaign, which spread through occupied Europe. Lord Beaverbrook's Tank Week for Russia, in the autumn of 1941, was another outstanding effort.

Definite war propaganda in Great Britain was initiated when the Foreign Office Publicity Department was inaugurated in June 1939. The department was embodied in the newly-created Ministry of Information when the war began in September. On the Home Front the Ministry spent £2,568,000 between September 1939 and May 1941 upon poster and newspaper propaganda on behalf of the various Government departments. Thus the public were instructed to "Eat National Wholemeal Bread," to "Keep Your Children in the Country," to "Save for Victory," etc.

Five-minute and other films were specially made for the Ministry of Food, the Ministry of Health and other departments, and happily supplemented poster and lecture propaganda. The full-length film "Target for Tonight," featuring the work of Bomber Command, was shown all over the world, and equalled in popularity the series of Russian films which did so much to restore confidence in the Russian war effort. News films, specially prepared on the fighting fronts in Northern France, Libya, Norway, Syria and elsewhere,

were widely circulated in the United States and the Dominions and did great service to the British cause, as did the films which revealed the damage done to British towns during the Battle for Britain.

In the early days of the war the greatest personal notoriety among broadcasters was that achieved by Germany's "Lord Haw-Haw of Zeesen," who was generally believed to be a renegade of British birth, William Joyce. Haw-Haw's chief was, of course, Dr. Joseph Goebbels, the Nazi Minister of Propaganda, the most cunning, as he was the most crooked, exponent of national advertising thus far revealed. Goebbels fully realized the value of "hot news," and never waited for verification of any happening calculated to help Germany's cause. At times German news reached Allied or neutral countries before it was released in Great Britain, and difficulties arose. The fact that the news was exaggerated or completely untrue made no difference to Goebbels. Always he was concerned to drive home the impression of Germany's ruthless power, and at times his treatment of neutral nations was astonishingly naïve. One broadcast from Munich in 1939 actually announced, " If we fail to find friendly neutrals, we make them friendly." The propagandist announcer went on to recall that Poland and Czechoslovakia " were restored to friendliness by force."

Propagandists of the Front Rank

International propaganda presents special difficulties and calls for the nicest discrimination. This was shown when a number of British authors and lecturers were sent to the United States to explain the British case against the Nazi regime, and thus prepare for America's entry into the war. In general, such efforts proved to be ill-advised, and better results were obtained when American authors and lecturers addressed their own people. The American, Quentin Reynolds, author of the Sunday evening postscript addressed to Dr. Goebbels in 1941, was a front rank propagandist on the Allied side. Miss Dorothy Thompson was another. A. P. Herbert's Eastertide postscript in rhyme, " Let Us Be Gay," was also memorable. Perhaps the most effective episode in Allied propaganda, however, was H. F. Knickerbocker's revelations in the early days of the war that the leaders of the Nazi Party had invested £6,974,000 abroad. The details of these infamous transactions, originally published in the Paris " Soir," were wirelessed and cabled all over the world and the moneys and insurance policies benefiting Goebbels, Goering, Ribbentrop, Hess, Ley and Himmler were set out in detail.

Of special value were the daily B.B.C. broadcasts in Arabic, transmitted over the Near East and answering the insidious propaganda which Italy broadcast during the early months of the war, when she was still nominally at peace with Britain and France. Nor must the secret wireless stations in Germany, Czechoslovakia and other occupied countries be forgotten. The internal propaganda did much to inflame the hatred of the suffering nationals against Nazi brutality. The danger which these secret broadcasters were facing hourly added to the drama, and thus to the effectiveness, of the propaganda.

Provence. Completed in 1915, this French battleship belonged to the Bretagne class. She had a displacement of 22,189 tons, carried a complement of 1,133, and her speed was approximately 20 knots. On July 3, 1940, the Provence was at Oran in North

THE FLAGSHIP HOISTS HER COLOURS
One of Britain's mightiest battleships, H.M.S. Queen Elizabeth was flagship of the Mediterranean Fleet. This photograph shows the hoisting of the colours in the presence of the Commander-in-Chief, Admiral Sir Andrew Cunningham. The band of the Royal Marines plays the National Anthem while the salute is given.
Photo, British Official

flag " in Syria. But pressure from the Pétain Government, through Gen. Weygand, caused a change of front, and four days later Gen. Mittelhauser had to order the cessation of hostilities. This done, he was recalled and replaced by Gen. Fougère. Puaux and the new C.-in-C. received the Italian Armistice Commission in July, and expressed their willingness to cooperate with the Italians in every way consistent with their loyalty to Marshal Pétain's Government. But German-controlled Vichy evidently felt that the Puaux regime was not strong enough, for more and more French dissentients slipped over the frontier into Palestine and Transjordan to continue the fight against the Axis. So in November 1940 he was dismissed and the post of High Commissioner given to Chiappe (*q.v.*), a former Chief of Police in Paris, known for his ruthless methods. *See* Syria.

Purchase Tax. The introduction of this tax was foreshadowed by the Chancellor of the Exchequer, Sir John Simon, in the House of Commons on April 23, 1940. It was to be levied on all sales (except food, drink, tobacco, foodstuffs, fuel, gas, electricity and water, etc.) by wholesalers to retailers. Designed to restrict internal spending, the tax, it was estimated, would yield about £40,000,000 in 1940–41. On Oct. 15, 1940, the House of Commons approved by 138 votes to 28 the introduction of the tax, and it came into force on Oct. 21.

Africa, along with other battleships, cruisers, destroyers and submarines of the French Fleet. She was badly damaged and put out of action when, following the French admiral's rejection of the British ultimatum, units of the Royal Navy opened fire. *See* Oran.

Przemysl. Situated on the River San, 60 miles west of Lwow in Southern Poland, this town, the centre of a valuable petroleum-producing area, was captured by the Germans on Sept. 9, 1939. At the partitioning of Poland between Germany and Russia on Sept. 29, 1939, Przemysl was assigned to the U.S.S.R. The place was the scene of bitter fighting between the Germans and Russians when the former invaded Soviet-Poland on June 22, 1941. The Russian forces retreated eastwards in the face of the Nazi onslaught, and Przemysl was occupied by the Germans.

Puaux, GABRIEL (b. 1883). He was French High Commissioner for Syria from the beginning of 1939 until November 1940. On June 23, 1940, the day after the signing of the Armistice with Germany, Puaux broadcast a proclamation from Beirut to the effect that Gen. Mittelhauser (*q.v.*), French C.-in-C. in Syria, had decided " to defend the honour of France and of her

 Queen Elizabeth, H.M.S. This famous British battleship, completed January 1915, was the flagship of Admiral Beatty when the German Fleet surrendered in November 1918. She was the first British warship to carry 15-in. guns and to be driven entirely by oil fuel. The Queen Elizabeth, of the class to which she gave her name, has a displacement of 30,600 tons, a main armament of eight 15-in. guns, and a normal complement of over 1,100. In January 1942 she was the flagship of the Mediterranean Fleet, then under the command of Admiral Sir A. Cunningham.

Queen Elizabeth, R.M.S. The largest ship in the world, the 84,000-ton Cunard White Star liner, sister ship to the Queen Mary, made one of the strangest " trial trips " in history. On Feb. 26, 1940, the Queen Elizabeth (*see* pp. 3683–4) was moved from her builders' down the narrow Clyde to the sea. No news was given to the world until the day before the vessel arrived in New York, having accomplished her maiden voyage across the Atlantic with part of her launching gear still attached to her hull. Fitted with a de-Gaussing cable (*see* illus. in p. 92), a safety device against magnetic mines, she safely reached harbour on March 7. Although little was heard of this great vessel after her arrival in New York, she was later used as a transport, possibly conveying some of the many thousands of reinforcements sent to Malaya in 1941. She took part in a naval engagement in the Mediterranean on Nov. 25, 1941, with H.M.S. Valiant and Barham, where the latter was sunk off Sollum.

BRITAIN'S CRACK LINER DOCKING AT NEW YORK

The Queen Elizabeth (84,000-ton Cunard Liner), largest ship in the world, was still on the stocks when war broke out. On Feb. 26, 1940, she made the dangerous trip across the Atlantic to berth in New York. Here tugs are seen towing her into dock ; the Queen Mary, the Normandie and the Mauretania are in the background.

Photo, Fox

Queen Mary, R.M.S.

Launched in 1934, this Cunard White Star liner of 81,235 tons, sister ship to the Queen Elizabeth, was lying in New York harbour at the outbreak of war and had to remain there at a monthly maintenance cost of some £5,000. On March 21, 1940, the Queen Mary (*see* p. 3685) left the security of New York harbour for a secret destination.

Queen's Messengers.

By consent of H.M. the Queen, the Ministry of Food convoys that carry food and comforts to badly bombed towns are called Queen's Messengers. Units consist of a water tanker holding 300 gallons, two food lorries each containing 6,000 meals, two kitchen lorries equipped with soup boilers, fuel and utensils, and three mobile canteens to distribute the food. Five motor cyclists, for making and maintaining contact with local authorities, complete the convoy. Of the fleet of eighteen Queen's Messengers ready for duty in 1941 the first was the gift of Her Majesty, and the remainder were presented by the American Allied War Relief Organization. They are attached to the headquarters of each divisional food area and stand ready to rush to succour the homeless people of a bombed town.

Quisling, MAJOR VIDKUN (b. 1887).

Leader of the Norwegian Nazi Party (Nasjonal Samling). Quisling was appointed Prime Minister of occupied Norway on Feb. 1, 1942, the title subsequently being changed to that of Minister-President.

For many months before the German invasion of Norway Quisling, an ardent admirer of Nazism and Fascism, helped by the members of his party, had been preparing the way for the enemy. At the beginning of April, 1940, he went to Berlin for his final instructions. On April 9, three days after his return to Oslo, Norway was invaded, and Quisling was immediately appointed Premier of the so-called National Government set up by the Germans. Public reaction, however, was so strong that after one week's premiership he resigned.

On Sept. 28, 1940, Quisling was nominated the sole political leader in Norway. So great was the loathing felt by the majority of Norwegians for him and his party that, despite the risk of severe punishment, they could not disguise their hostility. There were frequent clashes in the streets between loyalists and Quisling's brownshirts, or Hirdmen, anti-Quisling demonstrations in schools, while crowds of youths and girls shouted " Long live King Haakon ! Down with Quisling ! " before the latter's headquarters. On Dec. 1, 1940, an attempt was made to assassinate Quisling as he was walking at the head of a Nazi youth procession at Fredrikstad. The bomb which was thrown exploded immediately ahead, but he himself escaped.

Speaking on March 12, 1941, Quisling said that it was his intention to " change the Norwegian mentality " and to make the Norwegian nation " a Germanic outpost of the greater Germanic nation."

On becoming Prime Minister, Quisling seized powers previously vested in King and Parliament, with legislative powers overruling the Constitution. He stated that his foreign policy would be to make peace with Germany.

For the despicable part that Quisling played in betraying his country to the invader he was destined to give his name to all other similar traitors, no matter what their nationality. *See* Norway

Rabaul. Capital of New Britain, the largest island in the Bismarck Archipelago, which was mandated to Australia by the League of Nations. On Jan. 20, 1942, it was heavily attacked by waves of Japanese bombers escorted by fighters, based on an aircraft-carrier and on shore bases. Their main targets were the aerodrome and the harbour, where a merchantman was set on fire. Three of the attacking 'planes were shot down and one damaged, and the R.A.A.F. lost five. This was the first large-scale attack on Australian territory. It was followed by two heavy attacks on the morning of Jan. 22, and that afternoon eleven enemy vessels were sighted off the coast. The radio station ceased transmitting and it was correctly assumed that the town had been evacuated in face of a Japanese invasion. In the succeeding days the garrison put up a splendid fight, and was assisted by the R.A.A.F., which attacked Japanese transports, but the opposing forces were too numerous for them, Rabaul was in enemy hands by the end of the month, and it served as an air and supply base for Japanese attacks on New Guinea and Australia. Continuous bombing by the R.A.F. did considerable damage, and up to the end of June 1942 no further Japanese offensive materialised.

Raczkiewicz, WLADYSLAW. He became President of Poland on Sept. 30, 1939, in succession to Professor Moscicki, who resigned when the Polish Government was driven into exile. M. Raczkiewicz had formerly been Governor of the Corridor province of Pomorze, and had also held office as President of the Senate and twice as Minister of the Interior. His first act as President in 1939 was to form a " Cabinet of National Unity " under General Sikorski. The French town of Angers became the Polish headquarters until the French débâcle. The Government was then transferred to England, where M. Raczkiewicz and members of his Cabinet were welcomed by H.M. the King on June 21, 1940.

Raczkiewicz, Polish President.
Photo, Associated Press

Raczynski, COUNT EDWARD (b. 1891). He was Polish ambassador in London from 1934 onwards, and in that capacity delivered a stirring broadcast message to the British people on Sept. 9, 1939, following the German invasion of Poland. He also addressed a historic Note to the British and French Governments. After the establishment of the Polish Government in London in June 1940 he was appointed Acting Minister for Foreign Affairs in 1941.

Radiolocation. Method of detecting the presence of aircraft at a distance. It depends on the sending out of a wireless beam which is intercepted or reflected by aircraft in flight ; by timing the interval between the emission of the beam and the arrival back of the same beam reflected an estimate can be made of the distance of the aircraft sought ; while the bearing and altitude of the aircraft can be determined from the known direction of the beam which has intercepted the 'plane. Owing to security reasons little information about radiolocation has been made available, but in June 1941 it was officially announced that such a system was now out of the experimental stage and had been used in Britain in successfully

detecting enemy raiders approaching our shores ; it had made it unnecessary to maintain standing patrols of fighters to patrol vital areas (*see also* pages 137, 138).

On Feb. 27, 1942, there was a successful British combined attack on the enemy radiolocation station at Bruneval, 12 miles N. of Havre ; the station was destroyed. Later in the year the Germans put out a story of an aircraft locating device which detected the wave emission from the engine magneto (the sparks of which set up electro-magnetic disturbances), but this was probably a mere tale for Allied consumption. For many years there had been stories of inventions which by interference with the magneto from a distance were claimed to be able to stop internal combustion engines. *See* Air Defence.

Admiral Raeder, Nazi Naval C.-in-C.
Photo, Planet News

Raeder, GRAND ADMIRAL ERICH H. A. (b. 1876). C.-in-C. of the German naval forces from 1935. Admiral Raeder had had a long naval career and during the 1914–18 War was chief of staff to Admiral Hipper. Priding himself on maintaining the " high standards " of the German fleet created by Kaiser Wilhelm, he tried, in an interview with American correspondents in March 1940, to justify German unrestricted warfare at sea by assuming the British blockade to be illegal.

R.A.F. *See* Royal Air Force.

Rajputana, H.M.S. Formerly a P. & O. liner, this 16,644-ton armed merchant cruiser was a sister ship of the Rawalpindi (*q.v.*). It was announced by the Admiralty on April 23, 1941, that the Rajputana was torpedoed and sunk in the North Atlantic while on patrol duty. Forty lives were lost.

Ram, SUBADAR RICHPAL, V.C. The outstanding courage and devotion of this gallant Indian officer of the 6th Rajputana Rifles, Indian Army, gained for him in June 1941 the posthumous award of the V.C. On the night of Feb. 7–8, 1941, during a British attack on enemy positions at Keren, Eritrea, Subadar Richpal Ram, second in command of a leading company, insisted on accompanying the forward platoon and led its attack on the first objective. His company commander being then wounded, he assumed command, leading the attack of the remaining two platoons to the final objective. Under heavy fire he then, at the head of some thirty men, rushed the objective with the bayonet and captured it. Under his inspiring leadership the party beat back six enemy counter-attacks until their ammunition ran out and they were surrounded by the enemy. This officer then fought his way back to his battalion with a handful of survivors. Again, on Feb. 13, he led the attack of his company on the same position. In face of heavy and accurate fire he pressed on fearlessly, until his right foot was blown off. He then suffered further wounds, which proved fatal. While lying wounded he spurred his men on, inspiring them with his resolute spirit, courage, and determination.

Ramb I. Italian commerce raider of 3,667 tons, armed with 4·7-in. guns. It was announced on March 8, 1941, that she was sunk in the Indian Ocean by H.M. cruiser Leander (*q.v.*). Ramb I was flying the Red Ensign when sighted, but on being challenged she hoisted the Italian flag and opened fire. One hundred of her officers and men were rescued.

Ramillies, H.M.S. This 33,500-ton British battleship of the Royal Sovereign class, with a complement of over 1,000 and a main armament of eight 15-in. guns, was completed in 1917. While escorting convoys in the N. Atlantic towards the end of May 1941 she joined in the search for the German battleship Bismarck (*q.v.*).

Vice-Adml. Ramsay, hero of Dunkirk.
Photo, "Daily Mirror"

Ramsay, VICE-ADMIRAL SIR BERTRAM HOME, K.C.B. (b. 1883). Flag Officer commanding Dover from 1939. As commander of the naval forces operating from Dover, Vice-Adml. Ramsay organized the evacuation of British troops from Boulogne when, on the night of May 23–24, 1940, six destroyers succeeded in bringing off 4,600 soldiers under heavy fire and bombardment. He was responsible, too, for the organization, a few days later, of that great armada of ships of all kinds, from destroyers to motor boats, that evacuated several hundred thousand British and French troops from Dunkirk (*q.v.*). His brilliant services were recognized on June 7, 1940, by the award of the K.C.B.

Ramsgate. While London was still untouched by the blitzkrieg, this popular Kentish pleasure resort and fishing port felt its full force. A particularly heavy raid occurred on Aug. 24, 1940, when entire rows of houses were demolished, the local gasworks set on fire, and firemen machine-gunned by the raiders. By September 1940 over one thousand houses in the town were destroyed. One of the targets of the German bombers was the aerodrome at Manston, near Ramsgate, where considerable damage was done.

Despite the frequent bombing attacks the loss of life in Ramsgate was comparatively small, owing to its magnificent system of air-raid shelters. Providing refuge for 60,000 people, these shelters—the finest in the country—were excavated in the chalk on which the town is built. They lie more than sixty feet below the surface and have a total length of four miles. There are twenty-two entrances, and from every part of the town one can be reached in five minutes. Owing to the formation of the land no artificial ventilation is needed, for a natural current of air passes through the galleries.

Rangitane, S.S. This liner of 16,712 tons, belonging to the New Zealand Shipping Co., was attacked by a German raider in the Pacific and sunk on Nov. 26, 1940. With about one hundred passengers on board she was on her way from Australia to England

when the enemy vessel was sighted. Without warning the raider fired a shot which went through the steering-gear; other shells followed rapidly, killing and wounding some of the passengers and crew. After weeks of imprisonment in a German supply ship, survivors were marooned on the little South Sea island of Emirau (*q.v.*).

Rangitiki, S.S. This 17,000-ton P. & O. liner was one of the main targets of the German raider Admiral Scheer (*q.v.*), which attacked the Jervis Bay convoy in mid-Atlantic on Nov. 5, 1940. She was the largest ship in the convoy and the first to be fired on by the enemy, who, from a distance of about eight miles, may have taken her for the escort vessel, H.M.S. Jervis Bay (*q.v.*). A few splinters went through the Rangitiki's funnels from shells bursting in the water, and the bridge was smothered in spray and shell fragments, but no appreciable damage was done. Thanks to the heroic action of the Jervis Bay the Rangitiki returned safely to a West Coast port.

Rangoon. The capital and chief port of Burma, Rangoon lies some 21 miles from the mouth of the Rangoon River, and is an important centre of communications by water, road and railway (*see* page 3432). It was a main objective of the Japanese, since its capture enabled them to menace India and to cut the main line of Allied transport of supplies to China. The first of many Japanese bombing raids was made on Dec. 23, 1941. At the cost of many 'planes, the enemy inflicted considerable damage in these raids, and casualties were heavy. Japanese troops entered Burma from Siam on Jan. 17, 1942, and after successive advances they occupied Rangoon on March 8. A "scorched earth" policy had been adopted by the defenders and everything of value was destroyed. General Wavell declared the loss of Rangoon to be even more serious a blow than the loss of Singapore. "As in Malaya," he said, "reinforcements were insufficient, they arrived too late, and they were insufficiently trained." For 44 days the defenders

RAMSGATE'S BOMB-PROOF SHELTERS

Ramsgate was one of the first English towns to suffer the full force of the Nazi bombing. Though repeatedly blitzed, its inhabitants had the advantage of an absolutely safe and well-ventilated shelter tunnelled out of the cliffs; it extended for four miles, had 22 entrances, accessible from any part of the town, and housed 60,000 people.
Photos, Fox

A.R.P. COMES TO RANGOON

Rangoon was heavily attacked by Japanese bombers. Surface shelters, like the one shown here, were hurriedly erected, but casualties and damage were considerable. The capture of the city was a serious loss to the Allies, since it opened the gate to the Burma Road and to India.

Photo, British Newsreels

had heroically endured the strain of a terrific pounding and all the hardships entailed by the shortage of men and supplies. in face of an enemy three times as numerous and most efficiently equipped and supplied. *See* Burma.

Rashid Ali-al-Gailani (b. 1889). A strong supporter of the Axis Powers, Rashid Ali became Prime Minister of Iraq on March 31, 1940, when a new Government was formed on the resignation of the Cabinet under General Nuri es Said. Rashid Ali resigned the premiership on Jan. 31, 1941, after refusing to comply, in spite of the Anglo-Iraqi alliance, with the British request to sever relations with Italy.

On April 3, 1941, Rashid Ali carried out a coup d'état, engineered by German intrigue. At one sudden stroke, choosing a moment when Parliament was in recess and the Regent absent from the capital, this cunning politician, with the assistance of high officers of the Iraqi Army, turned out the Prime Minister, deposed the Regent, and seized power. He then re-established himself as Premier and installed a new Regent in the name of the six-year-old King Feisal II. Later, with the arrival of British troops in Iraq, Rashid Ali's government took the line that the landing of further troops would not be permitted until the first batch had passed out of the country. This was a strange interpretation of the terms of the Anglo-Iraqi Treaty and, on the arrival of fresh British troops, a clash followed, Rashid Ali appealing to Hitler for help against a British "invasion." After a month of intermittent fighting the revolt collapsed, and at the end of May the usurper fled into Persia.

In June 1941, when details of the negotiations between Rashid Ali and Dr. Grobba, the German Minister sent to Baghdad, were revealed in Iraq, it was discovered that the former had received a substantial bribe to ensure his silence. Irrefutable evidence in British hands showed also that every move by him was made with the avowed object of betraying the Moslem nations in the Middle East and their British and Indian allies into the hands of the Axis.

At an Iraqi court-martial which tried the ringleaders of the revolt on Jan. 8, 1942, Rashid Ali, then in Berlin, was sentenced to death. *See* Iraq.

Rationing. *See* Food.

Raven, H.M.S. Fleet Air Arm School. Carefully selected men are chosen for training at these schools, which, though on land, are named like ships, such as H.M.S. Peregrine and H.M.S. Kestrel (*q.v.*). One part of the course deals with the recognition of British and enemy 'planes, scale models being used for the purpose. Air gunnery and map-reading are other important features of the training. *See* Fleet Air Arm.

Ravenstein, GENERAL VON. The first German general to be captured during the war, General von Ravenstein had served with distinction during the campaign in France, where he was in charge of the motorized infantry which succeeded in crossing the River Meuse. He was appointed Major-General of the 5th Light Armoured (Colonial) Division, which was converted into the 21st Panzers, and was sent to Libya. He was taken prisoner in November 1941.

Rawalpindi, S.S. The first real naval engagement of the war took place between the Rawalpindi, an armed merchant cruiser of 16,697 tons, formerly a P. & O. liner, and the German "pocket" battleship Deutschland (*q.v.*). The Rawalpindi, manned by merchant seamen, naval reservists and men of the R.N.R. and R.N.V.R., and forming a part of the Northern Patrol engaged in contraband control, sighted the Deutschland S.E. of Iceland on Nov. 23, 1939. Her crew were ordered to action stations, and

RAWALPINDI IN DAYS OF PEACE

This British merchant cruiser, while on patrol off the Iceland coast, sighted the German pocket battleship Deutschland, which, supported by another warship, opened fire. The Rawalpindi fought gallantly against odds, refusing to surrender. She went down with her flag flying.

Photo, Planet News

an attempt was made to escape under cover of a smoke screen. But a second enemy ship was soon seen to starboard. The Deutschland signalled the Rawalpindi to stop and when she failed to do so fired a shot across her bows. This warning being rejected, the battleship opened fire with her 11-in. guns and shortly afterwards the second German ship started firing. In face of these overwhelming odds the Rawalpindi gallantly fought the enemy until all her guns had been put out of action and nearly the whole ship was ablaze. She finally went down with her flag flying. Over 260 officers and men were reported missing, including the commander, Captain E. C. Kennedy, who went down with his ship. A few survivors were rescued by the armed merchant cruiser Chitral and twenty-six were picked up by the Deutschland.

Reading, DOWAGER MARCHIONESS OF (STELLA), D.B.E. Chairman of Women's Voluntary Services for Civil Defence from June 1938, Lady Reading was awarded the D.B.E. for services rendered in this capacity. *See* Women's Services.

Reconnaissance Corps. The fastest-moving unit in the British Army is the Reconnaissance Corps, known to the men of the Army as "Recce." Formed at the beginning of 1941, it is a lightly armoured and very fast-moving force, and its task is to provide a modern equivalent of the old divisional cavalry. Each scout company of the Corps carries with it a platoon of motorized infantry to be used against parachute troops or other enemy pockets of resistance, and to give support until the main body of troops arrives. These infantrymen have to be more highly trained than infantry of the line, specialists in the art of guerilla warfare and capable of acting on their own initiative. The Corps makes use of a variety of mechanized transport : motor-cycles, lorries, Bren-gun carriers, armoured cars and scout cars, and each unit is self-contained, with its own automatic cookers, repair outfits, petrol carriers, and A.A. weapons. Like the British parachute troops, the men of the Recce Corps are picked men and all volunteers. The Reconnaissance Corps takes its place in the van of an attack, spying out the land, holding up the enemy and sending back information by radio. *See* Commando Troops.

Badge of the Reconnaissance Corps.

Red Cross, International. The International Red Cross Committee is composed entirely of Swiss citizens. There are 25 members and they serve for three years.

The Red Cross movement was the idea of Henri Dunant. He was appalled at what he saw at the battle of Solferino. He approached the Geneva Society of Public Welfare, and in 1863 a committee of five was set up. It convened the first Red Cross Conference, 1863. It was called the International Committee. The Committee's purpose is to relieve suffering caused by war. It is neutral, impartial, independent. In outlook it is international.

In September 1939 the Committee informed all national Red Cross societies that it was prepared to cooperate to alleviate suffering. The first step was personal representation in all belligerent countries. These are the eyes and ears of the Committee, people with freedom of movement and very special powers.

The chief work is for prisoners of war (*q.v.*). The Committee guards the provisions of the Prisoners of War Convention, making representations to the Power concerned where there are infringements of it. Representatives inspect prison camps. There is a Prisoners of War Central Agency at Geneva. The chief function of this Agency is to transmit information as to prisoners and the missing. There are 8,000,000 cards in its index of men in all theatres of war. The French Index alone occupies the whole of the vast Hall of the Palais du Conseil Général, Geneva.

If a prisoner of war dies, the Agency informs the relatives and sees to the return of the dead man's personal belongings.

Next, it provides relief for prisoners of war : food, clothing, medicine, toilet articles, and so on. Having limited financial resources for this purpose, it encourages national Red Cross Societies to raise funds. To French prisoners alone the Committee has distributed over 1,500 wagons of bread, clothes, medical stores and tobacco. It also provides books—250,000 volumes have been provided—sports equipment, musical instruments, and so on.

It repatriates the permanently disabled, treats enemy aliens as prisoners of war, assists refugees and organizes and runs a postal message scheme between relatives separated by residence in different countries at war. *See* illustration in page 361.

Red Cross Society. The British Red Cross Society and St. John perform eleven services to alleviate suffering caused by war. Their Joint War Organization is the only body authorized by government to send standard parcels to prisoners of war (*q.v.*). It sends also books, including Braille books and educational books covering over a hundred courses, and games.

It searches for British and Dominions missing men of the Services and men of the Merchant Navy through a Wounded and Missing Department. It searches also for civilians in enemy countries and for men of our allies. Its Postal Message Service brought from the Channel Isles alone 25,000 replies in three months.

In nursing and first aid it has trained 300,000 men and women, most of whom are in Civil Defence, hospitals or the Services. It is establishing hospitals and homes to accommodate 15,000 patients, and these will be staffed by Red Cross personnel. It has already taken over and adapted over 200 country houses.

There were in 1942 over 1,000 ambulances bearing the familiar red cross in service ; 350 were attached to military commands. Over 50 per cent were four- and two-stretcher ambulances. It runs X-ray mobile units, canteens, physio-therapy units, vans and motor cycles. The Society has eight large Central Depots and more than a hundred smaller depots where medical supplies are stored against emergency should normal communications break down. A.R.P. and kindred Civil Defence services are being augmented with ambulances, personnel, auxiliary hospitals, medical stores, clothing and cash grants. Sick and exhausted Civil Defence workers are looked after and an extensive Private Hospitality Scheme is managed.

A quarter of a million work-party members throughout the country are busy making garments and comforts, medical supplies and so forth for the Services.

The Society looks after the troops in the Middle East through branches that cover Egypt, Sudan, Abyssinia, Palestine, Cyprus and Malta. £125,000 worth of stores have been supplied to them. To these activities help to Russia has been added and £250,000 had been sent by early 1942, apart from the seven-figure response made to Mrs. Churchill's Help Russia Fund organized by the Society.

Regent, H.M.S. This British submarine, completed in September 1930, has a displacement of 2,030 tons and carries a complement of 50. Among her Mediterranean successes were the destruction of a 6,000-ton Italian supply ship (announced Oct. 25, 1940) and the sinking of another Italian supply ship, almost certainly the 2,472-ton Citta di Messina (announced Feb. 23, 1941). Her commander, Lt.-Cdr. H. C. Browne, was awarded the D.S.O., and members of the crew received other awards, in October 1941, for " daring, enterprise, and coolness in taking H.M. submarine Regent into the port of Kotor to try to embark the British Minister to the Government of Yugoslavia, and in keeping her there for nine hours though surrounded by large Italian forces."

Von. Reichenau,
German C.-in-C.

Reichenau, FIELD-MARSHAL WALTER VON (1884–1942). A typical member of the German High Command and an extremist Nazi, Field-Marshal von Reichenau was on the General Staff of the German Army during the war of 1914–18, and played an important part in the German campaigns in Poland, the Low Countries, and Russia in the present war. Shortly before his death he issued the notorious " No Pity " Order of the Day, discovered by the Red Army amongst other Gestapo papers at Klin after the Germans' retreat. In this he commands the German troops to be merciless in their dealings with the Russians, and describes the supply of food to local inhabitants and prisoners of war as " unnecessary humanitarianism." On Jan. 17, 1942, it was officially announced in Berlin that von Reichenau, commanding the German 6th Army in the Ukraine against Marshal Timoshenko, had died of a stroke while on his way from the front to Berlin. Hitler ordered a State funeral for him and eulogized him as " the standard-bearer of the thoughts of a new age " and " one whose name would live for ever in the history of the German people and its armed forces." But it was rumoured that he had been shot by the Gestapo.

Reims. This French town (see p. 3454) was the headquarters of the Advanced Air Striking Force from the autumn of 1939 until May 1940, when they were forced back into Central France and finally to England.

Lord Reith,
British Politician
Howard Coster

In June 1940 a battle raged here for some days until the French, wearied and outnumbered, withdrew. On June 12 the Germans occupied the town.

Reith, JOHN CHARLES WALSHAM REITH, 1ST BARON, P.C., G.C.V.O., G.B.E. (b. 1889). For many years Director - General of the B.B.C., Lord Reith was appointed Minister of Information on Jan. 5, 1940. He was Minister of Transport, May to Oct. 3, 1940. He then became Minister of Works and Buildings and First Commissioner of Works, which appointment he held until Feb. 11, 1942, when he was succeeded by Lord Portal.

Reitz, COL. DENEYS (b. 1882). Minister of Native Affairs, South Africa, from 1939, and Deputy Prime Minister. Col. Reitz was one of the Dominion representatives who arrived in Great Britain at the end of October 1939 to co-ordinate the Empire's war effort. In this connexion he took part in the Empire Conference held in London during November 1939.

Col. Deneys Reitz,
South African statesman.

Rendel, GEORGE WILLIAM, C.M.G. (b. 1889). British Minister to the Yugoslav Government in London from August 10, 1941. Mr. Rendel was British Minister to Bulgaria, 1938–41, and in that capacity he conveyed to the Bulgarian Premier on March 5, 1941, Britain's formal announcement of her breaking off relations with Bulgaria. At the same time he asked for his passports. On his arrival in Istanbul on March 11, with the Legation and Consular Staffs, he had a narrow escape from death when a bomb exploded at his hotel. Four people, including the British Military Attaché's Secretary and two Turkish detectives, were killed and several injured, but Mr. Rendel himself was unharmed. This design on his life apparently originated in Sofia, where two suitcases were surreptitiously added to the Legation party's luggage. One case, that taken to Mr. Rendel's hotel, exploded ; and in the other case it was discovered that an apparent electric battery was a T.N.T. bomb. Both bombs were presumably intended to explode in the train. The force of the explosion was enough to rock the hotel, a substantial modern building.

Renown, H.M.S. A veteran of Jutland, this famous British battle cruiser, completed September 1916, was practically rebuilt between 1936 and 1939 at a cost of over £3,000,000 — as much as she cost

BRITISH BATTLE CRUISER IN ACTION

Here is H.M.S. Renown, famous British battle cruiser, as she steams at 30 knots in the Mediterranean, scene of her triumphs against the ships of the Italian navy. The Renown is seen firing a salvo from her forward guns during one of her many engagements with the enemy.

Photo, British Official: Crown Copyright

originally. She has a displacement of 32,000 tons, a main armament of six 15-in. guns, and carries a complement of about 1,200. On April 9, 1940, Renown sustained some damage when engaged in a running fight off Narvik with the German battleship Scharnhorst and a heavy cruiser of the Hipper class. In the course of the nine-minute fight the Scharnhorst was hit and forced to retreat. There were no casualties on board the British ship. Renown, flying the flag of Vice-Admiral

SUNK BY JAPANESE AIR ATTACK

The sinking of H.M.S. Repulse off Malaya by Japanese aircraft was announced by Mr. Churchill on Dec. 11, 1941. The news of this disaster was a blow to the country, but the comparatively small loss of life showed how fine was the rescue work. The Repulse is here seen at Malta.
Photo, Planet News

Sir James Somerville, was one of the units which inflicted heavy damage on the Italian warships intercepted on Nov. 27, 1940, off Sardinia. She also took part in the bombardment of the naval base of Genoa on Feb. 9, 1941, and in the search for the Bismarck in May 1941.

Repulse, H.M.S. This 32,000-ton British battle cruiser, of the Renown class, was launched in 1916, saw service in the last war, and was extensively refitted a few years before the outbreak of the present war. She mounted six 15-in. guns and a secondary armament of 4-in. guns, and carried a normal complement of about 1,200. Previous to her tragic loss in December 1941 she was repeatedly reported as sunk by the German broadcasting stations.

Whilst carrying out operations on Dec. 10, 1941, against Japanese transports attempting to invade Malaya, the Repulse, with the modern battleship, H.M.S. Prince of Wales (q.v.), which was operating with her, was repeatedly attacked by Japanese bombers and torpedo aircraft. These attacks were delivered with great determination, direct hits being scored by bombers flying at a height of 15,000 feet. The antiaircraft guns of the British ships, though putting up a fierce barrage and bringing down at least seven enemy 'planes, were not adequate protection against such attacks from the air. Owing to lack of fighter support, which arrived about an hour too late, these two great warships were lost. Survivors clung to wreckage or drifted in lifebelts until rescued by destroyers. Of the crew of the Repulse 433 were lost. Out of a total complement for the two ships of nearly 3,000 men at least 2,330 were landed at Singapore. Among those saved was the captain of the Repulse. Capt. W. G. Tennant. *See* Malaya.

Reynaud, PAUL (b. 1879). Prime Minister of France, March to June 1940. An orator of renown and an economist of high reputation, Reynaud was Finance Minister in the Daladier Government until March 21. 1940, when he superseded Daladier as Prime Minister, with the object of facilitating the co-operation of the Socialist Party

**Paul Reynaud
French Prime Minister**
Photo, Topical Press

in the war ministry. On May 18 Reynaud became Minister of National Defence and, when the crisis deepened in June, he added the portfolio of Foreign Affairs. He resigned after the capture of Paris and was succeeded by Pétain (q.v.).

Reynaud was never in favour of complete surrender and after the loss of Paris urged that the French Government should be transferred to North Africa. He would have accepted Churchill's offer of total union between Britain and France, including the sharing of man-power, finance and production. On this aspect of the alliance some of his declarations were historic. He said : " The field of Franco-British collaboration should be extended even farther. Already we have at our disposal an arm which, after the war, will serve to produce a healthy Europe."

As early as December 1939 Reynaud had urged that what the democracies lacked for twenty years in order to win peace had not been material means but lucidity and daring. " Our will must be firmer than the enemy's ; our union more total."

Reynaud's Cabinet in 1940 was too large for wartime needs and partisan considerations weighed too greatly in its decisions, but it will be remembered as the last Government to represent the Third Republic. Even his political enemies in the Vichy Government did not dare to bring Reynaud before the Tribunal at Riom (q.v.), though he was under arrest and was among those whom Laval at the National Assembly of July 1940, threatened with trial, for " betraying the duties of the office with which they were charged."

Reynaud was the victim of a motoring " accident " in July 1940, which bore a strange resemblance to the Nazi attempt upon the Austrian Dr. Schuschnigg in 1935.

Rhineland. According to the provisions of the Treaty of Versailles the Rhineland was demilitarized. When in March 1936 Hitler marched his troops into the area and proceeded to fortify it, he had made an important move in his progress towards war.

There are valuable coalfields in the Ruhr district, which occupies most of the Northern Rhineland, and 75 to 80 per cent of German war industry was located there. The Ruhr (q.v.) was therefore constantly bombed by the R.A.F. Attention was also given to Rhineland targets farther south, notably Coblenz, Mainz, Frankfort-on-Main, Darmstadt, Mannheim

war effort. On the outbreak of war two-thirds of the man-power of Rhodesia volunteered at once for service and all the paramount chiefs of native tribes asked how they could serve. Rhodesia became a centre for the Air Training Scheme of January 1940, and three schools were set up, two being at Salisbury and Bula-wayo. On April 24, 1940, S. Rhodesia decided to adopt con-scription. The first contingent of the Rhodesian Territorial Forces arrived at Suez to join the Allied forces in the Middle East at the end of April. In

Ludwigshafen, Karls-ruhe and Freiburg. The chief objectives were railway junctions and marshalling yards, oil storage plants and re-fineries, and blast fur-naces ; among others were aircraft and motor factories and aluminium works, munition works, power stations, docks, water-ways, bridges and roads. For a period in Sep-tember 1940 incendiary leaves were showered on the Black Forest and the Thuringian and Grünewald forests and Hartz Mountains, where concealed dumps of am-munition were exploded.

RHODESIANS TAKE TO THE AIR

Rhodesian squadrons of the R.A.F. played a magnificent part in aerial warfare. Rhodesia was an Empire Air Training centre. A detachment of Askari troops is seen, above, mounting guard on machines at Cranbourne. Top, Mr. O'Keeffe, Rhodesian High Commissioner in London, welcomes at a British port the first contingent of Southern Rhodesian airmen joining the R.A.F.
Photos, British Official; Keystone

Rhodes. Italian island in the Aegean Sea, close to the Dodecanese (*q.v.*) and sometimes counted as one of the group. It has an area of 545 sq. m. and its only town is the capital, Rhodes. Important Italian naval, submarine and air bases are established here, and these were heavily attacked by British naval and air forces. On Sept. 5, 1940, a British battle squadron attacked the submarine base, while bombers raided the aerodromes of Maritza and Calato, inflicting much damage. In November 1940 Rhodes was bombarded by British ships and 'planes. During the night of March 15–16, 1942, British light naval forces shelled the city of Rhodes, when important targets, including the E-boat base and harbour installations, were hit. The British forces suffered no casualties, the enemy having been taken by surprise.

Rhodesia. Divided into Northern and Southern Rhodesia (*see* pp. 3466–9), this British territory in S. Africa made a magnificent contribution to the Empire's

August 1940 the first contingent of Rhodesian airmen arrived at a Scottish port on their way to join the Royal Air Force under the Empire Air Training Scheme. They were destined to become part of the technical and maintenance personnel of Rhodesian fighter and bomber units later formed in Britain. There were large numbers of Rhodesians in the forces operating in Western Abyssinia in 1941. *See* South Africa.

Ribbentrop, Joachim von (b. 1893). German Foreign Minister. Joachim von Ribbentrop (his father was plain Colonel Ribbentrop) has had two careers : first, as head of the famous German Champagne House, Henkell, the daughter of whose proprietor he married ; secondly, as one of the chief lieutenants of Hitler and a political power in the Nazi Party.

He served as Ambassador to the Court of St. James's from 1936 to 1938. His tenure of that office was characterized by vulgarity (he spent prodigious sums

Von Ribbentrop,
German Foreign Minister.
Photo, Wide World

on the German Embassy) and very bad manners. He was, in fact, the negation of everything implied by the word "diplomat," and when he was replaced the Corps Diplomatique were glad.

Back in Berlin, Ribbentrop became Hitler's chief adviser on foreign affairs, a sort of shadow Foreign Minister behind Von Neurath. Many thought him Hitler's "böser Geist"— evil spirit. In March 1938 Chamberlain was striving to settle Europe by means of appeasement. He had brought off one coup—an agreement with Grandi about the withdrawal of foreigners from Spain. He desired to talk with Ribbentrop. What, then, were the points at issue between Britain and Germany? he inquired. There were two, replied Hitler's expert: first, objection to the rude remarks made in the British Press about the Fuehrer; secondly, a desire for lebensraum.

That talk took place on March 9, 1938, at a moment when, as Ribbentrop well knew—since the event was the execution of his own policy—German troops were moving into Austria. The next day Lord Halifax taxed Ribbentrop with bad faith. His answer was the ultimatum to Austria and, despite all solemn pledges, the Anschluss was an accomplished fact, and the first grab of the many to follow efficiently made. That transaction was typical of every other deal made by Ribbentrop in the foreign field, and his name became synonymous with double-dealing, chicanery, browbeating of the weak and truculent insolence.

On Dec. 6, 1938, Ribbentrop went to Paris and signed with M. Bonnet a joint declaration to the effect that no territorial questions remained outstanding between the two countries. His crime against Czechoslovakia is too well known to need more than passing reference. First a false case was worked up, based on alleged maltreatment by the Czechs of the Bohemian minority; then Dr. Hacha, the President, was summoned to Hitler and brutally presented by Ribbentrop with a demand for the dismemberment of that State. It was to be carved into three States, and Bohemia and Moravia were to be Reich protectorates. Refusal would involve the utter destruction of Prague. For hours Dr. Hacha was browbeaten and bullied. This was on March 14, 1939. The next day the invasion followed.

That year, while Chamberlain was assuring the House of Commons that all was proceeding well with the Moscow talks, Ribbentrop told Count Ciano, Italy's Foreign Minister, that Germany had signed a trade pact with the U.S.S.R. On Aug. 21 the Commercial Treaty was openly announced, and a Non-Aggression pact as well, and Ribbentrop set out to Moscow to sign it.

From Ribbentrop's point of view, he was enjoying a series of brilliant successes, and his appetite was whetted accordingly. Poland was the next bite. He took it wolfishly. The technique was the same. Trumped-up minority persecution charges, "Jewish problems," and so on. Chamberlain, still without full appreciation of the kind of people he had to deal with, offered to mediate. Von Ribbentrop agreed. But the Polish plenipotentiary must be in Berlin in 24 hours. What would be the acceptable terms?

asked the British Ambassador. In rapid German, Ribbentrop gabbled through them. A written version? No! Had Poland seen the terms? No. That was on the night of Aug. 29. Three days later, before either Britain, the mediator, or Poland, the chief party, had so much as seen Germany's terms, Poland was invaded and despoiled.

In 1940 Ribbentrop made many visits to Rome, the first being on March 10. Britain had detained Italian ships carrying German coal to Italy. Ribbentrop tied Italy to the Nazi chariot with an offer of 12,000,000 tons per annum. Completely oblivious to the anger in the Vatican against the Nazi regime, Ribbentrop sought and obtained an audience of the Pope, his object being to swing the Papacy towards Germany. The interview was stormy and he left a chastened man.

Ribbentrop was present in the famous coach at Compiègne when the French capitulated. Shortly afterwards he announced the successful solution of the South-East European situation. Actually the facts were that representatives of Hungary, Rumania, Bulgaria and Slovakia had been summoned to Germany and given direct orders.

Among those about Hitler, Ribbentrop is at once the most detestable and the most dangerous man. But his loyalty to his chief is unquestionable, and he is likely to survive that relationship which has proved fatal to so many in the past.

Richelieu. France's finest battleship, the Richelieu, completed in April 1940, had a displacement of 35,000 tons, a main armament of eight 15-in. guns, and carried a complement of 1,670. After the French surrender she took refuge at Dakar (*q.v.*) in French W. Africa, where on July 8, 1940, a twofold attack was delivered upon her by the British Navy. She was first disabled by depth charges dropped under her stern; then severely damaged by torpedoes dropped by aircraft of the Fleet Air Arm. Some months later it was stated that the Richelieu had been repaired.

Riom Trial. The French "war guilt" trial opened at the old-world town of Riom, near Clermont-Ferrand, on Feb. 19, 1942. The President and judges were drawn from the Supreme Court of the Republic, and the principal accused were Edouard Daladier and Léon Blum, former Prime Ministers, and General Gamelin, ex-Generalissimo of the combined Anglo-French forces. Other accused were Guy la Chambre, Air Minister in the Daladier Government, Robert Jacomet, former Controller-General of Armaments, and Pierre Cot, Air Minister in the Blum Government. M. Cot, who was in the United States, was tried in his absence. Paul Reynaud, Prime Minister at the time of France's collapse, and Georges Mandel, his Minister of the Interior, who were also under arrest, were not charged at Riom.

The charges against the accused were: betrayal of the duties entrusted to them; and attempts against the security of the State.

The President of the Court was M. Caous, and the Prosecutor M. Cassagnau, Advocate-General of the Court of Cassation. The judgement of the Court was not subject to any appeal and, though it had no power to pass sentence of death, it could pronounce the banishment of any of the accused.

When the Court assembled General Gamelin announced that, after full reflection, he had decided to take no part in the discussions. "I have already been

THE RIOM TRIAL OPERATED IN FAVOUR OF THE ACCUSED

Seated in solemn state, the nine judges are seen in the Court Room at Riom, while the French Public Prosecutor sits on the left.   Riom is the judicial capital of Auvergne, where the Vichy Government set up its Court to try Daladier, Blum, Gamelin, Pierre Cot, La Chambre, and others held to be responsible for France's defeat.

Photo, Sport & General

condemned on political grounds without being able to put forward my defence. My most ardent wish is that the Army may remain a guarantee of the independence of our country. I ask my two counsel to join in my silence, actuated by the same patriotic motives."

The other defendants intimated that their general defence was that the military chiefs were responsible for the military disaster, owing to their faulty utilization of the war material at their disposal.

Following Gamelin, Léon Blum opened his defence, emphasizing that he and his fellow prisoners had been condemned in advance by a sentence of the Chief of State (Marshal Pétain), based on the advice of his political counsellors. "Were not the mistakes of the High Command the determining cause of defeat ? We have put this question for the last year without those who have conducted the inquiry being willing to take it into consideration."

Daladier, in his defence, took a similar line, adding that Germany, which in reality was responsible for the war, wanted by this trial to obtain an acknowledgement of her innocence. Twice the President of the Court threatened to hear the case in camera if Daladier persisted in accusing Germany. It is to be noted that the committal for trial, in terms, stated that none of the counts of the indictment dealing with the diplomatic relations of France or the conduct of military operations would be heard in camera.

In the course of Daladier's examination M. Caous pointed out that in September 1939 France had only 3,000 tanks against 7,000 tanks of Germany. Daladier admitted this, but declared that Germany attacked with a total of tanks about equal to the French total. He criticized the dispersion of the French armoured units and their "premature" use in Belgium.

Guy la Chambre was similarly cross-examined by the President of the Court regarding the alleged shortage of fighter and bomber aircraft. La Chambre's answer was that, before the war, production

was at the rate of 35 machines a month. During a month of war it rose to 300 a month. Personally, he reorganized aeronautical production to such a degree that he delivered 3,300 machines between January 1939 and March 1940.

General Mittelhauser, who commanded the French Army of the Alps, gave evidence as to the lack of officers, anti-aircraft equipment, ammunition and tanks, adding that the army suffered from an absence of liaison with the air force. "If Gamelin had received sufficient British help he would not have been obliged to put into the front line divisions so badly officered." At this point Gamelin intervened with the statement that there were 4,000 more officers in France than in Germany at the time of the mobilization.

General François, who commanded in the Longwy region, and General Besson, who commanded the French armies behind the Maginot Line, also gave evidence, their main point being numerical inferiority. General Besson concluded his evidence with an impression of the French spirit at the outbreak of war. He said : "People were gloomy. They did not know why they were going to fight. It seemed that since the 1930 call-up the destiny of France no longer mattered to the younger generation."

As the trial at Riom progressed it became plain that its course was very different from anything the Vichy Government or its German masters had visualized. What Hitler wanted was a public admission by the highest authorities in France that the war had been instigated by Frenchmen and not by Nazi Germany. Hitler was not in the least interested in any inquiry into the reasons for the French military defeat, which, in fact, was what the Riom Court was seeking to determine. By the middle of March angry comments were appearing in the German newspapers, describing the Riom trial as a farce. Unveiled threats were launched against the judges and the Vichy Government if they failed to meet German wishes.

Nor was Marshal Pétain any better pleased. In framing the indictment the purpose of the authorities at Vichy was to make the accused responsible for the collapse of France. The investigations were expressly confined to events between 1936 and 1940, 1936 being the year when Léon Blum formed the Popular Front. Above all, Pétain was most anxious that no attack upon himself should be allowed. With Germany and the Vichy Government alike disgruntled, a summary end to the Riom trial seemed possible at any time.

It came in April 1942, when Pétain capitulated to Germany and allowed Laval to become head of a reconstituted Vichy Government. Indefinite postponement was certain after Hitler's speech at Zeughas on March 15, in which he denounced the proceedings because " those responsible for the war were not mentioned in a single word." Hitler first demanded the dismissal of M. Barthélemy, Vichy Minister of Justice, and of M. Pucheu, Minister of the Interior, who were held responsible for the fact that Riom had not proved a war-guilt trial. If the 650 witnesses who were to have been examined had, in fact, been called, the trial might well have outlasted the war itself.

Ritchie, Lt.-Gen. Neil Methuen, d.s.o., c.b.e., m.c. (b. 1897). General Ritchie came into the public eye when he was appointed commander of the Allied forces in Libya in November 1941. At the outbreak of war he was Brigadier (Acting Major-Gen.) on the General Staff, and was appointed Deputy Chief of Staff (Middle East) in 1941. He received his C.B.E. for his part in the Dunkirk evacuation. He was made commander of the Eighth Army in Libya on Nov. 26, 1941, in succession to General Sir Alan Cunningham. When Tobruk fell on June 21, 1942, General Auchinleck took over command. *See* North Africa.

Lt.-Gen. Ritchie, commanded in Libya.
Photo, British Official

Robin Moor. An American freighter of 4,985 tons, the Robin Moor was sunk in the S. Atlantic by a German submarine on May 21, 1941. Despite the American flag painted on her side the submarine commander gave orders to the captain, Edward W. Myers, to abandon ship and to leave her lying as she was—a perfect target. Immediately the Robin

Moor's lifeboats were launched the enemy fired a torpedo at her, followed by shells, and she sank in twenty minutes. The submarine officer promised to wireless their position. Some weeks later thirty-five survivors were landed at Cape Town by a British ship and eleven more at Pernambuco by the steamship Osorio, thus accounting for all members of the crew and passengers. Considerable feeling was roused in the U.S.A. by the sinking of the Robin Moor.

Rodney, H.M.S. One of Britain's two most modern battleships, H.M.S. Rodney was completed in August 1927. She had a displacement of 33,900 tons, a main armament of nine 16-in. guns, and carried a complement of over 1,300. On April 9, 1940, during a German air attack on British naval units off Bergen, Norway, she was hit by a very heavy bomb. Her armour withstood the impact and little damage was done. In May 1941 the Rodney, which had been escorting convoys in the North Atlantic, proceeded to join in the search for the German battleship Bismarck (*q.v.*). When, with H.M.S. King George V, she engaged the enemy on May 27, the gunfire of the two British ships silenced the Bismarck.

Rommel, Field Marshal Erich. Commander-in-Chief of the Nazi forces in Libya, F. M. Rommel proved to be a worthy opponent for the picked British generals who took the field against him. He had risen from the ranks and won the personal friendship of Hitler, serving on the Fuehrer's staff during the invasion of Czechoslovakia and later during the invasion of Poland, and commanding a division during the French campaign. When the Italians were routed in Libya, Hitler sent his crack Afrika Korps, under Rommel, to stiffen resistance. The forces at Rommel's disposal were two

F. M. Rommel, Nazi C.-in-C.
Photo, Associated Press

Panzer divisions, one Italian armoured division, and several Italian infantry divisions. He conducted a vigorous campaign for the recapture of Libya during the spring of 1941, but was beaten back in the autumn. In May 1942 he started another offensive, took Tobruk on June 21 and three days later was well over the Egyptian frontier. *See* North Africa, Campaigns.

FRANKLIN D. ROOSEVELT, AMERICA'S LEADER

Under President Roosevelt's inspiring leadership America became united against the Dictators. He stood as a great figure among the United Nations after Japan had struck her treacherous blow against the U.S. on Dec. 7, 1941, and the eyes of all freedom-loving peoples were then turned towards him. See United States.

Roosevelt, Franklin Delano (b. 1882). President of the U.S.A. from 1933. The early months of the war were for President Roosevelt difficult ones. He had a clear insight into the general drive of world events towards war, and knew the need for his country to put her defences in good order. Yet he was faced with the powerful opposition of the Isolationists, led by the whilom hero Charles Lindbergh and Senator Wheeler. At the Democratic Convention, Chicago,

Wheeler secured a resolution on July 18, 1940, defining American 100 per cent Isolationism from all wars European, Asiatic and African.

On that date President Roosevelt, having been again nominated for re-election on the Democratic ticket, told his fellow countrymen that the United States faced the choice : Dictatorship or Civilization. On that plain, unqualified platform the President brought into his camp Col. Alfred Knox and Mr. Henry

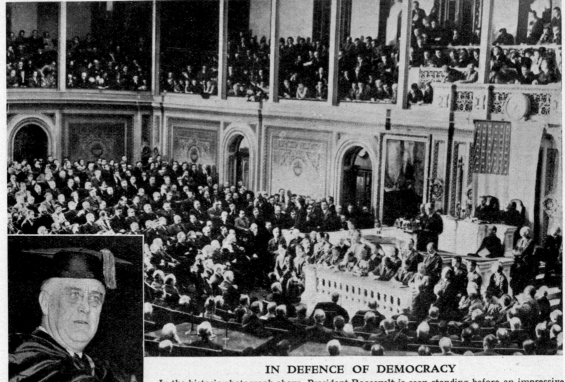

IN DEFENCE OF DEMOCRACY

In the historic photograph above, President Roosevelt is seen standing before an impressive row of microphones. He is asking Congress for a declaration of war against Japan, and within half an hour after he spoke war was declared against the aggressor. Inset, the President addressing the University of Virginia.

Photos, Keystone; Topical Press

Stimson, the one to the Admiralty, the other to the War Department.

Roosevelt's main preoccupation then was to succour Britain whilst he set turning the wheels of an ever-expanding war industry. On Sept. 2, 1940, Roosevelt made an agreement with Britain for Atlantic bases in exchange for fifty destroyers. On Sept. 16 he introduced compulsory military service. Thus Roosevelt was setting about the protection of the American Atlantic seaboard, recognizing the feasibility and possibility of aggression by Germany.

Seen in retrospect, these moves to secure cohesion of defence measures by Britain and the U.S.A. appear as the acts of a single national entity rather than the deals of separate sovereign States. Mr. Winston Churchill, speaking in the House of Commons on Aug. 20, characterized the agreements as decisive steps in the relations of the two countries. On Aug. 17 Mr. Mackenzie King, Canada's Liberal Premier, visited President Roosevelt and left with a Joint Commission of Common Defence outlined. Thus, bit by bit, the American continent was consolidating itself against the threat of major war.

That the President forced through his thorough-going programme of defence in the face of organized and German-inspired Isolationism; that he secured powers to run industry for war production; that he won to his side political opponents: all this revealed him as a forceful leader worthy, many thought, to be compared with the great Lincoln himself.

On Sept. 27, 1940, the Berlin Pact was signed. It constituted Germany, Italy and Japan as a coalition; and it was, clearly, the Totalitarian answer to the Anglo-American defence system. The pact bound Japan to attack the United States should that country enter into a state of war with the Axis partners. Mr. Churchill described it as a threat of violence, and added a characteristic comment. Now, however, the President had to turn thoughts and eyes from Atlantic to Pacific. On Oct. 9 Britain, the United States and Australia took counsel in Washington.

At Dayton, Ohio, on Oct. 12, the President spoke vigorously against the Three-Power (Berlin) Pact. He said: "No combination of dictator countries of Europe and Asia will halt us in the path we set ahead for ourselves." He enunciated the doctrine of totalitarian American defence: it was a restatement of the Geneva doctrine of collective security—one that may yet save the world of free men.

On Nov. 5 Roosevelt was re-elected President of the United States, the first President to serve a third term. For Britain, that re-election meant the continuance at the White House of a good friend of Great Britain. Thereafter occurred in the United States one of those swing-overs in politics that are as dramatic as they are psychologically obscure. Wendell Willkie, defeated presidential candidate, large, loose-limbed, good-hearted, declared: " He is my President as he is yours," words that were a sort of coda to the general national orchestration of pro-Roosevelt feeling.

Roosevelt continued to reveal himself as a strong man and a fearless. When Japan made a feint at

Eastern Asia with a vast troop concentration, obviously aimed at the Malay Peninsula and the Netherlands East Indies, Roosevelt calmly authorized a loan of $100,000,000 to China's General Chiang Kai-shek. As between the United States and Japan the temperature was rising steadily. On Dec. 22, 1940, the President put an embargo on iron and steel exports to Japan.

After his election Mr. Roosevelt went on holiday. He returned and called a Press conference, the method he has always preferred to get across ideas to the people. On Dec. 7 he told the press-men he was going to put before Congress a plan for all-out aid for Britain. The position of the United States was, by the end of 1940, that of a country participating in a war short only of armed intervention in it.

On Jan. 6, 1941, the President outlined to Congress the principles and policy he intended to apply and work out. He had become, clearly, a man of one idea, inflexible of purpose and case-hardened against attack. He saw that the world could not survive if the Totalitarian States beat Britain to her knees. He meant to help Britain. He intended to swing the United States over to a war footing. In his public utterances —and he has a voice clear and resonant, and strong with the speaker's sincerity—Roosevelt has uttered phrases as fine as any voiced by Mr. Churchill. Speaking on Jan. 20, he said : " Lives of nations are determined not by the count of years but by the lifetime of the human spirit, by the fullness of the measure of its will to live." Throughout the period under review, and up to the spring of 1942, Hitler lost no opportunity of abusing Mr. Roosevelt as a Jewish warmonger of the worst description.

On March 11, 1941, the Lease-Lend Act (p. 223) was signed by Mr. Roosevelt, and a fortnight later the Appropriation Act which provided the necessary funds. At the eleventh hour (as time was to prove) American Isolationists, who had seemed to be moderating their extremist views, suddenly attacked in force. The passage of both the above measures revealed the strength of this great President and his unswerving steadfastness of purpose.

President Roosevelt, the man who had refused to accept a decree of Fate that, in mid-life, he should surrender to the infantile paralysis that then rendered him physically useless, applied now the same indomitable will to the rousing of a half-awakened, half-aware America. In mid-April he " froze " the assets in America of the aggressor nations ; occupied West Indian bases, and, in July, put American troops on Iceland. On Aug. 14 he met Mr. Winston Churchill in mid-Atlantic and with him drew up the Atlantic Charter, a definition of common aims and ideals. On Sept. 11 the President, following the sinking of the U.S.S. Greer, issued

his historic order " Shoot First." On Oct. 9 he called on Congress to revise the Neutrality Act. On Nov. 6 he announced a loan to Russia and " all aid."

On Dec. 7 that which the President had foreseen as inevitable came to pass, and the United States, so long upon the fringe of it, was brought into the war by the Japanese attack on Pearl Harbour. On Dec. 26, at the President's invitation, Mr. Churchill addressed Congress in the Senate House, a signal honour.

The coming of total war gave the American public of all parties and racial origins the opportunity of examining the President's policy from 1939 onwards, retrospectively. It was then seen to be prescient and prudent wherever the fundamental interests of the United States were concerned.

From May 29 to June 4, 1942, Mr. Roosevelt had conversations with M. Molotov. Full understanding was reached on the question of a second front in Europe. Other activities and important utterances of Mr. Roosevelt appear under the heading United States.

Rosenberg, ALFRED (b. 1893). This Nazi " cultural leader " and Party " expert " on Russian affairs (himself a Balt) was appointed Minister for the occupied Russian territories in November 1941. When the Nazi political creed was in its early stages Rosenberg, an emigré from Bolshevist Russia, went to Munich, where he formed a close friendship with Hitler. On the Nazi Party's advent to power Hitler appointed him Director of Foreign Press, Director of Philosophical Outlook for the Reich, and editor-in-chief of a chain of official newspapers, most prominent of which was the " Volkischer Beobachter." From that time onward he was engaged in broadcasting the propaganda of a new doctrine.

Rostock. German port and commercial centre on the Baltic. The port, U-boat building yards and Heinkel factories were heavily bombed by the R.A.F. on four consecutive nights, April 23–26, 1942. Severe damage was inflicted, resulting in a complete stoppage of war supplies.

Rostov-on-Don. Capital of the North Caucasian area, Rostov-on-Don lies 27 miles inland from the mouth of the River Don, which flows into the eastern

WELCOMING THEIR DELIVERERS
These delighted inhabitants of Rostov-on-Don are hurrying to meet the Russian troops as they enter the town. The nightmare of the Nazi occupation and its attendant horrors is over at last, and down the wide thoroughfare crowd men, women and children, free citizens once more.

Photo, Associated Press

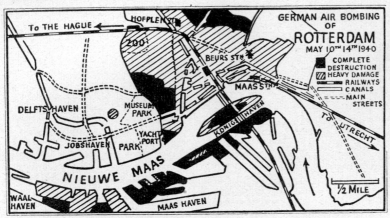

GERMAN AIR BOMBING
OF
ROTTERDAM
MAY 10TH 14TH 1940

COMPLETE DESTRUCTION
HEAVY DAMAGE
RAILWAYS
CANALS
MAIN STREETS

Areas of devastation wrought by the Germans in Rotterdam in May 1940.

tip of the Sea of Azov. Rostov is an important railway junction and industrial centre. A huge plant for the manufacture of tractors and agricultural implements was built here, to effect the mechanization of agriculture, which was part of the First Five-Year Plan. Production could be (and was) switched over to the manufacture of tanks and machine-tools. Rostov has additional importance from the fact that the oil pipeline from the Caucasus runs through it. It was therefore a main objective of the German armies under General von Kleist in their drive towards the Caucasus.

On Nov. 22, 1941, strong German forces, headed by tanks, succeeded in entering the city, at the cost of very heavy losses in men, tanks, guns and other equipment. The Russians bitterly contested their entry in house-to-house fighting, and carried out a "scorched earth" policy, which left nothing of value for the invaders. Marshal Timoshenko, newly in command in this area, rallied his troops for a terrific counter-attack, which regained the city on November 28. The retreating Nazis indulged in an orgy of murder and bestiality, looting and fire-raising, which their propaganda was afterwards compelled to try to justify by the argument that the civilian population, in defending their homes, were violating international law and needed exemplary punishment. The victorious Russian army pursued them as far as Taganrog, some 40 miles to the west, and drove them headlong along the road to Mariupol, in a thrust to clear the Crimean area. The German retreat from Rostov was Hitler's first major defeat in the field of battle.

Rotterdam. Chief port and second largest city in the Netherlands, Rotterdam (*see* p. 3537) was the scene of some of the fiercest fighting during the Nazi invasion. In the early hours of May 10, 1940, large numbers of German troops landed here from transports which had made their way down the coast during the night. Despite furious opposition by Dutch local forces they established themselves in the harbour area, and also, in conjunction with waves of parachutists, captured the airport of Waalhaven, some four miles south of the city. As in other places, the invaders were powerfully and cunningly aided by Nazi sympathizers amongst the Dutch civilian population. Directly Waalhaven was seized the R.A.F. bombed the aero-

PITIFUL SCENE OF DESOLATION AT ROTTERDAM

One of the most prosperous ports in the world, Rotterdam was bombed by the Nazis with Teutonic thoroughness, and the destruction of the city was comparable with the savage attacks against Warsaw and Belgrade. Here is the centre of the city after the Nazis had done their worst, a solitary house in a once-populous district testifying to their barbarian methods.

Photo, Wide World

drome and the German forces assembled there, destroying many of the troop-carrying 'planes on the ground. The Dutch, in a determined counter-attack, managed to gain a footing there again, but it was shortlived. The Germans poured in men by air and secured a hold on the airport that could not be loosed.

On May 14 Rotterdam suffered one of the most terrible air raids of the war, the centre of the city being completely devastated. Two squadrons of German bombers, meeting no opposition, flew backwards and forwards over the city and ploughed what were described as veritable furrows of destruction across its densely populated shelterless centre. In half an hour nearly two square miles were converted into a vast heap of rubbish and 30,000 people were killed, besides thousands more injured. That evening Gen. Winkelman announced that Rotterdam had surrendered and that, to save the civilian population, he had ordered the troops to lay down their arms.

After the German occupation of Holland the R.A.F. made frequent raids on oil depots, the docks, and enemy shipping and barge concentrations at Rotterdam. *See* Netherlands, Invasion.

Rouen. One of the chief ports of France, Rouen is about 80 miles from the mouth of the Seine and 87 miles N.W. of Paris. During the early months of the war General Gort established base reinforcement depots there. Following the German break-through in June, the advance guard of the Nazi troops reached Rouen on June 9, 1940, and the town remained in enemy occupation. It was an occasional target for the R.A.F., which bombed the shipyards and power station. On March 25, 1942, the shipbuilding yards at Le Trait, west of Rouen, were attacked.

Rovaniemi. An important railhead of Northern Finland, the town of Rovaniemi is within the Arctic Circle. It suffered heavily from bombing attacks by the Russians in the Russo-Finnish war.

BRITAIN'S UNCONQUERABLE AIR FORCE

" Never in the field of human conflict was so much owed by so many to so few."
Mr. Churchill's phrase thus aptly described the magnificent work of the R.A.F. during the never-to-be-forgotten days of the Battle of Britain. See Aircraft; Air War; Bomber, Coastal and Fighter Commands; also the various campaigns; and Colour Plate facing p. 16.

Royal Air Force. The Royal Air Force was twenty-one years old when the Second World War broke out. It came into existence on April 1, 1918, when the Royal Flying Corps and the Royal Naval Air Service were merged into a single service.

In the period between the war of 1914–1918 and the present conflict the R.A.F. underwent drastic changes ; a great reduction was made in its strength in the early post-war years, and then, when this policy had become plainly ill-advised, a belated expansion programme was formulated. The high standards which have been reached in the production of aeroplanes for the R.A.F. will go down in history, and they cast a clear light on the brilliance of British aircraft designers who, over a period of years, worked under difficult and often disheartening conditions.

PREPARING FOR ANOTHER FLIGHT
" All black " Hurricanes were thus camouflaged because their principal activity was night-flying over Britain and enemy-occupied territory. An armourer is seen re-ammunitioning the cannon of one of these machines.
Photo, Central Press

The peak of development of the single-seater biplane fighter, represented by the Hawker Fury and the Gloster Gladiator in 1935, preceded the advent of the low-wing monoplane fighter, which, it is no exaggeration to say, altered the course of the war in 1940. These machines were the Hawker Hurricane and the Supermarine Spitfire. The former was issued to service squadrons of the R.A.F. in the spring of 1938, and the Spitfire, closely related to the record-breaking S.6 Schneider Trophy seaplane, was delivered in July 1938.

Other aircraft which went into service shortly before the outbreak of war were the Army Cooperation Westland Lysander, the Armstrong-Whitworth Whitley (Mark V) heavy

A.C. Marshal Sir H. Dowding, built up air fighting force.
Photo, British Official

bomber, the Vickers-Armstrong Wellington heavy bomber, the Bristol Blenheim and Handley Page Hampden medium-heavy bombers, and the Short Sunderland general reconnaissance flying-boat. These aircraft were designed and equipped for specific purposes laid down by the Directorates of Military Cooperation, Bomber Operations, and Naval Cooperation, all part of the Department of Chief of Air Staff.

The Air Staff consists of the Chief, Vice-Chief, Deputy Chief, and Assistant Chiefs responsible for General Duties, Operational Requirements and Tactics, and Intelligence. In 1942 the Chief of the Air Staff was Air Chief Marshal Sir Charles Portal, K.C.B., D.S.O., M.C. The Vice-Chief was Air Chief Marshal Sir Wilfrid Freeman, K.C.B., D.S.O., M.C.

The R.A.F. is divided into nine commands at home. These consist of the Fighter Command, Bomber Command, Coastal Command, Army Cooperation Command, Balloon Command, Ferry Command, Flying Training Command, Technical Training Command, and Maintenance Command.

The Fighter Command, with the squadrons it controls, has made history from the first phase of the conflict. The defence of Britain against attack from the air was, and still is, its main function. The aerodromes where its squadrons are stationed are situated in prescribed sectors which are controlled by Group Headquarters. All sectors are interconnected by an intricate system of communication, and, through Operations Rooms, Command Headquarters is provided with a minute-by-minute tracing of every movement and development of air actions over this island.

The Air Officer Commanding-in-Chief of Fighter Command at the time of its inception was Air Chief Marshal Sir Hugh Dowding. He held this appointment from July 1936 until 1940, in which year the epic drama of the Battle of Britain was enacted, when the Hurricanes and Spitfires during the months of August, September and October accounted for 2,375 enemy machines. The defending squadrons lost 724 aircraft, but 374 pilots were saved (*see further* page 383). In 1942 the A.O.C.-in-C., Fighter Command, was Air Marshal Sir Sholto Douglas, K.C.B., M.C., D.F.C. Early in 1941 new duties were allotted the squadrons

of Fighter Command. With Hurricanes re-equipped with cannon and twelve machine-guns, they changed their tactics from the purely defensive to wider and offensive action against the enemy when they carried out " offensive sweeps " over occupied France. In the first months of 1941 assaults on enemy aerodromes, transport, gun emplacements, barracks, and assembled ground forces were pressed home with great tenacity and great effect. These attacks were achieved by flying at a low level, and later the Hurricanes were again modified so that they could carry two 250-lb. delayed-action bombs with which much execution was done at roof-top height. The cannon-equipped Hurricane was also employed in attacks on enemy shipping in the Channel, and the fire from the guns, which are of 20-mm. calibre, had the most devastating results.

In the first months of the war, when the enemy made tentative daylight bombing attacks on Scotland, the Hurricane and Spitfire pilots showed their unquestionable power as defenders of Britain. Then there was the Battle of Britain, when an unsurpassed gallantry and skill against tremendous odds stirred the whole civilized world. Thus did the R.A.F. play its part at home. From September 1939 until the capitulation of France units stationed in that country served with the same devotion to duty, efficiency and resolution. The squadrons formed what was known as the Advanced Air Striking Force, and though their operations were at first on a relatively small scale, there was plenty of evidence here too that the British air arm was superior to that of Germany. No greater proof is to be found than the R.A.F.'s part in the evacuation of the British Expeditionary Force at Dunkirk, when the squadrons which had been based in France joined home-based fighters in the unforgettable and unequal struggle which went on from May 29 until June 4.

Throughout the first twelve months of the conflict the Coastal Command and Bomber Command operated with ceaseless energy. The squadrons of Coastal Command, under the leadership of Air Chief Marshal Sir Frederick Bowhill, K.C.B., C.M.G., D.S.O., carried out daily patrols to protect shipping in all weathers. Using the American Hudson reconnaissance-bomber and the Short Sunderland general-reconnaissance flying-boat, British pilots and their crews flew far out over the wastes of the Atlantic and the North Sea, searching for and attacking U-boats and enemy surface raiders. Later, when the Command was expanded, strengthened and equipped with fresh long-range

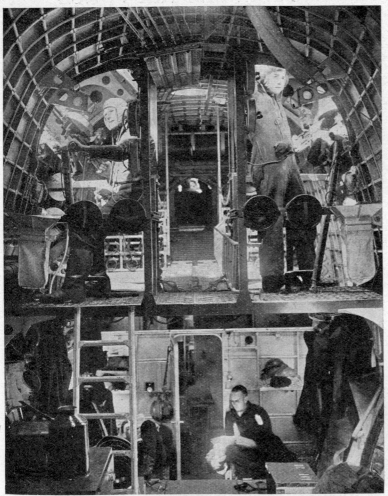

INSIDE A FLYING BOAT OF COASTAL COMMAND

R.A.F. Coastal Command played a splendid part in the protection of British convoys, patrolling enemy-occupied shores and attacking German shipping. Here is a view of the inside of one of the large flying-boats. The men above are gunners at their posts, while those below are off watch and are resting in the crew's quarters.

Photo, Fox

R.A.F. GUNNERS AND MECHANICS IN TRAINING

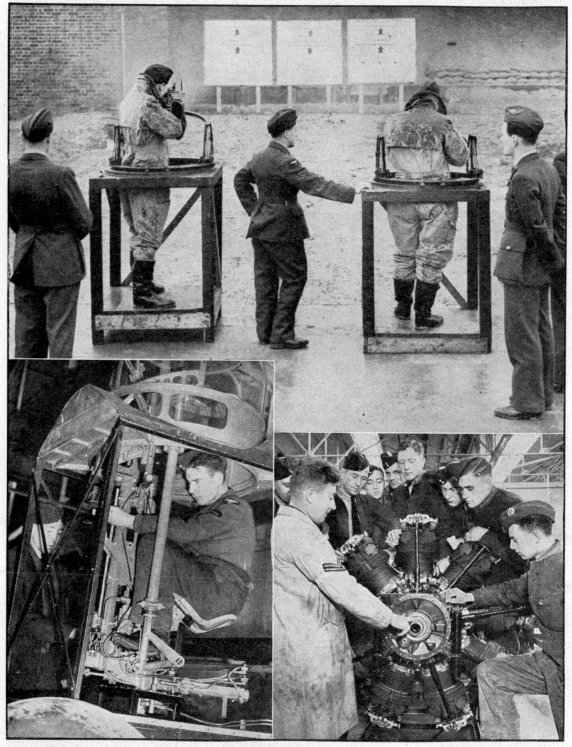

Officer trainees, who are undergoing instruction in gunnery at a West Coast aerodrome, are seen in the top picture putting in some target practice. Below, left, an unusual study of members of the R.A.F. ground personnel in the gun turret of a machine ; working of the gun turret is included in their training. Right, keen young trainees, newly drawn from all walks of life, at an engineering lecture, where they are learning to be fitters.

Photos, Keystone; Fox; Sport & General

aircraft, such as the American Catalina flying-boat and the huge four-engined Liberator bomber, this vital work was intensified, so that in two years no less than 40,000,000 miles had been flown on operational sorties. By September 1941, 240,000 tons of enemy shipping had been sunk and seriously damaged by bombs and torpedoes dropped by machines of the Coastal Command. Hudsons, Sunderlands and Catalinas were responsible for the tracking of the Bismarck, and one Hudson performed the unique feat of capturing a U-boat in September 1941. In searching for the Bismarck, in the last phase of the memorable chase, one Catalina flying-boat was in the air for nearly 21 hours.

The distinction of striking the first blow at the enemy in the Second Great War fell to squadrons of the Bomber Command. These units, equipped with Bristol Blenheims, went into action on the afternoon of Sept. 4, 1939, the destinations being Brunsbüttel and Wilhelmshaven, where German warships were bombed from a low altitude. The operation was the prelude to the gigantic task of bombing the enemy in his own territory. The fall of France, which deprived the R.A.F. of bases which would have provided the British bombers with starting points for short-range raids, and the entry of Italy into the war, placed

LOADING A STIRLING WITH BOMBS
Since March 1941, when it first came into service, this great four-engined bomber, the Short Stirling, has night and day carried the war into the enemy's own territory. Powered with Bristol Hercules engines of 1,400 h.p., it carries extremely heavy loads. Its manoeuvrability and powerful armament enable it to tackle fighter aircraft.
Photo, P.N.A.

incalculable obstacles in the way of Bomber Command. While the Luftwaffe was able to use aerodromes less than thirty miles away from England's coast-line, the R.A.F. had to fly distances of many hundreds of miles to reach its objectives in Germany, and over a thousand miles to strike at Italy from the air. Yet the long-term bombing policy was adhered to, and raids fraught with great difficulties and hazards were carried out. Berlin was attacked by R.A.F. bombers for the first time on the night of Aug. 25, 1940, and by the second anniversary of the outbreak of war the capital had been raided 48 times. Altogether in two years the Bomber Command units had assaulted 241 targets in Germany and there had been over 1,700 raids. On a number of occasions home-based bombers flew to Northern Italy and bombed Milan, Turin and Genoa. As well as these attacks on the homelands of the Axis, British airmen were also engaged in raiding places important to the enemy in Holland and Norway.

During 1941 the Bomber Command (A.O.C.-in-C., Air Marshal Sir Richard Peirse, K.C.B., D.S.O., A.F.C.—and later Air Marshal A. T. Harris, C.B., O.B.E., A.F.C.) received and placed in service two new types of four-engined heavy night-bombers, the Handley Page Halifax and the Short Stirling. Deliveries also began of the American four-engined bomber the Boeing Flying Fortress. Delivery of American bombers and flying-boats entailed further duties for men of the R.A.F., and as the need rose with the U.S. allotment of machines steadily increasing, the Ferry Command was formed. Pilots and air crews were transferred from various branches of both the R.A.F. and the Royal Canadian Air Force to this Command, and long-

R.A.F. Attacks on Enemy-Occupied Territory

Main Targets	Number of Attacks 1.1.40 to 31.12.41	1.1.42 to 31.8.42	TOTAL
Antwerp	32	4	36
Boulogne	123	9	132
Brest	97	15	112
Brussels	28	—	28
Calais	89	6	95
Cherbourg	67	8	75
Danzig	—	1	1
Dunkirk	83	14	97
Flushing	66	3	69
Gdynia	—	1	1
Le Havre	63	29	92
Lille	—	4	4
Lorient	53	1	54
Ostend	90	12	102
Rotterdam	79	2	81
St. Omer	22	9	31
St. Nazaire	23	14	37
Schipol	35	—	35
Stavanger	35	—	35
Texel	28	—	28
Waalhaven	21	—	21
Zeebrugge	15	—	15

Note.—Raids by Bomber and Coastal Commands are included.

READY FOR AN ENEMY SHIP
Here is a "tin fish" being loaded aboard a Bristol Beaufort in readiness for another attack on enemy shipping. This type of torpedo bomber of Coastal Command, in service since early 1940, took a very heavy toll of Axis ships.

Photo, British Official

equipment, and new fighters and new bombers were replacing some of those types which had done notable service. Progress was to be noted in particular in the design of night-fighter aircraft and a means of locating the enemy in darkness so that home defence was likely to be far more effective.

Details which later became known made it clear that the Battle of Britain will stand in the world's history as a milestone in the development of aerial combat. It was the first time that hundreds of bombers with hundreds of escorting fighters were used daily in single operations and the unparalleled prowess of the defensive fighters changed the whole complexion of the progress towards world-wide conquest. The young pilots of R.A.F. Fighter Command did, indeed, save the world.

range aircraft were flown direct from America to Britain with increasing frequency and noteworthy success. The Ferry Command, formed in 1941, was placed under the command of Sir Frederick Bowhill, whose position as A.O.C. Coastal Command was taken over by Air Chief Marshal Sir Philip Joubert De La Ferté, K.C.B., C.M.G., D.S.O.

From the day Italy entered the conflict the R.A.F. was faced with additional burdens, tasks and problems. In the African and Mediterranean theatres of war squadrons of the Middle East Command, under the leadership of Air Chief Marshal Sir Arthur Longmore, G.C.B., D.S.O., and later of Air Marshal A. W. Tedder, had to combat the Italian air force in Libya, Abyssinia, Eritrea and also Greece. With what success the British fought the Regia Aeronautica is plainly shown by the losses of aircraft of both sides between June 1940 and July 1941. They were: Italian, 2,617; British, 380. The invasion of Greece and Crete by the Germans, and the extension of the Luftwaffe's activities to Libya to support the sorely-pressed Italian forces, added to the immensity of the task of the Middle East Command. Yet through the aid of the U.S., which were supplying Britain's Air Force with more and more machines in Africa, numerical superiority was gained in the latter end of 1941, and this had a profound influence in the second British offensive in Libya. By the end of that year, when the war had spread to the Far East, the R.A.F. was operating over the Seven Seas. Squadrons were serving as far afield as in Iceland and Burma, North Russia and Libya and Malta.

At home important changes were being made in the

WOMEN WORK ON SPITFIRES
Members of the Women's Auxiliary Air Force perform most useful, varied, and often arduous tasks in the course of their day's work. Many are skilled engineers, such as those seen above fitting guns into the wings of a Spitfire.

Photo, "Daily Mirror"

In the epic struggle which lasted from Aug. 8 until Oct. 31, 1940, the enemy employed hundreds of JU 88, Heinkel 111, Dornier 17 and Dornier 215 bombers as well as his notorious dive-bomber, the JU 87. The protecting escorts consisted of hordes of ME 109 single-seat fighters and ME 110 long-range twin-engined fighter machines. From dawn to eye these aircraft of the Luftwaffe were faced continuously by Hawker Hurricanes, Supermarine Spitfires and, in small numbers, Boulton-Paul Defiant two-seater fighter aircraft. Throughout the eighty-five days of the critical struggle the R.A.F. was invariably outnumbered. Yet always the odds were accepted and when the protracted battle died away 2,375 German aircraft had been destroyed during the daylight hours. Others, the exact total of which will never be known, must have fallen as they fled towards the bases in France which they never reached.

The war in the air became increasingly complex in 1942 as the colossal struggle continued. The aircraft used by both sides became more formidable by reason of their heavier armament, the bomb load carried and the increased speed and range.

High Standards of Training

As always it was a battle of wits as well as of numerical strength. It was vital that Bomber Command should be re-equipped with new, heavy bombers in great numbers. And it was equally essential that pilots and aircrews should be fully trained to form the vast personnel needed to fly them. The production of aircraft and air training were, therefore, pressed forward at all possible speed. Experience showed, however, that too hurried a training of pilots, navigators, bomb-aimers and wireless operators and air gunners was uneconomic. There was a period when Britain's position in the war assumed the gravest aspect so that a certain reduction in air training was introduced. It became evident, however, that any curtailment of flying training meant an increase in casualties due to the consequent lack of skill and a loss of efficiency when the aircrews were sent into action. And so the normal curriculum was re-introduced. Under this training programme no bomber pilot was posted to an operational squadron until he had completed 250 to 300 hours in the air, flying solo. His training usually took fourteen months.

This rigorous instruction, unequalled by that of any other air force, was one of the keys to the triumphant progress of Bomber Command and in the long-drawn-out offensive against Germany. On the night of May 30, 1942, the biggest raid of the war was made by Bomber Command, when 1,130 aircraft blasted the industrial areas of Cologne. A high proportion of the attackers were the four-engined " heavies " (the Stirling, Halifax, and the renowned Lancaster, the last one of the greatest bombers ever produced). It was a massed attack in which the " cascade " bombing rendered impotent the German ground defence system. Our losses were light, numbering only 44.

Two nights later, 1,036 aircraft of Bomber Command continued the offensive against Western Germany, concentrating on industrial centres in the Ruhr. These early mass raids were the beginning of what became known as the Battle of the Ruhr, which continued with growing intensity. In the historic bombing attack on Cologne, it was estimated that the bombs were dropped at the rate of twenty tons a minute. The operation lasted for ninety minutes so that in that period ten aircraft were over the targets every minute. Reconnaissance photographs, only secured several days after the raid owing to the dense smoke, revealed that extremely heavy damage was spread over more than 5,000 acres. (See also pp. 137–138.)

The second big raid, made on June 1, 1942, was mainly against Essen. Of the 1,036 aircraft which took part in the assault, 35 were lost.

The growing striking power of Bomber Command was made even clearer on July 11, when several squadrons of Lancasters made a round flight of 1,750 miles to bomb Danzig in daylight. Most of the outward run was at only about 50 feet and severe weather was met. There was much trouble due to static electricity and icing. Some Lancasters got off their course and so did not reach their objective, but those which arrived at Danzig flew at heights of no more than 2,500 feet when the bombs were dropped. The operation was planned and carried out as part of the organised offensive designed to help defeat the enemy in the Battle of the Atlantic. It was followed by other long-range attacks by Bomber Command against U-boat building yards and component factories. The audacious Danzig raid, while being an outstanding exploit particularly because it was necessary to fly unescorted by fighter aircraft over hundreds of miles of enemy-occupied territory, was not the first important daylight operation made by Bomber Command in the Second World War. On Apl. 17, 1942, a force of twelve Lancasters, led by Squadron-Leader Nettleton, swept over France at a low level to assault the M.A.N. diesel engine works at the German town of Augsberg in the daytime. It was a magnificent achievement for which Nettleton was awarded the Victoria Cross. Unfortunately he was killed in action some time later.

R.A.F. Debts to Radar

Although not known at the time, much of the success of the R.A.F. in the defence of Britain from 1940, in the bombing of Germany, and in the Battle of the Atlantic after the spring of 1942, was due to the installation of ever-improving Radar devices. They were of particular importance in night work and in bad weather. Systems of warning of enemy approach, ground-controlled and aircraft interception, operating on micro-waves, provided the technical means by which, combined with the efficiency and gallantry of R.A.F. aircrews, Britain was saved.

Other Radar developments raised the bombing of Germany to a high scientific level (see pages 137–138). At sea Radar methods of detection of surface and undersea vessels eventually killed the U-boat. In the late summer of 1942 the American 8th Army Air Force, based in Britain, employing first R.A.F. and then their own Radar devices, began their series of daylight bombing raids which in the end devastated Germany.

In the Middle East the strength of the R.A.F. which from the earliest phase of the war against Italy had been meagre, was being built up by prodigious efforts. Its work stood in relief when Rommel's land forces at El Alamein were attacked from the air with shattering ferocity and the tide began to turn.

Books to Consult. A.B.C. of the R.A.F. (Amalgamated Press). British Fighter Planes and Bombers, C. G. Grey (Faber). The Royal Air Force in the World War, Capt. N. Macmillan (Harrap). Warfare in the Air : R.A.F. since the Battle of Britain, Sydney Veale (Pilot Press).

Royal Oak, H.M.S. This famous British battleship of the Royal Sovereign class had a displacement of 33,500 tons and a normal complement of over 1,000 men. She carried a main armament of eight 15-in. guns and twelve 6-in. guns. Completed in May 1916, she was withdrawn from the First Battle Squadron in 1934 and reconditioned at a cost of £1,000,000. During the war of 1914–1918 she was in action at the Battle of Jutland, and she was hit by an anti-aircraft shell during the Spanish civil war.

In the early hours of Oct. 14, 1939, the Royal Oak was sunk at anchor by a U-boat in Scapa Flow (*q.v.*). The submarine penetrated the defences of the landlocked anchorage, thought to be immune from such attacks, and fired a salvo of torpedoes at the Royal Oak. So far was it from the mind of those in command that the ship had been the subject of a submarine attack that they were taking precautions against a bombardment from the air, or alternatively examining the possibility of an internal explosion. Twenty minutes after the first torpedo was fired three or four more followed in quick succession, causing the ship to capsize and sink. As the Royal Oak was lying at the extreme end of the harbour it was impossible for the other vessels to come to the rescue before many officers and men were drowned. Altogether 24 officers and 786 men were lost out of 81 officers and 1,153 men.

H.M.S. ROYAL OAK IN SCAPA FLOW

This fine British battleship, which saw much service during the war of 1914–18, is here seen photographed only a few days before she was torpedoed. The Royal Oak was the first British battleship to be sunk in the present war.

Photo, Fox

Rubber. World rubber production is the child of the motor-car. Before the advent of the internal combustion engine the wild rubber of Brazil and Africa was sufficient for all needs. Then, about 1910, began the large-scale manufacture of motor-cars, all needing rubber tires, and thus the world's wild crop was found insufficient and large-scale planting began.

The following Table shows how a single great invention can conjure into existence a vast world industry.

	1910	1920	1930	1938
World Rubber Crop in tons ..	95,000	310,000	715,000	931,000
World Car Production	500,000	11,000,000	36,000,000	43,000,000

The sudden demand for rubber caused over-production. In 1934 and 1938 the chief producing countries, given here in order of importance—Malaya, Dutch East Indies, Ceylon, India, Burma, British North Borneo, Sarawak and Siam—agreed to limit production to keep world rubber stocks at a normal figure by adjusting in an orderly way supply to demand. Ninety-seven per cent of the world's total rubber crop is "Agreement rubber." The total produced by these countries was estimated for 1942 at 1,643,000 tons. A little wild rubber comes from Brazil and Africa.

The rubber richness of Malaya (651,000 tons for 1942) and of the Netherlands East Indies (650,000 tons for 1942) explains the covetousness of Japan for these territories, the world's greatest rubber producer. By the end of 1941 there were 8,700,000 acres devoted to rubber, an increase of 400,000 over 1938. The reason for this increase is war, for in war the consumption of rubber is enormous. For example, between 60 and 70 per cent of the world's total rubber product goes into tires in wartime.

The chief consumers of rubber, in order of importance, were in 1940 : the United States, 648,500 tons ; United Kingdom, 122,700 tons. In 1938 Germany imported 90,000 tons ; France (1938) 58,000 tons ; Canada (1940) 52,567 tons ; Japan (1939) 42,300 tons ; Italy (1938) 28,200 tons ; U.S.S.R. (1938) 26,800 tons. In each case these are the last official figures. The following consuming countries used between 7,000 and 10,000 tons : Belgium, Czecho-slovakia, South Africa, Argentina, Sweden, Poland and Austria.

In Mexico, a country outside the Agreement referred to, a special kind of rubber called guayule, a plant or shrub whose roots yield a high resin-content rubber, is exported. A rubber tree is tapped ; the little Mexican shrub is pulled up for the properties of its root.

In the U.S.S.R., where plant physiology has played so large a part since the Revolution, experts have been experimenting to produce a plant of a genus similar to that of the Mexican shrub in order to make the country independent of outside supplies of natural rubber. These experiments have been successful, and a plant something like a dandelion has been yielding rubber. Another interesting facet to the picture of the world rubber position is the increasing practice, particularly in the U.S.A., of using reclaimed rubber. No less than 25 per cent of all crude consumption in the States is reclaimed rubber.

Great Britain, following the usual practice of countries at war, has published no figures of the Empire's rubber production since war began. The supply is very large, as are the reserves.

The conquest of the Malay Peninsula and Netherlands East Indies, great rubber-growing areas, created a serious problem for the United Nations, for that conquest meant that 90 per cent of the total world rubber production was lost to them. As stated above, war creates a tremendous demand for rubber, and while there were certain areas of wild rubber available, the problem of conserving, salvaging (reconditioning) and of producing a synthetic material at once arose.

Germany, before the war, had to get her rubber by sea. She therefore made ready against the possibility of blockade by creating a great synthetic rubber (buna) industry, and beside it she built up a great reclaiming industry. Germany was said (U.S. Bureau of Commerce) to have produced 20,000 tons of synthetic rubber in 1939. The U.S.S.R. took similar precautions and has a vast synthetic rubber industry, producing 29,000 tons a year.

The United States, first in this field of applied science, has a huge industry, and in March 1942 drew up a programme, backed by the Reconstruction Finance Corporation, whereby leading rubber, oil and chemical corporations of the U.S.A. should pool plans, patents, technicians and supplies, including the heavy machinery needed in this industry. The aim was for 400,000 tons of synthetic rubber a year, and $400,000,000 were earmarked for this ambitious enterprise. Even so, the production of the tonnage aimed at would not do more than meet half the total rubber requirements of America.

The United Kingdom is alone in being without a synthetic rubber industry, nor do there exist in the British Isles facilities for bringing such an emergency industry into being at short notice. The difficulty lies in the very heavy type of plant needed.

The need for conserving this commodity in Britain was an urgent one. In December 1941 measures were taken to prohibit the use of rubber in the manufacture of certain articles, the list being extended in March 1942. A scheme to salvage rubber was inaugurated, and from March 7 the sale of tires was prohibited. Steps were being taken to obtain the maximum possible production in East and West Africa.

The effect of the Japanese control of this main source of the world's rubber supply has also a post-war bearing, for always when industry enters upon periods of expansion, as has been remarked above, the call for rubber increases in keeping. The post-war world, after its bout of destruction, will have much rebuilding and reconstruction of all kinds to do and much manufacture of commodities of all kinds. Then it will be found that a rubber shortage will act as a brake on progress : that is, unless a sound, economic substitute is meanwhile forthcoming.

Ruhr. The Ruhr district in the Rhineland extends roughly from Münster in the N. to Cologne in the S., and from Krefeld in the W. to Hamm in the E. It is traversed from S.E. to N.W. by the Rhine, and from E. to W. by the Ruhr, which enters the Rhine at Duisburg-Ruhrort. It is the most highly concentrated industrial area in Germany, based on the coalfields of the Ruhr basin.

As in the war of 1914–18, the Ruhr district was a great arsenal for the manufacture of munitions and armaments. The R.A.F. subjected it to constant bombing attacks, gradually increasing in intensity; the first heavy raid with 93 planes was on May 15–16, 1940. This was insignificant compared with what followed. By the end of April 1942 the Ruhr had been bombed over 400 times, and 1,500 objectives

had been successfully damaged These were railways and communications, docks and shipping, oil refineries and storage plants, munition factories, aircraft and motor works, power stations, military stores, aerodromes and seaplane bases. Hamm, an important railway junction with the largest marshalling yards in Germany, was heavily and persistently attacked ; the German transport system was thoroughly dislocated by these raids. Cologne, a vital centre of industry and another frequent target, suffered, on May 30, 1942, the first of the 1,000 bomber raids. Two nights later, the Krupps works at Essen, already badly damaged, were attacked by 1,036 bombers, with grim results. Gelsenkirchen, noted for its oil refineries, was repeatedly attacked, as were Duisburg-Ruhrort, Düsseldorf, Krefeld, Münster, Dortmund and many other towns, and the aqueducts and locks of Dortmund-Ems Canal were seriously damaged. Undoubtedly the havoc wrought by these raids was immense. See Table under Bomber Command, page 47.

Rumania. Rumania became involved in the war on the side of Nazi Germany through causes political, geographical and economic. An appreciation of these alone can make clear her action in virtually committing suicide, as a sovereign state, to become the despised subject of a voracious and all-consuming "ally."

The political causes were unstable government at home and the rise of a political party moulded on, and inspired by, the Nazi model, and known as the Iron

HITLER'S SATELLITES
Iron Guards stand rigidly to attention during a speech of General Antonescu. The Iron Guard leader, Horia Sima, is seen beside the General, and above the platform is a portrait of the leader, Corneliu Codreanu, arrested under a former regime and shot while trying to escape.
Photo, Keystone

Guard. Codreanu, its leader, was a violent anti-Semite. In 1938 King Carol, a play-boy with moments of political insight, assumed dictatorial powers rather than risk the collapse of a weak government— that of Goga, and known as the National Christian Front—*vis-à-vis* the powerful Iron Guard.

In the autumn of 1938 the King and Calinescu, his Minister of the Interior, "liquidated " the Iron Guard, who had become more turbulent. Codreanu was shot. In January 1939 a Grand Council took the place of the Parliament of the 1938 Constitution; under this the King possessed sole power to make laws. On Jan. 4 Calinescu, later to be Premier, organized the National Regeneration Party.

GERMANS ESTABLISHED IN RUMANIA

During 1940 the Nazification of Rumania became complete, the country being dominated by Germany, militarily as well as economically. By early October, when this photograph was taken, German A.A. guns were established in the oilfields.

Photo. Associated Press

Early in the year a German Economic Mission came to negotiate a trade agreement. While it was in Belgrade, news of the annexation of Bohemia was received and the trade negotiation became a bare-faced economic hold-up. The agreement which was concluded under duress on March 23, 1939, put economic chains on Rumania, who was pledged by its terms to work with the Germans for the development of the country's vast oil resources. The fear, first kindled by the Bohemian aggression, was intensified when Hungary, apt pupil in the school of Power Politics, annexed Ruthenia. The next shock was supplied by Italy, whose seizure of Albania on Good Friday caused Rumania to fear similar action by Bulgaria against the Dobruja.

Rumania's earlier efforts to put her own house in order, and to prevent others from entering it or interfering in its affairs, were foredoomed. Fear of the evil drew the evil feared. In August Hungary moved, and clashes between the troops of Rumania and those of Hungary occurred. Rumania suggested that standard preliminary to war, a non-aggression pact; Hungary declined. When Russia occupied Eastern Galicia, Rumania became fearful for Bessarabia.

On Nov. 13 Clodius headed a German Economic Mission to Bucharest which pressed, with threats, for larger supplies of oil. The Nazi economic grip was tightening; the threat of war increasing. On Jan. 18, 1940, Rumania agreed to supply Germany with 130,000 tons of oil a month. Rumania, a pygmy possessed of great treasure placed between two greedy giants, began feverishly to defend her frontiers. With the assumption of power by Gigurtu on June 1, 1940, the Nazification of Rumania was complete, for this pro-Nazi invited Germany to take over Rumania, openly proclaiming the country's adhesion to the Axis group and flooding it with Nazi military and civilian technicians. On June 26 Molotov presented his Note. The U.S.S.R. demanded Bessarabia. Carol appealed to Germany in vain. Rumania was forced to agree. Almost simultaneously, both Hungary and Bulgaria increased their warlike activities.

By Aug. 30 Rumania had ceded half Transylvania to Hungary, a transaction which represented obedience to orders given by Hitler and known as the Vienna Award.

In September Bulgaria demanded her pound of flesh and the Southern Dobruja passed to her.

Throughout these national humiliations the Rumanian army, over a million strong, struck no blow. On Sept. 20 Antonescu, who had assumed royal rights after Carol's abdication, Sept. 6, called in the Nazis to reorganize the Rumanian army. By the end of October there were no fewer than eighteen German Divisions in Rumania. On Nov. 19 the Iron Guard instituted a massacre of all opponents. The control of Rumania by Germany through her puppet, Antonescu, was complete by the end of 1940. In June 1941 Rumania declared war on Russia on Germany's orders and reoccupied Bessarabia and Bukovina and the city of Odessa. Fighting in South Russia, in which Rumanian troops suffered heavy losses, continued throughout 1942.

Absolute economic exploitation, complete political control, and the sufferings of an unwanted war were the rewards of Rumania as the "ally" of the Axis bloc. In addition she was, in March 1942, threatened with the loss of part of Transylvania to satisfy the increasing demands of Hungary.

Rundstedt, FIELD-MARSHAL VON. After commanding an army group during the Polish campaign, Field-Marshal von Rundstedt took part in the fighting in France, and was responsible for breaking through the French lines in the Ardennes and along the Meuse. When Germany attacked Russia, von Rundstedt was put in charge of the four armies thrusting through the Ukraine. At first considerable progress was made, but his opponent, Marshal Budenny, a fine strategist, was able to extricate the Soviet troops and afterwards to consolidate his lines, preparatory to the Russian counter-attack. In April 1942 von Rundstedt took over command of the German forces in France. He inspected all occupied coastal defences and organized measures to meet the threat of a United Nations' attack.

Von Rundstedt, German soldier.
Photo, E.N.A.

THE PRE-WAR POLICY OF SOVIET RUSSIA

Striving to maintain peace with other great Powers, Russia nevertheless prepared for any contingency. This article outlines the foreign policy pursued by the U.S.S.R. after the Munich crisis of 1938, and tells of her vast and secret preparations in the event of war.

Russia, Before Invasion. Fear, mutual distrust, double-dealing and blind self-interest were among the many unsatisfactory characteristics of European diplomacy immediately following the war. None of the Great Powers had, in this respect, a clean record, the acts of all being, at various times, likely to bring about the war which all, save Nazi Germany, feared.

Hitler's words, written and spoken, all breathed hatred of the political system of the Soviet Union and foreshadowed war between the two countries. For him Bolshevism was not so much a political system and way of life as an enormity which threatened the world. Russians were for him " unspeakable Asiatics."

Yet, in 1939, Nazi Germany, standing for a system based on the absolute will of one man, and the Soviet Union of Russian Republics, standing for the rule of the people, became friends and allies. It was one of the most astounding reorientations of international relations between two hostile powers in all recorded history.

RUSSIA ENTERS POLAND

Molotov, Soviet Foreign Minister, is seen above checking over the Russo-German plan for the demarcation of Poland; behind him stand Ribbentrop and Stalin. Below, peasants greet the Russian troops on their entry into Poland, September 1939.
Photos, Wide World; Planet News

The change began in 1938. On Sept. 29 Great Britain, France, Germany and Italy signed the Munich Agreement, agreeing to the cession to Germany of the Sudetenland by Czechoslovakia. Quite naturally, this looked like the first step towards reconciliation between the Nazis and the Democracies, and the isolation of the Soviet Union. It was known that Hitler had ambitions in the Ukraine and that Poland was coveting territory in northern Czechoslovakia ; Russia, therefore, had reason to suspect her neighbours and to fear for her western frontiers.

On Feb. 21, 1939, Russia openly repudiated any obligations between herself and France and England and announced her intention of acting without reference to either the Dictators or the Democracies. On March 10 Stalin summarized the Soviet Union's foreign policy as : Peace and trade with all friendly powers ; close cooperation with neighbours, provided her frontiers were not menaced ; support for the victims of aggression ; preparedness to fight, if necessary. Stalin expressed his contempt for the Democracies owing to their inaction in the face of the aggressor nations.

History may modify current opinion upon Russia's role at this time. On March 14 Germany, in flagrant breach of solemn pledges, marched into Czechoslovakia. Had Russia and the Western Powers entertained mutual respect and confidence for one another, the conference proposed by Stalin for a general European discussion of the menace of aggression would have taken place. That it did not was due in part to Britain's failure to participate. Lord Halifax, then Foreign Secretary, temporized and the occasion passed.

What Britain desired was assurance of Russian military help in the event of war with Germany. Lord Halifax was unable to secure any promise ; but on April 16, 1939, M. Litvinov, Soviet Foreign Commissar, went farther and suggested an open military alliance between the U.S.S.R., Great Britain and France. That offer was the measure of Russian distrust of Germany. Again, mutual mistrust hampered negotiations, which came to nothing. M. Litvinov was replaced by M. Molotov, the new Foreign Commissar assuring

Britain that Russia's anti-aggression policy still stood. Further proposals for staff talks also petered out. In May Stalin assured Col. Beck, Polish Premier, that if Germany invaded Poland the Soviet Government would adopt an attitude " bienveillante."

Rumour had by that month gained ground that Russia and Germany were secretly negotiating ; further assurances that this was not so were given by Moscow to Warsaw. Throughout those weeks Hitler intensified his verbal campaign against Poland. He demanded Danzig and the Polish Corridor (outlet to the Baltic for a land-locked State). He also strove to secure fortified points on the Baltic, clearly against Russia. Alarming rumours multiplied. On May 31 Molotov reproached the democracies, in particular for their betrayal of Czechoslovakia.

Nazi demands during these weeks became intensified. But the diplomatic machinery to cope with them was hopelessly clogged by mistrust. On June 12 a British Mission went to Moscow under Mr. Strang, Foreign Office expert, who was to act as Counsellor to our Ambassador. But negotiations lagged and Moscow accused Britain of bad faith and of having no desire to " do business." While these talks went on Moscow announced on Aug. 21 a Russo-German Pact of Non-Aggression. It was signed by Von Ribbentrop, Nazi Foreign Minister, two days later. Britain made her alliance with Poland on Aug. 25. On Sept. 1 Germany invaded Poland. On Sept. 17 Soviet troops entered Poland. Twelve days later Germany and the Soviet Union partitioned Poland. Twenty-six days after France and Britain had declared war on Germany, the country in whose defence they took up arms was destroyed. Soviet measures for defence against an ultimate clash with Nazi Germany began at once. They included military action in Finland (q.v.) and in the Baltic States, while in the Balkans diplomatic pressure was exerted for the cession by Rumania of Bessarabia, and continued throughout 1940.

After the partition of Poland both Germany and Russia, in spite of their pact of friendship, deemed it advisable to maintain large forces on their new frontier. Russia, however, did not mobilize her whole army ; relying on the covering force maintained in the newly acquired buffer zone, soon to include the Baltic States, Bessarabia and parts of Finland, to absorb the first shock of a possible German attack.

Russia : Strength in War. The Soviet Union withholds details of its strength in war. Estimates rest only on probabilities, and may fail to take account of the enormous and little publicized development within recent years. In 1936 Hitler told Lord Londonderry that he considered the U.S.S.R. to be the greatest military power in the world, having the strongest Army, Tank Corps and Air Force.

Military training, with subsequent refresher courses, is compulsory for all men between the ages of 16 and 60, and the U.S.S.R., with its population of nearly 200 million, has therefore a vast reservoir of man-power. The drafting of men into the Army is facilitated by the employment of women in industry, and in normal times amounts to at least 1,500,000 annually. At least 12 million men could be put into the field on the outbreak of war, with two years of intensive training in up-to-date methods of modern warfare ; a reserve of some 8 million could also be held available. There are a number of schools for the technical and higher training of officers which have evidently produced a

FINNS AND RUSSIANS AT HANGO

A condition of the Russo-Finnish peace treaty was the leasing to Russia for 30 years of the port and territory of Hango. Here is a photograph of Finnish soldiers (foreground) and Russian soldiers facing each other over the frontier.

Photo, Associated Press

remarkable advance in leadership. Equipment is of excellent quality.

The Soviet division numbers 18,000, and is more formidable than its German counterpart. Mechanization has been carried to a higher degree, and the supporting guns, tanks and aircraft are fully adequate to their tasks. Guns are often brought right up to the line instead of being husbanded in the rear. The Soviet tank is said to be superior in quality to the German product ; tanks of every type have been used, including monsters of 100 tons, carrying crews of 15 and capable of cruising at high speed. Amphibian tanks have not been overlooked ; the Russians were the first people to develop these. At a moderate estimate they probably had 10,000 tanks at the outbreak of the Russo-German war, besides a very considerable number of armoured cars.

This extensive mechanization has not excluded the vitally important cavalry. Soviet cavalry forces, both horsed and mechanized, are numerically equal to those of Germany, Italy, France and Poland combined.

A German estimate of the size of the Red Air Force in 1937 went as high as 17,000 front-line machines of various types. It is known that some 15,000 pilots were then in training. Russian factories were organized for mass-production of aeroplanes as early as 1936, and by 1939 were employing some 250,000 workers and turning out no fewer than 20,000 machines a year, a figure which was being stepped up. These 'planes have proved thoroughly efficient, and include new types of which the secret was well kept— for instance, the famous Stormovik dive-bombers. Parachute-jumping was developed in Russia earlier and on a greater scale than anywhere else ; at Kiev in 1935, during army manoeuvres, two infantry battalions, 1,200 men in all, were dropped from 'planes, with 16 light guns and 120 machine-guns, and took only eight minutes to land and assemble in formation.

Of the Red Fleet, little is authentically known, but in the list given in Jane's " Fighting Ships " for 1940, 416 units are recorded, including some which were under construction. The Soviet Union had embarked on a great shipbuilding programme ; in submarines, supremacy was already hers.

Defence is as well organized as attack ; the Soviet towns have an abundance of A.A. guns disposed in a zonal system, which were extremely successful in repelling attack and in shooting down attackers.

Behind the armed forces is the powerful civilian organization, Osoaviakhim, of more than 15 million men and women who in their spare time undergo training in the use of rifle and machine-gun, in parachute-jumping, in gas attacks and in street fighting. These are the backbone of the guerilla movement.

THE GERMAN ONSLAUGHT AGAINST RUSSIA

Hitler's sudden invasion of the U.S.S.R. marked a turning-point of the war. Along a vast front of 2,000 miles the enormous masses of the German and Russian armies fought a furious battle for supremacy in the greatest conflict of history. See also Crimea; Leningrad; Moscow; Sevastopol; Ukraine; etc.

Russia, War in. In May 1940 the British Government, noting the aid which Russia was giving Germany in the economic sphere, thought it advisable to establish a Trade Agreement, and talks, which had been begun the previous year and broken off after the Russian invasion of Finland, were now renewed. Sir Stafford Cripps was sent on this difficult mission, and as the Soviet Government refused to negotiate unless he was given ambassadorial status, Cripps succeeded Sir William Seeds as British Ambassador to the U.S.S.R., and continued to hold this post until January 1942. He did invaluable work in bridging the gulf of mistrust.

When on June 22, 1941, Germany, without any declaration of war, hurled her armies against Russia, Mr. Churchill in a world broadcast that evening declared that " we shall give whatever help we can to Russia and the Russian people." Sir Stafford Cripps, who had been in London for consultation, returned to Moscow on June 27 with a military mission, and on July 12 concluded a pact of mutual assistance.

READY TO FIRE

A big gun of a Soviet heavy artillery unit is here seen elevated at its firing position. Formidable weapons such as this hurled back the Nazi invaders on many fronts, taking a terrible toll of their ranks.

Photo, British Official

This proved to be no mere gesture; enormous quantities of war material of every kind were sent to Russia from Britain, and later from America, mainly in Allied shipping, throughout the campaign, and British air pilots took part in the fighting on the Moscow front and elsewhere.

Russia was by no means unprepared when Germany launched her treacherous and long-planned attack, but she was under the grave disadvantage of having to complete her mobilization. Germany, on the other hand, with her military resources on a complete war footing, had only to concentrate for attack. Her onslaught was therefore bound to achieve operational surprise and to confer the initiative on her.

It is hardly surprising that under these conditions the German High Command, and world opinion in general, expected a speedy Russian collapse. The fighting qualities of Russian soldiers were not underrated, but there were justifiable doubts whether their equipment would equal in quality and quantity that of the Germans, and whether the new industries of Soviet Russia would be capable of arming the vast manpower of the nation and of meeting the immense wastage of war. Few believed that in spite of their great development they would prove equal to the task.

The German attack developed in the form that had previously proved its effectiveness. Germany's primary military object was, of course, the rapid destruction of the Russian Army, taking full advantage of surprise and the initiative. The direction of the main German thrusts was, however, dictated by the chief political and industrial centres of the country.

German Plan of Campaign

The plan of campaign soon became apparent. From East Prussia one army under von Leeb advanced through Lithuania and Latvia, directed on Leningrad. Another group under von Bock took the direct line from Poland towards Moscow north of the Pripet marshes. South of the Pripet marshes von Rundstedt's group invaded the Ukraine, its left wing advancing towards Kiev; while farther south a force composed of German, Hungarian and Rumanian troops were intended to force the line of the R. Pruth, occupy Bessarabia and advance into the southern Ukraine, capturing the Black Sea ports and threatening the industrial regions of the Donetz Basin.

During the first week almost everything appeared to go according to plan in spite of fierce Russian resistance. By the end of the week practically the whole of Russian Poland had been occupied, and it was claimed that a large Russian force was surrounded at Bialystok. Von Leeb's group in particular made rapid progress through Lithuania. By the end of the second week there were indications, however, that Russia's resistance would be more formidable than was expected. Her troops were fighting not only with courage but with skill and initiative, always ready to counter-attack.

There had been a fierce tank battle east of Lwow in which both sides had heavy losses. Lwow, though surrounded, had held out firmly and some at least of the defenders had cut their way out—as was probably also the case where other forces became isolated. The earlier attempts to cross the Pruth into Bessarabia had definitely failed. North of the Pripet marshes, on the main road to Moscow, fighting was becoming fiercer, as the old frontier was crossed about Minsk. Even more important, it was apparent that the Russian air force had not suffered heavily in the initial attack on their aerodromes, and the Germans had not established air superiority to the same extent as in their previous campaigns. The Germans, in fact, soon discovered that they had miscalculated the strength and efficiency of the Russian air arm ; and it may have been this that caused the Germans to withdraw a large part of the Luftwaffe from the west and abandon intensive bombing of Britain.

Yet the speed of the German advance was impressive, though in many instances the line which it was claimed had been reached was only that attained by Panzer thrusts, while heavy fighting continued in a deep zone behind. Absence of well-defined linear advances and the depth of the zones of combat have, in fact, been a characteristic feature of the war, mainly owing to Russian tactics, which aim at separating the main infantry advance from the Panzer spearheads.

Towards the end of the third week, though fighting continued, there was a distinct pause in the German advance, which had now reached the so-called Stalin Line. That was a zone of considerable depth stretching from the Gulf of Finland and Lake Peipus in the north to the Black Sea. It was to some extent a fortified position consisting of numerous prepared centres of resistance and including some natural obstacles, chiefly rivers. It ran roughly parallel to the old Russian frontier at a short distance east of it. The line, however, primarily represented the position selected for the deployment of the main bodies of the first line Russian Army. It was with these troops that the Germans had now made contact, and they paused for a few days before delivering a major attack.

About the end of the third week (mid-July) the

The German advance in Russia to July 31, 1941.
Courtesy, Oxford University Press

attack was delivered, and no doubt it had considerable success. Panzer thrusts penetrated deep into the Stalin Line and the Germans claimed to be threatening Leningrad, to have captured Vitebsk and to be approaching Kiev. But the Russians stood their ground and prevented the German masses from supporting the Panzer thrusts. After another pause in the fourth week the attack was renewed, proclaimed by the Germans to be the decisive blow. Again the Panzer thrusts made progress and passed Smolensk, which was said to be encircled, but the Russians still fought fiercely and the main battle raged round Pskov (south of Lake Peipus), round Smolensk and some 80 miles short of Kiev. Farther south the Pruth had been crossed and most of Bessarabia occupied.

The German main effort at this period was towards Moscow, but already guerilla parties were giving

GERMANS PREPARE FOR BATTLE ON THE WAY TO MOSCOW

At the beginning of the campaign in Russia one of the German main thrusts was towards the capital, and above Nazi infantry are seen assembled before the attack on Brest-Litovsk, from which they advanced on the road to Moscow.

Photo, Keystone

Map legend:
- Frontier 1939-40.
- Main thrusts by Germans etc.
- Approximate Front 31 July.
- 31 August.
- Area occupied by Germans etc. by 31 August.

Stalin Canal to White Sea

To Murmansk 400 miles

FINLAND — Helsinki · Viipuri · Sortavala · Lake Onega · L. Ladoga · Kronstadt · Leningrad · Karelian Isthmus · Kingisepp · Novgorod · L. Ilmen · Tallinn · Lake Peipus · Lovat · Riga · LATVIA · Dvina · LITHUANIA · Vitebsk · Moscow · E. PRUSSIA · Vilna · Minsk · Vyazma · Smolensk · Warsaw · Bug · Brest-Litovsk · Mogilev · Bobruisk · Bryansk · Pripet Marshes · Gomel · Orel · POLAND · Vistula · Jitomir · Kiev · UKRAINE · Kharkov · HUNGARY · Dniester · S. Bug · Dnepropetrovsk · Zaporoje Dam To Caucasus · RUMANIA · Pruth · Nikolayev · Kherson · Sea of Azov · Odessa · BLACK SEA · CRIMEA

BALTIC SEA

AUGUST 1 - AUGUST 31

0   100   200   300   400   500 MILES

Progress of the war at five points during August 1941.
Courtesy, Oxford University Press

opened an offensive in Karelia and between Lakes Onega and Ladoga, threatening the southern stretches of the Murmansk railway and Leningrad itself. The attack on Murmansk definitely failed owing to difficulties of the rocky and marshy terrain and the action of the Russian warships and aircraft based on Murmansk. The more southern operation made some progress, but after the Finns had recovered their lost territory they showed little eagerness for further offensive action. The successful defence of Murmansk was of immense importance, as it was to become an important port of entry for Allied war material.

Fall of Smolensk and Retreat in Ukraine

To return to the main theatre. Early in August Hitler again proclaimed that the Russian Army east of Smolensk had been annihilated and published extravagant figures of captures during the first six weeks (June 22–August 4). Russian denials and counter-claims were more moderate, but no great reliance could be placed on either set of figures.

In the middle of the month it was admitted that Smolensk had been evacuated, which proved that the Stalin Line, such as it was, had been passed. Resistance east of Smolensk, however, continued, and German progress on that front was practically brought to a standstill by Timoshenko's central army, which had always shown readiness to counter-attack.

Meantime, however, the situation both in the north and the south was becoming serious. In the Ukraine, although the direct advance on Kiev had been checked, a thrust towards the south-east had reached the railway connecting Kiev and Odessa, outflanking the army behind the Dniester. Farther south, too, Rumanians and Germans had crossed the Dniester near its mouth, by-passing Odessa, and on August 16 occupied the naval base of Nicolaiev, which, however, was thoroughly demolished before evacuation.

trouble, Stalin's scorched earth policy was in operation and German complaints of bad roads were frequent. Evidently supply of their armies promised to be a major problem. The world, including Germany, had by now realized that Russia was much more tough than had been expected and her leaders had shown no sign of the moral paralysis which elsewhere the onslaught of the Reichswehr had caused. Possibly to allay doubts in the homeland, Hitler, about July 21, made his first claim to have achieved decisive victory, and to have split the Russian Army into disconnected fragments with no recognizable central control. In spite of that claim Russian resistance showed no signs of breaking, and in the fourth, fifth and sixth weeks fighting continued fiercely. Smolensk, although by-passed, held out and little progress was made towards Kiev or Leningrad. In the south, however, the Germans were advancing and the upper Dniester had been crossed. In Estonia, too, subsidiary operations of importance were developing; part of von Leeb's army was to clear the country and to capture the Russian naval base at Tallinn and the island of Oesel, from which Russian bombers raided Berlin.

Another subsidiary operation may at this point be mentioned. A Germano-Finnish force made an attempt to capture Murmansk and to interrupt the Murmansk railway in the neighbourhood of Kandalaksha on the White Sea. Other Finnish and German forces also

GUERILLAS NEVER GAVE IN

The Russians are well versed in guerilla tactics, and these intrepid fighters are a source of constant worry to the Germans, harrying them at every turn. Here is seen a small band of guerillas waiting to carry out some act of impeding the enemy.
Photo, Keystone

SOVIET TROOPS ROUND UP THE RETREATING GERMANS

These photographs, taken in the spring of 1942, record the success of the great Russian counter-offensive. The top photo shows Soviet troops advancing against German tanks, one of which is on fire ; the lower one shows a detachment of German troops, left as a rearguard to cover the retreat of an infantry battalion, surrendering in no uncertain fashion to the Russians advancing upon them.

Photos, Planet News

Budenny's southern army was now in full retreat towards the Dnieper, and the siege of Odessa had begun. In the north Voroshilov's army, covering Leningrad, was also under heavy pressure. After prolonged heavy fighting in the neighbourhood of Pskov the Germans succeeded in breaking through, reaching Staraya Russa, south of Lake Ilmen, by August 13, and Novgorod, north of that lake, about a week later. This movement threatened railway communications between Leningrad and Moscow. At the same time the Germans were advancing north and north-west, on both sides of Lake Peipus, to cut off the Russians in Estonia and directly threaten Leningrad. The Russian force in Estonia covering Tallinn became isolated, and at the end of August 1941 Tallinn itself was evacuated, leaving the whole of Estonia, except the island of Oesel, which held out till the end of September, in German occupation.

Situation After Ten Weeks

The general situation at the beginning of September showed the Germans halted on the Dnieper, across which Budenny's army had withdrawn, after suffering heavily, though they still held some small bridgeheads on the west bank. Odessa was standing siege bravely and, by denying its port to the Germans, added to their supply difficulties. Kiev was holding out, but was in danger of encirclement, as the Germans had crossed the upper Dnieper, north and south of the city. East of Smolensk the German drive towards Moscow had died down in face of Timoshenko's stubborn resistance. The immediate danger lay in the north, where the Germans had reached the outer defences of Leningrad, west and south of the city, and it was threatened, if not

with early capture, with the danger of complete isolation. The German thrust towards Novgorod had severed the most direct railway to Moscow, and counter-attacks by Voroshilov had been unsuccessful. The marshy and forest country to the east of the city made complete encirclement difficult, but the Germans pressed their direct attack hard, confidently claiming that the fall of the city was imminent. The inhabitants and garrison, however, fought back with the greatest courage and determination ; and since the Leningrad area contained great munition works and large resources of raw material, the partial loss of communication with Moscow was of less consequence. In the first week of September the Germans, however, completed the encirclement of the city until such time as the freezing of Lake Ladoga gave a new outlet to the east.

It seems probable at this time, although their offensive in the north and the south had important objectives, that the intention of the Germans was to draw Russian reserves to a flank before delivering a final decisive attack towards Moscow ; and their defensive attitude in the centre protected vast preparations required for a continuous effort. Timoshenko's counter-attacks, which had considerable success in driving the enemy back towards Smolensk, had not the character of a general offensive, but probably aimed mainly at disturbing German preparations, thus gaining time for Russian reserves to assemble.

Fall of Kiev

During September heavy autumn rain began to fall and it hampered German operations in the north, where, though heavy fighting continued, little progress was made. On the other hand, in the south the

SOVIET SUPERSPEED BOMBERS IN ACTION

The PE-2, twin-engined superspeed bomber of the Red Air Force, is here seen in action on the Moscow front. In accordance with the Soviet policy of closely guarding military secrets in wartime, the details of its actual performance are not published.
Photo, British Official

but, though parts of Timoshenko's army were isolated, they continued to resist and check the momentum of the German advance. Fighting was particularly heavy about Briansk, Vyazma and Orel. Orel and Briansk were evacuated, but Vyazma on the direct road to Moscow held out till it was far behind the forward limits of the German advance. On Oct. 12 the threat to Moscow became so apparent that women and children were evacuated. By the end of the third week of October Mojaisk and Malo Yaroslavets, 60 miles to the west and south-west of the city, were in German hands, while to the south and north wider pincer thrusts at Orel and Kalinin threatened the isolation of the capital. On Oct. 20 the Government transferred to Kuibyshev and a state of siege was proclaimed in Moscow.

Germans, who had been held up on the Dnieper, in front of Kiev and before Odessa, renewed their efforts, and a serious situation developed. A thrust south-eastwards from Gomel made rapid progress and forced the line of the Desna, outflanking Kiev from the north, while about the same time the Dnieper was crossed at Kremenchug, the nearest point to the great industrial towns of Poltava and Kharkov. After hard fighting Kiev was evacuated about Sept. 19—two months, it may be noted, after the Germans had first claimed to have entered the city. Farther south, the advance towards Kharkov was threatening, but was checked in the neighbourhood of Poltava. In the extreme south, however, the force that had crossed the lower Dnieper had advanced, and in the first week of October opened an attack on Perekop with the intention of invading the Crimea. To meet the threat Budenny launched a counter-move along the north of the Sea of Azov. It was a dangerous attempt in view of the great German forces to the north operating in the Donetz basin, and met with disastrous failure.

The Threat to Moscow

We must return now to the centre front. On Oct. 3 Hitler again claimed that the Russians were completely defeated, and at the same time he announced that the final decisive offensive was about to be launched. This was the signal for a renewed offensive in the centre on a broad front from Orel in the south to the Valdai hills. The Russian front was penetrated by Panzer formations,

Autumn rains had, however, now brought mud, and that, combined with the constant appearance of fresh Russian reserves, slowed down the German advance till it was practically brought to a standstill. Deep Panzer thrusts and long-range encircling movements were no longer possible and tanks were increasingly used merely to support infantry attacks. Under these conditions, and faced with forest country and the strong defences protecting the city, there is little doubt that at this time the German General Staff reached the conclusion that the capture of Moscow before winter set in was impracticable, and that they

SAILORS OF THE RED NAVY ON GUARD

The Russian Fleet, though an unknown quantity, is to the enemy a force to be reckoned with. Going silently and grimly about its vital task of sinking German warships, transports and supply ships, it guards a coastline thousands of miles long. Above, members of a naval gun crew are seen at their station on a Soviet warship.
Photo, British Official

WINTER WARFARE IN RUSSIA

This picture, radioed from Moscow, shows two groups of scouts (women were sometimes employed) proceeding on an assignment during the Red Army's triumphant offensive. The camouflage they wear renders them almost invisible against the snow.

Photo, British Official

wished to establish a well-organized winter position in which their troops would have shelter and be prepared to return to the offensive in the spring. Towards the end of October there was therefore a definite pause on the Moscow front, but, on the other hand, the offensive in the south was pressed with renewed violence.

Odessa and the Crimea

On Oct. 17 the evacuation of Odessa was announced. It had defeated a number of attacks most gallantly and inflicted heavy casualties, especially on the Rumanians. The evacuation, which took eight days to effect, was carried through without interference, and when the enemy entered the city they found the port and everything of value thoroughly scorched. Delayed action bombs, too, for a long time made life insecure for the new occupants. The evacuation was probably carried out mainly to relieve the Fleet of dangerous tasks and to provide reinforcements for the defence farther east, for both the Crimea and Rostov-on-Don were threatened.

At this time, too, the Russian Command was reorganized; Budenny and Voroshilov were relieved and given the task of training new armies. The whole front was divided into two; Timoshenko being given the southern half and Zhukov, the former Chief of Staff, the northern from Moscow inclusive.

Timoshenko's task was difficult. The German thrusts into the Donetz Basin, towards Rostov and into the Crimea, were being pressed hard. They had reached Kharkov and Stalino in the Donetz, Taganrog on the shores of the Azov Sea, and, forcing the Perekop defences, had entered the Crimea. Timoshenko appears to have put new heart into the defence and rapidly reorganized it, checking the advance in the Donetz, though heavy fighting continued and intensified whenever the weather improved. During the first three weeks of November the situation remained very

critical, especially in the far south, where the Germans appeared to be planning a winter campaign into Caucasia. They pressed on towards Rostov and the city was evacuated on Nov. 21, though the Don was not crossed; while in the Crimea the Kerch Peninsula, commanding the narrow entrance to the Sea of Azov, was captured and Sevastopol was closely besieged, ceasing therefore to be usable as a naval base. A combined attack from Rostov and across the Straits of Kerch into Caucasia was expected, though it would clearly take time to prepare, especially as the Black Sea Fleet could interfere with the collection of transports at Kerch.

Winter Attack on Moscow

We must now turn again to the Moscow front. Hitler, in spite of the views of the General Staff, was determined to take Moscow and to find winter shelter for his army there. The frosts and light snowfalls of early winter produced conditions in which tanks could again operate effectively, and he was willing to take the risk of failing to accomplish his object before heavy snow immobilized them. Failure would, of course, mean that his army would be condemned to suffer the rigours of winter without adequate shelter and completely unprepared to meet their terrors.

By the middle of November the offensive, which for some time had been mainly directed to secure positions round Kalinin to the north, and Tula to the south, of the city, as springboards for wide encircling movements, blazed up in full fury. In particular thrusts came from the north-west, by Volokolamsk and Klin; while, south of the city, Tula, which still held out, was bypassed by a dangerous thrust to the east, severing important railway communication of Moscow with the oil supplies and industrial centres of the south. But perhaps the greatest danger of all was the direct attack from the west along the main road from Mojaisk. In face of these dangers the troops and the civilian inhabitants of Moscow threw themselves into the struggle, sparing no sacrifice. The casualties on both sides were terrific; and we now know that the Germans, in places, came to within fifteen miles of the city, practically in its outskirts, before snow and intense cold left them incapable of further effort.

In the second week of December Stalin, who had remained in Moscow in supreme control of operations, judged the moment had come to launch his reserves in a winter counter-offensive; they had been carefully husbanded in anticipation of an opportunity arising, and included great masses of cavalry and numbers of ski troops, having a mobility in deep snow which the German mechanized forces could not equal. An even greater advantage was possessed by the Russians. They were warmly and suitably clothed for winter conditions, whereas the wretched men of the Reichswehr, promised a rapid success before winter, had only normal uniforms, worn-out boots and no gloves.

Reichswehr's First Big Defeats

Before following the course of the winter counter-offensive two important preliminary successes should be recorded. By a daring and skilful counter-attack in the last days of November Timoshenko threw the Germans out of Rostov in confusion and pursued them vigorously to Taganrog and beyond, capturing great quantities of material. This was the first really disastrous reverse the Reichswehr had suffered in the whole war and its moral effect was immense. German

Northern part of the front from Murmansk to Leningrad.

Navy had played an important role. In the Black Sea it closed what might have been a valuable channel of communication for the Germans, and it carried out effectively the evacuation of Odessa and other ports. In the Baltic, till the Estonian bases were lost, it stopped attempts by the Germans to use sea transport, and it made a valuable contribution to the defence of Leningrad. In the Arctic it was a main factor in defeating the attempts to capture Murmansk. Perhaps the most amazing features of the defensive war were the determination and effectiveness of the guerilla activities, despite ruthless German reprisals, and the wholesale application of the scorched earth policy.

Stalin's Winter Counter-offensive

Less virile leadership might well have been satisfied with the successful defence which had proved the Reichswehr was not invincible and had denied to Germany the economic benefits she had hoped to gain. A winter campaign would entail great hardships on the Russian Army, but M. Stalin, realizing that his opponents were exhausted and that for them winter would prove more terrible, seized the opportunity he had seen approaching. It is not possible to give the story of the great winter counter-offensive in detail. Winter conditions prohibited attacks on a maximum scale or rapid exploitation of victories. Results represent the sum of a vast number of offensive strokes.

Dec. 10, 1941, may be accepted as the opening date of the main counter-offensive. It soon became apparent that its first objective was to remove the threat to Moscow. The salients the Germans had established to the south of Moscow, east of Orel and Tula, and to the north of Moscow at Kalinin and Klin, had to be eliminated. The relief of Tula, which had held out against heavy attacks, and of Kalinin, which had changed hands several times, were of special importance. At the same time every effort was made to drive back the Germans on the Mojaisk road.

The counter-offensive had great immediate success. The Germans were undoubtedly taken by surprise, had had no time to consolidate their advanced positions, and their troops were perished with cold. By the middle of January 1942 a deep wedge had been driven into the German front south of Moscow, leaving Mojaisk in a dangerous salient and cutting the railway between Vyazma and Briansk. To the north the attack on the Kalinin-Klin salient had been equally successful. The Germans lost great quantities of material and suffered heavy casualties, though strong rearguards fought stubbornly. The Germans could not deny the sudden change, but at first proclaimed that it had been found impossible to continue the offensive under winter conditions and that their withdrawal was made to straighten and shorten the front for the winter.

Immediate danger to Moscow soon passed, but for a time the Germans clung to Mojaisk and did not withdraw till they had succeeded in evacuating much of the material accumulated there. They stood again at Ghatsk, some 50 miles to the west, and showed every intention of holding Rzhev and Vyazma in order to cover Smolensk and to provide a springboard for a renewal of an attack on Moscow in the spring. A great Russian thrust in the third week of January between Rzhev and the Valdai hills, combined with the thrust in the south between Vyazma and Briansk, produced, however, a great salient in the German front west of Moscow, and it threatened to interrupt the lateral railway between Smolensk and Leningrad. About the

rearguards maintained their position at Taganrog, but the town was by-passed and the counter-attack was soon to spread northwards.

Another important reverse was inflicted on the Germans in the north. Taking advantage of frozen ground, they had launched a long-range thrust to the east of Leningrad, and in the last days of November captured Tikvin on the important Leningrad-Vologda railway, presumably with the intention of making the isolation of Leningrad more complete, and, possibly, of securing a springboard for a spring offensive towards Vologda. Through Vologda all Allied supplies landed at Murmansk and Archangel had to pass, and its strategic importance was consequently great. Tikvin, however, was a dangerously advanced position and Russian counter-attacks by Dec. 9 heavily defeated and drove back the thrust. This was a notable success, opening the way for attacks against the German inner encircling position and making possible a railway connecting Leningrad with Vologda across the ice of Lake Ladoga.

In the defensive operations the Russian High Command had impressed the world with its efficiency, not only in strategical and tactical directions, but also, where weakness was expected, in administration. The test had been desperately severe, but at no time were there signs of the moral paralysis which the Panzer and Luftwaffe attacks had elsewhere caused. The tactical methods adopted to a very large extent robbed Panzer penetration of its terrors, and reserves were used with judgement and counter-attacks were delivered with determination. The Russian air force and anti-aircraft defences surprised all observers with the quality of their material and the skill of their handling. Nor should it be forgotten that the Russian

From Leningrad to the Crimea the shaded section shows Russian territory recaptured between Dec. 1941 and May 1942.
By courtesy of "The Illustrated London News"

same time Timoshenko launched a fierce drive south of Kharkov towards Dnepropetrovsk, threatening vital railway communications with the Crimea.

But by February 1942 the counter-offensive was losing some of its momentum. That was to be expected, for German resistance stiffened where it had time to consolidate defences. Moreover, as the Russians advanced, supply difficulties and the reconstruction of damaged roads and railways were bound to cause

delays. The counter-offensive thus became an operation of attrition—its main object once the threat to Moscow was removed. There can never have been any expectation that the whole German army would be forced to retreat ; but by harrying it, by depleting reserves designed for a renewal of the offensive, and by preventing the relief of troops exhausted by summer fighting and by winter hardships, the power of the German war machine could be reduced.

It is impossible to follow closely operations of that character, but certain notable results achieved may be recorded. Early in February the drive north of Rzhev made progress in a south-westerly direction, cutting the railway running west from that town, which, though then practically isolated, the Germans clung to desperately. This advance also began to threaten the railway between Vyazma and Smolensk. By the middle of March further advances in this region, combined with successes between Vyazma and Briansk, made the use of this railway precarious, and turned the Rzhev-Vyazma region into an immense pocket rather than a salient. In the third week of February, by a clever surprise outflanking movement, the German 16th Army at Staraya Russa was completely surrounded, and all through March German reserve divisions were flung into counter-attacks in attempts to relieve it; while transport 'planes, of which the Russian airmen took heavy toll, attempted to bring supplies to the beleaguered army.

Farther north, as the end of winter approached, which would break the Lake Ladoga route to Leningrad, the Russians renewed their great effort to open permanent communications with the city. The German investing front between Schlusselburg and Novgorod was, however, well dug in and progress was slow.

Brilliant Recapture of Kerch

In the Crimea, which, like the Murmansk and Finnish front, almost constituted a separate theatre of war, the counter-offensive had achieved a great measure of success. A combined operation which on the stormy night of Dec. 29, 1941, recaptured Kerch was a brilliant feat, reflecting the greatest credit on the Russian Navy. The result was to give the defenders of Sevastopol a respite, and the successful defence of that fortress denied Germany a base from which landing operations in Caucasia might have been launched.

By the beginning of March the Germans had abandoned all pretence that they were merely straightening their front, which had by then assumed a strangely irregular shape. Instead, they admitted they were fighting a great defensive battle and were employing more and more reserve divisions to check Russian encroachments and to bring relief to the partly encircled " hedgehog " key points to which they were clinging.

No doubt the counter-offensive had involved heavy Russian losses ; but many of the troops employed, the cavalry for example, could not be used with much effect in the summer. It must be admitted, however, that the winter had given the Germans a chance of reconstituting and re-equipping their Panzer divisions. By the end of March the thaw had set in and melting snow turned the ground into a morass in which large-scale operations increasingly became impracticable.

During April there was a heavy Russian offensive in Finland, lasting for two weeks, and another, employing Siberian troops, in Lapland. The German losses in the Leningrad area were particularly heavy in April, the Russians trying to push the enemy back from the vicinity of the beleaguered city. Smolensk was threatened by Russian pincer thrusts, and Hitler was forced to call up reserves intended for his great spring offensive in an effort to save his army there.

Spring passed without the development of a major German offensive, though signs that it would come in the summer were not lacking A violent attack to regain Kerch, started on May 5, indicated that a drive towards the Caucasian oilfields would mark its opening phase. After hard fighting the Russians evacuated their last positions at Kerch on May 23, and on June 5, to increase the value of the Kerch springboard, the Germans opened a final attempt to capture Sevastopol.

Meanwhile, however, to forestall and disrupt the orderly development of German plans, the Russians launched a new counter-offensive. Attacking on a 200-mile front north and south of Kharkov, Timoshenko took the Germans by surprise, penetrating in places to their second position, 40 miles in rear. Kharkov itself was too strongly defended to be seriously attacked, but its communications were threatened. Still more important, Timoshenko had become a serious menace to the left flank of any German drive towards the Caucasus. He had to be driven back. Operating in a pronounced salient, his left flank and communications were exposed, and against them von Bock rapidly organized a counter-stroke striking northwards from Izyum with troops that had been concentrated for his Caucasus operations. By May 31 the situation stabilized, leaving Timoshenko in possession of the ground he had won and retaining his menacing position. He had dislocated von Bock's plans and forced him to expend his reserves.

The extent of his success may be gauged from the fact that on June 11 another and more deliberate offensive was launched against him, only in turn to be brought to a standstill without achieving its object. But it was of such vital importance to the Germans to dislodge Timoshenko that on June 23 a third and still greater effort was made. This time Timoshenko was compelled to give ground, but only after inflicting immense losses.

On June 5 the Germans launched a full-scale attack on Sevastopol (q.v.). After its fall on July 3 a rapid advance in force from Kursk brought the Germans across the Don to Voronezh, which they claimed, prematurely, to have captured on July 7. This, the northern arm of von Bock's large-scale offensive aimed at the Caucasus, was held up by Russian counter-attacks, and on July 20 the defenders' position was definitely improved. The southern arm in the same period had made a deep incursion in the Donetz area, Voroshilovgrad falling on July 18 and the Moscow-Rostov railway being cut. The threat to Stalingrad and the Caucasus oil routes was obvious, but the Russians' vigorous stand in the North and their orderly retreat in the South clearly spoiled German anticipations.

The First Year of the Russian War

The first anniversary, June 22, 1942, of Hitler's treacherous invasion of their homeland saw the people and leaders of the great Soviet Union confident of final victory. While Germany was coming to the end of her man-power, taking skilled men from factories for the front line, the Red Army was becoming stronger and better organized. On all sectors of the front, with the exception of Kharkov and Sevastopol, the initiative was in Russian hands, and Soviet troops were driving the Germans out of fortified positions and liberating towns and villages.

The output of German industry was falling ; Russian industry increased its output of war material from month to month. Hitler's naïve hope of making peace with Britain by attacking the U.S.S.R. not only failed to materialize ; his attack, from the very first day, made the two countries friends and allies.

America, too, was giving increasingly large and valuable aid in war supplies.

Thus, after a year of total war on an unparalleled scale, a year that had brought bloodshed, destruction, and well-nigh intolerable suffering to the Russian people, they emerged calm and confident, grimly determined to oust the invader and to avenge the terrible crimes committed by the Nazis on women, children and old people in occupied Russia. On June 22 Moscow published a statement of German and Russian losses during the first year of war on the Eastern front. These figures—10,000,000 Germans killed, wounded, or missing (of which number it was claimed not less than 3,500,000 were killed), and 4,500,000 Russians killed, wounded, or missing— revealed the scale and ferocity of the fighting on this front, most of which took place in the open.

On May 26 a Treaty of Alliance between Great Britain and Soviet Russia, to remain in force for twenty years, was signed in London by Mr. Eden and M. Molotov. This Treaty confirmed the Anglo-Soviet alliance during the war ; provided that after the war mutual assistance would be rendered against further Axis aggression ; and for collaboration with the United Nations in the peace settlement, and during the reconstruction period, on the basis of the Atlantic Charter.

Books to consult : Why Russia Will Win, W. P. and Z. Coates (Eldon Press). Russia Fights On, Maurice Hindus (Collins). How Russia Prepared, Maurice Edelman (Penguin). Soviet Fighting Forces, Maj. A. S. Hooper (Muller). Strategy and Tactics of the Soviet-German War, Officers of Soviet General Staff (Hutchinson).

 St. Nazaire. French port on the Bay of Biscay at the mouth of the River Loire. It was the principal port for the landing of stores and vehicles for the B.E.F. in September 1939. In the harbour of St. Nazaire the Cunard White Star liner Lancastria (*q.v.*), which was engaged in evacuating troops in June 1940, was sunk by a German bomber. After the German occupation of France St. Nazaire became a U-boat base from which the enemy submarines set out on their Atlantic raids. The R.A.F. repeatedly attacked it.

On Mar. 28, 1942, a daringly spectacular raid by combined British forces was carried out, these forces consisting of light naval contingents, special service troops (including Commandos) and R.A.F. aircraft. The raid was directed primarily against the large dry dock and harbour installations. H.M.S. Campbeltown, ex-American destroyer (U.S.S. Buchanan), her bows specially stiffened and filled with five tons of high explosives with delay-action fuses, forced her way at a speed of 20 knots through the heavily guarded entrance to the dry dock and rammed the centre of the main lock gate. As soon as the destroyer was firmly wedged, special troops landed and set about the work of demolition, a motor launch having taken off the crew of the Campbeltown. The pumping station and dock operating gear were destroyed. A heavy explosion occurred as the British forces left the scene of operations and buildings on shore were blown to pieces. The entrance to the U-boat basin had been fired at by two delay-action torpedoes from a motor torpedo-boat. The British forces withdrew in motor launches, detailed to rejoin the destroyers. Some of our troops, after being isolated from the main force, put up a fierce resistance before they were made prisoners by the enemy. The naval forces were under the command of Commander R. E. D. Ryder, R.N., and special service troops were led by Lt.-Col. A. C. Newman, of the Essex Regt. The Campbeltown was commanded by Lt.-Cmdr. S. M. Beattie. Lt.-Cmdr. Beattie and Col. Newman were taken prisoner.

In May awards of the V.C. were made to Commander Ryder, Lt.-Cmdr. Beattie, and Able Seaman W. A. Savage (who was killed at his gun) in recognition of their great gallantry, and that shown by their ships' companies generally, in this raid.

St. Pierre. The small islands of St. Pierre and Miquelon, situated off the mouth of the St. Lawrence River, Newfoundland, constituted the last remaining parts of the former French Colonial Empire in North America. Vice-Adm. Muselier (*q.v.*), head of the Free French Navy, landed on the islands with a naval force on Dec. 24, 1941. He received an enthusiastic welcome from the 5,000 inhabitants, who, some three weeks earlier, had decided by a majority of 98 per cent in favour of Free France. His first step was to dismiss the Governor, a Vichy partisan, and to close the wireless station. The U.S. State Department issued a communiqué on Dec. 26 declaring the Free French action to be " contrary to the agreement between all parties interested " and " committed without the knowledge or consent of the U.S. Government."

St. Valery-en-Caux. This little French town on the Channel, situated on the Normandy coast between Dieppe and Fécamp, was the scene of fierce fighting and of an heroic stand by British troops in June 1940. On June 10 the 152nd and 153rd Brigades of the 51st (Highland Division) moved along the coast

BEFORE AND AFTER THE ATTACK

St. Nazaire harbour is seen (top) before the devastating British attack, with the lock gate to the Bassin de Penhouet (1) in position. Below, A shows the lock gate lying against the dockside ; B, the concrete dam ; C, the smashed machine house that operated the gates.

during the British retreat from the Somme to take up their final positions round St. Valery. A bridgehead was formed round the port, the southern portion being held by units of the French Ninth Corps. On June 11 the Germans launched heavy artillery attacks, assisted by very large numbers of aircraft, and that night our troops were ordered to withdraw to the beaches, there to await embarkation. It happened that at the same time a large number of other British troops were being embarked at Veules-les-Roses, 1½ miles distant, connected with St. Valery by a line of caves. This fact was unfortunately not known to the men at St. Valery, who could easily have marched there and been taken aboard the rescue ships.

The plan for embarkation at St. Valery miscarried, for the Germans forced back the French Ninth Corps and took the British positions in the rear. Harbour and beaches were already occupied by the enemy by the time our troops reached the rendezvous. The French capitulated, the town was handed over, and about 150 to 200 officers and 4,000 to 5,000 men of the B.E.F. were taken prisoner. A certain number eluded capture, hid in the caves and eventually made their way to Veules-les-Roses, where they discovered the British and French craft embarking troops under terrific enemy bombardment and dive-bombing.

Salazar, Antonio de Oliveira. Prime Minister and virtual Dictator of Portugal from 1932. On May 22, 1939, Dr. Salazar reaffirmed his country's fidelity to the Anglo-Portuguese pact, and after the outbreak of war in September the Portuguese Prime Minister adhered to a strictly neutral policy. A conference was held at Seville on Feb. 12, 1942, between Gen. Franco (q.v.) and Dr. Salazar, when it was stated that it had been agreed " to maintain the closest communication in order to safeguard the common interests of the two countries."

Dr. Salazar, Prime Minister of Portugal. Photo, Planet News

Salla. Centre of fierce fighting between the Finns and Russians during the Russo-Finnish war of 1939–40, Salla was the scene of a Soviet threat to Finland's " waist-line " early in December 1939. The Finns made repeated counter-attacks, but Salla was captured by the Russians on Dec. 12, 1939. The Finns claimed its recapture two days later. Salla passed to the U.S.S.R. at the conclusion of the war in March 1940. On July 8, 1941, the town was captured by the Germans during their campaign against Russia.

Salmijaervi. Small Finnish town situated 30 miles from the mouth of the Petsamo River. The Finns withdrew from this place on Dec. 15, 1939, after having totally destroyed the valuable British-owned nickel mines to prevent their use by the Russians.

Salmon, H.M.S. Completed in 1936, this submarine had a displacement of 670 tons and carried a complement of 40. In December 1939 she achieved some spectacular successes against the enemy. Her first exploit was to blow to pieces by torpedoes a large U-boat which was setting out upon a raiding foray against British shipping. On Dec. 12 the Salmon had the giant German liner Bremen at her mercy, but refrained from attacking the enemy ship since in the special circumstances to do so would have violated international law. On Dec. 14 the submarine attacked

a German cruiser squadron which, accompanied by the battle-cruisers Scharnhorst and Gneisenau, was making one of its rare excursions at sea. Two enemy cruisers were hit, one belonging to the Blücher and the other to the Leipzig class. The Salmon was hunted by the enemy with depth charges for two hours, but she escaped and subsequently returned to the scene. Her commander, Commander E. O. B. Bickford, was awarded the D.S.O. On July 21, 1940, the Salmon was reported overdue and was presumed lost.

Salonika. This famous Greek city and seaport on the Gulf of Salonika has a magnificent harbour. Both were repeatedly raided by the Italians at the beginning of April 1941. On April 6 the Germans made a lightning thrust through the Struma Valley in Northern Greece, with Salonika as their main objective. Fighting between the Greeks and powerful German forces was extremely fierce, but the weight of enemy numbers and equipment thrust aside Greek resistance. The Germans entered Salonika on April 9, but the stubborn defence by the Greeks in the area of the port made possible the rapid embarkation of substantial Greek forces in Eastern Macedonia. The city itself was not defended and all stores were either withdrawn or destroyed by April 9.

Salween, River. Rising in Tibet, this important river flows through China into the Shan States, then through Lower Burma to its mouth on the Gulf of Martaban, near Moulmein (q.v.). On Jan. 19, 1942, the Japanese advanced in the Tenasserim area, south of the Salween, and on Feb. 2 the enemy crossed the river, after capturing Moulmein on Jan. 30. British forces, having evacuated the town, took up positions west of the Salween. Fighting developed in the Paan area, about 30 miles north of Martaban, on the east bank of the Salween. Enemy forces were repeatedly bombed on the river by the R.A.F. and Indian Air Force, and Japanese columns were attacked between the Salween and Sittang rivers. See Burma.

San Diego. Situated on the Pacific coast, about 126 miles south of Los Angeles and almost on the Mexican border, San Diego is America's chief naval base in home waters.

Santi Quaranta. This Albanian port, situated on the Adriatic, was of considerable importance to the Italians as a base during the Italo-Greek war in 1940.

In December 1940 the Greeks advanced from the south and south-east of Albania, closed in on Santi Quaranta, after having stormed the heights which surrounded the town, and captured the place on Dec. 6. The Greeks withdrew from Santi Quaranta in April 1941, when the Germans invaded their country.

Sarajoglu, SHUKRI. Turkish Premier. As Foreign Minister he was responsible for the negotiation of the Treaty of Mutual Assistance between Great Britain, France and Turkey in 1939. In February 1940 he attended a meeting of the Permanent Council of the Balkan Entente at Belgrade, as a result of which Rumania, Greece, Turkey and Yugoslavia proclaimed the common interest of their States to maintain peace and order in S.E. Europe. Sarajoglu also took part in Anglo-Turkish staff talks in Ankara in January 1941. He was appointed Prime Minister on July 9 1942, following the death of Dr. Saydam, and retained the office of Foreign Minister. See Turkey.

Sarawak. British protected State in N.W. Borneo. It was reported from Singapore on Dec. 16, 1941, that the Japanese had effected landings at Miri and Lubong in Sarawak. Detachments of British troops had previously been withdrawn from these areas after totally destroying the oil refinery, wells and installations in the Miri and Seria oilfields, which had a normal capacity of about 1,000,000 tons a year. A Japanese cruiser covering the landings was bombed by a Dutch 'plane which scored a number of direct hits and left the ship ablaze. On Jan. 1, 1942, it was reported that British forces had been withdrawn from Sarawak and had been sent to West Borneo.

Sardinia. This Italian island (*see* p. 3593), situated in the Mediterranean, west of Italy, was used by the enemy as an air and naval base. Military targets on the island were bombed frequently, both by the R.A.F. and by Swordfish aircraft operating from the aircraft carrier Ark Royal (*q.v.*). On Nov. 27, 1940, there was a running fight off Sardinia, when British naval aircraft sighted enemy warships. Units of the Royal Navy, including the Ark Royal, the Berwick, and the Renown, set out to intercept the Italians. In the course of operations no damage was sustained by any British ship, and owing to the extreme range it was difficult to observe the damage inflicted on the Italians, who finally turned away and made off under cover of a smoke screen. It was believed that the Vittorio Veneto was hit by a torpedo and that several other vessels were damaged. On Aug. 1, 1941, British destroyers, assisted by naval aircraft, entered the roadstead of Alghero and the harbour of Porto Conte and bombarded the air bases, causing considerable damage. Other objectives of British bombers were the seaplane base and hangars at Elmas and the harbour and aerodrome at Cagliari.

Savage, MICHAEL JOSEPH (1872–1940). He was Prime Minister of New Zealand from 1935 to 1940. At the General Election of 1938 he was returned to power with the loss of only one seat. He died on March 26, 1940, and was succeeded by Mr. Fraser.

Savage, W. A., v.c., Able Seaman. It was announced on May 22, 1942, that Able Seaman Savage had been awarded the V.C. for gallantry at St. Nazaire (*q.v.*).

Saydam, DR. REYFIK. He became Turkish Prime Minister in January 1939, having previously been Minister of Health and Minister of the Interior. Saydam signed the Anglo-French-Turkish Pact for his country at Ankara on Oct. 19, 1939. On July 12, 1940, he reaffirmed Turkey's strict adhesion to neutrality, a speech provoked by Germany's attempts to undermine the confidence of the nation. He died on July 8, 1942, and was succeeded by M. Sarajoglu. *See* Turkey.

Scapa Flow. This famous anchorage in the Orkneys is an important naval base and during the war of 1914–18 was the principal base of the British Grand Fleet. On Oct. 14, 1939, a German submarine penetrated the defences of this landlocked harbour and sank the battleship Royal Oak (*q.v.*). Three days later Scapa Flow was twice raided within a few hours in daylight. Two bombs fell near the old battleship Iron Duke. On March 16, 1940, one hundred bombs were dropped by Nazi aircraft attempting to bomb units of the Royal Navy in Scapa Flow, but only one warship was slightly damaged, seven of the personnel being killed. When British fighters arrived the raiders turned tail and jettisoned their bombs, some of which fell on the five-cottage hamlet of Bridge of Waith, killing the first civilian to lose his life in a raid on Britain in the present war. *See* Scotland.

Scharnhorst. With her sister ship, Gneisenau (*q.v.*), the Scharnhorst was much in the news throughout this war. On Dec. 18, 1939, the Admiralty announced that H.M. submarine Salmon had engaged a naval squadron consisting of Gneisenau, Scharnhorst and several cruisers, of which two were hit. On April 9, 1940, Scharnhorst, with an escorting cruiser, was attacked in Norwegian waters. During a 9-minute fight she was hit by several salvoes and was forced to retire under a smoke-screen. She was bombed by

CREW JOINING THE SCHARNHORST
One of the most heavily bombarded battleships in the world, the Scharnhorst was successfully prevented by the R.A.F. from attacking British and Allied shipping for many months. Ratings are seen carrying their kit aboard the ship in 1939.
Photo, Planet News

naval 'planes on June 13, 1940, and a week later was torpedoed by H.M. submarine Clyde and also hit by three aerial bombs while coasting off Trondheim. She was towed into a floating-dock at Kiel to undergo repairs, and there was bombed and set on fire by aircraft of Coastal Command on July 2. Scharnhorst with Gneisenau afterwards berthed at Brest, where they were repeatedly attacked from March 30, 1941, onwards. For a short period she berthed at La Pallice, but was heavily bombed there on July 23 and 24, 1941. On her return to Brest she and her sister ship continued to be violently attacked. So serious was the effect of these raids that on Feb. 13, 1942, the two battleships, with the 10,000-ton cruiser Prinz Eugen and a very strong naval and aerial escort, ran the gauntlet of the English Channel and, though intercepted and considerably battered, succeeded in making Kiel. Here she was bombed again by the R.A.F. *See* Brest; Kiel; Gneisenau.

Scheldt, River. (ESCAUT). Rising in the Aisne Dept., France, this river flows through the Nord Dept., thence into Belgium and, after passing through Antwerp, divides into two main streams, one of which reaches the sea at Flushing and the other 15 miles to the north. The Scheldt held a place of importance in the strategy of the Allied armies in Belgium. It was the most westerly of three rivers flowing north in roughly parallel lines, the other two being the Dendre and the Dyle. When, owing to the German breakthrough at Maastricht, the British forces were compelled, on May 16, 1940, to withdraw from their positions on the Dyle, east of Brussels, they retired to the western bank of the Scheldt. Here seven divisions held the line, with two in reserve. At an important conference at Ypres on May 21 between Lord Gort, the King of the Belgians and Gen. Billotte it was agreed that the Scheldt line should be abandoned. *See* France, Defeat of.

Schicklgruber. It was as " Mr. Schicklgruber " that the American commentator Quentin Reynolds addressed Hitler in his famous broadcast to him in 1941. It is derived from the fact that Hitler's father was born under that name, though it was changed to Hitler as early as 1842.

Scotland. The war came to Scotland with a torpedo attack on the Royal Oak by a U-boat which penetrated the landlocked anchorage of Scapa Flow on Oct. 14, 1939. Eight hundred officers and men were lost with the battleship. On October 16, following reconnaissance, there was a bombing attack on Rosyth and the Forth Bridge. A bomb glanced off the cruiser Southampton and sank the Admiral's barge and a pinnace alongside. Another fell near the destroyer Mohawk, killing three officers and 13 ratings and wounding many others. Four Nazi machines were shot down. R.A.F. 'planes made contact with the enemy off the Isle of May, and for a while some of the air fighting took place over Edinburgh. No air raid alarm was sounded, but some citizens took cover while others watched the battle from the rooftops of the city. The Orkneys were again raided on Oct. 17, and the Shetlands on Nov. 13, their 12 bombs being the first to fall on British soil. By the end of January 1940 Scotland had made provision for 32,000 hospital beds and 20,000 girls had been recruited for the Nursing Reserve. It was hoped to bring 260,000 additional acres under the plough. So far as the Highlands were concerned the bulk of the men had gone into the Navy. Scots fishermen, in spite of bombs and torpedoes, played an important part in keeping up the food supply.

On March 16, 1940, the Naval base at Scapa Flow was again attacked with nearly a hundred bombs which damaged one warship slightly and killed 7 of the personnel and also James Isbister, the first British civilian to be killed in the Second Great War by the Germans. A year later, March 13-14, 1941, Clydeside experienced one of the heaviest raids of the war. Hospitals, churches and houses were wrecked. There were many casualties. Lord Reith, who visited the scene, said that the effect of the raid was worse than anything he had seen in any part of the country. Clydeside's answer was to increase the output of munitions from 10 to 16 per cent.

One of the most sensational events of the war had its setting near Glasgow on the night of May 10, 1941, when Hitler's deputy, Rudolf Hess (*q.v.*), was captured by a Scottish ploughman, David McLean, at Newton Mearns.

On the industrial front Scotland has been well to the fore. Ships and all the munitions of war flowed in an ever-increasing stream from the factories of Clydeside and the midland belt. The miners, likewise, in the west, centre and east have contributed their quota, no less than 25,000,000 tons, one-eighth of the nation's total output of coal.

SCOTTISH TROOPS IN ACTION. Highland regiments took part in Norway and Libya, at Dunkirk and in Crete. Other Scottish regiments were in Egypt, Iran, the Far North, and the Far East. In the Battle of France Scottish regiments put up a valiant fight. On May 10 the 51st (Highland Division) held a portion of the French line in front of the Maginot forts in the Metz area. Two of its brigades, however, had to surrender. The third, the 154th (Black Watch and Argylls), on May 27, 1940, held a line on the River Brezle, and went forward to the Abbeville area to defend the Somme bridgeheads. The division suffered heavy casualties on June 4, especially the 152nd Brigade (Seaforths and Camerons). But there was a highly successful attack by the Gordons in the Grand Bois. The position was captured, but overwhelming pressure forced a withdrawal to Brezle. On June 8 a further withdrawal to the line of Béthune took place. The following morning the 154th Brigade was detached and ordered to the Havre area. On June 10 the remaining two brigades moved back along coastlines via Dieppe and took up positions round St. Valery-en-Caux. Here heavy casualties were suffered by the 153rd Brigade (Gordon Highlanders and Black Watch), but the men held their line until increasing weight of fire accurately directed from the air made a withdrawal to the beaches inevitable. General Fortune gave a final order, dated June 11, that the utmost discipline must prevail while an effort was made to take off the division in boats. Though our retreat to St. Valery was carried out successfully, the French Ninth Corps was forced back, allowing the Germans to get behind the British positions and occupy the port. The French surrendered the town, and about 200 officers, including Major-Gen. V. M. Fortune, G.O.C. of the division, and 4,000 of our men, were taken prisoner with the French Ninth Corps.

On Dec. 11, 1940, Highlanders took part in Gen. Wavell's great Western Desert offensive against the Italians and captured Sidi Barrani. The town had been heavily bombed and bombarded from the sea and air and was then attacked by a British brigade including Highland troops in the centre. The Highlanders charged with their bayonets through a hail of bullets and gained a foothold on a low ridge commanding Sidi Barrani. Attacking again, they helped to take the town by storm and capture 15,000 Italian prisoners, including Gen. Gallina. In October 1941 the Black Watch arrived at Tobruk from Crete ; in November they made a heroic sortie through the enemy lines in an attempt to join up with the Eighth Army, advancing from Egypt.

At the beginning of February 1942 Highlanders took part in the Malaya fighting against the Japs. They were in action in the jungle round Ipoh, and the Gordons covered the withdrawal of our soldiers over the causeway into Singapore. *See* Great Britain.

Sedan. An historic town of France, Sedan fell to the Germans after the latter had crossed the River Meuse, by vital bridges left undamaged, near the town, on May 15, 1940. *See* France, Defeat of.

Sephton, PETTY OFFICER ALFRED EDWARD. He was posthumously awarded the V.C. for great courage

and endurance during a German dive-bombing attack on the cruiser Coventry off Crete on May 20, 1941. Two cruisers, the Coventry and Phoebe, went to the rescue of a British hospital ship, after she had radioed S O S, while a squadron of German 'planes were attacking her. Sephton, in one of the gun director towers, was critically wounded by machine-gun bullets from a low-

Petty Officer
A. E. Sephton, V.C.
Photo. " *Daily Mirror* "

flying Nazi dive-bomber. Despite great pain he carried on with his duties. He died later the same day.

Sevastopol. One of Russia's most important naval bases and home of the Black Sea fleet, Sevastopol, situated on the shores of the Southern Crimea, was first bombed by the Germans on June 22, 1941. The main German offensive against the Crimea began on Sept. 25, 1941, and by Oct. 28 the aggressors had reached the foothills of the Yaila Mountains, thus splitting the Russian forces into two, one body retiring along the railway from Simferopol

PREPARING TO STRIKE BACK IN THE CRIMEA

The defenders of besieged Sevastopol withstood a hard and bitter winter's fighting in 1941-42. Russian women are seen, top right, in a shelter, sewing underwear and warm clothing for their men. Marines of the Black Sea Fleet, above, are landing on the enemy-occupied shores of the Crimea from Soviet submarines.

Photos, Ministry of Information

towards Sevastopol. Bitter fighting developed round the great seaport in November, and for a time Sevastopol was cut off from the rest of the Crimea. The garrison repelled incessant German attacks, and launched counter-attacks against the enemy, aided by aircraft and the guns of the Black Sea Fleet. They inflicted heavy losses on the Germans and regained some miles of territory. The beginning of 1942 saw little change in the position. In February Russian forces landed at strategic points in the Crimea. Despite Nazi claims, Sevastopol continued to be a serious menace to the German plan of conquest in the Crimea. On April 30 it was estimated that the six months' siege of the city had cost the Germans some 45,000 casualties. The Black Sea Fleet continued to keep the port supplied. Early in June the Germans launched a fresh onslaught against Sevastopol, using 100,000 men and masses of guns and dive-bombers. The garrison fought heroically, but, outnumbered by seven to one and ceaselessly bombed and shelled, was forced to withdraw to the inner defence lines on June 24. The enemy flung in fresh reserves in their effort to take Sevastopol regardless of cost and on July 3 the city was evacuated after eight months' heroic defence, adding another epic to Russia's story. *See Crimea.*

Seyss-Inquart, ARTUR VON. Reich Commissioner for the Netherlands from May 29, 1940. A few weeks later he ordered thousands of Dutch subjects to be conscripted for heavy manual labour in Germany. Under a decree of Aug. 24, 1940, he was given the power of appointing high governmental and public officials, formerly the prerogative of Queen Wilhelmina. In 1938 he was Minister of Interior and Security in the reconstructed Schuschnigg Cabinet, Austria, and after the German occupation of that country in the same year he became Chancellor and Minister of Defence. In November 1939 he was the Deputy Governor-General of German-occupied Poland.

Shanghai. This Chinese seaport normally handles nearly half of the country's foreign trade. An International Settlement occupies some 9 sq. miles in the northern part of the city, and here British, French, and Americans have their quarters. When Japan entered the war, on Dec. 7, 1941, one of her first acts was to take over the International Settlement in Shanghai, an act which passed almost unnoticed, since it was dwarfed by the sensational bombing of Pearl Harbour (*q.v.*) on the same day. The British gunboat Peterel was sunk in Shanghai harbour two days later.

Shaposhnikov, MARSHAL BORIS MIKHAILOVICH (b. 1882). Chief of Staff of the Russian Army from October 1941. For the third time since 1928 Marshal Shaposhnikov was appointed to the post of Chief of Staff, and in that capacity he was, during the war, the most important man in Russia, second only to Stalin himself. He was responsible for the planning of the invasions of Finland and Poland, and of the Soviet defence against the German invasion in 1941.

Sheffield. This important centre of Britain's steel industry was heavily attacked by German aircraft and damage was done to factories, residential areas and business property. The first raids occurred on Dec. 12–13 and 15–16, 1940. The enemy adopted

SHEFFIELD WAS A MAJOR TARGET BUT INDUSTRY CARRIED ON

British cities suffered the full concentration of German fury during the winter of 1940–41, when Nazi bombers repeatedly attacked many of the chief provincial centres. The civil population stood up magnificently to this ordeal, and by 1942 Germany was being amply repaid for her ruthlessness. The first Nazi attacks on Sheffield were made during the middle of Dec. 1940. Here is a scene of devastation in the neighbourhood of Angel Street after demolition work had been carried out.

Photo, L.N.A.

the same technique as that employed against other British cities, showers of incendiaries being followed by H.E. bombs. Considering the scale of these raids casualties were not unduly heavy.

Shipping Ministry Of. This Ministry, set up in October 1939, was merged into the Ministry of War Transport (*q.v.*) on May 1, 1941.

Siam (THAILAND). In 1939 the familiar place-name Siam (*see* p. 3699) officially became Thailand, a name under which it was not easy to identify the country now generally known by its old name. Siam is inhabited by a race known as Thais, and the native name of the country—one of 200,000 square miles—is Muang-Thai, which means "Land of the Free," a claim now having a somewhat hollow sound. With the rest of the world, Siam awoke to national consciousness in a mood of optimistic ambition, with aspirations to become a sovereign state functioning fully as such and submitting to no foreign political pressure. One overt act to this end was the denunciation of all foreign treaties in 1936, to be recast in terms appropriate to the Siamese government's conception of the country's importance. After the abdication of King Prajadhipok in 1935 the policy was directed by the Premier, Luang Songgram.

Siam became involved in the war in Asia because of her geographical situation. The moves which involved her were as follows. First, Japan presented demands to the government of Indo-China directly France collapsed. On June 20, 1940, the French, under Japanese pressure, agreed to cut off supplies to China over the Haiphong-Kunming Railway, thus leaving a sole way of ingress to China, the Burma Road (*see* page 58). The Indo-China government permitted Japanese troops to land in the northern province of Kwangsi, and these were soon sent farther south to a terrain more adapted to tank warfare—for Japan's moves in this part of the Peninsula occupied by Siam and Indo-China were purely military in character. This deployment indicated the coming of a drive south down the Peninsula and not a drive north into China. Siam, at this point, made claims on certain Indo-China territory and there were armed clashes. Japan, as leading nation of East Asia, came forward

as mediator. On May 9, 1941, Siam and Indo-China signed a peace treaty under which Indo-China ceded to Siam the Paklai border territory, which was to be demilitarized. Japan secured from both countries " self-denying ordinances " under which they pledged themselves not to make any pacts with a third Power detrimental to Japan.

On July 28, 1941, Japan made a pact of military cooperation with French Indo-China and, on the plea that the war threatened the colony's security, began a military occupation. The reasons put forward by Japan for these measures were as fair at face value as

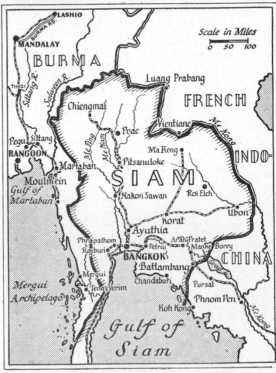

Siam in relation to French Indo-China and Burma.

WHEN MUSSOLINI'S MEN MARCHED AS PRISONERS INTO EGYPT
General Wavell's Army of the Nile swept swiftly forward to victory in the Western Desert, because its leader had learnt and even improved upon the lessons which the enemy had taught in other theatres of war. Here is a long column of Italian prisoners marching away from the ruins of Sidi Barrani. In some cases, only one soldier was necessary to guard a considerable number of prisoners, so dispirited were they by the turn of events.
Photo, British Official

foul in fact, and the pious fears expressed for the integrity of Siam in the face of British " aggression " merely masked the spring about to be made upon the tiny State. In her own interest, exclaimed Tokyo, Siam must give Japan military bases. Any such British designs on Siam were at once denied by the Foreign Secretary, Mr. Eden, in Parliament. Siam endorsed him, broadcasting : " The British have never been known to break such pacts "—a reference to the Siam-British non-aggression pact. Siam would resist any aggression and would do all things necessary to preserve her territorial integrity.

To understand why Japan was then casting greedy eyes on Siam it is only necessary to glance at the map and consider subsequent events, when all falls into a completed picture of a long-term military scheme. On Dec. 8, 1941, throwing off all pretence, her troops entered Siam and that country, after a resistance which " satisfied its honour," submitted. On Dec. 20, 1941, Siam made a forced alliance with Japan. The Japanese stated on July 11, 1942, that Indo-China had signed an agreement ceding N. and S. Laos and part of Cambodia to Siam.

The military occupation of Siam by Japan gave the latter country two great advantages : first, the obvious military one of a basis for an immediate invasion of Burma and a back-door entrance to Malaya ; secondly, complete control of the extensive rubber plantations of Siam and of the valuable tin mines of Indo-China. The exchanges between the small and militarily insignificant Siam and powerful Japan present a precise parallel with those that existed between Nazi Germany and, say, Czecho-slovakia—systematic false pretence and fraud with objectives to be secured by implied threats of force.

Sicily. On the Italian island of Sicily (*see* pp. 3704–6) were established many Italian and German air and sea bases. Lying in the middle of the Mediterranean, and dividing that sea into two parts, its position makes it of great strategical importance, chiefly for attacks against British Mediterranean shipping and as a base for air raids against Malta (*q.v.*), only 60 miles away. After Italy's entry into the war Sicily was a constant target for the R.A.F. Among the objectives bombed were aerodromes at Catania,

Marsala, Syracuse, Borizzo, Gerbini and Comiso ; power houses and munition factories at Licata ; the harbour at Palermo, which is the capital of the island ; docks and goods yards at Messina ; and the flying-boat base at Syracuse. In the Sicilian Channel, a stretch of water about 100 miles in width, separating Sicily from Tunis, there was a fierce combined naval and air action on Jan. 9, 1941. In this battle one Italian destroyer was sunk and at least twelve enemy aircraft shot down. H.M.S. Illustrious was hit and slightly damaged, and the cruiser H.M.S. Southampton (*q.v.*) damaged so badly that she was subsequently sunk by our own forces. *See* Italy ; Mediterranean.

Sidi Barrani. Situated on Egypt's Mediterranean coast, 60 miles E. of Bardia, the small village of Sidi Barrani was captured by Marshal Graziani's forces on Sept. 16, 1940. The Italian troops proceeded to dig themselves in, making no further attempt to advance. Except for attacks by the R.A.F. and British naval forces, activity was limited for the next few months to a few skirmishes between British mobile patrols and the enemy. In December 1940 the Imperial Army of the Nile, consisting of British, Australian, Indian and Free French forces, made a lightning counter-attack. Sidi Barrani was heavily bombed and bombarded from land, sea and air, and on Dec. 11, after three days' operations, it was once again in British hands. The Italians, driven out of their carefully prepared positions at Sidi Barrani and its protective screen of forts, surrendered. Thousands of prisoners, including three generals, Gallini, Pescatore and Mezzari, were captured, together with large quantities of war material. In a later campaign, when Rommel crossed the Egyptian frontier and rapidly advanced eastwards, German and Italian troops reached Sidi Barrani on June 24, 1942. *See* North Africa.

Sidi Omar. A Libyan frontier post on the Egyptian border, 30 miles S.W. of Sollum, Sidi Omar was captured by British forces on Dec. 16, 1940. It was recaptured during General Rommel's campaign in the following spring, but on Nov. 23, 1941, Indian troops took possession of it again, in the course of the second British advance into Libya. British armoured forces swept from Sidi Omar due west along Trigh-el-Abd, the Slave Road, a desert track to El Gobi, and then north to Tobruk. During Rommel's advance in June 1942, British troops withdrew from Sidi Omar to positions some way inside Egypt. *See* North Africa.

Sidi Rezegh. Situated 10 miles S.E. of Tobruk, this small Libyan town changed hands several times. During the first victorious British campaign it was captured by Jan. 6, 1940, as a preliminary to the capture of Tobruk. Though afterwards recaptured by General Rommel's forces, it was again taken by the British on Nov. 19, 1941. It became the scene of terrific tank battles, the British endeavouring to cut off the retreat of two Panzer divisions, which, however, succeeded in breaking through to the west and joining up with an Italian division (the Ariete). This engagement lasted for several days. Repeated German attempts to recover Sidi Rezegh were repulsed by the gallant stand of the South African Brigade, By Dec. 2 the town was in German hands, but it was won back within the week. Fighting again broke out in the region of Sidi Rezegh in June 1942. It was announced on the 19th that the town had been captured by Rommel's forces. *See* North Africa.

Siegfried Line. The construction of the Siegfried Line, Germany's reply to the Maginot Line (*q.v.*), was begun in 1938. It extended roughly along the German frontier from a spot some 15 miles east of Basle to Karlsruhe, then westward to the border of Luxemburg, and then east along the border of Belgium and Holland to the point where the Rhine enters Holland. To call it a line or a wall is misleading ; it was a zone of strong fortifications, sometimes two miles in depth, built of steel and concrete. The main part of it was underground, surmounted by some 12,000 concrete forts in which guns were mounted. There was a belt of anti-tank devices.

At the outbreak of war the Siegfried Line (officially known as the West Wall) was not completed ; ventilation was bad, the dug-outs were not yet habitable, the trenches were waterlogged. But when in the spring of 1940 Germany took the offensive on the Western Front, she was speedily victorious and could afford to let the Siegfried Line fall into disuse.

Sikorski, GENERAL LADISLAS (b. 1881). As Polish Prime Minister and Commander-in-Chief from

GIANT GUN OF THE SIEGFRIED LINE
The defences of the Siegfried Line lagged behind those of the Maginot, but Germany's defeat of France in 1940 rendered her West Wall superfluous as a defensive system. This photograph was taken inside the fortified emplacement of a huge Nazi gun in the Siegfried Line.
Photo, Keystone

the outbreak of the war, General Sikorski rendered exceptional service to his country, as might be expected from his previous record. This distinguished soldier and statesman was one of the leaders of the National Movement in Poland during the early years of this century. He held the rank of General from 1918, and received many decorations. For a period from 1922 to 1923 he was Prime Minister, and from 1924 to 1925 War Minister. When Poland was overrun by Germany he became Prime Minister and War Minister in the newly constituted Polish Government in exile. Paris was the new home of the Government, until the French débâcle ; it then came to London, and in 1941 the administration was reconstituted.

General Sikorski visited Canada and the U.S.A. during April and May 1941, negotiating for American aid under the Lease-and-Lend Act and for the establishment of training camps in Canada for Poles ; he also urged that after the war a Federation of Slavonic States should be organized, stretching from the Baltic to the Black Sea. In July 1941 he was in Russia,

DAMAGED TANKS IN THE DESERT
Tanks played a vital part in the desert warfare in the Libyan wastes ; both the Germans and the British threw in great numbers in an attempt to force a decision. These German tanks were knocked out at Sidi Rezegh by the South Africans.
Photo, Barnaby

General Sikorski,
Polish C.-in-C.
Photo. Fox

where he signed a treaty with the Soviet State, re-establishing diplomatic relations and obtaining the gradual release of Polish prisoners held in Russia. A Polish army was to be trained on Russian soil. By Stalin's invitation the General returned to Russia in December, to see for himself how these arrangements were being carried out. The Polish divisions already in Russia were moved to the Persian frontier, to be trained and equipped, and a further total of 25,000 Poles were made available for army service. In March 1942 General Sikorski was again in America to arrange for closer inter-allied cooperation.

Simon, Rt. Hon. John Allsebrook, p.c., k.c.v.o., 1st Viscount (b. 1873). Lord Chancellor from May 1940. He was Foreign Secretary in 1931, Home Secretary in 1935 and Chancellor of the Exchequer from 1937 to 1940 (*see* p. 3717).

Simon Bolivar. This Dutch liner of 8,309 tons was sunk by a German magnetic mine off the east coast of England on Nov. 18, 1939. Carrying a complement of about 400 passengers, the majority of whom were Dutch, she had left Amsterdam for the West Indies on Nov. 17. Over 120 lives were lost and many other passengers were seriously injured. The survivors were taken to London.

Simovitch, Gen. Dusan (b. 1882). He became Prime Minister of Yugoslavia as a result of the political coup d'état in March 1941. This was brought about through the signing away by her pro-Axis ministers of Yugoslavia's freedom to Germany. On March 27 Gen. Simovitch formed an All-Party Government. Before his nomination to the Premiership he was Chief of General Staff and subsequently Chief of the Air Force. On April 6 Germany attacked Yugoslavia without warning or declaration of war, and after the country had been overrun by the aggressors, Gen. Simovitch came to London with members of the Government. On Jan. 12, 1942, it was announced that Simovitch's Cabinet had resigned, and that Prof. Slobodan Yovanovitch had been appointed Prime Minister. Gen. Simovitch was offered an important post in the organization of the Yugoslav war effort.

Gen. Simovitch,
Yugoslav Premier, 1941.
Photo, "Daily Mirror"

Sinclair, Rt. Hon. Sir Archibald, k.t., p.c. (b. 1890). Secretary of State for Air from May 1940. He was Secretary of State for Scotland from 1931 to 1932, and in 1935 was chosen leader of the Liberals in the House of Commons.

Sir A. Sinclair,
Air Minister.
Photo, Lafayette

SINGAPORE FOUGHT ON TILL THE END

The speed of the Japanese drive through Malaya and the subsequent capitulation of Singapore were events that profoundly moved British and Allied opinion during the tragic month of Feb. 1942. But with the loss of Singapore the determination of the United Nations to defeat the enemy at all costs was strengthened. See Malaya ; Pacific.

Singapore. Singapore is an island off the south of the Malay Peninsula, separated from that mainland by a strait never more than one mile wide, and bridged by a rail-carrying causeway. On its north side a naval base was made at a cost of more than £3,000,000, and, excluding Australia, it was the only base east of Suez where Britain's great warships could be repaired and maintained. That is why its defence was vitally important to the Allied cause, and why its short siege and fall profoundly shocked the British Empire and her associate nations in arms

How was it possible for the Japanese forces, whose attack had long been expected, and, since February 1941, prepared against by reinforcements of Australian troops, to take this redoubtable fortress in eight days, when Hongkong, upon whose defence comparatively little had been spent, resisted for 19 days ?

When the clouds of battle rolled away from the stricken island it became possible to obtain in broad outline the sequence of events that ended with the entry into Singapore town of the first Japanese tanks, Feb. 15, 1942. It became possible, also, to see the causes which resulted in this major military and naval disaster. These were not one, but many.

On Feb. 4, sixty-three days after the launch of the southward drive down the Malay Peninsula, the order was given by the Japanese Commander-in-Chief, Yamashita, for a general assault on Singapore Island.

It was clear that the Japanese intended to make an attempt to land in force. For three days and three nights they pounded away with artillery of all calibres, and this hail of steel fell upon British, Australian and Indian troops already exhausted after fighting a continuous rearguard action down the Malay Peninsula. They were weary, dispirited, and, in the swamps and coconut plantations of the strait's southern shore, they had little or no protection.

Australian engineers had breached the causeway, but not sufficiently to prevent Japanese sappers making a swift repair and obviating the necessity for exclusively seaborne invasion. The first Japanese landed on the island on the night of Feb. 9. Nineteen hours later they had captured Tengan aerodrome. By Feb. 11 the first troops were infiltrating into the city. Four days later Lieut.-Gen. Percival, Commander-in-Chief under General Wavell, signed the surrender.

The Japanese claimed between 60,000 and 70,000 prisoners. Vast quantities of stores and equipment

Chief strategic points of the island of Singapore.
By courtesy of "The Observer"

others had not been fighting long enough, Japan brought to bear a tremendous air fleet. She needed no attempt at attack from the sea for which Singapore was so heavily prepared. From the start she obtained complete air ascendancy, firing and destroying large sections of the city. Scarcely a single Hurricane on the island survived that terrible week. Most of them were destroyed on the ground.

Next, the defenders found themselves deprived of the essential native labour for work behind the lines and at the naval base (where the normal 12,000 men diminished to 800 overnight). As the Governor, Sir Shenton Thomas, has told, the island was running short of water and food; and, as the generals have told, ammunition and petrol were also almost exhausted.

It was to save a million people from the peril of Japanese Bushido (chivalry), as exemplified by the atrocities committed in Hongkong, that the bitter cup of capitulation to such an enemy was drunk to the dregs. Between sixty and seventy thousand British, Australian and Indian troops and about a million civilians became the prisoners of the Japanese.

The consequences of the loss were at once apparent, particularly to Australia, for whom the fall of Singapore was a Dunkirk. It was realized that the illusion of the impregnable defence system, which should have

SINGAPORE'S FAMOUS CAUSEWAY

The fine causeway that connected Singapore with the mainland is seen above, a view taken from Johore Bahru looking across the Strait of Johore towards the island. Civil workers, right, are fighting the flames caused by Japanese bombers after a savage enemy raid on civilian homes at Singapore.
Photos, British Official; E.N.A.

also fell into their hands. To the outside world, the swift and tragic collapse seemed the more incomprehensible because it stood in such sharp contrast to the sustained defence put up by the American General MacArthur on the Bataan Peninsula in the Philippines.

Consider the facts. In the first place Singapore was prepared as a great naval base which would serve not only the British Empire but her obvious partner, sooner or later, the United States. But a great naval base minus great naval ships and their accompanying smaller craft is a stable without horses. It was not a fortress and had but minor defences against land attack from the north; there had been, apparently, no anticipation of invasion through the hills and plantations of Malaya and its big guns could only fire effectively seawards. Take, next, the character of the island. It is flat and open, offering no protection against concentrated artillery fire or air bombardment.

Against this vulnerability, defended by mixed troops of which some had been fighting too long and

received its death blow when the Germans swept over the Maginot Line, was finally gone.

Singapore taken, the conquest of the Netherlands East Indies (p. 305) followed speedily, and Japan stood with her feet astride the gateway from the Indian Ocean to the Pacific, master of the sea lanes, and in possession of a great naval base from which to organize her mass assaults upon Australia.

In the British House of Commons a call for an inquiry into the surrender of Singapore was demanded.

Book: Singapore and After, Lord Strabolgi (Hutchinson).

Sinkiang Road. From Alma Ata, capital of the Soviet province of Kazakstan, this is an excellent modern road, running N.E. to the Chinese province of Sinkiang. Across China it runs through desolate regions and is often no more than a track, but it is capable of bearing 3-ton lorries. It passes through Urumchi, capital of Sinkiang, and continues S.E. by way of Hami and Suchow to Langchow; there it becomes a modern highway again, proceeding past Chungtu, notable for its 1,000-acre aerodrome, to Chungking.

Sitwell, MAJ.-GEN. H. D. W. As G.O.C. British troops in Java, he defended the island vigorously but vainly against enormous odds, and in a spirited Order of the Day on March 2, 1942, declared " 'Attack' and not 'defence' must be our watchword."

Maj.-Gen.
H. D. W. Sitwell,
G.O.C. Java.
Photo, Lafayette

Skoplje (Uskub). Situated on the R. Vardar, in Yugoslavia, about 130 miles N.W. of Salonika, this town was captured by the Germans on April 9, 1941.

Slovakia. The Slovaks are a people of Slavonic race living in the northern area of the Carpathians. After centuries of Hungarian domination they were incorporated in the republic of Czechoslovakia, set up by Masaryk in 1918. A so-called People's Party, with clerical support, was formed by Father Hlinka and strove to obtain Slovak autonomy. In October 1938 the dismemberment of Czechoslovakia, following the disastrous Munich Pact, seemed to assist the aims of the People's Party, which began to organize Slovakia on Nazi lines, under the dictatorship of Father Tiso, who had succeeded to the leadership.

In March 1939 a revolt, instigated by Germany, broke out in Bratislava, the Slovak capital. This gave Hitler a pretext for declaring that Czechoslovak unrest was endangering Germany, and German troops invaded the country on March 14. The Czech provinces were annexed by Germany, and Ruthenia by Hungary, but Slovakia was proclaimed an independent state. She was, however, " protectively " occupied by German troops on the outbreak of war in September, and she had to cooperate in the war against Poland, although the Slovak Minister in Warsaw publicly declared that the Slovaks were in sympathy with the Poles. In February 1940 the Soviet Minister, M. Pushkin, made overtures based on the kinship of the Slavonic races, and these were favourably received by the Slovak Foreign Minister, M. Durchansky, but were opposed by M. Mach, Chief of the Hlinka Guard. Durchansky had to resign and Mach became Minister for Home Affairs. On July 28 Father Tiso, with Dr. Tuka (Prime Minister) and M. Mach, visited Salzburg and had conversations with Ribbentrop and with Hitler. Tuka afterwards said that Slovakia was, once and for all, under German influence, and there could be no chance for Communism; Germany would not interfere with religion. On Nov. 24, 1940, Slovakia joined the Axis Powers, becoming a puppet state run for Hitler's benefit. Since then the Slovaks have begun to realize their mistake, and look forward to the restoration of their freedom. *See* Czechoslovakia.

Smigly-Rydz, MARSHAL EDWARD (b. 1886). He assisted Pilsudski in 1919 and 1920 in establishing the Polish State and repulsing Russia, and when Pilsudski died in 1935 he designated Smigly-Rydz as his successor. Smigly-Rydz became Marshal and Inspector-General of the Polish army, and was virtual dictator of Poland, officially ranking next after the President. He directed the Polish resistance to German aggression in September 1939, and when the Polish armies were defeated he escaped to Rumania with members of the Polish Government. The Polish Government in France was critical of his management of the campaign and he was relieved of his duties in November 1939. Arrested in Bucharest in 1940 he escaped from Rumania but was caught by the Gestapo in August In July 1942, he escaped again.

Smith, F./O. THURSTON MEIGGS WETHERALL, D.F.C. One of the first five R.A.F. men to be decorated. He commanded a flying-boat of the Coastal Command in September 1939, and while on patrol over the Atlantic intercepted messages from the torpedoed merchantman Kensington Court (*q.v.*). Accompanied by a second flying-boat, he alighted on the water and rescued 20 of the ship's crew from a lifeboat containing 34, the remainder being picked up by his colleague.

Smolensk. This Russian city, on the R. Dnieper, some 250 miles S.W. of Moscow, is of considerable strategic importance. Following the German invasion of Russia on June 22, 1941, it was claimed on July 16 that Smolensk had been captured, but this was premature. German advance units were thrown back and there was very heavy fighting, several German

SMOLENSK WAS A KEY POINT

These Russian women are seen walking past a shattered church in Smolensk—the city that was so fiercely contended by Germans and Russians during Hitler's thrust to Moscow in August 1941.

Photo, Associated Press

divisions being annihilated. The Russians were, however, forced to evacuate the city on August 14, and in December Hitler established his headquarters there; but he was soon forced to withdraw to Minsk, in face of the Russian counter-attack. Soviet troops made a determined effort to recapture Smolensk.

Smuts, GEN. (FIELD-MARSHAL in the British Army) JAN CHRISTIAAN (b. 1870). Prime Minister and Minister of Exterior Affairs and Defence of the Union of South Africa from 1939. The earlier career of Gen. Smuts is told in Vol. 8, pp. 3731–32. Two days after war was declared in 1939 a piece of good fortune befell the British Commonwealth of Nations. General Smuts became Premier of South Africa, taking the place of Gen. Hertzog, who had proposed that the

GENERAL SMUTS IN CONFERENCE

Gen. Smuts, South African Premier, right, intently studies a map with Sir Alan Cunningham, during a visit to Kenya in 1941. South African troops fought with distinction in both Abyssinia and North Africa.

Photo, British Official

Union should take up a position of "modified semi-neutrality" (that was Gen. Smuts's description), and who was defeated in Parliament by 80 votes to 67. Smuts, in a powerful speech, urged that it would be wrong and even fatal not to sever relations with Germany. It was impossible to treat as a friend a country which was at war with Great Britain. South Africa must be for or against; it could not be neutral. Hitler aimed at dominating the world by force, and South Africans must either oppose him or range themselves on his side.

Two months later the Premier said the course taken had not been popular. Most people naturally wanted to keep out of war if they could. But the trouble he had been warned to look out for had not come ; the underground rumblings had ceased. He felt able, therefore, to promise on Feb. 7, 1940, that South African forces would go to the aid of other British communities as far as the Equator, though there would be no compulsion on them to do so. He would rely confidently on volunteers. As to pan-Africanism, he said (on March 20) that the idea of the United States of Africa might at present be Utopian, but there was nothing jingo or imperialistic in such an aim, and much might be done to bring the prospect nearer. The African natives, he added, could no longer be regarded merely as an aid to production. In another

speech at a later date he stated that white and black soldiers serving together had come to look on each other with mutual respect.

He was made Commander-in-Chief of all Union Defence forces on June 16, a post followed nearly a year later (May 24, 1941) by his appointment as Field - Marshal, partly in recognition of the fine work done by Union troops in the Abyssinian and Libyan campaigns. He lost no opportunity to urge his country to greater efforts in all directions and to keep their attention fixed on the real issue of the war—whether the world should consist of slave States or an international society of free nations.

A flying visit to the South African troops in Egypt during August gave him opportunity to express the opinion that the Middle East and the Mediterranean battlefields might become historic after those of Russia ; on them might be fought the Armageddon of the twentieth century. Of the rapid German successes in Russia he had spoken on July 14. They were spectacular, he admitted, but where and what was the end to be ? Though civilization might be frail and, like the sea, subject to tides of progress and recess, it could stand enormous strains and stresses, and history told clearly what had been the fate of would-be world conquerors. *See* South Africa.

Snapper, H.M.S. Belonging to the Shark class, this submarine was completed in 1935. Her displacement was about 670 tons, and she carried a complement of 40. During the Norwegian campaign in 1940 she sank four transport and supply ships, and her commander, Lt. W. D. A. King, was awarded the D.S.O. On July 7, 1940, the Admiralty announced that the Snapper had torpedoed five more enemy ships off Norway. On March 16, 1941, it was reported that she was overdue and presumed lost.

Sollum. On the Egyptian coast, just within the frontier and 15 miles south of the Libyan port of Bardia, stands the much-contested town of Sollum. When the Italians invaded Egypt in mid-September 1940 they advanced from Fort Musaid, a deserted frontier-post, and shelled Sollum for three days. On Sept. 13 they entered the town and found it deserted, the handful of British defenders having

ON THE QUAY AT SOLLUM

In spite of constant enemy air attacks Sollum, the strongly contested town just inside the Egyptian border, was long used by the British forces. Here is a scene taken at sunset, showing the quayside from which British supplies were sent to Libya.

Photo, British Official

withdrawn under cover of darkness. Graziani's troops continued their advance along the coast road, but in December the British forced them back, with the aid of naval bombardment, recaptured Sollum on Dec. 16 and proceeded to conquer Cyrenaica. In the course of Rommel's spectacular reconquest of the province for the Axis, Sollum fell to the Germans on April 14, 1941. The British counter-attacked and took the town on June 15, but German reinforcements were brought up and succeeded in regaining it two days later. A new British drive into Libya began on Nov. 11, 1941, when Sollum was by-passed and isolated, in an endeavour to cut off two German panzer divisions near Tobruk. On Jan. 12, 1942, Sollum was captured by the Transvaal Scottish Regiment, forming part of the 2nd South African Division. By June 25 it was again in German hands. *See* North Africa.

Somaliland, British. On Aug. 4, 1940, the Italians commenced an advance from Abyssinia into British Somaliland. Lack of cooperation on the part of the French at Jibuti, and the skilful organization of the Italians, hampered the comparatively small British force. Though strongly outnumbered, our troops at first successfully resisted an enemy attack on the Jugargan pass, between the Abyssinian frontier and Berbera, the capital of British Somaliland. The Italians, however, brought up reinforcements and the Empire forces withdrew on Aug. 19. It was subsequently decided to abandon the whole of the territory to the enemy. With the capture of Berbera the Italians claimed that the British would eventually be driven out of East Africa, and that the Red Sea would be closed to British trade. On March 15, 1941, a little fleet of British warships and troop carriers steamed towards the Somaliland coast. Two landings were made, and naval guns bombarded the capital. The taking of Berbera next day was followed by our capture of Hargeisa, an important stage in the progress of British columns advancing westwards towards the Abyssinian frontier. On March 24 a communiqué from Nairobi told how British Somaliland was once more under our complete control. *See* East Africa.

Somaliland, Italian. From July to December 1940 there was a gap of some 100 miles between the Italians and British on the Kenya-Italian Somaliland front. On Dec. 16 Gen. Cunningham opened an offensive, which in two months carried the Imperial forces past the Juba River. Composed of troops from South Africa, West Africa and East Africa, Gen. Cunningham's force delivered its first attack on Dec. 16, 1940, against El Wak, a frontier post in the bush. After its capture the invasion of Italian Somaliland was prepared and organized from points far to the south. First a number of frontier posts on the Kenya border were subdued, and then the Imperial forces swept on to Afmadu, 100 miles from the frontier. The S.A.A.F. bombed the place and the Italians withdrew on Feb. 10, 1941, rather than wait for the British onslaught which was timed for Feb. 12. In this action the King's African Rifles distinguished themselves. Kismayu at the mouth of the Juba was taken on Feb. 14, the enemy having withdrawn. The Royal Navy harassed the Italians who were moving along the road between Kismayu and Mogadishu, the capital, and on Feb. 26 Mogadishu itself was captured by Empire troops. The Italians surrendered in thousands, and only a small remnant endeavoured to escape along the road to Harar and Addis Ababa. *See* East Africa ; South Africa.

Somerville, VICE-ADM. SIR JAMES FOWNES, K.B.E., D.S.O. (b. 1882). C.-in-C. British Eastern Fleet from April, 1942. He carried out extremely courageous work in May 1940 when, as Deputy to the Vice-Admiral, Dover, he was instrumental in rescuing thousands of soldiers at Dunkirk. On July 3, 1940,

Sir J. Somerville, British Admiral.
Photo, British Official

he was in command at Oran (*q.v.*), and on Nov. 27, 1940, he achieved a spectacular success against the Italian Navy off Sardinia (*see* Cagliari). In the bombardment of Genoa on Feb. 9, 1941, his flagship, H.M.S. Renown, played a conspicuous part. It was in this ship that he commanded the force that took part in the pursuit of the German battleship Bismarck (*q.v.*) in May 1941. On April 13, 1942, he succeeded Vice-Admiral Sir Geoffrey Layton as C.-in-C. British Eastern Fleet.

Soong, T. V. (Sung Tsu-wen, b. 1891). This member of a famous Chinese family was appointed Foreign Minister in December 1941, in succession to Quo Tai-chi. Himself educated in America, he had done much to enlist American help for China against the Japanese. He was in Washington at the time of the treacherous Japanese attack on Pearl Harbour and other Allied outposts. On Feb. 27, 1942, he visited Toronto with a military mission, to arrange for Canadian help to China. Mr. Soong's family is one of the most influential in China ; there are three

THEY WELCOMED THE RETURNING BRITISH
After the British recaptured Berbera, capital of British Somaliland, in March 1941, the inhabitants proudly displayed the national flag—symbol of freedom that had been hidden during the Italian occupation. Here is a group of Somalis who had long awaited the day of liberation.
Photo. British Official

brothers (T. V., T. L. and T. A.) well known in public life, and three sisters, all, like their father before them, were educated in America and are Christians. Of T. V. Soong's sisters, the most famous is Madame Chiang Kai-shek ; another is wife of H. H. Kung, Finance Minister; the third is the widow of Dr. Sun Yat-sen, and herself a Chinese revolutionary leader.

Sortavala. Situated on the north shore of Lake Ladoga in Finland, this town was almost destroyed by Soviet aircraft during the Russo-Finnish war, 1939–40. At the conclusion of hostilities in March 1940 the Russian treaty stipulated that territory north and west of Lake Ladoga must be ceded to the U.S.S.R. Sortavala thus became part of the Soviet Union. Fighting between the Germans, Finns and Russians broke out in June 1941, and Lake Ladoga was again the scene of bitter warfare. The Finns claimed that they had recaptured Sortavala on August 16, 1941.

SOUTH AFRICA'S CONTRIBUTION TO THE WAR

Our brilliant victories against Mussolini's East African Empire and its subsequent destruction were due in no small measure to the fine work of the South Africans, who formed part of the Imperial force which routed the enemy there in 1941. See Abyssinia ; East Africa ; North Africa ; Somaliland.

South Africa. When war with Germany was declared in 1939 General Hertzog was Prime Minister of the Union. He resigned after the House of Assembly rejected his " Neutrality motion " and the Governor-General, the Hon. Patrick Duncan, refused his demand for a dissolution. Instead, General Smuts (*q.v.*) formed a Cabinet and selected a body of men who served the Union faithfully during the first two and a half years of the war, including the glorious months when the Active Citizens Force was " blooded " in the East African campaign of General Cunningham. The effort was the more remarkable because South Africa entered the war with its industry, as well as its army and air force, on a peace footing.

It is the measure of South Africa's potentialities and good fortune that in the opening years of the war the Union enjoyed a prosperity unique among the nations at war. Always money was abundant, and the weight of taxation was never oppressive. Moreover, supplies of South African gold were continually increased and furnished the most important source of purchasing power to Great Britain for orders in the United States which were not covered by the Lease-Lend Act. South African maize, dairy produce, wool, and sugar were among the primary products sold in bulk to the Mother Country.

This achievement would not have been possible if Smuts had not immediately realized the necessity for supplementing the available military personnel with a large body of civilian experts. In particular, he brought into being a special Civilian Directorate of Production, independent of military jurisdiction, under the leadership of Dr. H. J. van der Bijl, head of the South African Iron and Steel Corporation (Iscor). The Civilian Directorate did invaluable work in discovering the key men in mining, engineering, transport and industry, fitted to help in the war effort. Thus the secondary industries of the Union, which had a pre-war annual value of £188,000,000, were harnessed to war production. One outstanding product was the South African armoured car, thousands of which did service in the field, though the industry was entirely new to South Africa in 1939. Many of the heavy bombs used in East Africa were made in the South African Railways and Harbours workshops. The 3·7-inch howitzers, which figured prominently in the fighting, came from the central ordnance factory (Cofac).

When Smuts took up the reins of office he was faced with the inadequacy of the military preparations which he inherited from his predecessors in office. Very ingeniously, he did not propose a totally new scheme, but took over one which previous governments had fathered but had never carried into execution. This provided for three Active Citizen Force divisions totalling 67,000 men ; three special defence rifle brigades totalling 10,000 men ; and three defence rifle field forces totalling 60,000 men, a grand total of 137,000. The training of the three Active Citizen Force divisions proceeded intensively, and at the same time two mounted brigades were recruited, in order to give South Africa mobility in bush warfare.

The original military oath did not cover active service outside the Union. The Government, therefore, introduced a new voluntary oath, and four-fifths of the South African defence forces showed their willingness for every sacrifice by volunteering to serve " anywhere in Africa." These were the troops who wore the proud emblem of the orange tab on the shoulder strap. Women's Auxiliary Services and Women's Air Services were also incorporated in the Defence Force. Like the men, all women were expected to subscribe to the new oath to serve anywhere in Africa.

Thanks to this intensive organization, General Smuts was able to attend the farewell parade at Sonderwater Camp on July 14, 1940, which was the prelude to the departure of the troops next day for Gilgil in Kenya. By this time France had fallen and Italy was in the war. Road engineers got to work upon highways across the desert which ran from Habaswein to Wajir, 400 miles away, an oasis where for many centuries camel caravans had rested. Now the road was to be fitted for mechanized transport.

By December 1940 the troops were able to move on to Wajir and the campaign against the Duke of Aosta's troops in East Africa commenced in earnest. General Cunningham's troops were greatly outnumbered and only gained their astonishing victories by their greater mobility and their superiority in air power. The South African Air Force launched their bombs daily for months upon objectives which seemed so distant that the Italian commanders themselves wondered. The South African air fighters in a single raid again and again covered a distance greater than that between London and Berlin, and these flights were over uncharted deserts where a forced landing meant death by hunger or murder by hostile natives.

The opening fight in December 1940 was at El Wak, and the Transvaal Scottish, the Natal Carabineers, and a battalion of the Dukes had the place of honour, in company with men from the Gold Coast. On Christmas Day the Second and Fifth Brigades moved on to

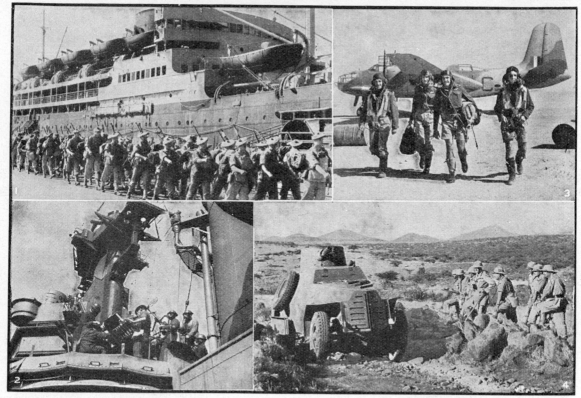

MEN OF THE UNION IN THE FIGHT FOR FREEDOM

1. South African troops marching along the quayside of a Union port en route for active service. 2. Members of the South African Division of the R.N.V.R. carry out gas drill in conjunction with pom-pom practice aboard their ship. The gun's crew wear gas masks. 3. The crew of an American Boston III 'plane, operating on the Libyan battlefront, leave their aircraft after desert patrol. 4. Officers in Kenya watch an armoured car returning after patrolling positions held by the Italians.
Photos, British Official; Fox

attack Marsabit, a forest-covered plateau, which represented the outpost of the territory from which the South Africans were to operate. Thence the Transvaal Scottish, the Transvaal Irish, and the Natal Mounted Rifles, together with armoured units, left the forest and plunged into the white wastes of the Chalbi Desert. Here the Fort of El Yibo, guarding vital wells, was taken by Natal troops in heat which reached 135°.

With this water supply secure, the conquest of Abyssinia may be said to have begun in earnest. The capture of the stronghold Mega, which was defended stubbornly by Blackshirts, was a feature in this section of the fighting.

Meanwhile, battalions of the Dukes, the Transvaal Scottish and the Natal Carabineers were advancing into Somaliland. Their first fight was on Feb. 10, 1941, at Afmadu, an important Italian administrative centre. Its capture opened the way to Kismayu, the third largest port in the territory, where the British Navy helped the South Africans to take five ships of 28,000 tons, apart from vessels sunk. By Feb. 14 all territory south of the Juba River was taken. "Hit them, hit them hard, and hit them again," was General Cunningham's Order of the Day, and the South Africans obeyed it to the letter. Within three days the Italian defences on the Juba had crumbled and the way to Mogadishu, the capital of Italian Somaliland, was open. It fell on Feb. 28. After the surrender of Addis Ababa on April 5, and of the Duke of Aosta on May 17, the South

Africans went on to take a gallant and valuable part in the Libyan campaign of Gen. Auchinleck.

The magnificent stand they made at Sidi Rezegh in November when, heavily outnumbered and faced with repeated tank, air and infantry attacks, they closed the exit to Rommel's retreating troops, cost them 1,200 casualties. In June 1942 they suffered a far more grievous loss at Tobruk. Few of the gallant defenders of that garrison, composed of the 2nd South African Division, Indian and U.K. troops, escaped capture by the Germans when Tobruk fell. Mr. Attlee sent a message of sympathy to Gen. Smuts, who replied : "Our sorrow will but harden our determination." Later Gen. Smuts broadcast a stirring appeal for more recruits to replace the losses at Tobruk.

South Africa did not participate in the Empire air training scheme in Canada, though many South Africans served with the Royal Air Force in Britain and France. South Africa came to the conclusion that training in Africa, under favourable conditions of climate and terrain, was preferable to training in another continent, having regard to the special commitments of the South African Air Force.

On the sea the Union made itself responsible for the defence of its Naval Station at Simonstown, and Union minesweepers and patrol boats kept guard over the 1,800 miles of South African coast line.

It is to be regretted that the record of South African sacrifice was dimmed by the cowardice of a few leaders,

AIRWOMEN OF THE UNION

Members of the South African W.A.A.F. are seen in an air-conditioned room wherein parachutes are stored. These women are parachute packers and are engaged in airing the unused parachutes lest the silk should deteriorate.

Photo, South African Official

among them General Hertzog, the ex-Prime Minister, and Dr. Malan, another Nationalist leader. In the autumn of 1940 Hertzog declared openly that Britain had lost the war. Dr. Malan's reaction to the fall of France was to argue that a victorious Germany would want a government in South Africa " which would be friendly disposed towards her." He added, " The Nationalist Opposition could provide a government which had already shown that it had no hostility towards Germany." On March 3, 1942, Dr. Malan demanded in Parliament that the Union should withdraw from the war. He said that in view of the enormous territorial gains by the Axis it was hopeless to expect the Allies to win. The Japanese danger to South Africa was a danger only so long as South Africa was in the war with the Allies. Happily, an insignificant minority supported Malan. Even Hertzog left the Nationalist Party after its congress at Bloemfontein in November 1940.

The trial of Robey Leibbrandt and sixteen other alleged Nazi agents, held at Pretoria in March 1942, was another incident in fifth column activities in South Africa. South Africa was to be congratulated that the whole movement was negligible in comparison with the splendid service which the Union rendered to the democratic alliance under Field-Marshal Smuts.

Book: South Africa Fights, J. S. M. Simpson (Hodder & Stoughton).

South America. South America's role during the first two years of the war was that of hapless victim. These republics, big and small, and most displaying some shade of the colour of democracy, were shops to which Europe looked for the replenishment of her larder shelves.

Britain's blockade of Germany bolted the door of the biggest European buyer, and South America found herself crammed with commodities, but minus customers to take them off her hands. This consequence was inevitable, but its interest lies not so much in the realm of international trade as in that of international relations. Argentina with 8,000,000 bushels of unsalable wheat in 1940, Peru with the bulk of a big cotton crop on her hands, and Chile without foreign buyers for her copper, were all in this sad case because of the war strategy of Britain. Yet not one of those hard-hit States raised its voice in protest against the blockade or the blockading Power. This surprising fact has great interest, for it demonstrates the world-wide character of the fear engendered by the dark deeds of Hitler Germany.

South America did not need to be persuaded of the extent of Germany's war aims, nor that such aims included the South American States. Nazi Germany supplied all the evidence of that. She did so through a campaign by the spoken and written word and by direct action.

The methods used included subornation by bribery of the Press and actual acquisition of newspapers and journals. The dissemination, through a very large Buenos Aires headquarters, of news services was a means of putting out Press propaganda. The cinema was corrupted by bribes, and, in one case, that of the showing of " The Great Dictator," actual official interference was resorted to (Uruguay).

Where Fascist Organizations Flourished

Actual Nazi parties were formed and actual training of a military kind was organized. The largest of these were the Chilean Fascist Vanguardia, Mexico's Falange Española and the vast underground subversive German organizations which permeated life at all points in Argentina, Brazil, Chile, Uruguay, and the rest. All these conspiracies had a single political objective : to prise the South American continent free from the United States and then to deal with the Republics by the method employed by Hitler in Europe.

The conduct of the Nazi agents became so outrageous in the days of the Nazi successes that the effect produced was the precise contrary of that intended : the consolidation of the whole western hemisphere against Germany's world domination designs.

At the Pan-American Conference, held in Havana, July 1940, 21 States found themselves in agreement under the presidency of Mr. Cordell Hull. The main issues dealt with were the disposition of the unsold products, and it was agreed to work together to effect this. An Advisory Committee was set up to this end.

Out of this conference, notable because it revealed a case of peoples thinking internationally despite continental interests—perhaps the next development of human relations—came the Act of Havana.

This pronouncement laid down a very important proposition, namely, that changes in the sovereignty of European-owned possessions in the New World were the business of the New World. It justified the setting up of American provisional governments in such cases. It was, obviously, aimed at Nazi aggression. A proviso for other action for self-defence left the United States free in the Caribbean Sea.

Meanwhile, though preoccupied with a war going none too well and suffering badly from air bombardment,

Britain sent, in December 1940, a Trade Mission under Lord Willingdon to South America to alleviate the blockade-created trade difficulties. Despite an outburst of Nazi anti-British propaganda, the Mission was received with the greatest friendliness everywhere.

Directly Japan struck at the United States, the Central American Republics, their Pacific seaboard and the Panama Canal imperilled, declared war.

For the rest, both North and South America became an undivided whole in sentiment and purpose vis-à-vis the Japanese aggressor. That all South America is solidly behind the United States is as certain as anything can be. Self-interest and common ideals of freedom cement two Continents.

Books to Consult: Inside Latin America, J. Gunther (Hamilton). Latin America, R. A. Humphreys (Oxford Pamphlet).

Southampton. The Germans concentrated on bombing this important seaport immediately they had established air bases in conquered France. The port was heavily raided on Aug. 13, 1940. Subsequent raids destroyed a large part of the centre of the city, where

THE KING VISITS SOUTHAMPTON
The King, accompanied by Mr. Herbert Morrison, Minister of Home Security, is seen making a tour of a badly bombed area of Southampton after a severe enemy raid. Soldiers meanwhile carry on with their work among the ruins.
Photo, Planet News

there were few targets of military importance. Shops and house property suffered in consequence. Southampton was raided severely for seven hours on Nov. 30, 1940, when many fires were started. Enemy attacks were made obviously with a view to terrorizing the civil population. Thousands of people lost their homes and many were killed and wounded, but the spirit of the inhabitants remained undaunted. On Dec. 5, 1940, King George toured the city and inspected some of the damage. Raids were resumed by the Germans in 1941 and 1942, though in many instances these were on a smaller scale.

Southampton, H.M.S. Completed in 1937, this British cruiser of 9,100 tons was damaged in the Firth of Forth on Oct. 16, 1939, during the first German air raid against Britain. Southampton, in company with Mohawk and Edinburgh, had just come in after convoy duty and had approached her moorings near the Forth Bridge. A bomb, glancing off her bow, fell into and sank the Admiral's barge and a pinnace

moored alongside. Both these vessels were empty. Bomb splinters, however, caused three casualties aboard the Southampton. She was the first British warship to be hit by a German bomb. On Jan. 9, 1941, she took part in a battle in the Sicilian Channel between British and Italian naval forces, the latter consisting of two destroyers. One of these, of the Spica class, was sunk. German and Italian aircraft, working from Italian bases, and including a number of dive bombers, made heavy attacks against the British ships. During the engagement the Southampton, commanded by Capt. B. C. B. Brooke, R.N., was hit and suffered casualties. So badly was she damaged that she was subsequently sunk by our own forces

Soviet-German Pact. Signed between Russia and Germany on Aug. 23, 1939, this Pact of Non-Aggression startled the world, for Hitler had ceaselessly vilified Communism as " the arch-enemy of mankind." The Pact, therefore, came as a shock both to the enemies and friends of the U.S.S.R. The chief provisions of the Pact were : (a) Both Powers bound themselves to refrain from aggressive action against each other. (b) Both Powers to abstain from participation in any grouping of Powers aimed directly or indirectly at either of them. (c) Both Powers to remain in future continuously in touch with each other by way of consultation. (d) The Pact to run for ten years, with provision for extending it a further five years. The Pact ended the Franco-Russian Alliance and was interpreted by many as an invitation to Hitler to invade Poland. With the prospects of peace now almost defeated, Britain pushed forward her measures for defence. Poland manned her frontiers and awaited the now inevitable German onslaught. On June 22, 1941, Hitler invaded the Soviet Union. *See* Russia.

Spaak, PAUL HENRI. Foreign Minister in the Free Belgian Government in Britain. He pursued a policy of strict neutrality as Foreign Minister in M. Pierlot's Cabinet after the outbreak of war in September 1939. In April 1940, when Germany invaded Norway, he was outspoken in his expressions of sympathy for that victim of Nazi aggression. Both he and the Prime Minister, M. Pierlot (*q.v.*), did their utmost to resist

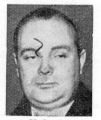

M. Spaak, Belgian statesman. *Photo, Wide World*

the tremendous onslaught in May 1940 when Germany invaded the country. In a final interview with King Leopold (*q.v.*) he begged him, but in vain, to hand over the command of the Belgian army to a general. With the King's capitulation on May 28 Belgian resistance came to an end. Thereupon the Belgian Cabinet reorganized itself in Paris, and after the collapse of France in June M. Spaak remained in that country until the end of August. Baudouin, French Foreign Minister, asked him for an undertaking not to go to Britain, but this was refused. After many difficulties, M. Spaak and M. Pierlot escaped to Spain and eventually arrived in London on Oct. 22, 1940.

Spain. The war policy of Spain between 1939 and 1942, though theoretically strictly neutral, had its origin in the help which Germany and Italy gave to General Franco during the Revolution of 1936. Associated with this sense of obligation to the Axis partners was the Falangist hatred of Communism, particularly in its Russian form. Spain was, therefore, quick to join the anti-Comintern Pact, though public opinion was momentarily shocked when Germany concluded her pact with Stalin in August 1939, previous to the declaration of war upon Poland in the following month. Spain preserved neutrality until the collapse of France in 1940, when a state of non-belligerency was substituted, based upon a general belief that the military success of Germany and Italy was now assured. Evidence of the changed attitude came on June 14, 1940, when General Franco occupied the Tangier Zone, in defiance of the convention with Britain and France dating from 1923 (modified 1928).

The Tangier Zone was expressly internationalized because it was recognized to be the African equivalent of Gibraltar. At the time of the occupation in June 1940 the move was regarded as a first step towards Spanish control of the Straits of Gibraltar, upon which the more extreme members of the Falangist Party were bent. The satisfactory result of the Battle of Britain, however, persuaded General Franco that the end of the British Empire was not yet. He was, therefore, content to accept the fact that Britain had not actively opposed the seizure of Tangier and made no further effort to break with her. Relations between the two countries were improved by the appointment of Sir Samuel Hoare as British Ambassador at Madrid in May 1940.

Empty 'Will to Empire'

The war policy of Spain is only to be understood in the light of the clause in the Falangist code which sets out : " We have a will to empire. We will not put up with international isolation or foreign interference." On the contrary, Spain has always been a poor country since it lost its overseas empire after the Cuban War of 1899. The economic aim of General Franco and his colleagues has been to increase internal production until the old-time empire can be revived, if not in America then in North Africa. The years of civil war further impoverished Spain, and most of the leaders are well aware that the country is in no condition to take up arms again or even risk a conflict with Great Britain and the United States by allowing a German army to pass through Spain for an attack upon Gibraltar or to pass into Morocco and Algeria.

During the war Gen. Franco had expressed himself as pro-Nazi and anti-British and anti-American (see p. 128, this vol.), and his brother-in-law, Señor Serrano Suñer, has been actively pro-Nazi. Franco is styled El Caudillo of Spain, " caudillo " being a diminutive derived from the word " caput," meaning " leader," and, as such, he is " responsible only to God and History." Suñer, however, is president of the political junta which rules Spain and became Minister of Foreign Affairs on Oct. 18, 1940. He has, therefore, been in a position to influence Spanish policy strongly in favour of the Nazis.

The Spaniards are a proud people, and it has long been galling to hold their Moroccan possessions by favour of France and Britain. It was, therefore, not surprising that the collapse of France seemed to give promise of a dominant position for Spain in the Western Mediterranean and also an influential position in a Latin bloc at the end of the war, which would suffice to keep a victorious Germany in a due place in the New Europe. Spain's final policy will be dictated by who is victor in the World War.

It is noteworthy that the terms of the armistice concluded between Germany and Vichy France expressly fixed the boundary between occupied and unoccupied France so as to include the railway connecting Spain and Germany, by way of Bordeaux and Tours. The line has carried iron from Bilbao and Santander, copper from Seville and zinc from Marcia and Santander, all welcome contributions to the Nazi war effort. *See* Franco ; Portugal.

Spearfish, H.M.S. Belonging to the Shark class, this submarine was completed in 1936, and had a displacement of about 670 tons. On April 11, 1940, she torpedoed and badly damaged the German pocket battleship Admiral Scheer. For this feat Lt.-Commdr. J. H. Forbes was awarded the D.S.O. On Aug. 28, 1940, the Spearfish was reported overdue and presumed lost.

Spitzbergen (Svalbard). Situated within 500 miles of the North Pole and some 360 miles north of Norway, Spitzbergen is an archipelago containing some of the richest coal deposits in the world. In 1938 the export of coal was 606,000 tons, there being six

SUPPLIES DENIED TO THE ENEMY

This vast column of smoke shows burning coal dumps—a source of enemy fuel which an Allied force destroyed after a daring landing on Spitzbergen in September 1941. The men in the foreground are members of the raiding party.
Photo, British Official

mining settlements inhabited all the year round by Norwegians and Russians. After the German occupation of Norway in April 1940 a small German military delegation visited Spitzbergen, and shortly before the Nazi onslaught against Russia in June 1941 reports reached Britain that the Germans were seizing the coal destined for the U.S.S.R. for their own transports operating along the Norwegian coast. An Allied expedition was therefore dispatched to Spitzbergen, a full report of which was given to the world on Sept. 8, 1941. The raiding forces were made up of Canadian, British and Norwegian troops under Canadian command, and the landing was completed without interference, possibly because the Germans were unable to spare the necessary naval force to oppose it. The mines were completely destroyed, and all the inhabitants, over 700 miners and their families, were brought back to Britain.

Spoleto, DUKE OF. King of Croatia. Younger brother of the Duke of Aosta (*q.v.*). After the Yugoslav capitulation a deputation of disloyal Croats, led by Anton Pavelitch (the assassin of King Alexander of Yugoslavia in 1934), made a formal request that the King of Italy should sponsor the new state of Croatia (formerly part of Yugoslavia) by choosing its ruler. The Duke of Spoleto assumed the title of King Aimone on May 18, 1941.

Stalag. A contraction for Stamlager, this official term is used to denote the type of camp used for privates and N.C.O.s who are prisoners of war in German hands. *See* Oflag; Prisoners of War.

JOSEF STALIN—BUILDER OF MODERN RUSSIA

For many years Stalin's was an enigmatic personality so far as the Western Democracies were concerned, but with the Nazis' attack on the U.S.S.R. in June 1941, Stalin emerged, not only as a supreme figure among his own people, but as an inspired leader among the United Nations. See Russia.

Stalin, JOSEF VISSARIONOVITCH (b. 1879). Chairman of the Council of People's Commissars and Head of the State, Union of Soviet Socialist Republics. Why Stalin accepted Hitler's offer of a non-aggression Pact a few days before the delivery of the German attack that had been planned to overrun Poland, an attack which compelled Britain and France as guarantors of Polish independence to go to its aid, is not clearly known. He may have been convinced of Hitler's good faith, as he declared he was in a speech made on July 3, 1941, just after the Nazi invasion of Russia had begun. He denied that the acceptance was a mistake. Such an offer could not be refused, he argued, even though it was made by " monsters and cannibals." At all events, he added, it had given Russia time to improve her armaments. To gain time may have been Stalin's motive. Or he may have believed that it was possible for his country to keep out of war.

What his agreement with Hitler actually did was to give the German army a free hand and enable it to subdue not only Poland, but Norway, Denmark, France, Holland, and Belgium as well. It was the removal of the need to fight on two fronts that made the German army leaders fall in with Hitler's itch for war. That Britain and France had any real concern about the Poles was ridiculed by Molotov, who must have been expressing Stalin's view, in a speech on March 29, 1940. He said that Germany had become a dangerous competitor with the two foremost imperialistic countries, Britain and France, which aimed at " smashing and breaking up Germany " and which were " intensely hostile " to the U.S.S.R.

This was after the Russo-Finnish war, during which British and French sympathies had been mainly on the side of the Finns, a small nation attacked by a very large one. The issues were not clearly understood. Stalin felt he must have better security from attack by an enemy coming through the Baltic countries. The Finnish frontier was only a few miles from Leningrad. Here was a danger, since this would probably be the point chosen for invasion. The Russian Government was misled into supposing that the mass of the Finnish people would collaborate with them, would throw up their caps and cheer Russian forces advancing into their country. So, when he had vainly tried to reach an agreement with the Finnish Government, dominated by Marshal Mannerheim, who had always shown marked Fascist sympathies, Stalin gave the word for troops to march, imagining they would have a triumphal procession. He was at once undeceived, and the immediate result of his error was a series of costly battles on a small scale, which gave

SOVIET DICTATOR

Wearing his unpretentious military jacket, Stalin is seen (above) giving instructions to Gen. Shaposhnikov at the time of the Russo-Finnish war of 1940. Shaposhnikov had the reputation of being " the brains " of the Red Army organization. Right, a recent photograph of Stalin.

Photos, British Official; E.N.A.

the impression that the Russian army had been hugely over-estimated. However, as soon as the army leaders had time to form a plan of campaign and to equip their troops for winter operations, the tide turned, and the war, which had begun on Dec. 2, 1939, ended on March 16, 1940, with the complete submission of the Finns to terms which were lighter than had been expected. Stalin obtained what he required and did not wish either to plunder or humiliate a beaten foe. During this episode Stalin had his 60th birthday (Dec. 21, 1939) and received a telegram from Hitler, conveying best wishes and hoping the Soviet Union would have a happy future. Stalin in reply said "the friendship between the Russian and German nations, cemented by blood, has every reason to be lasting."

Having secured the approach from Finland, Stalin turned to the other Baltic States, Estonia, Latvia, Lithuania, and was quickly able to get permission to send troops to occupy certain strategic points. Governments favourable to the U.S.S.R. were installed for the purpose of giving this ; the value of Stalin's foresight was seen when Germany invaded Russia. Before that happened Stalin became for the first time the holder of a post in the Government. Up to May 6, 1941, he had been Secretary to the Communist Party ; on that date he took the place of Molotov as Chairman of Commissars, which means Prime Minister, and became officially as well as actually head of the State. After the invasion he took over the Defence Ministry from Marshal Timoshenko, whom he sent to train new armies ; and when Moscow was in danger of being surrounded he took personal charge of the city's defence. He was credited also with planning the general strategy of the campaign, though this may have been an exaggeration. He became as much a hero in the world as he had been a bugbear.

He Faced Danger in Full Confidence

The disasters which befell the Russians during the months from June to November 1941 were not for a moment hidden from the nation. Stalin let them have the bitter truth ; he admitted that the U.S.S.R. was facing serious danger. But at the same time he declared that no armies were invincible and, although the enemy had the great initial advantage of a flying start, he was confident of final victory. He announced a policy of " scorched earth " and promised that conditions should be made intolerable for the Nazis in all the territory they overran. The encouragement he received from Mr. Churchill and America he acknowledged as " fully comprehensible and symptomatic." There was a warmer note in his acceptance of the proposal made at the Roosevelt-Churchill Atlantic Conference for a three-Power meeting in Moscow to discuss plans and allocate supplies. When the meeting took place (Sept. 1941) his calmness, close knowledge of conditions, and exact formulation of what he wanted made a very favourable impression on Lord Beaverbrook and the American representatives.

Just after the middle of October he announced that Moscow, then appearing to be in imminent peril, would be defended to the last, and sent his colleagues in the Government, as well as the diplomats, to Kuibishev, formerly Samara, on the Volga. By Nov. 6 he was able to state that Russian reserves were moving into line and that the enemy's strength was failing. In his talks with Mr. Eden during the latter part of December agreement was reached as to the necessity of utterly defeating Hitlerite Germany and making any repetition

of its aggression impossible, but as to the post-war organization it was merely given out that their exchange of views " would facilitate a future elaboration of concrete proposals." As the months went by and no proposals were made by the British Foreign Office, Stalin began to feel disappointment, and to doubt the British Government's desire to create a new social order. This came to a head in his address to the troops on Feb. 23, 1942, in which he looked forward confidently to the enemy being driven off Russian soil, though with great difficulty, but said nothing about what would happen after that had been accomplished ; did not threaten pursuit of the Nazis into Germany ; and made no mention of peace aims. He denounced as a stupid lie and senseless slander the statements in " the foreign Press " that the Russian aim was to exterminate the German people and destroy the German State. He did not identify Hitler's clique with the German people or the German State.

After the signing of the Anglo-Russian Treaty of Alliance, announced on June 11, 1942, Mr. Churchill, in a congratulatory telegram to Stalin, said : " I am very grateful to you for having done so much to meet us in the difficulties connected with our treaty."

Book : Landmarks in the Life of Stalin, E. Yaroslavsky (Lawrence & Wishart).

Stalino. A thriving industrial town in the Donetz Basin, 100 miles N.W. of Rostov, Stalino was the scene of bitter conflict during the German invasion of Russia. The Russians finally had to evacuate the town on Oct. 26, 1941.

Stanley, RT. HON. OLIVER FREDERICK GEORGE, P.C. (b. 1896). He was President of the Board of Education from 1935 to 1937, and President of the Board of Trade from 1937 to 1940. On Jan. 5, 1940, he succeeded Mr. Hore-Belisha as Secretary of State for War until May 10, 1940, when he was replaced by Mr. Anthony Eden.

Stannard, LT. R. B., R.N.R. On Aug. 16, 1940, it was announced that the second naval V.C. of the war had been conferred on Lt. Stannard for "outstanding valour and devotion to duty " at Namsos. The first British naval detachment landed at Namsos on April 14, and between then and May 2, when British troops were withdrawn, he made his gallant stand.

Lt. R. B. Stannard, awarded the V.C.
Photo, Topical Press

Enemy bombers had set fire to many tons of hand grenades on Namsos wharf. There was no water supply available, and Lt. Stannard ran H.M. trawler Arab's bows against the wharf and held her there. Sending all but two of his crew aft, he then endeavoured for two hours to extinguish the fire with hoses from the forecastle. After helping other ships against German air attacks he placed his damaged vessel under the shelter of a cliff, and landed his crew and those of two other trawlers, and established an armed camp. Here those off duty could rest while he attacked enemy aircraft which approached by day and kept anti-submarine watch during the night. Throughout a period of five days the Arab was subjected to 31 bombing attacks and the camp and gun positions ashore were repeatedly machine-gunned and bombed, yet the defensive position was so well planned that only one man was wounded. Lt. Stannard subsequently brought his damaged ship back to England.

Staraya Russa. Situated south of Leningrad and 10 miles south of Lake Ilmen, this Russian town was the scene of intensely bitter fighting between the German and Soviet forces during the opening months of 1942. On Feb. 25 the Russians completed the encirclement of the German 16th Army at Staraya Russa. Von Busch, the German commander, refused to surrender when called on, and three Divisions, including the SS " Death's Head " Division, were smashed by the Red Army, and 12,000 Germans killed. For some time the front in this sector had been indeterminate, and the town changed hands more than once. On Feb. 28 it was announced that the Russian army had reached the Don-Nevel railway, S.W. of Staraya Russa and only 80 miles from the Latvian border. Meanwhile, large German reinforcements made frantic efforts to extricate their 16th Army. A captured Nazi document showed that this trapped force had orders from Hitler—who promised to send munitions and supplies by air—to hold on at all costs. It was estimated that the Nazis had some 80,000 troops in this sector, and attempts to supply the beleaguered army from the air were frustrated by Soviet aircraft. By March 3 it was reported that the trapped forces were short of food, and by April 9 that German resistance was being gradually worn down. On April 24 Berlin claimed that their trapped 16th Army had been relieved and had contacted the main forces. Early in May strong Soviet attacks were reported in the Lake Ilmen area.

Adm. Stark, U.S. sailor.
Photo, Associated Press

Stark, ADMIRAL HAROLD R. (b. 1880). Chief of U.S. Naval Operations from Aug. 1, 1939. He was able to convince the House and Senate Committees that America should have a navy of paramount importance, both for Atlantic and Pacific defence, and a tremendous shipbuilding programme was begun. At the historic Atlantic Conference between Mr. Churchill, Mr. Roosevelt and their advisers in August 1941, Admiral Stark was one of those present. He was posted to London in March 1942 as Commander of U.S. Naval Forces in European waters.

Stavanger. An important port, situated on the Norwegian coast, Stavanger was occupied by German troops on the first day of the German invasion of Norway, April 9, 1940. The airport provided an excellent base for German aircraft to attack British shipping off the Norwegian coast, and was therefore the object of heavy attacks by the R.A.F. High and low level raids were made and enemy aircraft were machine-gunned. The Germans carried out repairs with great rapidity, but during the Norway campaign they did not once succeed in getting the aerodrome into full operation.

Staveren, REAR-ADM. J. J. A. VAN. On March 5, 1942, it was announced that he had succeeded Vice-Adm. C. E. Helfrich as Supreme Commander of the Allied naval forces in the South-West Pacific.

Stettin. Capital city of Pomerania, Stettin is one of Germany's chief ports, situated 30 miles from the mouth of the R. Oder and handling traffic from Berlin, 83 miles upstream. It has extensive docks and shipbuilding yards and is a centre for heavy industry (engineering and machinery) and an im-

portant railway junction. Though not within easy range of R.A.F. bombers, it was often attacked, owing to its use as a supply base for the Eastern Front.

Stilwell, LT.-GEN. JOSEPH W. (born 1883). American commander of Chinese forces in Burma. He was former Chief of Staff to Gen. Chiang Kai-shek, spoke Chinese fluently, and was a Far East authority. He arrived in Delhi on May 24, 1942, after an adventurous trek through central Burma, to consult with Gen. Wavell before returning to China.

Stimson, HENRY LEWIS (b. 1867). He became Secretary of War in President Roosevelt's Cabinet on June 21, 1940. Mr. Stimson was one of America's foremost supporters of the U.S. defence programme, and in important speeches on May 6 and 22, 1941, he urged the repeal of the Neutrality Act.

Mr. H. L. Stimson,
U.S. Secretary of War.
Photo, Wide World

Stone, LT.-GEN. R. G. W. H., D.S.O., M.C. (b. 1890). G.O.C. British troops in Egypt from February 1942. He was Military Attaché at Rome from 1935 to 1938, and from 1938 to 1940 Assistant Commandant of the Sudan Defence Force.

Strasbourg. The entire population (about 220,000) was evacuated from this Alsatian city early in September 1939. Situated on the Rhine, the Kehl Bridge connects the French side with the German, and after

STRASBOURG WAS A SILENT CITY

Here is a scene in the Place Kléber in the centre of Strasbourg as it appeared during September 1939, after the population had been evacuated. Stores, hotels and cafés are closed, streets are empty, the wide square deserted save for a party of Gardes Mobiles.
Photo, courtesy of the French Embassy

the outbreak of war this bridge was heavily protected by the opposing forces. The city itself is two miles distant from the Rhine and was France's nearest town of importance to the German frontier. Strasbourg was visited by Hitler after the collapse of France in June 1940, when he appeared in the triumphant role of conqueror. By July 1940 the Germanization of Alsace was reported to be in full swing. Only German-language papers were permitted to be published in Strasbourg and street names and names of shops and hotels were changed from French to German.

Strasbourg. This French battleship, a sister ship of the Dunkerque, was completed in 1938. She had a displacement of 26,500 tons, carried a complement of about 1,380, and her main armament consisted of eight 13-in. and sixteen 5·1-in. guns. The Strasbourg, although torpedoed by the Fleet Air Arm at Oran (*q.v.*) on July 3, 1940, escaped to Toulon.

Streicher, JULIUS. Known as " Jew-baiter No. 1," this notorious Nazi was for some time able to loose his evil instincts under the Hitler regime. Pandering to the Fuehrer's anti-Semitism, he conducted a virulent campaign against the Jews in his weekly paper, " Der Stürmer," which had a circulation of over 500,000, built up on pornography and racial hatred. On June 4, 1937, a Jewish youth, Helmut Hirsch, was beheaded for planning his assassination ; the evidence was never made public and was probably faked. Streicher founded what he called a " church," and at the summer solstice in 1937, and again in 1938, celebrated its pagan rites, amid Beltane fires, on the Hesselberg, a mountain which he declared sacred to Hitler. Streicher was considered to be the most hated of the Nazis, for his brutal face, his close-cropped head and his hulking figure gave him a sub-human aspect, in keeping with his character and mentality. In November 1940 it became known that he had been arrested for financial irregularities.

Strydonck, GEN. VAN. He was in command of the Free Belgian Forces in Britain.

Stülpnagel, GEN. VON. As head of the German delegation, Gen. von Stülpnagel attended the Franco-German Armistice Commission at Wiesbaden in June 1940, and was appointed Nazi Governor of Occupied France. When Germany took the offensive against Russia in the following year, he was given a command, side by side with Gen. von Reichenau, on the Southern front, and with the support of Gen. von Kleist's panzer divisions advanced beyond Zhitomir to Kiev, enabling the German hordes to sweep forward over a wide front beyond the Dnieper. He afterwards returned to his post as Nazi Governor of Occupied France.

Sturgeon, H.M.S. This small submarine, commanded by Lt. G. D. A. Gregory, D.S.O., encountered on Sept. 2, 1940, off the northern tip of Denmark, a 10,000-ton German transport carrying 3,000–4,000 troops, and, though operating under very difficult weather conditions, succeeded in sinking her. On Nov. 11 H.M.S. Sturgeon sank two supply ships off enemy-occupied territory, and on March 3, 1941, she sank an 8,000-ton tanker off the Norwegian coast.

RUTHLESS WAR UNDER THE SEVEN SEAS

Hitler promised Britain and the Allies a war of extermination on the high seas, and the Battle of the Atlantic was intensified in 1941 and 1942. Our reply was a greatly increased effort to keep open the ocean traffic lanes. America faced the same problems. See Atlantic ; Convoy ; U-boat.

Submarine Warfare. The Royal Navy, in consequence of Britain having worked for years, both by argument and example, to secure an international agreement to abolish the submarine, started the war with an underwater fleet that was quite inadequate. Ready for sea there were 24 of the ocean-going patrol type, 6 big minelayers, 15 seagoing and 12 coastal boats, many of the last two classes being obsolete. All except 7 in the Mediterranean and 15 in China were in home waters. The personnel was excellent in every way and the organization sound, but the composition of the fleet was criticized as being weak in the small, handy types particularly useful in the North Sea.

On the other hand, France had nearly a hundred of all types, completed or nearly so, including the 4,304-ton Surcouf, the biggest in the world, which was generally regarded as a failure. Poland had four, including the Orzel (*q.v.*), which soon became world-famous for her escape from the Baltic when her base was occupied and for subsequent dashing exploits before she disappeared with all hands. As their countries were subsequently invaded, Holland, Norway, Greece and Yugoslavia brought flotillas of varying size into the Allied service.

The strength of the German submarine fleet was not known to the public, but was believed to be about 70 units, mostly of 250, 500 and 710 to 750 tons surface displacement, the last-named quite capable of long cruises. In spite of Hitler's personal pledge that they would only be used in accordance with agreed rules of humanity, laid down by the civilized nations of the world, these were cynically disregarded at once and U-boats

BRITISH SUBMARINE ARRIVES HOME

H.M.S. Trident, which torpedoed and badly damaged the German cruiser Prinz Eugen on Feb. 23, 1942, off the coast of Norway after the latter's escape from Brest earlier in the month, is seen coming alongside her parent ship after a long patrol.
Photo, British Official

were stationed on the trade routes before the actual outbreak of war. They started operations with the sinking of the Athenia (q.v.) on Sept. 3, 1939, followed immediately by the Bosnia, Olivegrove, Pukkestan and others. Counter-measures were put in hand at once, but were handicapped by lack of material.

In the early days of the war our submarines were greatly hampered by lack of targets. Merchantmen on commercial work were not molested and neutral rights were scrupulously respected, even when the Bremen was escaping to Germany through neutral waters. The shallow entrances to the Baltic and the approaches to enemy bases were securely mined and German surface warships seldom ventured out into the North Sea. A cruiser of the Koeln type was torpedoed by the little Ursula and the Leipzig by H.M.S. Salmon in December 1939, while constant diving patrols were maintained off the enemy coasts.

The invasion of Denmark and Norway in April 1940 and the subsequent occupation of the Atlantic seaboard down to the Spanish border changed everything. Practically all enemy troops and munitions had to be carried by sea and ships on such service were legitimate targets, quite apart from the right of reprisal. In cooperation with the R.A.F., and with the French until their surrender, British submarines began to take a heavy toll in spite of powerful convoys. Dutch and Norwegian units soon helped gallantly and the losses became serious for Germany. Warship targets were found wherever possible ; H.M.S. Truant torpedoed the cruiser Karlsruhe when she was apparently safe inside a big minefield.

The collapse of France robbed us of French help except for the Surcouf and a few others, while the entry of Italy brought another 140 odd submarines of all types against us. Only a few of them were in the East African bases, and these failed to check the stream of men and munitions across the Indian Ocean and up the Red Sea, but the bigger Italian types soon appeared beside the Germans in the Atlantic. On the other hand, the Italian forces in North Africa and Greece required a constant stream of transports and supply ships, and British, Greek and Dutch submarines, with aircraft, sank a very large number of them and their protecting warships both on convoy and patrol duty. So successful were these operations that German stiffening had to be imported.

Losses of submarines were heavy (see Table, p. 422), and were published when confirmed, but no successful attacks on U-boats were announced until it was certain that the enemy could not learn anything from them. Certain exceptions were made — for instance, the ignominious surrender of the big Italian Galileo Galilei to H.M. trawler Moonstone (q.v.). Several on both sides were sunk by other submarines, which had been regarded as practically impossible.

All details of new construction and design were naturally kept secret, but from time to time the Admiralty mentioned new names in communiqués, honours and casualty lists, which proved that there was a steady flow of new units. The Upholder—in which Lieut.-Commander Wanklyn won his V.C.—Utmost, Unique, Union, Usk and Undaunted were presumably sisters, or similar, to the handy little vessels of the Unity class which had done such gallant work, but there was nothing to indicate the characteristics of the P.32 and P.33, which were both sunk. The Polish Navy received the Sokol to replace the lost Orzel.

CEASELESS VIGIL OF THE SEAS
This officer is looking through the periscope of a British submarine on the look-out for enemy ships during a patrol. Constant vigilance by our submarines was maintained from the outbreak of war.
Photo, Keystone

In 1940, in consequence of the growing efficiency of British convoys and other counter-measures, Axis submarines adopted what their propaganda described as the " Wolf-Pack " method of attack by several boats together. In this they were greatly assisted by wireless intelligence of the convoys' course from the Focke-Wulf long-distance 'planes and for a time they attained some measure of success, but counter-measures were soon devised.

When Japan extended the war into the Pacific in December 1941 it made a vast difference to the submarine war. She had an unknown number of submarines, certainly over 100, ranging from big ocean-going vessels to the miniature 2-man submarines which were carried by big ships to take part in the first treacherous attack on Pearl Harbour. Although they made good propaganda, their success was small and depended entirely on the element of surprise, which was only possible the first time they were used. The U.S. submarine fleet consisted of about 110 vessels built, and more than half that number building.

The Japanese immediately started a war on commerce in the Pacific, using gunfire very largely until American ships were armed and convoys started, and also carried out some " nuisance " bombardment of the American coast. In the South Pacific they were more successful in arranging submarine traps than their Allies, obviously benefiting from the intelligence work

VITAL WORK ABOARD A ' MOTHER ' SHIP

Scene of activity in a British submarine depot ship after the latter's charges have returned for a rest from their patrols. This photograph was taken in the torpedo shop, and men are seen at work on torpedo war heads.

Photo, Central Press

whom 1,800 were taken prisoner, wounded or killed. By May 22 fresh waves of parachutists had invaded this region. The British and their allies were hampered by having no aerodromes, but the Navy achieved magnificent work, sinking and scattering enemy convoys, thus preventing sea-borne landings by the enemy. On May 26 a penetration of the British positions at Suda Bay was made, and the Empire forces were compelled to withdraw to positions in the rear. Having captured Canea, the enemy was able to bring his fire to bear on the area, and on May 29 it was announced by British G.H.Q. that " in face of further attacks by German forces, our troops have withdrawn to position east of Suda Bay." On June 1 the Empire Force in Crete withdrew to Egypt. *See* Crete.

done by Japanese " fishermen " before the war. Simultaneously German and Italian submarines carried out an intensive campaign off the U.S. Atlantic Coast and in the West Indies, apparently to tie down U.S. naval forces and check their operations against the Japanese in the Pacific. As the Japanese overcame the barrier formed by Singapore and the Dutch East Indies their submarines worked into the Indian Ocean. On the other hand, the bigger U.S. submarines crossed the Pacific and sank ships close to the Japanese coast.

But Japan did not have it all her own way. On April 1, 1942, it was announced that a total of 25 Axis submarines had been sunk by U.S. Army and Navy forces, the latter being credited with 21. Of these 19 were in the Atlantic and two at Pearl Harbour. Several others were later sunk by the Allies off the Australian coast.

Suez Canal. This was a vital link in Allied communications, shortening the route from London to the Far East by some 5,000 miles (*see* pages 3880–3882). In 1939 the Canal carried a gross tonnage of 41¼ million. Of the 5,277 ships which passed through, 2,627 were British, and 135,696 troops, mainly British

British Submarine Losses—1940–1942			
Cachalot	P.32	Shark	Thistle
Grampus	P.33	Snapper	Triad
H.31	P.38	Spearfish	Triton
H.49	Perseus	Starfish	Triumph
Narwhal	Phoenix	Sterlet	Undaunted
Odin	Rainbow	Swordfish	Undine
Olympus	Regulus	Tarpon	Union
Orpheus	Salmon	Tempest	Usk
Oswald	Seahorse	Tetrarch	
Oxley	Seal	Thames	

Suda Bay. This fine, natural harbour on the north coast of Crete, situated between the towns of Canea and Retimo, has an area of 8½ sq. miles. British troops landed here early in November 1940, in order to assist Greece in her struggle with Italy. The British Navy occupied Suda Bay as a base, and on May 19, 1941, Nazi bombers swept across from their aerodromes in Greece and attacked targets in this area. Next day intense enemy bombing took place and German parachutists landed near Suda Bay. These numbered some 3,000, of

BOMBING A TARGET IN CRETE

Taken from a Stuka dive-bomber, this was how Suda Bay in Crete appeared to the enemy pilot during one of the German raids on the famous bay, used by the British as a naval base in May 1941. Bombs are seen bursting on shore works.

Photo, Keystone

KEY OBJECT OF ROMMEL'S DRIVE

Ships are seen, above, passing through the Suez Canal. This vital waterway was the object of innumerable Axis air attacks. Seated on the remains of a Heinkel bomber, left, is the Squadron Leader who brought down this enemy machine over the Suez Canal area and was awarded the A.F.C.

Photos, British Official; Fox

and Italian, were transported, either homeward or abroad. Anzac forces arrived in a fleet of luxury liners, convoyed by warships ; Maj.-Gen. B. C. Freyberg, V.C., commanded the New Zealanders, and Lt.-Gen. Sir Thomas Blamey the Australians. They were drafted for service in the Middle East, with Cairo as G.H.Q. The first arrivals were officially greeted by Mr. Anthony Eden on Feb. 12, 1940. Rhodesian troops followed in April. When Italy entered the war in June 1940 the Mediterranean route for merchantmen was discarded, and the products of the Eastern Mediterranean countries passed through the Suez Canal and round the Cape of Good Hope to reach Britain. After the conquest of Greece and Yugoslavia, the Germans began landing 'planes in Syria and launched their attack on Crete. " The drive for Suez has begun," they announced. It was intended that Rommel's forces should sweep east through Libya, so as to enclose Egypt and Suez in a gigantic pincer movement, which might have been assisted by the capture of Gibraltar and the bottling up of the British fleet in the Mediterranean. This threat was countered by the British occupation of Syria, and later of Persia and Iraq (potential danger-spots), by the clean-up of Abyssinia, Eritrea and Italian Somaliland, and by the establishment of an American base in Eritrea (*see* East Africa). By June 30, 1942, when Rommel was only 85 miles from Alexandria, the threat to Suez had become very grave. *See* North Africa.

Sumatra. The most westerly of the Dutch East Indies, Sumatra (*see* p. 3888), for about a half of its 1,000-mile length, lies along the western coast of the Malayan Peninsula, from which it is separated by the Malacca Strait, 30 miles to 195 miles in width. Soon after Japan's entry into the war on Dec. 8, 1941, it was threatened, on the one hand, by the Japanese advance through Malaya and, on the other hand, by the enemy landing in Sarawak. The first attack came on Dec. 28, when 17 Japanese 'planes raided the aerodrome of Medan, capital of the island. There were successive attacks on ports and aerodromes, especially at Palembang, on the S.E., and these culminated in a paratroop raid on Feb. 14, 1942, when 100 'planes dropped some 700 men in three groups, their purpose being to seize the oilfields. The Dutch defenders forestalled this by rigorously applying the " scorched earth " policy. Oil and installations to the value of over £5,000,000 went up in smoke. The annual output of Palembang (*q.v.*) was some $4\frac{1}{4}$ million tons, 55 per cent of the total for the Dutch East Indies, and this would have been invaluable for the Japanese. On Feb. 16, in spite of very heavy losses inflicted by Allied bombers, the Japanese succeeded in landing at Palembang, which then became a main objective for Allied raids. Fierce fighting continued, but the odds against the heroic Dutch were overwhelming. By March 13 Medan was captured, and on April 7 the Allied forces surrendered. *See* Java ; Netherlands East Indies ; Pacific

Suñer, RAMON SERRANO. Leader of the Falangists, Sr. Suñer was appointed Spanish Foreign Minister in October 1940 after his return from an extended visit to Germany and Italy. Reputed to be one of the most fervently pro-Axis Falange leaders, his speeches were anti-democratic in character. On the outbreak of the Russo-German war he declared, in an interview with a German Press correspondent, that the Falange were " taking up arms together with their German comrades in the European crusade against Asiatic barbarism." Before being appointed Foreign Minister he was, from August 1939, Minister of the Interior. *See* Spain.

Sunfish, H.M.S. Completed in 1937, this British submarine has a displacement of 670 tons and carries a complement of 40. Of the improved Swordfish design, this class of submarine is reputed to be a very handy craft, capable of making a " crash-dive " in thirty seconds. On April 10, 1940, the Sunfish torpedoed and sank a 3,000-ton German supply ship in Norwegian waters, and in the same month accounted for three more Nazi ships. In the course of an underwater patrol off the Norwegian coast in December 1940 she sank a German supply ship of about 4,000 tons and badly damaged a tanker that had been creeping along close to the shore.

Suomussalmi. Situated on Lake Kianta in the " waistline " area of Finland, this place was the scene of fierce fighting during the Russo-Finnish conflict. On Dec. 3, 1939, the Russians were reported to be advancing against Suomussalmi from their railhead at Ukhta. They made good progress, but disaster overtook them at Lake Kianta. This lake has two northern arms and the Russians advanced until they reached the westernmost. The territory here formed a natural trap, which some 15,000 Soviet troops entered in December. The Finns cut their opponents' supplies, and the intense cold reduced the Russians to breaking-point. They put up a stout resistance for three days, but on the fourth all was over. Thousands were killed, and the Finns claimed that the 163rd Russian Division of 18,000 men had been destroyed. Finnish losses were also heavy, but the Russian threat to Finland's waistline was temporarily removed. In January 1940 the Finns routed and destroyed the Russian 44th Division at Suomussalmi. When Finland joined Germany in attacking Russia in June 1941 this area again became involved in war.

Supply, Ministry of. Established in April 1939 with Mr. Leslie Burgin as its head, this Ministry was set up to direct and coordinate the production of munitions. Soon after the outbreak of war in September 1939 its activities became so vast that a Council of Supply was appointed, composed of " leaders in the civilian world of industry, commerce, and finance." Great changes were wrought in the nation's economy by the Ministry's activities. Much preparatory work had been done in the critical years just before the war, so that the change-over from peacetime industries to war production was carried out with the minimum of delay. Specialized machinery had been installed in readiness, buildings adapted, key men engaged. The Ministry of Supply was revealed as the world's biggest buyer of at least the heavier types of mechanized vehicles. Besides shells, guns and instruments, there was mass production of uniforms. Thousands of women were employed in making khaki clothing. In September 1939 some half-dozen contractors were satisfying the Army's clothing needs. Three months later the number had grown to over 500, and 1940–1942 saw an enormous increase in every branch of production and an ever-increasing speed-up of methods, from partial war to total war requirements. *See* Production, Ministry of.

Surabaya. City of Java and Dutch naval base. It was first raided by Japanese aircraft on Feb. 27, 1942, when attacks were made on the harbour. This raid proved abortive, as all bombs fell in the sea. By March 5 the position in Java had grown very serious, despite heroic Dutch and Allied counter-attacks against the invaders. The Japanese cut the island in two by occupying Surakata (Solo), the last rail-link between E. and W. Java, and Bodjonegoro, 50 W. of Surabaya, on the Batavia-Surabaya railway. On March 7 it was reported that Surabaya was closely besieged and that the collapse of the whole of Java was imminent. The kernel of the Dutch fleet had been lost in attempting to prevent enemy landings and in consequence the use of Surabaya as a naval base was lost. The Japanese claimed the capture of the town on March 10. The port was entirely wrecked. *See* Java; Netherlands East Indies; and illustration in page 206.

Surcouf. This French submarine was designed under the 1926 programme, but did not officially enter into service until 1934. The largest submarine in the world, the Surcouf represented an experimental type. She had a surface displacement of nearly 3,000 tons, a length of 350 feet and an armament which included two 8-in. guns. The submarine carried a complement of 150, and could dive in 2 minutes. After the collapse of France in June 1940 the Surcouf was at a British port. When it became clear that the Vichy Government intended to collaborate with Germany, and that the French fleet was in danger of being handed over to the Nazi conquerors, the British took control of two battleships, two light cruisers, a number of submarines and 200 smaller naval craft

THE GIANT SURCOUF WAS THE WORLD'S LARGEST SUBMARINE

Belonging to an experimental type not likely to be repeated, the French submarine Surcouf was reported lost on April 18, 1942, by the Free French authorities. Her trials included a cruise of 5,000 miles from Cherbourg to Agadir, Dakar and Konakri in Nov. 1932, and submergence for a period of 60 hours. Here is the Surcouf at sea, and this photograph gives a good idea of her immense length—350 feet.

Photo, Topical Press

lying at Portsmouth, Plymouth and Sheerness. In a scuffle due to a misunderstanding on board the Surcouf, Lt.-Commdr. Dennis Sprague, R.N., an able seaman, and one French officer were killed—practically the only incidents to mar an otherwise peaceful transfer. It was announced in April 1942 that the Surcouf was missing and must be considered lost.

Swansea. An important seaport and industrial town in South Wales, situated on the Bristol Channel, Swansea suffered heavily in the Nazi raids on Britain. A particularly violent attack took place on Jan. 17, 1941, when widespread damage was caused. In the following month, for three nights in succession—on Feb. 19, 20, and 21—many thousands of incendiaries and H.E. bombs were dropped indiscriminately on the town ; churches, hospitals, business premises, and houses, especially workers' dwellings, were destroyed or damaged, and casualties were heavy.

Sweden. In the first two and a half years of war Sweden maintained an uneasy neutrality, firmly announced but occasionally broken under Nazi pressure.

From the start the Swedish Riksdag (Parliament) emphasized the country's neutrality, and for this reason refused to sign a Pact of Non-aggression with Germany

But if Sweden by the spring of 1942 had escaped invasion, the war had brought both suffering and material loss. The period of military training was increased, armament production was stepped up, and the biggest budget in Swedish history was passed to provide for rearmament. Foreign trade was restricted by the British Navy, which intercepted ships bound for German ports, and by the activities of the German Fleet, which intercepted ships carrying Swedish cargoes to Britain.

When Russia attacked Finland in 1939 Sweden sang her neutrality chant ever louder, but her shivering was audible all over the world. The Russian invasion of Finland infuriated the Swedes, and both Press and people were for intervention. King and Riksdag opposed war firmly. But military aid was sent and more than 6,000 volunteers fought.

Fear of both Russians and Nazis dictated Sweden's refusal of passage for an Anglo-French Force to Finland in March 1940. When Finland gave up, Molotov's terms revolted Swedish sentiment and her Press became outspoken. The fall of Finland brought fear of aggression to obsession point.

It was in this mood that Sweden had to stand by impotently once more while Norway, comparatively poor and backward, fell to the Nazi invader. In addition, Sweden had a direct pistol threat in the port of Hangö, Finland, ceded by Finland to Russia and made into a fort. An attempt to form a Scandinavian alliance was prevented by Russia and Germany, and Sweden had to content herself with hoping for the best while preparing for the worst.

In January 1940 the Government took great emergency powers. Nazi headquarters were known to exist, but they were left untouched, though the Communists' were raided. Deep air-raid shelters to hold 30,000 were built for Stockholm's population. A new defence loan, 500 million kroner, was launched.

Then France fell and a wave of depression struck Sweden. The loan was a failure ; the Government was faced by a brutal demand by Germany for the passage of troops and materials through Sweden. The Riksdag consented in secret.

It took the success of Britain's R.A.F. to restore to Sweden a little of her ebbing courage. The improvement was evidenced by her point-blank refusal to join Hitler's New Order. Later, however, barter agreements were made with Germany, Denmark and Norway and, later still, a trade agreement was signed with Russia.

Swinton, PHILLIP CUNLIFFE-LISTER, 1ST VISCOUNT (b. 1884). On June 8, 1942, he was appointed to a newly created post, that of Minister Resident in West Africa. His most important task was to see to the effective working of defence measures. He was chairman of the United Kingdom Commercial Corporation from 1940.

Switzerland. The 4,300,000 inhabitants of Switzerland have long enjoyed democratic institutions, and their political sympathies with Britain, France and the United States in the struggle against Hitlerism are not to be doubted. In pre-war times the Social Democrats were the largest political party in the National Council. The pro-democratic hopes of Switzerland ended when France collapsed and the Confederation became a besieged country, so far as internal economy was concerned. Industrial self-sufficiency was impossible in a mountainous country which had no coal and very little iron. Switzerland was thus forced to sign an agreement with Germany which assured her limited supplies of iron and coal in exchange for exports of cheese, milk, butter and fruit. The industrial agreement was effective until the end of 1942.

Apart from internal needs, all Swiss factories had necessarily been working for Germany after June 1940, though little war material had been included in the exports. In a nutshell, the position was that Switzerland accepted stringent economic control from Germany in order to preserve her political freedom.

During the first nine months of the war, while the Maginot Line was still unbroken, an armed attack upon Swiss neutrality seemed possible at any time. It was known that the German general staff had detailed plans for a surprise attack, utilizing the cover of its ally, Italy. The scheme was that German troops should attack Zürich and Berne before the first lines of the Swiss defence could be manned. Then mechanized German divisions were to push on to the Jura Gap and thus threaten Lyons and other manufacturing centres in the Rhône Valley. Actually, the alternative attack through Holland and Belgium was adopted.

Nevertheless, the preservation of neutrality cast a staggering burden upon the Swiss. In three years from Germany's denunciation of the Locarno Pact Switzerland spent £46,000,000 upon reorganizing her army, and when the Second World War opened 480,000 fighting men were called up for the militia. In 1940 twenty-four per cent of the male population was mobilized. In Switzerland there are German-speakers, French-speakers and Italian-speakers, but in times of crisis all are defenders of the Confederation.

Switzerland suffered much from Nazi bullying. Thus Germany forbade her to charge economic freight rates for the German goods which pass over the Swiss railways. The war traffic between Germany and Italy is necessarily very heavy. Indeed, the threatened destruction of the Swiss tunnels is probably the real reason why Hitler and Mussolini refrained from attacking Switzerland in 1940. From the standpoint of the Democratic Alliance the great value

THE SYDNEY AS SQUADRON LEADER

H.M.A.S. Sydney, the Australian cruiser that sank the Italian Bartolomeo Colleoni in 1940, and was herself blown up in December 1941, is seen leading a cruiser squadron during naval manoeuvres in 1939.

Photo, Sport & General

of Swiss neutrality has been the preservation of the Confederation as a centre of Red Cross work, and the clearing of wounded and sick in the warring armies.

Sydney, H.M.A.S. Completed in 1935, and having a displacement of 6,830 tons, this cruiser was originally known as the Phaeton, but when taken over by the Royal Australian Navy she was renamed after the famous Australian cruiser of the last war. The Sydney, which joined the Mediterranean Fleet in June 1940, fought in every action that took place there up to her departure home for refitting in January 1941. The Italians claimed to have sunk her eight times. On July 19, 1940, she sank the Italian cruiser Bartolomeo Colleoni (*q.v.*) in a running fight N.W. of Crete. The enemy cruiser, which claimed to be the fastest in the world, possessed a speed of 37 knots against the Sydney's 32·5 knots. The Sydney's commander, Capt. J. A. Collins, was subsequently awarded the C.B. On Dec. 3, 1941, it was announced that the Sydney, after sinking the 9,400-ton German raider Steiermark (or Kormoran) on Nov. 19, blew up when flames from a fire amidships reached a magazine. It was also reported on the same day that a fund to raise at least £2,000,000 to purchase a new cruiser to replace the Sydney had been opened by the Lord Mayor of Sydney.

Sylt. This German fortified island in the N. Frisian group, connected to the mainland by the Hindenburg Dam, was the objective of R.A.F. attacks directed on the seaplane bases established there. During 1939, while the order prohibiting bombs on land targets remained in force, the British machines were not allowed to attack the enemy seaplanes while these were on the slipways. Reconnaissance flights by the R.A.F. were made on Sept. 9, 1939, and on Jan. 10, 1940, bombs were dropped, causing damage to the Hindenburg Dam. The object of the raids was to prevent German seaplanes from laying mines.

SYRIA WAS SWIFTLY FREED FROM AXIS CONTROL

Vichy-controlled Syria was a danger-spot to Britain and her Allies, and in June 1941 an Allied Army consisting of British, Anzac, Canadian and Indian troops, and a Free French force, crossed the border from Palestine. With Syria liberated from Axis control, the threat to Suez, Iraq and beyond was then averted.

Syria. During April–May 1941 the Axis started to penetrate the French mandated territory of Syria—and German warplanes to use Syrian airfields—with a view to making the country a base for operations against us in Iraq and the Middle East. The R.A.F. accordingly bombed the airfields, and on June 8 British Imperial and Free French forces, under General Sir Henry Maitland Wilson and General Catroux, entered Syria. Leaflets were dropped explaining that the Allies came as friends and that the independence of Syria and the Lebanon would be granted. Many Vichy officers and men came over to the Allied side.

The Allies relied on a war of manoeuvre, thus avoiding heavy casualties in a campaign between Frenchmen and between one-time French and British allies.

The initial phase of the campaign was confined to a direct northward push from our bases in Palestine and Transjordan. Three British columns operated simultaneously—one in the open country east of Mount Hermon, with Damascus as the first objective ; one up the central valley between Hermon and the Lebanon range, in the direction of Rayak ; and one along the coastal road, making for Beirut.

The Allied battle order was as follows : The eastern column was formed of the 5th Indian Brigade with

one field regiment of Royal Artillery, a squadron of the Royals and elements of the Transjordan Frontier Force. On their right were the Free French under General Catroux, and beyond them Colonel Collet's cavalry. In the central sector were the 25th Australian Brigade and the Royal Fusiliers. On the coast were the 21st Australian Brigade and the Cheshire Yeomanry.

The Vichy main defence was along the line Kiswe-Rachaya-Al Wadi-Jezzin-Sidon, with a second line along the Damour river on the coast, and other forces along the line Deir es Zor-Palmyra-Homs-Tripoli.

On June 9 the Indian Brigade with the Royals captured Dera'a, Sheikh Meskin and Ezra ; the Free French passed through them at Sheikh Meskin and pushed on towards Kiswe, where they were held. Colonel Collet's force reached Kiswe on June 11, but the Vichy position was too strong for a frontal attack.

In the centre the Royal Fusiliers captured Kuneitra on June 9, and the 25th Australian Brigade, starting from the Metulla salient, took Merj Ayun on June 11, after heavy fighting, and then advanced north to Nabatiyeh. On the coast the Cheshire Yeomanry brushed aside Vichy opposition at Ras Naqura, and with part of the 21st Australian Brigade pushed inland through the hills towards the upper valley of the

Litani, occupying Mazra'at ech Chouf and Mrousti, north of Jezzia. The rest of the 21st Australian Brigade captured Tyre and advanced to the Litani river at Mikiye, after overcoming stubborn resistance.

On the night of June 8–9 the Royal Navy landed a sea-borne detachment north of the Litani, in the face of heavy opposition, and on June 10 the Australians crossed the river and advanced five miles up the coast. Up to June 13 progress was generally good. Then Vichy resistance stiffened. The enemy withdrew his forward troops to his main defence lines. A flanking attack by tanks caused the Free French at Kiswe to withdraw. On June 15–16 the Vichy forces counter-attacked, driving two mechanized squadrons of the Transjordan Frontier Force out of Ezra. They then attacked Kuneitra with superior forces and compelled the garrison of Royal Fusiliers, who had run out of ammunition, to surrender. In the centre they obtained a foothold in Merj Ayun. On the coast they held up our advance to Sidon.

All this proved only a temporary set-back, as by June 17 Kuneitra was retaken by Australians and British, and Ezra by a mixed force of Free French and Transjordan troops. British and Australian forces took Jezzin on June 15. On the same day the Vichy forces evacuated Kiswe, and Sidon fell to a combined action by Australians and the Navy.

Meanwhile, our attack on Damascus made progress. The Indians and the Royals took Messe, after heavy fighting, while the Free French advanced by way of Al Qadem and threatened the Vichy flank. On June 21 they entered Damascus.

In the central sector Staffs. Yeomanry, Scots Greys and Australians battled round Merj Ayun. On the coastal sector we had advanced to just south of Damour. In the meantime a new factor was brought into play— a column consisting of Household Cavalry, Wilts and Warwickshire Yeomanry, the Essex Regiment, Royal Artillery, part of the Arab Legion, with R.A.F. and armoured cars, advanced across the desert. On June 22 it reached Palmyra—defended by pill-boxes held by German and Russian Foreign Legionaries. Part of our force encircled Palmyra, while patrols by-passed it and at Qariatein linked up with the Free French from Damascus. A second column from Iraq, the 10th Indian Division, advanced towards Deir es Zor on July 1.

On June 26 the Free French had captured Nebk. The Leicesters and Queens succeeded in holding the southern slopes of Jebel Mazar. In the central sector the Australians reoccupied Merj Ayun. The desert side was now practically clear of enemy forces except for the Damascus-Beirut road and the Beka'a down to Hasbaya and the Lebanon through Hasrout south of Bet ed din to the coast south of Damour ; and at the last-named there was a strong defence.

The war of manoeuvre conducted by the Allies soon made the Vichy position untenable. In the north the Indians cleared up the salient between Turkey and Iraq, while the main force advanced towards Aleppo. Farther south Palmyra surrendered on July 3. In the Damascus sector the 6th Division captured Jebel Mazar on July 10. On July 9 the Australians in the coastal area, supported by naval bombardment, captured the whole Vichy defence line on the Damour and advanced to within five miles of Beirut. On July 9 General Dentz, the Vichy High Commissioner, asked for an armistice, and at 9 p.m.

ALLIED ADVANCE INTO SYRIA

1. Inhabitants of Damascus cheer Free French soldiers as the latter draw up their armoured vehicle in one of the city's streets. 2. British troops enter Palmyra's classical colonnade in search of the enemy. 3. Gen. Catroux, with Gen. Sir Henry Wilson and Lt.-Gen. Lavarack, is seen on the balcony of Government House, Beirut.

Photos, British Official

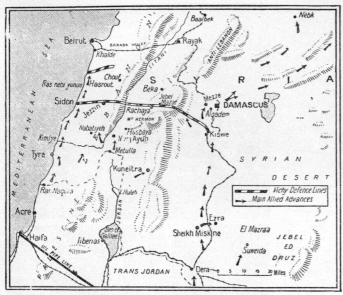

Allied advance against Vichy defence in Syria.

on July 11 the "Cease Fire" was sounded. By thus forestalling the Germans in Syria we obviated the Axis threat to our Middle Eastern and Egyptian areas, and prevented ourselves from being isolated from our Turkish ally. Thus we were able to preserve the whole politico-strategical structure of our Middle Eastern and Eastern Mediterranean policy—a great gain for a comparatively small expenditure.

 Taganrog. Russian town on the N.E. shore of the Sea of Azov, 50 m. west of the mouth of the Don. During the German thrust at Rostov the Russians evacuated it on Oct. 21, 1941, after inflicting 35,000 casualties. In a few weeks came the fierce counter-attack by Marshal Timoshenko. The Germans retreated west of Taganrog and, in their pursuit, the Russians bypassed the town. From then and in June and July 1942 Taganrog remained the centre of fierce fighting. *See* Russia ; Ukraine.

Tahiti. Largest of the Society Islands, in the South Pacific Ocean. It has an area of 600 sq. m., capital Papeete. The islands were annexed by France in 1880. When news came of the Pétain sub-servience to Germany a plebiscite was taken and the inhabitants, with scarcely an adverse vote, pledged allegiance to Free France on Sept. 3, 1940. On March 2, 1942, it was announced that the U.S.A. would cooper-ate with Free France in its defence.

Taipale. Finnish town ·on the Lake Ladoga shore of the Karelian Peninsula. The eastern bastion of the Mannerheim Line during the Russo-Finnish war, Taipale was, on Jan. 22, 1940, subjected to the fiercest bombardment of that war. From the early weeks of the war the Finns had spoken of Taipale as their Verdun, and it remained intact in spite of 117 attacks during the winter, the Russians sometimes advancing over the frozen lake. In fact, right up to the end of the war, on March 12, 1940, the Taipale sector held fast, the breaking-through of the Mannerheim Line being in the west. *See* Finland ; Karelian Isthmus.

Talisman, H.M.S. Submarine of 1,090 tons completed in 1940. She had one 4-in. gun and ten torpedo tubes. Her com-plement was 53. The Admiralty announced on Jan. 19, 1942, that this submarine had engaged in a dramatic fight with a U-boat in the Mediterranean, sinking it by gunfire. The Talisman also sank a 15,000-ton Italian troopship with four torpedoes in 12 minutes, and turned her guns on a destroyer which in the darkness her com-mander, Lt.-Comdr. F. Willmott, had mistaken for a U-boat. Her guns secured four direct hits within exactly four minutes after first sighting the foe, and 120 rounds from a Lewis gun had been sprayed over her decks before the crew of the submarine realized that she was fighting a destroyer. The enemy ship then tried to ram the Talisman, but missed her by 50 feet.

Tallinn (Reval). Capital of the Soviet Republic of Estonia (*see* Baltic States), Tallinn is an import-ant port at the southern entrance to the Gulf of Finland. Valuable as a naval base on the Baltic, it was ceded to Russia in September 1939. When the Germans attacked Russia Tallinn resisted strongly, the Germans losing 30,000 men before they captured it on Aug. 29, 1941. In the last few days of battle the city was an inferno, the Russians blowing up the quays and warehouses, German shells falling everywhere, while Russian warships and transports, with 50,000 men aboard, fought their way successfully out to sea. They took their part in the defence of Leningrad.

BRITISH SUBMARINE RETURNS FROM HER TRIUMPHS

H.M. Submarine Talisman achieved outstanding success in the Mediterranean. She sank four enemy ships, a U-boat, and fought a gun-duel with an Italian destroyer. Despite these daring and hazardous enterprises, the submarine is seen returning unscathed to her home base and her crew are lined up on deck. By attacking enemy ships in the Mediterranean the Talisman dealt a blow against Axis supplies en route for Libya.

Photo, British Official

Tangier. Seaport at the extreme north-west corner of Africa, on the Atlantic entrance to the Strait of Gibraltar. It was internationalized under a Convention signed in 1928 by Great Britain, France, and Spain (*see* p. 3939), the sovereignty of the Sultan of Morocco being recognized in the person of the Mendoub. A Frenchman acted as administrator, while Spain supplied the police. On June 14, 1940, Spanish troops entered the zone, " to ensure its neutrality," and on Nov. 4, 1940, Colonel Yuste, the officer commanding them, deposed the French administrator and dissolved the International Committee. On March 16, 1941, the Spanish authorities ejected the Mendoub and installed instead the German Consul, high-handed actions undoubtedly taken under pressure from the Axis. *See* Spain.

THE DEVELOPMENT OF TANK WARFARE

" Tanks—and more tanks !" was Britain's battle-cry after grim lessons learned in France in 1940, and production mounted until it was formidable. Tanks seek to outflank the enemy by superior speed and to break through by a combination of speed and momentum. See Mechanization and plates facing p. 432.

Tanks. The story of the invention of the tank and its use in the war of 1914–18 is told in pages 3940–41. The tank itself is but one of the armoured fighting vehicles which go to form the modern armoured division—a tactical fighting group exploited by Germany first in the swift conquest of Poland in September 1939. Hitler's Panzer divisions broke through the Dutch, Belgian and French defences in May 1940 and procured an equally swift victory for the invaders. For an account of the strategy of tank warfare and particulars of other armoured fighting vehicles *see* Mechanization, in this Volume.

At the beginning of the Second Great War the High Command of the Allies completely failed to realize that the tank had inaugurated a new era of land fighting by bringing into account a new and revolutionary weapon. This failure was the more surprising because so long ago as 1918 the tank played the decisive role in one of the great battles of the world. The German army then had washed forward over the face of France until by the spring its fringes reached Montdidier, Cassel and Château-Thierry. Yet by autumn that wave had been turned upon itself and rolled back by Marshal Foch, using tanks.

In Poland Germany defeated a nation of 35,000,000 people and its highly trained, brave and disciplined army of 1,250,000 men. Such a defeat demanded an **explanation**. which

Gen. (then Col.) de Gaulle supplied. The Germans had conquered Poland because they had applied the new tactics of battle, as propounded by the little-known French colonel. De Gaulle was the first soldier to understand the implications of the tank. After the Polish campaign he memorialized Daladier and Reynaud and Gamelin and Weygand, driving home the lessons of the new tank technique, but his representations were disregarded. Failure to digest the

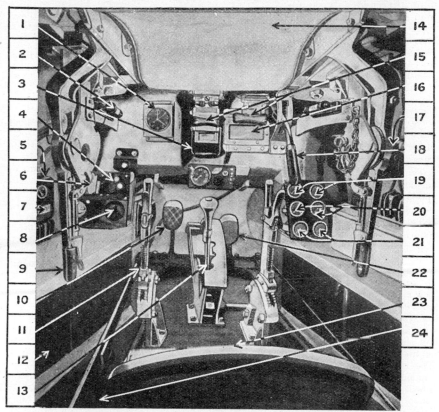

DRIVER'S COCKPIT OF A WALTZING MATILDA

1. Stop and trip time clock. 2. Festoon lamp. 3. Periscope. 4. Engine starter switch. 5. Ammeter. 6. Engine cut-out. 7. Electrical switch-box. 8. Side and tail lamp switch. 9. Driver's hood operating lever. 10. Gear change operating pedal. 11. Steering lever. 12. Accumulators. 13. Gear selector. 14. Driver's hood. 15. Brow pads. 16. Bullet-proof glass panel. 17. Series-parallel switch. 18. Lever operating visor. 19. Water temperature gauges. 20 and 21. Oil and air pressure gauges. 22. Throttle control. 23. Driver's seat. 24. Gear change operating rod.

Photo, British Official

lessons of the Polish campaign had far-reaching and disastrous consequences for the Allies.

The tank has brought war from the field of actual battle to workshop and factory, for without unlimited supplies of raw materials, large-scale heavy industrial plant, and a rich reservoir of highly trained workers tank warfare is not possible. For every pound of metal required to equip a rifle-carrying infantryman or sword-bearing cavalryman, the soldier who goes into battle as one of the crew of a modern tank requires tons of metal. This quantitative stepping-up has created vast economic and industrial problems, which only in 1941 and 1942 were grappled with seriously.

The development of tank warfare meant the coming of a new technique in battle tactics and general strategy, superseding all old military concepts.

Tank tactics consist in forcing a passage through the enemy lines of defence by a number of tanks in column, the spearhead being dive-bombing aeroplanes; other armoured and mechanized fighting vehicles, with light and heavy motorized formations of infantry and artillery, of course play an important part.

The soldier in a tank which has infiltrated into enemy territory finds himself protected by armour impervious to anything but a direct hit from a heavy or medium gun. He is sealed in against gas attack. He can talk by wireless with other tanks, with his base and—very important —with the aeroplanes hurtling through the air above his head. He can travel at speed over the worst of ground and overcome, by sheer strength and weight, all manner of obstacles. To cover his fast movements he can render himself invisible by ejecting a smoke screen. Last, he possesses immense fire-power.

Tank crews are carefully selected and trained. The soldier today must be a technician—not merely a specialist in one trade or one branch, but a handy man able to replace any other member of the crew.

The full extent to which mechanized warfare involved heavy industries became apparent soon after Russia was invaded by Germany, on June 22, 1941. Following a Three-Power conference at Moscow an agreement was signed under which Britain undertook to send tanks and other war material to assist her new ally in Eastern Europe. It was the call for tanks, and more tanks, which decided the British Government to extend the mobilization of man-and-woman power and apply more widely the principle of compulsion. By the end of 1941 there were over a million more munition workers than in 1918, and a million women. The target in tank production was increased to the immense figure of 30,000. Work on design was intensified, while all the ancillary problems of tank warfare (such as tank-gun calibre and anti-tank measures) were brought to the forefront of national effort.

The Libyan campaigns, with their ding-dong of advance and retreat, revealed the vital importance of fire-power. For in a battle between tank formations victory may well go to the force whose guns—whether borne on tanks, or swiftly mobile artillery, or in more or less static batteries—can pierce the armour of the enemy or deliver the coup de grâce of a direct hit by

superiority of range. The tank solved many long-standing military problems; but, in turn, it created problems of its own. The so-called " tank buster " is an attempt to solve the greatest of them—namely, fire that will put the machine out of action at longish range. It has been suggested that the armoured aeroplane carrying a large-bore cannon may be the answer. The U.S.S.R. air arm have craft of this type—the Stormovik armoured 'plane, with 37-mm. cannon in nose; and also the Stalin anti-tank 'plane with armour-piercing cannon. In late 1941 a Russian squadron so equipped claimed the destruction of 608 tanks in three months. The Beaufighter, used in Libya, also has a cannon (20-mm.), but this is not capable of knocking out a German Mark IV tank.

Tank design has developed largely on trial-and-error lines. The general tendency has been for a lowering of the main structure and the elevation of the commander's cupola. In early 1942 Britain was manufacturing five main types of tank (*see* table).

Some critics of design regard the 2-pounder gun now standard on British tanks as inadequate; the old

Four British Tanks

Name	Type	Weight tons	Speed m.p.h.	Armament	Crew	Notes
Valentine	Fighter	16	17	2-pdr. & Besa m.g.	3	Front line tank
Crusader	Cruiser	18	30	2-pdr. & 2 m.g.	5	Medium cruiser. high speed
Covenanter	Cruiser		High	2-pdr. & Besa m.g.	4	For scouting—fast as armoured car
Waltzing Matilda	Fighter and Assault	28	16	2-pdr. & Besa m.g. in turret	4	For attack on prepared positions

Note.—Details of the heavy " Churchill " tank not released.

Mark V star carried 4-pounders in 1918. German heavy tanks carry a 75-mm. gun. Main points of German tank design are greater weight, speed and fire-power : Mark III, 20 tons, 15 m.p.h., 1 gun, 2 machine-guns, crew of 5; Mark IV, 22 tons, 25 m.p.h., 1 75-mm. gun and 2 machine-guns.

The American type M 3, General Lee, was in action in North Africa. So was the 28-ton General Grant, which carrie s two guns, is heavily armoured and has a crew of 7. President Roosevelt, calling for 45,000 American tanks for 1942, announced a new model, M 4. A cast steel welded hull was one of many new features of this design.

Books to Consult : The Evolution of the Tank, Rear-Adm. Sir Murray Sueter (Hutchinson). Machine Warfare, Maj.-Gen. J. F. C. Fuller (Hutchinson).

Tanner, VAINO. Social Democrat leader and member of the Finnish Government. When Russia made her claims on that country M. Tanner went to Moscow three times in the autumn of 1939 in an effort to reduce them. When Russia began the war he became Foreign Minister in the new National Government. When Finland had to admit defeat M. Tanner again went to Moscow to make terms, broadcast to the Finnish nation on March 13, 1940. In the new Government then formed M. Tanner took the Ministry of Public Welfare. When Germany attacked Russia M. Tanner supported the Finnish Government's decision to help Germany. As Minister of Commerce he visited Germany, and publicly stated that Finland would not make peace with the present rulers of Russia.

Taranto. This port is the most important naval base in the south of Italy, lying sheltered in the north-eastern corner of the Gulf of Taranto between the toe and heel of Italy. It has an inner harbour, completely landlocked, and a very big outer harbour enclosed by a mole. Between these two harbours lies the town.

A large part of the Italian Fleet having been concentrated at Taranto in November 1940 to guard the passage of troops and supplies to the Italians fighting the Greeks in Albania on the Adriatic, Admiral Sir Andrew Cunningham, commanding our Mediterranean Fleet, was anxious to bring them to battle.

Accordingly it was decided to attack the Italian warships as they lay at anchor in the harbours of Taranto. Reconnaissance 'planes reported that there were six battleships—the new 35,000-ton Vittorio Veneto and Littorio, and four of the Cavour class,

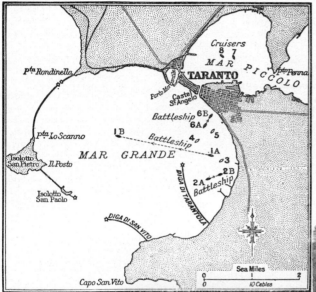

Our aircraft consisted of ten Glenn Martin Maryland bombers and eleven Fairey Swordfish torpedo 'planes. Rear-Admiral Arthur Lyster was in command of the aircraft carriers, which were protected by warships remaining well out to sea. The Marylands led the van, dropping flares to show the positions of the Italian warships and also of a balloon barrage. The Swordfish made a glide from 5,000 feet to between 50 and 100, dropped their torpedoes at the right moment, and climbed through the hail of shell which rose from all quarters of the land and water. All but two came safely out of this inferno.

Photographs taken from the air on the following and subsequent days showed the Littorio beached, with her forecastle under water, one battleship of the Cavour class sunk and a second beached, two cruisers with a heavy list, and two auxiliary ships with their sterns under water. Not long afterwards the majority of the surviving Italian ships stole away to Cagliari (q.v.), a more out-of-the-way base in Sardinia.

Tatarescu, GEORGE. Rumanian pro-French politician, leader of the Liberals. In 1937 he took an active part in suppressing the Iron Guard, becoming Prime Minister for a few

BRITISH VICTORY AT TARANTO

The plan left shows at A the positions of the Italian battleships at Taranto, when the British attack was made in November 1940. B depicts the positions to which damaged ships were towed. At 3, 4, and 5 are undamaged battleships. The Italian cruisers 7 and 8 show, in the reconnaissance photograph below, evidence of damage, and oil oozes from them.

Photo, British Official

reconstructed and modernized — in the outer harbour, and ten cruisers, eighteen destroyers, a seaplane carrier, and other smaller craft, including ten submarines, in the inner harbour. Not only were the shore batteries very powerful, but the warships were well equipped with the latest A.A. guns.

Aircraft of the Fleet Air Arm operating from the Illustrious and the Eagle, the youngest and the oldest aircraft carriers in the Fleet, were flown off to the attack on the evening of Nov. 11, 1940. There was little wind, some light from a moon three-quarters full, and just enough cloud to hide in.

weeks in November of that year. Tatarescu was again Prime Minister from Nov. 23, 1939, to July 4, 1940, when Gigurtu, the Fascist and friend of General Goering, succeeded him. Tatarescu's Government had stood for a policy of neutrality, national unity, and loyalty to the Balkan Entente. It was the last government in Rumania before the Axis domination.

Tedder, MARSHAL OF THE R.A.F. LORD ARTHUR W. K.C.B. (b. 1890). A.O.C.-in-C., R.A.F., Middle East. He served in the R.F.C. in the Great War. In 1938 he became Director-General of Research and in 1940 Deputy Air Member in the Ministry of Aircraft Production. Deputy A.O.C.-in-C. in the Middle East in 1940, in June 1941 he was promoted to the chief command. Elevated to the peerage in Jan. 1946.

Marshal of the R.A.F.
Lord Tedder
Photo, British Official

Teheran. Capital of Persia (q.v.). After having protested in vain against the infiltration of Germans into Teheran and other important Persian towns, the British and Russian Ambassadors, on August 25, 1941, presented Notes stating that they were taking military steps to check this hostile activity, at the same time assuring the Persian Government that they had no designs against the national independence. The Persians were dilatory, so on Sept. 17 British and Russian troops advanced to Teheran, armoured vehicles occupying the Skoda machine-gun factory east of the city and Russian parachutists taking charge of the barracks and airfields. On Sept. 16 Mohammed Riza Khan was sworn in as a constitutional ruler in place of Riza Pahlevi (q.v.), and by Sept. 20 all the Germans who were sheltering in their Legation were deported.

Teheran was at once made an important centre for the transport of supplies to Russia, a Directorate being set up there on Nov. 17 under Brig. Sir Godfrey Rhodes. The inhabitants of Teheran, who welcomed the new regime, shared in the cereals and other necessities provided by the Middle East Supply Centre. On Jan. 29, 1942, an Anglo-Soviet-Iranian Treaty of Alliance was signed at Teheran, in which the territorial integrity and independence of Persia were guaranteed and the withdrawal of the Allied forces six months after the end of hostilities promised. *See* Persia.

Teleki, COUNT PAUL (1879–1941). Hungarian statesman and Professor of Geography at Budapest University. Succeeding Dr. Imrédy as Prime Minister of Hungary on Feb. 16, 1939, Count Teleki, who was pro-British in sympathy, strove hard to maintain the Parliamentary institutions of his country, in spite of the fact that he had to keep on good terms with Germany and Italy. The Axis pressure intensified, and when a demand was made for Hungarian help in the attack on Yugoslavia, Count Teleki shot himself on April 3, 1941. *See* Hungary.

Tepelini. Important road and river junction in South Albania, 22 miles west of the Adriatic port of Valona. This Italian stronghold among the mountains was besieged by the Greeks during the first three months of 1941, the R.A.F. assisting with bombing. The capture of Klisura, 12 miles east, placed Tepelini in jeopardy, and the Italians brought up heavy reinforcements to drive back the Greeks. Mussolini himself was reported to have visited this battle front. Though they prevented the Greeks from capturing their stronghold the Italians lost three complete divisions in the conflict. The invasion of Yugoslavia and Greece by the Germans in April 1941 compelled the Greeks to retire from the Tepelini front.

Terboven. Gauleiter of Essen, Terboven was on April 27, 1940, appointed Reich Commissioner of Norway in the decree in which Hitler declared war on that country. Working through quislings and imported German police, he suppressed all Norway's free institutions, and in a speech on Oct. 5, 1941, he stated that it was a matter of complete indifference to Germany if a few thousands of Norwegian men, women and children starved during the war, and threatened that unless the Norwegians treated Germany's enemies as their own enemies the Reich would deprive Norway of independence for ever. A particularly mean order by Terboven on Sept. 26, 1941, was the requisitioning of all woollen blankets, with a penalty of three years' imprisonment if not handed over within four days.

Terijoki. Town situated on the shores of the Gulf of Finland in the south-east of the Karelian Peninsula. Here, on the outbreak of the Russo-Finnish war on Nov. 30, 1939, the Russians set up a so-called Finnish People's Government, headed by the Finnish Communist leader, Otto Kuusinen. With him Molotov signed a pact under which, among other terms, 23,000 square miles of the Karelian Peninsula were to to be ceded to the U.S.S.R.

Terror, H.M.S. This British monitor (armoured ship of low draught but high gun-power) was built (1915–1916) to bombard the German positions on

THIS WAR VETERAN OF 1915 DID GOOD SERVICE IN 1941

The famous British monitor, H.M.S. Terror, achieved magnificent successes against the Italians in 1940 and 1941 by constant bombardments of enemy positions along the Libyan coast. She was a sister ship of H.M.S. Erebus, and was begun in October 1915. Here the Terror is seen at anchor. She was sunk by air attack off Libya in June 1941.
Photo, Topical Press

FOUR LEADING EXAMPLES OF BRITISH TANKS

1. British "Covenanter" light cruiser tanks moving off to the forward area near Tobruk early in 1942. 2. "Valentines," 16-ton front line fighting tanks, advancing across country. 3. "Crusader," an 18-ton cruiser tank with the speed of a car, seen during a speed test. 4. Members of a Canadian tank corps in service with British armoured divisions are seen in their 28-ton Mark IV, "Waltzing Matilda."

Photos, British Official; Topical; Associated Press

HOW TANKS ARE REPAIRED IN THE FIELD

1. Fitting the tracks to a British "Valentine" tank. 2. Mounted on a conveyor, this British tank is being taken to repair workshops in Tobruk for overhauling. 3. A scene inside a tank repair shop in Tobruk in 1941, where the safety of the garrison depended on efficient machines. 4. Tank Corps students studying landscape targets. They learn to identify targets and then to fire quickly.

Photos, British Official; Fox; Topical

the Belgian coast. Drawing only 11 ft., yet carrying two high-angled 15-in. and eight 4-in. guns, this 7,200-ton veteran attacked the Italian positions between Sidi Barrani and Bardia on the North African coast early in December 1940. In addition to making the coast-road impassable and blowing up a stretch of 150 yards at what was known as Hellfire Corner with a direct hit, the Terror poured nearly 600 tons of high-explosive shells into Bardia while that stronghold was still resisting, and smashed up convoys of food and war materials approaching the outskirts.

In the naval bombardment of Jan. 19, 1941, which preceded the attack on Tobruk (q.v.), H.M.S. Terror took a giant's part. For two hours her 15-in. guns lobbed tons of high-explosive shells into the Italian lines and on to the two powerful shore batteries and the Italian cruiser San Giorgio, which, though aground in the harbour, continued to fire her 10-in. guns. All through the spring of 1941 H.M.S. Terror continued her career, until, on June 12, came the news that she had been sunk by air attack off the Libyan coast.

Tetrarch, H.M.S. Submarine of 1,090 tons, completed in 1940. She was one of the Triton class and carried one 4-in. gun and 10 torpedo tubes. Her complement was 53. This submarine accomplished much notable service. In June 1940 she sank a strongly escorted transport of 8,000 tons off Norway. Later she did great execution on Axis communications in the Mediterranean, sinking a 5,000-ton transport, two schooners, three caiques, two supply-ships and a tanker full of German troops. On Dec. 15, 1941, she was stated to be overdue and considered lost.

Texel. The most westerly of the Dutch Frisian Islands (q.v.). About 71 square miles in area, Texel was made a German seaplane base and was regularly attacked by British aircraft.

Thailand. *See* Siam.

Thanet, H.M.S. Destroyer of 905 tons, completed in 1919 ; her armament consisted of three 4-in. guns ; her complement was 98. Accompanied by the Australian destroyer Vampire, the Thanet was our first naval unit to engage the Japanese. On Jan. 26, 1942, off Endau, on the east coast of Malaya, these warships engaged in a running fight with a Japanese cruiser and three destroyers which were covering a landing of troops. One of the enemy destroyers was sunk and another damaged, but the Thanet was sunk.

Thermopylae. This Greek pass " between the mountains and the sea " was in this war once again the scene of a desperate fight to the death similar to that of which we read in page 4005. During the retreat south before the German invaders a body of Anzac troops stood fast here on April 25, 1941, and, though outnumbered by ten to one, put up an heroic resistance. British airmen who looked down on the scene after the battle declared that " German dead and wounded lay heaped on one another among their burned-out tanks and gun-carriages." It was believed that the total of German casualties in this 20th-century Thermopylae exceeded in number all the Imperial Forces then in Greece.

Thomas, SIR SHENTON, G.C.M.G. (b. 1879). Governor and C.-in-C. of the Straits Settlements and High Commissioner for the Malay States since 1934. Having served all his life in the Colonial Service, he was Governor of the Gold Coast before being transferred to Singapore. When the Japanese were investing that

city he carried on unperturbed to the last, his final message home, on Feb. 15, 1942, stating that the civilian population was " quiet but bewildered," and that the fire and telephone services were carrying on. Sir Shenton was made a prisoner when the Japanese captured Singapore on the following day.

Sir Shenton Thomas, Governor of Malaya.
Photo, Planet News

Tientsin. Second biggest Treaty Port in China (*see* p. 4016), at the junction of the Pei-ho River and the Grand Canal, 70 miles from Peking. The Chinese city was occupied by the Japanese in August 1937, but they respected the Foreign Concessions at that time. On Dec. 7, 1941, they occupied the British and U.S. Concessions, capturing and interning 200 American marines.

Tigris, H.M.S. Submarine of the Triton class, having a displacement of 1,090 tons, completed in 1940. She carried one 4-in. gun, 10 torpedo tubes, and had a complement of 53. Operating in the Arctic against the German sea route to Murmansk, in November 1941 the Tigris attacked a heavily escorted convoy of three supply ships, sinking two. She also sank three other enemy ships and severely damaged a sixth.

Tikhvin. Key town on the Leningrad-Vologda Railway, 110 miles S.E. of Leningrad. Named after its river, the Tikhvinka, a tributary of the Syas, it is famous for the barges constructed there, which bear the town's name. The Russians evacuated it in November 1941, but recaptured it on Dec. 8, after a strenuous ten days' struggle in which Gen. Merezhkov annihilated the German 18th Motorized, 12th Tank, and 60th Infantry Divisions, which were under the command of Gen. Schmidt. The Germans lost 7,000 killed, and the rest of the army threw away their arms and, clad in peasants' clothes, fled into the forests toward Budogorsk. The effect of this victory was to frustrate the drive to encircle Leningrad.

Timor. One of the Lesser Sunda Islands of the Malay Archipelago, lying about 300 miles N.W. of Darwin. Of its 13,330 square miles, the greater part belongs to Portugal ; 6,000 square miles in the S.W. are Dutch. The capital of the Portuguese territory is Dilly, that of the Dutch Kupang. As the last halting place of the air route to Australia, Timor had become a familiar name. In the course of trade talks in 1941 the Japanese had asked for privileges at the civil aerodrome on Timor, but the Dutch declined.

After war with Japan had broken out and Japanese submarines had been sighted in the neighbouring seas, the Government of the Dutch East Indies decided to occupy the Portuguese part of Timor because the garrison numbered but 400, of whom three-quarters were natives. So, on Dec. 18, 1941, Dutch and Australian forces were moved across the border. Portugal protested, but admitted that early in November she had accepted an offer of British help in the event of a Japanese invasion and on Dec. 8 had agreed to the Allies taking protective action in the event of attack. It was Jan. 23 before the 1,000 Portuguese troops sailed from Lourenço Marques, in Mozambique. On Feb. 20, 1942, the Japanese landed at both Dilly and Kupang, cynically stating that as far as Portuguese Timor was concerned their move was one of " self-defence," and her occupation was conditioned by Portugal maintaining a neutral attitude. Australian and U.S. 'planes were afterwards active in bombing Japanese airfields on Timor.

Timoshenko, MARSHAL SEMYON (b. 1894). A native of Bessarabia, this man, who was to become one of the most distinguished of Russia's military leaders, was conscripted into the Tsar's army in 1914. He had a natural genius for organization and rose to become Commander of the Kiev special military area, from which he was called in May 1940 to succeed Marshal Voroshilov (*q.v.*) as People's Commissar of Defence. On July 11, 1941, three weeks after Germany had struck her felon blow at Russia, the newly-formed State Defence Council appointed Timoshenko, at that time Commander-in-Chief of the Red Army, to command the western sector which comprised White Russia and Poland. Voroshilov commanded the sector to the north defending Leningrad, and Marshal Budenny (*q.v.*) the sector to the south covering the Ukraine. Though forced to give ground, Timoshenko succeeded in preventing the Germans from reaching Moscow, counter-attacking again and again until the ice and snow of the Russian winter slowed down the German mechanized forces and reinforcements arrived.

Marshal Timoshenko, C.-in-C. South Russia. Photo, Pictorial Press

The Germans, however, had made a deeper thrust in the southern sector, so on Oct. 22 a change was made in the commands, two being organized instead of three, the northern being placed under General Zhukov (*q.v.*) and the southern under Timoshenko. In that sector Taganrog (*q.v.*) and Rostov were about to fall. Yet within a month the whole position was reversed and

the German threat to the rich oilfields of the Caucasus frustrated. Timoshenko inspired fierce counter-attacks and the Germans and their Balkan Allies were soon in full flight westward, relentlessly pursued. The Kerch Peninsula was also freed from the enemy and the forces investing Sevastopol were unable to take that famous port. By the end of March 1942 Timoshenko's armies were capturing village after village on the outskirts of the key town of Kharkov, where on May 5, two German attacks were repulsed. On May 13, forestalling an enemy move against Rostov, he launched a major offensive in the Kharkov sector, aimed at destroying German man-power. Fierce fighting developed and Timoshenko advanced. On June 11 the Germans counter-attacked, recapturing certain positions, and on June 29 they launched an offensive at Kursk, 120 miles north of Kharkov, which Timoshenko still held on July 4. *See* Russia.

Tirana. Capital of Albania. Lying 30 miles due west of Durazzo on high ground above the River Rushka, Tirana has grown rapidly since King Zog became President in 1925 and King in 1928. In 1927 he had concluded a defensive alliance with Italy ; but without any warning, on April 7, 1939, Italian forces landed in Albania and captured the country, Victor Emmanuel being proclaimed King. An airfield was constructed near the capital, and when Italy made war on Greece this was one of the objectives of the Allied air forces ; otherwise Tirana's position in the east-central part of Albania placed her out of reach of the gallant Greeks in their courageous invasion before the Germans arrived. *See* Albania.

Tirpitz. German battleship, sister ship of the Bismarck. Completed in 1941, and listed as of 35,000 tons, this warship was believed to be much heavier, even 45,000 tons. Her armament was eight 15-in., twelve 5·9, and sixteen 4·1 guns, while she carried four aircraft. She was 792 feet long and had a speed of at least 30 knots. In August 1941 she was reported as having been seen off Tallinn, in the Baltic, but later she

THE TIRPITZ SUCCESSFULLY 'SPOTTED' BY THE R.A.F.
This photograph of the German battleship Tirpitz was taken by an R.A.F. reconnaissance aircraft as the British machine flew high above the enemy ship lying heavily camouflaged in Aas Fjord, Norway. The Tirpitz is seen protected by an anti-torpedo boom, stretching from amidships towards the shore. Floating camouflage lies on either side of her bow and stern, and thick white camouflage material is spread over the barrels of the 15-in. guns.
Photo, British Official

was stationed at Trondheim. Our reconnaissance 'planes sighted her proceeding in a northerly direction up the coast of Norway, and on March 9, 1942, she was attacked with torpedoes by our naval aircraft. This attack forced her to retire under a heavy smoke screen towards the coast, but the detailed results of the attack, in which two of our aircraft perished, were not at the time visible. At any rate, her first essay to attack our convoys in the North Sea was frustrated. The R.A.F. made an intensive search for her and she was spotted in April 1942 and photographed from a low height lying close to the sheer cliffs of Aas Fjord with an attempted effort at camouflage on either side of her bow and stern. Barges were alongside her, and an anti-torpedo boom protected her. On July 8 she was found in the Barents Sea and attacked by a Russian submarine (Capt. Lunin) and hit by two torpedoes. Later she went to a Norwegian fjord.

Tiso, Dr. Josef. President of Slovakia from Oct. 26, 1939, having been raised to that office from the Premiership, which he had secured on March 14, when his country proclaimed itself a republic independent of Czechoslovakia. History will record of this traitor to the great country which Masaryk and Benes built up after the Great War that he secured Slovakia's independence, but only for a day, for on March 15 he placed his country under the "protection" of Hitler. Dr. Tiso became prominent at the time of the Munich crisis. On Oct. 4, 1938, the day before the resignation of President Benes, Prof. Cermak, Slovak Minister in the Czechoslovak Cabinet, resigned, and the Slovak National Party at a congress at Zilina demanded complete autonomy within the republic. As a result, the new Prague Government appointed Tiso as Minister for Slovakia, with a Slovak cabinet of his own.

Tiso was not long in declaring to the press that he was in sympathy with the authoritarian States' methods for maintaining national discipline. Tiso's party worked for absolute independence and, to forestall this, the Czechoslovak Government dismissed him and placed him under police detention on March 10, 1939. Riots broke out in Bratislava and Tiso appealed to Hitler for help. Hitler responded at once by sending an aeroplane to fetch him for an interview, in the course of which Tiso telephoned to his successor to convene the Diet for the next day. At this Tiso was re-elected Premier and Representative of the independent Slovak State. This took place on March 14, and on the very next day President Hacha submitted to Hitler, while the German army entered Prague. On Aug. 28, 1939, Tiso issued a proclamation that German forces would use Slovakia as a jumping-off ground for invading Poland. His reward was the grant of some Polish territory and leave to be raised to the Presidency on Oct. 26. After that day Tiso showed himself an obedient vassal of his master.

Tmimi, El. Village in Libya on the coast road half-way between Gazala and Derna. Having changed hands more than once in the ebb and flow of the Battle of the Western Desert, El Tmimi was the scene of much fighting when the Germans drove back the British in the early months of 1942. In March the Germans made it the northern bastion of a secondary line of defence which ran south-west to Mekili.

FOR TWO HUNDRED DAYS TOBRUK HELD OUT

The defence of Tobruk was one of the epic sieges of history. For eight months, April 13 to December 8, 1941, when contact was made with the advancing 8th Army, the Imperial garrison held out against repeated enemy air and land attacks. But the British were again forced to retreat and Tobruk fell on June 21, 1942. See North Africa.

Tobruk. So long as British history lasts Tobruk will have a place in it, as Balaclava has, and Ladysmith, and the Revenge. Until a day early in January 1941 scarcely anyone had heard of this small coast town on the Mediterranean in Italian Cyrenaica. It lies less than a hundred miles from the frontier of Egypt. Not long after Gen. Wavell had begun his drive westward against the Italian forces under Marshal Graziani, preparations began to be made for its capture. It was important to have it in our hands, since its harbour is a good one, and, placed on the top of the bulge in the coast-line which occurs in this part of Africa, it has a commanding position. For some days it was shelled by the Navy and bombed by the R.A.F.; then on Jan. 21 the combined attack by sea, land and air was started. On the ground Australians led the way, showing their usual dash. There were Free French units in the assaulting columns also. So close was the cooperation between Navy, Army and Air Force, so excellent the staff work, and so determined the effort of all concerned, that by the evening of Jan. 22 Tobruk had surrendered. The total of prisoners was over 20,000, including a number of generals, one commanding a corps. It was reckoned that Graziani had, through this disaster, lost two-thirds of the force with which he opposed Wavell when the latter moved against him in December 1939. British casualties were surprisingly light.

At once the work of strengthening the defences, developing the port, and cleaning up the town was put in hand. One of the first things to be seen to was the water supply. This had been so poor that the Italians brought most of their drinking water by ship. Arrangements were made at the same time for collecting large supplies, so that Tobruk might serve as a base for Wavell's further operations. All this was very fortunate. At the time it was not foreseen that the place would have to stand a siege. Wavell's advance was aimed at continuing as far as Tripoli. But Germans arrived in large numbers, and in April the Axis forces began a drive forward which forced Wavell to give up most of the ground he had gained.

Tobruk stood firm. The enemy swept by to the south of it, intending to mop it up later. All through May 1941 attacks were made by land forces. They were all repulsed. The garrison made sorties at times, invariably sent Italians flying, and harassed Nazi troops by their rapid movements and fierce unexpected onslaughts. In these the Australians especially shone. Then in August and September the effect of heavy bombing and dive-bombing was tried. Enemy raids were frequent and severe.

Thanks to the Navy's command of the Mediterranean, it was possible to send reliefs so that tired men as well as wounded could be shipped back to Egypt and fresh ones brought in to take their places.

WHERE BRITISH HEROISM SO LONG WITHSTOOD AXIS PRESSURE

Here is an aerial photograph showing the harbour of Tobruk. The Italian cruiser San Giorgio was damaged by R.A.F. aircraft in January 1940 and was subsequently used as a fortress in the harbour. Shortly before the port fell to Imperial forces on Jan. 22, 1941, the cruiser was again badly damaged and set on fire. The ship is seen in the background and the huge pall of smoke shows burning petrol dumps.

Photo, British Official

In the course of the eight months during which the siege lasted (April 12–Dec. 10) 29,000 were landed at Tobruk and 33,000 taken away, and all that time an average of 142 tons of cargo—food, munitions and other necessary supplies—was delivered daily, 34,000 tons in all. A large part of these cargoes was carried in local patrol vessels, which had formerly been trawlers, drifters, and Norwegian whalers. Besides supplying the garrison with food, arms and ammunition, they swept mines and acted as anti-submarine escorts for merchant ships. The part which these crews of fishermen played in the defence of Tobruk was unspectacular, but very fine.

During the autumn, although artillery duels and patrol activities were constant, the enemy seemed to be less inclined to attempt the reduction of the fortress that had so long resisted and caused them such heavy losses. When winter began the garrison were in high spirits. The whisper went round that soon the British would be moving forward again. No one in Tobruk doubted that relief was near at hand. The battle of Sidi-Rezegh began. Success swayed now this way, now that. It was not such an engagement as the British commanders had expected. They supposed, so Mr. Churchill told the House of Commons, that the whole of the enemy armoured force would be encountered by the whole of ours, and that a few days would decide the result.

The campaign did not work out in that way. This first of tank battles on a large scale split itself up into many engagements. Von Rommel's army and air force were not wiped out. But in the course of

the many clashes that took place over a wide area the columns approaching Tobruk were steadily pushing on, New Zealanders being particularly active. And at the same time the defenders were pushing out to

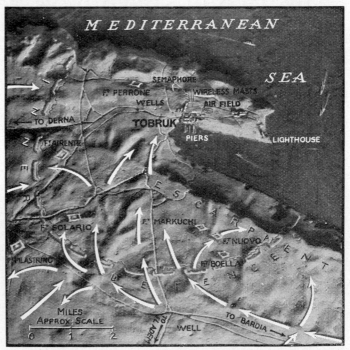

TOBRUK—KEY POINT IN LIBYAN DEFENCE

Tobruk, its fine harbour and the adjacent countryside are shown in this contour map, the arrows on which indicate the line of the British advance in 1941. The perimeter defences are clearly marked, as well as the roads leading from Bardia and El Adem.

Relief map by Félix Gardon

meet them. Day by day each of them gained a little ground, and in the last days of November they linked up, and very soon after that Tobruk was relieved, or, as the Prime Minister said "disengaged." The Eighth Army, thus joined by part of the troops from Tobruk, swept on westwards driving the enemy back as far as El Agheila, on the Gulf of Sirte. But by the end of May 1942, Rommel's heavily reinforced armies had turned the tide of battle once more, and the British were in retreat. After a disastrous encounter with enemy tanks and anti-tank guns starting on June 13, General Ritchie withdrew his main forces to the Egyptian frontier, leaving what was considered an adequate garrison in Tobruk. On June 20 the pursuing enemy turned and attacked Tobruk in full force from the south-east. The garrison fought hard, but unavailingly, against overwhelming odds, and early on June 21 surrendered. Rommel claimed the capture of 25,000 men and great quantities of material.

Dr. Todt,
Nazi military
engineer.
Photo, Mondiale

Todt, DR. FRITZ (1891–1942). Appointed Minister of Armaments and Munitions in the German Cabinet in 1940, Dr. Todt had been Inspector-General of Roads in the Reich since 1933. He was a very great military engineer, making the fullest use of modern machinery. It was the irony of Fate that he should perish in an accident to the most characteristic machine of his age, an aeroplane in which he was flying to the Russian Front.

Dr. Todt would have achieved fame even if there had been no World War, for his network of wide concrete roads (Autobahnen) was one of the wonders of Germany in the days of peace. In 1938 he was entrusted with the construction of the Siegfried Line (*q.v.*), and when war broke out he formed the organization of labourers behind the fighting lines known as the O.T. or Organisation Todt, into which hundreds of thousands of Germans were conscripted and also hundreds of thousands of foreign labourers. His work in France after it was overwhelmed was characteristic. Roads and railways had to be repaired, bridges rebuilt, and the local works and factories got into operation as speedily as possible. When these tasks were finished Dr. Todt built a chain of forts along the French and Netherland coasts. In the Russian campaign, too, his work behind the German lines, changing the gauge of the railways and so on, was speedy and invaluable to the supplies going forward to the 1,000-mile front. He was succeeded by Prof. Albert Speer.

Togo, SHIGENORI. Japanese Minister of Foreign Affairs, appointed Oct. 18, 1941. Mr. Togo was Japanese Ambassador in Berlin in 1937, and in Moscow, 1938–40. He married a German and became deeply imbued with the Axis mentality. When he became Foreign Minister he voiced his view of the new Tojo Government, which he had joined, through the Japanese " Times-Advertiser," which declared that the choice of a professional soldier as Premier was logical when Japan was encircled by hostile powers whose leaders had all had military experience. On Nov. 5 he sent Mr. Saburo Kurusu to join Admiral Nomura in Washington in deceiving the Roosevelt Government, and on Nov. 11 he received Sir Robert Craigie, the British Ambassador, who conveyed to him the warning Mr. Churchill had uttered in his Guildhall speech.

Tojo, GEN. HIDEKI. Prime Minister of Japan from Oct. 18, 1941, when he succeeded Prince Konoye. Tojo combined the Ministry of Home Affairs and War with the Premiership, having been Minister of War in Konoye's Cabinet. A silent and somewhat dour man, Gen. Tojo had become the chief power in the Forward Policy of Japan. A capable officer, he had, in 1938, been promoted over the heads of many seniors to be Inspector-General of Army Air Training, and he

Gen. Tojo,
Japanese Premier.
Photo, Wide World

devoted many years to organizing the area of Manchuria which borders on Siberia. By appointing three generals and two admirals to Cabinet office, he showed that the military party had won domination.

After his appointment he at once broadcast to the nation that, though filled with awe and trepidation, he had an iron will " to execute promptly the proper action, under the glory and grace of the Imperial Throne, and with the confidence and cooperation of the people," and to do his best to add to the brilliance of Japan's 3,000-year-old history. In other speeches Gen. Tojo emphasized that he was resolved to settle the China " incident," to set up the Greater East-Asia Co-Prosperity Sphere, and to expand to their utmost the industrial and munitions activities of the country. He congratulated Germany and Italy and expressed his hope that Japan would be associated with them in establishing the New World Order.

On Nov. 25 his representative in Berlin renewed Japan's adherence to the Anti-Comintern Pact, yet he gave assurances to Russia that this action did not imply any change in the neutrality pact with her. In his broadcast at the Declaration of War, and again in a speech in the Japanese Diet on Feb. 16, 1942, Gen. Tojo emphasized his intention to purge East Asia of all British and American interests.

Tokyo. *See* Japan.

Toulon. Naval port of France on the Mediterranean. Strongly fortified, with docks capable of taking the biggest battleships, Toulon became even more important to France when she established herself as a colonial power in North Africa. Under the French-German Armistice all ships based on Toulon were required to be recalled, except those employed in the protection of French colonial interests. Toulon is in Unoccupied France and the Allies have watched with anxiety to what extent the French would demobilize the warships at the port. It was to prevent the return of powerful French units to Toulon that the British Navy took action at Oran (*q.v.*), but when the Dunkerque, which had been driven ashore in attempting to escape to Toulon, succeeded in reaching that port under her own steam on Feb. 17, 1942, Mr. Sumner Welles, the American Minister, warned the French Ambassador in Washington that the Roosevelt Government, too, was watching future developments at Toulon with close attention. Other ships reported to be in harbour in mid-April 1942, when questions about the use of the French Navy by the Axis became acute, included the battleships Strasbourg and Provence, the heavy cruisers Algérie, Colbert, Foch, and Dupleix, four 6-in.-gun cruisers, destroyers, submarines and the seaplane tender Commandant Teste.

Tours. French city at the junction of the Rivers Cher and Loire, 145 miles S W. of Paris. When the German forces threatened Paris, the French Government and the Diplomatic Corps retired here in the beginning of June 1940, but on June 15 they hurried south to Bordeaux. On June 17 Marshal Pétain declared to his nation that he had asked for an armistice; three days later the Germans announced that they had reached Tours.

Tovey, ADMIRAL OF THE FLEET LORD JOHN. G.C.B.. (b. 1885) Commander-in-Chief of the Home Fleet from Dec. 2, 1940, succeeding Adm. Sir Charles Forbes. Admiral Tovey was Vice-Adm. commanding the destroyer flotillas in the Mediterranean when he received his promotion. He was in command of H.M.S. Onslow at the Battle of Jutland, and from 1932 to 1934 commanded H.M.S. Rodney. His new

Adm. of the Fleet Lord Tovey
Photo, Planet News

flagship was H.M.S. King George V, and it was from this ship (with the Rodney as her consort) that Admiral Tovey directed the long chase and destruction of the German battleship Bismarck (*q.v.*). He was promoted Admiral of the Fleet 1943, and raised to the peerage Jan. 1946.

Transjordan. Mandated Territory of 34,740 sq. m. situated east of Palestine, whose High Commissioner is also High Commissioner of Transjordan; pop. 300,000, mostly Arab Moslems. The native ruler is the Emir Abdullah Ibn Hussein. Amman is the capital, and is connected by good roads with Jerusalem, Deraa (in Syria), and Baghdad by way of Azrak across the desert. The R.A.F. has stations in Transjordan, while there is a Frontier Force under British officers. Under an agreement signed in 1928 Transjordan had received a very large measure of independence, and when, toward the end of 1941, the British Government asked that further troops should be raised in her defence, the Emir's Government willingly consented. Her helpful attitude during the rising in Iraq and the trouble in Syria (*q.v.*) proved a source of strength to the Allies.

Transport, MINISTRY OF WAR. Called at first the Ministry of War Communications, this was formed by amalgamating the Ministries of Shipping and Transport on May 1, 1941. Mr. Frederick James Leathers (*q.v.*) was made a Baron and appointed head of the Ministry, and under his control were all shipping, railway, port, road transport, and highway maintenance. The two Parliamentary Secretaries were Col. J. J. Llewellin (later Minister of Aircraft Production) and Sir Arthur Salter, who went to America to coordinate shipping activities. Under this Ministry were Regional Port Directors, Divisional Road Engineers, and Regional Transport Commissioners. **Lord**

Leathers was thus head of a Ministry which was of vital importance to the linking up of all our civil activities in wartime.

Transylvania. Province in the Carpathian Mts. transferred from Hungary to Rumania after the First Great War. Area 22,312 sq. m., population about 4,000,000. At a meeting at Vienna on August 30, 1940, Ribbentrop and Ciano awarded 17,300 sq. m. and 2,390,000 of the inhabitants, half of whom were Rumanian, to Hungary. In March 1942 Antonescu, the Rumanian Dictator, expressed dissatisfaction with this award. In June fighting was reported to have broken out between Hungarians and Rumanians in Transylvania.

Transylvania, H.M.S. Armed merchant cruiser of 16,923 tons, formerly belonging to the Anchor Line. This fine ship was torpedoed in the Atlantic, her loss, with 20 out of a complement of over 320, being announced on August 15, 1940.

Trident, H.M.S. Submarine of the Triton class, completed in 1939; she had a displacement of 1,090 tons, and carried one 4-in. gun and 10 torpedo tubes. Her complement was 53. Operating in Arctic waters against German troop transports and supply ships sailing to the Murmansk front, the Trident in November 1941 attacked a heavily escorted convoy of seven transports and supply ships, sinking three and damaging the other four so seriously that their loss seemed inevitable. An eighth vessel was attacked and damaged by gunfire. On Feb. 23, 1942, the Trident torpedoed and so seriously damaged the German cruiser, Prinz Eugen, off Norway that the latter had to be towed by tugs into Trondheim. It is believed that a German escorting destroyer was also hit. *See* illustration in page 420 of this volume.

Tripartite Pact. *See* Berlin Pact.

Tripoli. Seaport capital of the Libyan Province of Tripolitania, and also of Libya itself; pop., in 1938, 108,000, one-third being Italians. The Italians rapidly developed the port after they took it from the Turks

GERMAN TANKS PARADE IN TRIPOLI
Crowds line the streets of Tripoli to watch a display of German tanks. The statue in the foreground shows Mussolini decked out as a Roman warrior. His arm is raised in a triumphant gesture far above the spectators' heads.
Photo, Keystone

in 1911, and used it as the chief base in their campaign against Egypt in the summer of 1940. Tripoli was many times bombed from the air and shelled from the sea by our forces, while the stream of convoys crossing from the northern ports of the Mediterranean were attacked without cessation as they made for Tripoli, one ship in three being destroyed or damaged.

At dawn on April 21, 1941, the Mediterranean Fleet bombarded Tripoli for nearly an hour, pouring into the port over 500 tons of 15-in. and smaller shells sinking two and setting on fire three transports lying there, damaging a destroyer, and wreaking devastation on the Spanish Mole, the railway station, power plant, oil depot, and many military buildings. The shore batteries of the enemy proved ineffective, for our ships sailed away without damage or casualties. The R.A.F. had made many an attack on Tripoli prior to this great onslaught, and they did not let a week pass after it without dropping bombs on it, the famous Spanish Mole being their main objective. Its important aerodrome at Mellaha was also under constant attack by the R.A.F. *See* North Africa.

Tripolis. Sometimes referred to as Tarabulus, Tripolis is a rapidly growing town in Syria, 40 miles north of Beirut and two miles from the Mediterranean coast, its port, El Mina, being two miles distant. The town became famous in 1934 when the northern branch of the oil pipeline from Iraq reached it. With Homs, Damascus, and Merj-Ayoun-Sidon, Tripolis formed the quadrilateral on which the forces of Vichy France based their resistance to the British and Allied forces under Gen. Sir Maitland Wilson, a resistance which lasted but a short while. *See* Syria.

Tripolitania. Province of Libya (*q.v.*).

Triton, H.M.S. Submarine completed in 1938, and giving its name to a new class, a patrol type for general service. Of 1,090 tonnage, armed with one 4·1-in. gun and 10 torpedo tubes, and carrying a complement of 53, the submarines of this type have done good service in the war. The Triton was reported lost on Jan. 28, 1941, but she had previously sunk two Italian supply vessels, one being of 8,000 tons. *See* Talisman.

Tromsö. Ancient fishing town in Northern Norway, within the Arctic Circle. It is on an island of the same name and became important as the seaport for Spitzbergen (*q.v.*). The Germans made this port a seaplane base for attack on the Allied convoys to Murmansk.

Trondheim. A 1,000-year-old city of Norway, lying at the head of the ice-free Trondheim Fjord. It is the third biggest town in Norway and had been made into an air-base. It was occupied by the Germans on April 9, 1940, when they invaded the country, and was afterwards heavily bombed by the R.A.F., two cruisers and a transport being hit on June 11, 1940. It was to this port that the Prinz Eugen was towed after having been torpedoed by H.M.S. Trident on Feb. 23, 1942. It was heavily bombed on April 27 and 28, the Prinz Eugen being among the targets hit.

Truant, H.M.S. Submarine of the Triton class (*q.v.*). Completed in 1940, the Truant won early fame by braving the minefields of the Skagerrak and sinking the 6,000-ton German cruiser Karlsruhe during the attack on the Horten Fort near Kristiansand on April 9, 1940, during the German invasion of Norway.

While off Cape Spartivento, at the toe of Italy, on the night of Dec. 13, 1940, the Truant sank one heavily laden Italian transport, and possibly a second. On Dec. 15 she sank an Italian tanker off the Calabrian coast. Between these exploits the Truant rescued the captive British crew of the Haxby. This steamer had been sunk by a German raider and the crew transferred to the Norwegian merchantman Tropic Sea, which had also been captured and was being sent to Germany in charge of a prize crew. On patrol off Cape Finisterre, the Truant surfaced to investigate the Tropic Sea, whereupon the Germans scuttled the Norwegian boat, all on board taking to the boats. The Truant took on board the 24 British, and the Norwegian captain and his wife, all she had room for, but sent word to the R.A.F., who rescued the remainder.

In February 1941 the Truant did good work in attacking Italian convoys in the Mediterranean, torpedoing a ship of 3,500 tons. On March 17, 1942, it was announced that her commander, Lt.-Cmdr. H. A. V. Haggard, D.S.C., had been awarded the D.S.O. for bravery and enterprise during successful submarine patrols.

Tsolakoğlu, GEN. He was appointed head of a quisling Government of Greece by the Nazis on April 30, 1941, immediately after they had occupied Athens. Gen. Tsolakoglu had been dismissed from the Greek Army in disgrace at the close of the disastrous war with Turkey in 1920, but in 1927 he was restored to his military position. In establishing his regime the Germans spoke of it as " a Greek orientation of the Axis programme for a new European Order." His first compulsory task was to disband the gallant Greek army. Gen. Tsolakoglu proved powerless to prevent the wholesale looting of Greece or the appalling death-roll from starvation and disease which speedily followed the German occupation.

Tsouderos, GEN. EMMANUEL. Prime Minister of Greece. When, on April 18, 1941, M. Alexander Korizis died suddenly, King George, after assuming the Presidency of the Greek Cabinet for a day, appointed Gen. Tsouderos Premier, Foreign Minister, and Minister of Finance and National Economy. Two days after his appointment the Greek Army of Epirus was encircled and surrendered without any intimation to the new Greek Government. It was at once decided to remove the seat of Government from Athens to Crete. When Crete itself was overwhelmed the Premier accompanied King George to Egypt, and then by way of South Africa to London, where he arrived on Sept. 22, 1941. In London Gen. Tsouderos set about making preparations for the participation of all Free Greeks in the war, and as an earnest of the attitude of Greece towards her neighbours at its end he signed a pact with the Yugoslav Government at the Foreign Office on Jan. 15, 1942, establishing a Balkan Union embracing political, economic, and military questions. *See* Greece.

Gen. Tsouderos,
Greek Premier.
Photo, Planet News

Tsvetkovitch, DRAGISHA. Prime Minister of Yugoslavia from February 1939 to March 27, 1941. He was dismissed from office and arrested on account of his unpatriotic surrender to the Nazis when they were planning to invade Greece. In spite of warnings by Turkey and a strong note from the British Government, Tsvetkovitch, with his Foreign Minister, Cincar Markovitch, went to Berlin on March 25 and signed his country's adhesion to the Tripartite Pact. The documents he signed stated that the Axis Powers would not demand the passage of troops through Yugoslavia, but there was little doubt that there were secret terms. He returned to Belgrade to find his countrymen seething with anger, and early next morning King Peter (q.v.) assumed full powers and arrested the Prime Minister.

Tula. Russian town 121 miles south of Moscow, on the railway from Moscow to Kursk. Its munition factory was established by Peter the Great in 1712. In mid-November 1941 Tula was the centre of one of the most dangerous German efforts to capture Moscow before Christmas. Having failed in a frontal attack, the Germans were again unsuccessful from the north-west with the loss of 2,500 killed. The enemy, recklessly employing masses of tanks, succeeded in driving wedges into the Russian line hereabouts during the last week of November, but on Dec. 1 it was Russian successes that were being announced, General Zhukov, the new Commander-in-Chief on this sector, beginning to shatter the German hopes of winter quarters in the capital of Russia. On Dec. 12, indeed, the Soviet Information Bureau was able to state with accuracy " it is now obvious that this boastful plan for the surrounding and capture of Moscow has proved a complete fiasco." *See* Moscow ; Russia.

Tunisia. French colony in North Africa, lying between Algeria and Libya, and facing Sicily across the Mediterranean Sea. In its 48,300 square miles, which extend some 250 miles south into the Sahara, live 2,600,000 people, mostly Arabs, the Europeans numbering 108,000 French and 94,000 Italians. It has always been a sore point with Italy that France so easily secured the suzerainty of Tunisia in 1881, and won the loyalty even of the Italians who had already settled there. Tunisia is a vital factor in the war owing to the fact that her coast is pre-eminently suited to enable enemy ships from Italy to reach Tripoli by hugging the coast. The French, too, have converted Bizerta on the northern coast into a strong naval base. *See* North Africa.

Turin. Capital of the Piedmont Province of Turin, and the fifth biggest city in Italy (pop. 629,000). It stands on the banks of the River Po. Here are the Royal Arsenal, the Fiat motor works, iron and steel works, and many textile factories. On Nov. 8, 1940, the R.A.F., in a non-stop flight of 1,600 miles, dropped bombs on the Fiat works and the railway station. There was another big raid on Jan. 12, 1941, and another on Sept. 9 in which Stirlings and Halifaxes took part, causing enormous fires at the Royal Arsenal and straddling the railway station with sticks of heavy bombs from a low altitude. Whitleys took part in another successful raid during a moonless night in April 1942. These long-distance raids fulfilled the promise of Mr. Churchill that the Italian end of the Axis would be made to feel the weight of the R.A.F.

DESPITE AXIS INTRIGUE TURKEY WAS NEUTRAL

Although the Nazis had control of the Balkans, Turkey refused to be cowed. She preserved a strict neutrality, building up her army and defences to a high standard of efficiency, thus making clear her intention to contest every inch of her territory if attacked. See Balkans ; Syria.

Turkey in the War. Turkey succeeded in maintaining the cardinal points of her wartime policy—i.e. the alliance with Britain, together with non-belligerency —throughout the first two and a half years of the war, and was still doing so in the summer of 1942. This achievement was due mainly to two factors : (1) her steadfastness and foresight; and (2) Germany's belief that diplomacy rather than war would bring Turkey into the Axis orbit. How long the second factor would continue to operate it was, of course, not possible to say.

Turkish steadfastness consisted in remaining faithful to the fundamental lines of policy laid down by the late Kemal Ataturk, which was the maintenance of friendship with both Britain and Russia. Inspiring the continuance of this policy was the Turkish long-term belief in the eventual victory of the Allies. This enabled her to treat with Germany almost as an equal. So that when Germany pressed for a trade agreement Turkey was agreeable, but this did not permit the Germans to obtain the chrome supplies they wanted. And when Germany pressed for a treaty of friendship, Turkey was again agreeable, but this did not bring about the breaking of the Turkish alliance with Britain which the Germans wanted.

It was not always easy for Turkey to stick to her guns in this way. For instance, her alliance with Britain, which originally included one with France too, was

based on the idea of (1) Anglo-French war supplies, and (2) the safeguarding of the strategic position in the Near and Middle East by the Anglo-French forces. When France fell, this strategic conception collapsed. Moreover, France dropped out of the picture as a supplier of war material, and Britain, beset on many fronts, was not able alone to make up the deficit. Then came the Axis drive through the Balkans, the fall of Yugoslavia and Greece, and the defection of Bulgaria. There followed the Axis-instigated revolt in Iraq and the German penetration of Syria—events which bade fair at the time to isolate Turkey from her British ally. But Turkey stood the strain and remained firm. Later, the British action in putting down the Iraqi revolt and in turning the pro-Axis Vichy administration out of Syria, removed this threat of isolation.

Turkey's decision to remain a non-belligerent, unless actually attacked by the Axis, was based on an interpretation of the situation which caused her to feel that by these means—remaining a bastion of neutrality in the Middle East and building up her military strength against the day when the Axis might try to drive to the East and the South through her territory— she could best serve both her own interests and those of her British ally.

Germany therefore made unrelenting efforts, by mingled threats and bribes and intrigues, to induce Turkey to adopt at least a benevolent attitude towards

Axis designs. **Nazi intran-**
sigents from time to time
advocated a surprise attack
on Turkey, but von Papen,
the wily ambassador at
Ankara, always prevailed
on Hitler to believe that
the same ends could be
more easily achieved by
diplomatic means.

During the first half of
1942 the German attempt
to win over Turkey was
renewed with greater vig-
our. Turkey was offered
German "protection"
against the Russian
"Bolshevist menace,"
economic and political
collaboration with Hitler's
New European Order, and
a leading position in the
Middle East. At that time,
however, the Turks had not
shown any disposition to
depart from their established
policy — consisting of the
maintenance of peace with
Russia, the continuance of
the alliance with Britain,
and the preservation of
non-belligerency.

This non-belligerency was
of course conditional.
Turkey would fight not only
if directly attacked, but also if any hostile country
tried to force a passage through her territory, or if
any power tried to gain control of the Dardanelles.
Turkey contrived to maintain this policy because she
backed her diplomacy with the steady building up of
her defences, obtaining war material from Britain
and also from the U.S.A. under the Lease-Lend Act.

An attempt by Bulgaria in June 1942 to obtain
implicit recognition of the Bulgarian annexation of
Greek territory was foiled by Turkish firmness.

Turku (ABO). Seaport and former capital of
Finland, on the R. Aurajoki, 168 miles west of Helsinki
on the S.W. coast of Finland, opposite the Aaland
Islands. Constantly bombed by Soviet 'planes in the
Finno-Russian war, its historic castle was destroyed,
and a Red Cross ship sunk in its harbour. Early in
the German-Soviet war, June 1941, Turku was again
bombed, but on this occasion little sympathy was felt
for the inhabitants, who had welcomed the German
forces, which were the target of the Russian airmen.

Tweedsmuir, JOHN BUCHAN, 1ST BARON, P.C.,
G.C.M.G., C.H. (1875–1940). Governor-General of
Canada, 1935–1940. Born in Perth, as John Buchan
he became known as the writer of biographies of
Cromwell, Sir Walter Scott and others, poetry, and a
series of novels of which "The Thirty-Nine Steps"
and "Greenmantle" were best-sellers. Appointed
Governor-General of Canada in 1935, his devoted work
in the Dominion won universal praise, and there is no
doubt that his great tact and enthusiasm did much to
intensify the help which the great Dominion gave
to the Motherland in the war against Hitler. He died
on Feb. 11, 1940, at the summit of his career.

BRITON AND TURK ON THE FRONTIER
These Turkish soldiers are vitally interested in one of the Allied armoured cars that patrol
the Turco-Syrian frontier. The Turkish army was quick to realize the importance of speed
in manoeuvre in accordance with the progressive tendencies of the country.
Photo, British Official

 U-boat. The German submarine
(Unterseeboot, under-sea boat) bears,
instead of a name, the letter U followed
by a number. U-boats during the war
of 1914–18 were a serious menace, not
checked until the later stages (*see* p. 3877). In the
Second World War counter-measures were prompt
and efficient. The first week's sinkings were indeed
heavy, amounting to 65,000 tons, which was half of
the weekly losses in April 1917, the peak month of
the previous war. In the second week the total
dropped to 46,000 tons, and by the third it was down
to 21,000 tons. At least six U-boats were sunk during
this period, and the rate of 2–4 a week was
subsequently maintained.

On Sept. 28, 1939, Mr. Churchill, then First Lord of
the Admiralty, announced that the convoy system
was being adopted and that merchantmen and liners
were to be armed (*see* Convoy). Sinkings, of course,
continued, but the U-boats were themselves hunted
and destroyed in gratifying numbers. The most
effective weapon was undoubtedly the squadron of
fast-moving destroyers, which were able to surround
the area with depth-charges, while protecting themselves with a smoke-screen. Corvettes (*q.v.*), too,
were built in large quantities, and proved to be most
valuable. Patrolling 'planes, tracking U-boats, were on
several occasions able to destroy them by bombing.

In the spring of 1941 Hitler massed a great fleet of
U-boats, which was designed to destroy Allied shipping
at the rate of a million tons a month. During March
they were successful in sinking 124 ships, with a gross
tonnage of **515,763,** and in April the figures rose to

HOW ENEMY SUBMARINES CONCEAL THEMSELVES IN PORT

1. This German submarine is on the look-out, ready to submerge at the first sight of danger. 2. Watched by an interested crowd of soldiers, a U-boat enters its protective base on the German-occupied coast of France. 3. R.A.F. attacks on U-boat bases along the French coast so alarmed the Nazis that reinforced shelters were constructed for all submarines. This U-boat is seen in its " hide-out " while work proceeds in the dry dock.

Photos, Sport & General; Associated Press

135 ships, with a gross tonnage of 589,273. British counter-measures managed to reduce these losses progressively, and in July the gross tonnage was down to 164,000. Another peak period of losses came in December 1941, and Mr. A. V. Alexander told the House of Commons on Feb. 26, 1942, that U-boat construction had now reached an unprecedented level, in spite of which the British losses in convoy were less than one half of 1 per cent. The May sinkings, according to an American source, exceeded any in history. American ships built in June numbered 66, totalling 731,900 tons, but, stated the U.S. Maritime Commission, did not equal U-boat sinkings.

Germany is believed to have started the War with about 100 U-boats and it is impossible to estimate either losses or replacements, but one may perhaps assume that the latter have not exceeded the former. In addition to sinkings at sea, there have been British raids on submarine bases, notably on Kiel, Wilhelmshaven, Cuxhaven, Brest, Lorient and St. Nazaire, and on April 17, 1942, a daring and successful daylight attack was made on Augsburg, where half of the Diesel engines used for submarines were produced.

Udet, GEN. ERNST. An intrepid trick flyer, he was Germany's most famous air ace. Udet was chief of the Luftwaffe Ordnance Dept. and Goering's right-hand man on the home front. He was largely responsible for the building of Germany's air force before the war. On Nov. 18, 1941, it was announced that he had died from wounds after testing a secret weapon.

Ukraine. One of the constituent republics of the U.S.S.R., occupying 170,000 sq. miles and supporting a population of 32 millions, the Ukraine (*see* p. 4107) is immensely valuable, both for the fertility of its soil (the famous " black earth ") and for the wealth of its metallurgical deposits. When Hitler attacked the Soviet Union, the Ukraine was his main objective,

not only because of its intrinsic value, but because of its strategic position in relation to the drive to the East (Drang nach Osten) ; from the Ukraine he might hope to reach the Caucasus and the oilfields beyond.

The German thrust towards the Ukraine began in July 1941. Panzer divisions were used to crash through the flat wheatfields towards Kiev, the ancient capital of Russia, which was evacuated on Sept. 19 after very fierce fighting. The invaders then split their forces, one half being directed east towards Kharkov and the other half turning S.E. to Odessa, which was evacuated on Oct. 16. Stalino was captured four days later, Taganrog on Oct. 22, and Kharkov on Oct. 24.

As a result of this advance the enemy occupied practically the whole of the Ukraine, but gained little else. In the agricultural area the Russians had harvested their wheat, sugar-beet and other crops and sent them eastwards, together with their livestock, machinery and implements. Such property as could not be moved they destroyed. In the industrial regions a similar policy was pursued ; the machinery and other contents of huge industrial plants were transported to shadow factories farther east (*see* Urals and special map in page 449), and the buildings and installations were dynamited or fired. The most outstanding example of this destruction was the sacrifice of the Dnieper Dam and power stations.

At the end of November 1941 the Soviet counter-offensive began. The enemy were driven back from Rostov on Nov. 28, and next day were in headlong rout beyond Taganrog. By Jan. 27, 1942, the Russians had recaptured over 400 inhabited places in the Ukraine. On the Kharkov front they attacked throughout Feb. and March, and in May launched a heavy offensive, but in June the Germans attacked and the Russians, their armies still intact, were forced to withdraw. This saved Timoshenko's armies from the German threat of encirclement. In May and June there was fierce fighting on the Donetz front, where the Germans claimed to have crossed the river. New Nazi offensives N. and N.E. of Kharkov were launched on June 29 and July 3. *See* Russia.

United Nations. Term applied to the 26 Allied Nations at war with the Axis whose representatives signed the Declaration at Washington on Jan. 2, 1942, when the Grand Alliance against the aggressor States was formally concluded. *See p. 447.*

AMERICA JOINS IN THE FIGHT FOR FREEDOM

Hitler made one of his greatest blunders when he became involved in war with America, for her incalculable resources and unlimited supply of armaments threatened the ultimate doom of the Axis Powers. See Atlantic Charter; Guam; Hawaii; Lease-Lend Act; Neutrality Act; Pacific, War in; Pearl Harbour; Roosevelt, etc.

United States. American politics, both home and foreign, can be understood only when the fundamental difference between the great Republic and other sovereign states is kept in mind. Leaders of the world's other powers can, in moments of domestic trouble, appeal for national unity with some certainty of the response. In times of national danger they can make the tribal appeal to the spirit of the nation. In the United States it is otherwise, for she is an amalgam of many peoples, and, therefore, may become torn asunder politically by racial loyalties in moments of international clash.

In the last war the German people in the United States constituted a great problem, for they were numerous, powerful, and in sympathy with the "Vaterland." Strangely enough, history has not repeated itself: neither the German nor the Italian American population has aligned itself with the "Old Country," but, on the contrary, both have registered dislike of all that Totalitarianism represents.

The difficulties which confronted Roosevelt from 1939 onwards arose from financial, economic and political causes. First, he had to put over his New Deal. This was an attempt to graft on to the body of American capitalism the skin of social justice. Congress was hostile to this policy. The New Deal was the death sentence of the Era of the Millionaires. It spread the income jam on the national bread-and-butter fairly evenly, but the President's far-seeing schemes meant tapping the public pocket.

By inaugurating vast public works, including the construction of a system of inter-state motor highways, Roosevelt hoped to abolish the appalling unemployment—some 11 millions at the beginning of the year—which had come with the great depression in 1930. The policy called for a very deep dip into the Federal purse and was, for that reason, unpopular. And this ideal the President was striving to put over in a world where war darkened the horizon and made all social and economic reconstruction seem futile and vain.

In the last war it was a racial problem that the United States had to cope with; in this, a large block of opinion without particular affinity, but with a new world political outlook; it was a question of standing aside from any and every European or foreign conflict. The Isolationists feared that Roosevelt would land the country in a foreign war and for that reason were opposed to the China Loan of 25 million dollars and the

U.S. SHIPS FOR BRITISH BASES

Over-age U.S. destroyers are seen, left, steaming towards a British port. American marines and sailors, below, present arms as the Stars and Stripes are raised over the site of an American defence base on Little Goat Island, Jamaica—one of the places acquired in exchange for the 50 destroyers.

Photos, Wide World; Keystone

THEY HELPED BRITAIN'S WAR EFFORT
These American women are packing surgical instruments destined to equip a base hospital in Britain, at the "Bundles for Britain" warehouse in New York. The equipment for the hospital was purchased from the proceeds of a dance in New York. Shipping needs restricted these and other gifts in July 1942.   *Photo, Wide World*

sending of war material to assist her against the aggressor, Japan.

The termination of the Japanese Trade Treaty in July 1939 was another substantial straw moving in the strong breeze of things to come. Japan's retort that any attempt by the United States to strengthen her Pacific outposts—the island of Guam, for example —would be deemed an unfriendly act, troubled the Isolationists even more.

At that time there existed the so-called Neutrality Laws, which made illegal the supply to any belligerent of war materials. The object of the Act was the worthy twofold one of striving towards the limitation of future wars and the avoidance of embroilment of the United States. Yet, as events proved, the Neutrality Acts really served to help the aggressor States.

Roosevelt pointed out this fact to his 131 million fellow countrymen. With characteristic boldness the President made a start by permitting the French Military Mission to buy American war material. This angered the Isolationists and they misnamed this act, and the acts which followed it, economic sanctions against the Dictator countries. The Isolationists were chastened a little when Germany marched into Czechoslovakia in March. The President condemned this wanton aggression, and a 25 per cent tax on German imports underlined the verbal condemnation. It was a month later that Roosevelt addressed his peace plea to Hitler. The Isolationists persisted in their parrot cry "Keep Out !" and the interminable debates on the Neutrality Acts revision went on.

During these crucial months Roosevelt had had another problem to contend with, namely, the big strikes which took place and the opposition of the Union leaders. Here it is very interesting to note that whereas Labour's official leaders and their organizations were anti-Roosevelt, the rank and file of Labour, maybe with surer instinct, were behind him. The invasion of Poland brought about a modification of the opposition, but it was not until November that the arms embargo was lifted and the cash-and-carry system

made legal. This measure provided for cash transactions, the buyer to take the goods away.

The end of the year had brought about a considerable modification in the attitude of the majority of American people. They were beginning to realize what Totalitarianism really meant. Nevertheless, the Isolationists still held to their policy, and Lindbergh (*q.v.*), one-time national hero, was their spokesman.

The Isolationists, as many wrongly believed, did not represent a craven element, but rather the ignorant element, of the population. Lindbergh's oratory revealed his own educational limitations. He could not read nor interpret world events.

The New Deal, the obstinate depression which refused to be changed into a healthy young boom, Labour troubles and unemployment—still standing at the appalling figure of eight millions, roughly, one in sixteen of the total population—all sank into insignificance as political issues before the darkening world horizon. Now, somewhat larger than a man's hand, the war cloud lifted above the rim of the eastern horizon, coloured by the glow of burning cities.

Early in the New Year Roosevelt, to allay the general opposition to any measure likely to involve the country in the European turmoil, promised that never again should young American manhood be sent to be sacrificed on European battlefields. But the President added the warning that any nation might have to defend itself. Though it was revolutionary in character the Compulsory Military Training measure was passed, and, in addition, the compulsory training of people for essential defence work was provided for.

Roosevelt Prepares the Nation

During this period the President maintained his famous personal touch by regular "Fireside Addresses," whereby he chatted informally about affairs over the radio. He felt strong enough to press on his policy, namely, preparation against the possibility of ultimate embroilment in the spreading world war.

In the United States the year 1940 became one of feverish rearmament, and a great armaments industry sprang into being. It did so, not because of Roosevelt's rearmament policy, but under the stimulus of vast and ever-increasing British orders for armaments of all kinds. That in 1942 the United States, with a two-ocean war on her hands, could manufacture all types of war materials on a fabulous scale, was due to an armaments industry created by British cash.

The first estimate for war materials was $9,930,000,000, a fabulous figure that was to be eclipsed by the programme outlined by the President in person to Congress on Jan. 6, 1942, namely, $70,000,000,000. At that time the objective in aircraft production aimed at was put at 60,000 aeroplanes a year, which offered another dramatic contrast with the 125,000 to be delivered in 1943.

In May 1940 a Council of National Defence was set up with production-planning as its job, that term to include everything essential to enhanced production of war material, labour, transport, raw materials.

Men between twenty-one and thirty-five signed on for military service, the selection being by lot. This body of partly trained men would form a hard core for any vast conscript army that might later have to be raised. Foreign service was limited to the Philippines (*q.v.*), America's sole overseas possession.

When, in June, Italy stabbed France in the back, American feeling underwent a big change. Until

AMERICAN AIRCRAFT READY TO FIGHT WITH THE R.A.F.

U.S. aircraft, flown from California to New York, are seen above assembled at an airfield, ready to cross the Atlantic for service with the R.A.F. The 'planes with the three-wheel landing gear and single tail are Douglas DB-7A bombers, and those with double-tail surfaces are Lockheed Hudsons. American factories worked at full pressure, and an ever-increasing stream of supplies of all kinds reached Britain.

Photo, Planet News

then there had been many who were unperturbed by the possibility of the British Empire's defeat. Now Britain's role as defender of liberty was etched clearly against the war screen. Mussolini's act revolted American opinion and rallied the country, irrespective of party, behind the President.

In August fifty over-age U.S.N. destroyers were exchanged with Britain for bases on the Atlantic seaboard—in Newfoundland, Bermuda, the Bahamas, Jamaica, etc.

At that time the United States could not make cash loans to help Britain since the Johnson Act precluded it. This legal impediment was got round by a device. Britain was buying her war materials from the great engineering firms of America. Now the United States Government stepped in as buyer and, turning round, said, in effect: "We've bought all this and paid for it, but we don't need it all at the moment. Care to borrow it?" Unfortunately, the steps to make this legal change effective were long-drawn-out, and it was not until 1941 that patiently waiting Britain got the benefit of the deal.

In 1940 America's worries were not confined to events in the Old World. Japan for more than a quarter of a century had constituted a certain threat.

In March Washington refused to recognize Japan's North China fake State, and told Japan in undiplomatic language to keep out of the Dutch East Indies. War material was sent to China, but Japan got none.

Towards the end of the year feeling against Japan had hardened and the desire to help China was much stronger. On the emotional side the country was becoming more easily moved to intense feeling. This took the form of anti-communistic activities and a general round-up of foreign political organizations.

In March 1941, when the Lease-Lend Act became effective, Roosevelt still had great difficulties on his home front. He faced the opposition of the leaders of organized Labour who saw in the cry for maximum output for war their chance to press wages and conditions claims. In one case this opposition took the form of personal animosity. On the other hand, big industry demanded to have struck from it the shackles of the New Deal, curbing profits and providing guarantees for labour.

With outstanding courage and steadiness of vision the President continued to press for unity, for preparedness for the worst, for all aid to the Democracies. In July a Bill was steered through prolonging the period of military service of men then serving. A

ACT OF TREACHERY THAT PLUNGED THE FAR EAST INTO WAR

The photograph on the left gives a vivid idea of the intensity of the Japanese attack on the American base of Pearl Harbour on Dec. 7, 1941, as the magazine of the U.S. destroyer Shaw explodes. This ship was subsequently repaired and made her way safely to an American port. Right, a two-man Japanese submarine after being beached at Pearl Harbour. It was shelled by an aircraft tender, rammed by a destroyer and blasted by depth charges.

Photos, Associated Press; Keystone

Principal Types of U.S.A. Aircraft

No.	U.S. name	British name	Type	Engines h.p.	Speed m.p.h.	Bomb load or armament	Notes
A 20	Douglas	Havoc	Army light attack bmr.	2–1,606	400		Developed from DB 7 (below).
B 17 E	Boeing	F'ying Fortress	Army 24-ton bomber	4–1,200	325 max.	4–5 ton	Ceiling 40,000 ft. Crew 6-9.
B 19	Douglas	—	Army 82-ton bomber	4–2,000	200	18 ton	Range 7,750 miles. Guns in turrets.
B 24	Consolidated	Liberator	Army 20½-ton bomber	4–1,200	335	4 ton	3 turrets ; range 4,000 miles. Crew 9.
B 25	N. American	—	Army 13-ton med. bmr.	2–1,700	350	2 ton	Range under 1,500 miles.
B 26	Martin	Marauder	Army 13-ton med. bmr.	2–1,850	350	2 ton	Range under 1,500 miles. Very fast.
DB 7B	Douglas	Boston I	Army med. attack bmr.	2–1,050	315	—	Also Boston II with 1,600 h.p. engines. See A 20.
DB-8A5	Douglas	—	Army med. attack bmr.	1–1,200	265	5 m.g.	Used as British bomber.
EB-14B	Lockheed	Hudson	Army med. bomber	2–1,100	250	—	Medium range. Used Brtsh reconnaissance.
F4 F3	Grumman	Martlet	Navy fighter	1–1,200	350	6 m.g.	Fragmentation bombs.
F2A-2	Brewster	Buffalo	Navy fighter	1–1,200	360	6–8 m.g.	—
P 36A	Curtiss	Mohawk	Army pursuit	1–1,200	323	8 m.g.	—
P 38	Lockheed	Lightning	Interceptor pursuit	2–1,150	404	2 37mm. or 6 m.g.	Climbs 1 mile in first min.
P 39	Bell Airacobra	Caribou	Army pursuit	1–1,300	400	1 37mm. 4–6 m.g.	400 m.p.h. at 15,000 ft. Naval version, Airabonita.
P 40	Curtiss	Tomahawk	Army pursuit	1–1,050	330	2 37mm. 4 m.g.	P 40-F improved model (secret).
P 40D	Curtiss	Kittyhawk	Army pursuit	1–1,320	380	8 m.g.	Used as British fighter.
P 43	Republic	—	Army pursuit	—	—	—	Ceiling 7 miles.
P 47	Seversky	—	Army pursuit	1–2,000	400	6 m.g.	U.S. name " Thunderbolt."
PBM.1	Martin	—	Navy 20-ton bomber	—	—	—	Range 1,500 miles with full load.
PB2Y-2	Consolidated	—	Navy 25-ton patrol bmr.	4	225	—	Range 5,200 miles with 5-ton load.
PBY-5	Consolidated	Catalina	Navy flying bt.	2–1,200	200	3 m.g.	Time range 24 hours.
PB2X-2	Consolidated	—	Navy bomber	4–1,200	280 cruis. 335 max.	2–4 m.g.	Range 4,000 miles. 20½ tons gross weight.
SB2C-1	Curtiss	—	Navy scout & dive bomber	1–1,700	350 max.	1 ton bombs	" Helldiver," carrier borne, long range.
SB2U-3	Vought	Chesapeake	Navy scout	1–800	305	2 m.g.	—
SBD	Douglas	—	Navy scout & dive bomber	1–1,600	—	—	—
SBC-4	Curtiss	—	Navy scout & dive bomber	—	—	500–1,000 lb. bombs	Dives at 300 m.p.h.
—	Brewster	Bermuda	Navy dive bomber	1–1,700	325	4 m.g.	Similar to Curtiss SB2C.
TBD-1	Douglas	—	Navy torpedo plane	1–1,150	—	2,000 lb. torpedo	Attacks at 100 feet, carrier borne.
XF4-U	Vought-Sikorski	—	Navy fighter	1–2,000	400	2 cannon & 4 m.g. or 8 m.g.	Radius 1,000 miles, carrier borne.
XP-47B	See P47 (" Thunderbolt ') above						
XP-51	N. American	Mustang	Army scout	1–1,500	400	6 m.g.	—

Note. Letters and numbers indicate classes thus : ARMY : **A**, Attack (light bomber); **B**, Bomber; **DB**, Dive Bomber ; **P**, Pursuit (= British Fighter). NAVY : **F**, Fighter; **PB**, Patrol Bomber; **SB**, Scout Bomber; **TB**, Torpedo Bomber. **Makers** (last letters in certain designations) : **A**, Brewster ; **C**, Curtiss : **D**, Douglas ; **M**, Martin ; **U**, Vought ; **Y**, Consolidated ; **X**, Experimental.

month later came the historic and dramatic meeting of Roosevelt and Winston Churchill in mid-Atlantic, and the Atlantic Charter (*q.v.*), defining the mutual aims of the two great nations.

If one examines the acts of the United States up to this time they can be described only as those of a nation at war save in actual operations. Arms and money were being supplied in ever-increasing quantities to the Democracies. In April all Italian and German ships in United States ports had been seized. In May all assets of both those countries in America had been frozen. And, last, under the Lease-Lend arrangement, Germany's attempt to starve out Great Britain was being baffled by a steady stream of food supplies.

America's position, if by the middle of 1941 ever in doubt, was made doubly clear when, Russia becoming Germany's next victim, Roosevelt promised all aid to the Soviets also, and sent Averell Harriman to Moscow, where a £250,000,000 lease-lend credit was

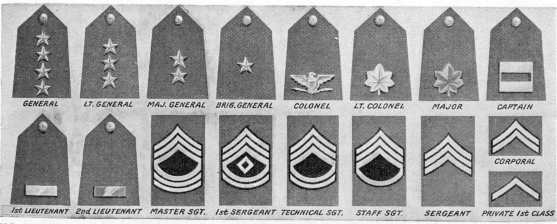

U.S. Army badges of rank range from the four stars of a general to the single stripe of a private. When the insignia is the same, silver denotes a higher rank than gold. The oak leaf of a lieut.-colonel and the bar of a first lieut. are silver, while those of a major and a second lieut. are gold.

arranged. In addition to wielding this economic and financial bludgeon against the Axis, America made naval and military moves in keeping. The exchanged Atlantic bases were occupied. American troops and naval units moved into Iceland and took over the sea area between that strategic point and the Atlantic seaboard. American merchantmen sailed armed and with orders to shoot U-boats at sight. It was war in everything but armed clash of big battle.

Last, in increasing numbers, there appeared in Britain, wearing the uniform of the R.A.F., pilots and observers carrying the additional device " U.S.A." In Northern Ireland (where, in January 1942, the first contingent of the American Expeditionary Force was to land), American technicians had been busy for many months, constructing airfields. In short, America was in the war in all save overt act.

This was to come in the last days of the year, a year which closed for America with one of the greatest disasters of her history. On Dec. 7, while her representatives were still at Washington, Japan launched a large-scale air attack on the United States naval base at Pearl Harbour (q.v.), Hawaiian Islands. Very heavy damage was done and the American Pacific Fleet was crippled for the time being at least. This atrocity committed, Japan formally declared war on both the United States and Great Britain.

In striking before declaring a state of war to exist, Japan followed the well-known Axis pattern of behaviour. Her blow at America was one that had been carefully prepared over a long period, and was the first of many designed to wrest from the United States the Philippine Islands and certain strategic islands in the Southern Pacific. And these objectives,

again, were but part of a large war picture which included the conquest of Hongkong and of Malaya, and even, apparently, envisaged the occupation of northern Australia, too.

The reaction of America to the heavy blow dealt her from the East consolidated public opinion and roused the whole country, which now stood solid, to the last Isolationist, beside that justified prophet of evils to come, the President. The entry of Japan into the world war fused in a single bloc the United States, Great Britain, China and the U.S.S.R. Her inital successes, gained by double-dealing and treachery, the policy of the militarist party, brought further reverses to America and hard blows at her prestige.

Accounts of the Japanese invasion of Pearl Harbour, of Guam, Midway Island and the Philippines are given under those headings.

On Dec. 22, 1941, Mr. Churchill, accompanied by the British Chiefs of Staff, arrived in the U.S.A. Announcing this visit Mr. Roosevelt said : " The present conferences should be regarded as preliminary to further conferences which will officially include Russia, China, the Netherlands and the Dominions. It is expected that there will be thus evolved an overall unity in the conduct of the war." On Dec. 26 Mr. Churchill addressed Congress.

Grand Alliance of the United Nations

The Grand Alliance against the Axis was one result of these conferences. This " Declaration of the United Nations," as it was officially styled, was signed at Washington on Jan. 2, 1942, by the representatives of 26 nations : the United States, United Kingdom, Soviet Union, China, Australia, Belgium, Canada, Costa Rica, Cuba, Czechoslovakia, Dominican Republic, Salvador, Greece, Guatemala, Haiti, Honduras, India, Luxembourg, Netherlands, New Zealand, Nicaragua, Norway, Panama, Poland, S. Africa and Yugoslavia. The text briefly is as follows : " Having subscribed to a common programme of purposes and principles embodied in the Atlantic Charter ; and being convinced that complete victory over their enemies is essential to defend life, liberty, independence, and religious freedom, and to preserve human rights and justice ; and that they are now engaged in a common struggle against savage, brutal forces seeking to subjugate the world ; each Government pledges itself to employ its full resources, military or economic, against those members of the Tripartite Pact and its adherents with which such a government is at war, and to cooperate with the Governments signatory hereto, and not to make a separate armistice or peace with the enemies. The foregoing Declaration may be adhered to by other nations rendering material assistance and contributions in the struggle for victory over Hitlerism." On June 2 Mexico joined the Grand Alliance.

The Aleutian Islands, lying off Alaska, and athwart the nearest trade route between N. America and Japan, were attacked and invaded by the Japanese in June 1942. On June 3 Dutch Harbour, one of the most important naval bases in the Aleutians and the key to Alaska's defences, was bombed by aircraft, presumably carrier-based. Ten days later the Japanese landed at Attu and Kiska Islands. Great quantities of American planes and equipment were immediately flown to Alaska for its defence.

On June 8, 1942, President Roosevelt sent to Congress the biggest War Appropriations Bill in American history, totalling more than £10,000,000,000, thus

U.S. SOLDIERS LAND IN AUSTRALIA
American soldiers step down the gangway from their ship at an Australian port. They are wearing a special type of steel helmet, designed to give maximum protection.
Photo, Keystone

U.S. TROOPS BRINGING IN PRISONERS

The Japanese believed in discarding everything save strict necessities in war, and here are some prisoners wearing only loincloths. They are being brought in for interrogation during the fighting on the Bataan peninsula.

Photo, Associated Press

bringing the projected American war expenditure to over £50,000,000,000. He asked for authority to transfer more than £3,000,000,000 of the new appropriation for lend-lease aid for America's allies.

Major-Gen. Dwight D. Eisenhower, newly appointed to the command of the European Theatre for U.S. Forces, arrived in England on June 26, 1942. On July 7 Maj.-Gen. Carl Spaatz was given command of the U.S. Air Force in the European Theatre.

Mr. Churchill visited America again in June 1942 for further discussions with President Roosevelt. On his return on June 27 a joint statement was issued simultaneously in Britain and the United States on the objects of these talks. The main points were : Coming operations to divert German strength from the attack on Russia ; new measures to reduce shipping losses ; and the methods to be adopted against Japan and to aid China. Speaking in the House during the War Debate on July 2 Mr. Churchill said : " The improvement in the position of Australia, New Zealand and India has been effected in the main by the brilliant victories gained by the U. S. Navy and Air Force over the Japanese in the Coral Sea and at Midway Island."

Books to Consult : Defence of the Western World, Hanson Baldwin (Hutchinson). U.S.A., D. W. Brogan (Oxford Press).

Upham, CAPTAIN CHARLES. An officer of the New Zealand Force, he was awarded the V.C. for gallantry during the German invasion of Crete, when he performed a series of remarkable exploits, showing outstanding leadership and tactical skill. Lieut. Upham commanded a forward platoon in the attack on Maleme on May 22, 1941, and fought his way forward for over 3,000 yards, unsupported by other arms.

Captain Upham, awarded the V.C.
Photo, British Official

Reported missing July 1942 and later a prisoner, he received his V.C. in May 1945.

Urals. Along the southern half of this mountain range (*see* p. 4142), which separates Europe from Asia, the U.S.S.R. has created a thriving new industrial region of vital importance to Soviet planning. Fear of war was the chief motive for this enterprise to provide for the continuance of the Soviet output independently of the more vulnerable western industrial areas. The site in the Urals was chosen because of the rich mineral deposits in that area. The Ural iron-ore deposits amount to at least half a billion tons, but the lack of coking coal had prevented development. There are, however, very extensive coalfields some 1,250 miles east, amounting to some 400 billion tons, in the Kuznetsk Basin in W. Siberia.

These two areas have therefore been linked by rail, and around the slopes of Mt. Magnitskaya in the Urals the world's largest iron and steel plant, Magnitogorsk, has been built, its factories, furnaces and power stations covering many square miles ; the workers' settlement is on the higher level, in pleasant and healthy surroundings. Between Magnitogorsk and the Kuzbas (Kuznetsk Basin) freight trains are incessantly bringing Kuzbas coal to Magnitogorsk and returning with Magnitogorsk ore for the Kuzbas, where a complementary industrial region has grown up around Stalinsk. Between these two focal points there is a vast network of subsidiary industrial plants and power stations, which has been extended southwards to link up with Karaganda and other cities of Kazakhstan, where copper is produced in abundance. There is another extension westwards from the Urals to Kuibishev, which is the centre of an important industrial system in the Middle Volga region.

Magnitogorsk Rose Out of Waste Land

This immense development has arisen since 1929, when the foundations of Magnitogorsk were laid in a waste land. In 1940 its output of ore was some 2¾ million tons, which equals the total output of the Ukraine mines, and throughout the entire Urals-Kuzbas area the output had exceeded 6 million tons. Much of this was converted into heavy machinery and machine-tools at factories within the area, under control of Uralmash, an organization which co-ordinates output. Uralmash, working according to the requirements of the Five-Year Plans, was to build up Soviet economic self-sufficiency and to ensure Soviet victory in the anticipated war with Germany.

Thus Chelyabinsk manufactured tractors and harvester combines, by mass-production methods, in order to hasten the mechanization of agriculture ; when war broke out, it could switch over to mass-production of tanks. Similarly, the truck works at Ufa could produce armoured cars and lorries ; the huge plant at Sverdlovsk could turn out armaments, and the great chemical works at Magnitogorsk and Berezhniki could manufacture explosives and, if necessary, poison-gas. Situated 1,500–2,000 miles from the western frontier, and even farther from the eastern frontier, these factories are remote from invasion and even secure from air attack.

Not content with this mighty achievement, the Soviet Union made plans for the removal, in time of war, of factories lying within range of attack from the west. Thus the machinery and other equipment of the Voroshilov plant at Dniepropetrovsk, together with the workers, were transported to the Urals, and other factories also moved east. Many thousands of railway wagons were required for this purpose, but within a couple of months the evacuated factories were settled in speedily erected shadow factories and were exceeding their former output. The local supplies of iron ore and coal were adequate for their needs, although not yet fully developed either in the Kuzbas cr in the supplementary coalfields of Chelyabinsk in the Urals proper.

The U.S.S.R. is well provided with nickel, and this is produced in the Urals. So, too, is aluminium. Plastics, of the bakelite type, and synthetic rubber are new industries, of especial value in time of war, which have grown up in this area. In the North Urals plywood factories have been established, utilizing the dense forests of birch.

In 1937 it was decided that the Urals oilfields must be developed as, in M. Molotov's words, " a second Baku," and by 1940 the output of oil was estimated at 5 million tons for the year.

Ursula, H.M.S. This is one of the three smallest submarines in the British Navy, displacing only 540 tons ; the usual displacement for an ocean-going submarine is 1,500 tons. The Ursula first distinguished herself on Dec. 14, 1939, when she sank an enemy cruiser of the Köln class (6,000 tons) at the mouth of the River Elbe. A naval expert said of this action :

" To penetrate right into the Heligoland Bight to the mouth of the Elbe, where

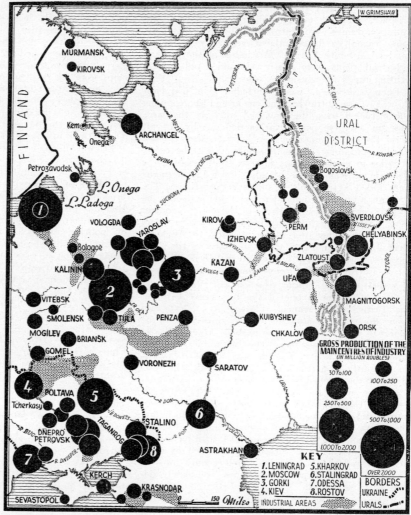

The Urals and the Ukraine constitute two of Russia's great industrial areas

German anti-submarine craft presumably teem, to penetrate a destroyer screen and torpedo the ship it protects, and finally to elude the inevitable counterattacks in the shallow waters of the Bight, are remarkable achievements." The D.S.O. was awarded to Lt.-Comr. G. C. Phillips, and the D.S.C. to Lt. J. D. Greene and Lt. Aston Piper.

U.S.A. *See* United States of America.

U.S.S.R. *See* Russia.

 Vaagso Island (*pron.* Vawg-sō). On Dec. 27, 1941, British military, naval and air forces combined in an assault against the islands of Vaagso and Maaloy, off the Norwegian coast. The raid was directed mainly against enemy shipping anchored off Vaagso, and was a fine example of service cooperation. Light forces of the Home Fleet bombarded enemy coastal defence batteries in Vaagso Fjord, thus enabling Commando and Norwegian troops to land on the island itself. There were two main military landings, one on Maaloy and the other on the town of South Vaagso. On

DESTRUCTION ON VAAGSO ISLAND

British soldiers, seen in the foreground, guard against snipers or surprise enemy attacks as an oil factory at Vaagso burns furiously. This photograph was taken during the British raid of Dec. 27, 1941.

Photo, British Official

Maaloy the entire garrison were either killed or taken prisoner, and oil tanks, military storehouses and munition dumps were destroyed. The British suffered some casualties before the Germans were finally subdued in South Vaagso. A wireless station and an industrial plant were destroyed, and hand-to-hand fighting raged fiercely in the streets.

Enemy shipping, which included five merchant ships, two armed trawlers and one armed tug, totalling about 16,000 tons, was smashed up. At the same time an offensive patrol was carried out by aircraft of the Bomber Command. R.A.F. 'planes also attacked Herdla aerodrome, about 100 miles down the coast, in order to prevent enemy aircraft from assisting the German garrison on the islands. Over 120 Germans were killed as a result of military operations. The German military commander was taken prisoner, as was the naval officer in charge of the convoy control port. Ninety-five Nazi naval and military prisoners and nine quislings were brought back to England. Brig. J. C. Haydon, D.S.O., was in charge of the Commandos, and the naval forces were led by Rear-Adm. H. M. Burrough, C.B. *See* Commandos; Lofoten Is.

Valetta. The Grand Harbour of Valetta, the capital of Malta, is one of the two great bases of the British Mediterranean Fleet. At Valetta are huge dock and victualling yards spread over the shores of the two arms of the harbour ; there are also magazines and storehouses. One of the most-bombed cities of the world, Valetta was attacked almost continuously from the entry of Italy into the war. Owing to the excellent shelters, most of them excavated from the rock, the casualties were not heavy in view of the frequency of the raids, but hundreds of houses and many fine buildings were wrecked, including the Opera House and the Museum. On July 26, 1941, it was announced that an attempted Italian naval raid on Valetta harbour was successfully repulsed by shore defences and the R.A.F., the whole enemy force of 17 E-boats and torpedo craft being completely destroyed. *See* Malta.

Valiant, H.M.S. Belonging to the Queen Elizabeth class, this British battleship was completed in 1916. She had a displacement of about 30,600 tons and carried a complement of 1,124–1,184. The reconstruction of this class between 1925 and 1933 involved an expenditure of about a million pounds per ship. In 1937 the Valiant was refitted and possessed a main armament of eight 15-in. guns. On March 28, 1941, commanded by Capt. C. E. Morgan, D.S.O., she played an important part in the Battle of Matapan (*q.v.*) when, in company with Warspite, Barham and the aircraft carrier Formidable, she destroyed the Italian cruisers Zara and Fiume. It was estimated that at least 75 per cent of her shells scored direct hits.

Lord Vansittart, British diplomat.
Photo, Vandyk

Vansittart, ROBERT GILBERT, 1ST BARON (b. 1881). From 1938, until he retired in June 1941, he was Chief Diplomatic Adviser to the Foreign Secretary ; he was then made Baron Vansittart of Denham. Labelled by its opponents Vansittartism, his contention was that the whole German people were responsible for the war and for Nazi methods of making war and holding down the peoples of occupied countries.

Vatican. At the beginning of 1939 the Nazi party had secretly decreed the downfall of the Catholic Church in Germany, a measure which was averted only by the personal efforts of Pope Pius XII (*q.v.*). The latter dispatched an emergency summons to the German bishops to assemble at Rome, and the strongest steps were then taken to urge the Italian and other Governments to intervene. Germany's persecution of the Catholic Church in Poland and her barbarous treatment of priests and nuns were strongly condemned by the Vatican wireless on Jan. 22, 1940. The German invasion of the Low Countries on May 10, 1940, was likewise denounced by the Papal organ " L'Osservatore Romano " (*q.v.*). Just before Italy's entry into the war in June 1940 it was reported that the Vatican wireless station would be allowed to broadcast the Pope's messages, but " L'Osservatore Romano," read by thousands of Italians for its frank and fearless views, must refrain from all comment on political events. On Aug. 2, 1940, the Pope instructed all Apostolic Nuncios and other Papal diplomats abroad, most of whom were Italian nationals, to take out Vatican citizenship in order to acquire greater freedom of action during the war. President Roosevelt had a special envoy to the Vatican, Mr. Myron Taylor. In March 1942 concern was expressed by both the British and U.S. Governments at the appointment of a Japanese " special " Ambassador at the Vatican. Shortly after this appointment China renewed her request for an exchange of diplomatic representatives with the Vatican, and this was granted on April 6.

Venice. Lying in a bay of the Adriatic Sea and built on over a hundred islands, this beautiful Italian city (*see* pp. 4157–60) served as a useful landmark to British pilots in finding near-by military objectives. One of these, Porto Marghera, an important dock and petroleum works centre on the mainland opposite Venice, was bombed heavily by the R.A.F. on Dec. 21, 1940, and in Jan. 1941. Another target was the oil tanks at Mestre, near Venice, which were set ablaze by French naval aircraft on June 13, 1940.

Verdun. A few days' fighting in the present war sufficed to bring about the fall of Verdun, the fortified city of Northern France whose fortresses were the scene of heroic French resistance in the war of 1914–18. It fell into German hands on June 15, 1940, and after the Franco-German Armistice became part of the occupied territory.

Vernon, H.M.S. Land establishment at Portsmouth. Here are the chief Torpedo School and Mine Experimental Department of the Navy. On Nov. 3, 1939, a party from the Vernon set out to investigate a new form of mine—the magnetic mine—which had been dropped on the shore near Shoeburyness by a German aircraft the previous day. Lt.-Cmdr. J. G. D. Ouvry (*q.v.*) and his party dismantled the machine. In recognition of their bravery Lt.-Cmdr. Ouvry and four others were decorated by the King on Dec. 19. *See* Mines and Minelaying.

'V' for Victory. This branch of democratic propaganda was the invention of a Belgian, Victor de Lavelaye, one-time leader of the Belgian Liberal Party. On Jan. 14, 1941, de Lavelaye broadcast an appeal to his countrymen in Belgium to write on their walls a V, the initial letter of the French " Victoire " and the Flemish " Vrijheid " (Freedom).

EUROPE'S SYMBOL OF FREEDOM

The famous V sign was prominently displayed throughout Britain following the launching of the "Victory Campaign" in June 1941. Here the sign is used as an effective decoration outside a London restaurant.

Photo, "Daily Mail"

Within a week the V sign had spread to occupied France and soon it was to be seen throughout German-occupied Europe.

The British " V " campaign was launched on June 27, 1941, when the famous but anonymous " Colonel Britton " took the air for the first time and introduced the morse equivalent of the ' V ' sign (. . . —; three short taps and one long one). Said Colonel Britton, " When you knock on the door, knock thus :

tap, tap, tap—and a long tap ! " At the same time, Colonel Britton recalled the opening bars of Beethoven's Fifth Symphony and reminded listeners all over Europe that the same conjunction of sounds suggested " Fate knocking at the door." The B.B.C. subsequently adopted the opening bars of the Fifth Symphony as its interval signal for European programmes. R.A.F. bombers reported " V " lights in France and the Low Countries, some of which were fifty to a hundred feet long and were manifestly part of the Victory campaign.

The best evidence of the success of the " V " campaign was the anger aroused in Germany. Dr. Goebbels tried desperately to kill the campaign by ridicule. Then he attempted to introduce a German variant, whereby the " V " would stand for a German " Viktoria," and not a democratic victory. *See* Propaganda.

Vian, REAR-ADMIRAL SIR PHILIP L., K.B.E., D.S.O. (b. 1894). As captain of H.M.S. Cossack (*q.v.*) Admiral Vian rescued three hundred British prisoners from the German prison-ship Altmark (*q.v.*) in February 1940. After this famous exploit his flotilla destroyed a whole German convoy off the coast of Norway, and in May 1941 he commanded the destroyer force that chased and attacked the Bismarck (*q.v.*) the

Adm. Sir P. Vian, British sailor.
Photo, British Official

night before she was sunk. Early in September 1941, in operations against German convoys supplying their troops on the Murmansk front, British naval forces under his command sank the German gunboat Bremse, and other vessels, without loss to themselves. Admiral Vian led the naval force that successfully protected an important convoy in the Mediterranean (*q.v.*) in March 1942, when strong Italian naval forces were sighted and engaged. A few days later, on March 28, he was awarded the K.B.E.

VICHY LAID FRANCE UNDER THE GERMAN HEEL

The Vichy Government was no more representative of the true France than the defeatists who composed its ranks were representative of the nation's will. The Germans sought to strengthen their dictatorship by installing Laval at its head in April 1942. See France, Occupied and Unoccupied; Laval; Pétain.

Vichy Government. The Government of France which negotiated the Armistice came into being on June 17, 1940. It was then sitting at Bordeaux, but the administrative centre was quickly moved to Vichy, a health resort about 75 miles north-west of Lyons, with a population of about 18,000. The Vichy administration made itself responsible for French affairs, at home and overseas, for the next two years. Essentially, Vichy represented a caucus of military and naval chiefs, headed by Marshal Pétain, who had convinced themselves, not only that France was defeated, but that Great Britain would be out of the war in three weeks. As one of them said at the time, " The English would have their necks wrung like a chicken," a dictum which led Mr. Churchill to make his memorable comment, " Some chicken ! "

An alternative to capitulation, rejected by the Vichy Government, was union with Great Britain, and a full and complete sharing of all munitions of

war, including financial resources. It was later revealed by Senator Charles Reibel that Weygand had advocated surrender to Germany as early as May 28, when he hoped to save Paris by accepting Germany's terms. M. Reynaud and M. Mandel, who were at the head of the Government, indignantly refused to forsake the British alliance. On June 13 the Reynaud Cabinet was still against surrender, though Pétain, Georges, Huntziger and other French generals now supported Weygand. On June 16 Reynaud resigned, and the Vichy Government thereupon negotiated the terms for the cease fire.

The policy which the Vichy Government pursued cannot be understood apart from the politics of the French Republic in the years immediately preceding the Second World War. Marshal Pétain held strong Fascist opinions long before the collapse of France. In his belief, democracy and social discipline were incompatibles, and as a soldier and a Catholic he was a stern disciplinarian. He described the authoritarian regime which he established at Vichy as "destined to permit a far more perfect realization of the ideals dear to Frenchmen than was possible under Parliamentary institutions." For the familiar Republican formula, "Liberté, Egalité, Fraternité," Pétain substituted the formula "Family, Work and Fatherland." In general, the wealthy upper middle class supported Pétain, partly because it feared that a British victory would bring the Socialist Popular Front once more to power in France. In order to emphasize the passing of Parliamentarianism all members of the two Houses of Parliament were forbidden to reside in Vichy, and were sent to the mountain spa of Mont-Dore.

In the sphere of local government the Vichy Government suppressed the departmental, cantonal and municipal assemblies, where the French tradition of local responsibility was likely to persist. At the same time Vichy dismissed large numbers of primary school teachers, and closed the primary teaching colleges, where such teachers had been trained, the reason being the dominance of Left political opinions in the teaching profession. Similarly, on Aug. 24, 1940, Vichy closed all ex-service men's associations, and substituted their own Légion Française des Combattants.

CHANGING THE GUARD AT VICHY

A scene outside the Hotel du Parc in Vichy, the building at which the Vichy Government had its headquarters. The ceremony of changing the guard took place before the main entrance of the hotel.

Photo, Keystone

The first Prime Minister under Pétain was Pierre Laval (*q.v.*), but his first term of office terminated suddenly on Dec. 13, 1940, owing to Laval's intrigues against the aged Marshal. Flandin, his successor, retained office only until Feb. 9, 1941, when the growing influence of Admiral Darlan (*q.v.*) sufficed to oust him. Gradually Darlan gathered authority into his own hands and, on Aug. 12, 1941, he was made Minister of Defence. Then Darlan, in his turn, was a victim of the machinations of Laval, who was restored to the Prime Ministership at Vichy on April 18, 1942, following upon Hitler's speech at the Zeughaus on March 15, in which he denounced the action of Pétain and the Vichy Government in connexion with the Riom trials (*q.v.*).

The Vichy Government, while under the direction of Pétain and Darlan, never had a clear-cut policy. Alibert wanted to restore the monarchy in France; Baudouin worked for a Latin alliance, including Spain and Italy, in the apparent hope that it would prove strong enough to counter even a victorious Germany; Pucheux and Benoist-Méchin favoured the most active collaboration with Nazi Germany, as did Marcel Déat. As the full significance of Vichy policy became plain, resignations from Pétain's National Council grew frequent, among them being those of André Siegfried and Cardinal Suchard.

By the end of 1941, owing to the weakness of Pétain, the concessions made by Vichy to Nazi Germany had greatly exceeded the terms laid down in the Armistice. At a meeting with the representatives of Nazi Germany at Montoire in 1940, Pétain and Laval agreed to give Germany the use of French factories for the making of armaments and, early in December 1941, Pétain and Darlan met Goering in the occupied zone and discussed the handing over of the French Fleet to Germany. Nothing but doubts as to whether the French naval ratings would obey such an order stopped Pétain from complete surrender to Goering's plans. As things were, Pétain and Darlan agreed to give Germany the use of French African air ports and shipping facilities, so that supplies from France could reach Rommel in Libya, by way of Tunis. The vessels St. Germain, Nantaise and Bougaroni carried Italian lorries from French ports, and the St. Etienne and the Cabyle provisions. Thus 2,000 lorries reached Rommel in 1941, as well as large quantities of petrol.

Laval Gains New Power by Intrigue

When Japan came into the war at the end of 1941, Vichy not only handed over certain French shipping in the Pacific to the Axis, but raised anxiety as to whether it would yield Madagascar to Japan, as it had yielded Indo-China. Noting that Pétain and Darlan were plainly susceptible to bullying, Laval made fresh contacts with Pétain in March 1942. It was stated that Pétain met Laval secretly in the forest of Randan and a final capitulation of Vichy to Nazi Germany was virtually agreed. Laval is said to have played upon the fears of the Marshal, telling him that Hitler had lost all confidence in the Vichy Government and had decided to make France pay dearly by forcing surrender of territory to the Axis. Moreover, the policing of France would be handed over to Himmler's Gestapo, and Hitler was threatening to cut off supplies. Whatever the truth may have been, early in April a German ultimatum was handed to Pétain, demanding the reinstatement of Laval with totalitarian powers within seven days, adding that, unless Pétain complied, Italy would seize Tunis, Corsica, Savoy and the Comté de Nice. Pétain, as usual, hesitated and at the last moment capitulated.

Laval broadcast an outline of his policy to the French people on April 20. It showed that Vichy's policy henceforward would be reconciliation and the fullest cooperation with Germany. Pétain and Darlan were both virtually ousted from the Vichy Government, though Darlan was Minister of Defence, with nominal control of the French Navy, under Pétain, and also had the promise of the reversion of the French Presidency if and when Pétain relinquished it. For his new Cabinet Laval could find few colleagues of repute and his only intimate was Cathala, his Minister of Finance. The Secretaries of State, all of them pro-German, were of more importance than the new Vichy Cabinet Ministers.

Curiously enough, Laval always had an obsession that his crooked courses against Great Britain could continue without disturbing good relations between

BOMBERS SET VIIPURI ABLAZE

Viipuri was one of Finland's chief ports and suffered severely as a result of Soviet air attacks during the Russo-Finnish war. This photograph was taken during one of the raids and houses are seen burning fiercely.

Photo, Associated Press

France and the United States. Throughout 1940 and 1941 the United States supplied French Northern Africa with much-needed food and only curtailed the supplies when it was plain that Germany was bene-fiting. The United States also supplied the French colony of Martinique with provisions, though the authorities there were plainly creatures of the Vichy Government and hostile to the Democratic Alliance. The Vichy Government sent the cruiser Emile Bertin to Martinique with large stores of gold after the collapse of June 1940.

Admiral Leahy, the United States Minister at Vichy, was recalled to Washington after Laval reassumed office. The attitude of America to France not only stiffened, but a break between the two nations was clearly threatened in consequence of Vichy's cowardly pliancy towards Germany. Roosevelt's broadcast on April 28 made it clear that the U.S.A. was concerned lest the Laval government might seek to force the French people to submit to Nazi despotism. The United Nations would take measures, if necessary, to prevent the use of French territory in any part of the world for Axis military purposes. These words were translated into action in Martinique and Madagascar.

Books to Consult: The Government of Vichy, Lt.-Col. Pierre Tissier (Harrap), The Shame of Vichy, Emrys Jones (Hutchinson). Pierre Laval, Henry Torres (Gollancz).

Victorious, H.M.S. A sister ship of the Illustrious, and one of Britain's most powerful aircraft carriers, the Victorious was completed in 1940. Her armament included sixteen 4·5-in. dual-purpose guns. She had a displacement of 23,000 tons, with a speed of 30 knots. Her naval torpedo aircraft were the first to disable the German raider Bismarck (*q.v.*) during the pursuit of the enemy ship in May 1941. This was the first intimation that Victorious was actually in commission. She subsequently took part in operations at Petsamo.

Viipuri (VIBORG). An important port on the Gulf of Finland, Viipuri was intensively bombed by Soviet aircraft during the Russo-Finnish war, one of the heaviest attacks occurring on Christmas Day 1939. By March 1940 the Russians held almost the entire eastern shore of the Gulf of Viipuri and heavy guns of the Red Army battered the city until little was left but smoking ruins. Soviet bombers completed the work of destruction, but although they suffered considerable losses the Russians were unable to capture Viipuri. On the cessation of hostilities on March 13, 1940, Viipuri and Viipuri Bay were ceded to Russia. When Germany attacked the U.S.S.R. on June 22, 1941, Finland joined the Nazis. On Aug. 24 the Finns announced that they had encircled Viipuri after capturing Kexholm. The recapture of the city itself was claimed on Aug. 30, 1941.

Vilna (WILNO). This city of N.E. Poland was annexed by the Poles in 1923, but was still regarded by the Lithuanians as their capital. The Germans bombed the place relentlessly in September 1939, it being estimated that 400 bombs were dropped on Vilna in one day; a total of 20,000 civilian deaths was reported up to Sept. 17. Vilna passed to Russia at the partitioning of Poland between Germany and the U.S.S.R. on Sept. 29, 1939. Russia returned the city to Lithuania on Oct. 10, 1939. On June 24, 1941, the Germans claimed to have captured Vilna after violent fighting in this area.

Vittorio Veneto. Belonging to the Littorio class, this Italian battleship was completed in April 1940 and had a displacement of 35,000 tons. She carried a complement of 1,600 and her main armament consisted of nine 15-in. and twelve 6-in. guns. During the battle of Matapan (*q.v.*) on March 28, 1941, the Vittorio Veneto was severely damaged as a result of hits from Fleet Air Arm and R.A.F. aircraft. Her speed was reduced from 30 knots to less than 15 and when last seen by British 'planes she was reported to be listing heavily and badly down by the stern.

Volokolamsk. An historic and important town about 75 miles N.W. of Moscow, Volokolamsk and its area were the scene of bitter and intense fighting between the Germans and Russians throughout November 1941. The Germans threw in enormous numbers of troops and equipment, including 1,800 tanks, regardless of the heavy losses inflicted upon them by the Red Army, in a frantic effort to reach the Russian capital. The Russians, contesting every inch of ground, fought heroically in an attempt to slow up the Nazi thrust. Both sides brought up reinforcements and the battle continued without respite, the Germans claiming to have captured the town on Nov. 30 and to have made deep penetrations beyond Volokolamsk. The Nazis were given no opportunity to consolidate their positions, however, for the Russians kept up their counter-attacks and recaptured a number of villages. On Dec. 20 Gen. Rokossovsky's forces recaptured the town as the result of a two-pronged drive after destroying enemy contingents. Five thousand Germans were killed in this battle, the German 291st Infantry Division being smashed. *See* Russia.

Voluntary Aid Detachment. *See* Women's Services.

Voroshilov, MARSHAL KLEMENT EFREMOVITCH (b. 1881). C.-in-C. of the Russian Northern Army. His heroic defence of Leningrad against the besieging

German forces during the autumn and winter of 1941–1942 was one of the greatest episodes of the war. Voroshilov was People's Commissar for Defence from 1925 to 1940, and on May 7, 1940, he was appointed Deputy-President of the Council of People's Commissars and Chairman of the Committee of Defence attached to that body. He was succeeded as Commissar of Defence by Timoshenko (*q.v.*).

Marshal Voroshilov,
Russian C.-in-C.
Photo, Pictorial Press

Vyasma. Situated 130 miles west of Moscow, on the road and railway to Smolensk, the Russian town of Vyasma was the centre of fierce fighting early in October 1941, during the German drive to the capital. On Oct. 13 the Russians announced its evacuation. Fighting again flared up in this sector in March 1942, when the Russians advanced towards the town. On March 18 the Germans counter-attacked in a desperate effort to keep open the Vyasma " pocket." Two hundred thousand Germans were believed to be almost surrounded in this area.

W.A.A.F. (Women's Auxiliary Air Force). *See* Women's Services.

Wainwright, MAJ-GEN. JONATHAN M. C.in-C. of American-Filipino forces in the Philippine Islands. Gen. Wainwright took over the command in March 1942, when Gen. MacArthur (*q.v.*) left for Australia to take full command in the S.W. Pacific. His forces on the Bataan Peninsula were at once subjected to heavier pressure by the Japanese, but when, on March 22, the Japanese Gen. Yamashita made a demand for the surrender of the army on the peninsula and the fortress of Corregidor in Manila Bay, Gen. Wainwright ignored it. By counter-attacks he won back some territory gained by a full-scale attack by the enemy, inflicting many casualties ; but early in April he was forced to withdraw his little army from the mainland to the island fortress, an operation he accomplished with success. *See* Corregidor ; Philippines.

Gen. Wainwright,
C.-in-C. Philippines.
Photo, Topical Press

Wake Island. Coral island in the Pacific, midway between the Philippines and Hawaii. It has an area of only one square mile, and was a U.S. naval and air refuelling base. The Japanese attacked it suddenly on Dec. 8, 1941 ; it had only 12 'planes and eight of them were put out of action that day. During the following fourteen days the garrison of fewer than 400 U.S. Marines put up an heroic resistance against continuous bombing by strong enemy air forces and shells from naval units. During this fortnight practically every installation on the island was destroyed or seriously damaged, and casualties were suffered by the Marine Corps, for the island is flat and affords no shelter. The defenders shot down many enemy 'planes,

sank a light cruiser and a destroyer, and damaged other destroyers before abandoning a hopeless resistance. On Dec. 21 the last two U.S. 'planes took the air and destroyed several Japanese aircraft before they were themselves shot down. The next day the enemy landed on the island.

On Feb. 24, 1942, units of the U.S. Pacific Fleet raided Wake Island. Naval aircraft dropped 219 bombs on the Japanese-occupied base, and cruisers and destroyers carried out heavy shelling. Two enemy gunboats were sunk, many prisoners being taken, three seaplanes were destroyed at their moorings, and fuel and munitions dumps, hangars, runways and storehouses were laid waste. The only U.S. loss was one aircraft.

On June 29 it was announced that U.S. navy aircraft from Hawaii, 2,000 miles away, had attacked Wake Island, damaging the airfield and shore installations. The enemy's A.A. and fighter defence were weak. *See* Pacific.

Wallenius, GEN. K. MARRTI. Commander of the Finnish armies operating in the north in the Russo-Finnish war. He had fought against the Bolsheviks in the civil war of 1918, and became Chief of the General Staff in Finland. A writer as well as a daring soldier, he was a newspaper correspondent at Berlin when the war broke out on Nov. 30, 1939. He hurried home to defend his country against the Russian advance on the Petsamo front, his ski-patrols penetrating for miles into Russian territory and disorganizing the Leningrad–Murmansk Railway. When on Dec. 14, 1939, the Russians used aircraft and brought up reinforcements Gen. Wallenius withdrew his forces gradually, after setting fire to the nickel works near Petsamo.

Wanklyn, LT.-CMDR. MALCOLM DAVID, V.C., D.S.O. In command of H.M. Submarine Upholder, operating in the Mediterranean, Lt.-Cmdr. Wanklyn was the first submarine officer to be awarded the V.C. in this war, the honour being announced on Dec. 11, 1941, " for outstanding valour, determination, and leadership." Many exploits stood to the credit of this daring sailor. The sinking of two enemy supply ships had won him

Lt.-Cmdr. M. D. Wanklyn, awarded the V.C.
Photo, British Official

the D.S.O. His supreme achievement, however, was on the evening of May 24, 1941, when he sighted and pressed home an attack on a convoy off Sicily strongly protected by destroyers. His listening gear was out of action and it was too dark to rely on his periscope. He did his best with the periscope, but just as he was about to fire an enemy destroyer dashed towards him, and he only just escaped being rammed. Adjusting his periscope, he aimed at and sank a big troopship, whereupon the destroyer counter-attacked by dropping 37 depth charges near the Upholder in the course of 20 minutes. He brought his submarine undamaged into harbour, to sally out again from time to time and to sink one destroyer, one U-boat, two large troopships, one tanker, and three supply ships, while one cruiser and one destroyer had probably been destroyed by his torpedoes. Upholder was reported lost on patrol on Aug. 24. 1942 and her crew missing.

Warburton-Lee, CAPT. B. A. W., V.C. (d. 1940). Heroic captain of the destroyer squadron in the Battle of Narvik (*q.v.*). Capt. Warburton-Lee

Capt. Warburton-Lee,
first V.C. of the war.
Photo, Vandyk

had served in destroyers for 32 years when he was awarded the first V.C. of the Second World War for his heroic action at Narvik.

The Germans having landed troops and sent warships into the long fjord on which Narvik lies, the Admiralty sent word of what had happened to Capt. Warburton-Lee, who, with his flag on H.M.S. Hardy, was patrolling at the mouth of West Fjord with four other destroyers. Reporting to Whitehall that the German force was bigger than suspected, he added that all the same he intended to attack at dawn. The Admiralty wirelessed at 1 a.m. next day (April 10, 1940) that they considered his proposed action so hazardous that he must be the sole judge of whether to attack or not, but that whatever happened they would support him. His reply was laconic—" Going into action."

With snow falling, so that the sides of the two-mile-long fjord were invisible from his bridge, he led his little flotilla in. Reaching the bay in which Narvik lies, he signalled the other ships to patrol outside while he swept into the harbour at 20 knots to find it filled with German vessels. He promptly turned to port and fired torpedoes at a large German destroyer. His manoeuvre brought into view two more destroyers, at which he launched more torpedoes, and ordered his 4·7 guns to fire. The fire was returned with vigour, and, the heavy shore batteries having joined in and the Hardy having fired her torpedoes, Capt. Warburton-Lee withdrew outside the harbour to enable his other destroyers to enter. When these had wreaked havoc with shell and torpedo, he took the Hardy in a second time, attacking the shore batteries. As he sailed out again six torpedoes passed close to his ship, but the enemy fire had slackened. However, he decided to steam in a third time, but as he did so he sighted three large German destroyers coming out against him. A terrific running combat ensued. The Hardy was soon hit, but continued to fire back from all her guns until a shell burst on her bridge, reducing it to a shambles. The captain was wounded in the face and thrown on to the deck below. Another shell burst in the engine-room, and it became obvious that the Hardy was doomed. Though mortally wounded, Captain Warburton-Lee determined at least to save the lives of his gallant men, so the Hardy was beached and the last order from his lips was, " Abandon ship. Every man for himself—and Good Luck." His final signal to his consorts was, " Continue to engage the enemy."

Mr. McCracken, the gunner and a rating lashed their captain to a stretcher, which they lowered into the icy waters and slowly towed to the shore. When they reached it he was dead.

War Cabinet, BRITISH. A War Cabinet confined to a few Ministers having proved invaluable in 1916–1918, immediately on the outbreak of the Second Great War Mr. Chamberlain reorganized his Government and appointed eight members to join him in a special Cabinet so that decisions could be taken swiftly. By June 1940 this War Cabinet had been reduced from nine members to five, each member presiding over a special Committee. When Mr. Churchill succeeded Mr. Chamberlain he enlarged the War Cabinet to eight, his seven colleagues being Mr. Attlee, Mr. Greenwood, Mr. Bevin, Lord Halifax, Lord Beaverbrook, Sir John

Anderson, and Sir Kingsley Wood. There was a general opinion in Parliament that this War Cabinet was too large, so on Feb. 19, 1942, Mr. Churchill reconstituted it with the following Ministers : Mr. Churchill, Prime Minister and Minister of Defence ; Sir Stafford Cripps, Lord Privy Seal and Leader of the House of Commons ; Mr. Attlee, Deputy Prime Minister and Dominions Secretary ; Sir John Anderson, Lord President of the Council ; Mr. Eden, Foreign Secretary ; Mr. Oliver Lyttelton, Minister of State ; and Mr. Bevin, Minister of Labour and National Service. Later two new members were added: Mr. Casey, Minister of State in the Middle East, and Mr. S. M. Bruce, Australian representative in London. The new system freed Mr. Churchill from frequent attendance at the House of Commons.

Ward, SGT. JAMES ALLEN, V.C. (1919–1941). New Zealand airman, the winner of the 7th V.C. awarded to the R.A.F. in the Second Great War. Returning from a raid on Münster on July 7, 1941, his aircraft was attacked by a Messerschmitt 110 over the Zuyder Zee and set on fire close to the starboard engine. Climbing through the narrow astro-hatch and breaking the fabric to make footholds, Sgt. Ward descended three feet into the wing and reached the rear of the engine.

Sgt. J. A. Ward, R. A. F.,
awarded the V.C.
Photo, British Official

Though there was a great risk of his being blown off the 'plane he succeeded in smothering the flames, and he then tried to push an engine-cover through a hole in the wing on to a leaking pipe where the fire had started. He did enough to save the 'plane, which reached home safely. For this courageous feat Sgt. Ward was awarded the V.C., being the first New Zealander to receive this honour in this war. Unhappily he failed to return from a raid in Sept. 1941, and was posted missing, presumed killed.

Warsaw. Capital of Poland, on the River Vistula ; population (1938) 1,265,000. Of this historic city in peacetime we read in page 4201, and in the story of Poland are recorded some of the terrible sieges that have marked its progress since it became· the national capital some 400 years ago. Yet no disaster has stricken it so terribly as that which shocked the whole of the civilized world in the opening stages of the Second Great War. After bomb and shell had done their worst to the streets and· buildings of Warsaw, the inhabitants were treated as few have been treated by their victors in modern times.

They had hoped for a peaceful solution of what appeared to them to be a mere political dispute, when on Sept. 1, 1030, the air raid sirens sounded for the first time and, looking up, they saw German reconnaissance 'planes over their city. At 9 a.m. a second wave of German aircraft came over, and these dropped bombs, both incendiary and explosive. Though Polish fighter 'planes went up and drove the bombers away, five or six further raids followed. On Sept. 2, 3 and 4 the Germans bombed without respite. On Monday, Sept. 4, however, the muttering of distant guns was heard and the Polish Government left Warsaw for a safer place to the east, having entrusted the city to the Mayor, M. Starzynski, and Gen. Czuma.

By the end of the week the German Army had fought its way to within five miles of the city, but its defences

SMOKE RINGS OF WAR ABOVE RAVAGED WARSAW

Warsaw suffered heavily in air raids from the outbreak of war until the enforced capitulation of the Polish capital. This photograph was taken just after an incendiary bomb had burst. A clearly defined smoke ring, such as nearly always occurs after the explosion of this type of bomb, is seen rising on the left. As a precautionary measure several of the horses in the foreground have been turned round in their shafts to prevent the animals bolting.

Photo, Planet News

held and the enemy pushed on east of them. They dared not leave such a centre in their rear, however, so they threatened to lay waste the city completely by bombs and shells regardless of the fate of civilians unless it was surrendered by the night of Sept. 17. Regarding Warsaw as the saviour of Poland's honour, Gen. Czuma and the Mayor refused the demand with scorn, the Mayor broadcasting a moving appeal for help to the peoples of the civilized world. Over 1,000 civilians were killed each day in the continual bombardment which ensued. Churches, hospitals, power stations, and finally the waterworks were destroyed, yet all were for resistance to the bitter end. The end came when the Germans captured the forts defending the city and, after 20 days of heroic defence, the Germans entered the smoking ruins on Oct. 1. Even on Oct. 5, when Hitler himself flew there to make a triumphal entry, the fires were still burning. The Gestapo then took charge and all Polish culture was uprooted, while thousands of innocent Poles were taken away to slave-labour in German factories and farms. Warsaw's streets were renamed and Herr Frank, the German Governor-General, proclaimed that the German flag would fly over Poland for ever.

All Warsaw's historical monuments were destroyed, including that of Chopin, whose music was strictly forbidden. All the treasures of the ancient Royal Castle of Zamek were transported to Germany and all high schools were closed, for the Herdenvolk (subject race) needed no cultural knowledge. Warsaw itself was divided into three areas : the best for German settlers, the second for Poles, and the third for Jews, 500,000 of whom were herded into a walled ghetto in medieval fashion, where they were allowed 60 grammes of bread daily, one half of that granted to the Poles.

In a statement to the U.S.A. in June 1941 the Polish Ambassador said " there is not a single principle of the right of human beings, nor a single clause of positive international law, which has not been ground under foot by the occupying forces."

Warspite, H.M.S. British battleship of the Queen Elizabeth class. Launched 1913 ; 30,600 tons ; eight 15-in. and eight 6-in. guns, and eight 4-in. A.A. guns; extensively modernized at a cost of £2,362,000 in 1937, with space for more aircraft than the four originally carried. The Warspite, under the command of Vice-Adm. Whitworth (*q.v.*), was sent by the Admiralty to support the attack on the German warships and shore batteries at Narvik which Capt. Warburton-Lee (*q.v.*) had made on April 10, 1940. Accompanied by a destroyer flotilla to sweep up mines, the Warspite proceeded up the fjord and sank four enemy destroyers in Narvik Bay (*see* p. 292, this vol.). Three others which fled up Rombaks Fjord were also destroyed. On the night of March 28, 1941, the Warspite, as flagship of Sir Andrew Cunningham, took a leading part in the naval victory of Cape Matapan, when her 15-in. guns sank the Italian cruiser Fiume, having made her burst amidships within seven seconds of her first broadside, and later her sister ship, Zara, on which was the Italian Admiral Cantoni.

War Transport, Ministry of. *See* Transport, War, Ministry of.

Waterhen, H.M.S. Destroyer launched in 1918 and handed over to the Royal Australian Navy in 1932. She displaced 1,100 tons and carried four 4-in. guns and a complement of 134. Her loss in the Mediterranean, due to an enemy bombing attack, was announced on July 5, 1941. All her officers and crew were saved. The Waterhen was the first warship of the R.A.N. to be lost by enemy action.

Wavell, Gen. Sir Archibald, g.c.m.g., m.c. (b. 1883). C.-in-C. India from July 1, 1941. Gen. Wavell served with distinction in both the South African and the First Great Wars, being Bt.-Lieut.-Col. in the Egyptian Expeditionary Force. In 1937 he returned to Palestine for a few months to command our forces there when the Arab-Jewish crisis was serious. In July 1939, when the war became imminent,

Gen. Wavell was appointed G.O.C. Middle East, with orders to prepare the defence plans of the forces stationed there and to coordinate their action in the event of war.

When, in May 1940, it seemed likely that Italy would enter the war, Gen. Wavell posted the British and Egyptian troops in their emergency stations, while the Egyptian Government evacuated the civilian populations from the frontier towns and villages. All was in readiness, therefore, when the first frontier incident occurred on June 13. The subsequent campaigns both in the Western Desert and in Abyssinia were directed by him with success; so hard did he hit the Italians in Libya that by Feb. 7, 1941, the important town of Benghazi was in his hands, while, in Abyssinia, on May 5, Haile Selassie (q.v.) was able to re-enter his capital.

Gen. Sir Archibald Wavell, C.-in-C. India.
Photo, British Official

On July 1 Gen. Wavell was appointed C.-in-C. India, exchanging with Gen. Auchinleck. There was immense responsibility, not only in India itself, but westward, to send help into Persia, and eastward, to meet the threat from Japan, Burma being added to his command a few days after he had attended an Allied Conference at Chungking, where, on Dec. 23, it was arranged that Chinese troops should serve under him in Burma. As a result of the intensity of the Japanese drive towards Singapore he was Supreme Commander of a Unified Command of the S.W. Pacific Area from Jan. 3 to March 2, 1942, when he reassumed his task as C.-in-C. India, being also made a member of the Executive Council of the Governor-General. The political crisis in that country added to his work of organizing India's defences against the rapid progress of the foe, but he found time to aid Sir Stafford Cripps in the complicated negotiations with the various Parties. He had already won their confidence by a candid statement at Delhi on March 13, in which he confessed that our setbacks were due to our "always having been behind the clock," adding that every preparation was being made in all three Services against any sea-borne attack by the Japanese.

Sir Archibald, of all our war-leaders, had a keen appreciation of what is required to vanquish the enemy, as his little book on Generals and Generalship, published in 1941, showed. He was also gifted with high qualities of statesmanship.

Welles, SUMNER (b. 1892). U.S. Under-Secretary of State from 1937. Mr. Welles had been associated with the Foreign Affairs department of America since 1915, and was especially successful in matters concerning Latin America. He was U.S. delegate to the Pan-American Conference at Rio de Janeiro in January 1942, at which the 21 American States decided to break off economic and financial relations with the Axis Powers, nine having already declared war against them. In his speech at this conference Mr. Welles declared that the security of 300,000,000 people of the Western

Sumner Welles, U.S. diplomat.
Photo, Wide World

Hemisphere, and the independence of each of the countries there represented, would be determined by whether the American nations stood together in that hour of peril.

At the beginning of 1940 President Roosevelt sent Mr. Welles to Europe on a " fact-finding " tour, during which he visited Count Ciano, Ribbentrop, President Lebrun, Lord Halifax, Gen. Sikorski, and other European leaders. When, in August 1941, Germany put pressure on the Vichy Government for more collaboration, Mr. Welles promptly stated that in future the attitude of the U.S. Government towards France would be determined by the effectiveness with which France defended her territory against the aggression of the Axis Powers ; and he protested vigorously against the handing over of Indo-China to Japan. When, in February 1942, there were rumours that Madagascar, too, might be made accessible to the Japanese, and that Tunisia was being made available for the transport of supplies to Gen. Rommel's forces in Libya, Mr. Welles made it clear to the Vichy Government that their relations with America rested on the formal assurance of neutrality and their promise not to relinquish control over the French Fleet and French possessions. One of his next steps was to recognize De Gaulle and to open an American Consulate at Brazzaville, in French Equatorial Africa, which acknowledged the authority of the Free French.

KEY TO THE WAR SITUATION IN WEST AFRICA

British possessions and Free French territories in West Africa formed an enormous bloc against Axis designs in that region. The speeding up of communications and the increasing flow of war supplies were made possible by the building of roads and improved facilities of ports. See Equatorial Africa.

West Africa. A glance at the map of West Africa supplies at once the key to the war situation there, for it reveals not only French West Africa but also Britain's West African possessions, Gambia, Sierra Leone, the Gold Coast and Nigeria. This vast coastline, stretching as it does, roughly, from Cape Blanco, where French Mauritania meets Spain's Rio de Oro, to the mouth of the Ubangi, upon which river stands Brazzaville (q.v.), the capital of French Equatorial

Africa (q.v.), boasts but few ports. Dakar (q.v.) is the northernmost of them ; Bathurst, Gambia, and some inferior ports in the Gulf of Guinea, and Loango, at the mouth of the Ubangi, make up the rest.

Even in times of peace the lack of ports was an impediment to trade. Cargoes have to be unloaded three miles off shore into surf boats beached by skilful native boatmen. In war this coast, facing across the South Atlantic towards South America, became of major importance, and the possession of its few ports, of which Dakar is the only one capable of taking a big ship, an equally urgent matter. For possession of the West African coastline means control of the South Atlantic, and that means control of one of Britain's major sources of seaborne supplies. The South Atlantic is the black spot for British shipping, and control of it is, therefore, a major affair of sea strategy.

That is one aspect of the West African problem. There is another. When war broke out practically all this seaboard was in the hands of allies—the French and British. That condition was drastically changed, and the British Navy, operating in waters thick with hostile craft, had to do so off a continental shore, vast stretches of which were Vichy-controlled. To have left the port of Dakar free would have been to run the danger of Vichy surrendering the giant battleship Richelieu, lying there, to Germany; so in 1940 the British blew off her propellers with a mine planted by a handful of ratings and one officer operating from a small boat with muffled engines. And it was for the same reason that the bombardment of the port was attempted by a combined Free French and British expedition, an enterprise now generally regarded as ill-advised and misconceived (see Dakar).

The result of these naval activities was the intensification of the bad feeling existing between a section of the French colonials and the British; roughly, the governmental officials and Governor-General Boisson, plus army, were fairly friendly towards the British and certainly not hostile towards the Germans; while to the naval people Britain seemed as much an open enemy as Nazi Germany herself. The sentiment of the French navy, which found its type in the arch-appeaser, Admiral Darlan, flows from an ancient grievance, for in history the British ships trounced the French so often that Britain became the traditional enemy of France afloat.

Nor was this all. The map reveals both the extent and the barren bleakness of the vast hinterland of the West African possession (it is half as large as the U.S.A.). Much desert, more semi-desert, and great areas made uninhabitable by the tsetse-fly render French West Africa dependent upon much imported food. Most of this, normally, came into the harbour of Dakar, but could do so no longer because the British Navy granted no navicerts to Vichy ships. So, too, with ships sailing from the West African port with such cargoes as peanuts (valuable for making margarine) for France. Though ostensibly destined for France, the bulk of such cargoes, it was found, went into Germany.

At any moment, therefore, possession of Dakar might become a strategical imperative, not alone for Britain, but for the United States, and an attempt upon it might come in a war notable for its dramatic developments.

An event which would bring such action closer would be the recall of the moderate Governor-General Boisson and the appointment of a naval man of Darlan's colour. That would hand over the French West African possessions to appeasers who came ever closer to Nazi Germany's side.

Britain possesses no West African port that is of any use to her Navy. This part of the coast is low, with beaches over which the breakers come in from the South Atlantic in vast cannonade. Even so, the West Coast is important and valuable, since from it the British could patrol the danger zones of the South Atlantic routes by air. In March 1941 an R.A.F. Coastal Command was established in West Africa to cover the South Atlantic. The personnel who established this air base had to contend with every manner of difficulty: the making of runways in the savannah, the extraction of oil from local ground nuts, the contriving of filter substitutes, and much else. In addition, they were exposed to disease and dependent on local native unskilled labour.

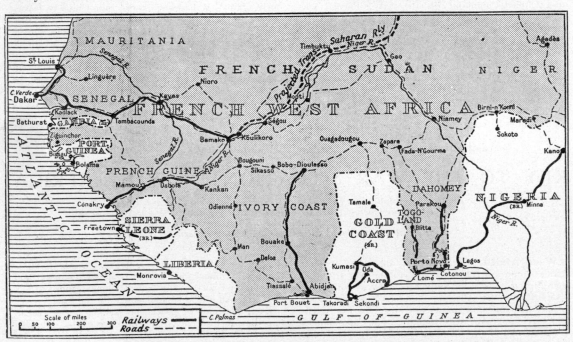

Vast in extent, French West Africa contains large tracts of desert, yet it is of great importance in the Allied plans.

By courtesy of " Foreign Affairs "

HEROIC FORT OF WESTERPLATTE

Hoisting the German flag over Westerplatte, the Polish fortified position near Danzig, which was magnificently defended by a small Polish garrison. The ruined wall testifies to the fierce bombardment launched by the enemy—an onslaught that resulted in the capitulation of the Poles.
Photo, Central Press

Even so, operational flying was maintained throughout the year uninterruptedly, despite electrical storms, tornadoes and the torrential rains of the rainy season. This Command has two main duties : to hunt and bomb U-boats and enemy surface craft, and to escort convoys, maintaining also constant air reconnaissance. The Command is now a separate one. It has also power boats, bomb scows and motor launches, and, inland, a radio station. Flying-boats and reconnaissance bombers are the main types of aircraft in use.

It is the long-range machines of this Command that have so often located and contrived the rescue of British seamen drifting, thirsty and starving, on rafts or in open boats, for this is the main graveyard of the Battle of the Atlantic.

This coast is also used by United States and British civil aircraft and is being increasingly used by United States bombers making the South Atlantic crossing, en route for North Africa.

On June 8, 1942, Lord Swinton was appointed Minister Resident of Cabinet rank in West Africa.

Western Approaches. Term given to the traffic lanes along which our island's supplies reach us across the Atlantic. The north-western approaches include the routes followed by vessels from Canada and the U.S., while the south-western include those from Central and South America, Africa, and the Far East. From the outbreak of the war surface raiders, U-boats, and 'planes have harried our shipping in this area, which may now be said to stretch from the coast of N.E. Africa to the Arctic, and to include the Bay of

Biscay, the English Channel, the Irish Sea and St. George's Channel, the North Sea and the open seas between Norway and Iceland, Iceland and the Faroes, the Faroes and the Orkneys, and the region beyond Ireland. So vital were unity of action and unity of command in this vast area, which increased in extent as time passed, that Adm. Sir Percy Noble was appointed Commander - in - Chief of The Western Approaches on March 14, 1941. *See* Atlantic, Battle of.

Western Desert. *See* Libya ; North Africa.

Westerplatte. Polish naval base and munitions store dominating Danzig from the promontory east of an old outlet of the Vistula and four miles north of the Free City. The Westerplatte was attacked by the Nazis from land, sea and air in the first days of the war, the German cruiser Schleswig-Holstein raining shells from close range. The heroic garrison held out under its commander, Maj. Koscianski, for a week, obeying the order broadcast to them from Warsaw by Marshal Smigly-Rydz : " Soldiers of the Westerplatte, fight ! Poland watches your gallant struggle with pride. Fight for Poland to the last man." The little company withstood the bombs from the air, the shells from the German warships, and at least a whole division of the German Army until the morning of Sept. 7, 1939, when, their ammunition exhausted, they surrendered to the captain of the Schleswig-Holstein. Even the Germans praised the gallant stand they had made. *See* Danzig ; Poland.

West Indies. *See* British Colonies.

Weygand, GEN. MAXIME (b. 1867). C.-in-C. of the French Army, May – June 1940 ; High Commissioner of French North Africa, Nov. 16, 1940, to Nov. 20, 1941. General Weygand was Chief of Staff to Marshal Foch in the First Great War, and he added to his fame by helping Gen. Sikorski to save Warsaw from the Red Army in 1920. He was High Commissioner of Mandated Syria from 1923 to 1924 and C.-in-C. of the French Army from 1931 to 1935. After Gen. Gamelin failed and was dismissed, the old and popular general was recalled from retirement to the supreme command on May 19, 1940. His efforts to hold up the German onslaught proved unavailing, and after the surrender of France he was appointed Minister of National Defence in Pétain's Government.

His admirers in this country were disappointed by

Gen. Weygand, French C.-in-C.

his appeals to the Colonial commanders to maintain confidence in Pétain's Government, though Gen. Noguès had declared that " not an inch of French territory would be yielded to Italy," and De Gaulle had formed the nucleus of a Free French Party. Gen. Weygand was one of the four members of the armed forces in the Authoritarian Government formed by Pétain on July 14, and about this time he is reported to have protested against the German infringement of the armistice respecting the seizure of French money.

Appointed C.-in-C. and High Commissioner of North Africa because his name carried weight with the armed forces there, he received power to expel any " dangerous person," and he paid visits to Senegal, Dahomey, the Ivory Coast, and the Niger Territory. Broadcasting from Algiers on Jan. 2, 1941, he spoke of the anguish that caused the French colonials to accept false news derogatory to Marshal Pétain, but his general attitude was much hated by the Germans. They hated him, too, because in a broadcast on Feb. 7 he denied the suggestion that Bizerta, the port of Tunis, was about to be handed over to Germany. There is little doubt that he detested the enemies of France, both within and without her borders, yet he probably did not trust Britain, for apparently he agreed with the decision to fight in Syria.

In July he was appointed Gov.-Gen. of Algeria, but was deprived of all military powers and subordinated to Admiral Darlan when that hater of Britain became second in the State to Pétain. The German masters of the Vichy Government then worked to have Weygand removed, and on Nov. 20, 1941, the aged general was dismissed from his post in North Africa, that post being abolished and replaced by a Secretariat directly under the control of Admiral Darlan.

White Russia (Byelo-Russia). Soviet Republic west of Russia proper, north of the Ukraine, and east of Poland; capital, Minsk; area, 59,022 sq. m. (in 1938); pop. 5,570,000. By the German-Soviet Treaty signed on Sept. 29, 1939, under which Poland was partitioned, White Russia received many thousands of square miles, her eastern boundary being extended to the River Bug, so that Brest-Litovsk became a frontier town and Bialystok came well within the new frontier. When, in June 1941, Germany tore up the Treaty and attacked her temporary ally, her forces speedily overran White Russia, though the crossing of the River Beresina was made difficult by the heroic resistance of the Russian army. In the spring of 1942 the Russian armies, in their counter-thrust on Smolensk, penetrated into White Russia beyond this town, which had been made a stronghold by the invaders.

Adm. Sir W. Whitworth, Second Sea Lord.
Photo, G.P.U.

Whitworth, Vice-Adm. Sir William Jock, k.c.b., d.s.o. Second Sea Lord of the Admiralty; appointed in succession to Adm. Sir Charles Little on May 20, 1941. At the beginning of the Second Great War Vice-Adm. Whitworth was in command of the Battle Cruiser Squadron, but he transferred his flag to the Warspite (*q.v.*) when that battleship was sent to destroy the German naval force which had occupied Narvik (*q.v.*). His daring entry of the mined fjord leading up to that port in snowy and misty weather was proof of his enterprising character, while his ordering of the successful action that followed won high praise from the Admiralty.

Wilhelmina, Queen of the Netherlands (b. 1880). When the dispute between Germany and Poland had reached its climax and war seemed inevitable Queen Wilhelmina, in association with Leopold, King of the Belgians, offered, on Aug. 29, 1939, to mediate between the two parties. But, Hitler having decided on the destruction of Poland, the Queen's good offices were ignored. On the same day she broadcast that " should the horrible possibility of a conflict materialize, Holland will maintain a strict neutrality with all the means at her command." Two months later she again endeavoured, but without success, to stay the conflict before it grew into a World War. Writing for King Leopold and herself, she offered to do all in her power to help the combatant nations to reach an agreement. On her

part, the Queen continued to act in the true spirit of neutrality, declining to approach the Allies for help in anticipation of any possible attack.

When, on May 10, 1940, the German ultimatum was delivered, some hours after the actual attack, Queen

Queen Wilhelmina of the Netherlands.
Photo, Wide World

Wilhelmina refused to submit, broadcasting to her people " a flaming protest against this unprecedented violation of good faith and violation of all that is decent between cultured States . . . I and my Government will do our duty. Do your duty everywhere and in all circumstances. Every man to his post." As if to wreak vengeance on her the Nazi parachutists, clad in uniforms not their own and armed with tommy-guns and grenades, sought to capture her; but she managed to escape in the nick of time and was conducted to a British warship which

had entered a near-by harbour. Brought at once to England, on the evening of May 15, she made a never-to-be forgotten broadcast, urging all Dutchmen never to submit to the Nazi ascendancy, for " morally we can never be conquered; our spirit will remain unbroken because our conscience is clear."

Having established her Government in London, Queen Wilhelmina vigorously appealed to her countrymen all over the world to stand fast; and the tenacity of her subjects in the East Indies against the Japanese bore proof of her inspiration. *See* Netherlands.

Wilhelmshaven. German naval base in Jade Bay on the North Sea, 41 miles west of Bremen. Its docks could accommodate the biggest battleships and its surroundings bristle with A.A. defences. Wilhelmshaven was an objective of intense bombing; from Sept. 4, 1939, to June 3, 1942, it was attacked 65 times. So great has been the damage wrought that this naval base is now of little use for Germany's bigger warships, though smaller craft seek its protection.

Mr. Wendell Willkie, American politician.
Photo, Keystone

Willkie, Mr. Wendell Lewis (b. 1892). Republican candidate for the U.S. Presidency, 1940. Mr. Willkie loyally worked for his successful rival in rousing his fellow-countrymen to the urgency of the war efforts, making a whirlwind tour of investigation in Britain in the spring of 1941. *See* Roosevelt.

Lt. E. C. T. Wilson, awarded the V.C.
Photo. " Daily Mirror "

Wilson, Lt. Eric C. T., v.c. Officer of the East Surreys, attached as Captain to the Somali Camel Corps. When, on Aug. 10, 1940, the enemy attacked the machine-gun post in the key position of Observation Hill above the Tug Argan Gap in British Somaliland, he inflicted so many casualties on them that they brought up a pack battery to within 700 yards and fired two shells through the loopholes of his post. Lt. Wilson was wounded severely in the shoulder, his Somali sergeant was killed at his side, and many of his men were wounded. The machine-guns had been blown off their stands, yet in spite of his pain Lt. Wilson replaced them and returned the enemy's fire. On the following two days, Aug. 11 and 12, although it had been impossible to tend his wounds, Lt. Wilson continued to man his guns, on which the field artillery of the Italians was now concentrating. Three days later, however, two of the machine-gun posts were blown in, but Lt. Wilson refused to give up the struggle until 5.0 p.m., when the enemy finally overran his post and he was taken prisoner. Promoted Captain, he got back to England in July, 1942, and then received his V.C.

Gen. Lord Wilson, G.O.C. 9th Army, Middle East.
Photo, British Official

Wilson, GEN. LORD HENRY MAITLAND, G.B.E., K.C.B., D.S.O. (b. 1881). Raised to peerage Jan. 1946. G.O.C. Ninth Army in Middle East. At the beginning of the war Gen Wilson was appointed G.O.C.-in-C. in Egypt, and led the British advance in the Western Desert to Benghazi, where he became Military Governor of Cyrenaica. When the Nazis invaded Greece Gen. Wilson commanded the British forces dispatched there, and when the French in Syria decided to resist the Allies he speedily defeated their forces, signing the Armistice Convention on July 12, 1941. On Dec. 4, 1941, it was officially announced at Jerusalem that Gen. Wilson, G.O.C. Syria and Palestine, had been appointed G.O.C. the newly-established Ninth Army in the Middle East. *See* North Africa, Campaign.

Winant, JOHN GILBERT (b. 1889). U.S. Ambassador to the Court of St. James's from Feb. 6, 1941. Mr. Winant had previously been Director of the International Office and Chairman of the U.S. Social Security Board. He was a personal friend of President Roosevelt. In

J. G. Winant, U.S. Ambassador to Britain.
Photo, Topical Press

all his speeches after he arrived Mr. Winant showed himself a true friend of this country and of the aspirations of its people. *See* United States.

Windsor, H.R.H. EDWARD, DUKE OF, K.G. (b. 1894). Formerly King Edward VIII of England. When the World War threatened, the Duke of Windsor emerged from his retirement to make a broadcast to America on May 8, 1939, urging the statesmen of the different countries to strive for peace, and not to regard themselves as " good Frenchmen, Italians, Germans, Americans, or Britons " only, but as good citizens of the world. In September he returned to England, where, having relinquished his rank of Field-Marshal, he was appointed a Major-General for service on the Staff in France. When France surrendered he made his way with the Duchess to Madrid and Lisbon, from which port he sailed to the Bahamas to take up the Governorship. His appointment to this post was announced by the Colonial Office on July 9, 1940.

Winkelman, GEN. HENRI GERARD. C.-in-C. of the Dutch Land and Sea Forces. General Winkelman, having previously organized the defences of Holland, withstood the German onslaught for four days, but on May 14, 1940, he broadcast that his troops had been obliged to lay down their arms, in order to save the civil population and to avoid further bloodshed. He was taken prisoner to Germany. *See* Netherlands.

Gen. H. G. Winkelman, Dutch C.-in-C.
Photo, Planet News

W.L.A. (Women's Land Army). *See* Women's Services.

Wolfenden, JOHN FREDERICK (b. 1906). Director of Pre-Entry Training, Air Ministry, from January 1941 to March 1942. Before this appointment he was headmaster of Uppingham School from 1934. *See* Air Training Corps.

Wolmer, ROUNDELL CECIL PALMER, VISCOUNT (b. 1887). In February 1942 Lord Wolmer was appointed Minister for Economic Warfare in succession to Dr. Hugh Dalton. Previous to this he was Director of Cement, Ministry of Works and Buildings, from 1940.

WOMEN ANSWER THE CHALLENGE OF WAR

Never before had women undertaken so many varied tasks in the country's defence. Thousands joined the three highly organized military services—the W.R.N.S., A.T.S. and W.A.A.F. Others performed important work in order to release men for active service.

Women's Services. There are three chief women's Services linked directly with the fighting forces and set up and designed to be complementary to Army, Navy and R.A.F. They are the Auxiliary Territorial Service (A.T.S.), the Women's Royal Naval Service (W.R.N.S.) and the Women's Auxiliary Air Force (W.A.A.F.). There are also a number of other women's Services associated with the fighting forces or of value to them as means whereby men are released for active service, namely, the Women's Voluntary Service, the Women's Land Army, the Mechanized

Transport Corps, and the several branches of nursing as set forth in detail below.

AUXILIARY TERRITORIAL SERVICE. This is the earliest in the present war and, perhaps, the most familiar of the women's war organizations. Though technically the A.T.S. came into being only in September 1938, its pedigree may fairly be traced to the Women's Auxiliary Army Corps (W.A.A.C.), a body brought into being in the last war to replace 12,000 soldiers in non-combatant jobs in France and, later, in the Home Commands. This Force was renamed Queen

Mary's Army Auxiliary Corps. Before demobilization 57,000 women had served as Waacs.

The A.T.S. was brought into being following Munich, as a Territorial Army ancillary. Its original personnel was composed of women with previous war service, and to these women goes the honour of having passed on the fine traditions of service learned before 1918.

By the summer of 1942 there were over 100,000 women in the A.T.S. and the enrolment of another 100,000 was planned. How this new army of women was being sought all knew who saw—and who did not ? —the clever posters displayed throughout the country.

The Chief Controller, Mrs. Jean Knox, summed up the purposes of the Service, saying : " This being a total war, the first in history, women fit in wherever

WOMEN OF BRITAIN IN A.A. DEFENCE
Members of the A.T.S. specially selected to train for A.A. duties listen attentively to the description of an anti-aircraft gun. Their duties include the working of predictors and height-finders—an essential factor in anti-aircraft defence.
Photo, British Official

they can be useful and replace men needed for rougher and tougher jobs. As I see it, the factor of women in war work of all kinds is going to swing the balance of this war."

Unlike our Russian allies, Britain still hesitates to place lethal weapons in the hands of her daughters, or to permit them to take part in actual fighting. Therefore, although women in the A.T.S. were on the fringe of the battle they were not yet in it, even though they located targets for A.A. guns and did such dangerous jobs as fitting detonators into finished bombs.

Unlike Wrens, who are not subject to Acts regulating the Royal Navy, the A.T.S. now comes under the Army Act. Officers hold the King's Commission and those who enrol do so for the " duration " and are liable for home or foreign service. It is of interest to recall that in 1940 the A.T.S. was among the last to leave Paris.

The age limits are 17½–43. Veterans of the last war are accepted up to 50. Discipline is exactly like that of the Army. Courts martial are held at which A.T.S. officers conduct both defence and prosecution. As with the Army of today, a citizen army, all commissions in the A.T.S. are from the ranks with the exception that women with science degrees or other high qualifications may go direct to the O.C.T.U.

The hours of work are not fixed but depend upon circumstances, but auxiliaries (privates) are entitled to 48 hours (pass out) per month, and 7 days privilege leave with pay every 3 months. Accommodation is usually

in requisitioned hotels or houses or barracks ; there is sharing of rooms, but no big dormitories. Personal belongings, flowers, etc., are encouraged. The uniform of the A.T.S. is smart. The tunic is square-shouldered with neat belted waist, the skirt panelled and slim fitting, the greatcoat unbelted but waisted. Colour is now supplied by the smart new field service cap in orange, brown and leaf-green. Scots units wear the tartan skirt. Discreet make-up is permitted. The food is good, plentiful and scientifically balanced.

When an auxiliary joins up she must go through the fixed basic training. This includes lectures on army organization, discipline, physical training, games. After preliminary training the recruits go on to special instructional centres where they get instruction in their own trades. Cadets for commission—two O.C.T.U.s handle 500 every six weeks—have lectures which include gas, psychology, army law, messing, quartering, welfare, hygiene and ceremonial.

Women at the Guns
The range of jobs done by auxiliaries has widened steadily. For example, in February 1940, 25,300 A.T.S. were working as follows : 11,500 clerks ; 6,000 orderlies ; 6,000 cooks ; 1,800 drivers. In 1942 jobs included confidential work of vital importance, calling for the highest standard of integrity, and high administrative posts. Auxiliaries are cooks, draughtswomen, clerks, pay-clerks, typists, and stenographers, convoy drivers and dispatch riders, switchboard operators and teleprinter operators, storewomen, orderlies, cinema projectionists and film librarians.

There are also special branches such as the Military Police Section, and Radiolocation and Anti-aircraft duties. The development of the last-named thrilled the A.T.S., for women for these duties needed characteristics usually regarded as masculine : manual dexterity and cleverness with gear and gadgets for the installation, maintenance and repair, the testing and so forth of apparatus. Another interesting job now being done by the A.T.S. is fire-control equipment by which targets are picked up by wireless in fog or at night working with camera and theodolite. Last there is work on Army Experimental Ranges. It is secret work, and of the highest importance. Auxiliaries on it wear blue reefer jackets and white skirts. This work includes testing new ammunition and other gunnery experiments.

The A.T.S. has a distinguished war record for courage and devotion to duty. On April 17, 1942, the first A.T.S. in the A.A. Command to be killed in action lost her life through a bomb-splinter as she stood at a predictor on a South Coast gun site during a raid. She was Pte. Nora Caveney, aged 18, formerly a worker in a silk factory. She was following an enemy 'plane and was " on target " when she collapsed. Another A.A. girl immediately took her place at the predictor, the other A.T.S. personnel kept on working with precision throughout the hour-long raid, and the guns continued firing without one moment's delay. Pte. Caveney was buried with full military honours.

In the A.T.S. is incorporated the First Aid Nursing Yeomanry, now called the Women's Transport Service. The F.A.N.Y. was founded in 1907, and served throughout the First Great War, being one of the first women's organizations to go overseas, where its members did valuable ambulance convoy work and nursing. The Corps subsequently carried on its training as a mechanical transport unit. In 1938 the Army Council invited its cooperation for the formation of the new

THE COUNTRY NEEDED THEM AND THEY CAME

1. Members of the W.V.S. are seen cutting up strips of material for camouflage netting.   2. A member of the Girls' Training Corps ; the V hat badge stands for the 5th group of the corps.   3. A Wren at work in a naval pinnace.   4. Nurses of the Civil Nursing Reserve training in an operating theatre.   5. Dispatch riders of the Women's Mechanized Transport Corps.   6. The Land Girl's armlet awarded to members of the W.L.A. after two years' service.

Photos, L.N.A.; Planet News; G.P.U.; Central Press; Sport & General

A.T.S., the "Fannys" being called upon to provide the personnel of all ranks required for the Motor Transport Companies to work with the Army. All these members were called up in September 1939, and some 2,000 are serving with the A.T.S. These drivers wear the name F.A.N.Y. underneath "Women's Transport Service" on the sleeve. In addition, a voluntary section of the Corps still exists whose members serve with the British Red Cross Society and the Polish Forces. They did admirable work in Finland in 1939–40 and in France before the Armistice.

WOMEN'S ROYAL NAVAL SERVICE. The W.R.N.S. is an auxiliary body like the A.T.S. It was set up to replace various categories of Naval Personnel in Shore Establishments, and thus to release men for active service. Its members perform no sea service, but in all its doings this Service conforms to naval usage and naval ways of speech. Many of its members are women with serving men-folk or with naval connexions. Though Wrens never go to sea, they often go ashore. Though they never board a ship, they always sleep below decks in cabins. When they keep house, they never use a kitchen, deigning only to work in galleys, like sailormen. In short, while still remaining outside the Senior Service in so far as they are not amenable to the disciplinary Acts governing the men in H.M. Royal Navy, the Wrens approximate their ways and days so far as possible to life aboard ship or in naval establishments.

There were, early in 1942, some 24,000 Wren officers and ratings. Entry is subject to fourteen days' probation, with notice on either side. The rating does not enlist: she enrols. That means that she is not subject to court martial, as is her sister of the A.T.S., but is exposed to the ignominy of an action in the civil courts should she default on her contract. Thus, since all rests upon esprit de corps, the Wrens have established a very high standard of conduct, and disciplinary troubles are virtually unknown.

Many Jobs for Women in the Navy

The Wrens accept ratings from 17½ to 45, women with special qualifications being taken up to 49. Recruits, having passed the character test and medical examination (strict), enter as either "Mobiles" or "Immobiles," the latter being for girls ordinarily resident near a naval establishment. Initial training in a Drafting Depot follows, and here the newcomer learns naval ways and naval talk. The categories of work done by this Service are wide and include the following. Clerical: confidential book corrector, mail clerk, shorthand typist, supply assistant, writer, recruiting assistant. Communications: coder, signal office watchkeeper, telephone switchboard operator, teleprinter, visual signaller, wireless telegraphist. Technical and Operational: aircraft checker, battery charger, cinema operator, meteorologist, parachute packer, plotter, radio mechanic or operator, photographic assistant. Domestic: cook, porter, laundry maid, steward, quarters assistant. Transport: motor driver, dispatch rider. Miscellaneous: maintenance staff, boats crew (harbour work only), gardener, messenger. The uniform is naval blue, with circular (bell-bottomed) skirt, the officer's hat being designed on those worn in the days of Nelson. Rank badges are of gold braid, and triangular.

As is now the rule throughout the fighting forces, promotion to commissioned rank is from the ranks

(R.N. excepted). In the Wrens outstanding women get commissioned rank very quickly.

The head of the Wrens is Mrs. Laughton Mathews, C.B.E., with the rank of Director. A recruit of the first day of the new Service, Mrs. Laughton Mathews was largely instrumental in building up the present organization. In the last war, as Miss Laughton, she received the M.B.E. for her work with the Women's Royal Naval Service.

WOMEN'S AUXILIARY AIR FORCE. As with the two Services already dealt with, the object of the W.A.A.F. is the replacement of men by women, in this case to release personnel for flying duties. Here, too, we find that the great organization of today has its origin in the last war, being the youngest of the three Sister Services (1918). Linking the present Service with the old W.R.A.F. is a small organization known as the Emergency Service. It was brought into being by a

VITAL WORK AT AN R.A.F. STATION
These three flight mechanics of the W.A.A.F. look very efficient in their dungarees. They are checking over a Miles Master III training aircraft before a flight.
Photo, Central Press

few clear-visioned women, one of whom, Air Commandant Katherine Jane Trefusis Forbes, C.B.E., was in 1942 its Director, her appointment dating from September 1938, when Dame Helen Gwynne-Vaughan was in command.

Recruits are accepted between the ages of 17½ and 44; they join for "duration" and must be prepared to serve anywhere at home or abroad. The status of the recruit is that of a serving airman, since the the W.A.A.F. is an integral part of the R.A.F. (Defence (Women's Forces) Regulations, 1941). The work done by the personnel covers nearly every activity of the Service bar actual flying, and includes over fifty trades, of which the following are examples: cine projector, clerk, cook, dispenser, fabric worker, flight mechanic, masseuse, parachute packer, pigeon keeper, radiographer, radio-wireless mechanic, tailor, tracer, workshop hand. The tendency is to increase the scope of the W.A.A.F.'s work, bringing her ever closer to her brother-in-arms. Thus, women are now handling balloons—no light job—and are on ground staff work in Sector stations, chiefly in Operations Room, where intelligence and quickness in uptake are essential qualities. At Fighter Stations, too, W.A.A.F.s act as plotters and carry on precisely as front-line troops during air raids. During the Battle of Britain they won golden opinions among the men of the R.A.F. for steadfastness under bombardment.

The recruit is first tested by a Central Trade Test Board on joining up, and then proceeds to appropriate training at a Depot, first general and disciplinary, next technical. The uniform is the familiar air-force blue belted tunic and short skirt, and round peaked cap. Promotion, normally, is from the ranks, recommended A.C.W.s (aircraft-women) going before a Selection Board. Student officers pass through the W.A.A.F. Training School. There are seven commissioned ranks : Assistant Section Officer, Section Officer, Flight Officer, Squadron Officer, Wing Officer, Group Officer, Air Commandant. Housing is in quarters, brick-built houses on R.A.F. stations ; in barrack blocks ; hostels ; billets and huts. Full provision is made for recreation, education, religious welfare and health. This Service makes a very direct appeal to girls and women with initiative and the spirit of adventure. In its ranks are women from all parts of the Empire, and many have gone overseas with the Air Forces of the Dominions.

MECHANIZED TRANSPORT CORPS. This Corps was started in February 1939 to supply a pool of skilled drivers for all organizations engaged on war work. Strength in March 1942, 2,800. Corps Commandant, the founder, Mrs. G. M. Cook. In December 1941 it came under the control of the Ministry of War Transport. Drivers are supplied to all government departments and ministries, the Royal Ordnance Factory, R.A.F. maintenance units, Home Guard, etc. The uniform is khaki, with blue distinguishing right arm brassards and Sam Browne belts.

Women in Green on the Home Front

WOMEN'S VOLUNTARY SERVICE. This Service is to the Home Office what the three auxiliary services are to the fighting forces. Its work is entirely with Civil Defence, a title that covers so wide a diversity of aid as organization of all war relief from U.S.A. and Canada, A.R.P. rest centres, care of air-raid casualties, supervision of over 100 country nurseries for evacuated babies, supply of personnel for Queen's Messengers Convoys, agency for nation-wide relief organization operating through county authorities, with village, town and country representation. The W.V.S. (Chairman, Dowager Marchioness of Reading, D.B.E.) acts as an advisory council on which 65 other women's organizations are represented. It would be true to say that no activity arising from war conditions as they affect the population is outside the purview of this remarkable organization of voluntary women workers who now number over a million. The uniform is bottle-green coat and skirt and burgundy-coloured blouse, bottle-green hat or beret. There are no " ranks," though designations attach to jobs, e.g. county organizer, regional administrator, centre leader.

NURSING AND FIRST AID. The chief ancillary nursing services in war are those of the British Red Cross Society, St. John's Ambulance Brigade, and St. Andrew's Ambulance Corps (Scotland). Training is part or full time, and service also. The character of this war, involving the setting up of many nurseries to deal with evacuated babies and small children, widened the scope of this type of national service. Also, the recruitment of young married women into war industry has made necessary organized crèches for their small children. These organizations give Child

Care training to girls from the age of 16 upwards. The training for the Detachment, as the hospital service is termed, involves examinations in first aid and home nursing, hygiene and sanitation, invalid cookery, A.R.P., child welfare. There are also clerical jobs. Members of the Red Cross Detachment have a large red cross on the apron and blue uniform. The St. John's Detachment nurses wear black and have the Maltese Cross or badge. The St. Andrew's Detachment have as badge the Cross of St. Andrew. These nursing services did much to make possible the successful handling of the victims of the great air raids.

From Farming to Forestry

WOMEN'S LAND ARMY. Here, again, is an organization designed to release able-bodied men for the fighting services. The W.L.A. is a section of the Ministry of Agriculture, and was formed before the war. The Hon. Director is Lady Denman. In 1942 there were over 21,000 volunteers on the land. Age limits are 17 to 40. Choice of work ranges from dairying to tractor-driving, market gardening to forestry. County rallies and competitions are organized. Women of the W.L.A. who carried on in Kent under fire, during the Battle of Britain, were awarded a special badge for courage. The uniform consists of corduroy breeches, green pullover, fawn shirt, brown felt hat, stockings, shoes, boots or gum boots, overall coat, dungarees and —latest addition—a coat similar to a British warm.

Books to Consult : She Walks in Battledress, A. Cotterell (Christophers). Feminine Plural, E. Somerset (Faber).

Sir Kingsley Wood, Chancellor of the Exchequer.
Photo, Barratts

Wood, SIR KINGSLEY (b. 1881). Chancellor of the Exchequer from May 1940. Before the war Sir Kingsley proved his administrative ability as Postmaster-General and Minister of Health. At the outbreak of war he was Secretary of State for Air. He held this vitally important office from May 1938 until April 1940, when, for a few weeks, he was Lord Privy Seal. From Oct. 3, 1940, until Feb. 19, 1942, Sir Kingsley was a member of the War Cabinet.

Woodhouse, CAPTAIN CHARLES HENRY LAWRENCE, C.B. For his gallant action as commander of H.M.S. Ajax (*q.v.*) in her epic fight with the Graf Spee in the Battle of the River Plate, December 1939, Captain Woodhouse was awarded the C.B. He served in the war of 1914–18 as lieutenant in H.M.S. Malaya at the Battle of Jutland.

Lord Woolton, Minister of Food.

Woolton, FREDERICK JAMES MARQUIS, 1ST BARON (b. 1883). Minister of Food from April 1940. For years one of the outstanding figures in the business world of the North of England, he was still Sir Frederick Marquis when, in 1939, he was made honorary adviser to the War Office and the Ministry of Supply on clothing for the army. Shortly afterwards he was appointed Director-General of Equipment and Stores on the Munitions Council, whence in April 1940 he was called by Mr. Chamberlain to take charge of the all-important new Ministry of Food, in which position he was confirmed by Mr. Churchill in the following month. *See* Food : in Wartime.

DURING A 'BAEDEKER' RAID

York's ancient Guildhall as it appeared on the night of April 28, 1942, after Nazi bombers had showered incendiaries on the building. The Germans made deliberate attacks on Britain's cultural heritage.

Photo, Keystone

Works and Buildings, Ministry of. This new Ministry, development of the Office of Works, was formed in October 1940. Its functions were to erect all civil works and buildings required by other Government Departments; to arrange with the Service Departments or the Ministry of Aircraft Production to erect non-specialized works and buildings; to license private building and decide as to the priority of air raid damage claims; to consult with the various Departments concerned with post-war reconstruction in town and country and subsequently advise the Cabinet on methods of dealing with this question. The first Minister of Works and Buildings was Sir John Reith; he was succeeded in February 1942 by Lord Portal.

W.R.N.S. (Women's Royal Naval Service). *See* Women's Services.

W.V.S. (Women's Voluntary Service). *See* Women's Services.

Ymuiden. Situated west of Amsterdam, this Dutch town and port played an effective part in hindering the German conquest of Holland in May 1940. A merchant vessel full of iron ore, together with a trawler, was sunk in the southern entrance to the port. Two floating docks collapsed, cranes, hoppers, dredgers and barges were sunk, and the lock gate machinery destroyed. A 12,000-ton liner was sunk at the other entrance to the harbour. The place was subsequently raided by the R.A.F. when the enemy-occupied docks, iron and steel works were bombed.

York. A "Baedeker" reprisal raid was carried out on York on the night of April 28, 1942, when the city was attacked by some 20 enemy aircraft, five of which were shot down. Considerable damage was done to ancient and historical buildings, but the number of casualties was fortunately not large. The raid took place by moonlight, bombs were released from a low altitude and many of the streets were machine-gunned.

York, H.M.S. Completed in 1930, this British cruiser had a displacement of 8,250 tons and carried a complement of about 600. On Oct. 12, 1940, H.M.S. Ajax (*q.v.*) attacked and crippled the Italian destroyer Artigliere during a sweep in the Mediterranean. The following day, as the damaged enemy ship was being towed by another Italian destroyer towards Sicily, the Artigliere was sunk by gunfire from the York, the latter commanded by Capt. R. H. Portal, R.N. On May 29, 1941, it was announced that the York had been sunk by continuous enemy dive-bombing while under repair at Suda Bay in Crete. Casualties amounted to two killed and five wounded.

Young, SIR MARK AITCHISON, K.C.M.G. (b. 1886). He was Governor and C.-in-C. of Tanganyika Territory from 1938 to 1941, and subsequently became Governor and C.-in-C. of Hongkong. Sir Mark displayed the utmost determination and courage during the powerful Japanese onslaught in December 1941. He refused to surrender to a Japanese ultimatum delivered on Dec. 13. Sir Mark's decision

Sir M. Young,
Gov. of Hongkong.
Photo, Elliott & Fry

received the approval of the British Government. On Dec. 25, however, the Governor was advised by the military and naval commanders that no further effective resistance could be made and the island of Hongkong (*q.v.*) was surrendered unconditionally.

HOW YUGOSLAVIA WAS OVERRUN IN TWELVE DAYS

Axis forces overwhelmed Yugoslavia in April 1941, but armed bands kept up guerilla warfare against the Nazi tyrants, and in Britain the Yugoslav Government continued the fight for freedom. By dismembering the country the Axis tried to split up national unity— with ill success.

Yugoslavia. Germany and Italy attacked Yugoslavia without warning on April 6, 1941. Bulgaria attacked a few days later. Hungary followed on. The Germans began with a savage air raid on Belgrade (*q.v.*). It was another "Rotterdam," a third of the capital being destroyed at one blow. This was the first intimation the Yugoslavs had that the Axis was at war with them.

The Germans then thrust into South Serbia (Yugoslav Macedonia) from their base in Bulgaria. They pushed their tanks and mechanized units through the tortuous mountain passes of Southern Serbia, accompanied by low-flying aeroplanes. The German plan to seek a major military decision in the first place, by the use of mechanized forces in a terrain like South Serbia, which was unsuitable for tank operations,

NAZI METHODS IN YUGOSLAVIA

1. Yugoslav soldiers set this block-house ablaze after holding out against the Germans ; the latter are seen watching the fire. 2. A crater caused by German bombs on a Yugoslavian railway track. 3. Yugoslav troops herded into a Nazi prison camp, after laying down their arms.
Photos, Keystone; Associated Press

instead of on the plainland of Croatia, which was ideal for tanks, came as a surprise to expert military opinion everywhere. In this the Germans repeated the feat which they had carried out at Sedan during the campaign in France. They had deliberately selected the most difficult and therefore the most unexpected point for their break-through.

The Yugoslav army in South Serbia had not the anti-tank guns to destroy the German mechanized divisions. They used mountain artillery to try to accomplish this purpose, but their batteries were smashed up by the low-flying German bombers, against which the Yugoslavs had no fighter 'planes at their disposal. The Yugoslavs, outnumbered in men and material, were unable to stem the tide of the German advance. They fought with their traditional bravery, their soldiers literally throwing themselves barehanded against the German tanks. But courage alone could not overcome the great odds. At a great battle near Skoplje the Germans succeeded in separating the Yugoslav army from the Anglo-Greek forces. This enabled the Germans to kill two birds with one stone : to turn southwards towards Salonika and prepare the way for smashing Anglo-Greek resistance, and to turn westwards towards Albania, where they succeeded in linking up with the Italians, thus saving the latter from annihilation at the hands of the Yugoslav forces operating in that country.

Weakness Caused by Pro-Nazi Regime

The Germans then invaded Yugoslavia from the north, advancing across the Croatian plains, whilst the Italians attacked through Slovenia. In the wake of the German and Italian armies, the Bulgarians attacked in the south and the Hungarians in the north.

The strategic disposition of the Yugoslav armies was far from good. This was due to the mistakes made by the previous regime, which General Simovitch's government had not the time to rectify to any appreciable extent. The Yugoslav armies had been thinned out in a cordon round the country's long frontiers, and were therefore weak in numbers at every vital point. They lacked concentration in what is known, in military terminology, as a " masse de manœuvre." Moreover, there had not been time for complete mobilization.

In the north, as in the south, Yugoslav bravery was overcome by superior weight of men and material. The Yugoslavs were further handicapped by Fifth Column defection on the part of certain Croatian units, although most of the Croatian regiments, like the Slovenes, fought bravely. The Serbs fought throughout with their traditional valour and tenacity. But at a great battle near Belgrade the Yugoslav flank was turned. The end had come.

Within the space of a fortnight Yugoslavia was invaded, occupied and dismembered. But her resistance had delayed Hitler's plan to attack Russia. Her heroism therefore had not been in vain. And with the closing of the chapter of her organized military resistance there opened the chapter of her guerilla resistance.

Yugoslavia : After the Conquest. After the Germans, Italians, Hungarians and Bulgarians had overrun Yugoslavia, the country was carved up, some of the territories being annexed outright, others being occupied.

Germany annexed more than two-thirds of Slovenia, and occupied Serbia to the limits of the 1912 frontiers, and also the Voivodina. In Serbia and the Voivodina a quisling administration was set up under German control, with the renegade Serbian General Neditch as Prime Minister.

Croatia was separated from the rest of what had once been Yugoslavia and made into an "Independent" State, under the Croat quisling, Ante Pavelitch, the hireling of Italy and Hungary who, some years before, had organized the murder of King Alexander of Yugoslavia at Marseilles. Nominally Croatia was made into a kingdom, with the Italian Duke of Spoleto as king. But the king has so far preferred to remain in Italy. Croatia is supposed to be an Italian sphere, but the Germans maintain garrisons at key points.

Italy annexed one-third of Slovenia and the hinterland of Fiume (Reka), thus adding another million and a half Slovenes and Croats to the already large Yugoslav minority in Italy. She also annexed large districts of the Dalmatian coast. The Province of Montenegro was occupied by the Italians, and, together with parts of South Serbia (Yugoslav Macedonia), put under a special administration charged with the task of preparing the creation of yet another vassal State under an Italian prince. At a later stage Italy occupied the rest of the Dalmatian coast.

Bulgaria annexed the greater part of Southern Serbia, with its principal town, Skoplje, thus bringing her new frontiers westwards to the Italian-occupied territory of Albania and Crnagora, and later occupied certain districts of East Serbia in the Morava valley.

Hungary annexed all the territories on the left bank of the Rivers Drava and Sava, including Backa, Baranya, Medjumurje and Prekomurje.

Yugoslavia has been divided up into fourteen parts. The table adjoined gives the general facts, and the accompanying map shows the general picture of the carve-up. The index figure of each territory given in the table has the corresponding figure on the political map.

The aim of the Axis in this dismemberment was to render permanently impossible the resurrection of a united Yugoslavia. Thus the Axis tried to devastate Slovenia by the deportation of the main part of the population to Serbia, Poland and Germany. In Croatia the Axis supported the hireling Pavelitch in his ruthless oppression of the population of Serbian extraction and also of the Croats themselves, most of whom refused to recognize the "New Order" of the Pavelitch regime. In Serbia, Hitler's Army and Gestapo conducted a savage war against the resisting population. The Bulgarians and Hungarians also showed that they have nothing to learn from their German masters in cruelty.

Hitler tried—but without success—to play off Serbs and Croats and Slovenes one against the other, with a view to sowing the seeds of dissension and thus preventing

Fourteen sections carved out of Yugoslavia by the Axis (see table below). Croatian boundaries not final.

The Break-Up of Yugoslavia

Index Figure on map	Occupied by	Square Kilometres	Population
1	Annexed by Germany	10,757	905,000
2	Annexed by Italy	4,490	245,000
3	Occupied by Hungary	950	96,000
4	Annexed by Italy	3,043	510,000
5	Occupied by Hungary	775	116,000
6	"Independent" Croatia	97,564	6,665,000
6a	Parts of Croatia occupied by Italy	28,813	1,213,000
7	Occupied by Hungary	10,023	707,000
8	Serbia (Neditch's Government)	67,664	4,849,000
9	Occupied by Bulgaria	27,312	1,158,000
10	Annexed by Italian Albania	8,459	452,000
11	Italian Montenegro	13,975	360,000
12	Croats and Slovenes annexed by Italy (1919)	—	600,000
13	Slovenes incorporated in Austria (1919)	—	120,000

Gen. Mikhailovitch, Yugoslav patriot. *Photo, G.P.U.*

them coming together again in a united revolt against the Axis. Similarly—but with more success—he played off his various allies and satellites, with a view to weakening their position and strengthening Germany's grip.

It is significant that whereas the Italian maps of dismembered Yugoslavia show the various territories under Axis control as "annexed," the German ones show them as "occupied."

All sections of the Yugoslav people, with the exception of the few quislings, were in revolt against the Axis rule. Passive resistance and active sabotage were continuous in Croatia and Slovenia. In Serbia and Montenegro, the Chetnik movement took the lead—i.e., the Serbian guerilla army under General Mikhailovitch, including some Croats and Slovenes, which, with its headquarters in the mountains, fought pitched battles with the occupying Axis troops and the troops of the quislings Pavelitch and Neditch. Large areas were under the control of the Chetniks, with the result that German and Italian rule became almost non-existent outside the larger centres of population. General Mikhailovitch maintained touch with the Yugoslav Government in London, which appointed him War Minister of the Free Yugoslav Forces.

The Axis retaliated by the murder and torture of hostages, wholesale killings throughout the country, and the literal blotting out of towns and villages by artillery fire and bombing. But none of these repressive measures succeeded in stopping either the sabotage or the active fighting of the Chetniks. This resistance on the part of the Chetniks had not only kept alive the active spirit of resistance in Yugoslavia ; it had also forced the Axis to maintain large bodies of troops in Yugoslavia which could have been employed against Russia or in the Middle East against Britain.

Book : The Land of Silent People, R. St. John (Harrap).

Yugoslavia : Free. After the conquest and dismemberment of Yugoslavia King Peter, General Simovitch (the Premier), and a number of Ministers and officials succeeded in reaching the Middle East. The King, General Simovitch, Dr. Nintchitch, the Foreign Minister, and others left the Middle East and arrived in London on June 21, 1941. Others went to the U.S.A. A Free Yugoslav Government was instituted in London and was recognized by the British Government.

On Jan. 9, 1942, changes took place in the Yugoslav Government. Dr. Slobodan Yovanovitch became Prime Minister and Minister of the Interior and among his Ministers were the following : Foreign Affairs, Dr. M. Nintchitch ; Vice-Presidents, Dr. Krnjevitch and Dr. Krek ; Finance, Dr. Sutey ; Justice, Dr. Gavrilovitch ; War, General Draja Mikhailovitch. Other Ministers were in the U.S.A.

In the Middle East, where Yugoslav land and air forces cooperated with the British, the Government Delegate and Commander was Colonel Rakitch. Yugoslav naval units also cooperated.

The Yugoslav Government in London maintained touch with the elements of resistance inside Yugoslavia, but its appointment to the post of War Minister of Gen. Mikhailovitch, leader of the Chetniks in Yugoslavia afterwards gave rise to considerable criticism. At this time the rôle of the Chetniks was not fully understood ; later allied recognition was withdrawn.

The Yugoslav Government in London showed its appreciation of the need for future Balkan cooperation against aggression from without by signing, together with the Free Greek Government in London, a Federative Agreement, whereby, after the war, Yugoslavia and Greece would enter into a close collaboration which, it was hoped, might provide the basis for some wider form of Balkan union.

King Peter, who became an undergraduate at Cambridge, was in 1941–42 regarded as the symbol of the continuity of the unitary Yugoslav ideal. In the Cabinet in London and amongst the officials were Serbs, Croats and Slovenes. Hitler's attempts to set the three sections of the Yugoslav people one against the other had, in any case, failed.

 Zhitomir. This town in the Ukraine, 80 miles S.W. of Kiev, was the scene of fierce and prolonged fighting, which began on July 23, 1941. Within the following three weeks it had been captured in the course of the German advance.

Zhukov, GENERAL GREGORY. This distinguished soldier, after fighting against the Japanese in Outer Mongolia, became leader of the Red Army during the occupation of Bessarabia. As the chief Soviet fortifications expert, he was made Vice-Commissar for Defence and was responsible for Moscow's outer defences when Hitler invaded the Soviet Union. On Feb. 24, 1941, at the age of 47, he was appointed Chief of the Soviet General Staff and was Military Commander in the Kiev district. When Marshal Timoshenko was transferred from the central sector to the southern, Zhukov succeeded him on Oct. 24, and in December conducted smashing counter-attacks on the Moscow front. In March 1942 the two wings of his army were converging on the Vyasma-Smolensk railway. By the end of June the situation in his sector had altered little.

Gen. Zhukov,
Russian C.-in-C.
Photo, Planet News

GREAT BRITAIN AND THE WORLD WAR : CHRONOLOGY

Principal Events, May to August, 1942

(Continued from page 156)

May 1942

1 **Mandalay evacuated. Air offensive begins against Malta.** Daylight sweeps and bombing raids by R.A.F. over France and occupied territory.

2 British troops on north bank of Irrawaddy withdrawn. Dr. Evatt arrives in Britain. U.S. lease lend extended to Iraq and Persia. Brazil and Paraguay break off relations with Hungary.

3 **Japanese capture Bhamo.** Night : First U.S. raids on Rangoon. Germans bomb Alexandria. Raid on Exeter.

4 **Japanese invasion fleet attacked off Solomon Is. by U.S.** naval and air forces. Japanese land on Corregidor. Mr. R. G Casey arrives at Cairo. Uruguay breaks off relations with Hungary. Night : Air raids on British south coast towns. R.A.F. bomb Pilsen and Skoda.

May 1942

5 **British land on Madagascar.**

6 Loss of H.M. destroyer Jaguar anned. Corregidor garrison surrenders.

7 **Battle with Japanese fleet resumed in Coral Sea.** Lord Gort transferred from Gibraltar to Malta as Governor and C.-in-C. British occupy Diego Suarez.

8 **German offensive in Kerch peninsula.** Japanese capture Akyab and Myitkina. Night : R.A.F. bomb Warnemunde.

9 **Japanese fleet in Coral Sea withdraws northwards,** having suffered heavy losses. U.S. aircraft carrier Lexington and a destroyer lost. U.S. negotiations with Vichy authorities in Martinique.

10 Mr. Churchill in a broadcast warns Germany of Allied retaliation if enemy uses gas against Russians.

May 1942

11 H.M. destroyers Lively, Kipling and Jackal sunk in Mediterranean by air attack. U-boat sinks freighter in St. Lawrence River.

13 **Timoshenko launches offensive in Kharkov region.** Russians on Kerch peninsula withdraw.

15 British forces retreating from Burma reach India. Costa Rica declares war on Hungary and Rumania.

16 **Germans capture Kerch.**

17 Loss of H.M. corvette Hollyhock anned. German cruiser Prinz Eugene attacked by Fleet Air Arm off Norway.

18 Admiral Sir Henry Harwood appointed to Mediterranean Command. Admiral Cunningham goes to Washington as head of Admiralty delegation.

19 United Nations Air Training Conference in Ottawa. **German counter offensive S.E.**

May 1942

of Kharkov. Night : R.A.F. raid Mannheim. Raid on Hull.

20 Russians attack at Taganrog.

21 Japanese offensive in Chekiang. **Heavy R.A.F. offensive in Libya.**

24 Gen. Stilwell reaches Delhi.

25 Night : R.A.F. begin series of raids on Messina.

26 **Anglo-Soviet treaty signed in London.** German offensive in Libya.

27 Reinhardt Heydrich, Gestapo chief in Prague, wounded by bomb and shots : dies June 4.

28 In Libya Germans withdraw through British minefields.

29 **In Libya, fierce tank battle in Knightsbridge region** Mexico declares war on Axis powers (as from May 22nd). Night : Raids by R.A.F. on Gennevilliers power station. Gnome-et-Rhone works and Goodrich factory near Paris.

May 1942

30 General Mason Macfarlane appointed Governor of Gibraltar. Chinese forces evacuate Kinhwa in Chekiang. Night: **Raid by 1,130 R.A.F. bombers on Cologne.**

31 Night: **Air raid on Canterbury.** Attack on Sydney harbour by 4 Japanese midget submarines; all sunk.

June

1 In Libya Germans widen gaps in British minefields. **Loss of H.M. cruiser Trinidad** announced. Daylight bombing raids on France and occupied territory. Night: Air raid on Ipswich. 1,036 R.A.F. bombers raid Essen.

2 U.S. lease-lend agreement with China. Night: Raid on Canterbury.

3 **Rommel's forces overrun British 150th Brigade near Knightsbridge.** Japanese aircraft bomb U.S. naval base of Dutch Island in Aleutians. Major G. Lloyd George appointed Minister of Fuel.

4 **Midway Island beats off Japanese air and sea attack.** British counter-attacks fail to halt Rommel's advance. **Commando raid on French coast between Boulogne and Le Touquet.** Anglo-Belgian military and economic agreement signed in London. Hitler visits Mannerheim in Finland.

5 Germans open heavy offensive in Sevastopol. **U.S.A. declares war against Hungary, Rumania and Bulgaria.** Warns Japan of retaliation in kind if gas is used against any of the United Nations. Night: Raid on Ruhr by R.A.F.

6 Night: R.A.F. raid on Emden. Germans raid Canterbury.

7 Rommel opens heavy attack on Bir Hakeim, held by Free French under Gen. Koenig.

8 Viscount Swinton appointed British Minister, in W. Africa.

9 Announced that H.M. submarine Turbulent had sunk an Italian destroyer and four ships in the Mediterranean.

10 German offensive by Von Bock on Kharkov sector. **In reprisal for death of Heydrich Germans destroy the village of Lidice, near Kladno, in Czechoslovakia**; all men shot, and women and children deported. Night: Garrison of Bir Hakeim withdrawn on C.-in-C.'s orders.

11 Night: American Liberators attack oilfields of Ploesti in Rumania.

12 Germans threaten Tobruk after a tank battle S.E. of Knightsbridge.

13 British tanks defeated with heavy losses at Knightsbridge. Rommel advances on Tobruk. **Japanese land on Attu, in Aleutians.** Loss of H.M. submarine Olympus announced.

14 In face of outflanking threat in Gazala sector, General Ritchie withdraws British forces there.

15 **British forces withdraw from Knightsbridge.**

16 **British convoy from Gibraltar fights its way, after continuous attack from the 13th, to Malta.** Another from Alexandria, is forced to turn back after four-day action.

June 1942

17 Ritchie's forces withdraw to Egyptian border. Garrison left in Tobruk. H.M. destroyer Wild Swan sunk by air attack in Atlantic.

18 **Two German columns advance towards Egyptian frontier.** Next day they turn west to attack Tobruk. Mr. Churchill arrives in U.S.A. Japanese invade Fukien.

19 **Mr. Churchill arrives U.S.A.**

20 Rommel attacks Tobruk in great strength. Japanese shell Vancouver Island.

21 **Germans capture Tobruk.** They advance east and occupy Bardia. Japanese land on Kiska, in Aleutians. Night: Air raid on Southampton.

23 Russians at Kharkov fall back.

24 **Rommel advances 50 miles into Egypt.** British evacuate Sollum and Sidi Omar and withdraw to Mersa Matruh.

25 Gen. Auchinleck takes over personal command from Ritchie. Major-Gen. Eisenhower appointed commander of U.S. forces in European theatre of war. Russians evacuate Kupyansk. Night: **1,000 bomber raid on Bremen.**

26 Night: Air raid on Norwich.

27 **Big Battle at Mersa Matruh.** Mr. Churchill arrives in Britain. Night: R.A.F. raid on Bremen. Luftwaffe raids Gibraltar.

28 German offensive at Kursk. Night: Air raid on Weston-super-Mare.

29 Germans enter Mersa Matruh; they bomb Alexandria. Night: R.A.F. bomb Bremen.

30 Germans reach El Daba.

July

1 **Germans reach El Alamein line;** heavy fighting. Gen. Auchinleck calls on 8th Army for a supreme effort. Anglo-Russian agreement for £25,000,000 to U.S.S.R.

2 Germans withdraw westward from El Alamein. British forces occupy Mayotte Island in Mozambique Channel.

3 **Russians evacuate Sevastopol.**

4 Germans reach the Don on a broad front. Russians retreat at Kursk and Byelgorod. In Aleutians, U.S. submarine sinks three Japanese destroyers, another on fire.

7 Heavy fighting in region of Voronezh, on the Don.

8. Russian submarine hits German battleship Tirpitz with two torpedoes in Barents Sea.

10 **British and Imperial forces counter-attack from El Alamein.** Russians evacuate Rososh; they counter-attack to relieve pressure on Voronezh.

11 **8th Army captures Tel el Eisa station.** Strong German attack reaches Voronezh.

12 Russians evacuate Kantemivorka and Lisichansk. Germans drive S.E. down the Donetz and E. towards Millerovo.

13 Russians evacuate Boguchar and Millerovo. **Stalingrad threatened by German drive.** Coal mines in Britain brought under government control.

14 Germans win back some ground at Tel el Eisa; our forces attack in centre and win back Ruweisat ridge. Free French movement changes name to " Fighting French."

July 1942

16 **R.A.F. bombs Lübeck and Flensberg in daylight.**

17 Russians hold Germans at Voronezh, but give ground in centre on Don. Australians advance S.W. from El Alamein and take a ridge.

19 Russians announce loss of Voroshilovgrad.

20 **8th Army attacks at night along 30 mile front.** Japanese land at Gona, New Guinea. U.S. submarines sink three Japanese destroyers at Kiska.

22 Russians make progress in Voronezh sector; they withdraw in Rostov area. Germans reach Tsymlyanskaya and Novocherkask.

23 **Russians hold positions on left bank of Don.**

24 **8th Army holds all Ruweisat ridge and Makhkhad ridge.** Germans claim Rostov.

25 **Japanese bomb Townsville, Queensland.** Germans cross Don at Tsymlyanskaya; advance from Kamensk towards Don elbow.

26 **Advance by 8th Army in northern sector.** Sweets rationing begins in England. Germans claim penetration of Russian lines S. of Chirskaya, W. bank of Don. Night: **Heavy R.A.F. raid on Hamburg.**

27 Russian evacuation of Rostov and Novocherkask. Germans claim Bataisk, 10 miles S. of the Don. **German aircraft bomb Stalingrad.** Timoshenko withdraws from lower Don and concentrates forces opposite Stalingrad.

28 Germans claim to have crossed lower Don in force, also entered Kalach. Russians hold enemy along the Chir River. Night: Heavy R.A.F. raid on Hamburg. German aircraft bomb Birmingham.

29 Fierce battle at Kletskaya, 80 miles N.W. of Stalingrad. In the Don elbow, Timoshenko sends in his reserves and halts German drive towards Volga.

30 Germans claim capture of Proletarskaya. **Canadian senate passes Conscription Bill.** Night: Germans bomb Midland towns.

31 Germans claim capture of Kushchovsk and to be advancing on a wide front towards Salsk. Night: **Heavy R.A.F. raid on Dusseldorf.**

August

1 German attack Don bend fails.

4 Germans advance in Caucasus and near Kotelnikovo. **They cross the Kuban River.**

5 Germans capture Kotelnikovo and Voroshilovsk.

6 Queen Wilhelmina addresses U.S. Congress at Washington.

7 **U.S. forces land in Solomons** (Guadalcanal-Tulagi area). Heavy fighting near Armavir.

8 **Russians fire Maikop oil wells.** Japanese counter-attack in Solomons is repelled.

9 Germans claim capture of Maikop and Krasnodar. In India, Gandhi and Congress members arrested.

11 Axis submarines attack British convoy from Gibraltar to Malta: **A/C Eagle lost;** also cruisers Cairo and Manchester and destroyer Foresight. Germans reach Caucasian foothills at Cherkessk. U.S. bombers attack Italian cruisers at Navarino. Night: R.A.F. heavy raid on Mainz.

August 1942

12 **Mr. Churchill arrives in Moscow for conference with Premier Stalin.** Russians in Cherkess regions withdraw: in Moscow sector they begin an offensive.

13 British naval force under Admiral Vian bombs island of Rhodes. Russians counter-attack in Stalingrad and Voronezh sectors. Germans claim the capture of Elista. They reach Mineralniye Vody and Georgievsk.

15 Russians driven back in Kalach and Kotelnikovo areas. Five **Brazilian ships sunk by U-boat.**

16 Russians report evacuation of Maikop.

17 **U.S. bomber force attacks Rouen.** U.S. marines raid Makin Island (Gilberts).

18 Gen. Alexander appointed C.-in-C. Middle East. Lieut.-Gen. Montgomery to command 8th Army. Germans cross Kuban at Krasnodar.

19 **British Special Service Troops and Canadians carry out reconnaissance in force at Dieppe:** Casualties being 3,350 out of 5,000 engaged. Destroyer Berkeley and 98 aircraft also lost. Russians evacuate Krasnodar.

20 **Loss of H.M.A.S. Canberra in Solomons announced.** U.S. bombers attack objectives in Amiens. Nearly 500 R.A.F. fighters carry out daylight sweeps over N. France.

22 Loss of H.M. submarine Upholder announced. Brazil declares war on Germany and Italy.

23 Gen. Sir H. Maitland Wilson appointed C.-in-C. Persia-Iraq Command. Germans claim Krimskaya and Kurchanskaya (Kuban sector). **R.A.F. daylight raid on Emden.**

24 Mr. Churchill returns to England. Night: Heavy R.A.F. raids on Wiesbaden and Frankfurt.

25 **H.R.H. the Duke of Kent killed in an aircraft crash.** Big naval battle in Solomons; six Japanese warships damaged. Germans within 40 miles of Stalingrad.

26 Japanese counter-attack on Guadalcanal beaten off. Six enemy ships sunk, **Japanese land at Milne Bay, in S.E. Papua.** Germans reach Mozdok.

27 In Moscow offensive the Russians isolate Rzhev. At Stalingrad they counter-attack to the N.W. Lord Moyne appointed Deputy Minister of State in Middle East. Night: **Heavy R.A.F. raids on Cassel and Gdynia.**

28 Russian offensive S. of Lake Ladoga. Night: Heavy R.A.F. raids on Saarbrücken and Nuremberg.

29 Japanese take off some of their troops from Milne Bay. Russians in Moscow area penetrate German line at Rzhev, also attack in Bryansk sector.

30 **Russians check enemy advance N.W. and S.W. of Stalingrad.** Night: Russian aircraft bomb Berlin, Koenigsberg, Danzig and Stettin.

31 **Rommel opens an offensive from El Hemeimat.**

For earlier chronology *see* Great Britain at War, pages 153-156.

The alphabetical arrangement of this Work ma... campaign, place, person or other subject connected w... CLASSIFIED INDEX of this Guide the reader is directed to all the articles ...mediate reference to any subject which he may wish to consult. See also List of Princ... In addition, by means at the beginning of the volume. Maps and Plans and Tables are ...iated with, any ...in page vii ...age viii.

	PAGE
Abyssinia	4
Addis Ababa ..	6
Amba Alagi ..	18
Aosta, Duke of..	20
Dessie	94
Gallabat	144
Gojjam	144
Gondar	144
Haile Selassie ..	167
Harar..	170
Moyale	286
Africa	
East Africa ..	99
Egypt	103
Equatorial ..	107
North Africa ..	312
South Africa ..	412
West Africa ..	457
See also under above	
individual headings	
Air War	13
Advanced Air	
Striking Force	7
Aircraft 7, *Col. Pl.*	
f.p. 16	
Air Component ..	7
Air Defence ..	11
Air Raids, Btn...	161
Air Transport	
Auxiliary.. ..	13
Battle of Britain	
157, 161	
Battle of London	232
Balloon Barrage	35
Belgium	40
Bomber Command	47
Bofors Gun ..	46
Coastal Command	78
Eagle Squadrons	99
Empire Training	106
Fighter Command	110
Fleet Air Arm ..	114
France	126
Germany	137
Gliders	140
Italy	196
Luftwaffe	11
North Africa ..	318
Observer Corps..	326
Radiolocation ..	366
R.A.F.	379
Albania, War in 15, 163	
Adriatic Sea ..	7
Chimara	68
Durazzo	98
Klisura	218
Koritza	219
Pogradets	353
Santi Quaranta	400
Tepelini	432
Tirana	434
Armies, Strength	22
Army, British ..	22
Battledress ..	38
B.E.F. Strength	55
Commandos ..	79
G.H.Q. Liaison..	139
Home Guard ..	176
Mechanization ..	259
Paratroops ..	338
Pioneer Corps ..	351
Reconnaissance	
Corps	369
Tanks	429
Atlantic, Battle of	95,
150, 152	
Anglo - American	
Agreement ..	19
Atlantic Bases ..	25
Convoys	80
Corvette	82
Graf Spee	6
Maritime Regt.	255
Merchant Navy	271
Mines	277
Navy, Royal 150,294	
Shipping,Min. 404,438	
Submarine War	420
U-boat sinkings	441
Western	
Approaches ..	459

	PAGE
Australia, in War	29
Coral Sea, Battle	86
Darwin, Port ..	92
Japan	197
Java, Battle ..	206
Malaya, and ..	244
Netherlands E.	
Indies	305
Pacific, War in	336
Port Moresby ..	358
Rabau	366
Balkan States ..	34
Albania	15
Adriatic Sea ..	7
Anglo-French-	
Turkish Pact ..	20
Bessarabia.. ..	44
Bulgaria	56
Croatia .. 85, 467	
Danube River ..	91
Greece	162
Hungary	181
Rumania .. 20, 386	
Transylvania ..	438
Turkey	440
Yugoslavia ..	467
Baltic States ..	36
Baltic Sea ..	36
Estonia	36
Latvia	36
Lithuania .. 36, 229	
Oesel	327
Vilna	453
Battle of Britain : *see* Air	
War ; Great Britain	
Belgium,Campaign	39
Albert Canal ..	15
Antwerp	30
Brussels.. ..	55
Dyle, River ..	99
Eben-Eymael ..	228
Leopold, King ..	226
Libre Belgique..	227
Liége	227
Louvain	239
Maastricht.. ..	241
Meuse River ..	275
Ostend	331
Scheldt River ..	401
Belgium, Free	
42, 351, 420	
Berlin : Raids, and	
war conditions 43,137	
Blockade : *See* Atlantic,	
Battle of and Eco-	
nomic Warfare	
British Empire	
Aden	54
Australia's Part	29
Bermudas ..	44
British Colonies	52
British Guiana ..	52
British Honduras	52
Burma	57
Canada	62
Ceylon	66
East Africa 53, 99	
Gibraltar ..	139
Hongkong ..	178
India at War ..	183
Malaya .. 54, 244	
Malta	249
Mauritius ..	54
Newfoundland ..	308
New Zealand ..	310
Northern Ireland	319
Rhodesia	54
Sarawak	400
Singapore ..	400
Somaliland, Brit.	411
South Africa ..	412
West Africa 53, 457	
West Indies 44, 52	
Burma	57
A. V. G. in ..	18
Burma Road ..	58
Chinese armies..	71
Indian reaction..	186
Moulmein ..	286
Rangoon	367
Salween River ..	400

	PAGE
Canada in the War	62
Alaska Road ..	15
Empire Air Tng.	106
Mackenzie King	217
China	68
Assam Road ..	59
Burma	57
Burma Road ..	58
Chiang Kai-shek	67
Chungking.. ..	72
Kowloon	220
Shanghai	403
Sinkiang Road ..	409
Tientsin	433
Civil Defence (Brit.)	74
Air Defence ..	11
Anderson Shelter	19
Bomb Disposal	46
Casualties	161
Nat. Fire Service	113
Commando Troops	79
Boulogne	49
Bruneval	55
Keyes, Sir Roger	215
Lofoten Is. ..	231
St. Nazaire ..	399
Vaagso Is. ..	449
Crete. *See* Greece	
Crimea. *See* Russia	
Czechoslovakia ..	88
Benes, Dr. E. 43, 89	
Brno, Moravia ..	55
Czech Legion ..	87
Heydrich .. 89, 174	
Lidice destroyed	89
Munich Agreement	286
Neurath, Baron	307
Pilsen	351
Prague	360
Slovakia	409
Denmark	93
Aalborg	1
Christian X, King	71
Copenhagen ..	81
Greenland	165
Iceland	182
East Africa, War in	99
Abyssinia	4
Aden	6
Afmadu	7
Amba Alagi ..	18
Aosta, Duke of	20
Asmara, Eritrea	24
Assab	24
Berbera	43
Dessie	94
Gallabat	129
Governments' part	53
Juba River ..	210
Kassala	212
Kenya	54
Keren, Eritrea ..	214
Kismayu	218
Massawa	256
Mogadishu.. ..	279
Somaliland.. ..	411
Egypt	103
Alexandria ..	16
Cairo	60
Halfaya	168
Mersa Matruh ..	275
North Africa,	
campaigns ..	312
Sidi Barrani ..	405
Sidi Omar.. ..	405
Sollum	410
Suez Canal ..	422
Eire .. 94, 96, 104	
Equatorial Africa	107
Brazzaville ..	50
Cameroons ..	61
Chad Territory	66
Free France ..	126
Gabun	129
Libreville ..	227
W. Africa	457
Finland	111
Aaland Islands ..	1
Hango	169
Helsinki	173
Karelian Isthmus	211

	PAGE
Kianta	216
Ladoga, Lake ..	221
Lotta Svard ..	239
Mannerheim,Mshl.	254
Mannerheim Line	254
Murmansk ..	289
Ohqvist, Gen...	327
Russia's policy..	389
Russia at war ..	392
Salla	400
Suomussalmi ..	424
Terijoki	432
Turku	441
Viipuri	453
France	120
Aisne, River ..	14
Alsace-Lorriane	16
Armistice Terms 21, 22	
Arras	24
B.E.F. in ..	55
Bordeaux	47
Boulogne	49
Brest	50
Bruneval	55
Calais, defence ..	60
Dunkirk	97
Free France ..	126
Lorient	239
Maginot Line ..	243
Maubeuge ..	258
Occupied France	127
Paris	341
Rouen	379
St. Nazaire ..	399
St. Valery	399
Toulon	437
Tours	438
Verdun	450
See also Equatorial	
Africa ; West Africa	
France, Vichy 127, 451	
Dakar, fleet at..	90
Indo-China ..	188
Laval, Pierre ..	222
Madagascar ..	242
Martinique ..	256
North Africa ..	319
Oran, action at	329
Petain, Marshal	346
Riom, Trials ..	373
Syria	426
Germany at War	132
Anti-Comintern	20
Augsburg ..	29
Axis, Berlin-Rome	32
Belgium, Invasion	39
Berlin	43
Berlin Pact ..	44
Bremen	50
Bremerhaven ..	50
Cologne, raids ..	91
Danzig	91
Denmark	93
Dortmund-Ems	
Canal	95
Europe at War	108
France, Defeat..	120
Greece, Invasion	162
Hamm, bombing	169
Heligoland ..	173
Hess, Rudolf ..	171
Hitler, Adolf ..	175
Hitler Youth ..	176
Jews	208
Kiel	216
Lebensraum ..	224
Lübeck	240
Luxemburg ..	240
Mannheim ..	255
Munich	286
Netherlands ..	301
Norway, Invasion	321
Oflag	327
Poland, Invasion	353
Poznan	360
Prisoners	361
Rhineland ..	371
Ruhr	386
Russia, Invasion	390
Siegfried Line ..	406
Soviet Pact 138, 415	

	PAGE
Stala..	
Sylt	417
U-boats	426
Wilhelmshaven	441
Yugoslavia ..	469
Great Britain ..	145
Air Defence ..	11
Air War on 157, 161	
Army.. 22, 259, 369	
Balloon Barrage	35
Bath	38
Birmingham ..	45
Black Market ..	46
Bristol	51
B.B.C.	51
Britain, Battle of	
157, 161	
Brit. Restaurants	55
Canterbury ..	63
Cardiff	64
Casualties, civi-	
lian	161
Censorship ..	65
Channel Islands	66
Chronology of	
Events .. 153, 161	
Civil Defence ..	74
Coastguard ..	79
Commandos ..	79
Cost of War ..	82
Coventry	82
Dover	96
Elizabeth, Queen	104
Emergency Powers	
Act	105
Ensa	107
Evacuation ..	109
Exeter	109
Faroe Islands ..	110
Fire Service ..	113
Food in Wartime	117
Forth, Firth of	119
George VI, King	131
Home Guard ..	176
Hull	180
Information, Min.	188
Lifeboat Insn...	228
Lightships ..	229
Liverpool ..	231
London, Battle of	232
Manchester ..	253
Merchant Navy	271
Munitions ..	286
Navy, Royal ..	294
Northern Ireland	319
North Sea ..	320
Norwich	325
Pioneer Corps ..	351
Plymouth ..	353
Police	357
Portsmouth ..	359
Production, Min.	362
Propaganda ..	362
Red Cross ..	369
R.A.F. .. 157, 379	
Scapa Flow ..	401
Scotland	402
Sheffield	403
Southampton ..	415
Supply, Min. of	424
Swansea	425
War Cabinet ..	455
Women's Services	461
Greece, Campaign	162
Albania	15
Athens	24
Corinth	81
Crete	83
Evzones	109
George II	131
German Invasion	162
Heraklion, Crete	173
Italian War ..	162
Klisura	218
Koritza	219
Larissa	222
Maleme, Crete ..	248
Patras	343
Salonika	400
Suda Bay, Crete	422
Thermopylae ..	433

PAGE

War ... 183
...man Is. ...
...am Road ... 19
Burma, Invasion 59
Ceylon ... 57
Italy at War ... 66
Adriatic Sea ... 194
Air War on ... 7
Albania Campaign 196
Axis ... 15
Brindisi ... 32
Dodecanese Is... 51
Genoa ...
Greece ... 99
Italian ... 312
Libyan, Battle 257
Mediterranean ... 264
Milan, raids 276
Mussolini ... 290
Naples ... 291
Pius XII ... 351
Sicily ... 405
Taranto ... 430
Turin ... 440
Vatican ... 331, 450
Venice ... 450
Japan ... 197
Australia ... 39
Aleutian Is. ... 448
Andaman Is. ... 448
Burma, Invasion 57
Ceylon ... 66
Coral Sea, Battle 86
China's fight ... 68
Corregidor ... 81
Hongkong ... 178
India ... 183
Java, Battle of... 206
Macassar Strait 242
Malaya, Invasion 244
Manila ... 253
Marshall Islands 255
Midway, Battle 276
Naval Losses ... 336
Netherlands E.
Indies ... 305
New Britain ... 308
New Guinea ... 308
New Zealand ... 311
Pacific, War 332, 333
Col. map f.p. 336
Pearl Harbour ... 343
Penang ... 345
Perak ... 345
Philippines ... 348
Port Moresby ... 358
Sarawak ... 400
Shanghai ... 403
Singapore ... 407
Tahiti ... 428
Tokyo bombed 336
U.S.A. ... 447
Wake Island ... 454
Latvia. See Baltic.
Libya. See North Africa
Lithuania. See Baltic.
London ... 232
See also Great Britain
Malaya ... 244, 334
Kota Bahru ... 219
Kuala Lumpur 220
... 247
Kuantan ... 220
Penang ... 345
Perak ... 345
Singapore 247,334,407
Malta ... 249, 450
Convoys ... 269
Mediterranean,
War in ... 263, 264
Adriatic Sea ... 7
Alexandria ... 16
Cagliari, Battle 60
Crete, Battle ... 83
Cunningham, Adm. 87
Cyprus ... 87
Dodecanese Is... 95
Egypt ... 103
Genoa ... 131
Gibraltar ... 139
Italy at war ... 191
Libya, campaign 312
Malta... 249, 450
Matapan, Battle 257
Navy, Royal ... 294
North Africa ... 313
North Africa, Fr. 319
Oran, action ... 329
Rhodes ... 372
Sardinia ... 401
Sicily ... 405
Spain ... 415
Suez Canal ... 422

PAGE

Tangier ...
Taranto, victory 439
Valetta (Malta) 430
Merchant Navy 450
Atlantic, Battle 271
Coastguards
Convoy ... 97
Corvette, war 102
DeGerps... ... 229
Dittme Rgt. ... 255
Mines ... 277
North Sea ... 320
Oropesa Float 330
Shipping, Min. of 404
Submarine War 430
U-Boat sinkings 441
Middle East. ... 276
Colour map f.p... 104
Alexandria ... 16
Auchinleck, Gen.
... 43, 313-318
Baghdad ... 32
Basra ... 38
Feisal II, King.. 110
Iraq ... 4, 189
Mosul ... 285
North Africa ... 312
Oil ... 327
Palestine ... 337
Persia ... 345
Suez Canal ... 422
Syria ... 426
Transjordan ... 438
See also Syria.
Navy, Royal ... 294
Abbreviations ... 2
Ark Royal, H.M.S. 20
Atlantic, Battle 25
Australian Navy 30
Convoy ... 80
Corvette ... 82
Courageous ... 82
DeGaussing ... 92
Depot Ship ... 93
Fleet Air Arm ... 114
King George V 217
Matapan, Battle 257
Mediterranean 264
Mines ... 277
Narvik ... 291
North Sea ... 320
Oran, action ... 329
Pacific, War ... 332
Plate, R. Battle 351
Prince of Wales 360
Renown ... 370
Repulse ... 371
Rodney ... 375
Royal Oak ... 385
Scapa Flow ... 401
Submarine war 430
Taranto, victory 430
Netherlands ... 301
Amsterdam ... 18
Flushing ... 117
Hague, The ... 167
Maastricht ... 241
Rotterdam ... 378
Seyss-Inquart ... 403
Wilhelmina, Q. 460
Netherlands East
Indies, ... 305, 335
Amboina ... 18
Bali ... 34
Borneo ... 48
Celebes ... 65
Japan ... 197
Java, invasion ... 204
Java Sea, Battle 206
Macassar Strait 242
Pacific, War 332, 335
Palembang ... 337
Sumatra 306,337,423
Surabaya ... 428
Netherlands, Free 304
Netherlands West
Indies ... 307
North Africa, War 312
Agheila, El ... 7
Alamein, El ... 318
Alexandria 43, 318
Auchinleck, Gen.
... 28, 316-318
Barce, Libya ... 37
Bardia ... 37, 315
Benghazi ... 43, 314
Capuzzo Fort ... 63
Cyrenaica ... 3, 37
Derna, Libya 93, 318
Egypt 103, 316, 318
Gazala, El... ... 130

PAGE

Halfaya ... 289
Jarab... ... 329
Barrani ... 405
Sidi Omar ... 405
Sidi Rezegh 317, 406
Sollum ... 410
Suez Canal ... 422
Tangier ... 429
Tmimi, El ... 435
Tobruk 315-318, 435
Tripoli ... 438
Tunisia ... 440
Norway ... 321
Aandalsnes ... 1
Altmark ... 17
Dombaas ... 95
Elverum ... 105
Free Norway ... 325
Hamar ... 168
Haakon VII ... 166
Kristiansund ... 220
Lillehammer ... 229
Lofoten Is., raid 231
Namsos ... 291
Narvik, Battles 291
Oslo ... 331
Quisling ... 365
Spitzbergen ... 416
Trondheim ... 439
Vaagso Is, raid... 449
Pacific, War 332, 333
Colour map f.p. 336
Aleutian Is. ... 448
Coral Sea ... 86, 336
Emirau ... 105
Guam... ... 166
Hongkong ... 178
Japanese attacks 333
Java Sea, Battle 206
Hawaii ... 171
Macassar Strait.. 242
Manila ... 253
Marshall Is. ... 255
Midway ... 276, 336
Netherlands E.
Indies ... 305
New Britain ... 308
New Guinea ... 311
Pearl Harbour ... 343
Philippines 334, 348
Sarawak ... 400
Tahiti ... 428
Timor ... 433
Wake Is. ... 454
Persia (Iran) ... 345
Caspian Sea ... 64
Iraq and ... 189
Oil ... 1, 327
Pahlevi ... 337
Teheran ... 432
Philippines ... 348
Corregidor... 81, 242
Manila ... 253
Pacific, War in... 334
Poland ... 353
Anglo-Polish
Agreement ... 30
Bialystok ... 45
Brest-Litovsk ... 51
Cracow ... 83
Danzig ... 91
Free Poland ... 356
Gdynia ... 130
Hel ... 172
Katowice ... 212
Lodz ... 231
Lublin ... 240
Lwow ... 241
Orzel, submarine 330
Vilna ... 453
Warsaw, siege 455
Westerplatte ... 459
Royal Air Force .379
Abbreviations ... 2
Aircraft 7, Plate f.p. 16
Air Training Corps 13
Air War ... 12
Britain, Battle of
... 157, 161
Camouflage f.p. 16, 61
Convoy ... 80
Glider Pilots'
Regiment ... 140
Gneisenau,
attacks 50, 142, 401
Netherlands,
campaign ... 302
Parachute Troops 338
Pigeons, Carrier 351

PAGE

...t... 142, 401
...achines ... 9
W.A.A.F. ... 435
See also Air War; Germany; Italy; Japan
Rumania ... 386
Antonescu, Gen. 20
Balkans ... 34
Bessarabia ... 44
Black Sea ... 46
Bucharest ... 55
Bukovina ... 56
Calinescu, A. ... 61
Cernauti ... 66
Constanza ... 80
Dobruja ... 95
Iron Guard ... 190
Michael I ... 275
Oil ... 328
Ploesti ... 353
Transylvania ... 438
Russia Before Invasion ... 388
Russia, War in ... 390
Aircraft ... 10
Anti-Comintern
Pact ... 20
Armed Strength 389
Baltic States ... 36
Baku ... 34
Batum ... 38
Black Sea ... 46
Caspian Sea ... 64
Caucasia ... 64
Crimea, 84, 214, 403
Finland, Invasion 111
Kalinin ... 211
Kaluga ... 211
Kandalaksha ... 211
Kerch (Crimea) 214
Kharkov ... 215
Kiev ... 216
Kronstadt ... 220
Kuibishev ... 220
Ladoga, Lake ... 221
Leningrad, siege 224
Minsk ... 279
Mojaisk ... 280
Moscow, defence 282
Moscow Three
Power Conference 285
Murmansk ... 289
Novgorod ... 325
Odessa ... 326
Orel ... 330
Petsamo ... 348
Poland, invasion 353
Rostov-on-Don 377
Sevastopol, siege 403
Smolensk ... 409
Soviet-German
Pact... ... 415
Staraya Russa ... 419
Stalin, Josef ... 417
Taganrog ... 428
Tikhvin ... 433
Tula ... 440
Ukraine ... 216, 442
Urals ... 448
Volokolamsk ... 453
Vyasma ... 454
White Russia ... 460
Scotland ... 402
Forth, Firth of.. 119
Gt. Btn. Air War 157
Orkney Islands 330
Scapa Flow ... 401
Shipping : see Merchant Navy
Siam ... 57, 188, 404
Malaya, and ... 244
Sicily ... 64, 195, 405
R.A.F. raids ... 196
Singapore
War 200, 247, 334, 407
Somaliland ... 411
See also East Africa
South Africa ... 412
Hertzog, Gen. ... 173
Rhodesia ... 372
Smuts, Gen. ... 410
South America ... 414
Montevideo ... 281
United Nations 447
Spain ... 415
Franco, Gen. ... 128
Suñer, R. S. ... 423
Tangier annexed 429
Submarine War ... 420
Corvette ... 82
Depot Ship 93, 422
Depth Charge ... 93
U-boat ... 441

PAGE

Sweden ... 425
Baltic Sea ... 36
Four-Power Con. 120
Hannson, P. A. 170
Lulea ... 240
Switzerland ... 425
Prisoners of War 361
Red Cross, Int. 369
Syria ... 426
Aleppo ... 16
Beirut ... 39
Damascus ... 91
Dentz, Gen. ... 93
Haifa ... 167
Tripolis ... 439
Tanks ... 429
Mechanization 259
North Africa 316-318
Tobruk 313-318, 440
Italian trenches 192
Turkey ... 440
Anglo-French-Turkish Pact ... 20
Papen, F. von ... 338
Sarajoglu, S. ... 400
Saydam, Dr. R. 401
Ukraine 94, 95, 442, 449
War in 392-4, 397-8
See also Russia.
U.S.A. ... 443
Aircraft ... 9, 446
Alaska Road ... 15
Anglo-American
Agreement ... 19
Atlantic Bases .. 25
Atlantic Charter 28
Bermudas ... 44
Canada ... 63
Coral Sea battle 86, 336
Corregidor... ... 81
Eagle Squadrons 99
Eisenhower, Gen. 448
Greenland ... 165
Guam ... 166
Hawaii ... 171
Hull, Cordell ... 180
Iceland ... 182
Isolationism ... 191
Japan ... 197
Java Sea, Battle 206
King, Adm. E. J. 217
Lease-Lend Act 223
MacArthur, Gen. 242
Macassar Strait 242
Marshall, Gen. ... 255
Marshall Is. ... 255
Martinique ... 256
Mexico ... 275
Midway Is. 276, 336
Moscow Con. ... 285
Neutrality Act.. 307
Oil ... 328
Pacific, War 332, 333
Panama Canal .. 338
Pearl Harbour ... 343
Philippines 253, 348
Roosevelt ... 375
Submarine War 421
Tahiti ... 428
Wake Island 336, 454
Welles, Sumner 457
West Africa ... 457
Brazzaville ... 50
Cameroons ... 61
Chad ... 66
Equatorial Africa 126
Gabun ... 107
Women's Services 461
Civil Defence ... 74
Elizabeth, Queen 104
George Cross and
Medal ... 132
Johnson, Amy ... 210
Knox, Jean, Mrs. 218
Mechanized
Transport 260, 466
Oliver, Dame ... 329
Police, Women's
Auxiliary.. ... 357
Queen's Messengers ... 365
Yugoslavia ... 467
Balkans ... 34
Belgrado ... 43
Croatia ... 85
Free Yugoslavia
... 407, 470
Monastir ... 280
Paul, Prince ... 343
Peter II ... 347
Skoplje ... 409
Spoleto, Duke of 417
Tsvetkovitch,
Dragisha ... 439